SIXTH EDITION

Trustees Handbook

A PRACTICAL GUIDE TO LABOR-MANAGEMENT EMPLOYEE BENEFIT PLANS

SIXTH EDITION

Trustees Handbook

A PRACTICAL GUIDE TO LABOR-MANAGEMENT EMPLOYEE BENEFIT PLANS

**Marc Gertner
Editor and Contributor**

International Foundation
EDUCATION – BENEFITS • COMPENSATION

Accomplish More.

The statements and opinions expressed in this book are those of the authors.
The International Foundation of Employee Benefit Plans disclaims
responsibility for views expressed and statements made in books published
by the International Foundation.

Copies of this book may be obtained from:

>Publications Department
>International Foundation of Employee Benefit Plans
>18700 West Bluemound Road
>P.O. Box 69
>Brookfield, Wisconsin 53008-0069
>(262) 786-6710, ext. 8240

Payment must accompany order.

Call (888) 334-3327, option 4, for price information or see www.ifebp.org/bookstore.

Published in 2006 by the International Foundation of Employee Benefit Plans, Inc.
©2006 International Foundation of Employee Benefit Plans, Inc.
Library of Congress Control Number: 2005928258
ISBN 978-0-89154-604-7
Printed in the United States of America

Table of Contents

Foreword		ix
Preface		xi
Contributors		xiii

Section I. Introduction

Chapter 1	History of Taft-Hartley Plans *Wayne Wendling, CEBS*	1
Chapter 2	Basic Concepts of Trusteeship *Marc Gertner*	8
Chapter 3	The Future Direction of Employee Benefits *Dallas L. Salisbury*	21

Section II. Fiduciary Duty and Responsibility

Chapter 4	Fiduciary Responsibility Under ERISA *Stephen M. Saxon and Jon Bourgault*	29
Chapter 5	Delegation of Responsibility *Thomas E. Funk and William H. Tobin*	43
Chapter 6	Trustees and Bargaining Parties *David W. Silverman*	50
Chapter 7	Fiduciary Responsibility in Investments *Rory Judd Albert*	59
Chapter 8	Legal Considerations of Real Estate Investment for Employee Benefit Plans *Neal S. Schelberg*	87
Chapter 9	Fiduciary Responsibility in Appointment, Monitoring and Removal of Trustees *Marc Gertner*	107
Chapter 10	Fiduciary Responsibility and Potential Liabilities in the Managed Care World *Thomas F. Fitzgerald, Robert A. Imes and Jon Bourgault*	113
Chapter 11	Utilizing Professional Advisors in Fulfilling Fiduciary Responsibility *Paul J. Ondrasik Jr. and Donald A. Walters*	122
Chapter 12	DOL and IRS: ERISA Enforcement Responsibilities *Bennett E. Choice*	134
Chapter 13	Accounting and Auditing *Robert B. Jones, CEBS*	138
Chapter 14	Reading and Understanding Employee Benefit Plan Financial Statements *David C. Lee and Michael A. Van Sertima*	142

Chapter 15	Internal Controls: An Overview	146
	Michael A. Van Sertima	
Chapter 16	Fiduciary Responsibility Issues in Connection With Payment or Reimbursement of Trustee Expenses	150
	Marc Gertner	
Chapter 17	Trustee Fiduciary Liability Insurance	157
	Jeffrey D. Mamorsky	

Section III. Design of Welfare Plans

Chapter 18	Managed Prescription Drug Benefit Programs	175
	Sean M. Brandle	
Chapter 19	Retiree Health Benefits	181
	Thomas F. Del Fiacco and Michael I. Helmer	
Chapter 20	Next Generation Health Plan Solutions: Trends in Multiemployer Health Plan Design	185
	Edward A. Kaplan	
Chapter 21	Recent Regulations in Compliance: HIPAA and COBRA	190
	Kathryn Bakich and Kaye Pestaina	

Section IV. Financing of Health and Welfare Plans

Chapter 22	Traditional Insurance Financing Methods	197
	Arthur L. Wilmes	
Chapter 23	Health Care Management Programs	203
	Arthur L. Wilmes	
Chapter 24	Self-Financing of Welfare Plans	222
	Arthur L. Wilmes	
Chapter 25	Savings Accounts and Consumer-Directed Health Plans	227
	Arthur L. Wilmes	
Chapter 26	Actuarial Analytics	232
	Arthur L. Wilmes	

Section V. Multiemployer Pension Plan Design

Foreword		239
Chapter 27	Design of Multiemployer Plans	241
	Daniel F. McGinn	
Chapter 28	Minimum Participation and Vesting, Postretirement Age Benefit Adjustments and General Benefit Distribution Rules	247
	Daniel F. McGinn	
Chapter 29	Joint and Survivor Pensions	253
	Daniel F. McGinn	
Chapter 30	Minimum and Maximum Funding of Defined Benefit Plans	256
	Daniel F. McGinn	

Chapter 31	Other Plan Design Considerations	258
	Daniel F. McGinn	
Chapter 32	Defined Contribution Plans—An Alternative to Defined Benefit Plans	261
	Daniel F. McGinn	
Checklist for Trustees		265

Section VI. Actuarial Considerations

Chapter 33	The Actuarial Process	267
	Ralph M. Weinberg	
Checklist for Trustees		273

Section VII. Mergers

Chapter 34	Pension Fund Mergers	275
	Barry S. Slevin	

Section VIII. Investment of Plan Assets

Chapter 35	Investment Fundamentals	283
	Eugene B. Burroughs	
Chapter 36	Investment Vehicles	288
	Eugene B. Burroughs	
Chapter 37	Developing Investment Policy	302
	Eugene B. Burroughs	
Chapter 38	Selecting an Investment Manager	306
	Eugene B. Burroughs	
Chapter 39	Performance Measurement	318
	Eugene B. Burroughs	
Chapter 40	The Role of the Investment Consultant	320
	Thomas A. Mitchell Sr., CEBS	
Chapter 41	The Utilization of Commission Dollars	330
	Thomas A. Mitchell Sr., CEBS	
Chapter 42	Participant-Directed Investing in Defined Contribution Plans	334
	Thomas A. Mitchell Sr., CEBS	
Bibliography		340
Checklist for Trustees		341

Section IX. Collections

Chapter 43	Collections.. *Ira R. Mitzner*	343

Section X. Administration of Taft-Hartley Plans

Foreword	....	351
Chapter 44	The Varying and Various Forms and Functions of Plan Administration .... *William J. Einhorn*	353
Chapter 45	The Administrative Manager's Relationship With the Plan Trustees, Plan Professionals, Participants and Other Parties...................................... *William J. Einhorn*	373
Chapter 46	Measuring and Evaluating the Cost of Plan Administration .... *William J. Einhorn*	387
Checklist for Trustees	....	395

Section XI. Communications

Chapter 47	Reporting and Disclosure Under ERISA .... *Lonie A. Hassel*	397
Chapter 48	Benefit Claims .... *Lonie A. Hassel*	401

Section XII. Trustee Effectiveness

Chapter 49	Trustees' Meetings.. *Timothy J. Parsons*	403
Chapter 50	Required Trustee Action Where Trustees Don't Agree on a Decision .... *Vivian C. Folk*	412

Appendixes

Appendix A	ERISA Sections..	417
Appendix B	LMRA of 1947, Section 302(c)	467
Appendix C	IRC Sections	469
Appendix D	Labor-Management Reporting and Disclosure Act of 1959, As Amended	567
Index	....	599

Foreword

One of the most awesome realizations of a newly appointed and seated trustee of an employee benefit plan subject to ERISA (and subject also to the Internal Revenue Code, the Taft-Hartley Act and many other federal enactments) is the enormity of the task he or she has accepted. Suddenly, the business manager of the local union, or the chapter manager, the carpenter or meat cutter, or the trucking executive or painting contractor has become an active, managing director of a multimillion dollar insurance-type business.

Immediately, the newly appointed and seated trustee must learn and use a whole new vocabulary. The terms *COB, subrogation, precertification, concurrent review, TMJ* and *TPA* must become a part of the new welfare trustee's basic vocabulary. His or her pension counterpart must now understand QDROs and joint and survivor annuities, equities and convertibles, GICs and BICs, inverse interest curves and risk/reward tradeoff, disintermediation and arbitrage, early retirement subsidies and actuarial equivalencies. The new trustees' left- and right-hand allies become fund counsel, the enrolled actuary, the administrative manager, the investment manager and the investment consultant.

Suddenly, the new trustee, who is accustomed to dealing with finances on a significantly smaller scale, has co-fiduciary responsibility for a multimillion dollar pension and welfare operation, with potential legal liability in eight figures. It is an awesome transformation.

To meet this crisis, the International Foundation of Employee Benefit Plans in 1970 published the first edition of the *Trustees Handbook*. Less than 300 pages in length, referencing only three major federal statutes and a dozen landmark court decisions, the book was an attempt to enable the newly designated trustee to bridge the enormity of the gap from labor or management representative to plan fiduciary.

The *Trustees Handbook* has been updated four times, the most recent being the fifth edition in 1998.

Recently, the directors of the International Foundation determined that it was necessary to publish a sixth edition. It was necessary to update the *Trustees Handbook* and to alert new trustees to the several new enactments of Congress in the decade. It was necessary to advise the trustees of the many important recent court decisions. A sixth edition was, in fact, due.

When I was first approached to serve as editor and principal contributor to this book, I was awestruck, as new trustees must be. It is an enormous work; it covers the entire gamut of Taft-Hartley pension and welfare plans. It goes from plan organization through design, funding and delivery of benefits. It covers the legal, actuarial, consulting, accounting and administrative disciplines. I wanted to say no. I finally agreed and, as I review the text for one final time, I am proud and happy I did.

There are many, many people who must be recognized in connection with this handbook. I appreciate the International Foundation Directors and the Executive Committee for their faith, trust, confidence and support so many times in so many different ways. I hope this work justifies the confidence they placed in me.

I am particularly indebted to my friend Claude Kordus, who was a major contributor to the initial *Trustees Handbook* in 1969-1970 and to the second edition, and who was the editor and principal contributor to the 1979 third edition. I have utilized much of Claude's organization of the *Trustees Handbook*.

I am particularly appreciative and indebted to the contributors to this important reference book. Those who have written entire sections or individual articles for sections are enumerated in the table of contents and at the outset of each article, as well as profiled in the contributors' section.

They are the leaders of the Taft-Hartley employee benefit industry. They are the elite, the crème de la crème, the best our industry has to offer. Each is a very busy person, personally and professionally, vocationally and avocationally. They all give of themselves, their time and their talent by speaking and writing for the International Foundation.

It was, in truth, an imposition to ask each to make the contribution to this sixth edition of the *Trustees Handbook.* Yet, each promptly accepted and very competently performed.

I have endeavored to acknowledge and thank each of them in person and by letter, initially and at the conclusion. Let me again thank each and every one of them. They are the *sine que non* not only of this *Trustees Handbook,* but also of the International Foundation of Employee Benefit Plans and of our Taft-Hartley employee benefits industry.

It is very common for editors and authors to dedicate their new work to a person or small group of persons who were integrally related to the work. As I near the end of a 38-year career as an attorney representing trustees of employee pension and welfare plans and look back thereon, the real heroes of the industry are the trustees of the plans. As noted above, the task is daunting, the responsibility enormous and the potential liability frightening. The trustees serve, and the overwhelming majority of them serve well.

They serve without pay. Most of the time they serve without appropriate recognition and appreciation from the brothers they serve. There are some meals, and maybe an occasional trip to an inviting locale for an educational seminar. Perhaps the greatest expression of appreciation comes from the periodic letters from spouses of members or from retirees. I remember one beautiful and heartfelt note from the spouse of a Toledo-area construction worker who had a long, painful and expensive bout with cancer. The words and appreciation were sincere: *Thank you, trustees and advisors, for seeing that my husband got the best care possible, without the necessity of selling the family homestead or depleting a lifetime of savings to pay for it.*

Then there was the letter from a retiree whom I helped by convincing the trustees and advisors of his retirement plan that he was entitled to a full pension. He told of his and his wife's happiness in their lives as retirees in Florida. In appreciation, he even invited me to come and fish with him.

Not all spouses or retirees take the time and trouble to write the trustees to express their appreciation, but they know it and feel it. This is the greatest reward a person involved in the Taft-Hartley employee benefits field can receive. This is what makes the long meetings and more common special meetings worthwhile. This is what makes wading through actuarial reports and legal opinions worthwhile.

As I prepare to leave this beautiful industry composed of thousands of saintly persons, I salute the thousands of trustees and dedicate this book to them—the real heroes of the Taft-Hartley employee benefits industry.

I wish to acknowledge with appreciation the cooperation and help I received from my colleagues in the employee benefits department of Shumaker, Loop & Kendrick, LLP—Gary R. Diesing, Vivian C. Folk and Susan D. McClay. They gave me great assistance in the hard work that is necessary to produce a book. They gave me time and counsel. They read articles and edited copy. Vivian also wrote an article.

A special thanks also to my longtime secretary and friend, Donna Lunsford. For the fourth time in less than 15 years, she did typing and related work to produce a sizable book.

Last, but most importantly, I wish to acknowledge and thank my wife Gerry, the pot of gold at the end of the rainbow, who ended a very dark and stormy period in my life. Without her encouragement and support, I could not have performed my role in this project.

Thousands of hours of labor were involved over the past year in the writing and publication of this sixth edition of the *Trustees Handbook.* Many people have made myriad contributions. The key test is whether this time and these efforts help new trustees accept and implement their awesome fiduciary duties. If those of you who read, reread and utilize this work find it worthwhile, then our efforts will have been worthwhile. We hope you will find it so.

Marc Gertner
Naples, Florida

Preface

The International Foundation of Employee Benefit Plans continues to fulfill its mission of education, which is the cornerstone of the Foundation. When the first meeting of the founders was held in 1954, the single objective in coming together was to provide a forum where trustees and administrators could exchange ideas and gain information to help them better manage the employee benefit plans they served. Trustees and administrators continue to join together to accomplish that objective through vibrant, ongoing education programs.

The *Trustees Handbook* supports that cornerstone of education. The book arose from the Trustees Institutes, which the Foundation began in 1967 and continues as an educational staple for trustees of multiemployer benefit plans. In tandem with these institutes, there arose the notion that there should be a manual for trustees—a book that would embody the principles, concepts, issues and problems dealt with in the institutes for trustees.

The *Trustees Handbook* debuted in 1970, with the advantage of broadening the audience served by the institutes and adding permanence to the information. Now in its sixth edition, the changes to each update of the *Trustees Handbook* mirror the growing, dynamic benefits industry.

The newest edition brings the volume up to date in an exciting period of change in employee benefits. At the forefront is the legal-legislative sphere: Major congressional enactments such as the Health Insurance Portability and Accountability Act are an annual occurrence; regulatory decrees come forth requiring vigilance; court decisions continually shape the legal framework. But other factors strongly influence the profession as well: Economic forces and business activity, a diverse workforce with changing values, trends in collective bargaining and technological advancements are among the obvious. To stand still as the landscape changes is to risk becoming obsolete. Education minimizes that risk.

The International Foundation has been fortunate to have Marc Gertner, a dedicated member, serving as editor of the *Trustees Handbook*. Mr. Gertner brings to the task a broad background and mass of knowledge in employee benefits, as well as a full grasp of contemporary and emerging issues. He is a retired partner in the Toledo law firm of Shumaker, Loop & Kendrick who practiced law in the multiemployer benefit plan sector for more than 45 years. He has served numerous times as a Foundation speaker and panelist, and has become well-known for his interest and expertise in the fiduciary obligations involved in benefit plan management. He is co-author of *The Annotated Fiduciary,* published by the Foundation, and served on a special committee that developed the first edition of *Investment Policy Guidebook for Trustees.*

Mr. Gertner was educated at Harvard and earned his law degree at Ohio State University. His range of professional activities has included the American Bar Association, Practicing Law Institute and Financial Analysts Federation. His expenditure of time and effort to prepare this edition of the *Trustees Handbook* was substantial. For that, he is accorded the esteem and gratitude of the Foundation, its officers and Board of Directors.

Serving as a benefit plan trustee is a high calling, involving significant legal and ethical responsibilities. The extent to which this book helps the individual trustee to effectively fulfill those responsibilities is the standard by which its success will be measured.

Michael Wilson
Chief Executive Officer
International Foundation of Employee Benefit Plans

Contributors

Rory Judd Albert is the co-chair of Proskauer Rose LLP's Labor and Employment Law Department, as well as the head of its Employee Benefits and Executive Compensation Law Group. He is serving a second term on Proskauer's six-person executive committee. Mr. Albert is a prolific author and speaker. He is a graduate of Massachusetts Institute of Technology and Columbia Law School. Mr. Albert has written articles for legal publications and for International Foundation publications. He has also served on the Foundation's Benefits Communication Committee.

Kathryn Bakich is national director of Health Care Compliance and a vice president at The Segal Company. She has published several articles about employee health and welfare benefits, and is the author of the *Employers' Guide to HIPAA Privacy Requirements* published in 2002. Ms. Bakich graduated from the University of Missouri in Columbia, Missouri with a J.D. degree, an M.A. degree in public policy and a B.A. degree in political science. She has been a frequent speaker at International Foundation programs.

Jon Bourgault is an associate with the Groom Law Group, Chartered of Washington, D.C., which specializes in employee benefits law. He received his J.D. degree from the New York University School of Law.

Sean M. Brandle is vice president of The Segal Company's National Health Practice. He chairs Segal's National Rx Consulting Group, providing guidance to Segal consultants regarding all aspects of prescription drug benefit plans. Mr. Brandle is often quoted in general business and employee benefit publications on prescription drug issues. He holds a B.A. degree in economics with business emphasis from Montclair State College.

Eugene B. Burroughs is an independent investment consultant and a chartered financial analyst. For 21 years, he was director of investments for the International Brotherhood of Teamsters. Mr. Burroughs has authored four books that have been published by the International Foundation. As an indication of his commitment to the goals of the Foundation education programs, Mr. Burroughs has accumulated thus far over 500 service credits on his participation roster. He presently serves as a member of the Foundation's Investment Management Committee.

Bennett E. Choice is a shareholder in the Employee Benefits Department of Reinhart Boerner Van Deuren s.c., a law firm based in Milwaukee, Wisconsin. He represents Taft-Hartley pension and health plan sponsors. Mr. Choice also serves as counsel for employee benefit plans sponsored by closely held businesses and tax-exempt entities. He obtained his bachelor of business administration degree in 1986 from the University of Iowa. Mr. Choice is a 1989 graduate of the University of Iowa College of Law. He has spoken at International Foundation conferences.

Thomas F. Del Fiacco is senior vice president and office head at The Segal Company's Minneapolis office. He serves as lead consultant to several multiemployer pension funds. Mr. Del Fiacco is a member of the American Academy of Actuaries and an enrolled actuary. He received a B.A. degree in mathematics from the College of St. Thomas in St. Paul, Minnesota. Mr. Del Fiacco frequently speaks at International Foundation conferences and is a member of the Foundation's Actuaries/Consultants Committee.

William J. Einhorn serves as the administrator for the Teamsters Health & Welfare and Pension Trust Funds of Philadelphia and Vicinity. He received both his B.A. and J.D. degrees from Temple University in Philadelphia. Mr. Einhorn, a frequent International Foundation speaker, has previously served in varying capacities with the Foundation, including as a Voting Member of its Board of Directors, Chair of its Administrators Committee, and as a member of its Accountants Committee, Financial Review Committee and Educational Program Committee.

Thomas F. Fitzgerald is a principal with Groom Law Group, Chartered of Washington, D.C. He specializes in various aspects of employee benefits law, particularly health care and litigation matters. Mr. Fitzgerald is a graduate of Georgetown University Law Center and received an M.B.A. degree from Loyola University. He has spoken at International Foundation programs and written for Foundation publications.

Vivian C. Folk is a partner in the Toledo office of the law firm of Shumaker, Loop & Kendrick. She has served as counsel to employee benefit plans and plan service providers. Ms. Folk is also an arbitrator for the American Arbitration Association Multiemployer Pension Plan Amendments Act Panel. She has taught employee benefits at the University of Toledo College of Law and for the Ohio Bar Association. Ms. Folk received a B.A. degree in philosophy from Ohio Wesleyan University and a law degree from Case Western University Law School. She is co-author of *The Annotated Fiduciary,* a textbook on fiduciary responsibility under ERISA, published by the International Foundation. Since 1977, Ms. Folk has spoken regularly at Foundation conferences.

Thomas E. Funk is a director of the law firm of Reinhart Boerner Van Deuren s.c. in Milwaukee, Wisconsin. He has served as legal counsel to trustees of Taft-Hartley plans throughout the country. Mr. Funk earned his B.A. degree at Valparaiso University and his J.D. degree at Northwestern University. He has served as an Advisory Director for the International Foundation and also served on the Attorneys Committee, Educational Program Committee, Constitution and By-Laws Committee and the Benefit Communications Committee.

Lonie A. Hassel is principal at Groom Law Group, an employee benefits law firm in Washington, D.C. She advises ERISA-covered single and multiemployer pension and welfare plans and public employee plans and plan sponsors on fiduciary and Title IV issues. Ms. Hassel defends and prosecutes individual and class actions involving fiduciary breach, benefit claims and Title IV of ERISA. She is a former assistant general counsel of the Pension Benefit Guaranty Corporation.

Michael I. Helmer is a consulting actuary in The Segal Company's Minneapolis office with experience in actuarial consulting for multiemployer, public sector, church and corporate health and welfare and pension plans. He received a B.A. degree in mathematics from Rutgers University in New Brunswick, New Jersey. Mr. Helmer is an enrolled actuary and a member of the American Academy of Actuaries.

Robert A. Imes is an associate with Groom Law Group, Chartered of Washington, D.C., which specializes in employee benefits. He is a graduate of Georgetown University Law Center.

Robert B. Jones, CEBS, is a senior vice president and the regional practice leader for Compensation Consulting for the Northeast Region for Aon Consulting in Conshohocken, Pennsylvania. He is a certified public accountant and received a B.A. degree from Dartmouth College and a law degree from Case Western Reserve University School of Law. Mr. Jones received his certified employee benefit specialist (CEBS) designation in the charter class of 1980, taught CEBS courses, and has been a fellow for 14 years in the International Society of Certified Employee Benefit Specialists. He has served as chairman of the board of ISCEBS and been active in ISCEBS chapters. Mr. Jones serves on the editorial board of *Benefits Quarterly.* He has served as an Advisory Director of the International Foundation. Mr. Jones is a Past Chair of its Accountants Committee and is the current Chair of its Continuing Education Committee, and a member of the Educational Program Committee.

Edward A. Kaplan is a senior vice president and national health practice leader at The Segal Company's National Health Practice. He created the *Segal Health Plan Trend Cost Survey* in 1996, which is now a standard in the industry. Mr. Kaplan holds a B.A. degree in economics from Rutgers University. He is often quoted in general business and employee benefit publications on managed care issues. Mr. Kaplan is a member of several pharmacy benefit industry advisory boards.

David C. Lee heads the Employee Benefits and Labor Group at Berdon LLP in New York City. He provides a full range of accounting and consulting services to benefit funds and labor unions, and helped revise nationally accepted accounting rules for auditing funds. Mr. Lee holds a B.A. degree in accounting from Pace University and is a CPA. A frequent moderator and guest speaker at International Foundation conferences, he has served on the Accountants Committee.

Jeffrey D. Mamorsky is a partner in the international law firm of Curtis, Mallet-Prevost, Colt & Mosle in New York City. A specialist in compensation and employee benefits law, he is a published author of books on ERISA and pensions. Mr. Mamorsky is also founder and editor in chief of the *Journal of Compensation and Benefits,* editor of the *Employee Benefits Handbook* and editor of the *Health Care Benefits Handbook.* He received a J.D. degree from New York Law School and an LL.M. in taxation from New York University School of Law. Mr. Mamorsky has been a speaker at International Foundation programs.

Daniel F. McGinn is president and chief actuary of McGinn Actuaries Ltd. in Anaheim, California. He serves primarily large multiemployer benefit plans. Mr. McGinn graduated with honors from Holy Cross College. He achieved fellowship in the Society of Actuaries, for which he served on the board of governors. Mr. McGinn has been a lecturer and an author of seven books on retirement systems, five published by the International Foundation, over a period of more than 40 years. He has served as a member and Chair of the Foundation's Actuaries Committee and, later, the Actuaries/Consultants Committee.

Thomas A. Mitchell Sr., CEBS, is a founding principal and vice chair of the Marco Consulting Group in Chicago. He has served the Taft-Hartley fund community, initially as an employee benefits fund administrator, and as an investment consultant. Mr. Mitchell's undergraduate studies were at Northeastern Illinois University. He has been a frequent speaker on a broad range of topics. Mr. Mitchell has served as a member of the International Foundation's Investment Committee and has been the committee Chair. He has written extensively on investment topics.

Ira R. Mitzner is a partner in the law firm of Dickstein Shapiro Morin & Oshinsky LLP and is partner in charge of employee benefit plan litigation for multiemployer plans in a wide variety of industries. He earned his J.D. degree at Georgetown University Law Center and his B.A. degree at Brown University. Mr. Mitzner currently is an Advisory Director of the International Foundation, as he has been in the past. He is also a Foundation speaker, member of the Educational Program Committee and Chair of the Attorneys Committee.

Paul J. Ondrasik Jr. is a partner in the Washington, D.C. law firm of Steptoe & Johnson, LLP, working primarily in the employee benefit plan field, with particular emphasis on ERISA litigation and the fiduciary responsibility area. He is a graduate of Princeton University and the University of Virginia School of Law and is a charter fellow of the American College of Employee Benefits Counsel. Mr. Ondrasik is a former Advisory Director of the International Foundation and currently serves on the Government Liaison Committee, of which he is a Past Chair. He has been a frequent speaker at Foundation programs and has served on the Attorneys Committee.

Timothy J. Parsons is a founding partner of Parsons Heizer Paul LLP of Denver, Colorado, a law firm specializing in employee benefits and ERISA. Mr. Parsons is also active in the Employee Benefits Committee of the Labor and Employment Law Section of the American Bar Association, where he is currently a co-chair of the Ethics Subcommittee. Mr. Parsons is a charter fellow of the American College of Employee Benefits Counsel. He is a graduate of Bowdoin College and the Georgetown University Law Center. A frequent speaker at International Foundation programs and a published author for the Foundation and other entities, Mr. Parsons has served as a member of the Foundation's Attorneys Committee, a member and Chair of the Benefit Communications Committee and a member of the Educational Program Committee.

Kaye Pestaina is a vice president and senior health compliance specialist at The Segal Company's National Compliance Practice in Washington, D.C. She works with compliance staff and benefit consultants across the country on legal and regulatory compliance matters pertaining to the design and administration of employee health and welfare benefit plans. Formerly with the Employee Benefits Security Administration as a senior health law attorney, Ms. Pestaina graduated from Cornell University with a B.A. degree in government and received her J.D. degree from Harvard Law School. Ms. Pestaina has been a speaker for the International Foundation, at the Annual Conference and for COBRA telewebs.

Dallas L. Salisbury is president and CEO of the Employee Benefit Research Institute (EBRI) in Washington, D.C. EBRI provides objective information regarding the employee benefit system and related financial security issues. He serves as a member of the advisory committee to the comptroller general of the United States and on the GAO Advisory Group on Social Security and Retirement. Mr. Salisbury is a fellow of the National Academy of Human Resources. Prior to joining EBRI, he held positions at the U.S. Department of Justice, the Employee Benefits Security Administration and the Pension Benefit Guaranty Corporation. Mr. Salisbury holds a B.A. degree in finance from the University of Washington and an M.A. degree in public administration from the Maxwell School at Syracuse University. He has been a speaker and author for the International Foundation since 1975, and has served for several years on the Foundation's Government Liaison Committee.

Stephen M. Saxon is a principal of the Groom Law Group, Chartered of Washington, D.C. His area of expertise includes the fiduciary responsibility and prohibited transaction rules, with an emphasis on pension investment issues. Mr. Saxon heads the firm's ERISA Title I practice group. He received his J.D. degree from Georgetown University Law Center. Mr. Saxon has served on the International Foundation's Government Liaison Committee and Attorneys Committee and has been a frequent speaker at Foundation programs.

Neal S. Schelberg is a partner in the Employee Benefits and Executive Compensation Law Group of Proskauer Rose LLP. He practices exclusively in the employee benefits law area and has had extensive experience in providing legal counsel to both sponsors and plan fiduciaries of single employer and multiemployer pension and welfare funds. Mr. Schelberg previously served as an attorney in the Office of the General Counsel of the Pension Benefit Guaranty Corporation. He received a J.D. degree from Hofstra University School of Law and an LL.M. degree from the Georgetown University Law Center. Mr. Schelberg has been active in International Foundation activities for over two decades, writing numerous articles and speaking at many Foundation programs. He has Chaired the Foundation's Continuing Education Committee and has been a member of the Attorneys Committee, Arbitration Committee and Educational Program Committee.

David W. Silverman, an attorney practicing in both New York and Washington, D.C., is a partner in the law firm of Granik Silverman & Hekker of New City, New York. He received his law degree and master's of law in taxation from New York University. Mr. Silverman's practice, predominantly in employee benefits litigation, includes appointment by several federal judges as a court-appointed independent fiduciary over plans placed in litigation by the U.S. Department of Labor. He has been a Director of the International Foundation for multiple terms representing management East. Mr. Silverman has served as Chair of the Foundation's Attorneys Committee, Chair of the Constitution and By-Laws Committee, and a member of the Financial Review Committee, Educational Program Committee and the Trustees Committee. He has spoken at Foundation Annual Conferences.

Barry S. Slevin is president of the law firm of Slevin & Hart, P.C., in Washington, D.C., and specializes in employee benefit law and related litigation. He is a member of the American Bar Association Section on Labor and Employment Law Committee on Employee Benefits. Mr. Slevin is a charter fellow of the American College of Employee Benefits Counsel and has testified before Congress on employee benefit matters. He is a member of the Attorneys Committee of the International Foundation. Mr. Slevin is a frequent speaker and author for the Foundation and others.

William H. Tobin is a shareholder in the law firm of Reinhart Boerner Van Deuren s.c. in Milwaukee, Wisconsin. He advises retirement and health and welfare plan sponsors and fiduciaries on their responsibilities under ERISA and on the administration of ERISA plans. Mr. Tobin received his undergraduate degree from Middlebury College and his law degree from the Boston University School of Law.

Michael A. Van Sertima is an audit manager with Schultheis & Panettieri, LLP of New York City. He specializes in performing financial statement, operational and internal control audits of employee benefit plans and labor organizations. Mr. Van Sertima earned a bachelor of science degree in accounting from the City University of New York. He is an adjunct lecturer in accounting and auditing at the City University of New York and is a member of the American Institute of Certified Public Accountants and the New York State Society of Certified Public Accountants. Mr. Van Sertima is an International Foundation speaker and author.

Donald A. Walters is president of Benefits Corporation of America in Trumbull, Connecticut. He received his LL.B. degree from the University of Georgia School of Law. Mr. Walters has been a frequent speaker at International Foundation programs since 1970 and is a former Advisory Director of the Foundation. He is a former member of the Administrators Committee, the Actuaries/Consultants Committee and the Investment Management Committee.

Ralph M. Weinberg is a principal and consulting actuary with Milliman and is the leader of the employee benefits practice in Milliman's Chicago office. He has experience in the design, funding, communication and administration of both qualified and nonqualified retirement plans. Mr. Weinberg is a member of the American Academy of Actuaries and an enrolled actuary under ERISA. He received his B.S. degree in actuarial science from the University of Illinois-Urbana, and did postgraduate work at DePaul University. Mr. Weinberg began speaking at International Foundation programs in 1975 and served several terms as an Advisory Director of the Foundation. He is a former Chair of the Continuing Education Committee and the Actuaries/Consultants Committee. Mr. Weinberg has written numerous articles on employee benefit topics.

Wayne R. Wendling, CEBS, is the senior director of research for the International Foundation in Brookfield, Wisconsin. He has over 25 years of experience in research and operations in the benefits and insurance industry. In addition to his experience with the Foundation, Mr. Wendling has held research positions with the American Medical Association, Upjohn Institute for Employment Research and St. Paul Travelers Insurance. He also was the vice president of Integrated Benefits and Managed Care for Orion Capital Companies and Royal & SunAlliance. Mr. Wendling has earned his Ph.D. degree in economics and the certified employee benefit specialist designation from the Foundation.

Arthur L. Wilmes is a principal with the Indianapolis, Indiana office of Milliman USA. His major area of expertise is individual and group health insurance and disability income. A fellow of the Society of Actuaries and a member of the American Academy of Actuaries, Mr. Wilmes is a graduate of Ball State University. He has been a speaker at International Foundation programs.

SECTION I
INTRODUCTION

Chapter 1

History of Taft-Hartley Plans

Wayne Wendling, CEBS

Multiemployer benefit plans are maintained pursuant to a collective bargaining agreement. More than one employer must participate in the plan for it to be considered multiemployer.

INTRODUCTION

Many writers will refer to the wage stabilization period of World War II and the subsequent *Inland Steel* case as the most significant impetus for the growth of employee benefits in the United States, and particularly among that segment of the workforce in which wages, salaries and the terms and conditions of employment are determined through the collective bargaining process. However, we would be remiss if we did not search back farther into the history of unions, guilds and benevolent societies to look for the antecedents of employee benefits.

The history of employee benefits is closely tied to the history of unions, and the benevolent societies formed from the crafts and guilds or mysteries that predated current craft unions. We can point to pre-Revolutionary times to see the precursors of the "benefit plan."

> The closest thing to trade unions before the Revolution were the benevolent societies for masters, journeyman and apprentices, formed in the few leading towns. Generally their purpose was that of "assisting such of their members as should by accident be in need of support, of the widows and minor children of the members." They paid sick benefits, provided funds for indigent members, occasionally loaned money, provided "strong boxes" for savings.[1]

As the quotation indicates, the benevolent society provided a financial safety net and assisted in the capital accumulation of its members.[2]

Taft-Hartley multiemployer plans are a specific response to the needs of a subset of the United States economy. They are particularly suited to unionized workers who have made a commitment to a craft and industry, as opposed to making a commitment to a specific employer. These plans also are well-suited to those employers in those industries since the multiemployer plan fosters a trained workforce committed to the industry, with the flexibility required by employers, and helps achieve scale in administration. However, because multiemployer plans represent a subset of the economy, legislation and the pursuant regulations may not account for the specific circumstances and needs of multiemployer plans.

Multiemployer plans have developed specific provisions to accommodate the unique needs of the workforce. The hours bank, in which workers can bank hours during peak economic activities to help them maintain eligibility during downturns, is just one example of adaptations to accommodate the specific needs of their industry. Within the building and construction trades, the demands of a specific building or construction project shift from one craft or trade to the next. Excavators and painters are not likely to be on the same project at the same time. Therefore, there is a need to rotate crafts from one project to the next depending on the specific needs of the project, and by moving from one project to the next, the individual tradesman or craftsman would also move from one employer to the next—whichever had project work.

Although some covered workers that tend to participate in multiemployer plans have regular 40-hour work weeks, many covered workers tend to experience wide fluctuations in work schedules. The construction and building projects tend to be sensitive to the economic cycle and seasonal demands, and therefore, must accommodate the swings in work availability so prevalent in the building and construction industries. Hospitality

Table I

MULTIEMPLOYER DEFINED BENEFIT PLANS INSURED UNDER PBGC

Pension Benefit Guaranty Corporation Insured Multiemployer Pension Plans

Year	Total PBGC Insured Plans	Plans >10,000 Participants	% of Total
1980	2,244	120	5.3%
1985	2,188	137	6.3%
1990	1,983	140	7.1%
1995	1,879	144	7.7%
2000	1,744	152	8.7%
2001	1,707	159	9.3%
2002	1,671	163	9.8%
2003	1,623	167	10.3%

Source: Pension Benefit Guaranty Corporation, *Pension Insurance Data Book*, 2003 edition.

Table II

PERCENT OF THE PARTICIPANTS IN MULTIEMPLOYER DEFINED BENEFIT PENSION PLANS WHO ARE CLASSIFIED AS ACTIVE PARTICIPANTS

Pension Benefit Guaranty Corporation Insured Multiemployer Pension Plans

Year	% Active Participants
1980	75.9%
1985	66.1%
1990	58.6%
1995	52.4%
2000	51.1%
2001	49.5%

Source: Pension Benefit Guaranty Corporation, *Pension Insurance Data Book*, 2003 edition.

sectors may also experience swings in activity due to tourist and convention activity.

Taft-Hartley multiemployer plans always have been a small but important subset of the benefits community. This is no more evident when examining defined benefit (DB) pension plans. In 1980 there were more than 90,000 single employer DB plans and 2,244 multiemployer DB plans covered under the Pension Benefit Guaranty Corporation (PBGC) insurance program. As of the last report of PBGC, the number of single employer DB plans hovered around 30,000 whereas the number of multiemployer DB plans stood at 1,623.[3] (See Table I.) In terms of the total number of DB plans, the multiemployer community has been more resilient than single employer plans; but multiemployer plans are facing continuing challenges as the percent of active participants in multiemployer plans continues to decline as shown in Table II. In some respects, the history of Taft-Hartley plans, and particularly the DB plan, is an example of the unintended consequences of corrective regulations.

OVERVIEW OF THE BEGINNINGS OF TAFT-HARTLEY PLANS[4]

"The very existence and continuation of jointly administered fringe benefit funds relies exclusively on the collective bargaining structure and process that creates the funds and sustains them." The history of Taft-Hartley plans, therefore, really begins with a history of collective bargaining.

Although legislative attempts to sanction collective bargaining can be traced back to the 1890s, collective bargaining was not fully protected until 1935. In that year, Congress passed the Wagner Act, which gives employees the right to self-organization and to bargain collectively through their representatives. (The Wagner Act is also commonly called the National Labor Relations Act.)

Unfair labor practices by an employer—including the refusal to bargain collectively over rates of pay, wages, hours of employment or other conditions of employment—such as pensions and welfare benefits—are prohibited under the Wagner Act.[5] The National Labor Board enforces the Act's provisions.

Although the passage of the Wagner Act was undoubtedly to labor's advantage, the Act's purposes were much broader. Objectives, say historians, included social and economic justice, industrial peace and effective collective bargaining. Increased wages obtained through effective collective bargaining, it was believed, would increase the demand for American products.[6]

In the years following the Wagner Act, the number of organizational strikes decreased, union participation increased, (from four million in 1935 to 16 million in 1948) and the number of collective bargaining agreements rose.[7] The pro-labor results of the Wagner Act, however, caused many employers to feel unfairly disadvantaged vis à vis unions.

The sentiment of management over the collective bargaining protections of the Wagner Act helped propel the Act's amendment. To balance the rights the Wagner Act provided employees in negotiating wages and other conditions of employment, Congress enacted the Taft-Hartley Act of 1947 (also called the Labor-Management Relations Act). Whereas the Wagner Act had originally restricted employer unfair labor practices, the Taft-Hartley Act prohibits union unfair labor practices (such as featherbedding, refusal to bargain in good faith and the closed shop) and gives employers certain bargaining rights.

The authority for Taft-Hartley plans is submerged within the extensive text of the Taft-Hartley Act. Actually, Taft-Hartley plans were created as an exception to a general rule: Employers cannot give money or anything else of value to employee representatives (individuals or unions). Employers can, however, contribute to jointly administered labor-management trust funds (Taft-Hartley funds) for the sole and exclusive benefit of employees, their families and dependents. Employer contributions to employee benefit plans that are unilaterally administered (solely) by unions are, in contrast illegal under the Taft-Hartley Act.[8]

Joint labor-management trust funds can be established for only certain purposes (see Table III). The number of purposes has grown, from generally just health and pension benefits under the Taft-Hartley Act of 1947 to educational scholarships, child care centers, legal services and financial assistance for housing added by subsequent amendments in the later 1950s, late 1960s, early 1970 and 1990.

Table III

PURPOSES OF TAFT-HARTLEY FUNDS

Medical/ Hospital Care	Pension	Occupational Illness/Injury
Unemployment Benefits	Life Insurance	Disability/ Sickness Insurance
Accident Insurance	Pooled Vacation/ Holiday/ Severance	Educational Scholarships
Child Care Centers	Legal Services	Financial Assistance for Housing

Jointly administered trust funds are proper only if (1) payments are by a written agreement with the employer, (2) the agreement provides for employers and employees to agree upon an impartial umpire for disputes (if no neutral parties are authorized to break deadlocks), (3) employers and employees are equally represented in fund administration and (4) the trust fund is audited annually. Any person involved in a financial transaction with a joint labor-management trust fund that is not permissible under the Act could face a fine, imprisonment or both.

The Taft-Hartley Act sets up a skeletal structure within which Taft-Hartley plans operate. The wider spectrum of considerations affecting all employee benefit plans, such as fiduciary responsibility, funding, and reporting and disclosure, was not addressed at the federal level until several years later.

KEY LEGISLATION FOR MULTIEMPLOYER BENEFIT PLANS

There were legislative initiatives dating back to 1921 that impacted benefit plans, including the 1942 amendments to the Internal Revenue Code and the Federal Welfare and Pension Plans Disclosure Act of 1958. However, the two most significant legislative initiatives for multiemployer plans were the Employee Retirement Income Security Act of 1974, and subsequent amendments (ERISA) and the Multiemployer Pension Plan Amendments Act of 1980 (MPPAA). Multiemployer plans have been impacted by other legislative initiatives such as COBRA (the Consolidated Omnibus Budget Reconciliation Act) and HIPAA (Health Insurance Portability and Accountability Act); ERISA and MPPAA are the most significant because of the distinctions they created for multiemployer plans. (It is important to note that although the focus will be on ERISA's impact on pension plans, ERISA also regulates welfare plans.)

EMPLOYEE RETIREMENT INCOME SECURITY ACT OF 1974

As Wendling wrote in 1989,[9]

The Employee Retirement Income Security Act of 1974 (ERISA) is the major piece of legislation affecting the private pension system. It set in motion subsequent pieces of legislation designed to accommodate new developments or correct flaws in earlier legislation.

The chief purpose of ERISA was to protect the interests of workers and their beneficiaries. The Act was instituted to ensure that:

- Workers and employees were not required to satisfy unreasonable age and service requirements before they could be eligible to participate in an employer- or fund-sponsored pension plan
- Individuals who work for a specified minimum period while covered by a pension plan receive at least some pension at retirement through vesting, benefit accrual and break-in-service provisions
- Promises are adequately funded by establishing minimum funding standards
- Monies set aside to meet future pension promises are invested as a prudent man would invest. Plan trustees were made personally liable for breaches of fiduciary responsibility in the operation of the plan.
- Employees and their beneficiaries know their rights under the plan by requiring employers to report and disclose plan provisions
- Benefits promised through DB plans are protected in the event of plan termination by establishing plan termination insurance
- Spouses of pensioners are protected through joint and survivor provisions.

The framers of ERISA originally envisioned that the plan benefit insurance program, PBGC, for multiemployer DB plans would operate in a manner similar to single employer DB plans. However, there also was an underlying assumption that multiemployer plans were more stable and less likely to terminate than single employer plans. Consequently, there was a separate multiemployer trust fund, and the premium rate for multiemployer plans was one-half the rate of single employer plans.

As McGill et al.[10] has pointed out, PBGC was not required to insure benefits of multiemployer plans that terminated before July 1, 1978 even though multiemployer plans were required to pay premiums into PBGC the day that ERISA became effective. Congress extended the date for mandatory coverage of multiemployer plans several times into 1980 until MPPAA was enacted.

Prior to MPPAA, an employer could withdraw from a multiemployer DB pension plan without any further financial obligation so long as the plan continued for another five years. When a plan terminated, only those employers still contributing and those who had contributed during the previous five years would be responsible for the pro-rata share of the plan's unfunded liabilities. Therefore, there was an incentive to withdraw from otherwise healthy DB pension plans, which ultimately threatened the health of these plans. *(It should be noted there has been a significant legislative initiative impacting employee benefits in almost every one of the years since ERISA.)*

MULTIEMPLOYER PENSION PLAN AMENDMENTS ACT OF 1980 (MPPAA)

MPPAA was designed to correct technical aspects of ERISA and its application to multiemployer plans. One of the underlying assumptions of ERISA was that multiemployer plans were inherently less risky than single employer plans because they depended on the financial performance of a number of employers. Therefore, if the financial fortunes of one employer declined, the economic activity and employment would be assumed by other employers serving that industry or region.

According to Wendling et al.,[11] MPPAA 1980:
(a) changed the definition of multiemployer plans to include all collectively bargained plans to which more than one employer contributed; (2) redefined the insured event to be plan insolvency; (3) reduced the benefit guarantees to plan participants; (4) changed the funding standards by

Table IV

PBGC MAXIMUM GUARANTEED BENEFITS (1980-2004)

Date of Plan Insolvency	Monthly Benefit Formula	Maximum Monthly Guarantee (30 Years of Service)	Maximum Annual Guarantee (30 Years of Service)
September 27, 1980 to December 21, 2000	The participant's years of service multiplied by the sum of: (1) 100% of the first $5 of the monthly benefit accrual rate Plus (2) 75% of the next 15 of the monthly accrual rate	$487.50	$5,850
On or after December 22, 2000	The participant's years of service multiplied by the sum of: (1) 100% of the first $11 of the monthly benefit accrual rate Plus (2) 75% of the next $33 of the monthly benefit accrual	$1,072.50	$12,870

Source: Pension Benefit Guaranty Corporation, *Pension Insurance Data Book,* 2003, Table M-15.
Note, there is no cap on the applicable years of service. 30 years was selected for illustrative purposes. The new guarantee does not apply to multiemployer plans that received financial aid from PBGC between December 22, 1999 and December 21, 2000. The old, lower monthly benefit guarantee continues to apply to the participants in those plans.

means of shortening the amortization period; (5) established withdrawal liability by which the withdrawing employer would be required to pay a portion of the plan's unfunded liability; and (6) raised the plan termination insurance premium.

MPPAA changed the onus for a potential unfunded liability to the withdrawing employer since that employer would be assessed a withdrawal liability, which would be equivalent to its pro-rata share of the projected unfunded liability. Therefore, there would be a cost to exit as opposed to an incentive to exit funds. MPPAA did create a free look period for employers in which to determine whether they wanted to become part of the multiemployer arrangement and therefore potentially assume the liability of other employers.

MPPAA also adjusted the benefit plan insurance program for multiemployer DB plans. The insurable event became plan insolvency and not plan termination. Insolvency occurred when it was deemed that plan assets will not be sufficient to pay the plan benefits expected to become payable over the next three years. Only basic benefits are insured; supplemental benefits are not insured. Benefits are not guaranteed until the plan or amendment to the plan has been in place for five years. Furthermore, a plan does not need to terminate to qualify for financial assistance; it must not be able to meet its basic benefit obligations.

The level of benefits insured is described in Table IV and the premium arrangement for multiemployer DB plans is described in Table V. It is noteworthy that the insured basic benefit level for multiemployer plans did not change for 20 years. In addition, premium levels did not change from 1988.

FROM LAW AND LEGISLATION TO PRACTICE

According to McGinn, multiemployer DB plan growth has been retarded by MPPAA[12]. The withdrawal liability provision, which was designed to ensure that leaving employers did not "put" the accumulated pension liabilities on remaining employers, actually discouraged new employers from participating in such plans and resulted in the steady decline of DB plans and the growth of defined contribution (DC) pension plans. However, it is probably fair to say ERISA deterred all DB pension plan growth and MPPAA stimulated DC pension plan growth among multiemployer plans.

Table V

PBGC'S HISTORIC PREMIUM RATES—MULTIEMPLOYER PLANS

For Plan Years Beginning	Premium Rate (per participant)
September 2, 1974-April 30, 1979	$0.50
September 1, 1979-September 26, 1980	$0.50 for plan years beginning in September 1979, growing gradually to $1.00 for plan years beginning September 1, 1980, to September 26, 1980
September 27, 1980-September 26, 1984	$1.40
September 27, 1984-September 26, 1986	$1.80
September 27, 1986-September 26, 1988	$2.20
On or after September 27, 1988	$2.60

Source: Pension Benefit Guaranty Corporation, *Pension Insurance Data Book,* 2003, Table M-16.

It is questionable whether the number of multiemployer DB pension plans would have grown after 1980 given the structural shifts in the U.S. economy and the decline of union representation in the private sector that characterized the U.S. economy. It probably is fair to say ERISA and MPPAA hastened the termination of DB pension plans and the substitution of DC plans in their place.

As indicated earlier, the framework for multiemployer plan formation was established in 1947 with the Taft-Hartley legislation in conjunction with the *Inland Steel* decision establishing the right to collectively bargain over benefits. Group health plan formation surged in the early 1950s and DB pension plan formation surged in the early 1960s. However, DC pension plan formation rose significantly in the 1980s, which would be consistent with MPPAA encouraging the substitution of DC pension plans for DB pension plans.

According to a representative sample of multiemployer plans, the primary growth of multiemployer health plans occurred from 1950 to 1961 and the primary growth period of DB pension plans took place between 1955 and 1963. In contrast, the primary growth period of multiemployer DC pension plans occurred from 1970 to 1985, with the greatest share of that growth taking place from 1979 to 1985 as the impacts of both ERISA and MPPAA were being understood by plan sponsors.[13] These patterns are represented in the figure.

As shown earlier in Table I, multiemployer DB pension plans have declined steadily since 1980. Part of the reason for the decline is most likely ERISA and MPPAA since those two legislative initiatives increased the cost of maintaining DB plans and also decreased the attractiveness of those plans to contributing employers. As a result, some of these plans have been terminated and no new participants are being covered under them. In addition, the consolidation of unions and collective bargaining arrangements also has contributed to the general decline in the *number* of DB plans. As noted in Table I, the percent of DB plans with more than 10,000 participants has increased from 5% of the total to over 10% of the total between 1980 and 2003 based on PBGC data. The growth in the relative importance of the large plans is less about organic growth of the underlying unions and regions, and more about the consolidation of locals and plans.

CONCLUSION

The antecedents of today's multiemployer health and welfare plans have a rich history that extends back 250 years, if not further. It is a rich history of providing sick benefits, a financial safety net and capital accumulation opportunities for their members, and a stable workforce to help those special industries grow and succeed. It also is an industry that is instructive of the law of unintended consequences. To what extent has ERISA and MPPAA improved retirement income security for employees? That is for others to answer; but the declining percent of active participants covered under DB pension plans suggests that one form of retirement income security will not be as strong in the future as it has been.

ENDNOTES

Author's Note: This article draws very heavily from previous writings of members of the research staff of the International Foundation of Employee Benefit Plans. We attempted to provide appropriate references where possible, and apologize in advance for any oversight. One study that is not cited specifically but did provide background information was the following: Terrance Davidson, "Characteristics of Multiemployer

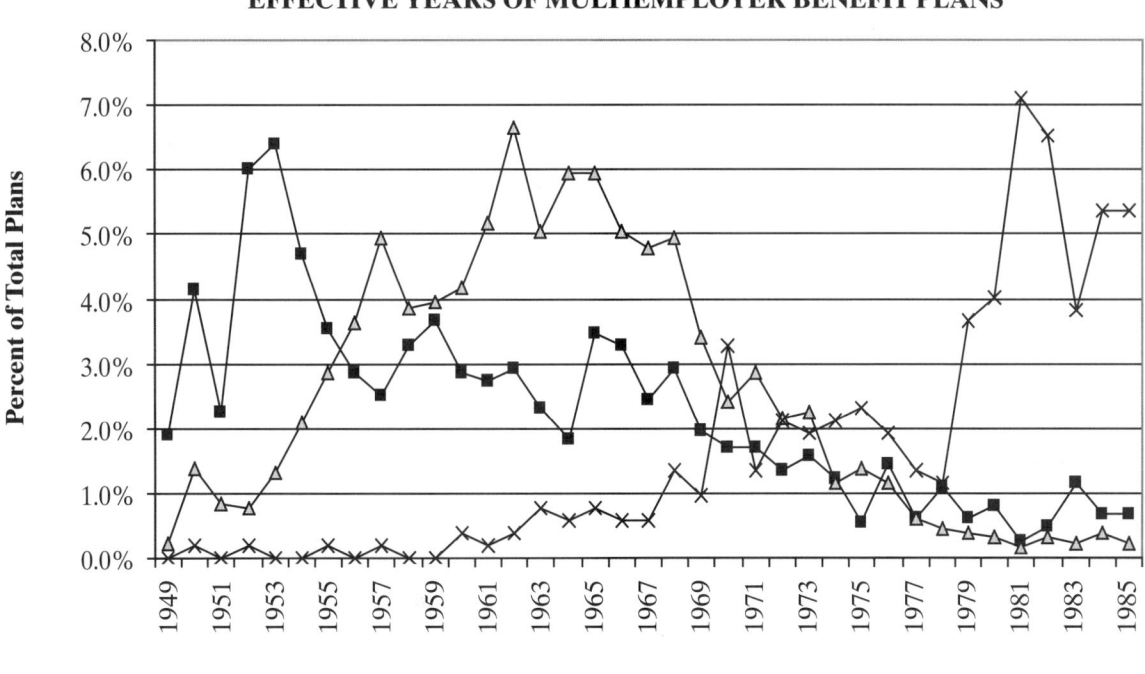

Figure

EFFECTIVE YEARS OF MULTIEMPLOYER BENEFIT PLANS

■ Health △ DB Pension ✕ DC Pension

Plans," *Basics,* Second Quarter, 1996, International Foundation of Employee Benefit Plans.

1. Philip S. Foner, *History of the Labor Movement in the United States: From Colonial Times to the Founding of the American Federation of Labor, Volume 1* (New York: New World Paperbacks, 1947, 26-27).

2. One group referenced providing these support services is the Benevolent Society of House Painters of New York. Philip S. Foner, *History of the Labor Movement in the United States: From Colonial Times to the Founding of the American Federation of Labor, Volume 1* (New York: New World Paperbacks, 1947, 26-27).

3. Pension Benefit Guaranty Corporation, *Pension Insurance Data Book,* 2003 Edition.

4. This section is taken from: Cynthia J. Drinkwater, "History of Taft-Hartley Plans, *Trustees Handbook: A Basic Text on Labor-Management Employee Benefit Plans,* Fifth Edition, Edited by Marc Gertner, International Foundation of Employee Benefit Plans, 1998.

5. Robert H. Boh, "Cooperative Action in the Construction Industry," *Employee Benefit Issues: The Multiemployer Perspective,* 1987 (Brookfield, WI: International Foundation of Employee Benefit Plans, 1988, 283).

6. The terms wages and other conditions of employment did not automatically include pension and welfare benefits. It was not until 1949, when the Supreme Court denied certiori in the landmark case of *Inland Steel Co. v. NLRB,* that pension plans became a mandatory subject of bargaining to include welfare plans, profit-sharing plans and stock purchase plans.

7. Benjamin J. Taylor and Fred Whitney, *Labor Relations Law,* 5th Ed. (Englewood Cliffs, NJ, Prentice-Hall, Inc., 1987), 163, 195.

8. Ibid., 194.

9. Wayne Wendling, "Overview," in *Employee Benefits Today: Concepts and Methods,* Claude Kordus, Editor (Brookfield, WI: International Foundation of Employee Benefit Plans, 1989, 9).

10. Dan M. McGill, Kyle N. Brown, John J. Haley and Sylvester J. Schieber, *Fundamentals of Private Pensions,* Seventh Edition, (Philadelphia, PA: University of Pennsylvania Press, 1996, 770-772).

11. Wayne Wendling, Connie Ann Crabb-Velez and Melody A. Carlsen, *The Regulatory Impact on Pensions* (Brookfield, WI: International Foundation of Employee Benefit Plans, 1986, 9, 10).

12. Daniel F. McGinn, *Multiemployer Retirement Plans: Handbook for the 21st Century* (Brookfield, WI: International Foundation of Employee Benefit Plans, 2004, xiv).

13. The International Foundation maintains a representative database of multiemployer plans. It does not contain data on all such plans nor is the data base a true random sample; but is generally representative of the industry.

Chapter 2

Basic Concepts of Trusteeship

Marc Gertner

In the third edition of the *Trustees Handbook,* the author, Claude L. Kordus, established a logical and understandable format for the book. The initial chapter dealt with "Basic Concepts." Thus, Mr. Kordus set forth a methodology to assist trustees in establishing their fiduciary priorities. In the fourth edition and again in the fifth edition, we found this organization and approach to be logical and we continued to follow it. In the preparation of this sixth edition of the *Trustees Handbook,* we looked at several different organizational approaches and plans. However, after study, we have concluded to continue the approach used by Mr. Kordus. In the first three chapters you will find the bare-bones basics and background for your role as a trustee and named fiduciary of your employee benefit plan(s) that are subject to the Employee Retirement Income Security Act of 1974 (ERISA) as amended. What follows in the next 48 chapters are the detailed and specific, substantive aspects of your role as a trustee and named fiduciary written by 35 different leaders of the Taft-Hartley industry, all experts of great renown in their respective fields. No other single work brings together such a wealth of knowledge, experience and expertise.

A threshold problem facing any new trustee is that there is no logical starting point. Once a person becomes a trustee, he or she becomes a named fiduciary charged by law with acting solely in the interest of plan participants and their beneficiaries. This includes a duty to maximize participants' benefits and defray the reasonable and necessary expenses of the plan. In addition, as a prudent plan fiduciary, that person must act in accordance with the plan documents.

We have had new trustees who have become so overwhelmed by their first trustees meeting that they wanted to resign immediately. They have had to review the annual actuarial report, reaffirm the actuarial assumptions and determine whether it was, in fact, prudent and proper to increase benefits and, if so, for whom and in what amount. They have had to meet with the plan's investment manager and analyze the manager's performance vis-à-vis the plan's investment objectives. They have had to hear claims and appeals on denials of welfare benefit applications before they fully comprehend the benefits provided by the plan.

Mindful of these and myriad other legal, accounting, actuarial, investment, administrative and practical issues that will come before the trustees, it is the purpose of this handbook to give the new trustee in this chapter a sense of the basic terms and concepts of Taft-Hartley employee benefit plans. The remaining chapters will be devoted to specific and substantive aspects of these plans.

LEGAL ASPECTS OF TRUSTEESHIP

One of the first lessons a new trustee learns is that much of what he or she can do, may do and cannot do is governed more by legal parameters to trustee conduct than by labor or management objectives, wants and needs of the plan participants, or the preferences of the trustees. Many trustees resent this. They argue, and with great logic, that they, the equal number of labor and management representatives, are the named fiduciaries and thereby are the only individuals charged by federal law and the plan documents to see to the administration of the plan. They argue, often with great emotion, that the plan participants are their members/employees and that they should have the discretion to design the plan and its benefits without the omnipresent pressure of the legal constraints on plan design and implementation.

By way of explanation, if not justification for the trustees' concerns, employee benefit plans are big business. In the private sector generally there are estimated to be in excess of 700,000 private pension plans and even more welfare plans that provide important benefits to millions of members/employees and their dependents.

In the total private sector, more than 79 million Americans participate in private pension plans and over 200 million Americans are covered by health and welfare plans.

The estimated value of assets of Taft-Hartley pension plans is over $500 million and growing. When we add the participation and assets of single employer, private sector and public plans, we are talking about the majority of the workforce in the country and over $7 trillion.

The assets of employee pension benefit plans represent the largest pool of private capital in the free world today. While history shows a small number of abuses in these plans, the impact of this small number is of a Draconian nature. Unfortunately, Congress has reacted to the substantial dollars involved and the egregiousness of the small number of abuses by creating a complex and comprehensive legal structure for the establishment, design and operation of pension and welfare plans.

The legal aspects of fiduciary responsibility in connection with investments, collections and other aspects will be considered in subsequent chapters. This chapter is directed to a discussion of general legal parameters.

THE TAFT-HARTLEY ACT

Any discussion of the organization of jointly trusted employee benefit plans inevitably starts with a discussion of the Labor-Management Relations Act of 1947, also known as the Taft-Hartley Act in honor of the two legislators who cosponsored this comprehensive labor reform bill. In fact, because all labor-management trust funds must be organized to comply with the Taft-Hartley Act, the shorthand name given to collectively bargained, multiemployer, jointly trusteed, labor-management plans is *Taft-Hartley plans.*

Section 302(a) of the act provides that no money or other thing of value shall pass from management to labor. On its face, this would appear to preclude an employer from making contributions required by a collective bargaining agreement to a pension, welfare or other fringe benefit plan. However, Section 302(c) of the Taft-Hartley Act provides the exception to the general prohibition of Section 302(a) and allows these payments if certain enumerated conditions are met, to wit:
1. Employers and employees must be equally represented in the administration of the plan.
2. The basis on which payments are to be made into the fund must be detailed in a written agreement.
3. There must be an annual audit of the income and assets of the plan.
4. There must be a procedure for selecting an impartial umpire to resolve any deadlock disputes that can result from the equal employer and union representation, or the district court of the United States for the district where the fund has its principal office must be given the power to appoint such an impartial umpire.
5. The plan must be operated for the sole and exclusive benefit of covered employees and their families.
6. Payments into the fund must be used for certain specified types of benefit programs.

In the event a plan does not meet these specific requirements of Section 302(c) of the Taft-Hartley Act, a structural violation is deemed to exist. The Taft-Hartley Act contains both civil and criminal sanctions.

In the more than 50 years since the enactment of the Labor-Management Relations Act of 1947, each of these provisions has been subject to judicial interpretation and amplification. For example, although the Taft-Hartley Act requires equal representation of labor and management in the administration of the plan, this has been construed to mean equal voting power rather than an equal number of trustees persons. There are some plans that have an uneven number of trustees by design and at a trustees' meeting frequently one side or the other has a trustee not present, even though a sufficient "number" is present to constitute a quorum. In such situations, the first requirement of Section 302(c) of the Taft-Hartley Act is met in that labor and management have equal voting power.

The requirement of a written agreement has been judicially construed to mean that there must exist between labor and management a collective bargaining agreement or its equivalent. In the landmark case of *Moglia v. Geoghegan,* 403 F.2d 110 (2d Cir. 1968), an employer had contributed to an employee pension benefit plan on behalf of Mr. Moglia for several decades. When Mr. Moglia expired, his widow applied to the plan for his pension. The trustees denied the benefit on the basis that Mr. Moglia's employer had never signed a collective bargaining agreement with the local union, even though it was admitted that the employer had throughout the years faithfully complied with all the terms of the bargaining agreements. The district court denied (and the court of appeals affirmed the denial) the application of Mrs. Moglia for benefits because of the violation of Section 302(c)(2) of the Taft-Hartley Act. The employer did not have a detailed writing setting forth the basis of payments into the plan; i.e., there was no collective bargaining agreement. This precedent has been affirmed in subsequent decisions.

This precedent is also of great significance when

plans desire to include and provide benefits to employees of the union, the employer association and/or the trustees. A participation agreement must be entered into between the trustees and the union or the employer association to afford the required written agreement.

The requirement of the Taft-Hartley Act for an annual audit has been supplemented by the provisions of ERISA but still is an important aspect of the protection. So, too, is a variety of techniques and methods to break deadlocks, such as the utilization of a permanent, standing, impartial umpire.

An important provision of Section 302(c) of the Taft-Hartley Act is the requirement that the plan be operated for the sole and exclusive benefit of the employees/plan participants and their families and dependents. This is a harbinger of the requirements of Section 404(a) of ERISA and provides an important guidepost to trustees in the performance of their fiduciary duties. It is, on its face, illegal conduct if action is taken because it is in the best interest of a union or employer association, the trustees or anyone other than the plan's participants and their beneficiaries.

This point was forcefully made in an opinion by Judge Gesell of the United States District Court for the District of Columbia in a landmark pre-ERISA case, *Blankenship v. Boyle*. In that case, there was a legal challenge by dissident union members to the conduct of the president of the International Mine Workers Union and the sole union trustee of its plan, who (1) deposited plan funds in a union-owned bank in a noninterest-bearing account to improve the operating income of that bank; (2) refused to pay claims to those eligible for benefits if their employers were delinquent, in an attempt to compel prompt and regular payment of employer contributions; (3) provided claim forms that implied union membership was required for benefits to be paid, in an effort to aid the union's organization efforts; (4) invested plan assets in stocks of utilities and then used the stock position to attempt to force organization and/or use of union-mined coal; and (5) increased pension benefits without adequate study to enhance his union political position. The court, in its opinion, 337 F.Supp. 296 (D.C.D.C. 1972) and 329 F.Supp. 1089 (D.C. D.C. 1971), ruled that the duty owed by the trustees of the plan was to the plan participants and their beneficiaries, not to the union or current union members. This concept has been amplified under ERISA and is at the core of the debates regarding employment generating investments.

This may be a difficult concept for some new trustees to grasp. They have been imbued with the concept that any activity that benefits the union or the association, which expands the scope of the industry—creating more jobs and more work—is valid. They see the billions of dollars of assets in the Taft-Hartley pension and welfare plans as means to these ends.

As sympathetic as one is to this approach, the provisions of both the Taft-Hartley Act and ERISA are clear: The named fiduciaries of employee benefit plans must exercise their duties "solely in the interests of the plan participants and their beneficiaries." Any compromise of this absolute standard of duty is a legal violation and erodes the underpinning of those entities that provide the retirement income and medical benefits for the members.

INTERNAL REVENUE CODE

A common denominator of all employee benefit plans subject to the Taft-Hartley Act and ERISA is that their trusts are tax exempt. In the case of a pension plan, this means that the plan has been determined to meet the requirements of Internal Revenue Code (IRC) Sections 401, *et seq.*, and the attendant trust is exempt under the provisions of IRC Section 501(a). In the case of a welfare plan, it means that the plan and its attendant trust have met the requirements of IRC Section 501(c)(9) and the regulations thereunder. There are other specific subsections under IRC Section 501 for apprenticeship, vacation and other plans.

The importance of establishing and maintaining this tax-exempt status cannot be minimized. The tax-favored position means that:

1. The employer is entitled to deduct its contributions to the plans.
2. Employees have no current income tax consequence on the contributions made to the plans on their behalf.
3. The earnings of the trust are tax exempt.

If a trust were to lose its tax-exempt status, it would constitute a per se breach of fiduciary duties by the trustees. It would undoubtedly cause a termination of the plan or, at the least, a significant diminishment in the value of the benefits that could be provided due to the requisite payment of federal taxes on the earnings of the plan. Thus, trustees must be mindful of the requirements of the IRC and the regulations thereunder to maintain this tax-exempt status. These requirements relate to who may or may not participate, when and under what conditions, the amount of and the funding of benefits, expenses of operation and administration, etc. In many ways, the IRC provisions parallel the provisions of ERISA and certain other federal statutes, but they have generally been construed to be separate and apart from the requirements of other federal statutes and are to be met in addition to those other provisions.

EMPLOYEE RETIREMENT INCOME SECURITY ACT OF 1974

On September 2, 1974 President Gerald R. Ford signed into law the Employee Retirement Income Security Act of 1974 (ERISA). This ended more than ten years of legislative study and consideration of the regulation and control of employee benefits. As a sidelight, the first "employee benefits bill" introduced in Congress by Senator Jacob Javits, then the junior senator from New York, dealt with portability of pension benefits—the ability of an employee who left one employer before being fully vested in a retirement benefit to take the money with him or her to the new employer to be used toward qualification for a pension through the plan of the new employer. One of the few, but very few, provisions that did not find its way into ERISA was portability of pension benefits.

Notwithstanding the fact that the news media in 1974 coined the phrase "national pension plan," ERISA governs not only employee pension benefit plans but also employee "welfare benefit plans." The term *welfare benefit plans* includes all hospital, medical, surgical, dental, life insurance, death benefits and related health and welfare benefits, as well as vacation, holiday, apprenticeship and related plans.

At the time of its enactment, a spokesman for the U.S. Chamber of Commerce said, "Never before in the history of socio-economic legislation have so few done so much for so many with such little regard for the near-term costs and long-term consequences." Within months of enactment, substantially everyone involved in the employee benefits industry agreed.

Now, more than 30 years later, most commentators believe this was a gross understatement. No other congressional enactment, no other court decision, and nothing in the history of employee benefits has rivaled the impact ERISA has had on the design, delivery, funding or administration of employee benefits.

Since ERISA was signed into law in 1974, it has undergone significant overhaul in all of the major tax legislation and legislation dealing with discrimination. Not only have participants' rights been continuously modified, but employers' obligations and limitations in terms of funding, deductibility of contributions and other related employer concerns have been affected. Primarily through the administrative and judicial systems, fiduciary obligations and actions that constitute prohibited transactions have been interpreted and, in many instances, expanded.

The following is, however, a brief outline of the major requirements of ERISA and the IRC that must be satisfied by any qualified plan, including multiemployer plans. These rules cannot be avoided by negotiation between unions and employers. It is intended to provide only a preview of the areas with which trustees must be concerned as the plan is interpreted.

Minimum Participation

- A plan cannot have a minimum participation age older than 21.
- A plan may require two years of service for participation if employer contributions are immediately 100% vested. If that vesting requirement is not satisfied, the plan can require only one year of service for participation.
- A cash or deferred plan must allow a participant to make deferrals after one year of service.

Maximum Age

- Employees may not be excluded from participation because of age under either a defined contribution plan or a defined benefit plan.

Minimum Vesting Schedules for Employer Contributions

- 100% vesting after no more than five years of service.
- Graduated seven-year vesting—20% after three years of service, with 20% per year additional vesting thereafter until 100% vesting is achieved after seven years of service.

Vesting of Participant Contributions

- A participant's rights to the accrued benefit derived from his or her own contributions must always be 100% vested. In defined contribution plans, a participant must be 100% vested in his or her own contributions plus earnings and gains in his or her account. In defined benefit plans, a participant is entitled to (1) his or her mandatory contributions, (2) interest calculated using the plan rate before the effective date of the new vesting rules imposed by the Tax Reform Act of 1986, and (3) interest calculated using the rate mandated by IRC Section 411(c)(2)(C)(iii) thereafter to the normal retirement age.

Year of Service/Hour of Service

- A 12-month period during which an employee completes at least 1,000 hours of service or an equivalent. Counted are hours for which an employee is (1) paid for performance of duties, (2) paid or entitled to payment but during which no duties are performed (such as vacation, holiday, illness, incapacity, jury duty, etc.) and (3) entitled to back pay.
- Equivalencies are described in Department of Labor regulations and are generally based on working time, periods of employment or earnings.
- Hours of service must be credited for certain maternity and paternity leaves but only for purposes of determining whether a break in service has occurred for participation and vesting purposes. These rules apply to an individual who is absent from

work (1) by reason of the individual's pregnancy, (2) by reason of the birth of a child of the individual, (3) by reason of the placement of a child in connection with the adoption of the child by the individual or (4) for purposes of caring for the child during the period immediately following the birth or placement for adoption.

Method of Benefit Payments

- A pension plan must provide a qualified joint and survivor annuity to a vested participant who retires or terminates from the plan and a qualified preretirement survivor annuity to the surviving spouse of a participant who dies before the annuity starting date.
- The plan may allow a participant to waive the qualified joint and survivor annuity form of benefit or the qualified preretirement survivor annuity form (or both) if the consent to the waiver is obtained from the participant's spouse. The waiver must meet the statutory requirements set forth in ERISA and the IRC.
- A qualified joint and survivor annuity is an annuity for the life of the participant with a survivor annuity for the life of the spouse that is at least 50% of the amount of the annuity that is payable during the joint lives of the participant and the spouse and that is the actuarial equivalent of an annuity for the life of the participant. A qualified preretirement survivor annuity is a survivor annuity for the life of the surviving spouse that is at least equal to the payment that would have been made under a qualified joint and survivor annuity if (1) in the case of a participant who dies after attaining the earliest retirement age under the plan, the participant had retired with an immediate qualified joint and survivor annuity on the day before his or her death or (2) in the case of a participant who dies on or before the date on which he or she would have attained the earliest retirement age, he or she had (a) separated from service on the date of death, (b) survived to the earliest retirement age, (c) retired with an immediate qualified joint and survivor annuity at the earliest retirement age and (d) died on the day after the day on which he or she would have attained the earliest retirement age.
- The plan may be drafted to require that the participant and the spouse have been married throughout the one-year period ending on the earlier of the participant's annuity starting date or the date of the participant's death.

Withdrawals From Multiemployer Plans

- If an employer withdraws from a multiemployer plan in either a complete or partial withdrawal, the employer will be liable to the plan for what is determined to be its withdrawal liability. The withdrawal liability of an employer is the employer's allocable amount of unfunded vested benefits adjusted by several factors, one of which is the *de minimis* rule, if any, adopted by the plan.
- A complete withdrawal occurs when an employer permanently ceases to have an obligation to contribute under the plan or permanently ceases all covered operations under the plan, with an exception contained in ERISA for work performed in the building and construction industry and for work performed in the entertainment industry.
- A partial withdrawal occurs on the last day of the plan year if there is a 70% contribution decline or there is a partial cessation of the employer's contribution obligation.
- A complete or partial withdrawal will not necessarily occur as the result of a bona fide, arm's-length sale of assets to an unrelated party if certain conditions are met:
  1. The purchaser has an obligation to contribute to the plan with respect to the operations for substantially the same number of contribution base units for which the seller had an obligation to contribute to the plan.
  2. The purchaser provides to the plan, for a period of five plan years commencing with the first plan year beginning after the sale of assets, a bond issued by a corporate surety company that is an acceptable surety for purposes of ERISA or an amount is held in escrow by a bank or similar financial institution satisfactory to the plan in an amount prescribed by ERISA.
  3. The contract for sale provides that if the purchaser withdraws in a complete or a partial withdrawal during the first five plan years, the seller is secondarily liable for any withdrawal liability it would have had to the plan with respect to the operations if the liability of the purchaser with respect to the plan is not paid. Failure to include language in the contract for sale automatically causes a withdrawal to have occurred if one would otherwise have occurred and withdrawal liability, if any, to be assessed.

Notice and Collection of Withdrawal Liability

- ERISA obligates an employer to respond to plan trustees' requests for such information as the trustees reasonably determine to be necessary to enable them to comply with the withdrawal liability provisions of ERISA.
- After the trustees have determined that a complete

or partial withdrawal has occurred, the trustees have an obligation to notify the employer of the amount of the liability, to specify a schedule for liability payment and to demand payment in accordance with that schedule.
- Contributing employers are given 90 days to request a review of the determination of the withdrawal liability and the schedule of payments and to identify inaccuracies.
- The plan trustees are obligated to review the matter and notify the employer of their decision, the basis for the decision and the reason for any change in the determination of the employer's liability or schedule of liability payments.

FIDUCIARY RESPONSIBILITIES

Fiduciaries

ERISA provides that each employee benefit plan shall, in its basic plan document, identify the named fiduciaries. These are the persons who are charged with the legal responsibility for the operation and administration of the plan. They are the "Harry S Trumans" of the plan, the persons with whom "the buck stops." In the context of Taft-Hartley pension and welfare plans, the equal number of labor and management representatives appointed by their respective bodies are the named fiduciaries of the plan.

ERISA also provides for other fiduciaries, sometimes referred to as *general fiduciaries*. These are defined as persons who possess or exercise any discretionary authority, control or responsibility in the management or administration of the plan, possess or exercise any authority or control in the management of plan assets, or have or exercise any discretionary authority or responsibility in the administration of the plan. This clearly encompasses investment managers; administrative managers and actuaries in many instances and in certain factual circumstances; and legal counsel to plans in certain instances.

Congress, in its wisdom, did not attempt to define fiduciary status by title but, rather, by the possession or exercise of authority vis-à-vis the plan (ERISA Sections 3(21)(A) and 402(a)). The Department of Labor has continued and expanded this approach. Thus, in *Donovan v. Williams,* 4 EBC 1237 (N.D. Ohio 1983), the union president, who was not a trustee and who had no documented role or responsibility in the operation or administration of the plan, was held by the U.S. District Court for the Northern District of Ohio, Eastern Division to be a fiduciary when he exercised control over the plan by directing the union trustees as to how to vote on matters before the joint board of trustees.

An essential duty of a trustee is to know who the fiduciaries of the plan are.

Parties in Interest

ERISA also creates a category of persons known as *parties in interest*. This includes all fiduciaries, service providers, the employer of employees who participate in the plan, the union whose employees participate in the plan, and certain officers, directors, shareholders and relatives of these persons and entities. ERISA's goal is to identify persons with a collateral relationship to the plan and its assets and to regulate in a limited degree their conduct vis-à-vis the plan and its assets.

General Fiduciary Duties

Jeffrey Clayton, former administrator of the Pension and Welfare Benefits Administration of the U.S. Department of Labor, speaking at the International Foundation's Annual Conference in New Orleans in November, 1983, stated that Part 4, Fiduciary Responsibility, was the most important section of ERISA and that the general fiduciary responsibilities set forth in Section 404(a) are the essential provisions of Part 4. As one can never sing the National Anthem, repeat the Lord's Prayer or salute the flag too often, a trustee of an employee benefit plan subject to ERISA can never read, reread, consider or discuss the general fiduciary duties in Section 404(a) of ERISA too often.

"Solely in the Interest"

The first of these general duties is to operate and administer the plan "solely in the interest of the plan participants and their beneficiaries." As was noted in the discussion of Section 302(c) of Taft-Hartley, this is the primary duty and responsibility of a fiduciary. This is the first commandment of plan trustees and a charge for which there is no exception or exclusion.

"To Maximize Benefits and Minimize Expenses"

As a corollary to the trustee's primary duty to act solely in the interests of plan participants, the trustee must do so for the purpose of maximizing benefits and defraying the reasonable cost of necessary expenses of the plan. This portion of ERISA Section 404(a) has two facets. First, in the discharge of their duties, the trustees must maximize benefits. This has had particular relevance in the several deadlocks and lawsuits involving benefit improvements to defined benefit pension plans that may have a correlative, negative impact on employer withdrawal liability. The result is predictable if one is knowledgeable of his or her fiduciary duties.

The second facet of ERISA Section 404(a)(1)(A) is that the trustees have a duty to minimize the necessary expenses of administration. The Department of Labor, in its enforcement of ERISA, has been particularly stringent in its examination and enforcement of this sanction, challenging fees to service providers, trustees' expenses for administration and so on.

"As an ERISA Prudent Man"

There has existed for several centuries in the common law of trusts the concept of *the prudent man*. The prudent man rule as adopted in ERISA Section 404(a)(1)(B) is not the common law prudent man rule for trustees generally. Rather, it is a rule designed to apply to fiduciaries of employee benefit plans rather than of personal trusts or charitable trusts. It requires that trustees act with the care, skill, prudence and diligence under the circumstances then prevailing that a prudent man acting in a like capacity (i.e., another trustee) and familiar with such matters (i.e., a knowledgeable fiduciary) would use in the conduct of an enterprise of like character and with like aims (i.e., a Taft-Hartley pension or welfare plan of comparable size, funding, etc.).

In conjunction with the "solely in the interest" test, the ERISA prudent man rule is the basis for substantially all litigation enforcement by the Department of Labor and by private persons. Unfortunately, the courts are increasingly interpreting and enforcing the prudent man rule as a prudent expert rule.

"By Diversifying Investments"

Somewhat surprisingly, Congress saw fit to specify diversification to avoid the risk of large losses as a specific general fiduciary duty as opposed to leaving it as a part of the prudent man rule. However, the subsequent litigation involving plan fiduciaries' investing 40-98% of their plan's assets in a single investment (or form or geographic area of investments) demonstrates the wisdom of the congressional intent. This is the common sense concept learned as children that you do not put all of your eggs in one basket. It is of particular importance to trustees in carrying out their duty to invest millions of dollars of plan assets to provide pensions and welfare benefits to their union brothers/employees/plan participants.

"In Accordance With Plan Documents"

The last of the five basic commandments of general fiduciary duty is that the trustees operate and administer the plan in accordance with plan documents, as long as those plan documents are in accordance with the law. This requires the trustees to have an intimate working knowledge of the terms, conditions and provisions of their plans, both pension and welfare, and to strictly operate and administer the plans in accordance therewith, provided those provisions are lawful.

DELEGATION OF FIDUCIARY RESPONSIBILITIES

Congress, in its wisdom, elaborated on a mechanism whereby named fiduciaries—the labor and management trustees of Taft-Hartley plans—could allocate or delegate a portion of their fiduciary responsibilities. By definition, trustees of plans are named fiduciaries of these plans. However, in actuality, the role of a labor or management trustee of a Taft-Hartley plan is, at best, avocational, on a part-time basis, without compensation.

When one begins to contemplate the duties of a trustee of an employee benefit plan in the 21st century, it is clear that there is an essential need for administrative managers, accountants, actuaries, lawyers, consultants, investment managers and other advisors to help operate and administer the plan—to shoulder certain of the responsibilities. The law provides that to the extent the plan documents allow for allocation or delegation of fiduciary duties, the trustees may do so and, so long as they do not violate certain minimum standards, they shall not be liable for the conduct of their delegatees.

The most important of the delegation provisions is with regard to an investment manager. It is clearly an awesome responsibility for a plumber, a transport company owner, a meatcutter or a general contractor to be responsible for the investment of millions of dollars of assets in stocks, bonds, guaranteed investment contracts, money market funds, etc. Prior to the enactment of ERISA, it was clear that trustees could engage investment advisors to assist them. What was not clear, however, was whether to the extent the layman trustee followed the advice of the professional investment advisor the trustee was immune from fiscal responsibility for any investment losses.

Under ERISA this is made clear. Again, to the extent the plan documents allow it, the named fiduciaries (that is, the Taft-Hartley trustees) may appoint an investment manager to manage the assets of the plan. The term *investment manager* is a term of art defined in ERISA and limited to certain specific individuals and entities who have certain qualifications and do certain acts. To the extent the trustees prudently select an investment manager, prudently establish investment guidelines for said manager, and prudently monitor the performance of the advisor, the laymen trustees are not liable for any investment losses. It is this provision that enables many laymen to serve as named fiduciaries of their plans, particularly multimillion dollar pension plans, with a feeling of security.

PROHIBITED TRANSACTIONS

Based on a few sordid incidents in history of Taft-Hartley pension plans prior to the enactment of ERISA, Congress adopted certain stringent provisions in ERISA Sections 406(a) and (b) prohibiting the plan or its fiduciaries from involvement in any categories of transactions that were defined and then identified as *prohibited transactions*.

ERISA Section 406(a) prohibits the plan from entering into certain types of transactions with parties in interest, including purchases or sales of property, contracts for goods and services, lending of money, etc. ERISA Sections 408(b) and (c) contain certain statutory exemptions to these prohibitions, and ERISA Section 408(a) allows a plan to obtain a specific administrative exemption as to a set of facts that without the exemption would constitute a prohibited transaction.

ERISA Section 406(b) deals with fiduciaries and prohibits them from any conduct that would amount to a self-dealing with the assets of the plan in the fiduciary's own interest or for his or her own account; or to serving in any capacity in a transaction where the fiduciary's interest could be adverse to the interests of the plan or its participants; or from receiving any consideration for his or her own account from any party dealing with such plans in connection with a transaction involving the assets of the plan. These are provisions that require a trustee—a fiduciary under ERISA—to observe the highest standards of care in his or her conduct as a trustee vis-à-vis plan assets.

TRUSTEE FIDUCIARY LIABILITY INSURANCE

ERISA also clarified that it is not improper for a plan to purchase trustee fiduciary liability insurance and to pay the premium on the basic policy with plan assets. The law requires that the contract of insurance provide for a right of recourse; i.e., if there has been a breach of fiduciary duty, there must be the right to sue the individual trustee or trustees responsible for the breach; but the insurance industry has designed policies and/or riders that cover the individual trustee for such recourse actions. The premium for a recourse policy, rider or endorsement cannot be paid with plan assets, but must be paid for directly by the trustee or the party appointing him or her. The premium is usually very modest.

At the same time, Congress mandated that exculpatory agreements (that is, contracts or provisions that hold that if a trustee acts in good faith, he or she shall not be liable for any errors) were illegal and unenforceable as against public policy.

REPORTING AND DISCLOSURE

More than ten years before the enactment of ERISA, Congress enacted the Welfare and Pension Plans Disclosure Act, which required a high degree of reporting and disclosure by plan fiduciaries to plan participants and the government. Many of these provisions were included and expanded in Part 1 of ERISA. The logic is that by telling plan participants everything there is to know about the plan, the plan participants will help police the operation and administration of the plan.

ERISA also sets forth a comprehensive scheme of documents and information that plan fiduciaries must report to the Department of Labor, the Internal Revenue Service and/or the Pension Benefit Guaranty Corporation.

DECISION MAKING ASPECTS OF TRUSTEESHIP

The discussion above is directed to the legal constraints that establish the parameters for trustee decision making. Within the broad range created by the legal parameters, there is the opportunity for the trustees to make a myriad of decisions. Thus, the serious trustee must be concerned not only with making legally supportable decisions but also with making decisions that are prudent and proper and in the best interests of the plan participants and their families.

How can one judge whether the best decision was made? A starting point would be to enumerate the basic tenets of the general fiduciary duties of ERISA and to test or measure each potential or actual decision against those criteria:

1. Was the decision solely in the interests of the plan participants and their beneficiaries or was it done to advance the interests of the union or of management or of an individual trustee?
2. Did the decision tend to maximize the benefits to the plan participants and minimize the reasonable and necessary expenses of administration?
3. Was the decision one that trustees of other comparably sized plans would make for their trusts?
4. Was the decision consistent with the plan documents?

With those tests, there are other more specific questions to be asked with regard to any decision making situation:

1. Does the decision lead to the best cost/benefit relationship?
2. Are the participants' needs best served?
3. Is the long-term solvency of the plan protected?
4. Are the current and potential economic fluctuations of the industry and geographical area recognized and provided for?
5. Will participants understand the benefit structures that result from the decisions made?
6. Is the decision made of the highest ethical quality so that full disclosure of the results can be made?
7. Does the decision lead to administrative procedures that insure a prompt response to participant problems?

As a new trustee will learn within months after being seated, he or she is, in effect, a member of the board of directors of a good-sized insurance company, taking in "premiums" in the form of employer and/or employee contributions, paying the costs of operation, and then returning these monies to the plan participants in the form of benefits. As businesses do not run themselves but need to be "managed" by their officers and directors, so too do employee benefit plans subject to ERISA not run themselves but need to be "managed" by the joint board of trustees.

A question we, as plan counsel, are frequently asked by new trustees, and one this book attempts to address, is: How do I, a plumber or a meatcutter, an electrical contractor or a timber operator, know how to run a major insurance-type business? Perhaps, when seated, you do not. However, in working with co-trustees, in utilizing your service providers, in reading, understanding and attempting to implement the lessons of this handbook, thousands of trustees like yourself will do so in the same successful manner as have trustees for the past 30+ years.

There are certain elements of effective decision making by trustees. We will attempt to touch on some of these.

CONCERN FOR OBJECTIVES

A principle that seems to be widely accepted is that the best decisions start with a clear-cut understanding of the objectives that the decision makers have for the activity with which they are dealing. These objectives are discussed in the subsequent substantive chapters. To illustrate the point, however, a few of them are noted here.

In the design of welfare benefits:
1. Where should the emphasis be placed when spending available dollars? Should you provide those benefits that most plan participants will utilize (prescription drugs, physical examinations, office visits) or those benefits that cost the most (orthodontics, organ transplants)? Do you spend your finite funds on the younger member (maternity and dependent coverage) or the older member (life insurance, Medicare wraparound)? Do you stress the basic, core benefits (i.e., hospital, medical, surgical) or do you include the collateral coverages (dental, eye care, psychiatric and substance abuse)?
2. Should spouses and dependents receive the same medical benefits as workers?
3. Should greater concern be shown for active or retired participants?
4. Should in-hospital or out-of-hospital benefits be emphasized?
5. Should catastrophic protection or "something for everyone" be emphasized?
6. Should full-time workers receive more benefits than part-time workers?
7. Should benefit design attempt to aid in the best structuring possible of the medical delivery system?

In the design of pension benefits:
1. When should participants be able to retire with full benefits?
2. Should a retired person drawing a pension be allowed to work and receive a paycheck also? Work full time? Work part time? Work only when the demand exists?
3. At what age should participants be allowed to retire with a reduced benefit?
4. Should retirement income or ancillary benefits be emphasized?
5. At what age should vested participants have a right to a pension?
6. How many hours of work in a year should entitle participants to full benefit accrual?
7. Should participants be induced to retire early through benefit enhancements?

In investing fund assets:
1. What rate of return should be expected?
2. How should rate of return be measured?
3. What actual rate of return will cause a review of alternative financing organizations?
4. What should be the ratio of equity versus fixed income investments?
5. How much risk should be taken to gain a given interest rate over a rate that is without risk?
6. To what extent should principal be absolutely protected?

Thus, every major decision that the trustees face should begin with questions concerning the objectives to be accomplished. Clearly, there will not always be total agreement among trustees on objectives, either at the onset of discussion or even at the time a vote is taken. If, however, the parties can reach a consensus upon the objectives or at least outline possible or alternative objectives and then discuss these, with the advice and input of the advisors, there is a greater probability that good decisions will be made.

THE DECISION MAKING PROCESS

Effective decision making begins with a clear understanding of objectives. It follows with an orderly process that takes into account all relevant aspects of a problem. In the abstract, as it is related to benefit design, for example, this process can be outlined as follows:
1. Defining objectives
   - What do we want to do?
   - What are the measurable limits for an acceptable solution?
2. Determining specifications. What alternatives fulfill the objectives?
3. Establishing costs. Based upon established funding assumptions and methods, what will the alternatives cost?
4. Selection of the best alternative. Based upon the

objectives of the trustees and the costs of various alternatives, what is the best alternative available?
5. Implementing the decision. Having decided upon a course of action, what steps need to be taken to get the selected alternative in operation? These steps will often encompass:
   - Drafting documents and, if a pension plan, getting governmental approval
   - Preparing communication material for distribution to participants
   - Preparing disclosure material for the government and participants
   - Establishing administration procedures and systems to carry out the program
   - Making arrangements with outside providers of services for benefit payments.

DECISION MAKING TOOLS

One of the early surprises that a new trustee has is the volume of tools available to him or her in the decision making process. These come from a variety of sources. For example, the official files, records and reports of the plan itself are important tools. These include:
1. Minutes of meetings
2. Annual and periodic financial statements
3. Reports of the administrative manager on fund operation
4. Annual financial reports of the certified public accountant
5. Annual actuarial reports
6. Special studies and reports of fund counsel, consultant, actuary, investment manager and/or administrative manager.

The larger problem is not the availability of this information as a tool to the trustee's decision making process but the time and willingness of the trustee to read and comprehend these materials. It is acknowledged that every person who is selected to serve as a trustee is an extremely busy person in his or her union and/or in his or her community, with his or her family, with his or her church and in other activities. Clearly, the designation to serve as a trustee of a Taft-Hartley plan is a great honor and one that most individuals are very reluctant to decline. However, if one is mindful of the general fiduciary duties, one cannot and should not accept a designation to serve as a trustee unless he or she is willing and able to spend the time and energy necessary to be an effective trustee. This means a commitment to:
1. Read all the materials submitted to the trustees in preparation for each meeting.
2. To the extent a trustee does not understand any of this information, to ask questions at the meeting until the trustee is satisfied that he or she does understand the information.
3. Be willing to challenge the advice of professionals but ultimately to accept sound professional advice of qualified professionals, even if it is contrary to a preconceived idea the trustee holds.

One of the purposes of this handbook is to help educate new trustees on the language of and the documents for plan administration to make it easier for them to read and comprehend these decision making tools.

ADEQUATE ADVICE

One of the more common frustrations of new trustees is the "Catch-22" position they quickly become aware of between the labor and management trustees and the professional advisors.

The law is very clear that the trustees are the named fiduciaries of the plans, i.e., those individuals charged by law with the duty to operate and administer the plan, those who are ultimately legally liable and responsible for the plan's operation and administration. The plan participants are their members or their employees. Yet, it does not take a new trustee very long to realize that they and their co-trustees could not operate and administer the plan for very long without a full cast of professional advisors: fund counsel, fund actuary/consultant, certified public accountant, plan administrative manager, investment manager and, in certain situations, others.

This creates a schizophrenic unhappiness with many new trustees. "It's our plan, for our members, with our money, and we'll run it" versus "we can't do it without you and we resent that we can't." The answer is merely to accept both as relevant facts and blend the two together, keeping in balance the named fiduciary role of the trustee with the necessary technical advisory role of the service providers.

What is essential and cannot be compromised is that the trustees must insist upon the engagement and maintenance of a complete group of the most competent professionals available to them. The attorney cannot also serve as the plan auditor nor can the administrative manager also serve as the investment manager. There is a unique and distinct role to be played by each professional, and as a trustee you must insist that each stays within the jurisdiction of his or her profession.

The second concept is that the trustees must insist that they hire and retain the best possible advisors. This seemingly simple and readily agreeable generalization, in fact, translates into thousands of hours of heated debate each year at trustee meetings throughout the country.

What it means is that the trustees may not be able to hire the union's accountant or the employer association's attorney because, although he is a "good old boy," he may not have any qualifications as fund counsel or fund auditor. The fact that a trustee personally uses and is happy with the investment services of an individual does not, per se, qualify that investment manager to serve as investment manager of the plan.

It is not uncommon that the best qualified service provider is one whose social, political or economic views are somewhat askance with those of all, or some, of the trustees. The answer is found in ERISA Section 404(a): In making your decision on engaging a complete group of the most competent professional advisors available to you, you must act "solely in the interest of plan participants" for the purpose of "maximizing benefits and minimizing expenses" and "as trustees of other comparable plans are doing." To a certain extent, the quality of the plan and its benefits are directly related to the quality of the plan advisors.

ETHICAL ASPECTS OF TRUSTEESHIP

Unfortunately, from time to time, trustees of Taft-Hartley plans and their advisors get so caught up with the legal constraints to the operation and administration of the plans, with the managerial methodology to be employed in the decision making process, with the objectives and alternatives and like considerations that they forget the ethical aspects of their trusteeship.

Frequently, we are asked why anyone would serve as a trustee to a Taft-Hartley plan. The hours that need to be invested are enormous and the pay is nonexistent. The rewards and recognition are modest and the legal exposure and potential financial exposure are great. Why, then, would anyone serve? The answer is that a trustee of a Taft-Hartley fund fulfills the highest ethical standard; he or she has a direct and material role in providing retirement income to his or her co-workers/employees and in seeing that their reasonable and necessary medical expenses are taken care of. What higher reward or satisfaction can any of us achieve?

Implicit in the general fiduciary duties of ERISA Section 404(a) is the concept of the ethical tone of a trustee. The trustee is to act solely in the interest of the plan participants, to maximize their benefits as a prudent person.

The history of the litigation involving Taft-Hartley plans in the first 30 years after the enactment of ERISA makes it clear that trustees who are aware of and guided by this ethical tone are not involved in litigation. Trustees who use their position to gain personal reward or political gain, who use greed, pride and self-aggrandizement as their guidelines do get involved in litigation.

Interestingly, the standard of fiduciary responsibility, the moral tone we are addressing, traces its origins to the writings of Chief Justice Benjamin Cardozo of the Court of Appeals of the State of New York in *Meinhard v. Salmon,* 164 N.E. 545 (N.Y. Ct.App. 1928), 20 years before the enactment of the Taft-Hartley Act and 46 years before ERISA:

> Many forms of conduct permissible in a work-a-day world for those acting at arms' length are forbidden to those bound by fiduciary ties. A trustee is held to something stricter than the morals of the market place. Not honesty alone, but the punctilio of an honor the most sensitive, is then the standard of behavior. As to this, there has developed a tradition that is unbending and inveterate. Uncompromising rigidity has been the attitude of courts of equity when petitioned to undermine the rule of undivided loyalty by the disintegrating erosion of particular expectations. Only thus has a level of conduct for fiduciaries been kept at a higher level than that troddened by the crowd.

It is a difficult concept and one that no amount of reading or training will provide. Trustees who have an ethical tone will, and do, make the most successful trustees.

OBSTACLES TO EFFECTIVE TRUSTEESHIP

The material presented above attempts to describe some of the most important aspects of trusteeship. This material, it is hoped, will be of value to the trustee who wishes to learn some of the ways in which the knowledge of facts or processes can add to his or her effectiveness. The contribution of the most serious trustee, however, can be hampered by certain attitudes or behavior patterns that detract from his or her efforts to operate in a totally legal, logical and ethical manner. The following material is presented to each trustee who is willing to examine his or her own performance.

Psychological Barriers

The Nitpicking Trustee

There is a type of trustee who has a compulsion to dig into every issue, every report and every discussion before the trustees and to examine all aspects of a subject, down to its most minute details. This trustee seems not to be able to establish priorities of importance because of his or her need to know everything about the operations of the trust, even though the decision involves expertise normally not possessed by the trustee, even though the trustee and his or her fellow trustees have exercised due care in the selection of various professionals to perform delegated acts, and even though due care has been used to supervise the acts of any professionals involved in the trust.

This particular type of trustee spends an unreasonable amount of time in meetings, and perhaps outside of meetings, reviewing relatively minor matters. This trustee will, for example, spend a great deal of time on small variations in elements of administration costs, variations that will be subject to audit and can be reviewed in some sort of overall way once a year.

The trustee who sees this tendency in himself or herself should attempt to develop priorities of importance. He or she should attempt to be comfortable with the delegation of authority that has occurred until such time as it becomes clear that there is a lack of capability on the part of the administrative manager, attorney, consultant, actuary or other professional working with the fund.

The Power Seeking Trustee

Men and women who have achieved roles of authority within their union or industry obviously have not been shrinking violets during their lifetimes. They have sought power and achieved it. While such personal efforts toward achievement can be recognized as a normal human tendency, when the person who seeks power cannot control the use of such power, that person can be more of a hindrance than a help in the effective operation of any organization.

This is true of joint labor-management trusts. There is the trustee who attempts and sometimes is successful in dominating meetings and dominating the decision making process. Not only is such personal behavior contrary to the spirit of the Taft-Hartley Act in that it reduces the bipartisan character of the joint labor-management trust, it also reduces the effectiveness of the board of trustees as a decision maker. No one person has all the answers to the problems that face a board of trustees. It is the input of the various persons on the board that usually will lead to the best possible decision. Whenever one person dominates a board, much of the contribution that other trustees could make is lost.

The Not-So-Humble Trustee

It was mentioned earlier that some trustees find it difficult to admit their lack of knowledge on certain issues and will not ask questions of the professionals who serve the board. Perhaps of all the behavioral habits discussed in this section, this is the most common and most harmful to the effective operation of a board of trustees. No trustee should expect to understand all the terminology of the various advisors who counsel the board. No trustee should expect to immediately understand such technical processes as actuarial valuations or financial audits. Yet, one soon learns that many trustees feel some sense of shame in disclosing their lack of knowledge.

It would be helpful to the operations of many trusts if each trustee could feel freer to discuss openly what he or she does not know as well as what he or she does know. A trustee should remember that often the question that he or she has is the same question one or more of the other trustees have.

Conflicting Duties as Barriers

Most of the trustees who manage funds are very busy people. The union trustees are usually fully occupied in the activities of a local, regional or national union organization. The management trustees are often directing a business or a trade association. When a person takes on the responsibility of trusteeship, too often it is done without full knowledge of the amount of work involved if a good job is to be done. Sometimes the best trustees are those who do not have the key roles in a union or business organization but are those whose roles may be somewhat less demanding.

In any case, the extensive liabilities and ethical responsibilities of trusteeship should be considered seriously before any person accepts the role of a trustee. If he or she is already overburdened by union or business activities, he or she should not attempt to act as a trustee of even the smallest fund but should seek others who have the time to give to the operations of the trust.

Even the smallest trust now involves a cash flow of several hundred thousand dollars, and the substantial funds have the cash flow of large businesses. In addition, the ERISA trust principles are the same, regardless of the trust size. No one would let a person who is already more than fully occupied run a large business or a large union. The same standard should be considered in the selection of trustees. It should be considered when an individual thinks of taking on trusteeship responsibilities.

Collective Bargaining Concerns as Barriers

Many people who are not actively and intimately involved in Taft-Hartley plans have condemned them as, on their face, impossible to operate. The most frequently stated reason for dooming this highly successful industry is the paradox created by the law that the trustees are appointed one-half from and by labor and one-half from and by management; however, once they are appointed and commence service as trustees and named fiduciaries, they must act with total disregard of their labor and management appointment and background as fiduciaries, acting solely in the interests of plan participants, as prudent persons. This is a potential weakness but, in most plans, the great strength of Taft-Hartley plans.

We are all, as human beings, the sum total of all of our background and experience. We are what we are, based in part, upon the part of the country in which we were born and raised, the socioeconomic class in which our parents raised us, the socioeconomic class we are in currently, the nature and extent of our religious and moral upbringing, the nature and extent of our educational experiences, etc. In this context, a person who has served for 25 years with devotion and dignity to the union movement or the management side cannot, merely by walking into the trustees' meeting, forget this background. He or she shouldn't! The great strength that the trustee brings to the Taft-Hartley trustee table is his or her knowledge and feeling for the industry and the people in it. The same holds true for management trustees.

From time to time, plans have experimented with "professional trustees." That is, labor and/or management have hired individuals whose specialty is the running of insurance type benefit plans, who are expert in reading actuarial reports and financial statements, who have personal knowledge of the legal precedents, who have hands-on training in the investment of millions of dollars. Invariably, these people are totally ineffectual as trustees because they do not know the individuals, the industry, the jurisdiction, and the wants and needs of the parties—those things the lay labor and management trustees *do* know intimately.

The overwhelming majority of trustees are able to separate their collective bargaining agreement duties and responsibilities from their trustee duties and responsibilities. It is, in truth, something that needs to be remembered. It is something that needs to be worked on. From time to time, the advisors, particularly fund counsel, have to intervene and restate the rule. The risk of occasional transformance of a trustees' meeting into a bargaining session is a lesser concern than the loss of the sense of the participants if nonbargaining representative trustees were utilized. As long as the new trustees are mindful of this point, it will not be a barrier to effective trusteeship.

SOURCES OF HELP

A final note might be helpful in covering the sources of help to which a trustee can look in his or her efforts to expand his or her knowledge, decision making skills and personal capabilities.

The International Foundation of Employee Benefit Plans sponsors not only an Annual Educational Conference but also many individual subject seminars and workshops. If one judiciously selects those programs that cover areas of information required by the specific trustee, these programs can be extremely useful in expanding the individual trustee's capabilities. In addition, the trustee can read extensively the literature distributed by the International Foundation, as well as other materials that cover the areas of concern of the specific trustee. The professionals working with a board of trustees can recommend these materials.

Perhaps one of the best ways for a trustee to expand his or her knowledge is to be inquiring and knowledge seeking during the regular meetings of a board of trustees. One of the best ways to expand knowledge is simply to ask questions, as indicated earlier. Other ways are to attend all the meetings of the board and get involved in various key issues by way of discussion. If a trustee does these things, he or she will build a background of information that will allow him or her to do the best job possible in protecting the interests of those who depend on the trust fund for their economic security.

Chapter 3

The Future Direction of Employee Benefits

Dallas L. Salisbury

INTRODUCTION

When American Express established the first private pension plan in 1875, it hardly could have projected where pensions would be today. The members of Congress who established Civil War veterans pensions would have been surprised by developments of the past century and one-half. The health system and the health insurance begun in the late 1930s would leave all administrators of that day in a state of disbelief. Even if we look at the "few" years since passage of the Employee Retirement Income Security Act of 1974 (ERISA), we find a world that looks very different, and one in which most of the changes would not have been predicted.

Employer sponsorship of annuity-only defined benefit (DB) plans has been in rapid decline since the early 1980s. Unions have negotiated "hybrid" designs to keep employers in the game. Both employers and unions are expanding defined contribution (DC) offerings in response to worker wishes and economic change. Employer sponsorship of retiree health insurance has also been in decline, and enactment of a drug benefit in Medicare is not likely to arrest that trend.

President Bush has put forth his own proposals that would accentuate these patterns, arguing for individual accounts in Social Security, new lifetime savings accounts and retirement savings accounts outside of the workplace, expansion of health savings accounts, and tax credits for individuals to purchase health insurance as long as they do not do it through an employer or a union.

Will these trend lines continue? What does the future hold for employee benefits?

TECHNOLOGY AS A FACILITATOR/ DRIVER OF CHANGE

Technology has been the primary facilitator/driver of these changes in culture and attitude and design. Without technological advances, we would not be living in a world that is now small, allows work to flow around the world instantaneously, allows any nation to compete, and makes the labor market worldwide when the issue of cost rises. Technology has brought a new form of world competition and a new employer and union focus on productivity and cost. This has in turn led to the rise of constant mergers, failures and a general feeling of the population that life is uncertain to a degree that if you do not look out for yourself, no one else will. The fear of job loss is high in this world, and it drives the actions of government, business and labor executives, as well as the rank and file.

A walk through any benefits conference exhibit hall brings you into direct contact with the ways in which technology has changed the form, nature, administration, communication and benefits, or employee benefits. The future direction of programs is made clear as well: the investment technology that allows any one of you to turn on a personal computer and check whether or not your investment consultant has been telling the story straight; the ability to use financial planning software to assess whether or not the combination of Social Security, a DB pension, what you have been putting into a DC savings program and your individual savings is going to be enough to allow you to retire, and when; the ability of workers to make a reassessment whenever an adjustment is made by Congress in the eligibility age for full Social Security or Medicare benefits, the benefit levels, the contribution limits for the 457, 403(b) or

401(k), etc.; workers' ability to visit retirement, investment and health care sites on the Internet that allow them to assess quality of mutual fund options, HMO options, or to research drugs and treatment options. Technology brings investment and actuarial forecasting to your desk. The Internal Revenue Code and all the pension and health regulations can now be carried around on one CD-ROM for reading on the airplane or at the beach. Informed decision making becomes much more possible, at much lower cost.

Technology has also made it possible for low-cost plan valuations to be undertaken, detailed asset and liability modeling on a continuous basis, health care driven by data, electronic records, bar code scanners, long-distance surgery making use of cameras and robots, individual accounts for savings, health and retirement with daily valuation and almost unlimited choices, and the "backbone" to move to what President Bush describes as the "ownership society" where every worker owns their own retirement and health benefits.

INFORMATION AS A FACILITATOR/ DRIVER OF CHANGE

The second facilitator/driver of change is the quality, quantity and availability of information. Health care and health insurance and health employee benefit choices, and DC individual accounts can only work with individual decision making with on-demand delivery of information. We see it around us each and every day: the data picture in *USA Today;* the ability to turn on CNN or C-SPAN and instantaneously get an assessment of legislative prospects; the ability to watch election outcomes as the wave of closing times moves across the United States, and then to go to the Internet to get up-to-the-minute vote counts; the information that you are able to obtain quickly on what's happening with the Supreme Court or a government agency on the Internet. And the list goes on.

Managed care as it is delivered today, with the data that is delivered today to make managed networks function, was not feasible 15 years ago. Nor were participant-directed DC plans with access to the open market, to thousands of mutual funds, with daily changes, and online Internet administration available with current technology. The speed of the technology and information trains is startling in terms of what it allows the benefit designers, the benefit sponsors and the benefit consumers.

New hospitals now opening underline how the relationship of the individual to the health system will change. Some will argue this makes involvement of the employer or multiemployer plan as a negotiator and representative all the more necessary. Others will argue it provides the basis for taking them out of the mix and turning full "ownership" and control over to the individual.

DEMOGRAPHICS AS A DRIVER OF CHANGE

Demographics is bringing about benefits change that will accelerate for at least the next 75 years. Growth of the nation's retiree population will change cost structures of both pension and health plans, particularly pay-as-you-go programs like Social Security and Medicare. As demographics-driven change occurs, it will spill over into employment-based programs. Social Security, under a good news scenario, will not have positive cash flow beyond 2018. According to bipartisan estimates, a doubling of the Social Security payroll tax from approximately 12% to 24% would be required to maintain the benefit promises that have already been made or benefit reductions of nearly 30%, if action is not taken soon. And that is before we move to the challenge represented by Medicare. The Medicare payroll tax would go from 3% to 9% to finance currently promised benefits, and that program is already in negative cash flow.

Benefit planners will need to focus on design. Implicit and explicit integration with Social Security will need to be considered as the retirement ages rise, benefit level rates of increase decline and Medicare premiums drive higher at a rapid rate. Should you have a retirement income objective, or should your focus be on facilitating the opportunity for retirement savings? Will you be able to accommodate people working until 70, 75 and beyond? Or how much more are you going to have to contribute in order to make your pension programs adequate to allow early retirement? Or how much more will your plan cost if you try to continue early retirement supplements and retiree health until Social Security full benefit payment and Medicare eligibility? The good news is that technology makes it extraordinarily easy to do the analyses. The bad news is that technology can't make the answers feel better.

THE GROWTH OF SMALL BUSINESS AS A DRIVER OF CHANGE

Another change of recent decades has been the growth of small business, the self-employed and the contingent worker, as employment in the largest organizations and union memberships have declined. Since small firms do not readily provide employee benefits, which large organizations do, we have seen pressure on both pension and health coverage. Due to the availability of low-cost approaches to retirement plan provision, with no employer contribution, overall plan availability has not declined, but coverage by traditional pension and health programs has. Health coverage has seen substantial declines, as has the generosity of health programs, and the downward trend is continuing. Demographics, technology, competition, union membership reductions and the "end of loyalty" promise to feed declines in voluntary employer-paid coverage in the future as well. Working longer becomes the only way to deal with longer lives if employment-based benefit programs are not in place to provide at least a floor of financial security.

INCREMENTAL HEALTH REFORM WILL BE ONGOING

As a result of changes in health delivery, health insurance payment and availability, pressures for incremental health reform continue. Initiatives like the expansion of government-financed coverage for children, partial portability when moving from an employer with health insurance, Medicare drugs and Medicare payment reform with a focus on "pay for performance," will be continuously built upon in the future. Comprehensive reform is unlikely as long as federal deficits persist, suggesting troubled decades ahead. Litigation and issues of quality and compliance will lead to continued consideration of rebalancing the role of the state in the regulation of self-insured health plans as compared to the federal role that has been dominant since the passage of ERISA in 1974. What will it mean for your plans? What will it mean for the flexibility to run them? What may it mean for taxes that you will be asked to pay to the state to finance state health reform? The answers are not certain, but there is certainty that change will occur. And, there is certainty that the cost of our health and retirement systems will continue to climb, with the major debate continuing to be "who pays."

"DO WE STILL WANT PENSIONS?"

ERISA defined both DB plans and DC plans as *pension plans* for the first time. The Revenue Act of 1978 clarified the status of pre-ERISA cash and deferred arrangements. Employee pretax salary reduction was clearly allowed, and the 401(k) revolution began. By the early 1980s, as job security was perceived to be on the wane, as the young baby boomers sought personal control, and as employers sought ways to limit contributions to a "budgetable" amount, they began to cut back on defined benefit plan formulas and expand defined contribution programs. The federal government did this for its employees in 1984, and the private sector has followed that lead with a vengeance.

Any debate of the past on pension plan type assumed certain things: first, that defined benefit plans paid benefits in the form of an annuity; second, because of lengthy vesting periods, that long service was rewarded financially, and retirement timing was something plan design should influence. As defined benefit plans have changed to lump-sum distributions and to individual accounts, what the debate is about becomes less and less clear. Plan type is actually a secondary issue.

Who bears longevity and investment risk (wins and loses) is the only clear and consistent difference between plan types and payment forms in this new age of technology and individual responsibility/control or "ownership."

We read much about a shift from defined benefit to defined contribution. We have experienced some shift across the economy, as unions have negotiated the addition of DC plans, and as state and local governments have slowly begun to debate and adopt similar changes. Exceptions like Procter & Gamble have always relied on profit-sharing plans, and not DB plans, as have some of our nation's largest companies that have only existed in a post-ERISA world: Microsoft, Wal-Mart, etc. What we are seeing as an ongoing direction is more and more focus on, and desire by the individual worker for, the individual account plan with a lump-sum distribution. Most often this plan is defined contribution. Why? Think back to presentations by former Secretary of Labor Robert Reich, joined by President Bill Clinton, talking about the changed America, the changed workplace, the end of job security, the necessities of constant retraining, and a focus on sabbaticals for retraining; speaking about the challenges of bringing people to the level of the technology jobs that Reich and Clinton saw as the economy of the future. What message do workers hear from media broadcasts each day? They hear the message that says "in the good old days" and then they flip the channel. And on the new channel they find the takeover artist from Wall Street talking about his obligation to the shareholder and in talking about the shareholder he mentions the California Public Employees Retirement System. In his obligation to the shareholder he mentions four different union-management pension funds that have invested in his takeover fund looking for maximum return. And the takeover artist says, "My community payment is jobs and the best return for my shareholders." It is not contribution to the United Way. It is not providing buildings and financing for the charities of the community. It is not to guarantee jobs to a particular segment of society. It is to create maximum return so that the trustees of activist pension funds will be happy. The takeover artist notes that it is for that reason, to better serve the pensioners of America, that they are announcing the elimination of 17,000 jobs in order to up the dividend next month that will fund those pension benefits of other workers in another part of the country. And what does that say to the worker today, on top of Bill Clinton and Robert Reich and Alvin Toffler discussing the new wave of America? It says, "I had better look out for myself. I had better be comfortable that there will be money there when I retire, and to be comfortable I need to be in charge." President Bush builds upon these themes with his vision of the "ownership society."

Listen to Professor Amatai Etzioni talk about the

fundamental change in America as a loss of community. He suggests a loss of community in our labor unions, our associations, our cities and in our rural communities. Employee benefit designs of the age may no longer benefit everyone. Individuals sense the message that I must look out for myself.

THE INDIVIDUAL OR THE GROUP?

For employee benefits and government programs the central design question has increasingly become one of the group or the individual. Individual empowerment has been the theme of much of the political discussion since 1980: expansion of individual retirement accounts, and health savings accounts, creation of lifetime savings accounts and retirement savings accounts, introduction or expansion of flexible benefit programs and choice by individual workers, rather than their being "dictated" to by the collective of the employer or the collective of the union, individual accounts as the "solution" for Social Security. And the beat goes on.

Those messages suggest more future directions for our employee benefit programs. The environment has brought with it a surge of employee interest in, and demand for, more individual choice, more push for the introduction of flexible benefit programs. We see a movement in defined benefit plans to mimic defined contribution plans, to provide an individual account so that the statement the individual gets has a dollar value instead of some eventual annuity. We see employee pressure for lump-sum distributions from both defined benefit and defined contribution plans. Should this take hold for the future it will produce a pension challenge of balancing the financing of pension programs, as instead of paying a check for each and every month for years, and gaining on investments all the time, a lump sum denies the plan investment gains. Is there any potential financial gain for the plan? Yes, since longer lives is one of the demographic facts of life today. We have seen examples in both the steel and airline industries of plans being moved to distress as a "rush on the bank" of those seeking lump sums drives a plan to termination.

Life extension can be good news, but if the actuaries did not foresee it, and a plan did not fund for it, it can cause plan costs to soar unexpectedly. Technology allows one to simulate alternative paths, but it cannot tell you which path will occur! And, plan fiduciaries have to want the truth badly enough to use assumptions that take future advances into account, rather than holding on to past patterns in an effort to keep the numbers low.

FUNDAMENTAL TAX REFORM COULD CHANGE ALL

President Bush would reform the tax system to bring down tax rates further. He might also change the tax treatment of all employee benefits. Individuals would find that all savings would be equally rewarded, where pensions now have an advantage. Economists suggest that if after tax money was used to pay for health insurance then individuals would only purchase as much health protection as they actually needed. In effect, reforms would lead to elimination of most employee benefits as we know them today. The tax reform issue is not generally discussed as an employee benefit issue, but it would overpower all the other drivers mentioned above.

Reports from the Government Accountability Office and the Congressional Budget Office make it clear tax revenue will have to increase substantially in the decades ahead if current benefit promises are to be kept. Reform of the tax treatment of employee benefits could hold down rate increases. Today's fiscal policies make future tax change inevitable.

REFORMS OF THE PAST ARE RESULTING IN MORE PENSION INCOME

When ERISA was enacted, there were just slightly more than 200,000 defined contribution retirement programs. Today there are over 700,000. In 1978, when the first 401(k) plans were established, fewer than 25% who were eligible chose to participate. By 1988, that had grown to 50% and by 2004 to 75%. The amount being contributed has been growing as well. We all experience the tremendous growth of financial planning columnists in the newspapers and magazines around the United States, the number of channels that any of us can tune into each and every day to hear the financial commentator on how much people need to save for retirement. As noted above, the Internet resources are now available. It is not, however, going to be as easy as a recent CNN special would have implied. A friendly stockbroker in his office on Wall Street looked into the computer and said, "Yes, any American willing to save $50 a month will be able to live an adequate retirement." The next clip on that CNN special took us to Palm Springs, California. They came up the long drive to a big home with a tennis court at the side. The camera zooms in across the swimming pool. Behind the pool is a stable filled with Arabian horses. The commentator says, "We've come here to Palm Springs to visit Joe who saved enough to retire at 50. He is enjoying every minute of it. We'll be back." And they flip to another segment with specialist Dorcas Hardy on the future of Social Security. And they said, "Dorcas, can we rely on Social Security?" And Dorcas said, "Not for too much." And they said, "Let's go back to Joe." They cut back to Palm Springs and asked Joe, "Do you worry about Social Security?" Joe said, "No, it didn't cover last year's utility bills." They then went back to the broker who said, "Well, maybe it will take $100 a month." Did all viewers find the show as unrealistic as

I did? Probably most. But the program made me think about savings, think about Social Security and think about the future. Ten years ago the show was about pension investing and "The Biggest Lump of Money in the World."

Today, the show is about you. Yesterday, you were told not to worry; it would all be taken care of. Today, you are told to pay yourself first, to save and to think about being prepared for change. Change is everywhere, and employee benefits are not being spared.

INDIVIDUALS ARE GETTING THE MESSAGE

Today, there are means to save. Payroll deduction is being used. Surveys like the EBRI Retirement Confidence Survey make it clear that individuals know they need to plan and to save. Participation rates in defined contribution plans continue to climb; contribution rates are on the rise; investment diversification is happening. Union and employer education is working, and its availability is on the rise as well. Interactive tools on the computer (www.choosetosave.org) or at the kiosk are joined by videos, audiotapes and workbooks and the "Ballpark Estimate" worksheet of our American Savings Education Council.

APPRECIATION AS THE "FUTURE" BENEFIT FOCUS

What of new employee benefits? In the beginning employee benefits were generally fully paid by the employer directly or through the negotiated wage package. Today, the emphasis is on facilitating action and obtaining appreciation, versus necessarily paying for economic security: plan sponsorship, payroll deduction, matching contributions, passing on the lower rates and broader eligibility that come with a group arrangement, etc.; providing the mechanism, for example, to help your workers get mortgage financing, for long-term care insurance coverage, for access to home health care and child care and elder care, auto insurance or group homeowner's insurance, and more. Cost might be limited to that of the administrative agent, or an employee fee might be charged to cover that expense as well. The goals are the facilitation, the delivery of benefits, the delivery of value and getting employee appreciation at low cost.

Appreciation and productivity return are becoming explicit goals for benefit programs. "Return on investment" measures are growing and new terms such as "presenteeism" are being coined. This has led to a new focus on measurement of delivery and measurement of value. The movement is toward vendor report cards and quality assessment in the health care area, toward implementation of Securities and Exchange Commission and Department of Labor communications goals for defined benefit and defined contribution plans, and more. There is a focus on understandability of information regardless of education level, provision of a videotape or an audiotape so that it can be put into the VCR at home or the car tape player and listened to without having to worry about appearing to not know. The TIAA-CREF "monopoly" game of retirement planning is an entertaining form that causes individuals to think, and to think aggressively, about what it is they should be doing to secure their future.

WHERE DO DEFINED BENEFIT PLANS FIT IN THE FUTURE?

Defined benefit plans have been through an extended period of being neither appreciated nor well understood. Fast vesting, combined with high rates of job turnover in almost every job setting, causes most workers to think they will not be around long enough to do well with a defined benefit plan. That employee never sees a TV ad about defined benefits but sees ads and articles daily about 401(k) plans. The extended period of low inflation has assured that appreciation of the ability of these plans to help people deal with postretirement inflation has not been present. By the time the first of the baby boomers are ready to retire in 2012 and 2013, they face the prospect of having been individualists, and of not having saved enough for retirement. So come about 2015, they will probably be coming to their unions and employers and saying, "You know that defined benefit plan we always told you we didn't like; well, we really think you better triple the benefits so that I can afford to retire. Let that baby bust group and those generation Xers figure out how to make up for the contributions." The response is not likely to be positive, because the funds will not be available. Long-service workers will be glad the defined benefit plan is available, but that is now down to 20% of workers, and mobile workers that left a defined benefit plan behind will wish they had stayed in one place longer. In short, defined benefit plans are not likely to go away for a long time, but they are not likely to grow either. And there is little prospect of the establishment of new defined benefit plans of size, and many employers are now closing plans to new hires. The essential shutdown of such plans will take 75 years, but it will eventually come. The managers who made the decisions will have retired decades before the plan is finally shuttered. The concerns noted above of competition, labor force work patterns, demographics, individual desire for control and the desire of employers to manage and predict costs, mean that new plans are not in the cards. The redefinition of job security, to a feeling of vulnerability, is driving individuals to say, "I don't want to make large contributions out of my compensation package so that others that went before me, that I never knew, can lead the good life." When they see the television program that has the retirees on the golf courses or deep sea fishing, their reaction is not, "Good gosh, I am happy for them, and I am glad I am helping to pay for their good life." Their sense of individualism is, "I can't afford to buy my children what they need; I can't afford to send my children to college. Why am I paying contributions so that they can lead the good life?" It could be an ugly period; it could be a period of rancor as we go through the process of adjustment. A likely result is many retirees going back to work in order to make ends meet. In fact, the Retirement Confidence Survey now finds that over 80% of boomers say they expect to work at least part time after they leave their primary job.

Management guru to labor and business Tom Peters is on the public television stage; he is hopping and bouncing and having a grand time. As he is hopping and bouncing and smiling, he is saying, "And your job is to reduce jobs. Your job is to increase profits. Your job is to get rid of those levels of individuals that you hired 20 years ago who did a great job for 15 years but whom technology has passed by; they have failed to keep up when the opportunity was provided. Let them go find something else. They are not your obligation. This is no longer a world of lifetime job security for anyone, and it was never such a world for most."

Defined benefit plans traditionally rewarded those who stayed for 25, 30 and 40 years. At the high point of job stability about one-third of workers remained with one employer for 25 years or more. Today it is less than a quarter of all workers, and only about 15% of private sector workers. Today, we design programs to get maximum productivity and maximum good feeling, and to accommodate the vast majority of workers, not the stayers. Today, most major employers want to be one of the two most profitable companies in America in their line of business, or they want to dump it.

Senate candidate Milt Romney in his debate with Senator Kennedy (D-Mass.) asked, "Senator, how can you hold me responsible for the fact that after I sold the company the new owners fired all the people?" The new efficiency. The new reality brought on by global competition. The new realm by the necessities of meeting the challenge of what others can do from new technology more efficiently. The message to individuals is a message that was communicated in a speech I heard in Nashville recently. A senior executive who was on the stage said, "Our human resources philosophy is a philosophy of the disposable employee." The *disposable employee.* We want them when we need them and, when the job is done, we want them to want to leave. So what does that mean that company's employee benefits approach and philosophy was? It was a philosophy of pure defined contribution. A philosophy of minimum health insurance and no family coverage. A philosophy of great total cash possibilities, but a low cash base and a huge performance layer of compensation. What is the message that this gives to the worker? What does it produce as attitude and demand? That is a message that leads the worker to say, "I'm nervous. I don't know if I will have a job tomorrow. I don't know if I will have jobs permanently. I do want Social Security; I don't want a defined benefit pension plan unless it is mandated and fully portable. I don't know if I will be here a year from now, let alone ten, let alone 20. Why should I trust?"

The other half of the loss of community is the loss of trust. Bill Clinton, on the day following the 1994 election, plaintively was not able to understand what had happened. "Don't people know the economy is better?" he said. "Don't people know unemployment is down? Don't people know economic growth is up? Don't they remember that I lowered their taxes? What is it?" One looking at that television performance might have said, "Mr. President, it's simple. It's the absence of the feeling of security. It's the absence of the feeling of having an employment home. It's the absence of any certainty whatsoever that, in the world that you and your Labor Secretary have so articulately described to us, one knows if he or she will have a job. It is an essence." I have a job today, but every channel I turn to tells me that it may be gone tomorrow. And at that point what does it say to individuals? It doesn't say, "Thank you for a low unemployment rate." It doesn't say, "Thank you that I am employed today." It says, "Will I be employed tomorrow and what is my level of angst and that potential, that absence of stability? Should I depend on my own ability to save and on Social Security, or should I rely on the future good will of future workers in a defined benefit plan?"

President Bush found in 2005 that support for Social Security was still very solid, as was support for making changes to assure solvency. He found that support for the "ownership society" focus on the individual was strong as well, since individuals have even less trust in institutions than they did in 1994. The message of today is increasingly one of trust in yourself, but in few others.

Employers in some cases have responded with a redesign of their plans to "hybrid" plans that communicate the defined benefit as an individual account balance. This has not been without controversy, and the legal status of such plans is still not clear. Congress has responded by moving to provide limited health care portability and health savings accounts. Discussion of retirement benefit portability is once again beginning. Workers want portability of all of benefit programs. Portability is something, within an industry, that multi-employer plans have done across America. With recent legislation for faster vesting, for redefinition of contract worker versus regular employee, and with change of focus, within-industry portability may not be enough.

HEALTH CARE REFORM IS IN THE BENEFITS FUTURE

Comprehensive health care reform will return to the national agenda as employers eventually ask the fundamental question: Why are we in the health business? The drivers mentioned above make the question one of *when,* not *if.* The response will either be an individual- and family-based system, a government program or a series of multiemployer plans to which the employer and individual will contribute.

Medicare will be at the center of this major reform. When later eligibility age arrives, when benefit reductions and means testing take hold, will employers and unions be able to afford to provide supplementation? What will be the structure of security that will work? The time for trustees to think about such issues is now, before Congress has acted and foreclosed trustee decision options.

SOCIAL SECURITY REFORM IS IN THE BENEFITS FUTURE

Social Security will be reformed. The age for early retirement, and for full benefits, are both likely to move higher. Benefit levels are likely to be reduced beyond the age reductions. How will this impact union and employer plan costs? How will it affect design decisions? How will it affect when individuals are willing to retire?

A mandatory defined contribution pension "tier" is likely to be legislated as well. The proposals discussed in the 1960s, again in the 1980s, and now as part of Social Security reform will not go away. Eventual enactment will be essential to assure a floor of future economic security. Politics may well delay action for many years, but it is likely in the years ahead.

Again, what does this mean for pension integration, plan design and plan investments? For the decision to sponsor a plan? For the decision of individuals to save? The time for trustees to think about such issues is now, before Congress has taken action and foreclosed trustee options.

EMPLOYEE BENEFITS HAVE MADE A DIFFERENCE: TELL THE STORY

The full family of employer and individual pension programs in America holds more than $11 trillion in assets today. Last year, the nation's retirees received over $300 billion in payments from these retirement income programs.

Plan participants are accumulating assets in defined contribution programs at the fastest rate of asset accumulation of any type of qualified plan in the history of the movement.

Health care programs sponsored by employers and unions are protecting nearly 64% of all nonelderly Americans. The number of uninsured is going up somewhat, but we still have an extraordinary health care insurance system in America. While alternatives may well be appropriate, moving from voluntary employment-based coverage to voluntary individual choice will increase the number of uninsured, not increase coverage.

Collective action has made these accomplishments possible. As we lose trust, and as we lose community, will we be able to get individuals to understand the value of the collective plan? Will we survive what Drucker termed "pension fund socialism?" This has been written about by others as pension fund involvement in corporate governance. What if the price of that pension fund activism is the loss of jobs, the termination of defined benefit pension plans, the elimination of retiree health care to trim cost?

In short, could the fiduciaries of employee benefit plans go down roads that lead to the undoing of the very programs and participants they seek to serve?

CONCLUSION

We are experiencing fundamental change in the design and orientation of employee benefit programs. This is because of technology, a changing philosophy in government, the messages of job insecurity and the ongoing loss of trust by individuals in both public and private sector institutions. We know with certainty the necessity for Social Security reform. Retirement age is already going up, benefit levels are likely to grow more slowly in the future, or come down in absolute terms if cash flow runs short. Action is inevitable. It may just not be timely. One can argue about when it will happen. One can argue about when it has to happen. But the numbers are clear, and we will have to redesign union/employer programs to deal with the changes already enacted and those yet to be enacted.

Medicare and the cost of retiree medical demand the same attention only sooner and with greater consequence. Medicare as we know it is not sustainable. The addition of prescription drug coverage only made the financing problem worse. Both parties know it. Both parties say it. We can argue about when the adjustments need to be made, but unions or employers that provide for retiree medical benefits have to figure out how to react to it. Those that do not provide retiree health insurance may not be able to get workers to retire.

The future of employee benefits will be based on education, on understanding, on advance planning and on strategic thinking. The future will belong to individuals like those reading this book. You are preparing to deal with the future. This book will help you do it.

SECTION II

FIDUCIARY DUTY AND RESPONSIBILITY

Chapter 4

Fiduciary Responsibility Under ERISA

Stephen M. Saxon and Jon Bourgault

One of the hallmarks of ERISA is the attempt by Congress to identify those persons and entities that are *fiduciaries* with respect to plans covered by ERISA, and to describe the responsibilities placed on plan fiduciaries. The trustees of Taft-Hartley pension and welfare plans are fiduciaries, and it is important for them to understand how ERISA's fiduciary responsibility rules apply to them. But it is equally important for trustees to understand how these rules apply to other fiduciaries, including the individuals and entities appointed by the trustees to manage the day-to-day operations of a plan. In particular, trustees are required to monitor the activity of other fiduciaries to ensure that they are complying with these rules.

Prior to ERISA's enactment, it was not always clear who was responsible for plan administration, investment, etc., or where liability should be placed in the event of wrongdoing. Congress sought to clarify this situation by enacting detailed provisions dealing with plan fiduciaries and their responsibilities. Congress relied on two primary sources in enacting ERISA's fiduciary provisions. First, Congress looked to the common law of trusts. The general fiduciary duties listed in ERISA are for the most part derived directly from trust law, and common law principles are therefore often useful tools for analyzing issues arising under ERISA's fiduciary provisions. Second, Congress drew from its experience with the Taft-Hartley Act (discussed in Chapter 1) in applying notions of fiduciary duty in an employee benefits context.

The first step in applying the fiduciary responsibility rules of ERISA is determining whether or not a person is an ERISA-covered fiduciary. As discussed more fully below, although trustees will always be fiduciaries to a certain extent, Congress generally chose to define *fiduciary status* in terms of the discretionary activities performed on behalf of the plan. As a result, fiduciary status (and exposure to fiduciary liability) may vary depending upon the actions undertaken on behalf of the plan.

Once fiduciary status is determined, the fiduciary is required to fulfill the fiduciary responsibilities set forth in ERISA. First, there are the general fiduciary duties derived from trust law and set forth in ERISA Sections 403 and 404. These are broad rules governing all aspects of fiduciary activity and have been the subject of extensive litigation since the enactment of ERISA. Second, there are the rules in ERISA Section 406 that prohibit a fiduciary from causing a plan to engage in transactions with so-called parties in interest. These prohibited transaction rules include per se prohibitions as well as conflict-of-interest and self-dealing provisions that complement the general fiduciary duty rules.

In the event that a fiduciary breaches one or more of these rules, the fiduciary will potentially be subject to a variety of civil penalties, excise taxes and liability. Consistent with its intent to clearly delineate the remedy for fiduciary wrongdoing, Congress mandated that a fiduciary must be *personally* liable. This is true whether the liability results from a fiduciary's own breach or from co-fiduciary liability imposed as the result of a breach of another plan fiduciary. Thus, as discussed below, a fiduciary cannot use plan assets to offset its fiduciary liability.

WHO IS A FIDUCIARY?

General Rules

In general, a *fiduciary* is a person in a position of trust. ERISA defines who is, and who is not, a fiduciary with respect to an ERISA-covered plan in terms of the functions performed by that person for the plan. In some instances, a person will become a fiduciary merely by occupying certain discretionary positions with respect to a plan. Most important of these is the plan's *named fiduciary*. ERISA requires that the documents governing a plan identify the plan's named fiduciary. This identification can be by name, title or position, or by a procedure described in the plan for naming the named fiduciary. For almost all Taft-Hartley plans, the named fiduciary will be the board of trustees. The named fiduciary is in essence the ultimate source of all fiduciary responsibility for the plan. Named fiduciaries may be granted certain powers that other plan fiduciaries may not exercise (including the power to appoint investment managers and the authority to make final claims determinations under the plan) and are subject to more potential liability. More specifically, named fiduciaries can appoint investment managers. In addition, the person responsible for final claims determinations must be a named fiduciary. By requiring the identification of the named fiduciary, Congress intended that plan participants would always have at least one clearly defined focal point for questions, complaints, appeals, etc., regarding plan operations.

The Department of Labor has by regulation expanded the number of categories of persons who become fiduciaries merely by occupying certain positions with respect to a plan. Thus, for example, the plan trustee will always be a plan fiduciary subject to ERISA. Even where the trustee acts pursuant to the direction of another plan fiduciary, such direction limits, but does not eliminate entirely, the trustee's exposure to potential liability but does not change the trustee's fiduciary status. See DOL Field Assistance Bulletin 2004-3 (Dec. 17, 2004).

Another designated fiduciary position is that of *plan administrator*.

Aside from these designated positions, ERISA, the courts and the Department of Labor have taken a functional approach to determining fiduciary status. Thus, ERISA states that the term *fiduciary* will include anyone who:
- Exercises any discretion or control over the management of a plan or the management or disposition of plan assets. This includes investment managers retained for the plan.
- Provides investment advice to the plan for a fee or
- Has any discretionary responsibility in administering the plan.

These definitions depend on the specific facts of the person's relationship to the plan. Thus, if a person has one of the defined relationships to an ERISA plan, the person will be a fiduciary whether or not he or she expressly agreed to be a fiduciary or, in some cases, is even aware of being a fiduciary to the ERISA plan.

Investment Advice

A person may become a fiduciary with respect to a plan if "he renders *investment advice for a fee* or other compensation, direct or indirect...." ERISA §3(21)(A)(ii) (emphasis added). The *for a fee* requirement is relatively easily satisfied, with both the courts and the Department concluding that *fees* include both direct or indirect compensation, including the receipt of commissions, even when paid by a party other than the plan.

The Department of Labor has issued a regulation under Section 3(21) of ERISA defining *investment advice*. 29 CFR §2510.3-21(c). Under the regulations, *investment advice* is defined as (1) providing advice as to the value of securities or other property, or making recommendations as to the advisability of investing in securities or other property; and (2) providing such advice (a) on a regular basis, (b) pursuant to a mutual understanding that the advice will serve as the primary basis for an investment decision and (c) individualized to the specific plan. The courts have generally required that each of the criteria in the Department's "investment advice" regulation be satisfied in order to confer fiduciary status. Thus, where a communication does not constitute either "advice" or a "recommendation," the criteria of the investment advice regulation will not be satisfied. Moreover, a person will not be a fiduciary by virtue of providing "investment advice," if advice or recommendations are not provided on a "regular basis," i.e., on more than just one or two occasions. Similarly, where advice or recommendations are not "individualized" (such as in the case of a generalized marketing presentation), a person will not be found to have provided investment advice. Finally, courts generally will not find investment advice in the absence of a "mutual agreement" to provide investment advice that will be "a primary basis" for investment decisions. Consistent with these requirements, the Department of Labor has determined that, where a plan permits participants to direct the investment of funds on their behalf, the fact that an investment advisor or other party provides investment education to participants will not necessarily cause that party to become a fiduciary. DOL Interpretive Bulletin 96-1 (June 11, 1996).

Delegation and Allocation of Fiduciary Authority

As noted above, Congress was concerned that it was not always possible to determine the identity of responsible plan fiduciaries under the law prior to ERISA. As a result, ERISA specifies the ways in which fiduciaries could allocate and delegate fiduciary authority, and the effects of each such allocation and delegation. For example, ERISA permits the plan to allocate, or to specify procedures for allocating, fiduciary responsibilities among a plan's named fiduciaries. In addition, ERISA permits the allocation and delegation by named fiduciaries of duties not involving "trustee responsibilities." *Trustee responsibilities* are those responsibilities for the management or control of the plan's assets that are provided in the trust agreement, including investment management responsibilities.

In the absence of an effective allocation or delegation of fiduciary responsibilities, each named fiduciary is jointly and severally responsible with the other named fiduciaries for controlling and managing the operation and administration of the plan. For example, if a plan administration committee appointed as a *named fiduciary* for purposes of making claims determinations under a plan breaches its fiduciary duties in performing that function, a trustee appointed as another *named fiduciary* but whose responsibilities are not circumscribed by an effective allocation would also be fully liable for the damages resulting from that breach, even if the trustee never actually participates in the claims process.

ERISA provides three methods through which named fiduciaries can reduce this broad liability by allocating responsibilities among themselves, or by designating others to carry out their responsibilities. First, the plan can provide procedures for the allocation of responsibilities among named fiduciaries. Second, the plan can provide procedures whereby a named fiduciary can designate persons other than named fiduciaries to carry out fiduciary responsibilities on its behalf. Finally, a named fiduciary can appoint an *investment manager* to manage some or all of the assets of the plan.

Allocation Among Named Fiduciaries

If fiduciary responsibilities are allocated among named fiduciaries in accordance with plan procedures, a named fiduciary will not be liable for the acts and omissions of other named fiduciaries, except as provided in ERISA's general co-fiduciary rules, set forth in Section 405 of ERISA, which always apply to plan fiduciaries. As discussed more fully below, ERISA's co-fiduciary rules provide that one plan fiduciary will be liable for the breach of another fiduciary, if the first fiduciary actively participates in the breach, conceals the breach, makes it possible for the breach to occur as a result of its own breach, or fails to take reasonable steps to correct the breach.

Designation of Others to Carry Out Named Fiduciary Activities

Other than general co-fiduciary liability, a named fiduciary will not be liable for the acts and omissions of a person who is not a named fiduciary but who is designated by the named fiduciary to carry out its responsibilities (other than trustee responsibilities). Of course, the named fiduciary must still prudently select and monitor the actions of the designated person.

Appointment of Investment Manager

ERISA allows a named fiduciary to appoint an investment manager to manage or control plan assets. An *investment manager* under ERISA is any fiduciary who:
- Has the power to manage, acquire or dispose of any assets of a plan
- Is (1) registered as an investment advisor under the Investment Advisors Act of 1940 or (2) a bank or (3) a qualified insurance company
- Has acknowledged its fiduciary status in writing.

ERISA §3(38).

Whereas named fiduciaries may be appointed only by an employer or employee organization, investment managers may be appointed by any named fiduciary, but only if the plan documents so provide. Under certain circumstances, a person can serve both as a named fiduciary and as an investment manager.

Neither the plan trustee nor the named fiduciary is liable for the acts or omissions of an investment manager that has been properly appointed. ERISA §405(c)(2). Of course, the named fiduciary appointing the investment manager remains responsible for the prudent selection and monitoring of the investment manager. In addition, the general co-fiduciary liability principles discussed above would be applicable.

GENERAL FIDUCIARY DUTIES

ERISA's general fiduciary duty provisions, contained primarily in ERISA Section 404(a), are first and foremost just that—general provisions. Unlike the exacting specificity of ERISA's reporting and disclosure provisions or the per se prohibitions in ERISA Section 406(a), ERISA Section 404(a) establishes broad standards of fiduciary conduct the application of which vary from situation to situation. These standards are derived from the common law of trusts, but are intended to be broader in application than those common law rules. As guideposts for fiduciary compliance, the rules in Section 404(a) are often troublesome and inexact. As protections for plan participants and beneficiaries, however, these rules have been viewed as vital.

The rules in ERISA Section 404(a) are interdependent, and it is often difficult to discern in application where one standard ends and another begins. However, Section 404(a) basically establishes five rules governing the conduct of ERISA-covered fiduciaries. First, Section 404(a)(1) requires a plan fiduciary to act solely in the interest of plan participants and beneficiaries. Second, a plan fiduciary is required by ERISA Sections 404(a)(1)(A) and 404(c)(1) to hold and deal with plan assets for the exclusive purpose of paying benefits and defraying reasonable cost of plan administration. Third, a plan fiduciary must, pursuant to ERISA Section 404(a)(1)(B), act prudently. Fourth, Section 404(a)(1)(C) requires that a plan fiduciary diversify plan investments. Finally, a plan fiduciary must under Section 404(a)(1)(D) act in accordance with plan documents, but only to the extent that the plan documents are consistent with ERISA.

Solely in the Interest

Before the enumeration of any specific fiduciary duties, Section 404(a)(1) of ERISA provides that a fiduciary must discharge its duties with respect to a plan "solely in the interest" of the plan's participants and beneficiaries. This standard is drawn directly from the common law of trusts, which required a trustee to administer a trust with a duty of undivided loyalty to the trust beneficiaries. The common law duty of loyalty was viewed as inherent in the trust relationship and the basic duty of the trustee.

The duty of loyalty was applied strictly at common law. In perhaps the most famous formulation of this duty, Justice Cardozo in *Meinhard v. Salmon*, 249 N.Y. 458, 164 N.E. 545, 546 (1928), stated that the standard of conduct applicable to a trustee was "[n]ot honor alone, but the punctilio of an honor the most sensitive. . . ." More recently, the Supreme Court in *N.L.R.B. v. Amax Coal Co.*, 453 U.S. 322, 330 (1981), applied this strict standard to employee benefit plans under the Taft-Hartley Act before enactment of ERISA by noting that "a trustee bears an unwavering duty of complete loyalty to the beneficiary of the trust, to the exclusion of the interests of other parties."

At common law, the duty of loyalty was the primary means of preventing fiduciary self-dealing. In adapting trust law to employee benefit plans, Congress enumerated and specifically prohibited many of the abuses formerly governed only by the duty of loyalty at common law. This greater specificity raises the issue of whether the duty of loyalty as embodied in Section 404(a)(1) has a significant independent existence within ERISA.

The answer to this question must be a resounding "yes." The structure of the statute itself, as well as court decisions and governmental pronouncements, all indicate that the solely-in-the-interest standard continues to be the central duty for ERISA fiduciaries. The statute lists the solely-in-the-interest standard first and does not relegate this standard to a particular subsection, apply it only in a specific situation, or permit any specific exceptions from its coverage. Indeed, both courts and the Department of Labor have indicated that Section 404(a)(1) itself imposes a separate duty of loyalty on ERISA fiduciaries.

The application of this and the other general fiduciary duties in ERISA Section 404 to plan investments is detailed in other chapters. This duty is not, however, limited to the investment context. For example, persons may be called upon to act as trustees for a number of plans that often cover different groups of participants and beneficiaries. Attempts by such trustees to differentiate among these groups may result in a breach of this duty of loyalty. For example, a breach of this duty would occur if the trustees of a multiemployer plan attempted to retroactively cancel service credits of participants of employers that have withdrawn from the plan. Similar breaches occur where trustees for two plans having similar participant populations consistently prefer the interests of one plan over the other in business dealings, or where apprentices in an apprenticeship program must repay the costs of their training unless they go to work for unionized employers.

Fiduciaries may also attempt to differentiate among participants as to the amount, type and timing of distributions. Courts have viewed these attempts in varying ways. For example, a breach does not occur simply because the right to a lump-sum distribution is restricted only to participants with smaller vested benefits. Further distinctions among participants in relation to benefit distributions may be more troublesome. For example, there is ordinarily no breach in conditioning accelerated lump-sum distributions on execution of a covenant not to compete where the plan has a substantial investment in company stock, courts have not approved distinctions of this type or delays in distribution where fiduciaries have failed to offer any explanation as to how their actions benefit the plan, or have admitted that they intended to punish participants who transferred to a competitor.

Exclusive Purpose

Sections 403(c)(1) and 404(a)(1)(A) provide that the assets of a plan shall be held for the exclusive purpose of providing benefits to participants and beneficiaries. Similarly, Section 401(a) of the Code provides that a qualified trust must be for the exclusive benefit of employees and beneficiaries. For purposes of this discussion, we refer collectively to these provisions as the *exclusive purpose rule*.

Courts have recognized that the exclusive purpose rule to a large extent overlaps with the requirement in ERISA Section 404(a)(1) that a fiduciary act solely in the interest of the plan and its participants and beneficiaries. As a result, much of the interpretive guidance provided with respect to the solely-in-the-interest standard apply with equal force to analyses under Section 404(a)(1)(A)'s exclusive purpose rule. Thus, the exclusive purpose rule in Sections 403(c) and 404(a)(1)(A) of ERISA, along with the solely-in-the-interest requirement, establishes a duty of loyalty owed by plan fiduciaries to plan participants and beneficiaries. However, the exclusive purpose rule also has certain specific applications, in part because its focus is restricted to the provision of benefits and payment of administrative expenses.

The exclusive purpose rule, like the other fiduciary duty rules in Section 404(a)(1) of ERISA, was based on prior law, and can be interpreted consistently with those preexisting legal standards. In the case of Section 404(a)(1)(A), the most relevant legal antecedents are Section 401(a) of the Internal Revenue Code and Section 302(c)(5) of the Taft-Hartley Act.

In adapting the preexisting law to the special purposes of employee benefit plans under ERISA, Congress created a two-prong test for the application of the exclusive purpose rule in ERISA Section 404(a)(1)(A). Under this approach, a fiduciary can satisfy Section 404(a)(1)(A) if the fiduciary acts for the purpose of *either* providing benefits as required by Section 404(a)(1)(A)(i) *or* defraying reasonable administrative costs as required in Section 404(a)(1)(A)(ii).

Provision of Benefits

A fiduciary satisfies the requirement of Section 404(a)(1)(A)(i) by managing and investing plan assets for the exclusive purpose of providing benefits. Thus, for example, a violation of this standard will occur where a fiduciary uses plan assets for the fiduciary's personal interests, or the interest of another party in interest. Similarly, a violation of the exclusive purpose standard will occur where plan assets are used to pay benefits to persons who are not eligible for benefits under the plan.

A particularly interesting variation on the application of the exclusive purpose rule occurs when a plan fiduciary proposes to make a socially responsible investment. The economic benefits of that investment flow to plan participants, but the investment also leads to benefits for nonparticipants—namely, society at large. In such cases, the Department of Labor has taken the position that a plan fiduciary may not sacrifice investment performance in order to achieve a social policy goal. However, where a fiduciary has identified two or more investments that are economically equal from the plan's point of view, the fiduciary may at that point consider the noneconomic, social policy factors in choosing an investment for the plan. This is consistent with the general rule that other parties may properly receive incidental benefits from plan investments, so long as the paramount goal in selecting those investments is, first and foremost, the financial well-being of the plan and its participants.

Reasonable Administrative Costs

In order to determine whether a fiduciary is acting for the exclusive purpose of defraying reasonable costs of plan administration, two determinations are necessary. First, the fiduciary may use plan assets to pay only those expenses properly chargeable to the plan. Second, even where the expenses are of the type that the plan may pay, the fiduciary may use plan assets only to pay expenses that are reasonable in amount.

With regard to the types of expenses that may be paid out of plan assets, the first focus of inquiry is the plan document itself. If the plan specifies that the plan sponsor will be responsible for paying certain expenses, the use of plan assets to pay those expenses will be a breach of Section 404(a)(1)(A)(ii).

Even where the plan permits the use of plan assets to pay administrative expenses, not all expenses related to the plan will qualify as expenses of administering the plan under Section 404(a)(1)(A)(ii). For example, services provided in conjunction with the establishment, termination and design of a plan ordinarily relate to the business activities of the plan sponsor. The Department of Labor has concluded that expenses related to these types of services will not constitute expenses of plan administration, and as a result cannot be paid from plan assets. However, the Department has also recognized that in the context of multiemployer plans, the responsibility for making decisions about the design of a plan will fall to the board of trustees, and not to the unions or employers that are ultimately the sponsors of the plan. Under those circumstances, if the plan documents provide that the trustees are acting in a fiduciary capacity when they take such actions, the cost of such an action can be paid from plan assets. Field Assistance Bulletin 2002-2 (November 4, 2002).

Where an expense is properly payable out of plan assets, a fiduciary also has a duty to inquire as to the reasonableness of the amount of the expense. In most situations, the reasonableness of administrative expenses can be determined by comparing the amount of the expenses with the scope and quality of services received. In more egregious situations, the absolute amount of plan assets committed to administrative expenses will indicate that a breach has occurred.

Prudence

ERISA Section 404(a)(1)(B) requires a plan fiduciary to discharge its duties with respect to a plan:
> with the care, skill, prudence, and diligence under the circumstances then prevailing that a prudent man acting in a like capacity and familiar with such matters would use in the conduct of an enterprise of a like character and with like aims.

ERISA's prudence standard is derived directly from the common law duty imposed on trustees in investing trust assets. At common law, this standard required a trustee to use the level of skill of a man of ordinary intelligence, although the trustee is bound to use a greater level of skill if he possesses it. Also at common law, the prudence of an investment was examined at the time the investment was made.

The common law prudence standard has been codified by most states through varying statutory pronouncements. These variations led Congress to recognize the need for a uniform, federal prudence standard to apply to employee benefit plans. Nevertheless, precedent derived from the common law of trusts is relevant to the prudence inquiry so long as those standards are applied in light of the special characteristics of employee benefit plans.

Much has been made of the possibility that Congress, in reformulating the common law prudent man rule to fit the particular needs of employee benefit plans, may have increased the level of care owed by plan fiduciaries. The common law of trusts required the level of skill of an ordinary person. ERISA Section 404(a)(1)(B) defines the *prudence standard* in terms of a "prudent man acting in a like capacity and familiar with such matter. . . ." Courts have noted that this provision establishes an extremely high standard for plan fiduciaries.

Does this high standard require a fiduciary to act as a *prudent expert*? Courts have generally said no, but have emphasized the importance of expertise in satisfying the prudence standard. Section 404(a)(1)(B) is technically designed to establish a flexible standard, the application of which may vary in different situations. Particularly in the investment area, however, prudence requires that fiduciaries either possess the expertise necessary to analyze investment opportunities, or seek outside experts to assist them.

Procedural Prudence

The prudence standard at common law was a test of conduct rather than result. As interpolated into ERISA, this has become known as the *standard of procedural prudence.*

A clear expression of this standard is found in the Department of Labor's regulation addressing an ERISA fiduciary's duty of prudence when investing plan assets. The Department stated that a fiduciary will satisfy the prudence requirement when investing plan assets if the fiduciary:

(A) has given appropriate consideration to those facts and circumstances that, given the scope of such fiduciary's investment duties, the fiduciary knows or should know are relevant to the particular investment or investment course of action involved . . . and (B) has acted accordingly.
29 CFR §2550.404a-1(b)(1).

In the Department's view, *appropriate consideration* includes (but is not limited to):

a determination by the fiduciary that the particular investment or course of action is reasonably designed . . . to further the purposes of the plan, taking into consideration the risk of loss and the opportunity for gain (or other return) associated with the investment or investment course of action . . . and (B) consideration of the following factors . . .

(i) The composition of the portfolio with regard to diversification;
(ii) The liquidity and current return of the portfolio relative to the anticipated cash flow requirements of the plan; and
(iii) The projected return of the portfolio relative to the funding objectives of the plan.
29 CFR §2550.404a-1(b)(2).

Although acknowledging that this regulation is merely a safe harbor and that other means of satisfying the prudence requirement in the investment context might therefore exist, the Department adopted this regulation in the face of some negative public comments in order to provide necessary guidance to fiduciaries in the satisfaction of their statutory duties. Indeed, the Department specifically refused to develop a "legal list" of appropriate plan investments, and rejected the urgings of some commentators to rule that certain types of investments were per se imprudent. The Department's focus remained firmly on the procedures followed by the plan fiduciary in making its investment decisions. Similarly, the Department recently stressed that when considering the appropriate response to allegations of improper conduct by mutual fund providers, fiduciaries fulfill the prudent investor rule by engaging in a "deliberative process" before deciding on a course of action.

Prudence in Noninvestment Contexts

The prudence requirement does no apply only to plan investments. The Department of Labor has noted that although the regulation deals only with investment activities, the prudence requirement applies to a fiduciary's exercise of all of its duties. One area that has attracted particular attention from the courts is the application of the prudence rule to the selection and monitoring of plan service providers. Those courts that have considered this issue have uniformly agreed that the prudence requirement applies to these activities.

As a threshold matter, a plan fiduciary must first determine whether the type of service to be provided would be necessary and helpful to the plan's participants and beneficiaries. If the answer is affirmative, the plan fiduciary must then select a person to provide that service. In order for a fiduciary to fulfill its prudence obligation in choosing a service provider, a fiduciary must inquire into the qualifications of a candidate and must follow accepted industry procedures for selecting a candidate.

Prudence in the choice of a service provider does not end a fiduciary's duty. The selecting fiduciary must also monitor the performance of the service provider. ERISA does not explicitly require that fiduciaries periodically review the performance of plan service providers. However, the monitoring function is central in two ERISA provisions that contemplate the appointment of persons to carry out plan functions. First, Section 405(d)(1) of ERISA permits the delegation of investment management authority to an investment manager as defined in ERISA Section 3(38). In connection with the appointment and review of such service providers, ERISA's legislative history notes:

> In order to act prudently in retaining a person to whom duties have been delegated, it is expected that the fiduciary will periodically review this person's performance. Depending upon the circumstances, this requirement may be satisfied by formal periodic review . . . or it may be met through day-to-day contact and evaluation, or in other appropriate ways. Since effective review requires that a person's services can be terminated, it may be necessary to enter into arrangements which the fiduciary can promptly terminate (within the limits of the circumstances).

H.R. Rep. 1280, 93d Cong., 2d Sess. 301.

Second, Section 408(b)(2) of ERISA provides an exemption from the prohibited transaction provisions of ERISA for the retention of parties in interest to provide services to a plan if, among other things, the services are provided pursuant to a reasonable arrangement. In the legislative history, Congress noted that one hallmark of a reasonable arrangement would be the plan's ability to terminate the contract or arrangement on relatively short notice if the contract or arrangement had become disadvantageous to the plan. Such a formulation naturally presumes that appropriate plan fiduciaries will be reviewing the arrangement to determine if it has begun to operate to the plan's detriment.

Expanding on the legislative history, the Department of Labor early in its stewardship of ERISA addressed the duty to monitor service providers. In Interpretive Bulletin 75-9, the Department stated:

> At reasonable intervals, the performance of trustees and other fiduciaries should be reviewed by the appointing fiduciary in such a manner as may reasonably be expected to ensure that their performance has been in compliance with the terms of the plan and statutory standards, and satisfies the needs of the plan. No single procedure will be appropriate in all cases; the procedure adopted may vary in accordance with the nature of the plan and other facts and circumstances relevant to the choice of the procedure.

29 CFR §2509.75-9.

Courts have also recognized that a prudent plan fiduciary must review the performance of plan service providers and should be guided by generally accepted standards in conducting such review.

Diversification

Section 404(a)(1)(C) requires a fiduciary to fulfill his or her duties with respect to a plan by diversifying plan investments unless it is "clearly prudent" under the circumstances not to do so. The statute states that the purpose of this restriction is to allow fiduciaries to "minimize the risk of large losses" that would result from an undue concentration of plan investments.

The diversification requirement is drawn directly from the common law of trusts. As in the case of the other fiduciary duties in Section 404(a)(1), Congress expanded upon this common law duty to fit the particular needs of employee benefit plans. Thus, for example, Section 404(a)(2) of ERISA provides an exemption from the diversification requirement for certain eligible individual account plans.

ERISA contains additional provisions demonstrating Congress' concern with diversification. Specifically, ERISA Section 407(a) contains a limited exemption for plan investments in real property leased to the employer and securities issued by the employer. Such real property (called *qualifying employer real property*) is a permissible investment only if, among other things, the real estate is geographically dispersed. Employer securities eligible for plan investment (called *qualifying employer securities*) must be either stock that meets certain diversified ownership criteria, or debt obligations that are "marketable obligations" meeting certain diversified holding requirements.

ERISA's Conference Report indicates that diversification is a case-by-case determination that cannot be stated as a fixed percentage of plan assets. The report indicates that fiduciaries should diversify in view of the number and type of investments held, and whether the value of such investments depends totally on the success of one enterprise or the economic conditions in a single geographic area.

Although Congress refused to specify percentage limitations for compliance with the diversification requirement, Congress did provide a list of factors relevant to the diversification determination in each case:

> The factors to be considered include (1) the purposes of the plan; (2) the amount of the plan assets; (3) financial and industrial conditions; (4) the type of investment, whether mortgages, bonds or shares of stock or otherwise; (5) distribution as to geographic location; (6) distribution as to industries; (7) the dates of maturity.

H.R. Rep 93-1280, 93d Cong., 2d Sess. p. 304.

Congress also recognized that many plan fiduciaries would invest plan assets largely or totally in pooled investment vehicles or mutual funds. In such cases, the diversification requirement would be met if the underlying assets of the pooled investment vehicle or mutual fund are themselves diversified. Similarly, a plan may invest all of its assets in insurance contracts and still satisfy the diversification requirement where the insurance company's investments are diversified.

A major condition placed on the diversification requirement is that a fiduciary must diversify plan assets unless it is "clearly prudent" not to do so. Congress indicated that the use of the term *clearly prudent* was not intended to establish a higher standard of prudence to be applied in determining diversification. Rather, Congress used the term to assure that, once a plaintiff has demonstrated a failure to diversify plan investments, the burden of proof will shift to the fiduciary to prove the prudence of the failure to diversify. A fiduciary must meet this burden not only by showing the prudence of each nondiversified investment made, but also by demonstrating that the plan has not been exposed to any significant risk of large losses as a result of the failure to diversify.

In Accordance With Plan Documents

The last of the major fiduciary duties listed in ERISA Section 404(a) is the requirement that a plan fiduciary act in accordance with the plan documents. Specifically, Section 404(a)(1)(D) requires a fiduciary to discharge his or her duties:

in accordance with the documents and instruments governing the plan insofar as such documents and instruments are consistent with the provisions of this title and title IV.

The requirement that a fiduciary act in accordance with governing documents and instruments is derived from the common law of trusts. At common law, the trustee was bound to comply with the terms of the document creating trustee status, unless such compliance would itself require illegal acts on the part of the trustee.

As in the case of the other fiduciary duties listed in Section 404(a) of ERISA, Congress modified this common law requirement to fit the particular needs of employee benefit plans and their participants and beneficiaries. Essentially, the requirement in Section 404(a)(1)(D) fulfills two purposes. First, it is the necessary extension of the requirement in ERISA Section 402 that all plans be governed by a written document. Second, requiring adherence to plan terms was considered central to ERISA's purpose of protecting participants and beneficiaries of employee benefit plans. The common law exception for situations in which obedience to trust documents would require illegal acts has been converted to the exception in Section 404(a)(1)(D) for situations in which plan documents conflict with the requirements of Titles I and IV of ERISA.

The application of Section 404(a)(1)(D) hinges on identifying the "documents and instruments governing the plan" and therefore governing fiduciary activity. However, Congress provided no guidance as to which documents and instruments fall within Section 404(a)(1)(D). Congress identified with some specificity the documents and instruments subject to other ERISA provisions. For example, the reporting and disclosure provisions of Subtitle B of Title I of ERISA detail the contents of a plan's summary annual report and summary plan description.

Similarly, ERISA Section 402(a) requires that a plan must be established pursuant to a "written instrument" that must identify one or more named fiduciaries of the plan. Additional content requirements for this "written instrument" are set forth in Section 402(b) of ERISA, pursuant to which a plan must state its funding policy, any procedures for allocating administrative responsibilities, its amendment procedures, and the basis on which payments are made to and from the plan.

ERISA also recognizes the existence of a trust agreement separate from the written instrument establishing the plan. ERISA Section 403(a) states that a trustee may be named either "in the trust instrument or the plan instrument described in section 402(a)."

The term *documents and instruments governing the plan* is, unfortunately, undefined. To be sure, the written instrument establishing a plan will qualify as one of the documents and instruments subject to Section 404(a)(1)(D). Similarly, the trust agreement pursuant to which plan assets are held will be an instrument within the coverage of Section 404(a)(1)(D). Aside from these two obvious categories, the courts and the Department of Labor have identified a wide variety of documents that they will for certain purposes view as documents and instruments governing a plan. Among such documents are collective bargaining agreements, investment management agreements, investment guidelines and, in some cases, summary plan descriptions.

Once a fiduciary has identified those documents and instruments governing the operation of the plan, the fiduciary is bound to act in accordance with those documents and instruments only to the extent that those documents and instruments are consistent with the provisions of Title I and Title IV of ERISA. Fiduciaries are at the same time liable for determining whether the plan would require actions in violation of ERISA. Clearly, compliance with terms that are made illegal by ERISA would be a breach of Section 404(a)(1)(D). Other situations are less clear-cut. Where interpretation of plan provisions is required, a fiduciary will generally not be viewed as breaching Section 404(a)(1)(D) merely by incorrectly construing plan documents; additional action to enforce the incorrect interpretation would be required for a breach to occur.

Proxy Voting

The Department of Labor has provided extensive guidance regarding the role of governing plan documents in situations involving the voting of proxies appurtenant to securities held by a plan. As interpreted by the Department, Section 404(a)(1)(D) requires specific delineation of the authority to vote proxies and strict adherence to the literal plan language conferring such authority.

The Department in 1988 recognized that proxies appurtenant to shares held by a plan are themselves plan assets, and the management of such proxies is subject to ERISA's fiduciary duty provisions. In Interpretive Bulletin 94-2, the Department affirmed the rule that when a named fiduciary has delegated investment management authority to an investment manager pursuant to ERISA Section 402, 405 and 3(38), the exclusive responsibility to vote proxies would also be delegated. The named fiduciary could retain the right to vote proxies only if it explicitly reserved that right in its delegation of investment management authority. In any situation in which the plan documents do not expressly preclude the investment manager from voting proxies, ERISA requires that the right to vote proxies must rest exclusively with the investment manager.

The Department has expanded this rationale to participant voting in tender offer situations.

This is not to say that a fiduciary must follow all plan terms regarding proxy and other participant voting issues in all cases. As early as 1984, the Department noted that plan terms regarding pass-through voting could not be enforced if, under ERISA Section 404(a)(1)(D), such terms conflict with Title I or IV of ERISA. In particular, the Department has taken the position that a plan fiduciary may not avoid responsibility for voting shares even where the plan document stipulates the method in which the fiduciary must vote unallocated shares or shares as to which no participant instructions have been received. Thus, for example, if following plan provisions would require a fiduciary to vote unallocated or nonvoting allocated shares in an imprudent manner, Section 404(a)(1)(D) would require prudence concerns to override the plan's terms. Thus, the overriding concern in voting shares must at all times be the financial well-being of the plan's participants and beneficiaries, without consideration to the interests of any other party.

Collectively Bargained Plans

Despite the fact that collective bargaining agreements are plan documents governing a plan, courts have identified a number of areas in which the fiduciaries of such plans may ignore collectively bargained terms in order to assure ERISA compliance. For example, it is well established that a fiduciary may refuse to accept contributions at a collectively bargained rate when to do so would imprudently endanger the financial status of the plan.

Similarly, courts have declared inoperative amendments to collectively bargained plans that purport to confer life tenure on a plan's board of trustees. Amendments such as these are usually developed by the board of trustees because the board is ordinarily vested with amendment authority in the case of collectively bargained plans. Such provisions are contrary to a fiduciary's duty of loyalty to the plan under ERISA Section 404.

The Department of Labor has also limited the extent to which a board of trustees can amend a collectively bargained plan to admit new participants. In Advisory Opinion 91-15A, the Department addressed a situation in which plan trustees proposed amending a plan to include employees of the union and of several other union-sponsored plans as participants. Because these new participants would be permitted to participate on a more favorable basis than existing participants, the Department concluded that the proposed amendment would violate Sections 404 and 406 of ERISA and would therefore be ineffective.

Collectively bargained multiemployer plans are also unusual in that the named fiduciary—that is, the board of trustees—also often engages in acts that would be the province of the employer or other plan sponsor in a single employer context. These acts, referred to as *settlor functions,* include among other things amending the plan to change eligibility requirements or benefit levels. The normal rule is that when a plan sponsor engages in settlor functions, the sponsor does not owe a fiduciary duty to plan participants. For multiemployer plans, however, the question of whether plan trustees owe a fiduciary duty to participants when engaging in acts that otherwise would be considered settlor functions is controlled by the plan documents. The Department of Labor has determined that if the plan documents do not dictate that the trustees act in a fiduciary capacity when amending the plan, the trustees will not be subject to fiduciary liability as a result of any amendment. Field Assistance Bulletin 2002-2 (November 4, 2002). The advantage of not being a fiduciary when amending the plan is that the trustees could make changes that are harmful to the interests of some participants without fearing liability for those changes. The disadvantage is that the trustees may not use plan assets to pay for the costs of these nonfiduciary acts.

PROHIBITED TRANSACTIONS

The general fiduciary duty rules of Sections 403 and 404 of ERISA are supplemented by the prohibited transaction rules of Sections 406 and 407 of ERISA. As described more fully below, ERISA Section 406(a) establishes a number of per se prohibitions preventing fiduciaries from causing plans to engage in transactions with "parties in interest." Section 406(b) prohibits self-dealing and conflicts of interest involving plan fiduciaries. Section 407 provides rules governing plan investments in securities issued by employers of employees covered by the plan.

Parties in Interest

A prerequisite to applying ERISA's prohibited transaction rules is the identification of the "parties in inter-

est" with respect to the plan. ERISA Section 3(14) states that a *party in interest* with respect to a plan includes:
- (A) any fiduciary (including, but not limited to, any administrator, officer, trustee or custodian), counsel, or employee of such employee benefit plan;
- (B) a person providing services to such plan;
- (C) an employer any of whose employees are covered by such plan;
- (D) an employee organization any of whose members are covered by such plan;
- (E) an owner, direct or indirect, of 50 percent or more of—
  - (i) the combined voting power of all classes of stock entitled to vote or the total value of all shares of stock of a corporation;
  - (ii) the capital interest or profits interest of a partnership; or
  - (iii) the beneficial interest of a trust or unincorporated enterprise which is an employer or an employee organization described in subparagraph (C) or (D);
- (F) a relative (as defined in paragraph (15)) of any individual described in subparagraph (A), (B), (C) or (E);
- (G) a corporation, partnership, or trust or estate of which (or in which) 50 percent or more of—
  - (i) the combined voting power of all classes of stock entitled to vote or the total value of shares of all classes of stock of such corporation;
  - (ii) the capital interest or profits interest of such partnership; or
  - (iii) the beneficial interest of such trust or estate, is owned directly or indirectly by persons described in subparagraph (A),(B),(C), (D) or (E);
- (H) an employee, officer, director (or a person having powers or responsibilities similar to those of officers or directors) or a 10 percent or more shareholder directly or indirectly of a person described in (B), (C), (D), (E) or (G), or of the employee benefit plan; or
- (I) a 10 percent or more (directly or indirectly in capital or profits) partner or joint venturer of a person described in subparagraphs (B), (C), (D), (E) or (G).

The provisions of Section 3(14) of ERISA are interpreted and applied in a strict and literal manner, and party-in-interest status will not result unless one of the relationships enumerated in Section 3(14) is found. For example, because Section 3(14)(G) requires a 50% ownership interest, ownership of up to 49.9% will not cause party-in-interest status under that section. In addition, we note that, in calculating the ownership percentages under ERISA Section 3(14), interests held by a group trust, bank collective investment fund or insurance company separate account are attributed to the plans participating in the trust, fund or account rather than to the managing trustee, bank or insurance company.

Per Se Prohibitions—Section 406(a)

ERISA Section 406(a) absolutely prohibits certain categories of transactions between a plan and a "party in interest." As discussed below, the fiduciary authorizing a prohibited transaction and the party in interest will be liable for losses, in the case of the fiduciary, and excise taxes or civil penalties, in the case of the party in interest. The transaction may also be rescinded and any profits of the fiduciary disgorged. It should be noted that even a transaction with a party in interest that is beneficial to the plan will be prohibited under these per se rules.

Absent exemptive relief, the following transactions are per se prohibited transactions under ERISA Section 406(a).

A Sale or Exchange of Property
Between a Plan and a Party in Interest

For example, this section would prohibit the sale of stock or real estate by the plan sponsor to the plan. Similarly, the sale of a bond to the plan in a principal transaction by a broker who provides other services to the plan would be prohibited.

A Loan or Other Extension of Credit
Between a Plan and a Party in Interest

For example, a prohibited transaction would occur where a plan sponsor advances funds to a plan to effect daily securities transactions. The plan's purchase of a bond *issued* by a provider of services to the plan or by the plan sponsor would also be prohibited. A guaranty issued to a plan by a party in interest could also be viewed as a prohibited extension of credit.

The Provision of Services, Goods or Facilities
Between the Plan and a Party in Interest

For example, a prohibited transaction will occur upon a plan's renewal of its contract with an investment manager. Once the manager begins to provide services, it becomes a "party in interest." Thus, any renewal of a contract is the provision of services by a party in interest.

The Transfer of Plan Assets to or for
the Use or Benefit of a Party in Interest

An example of this type of prohibited transaction occurs where a plan fiduciary causes the plan to purchase the plan sponsor's stock from an unrelated party in order to assist the plan sponsor in blocking a takeover attempt.

Section 406(a) states that these listed prohibited transactions can occur either directly or indirectly. The Department of Labor has indicated that an indirect prohibited transaction will occur where there is an arrangement to confer a prohibited benefit on a party in interest. Thus, for example, the sale of a plan asset to a third party straw man, who in turn sells the asset to a party in interest, will result in an indirect prohibited transaction under Section 406(a)(1)(D).

Prohibited Conflicts of Interest

In addition to transactions between the plan and "parties in interest," ERISA Section 406(b) also prohibits self-dealing and other conflicts of interest by plan fiduciaries. The prohibitions in Section 406(b) complement the general fiduciary duty rules in ERISA Section 404 and are interpreted in a manner consistent with the general fiduciary provisions. As distinct from the per se prohibitions in Section 406(a), Section 406(b) generally requires the analysis of all surrounding facts and circumstances to determine if a prohibited conflict or self-dealing exists. This requires an additional level of care from fiduciaries to avoid violations of Section 406(b).

Fiduciary Self-Dealing

ERISA Section 406(b)(1) states that a fiduciary may not deal with the plan's assets in his own interest or for his own account. The Department of Labor has explained this provision as meaning that a fiduciary should not act in any transaction in which he has an interest that could affect his best judgment as a fiduciary. Application of this provision requires an identification of the fiduciary's interest and the determination of whether that interest rises to the level of affecting the fiduciary's judgment. For example, courts have agreed that a fiduciary's receipt of an incidental benefit from a transaction that otherwise is primarily for the benefit of a plan will not violate Section 406(b)(1).

Situations involving fiduciary fees and fee structures often raise issues under Section 406(b)(1). Clearly, a fiduciary may not exercise any discretion to affect the amount or timing of his or her fees. This precept has caused the Department to indicate that certain performance fee arrangements may result in fiduciary self-dealing where, for example, the fiduciary's determination of whether to sell assets and which assets to sell directly affect the timing and amount of a performance fee.

Similarly, the Department of Labor has indicated that a fiduciary may not hire itself or its affiliate to provide services to the plan unless (1) the fiduciary charges no additional fee; or (2) the fee is limited to recoupment of "direct expenses" in providing the service. This "direct expenses" exception has been recognized as allowing fiduciaries to recoup certain costs (including employee salaries) where the fiduciary keeps records sufficient to indicate that the cost would not have been incurred but for the provision of services to the plan.

Fiduciary Conflict of Interest

Section 406(b)(2) states that a fiduciary may not represent or act on behalf of a party with interests adverse to those of the plan in a transaction involving plan assets. This section requires both the identification of an adversity of interests, as well as action by a fiduciary on behalf of a party other than the plan. Both of these are essentially factual determinations.

An adversity of interests most clearly exists when the fiduciary acts on both sides of the transaction. For example, a corporate official of the plan sponsor who is a plan fiduciary may not represent both the corporation and the plan in negotiating a sale of property between the sponsor and the plan. Other situations are less clear. Thus, the investment of plan assets on the same terms as a fiduciary's investment (for example, in the purchase of separate limited partnership interests in the same partnership) would not without more constitute a violation of Section 406(b)(2) because there is no present adversity of interests involved.

In the presence of an adversity of interests, a fiduciary can take a number of steps to avoid acting on behalf of an adverse party. The fiduciary facing the conflict can be removed from the decision making process through the appointment of an independent decision maker. Similarly, the fiduciary may be able to recuse itself from the matter involving the adversity and thereby avoid a violation of Section 406(b)(2).

Kickbacks

ERISA Section 406(b)(3) prohibits a fiduciary from receiving any consideration for his or her personal account from any party dealing with the plan in connection with a transaction involving plan assets. This rule clearly prohibits traditional kickbacks, but it also prohibits less obvious transactions. For example, a plan sponsor that invests plan assets with an investment manager may not receive a discount from that manager on other services provided to the company rather than the plan.

In light of the potentially serious nature of many Section 406(b)(3) violations, the Department of Labor rarely grants exemptions to transactions prohibited by this section. For the same reason, however, the Department and the courts have carefully studied transactions and have narrowly interpreted the requirement that payments be made "in connection with" a transaction involving plan assets. For example, the payment of a trustee's fee by a plan sponsor rather than by the plan will not involve a violation of Section 406(b)(3). As a result, a fiduciary receiving a payment from a third party has the opportunity of showing that payments were made for services other than a transaction involving plan assets. As a result, a fiduciary receiving a payment from a third party has the opportunity of showing that payments were made for services other than a transaction involving plan assets. Similarly, the payment of 12b-1 or shareholder servicing fees to a service provider, including a fiduciary, from a mutual fund, will not necessarily involve a violation of Section 406(b)(3) where the payment has been disclosed to the plan's fiduciary and the service provider has not caused the plan to invest in the mutual fund paying the fees. DOL Advisory Opinions 97-15A and 97-16A (May 22, 1997).

Employer Securities and Real Property

ERISA Sections 406(a)(2) and 407 prohibit a plan from holding "employer securities" or "employer real property" unless the securities and real property are "qualifying." *Employer real property* is real property leased to the plan sponsor or an affiliate. *Employer securities* are securities issued by the plan sponsor or an affiliate. ERISA §§407(d)(1), (2). *Qualifying employer securities* include stock, marketable obligations and certain limited partnership interests if immediately following the acquisition no more than 25% of the stock is held by the plan *and* at least 50% of the outstanding stock is held by persons independent of the issues. *Qualifying real property* must be dispersed geographically and be suitable for more than one use. If the plan is not an individual account plan, no more than 10% of the plan assets are invested in employer securities and employer real property. In addition, a plan may not purchase employer securities or real property from a party in interest, such as the employer, absent an exemption. Such exemptive relief is provided by ERISA Section 408(e) for a plan's purchase or sale of qualifying employer securities or qualifying employer real property if (a) no commission is charged, (b) the compensation is adequate and (c) the 10% limit applicable to nonindividual account plans is observed.

Statutory and Administrative Exemptions

Aware of the potential breadth of the prohibited transaction provisions, Congress included in ERISA a number of statutory exceptions applicable to transactions that, in Congress' view, were common in the marketplace and posed no threat of abuse. For additional flexibility, Congress also gave the Department of Labor the authority to grant administrative exemptions provided the Department concluded that granting an exemption was (1) administratively feasible; (2) in the interests of the plan and its participants and beneficiaries; and (3) protective of the rights of the plan participants and beneficiaries. Pursuant to this authority, the Department has over the years granted exemptions not only for individual transactions, but for a wide range of classes of transactions. Summarized below are some of the more important statutory exceptions and administrative class exemptions.

Provision of Services by a Party in Interest

A party in interest may provide (and be paid for) services to a plan if (1) the services are necessary for the operation of the plan, (2) they are supplied under a reasonable arrangement (which includes the plan's right to terminate without penalty on reasonably short notice) and (3) the plan pays no more than reasonable compensation. ERISA §408(b)(2). This exemption does not provide relief for self-dealing (e.g., it does not allow a fiduciary to cause the plan to pay itself additional fees). It is important to be aware that the payment of fees for a service may not always involve the direct transfer of funds from the plan to a party in interest. For example, a trust company may receive a portion of its compensation in the form of fees paid by mutual fund companies. DOL Advisory Opinion 2003-09A (June 25, 2003). Similarly, a bank may receive a portion of its compensation by being allowed to retain the "float" that is earned on funds in a general transfer account. DOL Field Assistance Bulletin 2002-3 (November 5, 2002). Such alternative compensation methods are proper where they have been disclosed to the appropriate fiduciary and the fiduciary has considered such compensation as a portion of the overall cost to the plan of receiving services from the party in interest.

Interest-Free Loans

Prohibited Transaction Exemption (PTE) 80-26 permits a party in interest to make an interest-free, unsecured loan to (or guarantee the debt of) a plan. The loan proceeds may be used only for (1) payment of the ordinary operating expenses of the plan (including benefit payments), or (2) for a term of three business days, for purposes incidental to the operation of the plan. On December 15, 2004, the Department of Labor proposed an amendment to PTE 80-26 which would eliminate the requirement that such a loan must be for no more than three business days. 69 *Fed. Reg.* 75088. Before entering into such a loan, a plan fiduciary should determine whether this amendment has been adopted.

Qualified Professional Asset Managers (QPAMs)

PTE 84-14, the QPAM exemption, generally permits most party-in-interest transactions that would otherwise be prohibited if, among other conditions, the assets involved in the transaction are managed by a QPAM. A *QPAM* is a bank, savings and loan or insurer meeting minimum capitalization requirements or a registered investment advisor with minimum capital and assets under management. This exemption provides no relief for self-dealing violations of Section 406(b). Nor does it cover transactions between a fund and the QPAM or persons who have appointment authority over the QPAM (e.g., employers).

Securities Lending

PTE 81-6 permits a plan to lend securities to banks and broker-dealers who are parties in interest if certain conditions are met. PTE 82-63 covers the payment of compensation for securities lending services to a fiduciary upon approval of an independent plan fiduciary. The Department of Labor announced on October 23, 2003 that it was considering an amendment to this PTE which would extend it to certain foreign banks and broker-dealers and would allow a plan to accept additional types of collateral when loaning securities. 68 *Fed. Reg.* 60715.

Short-Term Investments

PTE 81-8 permits a plan to invest in bankers acceptances, commercial paper, repurchase agreements and certificates of deposit that might otherwise be prohibited as party-in-interest transactions. There are specific conditions for each type of investment.

Investments in a Bank Collective Fund or Insurance Company Pooled Separate Account

ERISA Section 408(b)(8) allows a plan to purchase units in a bank collective fund or pooled separate account maintained by a party-in-interest bank or insurance company if certain conditions are met. The Department of Labor has recently confirmed that this exemption covers the prohibitions of both Section 406(a) and 406(b). See DOL Adv. Opinion 96-15A (Aug. 7, 1996).

Transactions by a Bank Collective Fund or Pooled Separate Account

An insurance company pooled separate account or a bank collective fund in which plans invest is deemed to hold plan assets. Thus, in order to engage in transactions with parties in interest with respect to any investing plan, the account or fund must comply with PTE 90-1 or PTE 91-38. These class exemptions do not exempt self-dealing violations by the managers of the account or fund.

Broker-Dealer Exemption

PTE 75-1 provides relief for agency, principal, market-making and underwriting transactions and for extensions of credits to a plan by a broker-dealer. Under the exemption, (1) a fiduciary broker may effect or execute securities transactions for the plan, (2) certain agency cross transactions may be effected if the broker does not have discretion on both sides, (3) securities may be bought or sold in principal transactions between a plan and a party-in-interest broker, bank or reporting dealer and (4) certain market-making and underwriting transactions between plans and fiduciary broker-dealers are authorized. On April 28, 2004, DOL proposed an amendment to PTE 75-1 that would expand the breadth of the transactions covered under the exemption. 69 *Fed. Reg.* 23216 (April 28, 2004). If adopted, this amendment will make it easier for plans to engage in transactions with parties in interest who are fiduciaries with respect to certain assets but only service providers with respect to others.

Insurance Agents, Consultants and Mutual Fund Underwriters

PTE 84-24 provides relief for certain transactions with insurance companies, mutual fund underwriters, insurance agents and consultants. This exemption allows fiduciary salespersons to provide investment advice to plans and receive commissions on plan transactions if certain conditions are met. It also authorizes sales of insurance or mutual fund shares to plans by party-in-interest insurers or underwriters. On September 14, 2004, DOL proposed an amendment to PTE 84-24 that would make clear that the exemption is available for transactions involving plans participating in a collective trust and the trustee of the trust (or its affiliate) so long as the trustee does not act as a fiduciary in connection with the subject transaction under PTE 84-24. 69 *Fed. Reg.* 55463 (Sept. 14, 2004). Again, this amendment—if adopted—will make it easier for plans to engage in transactions with parties in interest that would otherwise have been prohibited.

LIABILITY FOR FIDUCIARY VIOLATIONS

ERISA provides that when a fiduciary breaches its fiduciary duties, the fiduciary is personally liable to make good any losses suffered by the plan as a result of the breach. As noted above, Congress mandated that this liability be imposed personally on the fiduciary so that plan assets could not be used to pay for the fiduciary's liability. The fiduciary is also personally liable to restore to the plan any profits that the fiduciary made through the use of plan assets in violation of its fiduciary duties. The breaching fiduciary can also be subject to equitable (nonmonetary) relief such as removal from its position as a fiduciary and an injunction preventing the person from serving in a fiduciary capacity for any other plan.

In the event of a fiduciary breach, the fiduciary can be sued by the Department of Labor, plan participants and beneficiaries and other plan fiduciaries. If any of these parties prevail, they may be awarded attorney fees and court costs. Where the Department of Labor is involved in the lawsuit, the fiduciary may also be assessed a civil penalty equal to 20% of the amount recovered on behalf of the plan.

Where the fiduciary violation also involves a prohibited transaction, additional penalties apply. In the case of a qualified pension plan, the party in interest involved in the transaction (which includes the fiduciary in the case of fiduciary self-dealing) is liable for an excise tax equal to 15% of the amount involved in the transaction for each taxable year in which the transaction remains uncorrected. If the transaction is not corrected despite requests from the IRS, the excise tax can increase to 100% of the amount involved. Similar civil penalties are imposed by the Department of Labor in the case of welfare plans and pension plans not subject to the qualification rules in the Internal Revenue Code.

Co-Fiduciary Liability

A fiduciary is not only liable for losses arising out of its own activities, but also for a breach of duty by a second fiduciary where the first fiduciary knowingly participates in or conceals a breach, enables the second fiduciary to commit a breach, or has knowledge of a breach and fails to make reasonable efforts to remedy the breach. ERISA §405(a).

A person generally will not be liable for a breach of fiduciary duty that was committed before the person became a fiduciary, or after the person ceased to be a fiduciary. ERISA §409(b). However, a fiduciary may be held liable for its own subsequent breach of fiduciary duty where it knows of a breach of fiduciary duty by a predecessor and fails to take reasonable actions to remedy the breach. Such reasonable steps may include examining and rescinding the prior actions of a predecessor if those actions violated ERISA.

The Department of Labor has indicated, however, that where a fiduciary is aware only that a breach of fiduciary duty may have taken place, the fiduciary need not take steps to further investigate the potential breach, but rather may satisfy its duty to the plan by notifying the plan trustees of the information it has. The Department further indicated that a fiduciary is not required to implement special procedures for the sole purpose of evaluating whether a given transaction constituted a breach of fiduciary duty.

If an entity is not deemed to be a fiduciary, it will not be liable for participating in a fiduciary's breach of duty, even if it was aware that the fiduciary's activities constituted a fiduciary violation. This does not mean that a nonfiduciary will always escape liability for fiduciary breaches. If the fiduciary breach involves a prohibited transaction under Section 406(a) of ERISA and the nonfiduciary was the "party in interest" involved in the transaction, the nonfiduciary party in interest could be compelled to rescind the transaction.

Fiduciary Insurance and Indemnification

ERISA declares as void and against public policy any provision in a plan document or other agreement that purports to relieve a fiduciary from personal liability in the event of a fiduciary breach. This is not to say that a fiduciary can take no steps to protect itself from liability. A fiduciary can purchase fiduciary liability insurance. Plan assets can be used for the purchase of such insurance provided that the policy provides recourse against the fiduciary. In such cases, the fiduciary will ordinarily purchase a nonrecourse rider with its own assets.

A fiduciary may also seek indemnification in order to limit its exposure to fiduciary liability. Plan assets can be used to provide indemnification only if the plan so provides and then only if there is no fiduciary breach involved. For example, a fiduciary can receive from a plan reimbursement of court costs, attorney fees and other expenses incurred in successfully defending a suit for fiduciary breach.

Chapter 5

Delegation of Responsibility

Thomas E. Funk and William H. Tobin

INTRODUCTION

Anyone familiar with employee benefit plans knows that the operation and administration of such plans involves myriad duties and responsibilities. Fiduciaries must collect contributions, develop benefit plans, make payments to beneficiaries and invest plan assets, among many other integral duties of employee benefit plan administration.

If fiduciaries of employee benefit plans were required to personally perform all these functions, they would have to possess the skills and knowledge of an attorney, actuary, administrator, accountant and investment advisor. No such person exists! Most fiduciaries will not have the expertise necessary to carry out their fiduciary responsibilities in administering a plan without the use of experts or delegates. In fact, to attempt to administer a plan without the assistance of qualified experts and delegates risks a breach of the fiduciary's responsibilities under the Employee Retirement Income Security Act of 1974, as amended (ERISA). Consequently, a primary function of a fiduciary will be delegating responsibilities or duties to the extent authorized and in accordance with a procedure set forth in the plan document and to monitor those persons to whom the fiduciary delegates duties. A fiduciary may limit his or her liability if he or she properly selects and monitors delegates and advisors.

> Upon proper allocation or delegation, fiduciaries will not be liable for the acts or omissions of the persons to whom duties have been allocated or delegated.... [I]n implementing the procedures of the plan, plan fiduciaries must act prudently and in the interests of participants and beneficiaries. The fiduciaries also must act in this manner in choosing the person to whom they allocate or delegate their duties. Additionally, they must act in this manner in continuing the allocation or delegation of their duties.
>
> ERISA Conf. Report at 301, 1974 U.S.C.C.A.N. at 5,081-82.

The question, then, is the extent to which the law allows fiduciaries of employee benefit plans to delegate their duties and responsibilities to others and whether they can still be held liable for the acts delegated.

This chapter will review the legal guidelines that apply to the delegation of responsibility by fiduciaries of employee benefit plans. The extent to which the law allows such delegation will be analyzed, together with the concurrent question of the effect of such delegation on the potential liability of the fiduciary. ERISA clearly contemplates and allows for the allocation and delegation of fiduciary and trustee responsibilities.

For purposes of this chapter, the term *fiduciary responsibility* will mean any discretionary authority or discretionary responsibility in the administration or management of a plan, and the term *trustee responsibility* will mean authority or control respecting management or control of the assets of a plan.

TRUSTEE RESPONSIBILITIES

With respect to trustee responsibilities, ERISA Section 403(a) requires that all assets of an employee benefit plan be held in trust by one or more trustees. Such trustees have exclusive authority and discretion to manage and control those assets.

In the context of a Taft-Hartley plan, the employers and unions which sponsor the plan appoint individuals to serve as members of the plan's joint board of trustees. These trustees have this exclusive authority and discretion. ERISA explicitly permits the named fiduciaries to delegate this authority to an investment manager. (In Taft-Hartley plans, the joint board of trustees is also the named fiduciary; thus the board can appoint an investment manager.) ERISA §402(c)(3).

In general, an *investment manager* for ERISA purposes means an investment advisor under the Investment Advisers Act of 1940 (or a bank or an insurance company) that acknowledges in writing that it is a fiduciary with respect to the plan. Note that the named fiduciary may hire a professional to invest assets of the plan, but such a professional will not in all cases assume fiduciary responsibility for investment of the assets. For example, investments in mutual funds do not generally transfer fiduciary responsibility to the mutual fund manager. Trustees and their advisors should carefully review all documentation detailing the arrangement to assess the relative responsibilities. If the investment professional does not assume fiduciary responsibility, such responsibility will continue to reside with the trustees.

FIDUCIARY RESPONSIBILITIES

As to fiduciary responsibilities, ERISA Section 405(c) provides that the instrument under which the plan is maintained may expressly provide procedures for named fiduciaries to designate persons other than named fiduciaries to carry out fiduciary responsibilities under the plan.

Again, as previously noted, in the context of a Taft-Hartley plan, the members of the joint board of trustees are the named fiduciaries. An adjunct to delegation of fiduciary responsibility is the allocation of such responsibilities among named fiduciaries.

Allocation of fiduciary responsibilities typically involves a situation in which, in the context of a Taft-Hartley board of trustees, the board fixes certain responsibilities in some but not all members of the board. An example would be a board's appointment of a delinquency committee consisting of two individual trustees who would be responsible for monitoring the collection of all required employer contributions.

Again, it should be emphasized that, for a delegation or allocation of fiduciary responsibility to conform to the requirements of ERISA, the plan document must specifically allow and provide a procedure for it.

RULE OF PRUDENCE IN DELEGATION

Having determined that the law permits delegation and allocation of responsibilities, the next logical inquiry is the legal consequence of such delegation or allocation. One might ask: Does the act of delegating or allocating relieve the fiduciary of any responsibility or liability for the delegate's conduct? Again, ERISA addresses this question.

Prudence in Selection of Delegate

Section 405 of ERISA provides that a fiduciary will *not be liable* for an act or omission of a person to whom responsibility has been delegated or allocated if, in making the delegation, the fiduciary acted prudently and in the interest of participants and beneficiaries.

This means that, like any other act of a fiduciary, the general ERISA standards that govern fiduciary conduct apply to the act of delegating or allocating responsibility. Stated broadly and succinctly, these standards are that a fiduciary must discharge his or her duties solely in the interests of the participants and beneficiaries and in accordance with ERISA's *rule of prudence.* More specifically, this requires that the fiduciary act prudently in choosing the delegate person or firm and also act prudently in continuing this delegation.

In Accordance With Plan Documents

The plan documents are a focal point in determining when and how fiduciaries can delegate duties. The plan must authorize delegation and contain a procedure for making a delegation, and the fiduciary must act in accordance with the delegation procedures. If not, a court could determine the fiduciary breached his or her fiduciary duties under ERISA by not operating the plan in accordance with its terms. *Sandoval v. Simmons,* 622 F.Supp. 1174, 1216 (C.D.Ill. 1985) (fiduciary breach due to failure to follow delegation procedures in plan document). Also, and perhaps more importantly, the named fiduciaries will not be shielded from liability for breaches of a delegate if the document under which the plan is being maintained does not permit such delegation or if the delegation was improper. If the named fiduciary fails to comply with the various requirements in the plan in attempting to delegate responsibility, the delegation fails and the fiduciary has not transferred fiduciary responsibility.

> If the instrument under which the plan is maintained does not provide for a procedure for the designation of persons who are not named fiduciaries to carry out fiduciary responsibility, then any such designation the named fiduciaries may make will not relieve the named fiduciaries from responsibility or liability for the acts or omissions of the persons so designated.
>
> DOL Reg. §2509.75-8 (FR-14).

Prudence in Monitoring

A fiduciary's responsibilities continue after the delegate's appointment. A fiduciary has a duty to monitor the delegate's performance and to withdraw responsibilities from the delegate if and when it becomes clear that the delegate is not performing his or her duties properly.

Thus, effective delegation requires a fiduciary to monitor the delegate's performance and to withdraw responsibilities from the delegate if and when it becomes clear that the delegate fails to perform its duties properly. Thus, effective delegation requires a fiduciary to monitor the delegate. In reviewing this prudence requirement, the Conference Committee joint explanation of ERISA Section 405 states:

> In order to act prudently in retaining a person to whom duties have been delegated, it is expected that the fiduciary will periodically review this person's performance. Depending upon the circumstances, this requirement may be satisfied by formal periodic review (which may be by all the named fiduciaries who have participated in the delegation or by a specially designated review committee), or it may be met through day-to-day contact and evaluation, or in other appropriate ways. Since effective review requires that a person's services can be terminated, it may be necessary to enter into arrangements which the fiduciary can promptly terminate (within the limits of the circumstances).

Document All Delegation

It is important to create a "paper trail" or record supporting the fiduciaries' decision to delegate or allocate responsibilities. In the event of an audit by the DOL or IRS, the fiduciaries will be required to demonstrate the appropriate delegation. Accordingly, fiduciaries should document the process followed in selecting, retaining and monitoring a delegate, including the basis for the decision, the factors reviewed and the care given the decision. This will provide an "institutional memory" of the decision.

Effect of Delegation

If fiduciaries allocate or delegate responsibility in accordance with such a procedure and within the express provisions of the plan, then the fiduciary who delegates such duty will not, with certain exceptions, be liable for the act or omission of the delegate. ERISA §405(c)(2).

However, a fiduciary could be liable to the extent the named fiduciary does not exercise prudence with respect to (a) the initial allocation or delegation, (b) the continuation of the allocation or delegation or (c) the establishment or implementation of the delegation procedures.

Further, in the context of allocation, the general co-fiduciary rules of ERISA apply. This means that, even if a fiduciary has allocated a responsibility to another fiduciary, he or she *will still be liable if*:

1. Because of his or her failure to act prudently, he or she enables the other fiduciary to commit a breach
2. He or she has knowledge of a breach by another fiduciary and fails to make reasonable efforts to remedy the breach or
3. He or she conceals a breach of another.

ERISA PROCEDURES FOR DELEGATION—COURT DECISIONS

Numerous cases, many of which relate to the investment of the assets of an employee benefit plan, demonstrate the importance of adhering to the requirements of ERISA in the area of delegation.

Written Delegation

In one case, *McManus & Pellouchoud, Inc. Employees' Profit Sharing Trust v. L.F. Rothschild,* 1989 U.S. Dist. LEXIS 10098 (N.D.Ill. 1989), the trustees (who were also the named fiduciaries) delegated authority to the defendants to manage the trust's investments.

However, under ERISA (as previously noted), for a fiduciary to effectively transfer responsibility for the investment of plan assets, the responsibility must be transferred to a firm or person that qualifies as an investment manager and acknowledges *in writing* that it is a fiduciary with respect to the plan.

In this case, the defendant had not signed any such written acknowledgment. The court, therefore, concluded that the trustees retained responsibility with respect to investment of the trust assets. As a result of the delegation not conforming to the requirements of ERISA, the trustees remained fully liable for the acts of the firm to which they had delegated investment responsibility.

In the case of *Schetter v. Prudential-Bache Securities, Inc.,* 695 F.Supp. 1077 (E.D.Cal. 1988), the issue involved the mishandling of a brokerage account by a broker and the brokerage house that employed the broker. Because the broker gave investment advice to trustees of a plan, the trustees asserted that the broker was liable for a breach of fiduciary duty because the plan lost money. However, this court stated that the only method available for delegation of investment responsibility is with the appointment of an investment manager. Again, in this case the court found that the broker was not an investment manager because the broker had not acknowledged his status as such in writing.

Both of the above cases indicate that, when attempting to delegate trustee responsibility, the requirements of ERISA must be strictly adhered to. The courts will not relieve a trustee of liability if the provisions of ERISA are not followed exactly.

Duties Assigned

Court cases also make clear that fiduciaries should

ensure that all duties are being performed by the appropriate party. For example, in *Bass v. Prudential Insurance Co.,* 14 EBC 1837 (D.Kan. 1991), an employer claimed it had no duty to notify a participant that his benefit claim had been denied. The employer believed it had delegated that responsibility to its insurer, Prudential. However, the court determined that the plan documents specifically assigned this duty to the employer. Thus, the employer breached its fiduciary duty by failing to notify the claimant. Fiduciaries should document that all fiduciary obligations have been assigned to specific parties (either in the plan documents or by action of the plan sponsor or a fiduciary), and that each party is performing all obligations that have been delegated to that party.

Selection

The case of *Whitfield v. Cohen,* 682 F.Supp. 1888 (S.D.N.Y. 1988), is a good example of the importance of the rule of prudence in the selection of the firm or person to whom responsibility is being delegated. In the *Whitfield* case, the court held that the fiduciary's evaluation of the firm to invest the assets of the plan "fell far short of the careful inquiry required of a trustee." This conclusion was based upon the trustees' failure to determine the investment experience of the firm or any of its employees, the educational credentials of any of the firm's employees, whether the firm was registered as an investment advisor, the identity of other clients of the firm in order to obtain references, the nature of the investments to be made by the firm on behalf of the plan, and the fees to be paid to the firm.

Martin v. Hairline, 15 EBC 1138, 1148 (N.D.Ut. 1992), also illustrates potential liability in the selection of a delegate. The appointing fiduciary had violated his fiduciary responsibilities in the appointment of a trustee, in part due to the fiduciary's "failure to conduct any independent investigation into [the delegate's] qualifications to serve as a fiduciary."

Duty to Monitor Performance

A case that addressed the duty to monitor after delegation was *Brock v. Berman,* 673 F.Supp. 634 (D.Mass. 1987). In this case, the secretary of labor alleged that the board of directors of a company responsible for appointing an investment manager failed to properly monitor the investment manager's activities. The court concluded that the board of directors, as the named fiduciary, retained responsibility for determining whether the continued retention of the investment manager was appropriate.

The *Whitfield* case also provides a good example of the duty to monitor performance. In this case, the plan's fiduciaries had selected an agent (who did not qualify as an investment manager) to manage the assets of the plan. The court ruled that the fiduciary had a duty to monitor the agent's performance with reasonable diligence and to withdraw the investment if it became clear or should have become clear that the investment was no longer proper for the plan.

Similarly, in *Mazur v. Gaudet,* 14 EBC 2844 (E.D.La. 1992), the court determined that the individual members of a plan's board of trustees were subject to co-fiduciary liability by failing to properly monitor the actions of a co-trustee to whom investment authority had been allocated. As a result of the board members' lack of oversight and failure to independently review the investment actions of the co-trustee (who was solely responsible for investing the assets), the co-trustee embezzled $2.6 million.

The *Brock, Mazur* and *Whitfield* cases make it clear that monitoring the activities of the person or firm to whom responsibility has been delegated is essential to protecting a fiduciary from liability for the actions of others.

Duty to Train and Inform

The fiduciary responsibility to appoint and monitor a fiduciary may also be accompanied by the responsibility to adequately train the fiduciary. In *American Fed. of Unions Local 102 Health and Welfare Fund v. Equitable Life Assur. Soc. of the U.S.,* 841 F.2d 658 (5th Cir. 1988), an insurance agent appointed by the trustees as administrator for a health plan was found to have breached his fiduciary duty. Efforts to hold the insurance company responsible failed because the court held the plan's trustees responsible for training the agent.

The courts have also entertained claims that the duty to monitor includes a duty to supply the delegate with information. In *In re Sprint Corporation ERISA Litigation,* 2004 WL 1179371, *21 (D.Kan. 2004), the district court declined to dismiss the case and allowed discovery to proceed because the plaintiffs might be able to prove a set of facts that would entitle them to relief under the theory that the failure to monitor the delegate and inform it of critical information pertaining to employer stock constituted a breach of the named fiduciary's duties.

HOW TO ESTABLISH PRUDENCE IN SELECTION AND RETENTION

With the foregoing legal framework as the background, the inquisitive fiduciary would question: What does all this mean in the real world of the operations of my plan? What do I do now?

The answer is that a fiduciary of an employee benefit plan should be comforted by the knowledge that the law recognizes that fiduciaries need the assistance of others in carrying out their fiduciary responsibilities, and it provides protection from the acts or omissions of those to whom responsibility has been delegated if their selection and retention were prudent.

Although there are no clear, concise rules that can be set forth with the guarantee that, if followed, the fiduciary will be fully insulated from any risk of liability, it would be beneficial to explore the major operational areas of an employee benefit plan and to then review how fiduciaries can attempt to establish their prudence in selecting and retaining others to assist them in carrying out their responsibilities in each of these areas.

The operations and administration of an employee benefit plan can be divided into four major areas: recordkeeping, collections, providing benefits and investing. In all of these areas, the average fiduciary will probably not be qualified to perform all of the necessary tasks that will be required; instead, certain professional skills or experience will be needed. Thus, the fiduciary will be required to seek assistance. In obtaining this assistance, the law requires that the fiduciary be prudent in selecting those persons or firms to provide such assistance.

There are some general rules that can be suggested for fiduciaries to follow in establishing this requisite prudence. In all areas, the fiduciaries should document in the plan's records the process followed in selecting the person or firm, the information regarding the firms solicited, the experience of the candidates and the basis for selection. In other words, the fiduciary should create a written record establishing the prudence of the selection process.

In many cases, this may require that the fiduciaries undertake a formal competitive bidding process. After the person or firm has been retained, the fiduciaries will then have to establish techniques and procedures to assure that the delegate performs the assigned tasks timely and properly. This latter responsibility, of course, relates to the fiduciaries establishing their prudence in continuing to retain the person or firm selected. The fiduciary should continue to create a written record establishing prudence in the retention process.

Failure to adequately document can create significant burdens for fiduciaries attempting to defend decision making. In *In re Unisys Savings Plan Litigation,* 74 F.3d 420 (3rd Cir. 1996), the court denied summary judgment because the plan did not adequately document its investigation into certain insurance contracts before investing. Three years later, after a ten-day bench trial and another appeal, the court found sufficient evidence of a prudent investigation prior to investment in the insurance contracts. *In re Unisys Savings Plan Litigation,* 173 F.3d 145 (3rd Cir. 1999). However, the failure to adequately document the fiduciaries' investigation resulted in three years of litigation and legal fees.

The following describes the major operational areas of a plan and provides suggestions as to how in each area fiduciaries can document their prudence in continuing to retain those selected by them to provide assistance.

Recordkeeping

The records that need to be maintained in the operations of an employee benefit plan are numerous and diverse. In general, they include all necessary financial records to account for all payments to and from a plan and all of its assets and liabilities. This, of course, entails the maintenance of a plan's financial statements. The reporting and disclosure requirements of ERISA can also be included within the recordkeeping area. Recordkeeping for employee benefit plans further encompasses the need to maintain records necessary to establish a person's entitlement to benefits from the plan.

The recordkeeping aspects of the operations of an employee benefit plan involve two types of professionals that can assist the fiduciaries in carrying out their responsibilities: administrators and accountants. Either third party contract administrators (firms that are independent of the plan and contract with the plan to provide administrative services) or salaried administrators (individuals who are employees of the plan) may serve as administrators.

Fiduciaries may wish to consider the following to verify that the administrator is adequately performing his or her tasks:

1. The auditor should review and comment upon the adequacy of the financial recordkeeping systems and procedures of the administrator. The auditor can often perform this review in conjunction with providing a management letter to the board of trustees in which the auditor presents a written report on these matters.
2. The auditor or the actuary should review the record systems for establishing eligibility for benefits. In pension plans, the auditor or actuary would review the systems for keeping track of the vesting and benefit credits each plan participant earns annually.

Further, so as to relieve themselves of the responsibility for compliance with ERISA's reporting and disclosure requirements, the trustees should consider delegating these functions to either the administrator or accountant. For example, with respect to ERISA's government reporting requirements, the fiduciaries may delegate responsibility for timely filing of all government reports to either the administrator or accountant. If so delegated, the fiduciaries should then verify that the delegate timely filed the required reports. As to ERISA's requirements with respect to disclosure to participants, such as the summary annual report and the summary plan description, the fiduciaries may also relieve themselves of this responsibility by delegating this task to the administrative manager.

Collections

The fiduciaries of a Taft-Hartley plan are required to collect all monies owed to the plan by participating employers. To assure themselves that such contributions are being paid, the trustees could take the following actions:

1. Adopt delinquency rules and procedures that provide for:
   a. The written notices that are to be given by administrative personnel to employers delinquent in their contributions to the plan
   b. The assessment of interest and liquidated damages against delinquent employers
   c. Referral of the collection to legal counsel on a timely basis.
2. Retain an accounting or other firm to audit the payroll records of participating employers to confirm that employers make all contributions to the plan as required by the employer's collective bargaining agreement.

Providing Benefits

This is a broad area that includes the design of the plan's benefit program, the funding of the program and the payment of benefits.

With respect to design and funding, the trustees will certainly require the assistance of a consulting/actuarial firm. These aspects of a plan's operations are among the most technical.

As a practical matter, after the trustees have prudently selected the firm to provide these services, it will be difficult for the fiduciaries to monitor the technical adequacy of their performance. The trustees should, however, at a minimum insist upon timely, written reports from the professional firms and make certain that the substance of those reports is understandable. In pension plans, the trustees may wish to have legal counsel confirm that the funding status of the plan is in compliance with all legal requirements.

Payment of benefits is usually a task delegated to the plan's administrative manager. The trustees may wish to monitor the performance of this task by having the consultant or auditor review or audit the claim payments to assure that they are being paid in accordance with the plan's written benefit program and eligibility rules.

Investments

This is probably the area of most concern to the average trustee. Responsibility for investment of millions of dollars can be overwhelming. Again, in this area it is important trustees understand that the law clearly allows for the delegation of responsibilities for investments to qualified investment managers and provides that the trustees will not be responsible for these investments if the trustees are prudent in selecting, retaining and monitoring the investment manager.

The trustees should retain an investment consultant to counsel the trustees and assist in the selection and retention of investment managers and the creation and maintenance of investment guidelines and objections. Note that the trustees must comply with their fiduciary duties in the selection and monitoring of the consultant. The agreement should appoint the consultant as a fiduciary in accordance with the same methods and procedures outlined in this chapter for the appointment of any fiduciary delegate. The named fiduciary may even appoint a delegate to handle all trustee responsibilities related to the investment of plan assets.

A properly drafted investment manager agreement is key to allocating fiduciary responsibilities to an investment manager. The agreement with the investment manager should document the basis for the relationship, and should address such issues as acknowledgment of fiduciary status, a description of the scope of the engagement, style of management, applicable benchmarks, reporting obligations, fees, ERISA qualifications, compliance with bonding requirements, and any other representations or warranties required of the manager. Remember, proxy voting responsibility accompanies the investment in publicly traded securities. The duty to monitor an investment manager includes the duty to monitor the manager's proxy voting (or proxy voting service if a proxy voting service is retained). Therefore, the agreement should require the manager or service to provide proxy reports.

The monitoring of an investment manager can be best accomplished in the following fashion:

1. The trustees should, in concert with the investment manager, establish a written statement of investment objectives and guidelines.
2. The trustees should, with the assistance of the investment consultant, periodically (at least twice a year) meet with the investment manager and compare the performance of the manager against the plan's guidelines and objectives and against the performance of other investment managers.

With regard to individual account plans, such as money purchase pension plans and 401(k) plans, if the plan can satisfy ERISA Section 404(c), it may protect fiduciaries from liability. Under ERISA Section 404(c), if plan participants or beneficiaries are able to and actually exercise control over the assets allocated to their accounts, no fiduciary will be liable for any loss or by reason of any breach resulting from the participant's exercise of control. In essence, the fiduciary is able to delegate some fiduciary responsibility to the participants themselves. Fiduciaries should investigate the applicability of ERISA Section 404(c) as a potential shield against liability for investment losses. However, fiduciary responsibilities continue to attach to both the initial designation of investment alternatives and investment managers in the ongoing determination that such alternatives and managers remain suitable and prudent investment alternatives for the plan. *Tittle v. Enron Corp.,* 284 F.Supp. 2d 511, 574-79 (S.D.Tex. 2003).

CONCLUSION

With respect to all of the areas of a plan's operations, it is important to understand that not all of the responsibilities or functions that the trustees may be delegating to others are fiduciary in nature. For example, if an attorney is retained solely for the purpose of rendering a legal opinion, that attorney, in providing that opinion, would not be acting as a fiduciary.

However, whether or not the function or task the fiduciary delegates or assigns is fiduciary in nature, ERISA's rule of prudence requires the fiduciary, in all cases, to exercise prudence in selecting the person or firm to perform the task and, with respect to situations involving an ongoing delegation, prudently to monitor the performance of the delegated task.

Of course, the nature of the delegated task and the level of expertise or skill required to perform that task affects the degree to which fiduciaries can monitor the performance of others. In all cases, the trustees are well advised to create a written record in the minutes of their meetings or elsewhere of the basis and rationale for their decision to select persons to provide services to the plan and of the trustees' review of the delegated performance.

With the exercise of a reasonable amount of common sense, effort and reason, fiduciaries can easily satisfy ERISA's requirements respecting delegation of trustee and fiduciary responsibilities and rest assured that they fully satisfy the requirements of the law.

Chapter 6

Trustees and Bargaining Parties

David W. Silverman

The starting point of a discussion of trustees and bargaining parties begins with the passage of the Taft-Hartley amendment to the Labor-Management Relations Act (LMRA) (§302). From 1946 on, within the multiemployer setting, trustees and collective bargaining parties, as a general rule, were usually one and the same. The bargaining parties for the union may appear as trustees, and the bargaining parties for management may likewise appear as trustees of the designated employee benefit funds that were created by and through the collective bargaining agreement. This dual representation by bargaining party and trustee has resulted in the use of the term, the *two-hatted trustee;* that is, the trustee wears one hat when serving as a fiduciary in administering the trust fund and wears another hat when engaged in the business of the union and/or management. Problems and liabilities arise when the individual wears both hats at the same time, or dons the trustee hat for plan sponsor business, either union or management, or vice versa, dons the union or management plan sponsor hat for trustee business. In today's litigious world, the two-hatted trustee steps into an area full of potential liability. The purpose of this chapter is to explain that in the avoidance of risk and personal liability, the two-hatted trustee must receive impartial expert advice and understand that advice. Any action should be documented and a paper trail of the decision made and preserved. All of these steps, together with an adequate policy of fiduciary liability insurance, will contribute to a restful night's sleep for the two-hatted trustee.

BACKGROUND

Starting with the *Amax Coal*[1] case, the U.S. Supreme Court held there was no conflict of interest with respect to an individual who occupies a position as trustee and also a position as a member of either a union or a management bargaining association or employer. When sitting as a trustee on a jointly administered fund, the trustee is not a representative of the appointing authority (either management or labor), but is a designee of that authority whose duties are completely independent of those of a bargaining representative of either management or labor. Rather, the trustees operate under a detailed written agreement, which is itself the product of bargaining between the representatives of the employees and those of the employer. Indeed, the trustees have an obligation to *enforce* the terms of the collective bargaining agreement regarding employee fund contributions against the employer "for the sole benefit of the beneficiaries of the fund." Disputes between benefit fund trustees over the administration of the trust cannot, as can disputes between parties in collective bargaining, lead to strikes, lockouts or other exercises of economic power. Rather, whereas Congress has expressly rejected compulsory arbitration as a means of resolving collective bargaining disputes, §302(c)(5) explicitly provides for the compulsory resolution of any deadlocks among welfare fund trustees by a neutral umpire.[2]

This wall of demarcation between the duties as trustee and duties as a bargaining agent will not protect an employer (or a union) from giving false information to or withholding information from the participants to accomplish a business purpose. Such actions to the detriment of the participants are actionable under the Employee Retirement Income Security Act of 1974, as amended (ERISA). In its decision in *Varity v. Howe*,[3] the Supreme Court held that a representative of management, who was not a trustee, could not through trickery, falsehoods and misleading statements mislead participants as to their benefits, for to do so made the employer a fiduciary. Such statements were therefore in violation of the fiduciary duties outlined in §404 of

ERISA and were actionable on the part of the participants under §502(a)(3) of ERISA.

WHO SETS THE BENEFITS?

In examining the relations between the trustees and the bargaining parties, it is critical to understand what powers the bargaining parties give to the trustees. Do the bargaining parties merely agree that a specified dollar-and-cents amount will be paid to the employee benefit fund? Consequently, the employee benefit fund by its trustees determines what benefits will be provided from the contributions received. If the setting of benefits is done by the trustees of the plan, making use of the monies as set forth in the collective bargaining agreement, then their choice as to what benefits will be provided is their choice alone. In the *Sinai Hospital*[4] case, the bargaining parties could not direct the trustees as to how they would expend the contributions received. The expenditure of the money by the trustees would be in accordance with their statutory duty to act solely and exclusively for the benefit of the participant.

On the other hand, parties may agree in the collective bargaining agreement that it is the bargaining parties, and not the trustees, who set the benefits. In *United Mine Workers v. Robinson*,[5] it was the bargaining parties who determined the benefits and they therefore were not subject to the constraints that would be applicable to the fiduciary duty of trustees in setting such benefits.

THE TRUSTEES' POWER TO CREATE DEBT

The trustees of a defined benefit (DB) pension plan, together with their expert actuaries, make a determination as to the extent of a benefit that could be purchased with the monies being contributed pursuant to the collective bargaining agreements. The trustees' decision as to the extent of the benefit is treated by most circuit courts as a plan sponsor decision, which decision is thereby outside the governing terms and conditions of ERISA. A few circuits hold the decision as to what benefits will be provided by a multiemployer plan is a fiduciary decision subject to the rules of fiduciary conduct.[6] Whether one follows the majority or the minority view does not do away with the right of the trustees to create debt in the DB pension plan. Every time a trustee votes to give a benefit in excess of what the current contributions to, and the available assets in, the fund, that excess benefit creates a debt which has to be paid over a statutory period of time. When trustees create a debt by promising a benefit in excess of what current assets and contributions could purchase, the debt created is shared by all contributing employers and becomes a portion of withdrawal liability, either actual or incurred. The bargaining parties as well as the trustees should be made aware of their power to promise benefits in excess of present assets and contributions because their actions impact upon each contributing employer.

A general example might be as follows: When one acquires a home, the bank loans the money to be paid over a set term. If each payment is made, the mortgage at the end of the term is satisfied. However, if one sells the house before the term is over, the mortgage must be satisfied. The value of benefits in excess of assets is the mortgage that any withdrawing employer must satisfy on withdrawal or on termination of the plan.

THE BARGAINING PARTIES CAN TRANSFORM AN OBLIGATION TO PAY INTO A FIDUCIARY OBLIGATION

The collective bargaining agreement contains a promise to pay contributions as set forth therein. That is a contractual promise, binding on the corporate signatory and, as a general rule, is a corporate debt whose payment is not a personal obligation of the corporate signatory. In agreeing to make a contribution based upon each hour of work performed by a participant or upon weekly or monthly payroll, the collective bargaining parties can transform a management contributor who fails to make a contribution on time into one holding trust fund assets. The collective bargaining agreement can provide that the fund contributions are considered trust assets when due, and thus failure to pay when due transforms the management contributor into a holder of trust assets, with the failure to pay being a breach of fiduciary duty actionable under ERISA's fiduciary provisions.

Principles of general trust law may also be helpful. ERISA provides that those who have control of trust fund assets are fiduciaries. General trust law provides that if the agreement entered into between labor and management provides that title to all of the monies paid or due and owing to the fund are vested in and remain exclusively with the trustees of the trust, then the failure to pay when due would be a breach of fiduciary duty. The breach would be incurred because the corporate officer who had the authority to pay exercised control over monies of the trust fund. Failure to remit when due causes those in control of corporate monies to be exercising control over fund assets for the monies are immediately vested in the trust fund. Therefore, failure to pay is retention of funds in violation of §404 of ERISA and accords to that corporate officer the status of trustee in breach of his fiduciary duties, causing damage to the trust. The agreement can provide that the funds, when due, shall be deemed trust assets whether or not collected, which may afford the status of fiduciary to the corporate officer who used the monies for other purposes. Many cases are now being argued on the grounds that the specific language as to the status of contributions when due is a matter of contract. Collective bargaining agreements that characterize contributions when due to be an asset of the trust fund may very well make those corporate personnel who use the funds for other purposes personally liable as fiduciaries.[7]

APPOINTING TRUSTEES AND THE DUTY OF MONITORING BY BOTH LABOR AND MANAGEMENT

The starting point for entry into the legal minefield of the two-hatted trustee is the parties who have the power to appoint or remove a trustee to a Taft-Hartley trust, whether labor or management or by the single employer appointing a trustee to the company plan. The appointing authority, by making the appointment (or exercising the same power to remove a trustee) to that extent, exercises fiduciary power. As such, whoever appoints or removes does so with a single objective of exercising the power of appointment or removal by determining what is in the best interests of the plan's participants or their beneficiaries.[8]

To the trustee appointed, his or her fiduciary duties commence upon acceptance. There is no break-in period or learning period that might excuse a breach of fiduciary duty.[9] The trustee's obligations cease when he or she has been replaced, not when he or she resigns.[10] However, the Taft-Hartley trustee, whether appointed by union or management, serves only until the appointing authority replaces him or her and is totally without job security.[11] An appointment to fiduciary duties of any person employed by any contributing employer or bargaining union is by statute prevented from charging or being paid for the services rendered.[12] (Fair and reasonable expenses actually incurred may be reimbursed.)

The bargaining party as an appointed trustee is most probably aware of the fiduciary responsibility in the administration of the employee benefit plan. However, that same individual, if a union representative or representative of a management bargaining group or a corporate officer, also has fiduciary duties to union or management by virtue of other federal statutes and case law.

This twofold fiduciary responsibility can produce conflicts. Legally, it should not produce conflicts because the law draws a clear line of demarcation between collective bargaining functions and trustee functions. The failure to acquit fiduciary duty in union or management functions leads to litigation alleging the breach of the duty of fair representation.[13] The failure to acquit trustee fiduciary functions leads to litigation under ERISA for personal liability.

Though court decisions which deal with the "duty of monitoring" are sparse within the multiemployer area, it is necessary to point out that Congress, when it passed the fiduciary responsibility sections of ERISA (§404, etc.), made no distinction between the single employer plan and the multiemployer plan. The fiduciary duties are the same. The question of the duty of monitoring arises by virtue of the fact that when management and/or the union exercises its authority to appoint a trustee, that appointment is a fiduciary act. Since the act is fiduciary in nature, there is a concomitant obligation to determine at reasonable times whether the appointee is properly performing his or her fiduciary duty. There is authority on the part of the union and/or management to terminate the appointment and, therefore, appointment and/or termination, when exercised, constitutes a fiduciary because it affects the administration of the trust fund. The duty of monitoring the appointees is a fiduciary obligation of the appointing authority, whether management or union. Such appointment is made with full knowledge that the appointee is judged by expert standards from the moment the appointee assumes trusteeship. The failure to monitor will cast the appointing authority into litigation, with the claim being that the appointing authority has breached its fiduciary duty by allowing its appointee to damage the trust fund, thereby casting the appointing authority and/or its members into liability under §404 of ERISA.[14]

BASIC FIDUCIARY DUTIES UNDER ERISA

Section 404

The language defining *fiduciary duty* is set forth in basically three sections of ERISA, namely, §§404, 405 and 406. An examination of §404 clearly indicates it is structured in terms of concepts of what should be done, not requiring specific acts or a series of prohibitions. The conceptual terms in §404 leave to the court or administrative agency the decision as to whether the facts presented fit into the concepts set forth in the statute. Section 404 provides the following basic concepts, the violation of which creates fiduciary liability.

The fiduciary shall discharge his duties "solely in the interest of the participants. . . ."

What is *solely in the interest of the participants*? Trying to fit the trustee's actions into the words of the statute is achieved by the court finding the appropriate compliance with the balancing of the individual interest of a participant pursuant to the plan document and the general overall interest of all of the other participants. In so doing, however, the trustee acts with the exclusive purpose of providing benefits to participants. Providing benefits may create a conflict between the claim of an individual participant and the interest of the remaining participants, but actions that are motivated by allowing a benefit to a third party other than the participant must be avoided. A third party is clearly the labor organization or a management group or contributor, as well as others.

ERISA §404 continues with its conceptual language that, in administering the fund, the trustees must do so with the care, skill, prudence and diligence "under the circumstances then prevailing that a prudent man acting in a like capacity and familiar with such matters would use in the conduct of an enterprise of like character and with like aims." Who is this prudent man acting in a like capacity and familiar with such matters?

One of the early decisions under ERISA that took into consideration this "prudent man acting in like capacity" requirement was the *Donovan*[15] case. In *Donovan,* decided in 1981, the court found that the trustees' decision in granting a loan was imprudent and the loss on the loan was chargeable to the trustees as their personal obligation. The investigation into the propriety of granting the initial loan and its extensions was found by the court to be insufficient, applying this conceptual language. The court held that the trustees, either singly or as a group, did not constitute a person "familiar with such matters." In order to acquit their duties, the trustees "[were] compelled to take reasonable and sufficient steps to obtain the most suitable person they could reasonably be expected to obtain, given all of the circumstances," to apprise them as to the advisability of making the loan. The court found that the generally accepted industry standards for selecting a consultant to perform a feasibility study with respect to the loans and their extension were known or should have been known to the trustees. The trustees therefore violated their fiduciary duty in failing to select an expert who possessed the background required by industry standards of an investment banker or other professional familiar with real estate loans.

The trustees violated their fiduciary responsibility, for their actions failed to conform to what the prudent man would do in two separate ways. First, they did not select an expert in accordance with generally accepted industry practice. Second, the expert relied on by the trustees, having failed to meet generally accepted industry standards, did not qualify as an expert; therefore, the advice to make the loan was insufficient to justify the trustees' reliance and to meet their fiduciary duty. Investments are made on their merit, not to meet a bargaining party's wish or some other agenda.

Section 405

Section 405 of ERISA deals with liability for breach by a co-fiduciary. As such, it is written in part in conceptual language as is §404, but it also contains specific language with respect to certain transactions that are to be avoided. Section 405 provides that in addition to any liability that a fiduciary may have, the fiduciary may be liable for a breach of fiduciary responsibility of another fiduciary under three enumerated circumstances. Under §405, the fiduciary cannot participate "knowingly in, or knowingly undertake [] to conceal, an act or omission of such other fiduciary, knowing such other act or omission is a breach."

How does the trustee know? The answer in a co-fiduciary setting is, he or she has a duty of inquiry: a duty of inquiry into what your fellow trustee is doing or has done. If a fellow trustee did it or is about to do it, you may not make friends or influence people, but as a trustee you have an obligation to inquire and investigate. The failure to do so creates your own liability in case of loss.[16]

As an example, in *Buse v. The Vanguard Group of Investment Companies,*[17] the court did impose fiduciary liability upon Vanguard Group because of its failure to investigate the validity of an instruction it had received from a plan administrator. The court said, "Simply stated, a trustee does not act in good faith when it follows a fraudulent instruction that requires it to violate both its own trust agreement and the law." As a trustee, your fiduciary responsibility is not acquitted even if the requested action is in writing and executed by your fellow fiduciary or trustee.

Section 406

The third fiduciary section that imposes requirements upon trustees is §406 of ERISA, which deals with prohibited transactions. This section is the clearest and, although capable of being expanded by some conceptual language, is structured more in the nature of "do not." Section 406 provides the fiduciary shall not cause the plan to engage in a transaction if the fiduciary knows or should know that such transaction would be a sale or exchange of any property between the plan and a party in interest. People who constitute *parties in interest* are defined in §3(14) of ERISA and include plan fiduciaries, service providers to the plan, those employees or employers who are covered by the plan, and corporations and business entities that deal with the plan. The prohibitions under §3(14) extend to the lending of money or other extension of credit, the furnishing of goods and services between the plan and parties in interest, and other acts that deal with transactions between the plan and parties in interest. These transactions, by their very term, are prohibited, and the motive for, or the profit that would be made by, the fund as a result of its entering into such a transaction is totally immaterial. Under the circumstances, if it is a prohibited transaction, it is exactly as the statute says: prohibited.

There are further don'ts for a fiduciary that prohibit the fiduciary from dealing with the assets of the plan for his or her own interest or account. The fiduciary is forbidden to act on behalf of a party whose interests are adverse to the plan, nor can the fiduciary receive any money for his or her own personal account as a result of a dealing with the plan. Profit to the plan or the lack of any evil motive or intent is immaterial in the determination of whether the action is prohibited pursuant to §406.

No hard-and-fast rules can be imposed to traverse this minefield of potential personal liability. President Harry Truman had a sign on his desk that read, "The Buck Stops Here." But as president, he couldn't be sued if his decision, judged by hindsight, was incorrect, nor did an impulsive act in the administration of his office carry personal responsibility. The trustee's acts, unless properly documented by thorough investigation of alternative courses of conduct laid out by experts, do carry personal responsibility.

ADVICE FOR THE TWO-HATTED TRUSTEE ON AVOIDING LIABILITY

The best answer to the trustee who is not only the final decision maker but also the only decision maker was set forth in the *Howard* case,[18] where the court advised trustees on investigation required for expenditure of funds in the following language: "Although securing an independent assessment from a financial advisor or legal counsel is evidence of a thorough investigation, it is not a complete defense to a charge of imprudence. As Judge Friendly has explained, independent expert advice is not a 'whitewash.' The fiduciary must (1) investigate the expert's qualifications, (2) provide the expert with complete and accurate information, and (3) make certain that reliance on the expert's advice is reasonably justified under the circumstances. The focus is on the thoroughness of the investigation. An independent appraisal 'is not a magic wand that fiduciaries may simply wave over a transaction to ensure that their responsibilities are fulfilled. It is a tool and, like all tools, is useful only if used properly.' To justifiably rely on an independent appraisal, a conflicted fiduciary need not become an expert in the valuation of closely held corporations. But the fiduciary is required to make an honest, objective effort to read the valuation, understand it, and question the methods and assumptions that do not make sense. If after a careful review of the valuation and a discussion with the expert, there are still uncertainties, the fiduciary should have a second firm review the valuation."

To the two-hatted trustee, there is a requirement of vigilance to be sure that an expenditure or investment is strictly in the best interests of the fund and its participants.

BARGAINING PARTIES VS. TRUSTEE ACTIONS NO DUTY TO PROVIDE BENEFITS

Traversing the legal minefield for the two-hatted trustee is made more difficult by virtue of the court holdings that start with the clear legal principle that no employer or union is required to establish a benefit plan. If the party or parties so choose to create an employee benefit plan, the parameters of that plan are solely within the discretion of either the company establishing the plan or the bargaining parties who negotiated the plan. It is in the administration of the plan that the requirements of ERISA and other employee benefit legislation attach. It is easy to say that when a bargaining party is engaged in union or management business, the bargaining party is free of the restrictions placed on his or her conduct by ERISA. Bargaining parties are free to obtain their respective goals without the constraints of their ERISA fiduciary obligations. The contrary is likewise true that when the bargaining party is acting as an ERISA trustee, his or her obligation is solely and exclusively for the best interests of the participant free of any claim or loyalty or benefit to the bargaining party. The hard part of the problem is to determine when one is acting as a bargaining party or a trustee under ERISA and then to determine whether the action approved was for the benefit of the proper party; i.e., bargaining party or participant. This hard decision has been made by numerous courts where the bargaining party trustee has been a defendant.

As an example, in an action by union trustees against management trustees where the claim was that the management trustees were allegedly promoting nonunion and double-breasted operations, the court in *Jordan v. Sundt*[19] held that the management trustees as officers of the management bargaining association were not violating their fiduciary duty. Management trustees may engage in acts that take place within the employer association and that do not involve dealing with plan assets, but which may ultimately rebound to the diminishment of the plan funding. These decisions, taken in a bargaining context, are not covered by their fiduciary responsibility as benefit plan trustees. A fiduciary may serve as an officer, employee, agent or other representative of a union or an employer. Since the fiduciary may hold such a position, then he or she may fulfill the responsibility of either position. Therefore, to require a negotiator to negotiate only in the best interests of the plan would correspondingly require that negotiator to breach the trust of the labor union or management group represented.

This line of legal reasoning was applied to a claim by the United Independent Flight Officers.[20] Their participants in the benefit fund claimed that as a result of collective bargaining, they lost a benefit in their pension plan. The court held that a union may always compromise with an employer and mediate among various interests of the employees that the union represents. The administrator of a plan is a fiduciary only to the extent that he or she is engaged in administration of the plan. The liabilities in administration do not extend to negotiating the terms of the governing collective bargaining agreement. Such negotiations are clear and distinct from the transaction affecting land, property, money or other trust assets of the benefit fund. The union is not restricted from pursuing reasonable business behavior in negotiations even though it concerns pension benefits, and such behavior in negotiation is not covered by ERISA. Since conflicting duties are imposed upon negotiators and fiduciaries, neither a union nor an employer is an ERISA fiduciary simply because the union or employer is negotiating the terms and conditions of future pension benefits, at least where those benefits are not protected under the ERISA vesting and non-forfeitability provision.

Summarizing this general principle for the two-hatted trustee, one court stated[21] that to require the negotiator to consider only the best interests of the plan at the negotiation table would be to require the negotiator to breach the trust of his or her own constituents. This the court refused to do.

This dichotomy of approach was tempered in recent litigation involving the Michigan Bell Telephone Co.[22] The court was once again faced with deciding what was a management act in amending its pension plan, as compared to what would be the fiduciary responsibility in the event that the proposed action should be termed administration of the plan. The case dealt with whether or not an employee was entitled to an enhanced pension or "golden window" as an inducement to his early retirement. The court stated that before it could determine whether a fiduciary violated his duties, it must first determine if the party was acting as a fiduciary when he engaged in the disputed conduct. The court pointed out that the plan fiduciaries have a duty to avoid placing themselves in a position where their acts as officers or directors of a company will prevent their functioning with the complete loyalty demanded of them as trustees of a pension fund. This might, in certain instances, require them to step aside or to at least seek independent advice as to whether there is a potential conflict. However, not every decision that could impact a plan participant required the exercise of fiduciary responsibility. The court held that the plan design or what is termed settlor functions, which relate to the formation, design and termination of the plans, are not fiduciary activities;[23] such activities are free of the fiduciary responsibility as set forth in ERISA.

The court in making its determination that the golden window which was offered for early retirement could not be characterized in the usual form of plan formation or a plan sponsor's decision adopted the following test: "If a neutral third party, e.g., a bank, had been the plan fiduciary of MIPP (the golden window), could it have made the decision to offer MIPP benefits?"

The answer, the court stated, was clearly "no." If an independent trustee offered such a golden window, it would have constituted an unacceptable interference with Michigan Bell's (the employer's) business affairs. It is not the function of a fiduciary to make revenue projections, determine levels of employee surplus and inform management which of the multitude of costs and employee reduction methods available will be used to solve the problem. The U.S. District Court before whom the participants brought the case stated, "ERISA cannot be interpreted to put corporations with early retirement incentive programs into a straightjacket by requiring (advance) publication of the precise conditions under which such incentives will be offered."

The case then proceeded on appeal to the U.S. Court of Appeals for the Sixth Circuit.[24] The court of appeals reviewed the holding of the lower court, which did not want to place the corporate employer in a straightjacket and held that early retirement incentives were business decisions. The essence of the decision was that, as a matter of law, there was no responsibility on the part of the corporate employer to notify anybody as to what was being discussed in corporate circles as to future golden windows. The court of appeals refused to recognize such a black-and-white rule but held that when misleading communications to plan participants regarding the administration of the plan eligibility rules were made by corporate officers who also were plan fiduciaries, such misleading communications could support a claim for breach of fiduciary duty. Therefore, the corporate officer or bargaining party who also serves as a trustee when engaged in corporate or bargaining party business cannot lie or misrepresent to plan participants. The court further held "[t]hat when serious consideration was given by (the employer) to implementing (the golden window and offering it in the future) . . . then the employer as the plan administrator (and) the plan fiduciary, have a fiduciary duty not to make misrepresentations, either negligently or intentionally, to potential plan participants. . . . "

The obvious conclusion therefore is that when trustees are acting in their business capacity and in that capacity are dealing with their corporate or union objectives, they cannot mislead a participant or make false or negligent statements concerning the future of the plan. The *Varity* case is the most recent decision by the U.S. Supreme Court on the issue of which hat is being worn and the consequences of making promises under the wrong hat.[25] Many cases have commented on when there is a fiduciary duty of disclosure, especially when dealing with benefit improvements.[26]

ACTING IN THE INTEREST OF THE UNION

The courts have also decided cases that pose the contrary problem; namely, when do trustees in the performance of their duties as fiduciaries of a benefit plan act in the interest of their corporate or union employer? In

1984, the U.S. Court of Appeals for the Second Circuit held in litigation involving the truck drivers of Local 449[27] that the National Labor Relations Board could not find the trustees of a statewide pension and retirement fund to be union agents. As such, the trustees did not commit an unfair labor practice and violate §8(b)(3) of the National Labor Relations Act. Section 8(b)(3) provides that it is an unfair labor practice for one bargaining party to force the other to agree to a midterm modification of their collective bargaining agreement. The issue involved was whether the trustees could properly refuse to take contributions from employers that had not signed an amendment to the labor management contract by which contributions were to be made to the fund on behalf of seasonal and part-time employees. Before the midterm amendment insisted upon by the trustees, seasonal and part-time employees were not covered by the fund in accordance with the existing collective bargaining agreement.

The court agreed with the National Labor Relations Board that the trustees by their actions were coercing the employers to accept a midterm modification of the collective bargaining agreement. The court had no difficulty in holding that had the union performed the same act, it would have been a violation of the Taft-Hartley Act. In order to find the trustees liable of a labor law violation, however, the trustees must have been acting as an agent of a bargaining party or, in this case, the union. The court could find no evidence that the union sought and failed to accomplish such coverage for seasonal and part-time employees in its collective bargaining. The court could not find from the evidence that the union, being unsuccessful in collective bargaining to secure coverage for the part-time or seasonal workers, had trustees now acting as agents to accomplish for the union what it could not obtain in collective bargaining. The court took the position that, based upon the evidence presented to it, the trustees were seeking their own goals and they were merely trying to establish a funding policy and give credit for hours worked. In order for the unfair labor practice to hold against the trustees, they must be held as an agent of a bargaining party; namely, be under the bargaining party's control. The mere fact that the interests of a bargaining party and the trust fund might coincide was not sufficient to hold the trust fund as an agent of the bargaining party. The court pointed out certain instances where the trust fund might be held to be an agent of a bargaining party and therefore subject to remedial measures contained in the Taft-Hartley Act. However, in view of the decision in *Amax Coal*,[28] where the functions of trustees and the function of bargaining parties were not to coalesce unless direct agency were shown by control of one of the bargaining parties, the trustees were not amenable to the jurisdiction of the National Labor Relations Board. Correspondingly, a union may not use a trust fund issue to clothe what would otherwise be an unfair labor practice.[29]

Other instances where the trustees have been acting not for the benefit of the participants of the fund but for the benefit of a bargaining party was set forth in a decision involving the Masters, Mates and Pilots Pension Plan.[30] The issue in the case was the suspension of benefits upon the return to employment of a retiree. If the retiree went to work for a union contributor to the fund, upon the termination of that employment, the time period prior to the resumption of benefits was materially shorter than if the participant have gone to work for a nonunion employer. The alleged purpose of the board of trustees was to discourage the most experienced pensioners from seeking employment with noncontributing employers. The second purpose was to encourage new employers to recognize the union and consequently be responsible for contributions to the pension plan. The plan also attempted to place the legitimacy of its actions on grounds of financial integrity. The court held that the explanation offered was an after-the-fact explanation and not a factor taken into consideration at the time the rules concerning reretirement were adopted. The court held that the difference between a pensioner returning from covered employment as compared to a pensioner returning from employment with a nonunion operator had nothing to do with preserving the financial integrity of the plan. Since the fiduciary is the fiduciary for all of the participants and not just some of them, the trustees were using their position to further the goals of the union by restricting retirees from accepting further employment with nonparticipating, nonunion companies. The court held that the trustees, by placing their loyalty with the bargaining party, had breached their fiduciary duties.

ACTING IN THE INTEREST OF MANAGEMENT

Trustees can act for the benefit of the management as well. In the *Bierworth* case,[31] the trustees of the pension fund who were also senior officers of the Grumman Corporation were vigorously contesting a takeover attempt by LTV. In the process of contesting the takeover attempt, the trustees decided that the trust fund would buy additional shares of stock of Grumman Corporation, which would then be voted by the trustees who were also Grumman executives, to further hinder LTV'S takeover attempt. Grumman stock, however, had risen substantially in cost as a result of the tender offer and the purchase was made at the increased cost. The principle established by the *Bierworth* case was that the trustees breached their fiduciary duty by purchasing, for the retirement fund, additional Grumman shares for reasons that were not in the best interests of the participants. Not only did the corporate officers-trustees fail to make adequate inquiry into the value of that which they were buying, but they also failed to obtain independent legal advice with respect to the acquisition of additional securities. The Court held the officers and trustees were placed in such a conflict-of-interest position that it was difficult to see how they could argue that the acquisition of additional shares of Grumman stock was solely in the interests and solely for the benefit of the participants in the funds. The Court held under the circumstances that the acquisition of additional securities was done in bad faith, because there was only one goal and that was the corporate goal to defeat the tender offer by LTV. The trustees were personally responsible for any loss sustained because of the stock purchase and were subject to the IRS penalties for partaking in a prohibited transaction.

Similarly, in older cases involving the Taft-Hartley Act, the trustees had made a conscious choice as to whether or not they should pursue collection against marginal coal mine operators and thereby run the risk that the mine would close or whether they should close their eyes to the delinquent contributions of the marginal operators, but at least the participants would have a paycheck at the end of the week. The court held the fund's choice of ignoring delinquencies of marginal operators was a breach of their fiduciary duty.[32]

Trustees operating for the interest of a bargaining party rather than for the participants of the fund was the subject of a decision in the Third Circuit involving the New Jersey Brewery Employees Welfare Fund.[33] The issue before the court was the proper manner in which surplus funds of a welfare fund were to be distributed. The fund was going out of business and the termination date was not far off. During this period, several large refund checks were received from Blue Cross/Blue Shield, which precipitated the fund into the unique position of having far more assets than liabilities. A decision was made to the effect that current contributions set forth in the collective bargaining agreement would be waived and the excess funds created by the unexpected refunds would be used in place of bargained-for contributions. This, the court stated, was a decision made not for the benefit of participants, but a decision made for the benefit of one of the bargaining parties. The court refused to determine the propriety of the actions of the trustees by use of the "arbitrary and capricious" rule, which is a far more lenient legal doctrine to uphold the trustees' actions, but rather judged the trustees' actions under strict fiduciary standards. The court, however, did set up some guidelines that might be used when a trustee is faced with the potential question as to whether or not his action is for the benefit of a bargaining party or one that is for the benefit of the participant. The court stated that in determining a claim of breach of fiduciary duty dealing with actions that benefit a bargaining party, the trustee's explanation of his conduct is far more rigorous. The court stated, "We must consider, for example, whether the employer trustees voted as they did on the instruction of the employers; whether they took time to investigate the merits of alternative courses of conduct; and whether they consulted with others, for example, their attorneys. We do not intend this list of considerations to be exhaustive."

The court considered truly independent advice as a necessary ingredient in the trustee's justification of his conduct. Truly independent advice is the best defense to any claimed conflicts involving a trustee who is also a negotiating party.

Notwithstanding the legal right of a trustee to be a representative of management or a representative of labor, or the right of a fiduciary or trustee to be a member of corporate management, this right is always subordinate to the obligation that each action taken during the administration of the benefit plan must be solely and exclusively for the interest of the beneficiaries thereof. Any deviation from this duty results in a breach of fiduciary duties with its consequent personal liability for reimbursement of such losses under ERISA.

CONCLUSION

To the trustee who serves as a bargaining party, each and every act bears the potential for conflict. Therefore, the first advice that can be given to the dual or two-hatted trustee is to be aware of the potential conflict. Negotiate a collective bargaining agreement that clearly sets forth the obligations to contribute the amounts and on whose behalf. The failure to do so has been discussed in a recent Circuit Court holding that participation agreements with the fund cannot "serve as an alternative source for collective bargaining terms."[34] Assuming awareness, the dual trustee may then seek advice as to what would be the proper course of conduct. The advice received must be from those who do not bear a dual loyalty but whose only loyalty is to the fund. If a potential course of action in the exercise of the fiduciary duty as a bargaining party or in the exercise of the fiduciary duty as a fund trustee will either benefit or harm the bargaining parties or the trust, then independent advice from professionals not otherwise involved is the best way to avoid litigation and potential liability. To the dual trustee, awareness of potential conflict, seeking impartial advice, understanding such advice, documentation and paper trailing the decision, together with an adequate policy of fiduciary liability insurance, constitute the best defense to any potential challenge of their action.

ENDNOTES

1. *NLRB v. Amax Coal Co.,* 453 U.S. 322 (1981).
2. *NLRB v. Amax Coal Co., supra.*
3. *Varity Corp. v. Howe,* 516 U.S. 489 (1996).

4. *Sinai Hospital of Baltimore, Inc. v. National Benefit Fund for Hospital & Health Care Employees,* 697 F.2d 562 (4th Cir. 1982).

5. *United Mine Workers of America Health & Retirement Funds v. Robinson,* 455 U.S. 562, 102 S.Ct. 1226 (1982).

6. *Burke v. Bodewes,* 250 F.Supp. 2d 262 (W.D.N.Y. 2004).

7. *Connors v. Paybra Mining Co.* 807 F.Supp. 1242 (S.A.Va. 1992); *Hanley v. Giordano's Restaurant, Inc.,* 1995 WL 442143 (S.D.N.Y.1995); *Blatt v. Marshall and Lassman,* 812 F.2d 810, 813 (2nd Cir. 1987); *PMTA-ILA Containerization Fund v. Rose,* 1995 WL 461269 (E.D.Pa. 1995); *Curcio v. John Hancock Mut. Life Ins. Co.,* 33 F.3d 226 (3rd Cir. 1994); *U.S. v. Panepinto,* 818 F.Supp. 48 (E.D.N.Y. 1993).

8. 29 CFR §2509.75-8 at D4; *O'Neill v. Davis,* 721 F.Supp. 1013 (N.D.Ill. 1989).

9. *Free v. Briody,* 732 F.2d 1331 (7th Cir. 1984).

10. *Chambers v. Kaleidoscope Inc.,* 650 F.Supp. 359 (N.D.Ga. 1986).

11. *Mobile, Alabama-Pensacola, Florida Bldg. & Constr. Trades Council v. Daugherty,* 684 F.Supp. 270 (S.D.Ala. 1988).

12. 29 U.S.C. §1108(C)(2); ERISA §408(C)(2); Opinion # 83-13A DOL 8/29/88.

13. *Moldovan v. Great A&P,* 790 F.2d 894 (3rd Cir. 1986), 104 L.C. 11,923, *cert. denied,* 108 S.Ct. 1074.

14. See *Title v. Enron Corp.,* 284 F.Supp. 2d 511 (S.D.Texas 2003). See also *Baker v. Kingsley,* 387 F.3d 649 (7th Cir. 2004); *In re WorldCom, Inc. ERISA Litig.,* 263 F.Supp. 2d 745 (S.D.N.Y. 2003); *In re Sprint Corp. ERISA Litig.,* 2004 U.S. Dist. LEXIS 9622 [33 EBC (BNA) 1287] (May 27, 2004), decided, dismissed by, in part *In re Sprint Corp. ERISA Litig.,* 2004 U.S. Dist. LEXIS 19125 (D.Kan., Sept. 24, 2004); and *Hill v. BellSouth Corp.* 313 F.Supp. 2d 1361 (N.D.Ga. 2004).

15. *Donovan v. Mazzola* [2 EBC 2115] (N.D.Ca. 1981).

16. *Firstier Bank, N.A., Omaha v. Zeller,* 16 F. 3d 907 (8th Cir. 1994).

17. *Buse v. The Vanguard Group of Investment Companies* 1996 U.S. Dist. LEXIS 9152 [20 EBC 1524] (E.D.Pa. 1996).

18. *Howard v. Shay,* 100 F.3d 1484 (9th Cir. 1996).

19. *Jordan v. Sundt,* 1985 U.S. Dist. LEXIS 22858 (W.D. Wash. 1985).

20. *United Independent Flight Officers v. United Air Lines,* 756 F.2d 1274 (7th Cir. 1985).

21. *Evans v. Bexley,* 750 F.2d 1498 (11th Cir. 1985).

22. *Ogden v. Michigan Bell Telephone Co.,* 657 F.Supp. 328 (E.D.Mich. 1987).

23. 13 B&A Pension Report of 472 (1986), reporting on the position of the Department of Labor.

24. *Berlin v. Michigan Bell Telephone Company,* 858 F.2d 1154 (6th Cir. 1988).

25. *Varity Corp. v. Howe* 516 U.S. 489 (1996).

26. *Varity Corp. v. Howe, supra; Ballone v. Eastman Kodak Co.,* 109 F.3d 117 (1997); *Estate of Becker v. Eastman Kodak Co.,* 120 F.3d 5 (1997); *Mullins v. Pfizer Inc.,* 23 F.3d 663 (1994); *Pocchio v. NYNEX Corp.,* 81 F.3d 275 (1996).

27. *NLRB v. Truck Drivers Local 449,* 728 F.2d 80 (2nd Cir. 1984).

28. *NLRB v. Amax Coal Co.,* note 1, *supra.*

29. *NLRB v. Construction & General Laborers' Local 1140* 887 F.2d 868 (8th Cir. 1989).

30. *Deak v. Masters, Mates and Pilots Pension Plan* 821 F.2d 572 (11th Cir. 1987).

31. *Donovan v. Bierworth,* 680 F.2d 263 (2nd Cir. 1982), *affirming with modification,* 538 F.Supp. 463 (E.D.N.Y. 1981), *cert. denied,* 459 U.S. 1069, 103 S.Ct. 488 (1982).

32. *Nedd v. United Mine Workers,* 556 F.2d 190 (3rd Cir. 1978), *cert. denied,* 434 U.S. 1013 (1978).

33. *Strubble v. New Jersey Brewery Employees Welfare Fund,* 732 F.2d 325 (3rd Cir. 1984).

34. *N.Y. State Teamsters Conference Pension & Retirement Fund v. UPS,* 382 F.2d 272 (2nd Cir. 2004).

Chapter 7

Fiduciary Responsibility Issues Relating to the Investment of ERISA Plan Assets

Rory Judd Albert*

INTRODUCTION

Previous chapters have delineated the general fiduciary responsibilities relating to the establishment, operation and administration of an employee benefit plan subject to the Employee Retirement Income Security Act of 1974, as amended (ERISA). In this chapter, we will explore how these responsibilities impact directly upon one of the most critical fiduciary obligations under ERISA—the fiduciary's duty to invest plan assets prudently and in the best interests of a plan's participants (and their beneficiaries).

The chapter begins, by way of refresher, by discussing ERISA's basic fiduciary requirements. Most important, of course, is the duty to invest plan assets in accordance with ERISA's extremely stringent "prudent person" standard. Indeed, if only one term could be used to describe the essence of a fiduciary's responsibility under ERISA with respect to plan investments, it would be prudence. Every decision made by a fiduciary affecting plan assets, whether directly or in an oversight capacity, must be the product of a thorough, diligent and, above all, prudent investigation that has taken into account every consideration reasonably related to the investment decision. An intentional or even inadvertent failure to do so can trigger ERISA's enforcement and penalty provisions, the latter of which can be quite severe given the potential magnitude of investment losses.

This chapter also discusses exactly who is a fiduciary with respect to plan investments. As will be explained below, fiduciaries are those persons or entities who are "named fiduciaries," as well as those who exercise "discretionary authority and control" over plan assets. Of course, the determination of precisely who is a "named fiduciary," and who exercises "discretionary authority and control" raises the issue of the proper delegation of investment management authority.

This chapter will also discuss one of ERISA's most generous provisions—the broad power to delegate investment responsibilities, which allows plan fiduciaries to meet their duties to the plan while permitting them to avoid having to become expert investment advisors themselves. Fiduciaries with delegating authority, however, may not exercise this power blindly. In consideration of this fact, this chapter provides significant detail on the procedures fiduciaries should employ in selecting and monitoring those individuals and entities to whom investment management responsibility and/or advisory authority for plan assets is delegated.

After providing a detailed overview of the investment process, the chapter proceeds to address several miscellaneous topics related to plan investments. They are soft dollar arrangements, proxy voting, insurance and annuity products, guaranteed investment contracts and "social"/economically targeted investments.

One final, but important, point. While this chapter discusses fiduciary responsibilities generally, delegating fiduciary responsibility, developing investment policy, and selecting and monitoring the performance of an investment manager, the reader should be aware that each of these topics is covered more fully in separate chapters. Such redundancy, however, is not inappropriate, as the analyses contained herein provide the legal framework within which ERISA plan fiduciaries should operate when making all plan-related decisions, not merely those related to investments. Adherence to this

---

*Mr. Albert wishes to gratefully acknowledge the invaluable assistance received from Gia Brock in the preparation of this chapter.

method of procedural prudence will assist fiduciaries in meeting all of their obligations to the plan and in preventing them from having to contend with ERISA's rather draconian penalty provisions.

"SETTING THE SCENE"—THE ROLE OF THE FIDUCIARY IN TODAY'S POLITICAL AND ECONOMIC WORLD

The Opportunity of the Moment

The world of employee benefit plan funding and finance is currently a world of risk. The past several years have engendered massive economic losses, as well as a reduced level of confidence in the financial system and in those who manage it. The fact that participants bear the risk of investment losses—especially under DC plans, such as a 401(k) plan—is a new and very disturbing concept for many. Thus, it is more critical today than ever for ERISA plan fiduciaries to keep abreast of economic and legal developments and, most importantly, to proactively anticipate situations that may pose substantial risks as well as those that present opportunities—especially issues such as investment manager selection, fiduciary liability, participant education and investment diversification.

The Danger of the Moment

Employee benefit plan fiduciaries are being held accountable to increasingly strict standards. The Sarbanes-Oxley Act, signed into law on July 30, 2002, imposed increased sanctions on criminal violations of ERISA. The new law also tightened the restrictions on 401(k) blackout periods, requiring advance notice to participants of times that they will be unable to make any changes to their investments and limiting insider trading. In addition, premiums for "fiduciary liability," and other insurance for officers, directors, trustees and other plan fiduciaries are rising precipitously. Since September 11, 2001, premium rates have almost doubled in some cases—particularly for those that invest a significant percentage of their employee benefit plan's assets in company securities.

Some experts even argue that ERISA, now over 30 years old, is due for a significant overhaul that would shift the major responsibilities for the design and maintenance of retirement plans to nonemployer, independent entities (e.g., insurers, banks or other organizations). Under such a scenario, employers would no longer serve as plan sponsors and fiduciary responsibilities would be fully assumed by the external vendors, who would also handle participant claims and disputes over benefits.

New Directions in Investment Strategy

The search for the best individuals to manage employee benefit plan assets is one of the most important tasks a plan fiduciary can undertake. Conventional wisdom reflects that only one in four professional fund managers ever outperforms the index. The search is further complicated by the nation's recent tide of corporate scandals that occurred in the early part of this decade.

Funds are under increasing pressure to boost returns in order to pay benefits. In this context, investment professionals are placing increased emphasis on private equity, hedge funds, venture capital and other "alternative" forms of investments. Hedge funds are a booming asset class, currently attracting record cash flows. Up to 50% of equity trading revenues at an investment bank may be generated by hedge fund activity. Consequently, many institutional investors are seeking to educate themselves about hedge funds and trying to determine how a hedge fund strategy would fit in with their overall portfolios.

One of the most attractive benefits of a hedge fund—especially a hedge fund of funds—is that it offers low correlation to more traditional investments such as stocks. Low correlation means increased diversification and increased protection from downside risks. There is also an argument that loosely regulated hedge fund investment pools are better equipped to boost returns in a volatile market environment. However, one of the concerns is with the unregulated nature of the hedge fund sector. The Securities and Exchange Commission (SEC) has suggested subjecting hedge funds to regular inspections and compelling the funds to provide more information about their operations to investors and regulators.

An equally significant question relating to issues in investment of plan assets today is whether and how much to invest in company stock. Particularly in DC plans, employer stock often constitutes a significant percentage of the assets held. The Enron collapse led to increased scrutiny on the holding of employer stock in employee retirement plans. As of December 31, 2000, Enron stock constituted 62% of the assets in Enron's 401(k) plan. For example, in some large companies, the percentage of total 401(k) assets in employer stock even exceeded 90% (for example, Procter & Gamble 94.65%; Sherwin-Williams 91.56%; Abbot Laboratories 90.23%). Some companies voluntarily limit the amount of employer stock held in their retirement plans, but most do not. The aggregate percentage of 401(k) assets in company stock is 19% and has stayed relatively constant since Enron. However, as a result of the significant losses sustained by Enron participants, Congress has begun to consider imposing limits on the percentage of employer stock that could be held in company pension plans.

It is against this current backdrop that we now proceed to examine ERISA's rules as they relate to employee benefit plan investments.

"SETTING THE STAGE"— GENERAL FIDUCIARY ISSUES RELATING TO INVESTMENTS OF PLAN ASSETS

Basic ERISA Fiduciary Rules

The cornerstone of ERISA's fiduciary responsibility provisions is set forth in Part 4 of Title I of ERISA, where Section 404(a)(1) imposes four duties on the fiduciary of an employee benefit plan. Those duties are to act solely in the interest of plan participants and beneficiaries; to act prudently; to diversify plan assets; and to act in accordance with plan documents. Specifically, the statute requires that:

(a)(1) a fiduciary shall discharge his duties with respect to a plan solely in the interest of the participants and beneficiaries and—
  (A) for the exclusive purpose of:
    (i) providing benefits to participants and their beneficiaries; and
    (ii) defraying reasonable expenses of administering the plan;
  (B) with the care, skill, prudence, and diligence under the circumstances then prevailing that a prudent man acting in a like capacity and familiar with such matters would use in the conduct of an enterprise of a like character and with like aims;
  (C) by diversifying the investments of the plan so as to minimize the risk of large losses, unless under the circumstances it is clearly prudent not to do so; and
  (D) in accordance with the documents and instruments governing the plan insofar as such documents and instruments are consistent with the provisions of [Titles I and IV of ERISA.]

Definition of a *Fiduciary*

Before discussing how each of these specific duties impacts on a fiduciary's duty to invest plan assets, it is important to understand exactly *whom* these requirements apply to. The concept of a fiduciary derives from trust law, and it refers to a person having a duty, created by his undertaking, to act primarily for another's benefit in matters connected with such undertaking. ERISA incorporates this concept, and in Section 3(21)(A) provides a definition that is simultaneously broader and more specific than the common law. Under ERISA's definition, a *fiduciary* is any person who:
  1. Exercises any discretionary authority or discretionary control regarding management of the plan
  2. Exercises any authority or control (discretionary or otherwise) regarding management or disposition of its assets
  3. Renders investment advice regarding plan assets for a fee or other compensation, whether direct or indirect, or has any authority or responsibility to do so; or
  4. Has any discretionary authority or discretionary responsibility in the administration of such plan.

Federal courts addressing the issue of who is a fiduciary under ERISA have uniformly held that Section 3(21)(A) should be liberally construed,[1] and that fiduciary status turns "on the function performed, rather than on the title held."[2] Under this standard, neither the absence of a formal appointment[3] nor a person's subjective belief that he is not a fiduciary[4] will influence a court's determination or enable that person to avoid fiduciary liability under ERISA. Thus, in addition to the plan's "named fiduciaries" (i.e., the administrator and trustees),[5] the fiduciaries of a plan may include employers,[6] members of an employer's board of directors,[7] the members of an employer's plan investment or administration committees,[8] investment managers, investment advisors,[9] insurers with authority to determine eligibility or interpret plan provisions, accountants[10] and each person who selects, appoints, supervises or monitors such individuals.[11]

Officials of the company sponsoring an ERISA plan are fiduciaries to the extent that they retain authority for the selection and retention of plan fiduciaries because, to that extent, they have retained discretionary authority or control respecting management of the plan.[12] However, a plan sponsor does not become a fiduciary solely as a result of the establishment, amendment or termination of a plan. These so-called "settlor" functions are not subject to the ERISA fiduciary rules.[13]

Notably, the rules relating to and impacting investments in employer stock are often set by the settlor under the terms of the plan (e.g., whether the employer stock fund must be offered as an investment option; whether the employer match must be invested in employer stock; how long participants must hold employer stock, etc.). This is settlor conduct, in which the employer as plan sponsor, but not in a fiduciary capacity, acts in its own interest and, therefore, unrestrained by ERISA's fiduciary duties.[14]

Despite the expansive definition, there are some limits as to who may be considered an ERISA fiduciary, especially with respect to service providers. For example, one court has held that insurance sales agents promoting a welfare plan who have no significant control over the plan are not fiduciaries.[15] Similarly, the U.S. Department of Labor (the Labor Department), the federal agency charged with the interpretation and enforcement of ERISA's provisions, takes the position that an entity that performs only nondiscretionary administrative and recordkeeping services pursuant to detailed administrative guidelines is not a fiduciary.[16] The Labor Department adheres to this position, even where the entity being paid for its services is an affiliate under common control with the plan's investment manager.[17]

The Prudence Standard

Section 404(a)(1)(B) of ERISA provides that a fiduciary shall discharge his duties with respect to a plan "with the care, skill, prudence, and diligence under the circumstances then prevailing that a prudent man acting in a like capacity and familiar with such matters would use in the conduct of an enterprise of a like character and with like aims." The standard for prudence depends on the circumstances. "The scope of the fiduciary's duty of prudence is ... limited to those factors and circumstances that a prudent person having similar duties and familiar with such matters would consider relevant, whether the context is one of plan investments or otherwise."[18] The courts generally have held that "ERISA's prudence standard 'is not that of a prudent lay person but rather that of a prudent fiduciary with experience dealing with a similar enterprise.'"[19] Implicit in this provision are two tests, one relating to *procedural* prudence, the other to *substantive* prudence.

Procedural prudence, which is measured at the time an investment decision is made, without regard to the "20-20" nature of hindsight, focuses on the fiduciary's *methodology* in selecting a particular investment. "When applying the prudence rule, the primary question is whether the fiduciaries, 'at the time they engaged in the challenged transactions, employed the appropriate methods to investigate the merits of the investment and to structure the investment.'"[20] Accordingly, whether a fiduciary breaches his duty to the plan is not necessarily a function of the investment's performance, but turns instead on the steps the fiduciary took or failed to take in reaching and implementing the investment decision. Proper methodology will be explored in detail in the sections that follow.

Substantive prudence, on the other hand, focuses on the actual merits of the fiduciary's decision (also at the time the investment decision is made). According to the Labor Department, this means that the scope of the fiduciary's duty of prudence is "limited to those factors and circumstances that a prudent person having similar duties and familiar with such matters would consider relevant, whether the context is one of plan investments or otherwise."[21] In practical terms, this means that a fiduciary must give "appropriate consideration" to the following criteria in making investment decisions:

1. The investment must fit within the context of the plan's overall portfolio.
2. The design of the portfolio, including the investment, must be reasonable for the purposes of the plan.
3. The risk of loss and opportunity for gain (or other returns) must be favorable, relative to alternative investments.
4. The investment must fit into the diversification scheme of the portfolio.
5. The investment must not affect adversely the liquidity and current return of the entire portfolio relative to anticipated cash flow requirements of the plan.
6. The investment must take into consideration the projected return of the portfolio relative to the funding objectives of the plan.[22]

As long as there is no conflict of interest that would impair the fiduciary's exercise of independent judgment, a fiduciary who considers these substantive factors (substantive prudence) and does so using proper procedures (procedural prudence) will satisfy the prudence requirement in most cases.[23] In sum, the test of ERISA prudence "focuses on the [defendant]'s conduct in investigating, evaluating and making the [challenged] investment."[24]

Based on the foregoing, and given the very special characteristics of employee benefit plans, "ERISA's prudence standard 'is not that of a prudent lay person but rather that of a prudent fiduciary with experience dealing with a similar enterprise.'"[25] In fact, some courts and commentators have explicitly stated that the standard is that of a prudent "expert."[26]

Interestingly, courts have recently crafted a nexus between the prudence requirement and fiduciary status, demonstrating in the process that the fiduciary status of a service provider is not dependent solely on the level of activity it performs for the plan. In *Glaziers & Glassworks Union Local No. 252 Annuity Fund v. Newbridge Securities, Inc.,* 93 F.3d 1171, 1183 (3d Cir. 1996), the Third Circuit Court of Appeals held that a securities brokerage firm that had been retained as an investment manager had a duty to disclose material information to the benefit plan even after its relationship with the plan had terminated. The court explained that, while fiduciary relationships generally are consensual in nature, "once a fiduciary relationship exists, the fiduciary duties arising from it do not necessarily terminate when a decision is made to dissolve the relationship." Finding that the investment manager had a continuing duty to disclose certain material information to the plan that the plan did not know but needed to know for its own protection, the court held that "an ERISA fiduciary's obligations to a plan are extinguished only when adequate provision has been made for the continued prudent management of plan assets."

Fiduciary Liability

If the "carrot" that ERISA dangles in front of benefit plan fiduciaries is the knowledge and satisfaction that they are acting in the plan's participants' best interests,

the "stick" is most certainly the penalty provisions found in Section 409. As too many fiduciaries have learned all too late, a violation of ERISA's fiduciary duty rules results in the imposition of severe and, in certain cases, draconian penalties. Indeed, those fiduciaries who cause plans to incur losses are *personally liable* for such losses. Among the penalties that may be imposed under Section 409 for breaching any of the responsibilities, obligations or duties imposed upon a fiduciary are:
1. *Personal liability* to reimburse the plan for any losses resulting from each breach
2. The possible imposition by the U.S. secretary of labor of an *additional 20% penalty* on the amount involved
3. Responsibility for *restoring to the plan any profits* made through use of plan assets
4. Other *equitable or remedial relief* as the court deems proper, such as:
   (a) Liability for claimant's attorney fees or
   (b) Removal from his or her fiduciary position (but only if the breach is substantial or repeated).[27]

"Losses" to the Plan Resulting From Breach of Fiduciary Duty

Courts have adopted a "but for" approach to assessing monetary damages for breaches of fiduciary duty. Liability is imposed in the amount that would restore the plan to the position it would have been in "but for" the breach.[28] For example, courts have held that "even if losses attributable to the breach are more than balanced by gains resulting from appropriate investments, the plan beneficiaries are entitled to 'the greater profits the Plan might have earned if the Trustees had invested in other plan assets' rather than the impermissible assets."[29] Similarly, where investments are alleged to have been improper, loss to plaintiffs may be measured by the difference between the actual performance of the investments and how alternative investments made by a reasonable investor would have performed.[30]

Hence, even if an improper decision results in a positive investment return, damages will nevertheless be assessed if a prudent decision would have resulted in an even greater return.[31] Many courts hold that "[I]f, but for the breach, the Fund would have earned even more than it actually earned, there is a 'loss' for which the breaching fiduciary is liable."[32] The burden is on the breaching fiduciary to prove that the funds would have earned less than the most profitable investment, and "any doubt or ambiguity should be resolved against them."[33]

Co-Fiduciary Responsibility and Liability

Even where a fiduciary has not directly caused a plan to suffer a loss, liability may still be imposed for actions the fiduciary failed to take. Section 405(a) of ERISA provides that a plan fiduciary is liable for *another fiduciary's* breach of duty with respect to the same plan if he or she:
1. Participates knowingly in, or knowingly undertakes to conceal, an act or omission of such other fiduciary, knowing such act or omission to be a breach of fiduciary responsibility[34]
2. By failing to fulfill his or her own fiduciary responsibilities, has enabled the other fiduciary to commit such breach[35] or
3. Has knowledge of a breach by such other fiduciary and fails to make reasonable efforts under the circumstances to remedy the breach.[36]

ERISA also makes clear that where assets are held by two or more trustees, each fiduciary shall use reasonable care to prevent a co-trustee from committing a breach, and shall jointly manage and control plan assets unless specific duties have been allocated among them.[37]

In the absence of conduct that falls within Section 405(a), however, the liability of a fiduciary who is not a "named fiduciary" is generally limited to the functions he or she performs with respect to the plan, and he or she will not be personally liable for all phases of the management and administration of the plan.[38] In fact, some courts have held that a fiduciary may bring a suit for indemnification against a co-fiduciary predicated on the latter's violation of the terms of the plan.[39]

Delegation of Fiduciary Responsibilities

As already discussed, ERISA measures a fiduciary's conduct against that of an objective "prudent expert." Not all fiduciaries, however, can be experts in each and every endeavor associated with employee benefit plans. ERISA recognizes this limitation and grants fiduciaries broad power to delegate their responsibilities accordingly. Thus, in addition to being able to delegate responsibility for plan administration and benefits determination, fiduciaries can delegate investment management authority.

Plan documents may provide for the allocation of responsibilities among named fiduciaries, and may authorize named fiduciaries to delegate nontrustee fiduciary responsibilities to others. However, "trustee responsibilities" relating to the management or control of plan assets may not be allocated unless such authority is delegated to an investment manager.[40]

For example, if an employer prudently allocates fiduciary responsibilities among named fiduciaries according to plan procedures designed for that purpose, the employer will not be liable for the acts and omissions of other named fiduciaries, except as provided in ERISA's co-fiduciary rules.[41] Similarly, named fiduciaries will not be liable for the acts and omissions of a person who is not a named fiduciary in carrying out the responsibilities delegated to such person[42] provided, of course, that the named fiduciary prudently selects and monitors the actions of such individual.

Delegation to an Investment Manager

Section 3(38) of ERISA defines an investment manager as either (i) an investment adviser registered under the Investment Advisers Act of 1940; (ii) a bank, as defined in the Investment Advisers Act of 1940; or (iii) an insurance company qualified under the laws of more than one state to manage, acquire or dispose of plan assets. Plan fiduciaries who appoint an ERISA-qualified investment manager to manage the plan's assets relieve themselves, the plan's sponsoring employer(s) and all other fiduciaries (other than the investment manager) from liability for the acts or omissions of the investment manager with respect to the investment of plan assets under the control of the investment manager.

The caveat, however, is that fiduciary liability will not be avoided with respect to the acts and omissions of the investment manager if the:
1. Appointment was imprudent
2. Fiduciary fails to monitor the conduct of the appointee
3. Fiduciary would be liable as a co-fiduciary under Section 405(a) of ERISA.[43]

Oftentimes, investment management agreements between a plan and the investment manager explicitly provide for the investment manager to declare that it is a "fiduciary" under ERISA with respect to the plan. Other times, however, an investment advisor, bank or insurance company has no intention of being an "investment manager" or a fiduciary, and therefore has made no such declaration.[44] The statute, 29 U.S.C. §1002(21)(A)(ii), as interpreted by the Department of Labor's regulations, 29 CFR §2510.3-21, and by recent case law,[45] requires that the investment advisor, in order to be deemed a fiduciary, actually must be rendering advice pursuant to an agreement, be paid for the advice, and have influence over the plan's investment decisions.[46]

Courts frequently take the position that banks not exercising "discretionary authority and control" over a plan's assets, but instead acting as custodians or servicing agents, are not fiduciaries with respect to the assets they hold.[47] For instance, a bank that lends money to a plan and takes as security certain plan assets is not a fiduciary where clear standards circumscribe the bank's discretion with respect to the plan's assets.[48] Similarly, a bank is not a fiduciary where it merely acts as the servicing agent for a specific investment and is not involved in the plan's administration, management or in making the plan's investment policy and decisions.[49] Nor is a bank a fiduciary where it performs only ministerial services, i.e., receiving payments, paying administration fees and transferring funds between accounts, but not exercising any judgment.[50] Essentially, a bank whose duties are limited to the simple maintenance of an account and the preparation of records associated therewith, and that makes payments and expenditures solely at the direction of a plan's trustees, will not be deemed a fiduciary. The Labor Department's position is consistent with that of the courts.[51]

However, if a bank exercises investment discretion over plan assets or has discretionary authority in the administration of plan assets, it will be deemed a fiduciary to the extent of its discretion and authority. Thus, a bank that sells annuity contracts to a plan and establishes a trust to facilitate the marketing of an annuity is a fiduciary where it has discretionary authority to appoint the administrator of the trust.[52] Again, the Labor Department's position is consistent with that of the courts.[53]

With respect to insurance companies, courts generally predicate fiduciary status on the company's discretion to manage and dispose of plan assets in order to pay benefits under the plan and its discretion to grant or deny claims.[54] For example, one court found that the insurer's agent was a fiduciary where he had the authority to grant or deny claims, manage and disburse fund assets and maintain claim files, even though the trustees had final authority to grant or deny claims and improve investments.[55] However, the courts have refused to impose fiduciary duties on insurance companies who merely sell their products or services to a pension plan unless the insurer assumes decision-making control over the administration of the plan or the disposition."[56]

Delegation of Investment Duties to Plan Participants: Participant-Directed Trusts

Where a plan consists of individual accounts—for instance, money purchase pension plans, profit-sharing plans or 401(k) plans—Section 404(c) of ERISA provides *optional* rules for relieving a fiduciary of liability for investment decisions that are "passed through" to plan participants. Under this section and the Labor Department regulations issued thereunder,[57] a participant or beneficiary will not be deemed a fiduciary by exercising investment discretion and control, and any person who is otherwise a plan fiduciary will not be liable for any loss resulting from the participant's or beneficiary's exercise of control over his or her account *if* a plan that provides for individual accounts:
1. Permits a participant or beneficiary to exercise independent control over the assets in his or her account
2. Offers the participants an opportunity to select, from a *"broad range of investment alternatives,"* the manner in which such assets will be invested

3. The participants or beneficiaries actually exercise such control.

The key to 404(c) protection is giving the participants the power to direct their investments themselves, so that it is not the plan fiduciary's duty to do so. Notably, the regulations issued by the Labor Department require the fiduciaries to disclose, and continue to disclose, the financial information necessary in order for the participant to make an informed decision. Though it always depends on the facts and circumstances of each particular case, a participant's or beneficiary's exercise of control is not independent in fact if:

1. The participant or beneficiary is subjected to improper influence by a plan fiduciary or the plan sponsor with respect to the transaction
2. A plan fiduciary has concealed material nonpublic facts regarding the investment from the participant or beneficiary,[58] unless the disclosure of such information by the plan fiduciary to the participant or beneficiary would violate any provision of federal law or any provision of state law which is not preempted by ERISA or
3. The participant or beneficiary is legally incompetent and the responsible plan fiduciary accepts the instructions of the participant or beneficiary knowing him to be legally incompetent.[59]

DOL Reg. §2550.402c-1(b). The Labor Department regulation is designed to ensure that before a fiduciary can be relieved of investment responsibility by reason of a participant's election to direct the investments in the participant's account, the fiduciary must give the participants the opportunity to make well-informed investment choices.[60] The Labor Department recently issued an opinion letter stating that the delivery of a profile (designed to comply with Section 10(b) of the Securities Act) by an identified plan fiduciary or designee to plan participants or beneficiaries satisfies the requirements of the 404(c) regulations because it provides a clear summary of key information about a mutual fund that is useful to such participants and/or beneficiaries.[61]

Essentially, Section 404(c) allows asset management by participants without subjecting anyone to fiduciary liability. However, if a participant fails to affirmatively exercise investment control, Section 404(c) would not apply and the plan fiduciaries must manage the assets.

Oftentimes, a fiduciary *may decline* to implement a participant's or beneficiary's investment instructions. Instructions may be ignored, for instance, if they:

1. Would result in a prohibited transaction
2. Would generate income that would be taxable to the plan
3. Would not be in accordance with the documents and instruments governing the plan
4. Would cause the fiduciary to maintain the indicia of ownership of plan assets outside the jurisdiction of the United States district courts
5. Would jeopardize the plan's tax-qualified status
6. Could result in a loss in excess of the participant's or beneficiary's account balance.

In addition, the Labor Department issued an opinion letter stating that trustees may refuse to *continue* to carry out a participant's or beneficiary's *last* affirmative exercise of investment control if continuing to follow the last directive would no longer be prudent *and* the trustees can no longer locate the participant or beneficiary.[62] In this situation, a plan does not lose its status as a Section 404(c) plan merely because the fiduciaries decide to override the last investment directive of a missing participant or beneficiary. However, the transactional relief afforded by Section 404(c) would not be available with respect to investment decisions made by plan fiduciaries on behalf of missing participants and beneficiaries; rather, the general fiduciary standards of Title I of ERISA apply.

Some employers and benefit plan practitioners have questioned whether the benefit of satisfying Section 404(c) is worth the administrative difficulties entailed in complying with the regulations. After all, the "opportunity to exercise control" and "broad range of investments" tests[63] found in the Labor Department regulations impose exacting requirements laden with investment vehicle selection and information distribution requirements; and compliance with these provisions oftentimes entails amending the plan and establishing new administrative practices—all with attendant additional costs. Finally, beyond the requirements of Section 404(c) and the Labor Department regulations, the fiduciary must still act prudently in selecting and monitoring plan investments, properly implementing participant investment decisions, disseminating required information and avoiding prohibited transactions.

THE INVESTMENT PRODUCT—GENERAL LEGAL CONSIDERATIONS

The Fiduciary's Independent Investigation

One of the hallmarks of prudence under ERISA is whether the fiduciary undertook a thorough and complete investigation before embarking on a particular course of investment action.[64] "A fiduciary's independent investigation of the merits of a particular investment is at the heart of the prudent person standard."[65] If a fiduciary fails to undertake the appropriate investigation before making an investment decision, the question is "whether, considering the facts that an adequate and thorough investigation would have revealed, the investment was objectively imprudent."[66]

Note that a fiduciary's duties with respect to plan investments do not end after he or she has selected the investment options. Fiduciaries should monitor investments with reasonable diligence and, if necessary, dispose of improper investments.[67]

The fiduciary's first step in the prudent investment of plan assets entails the establishment of prudent investment objectives and strategies. In doing so, fiduciaries must fully consider both broad concepts and specific details. Factors that must be considered, for instance, include:

1. The nature of the plan
2. The purpose of the plan and the employer's aim in offering the plan (taking into account the age, income levels and investment needs of participants)
3. The plan's funding characteristics and funding provisions
4. The size of the plan
5. The plan's liquidity requirements and
6. Acceptable risk-to-return ratios.

In addition, the following factors, among others, should be considered with respect to the investment of plan assets:

1. Whether the particular investment or investment course of action is reasonably designed, as part of the portfolio, to further the purposes of the plan, taking into consideration the risk of loss and the opportunity for gain (or other return) associated with the investment or investment course of action
2. The composition of the portfolio with regard to diversification
3. The liquidity and current return of the portfolio relative to the anticipated cash flow requirements of the plan
4. The projected return of the portfolio relative to the funding objectives of the plan.[68]

After weighing the foregoing considerations, fiduciaries should then prepare a written statement describing the plan's investment objectives, complete with guidelines and general instructions concerning various types or categories of investment management decisions. The investment guidelines may include restrictions, for instance, on:

1. The types of investments (e.g., no foreign securities or venture capital issues)
2. Asset allocation requirements (e.g., limiting plan investments in equities to a specific percentage of the portfolio)
3. Minimum bond quality grades (e.g., no more than a certain percentage of the total fixed income portfolio should be invested in bonds rated less than "A")
4. Proxy voting decisions (e.g., criteria regarding the support of or opposition to recurring issues, such as proposals to create classified board of directors), etc.

Although ERISA does not specifically require that plan fiduciaries prepare statements of investment policy, the Labor Department takes the position that a named fiduciary's authority to issue statements of investment policy to investment managers is inherent in the named fiduciary's authority under the terms of the plan to appoint investment managers.[69] In addition, the regulations specify that such a statement "is consistent with the fiduciary obligations" embodied by the duty of prudence and the "exclusive purpose" rule.[70]

The Labor Department believes that such statements serve a legitimate purpose in many plans by helping assure that the investments are made in a prudent and rational manner and are designed to further the purposes of the plan and its funding.[71] Recent federal cases are consistent with this view.[72] However, the Labor Department also takes the position that a named fiduciary's determination of the terms of a statement of investment policy represents an exercise of fiduciary responsibility. Accordingly, such statements need to take into account factors such as the plan's funding policy and its liquidity needs as well as issues of prudence, diversification and other fiduciary requirements.

Assuming that a plan has a written statement of investment policy, it would be advisable for it to contain a statement of proxy voting policy in order to increase the likelihood that proxy voting decisions are consistent with other aspects of the investment policy. In addition, if a plan has many investment managers, a written proxy voting policy may prevent the investment managers from taking conflicting positions on a given issue.

Prudent Investment Strategies and Decisions

As discussed earlier, the standard for prudence under Section 404 depends on the circumstances existing at the time a fiduciary makes an investment decision. This means that the scope of the fiduciary's duty of prudence is "limited to those factors and circumstances that a prudent person having similar duties and familiar with such matters would consider relevant."[73] The legislative history accompanying ERISA reflects that the expertise required of a plan fiduciary varies with the size and scope of the plan. Thus, individuals managing larger plans with enormous assets are required to exercise a more professional approach to investment management than individuals administering small plans with limited portfolios.

Given the fact that ERISA has been extant for three decades, and there are literally trillions of dollars committed to ERISA plan investments, it is surprising to note that there remain relatively few reported cases involving the issue of whether an investment is prudent. However, in those cases addressing the subject, the fiduciary's failure to live up to his duties is easily identified.[74] For example, one court found that an investment manager's decision to invest one-third of a welfare fund's portfolio in highly volatile inverse floaters was a violation of ERISA's prudence standard.[75] In another, perhaps less obvious, decision an ESOP trustee was held not imprudent in the sale and buy-back of the ESOP's closed corporation stocks because opinions reasonably differed as to the stocks' value and a prudent fiduciary in the trustee's place would have bought the stocks back at the price that the trustee paid.[76]

As these cases demonstrate, courts have developed general standards for determining whether a fiduciary acted prudently in designing investment strategies and in making investment decisions. Essentially, the proper test is whether the fiduciary:
1. Employed proper methods to investigate, evaluate and structure the investment
2. Acted in a manner as would others who have a capacity and familiarity with such matters
3. Exercised independent judgment when making investment decisions.[77]

Analyzed under these criteria, fiduciaries must be able to establish that, in effecting investment decisions, they:
1. Diligently conducted an impartial, arm's length study of the advantages and disadvantages of the particular transaction
2. Utilized acceptable standards in retaining qualified experts and consultants[78]
3. Relied on complete and up-to-date information.

Finally, the fiduciary's investment decisions must be made in accordance with the plan documents. Investment decisions that are not permitted by the plan are flatly prohibited by ERISA, notwithstanding argument that an investment manager's investments were prudent.

Retention of an Expert

Courts recognize that not all plan fiduciaries can be experts in every phase of an employee benefit plan's investments and administration, nor can they be knowledgeable in the entire range of activities integral to the operation of a plan. Therefore, fiduciaries have an *affirmative duty* to seek the advice and counsel of independent experts when their own ability is insufficient under the circumstances.[79] Fiduciaries responsible for delegating investigative authority must ensure that the consultants they retain are qualified in the subject area of the transaction and must provide those consultants with accurate information.[80]

However, mere reliance on an expert's opinion will not relieve the fiduciary of his independent duty to investigate.[81] The fiduciary must:
1. Investigate the expert's qualification
2. Provide the expert with complete and accurate information
3. Ensure that reliance on the expert's advice is reasonably justified under the circumstances.[82]

Except where properly delegated to an investment manager, authority over investment decisions remains with the plan's fiduciaries.[83] Accordingly, the advice of experts should set forth adequately the benefits and risks of a particular transaction in a form that is comprehensible and should provide sufficient analysis and grounds for making informed decisions.

Diversification of Plan Investments

ERISA requires the fiduciary responsible for plan investments to diversify the plan's investment portfolio so as to minimize the risk of large losses to trust principal, unless under the circumstances it is clearly prudent not to diversify. The theory behind the diversification requirement is that potential losses in one area of the plan's portfolio due to a particular economic event will be offset by gains in another area.[84] Moreover, even where such a loss is not offset, its impact is limited to a relatively small portion of the fund.[85]

Diversification is usually achieved by limiting the proportion of trust assets invested in any one type of investment and instead committing the assets to different classes of investments that are characterized by different types of risks. In order to achieve this goal, ERISA does not tell plan fiduciaries how to diversify their plans' portfolios. Rather, diversification "depends upon the facts and circumstances surrounding each plan and investment."[86] According to the Conference Report in the legislative history, fiduciaries should consider the following factors:
1. The purpose of the plan
2. The amount of plan assets
3. Financial and industrial conditions
4. The type of investment, whether mortgages, bonds or shares, or stock or otherwise
5. Distribution as to geographic location
6. Distribution as to industries
7. The dates of maturity of the investment and loan maturity dates.[87]

Cases bear testimony to the fact that diversification is literally a "facts and circumstances" test. For example, whereas one case has held that a concentration of 36% of the plan's assets in one form of investment may be a violation of ERISA §404(a)(1)(C),[88] another declined to find a breach where the sole trustee and administrator of the plan invested 63% of the plan's assets in a single parcel of undeveloped real estate.[89] In yet a third case, the court found no breach where a plan invested 90% of its assets in only three investments.[90]

In a recent district court case, the participants alleged the trustee breached his fiduciary duty by his increased use of margin debt coupled with his decrease in diversification of the plan's assets. The court found that, although the trustee clearly invested the assets of the plan aggressively, he invested prudently as a man of like capacity and familiar with the plan would have invested with an aggressive investment strategy to maximize profits pursuant to ERISA §404(a)(1)(B).[91] The court further found that, although the plan's assets were not diversified to minimize the risk of all large losses, under the circumstances the trustee was clearly not imprudent in his aggressive investment strategy, pursuant to ERISA 404(a)(1)(C), because he invested in 20 different stocks.[92]

Moreover, case law makes clear that both *individual* investments and the asset allocation of the plan's *entire* investment portfolio are evaluated for diversification. Thus, even where "evidence supports that each loan was prudent," such a finding "is not dispositive of the diversification inquiry."[93]

Based on the foregoing, fiduciaries should be wary of creating portfolios with the following characteristics:

1. Disproportionately heavy investments in a security of a single issuer
2. Securities dependent upon the success of a single enterprise
3. Securities dependent upon conditions in one locality
4. Stock of corporations engaged in one industry
5. Mortgages concentrated in one geographic allocation
6. Mortgages on one particular class of property.

Communications to Plan Participants

Prudent selection of investment options by plan fiduciaries assists participants in meeting their individual investment goals. However, the fiduciaries' responsibility to the plan's participants also entails ensuring that the participants have adequate information upon which to base their personal decisions. This information includes (1) accurate and understandable descriptions of investment options and objectives; (2) projections of long-term results; (3) consistent, frequent and useful performance reports; and (4) assistance in identifying individual retirement needs, potential shortfalls and the disadvantages of certain investment options. Notably, employers can have a significant impact on the effectiveness of a plan simply by taking an active role in communicating accurately to participants the plan's objectives, strategy and investment options.

PRUDENT SELECTION OF AN INVESTMENT MANAGER

When plan fiduciaries choose to delegate investment management authority to an investment manager, the choice of the investment manager must be prudent. Although this topic will be addressed in much greater detail in Chapter 38, a brief synopsis is warranted here.

As a general proposition, fiduciaries should consider four factors in selecting an investment manager. They are:

1. The manager's ability to effectively manage the type of fund involved
2. Whether the manager's organization and investment philosophies are consistent with the needs of the plan
3. Whether the manager has performed well in managing similar investments for plans
4. The manager's track record for meeting the stated objectives of plans he or she has managed.

Given these broad parameters, the fiduciary's initial task is to investigate prudently the investment manager's experience, qualifications and investment approach. Prudent investigation begins by identifying a range of candidates whose expertise is consistent with the proposed investment guidelines or investment style and by documenting the process by which such candidates are selected.

As part of the selection process, plan fiduciaries should solicit a wide range of information from each candidate that is being considered for retention as an investment manager. For instance, each candidate should be asked to provide:

1. A description of the precise services that the manager is prepared to offer
2. A history of the manager's experience in the investment management business, including the total amount of assets under its control
3. A statement of the manager's investment approach or philosophy, and whether the manager has any internal investment guidelines
4. The number of retirement plan accounts and other accounts under the manager's management and their total current fair market value
5. A detailed schedule of investment management fees
6. A description of the manager's current staffing, and details as to the general experience and educational qualifications of the individuals who would be primarily responsible for the plan's account
7. The name of any individuals who would be actively involved in handling the pension plan's account and details as to the experience and educational qualifications of such individuals
8. A statement as to whether members of the staff would be available to meet with the plan fiduciaries on a regular basis
9. A description of how policy is established by the manager and how it will be implemented with respect to the plan assets in question
10. A summary of any investment policy the manager recommended for pension plan assets placed under its management

11. A tabulation of time-weighted annual rates of total investment return on the combined results of all retirement plan equity portfolios under management for each of the previous five to ten years, and cumulatively for that period
12. A tabulation of time-weighted annual rates of total investment return on the combined results of all retirement plan portfolios under management for each of the previous five to ten years, and cumulatively for that period
13. The dollar amount of the manager's fiduciary liability insurance and fidelity bond policies
14. The existence of any current or past litigation involving claims against the manager or any of its principals or investment professionals, and whether the manager or any of its principals or professionals has ever been held in violation of any federal or state laws
15. Whether the manager, or any of its principals, has ever undergone bankruptcy, liquidation, reorganization or similar proceedings; has had its registration or license revoked or activities restricted; has ever been sued by a client or the Securities and Exchange Commission; or has ever been denied fiduciary liability or fidelity insurance
16. Whether the manager is registered with the Securities and Exchange Commission under the Investment Advisers Act of 1940, and the date of its initial registration
17. Whether the manager is affiliated (or has any business relationship) with the broker-dealer it uses that could affect its investment decisions
18. Financial information relating to the manager, including its most recent balance sheet
19. The manager's policy with respect to the voting of proxies appurtenant to investment securities (see discussion above)
20. A description of the manager's business structure, principal owners and affiliates
21. The procedure to be employed by the manager to comply with ERISA's prohibited transaction restrictions and whether the investment manager is a qualified professional asset manager.

The foregoing list is not exclusive. Thus, where the particular circumstances warrant, additional information should be solicited. Moreover, the fiduciary's investigation should not stop upon receiving answers to the foregoing inquiries. Instead, plan fiduciaries should independently evaluate the manager's qualifications by:

1. Examining the manager's experience in the particular area of investments under consideration, as well as its experience with other ERISA plan assets
2. Making an independent assessment of the manager's qualifications. This may be accomplished by:
   (a) Determining that the manager is widely known and well respected (as is the case with a major financial institution)
   (b) Securing and calling existing client references
   (c) Seeking the advice of a professional third-party consultant who is knowledgeable in such matters
   (d) Utilizing the Internet as a resource to gather information regarding the manager.
3. Evaluating the record of the manager's past performance with investments of the type contemplated and by reviewing a sample portfolio managed by the manager for a similarly situated client
4. Evaluating the credentials and performance of the principals of the manager
5. Inquiring of the U.S. secretary of labor, and the Securities and Exchange Commission, as to whether any enforcement actions have been initiated during the previous five to ten years with respect to the manager, or any of its principals or investment professionals.

COMMUNICATION OF THE PLAN'S INVESTMENT OBJECTIVES

Preliminarily, the plan fiduciaries responsible for the investment of plan assets, or their authorized representatives, should identify an investment style for that portion of the plan assets to be committed to the investment manager for the plan. Once an investment style has been selected, the fiduciary responsible for appointing the manager should establish a clear understanding with the manager as to:

1. The rate of return sought through management of the plan assets
2. The level of acceptable risk tolerance and diversification latitude
3. The scope of the manager's discretion to acquire and maintain particular forms of assets and to determine the amounts of each type of asset
4. The time frame for measuring performance
5. The procedures to be used in monitoring and evaluating the performance of the manager
6. A clearly defined list of investment restrictions concerning, for example:
   (a) Venture capital investments
   (b) Bond quality grades
   (c) Uncovered options
   (d) Short sales
   (e) Futures contracts
   (f) Restricted stock or private placements

(with the possible exception of Section 144A securities)
(g) Margin transactions (or any other borrowing of money)
(h) Volatile "derivative" instruments.

The foregoing is not an exhaustive list and, depending on the particular characteristics of the portfolio, some (or all) of the foregoing types of investments may, under certain circumstances, be appropriate.[94]

Negotiating the Investment Management Agreement

Once an investment manager has been selected, the fiduciary responsible for the appointment has a duty to ensure that the manager has a clear understanding of the fiduciary's expectations.

In terms of specific provisions of the agreement, one of the most important is the ability of plan fiduciaries to terminate the investment manager's services with little or no advance notice (i.e., under most circumstances, not more than 30 days), with any fees paid in advance to the manager prorated to the date of termination.[95] In this way, fiduciaries can protect their plans upon the first true signs of inadequate performance.

Additionally, the agreement should contain several essential representations and warranties on the part of the investment manager stating that it:

1. Is an investment advisor registered with the SEC under the Investment Advisers Act of 1940
2. Is an investment manager within the meaning of ERISA Section 3(38)
3. Acknowledges being a fiduciary (within the meaning of Section 3(21)(a) of ERISA) with respect to the plan's assets under investment
4. Has obtained a bond in accordance with ERISA Section 412
5. Maintains fiduciary liability insurance in an amount determined by the plan fiduciaries to be sufficient under the circumstances (the question of whether fiduciary liability insurance should be required at all may depend on the manager's size, stature, background and experience)
6. Has made all necessary filings and obtained all requisite approvals from all relevant government agencies
7. Will maintain the indicia of ownership of the plan's assets in the United States or else comply with the requirements of ERISA Section 404(b) and the regulations thereunder
8. Has obtained the appropriate authorization to execute the agreement
9. Will indemnify the plan fiduciaries from any damages arising out of a breach by the manager of its agreement and/or its investment management duties (reciprocal indemnity, from plan fiduciaries to manager, should be avoided wherever possible)
10. Will promptly advise the plan fiduciaries of any change in the ownership or management of the manager
11. May not assign the agreement to a third party without the advance written consent of the plan fiduciaries
12. Shall not effect any transaction that directly or indirectly will cause the plan (or any fiduciary thereof) to enter into a prohibited transaction under Section 406-408 of ERISA or Section 4975(c) of the Code (including any broker/dealer transactions with an affiliate of the manager, which is not the subject of a prohibited transaction exemption)
13. Agrees that each of the foregoing representations are to be "continuing" in nature.

If the investment manager's fees are to be paid directly from plan assets (rather than by the sponsoring employer(s)), the plan fiduciaries have a duty to ascertain the reasonableness of the fees to be paid in relation to the amount of plan assets to be invested with the investment manager, in comparison to fees charged by comparable advisors.

Finally, plan fiduciaries should have legal counsel analyze the specific details of the investment management agreement, offering memorandum, subscription agreement or other documents that set forth the terms of the relationship between the plan and the investment manager.

MONITORING THE INVESTMENT MANAGER

A fiduciary's duties with respect to plan investments do not end after he or she has selected the investment options. Quite the contrary, fiduciaries must monitor investments with reasonable diligence and, if necessary, dispose of improper investments.[96] The Labor Department has described a fiduciary's duty to monitor the actions of those individuals to whom employee benefit plan fiduciary responsibilities have been delegated as follows:

At reasonable intervals the performance of trustees and other fiduciaries should be reviewed by the appointing fiduciary in such manner as may be reasonably expected to ensure that their performance has been in compliance with the terms of the plan and statutory standards, and satisfies the needs of the plan. No single procedure will be appropriate in all cases; the procedure adopted may vary in accordance with the nature of the plan and other facts and circumstances relevant to the choice of the procedure.[97] For example, in one recent case, the purported ignorance of mismanagement by investment managers was not a defense to a breach of fiduciary duty since appropriate monitoring would have alerted the fund administrators of the situation and imposed on them the responsibility to take corrective action.[98] However, in another case, the court limited its assessment of the board of director's fiduciary duty to the specific responsibilities of appointment and removal of the investment committee members identified in the plan and failed to impose a duty to monitor the actions of the committee.[99]

Thus, while precaution in selecting and monitoring an investment manager is always necessary, the level of precaution used should reflect in significant part the percentage of fund assets dedicated to the investment manager. Insofar as plan fiduciaries are capable of reviewing the investment reports of an independent custodian responsible for valuing fund assets and reporting all investment transactions, an added layer of precaution is added to the monitoring process.

A fiduciary's principal means of ensuring an investment manager's compliance with the plan's funding objective and policy is to require a periodic accounting and report on the plan's investments. These reports, which should be prepared and reviewed on at least a quarterly basis, enable fiduciaries to determine whether the original plan investment objectives, and the objectives set forth in any investment guidelines, are being achieved. Also, they help to determine whether modifications in underlying plan objectives or investment strategies are warranted. At minimum, the content of the accounting should include:

1. An inventory and description of the cash and each security and other investment held
2. The fair market and book value of the investments (where an investment consists of securities not regularly traded on a national securities exchange, a detailed description of the financial condition of the issuer of such securities, including applicable financial statements, should be provided)
3. A calculation of the investment income, capital appreciation or depreciation (both realized and unrealized) and investment return for the period in question (it probably also would be useful to have the investment return computed on a quarterly, annual and from-inception basis)
4. A list of the proxies appurtenant to the investment account and detailed information with respect to the manner in which such proxies were voted by the manager (and the precise reasons for each such vote)
5. A breakdown of all fees (from whatever sources) received by the investment manager in connection with the investment of trust assets, including brokerage commissions.

In addition to reviewing the periodic accounting reports, fiduciaries should regularly review the investment manager's proxy voting procedures, brokerage and trading practices, communications procedures and fee computation. Finally, fiduciaries should meet with the investment manager (at least annually) to review both the status and performance of the plan's investments, as well as to review the investment manager's performance. In focusing on the investment manager's performance, consideration should be given to any significant changes in its corporate or capital structure, investment style, brokerage affiliation or practices, investment process or professional staff.

Fiduciaries should consider retaining an independent investment consulting or monitoring firm to assist in all or a portion of the foregoing monitoring activities.

At the very least, the delegating fiduciary should review periodically (at least quarterly, or more often if necessary) the accounting and reports provided by the investment manager for the purpose of confirming the adequacy of their content; the investment manager's performance during the period; the accuracy of the asset valuation method; whether the investment manager has managed the portfolio consistent with any investment guidelines and the investment manager's stated investment philosophy and style; and for the purpose of generally comparing them in material respects with information provided by the plan's custodian including the custodian's statement of transactions; the rate of return earned by the investment manager during the period in question on an overall basis, and by asset class; where investments are in more than one sector, by sector; and whether that rate is reasonable (as an absolute number and when compared to other comparable investment managers appropriate indices or benchmarks) and, if not, whether the continued retention of the investment manager is prudent.

The fiduciary should meet with the investment manager periodically (at least annually) to review the status and performance of the plan's investments, as well as to review the investment manager's performance and any significant changes in its corporate or capital structure, investment style, brokerage affiliation or practices, investment process or professional staff.

Also, he or she should periodically (at least annually) review the voting procedure pursuant to which the investment manager votes proxies, in addition to the manner in which proxies were voted in specific situations; review periodically the investment manager's practices regarding brokerage and trading, including brokerage costs, use of soft dollars, quality of securities, execution and portfolio turnover; establish and review, at least annually, the procedures for communicating information regarding investments and investment managers among the trustees, the plan's staff and the plan's service providers (including but not limited to the plan's attorneys, actuaries and custodial trustees); and verify, at least quarterly, the accuracy of the fee computation.

Of course, an investment manager's services should be terminated as soon as prudently possible if its performance is unsatisfactory.

SOFT DOLLAR ARRANGEMENTS

A *soft dollar arrangement* is an arrangement whereby a brokerage firm provides to an investment manager or other plan fiduciary additional services over and above basic brokerage services at no additional charge in exchange for a commitment from the investment manager or other fiduciary to execute a specified percentage of the plan's trades through the brokerage firm. Plans enter into soft dollar arrangements to obtain additional services—such as research services—that the plans might not otherwise be able to afford. By directing trades through a specified broker-dealer, the plans can acquire these additional services without spending "hard" dollars.

With the enactment of ERISA, there was concern that the use of soft dollars would violate the fiduciary responsibility provisions because the investment manager is paying more than the true cost of execution in order to obtain services it will use in managing plan assets. Partially in response to this concern, the Securities and Exchange Commission (SEC) issued an Interpretative Release under Section 28(e) of the Securities Exchange Act of 1934, which provides a safe harbor for persons who exercise investment discretion over beneficiaries' or clients' accounts to pay for "research and brokerage services" with commissions generated by account transactions.[100]

Section 28(e) provides that no person who exercises investment discretion with respect to an account shall be deemed to have acted unlawfully or to have breached a fiduciary duty under state or federal law solely by reason of his having caused an account to pay more than the lowest available commission. This favorable treatment is only available if the person with "investment discretion" determines in good faith that the amount of the commission is reasonable in relation to the value of the "brokerage and research services" provided. A person has "investment discretion" when he or she is authorized to determine what securities or other property will be purchased or sold by for the account.

A person provides "brokerage and research services" to the extent he (1) furnishes advice as to the value of securities, the advisability of investing in, purchasing or selling securities, or the availability of securities or purchases or sellers of securities; (2) furnishes analyses and reports concerning issues, industries, securities, economic factors and trends, portfolio strategy and the performance of accounts; or (3) effects securities transactions (and required or incidental functions such as clearance, settlement and custody) under SEC rules or the rules of a self-regulating organization governing such transactions.

Clearly, the safe harbor is a narrow provision, leaving many transactions outside of its protective reach. However, if a transaction falls outside the safe harbor of Section 28(e), such as directed brokerage, then ERISA Technical Release 86-1 provides that the decision as to brokerage and its cost are subject to the fiduciary responsibility provisions of ERISA, including the prohibited transaction rules. Specifically, Technical Release 86-1 provides that an investment manager may enter into soft dollar arrangements to procure goods and services on behalf of the plan for which the plan would otherwise be obligated to pay, but only if (1) the total compensation paid to the broker-dealer is reasonable and (2) best execution is obtained. The term *best execution* means trades that are executed in such a manner that the total cost in each transaction is the most favorable under the circumstances.

In this situation, the determination of whom to utilize for brokerage and how to pay for services must be made prudently and exclusively for the affected plan, i.e., appropriate and helpful to the plan. Moreover, the trustees must monitor the service provided by the broker-dealer to assure that the best execution is being obtained. The Labor Department has clarified that best execution clearly goes beyond commission cost and includes the actual price of the security.

The SEC has issued findings that reiterate and further explain its 1986 Interpretive Release and provided for a clearer explanation as to the reach of the safe harbor.[101] It found, among other things, that the types of products available for purchase with soft dollars have greatly expanded since 1986. Because industry participants are now grappling with decisions as to whether these various products are "research" or "brokerage" within the safe harbor or whether these products should be considered part of advisers' overhead expenses to be paid for by advisers with hard dollars, it recommended that the SEC reiterate and provide further guidance with respect to the scope of the safe harbor, particularly concerning (a) the use of electronically provided research and the various items used to send, receive and process research electronically and (b) the use of items that may facilitate trade execution.[102]

Prohibited Transactions Issues Relating to Soft Dollar Arrangements

A soft dollar arrangement might benefit a party in interest and/or a fiduciary, such as a participating employer or a union in violation of Sections 406(a)(1)(c) and/or 406(b)(1) of ERISA. For example, an employer that is the named fiduciary for its plan and does not exercise investment discretion with respect to the plan would normally be prohibited from directing the plan's trades through a broker-dealer that agrees to utilize a portion of the brokerage commissions received from the plan to procure goods and services for the benefit of the employer.

A soft dollar arrangement could also violate Section 406(b)(1) of ERISA if it is used to benefit a party who is responsible for directing a transaction. For example, it may be a prohibited transaction for a plan's investment manager to direct transactions to a specified broker-dealer in exchange for bookkeeping services to be provided to the investment manager that do not benefit the plan. In order to fall within the prohibited transaction exemption set forth in Section 408(b)(2), plan fiduciaries must be able to demonstrate that the plan has paid no more than reasonable compensation for investment transactions.

Actions to Consider When Entering Into Soft Dollar Arrangements

Given these legal parameters, fiduciaries should undertake several actions when considering soft dollar arrangements. First among them is to measure the actual cost of transactions. Second, they should require accounting from investment managers of all services received from a brokerage firm under a soft dollar arrangement. Third, fiduciaries should require all investment managers to obtain best execution. In addition, fiduciaries should consider retaining a monitoring service to measure the "best execution" and commission costs paid by the plan. The plan can then disclose the results of the study to its investment managers to obtain their written comments on any deviations from the norm. Finally, they should consider directing at least a portion of trades to lower cost brokers.

Recapture Arrangements

A *recapture arrangement* is a type of soft dollar arrangement whereby a portion of brokerage commissions is rebated to the plan or to some other service provider to defray the costs of those services. Recapture agreements enable the plan to obtain a tangible monetary benefit in exchange for its directed transactions, which may, in certain instances, outweigh the benefits the plan may receive through a typical soft dollar arrangement. The same fiduciary issues that govern typical soft dollar transactions—including the prohibited transactions issues—apply to recapture arrangements.

PROXY VOTING

Shareholders of companies are provided the right to vote on certain corporate issues. The voting procedure in connection with this right is referred to as the *voting of proxies* or *proxy voting*.

Labor Department Position

The Labor Department takes the position that the fiduciary act of managing plan assets includes the voting of proxies appurtenant to the shares of stock owned by the plan, and therefore, at least initially, plan fiduciaries have the exclusive authority and responsibility for voting proxies.[103] However, where the plan delegates authority to an investment manager to acquire or dispose of the plan's assets, it generally delegates its authority to vote proxies as well. This holds true unless the plan document permits the trustee or other fiduciary to vote proxies and the investment management agreement expressly precludes the investment manager from voting proxies.

If the plan has appointed an investment manager, and the plan has not reserved the right to vote proxies, the investment manager has a fiduciary duty to (1) confirm that it has received the proper number of proxies, (2) vote the proxies and (3) maintain accurate records as to the voting of proxies, as well as the rationale for the vote.[104] Moreover, if an investment manager has been appointed, the plan's fiduciaries may not make a decision on how to vote proxies appurtenant to shares being managed by an investment manager, unless the right to vote proxies is reserved to the trustees or named fiduciary. Thus, where authority has been delegated, other than monitoring proxy voting procedures and the voting of specific proxies, plan fiduciaries will be relieved of liability for the improper exercise of proxies by the plan's investment managers.

DOL Interpretive Bulletin 94-2 (July 29, 1994) confirms the approach discussed above, which is derived from Labor Department letters to private individuals. The bulletin clarifies that when delegating investment management authority to an investment manager, the named fiduciary may reserve the right to direct a trustee regarding the voting of proxies relating to specified shares of stock or issues. The fiduciary may also reserve this right to another named fiduciary if the plan provides for procedures for allocating fiduciary responsibilities among named fiduciaries.[105]

Other Actions to Consider in Connection With Proxy Voting

Several other actions must be considered in connection with proxy voting. For instance, fiduciaries should carefully review plan documents and investment management agreements to ensure that they are not precluded from delegating voting authority to an investment manager. Fiduciaries should negotiate investment management agreements with specific language delegating to the investment manager the fiduciary duty to vote proxies or specific language retaining the fiduciary duty to vote proxies. These guidelines should include a specific set of procedures for voting proxies that separate issues involved in proxy voting into established categories (i.e., routine matters, nonroutine matters, corporate governance matters and social issues). Fiduciaries should also establish procedure for monitoring and reviewing proxy voting activity. In this regard, they should consider establishing an internal proxy monitoring or corporate governance committee, or retaining an outside evaluator to help with this task.

Finally, when a named fiduciary reserves the right to vote employer securities (e.g., in an ESOP) and such right is not passed through to plan participants and beneficiaries (provided that pass-through voting is not legally required),[106] fiduciaries should exercise extensive caution in voting employer securities in order to avoid prohibited transactions under Section 406(b) of ERISA and conflicts of interest.

INSURANCE AND ANNUITY PRODUCTS

Annuity Contracts and Their Impact on Plan Participants

Annuity contracts are typically purchased by a plan fiduciary to guarantee the payment of benefits either under a terminated or ongoing pension plan (i.e., for participants who are retiring or separating from service with accrued vested benefits). Such annuities are commonly known as *benefit distribution annuities*. Plans also sometimes purchase annuities for investment purchases.

An annuity's most distinguishing feature is that, upon its purchase by a plan, liability for benefits promised under the plan is transferred from the plan to the insurance company selling the annuity. Indeed, once the annuity contract is issued, the individuals covered under such contract cease to be plan participants. The Labor Department, the Internal Revenue Service and the Pension Benefit Guaranty Corporation (PBGC) each has recognized that an individual ceases to be a plan participant if the full benefit rights of such individual are fully guaranteed by an insurance company, thereby extinguishing the plan fiduciary's liability to that participant for the payment of the pension benefit.[107]

Prudent Selection of an Annuity Provider

At this point in the chapter, it should be axiomatic that a plan's selection of an annuity provider must be made in a prudent manner consistent with general principles discussed above. As with the selection of any other type of investment vehicle, it is the fiduciary's process in selecting and purchasing annuities, rather than the ultimate result of the fiduciary's decision (e.g., the collapse of the insurer), that determines whether or not the fiduciary's selection of an annuity provider satisfies ERISA's prudence requirements. Accordingly, fiduciaries must, among other things:

1. Inquire as to the company's strength
2. Assess the insurer's administrative abilities
3. Assess the insurer's claims paying ability
4. Retain qualified experts and consultants.

As the Labor Department cases evidence, consideration only of the company's financial strength is inadequate. Indeed, the complaints in recent Labor Department cases assert that it is insufficient for a plan fiduciary to rely on rating services, even if a company's rating is high, rather than independently evaluating the solvency of a company offering an annuity product to the pension plan. Moreover, where fiduciaries of plans have investments in insurance companies that are *known* to be experiencing economic difficulties, they must take actions to understand all facts relating to the troubled investment (including the nature of the plan's investment and the plan's contractual rights and obligations) and, further, must evaluate and monitor the investment scrupulously, as well as the regulatory developments governing the insurance company and the particular investment.

Selection of an Insurance Product

The highly publicized problems of insurance companies, particularly Executive Life Company of California, Executive Life Company of New York and Mutual Benefit Life in New Jersey and, most recently, Confederation Life, and the concomitant inability of those carriers to satisfy their annuity liabilities because of high-risk/high-yield debt securities (i.e., junk bonds), or troubled real estate loans, or a combination of both, have substantial implications for pension plans, their sponsors, plan fiduciaries and participants.

The PBGC, for instance, takes the position (in connection with a terminated plan) that once a plan sponsor has purchased irrevocable commitments from an insurance company authorized to do business in a state or the District of Columbia, the plan sponsor satisfies its obligations under Title IV of ERISA (i.e., ERISA's plan termination insurance provisions).[108] This is so even if the insurance company is unable to pay the benefits it has guaranteed under the annuity contract. In a May 1991 opinion letter, the PBGC enunciated this position in connection with annuity contracts issued by Executive Life, which reduced the payments under such contracts by 30%. That is, Executive Life, under court order, paid only 70% of the amounts owed under retirement annuity policies. The PBGC has opined that the plan sponsor has no liability for the difference once the annuity contract is purchased.[109]

The PBGC also takes the position that, once an irrevocable annuity contract is purchased from an insurance company, if the insurance company is unable to satisfy its commitments, the PBGC will not pay such benefits. It bases its position on the fact that the insurable event under ERISA is plan termination. The final distribution of assets (i.e., purchase of annuity contract) extinguishes the PBGC's statutory guarantee obligation. This position is directly contrary to the PBGC's earlier position in 1981, in which it advised that it generally would guarantee the retirement benefit if the insurance company was unable to pay the benefit under the annuity.

Thus, assuming the plan fiduciary was prudent in its selection of the insurance company, the plan sponsor should be relieved from any further benefit liabilities. But, if the plan fiduciary was *not prudent* in selecting an annuity provider, the fiduciary may be liable. Indeed, the Pension Annuitants Protection Act of 1994, which amends ERISA Section 502(a),[110] clarifies that former participants or beneficiaries of terminated pension plans have standing to seek relief where a fiduciary breach has occurred involving the purchase of insurance contracts or annuities in connection with their termination as plan participants.

Concerns about the financial condition of certain insurance carriers and the security of the pension benefits promised to participants and beneficiaries under benefit distribution annuity contracts purchased on their behalf from those carriers have not gone unheeded by the Labor Department. Indeed, the Labor Department has brought numerous lawsuits against employers whose plans purchased annuities on the grounds that the plan fiduciaries failed to follow adequate procedures designed to select the safest available insurance carrier when choosing an annuity provider.[111] Notable examples include cases that have been brought against employers purchasing annuities from Executive Life Insurance Companies, including Pacific Lumber Co.; Magnetek, Inc.; Smith International Inc.; Geosource, Inc.; American National Car Company; AFG Industries, Inc.; and Ray-mark Industries, Inc.

In addition to actively prosecuting individual cases, the Labor Department has issued an interpretive bulletin relating to fiduciary standards governing the selection of annuity providers,[112] keeping its regulation setting forth the minimum standards intact.[113] With respect to a benefit distribution annuity purchased in anticipation of plan termination, the bulletin provides that the termination will not constitute a valid standard termination under Title IV of ERISA unless the plan administrator selects the insurer in accordance with the fiduciary standards of Title I of ERISA.

According to the Labor Department, ERISA's fiduciary rules require, at a minimum, that plan fiduciaries conduct an "objective, thorough and analytical search" for the purpose of identifying and selecting providers from which to purchase annuities. In conducting such a search, a fiduciary must evaluate various factors that relate to the potential annuity provider's claim paying ability and creditworthiness, including:

1. The quality and diversification of the annuity provider's investment portfolio
2. The size of the insurer relative to the proposed contract
3. The level of the insurer's capital and surplus
4. The lines of business of the annuity provider and other indications of an insurer's exposure to liability
5. The structure of the annuity contract and guaranties supporting the annuities, such as the use of separate accounts
6. The availability of additional protection through state guaranty associations and the extent of their guaranties.

Unless fiduciaries possess the necessary expertise to evaluate such factors, fiduciaries must obtain the advice of a qualified, independent expert. Finally, as an added enforcement measure, the PBGC has announced proposed rules regarding the termination of single employer plans, in which the PBGC stated that as part of its standard termination audit program, it intends to audit insurer selections for compliance with these fiduciary standards and to take appropriate corrective action where necessary.[114]

GUARANTEED INVESTMENT CONTRACTS

One of the investment vehicles often chosen by plan fiduciaries is contracts issued by an insurance company (GICs) or a bank (BICs) that "guarantee" the return of principal and pay a fixed rate of interest.

Fiduciary Issues Relating to GICs

As with all investment decisions, a fiduciary purchasing a GIC is subject to the fiduciary obligations imposed under Section 404 of ERISA. Not surprisingly, the test of prudence with respect to GICs is "whether the individual trustees, at the time they engaged in the challenged transactions, employed the appropriate methods to investigate the merits of the investment and to structure the investment."[115] According to the Labor Department, a fiduciary would not be acting prudently if he or she chose a GIC that provided the plan with "less return, in comparison to risk, than comparable investments available to the plan, or if it involved a greater risk ... than other investments offering a similar return."[116] Thus, in deciding whether to invest plan assets in a GIC or which insurer to use, the fiduciary must investigate the options, assess the prudence of his or her decisions and adequately investigate the soundness and stability of the insurance company.[117]

By way of example, investment in a GIC that has a single, rather than staggered, maturity date, may result in a breach of fiduciary duty since such an investment may not address the plan's cash flow needs. Applying principle to fact, one court held that it was a breach of prudence and diversification duties to invest 70% of plan assets in long-term bonds with nonstaggered maturity dates that had to be sold at a loss in order to cover benefit distributions.[118]

Factors to Consider When Selecting a GIC

In choosing GICs as an investment option, plan fiduciaries should consider several important points. First of these is that although the word *guaranteed* is prominently featured in the GIC name, GICs are *not* guaranteed by either the federal (or any state) government or by plan fiduciaries; they are simply another type of investment. This lack of guaranty leads to the next point, which is that the security of a GIC depends entirely on the financial stability of the issuer. Put another way, GICs are subject to default risks. In the event the issuer fails, participants and beneficiaries may not receive the stated interest rate and may even lose part or all of the original investment.

The next factor to consider is that GICs, like other investments, have investment risks that will affect whether participants will receive the benefits to which they are entitled. One of these risks is that the investments underlying GICs—typically private placement bonds, mortgages and real estate—inextricably link the underlying investments to the real estate industry. Over a long period of time, the fixed income return on GICs may not compare with the return that may be obtained from equity investments.

Finally, many GICs impose penalties for early withdrawal. Such a withdrawal may occur, for example, in the event of a mass layoff or division shutdown. Therefore, it is essential to review GIC provisions and clarify the events that trigger such penalties. Participants should be advised as to the situations in which they will bear the penalty.

Here it should be recalled that the plan's fiduciaries may not be the only fiduciaries with respect to a GIC. Under Section 3(21)(A) of ERISA, the insurance company may be a fiduciary, even without a formal designation or title, if it exercises authority or control over the plan or its assets. Since the insurance contract is a plan asset, exercising discretionary authority over the insurance contract will make the insurer a fiduciary.[119]

Guidelines for Fiduciaries

In reaction to the relatively recent financial difficulties in the insurance industry, plan fiduciaries might want to consider substituting other fixed income investment options (i.e., government bonds, high-quality corporate debentures, money market funds, etc.) for GICs. However, rather than eliminate GICs entirely, plan fiduciaries should:

1. Evaluate and adjust, if necessary, the performance goals and strategies of the plan
2. Investigate methods to enhance the security and performance of GICs
3. Engage in the prudent selection of GICs and other insurance products by soliciting and comparing several bids
4. Implement guidelines to ensure the prudent selection of annuity providers and GIC issuers
5. Beware of replacing the default risk associated with GICs with an increased market risk
6. Consider making shorter term commitments, diversifying investments among various insurance carriers and avoiding placing all investments in one insurance company
7. Review all insurance, annuity and related contracts and other documentation on a periodic basis.

In selecting an issuer, plan fiduciaries should also consider the factors set forth in the discussion relating to the selection of an investment manager.

Communicating the Nature of GICs to Plan Participants

Plan fiduciaries should review all plan communications and materials to ensure that they contain adequate and accurate descriptions of the plan's GICs and other investment options. In doing so, fiduciaries should seriously consider eliminating the term *guaranteed*, thus avoiding any suggestion of guaranteed rates or return of principal or any misconception that the insurance product is guaranteed by the plan sponsor or other plan fiduciaries. Terms such as *fixed income fund* or *stable value fund* should be used instead. As a result, participants will not be misguided as to the risk of default and other potential investment risks inherent in GICs. Also, because no rate is guaranteed, when projecting annual rates for a GIC, plan fiduciaries should communicate to participants, in addition to the current rate of return, a history of rates of return and the rates of other accounts with similar liquidity. This will provide a basis for comparison for the plan participants.

Information should be made available to plan participants regarding the quality of the GIC offered by the plan. For example, participants should be advised, among other things, as to:

1. The number of issuers represented in the portfolio

2. The percentage of the portfolio that is held by any single issuer
3. The average maturity of all contracts in the portfolio
4. The quality standards used to determine whether an issuer may be included in the portfolio.

Plan participants should be made aware, in clear and concise terms, of the action that will be taken in the event that the issuer defaults on its obligations or otherwise fails.

Plan fiduciaries should also clarify the alternatives to GICs that are offered by the plan. Such clarification should include an explanation as to how and when transfers may be made from a GIC to another option, as well as a description of any risks associated with such a transfer. Plan investment guidelines may have to be revised so as to permit other high-quality, stable value investments, in addition to GICs, that are consistent with the fund's objectives.

Finally, and perhaps most importantly, plan fiduciaries should consider retaining outside investment experts to assist plan participants in understanding the relative security of their GIC portfolio, notwithstanding the events in the insurance industry.

SOCIAL INVESTMENTS— ECONOMICALLY TARGETED INVESTMENTS

The primary objective of a pension plan is to provide "employee retirement income security." To meet this objective, plan assets must be invested in a manner that satisfies ERISA's requirements of loyalty, prudence and diversification. As explained in this section, a plan's assets can be invested in a manner that satisfies these requirements and achieves a broader social goal as well.

Social Investing

Social investing has been defined as investing where the principal impetus is not to maximize investment returns to benefit plan participants or their beneficiaries, but to further some other "social" policy or goal. *Social investing* should be distinguished from *socially sensitive* or *socially responsible* investing in which investments are selected based upon the traditional due diligence analysis of financial/economic factors and only then are noneconomic factors considered as secondary considerations. Socially sensitive investing will be discussed later on in this section.

Examples of social investments range from community projects (such as low-income housing or below-market interest rate mortgages) to investments in environmentally sound products. Social investments may include those designed to spur local economies, increase the use of union labor and provide jobs to certain groups (including groups primarily comprised of participants in the plan that is making the investment). A social investment strategy may also take the form of abstaining from investing in a particular opportunity, such as a company doing business in a country that supports political (or other) policies with which the fiduciaries of the plan do not agree philosophically, or companies that manufacture products that are deleterious to human health (e.g., cigarettes) or environmentally harmful (e.g., certain sectors of the chemical industry).

There are no statutory provisions in ERISA or regulations issued by the Labor Department that specifically address whether plan fiduciaries may make investment decisions based on social policy concerns. There are, however, opinion letters, commentaries and a Labor Department interpretive bulletin, all of which indicate that plan fiduciaries may not implement an investment policy that has social underpinnings, unless the policy also satisfies ERISA's exclusive benefit rule, duty of prudence and diversification requirement.

In at least one early advisory opinion letter, for instance, the Labor Department approved social investing where the projected economic return of the investment was comparable to, or better than, alternative investments.[120] In that letter, the Labor Department stated that a "decision to make an investment may not be influenced by a desire to stimulate the construction industry and generate employment, unless the investment, when judged solely on the basis of its economic value to the plan, would be equal or superior to alternative investments available to the plan." In most situations, however, a fiduciary who pursues an investment strategy that forgoes maximization of investment return in favor of furthering a social policy or goal violates his or her fiduciary duties under ERISA. In other words, the establishment of an investment strategy that utilizes social or moral criteria in choosing investment opportunities and does not utilize economic factors as a primary consideration in making investment decisions, in most instances would violate ERISA.

ERISA Advisory Opinion Letter No. 98-04A (May 28, 1998), issued to the Calvert Group Ltd., dealt with investment in socially responsible funds. Citing DOL Reg. §2509.94-1, the Labor Department stated that it "has expressed the view that the fiduciary standards of sections 403 and 404 do not preclude consideration of collateral benefits, such as those offered by a 'socially-responsible' fund, in a fiduciary's evaluation of a particular investment opportunity. However, the existence of such collateral benefits may be decisive only if the fiduciary determines that the investment offering the collateral benefits is expected to provide an investment return commensurate to alternative investments having similar risks."[121]

The Labor Department has issued a series of opinion letters and information letters dealing with investment in real estate mortgages based on various social purposes which came to similar conclusions.[122] If the fiduciary reasonably believed, after taking the proper steps to assure compliance with both the procedural and substantive components of his or her fiduciary duties, that the return of a socially screened fund, relative to the risk, was at least equal to that otherwise available, taking into account social considerations in choosing between socially screened funds and other fund, it would clearly be appropriate under current law.

However, DOL Reg. §2509.94-1 does not provide support for the proposition that a fiduciary can consider social consequences if the likely returns (after considering transaction and market impact costs), relative to risk, of a socially screened fund are even slightly less than those of otherwise available investments. Indeed, ERISA Advisory Opinion 98-04A specifically provides that, "A decision to make an investment, or to designate an alternative investment alternative, may not be influenced by non-economic factors unless the investment ultimately chosen for the plan, when judged solely on the basis of its economic value, would be equal to or superior to alternative available investments."[123]

Despite the possibility that a policy of social investing may be permissible if plan fiduciaries give primary weight to the economic benefit to the plan of such investments, comments made during the last few years by senior staff members of the Labor Department and the PBGC indicate that these individuals are not convinced that utilization of a social investment strategy comports with the ERISA obligations to invest plan assets for the "exclusive benefit of plan participants" or with their interpretation that ERISA requires plan fiduciaries to maximize investment returns for the sole benefit of plan participants.

Given the foregoing background, and in recognition of the fact that there is scant judicial or authoritative administrative pronouncements regarding social investing, fiduciaries should proceed very cautiously in pursuing a strategy of social investing. Fiduciaries that implement investment policies that incorporate social or moral criteria as a primary or material consideration (ahead, or in lieu, of prudent economic analyses) could be subject to legal challenge by the Labor Department or by plan participants and their beneficiaries. Thus, after prudent consideration of all the relevant economic factors, it is especially important for plan fiduciaries to document the analysis behind their decision to implement a policy of "social investing." Absence of documentation regarding such investments will, in most instances, violate ERISA's "procedural" prudence requirement and will leave the investments open to challenge by the Labor Department and, possibly, plan participants.

A policy of social investing has been implemented by a number of employee benefit funds that are not covered by the requirements of ERISA, such as public pension funds.[124] Indeed, some states have enacted statutes that actually require pension plans to implement and follow a policy of social investing. Plans that are not subject to ERISA's fiduciary requirements may implement a policy of social investing, provided, of course, that other statutory provisions regulating such plans do not otherwise preclude social investment policies.[125]

Economically Targeted Investments (ETIs)

In an effort to distinguish certain socially sensitive investments from purely social investments, plan fiduciaries, unions, plan sponsors and the Labor Department have shifted their focus from scrutinizing the underlying merits of social investments (which are generally impermissible under ERISA) to sanctioning certain economically targeted investments (ETIs), which are more likely to be acceptable under ERISA. Unlike social investing, ETIs are not used to further some social, moral or other noneconomic goals, but rather are used to further a particular economic achievement that, in turn, may provide collateral benefits to certain targeted groups (such as union members, plan participants, communities in which the plan operates, etc.).

Until recently, ETIs generally were viewed as a type of investment where plan assets are invested to further a particular economic goal such as the creation of jobs or affordable housing. In June 1994, however, the Labor Department released an interpretative bulletin relating to the fiduciary standards to be employed under ERISA in evaluating ETIs for ERISA plans.[126] The Labor Department released this bulletin primarily to eliminate the misperception that plan investments in ETIs are incompatible with ERISA's fiduciary obligations.

Semantics aside, the Labor Department's current position is that, under ERISA, investments that further a societal goal *and* that meet ERISA's prudence requirements are acceptable. Thus, fiduciaries can select an investment course of action that reflects noneconomic factors, provided that the application of such factors follows primary consideration of a broad range of investment opportunities that are equally advantageous economically. Stated simply, if two investments are equally attractive for financial reasons, it is acceptable to choose one of the two based on socially useful reasons.[127] As noted previously, public employee funds are creatures of state legislatures and are not subject to ERISA. Some states have enacted statutes actually requiring the social investment of pension assets. Moreover, although several states have patterned their employee benefit plan fiduciary responsibility rules after ERISA's fiduciary provisions, standards under state laws that govern fiduciaries of some state plans may be less restrictive than ERISA. Generally, public employee funds have more latitude than ERISA funds to consider socially useful investments.

Types of Economically Targeted Investments

According to the Labor Department, ETIs fall within a wide variety of asset categories, including real estate, venture capital and small business investments. An ETI could, for example, provide collateral benefits to union members or finance construction projects. Some recent examples of ETIs include:

1. A new Housing and Urban Development (HUD) program designed to attract pension capital for affordable housing and community development whereby HUD makes available to pension funds, on a competitive basis, project-based rental assistance to support construction and rehabilitation of affordable, multifamily housing
2. HUD is currently designing a new plan to encourage targeted pension fund investments in low- and moderate-income housing through Federal Housing Administration mortgage sales programs.
3. Investments in affordable single family housing projects in California by the California Public Employee Retirement Systems. Other state pension systems have invested in similar single family housing projects.
4. Investments in fixed rate, long-term Colorado Housing and Finance agency bonds by Colorado Prime Employees' Retirement System, which are used to finance small business loans within the state
5. Creation of funds with unique financing techniques such as loan funds operated by municipalities and community groups to promote small business loans or loan funds to build low-income housing whereby the pension fund may receive government-backed debt securities (which are exchanged for the loan).

Standard of Conduct Applicable to Investments in ETIs

Under ERISA, a plan fiduciary may invest plan assets in an ETI, provided that the fiduciary determines that such investment is appropriate for the plan by applying the same factors that a prudent fiduciary would use in determining whether any other type of investment is appropriate for the plan. The requirements of Sections 403 and 404 of ERISA do not prevent plan fiduciaries from deciding to invest plan assets in an ETI, *provided that* the ETI has an expected rate of return that is commensurate to rates of return of alternate investments with similar risk characteristics that are available to the plan *and* if the ETI represents an otherwise appropriate investment for the plan (considering such factors as diversification and the plan's investment guidelines or policy).

The Labor Department recognizes that nothing in ERISA precludes plan fiduciaries from considering ETIs even though certain ETIs may require a longer period of time to generate significant investment returns, may be less liquid and may not have as much readily available information on their risks and returns as other asset categories.[128] However, a violation of ERISA would occur if a plan fiduciary is willing to accept rates of investment return that fall below conventional investments or entail greater risks to secure collateral benefits. In order to properly evaluate an ETI, most plan fiduciaries will be well advised to seek special advice from investment experts who are familiar with ETIs and are able to analyze them from a risk and return perspective.

CONCLUSION

The investment of plan assets is one of the (if not *the*) most important duties assumed by a plan fiduciary. While we have endeavored to set forth the salient legal—and practical—considerations attendant to this critical duty, fiduciaries will be well served if they derive only two pieces of wisdom from this chapter. First, act prudently, and be sure to be cautious and diligent every step of the way in effectuating investments for ERISA plan assets. Second, seek professional advice whenever appropriate. Trained experts are available to assist fiduciaries from the initial step of designing investment objectives to selecting an investment manager, and then to monitoring investment performance. Adherence to these guiding principles will help ensure that fiduciaries meet their obligations under ERISA when it comes to plan investments while avoiding (what can be some) draconian penalties.

ENDNOTES

1. *Thomas, Head & Greisen Employees Trust v. Buster*, 24 F.3d 1114, 1117 (9th Cir. 1994), *cert. denied*, 513 U.S. 1127 (1995).
2. *Blatt v. Marshall & Lassman*, 812 F.2d 810, 812 (2d Cir. 1987); *Adamczyk v. Lever Bros. Co., a Div. of Conopco*, 991 F.Supp. 931, 936 (N.D.Ill. 1997) ("the definition of [fiduciary] is a functional one: a person may be a fiduciary for the purposes of plan management or administration but not for other purposes"); *Acosta v. Pacific Enterprises*, 950 F.2d 611, 617 (9th Cir. 1991) (stating that "a person's actions, not the official designation of his role," determine fiduciary status).
3. See *Stein v. Smith*, 270 F.Supp. 2d 157, 165 (D.Mass. 2003) ("Under ERISA, a person . . . can be a fiduciary by virtue of being either named as such or by acting in a fiduciary capacity with regard to an ERISA plan."); see also *Donovan v. Mercer*, 747 F.2d 304 (5th Cir. 1984) (formal appointment is not a prerequisite to fiduciary liability).
4. See *Bd. of Trustees of Bricklayers and Allied Craftsmen Local 6 of New Jersey Welfare Fund v. Wettlin Assocs., Inc.*, 237 F.3d 270, 271 (3d Cir. 2001) (despite claims that its control of

welfare and pension plan assets was purely ministerial, third party administrator's ability to "determin[e] the legitimate expenses of the fund, wr[ite] checks, and disburs[e] assets from the fund's bank account," represented sufficient authority and control over plan assets to sustain complaint alleging that administrator was an ERISA fiduciary); see also *Farm King Supply, Inc. Integrated Profit Sharing Plan and Trust v. Edward D. Jones & Co.,* 884 F.2d 288 (7th Cir. 1989) (fiduciary status is determined by objective standards; "it matters not that the person may subjectively believe that he or she is not a fiduciary as long as the requirements under the regulations are met").

5. See *Administrative Committee v. Gauf,* 188 F.3d 767 (7th Cir. 1999) (named plan administrator, who is given express authority "to resolve all questions concerning the administration, interpretation, or application of the Plan," is fiduciary).

6. See *LoPresti v. Terwilliger,* 126 F.3d 34, 40 (2d Cir. 1997) (company's co-owner, who signed company checks payable to pension fund, was an ERISA fiduciary with respect to the pension fund because in commingling plan assets with company assets, and using plan assets to pay company creditors, he "exercised...authority or control respecting disposition of [plan] assets).

7. See *Newton v. Van Otterloo,* 756 F.Supp. 1121, 1132 (N.D.Ind. 1991) (power to appoint and remove fiduciaries makes company's board of directors fiduciaries); *Martin v. Harline,* 15 EBC 1138 (D.Utah 1992) (member of employer's board of directors was a fiduciary because he had discretion to act with respect to employer's ESOP and, thus, was jointly and severally liable for any losses resulting from fiduciary breach).

8. See *Bd. of Trustees of Bricklayers and Allied Craftsmen Local 6 of New Jersey Welfare Fund v. Wettlin Assocs., Inc.,* 237 F.3d 270, 271 (3d Cir. 2001) (despite claims that its control of welfare and pension plan assets was purely ministerial, third party administrator's ability to "determin[e] the legitimate expenses of the fund, wr[ite] checks, and disburs[e] assets from the fund's bank account," represented sufficient authority and control over plan assets to sustain complaint alleging that administrator was an ERISA fiduciary). But see *CSA 401(k) Plan v. Pension Prof'ls, Inc.,* 195 F.3d 1135 (9th Cir. 1999) (defendant appellee, third party administrator, did not exercise discretionary authority over plaintiff appellant, pension plan, and was not liable as a fiduciary under ERISA).

9. *Wolin v. Smith Barney, Inc.,* 83 F.3d 847, 849 (7th Cir. 1996) (in order to be deemed a fiduciary, investment advisor must be rendering advice pursuant to an agreement, be paid for the advice and have influence approaching control over the plan's investment decisions).

10. See *Martin v. Feilen,* 965 F.2d 660 (8th Cir. 1992), *cert. denied,* 113 S.Ct. 979 (1993) (accountants were fiduciaries by reason of their control of plan assets); *Pension Plan of Public Serv. Co. of New Hampshire v. KPMG Peat Marwick,* 815 F.Supp. 52 (D.N.H. 1993) (auditing firm was not a fiduciary because it had no control over plan assets and had not performed in any capacity beyond that of an independent auditor).

11. *Newton v. Van Otterloo,* 756 F.Supp. 1121, 1132 (N.D. Ind. 1991) (power to appoint and remove fiduciaries makes company's board of directors fiduciaries).

12. 29 CFR §2509.75-8 at D-4; see *In re WorldCom, Inc., ERISA Litig.,* 263 F.Supp. 2d 745 (S.D.N.Y. 2003) (mere authority to act as a fiduciary is insufficient if the person did not engage in the responsibilities of a fiduciary and was not formally named as a fiduciary); *Rankin v. Rots,* 278 F.Supp. 2d 853 (E.D.Mich. 2003) (CEO may not be held liable merely as a result of his position as head of the company named as the fiduciary of the plan but allegations of controlling the plan's assets and selecting the members of the investment committee are sufficient to assert a fiduciary duty and survive dismissal).

13. See *Walling v. Brady,* 125 F.3d 114 (3d Cir. 1997); *Bennett v. CONRAIL Matched Sav. Plan Admin. Comm.,* 168 F.3d 671, 674 (3d. Cir. 1999) (quoting *Payonk v. HMW Indus.,* 883 F.2d 221, 225 (3d Cir. 1989), "when employers wear 'two hats' as employers and administrators' . . . they assume fiduciary status "only when and to the extent" that they function in their capacity as plan administrators, not when they conduct business that is not regulated by ERISA' ")); DOL Letter to Kirk F. Maldonado, dated March 2, 1987, reprinted in *BNA Pension Reporter,* April 6, 1987.

14. See, e.g.,*Sprint Corp ERISA litigation,* 2004 WL 1179371 at *8 (D.Kan. May 27, 2004) (defendant acts in settlor capacity when setting the plan terms regarding the company stock); see also *Steinman v. Hicks,* 352 F.3d 1101, 1105 (7th Cir. 2003) (observing that a trust to trust transfer is not a fiduciary act). Prior to the *Steinman* ruling, a district court in the Seventh Circuit applied a contrary rule. See *Nelson v. IPALCO Industries Inc.,* 29 EB Case 2665, 2003 WL 402253 at *6-*7 (S.D.Ind. Feb. 13, 2003) (in merger, plan amendment converting existing plan assets from the acquiring to the acquired company's stock was a fiduciary act).

15. *Gabner v. Met. Life Insurance Co.,* 938 F.Supp. 1295, 1305-1306 (E.D.Tex. 1996).

16. Therefore, a person who performs purely ministerial functions for an employee benefit plan within a framework of policies, interpretations, rules, practices and procedures made by other persons is not a fiduciary because such person does not have discretionary authority or discretionary control respecting management of the plan; does not exercise any authority or control respecting management or disposition of the assets of the plan; and does not render investment advice with respect to any money or other property of the plan and has no authority or responsibility to do so. 29 CFR §2509.75-8 at D-4; DOL Advisory Opinion No. 97-16A, Letter to Stephen M. Saxon (May 22, 1997); see also *Pension Plan of Public Serv. Co. of New Hampshire v. KPMG Peat Marwick,* 815 F.Supp. 52 (D.N.H. 1993) (auditing firm was not a fiduciary because it had no control over plan assets and had not performed in any capacity beyond that of an independent auditor).

17. Id.; see also *Geller v. County Line Auto Sales,* 86 F.3d 18 (2d Cir. 1996) (employers that merely sent reports to plan trustees, guaranteed employee eligibility and remitted premiums to trust performed purely ministerial duties and were not ERISA fiduciaries with respect to the multiemployer pension plan).

18. 44 *Fed. Reg.* 37,222-23 (July 20, 1979) (DOL release accompanying DOL Reg. §2550.404a-1(b)); see also *Metzler v. Graham,* 112 F.3d 207, 209 (5th Cir. 1997).

19. *Whitfield v. Cohen,* 682 F.Supp. 188, 194 (S.D.N.Y. 1988) (quoting *Marshall v. Snyder,* 1 Employee Benefits Cas. (BNA) 1878, 1886 (E.D.N.Y. 1979)).

20. *California Ironworkers Field Pension Trust v. Loomis Sayles & Co.,* 259 F.3d 1036, 1043 (9th Cir. 2001). "A fiduciary's independent investigation of the merits of a particular transaction is at the heart of the prudent person standard." *Henry v.*

Champlain Enters., 334 F.Supp. 2d 252(quoting *Whitfield v. Cohen,* 682 F.Supp. 188, 194 (S.D.N.Y. 1988)).

21. 44 *Fed. Reg.* 37,222-23 (July 20, 1979) (DOL release accompanying DOL Reg. §2550.404a-1(b)); see also *Chao v. Trust Fund Advisors,* 2004 U.S. Dist. LEXIS 4026, 4034 (D.D.C. 2004) (In applying ERISA's prudent person standard in other cases, courts have recognized that "ERISA's prudence standard is not that of a prudent lay person but rather that of a prudent fiduciary with experience dealing with a similar enterprise.") (citing *United States v. Mason Tenders District Council of Greater New York,* 909 F.Supp. 882, 886 (S.D.N.Y. 1995)).

22. See DOL Reg. §2550.404a-1(b).

23. *Chao v. Trust Fund Advisors,* 2004 U.S. Dist. LEXIS 4026, 4034 (D.D.C. 2004) (citing *Katsaros,* 744 F.2d at 279).

24. *United States v. Mason Tenders District Council of Greater New York,* 909 F.Supp. 882, 886 (S.D.N.Y. 1995).

25. *Whitfield v. Cohen,* 682 F.Supp. 188, 194 (S.D.N.Y. 1988) (quoting *Marshall v. Snyder,* 1 EBC 1878, 1886 (E.D.N.Y. 1979)); accord *Chao v. Trust Fund Advisors,* 2004 U.S. Dist. LEXIS 4026, 4034 (D.D.C. 2004).

26. See *In re Bicostal Corporation,* 191 B.R. 238 (Bank. M.D.Fla. 1995), order reversed in part by 202 B.R. 988 (M.D.Fla. 1996) (Section 404(a)(1)(B) explicitly holds fiduciaries to the standard of a prudent expert, rather than that of a prudent layman); cf. *Donovan v. Cunningham,* 716 F.2d 1455 (5th Cir. 1983), *cert. denied,* 467 U.S. 1251 (1984) (emphasis of Section 404 is on flexibility; level of knowledge required by fiduciary varies with nature of the plan). But see *Thompson v. Avondale Indus.,* 29 Employee Benefits Cas. (BNA) 2865, 2872 (E.D.L.A. 2003) ("The reference in 29 U.S.C.S. §1104(a)(1)(B) to a prudent man "familiar with such matters" does not create a "prudent expert" under ERISA, and prudent fiduciaries are entitled to rely on the advice they obtain from independent experts. On the other hand, subjective good faith—a pure heart and an empty head—is not enough.) See also Edward J. Farragher and Robert Kleinman, "How Pension Funds Make Real Estate Investment Decisions," *Real Estate Review* (Winter 1996) (prudent expert).

27. See *Martin v. Feilen,* 965 F.2d 660 (8th Cir. 1992), *cert. denied* 113 S.Ct. 979 (1993); *Tittle v. Enron Corp.,* 284 F.Supp. 2d 511 (S.D.Tex. 2003) (named fiduciaries, and those who assume fiduciary duty through their actions, are equally subject to liability); *Oscar A. Samos, M.D., Inc. v. Dean Witter Reynolds, Inc.,* 772 F.Supp. 715 (D R.I. 1991); cf. *Tittle v. Enron Corp.,* 284 F.Supp. 2d 511 (S.D.Tex. 2003) (service providers and employers of plan participants, although not fiduciaries, may be liable for equitable relief if they knowingly assist in a fiduciary's breach).

28. *California Ironworkers Field Pension Trust v. Loomis Sayles & Co.* 259 F.3d 1036, 1046 (9th Cir. 2001).

29. Id. (quoting *Donovan v. Bierwirth,* 754 F.2d 1049, 1056 (2d Cir. 1985) (measure of loss requires a comparison of what plan actually earned with what it would have earned had the funds been available for other purposes).

30. *Liss v. Smith,* 991 F.Supp. 278 (S.D.N.Y. 1998); *Harley v. Minnesota Mining and Mfg. Co.,* 42 F.Supp. 2d 898 (D.Minn. 1999) (loss to be determined by comparing plan's actual profit to the potential profit that could have been realized in the absence of breach), *cert. denied,* 537 U.S. 1106.

31. See *Dardaganis v. Grace Capital, Inc.,* 889 F.2d 1237 (2d Cir. 1989) (despite fact that plan assets increased during investment manager's tenure, investment manager liable where it failed to follow trustees' instructions to limit equity investments to 50% of plan assets, the presumption being that, but for the breach, the funds would have been invested in the most profitable of the alternatives).

32. *Toussaint v. James,* 30 Employee Benefits Cas. (BNA) 2793, 2795 (S.D.N.Y. 2003) (citing *Dardaganis v. Grace Capital, Inc.,* 889 F.2d 1237 (2d Cir. 1989)). See, e.g., *Harris Trust & Savings Bank v. John Hancock Mutual Life Ins. Co.,* 122 F.Supp. 2d 444, 465 (S.D.N.Y. 2000) (quoting *Donovan v. Bierwirth* 754 F.2d 1049, 1056 (2d Cir. 1985) ("We hold that the measure of loss applicable under ERISA section 409 requires a comparison of what the Plan actually earned on the Grumman investment with what the Plan would have earned had the funds been available for other Plan purposes.")).

33. Id.; see also *Leigh v. Engle,* 727 F.2d 113, 138-39 (7th Cir. 1984) ("[w]e believe that the burden is on the defendants who are found to have breached their fiduciary duties to show which profits are attributable to their own investments apart from their control of the ... trust assets. It is conceivable that the defendants who have breached can show they received no benefit at all from the use of the trust assets. In any event, while the district court may be able to make only a rough approximation, it should resolve doubts in favor of the plaintiffs.").

34. See *Wright v. Heyne,* 2001 U.S. Dist. LEXIS 22657 (S.D. Ohio Nov. 28, 2001) (The action, brought by plan trustees against investment advisors for breach of fiduciary duties under ERISA, was untimely because the trustees had actual knowledge of the alleged wrongdoing more than three years before filing suit); see also *Davidson v. Cook,* 567 F.Supp. 225 (E.D.Va. 1983), *aff'd,* 734 F.2d 10 (4th Cir.), *cert. denied,* 469 U.S. 899 (1984) (fiduciary who does not possess actual knowledge of a co-fiduciary's participation in, or concealment of, a breach of fiduciary duty is not necessarily liable for the acts or omissions of the co-fiduciary).

35. Every fiduciary must exercise prudence to prevent his or her co-fiduciaries from committing a breach of fiduciary responsibility, and must jointly manage and control plan assets unless specific duties have been allocated among them. ERISA §405(b)(1)(A),(B); see also *Silverman v. Mutual Ben. Life Insurance Co.,* 941 F.Supp. 1327, 1335 (E.D.N.Y. 1996) (even where a fiduciary has knowledge of a co-fiduciary's breach of duty, the fiduciary's failure to act with reasonable diligence is not tantamount to concealment, and no liability will be imposed where plaintiff fails to demonstrate how co-fiduciary enabled plan trustees to commit breach of their fiduciary duty).

36. See *Reich v. Hall Holding Co.,* 990 F.Supp. 955 (N.D.Ohio 1998) (holding that proof of harm or loss resulting from a prohibited transaction was not necessary to establish a violation under §406.) The court found that the companies caused the ESOP to engage in a prohibited transaction in violation of §406, by failing to conduct a prudent and independent investigation to determine the fair market value of the certain stock purchased by the ESOP. Id.; see also *Etter v. J. Pease Construction Co., Inc.,* 963 F.Supp. 1005, 1010 (7th Cir. 1992) (plan need not suffer some sort of injury for court to find that transaction is prohibited under §406); *Raff v. Belstock,* 933 F.Supp. 909, 916 (N.D.Calif. 1996) (whether §406(b) has been violated "does not depend on whether any harm results from the transaction"); *Freund v. Marshall & Ilsley Bank,* 485 F.Supp. 629, 640-641 (W.D.Wis. 1979) (ERISA imposes a duty on a fiduciary to take

affirmative actions to remedy breaches by another fiduciary, for instance, monitoring the conduct of another trustee and to intervene if he or she suspects improprieties).

37. ERISA §405(b)(1)(B).
38. 29 CFR §2509.75-8 at FR-16. Cf. *Birmingham v. So-Gen-Swiss Int'l Corp. Retirement Plan,* 718 F.2d 515, 521-522 (2d Cir. 1983) (the very purpose of designating a named fiduciary is to focus liability for mismanagement with a measure of certainty by limiting the exposure of liability to that named individual).
39. *Maher v. Strachan Shipping Co.,* 817 F.Supp. 43, 45 (E.D.La. 1993) (holding that a co-fiduciary can maintain a cause of action for indemnification under ERISA); *Youngberg v. Bekins, Co., et al.,* 930 F.Supp. 1396, 1398 (E.D.Cal. 1996) (holding ERISA'S "catchall" section, which provided equitable remedy for redressing violations of plan or to enforce plan, permitted employer's suit for indemnification against insurer). In contrast, the Ninth Circuit has held that breaching fiduciaries have no right to contribution under ERISA. *Concha v. London,* 62 F.3d 1493, 1500 (9th Cir. 1995); *Kim v. Fujikawa,* 871 F.2d 1427, 1432-33 (9th Cir. 1989).
40. ERISA §405(c)(1).
41. 29 CFR §2509.75-8 at FR-13.
42. 29 CFR §2509.75-8 at FR-14.
43. ERISA §405(d)(1).
44. See, e.g., *Wolin v. Smith Barney,* 83 F.3d 847, 849 (7th Cir. 1996); *Farm King Supply, Inc. Integrated Profit Sharing Plan and Trust v. Edward D. Jones & Co.,* 884 F.2d 288 (7th Cir. 1989); *Thomas, Head & Greisen Employees Trust v. Buster,* 24 F.3d 1114, 1117-20 (9th Cir. 1994). See also 29 CFR.. §2510.3-21.
45. See, e.g., *Wolin v. Smith Barney,* 83 F.3d 847, 849 (7th Cir. 1996); *Farm King Supply, Inc. Integrated Profit Sharing Plan and Trust v. Edward D. Jones & Co.,* 884 F.2d 288 (7th Cir. 1989); *Thomas, Head & Greisen Employees Trust v. Buster,* 24 F.3d 1114, 1117-20 (9th Cir. 1994).
46. For instance, the Seventh Circuit held in *Wolin v. Smith Barney,* 83 F.3d 847, 849 (7th Cir. 1996), that an investment advisor, in order to be deemed a fiduciary, must be rendering advice pursuant to an agreement, be paid for the advice and have influence approaching control over the plan's investment decisions.
47. *O'Toole v. Arlington Trust Co.,* 681 F.2d 94 (1st Cir. 1982) (holding that the appellee bank's responsibilities as the depository for the funds do not include the discretionary, advisory activities required by the statute) (citing *Robbins v. First American Bank of Virginia,* 514 F.Supp. 1183, 1189-91 (N.D.Ill. 1981)).
48. *Useden v. Acker* 947 F.2d 1563 (11th Cir. 1991), *cert. denied,* 113 S.Ct. 2927 (1993).
49. *Int'l Ass'n of Heat and Frost Insulators Local 17 Pension Fund v. Am. Nat'l Bank & Trust,* 13 F.Supp. 2d 753 (N.D.Ill. 1998) (bank that performed actuarial and portfolio management services for a pension fund's dedicated bond portfolio was not a fiduciary).
50. *Robbins v. First Am. Bank,* 514 F.Supp. 1183, 1190 (N.D.Ill. 1981); *Hibernia Bank v. International Bd. of Teamsters,* 411 F.Supp. 478 (N.D.Cal. 1976).
51. See *Manufacturers & Traders Trust Co.,* DOL Adv. Op. Ltr. No. 88-2A (Feb. 2, 1988); Futures Industry Associations, Inc., DOL Adv. Op. Ltr. No. 82-049A (Sept. 21, 1982); Home Savings and Loan Association, DOL Adv. Op. Ltr. No. 77-11 (Jan. 5, 1977).

52. *Associates in Adolescent Psychiatry, S.C. v. Home Life Ins. Co.,* 941 F.2d 561 (7th Cir. 1991), *cert. denied,* 112 S.Ct. 1182 (1992).
53. See Bank of Prattsville, DOL Adv. Op. Ltr. No. 88-09A (Apr. 5, 1988); Krehbiel & Hubbard, Inc., DOL Adv. Op. Ltr. No. 82-052A (Sept. 28, 1982); Affiliated Hospitals of San Francisco, DOL Adv. Op. Ltr. (WSB) No. 80-98 (Oct. 1, 1980). Cf. AmSouth Bank N.A., DOL Adv. Op. Ltr. No. 86-28A (Dec. 11, 1986).
54. See *Midwest Cmty. Health Serv., Inc. v. Am. United Life Ins. Co.* 255 F.3d 374, 376 (7th Cir. 2001) (noting that an "insurer's discretionary authority or control over group insurance contracts purchased by employee benefit plans subjects the insurer to ERISA fiduciary standards"); *Sixty Five Sec. Plan v. Blue Cross & Blue Shield,* 583 F.Supp. 380 (S.D.N.Y. 1984), *reh'g denied, certif. granted,* 588 F.Supp. 119 (S.D.N.Y. 1984) (fiduciary status found where Blue Cross assessed reasonableness of plan participants' length of hospital stay, denied and granted claims, and negotiated plan's hospital rates).
55. *American Federation of Unions Local 102 Health & Welfare Fund v. Equitable Life Assurance Soc'y,* 841 F.2d 658 (5th Cir. 1988).
56. *Fechter v. Connecticut General Life Ins. Co,* 800 F.Supp. 182, 197 (E.D.Pa. 1992) (holding that the defendant insurance company did not exercise discretionary control over the disputed terms of the guaranteed cost contract that it sold to the plan or over the distribution of the plan's assets, and provided actuarial calculations only as an actuary rendering professional advice, not in any fiduciary capacity).
57. See DOL Reg. §72550.404c-1.
58. Interestingly, in the recent wave of Enron litigation, the Labor Department's Section 404(c) regulation (DOL Reg. §2550.404(c)-1) played a part in the ENRON defense. Employers are not required to avail themselves of ERISA 404(c), but ENRON attempted to do so, in the case of the nonmatching contributions in its 401(k) plan. However, the 404(c) defense failed, in part because, although there are quite elaborate protections built into the 404(c) regulations, no matter how comprehensive, they are ineffective against outright fraud.
59. DOL Reg. §2550.404c-1(c)(2).
60. Under the Labor Department regulations, a "participant or beneficiary shall be provided, either directly or upon request, the following information, which shall be based on the latest information available to the plan: copies of any prospectuses, financial statements and reports, and of any other materials relating to the investment alternatives available under the plan, to the extent such information is provided to the plan." 29 CFR 2550.404c-1(b)(2)(i)(B)(2)(ii).
61. See DOL Adv. Op. Ltr. No. 2003-11A (Sept. 8, 2003).
62. See DOL Advisory Op. No. 96-02A (Feb. 9, 1996).
63. See DOL Reg. §2550.404c-1(b)(2) and (3).
64. *Harley v. Minnesota Mining and Mfg. Co.,* 42 F.Supp. 2d 898, 906 (D.Minn. 1999) ("Under this standard, a fiduciary is obligated to undertake an independent investigation of the merits of an investment and to use appropriate, prudent methods in conducting the investigation."), *cert. denied,* 537 U.S. 1106 (2003); *Fink v. National Sav. & Trust Co.,* 772 F.2d 951, 957 (D.C. Cir. 1985).
65. Id. See also *Liss v. Smith* 992 F.Supp. 278, 297 (S.D.N.Y. 1998) (quoting *In re Unisys Savings Plan Litig.,* 74 F.3d 420, 435 (3d Cir.), *cert. denied,* 117 S.Ct. 56 (1996)) ("It is by now black-

letter ERISA law that 'the most basic of ERISA's investment fiduciary duties [is] the duty to conduct an independent investigation into the merits of a particular investment.' ").

66. *Whitfield v. Cohen* 682 F.Supp. 188, 195 (S.D.N.Y. 1988); *Reich v. Hall Holding Co., Inc.*, 990 F.Supp. 955, 966 (N.D.Ohio 1998) (quoting *Kuper v. Iovenko*, 66 F.3d 1447, 1458 (6th Cir. 1995)), *aff'd sub nom., Chao v. Hall Holding Co., Inc.*, 285 F.3d 415 (6th Cir. 2002),*cert. denied*, 537 U.S. 1168 (2003) ("in an effort to hold the fiduciary liable for a loss attributable to [an] investment decision, a plaintiff must . . . demonstrate that an adequate investigation would have revealed to a reasonable fiduciary that the investment at issue was improvident.").

67. *Hunt v. Magnell*, 758 F.Supp. 1292 (D.Minn. 1991); *Harley v. Minnesota Mining and Mfg. Co.*, 42 F.Supp. 2d 898, 906 (D.Minn. 1999) ("Once the investment is made, a fiduciary has an ongoing duty to monitor investments with reasonable diligence and remove plan assets from an investment that is improper."), *cert. denied*, 537 U.S. 1106.

68. 29 CFR §2550.404a-1(b).

69. DOL Interpretative Bulletin 94-2 (July 29, 1994); ERISA §402(c)(3).

70. 29 CFR §2509.94-2.

71. DOL Interpretative Bulletin 94-2 (July 29, 1994); ERISA §402(c)(3).

72. *White v. Martin*, 286 F.Supp. 2d 1029, 1033 (D.Minn. 2003) (recognizing the benefits of creating a statement of investment policy, but refusing to find mandatory statement of investment policy); but see *Liss v. Smith*, 991 F.Supp. 278, 296 (S.D.N.Y. 1998) ("[t]he maintenance by an employee benefit plan of a statement of investment policy designed to further the purposes of the plan and its funding policy is consistent with the fiduciary obligations set forth in ERISA.").

73. 44 *Fed. Reg.* 37,222-23 (July 20, 1979) (DOL release accompanying DOL Reg. §2550.404a-1(b)).

74. See, e.g., *In re Unisys Savings Plan Litig.*, 74 F.3d 420 (3d Cir.), *cert. denied*, 117 S.Ct. 56 (1996) (it is a breach of the prudence standard if a plan administrator, without conducting an independent investigation, passively accepts a consultant's positive appraisal of a debt investment in a corporation that subsequently becomes bankrupt); *Meyer v. Berkshire Life Ins. Co.*, 250 F.Supp. 2d 544 (D.Md. 2003) (violation of fiduciary duty of prudence demonstrated by insurance investor's choice of conservative investments without regard to plan's risk preference, frequent transfer of funds, and inability to identify reasons for investment selections); *White v. Martin*, 286 F.Supp. 2d 1029, 1039 (D.Minn. 2003) loss occurring over two years to plan with significant investment in one company by managing trustee, the employer's wife, was not indicative of fiduciary breach because of lack of proof that the investments "were improper, imprudent, or represented an unduly large portion of the Plan's assets"); *Harley v. Minnesota Mining and Mfg. Co.*, 42 F.Supp. 2d 898 (D.Minn. 1999) (summary judgment precluded based on genuine issues of material fact as to whether employer conducted sufficient investigation or undertook reasonably prudent efforts to monitor investments), *cert. denied*, 537 U.S. 1106 (2003); *Liss v. Smith*, 991 F.Supp. 278 (S.D.N.Y. 1998) (trustees demonstrated no deliberation or investigation as to the safety of an investment and breached the prudence standard when it approved the purchase of collateralized mortgage obligations constituting over 25% of plan assets on the day following receipt of broker's recommendation); *Board of Trustees of the Local 295 v. Callan Assocs., Inc.*, 1998 U.S. Dist. LEXIS 8196 (S.D.N.Y. 1998) (investment consultant did not breach the prudence standard in deciding to transition assets in cash rather than in kind to a new investment manager, even though the pension fund sustained over $1.15 million in losses from an unexpected shift in interest rates), *aff'd*, 175 F.3d 1007 (2d Cir. 1999); *Reich v. Hall Holding Co., Inc.*, 990 F.Supp. 955 (N.D. Ohio 1998) (ESOP plan administrators breached the prudence standard by relying on a stock valuation based on ownership of 100% of the company and, as a result, paying more than adequate consideration for their minority stake), *aff'd sub nom., Chao v. Hall Holding Co., Inc.*, 285 F.3d 415 (6th Cir. 2002), *cert. denied*, 537 U.S. 1168 (2003); *In re Bicostal Corporation*, 191 B.R. 238, 244 (asset manager's "lackadaisical approach" in her use of plan assets to finance a real estate developer's purchase of property was "nothing short of gross negligence" where plan's actuary, accountant, counsel and professional investor advised against the investment); *GIW Indus., Inc. v. Trevor, Stewart, Burton & Jacobsen, Inc.*, 895 F.2d 729 (11th Cir. 1990), *aff'g*, 10 EBC 2290 (S.D.Ga. 1989) (investment manager held imprudent where he failed to conduct appropriate investigation of plan's cash flow needs and failed to diversify investments resulting in plan's loss of $537,000 upon liquidation of investments in order to meet cash flow needs); *Katsaros v. Cody*, 744 F.2d 270, 279 (2d Cir.), *cert. denied*, 469 U.S. 1072 (1984) (trustees breached prudence standard in connection with $2 million loan to bank, where they considered only information presented by interested parties who sought loan, and failed to conduct an independent investigation); *Donovan v. Mazzola*, 2 EBC 2115 (N.D.Cal. 1981), *aff'd*, 716 F.2d 1226 (9th Cir. 1983), *cert. denied*, 464 U.S. 1040 (1984); *Marshall v. Glass/Metal Assoc. and Glaziers and Glassworks Pension Plan*, 507 F.Supp. 378, 383 (D.Hawaii 1980). Compare *Metzler v. Graham*, 112 F.3d 207 (5th Cir. 1997); *Etter v. Pearse Construction Co., Inc.*, 963 F.2d 1005 (7th Cir. 1992); *Reich v. King*, 867 F.Supp. 341 (D.Md. 1994); *Jones v. O'Higgins*, 11 EBC 1660 (N.D.N.Y. 1989). In these cases, a plan potentially in violation of Section 404 on nondiversification grounds was found not to violate ERISA because under the particular facts and circumstances the investment decisions had been prudently made. See also *DeBruyne v. Equitable Life Assurance Soc'y*, 920 F.2d 457 (7th Cir. 1990), *aff'g*, 720 F.Supp. 1342 (N.D.Ill. 1989) (investment manager did not act imprudently despite fact that fund lost 18% in 1987 stock market crash).

75. *California Ironworkers Field Pension Trust v. Loomis Sayles & Co.*, 259 F.3d 1036 (9th Cir. 2001).

76. *Herman v. Mercantile Bank, N.A.*, 143 F.3d 419 (8th Cir. 1998).

77. *Jones v. O'Higgins*, 11 EBC 1660, 1667 (N.D.N.Y. 1989), citing, inter alia, *Katsaros v. Cody*, 744 F.2d 270, 279 (2d Cir.), *cert. denied*, 469 U.S. 1072 (1984).

78. Depending on the jurisdiction in which the plan operates, a fiduciary's investigative conduct may even have to satisfy prevailing industry standards. Compare *Jones v. O'Higgins*, 11 EBC 1660, 1668 (N.D.N.Y. 1989) (To find the defendant liable, this court would have to be provided with evidence that the defendant acted imprudently within the standards of the investment industry) with *GIW Indus., Inc. v. Trevor, Stewart, Burton & Jacobsen, Inc.*, 10 E.B.C. 2290, 2304 n.23 (S.D.Ga. 1989) (While investment management industry custom and practice enter into an evaluation of prudence, the particular obligations

of a fiduciary under ERISA are not controlled by the investment management industry but by statute), *aff'd*, 895 F.2d 729 (11th Cir. 1990).

79. "ERISA encourages fiduciaries to seek the advice of qualified experts in order to satisfy this procedural standard of prudence." *King v. Guynn*, 1992 U.S. Dist. LEXIS 21582 at *35 (E.D.Va. 1992). See also *Katsaros v. Cody*, 744 F.2d 270, 279 (2d Cir.), *cert. denied*, 469 U.S. 1072 (1984) (trustees breached ERISA's prudence standard in connection with $2 million loan to bank, where trustees considered only information presented by bank holding company president who sought loan, and failed to conduct an independent investigation); *Donovan v. Tricario*, 5 EBC 2057, 2064 (S.D.Fla. 1984) (fiduciaries violated prudent man standard in connection with plan's purchase of individual whole life insurance, without initiating competitive bids, and without obtaining expert advise on the prudency of whole life benefits, causing the plan to incur investment costs 300% to 400% greater than that of group insurance); *Diamond v. Retirement Plan* 582 F.Supp. 892 (W.D.Pa. 1983) (failure to seek independent advice, and reliance on a mere belief that investment is "wise," constitutes breach of "prudent man" duty).

80. See *Donovan v. Cunningham*, 716 F.2d 1455, 1474 (5th Cir. 1983), *cert. denied*, 467 U.S. 1251 (1984) (An independent appraisal is not a magic wand that fiduciaries may simply wave over a transaction to ensure that their responsibilities are fulfilled.... ERISA fiduciaries ... are entitled to rely on the expertise of others ..., but are responsible for ensuring that information is complete and up to date).

81. See, e.g., *Eyler v. C.I.R.*, 88 F.3d 445, 456 (7th Cir. 1996) (reliance on counsel's advice, at best, is but a single factor to be weighed in determining whether ESOP's fiduciary breached duty in determining merits of investment).

82. *Chao v. Hall Holding Co., Inc.*, 285 F.3d 415, 430 (6th Cir. 2002) (quoting and adopting the standard for fiduciary reliance on experts outlined in *Howard v. Shay*, 100 F.3d 1484, 1489 (9th Cir. 1996), *cert. denied*, 520 U.S. 1237 (1997)), *cert denied*, 537 U.S. 1168 (2003). But see *In re Unisys Savings Plan Litig.*, 173 F.3d 145 (3d Cir. 1995) (reliance on the Standard & Poor's "Triple A" rating of an investment was neither unreasonable nor imprudent).

83. See, e.g., *Liss v. Smith*, 991 F.Supp. 278 (S.D.N.Y. 1998) (trustees are obligated to seek independent advice where it is essential, but ultimate decision-making authority and responsibility for investments rest with the trustees); *Donovan v. Tricario*, 5 Employee Benefits Cas. (BNA) 2057, 2064 (S.D.Fla. 1984), *aff'd sub nom Brock v. Tricario*, 768 F.2d 1351 (11th Cir. 1985) ("mere retention of an expert cannot be permitted to protect defendants against claims of failure to discharge their own fiduciary responsibilities. Expert advice must be considered as carefully as any other information that the trustees have available to them when making decisions to commit plan assets.").

84. See *Donovan v. Guaranty Nat'l Bank*, 4 EBC 1686, 1688 (S.D.W.Va. 1983).

85. *Id.*

86. *Marshall v. Glass/Metal Association and Glaziers and Glassworks Pension Plan*, 507 F.Supp. 378, 383 (D.Hawaii. 1980).

87. H.R. Rep. No. 93-1280 (1974), reprinted in 1974 U.S.C.C.A.N. 5038, at 5084-5085.

88. See *Marshall v. Teamster Local 282 Pension Trust Fund*, 458 F.Supp. 986 (E.D.N.Y. 1978).

89. See *Metzler v. Graham*, 112 F.3d 207 (5th Cir. 1997).

90. See *Jones v. O'Higgins*, 11 EBC 1660 (N.D.N.Y. 1989) (no breach where 90% of plan assets invested in only three investments).

91. *Simons v. Barnette*, 2003 U.S. Dist. LEXIS 25008 at *1 (M.D.Fla. 2003); see also *Lanka v. O'Higgins*, 810 F.Supp. 379 (holding that no authority was found to support the co-trustees' expert's per se imprudence contention that the mere employment of the "contrarian method" was imprudent and a breach of fiduciary responsibility).

92. *Simons v. Barnette*, 2003 U.S. Dist. LEXIS 25008 at *1 (M.D.Fla. 2003).

93. See *Brock v. Citizens Bank of Clovis*, 1985 WL 71535 (D.N.M. 1986).

94. See also *In re Unisys Savings Plan Litig.*, 74 F.3d 420 (3d Cir. 1996) (fiduciary has an obligation to impart material information to participants sufficient to apprise the average plan participant of the risks associated with the plan's investments), *cert. denied*, 117 S.Ct. 56 (1996).

95. But see *Bona v. Barasch*, 2003 U.S. Dist. LEXIS 8760 (S.D.N.Y. 2003) (failure to specifically state the ability to terminate an agreement on short notice is not an ERISA violation, if the agreement does not prevent such termination).

96. *Harley v. Minnesota Mining & Mfg. Co*, 42 F.Supp. 2d 898 (D.Minn. 1998), *aff'd on other grounds*, 284 F.3d 901 (8th Cir. 2002), *cert. denied*, 123 S.Ct. 872 (2003) (ongoing duty to monitor investments); *Glennie v. Abitibi Price Corp.*, 912 F.Supp. 993 (W.D.Mich. 1996) (fiduciary's duty to monitor an "ERISA plan's investment is separate and distinct from duty to administer plan assets prudently, thus, a fiduciary's responsibilities with respect to an ERISA investment does not terminate upon conclusion of appropriate investigation and purchase of asset"); *Liss v. Smith*, 991 F.Supp. 278, 299 (S.D.N.Y. 1998) (noting that fiduciaries breached their duty to monitor the performance of the plan's broker); *Hunt v. Magnell*, 758 F.Supp. 1292, 1299 (D.Minn. 1991) ("ERISA's fiduciaries must monitor investments with reasonable diligence and dispose of investments which are improper to keep."); *Whitfield v. Cohen*, 682 F.Supp. 188, 196 (S.D.N.Y. 1988) (Cohen had a duty to monitor Penvest's performance with reasonable diligence and to withdraw).

97. ERISA Interpretative Bulletin 75-5, FR-17 (June 25, 1975); 29 CFR §2509.75-8 (1975). See *Leigh v. Engle*, 858 F.2d 361 (7th Cir. 1988), *cert. denied sub nom. Estate of Johnson v. Engle*, 489 U.S. 1078 (1989) (fiduciaries who were aware that the plan administrators were making investment decisions out of personal motivations breached their supervisory duties when they failed to take any action to rectify the situation); *Tittle v. Enron Corp.*, 284 F.Supp. 2d 511, 553 n.59 (S.D.Tex. 2003) ("the exercise of power to appoint, retain and remove persons for fiduciary positions triggers fiduciary duties to monitor the appointees"); *Whitfield v. Cohen*, 682 F.Supp. 188, 196 (S.D.N.Y. 1988) ("fiduciary must ascertain within a reasonable time whether an agent to whom he has delegated a trust power is properly carrying out his responsibilities"); see also *Martin v. Harline*, 15 Employee Benefits Cas. (BNA) 1138 (D.Utah 1992) (fiduciary's failure to conduct periodic reviews of an investment manager's performance after his appointment constitutes a breach of his ERISA duty); cf. *In re McKesson HBOC, Inc. ERISA Litig.*, 29 Employee Benefits Cas. (BNA) 122 (N.D.Cal. 2002) (duty to monitor an investment committee's performance

does not impose a similar duty to review 401(k) participants' personal investment choices).

98. *Saxton v. Cent. Pa. Teamsters Pension Fund* 2003 U.S. Dist. LEXIS 23983 (E.D.Pa. 2003) (ignorance of mismanagement by investment managers was not a defense to a breach of fiduciary duty since appropriate monitoring would have alerted the fund administrators of the situation and imposed on them the responsibility to take corrective action).

99. *Crowley v. Corning, Inc.*, 234 F.Supp. 2d 222 (W.D.N.Y. 2002).

100. S.E.C. No. 34-23170 (Apr. 23, 1986), 35 S.E.C. Docket 703, 51 *Fed. Reg.* 16004, 1986 WL 72981.

101. Inspection Report on the Soft Dollar Practices of Broker-Dealers, Investment Advisers and Mutual Funds, The Office of Compliance, Inspections and Examinations, S.E.C., September 22, 1998, available at http://www.sec.gov/news/studies/softdolr.htm#recm.

102. Id.

103. See DOL Letter to Helmuth Fandl, Chairman of Retirement Board of Avon Products, Inc. (Feb. 23, 1988).

104. See DOL Letter to Robert A. G. Monks, Institutional Shareholders Services, Inc. (Jan. 23, 1990).

105. The Labor Department has also stated that the decision to tender shares of stock in a tender offer is a fiduciary act. However, there is not an automatic requirement that fiduciaries must accept a tender offer when the offer represents a premium over the prevailing market price.

106. See, e.g., "Labor Department Guidance on Voting Provisions in Collectively Bargained Employee Stock Ownership Plans," 22 *Pen. & Ben. Rep.* (BNA) 2249, 2250-51 (Sept. 28, 1995). The Labor Department addressed a directed trustee's role where an ESOP plan granted plan participants the authority to direct the trustee regarding the tendering of stock or proxy voting of stock allocated to their own accounts. As such, the participants were fiduciaries for the limited purpose of giving such directions. The letter states that the trustee can satisfy §403(a)(1) and assure itself that a participant's instructions are proper and not contrary to ERISA and the plan if it follows procedures to ensure that the eligible individual account plan's provisions are fairly implemented; the directing participant has not been subject to coercion or undue pressure in its decision; necessary information was provided to the participant; and that clearly false information or misleading information is not distributed to the participant, or that any false or misleading information that may have been distributed by other parties is corrected. Id. at 2250. Furthermore, DOL stated that the fact that the named fiduciary-participant issues such a direction with respect to a tender offer or proxy vote related to stock in its individual account "does not diminish the trustee's duty to diligently investigate and evaluate the merits of the course of action required by the plan document to determine that the instructions are consistent with titles I and IV [of ERISA]."

107. See PBGC Adv. Op. Ltr. No. 911 1991 PBGC LEXIS 3 (Jan. 14, 1991); 29 CFR §2510.33(d)(2)(ii).

108. See PBGC Adv. Op. Ltr. No. 859 1985 PBGC LEXIS 24 (Apr. 5, 1985); PBGC Adv. Op. Ltr. No. 8528 1985 PBGC LEXIS 6 (Dec. 3, 1985); ERISA §4041(b)(3).

109. See PBGC Adv. Op. Ltr. No. 914 1991 PBGC LEXIS 4 (May 3, 1991).

110. Pension Annuitants Protection Act of 1994, Pub L. No. 103-401 (Oct. 22, 1994).

111. See *Martin v. BMC Industries, Inc.*, 19 Pens. Rep. 630 (D.Minn. 1992); *Martin v. Geosource Inc.*, 18 Pens. Rep. 2012 (S.D.Texas 1991); *Martin v. AFG Industries, Inc.*, 18 Pens. Rep. 1242 (N.D.Texas 1991) (fiduciaries failed to implement a meaningful bid process or meaningful analysis of Executive Life's creditworthiness or claims paying ability); *Martin v. Magnetek*, 18 Pens. Rep. 991 (E.D.Wis. 1991); and *Martin v. Pacific Lumber Co.*, 18 Pens. Rep. 991 (N.D.Cal. 1991). The complaints in these cases charge that it is insufficient for a plan fiduciary to rely on the rating services, all of which initially rated Executive Life very highly, rather than independently evaluating the solvency of a company offering a pension plan. See also *Martin v. StrouseAdler* (D.Conn. 1991) (complaint alleges that the fiduciaries violated ERISA's exclusive purpose and fiduciary duty provisions by causing the plan to purchase annuities from Presidential Life Insurance Company to fund benefits upon plan termination when the plan had sufficient assets to purchase annuities from a more secure insurance carrier).

112. Interpretative Bulletin No. 95-1 (March 6, 1995).

113. See 29 CFR §2510.3-3(d)(2)(ii).

114. See 62 *Fed. Reg.* 60424-216, Final Rule of PBGC for termination of single employer plans (amending termination regulation to extend deadlines, to otherwise simplify the termination process, and to ensure that plan participants receive information on state guaranty coverage of annuities).

115. *Katsaros v. Cody*, 744 F.2d 270, 279 (2d Cir.), *cert. denied*, 469 U.S. 1072 (1984); see also *In re Unisys Savings Plan Litig.*, 74 F.3d 420, 435 (3d Cir.), *cert. denied*, 117 S.Ct. 56 (1996) (fiduciaries were obligated to impart to plaintiffs material information within their knowledge that was sufficient to apprise plaintiffs of the risks associated with the GIC investments at issue).

116. DOL Adv. Op. Ltr. (WSB) No. DL0014 (Mar. 4, 1985).

117. See *Whitfield v. Tomasso*, 682 F.Supp. 1287 (E.D.N.Y. 1988) (trustees breached fiduciary duties of prudence and diversification by investing substantial amount of plan assets in questionable insurance company; trustees did not investigate financial soundness of company, did not review ratings and did not consult an expert).

118. See *GIW Indus., Inc. v. Trevor, Stewart, Burton & Jacobsen, Inc.*, 895 F.2d 729 (11th Cir. 1990), *aff'g*, 10 EBC 2290 (S.D.Ga. 1989); cf. *In re Unisys Savings Plan Litig.*, 74 F.3d 420, 435 (3d Cir.), *cert. denied*, 117 S.Ct. 56 (1996).

119. See *Chicago Bd. Options Exchange, Inc. v. Connecticut Gen. Life Ins. Co.*, 713 F.2d 254, 259 (7th Cir. 1983) (insurer had unilateral power to amend contract). See also *Harris Trust & Savings Bank v. John Hancock Mut. Life Ins. Co.*, 114 S.Ct. 517 (1993), affirmed in part and reversed in part, 302 F.3d 18 (2d Cir. 2002) ("To the extent that the insurer engages in the discretionary management of assets attributable to that phase of the contract which provides no guarantee of benefit payments or fixed rates of return, it seems to us that the insurer should be subject to fiduciary responsibility.") (insurance company was not a fiduciary in regard to guaranteed group annuity contract where it did not exercise any discretionary authority or control over the management or disposition of the policy itself; however, fiduciary duties were implicated with respect to portion of plan assets that were not guaranteed). But see *Mack Boring & Parts v. Meeker Sharkey Moffitt*, 930 F.2d 267 (3d 1991) (appellee insurer was not an ERISA fiduciary by virtue of ERISA's guaranteed benefit policy exception under §1101(b)(2) because the ac-

count at issue was a general account insurance contract in which the issuing insurance company guaranteed to the plan participants a fixed amount of benefits, payable at a clearly stated time, without variable, and therefore not subject to plan asset treatment).

120. See DOL Adv. Op. Ltr. No. 85-36A (Oct. 12, 1985).

121. ERISA Advisory Opinion Letter No. 98-04A (May 28, 1998).

122. See, e.g., ERISA Opinion Letter Nos. 88-16A and 85-36A, and information letters issued to Prudential Life Insurance Company of America (January 16, 1981); Electrical Industry of Long Island (March 15, 1982); Union Labor Life Insurance Company (July 8, 1988); and General Motors Corporation (May 14, 1993).

123. ERISA Advisory Opinion Letter No. 98-04A (May 28, 1998).

124. See, e.g., *Barrington Police Pension Fund Trustees v. Illinois Ins. Dep't,* 13 EBC 1999 (Ill.App.Ct. 1991) (public pension fund may invest in residential real estate mortgages that benefit fund participants and the local community).

125. See, e.g., *Withers v. Teachers' Retirement Sys. of City of New York,* 447 F.Supp. 1248 (S.D.N.Y. 1978), *aff'd,* 595 F.2d 1210 (2d Cir. 1979) (public pension plan trustees' decision to purchase highly speculative city bonds to stave off city's potential bankruptcy was prudent). See also *Board of Trustees of the Employees' Retirement Sys. v. Mayor of Baltimore City,* 11 EBC 1521 (1989), *cert. denied* 493 U.S. 1093 (1990).

126. DOL Interpretative Bulletin 94-1; DOL Reg. §2509.94-1, 59 *Fed. Reg.* 32606 (1994).

127. See Jane Elizabeth Zanglein, "Protecting Retirees While Encouraging Economically Targeted Investments," 5-WTR *Kan. J.L. & Pub. Pol'y* 47 (Winter 1996); "High Performance Investing: Harnessing the Power of Pension Funds to Promote Economic Growth and Workplace Integrity."

128. It should be noted that ETIs were recently faced with legislative resistance. Members of Congress, in both the House of Representatives and the Senate, introduced bills in 1995 (the Pension Protection Act of 1995, HR 1594, S 774) that would have prohibited the use of federal funds to promote or subsidize ETIs and that would have specifically prohibited federal funding for the ETI clearinghouse that had been established pursuant to a contract awarded by the Labor Department shortly after it issued Interpretative Bulletin 94-1. However, neither bill was ever enacted into law.

Chapter 8

Legal Considerations of Real Estate Investment for Employee Benefit Plans

Neal S. Schelberg

INTRODUCTION

Deciding where and how to invest the assets of an employee benefit plan is among the most difficult and important tasks facing a fiduciary under the Employee Retirement Income Security Act of 1974, as amended (ERISA). Typically, a plan fiduciary invests plan assets in various sectors of the economy through vehicles such as stocks, bonds, guaranteed investment contracts (GICs) and money market instruments. With the assistance of an astute investment manager, these investments should help the plan fiduciary meet the plan's funding needs and obligations.

Chapter 7 contains a comprehensive review of the legal requirements under ERISA for the investment of plan assets. The primary focus of this chapter will be on the application of those basic legal principles to direct and indirect investments in real estate.

The real estate markets present plan fiduciaries with investment opportunities and strategies that may complement the plan's other investments. Real estate investments may take many different forms and may be comprised of a variety of different types of properties, vehicles and positions. They may include direct investments where the plan holds real property, for example, through either direct ownership, limited partnerships or tax-exempt holding companies that own undeveloped land primarily for capital appreciation but also for the income stream generated after the property is developed. Or, they may take the form of indirect investments in real property in which the plan's investment is not directly related to any particular parcel of real estate, but derives its value from some underlying interest in real property, for example, insurance company separate accounts, common trusts, group trusts or real estate investment trusts (REITs) that invest in real property.

On the other hand, some plan fiduciaries see real estate investments solely as a debt investment. Rather than own the asset (or the security that represents an undivided share of the underlying real property), a plan may serve as a lender and provide a loan in which the borrower agrees to repay the amount borrowed on a schedule and pledges the property as collateral to secure the loan.

ERISA's principal thrust in the investment area is on the process that plan fiduciaries must follow in deciding whether and where to invest plan assets. This same searching process must be followed in making real estate investments. Indeed, in view of the unique characteristics of some real estate investments, the process that must be followed to satisfy a fiduciary's responsibilities under ERISA may require additional steps to be taken and factors to be considered. These considerations as well as other related legal requirements under ERISA are addressed in this chapter.

The chapter also addresses the topic of socially sensitive investing and economically targeted investments (ETIs). In past years, ETIs have gained much currency. ETIs are broadly defined as "investments selected for the economic benefits they create apart from their investment return to the employee benefit plan."[1] In the real estate context, an ETI might include a pension fund's financing of low-income housing or below-market interest rate mortgages; or it might entail a pension fund's investment in local construction projects designed to create jobs and increase the use of unionized labor (which would directly benefit plan participants through increased employer contributions into the trust fund), i.e., so called employment-generating real estate investments. As will be discussed in this chapter, regardless of the societal goal of the ETI, it is crucial that the fiduciary's primary motivation in making the investment is the maximization of investment returns to plan participants or their beneficiaries. According to the United States Department of Labor (DOL), so long as a fiduciary satisfies ERISA's fiduciary standards and does not engage in a prohibited transaction, investments that also further a societal goal are permissible.[2]

Also considered in this chapter are the ERISA fiduciary issues relating to Taft-Hartley "housing trust funds"—which do not technically involve an *investment* in real estate by plan fiduciaries, but raise analogous ERISA fiduciary concerns since it involves the use of plan assets. The 1990 amendments to the Labor-Management Relations Act of 1947, as amended (LMRA) authorized the establishment of this new type of trust fund under which plan fiduciaries accept employer contributions made pursuant to the terms of a collective bargaining agreement between an employer and a labor union for the purposes of providing housing assistance to employees and their families.

WHY INVEST IN REAL ESTATE?

Direct Investments in Real Estate and Real Estate-Related Securities

Direct equity investments in improved or unimproved real estate may serve to enhance an employee benefit plan's overall investment strategy. Many of the benefits of real estate as an asset class are a function of real estate's uniqueness among investment vehicles as a fixed, tangible asset. First, real estate is inherently valuable and has longevity and little risk of long-term depreciation.[3] Land likely will always be in demand, and the uses to which it can be adapted can usually be changed. Second, real estate has historically been, and continues to be, a good hedge against inflation. While the real estate market clearly is affected (and in some cases driven) by the overall strength of the economy, the tangible, enduring nature of real estate and its finite supply generally will ensure its demand.

Real estate's physical stability may translate into financial stability as well. The contractual nature of real property leases tends to stabilize investment returns since the parties can renegotiate and restructure their leases and loans in response to contingencies (e.g., the bankruptcy of the lessee) or as a result of external market forces (e.g., changes in the real estate market—a glut or surplus of rentable space).[4] In addition, real estate investments as an asset class have historically generated high risk-adjusted returns when compared to those for stocks and bonds. Returns on real estate investments generally run countercyclical to other types of investments since market factors that depress the value of other investments generally either have no impact on real estate investments or, indeed, may actually increase their value.[5] Accordingly, such investments offer a means of stabilizing an investment portfolio by reducing its volatility and shielding a plan from losses in other markets. Finally, real estate investments help plans to satisfy ERISA's diversification requirement.

Despite these virtues, direct equity investments in real estate may present plan fiduciaries with some distinct drawbacks. The first and foremost is that real estate is less liquid and carries higher costs of acquisition or disposition than other types of investments. For example, because a transaction involving the sale of an office building or a shopping center is extremely complicated, time-consuming and expensive, it is not an efficient means of raising cash. Thus, a plan that must satisfy stringent cash flow needs (e.g., benefit payments, administrative expenses, etc.) from its investments may be unable, as a practical matter, to invest in real estate unless it also has other, more liquid investments from which to draw. Also, because of its relative illiquidity, plan fiduciaries lose the flexibility to liquidate a real estate investment on short notice to take advantage of other investment opportunities. In sum, real estate investments should be viewed as long-term in nature and should not be relied upon as a source of capital or to solve short-term liquidity needs.[6]

Third, unlike securities that are traded on the national exchanges, real estate has no comparable central marketplace where the value of the asset is determined by efficient market forces and where transactions can be readily effected. Instead, the real estate "market" is the sum total of individual, isolated private transactions, subject to both local and national economic forces as well as personal preferences. As a result, real estate values are not set in "real time," as are publicly traded securities, but instead are established by market appraisals. However, as discussed below, the growing popularity of commingled real estate investment funds (such as REITs) may eventually establish a public real estate marketplace that provides a liquid, readily accessible arena for real estate investments.

Economically Targeted Investments (ETIs)

Another reason for making real estate investments is that, in addition to serving their primary goal of satisfying a plan's investment needs, they may offer the opportunity to further societal goals. ETIs come in several forms—some involving real estate, others not. Regardless of the vehicle, however, all ETIs are structured to provide economic benefits apart from the investment returns they generate for the plan. In those ETIs that do involve real estate, the collateral economic advantages sought to be achieved often include combinations of the following: the creation of construction jobs and an overall increase in the use of unionized labor; increased access to housing mortgages; increased availability of affordable housing; improved social service facilities; and a modernized infrastructure.[7]

Some plan fiduciaries are apprehensive about investing in ETIs, believing (incorrectly) that they are unlawful under ERISA and will subject fiduciaries to personal liability. Also, there has been some negative press coverage accompanying some ETIs that have failed to produce the intended results. Since perceptions often create reality, some employee benefit plan fiduciaries have been, and continue to be, reluctant to commit assets to ETIs.

As will be discussed below, however, the DOL, the government agency charged with administering and enforcing ERISA's fiduciary provisions, has clearly communicated the permissibility of ETIs as investment vehicles, declaring that the "fiduciary standards applicable to ETIs are no different than the standards applicable to plan investments generally."[8] So long as ERISA's standards are met, an ETI will be an appropriate investment vehicle.

Taft-Hartley Housing Trust Funds

Some collective bargaining parties have created trust funds to assist members in acquiring real estate. Through these trusts, plan fiduciaries cannot make direct equity investments in real estate, nor can they act as a lender by utilizing plan assets to make mortgage loans to members. Thus, these trusts do not involve *investments* in real estate. However, because they use plan assets to provide benefit payments to members to facilitate their housing purchases, many of the same ERISA fiduciary principles that are applicable to investments apply to housing trusts.

Section 302 of LMRA prohibits payments by employers to representatives of their employees for purposes other than those specified under Section 302(c). In 1990, Congress amended Section 302(c)(7) of LMRA to permit employer contributions to trust funds established for the purpose of providing housing assistance to employees and their families.[9] According to the bill's legislative history, "[f]inancial assistance for employee housing means financial assistance to individuals for mortgage collateral, closing costs, down payments or other similar purposes."[10] However, such assistance does "not include the direct sale of property by a housing trust to an employee under circumstances which would violate provisions of ERISA which prohibit the transfer of plan assets to parties in interest."[11] Potentially, housing trusts can serve as a significant catalyst to spur real estate purchases by assisting plan members in their housing purchases.

TYPES OF REAL ESTATE

This section discusses several types of real estate investments categorized as: (1) equity investments and (2) debt investments.

Equity Investments

1. *Raw Land.* This is the most basic form of real estate investment. Plan fiduciaries may buy a piece of land and, without developing it, wait for it to appreciate in value and then sell it for a gain. Or the plan may buy the raw land and develop it for residential or commercial purposes. These forms of real estate investment may be ill-suited for many employee benefit plans. The ownership of the real estate will probably be a cash drain on the plan, as there are real estate taxes to be paid regardless of what happens to the property, and there will probably be a period of time when there is no investment income generated (including any rental income). Also, most plan fiduciaries do not have the expertise to find and evaluate a suitable real estate investment. Thus, it is likely that the plan fiduciaries will need to retain professional advisors and consultants. This process may be expensive and time-consuming. Similarly, if the investment in raw land is made with the eye toward developing it, architects, engineers and other professionals also will be required to assist the fiduciaries in this project.

2. *Commercial Real Estate.* A plan can purchase an interest in commercial property with the intent of earning (through rents) a return on its investment in the form of an income stream. Typically, however, plan fiduciaries will not have the expertise to manage the property and will have to hire a professional property management firm. Management of commercial real estate is a very sophisticated business, which can easily make or break a project.

3. *Commingled Funds.* A plan can also *indirectly* invest in real estate by purchasing, together with other investors, a share or unit in a common, pooled investment vehicle that utilizes the invested assets to purchase real property. One example of a commingled fund is a REIT, which is a stock holding company that buys and manages real estate mortgages. Another example is a pooled ETI, the most basic of which is a commingled account (fund). Such funds are useful alternatives where the plan fiduciaries believe that the benefit plan is not big enough or experienced enough to handle a real estate development directly. These funds are open ended, meaning they are always available for contributions and cashouts. Income takes two forms: income from mortgage or rental payments, and appreciation on the underlying property or mortgages—depending on whether the fund owns property (has an equity interest) or lends money on property. Income is typically reinvested and is reflected in higher unit values of the commingled fund. Importantly, there is no income stream to the fund unless a cashout is requested, but these commingled funds are relatively illiquid. If the fund has the cash to honor a redemption request, it will (usually quarterly). Otherwise, the plan investor will have to wait until the cash is available.

Debt Investments

1. *Mortgage Loan Programs.* Both ERISA in Section 408(b)(1) and the Internal Revenue Code in Section 4975(d)(1) permit a plan to make loans to participants and their beneficiaries. Such loans (1) must be available to all participants and beneficiaries on a reasonably equivalent basis; (2) are not made available to highly compensated employees under terms more favorable than those offered to nonhighly compensated employees; (3) are made in accordance with the terms of the plan; and (4) are adequately secured. In addition to these requirements, the general duties of prudence and loyalty under ERISA must be met.

2. *Commercial, Single Family and Multifamily Residences.* With this type of investment, the plan is typically a lender (rather than an owner) although, depending on the nature of the mortgage, the plan may have an equity interest and participate in the increase in the value of the property as well. Accordingly, the investment normally takes the form of a loan in which a construction, interim or a permanent mortgage is pledged as security by the borrower.

A plan may become an equity owner of real estate by purchasing it on the open market or acquiring it from a contributing employer. If the real estate is purchased on the open market, the plan fiduciaries must satisfy ERISA's general fiduciary requirements but should not ordinarily give rise to prohibited transaction issues. Where, however, an ERISA plan seeks to acquire real property from a contributing employer, the ERISA fiduciary and prohibited transaction provisions, which are discussed below, may be implicated.

APPROPRIATE ALLOCATION

Assuming a decision has been made to proceed with a real estate investment program, the plan fiduciary must determine what percentage of the plan assets should be invested in real estate. In making this allocation decision, ERISA's prudence and diversification rules dictate that the plan fiduciaries consider the financial, actuarial and investment needs and characteristics of the plan. Particularly in view of the illiquid nature of real estate as an asset class, the financial condition of the plan must be carefully reviewed before allocating plan assets to real estate investments. However, most investment consultants believe that if real estate investments are to have an impact on the plan's overall investment performance, they should constitute between 5% and 20% of the plan assets, with the majority targeting 10% as a goal.[12]

PLAN ASSETS

ERISA requires that plan fiduciaries hold "plan assets" in trust, exercise fiduciary responsibility with respect to them and not engage in prohibited transactions. Since by its very terms ERISA applies only with respect to a plan fiduciary's management, control and investment of plan assets, before discussing ERISA's fiduciary duty requirements it is appropriate to consider the application of the plan asset rules to the types of real estate investments described in the preceding section.

As a general rule, any type of property to which a plan holds legal title is a plan asset. In the case of direct real estate investments, the real property, whether developed or undeveloped, is the asset. However, where a plan invests in another entity, the plan assets will generally include its investment in that entity, but will not, solely by reason of such investment, include any of the underlying assets of the entity. That is, there is no "look-through." Where the look-through rule does apply, however, a plan's assets include not only the plan's equity interest in another entity, but also an undivided interest in each underlying asset held by the entity. Thus, any person with authority or control over the management of the underlying assets, or any person providing investment advice for a fee concerning such assets, is a fiduciary of the plan.[13]

In general, the look-through rule applies if the plan's equity interest in an entity is neither (1) a publicly offered security, nor (2) a security issued by an investment company registered under the Investment Advisers Act of 1940. Under the DOL regulations, an equity interest is any interest in an entity other than an instrument treated as indebtedness under local law and that does not have any substantial equity features such as an undivided ownership interest in property. A *publicly offered security* is a security that is freely transferable, part of a widely held class of securities (i.e., owned by 100 or more investors who are independent of the issuer and each other), and covered under certain federal securities registration rules.[14]

The DOL regulations also provide that equity investments in (1) "operating companies" and (2) an entity where the equity participation by "benefit plan investors" is not significant (i.e., 25% or more of the value of any class of equity interest is held by a pension or welfare plan, individual retirement account or annuity) are generally exempt from the look-through rules. As noted above, if the investment is exempt from the look-through rules, then only the investment in the entity, and not the underlying assets owned by the entity, is treated as a plan asset (subject to ERISA's trust, fiduciary obligation and prohibited transaction provisions), even where the investment is not a publicly offered security or a security issued by a registered investment company.[15]

Under the DOL regulations, an operating company, which is generally exempt from the look-through rule, is defined as—

1. An entity that is primarily engaged in producing or selling a product or service other than the investment of capital
2. A real estate operating company (REOC)
3. A venture capital operating company (VCOC).[16]

In the real estate context, the primary entity subject to these rules is a REOC. An entity is a REOC if—

1. At least 50% of its assets (valued at cost) are invested in real estate that is managed or developed
2. The entity has the right to substantially participate directly in the management or development of the eligible real estate
3. The entity actually engages directly in real estate management or development.[17]

The DOL regulations contain the following examples of these rules.[18] Plan P invests (pursuant to a private offering) in a Limited Partnership W that is engaged primarily in investing and reinvesting assets in equity positions in real property. The properties acquired by Partnership W are subject to long-term leases, under which substantially all management and maintenance activities with respect to the property are the responsibility of the lessee. Partnership W is not engaged in the management or development of real estate merely because it assumes the risks of ownership of income producing property, and Partnership W is not a real estate operating company. If there is significant equity participation in Partnership W by benefit plan investors, Plan P will be considered to have acquired an undivided interest in each of the underlying assets of Partnership W. Accordingly, any person with effective control over any assets of Partnership W (including lessees and their agents) will be an ERISA fiduciary of Plan P with respect to such assets.

By contrast, assume that Partnership W owns several shopping centers in which individual stores are leased for relatively short periods to various merchants (rather than owning properties subject to long-term leases under which substantially all management and maintenance activities are the responsibility of the lessee). Partnership W retains independent contractors to manage the shopping center properties. These independent contractors negotiate individual leases, maintain the common areas and conduct maintenance activities with respect to the properties. Partnership W has the responsibility to supervise and the authority to terminate the independent contractors. During its most recent valuation period, more than 50% of Partnership W's assets, valued at cost, are invested in such properties. Partnership W is a real estate operating company. The fact that Partnership W does not have its own employees who engage in day-to-day management and development activities is only one factor in determining whether it is actively managing or developing real estate. Thus,

Plan P's assets include its interest in Partnership W, but do not include any of the underlying assets of Partnership W. Accordingly, persons with effective control over the assets of Partnership W (including the independent contractors) will not be fiduciaries of Plan P by reason of Plan P's investment in Partnership W.

Accordingly, as a threshold matter, the plan fiduciaries should determine whether or not plan assets are involved in the proposed investment and, if so, whether ERISA's trust, fiduciary and prohibited transaction rules are implicated.

MAKING INVESTMENT DECISIONS

By their nature, plan investments may raise ERISA fiduciary duty and prohibited transaction issues. Both are traps for the unwary. If the DOL challenges an investment program, it generally will do so under Section 404 of ERISA (fiduciary duties), Section 406 of ERISA (prohibited transactions), or both.

As was discussed in Chapter 7, the DOL is primarily concerned with the process that plan fiduciaries undertake in making investment decisions. This proposition is equally true in formulating investment decisions regarding real estate. Indeed, given some of the unique characteristics of real estate investments discussed above, this proposition applies *a fortiori*. To avoid (or minimize) Section 404 and 406 violations, the plan should have clear standards and guidelines with respect to the following:

1. The types of real estate investments that will be made
2. The percentage of plan assets that will be invested in real estate
3. The selection and retention of investment managers
4. The methodology and the frequency for valuing real estate assets
5. The standards for evaluating the performance of the plan's investment managers and the investments under his control
6. The level of fiduciary responsibility that will either be retained or delegated by the plan fiduciaries.[19]

Establishing Real Estate Investment Guidelines

Before actually committing plan assets to real estate investments, plan fiduciaries should establish prudent written investment objectives and strategies that take into account the particular attributes of this asset class. Establishment of these guidelines may be among the most difficult, yet important, tasks facing a plan fiduciary since it defines the plan's risk tolerance and investment return objectives.

ERISA does not specifically require plan fiduciaries

to prepare statements of investment policy that provide those individuals who are responsible for plan investments with guidelines and general instructions concerning various types of categories of investment management decisions. The DOL, however, has underscored its view that such statements serve an important purpose in many plans by helping assure that the investments are made in a prudent and rational manner, and are designed to further the purposes of the plan and its funding.[20] It is particularly important for plan fiduciaries to prepare (and where guidelines exist, to review) investment guidelines where a real estate investment is being considered to ensure that such investment's role in the plan's overall investment strategy is clearly defined, and the plan fiduciaries clearly enumerate their investment needs, risks and tolerances.

In establishing plan objectives, the following factors (among others) should be considered—
1. Nature of the plan
2. Purpose of the plan, taking into account the age, income levels and investment needs of plan participants
3. Plan funding characteristics and funding provisions
4. Size of the plan
5. Plan liquidity requirements
6. Acceptable risk-return ratios
7. Debt or equity/investments
8. Location and economic diversification
9. Length and terms of leases that will be necessary to ensure an adequate return on the investment
10. Type and diversity of tenants
11. Borrower or tenant's creditworthiness.[21]

Selecting a Real Estate Investment Manager

Among other issues, ERISA's test of prudence focuses on a plan fiduciary's conduct in investigating, evaluating, selecting and monitoring an appropriate investment manager for investing plan assets. In selecting an investment manager, due consideration should be given to—
1. The manager's ability to effectively manage the type of investment
2. Whether the manager's organization and investment philosophies are consistent with the needs of the plan
3. Whether the manager has performed well in managing similar investments for other plans
4. The manager's track record for meeting the stated objectives of plans he has managed.[22]

In making these determinations, the fiduciary should undertake several tasks. Among them are a thorough investigation of the investment manager's experience, qualifications and investment approach. In selecting a final candidate to manage the plan's real estate investments, plan fiduciaries should identify a range of candidates and document the process by which such candidates are selected. This process should include not only questioning of the candidates on their views on a whole range of highly detailed and particularized topics relating to their investment approach and philosophy, but should also include the communication to the candidates by the fiduciaries of the plan's objectives. Finally, the fiduciaries must negotiate an investment management agreement with which they (and their counsel) are comfortable.

Valuing Plan Assets

In order to determine whether a plan is properly funded, whether adequate contributions are being made, whether benefits can be improved, and for a variety of other purposes, Section 103(b) of ERISA requires that a plan must publish an annual report containing a statement of the plan assets and liabilities "valued at their current value." Current value is defined under Section 3(26) of ERISA as:

> fair market value where available and otherwise the fair value as determined in good faith by a trustee or a named fiduciary . . . pursuant to the terms of the plan and in accordance with regulations of the Secretary [of Labor], assuming an orderly liquidation at the time of such determination.

In other words, ERISA requires a plan to "mark to market" its investments on a regular basis. That is, the current value of all investments (including a plan's real estate investments) must be reflected in the plan's annual report (Form Series 5500) that must be filed with the DOL by the plan administrator on an annual basis. The failure to file an annual report that conforms to the requirements set forth in the DOL regulations, including the valuation provisions, can subject the plan administrator to severe penalties under Section 502(c)(2) of ERISA and, for certain plans, under Section 6652 of the Internal Revenue Code.

Adjusting the books of the plan to reflect the current value of both its equity and debt real estate investments is difficult because of (1) real estate's illiquidity and (2) the absence of a public market for real estate investments, such as exists for stock and bond investments. Thus, to establish the value of real estate investments, a plan must retain an appraiser who formulates an opinion as to its value based on various methodologies and approaches. The plan fiduciaries, as well as the plan auditor that certifies the plan's financial statements, must be satisfied that the appraiser's approach and methodology in valuing the investment are sound, reliable and consistent with the terms of the plan, and that the appraisal indeed reflects the current value of the real property.

Evaluating the Investment Manager's Performance

The DOL has described a fiduciary's duty to monitor the actions of those individuals to whom employee benefit plan fiduciary responsibilities have been delegated—

At reasonable intervals the performance of trustees and other fiduciaries should be reviewed by the appointing fiduciary in such manner as may be reasonably expected to ensure that their performance has been in compliance with the terms of the plan and statutory standards, and satisfies the needs of the plan. No single procedure will be appropriate in all cases; the procedure adopted may vary in accordance with the nature of the plan and other facts and circumstances relevant to the choice of the procedure.[23]

While some level of precaution is always needed in connection with the selection and monitoring of an investment manager, the amount used should reflect in significant part such factors as the type and complexity of the investment vehicle, the relative difficulty in valuing the investment and the percentage of plan assets that are managed by the investment manager. In view of the unique characteristics of real estate as an asset class, the plan fiduciaries should carefully engage an investment manager that specializes in the particular type of real estate investment being considered and must establish (in consultation with the investment manager) specific guidelines, benchmarks and procedures for evaluating the performance of the investment manager.

FIDUCIARY DUTIES

Part 4 of Title I of ERISA (Section 404) imposes four broad duties on the fiduciary of an employee benefit plan—to act solely in the interest of plan participants and beneficiaries; to act prudently; to diversify plan assets; and to act in accordance with plan documents. In pertinent part, the statute requires that—

(a)(1) a fiduciary shall discharge his duties with respect to a plan solely in the interest of the participants and beneficiaries and—
  (A) for the exclusive purpose of—
    (i) providing benefits to participants and their beneficiaries; and
    (ii) defraying reasonable expenses of administering the plan;
  (B) with the care, skill, prudence, and diligence under the circumstances then prevailing that a prudent man acting in a like capacity and familiar with such matters would use in the conduct of an enterprise of a like character and with like aims;
  (C) by diversifying the investments of the plan so as to minimize the risk of large losses, unless under the circumstances it is clearly prudent not to do so; and
  (D) in accordance with the documents and instruments governing the plan insofar as such documents and instruments are consistent with the provisions of [Titles I and IV of ERISA].

Before considering how each of these duties applies specifically to real estate investments, it is important to keep in mind several general principles. First and foremost is the "big picture" of ERISA's fiduciary duty requirements: that ERISA requires *procedural* prudence measured at the time the investment is made, without regard to hindsight.[24] Accordingly, whether a fiduciary breaches his fiduciary duty to the plan generally is not a function of the performance of the investment; rather, it will turn on the steps the fiduciary took (or failed to take) in reaching and implementing the investment decision.

Next, plan fiduciaries may delegate some of their duties to investment managers, thereby shielding themselves to some degree against potential fiduciary liability. However, in order to so delegate, the plan documents and governing instruments must explicitly set forth the procedures permitting such delegation. Failure to set forth such a procedure, or failure to follow it—for instance, exercising discretionary authority over an investment decision after full authority has been delegated to an investment manager—may result in a legally ineffective delegation of investment authority.

Third is the fact that fiduciary duties under ERISA with respect to ETIs are identical to those involved in all other types of plan investments. In June 1994, the DOL released Interpretative Bulletin 94-1 relating to the ERISA fiduciary standards for evaluating ETIs under ERISA plans.[25] The bulletin was intended primarily to eliminate the misconception that plan investments in ETIs are incompatible with ERISA's fiduciary obligations. The DOL stated that, under ERISA, investments that meet ERISA's prudence requirements, but that collaterally also further a societal goal, are permissible. Thus, fiduciaries can select an investment course of action that reflects economic factors outside of the plan's benefit, provided that the application of such factors follows primary consideration of a broad range of investment opportunities that are equally advantageous economically. Stated simply, if two investments are equally attractive for financial reasons, it is acceptable to choose one over the other based on socially useful reasons.[26]

Finally, it should be pointed out that the establishment of a Taft-Hartley housing trust raises some, but not all, of the fiduciary duties attendant to making investments with plan assets. A housing trust fund is a welfare benefit plan covered by Section 3(1) of ERISA. That section defines an employee welfare benefit plan to include any plan, fund or program established or maintained by an employer, employee organization or both for the purpose of providing its participants with any benefit described in Section 302(c) of LMRA. Accordingly, the fiduciary duties enumerated in Part 4 of Title I of ERISA (Section 404) apply to the provision of benefits from a housing trust. However, as indicated in the legislative history, those "fiduciary rules will, however, apply somewhat differently in the context of a provision of a benefit as opposed to decisions concerning the safeguarding and investment of plan assets."[27] Consequently, neither the diversification requirements of Section 404,[28] nor the prohibited transaction restrictions of Section 406, are applicable. However, the rules governing the administration of other types of Taft-Hartley trusts—joint administration by employer and employee representatives, for example—must all be followed.

Exclusive Benefit Rule

In significant ways, ERISA's exclusive benefit requirement codifies what has been the operative common law rule for several hundred years—that a fiduciary owes a duty of undivided loyalty to the trust. The crucial test is always, "Was an investment decision made for the primary purpose of benefitting plan participants?"

Application of the exclusive benefit rule takes many forms. In one respect, it prevents plan sponsors from taking actions that, although *ultimately* benefitting plan participants, serve primarily to benefit the plan sponsor. In another form, it prevents trustees serving as fiduciaries for more than one plan from subordinating the needs of one plan to those of another. The exclusive benefit rule also prevents trustees from engaging in pure social investing—making an investment to further socially desirable goals that, when analyzed on a risk-to-return ratio, is less prudent than other available investment options. Finally, the rule prevents trustees from using plan assets to further their own financial interests.

The seminal case holding that trustees must focus on the interests of plan participants instead of on the interests of the plan sponsor is *Blankenship v. Boyle*, 329 F.Supp. 1089 (D.D.C. 1971). In *Blankenship*, the trustees of the United Mine Workers Welfare and Retirement Fund invested a portion of the plan's assets in common stock of certain electric companies. The court ruled that the trustees breached their fiduciary duty because the primary purpose of the investment was to force the utility companies to purchase coal supplied by coal companies that were organized by the United Mine Workers. Arguably, the purpose—increased contributions to the trust fund that were based on the tonnage of coal mined—served the interests of plan participants and beneficiaries. Nonetheless, the court held that the trustees were acting primarily for the benefit of the United Mine Workers and union-organized coal companies, rather than in the sole interest of the participants of the plan.

Another example of this principle is *Donovan v. Bierwirth*, 538 F.Supp. 463 (E.D.N.Y. 1981), *aff'd, modified on other grounds*, 680 F.2d 263 (2nd Cir.), *cert. denied*, 459 U.S. 1069 (1982), which arose out of the attempt by LTV Corporation to buy a controlling interest in the Grumman Corporation. The DOL alleged that the trustees of the Grumman Corporation Pension Plan breached their fiduciary duty under ERISA by using plan assets primarily to purchase Grumman stock in an effort to fend off the hostile takeover effort by LTV.

In ruling that the trustees of the Grumman Corporation Pension Plan violated ERISA, the Court of Appeals for the Second Circuit emphasized that, when a fiduciary has dual loyalties—a loyalty to the pension plan and a loyalty (in this case) to the corporation—the investment decision must be both intensive and scrupulous and must be discharged with the greatest degree of care. The trustees of the Grumman plan stated that they believed that Grumman stock presented a unique and substantial opportunity for long-term appreciation, and that their decision to buy the stock was designed to further the purposes of the plan and the interests of its beneficiaries. The court concluded that the main efforts of the trustees were not devoted to the participants' best interest but, instead, were devoted to defeating the takeover effort and that the decision to purchase Grumman shares was made without sufficient inquiry into the facts.

The second category of cases—those holding that the trustees of related plans cannot subordinate the interests of the participants of one plan to those of another—is typified by *Donovan v. Mazzola*, 2 EBC 2115 (N.D.Cal. 1981), *aff'd*, 716 F.2d 1226 (9th Cir. 1983), *cert. denied*, 464 U.S. 1040 (1984). There, the defendants, who were the trustees of both the Local Union 38 Pension Fund and Local Union 38 Convalescent Fund, approved six transactions challenged by the DOL, three of which raised exclusive benefit issues. Those transactions were: (1) a $1.5 million loan from the pension fund to the convalescent fund, which was secured by a hotel owned by the convalescent fund that was both losing money and subject to prior liens, and which was intended to alleviate the operating losses experienced by the hotel and other properties owned by the convalescent fund; (2) an extension of credit to the convalescent fund in the form of a six-month moratorium on repayment of the $1.5 million loan that no "reasonably competent real estate lender, standing in a like position to the pension fund trustees at the time" would have granted without further consideration or security from the borrower; and (3) an additional extension of credit to the convalescent fund, without further consideration or security, to repay a preexisting $500,000 loan. In explaining that these three transactions violated Section 404(a)(1)(A), the court stated that the trustees "have consistently transacted business with and for the Convalescent Fund at all relevant times for the purpose of aiding the Convalescent Fund at the expense of the Pension Fund.... [T]hey acted on both sides of the transaction and sought to benefit the Convalescent Fund rather than to protect the best interests of the Pension Fund." *Id.* at 2133-34.

The third category is cases interpreting the exclusive benefit rule as it pertains to "social investing." Simply stated, pure social investing is inconsistent with ERISA's fiduciary principles. The more significant the collateral or incidental benefits become, the more likely the transaction will be viewed as an ERISA breach of fiduciary duty. As the district court in *Marshall v. Glass/Metal Association and Glaziers and Glassworks Pension Plan,* 507 F.Supp. 378 (D. Haw. 1980) explained, the trustees failed to follow the procedures of a prudent lender even though they "vigorously defended" the proposed real estate project on the grounds that the plan's loan would "provide a high rate of interest to the Plan, as well as job opportunities for construction workers and recreational facilities for residents...." *Id.* at 383, 384. Holding that the trustees violated their fiduciary duty, the court succinctly stated the plan fiduciaries' role: "the job of the trustees in this situation is not to adopt the borrower's enthusiasm for his project, but to evaluate the prospective risks and returns to the Plan."

With respect to *socially sensitive* investments, however, courts and the DOL have generally reached the conclusion that, as long as the primary purpose of a fiduciary's action is solely in the interest of the participants, the fact that other parties gain a collateral or incidental benefit is not a breach of fiduciary duty. It is this interpretation that makes ETIs possible.[29]

Finally, the case of *Metzler v. Graham,* 112 F.3d 207 (5th Cir. 1997) focuses on the aspect of the exclusive benefit rule that prohibits fiduciaries from using plan assets to further their own interests. In *Metzler*, the defendant-appellee Graham was the president and sole owner of GAI, and served as the sole trustee and administrator of a defined contribution benefit plan established to provide retirement, death and disability benefits to the employees of GAI. Before 1985, the plan assets consisted of short-term certificates of deposit and U.S. Treasury securities, cash and cash equivalents, 20% of which was personally owned by Graham in his pension plan account. In April 1985, Graham used plan assets to purchase a lot of undeveloped land (the property) for $1.65 per square foot. Contemporaneous independent appraisals valued the property between $2 and $2.75 per square foot. Although Graham intended to resell the property shortly after its purchase, the subsequent sale never occurred; and while the property maintained its value and no participants lost any benefits due to the purchase, the plan paid maintenance and taxes on the property, but earned no income from it.

In bringing its breach-of-loyalty charge against Graham, the DOL alleged that Graham had made the purchase primarily to increase the value of two adjacent parcels of property, which he personally owned. Rejecting the DOL's charge and holding that Graham did *not* violate ERISA, the Fifth Circuit affirmed the district court's opinion that

> merely because Graham was a partner in other real estate investments in the area[,] it was not a breach of his fiduciary duty to acquire the land on behalf of the Plan, nor was it, under the specific facts of this case, a breach of his fiduciary duty to try to market the Plan's Property in a package along with the property he had an interest in, since doing so provided a larger market of potential purchasers... [In fact,] Graham's control of the adjacent parcels actually inured to the benefit of the Plan.
>
> *Id.* at 212-213.

In further support of its holding, the court assessed the prudence of Graham's decision-making process, pointing out that he made full disclosure to, and sought approval by, plan participants; consulted with an independent appraiser, as well as the plan's actuary, accountant and lawyer; and utilized his own skills as a sophisticated real estate investor to undertake an independent analysis. Comparing *Graham* to *Bierwirth,* the court stated that *Bierwirth* "involved the commitment of plan assets to corporate control contests in which the plan trustees' jobs were at stake." *Id.* at 213. In the court's view, Graham's ownership of adjoining property had not nearly as much potential for conflict. Accordingly, the *Graham* court determined that "[t]he level of precaution necessary to relieve a fiduciary of the taint of a potential conflict should depend on the circumstances of the case and the magnitude of the potential conflict."[30]

Prudent Man Rule

Section 404(a)(1)(B) of ERISA states that a fiduciary shall discharge his duties with respect to a plan "with the care, skill, prudence, and diligence under the circumstances then prevailing that a prudent man acting in a like capacity and familiar with such matters would use in the conduct of an enterprise of a like character and with like aims." Under the common law prudent man rule, the standard by which a person's prudence was measured was that of an ordinary layperson. However, courts and commentators have interpreted ERISA's prudence standard differently, stating that Section 404 of ERISA takes into account the very special characteristics of employee benefit plans. Accordingly, under ERISA the test is that of a "prudent expert."[31]

It is also clear that ERISA's prudence requirement is

a rule of methodology, not of result. Methodology refers to *how* a decision is made, and it entails the range of considerations that a prudent fiduciary should evaluate when committing plan assets to an investment. Using this analysis, it becomes clear that if the plan fiduciaries properly identify issues facing them; engage qualified experts when needed; receive from these experts written reports and opinions; study the reports and opinions; question the experts so that the fiduciaries fully understand not only the conclusions, but also how the conclusions were reached; properly consider the alternatives; and then adopt a course of conduct that is reasonable under the circumstances, they likely have acted prudently.[32]

Such prudent behavior, for the most part, shields fiduciaries from potential fiduciary liability. This is because courts, evaluating the decision-making process at the time the decision was made, rather than with hindsight, generally will not second-guess a prudently made investment, even if the investment performance turns out to be negative. As will be demonstrated below, courts grant wide latitude to plan fiduciaries who act in a well-reasoned, methodical, deliberative manner. However, they are quick to find a violation where fiduciaries fail to act in this fashion.

Marshall v. Glass/Metal Association and Glaziers and Glassworks Pension Plan, 507 F.Supp. 378 (D. Haw. 1980) (discussed in the previous section in connection with the exclusive benefit rule) provides a striking example of trustees who acted in an imprudent manner and thus failed to perceive the dangers to which they were exposing the plan. In *Glass/Metal,* a real estate developer requested a $750,000 loan (which constituted 23% of the plan assets), to finance the development of a time-sharing condominium venture. The *known* risks inherent to the project were numerous: Construction had stopped years earlier, allowing the existing structures to deteriorate substantially; the mortgage on the land upon which the condominiums would be built was in default and a foreclosure proceeding had begun; the developer was in Chapter 11 bankruptcy; and a construction loan, which would have been used to repay the plan's loan (which itself would have been used to remove the developer from bankruptcy), was contingent on both the plan's loan and the developer's successful efforts to presell (for cash) a certain percentage of time-share units in local property to local residents—a difficult endeavor since there was no proven market. In addition, the trustees had no experience in a real estate loan and only minimal experience in lending or finance.

In establishing its case for a violation of ERISA's prudence requirement, the DOL offered the testimony of an experienced real estate investor who testified that an experienced lender would have analyzed the loan by examining: (1) the borrower's financial capability and track record; (2) the market for the project to be financed by the loan; (3) the economic feasibility of the project; (4) the value and liquidity of the collateral for the loan; and (5) the existence and availability of other financing as a source of repayment for the loan. The trustees undertook none of this due diligence, however, and instead relied on the borrower's "sketchy" marketing information "reflecting largely the natural optimism of a developer and salesman." *Id.* at 382. Accordingly, the court held that the proposed loan violated ERISA because a commitment of 23% of the plan assets to a "single, speculative real estate venture" laden with risks that would have caused an experienced lender to balk would have "subject[ed] a disproportionate amount of the trust assets to the risk of a large loss." *Id.* at 381, 384.

Donovan v. Mazzola, 2 EBC 2115 (N.D.Cal. 1981) (discussed in the previous section in connection with the exclusive benefit rule), similarly serves as another example of a case involving real estate where the plan fiduciaries failed to act prudently by not undertaking a complete review of the circumstances before making a loan. In *Mazzola,* the court held that the trustees breached their fiduciary duty both by paying a physician $250,000 to conduct a feasibility study on converting a hotel into a more profitable enterprise, and by granting a $2.25 million construction loan to convert another hotel into a recreational exercise facility. Regarding the feasibility study, the court found that the physician was unqualified to issue such a report, and that a qualified expert could have written such a report for $50,000 to $100,000. As for the loan secured by the hotel-soon-to-be-spa, the record showed that it was undertaken without financial statements of the borrower, accurate cost figures, a complete market study, or architectural and engineering plans.

Most recently, in *In re Bicoastal Corp.,* 191 B.R. 238 (Bankr. M.D. Fla. 1995), the court found that the plan investment manager's "lackadaisical approach" in her use of plan assets to finance a real estate developer's purchase of property was "nothing short of gross negligence." *Id.* at 244. *Bicoastal* involved a dispute that began when the plan's custodian first refused on its own accord, and then was instructed by the plan to ignore the instructions of its prior investment manager, to transfer $44 million in plan assets to close a real estate deal. Bicostal's successor entity (and current sponsor of the plan) brought this action to recoup litigation costs incurred by the plan and its custodian in defending the developer's action for specific performance on the grounds that these costs were administrative expenses arising out of the previous asset manager's breach of fiduciary duty.

In *Bicoastal,* a real estate developer (Bullard) approached the pension plan's president, CEO and named fiduciary for asset management (Redmond) with the suggestion that the plan purchase two pieces of real estate, one in Osceola, Florida, known as the "Gateway" property, and one in Jacksonville, Florida, known as "Queen's Harbor." The plan financed Bullard's purchase of the Gateway property, taking back a note and mortgage. Bullard defaulted on the Gateway loan, and the plan was forced to foreclose on the property. Prior to Bullard's default on the loan, Victoria Clear replaced Redmond as the asset manager of Bicoastal's pension plan.

After Clear took over as asset manager, she contacted the plan's enrolled actuary to discuss whether it would be prudent to make a substantial investment of plan funds in the Queen's Harbor project. The actuary advised Clear that such an investment was "not wise," owing to the plan's current financial circumstances, which included Bicoastal's pending bankruptcy, pending litigation and the possible existence of a funding deficiency in the plan. The actuary recommended that plan assets be kept liquid by investing only in short-term investments. The actuary then wrote Redmond, Clear, the plan's auditor and its general counsel, outlining the potential downsides of a long-term investment. He stated that the plan "should focus on short-time horizon investments until 'near term uncertainties settle and the threat of termination ceases.'" *Id.* at 240.

Despite this advice, all of which was given *subsequent to* Bullard's default on the Gateway loan, Clear executed a contract with Bullard on behalf of the plan to purchase the Queen's Harbor property for $38.5 million. The contract provided no legal description of the property. Furthermore, Clear agreed that the plan would loan Bullard an additional $5 million for the development of a country club on the property. This loan failed to specify an interest rate, repayment schedule or other customary terms. Based on these facts, the court stated that Clear breached her duty as the named fiduciary for asset management.

Finally, in *United States of America v. Mason Tenders District Council of Greater New York,* 90 F.Supp. 882 (S.D.N.Y. 1995), trustees of a pension fund were found to have breached their fiduciary duties under ERISA by making extremely questionable investments in two properties that were purchased for much larger amounts than their fair market value. On behalf of the pension fund, the trustees purchased an office building in New York City for $24 million, which was $16.5 million more than the seller had paid for the building less than ten months earlier. Also, the trustees purchased a residential property in Florida with pension fund assets for the price of $1.45 million, $600,000 more than the valuation contained in any contemporaneous valuation of the property.

Noting that the test of prudency under ERISA "focuses on the trustee's conduct in investigating, evaluating and making the investment," the court held that the trustees' failure to obtain any valuation or appraisal of the New York building or otherwise seek to ascertain its value before approving the pension fund's purchase of it, constituted a breach of fiduciary duty. Also, the trustees' failure to utilize a qualified professional asset manager (QPAM)[33] to assist in the purchase—which was a condition for coverage under the pension fund's fiduciary liability insurance policy—also constituted a breach of the ERISA fiduciary duty of prudency.

Similarly, with respect to the Florida property, the trustees' failure to investigate the value of the property (and even read a letter assessing its value at $600,000 less than the $1.45 million purchase price) caused the pension fund to overpay for it. In holding that the trustees breached their fiduciary responsibility, the court rejected the trustees' defense that they relied on counsel and acted in good faith. The court noted that neither good faith alone nor reliance on counsel is a defense to a breach of fiduciary duty under ERISA.

Each of these cases, however, should be contrasted with *Etter v. J. Pease Construction Co.,* 963 F.2d 1005 (7th Cir. 1992), *Metzler v. Graham,* 112 F.3d 207 (5th Cir. 1997), and *Reich v. King,* 867 F.Supp. 341 (D.Md. 1994). In these three cases, plan fiduciaries were found *not* to have violated ERISA because, under the particular facts and circumstances, the investment decisions had been prudently made and the failure to diversify was also prudent.

In *Etter,* the trustees, who managed and invested primarily their own money since they comprised a majority of the plan beneficiaries, invested 88% of the plan's net assets ($112,850 out of $127,993), along with $407,356 of their own money, in a local real estate venture. Eighteen months later, when the plan and the trustees sold their interests for $910,000, the plan realized a profit of $109,567—or a 97% return on its investment. The district court found that there was no breach of fiduciary duty. The court also held that the investment was not a prohibited transaction (i.e., no self-dealing and no transfer of plan assets for personal use).

Evaluating the prudence of the investment on the facts presented, the district court found that while the trustees were not "sophisticated investors," they were experienced in real estate and knew the local market and development potential in the county. As part of their due diligence, all of the trustees visited the parcel personally, inquired about an adjacent golf course that was being constructed by a reliable developer, investigated the possibility of annexation by a local village, and reviewed both aerial photographs and local floodplain maps. In addition, the trustees considered several other properties before committing to the investment. Thus, given the reasonable investigation, the Seventh Circuit affirmed the district court's finding that, under the circumstances, it was clearly prudent not to diversify.

As discussed above in *Graham,* as sole trustee and administrator of the plan, Graham invested 63% of the plan assets in a single parcel of undeveloped real estate.

Despite the large concentration of the plan's assets in a single investment, the court concluded that Graham had exercised proper due diligence and prudence and that at no relevant time had there been a risk of large loss to the plan that would have impaired the plan's ability to pay benefits. The district court found that in purchasing the property, Graham was attempting to increase the return on the plan's investments that previously had been entirely in short-term monetary or cash equivalent instruments. The court also found that Graham was very knowledgeable in commercial real estate development (especially in the local market); that he had discussed the investment with the plan's counsel, actuary, major participants (who also had considerable experience in local commercial real estate development); and that he gave proper consideration to an independent appraisal that valued the property significantly higher than the purchase price. As to the risk of large losses, the court considered (1) the relatively young age of the plan participants; (2) the portfolio's prior lack of real estate holdings and thus its need for a hedge against inflation; (3) the significant gap between the purchase and the contemporaneous appraisal prices; and (4) Graham's real estate expertise. The court found that these factors supported the conclusion that "the investment did not carry a 'risk of large loss' at any relevant time."

King involved the plan trustees' investment of 70% of the plan assets in residential real estate mortgages in one county. The trustees conceded that this investment failed to satisfy, at least initially, ERISA's diversification requirement. However, in support of their investment, the trustees offered expert testimony from the president of a local bank, a private investment management consultant and an employee benefits consultant. The first expert testified that based on the loans' low loan-to-value ratios, their status as five-year "balloons," the good payment histories of borrowers, Mr. King's knowledge of the local real estate market, the fact that 60% of the bank's assets are invested in similar mortgage loans in the same geographic area and that the loans were marketable, they did not carry a risk of large losses. The second and third experts testified more generally about mortgage-backed investments and statistical comparisons on investment returns, respectively. As is more fully discussed in the next section relating to diversification, the court held that the plan proved that the plan's lack of diversification was clearly prudent and not in violation of Section 404(a)(1)(C).

Diversification

The third requirement of ERISA's fiduciary provisions is the duty to diversify plan assets. The diversification requirement exists to minimize the risk of large losses to trust principal—a goal that is usually achieved by limiting the proportion of trust assets invested in any one type of investment and instead committing the assets to different classes of investments that are characterized by different types of risks. By diversifying into different types of investments, the potential losses that might occur in one portion of the portfolio due to a particular economic event will be offset by gains in another area.[34] Furthermore, even if such a loss is not offset, its impact is at least limited to a relatively small portion of the fund. The diversification provision can be viewed as a subset of the prudence requirement, although it may have been separately stated in ERISA for purposes of emphasis.

Since diversification is concerned with minimizing risks, an initial step is to identify risks associated with various types of investments. With respect to equity investments in real estate, the two overarching risks are that economic forces will depress property values, thereby affecting resale value and that, where the property is being developed for residential or commercial purposes, it will fail to produce an acceptable income stream.

As to debt investments in real estate such as mortgages, courts have recognized that there are four attendant risks: default risk, interest rate risk, inflation risk and liquidity risk.[35] *Default* risk is the risk that payments will not be made timely or that it will be necessary to foreclose on the mortgaged property for repayment of the loan. *Interest rate* risk is the risk that the lender's cost of funds will approach or exceed the interest rate charged to the borrower. *Inflation* risk is the risk that the expected real rate of return on a mortgage will not be realized because of unanticipated inflation. Finally, *liquidity* risk refers to the risk that there is no secondary market for the plan's mortgages, which could result in losses if the plan were suddenly forced to sell the loans at below face value. Based on the recent cases, it appears that courts will not find an ERISA violation where the only evidence offered against the challenged loan is "textbook type theories that appear far removed from the actual realities of [the] mortgages. . . ."[36] Specific facts demonstrating that these risks outweighed the potential rewards in making the loan are necessary.[37]

By design, ERISA's diversification requirement contains no specific percentage limits on any one type of investment. Instead, Section 404(a)(1)(C) imposes "a requirement of diversification that depends upon the facts and circumstances surrounding each plan and investment."[38] According to ERISA's legislative history, in considering the diversification requirement fiduciaries should review the following factors:

(1) the purposes of the plan; (2) the amount of plan assets; (3) financial and industrial conditions; (4) the type of investment, whether mortgages, bonds or shares of stock or otherwise; (5) distri-

bution as to geographical location; (6) distribution as to industries; (7) the dates of maturity.[39]

The legislative history also explains that if a trustee "is investing in mortgages on real property he should not invest a disproportionate amount of the trust in mortgages in a particular district or on a particular class of property so that a decline in property values in that district or of that class might cause a large loss."[40]

In connection with the diversification rules, one crucial point that is not found in the legislative history, but certainly appears in case law, is the fact that both the individual investments and the asset allocation of the plan's entire investment portfolio must be evaluated for diversification. Indeed, as one court noted, even where evidence supports that each loan was prudent, such a finding is not dispositive of the diversification inquiry.[41]

The DOL and individual plan participants have brought numerous cases against the trustees of various plans alleging that the real estate investment at issue, whether in the form of a mortgage-backed loan or a direct purchase of land, violated both the diversification and prudence requirements of Section 404 of ERISA. The reason for this is that, as noted above, while diversification and prudence are each distinct requirements, they are clearly interrelated rules. Indeed, Section 404(a)(1)(C) states explicitly that a fiduciary must "diversify the investments of the plan so as to minimize the risk of large losses, unless under the circumstances it is clearly prudent not to do so."

Following this statutory language, courts have engaged in a two-step burden shifting analysis. First, to establish a violation, a plaintiff must demonstrate that the plan's investment portfolio is not diversified on its face. Then, once the plaintiff has established a failure to diversify, the burden shifts to the defendant to show that under the circumstances it was clearly prudent not to diversify. Thus, even if a plan is not diversified on its face, it does not violate the diversification requirement if, under the facts and circumstances, it was clearly prudent not to do so.

For ERISA diversification purposes, plans can be divided into three categories. First, there are those plans whose asset allocation satisfies the diversification requirement. With respect to these plans, it is important to recognize that merely because the plan investments are diversified does not assure that they necessarily comply with the other ERISA requirements contained in Sections 404 and 406. Next, there are plans that are not diversified on their face, but under the circumstances such nondiversification is clearly prudent. Finally, there are plans that are not diversified, and under the circumstances such nondiversification is not prudent. Plans in this category violate ERISA's diversification requirement.

As mentioned in the previous section regarding prudence, *Etter, Graham* and *King* each provide an example of a plan that, while not diversified on its face, was found *not* to violate the diversification requirement because under the particular facts and circumstances it was clearly prudent not to diversify. In analyzing these decisions, a common theme emerges. Often the trustees were experienced in real estate and knew both the local market and its development potential. They often visited the site personally, inquired about current and future development or municipal use of adjacent and nearby land. They discussed the investment with their plan's actuary, counsel, auditor and sometimes even their participants. They gave due consideration to independent appraisals. When acting as a lender, they considered the payment histories of their borrowers, the loan-to-value ratios of the loans and the practices of other local lenders. And, of course, they always considered several other properties before committing to the investment.

These prudent measures should be contrasted with the actions of the trustees in *Donovan v. Mazzola,* 716 F.2d 1226 (9th Cir. 1983), in which the DOL challenged two transactions (among others) for violating ERISA's diversification requirement. The first transaction was a $1.5 million loan secured by a hotel; the second was a $650,000 loan secured by a hotel being converted into a health spa (for which the plan also made a $2.25 million construction loan). Evaluating these transactions, the district court stated that:

Taken alone, the $1.5 million loan, representing 12% of the Pension Fund assets, subjected too large a portion of the over-all portfolio to a common set of risks associated with the Clear Lake property at a time when a broad range of other investment possibilities requiring a smaller investment outlay of funds were available in securities, fixed income instruments and real estate. When viewed in conjunction with other monies loaned by the Pension Fund to the Convalescent Fund, the $1.5 million loan violated §1104(a)(1)(C) by subjecting a disproportionate amount (approximately 53%) of Pension Fund assets to a common set of risks associated with the same capital market, vehicle, geographic area, product type and property.

Id. at 2136.

With respect to the $1.5 million loan, the trustees violated Section 404(a)(1)(A) and (B) (1) because they failed to ascertain the identity and value of the loan security; (2) because on the date the loan was made, based on existing information, they knew or should have known the loan presented an unreasonable risk of not being timely and fully paid without resort to the collateral; (3) because they granted the loan below the prevailing interest rates for comparable mortgages at that time; (4) because they acted on both sides of the loan transaction; and (5) because they had consistently transacted business with and for the Convalescent Fund at all relevant times for the purpose of aiding the Convalescent Fund at the expense of the Pension Fund.

The making of the $650,000 loan violated the requirements of Section 404(a)(1)(C) of ERISA by investing a disproportionate amount of plan assets in the real estate market, in mortgages, in Northern California resorts and in the health spa as an individual property. Viewed only in connection with the $2.25 million S&F loan, the $650,000 loan committed too large a portion of the pension fund assets (about 14.5%) to a common set of risks linked to the spa at a time when other investment possibilities were available in securities, fixed income instruments and real estate. Viewed in conjunction with other mortgages in the pension fund portfolio, the $650,000 loan violated Section 404(a)(1)(C) by exposing too large a percentage (approximately 76%) of assets to a common set of risks tied to the same capital market and vehicle (real estate mortgages), by exposing approximately 47% of the assets to the common set of risks associated with Northern California real estate, and by exposing approximately 73% of the assets to the common risks associated with the hotel, resort and recreation property.

In making the $650,000 loan to S&F, the trustees violated Section 404(a)(1)(B) by both (1) failing to follow reasonable procedures for underwriting the loan and (2) actually making this unreasonably risky loan, which a reasonably competent lender in their position would not have made.[42]

Plan Documents

The final aspect of ERISA's fiduciary duty requirement is to act in accordance with the documents governing the plan. Although this requirement seems obvious and straightforward, if overlooked, it can clearly cause problems. Plan documents for this purpose may include, not just the plan description and summary plan description, but also the plan's trust indenture, the collective bargaining agreements under which the plan is maintained, insurance contracts and other ancillary documents. Thus, for example, before embarking on real estate investments, plan fiduciaries should ensure that the plan's trust agreement authorizes such investments. If not, the fiduciaries may wish to consider making the appropriate amendments. In addition, in the course of making such amendments, the plan fiduciaries will want to review (and revise where necessary) the plan's investment guidelines to determine whether they are clearly authorized to make the contemplated real estate investment. For example, as will be discussed below, an eligible individual account plan that is otherwise permitted to invest in qualifying employer real property may do so only if the plan documents *explicitly* provide that the plan may acquire and hold it.

Fiduciary Duties Regarding ETIs

Under ERISA, a plan fiduciary may invest plan assets in an ETI, provided that the fiduciary determines that such investment is appropriate for the plan by applying the same factors that a prudent fiduciary would use in evaluating any other type of plan investment. Thus, the analytical framework for the rigorous, searching analysis of the relevant aspects of all investments must be used equally in evaluating the investment in an ETI.

The DOL has consistently taken the position that collateral benefits may be considered when making an investment decision so long as the investment places the interests of plan participants and beneficiaries first. For instance, in response to an inquiry concerning a plan's investment in a mortgage pool for union-built properties, the DOL stated that—

> in deciding whether and to what extent to invest in a particular investment, a fiduciary must ordinarily consider only factors relating to the interests of plan participants and beneficiaries. . . . A decision to make an investment may not be influenced by a desire to stimulate the construction industry and generate employment, unless the investment, when judged solely on the basis of its economic value to the plan, would be equal or superior to alternative investments available to the plan.[43]

Thus, so long as the primary objective of an ETI is to seek competitive rates of return for the plan, the prudence and exclusive benefit rules will not prevent the plan from investing in ETIs. The DOL clarified its position by issuing Interpretive Bulletin 94-1, in which it stated that "[t]he fiduciary standards applicable to ETIs are no different than the standards applicable to plan investments generally."[44]

The fiduciary requirements of Sections 403 and 404 of ERISA, then, do not prevent plan fiduciaries from deciding to invest plan assets in an ETI, *provided that* the ETI has an expected rate of return that is commensurate to rates of return of alternate investments with similar risk characteristics that are available to the plan *and* if the ETI represents an otherwise appropriate investment for the plan (considering such factors as diversification and the plan's investment guidelines or policy). However, the plan fiduciaries cannot choose to invest in an ETI without evaluating "the availability, riskiness and potential return of alternative investments."[45]

Further, the DOL recognizes that plan fiduciaries can consider an ETI even where it may require a longer period of time to generate significant investment returns, may be less liquid and may not have as much readily available information on its risks and returns as other asset categories. However, a violation of ERISA would occur if a plan fiduciary is willing to accept rates of investment return that fall below conventional investments or entail greater risks to secure collateral (i.e., noneconomic) benefits.

Fiduciaries can obtain data on ETIs through the ETI clearinghouse. The clearinghouse is a central information repository for plan sponsors on ETIs that the DOL established by contracting with a securities advisory corporation. However, in evaluating ETIs, most plan fiduciaries will be well advised to seek specialized advice from investment experts who are familiar with ETIs and who are able to analyze them from a risk and return perspective. Finally, fiduciaries must remember to act only in accordance with the plan provisions and guidelines they establish for themselves.

PROHIBITED TRANSACTIONS

Buttressing ERISA's fiduciary provisions are the prohibited transaction rules.[46] As with all investments under ERISA, real estate investments must not constitute a violation of the statute's prohibited transaction rules.

Briefly stated, the prohibited transaction rules are designed to prevent individuals with close relationships to an employee benefit from benefitting from such relationships. Also, these rules exist to prevent fiduciaries from engaging in transactions constituting conflicts of interest.

Sections 406 and 407 of ERISA contain the prohibited transaction provisions. In Section 406 the rules are divided into two categories: (1) prohibitions of certain transactions between plans and parties in interest—sale or exchange of property, lending of money or other extension of credit, furnishing of goods or services; and (2) prohibitions on the conduct by a fiduciary that could result in a conflict of interest. In connection with real estate transactions, these rules contain *special provisions* relating to employer real property.

Section 406 provides in pertinent part:

(a)(1) A fiduciary with respect to a plan shall not cause the plan to engage in a transaction if he knows or should know that such transaction constitutes a direct or indirect—

(A) sale or exchange, or leasing, of any property between the plan and a party in interest;

(B) lending of money or other extension of credit between the plan and a party in interest;

(C) furnishing of goods, services, or facilities between the plan and a party in interest;

(D) transfer to, or use by or for the benefit of, a party in interest, of any assets of the plan; or

(E) acquisition, on behalf of the plan, of any employer security or employer real property in violation of Section 407(a).

It is important to remember that these rules are absolute. It is no defense that a prohibited transaction was good, fair, reasonable, appropriate or was without harm or was a benefit to the plan. It is also important to note that Section 406(a)(1)(D), relating to the transfer of plan assets, is not implicated in the case of a Taft-Hartley housing trust that provides financial housing assistance to its participants. As indicated in the legislative history, Congress exempted housing assistance grants from the prohibited transaction rules.

Parties in Interest

As noted above, Section 406(a) prohibited transactions involve specified transactions with plan assets between the plan and a party in interest. Thus, before embarking on any real estate investment (as with any investment), the plan fiduciaries should develop a checklist of the parties involved in the investment program to determine if there are any "parties in interest," as that term is defined in Section 3(14) of ERISA. A partial list of common parties in interest includes—

1. The named fiduciaries of the plan, other plan fiduciaries and parties in interest
2. The union including employees and officers of the union
3. Contributing employers, the management association, or both, and each of their 10% shareholders, officers, directors and employees
4. Service providers—the accountant, actuary, attorney, consultant and administrative manager, trustee, custodian, etc.

In the context of typical real estate transactions, ERISA provides two particularly important statutory exemptions and several administrative exemptions from the prohibited transaction rules. An extremely useful exemption is applicable where plans contract with a party in interest for office space. Under Section 408(b)(2) of ERISA, a lease for office space by a party in interest to a plan is not prohibited where the arrangement is necessary for the establishment and operation of the plan, and if no more than reasonable compensation is paid for the space. In the case of collectively bargained multiemployer plans, both Prohibited Transaction Class Exemption (PTCE) 76-1[47] and PTCE 77-10[48] provide relief from the prohibited transaction rules in connection with the provision of office space by a plan to a party in interest, such as where a plan leases office space to or from a related plan or to an affiliated union.

Where a plan seeks to invest in employer real property, the transaction must satisfy special statutory requirements to avoid violation of the prohibited transaction provisions. An ERISA plan that invests in employer real property may only invest in qualifying employer real property (QERP). In broad terms, under Section 407 of ERISA, a plan may not acquire or hold QERP if the total fair market value of such assets exceeds 10% of the total fair market value of all of the plan assets at the time of acquisition. However, an eligible individual account plan (e.g., a profit-sharing, stock bonus, thrift or savings plan or employee stock ownership plan (ESOP)) may acquire or hold more than 10% of the value of the plan assets in QERP without violating ERISA's diversification requirements. In addition, under Section 408(e) of ERISA, a plan's sale, acquisition or lease of QERP must be for "adequate consideration," and no commission may be charged.

QERP consists of any parcels of real property and related personal property that are owned by the plan and leased to an employer of employees covered by the plan (or to an affiliate). Real property that is owned by *the employer* and leased to the plan is not employer real property. QERP is defined as parcels of employer real property that (1) are geographically dispersed, (2) are suitable for multiple uses, (3) may be leased to an employer, and (4) whose acquisition and retention comply with the fiduciary provisions of ERISA, other than the diversification requirements.

In a typical transaction, a plan may acquire real property from the employer either by purchasing unencumbered property at a price not exceeding fair market value, or by receiving the real property as a contribution to the plan.[49] The plan then may lease the real property back to the employer and must receive rental income that provides the plan with no less than adequate consideration for such lease. As is noted above, although a properly structured transaction may avoid prohibited transaction violations, the transaction must also satisfy ERISA's fiduciary standards.

The prohibited transaction rules must also be considered where the plan is acting as a lender providing a construction loan to a contributing employer. This may occur, for example, to generate work for local contractors—who also are contributing employers—that, in turn, results in the creation of jobs for members of the bargaining unit, who also are plan participants.[50] Such loans constitute an extension of credit between the plan and a party in interest (the contributing employer), and a transfer of plan assets to a party in interest, which are impermissible under the prohibited transaction rules, absent an administrative exemption.

PTCE 76-1[51] provides such relief. Under this PTCE, the DOL has exempted from the prohibited transaction provisions of ERISA construction mortgage loans in which the borrower is a contributing employer, if several conditions are met. Those conditions are that—

1. The loan must be a construction loan.
2. The decision to make the loan must be made by a bank or savings and loan association.
3. The plan and the employers cannot exercise controlling influence over the management or policies of the bank or savings and loan.
4. The loans must meet the guidelines the bank has established for making loans with its own funds.
5. There must be a commitment for permanent financing.
6. One loan cannot exceed 10% of plan assets.
7. All loans cannot exceed 35% of plan assets.

PTCE 76-1 has been used by many plans to become involved in construction lending. These construction loan programs generate job opportunities, but may also present good investment opportunities.

Another PTCE extremely useful for real estate investments is PTCE 84-14,[52] relating to qualified professional asset managers (QPAMs). The QPAM exemption allows fiduciaries to segregate a portion of their plan assets and place them under the exclusive management and control of a QPAM, who then makes the real estate investments. As with PTCE 76-1, the QPAM exemption avoids many[53] prohibited transaction problems under the party-in-interest provisions of Section 406 of ERISA.[54]

PTCE 84-14 is only applicable to QPAMs that are independent of the parties in interest. Under PTCE 84-14, a QPAM may include a bank, savings and loan association, insurance company or an investment advisor registered under the Investment Advisers Act of 1940 that has under its management and control client assets in excess of $50 million and that meets certain other net worth or equity capital standards. The entity must acknowledge in writing that it is a fiduciary. PTCE 84-14 will not apply, however, to any transaction with a party in interest or its affiliate if the party in interest (or its affiliate) had authority to appoint or terminate the appointment of the QPAM or to negotiate the terms of the QPAM's management agreement.

For the QPAM exemption to apply, the terms of the transaction must be negotiated on behalf of the plan by the QPAM (or under its direction in certain circumstances), and must be at least as favorable to the plan as the terms generally available in an arm's length transaction between unrelated parties. Also, to ensure that no single plan unduly influences the QPAM, its assets (when combined with the assets of similar plans of related employers) may not represent more than 20% of the total client assets managed by the QPAM at the time of the transaction. Finally, the exemption requires that neither the QPAM nor any owner, direct or indirect, of a 5% or more interest in the QPAM or an affiliate be a person who within the ten years preceding the transaction has been convicted or released from prison for certain enumerated crimes.

Recently, the DOL issued PTCE 96-23,[55] a new class exemption regarding the use of in-house asset managers

(INHAMs). PTCE 96-23 allows plans to enter into transactions with a party in interest (who is such solely by reason of its providing services to the plan, and is neither the INHAM nor a party related to the INHAM) provided that an INHAM has discretionary authority or control with respect to the plan assets involved in the transaction and additional conditions are satisfied. Those conditions include the following—

1. The terms of the transaction are negotiated on behalf of the plan by, or under the authority or general direction of, the INHAM; and either the INHAM or a property manager acting in accordance with written guidelines established and administered by the INHAM makes the decision on behalf of the plan to enter the transaction.
2. The transaction is not described in PTCE 81-6[56] (relating to securities lending arrangements); PTCE 83-1[57] (relating to acquisitions by plans of interests in mortgage pools); or PTCE 88-59[58] (relating to certain mortgage financing arrangements).
3. The transaction is not part of an agreement, arrangement or understanding designed to benefit a party in interest.
4. At the time the transaction is entered into, and at the time of any subsequent renewal or modification requiring the INHAM's consent, the terms of the transaction are at least as favorable to the plan as would be an arm's length transaction between unrelated parties.
5. An independent auditor with appropriate technical training or experience and proficiency with ERISA's fiduciary responsibility provisions must test an INHAM's practices against its written policies and procedures as well as the objective requirements of the exemption.

The exemption also provides that, notwithstanding the foregoing, a transaction involving an amount of $5 million or more, which has been negotiated on behalf of the plan by the INHAM, will not fail to satisfy the requirements of the exemption solely because the plan sponsor or its designee retains the right to veto or approve the transaction.

In addition to the general exemption, PTCE 96-23 also provides two specific exemptions with respect to real estate. The first provides that office or commercial space owned by a plan and managed by an INHAM may be leased to an employer (any of whose employees are covered by the plan or an affiliate), without constituting a prohibited transaction provided that, in addition to the requirements of the general exemption, the plan acquires the property subject to an existing lease with the employer through a foreclosure proceeding; the INHAM exercises discretionary authority in deciding on behalf of the plan to foreclose; certain conditions tied to the duration or renewal of the lease are met; and the amount of space covered by the lease does not exceed 15% of the property's rentable space.

The second special exemption provides that a plan may lease residential space to a party in interest without engaging in a prohibited transaction if, in addition to the requirements of the general exemption, the party in interest is an employee of an employer (any of whose employees are covered by the plan or an affiliate); the employee lacks discretionary authority and control with respect to the investment of plan assets; the employee is neither an officer, director nor 10% shareholder of the employer or an affiliate; the transaction was comparable to an arm's length transaction between unrelated parties; and the amount of space covered by the lease does not exceed 5% of the property's rentable space (and the aggregate space leased to all covered employees cannot exceed 10% of such rentable space).

The DOL has also issued PTCEs 83-1[59] and 88-59,[60] that permit, respectively, plan investments in first and second mortgage pools and pass-through certificates evidencing interests therein. Plans may invest in the pass-through certificates when the pool sponsor, trustee or insurer is a party in interest who plans to enter into several types of residential mortgage arrangements, including those relating to multifamily residential loans. In particular, under PTCE 88-59, plans are permitted to issue mortgage commitments, and to receive a fee therefore, to purchasers of residential dwelling units.

Where a transaction does not fall within the requirements of a PTCE, the plan fiduciaries may wish to seek an individual administrative exemption from the DOL. An individual exemption applies only to (and can only be relied upon by) the specific parties in interest named or otherwise defined in the exemption granted by the DOL involving real estate issues that typically require the involvement of an independent fiduciary to oversee the initial and ongoing phases of the transaction.

In several other prohibited transaction exemptions the DOL has permitted plans to sell illiquid real estate holdings to interested parties in order to acquire plan assets that were more amenable to individual investment decision making on a self-directed basis. For example, in PTCE 96-13,[61] the DOL authorized a proposed cash sale of improved real property by the plan to the sponsoring employer's sole shareholder, who also served as plan administrator. The plan intended to invest the proceeds in marketable securities, which would facilitate the establishment of participant-directed individual plan accounts.[62]

Recently, the DOL issued PTCE 2004-7,[63] a new class exemption allowing individual account plans sponsored by real estate investment trusts (REITs) or its affiliates to acquire, hold and sell certain publicly traded shares of beneficial interest in a REIT that is structured under state law as a business trust (trust REIT). As noted above, Section 407(a) of ERISA states that a plan may not acquire or hold an employer security that does not constitute a "qualifying employer security." Prior to PTCE 2004-7, it was not clear whether shares issued by trust REITs constituted "qualifying employer securities" under Section 407(d)(5) of ERISA. PTCE 2004-7 specifically allows individual account plans sponsored by REITs to acquire, hold and sell such shares if certain conditions are satisfied (e.g., the participant must have discretionary authority to direct the trustee to sell shares purchased by his account no less frequently than monthly). PTCE 2004-7 also describes the conditions for retroactive relief for transactions occurring up to six years prior to the date of the final exemption.[64]

Conflicts of Interest

The second type of prohibited transaction under Section 406(b) of ERISA involves the conflict-of-interest provisions. Fiduciaries cannot act where they are in a conflict-of-interest position or where there is the potential for self-dealing. As with ERISA's exclusive benefit rule, under the Section 406(b) prohibited transaction provisions, a fiduciary cannot have dual loyalties.

Some potential real estate investments, particularly those involving employment generating investment programs, raise questions under the conflict-of-interest provisions of Section 406(b). Because the facts in each of these cases are unique, the DOL has not issued prohibited transaction class exemptions, rather dealing with these issues on a case-by-case basis.

Specific steps can be taken to minimize the possibility of violating the conflict-of-interest prohibited transactions. For example, if a fiduciary (i.e., a trustee) has an interest in an employer involved in a construction project that is to be financed by a loan from the plan, or if the plan is considering participation in the loan, the fiduciary should—

1. Avoid any participation in the discussion and consideration of the proposed loan (and consider physically absenting himself from the room during these discussions)
2. Abstain from voting on whether to make the loan
3. State in the minutes that the fiduciary has not discussed the proposed loan with any other trustee, has not participated in the plan's deliberations relating to the loan or attempted to exert any influence on any trustee regarding the loan.

CONCLUSION

Investments in real estate may play an important role in an employee benefit plan's investment portfolio. However, given the unique characteristics of this asset class, the investment decision must be approached carefully and scrutinized thoroughly to determine whether it is an appropriate investment vehicle for the plan. Most plan fiduciaries will lack the specialized knowledge and experience to invest in many real estate investments. To satisfy ERISA fiduciary requirements, plan fiduciaries should seriously consider retaining a professional advisor with specific expertise in the contemplated real estate investment.

ENDNOTES

1. DOL Interpretive Bulletin 94-1, 59 *Fed. Reg.* 32,606 (June 23, 1994), codified in 29 CFR §2509.94-1 (1994).
2. ETIs should be contrasted with pure *social investing* (i.e., investing where the principal impetus is not the maximization of investment returns to benefit plan participants or their beneficiaries, but to further some other social policy or goal). Any investment policy that incorporates social or moral criteria as a primary or material consideration ahead, or in lieu, of prudent economic/investment analysis could be subject to legal challenge on the grounds that the fiduciary violated his or her duties under ERISA (i.e., the exclusive benefit rule, duty of prudence and diversification requirement). See DOL Reg. §2550.404a-1(b)(2).
3. See Robert L. Johnson Jr. and Peter R. Shepard, "Defined Contribution Pension Plans: Can the Real Estate Industry Tap This Growing Pool of Capital?," *Real Est. Rev.,* Spring 1997, at 6, 10.
4. See Bruce J. Korter, "Why Invest in Real Estate Today?," *Employee Benefits Journal,* March 1997, at 16, 16 (citing *The Handbook of Real Estate Portfolio Management,* (Joseph L. Pagliari Jr. ed., 1995)).
5. Id.
6. The DOL has provided administrative relief to some plans with illiquid real estate investments by granting exemptions from ERISA's prohibited transaction rules. For example, the DOL has granted requests by plans to sell illiquid real estate assets to parties in interest, a practice normally prohibited under Section 406 of ERISA. In Prohibited Transaction Exemption (PTE) 96-18 (61 *Fed. Reg.* 11,878 (Mar. 22, 1996)), a plan was given permission to transfer an illiquid parcel of improved real property to the sponsoring employer. Under the terms of the proposed sale, the plan would (1) receive the greater of the fair market value as represented by an average of values provided by three appraisal approaches or the fair market value of the plan's leased fee interest in the property at the time of sale, as determined by a qualified independent appraisal, and (2) not pay any commissions or expenses related to the transaction. See also PTE 96-91 (61 *Fed. Reg.* 66,333 (Dec. 17, 1996)) and PTE 96-24 (61 *Fed. Reg.* 18,159 (Apr. 24, 1996)) (each requiring fair-market valuation and no payment of fees).
7. See Jayne Elizabeth Zanglein, "High Performance Investing: Harnessing the Power of Pension Funds to Promote Economic Growth and Workplace Integrity," 11 *Lab. Law.* 59, 62-67 (1995). Although the scope of this chapter is limited to real estate investments, it should be noted that "social investing" is not so confined. ETIs may also utilize plan assets to fund small business loans, venture capital financing and private placements.

8. DOL Interpretive Bulletin 94-1, *supra* note 1.

9. See Pub. L. No. 101-273 (1990), reprinted in, 1 *U.S. Code Cong. & Admin. News,* 1990, at 104 Stat. 138 (West 1990).

10. H.R. Rep. No. 101-441 (1990), reprinted in, 4 *U.S. Code Cong. & Admin. News,* 1990, at 143, 145 (West 1990).

11. Id.

12. See Korter, *supra* note 5, at 16.

13. DOL Reg. §2510.3-101(a)(2).

14. DOL Reg. §2510.3-101(a)(2) and (b)(1)-(3).

15. DOL Reg. §2510.3-101(c)(1) and (f)(1).

16. DOL Reg. §2510.3-101(c), (d), and (e).

17. DOL Reg. §2510.3-101(e).

18. DOL Reg. §2510.3-101(j)(7) and (8).

19. See Stanley L. Iezman, "Complying with ERISA: A Primer for Pension Plan Trustees," *Real Est. Rev.,* Spring 1997, at 18, 18-19.

20. See DOL Interpretive Bulletin 94-2, 59 *Fed. Reg.* 38,860 (June 29, 1994), codified in 29 CFR §2509.94-2 (1994).

21. Iezman, *supra* note 20, at 19.

22. Id. at 20.

23. DOL Interpretive Bulletin 75-5 (June 25, 1975), codified in 29 CFR §2509.75-8 (1975). See *Whitfield v. Cohen,* 682 F.Supp. 188, 196 (S.D.N.Y. 1988) ("fiduciary must ascertain within a reasonable time whether an agent to whom he has delegated a trust power is properly carrying out his responsibilities"). See also *Martin v. Harline,* 15 EBC 1138 (D.Utah 1992).

24. See *Metzler v. Graham,* 112 F.3d 207, 209 (5th Cir. 1997).

25. DOL Interpretive Bulletin 94-1, *supra* at note 1.

26. It should be noted that many ETIs have been sponsored, established or invested in by public employee benefit funds. These plans typically are creatures of state legislatures or other governmental authorities and, as governmental plans, generally are not covered by ERISA. In fact, some states have enacted statutes *requiring* social investing of pension assets. See Zanglein, 11 *Lab. Law.* 59, 83-84. For example, in 1987 Missouri enacted legislation that required its State Employees Retirement System to invest 3-5% of its assets in small Missouri businesses. Moreover, although several states have patterned their employee benefit plan fiduciary responsibility rules after ERISA's fiduciary provisions, fiduciary standards under some state laws may be less restrictive than under ERISA. Thus, the experience of these governmental plans in the investment in ETIs does not necessarily serve as a model for ERISA benefit plans.

27. H.R. Rep. No. 101-441 (1990), reprinted in 4 *U.S. Code Cong. & Admin. News,* 1990, at 143, 148 (West 1990).

28. Notably, the diversification requirement is not implicated in the case of a Taft-Hartley housing trust. In the language of the legislative history of the 1990 amendments to LMRA, the

> diversification requirement of Part 4 (of the Title I fiduciary provisions of ERISA) is a requirement concerning the investment of plan assets, and is not applicable to the mere pay out of plan benefits. Nothing [in the bill] would require plans to provide a housing benefit in the form of a plan investment. Thus, in administering such benefits, a fiduciary would not necessarily be concerned with the diversification requirement relating to the investment of plan assets. *Id.*

29. See *Donovan v. Walton,* 609 F.Supp. 1221 (S.D. Fla. 1985), *aff'd sub. nom. Brock v. Walton,* 794 F.2d 586 (11th Cir.

1986); *Bierwirth,* 680 F.2d at 271; *Morse v. Stanley,* 732 F.2d 1139 (2d Cir. 1984). See also DOL Interpretive Bulletin 94-1, *supra* at note 1; DOL Op. No. F-3353 A (July 8, 1988).

30. In several recent rulings, the DOL has granted prohibited transaction exemptions allowing plans to take advantage of enhanced land values arising from consolidated ownership of adjacent property on facts similar to these presented in *Graham.* These exemptions permitted plans to purchase or sell adjoining parcels of property to interested parties. Exempted sales or exchanges by plans commonly provided for receipt of a premium over market price from the interested parties acquiring adjacent lots. See PTE 96-60 (61 *Fed. Reg.* 40,000 (July 31, 1996)); PTE 95-12 (60 *Fed. Reg.* 8,095 (Feb. 10, 1995)); PTE 94-72 (59 *Fed. Reg.* 51,213 (Oct. 7, 1994)); PTE 92-80 (57 *Fed. Reg.* 47,353 (Oct. 15, 1992)). But see PTE 94-65 (59 *Fed. Reg.* 45,733 (Sept. 2, 1994)) (plan would not receive premium since purchaser-employer's adjacent property had been on market for eight years but sale would still permit plan to unload an illiquid asset that had not significantly risen in value). On the opposite end are transactions such as that authorized in PTE 96-42 (61 *Fed. Reg.* 25,912 (May 23, 1996)) where the plan proposed to exchange adjacent lots with the owner and his spouse. The plan would receive Lot 1 plus a cash payment of the difference in fair market value between Lots 1 and 2, and be freed from involvement in the improvement project devised by the owner and spouse for Lot 2. In their request for an exemption, the owner and spouse represented that the transaction would improve the marketability of both lots.

31. See *In re Bicoastal Corp.,* 191 B.R. 238, 243 (Bankr. M.D. Fla. 1995), *rev'd on other grounds,* 202 B.R. 998 (M.D. Fla. 1996) (Section 404(a)(1)(B) explicitly holds fiduciaries to the standard of a prudent expert, rather than that of a prudent layman). Cf. *Donovan v. Cunningham,* 716 F.2d 1455 (5th Cir. 1983), *cert. denied,* 467 U.S. 1251 (1984) (emphasis of Section 404 is on flexibility; level of knowledge required by fiduciary varies with nature of the plan). See also Edward J. Farragher & Robert Kleiman, "How Pension Funds Make Real Estate Investment Decisions," *Real Est. Rev.,* Winter 1996, at 17, 17 (prudent expert).

32. See *Chao v. Trust Fund Advisors,* 2004 U.S. Dist. Lexis 4026 *5 (D.D.C. 2004).

33. See the discussion relating to QPAMs in footnotes 52-54 and the accompanying text, infra.

34. See *Donovan v. Guaranty Nat'l Bank,* 4 EBC 1686, 1688 (S.D. W. Va. 1983).

35. See, e.g., *Graham,* 112 F.3d at 211 n.8; *King,* 867 F.Supp. at 344 n.3; *Brock v. Citizens Bank of Clovis,* No. Civ. 83-1054 BB, 1985 WL 71535, at *4 (D.N.M. Dec. 20, 1985).

36. *King,* 867 F.Supp. at 345.

37. Id. at 344.

38. *Glass/Metal,* 507 F.Supp. at 383.

39. H.R. Rep. No. 93-1280 (1974), reprinted in *Pension & Benefits Law,* 1013, 1034 (RIA 1997).

40. Id. at 1034-35.

41. *Citizens Bank,* 1985 WL 71535, at *3.

42. See also *Brock v. Wells Fargo Bank,* 7 EBC 1221 (N.D.Cal. 1986) (trustees preliminarily enjoined from lending $4.5 million in pension funds (10-14% of total assets) to real estate developer where evidence strongly suggested that trustees did not study investment with care required under ERISA, where trustees did not appraise property or adjust appraisal to

reflect problems including lack of permits and other land use approvals, where trustees conducted no market survey, and neglected to examine possible competition, and where trustees did not consider plans for property in event of default).

43. DOL Op. No. F-3353 A (July 8, 1988).
44. DOL Interpretive Bulletin 94-1, *supra* at note 1.
45. DOL Op. No. F-2980 A (Mar. 4, 1985).
46. Section 4975 of the Internal Revenue Code contains prohibited transaction provisions analogous to the ERISA requirements that are applicable to certain qualified pension plans, IRAs, individual retirement annuities and other plans.
47. 1976-1 C.B. 357 (Jan. 1976).
48. 1977-2 C.B. 435 (July 1977).
49. See DOL Interpretive Bulletin 94-3, 59 *Fed Reg.* 66,735 (Dec. 28, 1994), codified in 29 CFR §2509.94-3 (1994) (setting forth the DOL's view that in-kind contributions (i.e., any property other than cash) that reduce an employer's contribution obligation to the plan constitute prohibited transactions under Section 4975(c)(1)(A) of the Internal Revenue Code and Section 406(a)(1)(A) of ERISA. Although the Supreme Court in *Commissioner v. Keystone Consolidated Industries, Inc.,* 508 U.S. 152 (1993) held only that an employer's contribution of unencumbered real property to a tax-qualified defined benefit pension plan in satisfaction of the employer's funding obligation is a "sale or exchange" prohibited by Section 4975(c)(1)(A) of the Code, the Interpretive Bulletin is broader than *Keystone,* applying equally with respect to in-kind contributions to plans other than defined benefit pension plans and in-kind contributions that are in excess of the statutory minimum funding obligations of Section 302 of ERISA and Section 412 of the Code. Finally, the Interpretive Bulletin reaffirms the DOL's position that the decision to accept a contribution is a fiduciary decision subject to Section 404 of ERISA.
50. See, e.g., Union Labor Life Insurance Company's (ULLICO) Mortgage Separate Account "J for Jobs" program. J for Jobs is an open-ended commingled mortgage account consisting of the pension investments of over 170 Taft-Hartley pension plans. They utilize those pension assets to provide developers financing for commercial real estate projects, with the stipulation that all work must be 100% union built. See also Zanglein, 11 *Lab. Law.* 59, 70.
51. 1976-1 C.B. 357 (January 1976).
52. 49 *Fed. Reg.* 9,494 (March 13, 1984).
53. The QPAM exemption does not provide relief from the prohibited transactions under Section 406(a)(1)(E) (acquisition on behalf of the plan of any employer security or employer real property in violation of Section 407(a)), 406 (a)(2) (holding employer securities or employer real properties that violates Section 407(a)) and 406(b) (conflicts of interest).
54. Fiduciary liability insurance carriers have begun requiring the use of a QPAM for coverage under errors and omissions policies in connection with breaches of fiduciary duty involving investments (particularly real estate investments). Under such policies, to preserve insurance coverage, plan fiduciaries will want to utilize a QPAM, even where no possible transaction between a plan and a party in interest is involved.
55. 61 *Fed. Reg.* 15,975 (Apr. 10, 1996).
56. 46 *Fed. Reg.* 7,527 (Jan. 23, 1981).
57. 48 *Fed. Reg.* 895 (Jan. 7, 1983).
58. 53 *Fed. Reg.* 24,811 (June 30, 1988).
59. 48 *Fed. Reg.* 895 (Jan. 7, 1983).
60. 53 *Fed. Reg.* 24,811 (June 30, 1988).
61. 61 *Fed. Reg.* 10,025 (Mar. 12, 1996).
62. See also PTE 96-86 (61 *Fed. Reg.* 59,467 (Nov. 22, 1996)); PTE 96-51 (61 *Fed. Reg.* 36,766 (July 12, 1996)); PTE 96-15 (61 *Fed. Reg.* 10,034 (Mar. 12, 1996)).
63. 69 *Fed. Reg.* 23,220 (April 28, 2004).
64. This exemption is generally similar to an individual exemption that was previously granted by the DOL. See *Crown American,* PTE 97-64 (yw FR 66690 (12/19/97)).

Chapter 9

Fiduciary Responsibility in Appointment, Monitoring and Removal of Trustees

Marc Gertner

Although hundreds of books and articles have been written and thousands of speeches have been given over the past 20 years on the fiduciary aspects or fiduciary responsibility of almost all phases of the operation and administration of employee benefit plans subject to ERISA, very little has been written or said about the fiduciary aspects of the appointment, monitoring and removal of Taft-Hartley trustees. Many knowledgeable trustees and service providers do not even realize that the appointment, monitoring and removal processes have fiduciary considerations. If the trustees are the named fiduciaries of their plans, they must be knowledgeable in this area.

FIDUCIARY CONSIDERATIONS IN APPOINTMENT OR REMOVAL OF TRUSTEES

The matter of the appointment and removal of trustees is always contained in the agreement and declaration of trust that governs the operation of the plan. The most common provisions are that the local union (or equivalent) has the power to appoint and remove the union trustees and the employer association (or equivalent) has the same powers with regard to the employer trustees. Frequently, this is all that is said or considered with regard to this vital aspect of the plan's organization and operation.

Under these facts, the employer association and the local union, as plan co-sponsors, are fiduciaries, albeit limited fiduciaries. In the matter of the appointment of their respective trustees and in monitoring those appointees, the sponsors have fiduciary status.

The authority for this is Department of Labor Regulation Section 2509.75-8, D-4. This is part of a question and answer interpretive bulletin originally issued October 6, 1975. The question posed was:

D-4 Q: In the case of a plan established and maintained by an employer, are members of the board of directors of the employer fiduciaries with respect to the plan?

The answer is:

A: Members of the board of directors of an employer which maintains an employee benefit plan will be fiduciaries only to the extent that they have responsibility for the functions described in section 3(21)(A) of the Act. *For example, the board of directors may be responsible for the selection and retention of plan fiduciaries. In such case, members of the board of directors exercise "discretionary authority or discretionary control respecting management of such plan" and are, therefore, fiduciaries with respect to the plan. However, their responsibility, and, consequently, their liability, is limited to the selection and retention of fiduciaries* (apart from co-fiduciary liability arising under circumstances described in section 405(a) of the Act)....

The IRS notes that it would reach the same answer to this question under section 4975(e)(3) of the Internal Revenue Code of 1954. [Emphasis added.]

To the extent an association or a union, by either the chief executive officer, the board of trustees, the executive board or whomever, possesses or exercises the legal authority to appoint (and to continue the appointment of) trustees, he, she, it or they are ERISA Section 3(21)(A) fiduciaries, albeit with an area of fiduciary responsibility limited to the selection, monitoring and/or removal of their named fiduciaries.

This means that with regard to the appointment and

retention of trustees, the appointing person or body must comply with ERISA Section 404(a). That is, the appointer must act solely in the interest of the plan's participants, to maximize benefits and minimize the reasonable and necessary expenses of administration, as ERISA prudent men in accordance with the plan document.

INTERFERENCE WITH RESPECTIVE RIGHTS OF APPOINTMENT

One of the very few restrictions imposed by ERISA, Taft-Hartley, etc., upon the discretion of unions and associations in their selection of trustees, one of the first and most explicit, is found in *Quad City Builders Association, Inc. v. Tri City Bricklayers Union No. 7, AFL-CIO*, 431 F.2d 999 (8th Cir. 1970). This was an action brought by the builders' association for declaratory judgment that the trust fund, which was established by the union and several mason contractors and which was contributed to by the association, was being administered in violation of the statute. The District Court for the Southern District of Iowa (302 F.Supp. 1031) entered a judgment for the association, which the union appealed. The court of appeals held, *inter alia*, that the trust fund did not comply with the statute requiring that employees and employers be equally represented in the administration of a health and welfare fund.

The court held that where, under a collective bargaining agreement, the builders' association was required to contribute to a health and welfare fund, which by prior trust agreement was administered by three representatives from union and three from ten mason contractors, eight of which were union members who at times served as employees, the election of management trustees by the ten mason contractors did not conform to the equal representation requirement of the statute. Therefore, the court held that the two nonunion mason contractor trustees were enjoined from acting as employer trustees unless and until reappointed by fair election proceedings conforming to statute.

Finally, the court ruled that any plan for electing the management trustees of the health and welfare fund should be so designed that active union members, who at times serve as employers and at times serve as employees, do not have a dominant voice in the election of the management trustees.

The U.S. District Court for the District of Columbia, in *Mason Contractors Association of America v. International Council of Employers of Bricklayers & Allied Craftsmen*, 853 F.Supp. 515 (D.C. 1994), questioned the validity of *Quad City Builders* and *Mobile Mechanical*. Although the court in *Mason Contractors* refused to render an opinion on the issues because the court found that it did not have jurisdiction, *Mason Contractors* recognized that the factual situation presented gave rise to the potential for union control over management trustees. The court refused to render a decision on whether such potential was sufficient to violate the equal representation rule of the Labor-Management Relations Act of 1947 (LMRA), but stated that there was no evidence to support a finding of actual dominion or control by the union. The court in *Mason Contractors* also walked through a discussion of the *Amax* and *Demisay* cases (discussed below). The *Mason Contractors* case also refused to follow and rejected a *per se* violation rule established in the *Associated General Contractors* case (discussed below) that, whenever employer trustees representing rival associations not a party to the original trust are added to the board of trustees without the consent of the original employer association, it is a *per se* violation of LMRA Section 302(c)(5).

Local 144 Nursing Home Pension Fund v. Demisay, 508 U.S. 581 (1993), involved a jurisdictional issue and did not directly reach a determination on the selection of trustees. In *NLRB v. Amax Coal Company*, 453 U.S. 322 (1981), the court noted in the dissenting opinion that the equal employer representation rule was intended to offset possible union dominance of the fund and to prevent mismanagement or misuse of the fund by union officials—not to simply provide the employer with a voice, but to ensure that contributions are used for the welfare of employees. Although the holdings of these cases are not directly relevant, each of these cases is a Supreme Court case that deals in part with the equal representation rule under LMRA Section 302(c)(5).

In *Denver Metropolitan Association of Plumbing, Heating, Cooling Contractors v. Journeyman Plumbers & Gas Fitters Local No. 3 & Pipefitters Local No. 208*, 586 F.2d 1367 (10th Cir. 1978), members of an employer's negotiating association brought action challenging contributions made to pension funds by employers that were not members of the association. The District Court for the District of Colorado entered judgment in favor of the unions, and the employers appealed. The court of appeals held that: (1) The contributions did not violate the collective bargaining agreement or the trust agreements; (2) the contributions were being made as specified in written agreement as required by statute; and (3) the fact that the nonmember employers did not have a voice in the selection of the employer trustees did not violate the statutory requirement that employees and employers be equally represented in the administration of such funds.

In dictum, the court held that the
Purpose of statutory provision for equal employer-employee representation in trust funds is to protect the interest of employees from exploitation by unscrupulous union officials. . . .

So long as employer trustees are totally independent of the domination of the unions, there is no reason why each contributing employer must be a direct participant in the trustee selection process if the employer is willing to contract away that right; provisions of Labor Management Relations Act were not violated by the fact that contributions to the funds were being made by employees who were not members of the employer's negotiating association and who had no voice in the selection of the employer-trustees....

In *Ader v. Hughes,* 570 F.2d 303 (10th Cir. 1978), an appeal was taken from an order of the District Court for the District of Colorado holding that a dispute regarding the amending of a union welfare trust agreement, as to which the trustees were deadlocked, was a matter of trust "administration," which must be allowed to go to an impartial umpire.

The court ruled on a collateral issue, as follows: The legality of the amendments were not an issue before the district court. The parties did not make them an issue. The amendment dealing with employer trustee appointment is an attempt at union participation in the choice of an employer representative. Such participation has been forbidden elsewhere as contrary to the scheme of the LMRA. See *Associated Contractors v. Laborers, supra; Quad City Builders Association v. Tri City Bricklayers Union No. 7, AFL-CIO,* 431 F.2d 999 (8th Cir. 1970). Without the benefit of arguments on the question, however, we are not in a position to judge the legality of the proposed amendments.

In *Holcomb v. United Automotive Association of St. Louis, Inc. et al.,* 852 F.2d 330 (8th Cir. 1988), a beneficiary of a pension plan, established by the trust agreement executed by the union and the employer association, brought an action for declaratory injunctive relief alleging the plan was administered and maintained in a manner violating ERISA and the structural requirements of the Labor-Management Relations Act of 1947 (LMRA), as amended. On cross-motions of plaintiff and defendants for summary judgment, the district court granted the motions in part and denied in part, and an appeal was taken. The court of appeals held that: (1) The equal representation provision of LMRA was applicable to the employer trust fund and pension plan, and (2) the pension plan violated the structural requirements of LMRA, where the union had no representation among trustees.

In *Kyhl v. A-One Plumbing, Inc. et al.,* 679 F.Supp. 991 (E.D.Mo. 1988), the court held that "unequal" representation in the administration of the employee trust fund could not excuse the employers' failure to make required contributions to the employee benefit fund in a collection action and if the trust fund did indeed violate the equal representation requirements of LMRA, the employers could, and should, file a suit for injunctive relief.

In the important and oft-cited *Mobile Mechanical Contractors Association, Inc. v. Carlough,* 456 F.Supp. 310 (S.D.Ala. 1978), the court held:

... To allow the union to participate in any degree in the selection of employer trustees is unlawful under Section 302. *Blassie v. Kroger Co.,* 345 F.2d 58, 72 (8th Cir. 1965); *Quad City Builders Association v. Tri City Bricklayers Union No. 7, AFL-CIO,* 431 F.2d 999, 1003 (8th Cir. 1970).

On a hearing on preliminary injunction in *Mobile Mechanical,* the court quoted extensively and with approval from the *Quad City* opinion. See also *Motor Carriers Labor Advisory Council v. Trucking Management, Inc.,* 711 F.Supp. 216 (E.D.Pa. 1989).

Another landmark case in point is *Associated Contractors of Essex County, Inc. v. Laborers International Union of North America,* 559 F.2d 222 (3rd Cir. 1977). In this case, an employers' association and its trustees on the boards of employee welfare and pension funds brought an action under LMRA challenging the validity of amendments to the trust agreements and actions taken pursuant thereto. The district court entered partial summary judgment for defendants, and plaintiffs appealed. The court of appeals held, *inter alia,* that the equal representation clause of the act was violated when the employer trustees representing a rival association, not a party to the original trust agreement, were added to the board without the consent of the original employer association.

The court stated that the

Goal of equal representation in administration and control of [employee welfare and pension] trust funds is defeated if union in any degree participates in choice of employer representatives or by any arrangement which creates possibility of union domination; essence of equal representation is that each side have veto power on any proposed action.

The rule is clear. Neither side can have any voice, any role or any authority in the appointment of trustees by the other side of the table. Subject to this rather obvious and not very profound limitation, the basic rule of selection of trustees by unions and associations is that they may pick anyone they want, subject to their fiduciary duties under Section 404(a) and subject to the rule in *Quad City.*

TENURE OF APPOINTMENT

Generally, nothing is said in the trust agreement beyond the fact that the trustee shall serve until death, disability, retirement or removal by the appointing plan sponsor. In recent years, the tenure of the appointments has drawn increased scrutiny by the courts and has resulted in a corollary rule that lifetime appointments (i.e., appointments without removal rights at the will of the appointing party) violate the Taft-Hartley Act and

ERISA. In *Teamsters Local No. 145 v. Kuba,* 631 F.Supp. 1063 (U.S.D.C. Conn. 1986), the local union sought to permit replacement of union representatives on the board of trustees of a local health services and insurance fund. The dispute was between rival factions of Teamsters Local No. 145. The trust agreement governing the subject health and welfare plan provided for governance by a four-person board of trustees, two to be appointed by the local union and two to be appointed by the contributing employers. The trust agreement originally provided that trustees would serve until death, disability, resignation or removal. On June 15, 1985, the trustees voted to amend the trust agreement to provide that each trustee would continue to serve until death, incapacity or removal for "proper and just cause only."

In considering whether the June 15, 1985 amendment constituted a structural violation of Section 302(c)(5) of LMRA, the court noted that there was authority for the propositions of law that:

(a) the court has authority to examine the amendment, its purposes and effects to determine whether it is arbitrary or unreasonable or, stated differently, whether the amendment was devoid of any rational nexus or relationship to the requirements of Section 302(c);

(b) the court must disallow the amendment if it has no rationale nexus to the requirements of Section 302(c), but actually frustrates those requirements.

The court, in a deliberate and considered opinion, concluded that the "for proper and just cause" amendment provided sufficient potential for abuse to make it a violation of LMRA Section 302 and, further, that it was devoid of a rational nexus or relationship to the requirements of Section 302.

Partenza v. Brown, 14 F.Supp. 2d 493 (S.D.N.Y. 1998), cites and supports the *Kuba* case and bolsters the notion that indefinite tenure and removal "only for just cause" are violations of ERISA. In addition, the case held that a cumbersome and time-consuming removal process contributes to the factual basis for the violation of the ERISA prohibition on excess entrenchment of trustees. *Partenza* also cites and supports the *Daugherty* case (discussed below) and supports but distinguishes the *Joint Council 18* case (discussed below) on its facts. *Partenza* also cites *Levy v. Local Union No. 810,* 20 F.3d 516 (2d Cir. 1994), a Second Circuit case that is similar in holding to the *Daugherty* case.

In *Mobile, Alabama-Pensacola, Florida Building and Construction Trades Council v. Daugherty,* 684 F.Supp. 270 (D.C.Ala. S.D. 1988), union members who were business representatives of local unions brought action to remove trustees of the local's pension and welfare plans following the election of new trustees. Initially, the employer association and the building trades council had the power to appoint and to remove trustees of the companion pension and welfare plans. Later, the respective trust agreements were amended to provide that trustees would serve until death, incapacity, resignation or removal for misfeasance, malfeasance or nonfeasance in the execution of the trust pursuant to an elaborate procedure set forth in the agreement.

The court, with excellent analysis and citation of authority, concluded:

19. Under either plan (welfare or pension) the trustees are appointed for lifetime tenures absent incapacity, resignation or removal for malfeasance, misfeasance or non-feasance. Based upon the DOL Pension and Welfare Benefits Opinion Letter 85-41A and the deference to be accorded such opinion, this Court HOLDS THAT THE WELFARE AND PENSION PLANS' PROVISIONS FOR THE LIFETIME APPOINTMENT TENURES FOR THE TRUSTEES (UNION TRUSTEES AND EMPLOYER TRUSTEES ALIKE) ABSENT INCAPACITY, RESIGNATION, OR REMOVAL FOR MALFEASANCE, MISFEASANCE OR NON-FEASANCE ARE CONTRARY TO THE POLICIES OF ERISA AND ARE THUS LEGALLY VOID.

684 F.Supp. at 278-79 (capitalization by the court).

Later, the court repeated its opinion:

25. The Court HOLDS THAT A LIFETIME TERM OF APPOINTMENT FOR A PENSION PLAN OR WELFARE PLAN TRUSTEE VIOLATES THE FIDUCIARY RESPONSIBILITY PROVISIONS OF ERISA.

684 F.Supp. at 280 (capitalization by the court).

The court discussed at length and quoted from the *Kuba* decision, *supra,* and concluded as follows:

28. This Court holds that the Plans' provisions that trustees can be removed only upon death, resignation, incapacity, or malfeasance, misfeasance, non-feasance or conviction of a felony "clearly poses sufficient 'potential of abuse' to render [them] unenforceable under section 302" of the LMRA. This Court holds that for the plans *sub judice* to comply with §302(c)(5) of the LMRA the trustees must be removable *at will* by the group which the trustee represents, i.e., the Mobile, Alabama-Pensacola, Florida Building and Construction Trades Council should be able to remove at will the Union-appointed trustees and the Mobile Chapter of the Associated General Contractors of America, Inc. should be able to remove *at will* the Employer-appointed trustees. 684 F.Supp. at 280 (emphasis by the court).

An interesting case in point is *International Brotherhood of Teamsters Joint Council 18 v. New York State Teamsters Council Health and Hospital Fund,* 903 F.2d

919 (2d Cir. 1990). This case involved a collectively bargained, jointly trusteed, employee welfare benefit plan. Initially, Joint Council No. 18, I.B.T. selected all union trustees for terms of four years. Employer trustees were selected by and subject to removal by participating employers. In February 1988, the trustees amended the procedures for selecting and removing trustees. Whenever a vacancy exists for a union trustee, the three New York State joint councils nominate a potential new union trustee, who is then selected by the majority vote of the existing union trustees. Union trustees continue to serve for four-year terms "unless removed by the unanimous vote of the remaining existing employee trustees." Employer trustees serve without time limit on their terms but are subject to removal by a vote of two-thirds of the contributing employers.

The court found no violations of Section 305(c)(5) or of ERISA under the amendment and the changed procedures. The court also distinguished both *Kuba* and *Daugherty,* holding as follows:

> Seeking to support their argument that the amendment violates the "equally represented" standard of §302, Joint Council 18 and Olivadoti point to two district court cases: *Mobile, Alabama-Pensacola, Florida Building and Construction Trades Council v. Daugherty,* 684 F.Supp. 270 (S.D. Ala. 1988), and *Teamsters Local No. 145 v. Kuba,* 631 F.Supp. 1063 (D.Conn. 1986). However, in both these cases, where courts rejected amendments to provisions for appointment and removal of trustees, employee trustees had adopted provisions designed to prevent their own removal. The amendment that Joint Council and Olivadoti contest has the opposite effect—it makes easier the removal of employee trustees and is therefore consistent with the objectives of §302.

Also of interest and support of this position are *Associated General Contractors of Essex County v. Laborers International Union of North America, Local 32, 699 and 112 et al.,* 559 F.2d 222 (3rd Cir. 1977); *Nixon v. O'Callaghan,* 392 F.Supp. 1081 (D.C.S.D.N.Y. 1975). (When an action is commenced in federal court alleging that trustees of a Taft-Hartley employee benefit plan and trust have enacted a regulation which, on its face or as applied, is in contravention of the "structural" requirements of LMRA, the courts have the inherent power to examine the regulation, its purposes and effects, and determine whether it is arbitrary and unreasonable; that is, whether the regulation is devoid of any rational nexus or relationship to the requirement of the statute.)

The Department of Labor is in accord with these decisions. In Advisory Opinion 85-41A, the Department stated:

> . . . However, the Department is generally of the view that a lifetime term of appointment for a pension fund trustee would be inconsistent with ERISA's fiduciary responsibility provisions.

Later, the Department added that:

> The Department believes the principles outlined above may be frustrated where a plan sponsor that appoints a trustee can appoint a successor trustee only upon successfully bringing such charges as misfeasance or incapacity to perform the duties of the position. Under section 404(a)(1)(D) of ERISA, fiduciaries are required to act in accordance with the plan documents and instruments, but only insofar as they are consistent with titles I and IV of ERISA. Thus, in the Department's view, the fiduciaries of a plan cannot lawfully rely upon a plan provision to the extent it would purport to establish a trustee's term of appointment as lifetime.

> We do not intend to suggest that trustees should serve only at will. Limited terms, such as for a specified number of years, that are reasonable under the facts and circumstances of the plan generally would be consistent with ERISA.

DUTY TO MONITOR TRUSTEES

Generally, there is a paucity of authority on the issue of appointment, removal and monitoring of named fiduciaries. In Department of Labor Regulation §2509.75-8, FR-17, the question is asked:

FR-17 Q: What are the ongoing responsibilities of a fiduciary who has appointed trustees or other fiduciaries with respect to these appointments?

A: At reasonable intervals the performance of trustees and other fiduciaries should be reviewed by the appointing fiduciary in such manner as may be reasonably expected to ensure that their performance has been in compliance with the terms of the plan and statutory standards, and satisfies the needs of the plan. No single procedure will be appropriate in all cases; the procedure adopted may vary in accordance with the nature of the plan and other facts and circumstances relevant to the choice of the procedure.

In addition, there are analogies in the common law and under ERISA that provide insight into the issue.

The first analogy is to the liability or absence of liability of one engaging a true independent contractor to provide a service. In most jurisdictions, if the owner-employer exercises prudence and due care in selecting and engaging a true independent contractor to practice the latter's profession, the owner-employer is not liable for the acts or omissions of the independent contractor. The test for the hirer is prudence and due care in the selection process, not the ultimate conduct. The same is true of labor and management plan co-sponsors in the trustee selection process.

Another test, and one closer to home for most Taft-Hartley named fiduciaries, is the analogy to ERISA Section 405 (d)(1) and (2). If the plan document allows it, the trustees may designate an ERISA Section 3(38) investment manager to manage plan assets. To the extent they do so, the trustees are entitled to the benefit of the exculpation language in Section 405(d)(1), to wit:

> (d)(1) If an investment manager or managers have been appointed under section 402(c)(3), then, notwithstanding subsections (a)(2) and (3) and subsection (b), no trustee shall be liable for the acts or omissions of such investment manager or managers, or be under an obligation to invest or otherwise manage any asset of the plan which is subject to the management of such investment manager.

This exculpation is subject to the provisions of Section 405(d)(2), to wit:

> (2) Nothing in this subsection shall relieve any trustee of any liability under this part for any act of such trustee.

This has generally been accepted to mean that if the trustees exercise prudence:

1. In the selection of the investment manager
2. In developing investment guidelines for the investment manager to follow and
3. In monitoring the performance of the investment manager,

then, and in those events, the trustees have fulfilled their general fiduciary duties and are entitled to the exculpation provisions of Section 405(d)(1). By analogy, if the union and the associations, in connection with trustee selection, exercise Section 404(a)(1)(B) prudence:

1. In selecting a trustee
2. In creating the scope and sphere of the trustee's conduct and
3. In monitoring the performance of the trustee,

THEN, and in that event, the trustees have no liability.

Liss v. Smith, 991 F.Supp. 278 (S.D.N.Y. 1998), dealt with fiduciaries who had engaged in repeated and significant fiduciary violations. In part, the court's holding supported the principle that an individual with the authority to appoint and remove trustees may be held liable for the fiduciary breach of those trustees over which he or she holds the appointment and removal powers based on such powers. The court held that the power to appoint and remove trustees carries with it the concomitant duty to monitor their performance and to take action upon discovery of improper performance. Under the *Liss* holding, a failure to monitor appointees and to remove nonperforming fiduciaries renders the appointing fiduciary jointly and severally liable for the appointee's breaches. The opinion supports and refers favorably to the *Daugherty* and *Joint Council 18* cases.

In *Howell v. Motorola,* 337 F.Supp. 2d 1079, at 1095-1099 (N.D. Ill. 2004), the court found that the weight of authority imposes a duty on those with the power to appoint, retain and remove plan fiduciaries to monitor such fiduciaries and possibly to even prevent wrongful conduct. The court rejected the argument that those with appointment power were simply required to appoint persons with the appropriate level of education, knowledge and experience. In *re AEP Litigation,* 327 F.Supp. 2d 812, at 832-833 (S.D. Ohio 2004), stated that "there can be no doubt that the ERISA statutory scheme imposes a duty to monitor upon fiduciaries when they appoint other persons to make decisions about the plan." The court recognized that the duty to monitor is implicit in the power to appoint and remove plan fiduciaries.

In our experience, only a very, very small number of Taft-Hartley plan sponsors in fact monitor the fiduciary performance of the trustees they appoint. Those that do, do so only in a very informal manner. The issue of an alleged breach of fiduciary duty with regard to the failure to monitor the trustees appointed by the plan's sponsors is paramount in a major ERISA proceeding in federal court in Detroit.

All plan sponsors of all Taft-Hartley employee benefit plans would be well advised to review and, to the extent necessary, revise the steps and procedures they currently employ in the appointment, monitoring and removal of trustees of Taft-Hartley plans.

Chapter 10

Fiduciary Responsibility and Potential Liabilities in the Managed Care World

Thomas F. Fitzgerald, Robert A. Imes and Jon Bourgault

As fiduciaries of welfare plans subject to the Employee Retirement Income Security Act of 1974 (ERISA), multiemployer fund trustees face the difficult task of establishing efficient cost-containment and administrative strategies for their plans in ways that pose the fewest legal risks to plans and fiduciaries. This chapter discusses some current fiduciary issues relating to plan design, claims decision making, plan service provider selection and other matters of interest to plan trustees.

PLAN DESIGN

Given that health plan costs are continuing to rise rapidly, plan trustees often find it necessary to review their plans' designs and make changes. While making plan amendments generally is not considered a fiduciary activity under ERISA, implementing the changes may carry fiduciary obligations. Moreover, plan amendments affecting plan benefits are subject to federal law requirements as well as state law requirements if the plan funds its benefits through the purchase of insurance.

Fiduciary Versus Settlor Acts

Generally speaking, plan design decisions under ERISA are regarded as settlor, rather than fiduciary, acts. As such, plan trustees wear their employer and union representative "hats" rather than their ERISA fiduciary "hats" when they make plan design determinations. For example, in *Curtis-Wright v. Schoonejongen,* 514 U.S. 73 (1995), a group of retirees challenged their former employer's decision to amend its retiree health plan by eliminating benefits in certain instances. In its opinion, the Supreme Court emphasized that "[e]mployers or other plan sponsors are generally free under ERISA, for any reason at any time, to adopt, modify, or terminate welfare plans." Subsequent cases have made clear that these settlor decisions ordinarily do not subject the plan sponsor to fiduciary liability under ERISA. *Hughes Aircraft Co. v. Jacobson,* 525 U.S. 755 (1999); *Lockheed Corp. v. Spink,* 517 U.S. 882 (1996).

In the past, some authorities had held that plan design decisions made by multiemployer plan trustees (in contrast to decisions made by single employer plan trustees) could be fiduciary in nature because multiemployer trustees administer the plan asset pool to which separate employers have contributed. Thus, under this view, the trustees exercised discretion over what are necessarily plan assets. E.g., *Siskind v. Sperry Ret. Program, Unisys,* 47 F.3d 498 (2d Cir. 1995). However, following *Curtis-Wright, Hughes* and *Lockheed,* courts have tended to reject this distinction and regard plan design changes made by multiemployer plan trustees as settlor in nature. E.g., *Hartline v. Sheet Metal Workers' Nat'l Pension Fund,* 286 F.3d 598 (D.C.Cir. 2002); *Walling v. Brady,* 125 F.3d 114 (3d Cir. 1997). Nonetheless, in Field Assistance Bulletin 2002-2 (Nov. 4, 2002), the Department of Labor (DOL) stated that, in the multiemployer plan context, acts that are ordinarily settlor in nature will be regarded as fiduciary in nature if relevant documents such as collective bargaining agreements, trust documents and plan documents indicate that the plan trustees act as fiduciaries in making these determinations. On the other hand, if the relevant documents are silent, the trustees' act will be regarded as settlor. *Id.*

In addition, it should be noted plan design decisions that ordinarily would be viewed as settlor in nature if made by the plan trustees may be viewed as fiduciary in nature if unilaterally made by a plan service provider. For example, it has been alleged in some recent class actions that pharmacy benefit managers (PBMs) acted as fiduciaries by exercising final control over the drug formulary offered by the plans.

Benefit Design

There are a number of benefit features plan trustees may consider adopting in order to control plan costs. For example, these may include plan provisions that impose waiting periods before preexisting conditions are covered, create cost-sharing requirements (e.g., copayments and coinsurance), limit out-of-network coverage, and/or exclude certain benefits altogether (e.g., cosmetic surgeries and experimental treatments). It is important to note the plan's freedom in designing benefits may be constrained by substantive mandates contained in federal law including, but by no means limited to, preexisting condition limitations and mental health parity requirements. ERISA §§701, 712.

If the plan insures its benefits, state law requirements may also apply since ERISA §514 saves state insurance law mandates from federal preemption. For example, in *Kentucky Association of Health Plans, Inc. v. Miller*, 538 U.S. 329 (2003), the Supreme Court upheld a state "any willing provider" (AWP) law as a saved insurance law. The Kentucky AWP statute had prohibited health insurers from discriminating against any providers practicing in the plans' geographic service area that were willing to abide by the insurers' terms and conditions for network participation. In effect, the Kentucky law hindered insurers in restricting the size of their provider networks. See also *Met. Life Ins. Co. v. Mass.*, 471 U.S. 724 (1985) (state law mental health mandates saved from ERISA preemption).

Disclosing Plan Benefits

Of course, implementing a plan design change may carry fiduciary implications since this is a matter of plan administration. E.g., DOL, *Guidance on Settlor v. Plan Expenses*, available at: www.dol.gov/ebsa/regs/AOs/settlor_guidance.html. In particular, care should be taken to accurately disclose plan terms in summary plan descriptions (SPDs) and other plan communications in a manner that is easily understood by plan participants. Cf. 29 CFR §2520.101-2. In that regard, participant cost-sharing requirements continue to spur class action lawsuits. One variation on this theme involves plans that provide for participant cost-sharing based on a percentage of the provider's usual and customary charges, rather than a percentage of the discounted charges that the plans actually pay to network providers. Plaintiffs have claimed they were misled about copayment responsibilities and that they should have had their percentage copayments based on the discounted charges. E.g., *Corsini v. United HealthCare Services, Inc.*, 145 F.Supp. 2d 184 (D.R.I. 2001). Other cases have involved claims that plan communications failed to clearly disclose that sometimes participant copayments would exceed a prescription drug's actual costs, and that participants were entitled to the excess of the copayment over the drug's cost. *Alves v. Harvard Pilgrim Health Care, Inc.*, 204 F.Supp. 2d 198 (D.Mass. 2002), *aff'd*, 316 F.3d 290 (1st Cir. 2003). The key to avoiding these types of controversies is to ensure that plan communications are clearly written and not ambiguous. For example, some plans now provide for flat dollar copayments (e.g., a $10 copayment for certain services) to avoid disputes over whether a percentage copayment is based on billed or discounted charges.

CLAIMS DECISIONS

Deciding claims and resolving benefit disputes present a number of challenges for plan trustees. In any event, though, courts typically give a good deal of deference to a plan's benefit decisions and ERISA provides substantial protection to those persons involved in the claims decision process.

Fiduciary Status of Claims Decision Maker

As noted by the Supreme Court, the language of ERISA §503 "strongly suggests that the ultimate decision maker in a plan regarding an award of benefits must be a fiduciary and must be acting as a fiduciary when determining a participant's or beneficiary's claim." *Aetna Health, Inc. v. Davila*, 542 U.S. 200 (2004). See also *Varity Corp. v. Howe*, 516 U.S. 489 (1996) (fiduciary duties apply "with respect to the interpretation of plan documents and the payment of claims"). In addition, the DOL claims procedure regulation implementing §503 appears to require that even persons deciding first-level appeals as part of a two-level appeals process be named fiduciaries. 29 CFR §2560.503-1(h).

With respect to initial benefit determinations, some federal courts of appeal and DOL generally regard these decisions as "ministerial" rather than fiduciary acts because the claims processor's discretion is limited. E.g., *Blue Cross & Blue Shield of Ala. v. Sanders*, 138 F.3d 1347 (11th Cir. 1998); *IT Corp. v. Gen. American Life Ins. Co.*, 107 F.3d 1415, 1420 (9th Cir. 1997); 29 CFR §2509.75-8, D-2. Nonetheless, other courts have held that a person without appeal responsibility for denied claims, but with final authority in connection with claims that are granted on the initial benefit determination, acts as a fiduciary. E.g., *Klosterman v. Western Gen. Mgmt., Inc.*, 32 F.3d 1119 (7th Cir. 1994); *Fed'n of Unions Local 102 Health & Welf. Fund v. Equitable Life Assur. Soc'y*, 841 F.2d 658 (5th Cir. 1988).

In practice, self-funded plans address the need for a named fiduciary for claims appeals in a variety of fashions, generally depending on the level of involvement the trustees want in the process. In some cases, the plan trustees or a committee composed of trustees make all appeals decisions. Alternatively, the trustees may designate the plan's third-party administrator as the named fiduciary for appeals. See ERISA §402(b) (allowing delegation of fiduciary responsibilities). And finally, if a two-level appeals process is provided by the plan, the trustees may direct the third-party administrator to handle the first level, while they handle the second (final) level of appeals. Of course, if the plan is insured, the insurer typically acts as the plan's fiduciary for all appeals.

Claims Procedure

Both initial benefit determinations and appeals decisions are governed by the DOL claims procedure regulation. 29 CFR §2560.503-1. The claims procedure regulation as originally promulgated in 1977 provided one time line for all types of ERISA-covered claims—pension, health, disability, etc.—regardless of the urgency in determining such claims. However, with the rise of managed care practices in the 1980s and 1990s, it became increasingly clear that a one-size-fits-all claims procedure was not as practical as it had once been, especially with respect to health claims. Thus, DOL revised the claims procedure regulation, effective for plans no later than January 1, 2003. The revised procedure set forth special time frames for deciding health and disability plan claims that differed from those used for all other types of claims (e.g., pension and life insurance). In particular, initial benefit determinations and appeals for health claims are now subject to different time limits depending on whether the claims were preservice, postservice, concurrent care or urgent care.

Of particular relevance to fiduciaries making appeals decisions, urgent care claims must be decided within 72 hours, preservice claims within 30 days and postservice claims within 60 days. If a multiemployer plan has a board of trustees or a committee that meets at least quarterly to hear appeals, postservice claims generally must be heard at the board's next meeting, unless the appeal request comes within 30 days before the board's meeting. In that case, the appeal may be deferred until the next quarterly meeting. If special circumstances (such as the need to hold an oral hearing) so require, an appeal may even be deferred to the third quarterly meeting after the appeal request has been received, provided the claimant is given notice of the special circumstances and the date by which the appeal will be made. As a practical matter, the strict time frame for deciding urgent care appeals has caused many plans to consider delegating responsibility for at least these decisions to their third-party administrators.

External Review

In the second half of the 1990s, states increasingly began to require that health insurance policies allow covered persons to have independent medical experts, outside of their insurers, review health claims that were denied based on medical necessity grounds or experimental status. Initially, there was some question whether these laws were preempted under ERISA §§502 or 514. In *Rush Prudential HMO, Inc. v. Moran,* 536 U.S. 355 (2002), the Supreme Court ruled that the Illinois external review statute was an insurance law saved from ERISA preemption under §514 and that it did not create an alternative enforcement mechanism to §502(a)(1)(B). In that regard, the Court noted that the external review decision would be enforced through an ERISA claim for benefits. Cf. *Hawaii Mgmt. Alliance Ass'n v. Ins. Comm'r,* 100 P.3d 952 (2004) (ERISA preempts state law purporting to enforce external review decisions through state law remedy).

Currently, some self-funded plans voluntarily provide for external review after a participant exhausts the appeals process under ERISA §503. These plans typically view external review as providing participants and the plans themselves with a useful means for resolving benefit disputes without having to resort to expensive and time-consuming litigation. It is important to note that the DOL claims procedure provides that self-funded plans cannot require that plan members participate in additional levels of appeal such as external review. If members do elect external review, no fees may be charged to them for the review, and the plan must waive any statute of limitations or other timeliness defense it may have while the review is pending. 29 CFR §2560.503-1(c)(3).

Judicial Review of Claims Decisions

Courts typically give considerable deference to the benefit decisions made by plan fiduciaries when participants sue for benefits under ERISA §502(a)(1)(B). In *Firestone Tire & Rubber Company v. Bruch,* 489 U.S. 101 (1989), the Supreme Court held that where the plan documents confer discretion on a plan fiduciary to determine eligibility or construe terms, the fiduciary's decision is typically reviewed only to determine whether the decision was an "abuse of discretion" or "arbitrary and capricious." In other words, a court's review in this circumstance is limited to whether the fiduciary's decision was reasonable or was supported by substantial evidence. In contrast, if no discretion has been granted by plan documents, the court's review will be "de novo," or without any deference to the decision made by the plan fiduciary.

Following *Firestone,* many courts exerted significant efforts in deciphering whether plans contained appropriate language granting discretion to plan administrators in making benefit decisions. In *Herzberger v. Standard Ins. Co.*, 205 F.3d 327 (2000), the Seventh Circuit suggested the following safe harbor language be used in plan documents to make clear when discretion has been granted: "Benefits under this plan will be paid only if the plan administrator decides in his discretion that the applicant is entitled to them."

In addition, the lower courts have taken note of *Firestone's* dicta suggesting that if a fiduciary operates under a conflict of interest, this fact should be taken into consideration in determining the level of deference owed to the fiduciary's benefit decision. E.g., *Torres v. Pittston Co.*, 346 F.3d 1324 (11th Cir. 2004). Courts differ in their evaluation of the benefit determination of a conflicted fiduciary; some adopt a "sliding scale" approach under which a deferential standard is always applied but deference to the fiduciary's decision is decreased in proportion to the seriousness of the conflict. E.g., *Martin v. Blue Cross & Blue Shield of Va., Inc.*,115 F.3d 1201 (4th Cir. 1997). Other courts apply a "presumptively void" test, under which, if a claimant shows material, probative evidence suggesting a fiduciary's self-interest amounted to a breach of fiduciary duty, the fiduciary must then come forward with evidence that the conflict of interest did not cause the benefit denial. Otherwise, the fiduciary's decision is reviewed de novo. E.g., *Atwood v. Newmount Gold Co., Inc.*, 45 F.3d 1317 (9th Cir. 1995). When there is no conflict, a plan fiduciary's discretionary denial of a benefit claim is reviewed to determine only if the denial is reasonable or supported by substantial evidence.

Liability for Erroneous Claims Decisions

ERISA only permits participants suing for benefits denied by their plans to recover the costs of the denied benefits and, possibly, attorney fee. ERISA §502(a)(1)(B), (g)(1). As such, plan liability for wrongly denied claims is extremely limited since ERISA does not authorize participants to seek consequential or punitive damages. However, critics have long claimed ERISA's remedies are inadequate, especially in situations where denied health claims cause participants to suffer economic damages such as lost wages and additional medical expenses. The lack of an ERISA remedy for these types of injuries has caused some plan participants to seek state law remedies, typically claiming that claims denials based on their plans' medical necessity or experimental treatment exclusion were negligently made. As discussed below, the Supreme Court recently reconfirmed that any state law causes of action that duplicate, supplement or supplant the exclusive remedies provided under ERISA §502 are completely preempted. *Aetna Health Inc. v. Davila*, 542 U.S. 200 (2004). See also *Pilot Life Ins. Co. v. Dedeaux*, 481 U.S. 41 (1987) (state bad faith claim for denied insurance benefit preempted by ERISA).

In *Davila*, the plaintiff's physician prescribed Vioxx, but the plan refused to cover it. The plan did, however, offer to cover similar, less-costly medications included on its prescription drug formulary. Rather than appeal the denial for Vioxx, Davila took another medication that caused a severe reaction forcing him to require extensive treatment and surgery. Davila sued in state court under the Texas Health Care Liability Act (THCLA), which required health maintenance organizations (HMOs) to "exercise ordinary care when making health care treatment decisions" and made them liable for damages "proximately caused" by failures to satisfy this standard of conduct. Tex. Civ. Prac. & Rem. Code Ann. §§88.001-88.003.

In deciding *Davila*, the Supreme Court held that ERISA completely preempts a state law claim if a plan participant could have sought relief under ERISA and the claim implicates no other independent legal duty. With respect to the case at hand, the Court explained that THCLA liability could only exist because of the HMO's duties to interpret and determine coverage under the plaintiff's ERISA plans. The Court noted that the plaintiff's HMO had not been responsible for treatment, and that his plan's utilization review decision was purely a benefit eligibility decision. As such, this type of decision was not subject to state law remedies (e.g., malpractice claims), even though medical judgment may have been exercised in making it.

Prior to *Davila*, the courts of appeal had been split on whether state law actions could lie against HMOs making medical necessity decisions. For example, in *Cicio v. Does*, the plaintiff's husband had sought plan coverage for a double stem cell transplant to treat his cancer. 321 F.3d 83 (2d Cir. 2003). The plan's medical director denied coverage for this procedure on the grounds that it was experimental, but instead volunteered that, based on the patient's condition, coverage would be available for a single stem cell transplant. However, by the time this decision was made, the plaintiff's husband was no longer a candidate for any stem cell transplant. The husband died shortly thereafter. The plaintiff then sued the HMO and its medical director on medical malpractice, negligence and other grounds. The Second Circuit initially ruled that the plaintiff's state law action was not preempted by ERISA. The court reasoned that by denying one treatment and authorizing another the treating physician had not requested, the medical director had engaged in a patient-specific treatment decision rather than simply making a benefit coverage determination.

Following *Davila*, *Cicio* was remanded to the Second Circuit. On reconsideration, the court noted that neither the HMO nor its medical director actually had been involved in treating the deceased. As such, it held that any malpractice cause of action against the HMO or medical director would impermissibly supplement ERISA's exclusive remedies for denied benefits and was therefore preempted. 383 F.3d 156 (2004). The *Cicio* court's post-*Davila* decision is consistent with the stances taken by other courts of appeals even prior to *Davila*. E.g., *Hull v. Fallon*, 188 F.3d 939 (8th Cir. 1999) (malpractice suit against a plan and its medical director preempted because the plaintiff did not have a medical treatment relationship with either party; the plan and medical director merely made coverage decisions); *Jass v. Prudential Health Care Plan, Inc.*, 88 F.3d 1482 (7th Cir. 1996) (negligence suit against a plan and its review nurse preempted because the nurse provided no treatment to plaintiff).

As noted earlier, there is considerable debate whether ERISA provides adequate remedies to persons whose benefit claims are wrongly denied. In recent years, Congress has considered, but has never enacted, "patients bill of rights" legislation that would have amended ERISA's remedies to provide for economic damages and limited noneconomic damages under some circumstances when health benefits are denied. Although the push for legislative action seems to have died down somewhat, it is possible that the *Davila* decision could spur new interest in this. In addition, a concurring opinion in *Davila* questioned whether ERISA §503(a)(3), which provides a "catch-all" remedy enabling participants to obtain appropriate equitable relief, could provide a vehicle for participants to obtain consequential damages in addition to their denied benefits. Although DOL seems to support this view, none of the lower courts have yet adopted it.

Finally, while persons involved in making plan benefit decisions are immune from state law liability, it is important to note that medical providers actually treating participants are, of course, subject to state law malpractice liability. *Pegram v. Herdrich*, 530 U.S. 211 (2000) (holding that treating physician is not an ERISA fiduciary).

CONTRACTING WITH PLAN SERVICE PROVIDERS

One of the greatest challenges facing plan fiduciaries is choosing and contracting with service providers. With respect to a health plan, trustees may need to contract with one or more of the following entities to provide specialized services to their plan: insurance companies, HMOs, TPAs, preferred provider organizations (PPOs), PBMs, utilization review firms and subrogation firms.

Selecting and Monitoring Service Providers

Selecting plan service providers is a fiduciary act on the part of plan trustees because it is the exercise of discretion over plan assets and plan management. For example, in *Reich v. Lancaster*, the court found the defendant exercised discretion over plan assets by recommending particular insurers for the plan, which the plan's other fiduciaries accepted without question. 55 F.3d 1034 (5th Cir. 1995). See also *Whitfield v. Tomasso*, 682 F.Supp. 1287 (E.D.N.Y. 1988) (selection of administrative services provider); *Brock v. Hendershott*, 8 E.B.C. 1121 (S.D.Ohio 1987) (same), *aff'd*, 840 F.2d 339 (6th Cir. 1988).

In recent years, it has become clearer that the selection of network health care providers for ERISA health plans also may cause the selector to act as an ERISA fiduciary. DOL Info. Ltr. to D. Ceresi (Feb. 19, 1998). Similarly, the courts have found that a person acts as a fiduciary when negotiating discounted rates for a plan with health care providers. *Everson v. Blue Cross & Blue Shield of Ohio*, 898 F.Supp. 532 (N.D.Ohio 1994); *Forsyth v. Humana, Inc.*, 827 F.Supp. 1498 (D.Nev. 1993). In one recent case, DOL argued, and the court agreed, that a company's selection of medical and pharmacy network providers on behalf of a plan (among various other acts) gave rise to fiduciary status. *Chao v. Crouse*, 346 F.Supp. 2d 975 (S.D.Ind. 2004).

Trustees must select service providers prudently and solely in the interests of plan participants and beneficiaries. Further, trustees must act for the exclusive purpose of paying benefits under the plan and defraying only reasonable plan administrative expenses. ERISA §404(a)(1)(A), (B). Courts have consistently construed these requirements stringently, saying that plan fiduciaries must act with an "eye single" to the interests of participants and beneficiaries. *Gregg v. Transp. Workers of America Int'l*, 343 F.3d 833 (6th Cir. 2003).

In assessing whether fiduciaries have met their fiduciary obligations in selecting service providers, courts generally focus on the procedures employed by fiduciaries in making their decision. E.g., *Howard v. Shay*, 100 F.3d 1484 (9th Cir. 1996) (fiduciary use of appropriate methods to investigate merits of decision). Moreover, it is not enough to act prudently; the decision-making process must be documented. Maintaining records is itself regarded as an element of prudence and, as a practical matter, a lack of records may make it impossible to later prove careful decision making by the fiduciary. Fiduciaries must conduct and document an objective, thorough and analytical search while identifying and selecting service providers. If fiduciaries have insufficient expertise to make a particular decision, they may have the duty to obtain appropriate assistance.

When selecting a health care delivery system for a plan, trustees must thoroughly evaluate the merits of each potential service provider. DOL has expressed the view that when selecting health care providers, fiduciaries may take into account both the costs and quality of medical care expected, and that the lowest cost provider need not be selected. DOL Info. Ltr. to D. Ceresi. Cf. 29

CFR §2509.95-1 (noting that, in retirement plan context, factors such as the quality of an insurer's investment portfolio and insurer's size may be relevant in choosing an annuity provider). If, after an objective and thorough search and analysis, the trustees have identified more than one appropriate service provider, the trustees may consider other factors while making a decision, such as whether a service provider employs union workers. Trustees should note, however, that satisfying this test may be difficult in light of the trustees' competing and possibly conflicting interests. E.g., *Davidson v. Cook,* 567 F.Supp. 225 (E.D.Va. 1983), *aff'd mem.,* 734 F.2d 10 (4th Cir. 1983). Cf. 29 CFR §2509.94-1 ("socially-responsible" investment must meet same fiduciary standards as other investments); DOL Adv. Op. 98-04A (May 28, 1998) (same).

Once a service provider has been selected, trustees must take into account their continuing obligation to monitor the service provider's performance. Cf. 29 CFR §2509.75-8, D-4 (noting fiduciary responsibility in deciding whether to retain fiduciary service providers). Some plans conduct periodic requests for information or proposals to stay informed about offerings from other service providers, even if they are generally satisfied with their current service providers' performance. In addition, health plans are increasingly auditing their TPAs to detect systematic errors and measure their accuracy rates against industry standards. (Vanessa Fuhrmans, "Oops! As Health Plans Become More Complicated, They're Also Subject to a Lot More Costly Mistakes," *Wall Street Journal,* January 24, 2005, at R4.)

Compensating Service Providers

Service provider compensation also raises some special concerns in the health plan context. ERISA §406(a)(1)(C) prohibits fiduciaries from causing their plans to enter into transactions that constitute the furnishing of goods and services between the plans and parties in interest. Significantly, parties in interest include plan service providers. Since ERISA §406(a)(1)(C) has the obvious effect of barring all contracts between a plan and a service provider, §408(b)(2) provides a statutory exemption from this prohibition so long as: (1) The services are necessary for the establishment or operation of the plan; (2) the services are furnished under a contract or arrangement that is reasonable; and (3) no more than reasonable compensation for the services is paid from plan assets. 29 CFR §2550.408b-2(a). See *Gilliam v. Edwards,* 492 F.Supp. 1255 (D.N.J. 1980); *Marshall v. Kelly,* 465 F.Supp. 341 (W.D.Okla. 1978). Plan assets can include amounts held in a plan's trust, as well as amounts that represent the return of plan assets from a third party. E.g., DOL Adv. Op. 99-08A (May 20, 1999) (amounts held in trust); DOL Adv. Op. 2005-08A (May 11, 2005) (return of premiums to plans due to state law limiting insurer's surplus). Whether compensation is reasonable is subject to a "facts and circumstances" test. 29 CFR §2550.408c-2(b)(5).

DOL has made clear that in determining whether a service provider's compensation is reasonable, a fiduciary should take into account the total compensation that the service provider receives in connection with the services arrangement, even if some amounts are received indirectly by the service provider from the plan. Cf. DOL Adv. Op. 97-16A (May 22, 1997) (administrative fees paid by mutual fund to plan service provider viewed as part of compensation paid by plan); DOL Adv. Op. 95-17A (June 29, 1995) (same). For instance, in addition to the monthly administrative fees directly paid by a plan, service providers may also receive indirect compensation from health care provider discounts, prescription drug rebates, the sale of de-identified claims data, interest or "float" earned on benefit checks that have not yet been cashed by health care providers or plan participants, and percentage fees charged for overpayment and subrogation recovery services. When contracting, trustees should inquire about these indirect sources of compensation and demand as much transparency as possible.

Of course, nothing precludes a plan from authorizing a service provider to retain indirect compensation as part of its overall compensation. Indeed, some courts have recognized that TPAs do not violate any fiduciary obligations when they retain amounts such as provider discounts or float pursuant to their administrative service agreements with plans. E.g., *Seaway Food Town, Inc. v. Med. Mut. of Ohio,* 347 F.3d 610 (6th Cir. 2003); *Guardsmark v. Blue Cross & Blue Shield of Tenn.,* 313 F.Supp. 2d 739 (W.D.Tenn. 2004). In contrast to situations involving self-funded plans, these indirect compensation issues are not as problematic with insured plans because insured claims typically are paid from insurer assets, not plan assets. Thus, the insurer has a clearer right to retain any discounts or float that may be generated in connection with these claims. E.g., *Marks v. Independence Blue Cross,* 71 F.Supp. 2d 432 (E.D.Pa. 1999).

Although the courts in *Seaway Food Town* and *Guardsmark* accepted somewhat generalized disclosures as being sufficient to enable fiduciaries to approve these types of compensation arrangements, DOL believes more detailed disclosures are required. In Field Assistance Bulletin 2002-3, DOL outlined its views concerning the retention of float as part of service provider compensation. First, DOL advised plan fiduciaries to examine whether comparable service arrangements are available with other providers that would credit float to the plan, rather than to the providers. Second, fiduciaries should consider the conditions under which float will be earned by the service provider. For example, service provider contracts should specify these circumstances and impose limits, where possible. Moreover, fiduciaries should review reports concerning checks that go uncashed for long periods of time. Third, DOL stated fiduciaries should request information concerning the interest rates the service provider expects to earn (e.g., a statement such as "money market rates" may be adequate). Finally, DOL points out a fiduciary's obligation to monitor service provider compensation is an ongoing duty and does not only apply at the beginning of a service relationship with a plan.

Limitations on Service Provider Liability

ERISA §410 provides that any agreement purporting to relieve a person from its fiduciary responsibilities or liabilities resulting from breaches is void. However, employers and fiduciaries are not precluded from purchasing insurance for or indemnifying fiduciaries in case of losses resulting from breaches. Id.; 29 CFR §2509.75-4. In addition, DOL has indicated that liability limits and indemnification provisions in service provider contracts are not per se imprudent under ERISA. DOL Adv. Op. 2002-08A (Aug. 20, 2002). Fiduciaries may be able to agree to limitation of liability provisions that invoke negligence and unintentional malpractice standards, but these provisions must be considered in the context of the agreement's overall reasonableness and the potential risks these provisions pose to plan participants. Fiduciaries also should assess whether the plan can obtain similar services elsewhere at a comparable cost without agreeing to such limitations of liability. DOL has stated it would be imprudent for a fiduciary to agree to provisions that purport to relieve service providers from liability for fraudulent acts or willful misconduct.

Special Considerations With Insurance Brokers

Recently, state attorney generals and insurance regulators have been closely scrutinizing certain insurance broker commission arrangements, focusing on improper disclosure, "bid-rigging" and kickback allegations. The sale of health and other insurance policies to employee benefit plans has drawn some attention, even though most of these state investigations have focused largely on the sale of property and casualty insurance. In any case, these allegations against the insurance brokers underscore the importance of plan trustees requesting and reviewing information concerning the payments brokers receive from insurers so that the trustees can determine the reasonableness of the brokers' compensation under ERISA §§406 and 408. The National Association of Insurance Commissioners (NAIC) recently released a model state law concerning broker fee disclosure which, if actually enacted by the states, could facilitate trustees' ability to obtain information on these fees.

In addition, DOL recently reinforced existing guidance concerning the reporting of insurance broker fees on Schedule A of the Form 5500, the annual report that plan administrators must file each year concerning their plans. ERISA §103(a)(2), (e); Adv. Op. 2005-02A (Feb. 24, 2005). As part of the Form 5500 requirements, insurers have a duty to provide plan administrators with the insurance policy-related information needed to complete the form, including information on broker compensation. In summary, Advisory Opinion 2005-02A emphasized that the broker compensation that must be reported on Form 5500 is very broad and includes commissions on paid single contracts, complex commissions paid across multiple contracts, and even noncash compensation such as prizes, trips and stock awards. In cases where complex formulas are used to determine broker commissions, insurers are permitted to use any reasonable method to allocate the portion of a commission to assign to a given customer, so long as the methodology is disclosed to the customer. DOL also noted the Form 5500's "override exception," allowing compensation to general agents not to be reported, should be narrowly construed and that a "general agent" never included a broker representing insureds. While this guidance is helpful to plan trustees, it should be noted that insurers have up to 120 days after the end of the plan year to provide the Form 5500 information. As noted earlier, plan trustees should inquire upfront about broker commissions in order to have information concerning these compensation practices at the initiation of a relationship.

Special Considerations With PBMs

In recent years several ERISA class actions have been filed alleging that PBMs serve as plan fiduciaries and engage in a variety of practices that give rise to prohibited transactions under ERISA §406. E.g., *In re: Medco Health Solutions, Inc. Pharmacy Benefit Mgmt. Litig.*, Civ. No. 03-MDL1508 (CLB), 2004 WL 1243873 (S.D.N.Y. May 25, 2004) (the *Gruer* litigation). The plaintiffs in these cases typically allege the PBMs are plan fiduciaries since they exercise discretionary authority and control over plan administration and plan assets in negotiating contracts with drug manufacturers and pharmacies, retaining rebates and other amounts received from manufacturers, and designing drug formularies. However, few of these cases have progressed to the point where the courts were required to rule on a PBM's fiduciary status. In one of the few cases, *Bickley v. Caremark, Rx, Inc.*, 361 F.Supp. 2d 1317 (N.D.Ala. 2004), the court ruled that the PBM was not a fiduciary due to its negotiation of drug manufacturer contracts and undisclosed retention of rebates. Nonetheless, the *Bickley* court's holding was predicated on the mistaken belief that plan assets had not been used to pay for drug benefits under the plan. Thus, it is difficult to draw clear conclusions from *Bickley* since the court might have ruled differently if it had had a correct understanding of the case's facts.

With respect to ERISA violations, plaintiffs in these cases typically allege the PBMs violate their fiduciary duties of prudence and loyalty under ERISA §404, as well as §406's specific prohibitions on self-dealing transactions and kickbacks from third parties. The alleged PBM practices constituting these violations include: (1) PBMs fail to disclose to plans the existence of and fail to pass through rebates and other amounts they receive from drug manufacturers; (2) PBMs structure their drug formularies in order to maximize the amount of rebates and other payments they receive from drug manufacturers, even when this results in increased costs to ERISA plans; (3) PBMs negotiate and/or create pricing spreads for their own benefit in their contracts with outside pharmacies and/or their in-house mail-order pharmacies; and (4) PBMs engage in coercive activities to steer physicians and pharmacies to prescribe or dispense drugs that produce the most rebates for PBMs.

In light of all this controversy, plan trustees should request and review as much information as possible concerning the rebates and other payments the PBMs receive from drug manufacturers. This applies both to initial contracting as well as periodic monitoring during the course of the agreement. Trustees should explore the extent to which PBMs are willing to pass through rebates and other amounts received from manufacturers to the plan. Trustees should also inquire whether the PBM engages in drug-switching in order to increase the rebates and other amounts the PBM receives from the manufacturer. If trustees agree to a "rebate guarantee" arrangement with a PBM, in which the PBM agrees to pay a per drug amount to the plan rather than forward actual rebates to the plan, trustees should still monitor the actual rebate amounts received from manufacturers, to the extent possible.

Although PBMs seem to be becoming more open about their operations and financial arrangements, transparency is still lacking in many instances. The state of Maine has enacted a statute that would require PBMs providing services to Maine-based customers to provide certain types of disclosures. Unfair Prescription Drug Practices Act (UPDPA), 22 Me. Rev. Stat. Ann. §2699. UPDPA requires that PBMs disclose: (1) all arrangements by which they receive remuneration from drug manufacturers and labelers; (2) information about drug-switching practices; and (3) upon request, all financial and utilization information concerning a plan's covered individuals. UPDPA also creates a state law fiduciary standard of conduct for PBMs and requires the pass-through of certain amounts received by PBMs from drug manufacturers.

UPDPA recently withstood an ERISA preemption challenge in the U.S. District Court for the District of Maine. *Pharmaceutical Care Mgmt. Ass'n v. Rowe,* Civ. No. 03-153-DBH (D.Me. April 13, 2005); adopting the magistrate's proposed decision available at: 2005 WL 757608 (Feb. 2, 2005). The plaintiffs appeared to have argued that PBMs are not ERISA fiduciaries because they do not exercise discretion over plan administration or assets. The court agreed, and then proceeded to decide that UPDPA's remedies for state law fiduciary misconduct were not preempted by ERISA's §502 remedies for similar misconduct. Furthermore, the court held that UPDPA did not "relate to" ERISA plans and thus was not preempted by ERISA §514. The court explained that UPDPA does not mandate any particular benefits that plans must offer, even though it imposes administrative and fiduciary duties on PBMs.

A number of other states have considered legislation similar to the Maine UPDPA, but only the District of Columbia actually has enacted it. Following *Rowe,* it is possible that other states now may act and trustees would have access to more information on PBM practices and compensation.

SUBROGATION AND REIMBURSEMENT RIGHTS

Plan fiduciaries often face the decision whether to seek reimbursement from participants' recoveries against third parties (e.g., tortfeasors or their insurers) for medical expenses the plan paid on the participants' behalf, even though the third parties were responsible for the injuries. For many years, plan fiduciaries used ERISA §502(a)(3), which authorizes fiduciaries to bring lawsuits to obtain "appropriate equitable relief" to enforce their plans' subrogation and reimbursement provisions. However, the Supreme Court's decision in *Great-West Life and Annuity Insurance Co. v. Knudson,* 534 U.S. 204 (2002), has undermined plans' ability to administer these provisions under §502(a)(3).

In *Knudson,* the plan sought to make a recovery from a participant when the participant was not in possession of the damages recovered from the third party. Instead, the damages had been paid over to a trust established for the participant's benefit. The Supreme Court determined that a claim to repay money asserted directly against the participant was a claim for "legal" relief and that ERISA only authorized traditional "equitable" relief. The Court left open the possibility that reimbursement claims, if pled differently, could be "equitable" claims permitted by ERISA.

Since *Knudson,* health plans have sought to enforce reimbursement provisions by characterizing their claims as equitable relief in order to fit within the parameters of ERISA §502(a)(3). The Seventh Circuit has found that reimbursement claims can be equitable, but only if the following factors are met: (1) There are identifiable funds (e.g., the damages award is held in a bank account that has not yet been disbursed to the participant); (2) a plan fiduciary sues the person who actually holds the funds (which may or may not be the participant); and (3) the plan contains a provision stating it is entitled to the funds. *Admin. Comm. of the Wal-Mart Stores Inc. Associates' Health & Welfare Plan v. Varco,* 338 F.3d 680 (7th Cir. 2003). See also *Aerospace Employee Welfare Benefits Plan v. Ferrer, Poirot & Wanbrough,* 354 F.3d 348 (2003) (same).

In contrast, the Sixth Circuit has characterized all attempts to enforce reimbursement provisions as actions to remedy breaches of contract, even when the participant possesses or controls an identifiable fund. As such, the relief sought is never equitable, and thus is not authorized by ERISA §502(a)(3). *QualChoice, Inc. v. Rowland,* 367 F.3d 638 (2004). The Ninth Circuit has taken the same position. *Providence Health Plan v. McDowell,* 385 F.3d 1168, 1174 (2004); *Westaff v. Arce,* 289 F.3d 1164 (2002). In addition, the *McDowell* court held, contrary to prior precedent from other courts and even within the Ninth Circuit, that subrogation claims do not "relate to" ERISA plans, thus permitting plans to bring such claims in state court without plaintiffs being able to object on preemption grounds.

Given the confusion that now surrounds *Great-West,* it is likely the Supreme Court will need to weigh in or legislative reforms will be required in order for plans to once again be able to uniformly administer their subrogation and reimbursement provisions throughout the country. In the meantime, uncertainty concerning a plan's ability to enforce these provisions could hurt the plan's ability to obtain full reimbursement when settling such claims with participants.

Chapter 11

Utilizing Professional Advisors in Fulfilling Fiduciary Responsibility

Paul J. Ondrasik Jr. and Donald A. Walters

INTRODUCTION

As we noted in the last edition of the *Trustees Handbook,* professional advisors to employee benefit plans are much like spouses—you can't live with them, and you can't live without them. This age-old adage is even more true today. The administration of the modern employee benefit plan is more complex and time-consuming than ever before. The assets of these plans have grown tremendously; novel and increasingly sophisticated investment options, vehicles and techniques for managing those assets are constantly introduced. The provision of adequate medical coverage in the face of increasing costs and competing demands remains a daunting and perplexing task. The legal and regulatory environment in which plans operate is subject to change on seemingly a daily basis and is confusing even to the regulators themselves.

Given these complexities, it is not surprising that trustees of multiemployer plans have turned with increasing frequency to professional advisors for assistance in discharging their plan duties. Virtually all trustees have full-time jobs with other responsibilities and demands on their time and attention. While they are undoubtedly dedicated to their plans and the plans' participants and beneficiaries—indeed, the satisfaction they derive from serving those constituents is often their *only* plan reward—service as a trustee is an avocation; it is secondary to what they do for a living. As a result, no matter how hard they work or how bright they are, it is very difficult for them to bring to every aspect of their trustee responsibilities the same degree of expertise that can be expected from a professional operating within his or her area of professional concern.

At the same time, however, in turning to professionals for assistance, trustees cannot forget one important fact—the ultimate responsibility, and ultimate liability, for proper administration of the plan largely remains with them. In the final analysis, it is *your* fund; *you,* and not your professional advisors, are responsible for its successful operation; the fund's participants and beneficiaries will be looking to *you,* and not your professional advisors, for answers.

This chapter is intended to give you a better understanding of your relationship with your professional advisors, from both a legal and a practical perspective. At the outset, it provides you with an overview of the general legal standards that govern this area, with particular focus on the fiduciary issues that arise in connection with the selection and monitoring of these professionals. It then identifies the common members of your professional advisor "team" and offers you a brief description of the types of services you can expect each member to provide. We hope that it will suggest some practical aids and guides that will assist you in discharging your duties when you retain and use professional advisors and, at the same time, assist you in obtaining the maximum benefit of their services.

THE GOVERNING LAW—ERISA

The governing law in this area is the Employee Retirement Income Security Act of 1974, which is universally referred to by its acronym ERISA. The responsibility for ERISA's administration and enforcement lies largely with the Department of Labor (the DOL, or the Department).

ERISA permits you to use plan advisors and, in many cases, encourages their use. In fact, in certain areas, the use of professional advisors is a practical necessity if you are to fulfill your duties and, at the same time, avoid liability. This is particularly true when you are involved in important plan decisions in areas in which you lack expertise or in which you face a potential conflict of interest. The DOL has taken the position that ERISA's prudence standard amounts to a "prudent expert" standard, i.e., that your actions should be judged against those of an expert in the particular endeavor involved; and a number of courts have adopted this approach. As a result, if your decisions are later challenged in court on breach-of-fiduciary grounds, you undoubtedly will be faced by testimony from experts detailing what they would have done under similar circumstances. The fact that you have consulted an expert, and acted accordingly, in making the decision in question is the best means for countering evidence of this type.

At the same time, the use of professional advisors is not without pitfalls of its own. The DOL is paying greater attention to service arrangements, given the volume of plan dollars that are spent on such matters. For example, it is interested in knowing whether the services you are buying are appropriate as well as whether the fees paid for those services are reasonable. If they are not, you can face liability.[1]

The Department is also paying greater attention to selection and monitoring issues. Why? In some cases, these issues give the Department a basis for "upstreaming liability," to hold you as trustees responsible for your advisors' actions. If you as trustees failed to discharge your own responsibilities—if you have acted inappropriately—in selecting or monitoring those advisors, you can face potential liability for their actions.[2]

Obviously, you are not looking for this type of exposure when you enter into a service arrangement. Professional advisors should be a source of assistance and comfort to you in the discharge of your own fiduciary responsibilities. They should *not* be a source of potential liability. As a result, it is important that you have a basic understanding of your own legal duties and responsibilities in this area. With this in mind, we turn now to an overview of the governing legal standards.

BASIC FIDUCIARY STANDARDS

Any discussion of these issues must begin with a review of your basic ERISA fiduciary responsibilities. While often overlooked in this context, these rules are fully applicable in your relationship with your professional advisors. Your responsibilities here flow from your status as the "named fiduciary" for your plan. In the Taft-Hartley setting, the role of named fiduciary is played by you, the board of trustees. It is an extremely important role because, as named fiduciary, you have ultimate responsibility for the control and management of the operation and administration of your plan. See ERISA 402(a). In short, you are the Harry S. Truman of plan fiduciaries—the "buck stops with you."

In performing this key role, you are fully subject to ERISA's fiduciary rules. These include the basic fiduciary duties set out in §404 of ERISA that are covered elsewhere in this handbook—your duty to act "solely in the interest of," and thus with "undivided loyalty" to, the plan's participants and beneficiaries; your prudence obligation; and your duty to adhere to the plan documents unless they are inconsistent with ERISA. You also have a duty to avoid prohibited transactions under ERISA §406. This includes the duty to avoid plan transactions with "parties in interest"—i.e., parties with specified relationships to the plan that could give rise to a conflict of interest (see ERISA §3(14))—in the absence of an exemption from these rules. It also includes the duty to avoid self-dealing on your own part when you are engaged in plan-related transactions.

ERISA exposes you to significant personal liability and penalties in the event you violate these duties. For example, if you breach your fiduciary responsibilities and, as a result, the plan suffers a loss, you can be held personally liable to make good that loss. ERISA §409. Likewise, if you profit personally from your breach of duty, you can be required to disgorge those profits to the plan.[3] You are also subject to the "equitable powers" of the court and, in an appropriate case, could be removed from your position as a trustee, or have your authority circumscribed. Moreover, under ERISA's cofiduciary provisions, you can, in certain circumstances, find yourself responsible for the fiduciary breaches of your fellow fiduciaries. ERISA §405(a). In sum, you could be damaged—and damaged significantly—both in your pocket and in your reputation, if you fail to discharge your responsibilities in the manner ERISA commands.

THE EFFECT OF USING PROFESSIONAL ADVISORS

Fortunately, ERISA does not require you to do everything yourself. In fact, the act specifically contemplates that you will use others, including professional advisors, to assist you in discharging your responsibilities to the plan. In this regard, ERISA specifically provides that the plan can authorize you to retain advisors at plan expense. ERISA §402(c)(2). It also makes clear that you can allocate and delegate, i.e., turn over, fiduciary duties to others. Of particular significance is your ability to delegate investment management responsibilities to an *investment manager* within the meaning of the act. ERISA §402(c)(3). The key here, however, is your plan document. Do your plan documents—trust agreement and/or plan—authorize you to retain these professionals and pay them from plan assets? Do they allow you to allocate or delegate your duties to others? You must have that authority in your documents. Thus, to protect yourself in the first instance, it is extremely important that you familiarize yourself with the documents governing your plan and, in particular, your trust agreement.

If you have this authority, what happens, from a legal perspective, when you use professional advisors? What impact does it have on your own responsibilities under ERISA? The answer really depends on what you are trying to accomplish when you look to a third party advisor. On the one hand, you may be attempting to allocate or delegate—to turn over—one of your fiduciary responsibilities to the advisor. Alternatively, you simply may be seeking advice and guidance from the advisor in connection with a plan decision you will make on your own. In the former situation—the allocation and delegation situation—you are actually transferring your fiduciary responsibility to the third party. In the advice situation—the nondelegation situation—you are not. You are retaining full fiduciary responsibility for the decision yourself, and that is an important point you should always remember. Each of these situations is addressed in more detail below.

Delegation

ERISA permits you, as fiduciaries, to allocate fiduciary duties among yourselves or to delegate those responsibilities to a third party, provided that certain requirements are satisfied. See ERISA §405(c). If you make that allocation or delegation in accordance with those rules, you, as a fiduciary, generally will have no responsibility—and importantly no liability—for the performance of the duty in question. In effect, you have transferred that duty to a third party.

The rules governing allocation and delegation of fiduciary responsibility are set out in §405(c) of ERISA. Under these rules, the first and foremost requirement is that your plan documents *must* set forth a procedure that authorizes and enables you to allocate or delegate fiduciary responsibilities. Thus, once again, your plan documents are the key; an express procedure in your plan is the essential prerequisite to any allocation or delegation of fiduciary responsibility. ERISA §405(c)(1).

The remaining requirements focus on your own conduct in initially making the allocation and delegation and, thereafter, in permitting that allocation or delegation to continue. To make an effective allocation or delegation of fiduciary duties, ERISA requires that you act in accordance with your own fiduciary responsibilities in establishing and implementing the procedure and in making the allocation or delegation. In other words, you must act prudently and otherwise in accord with your own ERISA duties in selecting the party who will perform the fiduciary acts in question. In addition, you must adhere to your own fiduciary duties in allowing the allocation or delegation to continue. Thus, you must monitor prudently the party's activities and performance in order to determine whether the party should be allowed to continue performing the responsibilities involved. See ERISA §405(c)(2).

Several additional requirements must be satisfied when you are attempting to delegate investment management responsibilities to an investment manager. Those additional requirements are as follows:

- The plan documents must specifically permit you to delegate investment management responsibilities to an *investment manager* within the meaning of ERISA. ERISA §402(c)(3).
- The party to whom you delegate that investment discretion must meet ERISA's definition of an *investment manager*. That means the party must be a registered investment advisor under the Investment Advisors Act of 1940, a bank or an insurance company qualified to engage in such business under the laws of more than one state. ERISA §3(38).
- That party must acknowledge in writing its fiduciary status to your plan.

What happens if you meet these requirements, and thereby make an effective delegation of fiduciary responsibility to the third party? In that case, you generally will have no liability for the third party's acts or omissions in carrying out that delegated duty, unless (a) You violated your own ERISA fiduciary responsibilities in making the selection or continuing it; or (b) you find yourself subject to liability under ERISA's co-fiduciary responsibility rules. Accordingly, to avoid potential liability in this area, you should review your plan documents to ensure that you have the authority, i.e., the power, to make a delegation. In addition, you should have procedures in place to ensure that you properly discharge your fiduciary responsibilities both in selecting and in monitoring the professional.

Advice

Let's look now at the second situation—the nondelegation situation—where you are simply looking to your professional advisors for advice. This is the most typical way you will use your professional advisors outside the investment management context. Here, there is *no* transfer of fiduciary responsibility to your advisor. You remain fully responsible for the performance of the fiduciary duties in question. Moreover, reliance on professional advice is *not* a defense in the event of a fiduciary challenge![4]

This, however, does not mean that you should not look to your professional advisors for advice and guidance. Their input obviously can be quite helpful in assisting you to make an appropriate decision. Moreover, even though such advice is not an absolute defense in the event of fiduciary challenge, the fact that you have consulted with your advisors and obtained professional advice can be very strong evidence of proper fiduciary behavior.

In fact, in many cases it can be conclusive evidence that you have discharged your responsibilities in accordance with ERISA's fiduciary rules. This is particularly true if you are acting in an area in which you lack experience or expertise or if you find yourself in a potential conflict-of-interest situation. In these situations, it is very important to seek out professional advice so no one can suggest later that you acted without consideration of factors that would be important to experienced parties faced with the same decision or without an understanding of what your fiduciary duties would be under the circumstances.[5] However, for it to be effective evidence, your reliance on that advice—your use of that advice—must be reasonable; it cannot be blind. Thus, you should question your advisors to make sure the advice they are giving you makes sense and that you understand what they are telling you. And, if it's an important decision, have those advisors put their advice in writing.

THE SELECTION AND MONITORING PROCESS

As indicated above, the effective use of professional advisors, in large part, turns on the satisfaction of your own fiduciary obligations in selecting them and then reviewing their performance. How do you fulfill your own duties in these areas? The key here is paying close attention to your basic prudence obligation as a trustee. This, of course, should be no surprise. Generally, when you enter into a relationship with an advisor, you can expect to spend significant plan dollars on his or her services. If you are spending plan dollars, you ought to look at that decision as an investment decision and treat it with the same importance. As a result, you should have in place an effective procedure, both for selecting your professionals and for monitoring their performance.

Why is the implementation of such a procedure important? The adoption of and adherence to procedures has become a key component of your prudence obligation, as interpreted by both the courts and the Department of Labor. In many respects, that prudence obligation has evolved into a "procedural prudence" standard, that focuses not so much on results, but on the quality and thoroughness of your decision making process.[6] Having and following a procedure demonstrates that you did not approach your decision in a haphazard fashion, but rather in a reasonable, responsible and thoughtful way. Moreover, it helps ensure that you do, in fact, consider and evaluate the factors that are important to the decision you are making on behalf of the plan, and then make a reasoned decision based on all the appropriate information.

Selection Procedures

Unfortunately, ERISA itself offers little concrete guidance on just what should be included in these sorts of procedures. As a result, there are no hard-and-fast rules here; what is appropriate really turns on the facts and circumstances of each situation. However, it would appear that any prudent selection process would have a number of basic elements. They are as follows:

- *Preparation of specifications for the position you are seeking to fill.* What are your requirements? What services do you expect the professional to provide? What basic qualifications do you expect the professional to have?
- *Identification of appropriate candidates for that position.* You have a wealth of information generally available to you to help you identify candidates. For example, you can consult with other funds in your area or your other professional advisors to obtain recommendations. In an appropriate case, you might consider employing the services of a professional search firm. If you are looking for an investment manager and have already employed an investment consultant, that consultant might perform an initial search for and screen of potential candidates.
- *Solicitation of bids and proposals from the candidates.* Those proposals should set forth the candidates' qualifications, the manner in which they propose to provide the service, their proposed fees and references.
- *Conduct interviews with the candidates.*
- *Compare fees and never forget to check references.*
- *Make a reasoned decision based on the information you have obtained and document that decision.*

Monitoring Procedures

The monitoring process is equally undefined under ERISA. Indeed, the DOL has issued a regulation that offers very little guidance on the subject other than to state that "at reasonable intervals" performance should be "reviewed . . . in such manner as may be reasonably expected to ensure that [the party's] performance has been in compliance with the terms of the plan and statutory standards, and satisfies the needs of the plan." 29 CFR §2509.75-8 (FR-17). However, even here the Department's regulation does suggest some basic elements of a monitoring process.

- *Conduct reviews at regularly scheduled intervals.* Establishing a schedule helps ensure that performance, in fact, is reviewed.
- *Establish standards against which the performance of the professionals is judged.*

In short, once you employ the professional, don't forget about him or her. The existence of a procedure prevents this from occurring.

DOL Guidance in the Investment Management Area

While ERISA itself offers little guidance concerning

the selection and monitoring process, the Department has suggested, in more concrete terms, what it believes appropriate selection and monitoring procedures should include in the investment management context. This guidance was not issued in the form of regulations. Rather, it can be derived from the terms of consent judgments entered into by the Department in settling litigation involving investment matters arising in the multiemployer plan context.[7] Those consent judgments set forth detailed requirements that the Department required the trustees of the plans in question to follow on a going-forward basis in selecting and monitoring the performance of investment professionals for those funds.

Before proceeding to the factors set forth in those consent judgments, a number of general observations are in order. First, these consent judgments emphasize the importance of establishing formal procedures in the investment context. Second, the detailed and sophisticated types of information these consent judgments would have the plan's fiduciaries review underscore how ERISA's prudence standard has come to be viewed, at least in some circles, as a prudent expert test; and they indicate that the investment area is one that particularly lends itself to the use of professional advisors, such as investment consultants and performance monitoring firms, to assist trustees in performing their selection and monitoring duties. Many trustees simply do not possess the investment experience or expertise to make meaningful use of this information without professional assistance. The fact that the investment arena is also the source of greatest potential liability to plan fiduciaries in view of the magnitude of plan dollars at stake also supports this conclusion.

Finally, it should be noted that the terms of these consent judgments are not legal requirements that all trustees must follow; and, indeed, the procedures they set forth may not be appropriate or realistic for all funds. Nonetheless, they do provide trustees with an appropriate checklist against which to compare their own selection and monitoring procedures. Obviously, the closer trustees conform their procedures to those set forth in these consent judgments, the less likely the Department or some other plaintiff could mount a successful fiduciary challenge against them.

With that background, let's look at what those consent judgments reveal, first with respect to the selection of investment managers. In this area, they indicate that the key feature of the selection process is the collection and evaluation of relevant information concerning the potential investment manager and its capabilities and practices in the investment area. In this regard, they indicate that the information to be collected and evaluated should include the following:

- Whether the candidate qualifies as an investment manager pursuant to ERISA §3(38)
- The business structure and affiliations of the candidate
- The financial condition and capitalization of the candidate
- A description of the investment style proposed by the candidate
- A description of the investment process to be followed by the candidate
- The identity, experience and qualification of the professionals who will be handling the plan's portfolio
- Whether any relevant litigation or enforcement actions have been initiated within a reasonably relevant time period against the candidate, the candidate's officers or directors, or the candidate's investment professionals who have responsibility for the plan's portfolio
- A description of the experience and performance record, over an appropriate period of time, of the candidate and its investment professionals, including experience managing other tax-exempt and employee benefit plan assets
- Whether the candidate has and would propose to utilize the services of an affiliated broker/dealer and, if so, the types of transactions for which such affiliates would be used and the financial arrangement with the broker/dealer
- The procedures to be employed by the candidate to comply with ERISA's prohibited transaction restrictions, including whether the candidate is a qualified professional asset manager
- Whether the candidate has the bonding required by ERISA
- Whether the candidate has fiduciary liability or other insurance that would protect the interests of the plan in the event of a breach of fiduciary duty
- The proposed fee structure
- The identity of client references
- The total amount of assets under the control of the candidate
- The candidate's policy with respect to the voting of proxies
- Any other appropriate and relevant information.

The consent judgments expect that this information will be evaluated by the trustees and that interviews will be conducted with the candidates under serious consideration. As noted earlier, given the sophistication of much of this information, many trustees—if they follow this course—would find the use of an investment consultant quite helpful. Finally, the consent judgments would require that the information reviewed be verified with reliable independent sources. Indeed, they go so far as to require that inquiries be made both to the Department and the Securities and Exchange Commission as to whether enforcement actions have been initiated against the candidate, the candidate's officers and directors, or the candidate's investment professionals who will have responsibility for the plan's portfolio.

The monitoring procedures set forth in these consent judgments are equally detailed and require the review and evaluation of similarly sophisticated investment information. In this regard, they indicate that the investment manager monitoring process should include the following:
- A review, at least quarterly, of the portfolio of the investment manager for compliance with its investment guidelines
- A review, at least quarterly, of the basis on which assets under the investment manager's control are valued
- A computation, on a quarterly basis, of the rate of return for the investment manager on an overall basis, by asset class and, where investments are in more than one industry sector, by sector
- A comparison, at least quarterly, of the investment results of the investment manager with appropriate indexes or benchmarks
- A review, at least annually, of the investment manager's practices regarding brokerage and trading, including those regarding:
  —Brokerage costs
  —Use of soft dollars
  —Quality of securities' execution
  —Portfolio turnover
- A verification, at least quarterly, of the investment manager's fee computation
- A review, at least annually, of the investment manager's proxy voting policies and performance
- A meeting with the investment manager, at least annually, to review the manager's investment performance and any significant changes in corporate or capital structure, investment style, brokerage affiliation or practices, investment process and professional staff
- The development, and a review at least annually, of procedures for communicating information regarding the plan's investments and the investment manager among the plan's trustees, the plan's staff and the plan's service providers (including, but not limited to, the plan's attorneys, actuaries and custodial trustees)
- A review, at least annually, of the plan's cash management and short-term investment procedures and performances, as well as the overall performance of the plan's custodial trustee(s).

In addition, a mechanism should be established that allows the investment manager's services to be terminated as soon as prudently possible, if the investment manager's performance is determined to be unsatisfactory or it is determined that the investment manager has violated its investment guidelines. This should be addressed in your contract with the investment manager.

Any detailed analysis of the various components of the selection and monitoring procedures set forth in these consent judgments is well beyond the scope of this chapter. However, the approach taken by the Department illustrates that the legal environment in which you operate as a trustee is increasingly complex and regulated. We now turn to your professional advisors themselves and some practical considerations that may assist you in using their services to meet both your needs and those of your fund's participants and beneficiaries.

PROFESSIONAL ADVISORS— SOME PRACTICAL CONSIDERATIONS

In dealing with your professional advisors, it is important to keep one fact in mind—there is no substitute for good judgment and common sense on your part. Obviously, the advice of your fund's professional advisors, based on their expertise and experience with similar funds, can be very helpful. However, as trustees, your knowledge of your own industry and local conditions is tremendously important. Therefore, seek the guidance of professional advisors, but apply their input to your own knowledge of the issues involved. As noted earlier, do not follow their recommendations blindly.
- Question the advisor, on the record, concerning the development of his or her opinion and recommendations and, where appropriate, get the advice or recommendation in writing.
- Weigh the professional's recommendations in light of your personal knowledge of the facts and circumstances of the issue at hand and the local industry.

And *remember* that no matter how qualified your advisors might be, it is *your* fund and *you* bear the ultimate fiduciary responsibility for its successful operation.

WHO ARE THESE PROFESSIONAL ADVISORS?

As has been noted in previous editions of *The Trustees' Handbook,* the spectrum of jointly negotiated benefits continues to expand. Hence, many professional advisors have developed an expanded area of expertise. At the same time, new advisors have emerged who offer an expertise focused on the expanded area of benefits. An example of this evolution is the negotiated 401(k) plan which was nonexistent only a few years ago. The establishment of 401(k) plans gave rise to the immediate need of professional advice in the:
- Evaluation of a broad range of investment alternatives
- Selection of an appropriate package of investment vehicles from which plan participants could select
- Monitoring of the ongoing performance of each of the investment vehicles offered.

With trustees facing the fiduciary responsibility attendant to these differing areas of technical expertise, the community of professional advisors responded immediately. Some established professionals' range of expertise was such that they were qualified to immediately step forward offering the required advisory services. Some who had not previously served as a professional advisor to multiemployer fund trustees found their expertise was needed by 401(k) trustees, and they came forward offering advisory services.

Whether or not the future of jointly negotiated benefits will see the introduction of additional benefits, it is likely the evolution of legislative, judicial and bureaucratic interpretations and mandates will alone require expanded areas of professional expertise. Thus it will be necessary that trustees continually evaluate the advisory services required and those advisors rendering these services.

Recognizing the foregoing caveat that "professional advisors to multiemployer trustees" is not a static community, the following brief description of the professional services that are commonly used by trustees of multiemployer funds is simply those in place in early 2005.

Administrator

There continue to be two basic approaches to the administration of a multiemployer fund: self-administration and administration by a third party, or contract, administrator (TPA).

Self-administration now takes on two forms. Traditional self-administration entails the trustees hiring their administrator and his or her staff as employees of the board(s) of trustees. (Oftentimes, a family of funds—health and welfare, pension, vacation and 401(k)—will jointly employ a staff that will administer all of the funds of a given local union or given collective bargaining parties.) However, some such staffs process health and welfare claims while others turn to insurance companies, PPOs or HMOs to provide claims processing services. (Even where the staff processes health claims, PPOs often reprise claims and submit them to the fund office for payment.)

TPAs are service provider companies that are hired by the trustees to administer the fund(s). In a health and welfare fund that utilizes a PPO, they too will typically receive reprised claims from the PPO, which they will then process.

In years past, it was not uncommon to hear arguments as to which of these two approaches provided better administration. These are rarely heard any more, since it is generally conceded that they can be equally as good (or bad). Both approaches continue to be widely used; and, for the greater part, the factor that most influences trustees to take one over the other is the comfort level of trustees. Some trustees favor the exclusive focus of a self-administration staff on their fund or family of funds. Other trustees favor what they perceive to be more objective administration by a TPA.

The issue of cost (i.e., which approach will be the least expensive) still remains unanswered. Sometimes self-administration will be less expensive, and sometimes a TPA will be less expensive. It will vary from fund to fund. The only way to be sure in a given situation is to take bids from TPAs and compare their costs with those of self-administration. However, great care must be taken to be sure that all costs reflect the provision of all of the required services.

Whatever the approach taken, it is the job of the administrator to receive the employer contributions, keep the records of employees' work in covered employment, maintain the eligibility rolls, verify eligibility for benefits or pay benefits and, in general, maintain all the records of the fund.

Fund Auditor

As previously indicated, the law requires an annual audit of multiemployer funds. These are typically conducted by a CPA or a licensed auditor who serves as the fund auditor.

In addition to the annual fund audit, a fund will periodically require payroll audits of participating employers. The American Institute of Certified Public Accountants (AICPA) has taken the position that a multiemployer benefit fund must audit each participating employer over a period of years to determine that all employers are making contributions to the fund in accordance with the collective bargaining agreement(s).

From time to time the trustees will wish to have an employer audited for cause. In other words, the trustees might have reason to believe that the employer is not making contributions in accordance with the collective bargaining agreements (e.g., where an employer is known to be using workers in covered employment, but is not making contributions to the fund on their behalf or is not contributing on all hours worked).

The more predominant approach is to have the fund auditor perform both of these functions (i.e., annual audit of the fund itself and the payroll audits of participating employers). However, this does not necessarily have to be the case. There are some geographical areas in which all or a number of building trades benefit funds have entered into a cooperative agreement on audits and have retained a single firm to conduct the audits for all the funds. The rationale for this approach is that, if a contractor is delinquent to the benefit funds of one trade, it likely is delinquent to the benefit funds of other trades whose members it employs. Therefore, when the auditor goes in to audit for one fund, he or she audits for all funds; and the proportionate cost is far less for each fund.

Fund Counsel

Fund counsel is, of course, the attorney who is retained by the board of trustees for legal advice. Most frequently, the trustees retain a single attorney to serve as fund counsel for the entire board of trustees, but some funds employ co-fund counsels.

In a co-fund counsel situation, the more common approach is for the employer trustees to select an attorney and for the union trustees to select another attorney, who both then serve as co-counsel to the fund.

From time to time, a question is raised as to whether the use of co-fund counsels is imprudent or otherwise violative of ERISA. ERISA does not, on its face, prohibit co-fund counsels. Additionally, to the best of the authors' knowledge, no court has ever held that the employment of co-fund counsels was either illegal or imprudent. Finally, since the use of co-counsels existed prior to ERISA's enactment, it is noteworthy that the Department has never formally challenged or questioned this practice.

Notwithstanding the foregoing, ERISA's prudence standard should be considered by a board of trustees in employing co-counsel. Those standards would seem to require that:
1. Each fund counsel represent the full board of trustees even though he or she might have been designated by one side of the board only
2. Legal work be divided between the co-fund counsels to preclude a duplication of services
3. The combined legal fees of the co-counsels be reasonably comparable to legal costs the fund would have incurred had the trustees chosen to have a single fund counsel.

Another question that often arises is whether it is proper for the union's attorney or the management association's attorney to serve as fund counsel. The simple fact that an attorney serves one of the parties to collective bargaining should not disqualify that attorney from serving as fund counsel as long as he or she is knowledgeable about ERISA, employee benefits and the law governing the trustees of multiemployer benefit funds. Clearly, there are attorneys and/or law firms representing either the union or the employers that possess the qualifications necessary to serve objectively as the fund counsel to the board of trustees. Similarly, there are law firms practicing in the multiemployer fund area that will not serve the board of trustees of a fund if they represent any single employer or the association or the union.

Investment Consultant

As noted, the investment consultant is new to our list of typical professional advisors.

In order for trustees to effectively delegate their fiduciary responsibility for the investment of fund assets, ERISA requires, among other things, that the investment manager's performance be the subject of continuing review. At the time of the enactment of ERISA, and for a number of years thereafter, the majority of multiemployer pension funds had a very basic investment policy calling for X% of the assets to be invested in fixed incomes and Y% to be invested in equities. As a result, reviews of investment performance were, for the most part, basic and unsophisticated. However, as trustees began to become familiar with alternative asset classes, risk/reward ratios, and the balancing techniques attributable to a studied and broader spectrum of asset allocation, the need for a more sophisticated process of evaluating the performance of investment managers became clear. Thus, professional investment performance measurement companies expanded into the multiemployer arena; consulting firms developed this expertise; and new investment consulting firms were born.

Today these companies offer a wide range of services, including:
- Asset allocation studies (i.e., studies that quantify the probable long-term impact on investment performance by using varying investment strategies and asset allocation models)
- Investment manager searches
- Investment performance measurement reports (i.e., analysis of the investment manager's performance as compared with that of similar managers or indexes, together with their sector and company selection)
- Custodian performance
- (In many cases) proxy voting.

Originally these services were directed toward pension funds only, but a growing number of larger health and welfare fund trustees are turning to investment consultants to assist them in improving the yield on the investment of fund reserves.

Investment Manager

ERISA, as noted earlier, clearly permits a board of trustees to delegate its fiduciary responsibilities for the investment of fund assets, provided that such responsibilities are delegated to an *investment manager* as defined by the act. To meet that definition, an investment manager must be:
1. A national bank
2. An insurance company doing business in more than one state; or
3. An investment manager registered under the 1940 Investment Advisors Act.

If the firm retained as an investment advisor does not qualify as an *investment manager* under this definition, the trustees would not have the ability to delegate to that firm their fiduciary responsibility for investment—

even if that firm employed the brightest investment advisors with the best investment record in the industry. That does not mean the board of trustees could not use that firm in the investment of the fund's assets; the trustees simply would not enjoy the ability to delegate to it their fiduciary responsibility for investment.

It is also very interesting to note that, while the employing of an investment manager typically arises in the pension fund context, the trustees' fiduciary responsibility for the investment of plan assets exists in any and all ERISA-covered benefit plans. Therefore, the trustees of a health and welfare fund have the same responsibility as the trustees of a pension fund insofar as the investment of plan assets is concerned.

Nevertheless, the relatively small size of health and welfare fund assets is such that the investment of these assets often is performed by the board of trustees rather than through an investment manager. There is nothing wrong with this approach. Where the fund's cash flow and/or liquidity requirements limit the available investment vehicles to short-term, guaranteed interest instruments, the trustees can generally accept this responsibility and typically save money on investment management fees in the process. A decision to take this approach largely depends upon the trustees' willingness to accept the fiduciary responsibility.

Consultant and Actuary

The actuary and the consultant serving companion funds are often employees of the same actuarial and consulting firm. Thus, from time to time there is some confusion as to the services they provide. However, they are separate and distinct.

The actuary is a sophisticated mathematician. He or she determines the amount of monthly pension benefits that can be provided for a given contribution rate. The annual actuarial valuation of a defined benefit pension plan, which the actuary produces, addresses all of the technical issues of the funding of a pension plan that are required by the Internal Revenue Service. In addition, he or she develops the mathematics of withdrawal liability, if any.

The consultant, on the other hand, typically advises and assists the trustees of multiemployer funds (including defined benefit pension plans) on all matters that do not fall within the specific expertise of other professional advisors utilized by the trustees. These services include questions of plan design, eligibility rules and a myriad of other issues facing the trustees in the ongoing operation of the fund. He or she is also a resource of information as to how the trustees of other funds have addressed issues similar to those with which the trustees are concerned.

Do these separate roles mean that the consultant must be a separate and distinct person from the actuary? Not necessarily. Some pension funds have an actuary who serves as both the actuary and the consultant. In addition, an actuary will sometimes serve as consultant to a health and welfare fund. At the same time, it is not unusual for a consultant to serve the trustees of all funds and to have the actuarial valuations prepared by an actuary who rarely, if ever, meets with the trustees. In those instances, the consultant would present to and discuss with the pension fund trustees the actuarial valuation.

Which is the better approach? Again, there is no clear answer. Since the consultant will typically be involved with and advise on all those things that come before a board of trustees—both health and welfare and pension—that are not clearly and exclusively the concern of another professional advisor, all actuaries would not have the experience with or knowledge of actuarial science to effectively serve the trustees' needs in handling basic pension fund issues with them in the absence of an actuary.

There also are some consultants and/or actuaries who combine their practice with plan administration. Is this legal or proper? There is nothing illegal about a multiple practice firm that includes administration. Certainly, it should be recognized that serving as either a TPA or a consultant and/or actuary are demanding jobs in and of themselves. Combining these disciplines in a single firm simply compounds the responsibilities. At the same time, there is an area of potential conflict of interest when an individual consultant or consulting firm is called upon to advise trustees on such matters as eligibility rules and plan design when those specific provisions could have an impact on that same person's or firm's work as an administrator. Nonetheless, there are firms that offer both services and do both quite well.

401(k) Consultant

This "newest" of professional advisors necessarily addresses areas of defined and potential trustees' liability exposure. The defined exposure was previously addressed as needed areas of professional advice, i.e., evaluation and selection of investment vehicles. The monitoring of the performance of the selected investment vehicles is less clear, and we therefore refer to it as an area of potential liability exposure. However, though some debate any notion that trustees have a fiduciary duty to monitor the performance of selected investment vehicles, it would appear that given the current climate of consumer and stockholder advocacy, trustees would be well advised to take this additional step. Even though ERISA provides trustees some relief from their fiduciary responsibility for the investment of (pension) plan assets when the plan provides for and the participant elects to direct the investment of "his own" plan assets, we are concerned with the court's (or a jury's) response to a participant's complaint that the trustees offered (in the 401(k) plan) investment funds that had posted investment results over a period of years that were substantially below those realized by the majority of investment funds utilizing the same investment styles and classes.

Since most trustees have full-time jobs unrelated to the investment and other issues confronting plan trustees, few could be expected to have the time and expertise to do the amount of research required to prudently exercise these evaluation, selection and monitoring responsibilities. Therefore, it is essential that the trustees retain a 401(k) consultant who, in addition to being proficient in basic structural requirements and fiduciary responsibility, has the demonstrated expertise to objectively provide these services. At the same time, it would appear likely that as negotiated 401(k) plans mature, trustees are going to be required to provide more and better programs and materials designed to better educate participants in investments. Clearly the 401(k) consultant should provide guidance in this important area.

SUMMARY

Again, as the scope of multiemployer funds continues to grow and mature, the desirable—not required—areas of professional expertise also expand. Included for the first time in our list of professional advisors is 401(k) consultant. There are professionals of other disciplines now serving some funds who might well be universally used in the coming years. The fact that they are not specifically included here does not mean that the services they offer are not worthwhile. It simply means that at this time they are not as widely used as those previously discussed.

DO ALL FUNDS NEED EACH OF THESE PROFESSIONAL ADVISORS?

The easy answer to the foregoing question is "no." There are many multiemployer health and welfare funds that do not have an investment manager. Similarly, since health and welfare funds do not require an actuarial valuation, it is clear that they do not necessarily have to employ an actuary.

Because an annual audit of all funds is required by law, it is equally clear that the fund auditor is the one professional advisor who absolutely must be retained by all funds.

What about the others? Obviously, someone has to administer the plan. Consequently, almost all funds will use either a TPA or their own employees as fund administrator.

What about fund counsel? While there are a number of funds that do not employ the services of legal counsel, most boards of trustees believe, and the authors agree, that such an approach presents unacceptable risks. The law is continually being changed by new legislation, the issuance of regulations by federal agencies and court decrees. Given this constant change and the significant responsibilities and exposure the law imposes on them, most trustees believe it is imperative that they retain fund counsel to advise them of their legal rights, duties and responsibilities.

There are also funds that do not have consultants but, instead, rely on the administrator to assist them with matters of eligibility rules, benefits, cost-containment initiatives and so on. However, here again, most trustees believe it is essential that they retain a qualified consultant. The same can be said about investment managers in the pension fund context. While not essential, the trustees of pension funds of any appreciable size have turned to investment managers to perform the investment management function. Similarly, the investment consultant has become almost universally used by pension funds.

In a defined benefit pension fund, an actuary is required to determine the benefits that can be provided and to do the actuarial valuation.

It is our sense that the trustees of a 401(k) plan (or for that matter, the trustees of an annuity fund that allows participant-directed investments and provides an array of investment funds from which to select) who do not have a qualified 401(k) consultant, are taking on an inordinate risk. Even so, some trustees rely on the "packages of funds" to advise them and forgo a consultant. Unfortunately, few of the packages provide a monitoring service that sufficiently identifies unacceptable performance combined with recommended remedial action within an acceptable time frame.

Perhaps the best way of analyzing the necessity of these various professional services is to consider this issue in hindsight and in the context of a fiduciary challenge of the trustees' actions. In other words, in what position will the trustees find themselves if they fail to employ one or more of these advisors and then encounter difficulties (or the plan sustains losses) in areas in which such an advisor would have provided advice and assistance?

As noted earlier in this chapter, and as discussed more fully elsewhere in this handbook, courts generally judge trustees' performance against a prudent expert standard; i.e., they expect trustees to discharge their fund responsibilities in the same manner as a professional in such matters. Trustees, therefore, should assess their own capabilities and experience and ask themselves whether they could satisfy this standard. Put another way, they should, in effect, ask themselves whether they can afford to be without professional assistance in these basic areas. In answering these questions, few trustees find they are prepared to accept this risk.

WHERE DO YOU FIND THEM, AND WHO IS GOOD?

Of the two foregoing questions, the first is easier to answer.

The trustees of a fund of any substantial size really do not have to look for professional advisors. Those advisors find their way to the trustees. Consequently, the trustees of such funds typically have a long list of available names of persons and companies who are more than anxious to provide whatever professional service might be required.

Nevertheless, there are many small and medium sized funds that, though called on frequently by professional advisors, will not have on file an adequate list of potential candidates for all of the services they might consider from time to time. Similarly, trustees might wish to explore candidates other than those who have solicited their business. Where should they turn for the names of additional candidates?

As in many cases, this is an area where an enormous amount of time and effort can be spent pursuing absolute answers when common sense offers the best and most practical solution. Trustees sometimes fail to recognize that they have available a wealth of information on such matters.

By virtue of their position, the union trustees of multiemployer funds will have corresponding trustees on multiemployer funds in other cities. For example, the union trustees of the Paperhangers Health and Welfare Fund of Hahira, Georgia can easily determine the names of the union trustees of the Paperhangers Health and Welfare Funds in Jacksonville, Atlanta and other cities in the area. Similarly, through their contractors association, the employer trustees on the same Hahira fund will be able to identify the employer trustees on other funds.

With this information, either group of trustees can contact their brother and sister trustees in other cities and ask them who they use as professional advisors. They also can solicit information concerning the quality of service, including the appropriateness and timeliness of responses to questions raised by the trustees. Should a greater number of prospective providers be desired, the same questions could be asked of trustees of funds of other trades or unions. For example, the trustees of a retail food fund might ask the trustees of a building trades or service employees fund.

In addition to consulting with the trustees of other funds in the immediate geographic area, there is no reason not to reach out and ask similar questions of fund trustees in other sections of the United States or to ask them of the international unions or the national association headquarters. The simple fact that a given service provider does not have an office in the immediate area in which the fund is located does not mean that it could not be considered. For example, there are attorneys, accountants, consultants and actuaries who serve funds over a wide geographic area. Indeed, even though administrators typically are domiciled in a particular area, they might be interested in establishing an office in a new city if a fund were desirous of their services. The bottom line is that the trustees have nothing to lose by contacting these people to determine whether or not they would be interested in serving as professional advisors to the specific boards of trustees.

Interestingly, trustees often overlook one of the better sources of information available to them—their other professional advisors. Most professional advisors serve as advisors to more than one fund. As a result, they frequently will have worked with a number of people who share the same professional disciplines with whom they have not worked directly. Therefore, when seeking out candidates, it always makes sense to turn to the other professional advisors and ask them who they work with on other funds or who they know of that might provide good services.

COST

As we all know, the cost of professional services varies widely. Not only does it vary by discipline, it also varies significantly within disciplines. In addition, there can be a tremendous variation based on the geographical area in which the services are performed.

The unfortunate truth is that there are no good rules of thumb as to what trustees should be paying for any given professional service. The highest bidder could in fact offer mediocre services, reflecting a limited knowledge of the field. The lowest bidder could be accurately reflecting the value of the services he or she would provide as opposed to other service providers. There are no absolutes to enable the trustees to know ahead of time who will provide the best service.

Again, common sense offers trustees the best guide. In addition to comparing prices, trustees should talk to clients of the prospective advisors and ask them about the quality of service they receive for the fees charged. They should talk to their other professional advisors about what other funds are paying for the services in question. They should solicit similar information from trustees of other funds and the other sources previously noted. Finally, they should not be afraid to negotiate.

This commonsense approach frequently will provide the trustees with a very clear picture of which provider is most likely to render the services the trustees desire and, at the time, enable them to secure those services at an appropriate and reasonable price.

ENDNOTES

1. See, e.g., *Dole v. Formica,* 14 EBC 1397 (N.D.Ohio 1991); *McLaughlin v. Tomasso,* 9 EBC 2438 (E.D.N.Y. 1988).
2. See *Martin v. Harline,* 15 EBC 1138 (D.Utah 1992); see

also Letter from Olena Berg, former Assistant Secretary for Pension Welfare Benefits, U.S. Dept. of Labor, to Comptroller of Currency (Mar. 21, 1996).

3. In addition, if the Department recovers these amounts for the plan, either through litigation or a settlement, you face an additional civil penalty equal to 20% of the recovery amount. ERISA §502(l).

4. See *Donovan v. Tricario,* 5 EBC 2057 (S.D.Fla. 1984).

5. See *Katsaros v. Cody,* 568 F.Supp. 360 (E.D.N.Y. 1983), *aff'd as modified,* 744 F.Supp. 270 (2d Cir.), *cert. denied,* 409 U.S. 1072 (1984); *Donovan v. Bierwirth,* 680 F.2d 263 (2d Cir. 1982).

6. See, e.g., *Fink v. National Savings Trust Co.,* 772 F.2d 951 (D.C.Cir. 1985); *Katsaros v. Cody, supra*; see also 29 CFR §2550.404a-1(b)(1).

7. See Consent Judgments in *Arizona State Carpenters Pension Trust Fund v. Miller,* No. Civ. 89-0693 (D.Ariz., 11/1/94) and *In re Masters, Mates & Pilots Pension Plan and IRAP Litigation,* Lead File No. 85 Civ. 9545 (VLB) (S.D. N.Y. 12/15/92).

Chapter 12

DOL and IRS: ERISA Enforcement Responsibilities

Bennett E. Choice

The Employee Retirement Income Security Act of 1974 (ERISA) provides comprehensive rules governing the establishment and administration of employee benefit plans, including retirement plans and health and welfare plans. The administration of ERISA is divided among the Department of Labor (DOL), the Department of the Treasury (Treasury) and the Pension Benefit Guaranty Corporation (PBGC).

ERISA's provisions initially caused bureaucratic confusion due to overlapping jurisdictional and regulatory authority between DOL and Treasury. Reorganization Plan No. 4 of 1978 (reorganization plan) helped eliminate much of the overlap involved with administering ERISA. Pursuant to the reorganization plan, DOL received responsibility for enforcing ERISA's disclosure, reporting and fiduciary obligations, as well as responsibility for issuing individual and class-prohibited transaction exemptions and interpreting plan investment rules. Under the reorganization plan, the Internal Revenue Service (IRS), an agency within the Treasury, received responsibility for enforcing ERISA's vesting, minimum participation and funding requirements.

PBGC was established pursuant to ERISA and is responsible for insuring pension benefits provided by defined benefit (DB) pension plans. Sponsors of DB plans pay premiums to PBGC annually; in return, PBGC guarantees benefits provided by such plans (up to a statutory maximum). PBGC is responsible for overseeing this program as well as processing terminations of DB pension plans.

This chapter provides an overview of ERISA enforcement responsibilities and the organizational structure of DOL and IRS, as well as highlights of recent enforcement initiatives.

DEPARTMENT OF LABOR

DOL administers and enforces more than 180 federal laws, including significant portions of ERISA. DOL has principal jurisdiction over ERISA Title I, which requires persons who manage and/or control plans and/or plan assets to manage plans for the exclusive benefit of participants and beneficiaries; carry out their duties in a prudent manner; comply with plan documents; refrain from conflict of interest transactions expressly prohibited by ERISA; use plan assets to pay plan benefits and appropriate plan expenses; and fund benefits in accordance with ERISA and plan rules. ERISA Title I also requires plan fiduciaries to report and disclose information to participants, beneficiaries and DOL. The reporting and disclosure provisions of ERISA require plans to provide the following types of information to participants:

- Summary plan description
- Summary annual report
- COBRA notice and HIPAA certificates (health plans)
- Form 5500 (on request)
- Plan document (on request)
- Blackout notice (participant-directed plans)
- 404(c) disclosure (optional for participant-directed plans)
- Notice of benefit reductions (pension and health plans).

In addition, ERISA's reporting and disclosure requirements obligate plan sponsors to file an annual report (Form 5500) with DOL annually.

DOL established the Employee Benefits Security Administration (EBSA) to carry out ERISA enforcement responsibilities. Prior to February 2003, EBSA was known as the Pension and Welfare Benefits Administration.

EBSA has 15 field offices located throughout the country, including ten regional offices and five district offices. EBSA's national office is located in Washington, D.C. The national office is responsible for operational oversight, review of the field offices, enforcement policy, program direction and issuing various rulings.

EBSA issues general publications (and posts information on its Web site) intended to assist employers and employees in understanding their obligations and rights under ERISA. For example, EBSA has posted information on plan expenses so that employees understand the costs associated with their decisions, and to help employers understand their obligations when using plan assets to pay plan expenses. In addition, EBSA provides technical assistance to individuals, employers and plan administrators on fiduciary, reporting and other issues. Any individual or organization can request an advisory opinion or information letter from EBSA regarding the interpretation or application of ERISA's provisions within the DOL's jurisdiction.

Administrators, employers, trustees, service providers and/or other fiduciaries of employee benefit plans most often encounter EBSA by either (1) requesting an interpretative ruling regarding ERISA's provisions, (2) requesting a prohibited transaction exemption or (3) through the EBSA enforcement program.

One responsibility of the EBSA enforcement program is conducting audits of employee benefit plans throughout the country. These audits focus on compliance with Parts 1 and 4 of ERISA Title I, which deal with reporting and disclosure rules, establishment of the plan and trust, fiduciary duties, the existence of prohibited transactions and the bonding requirement. A particular area of focus relates to the investment of plan assets.

Sometimes EBSA audits may be generated randomly. However, it is more likely a specific event or factor will trigger an EBSA audit. For example, EBSA may initiate an audit based on a complaint submitted by a plan participant or by discrepancies in Form 5500 returns. For example, if the Form 5500 indicates the plan does not maintain a fidelity bond, or reports unusual investment activity, EBSA may select the plan for audit. EBSA also may initiate an audit based on a referral from another governmental agency, such as IRS, PBGC or the Securities and Exchange Commission.

In addition, certain EBSA initiatives intended to facilitate ERISA compliance may trigger an audit. For example, a more recent EBSA initiative (aimed at safeguarding employee contributions to 401(k) plans) investigates situations in which employers improperly delay depositing 401(k) employee contributions into the trust. EBSA found widespread noncompliance with the requirement that employers deposit 401(k) contributions timely.

With respect to the audit process itself, EBSA first sends a letter that alerts the plan to the pending audit and requests certain information for review prior to an onsite visit. Such requested information typically includes past Form 5500 returns, plan documents, participant disclosures and other related plan records. During the onsite visit, an EBSA investigator usually interviews fiduciaries and other plan officials and employees, and the EBSA investigator may request and review additional plan documentation. ERISA also authorizes EBSA to use its subpoena power in conducting audit investigations.

After completing an audit, EBSA generally notifies the plan fiduciaries of the investigator's conclusions. If the investigator concludes a fiduciary breach has occurred, EBSA typically requires correction of the breach. In addition, EBSA may impose civil and/or criminal penalties depending on the nature of the violation. ERISA also authorizes DOL to remove a fiduciary who caused a breach.

ERISA authorizes DOL to assess civil penalties against parties in interest (generally the plan sponsor, the fiduciary and certain related parties) who engage in prohibited transactions with employee benefit plans. A prohibited transaction is generally a conflict of interest transaction. The penalty starts at 5% and increases to 100% of the amount involved in the transaction. A parallel provision in the Internal Revenue Code (Code) imposes an excise tax against disqualified persons (generally defined the same as parties in interest) who engage in prohibited transactions. ERISA also requires DOL to assess a mandatory civil penalty equal to 20% of the amount recovered with respect to fiduciary breaches that result in either a settlement agreement or a court order. In addition, ERISA provides that a plan fiduciary is personally liable to restore any plan losses or profits made due to a fiduciary breach.

EBSA has established two compliance programs to help plan fiduciaries voluntarily correct certain ERISA violations. First, the Delinquent Filer Voluntary Compliance Program allows plan administrators to pay reduced civil penalties for voluntarily complying with annual reporting requirements (typically filing overdue Form 5500 returns). Second, the Voluntary Fiduciary Correction Program permits plan administrators to identify and correct 15 specific transactions, including prohibited purchases, sales and exchanges, improper loans and delinquent participant contributions. A plan sponsor can use these programs to voluntarily correct a defect and avoid more serious penalties.

In addition to auditing plans and fiduciaries, EBSA has also focused investigations on persons or entities that provide services to employee benefit plans, such as third-party administrators, insurance brokers, investment providers, accountants and actuarial consulting firms. This has provided another avenue for EBSA to monitor and enforce compliance with ERISA.

As an example of recent enforcement activity, in fiscal year 2004, EBSA closed 4,399 civil investigations, and nearly 70% of those investigations resulted in correction of violations under ERISA. In addition, criminal investigations led to the indictment of 121 individuals during that year.

INTERNAL REVENUE SERVICE

IRS has primary responsibility for enforcing ERISA's vesting, minimum participation and funding requirements. IRS also determines whether a plan meets the tax-qualification requirements. Tax-qualified retirement plans are eligible to receive favorable tax treatment under the Code.

IRS has both a national office and regional offices. The IRS Restructuring and Reform Act of 1998 prompted the most comprehensive reorganization of IRS in nearly 50 years. IRS was reorganized into four major operating divisions, including the Tax Exempt and Government Entities Division (TE/GE Division). Under the TE/GE Division, the Office of Employee Plans and Exempt Organizations oversees the Employee Plans Examination Program, which is responsible for ERISA enforcement and tax-qualification determinations.

Plan sponsors, administrators and service providers most often encounter IRS enforcement agents through plan audits. These audits typically involve potential prohibited transactions (conflict of interest transactions) or tax-qualification issues. An IRS audit may result from an independent investigation by IRS or a referral from another agency, such as DOL. Audits are also generated randomly.

IRS issues substantive rulings necessary to promote a uniform application of tax law, including notices, announcements and revenue procedures. IRS also issues private letter rulings (applying tax laws to specific facts submitted by taxpayers) and revenue rulings (providing broad application of tax laws).

IRS is responsible for determining the existence of prohibited transactions with respect to retirement plans and levies nondeductible excise taxes on such transactions. If a prohibited transaction occurs, a plan fiduciary must correct the transaction, file a Form 5330 with IRS and pay the applicable excise tax. This tax equals 15% of the value of the transaction for each year of its existence.

IRS also determines the tax-qualified status of retirement plans. Tax-qualified plans are eligible to receive favorable tax treatment under the Code (i.e., employer contributions to the plan are deductible by the employer, earnings on the contributions accrue tax free until distributed and employees are not taxed on their benefits until distributed). A plan must satisfy numerous requirements, both in form and operation, to maintain its qualified status. For example, the plan must be in writing and satisfy requirements relating to the timing and amount of contributions and distributions.

A plan may become disqualified for many reasons, including failing to administer the plan in accordance with its terms, violating nondiscrimination rules, making employer contributions in excess of specified limits, excluding eligible employees from plan accruals and failing to make minimum required distributions. Disqualification of a plan results in devastating tax consequences for the participants, the trust and the sponsoring employer. Such consequences may include the employer losing prior deductions, participants being taxed immediately on vested amounts and the trust becoming taxable. This would require the affected parties to file amended returns for the applicable years.

Given the severity of plan disqualification, IRS has established the Employee Plans Compliance Resolution System (EPCRS) as an alternative to plan disqualification. *EPCRS* is a comprehensive system of correction programs that enables sponsors of retirement plans that have experienced compliance violations to preserve the tax-qualified status of their plans. Under EPCRS, a plan sponsor can avoid disqualification if it corrects its defect in the prescribed manner.

EPCRS contains three subprograms for correcting different types of qualification issues: the Self-Correction Program (SCP); the Voluntary Correction Program (VCP); and the Correction on Audit Program (CAP). SCP is available for correcting nonegregious, operational failures and does not require any fee or filing with IRS. Thus, under SCP, a sponsor can self-correct a defect on its own without IRS involvement. VCP is available to correct several failures (including egregious failures) but requires paying a fee and filing with IRS. CAP is available for correction of failures discovered by IRS during an audit. Under CAP, the sponsor must pay a sanction amount to IRS and correct the defect. The applicable sanction depends upon the nature, extent and severity of the failure. EPCRS has proven beneficial for IRS since it has encouraged plan sponsors to correct defects, and it is beneficial to plan sponsors because it provides an alternative to disqualification.

IRS has published a guide intended to help multiemployer benefit plans prepare for an IRS audit. In this guide, IRS listed several recurring issues it has encountered during such examinations. Pursuant to this guide, fiduciaries of multiemployer plans should be aware of the following key issues:

- Plans have failed to make required distributions to participants as required under Code Section 401(a)(9). Plan administrators should be more proactive with respect to monitoring the required minimum distribution requirements.
- Plans are failing to meet the Code's "definitely determinable" benefit requirements (primarily an issue for DB plans).

- The required actuarial adjustments or interest-adjusted back payments are not being paid to participants whose retirement benefits first commenced after the "normal retirement date" as stipulated in the plan.
- Errors are made when participant benefits are calculated, often because (1) benefit provisions in the plan are misapplied, (2) applicable law is not understood, (3) faulty participant data is used and/or provided by employer and (4) combinations of all the above.
- Vesting has been miscalculated due to use of an incorrect vesting schedule or due to errors when calculating a participant's vesting percentage.
- Plans subject to Code Section 412 minimum funding requirements are failing to receive the necessary contribution amounts within the required period of time.
- Employers responsible for excise taxes that result from prohibited transactions or funding deficiencies are not filing the applicable excise tax return (Form 5330) and/or paying the excise tax.
- Plans have exceeded the statutory limitations imposed on annual additions and benefits by Code Section 415.

CONCLUSION

IRS and DOL have primary responsibility for enforcing ERISA. Of course, there are other relevant state and federal laws that apply to benefit plans, including the Code, HIPAA, the Taft-Hartley Act, FMLA and a host of others. Some of these laws are administered by IRS or DOL; others are enforced by other agencies, such as Health and Human Services or EEOC. Consequently, it is important to understand that, while IRS or DOL will have the most significant oversight of employee benefit plans, fiduciaries may have contact with other agencies.

For example, the Office of Civil Rights (OCR) is responsible for enforcing HIPAA privacy obligations that became effective with respect to health plans over the past several years. Fiduciaries are already witnessing complaints that are leading to contact with OCR. Also, EEOC is responsible for enforcing workplace discrimination laws, and this has impacted health plans in areas such as retiree health eligibility rules and coverage of fertility treatment.

Ultimately, however, fiduciaries will have the most interaction with IRS or DOL as they enforce the qualification rules under the Code and the fiduciary and reporting and disclosure rules under ERISA.

Chapter 13

Accounting and Auditing

Robert B. Jones, CEBS

INTRODUCTION

The purpose of this chapter is to introduce the two fields of accounting and auditing in the context of multiemployer plans.

It is important for fund trustees to be able to distinguish between the two fields of accounting and auditing. The distinction is a little bit like the difference between a baseball team's manager and the head statistician.

The fund accountant is responsible for establishing a system of internal control over the assets and for gathering and recording the fund's financial activities.

The fund auditor is responsible for actually auditing the system of internal control and the financial statements prepared by the trustees (by their accountant) so that the auditor can express his or her opinion as an *independent outside expert* as to the fairness of presentation of the financial statements. However, the auditor is not the guarantor of the integrity of the financial statements—merely rendering an opinion as to whether they have been prepared in accordance with generally accepted accounting principles (GAAP) and generally accepted auditing standards (GAAS).

WHAT ARE THE REQUIREMENTS TO BE AN AUDITOR?

The fund auditor should have established his or her credentials by having passed (achieved a grade of 75% in all four parts) the uniform, certified public accountant (CPA) examination in his or her state of practice. This is a rigorous three-day examination held semi-annually that tests the accountants' knowledge of accounting, auditing, income tax and business law. This requirement is an important rite of passage for all junior accountants and is often a criterion for promotion in many firms.

Further, any person who holds himself or herself as a CPA must have a minimum number of hours of continuing professional education each year. (In fact, there has been a bill on Capitol Hill for the past few years that would require additional industry specialized training for accountants who audit employee benefit plans. The industry is definitely moving in the direction of more specialized training as the professional environment becomes more demanding.)

A CPA must also keep abreast of current trends in the industry and must, at all times, follow the requirements of GAAS in the conduct of the audit. Additionally, a CPA must satisfy himself or herself that the client has prepared the financial statements of the fund in accordance with GAAP.

The auditor must also be aware of the pronouncements from the Financial Accounting Standards Board (FASB) to be certain that the fund financial statements are prepared in keeping with said pronouncements. (To date there have been over 150, and the FASB is a little bit like Congress in that it keeps legislating new rules and regulations.)

Included in the store of knowledge that the auditor must possess is a working knowledge of the Employee Retirement Income Security Act of 1974 (ERISA), the Multiemployer Pension Plan Amendments Act of 1980 (MPPAA) and various tax laws as they affect pension and welfare funds. This does not mean that the auditor should be looked to for legal answers or interpretations. That is the function of the fund attorney.

In like manner, while the auditor is primarily a "numbers person," he or she should not be looked to for actuarial interpretations or calculations, as that is also not the auditor's main area of expertise.

That is normally the province of the fund actuary or benefits consultant.

Similarly, the area of investments is not normally

the province of the auditor, although many people mistakenly interpret the role as including this field. Under ERISA, because the accountant does not normally exercise discretionary authority, he or she would not be considered a *fiduciary* in the normal course of events.

Under ERISA, the term used is *independent qualified public accountant (IQPA)*.

WHAT IS THE REGULATORY ENVIRONMENT OF EMPLOYEE BENEFIT PLAN AUDITS?

ERISA Section 103 states that every employee benefit plan must have an audit by an independent qualified public accountant. Generally, this means plans with greater than 100 participants as of the beginning of the plan year. The Department of Labor (DOL) and the Internal Revenue Service (IRS) share joint responsibility for ensuring that the annual return reports—the Form 5500 series—are filed on a timely and complete basis. The DOL maintains an office with several CPAs within the Division of Reporting and Compliance that maintains regulatory supervision over the employee benefit plan audits within the United States. The DOL, in conjunction with the trade association for accountants—the American Institute of Certified Public Accountants (AICPA)—refers problem cases to the AICPA for followup and, in extreme cases, disciplinary action by the states. An improper or nonexistent audit can constitute an incomplete filing of the Form 5500, which can cause significant penalties per day (as indexed) per plan.

Note that the DOL maintains a delinquent filer voluntary compliance (DFVC) program for plan sponsors that have not completed the audit in a timely basis that provides for a substantially reduced penalty structure.

The IRS has also indicated that it will attempt to audit a number of multiemployer plans in the future; therefore, not only is a regular plan audit as discussed above and below a required step, but an operational review may be an important step as well to obtain assurance that the plan is being run properly. Often, accountants can, in conjunction with fund lawyers, perform this operational review.

WHAT ARE THE DUTIES OF THE AUDITOR?

As we noted above, the auditor is generally responsible for auditing the financial statements of the fund. Based on various audit steps, the auditor expresses an opinion as to the fairness of presentation of those financial statements prepared by the management of the fund. That opinion can be one of four types: unqualified, qualified, adverse or disclaimer.

Unqualified Opinion

Unqualified means the auditor found nothing of material significance in the course of the audit that would cast doubt on the fairness of presentation of the financial information contained in the financial statements and footnotes. (This is the most common form of plan audit.) *Fairness* is used in the sense that nothing unfair or misleading is contained in the statements, nor have there been any material facts that have not been disclosed in the statements or footnotes. (This is also called a *clean opinion* by the auditing profession.)

Qualified Opinion

Qualified means that the auditor was limited in some area of the audit, such as not being permitted to perform payroll audits or review investments because they were with a bank or insurance company (ERISA Section 103(a)(3)(A)). This is the second most common category in employee benefit audits. However, even though qualified opinions are extremely common (based on the number of bank-trusteed or insurance company-managed plans), this does not mean that the auditor does not audit payables or plan transactions—a significant audit responsibility exists. (There has been proposed legislation that would eliminate the "limited scope" audit protection but, to date, nothing has passed.) One of the main reasons for limited scope originally was to avoid the extra work of auditing funds whose assets were managed by entities that were, in turn, audited by state regulatory authorities.

Adverse Opinion

Adverse means the auditor takes exception to the presentation of the financial information because, in his or her judgment, it is not fairly presented. An adverse opinion would constitute a red flag to the regulatory authorities—the DOL and the IRS and would invite a regulatory inquiry.

Disclaimer Opinion

Disclaimer means the records are such, or the difference of opinion between the fund accountant and the fund auditor is of such magnitude, that the auditor disclaims the expression of any opinion. A disclaimer of opinion would also be required if the auditor was in fact not independent. It is important to note that this type of audit would normally cause the DOL, upon review of the audited financial statements, to make an inquiry as to the reason for the disclaimer.

WHAT ARE THE MAIN STEPS IN THE AUDIT?

The first step in preparing for an audit is to write an audit program. This is like a work plan for any consulting project. The purpose of the audit program is to outline the main areas that the auditor wishes to review or test based on his or her knowledge of the client; results of the prior year audit; changes in the plan; changes in the laws, such as ERISA or MPPAA; and similar matters of financial importance.

Upon arriving at the client's office, the auditor should then review the system of internal control to determine that it is still being followed and/or ensure that any changes suggested at the time of the last audit have been implemented. Based on this review, the auditor can determine the scope of the audit. As discussed above, if the assets are managed by a bank trust department, the scope of the audit will probably be limited.

Having determined the scope of the audit, the auditor will then test, recalculate, observe and/or confirm those items on the balance sheet or the income statement that, in his or her judgment, are of material significance. In broad terms, those items are:
- Cash
- Receivables
- Investments
- Other assets
- Payables
- Other liabilities
- Contributions
- Investment income
- Other receipts
- Claims paid
- Administrative expenses.

Other areas of interest to the auditor are:
- Tax status
- Prohibited transactions
- Subsequent events that affect the financial statements.

Again, the auditor cannot serve as the guarantor of the favorable tax-exempt status of the plan being audited, the same way that an auditor of a public company generally cannot act as a guarantor against fraud or misdeeds. However, the requirement of the *AICPA Audit Guide* is that the auditor should satisfy himself or herself that the plan is being maintained as a qualified plan (in the case of a pension plan) or a qualified trust (in the case of a Section 501(c)(9) trust or voluntary employees' beneficiary association (VEBA)) by taking certain steps and doing some due diligence.

The final step of the audit procedure before issuing the audit report is to obtain a client representation letter (the client rep letter). This document is probably the most misunderstood of all the letters that the auditor requires (with the lawyer's letter running a close second).

The client representation letter is designed to establish certain basic facts regarding the financial statements, as well as who is accepting responsibility for what. The trustees, as management, are asked to acknowledge that they have primary responsibility for the financial statements and that, to the best of their knowledge, the statements are correct. The letter does not change or add to the traditional, fundamental responsibilities of either party. It simply clarifies these roles.

It is well worth the time and effort for the trustees to discuss with the auditor the meaning of the terms and phrases in the letter so there will be no misunderstanding as to their meaning and possible impact on the audit. Without the letter, the auditor cannot issue a clean (unqualified) opinion. Keep in mind the words that should appear in the opening paragraph of the letter: "We confirm, to the best of our knowledge and belief. . . ." Again, it is important to note that the representations *do not constitute a guarantee* that the information given is correct but, rather, that it is in good faith and based on the trustees' best knowledge and belief.

WHAT QUALITIES SHOULD A FUND LOOK FOR IN A GOOD AUDITOR?

To properly exercise their fiduciary responsibility and fund governance, fund trustees should ask at least the following questions (not meant to be an all-inclusive list):
- What is the experience level of the fund auditor(s)?
- What qualified references does the fund auditor have?
- What continuing education programs and training programs exist at the audit firm?
- Has the fund auditor participated in the DOL's employee benefit plan audit specialization program?
- How many years of experience and how many audits has the person/firm performed?
- What quality control measures and procedures exist at the audit firm?
- Has the firm received a regulatory sanction/disciplinary action/inquiries or suspension from the governing bodies?
- What turnover has existed in personnel at the audit firm?
- What emphasis is placed on employee benefit plan auditing at the firm?

Generally these are questions that should be asked by any plan fiduciary in selecting, reviewing and monitoring a service provider.

CONCLUSION

Due to space limitations, it would not be physically possible to describe the entire audit process. The best book to review on this subject is the annual volume of the AICPA—*Audits of Employee Benefit Plans,* generally published in early May of each year. Another excellent source of information is the *Audit Risk Alert* prepared annually by the staff at the DOL, which outlines areas of common misunderstanding and highlights traps for the unwary. Each auditor would be wise to review this document!

It is not the purpose of this chapter to go through an entire audit step by step but, instead, to explain for trustees the main areas of the auditor's responsibility.

Trustees are encouraged to ask their auditor for an explanation of the tests and procedures being used in the audits so they can have an understanding of what their audit report covers. A good auditor will also provide management letter comments either in writing or orally to describe improvements in fund operations, technology, procedures or personnel that the fund could take to better and more securely provide employee benefits to participants and their beneficiaries.

Chapter 14

Reading and Understanding Employee Benefit Plan Financial Statements

David C. Lee and Michael A. Van Sertima

If your employee benefit plan has more than 100 participants, chances are you've had to work your way through the audited financial statements you're required to include with your Form 5500 filing. These statements contain a wealth of information about the financial health of your plan, and understanding them is an important fiduciary responsibility. To strengthen your grasp of financial statements, this chapter gives an overview that will make a plan's financial statements more informative, explains their basic structure and provides information on some of the more arcane aspects (such as actuarial tables). While this chapter focuses on Taft-Hartley (multiemployer) plans, much of it applies to other types of employee benefit plans.

Generally speaking, financial statements must be submitted with Form 5500 for employee benefit plans with more than 100 participants. What's more, an independent qualified public accountant—that is, a certified public accountant (CPA)—must audit the financial statements. The audit is required to be performed according to generally accepted auditing standards (GAAS). And, when Department of Labor (DOL) regulations call for supplemental schedules, the Employee Retirement Income Security Act (ERISA) also requires an audit report on those schedules. Sometimes the two audit reports are combined.

The purpose of financial statements is to tell fiduciaries, managers and other interested parties about the plan's ability to pay benefits. Ultimately, the financial statements are management's responsibility, even though the auditor helps to prepare them or even performs all of their preparation. The auditor is responsible for the audit report, which provides an opinion as to whether the financial statements are free of material misstatements. The auditor does not, however, guarantee the *accuracy* of the financial statements, but merely provides reasonable assurance that they are fairly stated.

It is important to keep in mind that "one size does *not* fit all." That is, there are different reporting requirements for defined benefit (DB) plans and defined contribution (DC) plans. For instance, you won't find benefit obligations listed in the statements of a DC plan such as a 401(k) plan or an annuity plan, since the net assets available for benefits of a DC plan are equivalent to its obligations for benefits. These plans maintain an account for each participant. Such an account is credited with contributions, investment income and gains; and it is debited (charged) with distributions, investment losses and expenses. At any one time, the sum of the balances in these individual participant accounts represents the total benefit obligation to participants.

On the other hand, DB plans, whether pension or health and welfare, must present benefit obligations and the changes in those benefit obligations in their financial statements in one of three ways.

1. As separate statements, i.e., two statements in addition to the statement of net assets available for benefits and statement of changes in net assets available for benefits. These additional statements are the statement of benefit obligations and statement of changes in benefit obligations.
2. Combined with the statement of net assets available for benefits and the statement of changes in net assets available for benefits, i.e., the statement of benefit obligations and the statement of changes in benefit obligations are superimposed on the statement of net assets available for benefits and the statement of

changes in net assets available for benefits, respectively.
3. Reported as a disclosure in the notes to the financial statements.

What do financial statements consist of? To give information about its resources and obligations, a plan's financial statements will include:
1. A statement of net assets available for benefits
2. A statement of changes in net assets available for benefits
3. A statement of benefit obligations
4. A statement of changes in benefit obligations
5. Notes to the financial statements.

Items 3 and 4 apply to DB plans only.

STATEMENT OF NET ASSETS AVAILABLE FOR BENEFITS

The corporate equivalent of this is the balance sheet. This statement shows the assets and liabilities of the plan. The liabilities in this statement, however, are not obligations to members for benefits, but instead are comprised of items such as amounts owed to vendors for operational and administrative expenses. Some key items shown on this statement are:
1. Investments—shown at fair value. In the case of securities that are traded, fair value means the quoted market prices of those securities. Investments for which quoted market prices are not readily available are valued using alternate methods: For example, real estate is valued through professional appraisal.
2. Contributions receivable from employers and, if it's a contributory plan, from employees
3. Property assets such as land and building, office furniture and equipment, etc. It is important to note how real estate is shown. It can be presented under property assets at historical cost after depreciation is factored in or under investments at appraised value. How it is reported depends on how it is used. If it serves primarily to house the operations of the plan and related entities such as other plans, then real estate is presented as a property asset. If it is held as an investment property, for instance, to generate rental income from unrelated third parties, then it should be shown in the investment section described above.
4. Amounts due to and from related entities. This item almost always appears if there is an administrative expense-sharing arrangement among related entities. Trustees need to ensure that balances owed by or to a related entity are collected or paid in a timely fashion. It's a very good idea—one that can save you much grief later on—to have an actual written expense-sharing agreement in place and to update it periodically.
5. Amounts due to and from brokers for investment trades executed at year-end but settled afterward
6. Operating liabilities—accounts payable and accrued expenses. Examples include amounts owed for rent, salaries and professional fees.
7. Net assets available for benefits. This important category deserves special attention. It presents total assets less total liabilities. This number, when compared with the benefit obligations, provides information on the financial status of a DB plan. In the case of a DC plan, the net assets balance approximates the sum of the participants' account balances.

STATEMENT OF CHANGES IN NET ASSETS AVAILABLE FOR BENEFITS

Here is where you find a summary of the plan's financial activity—essentially, its income and expenses—for the fiscal year. The corporate equivalent is the income statement. This statement shows additions (income) to and deductions (expenses) from the net assets available for benefits. In this statement you'll see, among other things:
1. Net appreciation or depreciation in the fair value of investments. This is just fancy language for realized and unrealized investment gains and losses. A gain or loss is realized only when a security is sold. If the investment's market value changes and it is still owned by the plan, i.e., if it has not been sold, the gain or loss is unrealized.
2. Interest and dividends earned on investments
3. Investment expenses such as fees paid to investment advisors, managers and custodians
4. Employers' (and employees') contributions
5. Benefit expenses. Note that this item is always shown on a cash basis even though the statements may be on a modified cash or accrual basis.
6. Administrative expenses such as salaries paid to plan personnel, office expenses, etc.
7. Net increase or decrease in net assets, or total additions (income) less total deductions (expenses). This is, in effect, the bottom line of the plan, telling you how well or poorly the plan has done financially.

STATEMENT OF A PLAN'S OBLIGATIONS

As mentioned above, DB plans do not include obligations for benefits in the statement of net assets available for benefits (balance sheet). Often, you'll find those obligations presented in a separate statement. Sometimes they appear combined with information in another statement or in the footnotes to the statements. But in all cases, the presentation must show the various components of benefit obligations.

For example, a health and welfare plan statement would show some or all of the following benefit obligations:

1. Claims payable—These are claims that have been processed for payment but not paid as of the end of the plan's accounting period.
2. Claims incurred but not reported (IBNR)—These are claims that have been incurred by participants and their dependents but have not been reported to the plan, that is, claims of which the plan is as yet unaware (sometimes referred to as pending and unrevealed claims). How can unknown claims be shown? Generally accepted accounting principles (GAAP) require that such claims be estimated and reported. This amount is combined with claims payable and reported as a single total.
3. Accumulated eligibility credits (AEC)—This is an estimate of a plan's obligation to provide benefits to participants following their termination of employment. Where such coverage is provided, it is usually extended for a period of time—typically 30 to 90 days following termination—that varies with the industry involved. Note that this is different from the Consolidated Omnibus Budget Reconciliation Act (COBRA) coverage.
4. Postretirement obligations—These must be estimated and reported if the plan provides health and welfare benefits to retirees or their dependents. For a plan this is a large amount, often well in excess of the plan's net assets available for benefits. Unlike pension benefits, however, these benefits are not vested, and they may be modified or even terminated, depending on the financial condition of the plan.

Since the last three items involve some degree of estimation, an actuary or benefit consultant usually provides the information for them. GAAP and GAAS dictate how this information is used and reported.

BENEFIT OBLIGATIONS OF A PENSION PLAN

Measurement of accumulated plan benefits (pension liabilities) is also prepared by an actuary and presented in an annual actuarial valuation. Some of this information appears in the financial statements. Accumulated plan benefits, i.e., the pension liabilities, should be reported in three categories: vested benefits of participants currently receiving benefits, other vested benefits and nonvested benefits.

FOOTNOTE DISCLOSURES

Too often, readers of financial statements hurry past the footnote disclosures. That's a mistake. Even though footnotes may seem dry and dense, they are a treasure-trove of information and an integral part of the financial statements. They play an important role in presenting and explaining the whole picture.

Related party transactions. Both accounting standards and ERISA require that transactions involving related parties (referred to as parties in interest, under ERISA) be reflected in footnotes to the financial statements. Parties in interest include fiduciaries or employees of the plan and a union whose members are participants of the plan. Examples of these transactions include expense-sharing arrangements among related plans and transactions with a contributing employer.

Nonexempt (prohibited) transactions. ERISA generally prohibits transactions between a plan and a party in interest. But there are exemptions which permit certain transactions with parties in interest such as the provision of accounting and legal services. If a prohibited transaction has occurred, it should be disclosed in the footnotes to the financial statements. Additionally, prohibited transactions must be disclosed in Part III (nonexempt transactions) of Schedule G of Form 5500, and the auditor's report must state an opinion whether the information reported on Schedule G is fairly stated.

Benefit obligations. For DB pension and welfare plans, the footnotes must disclose additional information from the actuary's valuation. As mentioned previously, disclosure in the footnotes is one method of presenting the information related to the liabilities for benefits. Regardless of the method of reporting the amounts, additional information must be disclosed for benefit obligations, including:

- The method and significant assumptions used in calculating the accumulated plan benefits of a pension plan and the postretirement benefit obligations of a health and welfare plan
- For a pension plan, whether minimum funding requirements were met.

Subsequent events. This footnote will tell you about significant events that occurred after the end of the fiscal year such as a decision to terminate or merge the plan or a large employer going out of business.

Plan amendments. GAAP requires the disclosure of significant plan amendments such as those pertaining to participants covered, vesting and benefit provisions.

Investments (GAAP). Individual investments that are equal to or greater than 5% of net assets available for benefits at the end of the plan year must be disclosed in the notes. This should not be confused with the ERISA requirement to list investments held at the end of the plan year, which is one of the supplemental schedules (see below). Additionally, the appreciation or depreciation in the fair value of investments must also be disclosed by category of investment—common stock, corporate debt instruments, governmental securities, and so forth.

Reconciliation between the financial statements and Form 5500. Financial statements and Schedule H of Form 5500 report some information differently. For example, real estate held as an operating asset is reported at depreciated historical cost in the financials, as required by GAAP, but at fair market value in Schedule H. For example, a building purchased for $50,000 might appear in the financials at a depreciated value of $40,000 and in Schedule H at $200,000, today's market value. This difference makes net assets available for benefits per the financials different from net assets as reported in Schedule H. So a reconciliation is required to be included as a footnote disclosure in the financial statements.

Another example is, in the case of a health and welfare plan, the net assets balance shown in Schedule H has been reduced by benefits payable and benefits incurred but not reported, as mentioned above. Since such liabilities are not included in the statement of net assets available for benefits, the statement and the schedule will show different results. ERISA requires these differences to be explained in the notes to the financials.

ERISA SCHEDULES

In addition to what GAAP requires, ERISA requires the following supplemental schedules be included in the annual report whenever they apply:
- Schedule of assets held for investment purposes and a listing of securities and other investments held at the end of the year. Real estate and participants' loans should be included.
- Schedule of reportable transactions. Certain transactions over a 5% or greater threshold involving securities and individuals are reported here.
- Schedule G of Form 5500
  —Part I—Schedule of Loans or Fixed Income Obligations in Default or Classified as Uncollectible
  —Part II—Schedule of Leases in Default or Classified as Uncollectible
  —Part III—Nonexempt Transactions. All nonexempt (prohibited) transactions are required to be reported, regardless of materiality.

AUDITORS' REPORTS

Supplemental Schedules

In addition to issuing a report on the basic financial statements, the auditor must also report on the above ERISA supplemental schedules. These reports may be combined or issued separately.

Basic Financial Statements

An auditor may issue several types of report (opinion), depending on the degree to which the financial statements adhere to GAAP and ERISA, and the extent to which the information required by the auditor was obtained. But DOL will accept only two types of audit opinion—a report with an unqualified or "clean" opinion, or a report with a disclaimer of opinion due to limited scope. An auditor issues a report with a disclaimer due to limited scope when a plan opts not to have audit procedures performed on its investment-related balances in the financial statements. ERISA allows this choice, if certain conditions are met with respect to the bank or insurance company that has custody of a plan's investments. In this case, an auditor would not be able to provide any opinion on the financial statements as a whole since the auditor had not performed any audit procedures on a highly material part of the statement, the investment-related balances.

DOL will reject a Form 5500 if it contains an adverse opinion, i.e., an opinion that the financial statements are not fairly stated as a whole, or an opinion that was qualified because of departures from GAAP or a restriction on the scope of the audit. A qualified opinion indicates that except for a specific reason, the financial statements are fairly stated.

CONCLUSION

As you can see, a step-by-step reading of the financial statements will give you a solid grasp of the financial health of your plan. That's what financial statements are designed to do—to provide an understanding of the financial condition of a benefit plan or other entity. They seek to capture important financial information in a way that is clear and useful. A careful reading will provide information you need to make prudent decisions for the plan and for the participants and beneficiaries it serves.

Chapter 15

Internal Controls: An Overview

Michael A. Van Sertima

INTRODUCTION

A plan's management should view an effective system of internal controls as one of the mechanisms for meeting its fiduciary responsibilities. Accounting internal controls do not usually come up for discussion among trustees and those charged with the day-to-day administration of an employee benefit plan, unless fraud against the plan is discovered. While trustees and plan professionals get involved in reviewing audited financial statements and other financial reports, very little attention is usually paid to internal control matters. This chapter will discuss, among other topics, the nature, purposes and limitations of internal controls; who is responsible for implementing and maintaining internal controls; the impact of third parties processing transactions; and how the auditor can assist the plan's management with respect to internal controls. It is meant to provide an overview for non-accountants involved in the administration and servicing of Taft-Hartley employee benefit plans.

DEFINITION

Internal control is defined in the auditing literature (AU Section 319, *Consideration of Internal Control in a Financial Statement Audit*) as "a process—effected by an entity's board of directors, management, and other personnel—designed to provide reasonable assurance regarding the achievement of objectives in the following categories: (a) reliability of financial reporting, (b) effectiveness and efficiency of operations, and (c) compliance with applicable laws and regulations."

THE AUDITOR'S RESPONSIBILITY VS. MANAGEMENT'S RESPONSIBILITY

Inherent in the above definition is plan management's responsibility to implement and maintain effective internal controls to ensure financial statements are free of material misstatements and the assets of the plan are adequately safeguarded from misappropriation. Management should implement and maintain effective internal controls that provide reasonable assurance that adequate controls exist over the plan's books and records, and its assets. An example of a basic internal control is the proper authorization of transactions.

The auditor's role with respect to internal controls is to gain an understanding so as to plan the audit of the entity's financial statements. Ensuring effective internal controls are in place is one of the day-to-day functions of management, and the auditor cannot take on that responsibility. To do so would breach the independence rules, which are at the core of the auditing profession.

It is important to note the auditor is not required to test internal controls in the course of performing an audit of financial statements. Generally accepted auditing standards require only that the auditor obtains an understanding of internal controls. So how does an auditor conclude whether or not the financial statements are fairly stated if, in certain cases, there will be no testing of internal controls? The answer is simply the auditor has other tools at his or her disposal.

Some elaboration of the preceding discussion would be helpful. It would be virtually impossible to perform an effective audit of a relatively large entity (for instance, General Motors or a multibillion-dollar employee benefit plan) without performing tests of its internal controls. The complexity of the organization and the volume of transactions would be such that the auditor would have to evaluate the way processing takes place through the system of internal controls, to determine the degree of reliability to be placed on the accounting information produced by the entity. The auditor would, therefore, test internal controls to determine their effectiveness and thus be assured the system of internal controls facilitates reliable processing of data, which is then summarized to produce financial statements that are free of material misstatements.

On the flip side of this are numerous situations in which an entity is considered small or not complex. In these situations, it is usually not economically feasible for the auditor to test internal controls. This can be appropriately bypassed and compensated for by the performance of other procedures. This does not mean the auditor ignores internal controls in the case of a relatively small entity. As previously mentioned, an audit would be substandard if the auditor did not obtain an understanding of the entity's internal controls. This understanding is obtained so the auditor can plan what types of procedures to perform and choose the extent to which they're needed and when to perform them.

THE ENGAGEMENT LETTER

The auditor's standard *engagement letter,* which is the contract between the auditor and the plan for the performance of the audit, makes clear the responsibilities of the auditor and those of plan management. It specifically states that, among other things, management is responsible for:
- The establishment and maintenance of adequate records and effective internal controls over financial reporting
- The design and implementation of programs and controls to prevent and detect fraud.

The standard letter also states the auditor will obtain an understanding of the internal controls only as is necessary to plan the audit of the financial statements. It goes on to say the audit is not designed to provide assurance on internal controls or to identify significant shortcomings in their design or operation.

THE MANAGEMENT LETTER

While only limited procedures on internal controls are performed in the course of a financial statement audit, the plan's management can still derive benefits from those procedures. By obtaining an understanding of the plan's internal controls, the auditor can identify weaknesses that can be remedied in a cost-effective way, even in a relatively small plan.

These findings, together with recommendations, should be communicated to the plan's management, either in writing or informally. When disseminated in writing, such correspondence is called a *management letter.* It is important to note this communication is not intended to be a comprehensive report on internal controls. It is only meant to bring to management's attention matters encountered as a consequence of obtaining an understanding of the internal controls to plan the audit of the financial statements. An accountant would have to perform a special audit in order to opine on the state of an entity's internal controls. The procedures performed for this type of engagement are broader in scope and will include testing of the internal controls to evaluate their effectiveness.

THE OBJECTIVES OF INTERNAL CONTROLS

Reliability of Financial Reporting

Generating reliable financial data is a must for the smooth operation of a plan (internal use) as well as to ensure the numbers included in regulatory filings (e.g., Form 5500) are fairly stated (external use).

Typically, plan management reviews both financial and nonfinancial data to monitor the operations of a plan. Management must be assured that the data on which they base decisions are reliable. This is extremely important, especially in cases where a decision is to be made as to whether certain operations (e.g., processing of medical claims) should be outsourced. Although annual audited financial statements provide a wealth of information about a plan's assets, liabilities, income and expenses, a sound system of internal control will provide additional reliable internal reporting.

Safeguarding Assets

This is an objective most can relate to; it has to do with preventing and detecting the misappropriation of the plan's assets. Adequate internal controls should be in place to safeguard the plan's assets against unauthorized use and disposition. Examples of such controls are requiring the use of two signatures on checks and board of trustees' authorization of payroll increases, conference expenses, capital expenditures and the write-off of uncollectible receivables.

Related to this objective is the safeguarding of a plan's records. Proper measures should be in place to prevent the destruction or loss of a plan's records and to recover the records in case either occurs.

The Effectiveness and Efficiency of Operations

In the course of performing the financial statement audit, the auditor may bring to management's attention matters which, while not affecting the maintenance of reliable books and records, impact the operations of the entity. These could be duplicate operations or operations that are not needed, for instance, maintaining detailed investment records at the plan office. This may not be necessary if the information is, or could be, provided by a benefit plan's investment custodian. Duplicate operations could come about where a plan grows in size and complexity due to mergers, for example, and little or no attention is paid to combining or coordinating operations. Suggestions for improvement in the efficiency of operations of the entity are usually included in the management letter. A comprehensive review of operations, whether done internally or by the plan's independent CPA, could be beneficial in identifying areas where some streamlining and cost savings could be accomplished.

Compliance With Applicable Laws and Regulations

A plan should have systems, policies and procedures in place to prevent and detect noncompliance with laws, rules and regulations pertaining to plan operations. Think ERISA and HIPAA. Written policies on the sharing of common administrative expenses, collection and delinquency, and reimbursement of trustees' expenses should be in place. Of course, these policies should meet the pertinent legal requirements and be followed.

Similarly, checks and balances should be in place to ensure there is compliance with the requirements of HIPAA.

INHERENT LIMITATIONS OF INTERNAL CONTROLS

Regardless of how well designed and smoothly operated a system of internal controls is, it can only provide reasonable—not absolute—assurance that the objectives of the plan will be attained. Surveys have indicated two of the main reasons why frauds occur are management override of internal controls and collusion. So it is no coincidence two key inherent limitations of a system of internal controls are:

- **Management override.** Internal controls can be circumvented by management pressuring a subordinate to record improper accounting entries. This may be done to conceal the misappropriation of assets, or to misrepresent the information reported in the financial statements, i.e., "fudging the numbers." For example, in order to show a better bottom line, management directs expenses for repairs and maintenance be recorded as additions to fixed assets, thus delaying the recognition of a portion of the expense.
- **Collusion.** In smaller organizations, for instance, where a bookkeeper who is inadequately supervised and monitored does the banking, maintenance of the books and records, etc., there is susceptibility for the perpetration of fraud by that person because of the lack of segregation of duties. However, this vulnerability does not necessarily disappear in larger organizations, where there may be layers of supervision, and checking and cross-checking taking place. It is extremely difficult, despite the segregation of duties that may exist in a larger entity, to prevent and uncover fraud, if there is collusion between two or more individuals. This collusion may be internal, involving employees only, or a combination of internal and external, involving an employee and a vendor.

COST/BENEFIT

The cost/benefit factor in the design and implementation of internal controls should always be considered. Every procedure that is put into place comes with a cost. It is important to keep in mind what the plan hopes to achieve. To an extent, this is a subjective process and the particular circumstances and risks of errors or fraud must be carefully considered. This is an area where management can consult with the plan's professionals.

SERVICE ORGANIZATIONS

It is quite common for plans to outsource some of their transaction processing and recordkeeping. For example, a custodian bank is given physical custody of the investments and maintains the records of transactions affecting those investments. Other examples of service organizations are a pharmacy benefit manager (PBM); an insurance company that provides administrative services only (ASO) in the area of health claims processing; a recordkeeper (a financial institution such as a mutual fund company, bank or insurance company that maintains participant account balances) of a participant-directed defined contribution retirement plan; and a dental claims processor. In some cases, a third-party administrator (TPA) is hired to assume all or substantially all the administrative functions, sometimes including the bookkeeping.

Whenever services are outsourced, the internal controls in operation at the service organization are considered a part of the plan's internal controls. For this reason, the plan auditor is required to obtain an understanding of those internal controls to plan the financial statement audit. It would be helpful for plan management, in the course of hiring a service organization or anytime thereafter, to ask about the internal controls in place at the service organization. Many of the larger service organizations hire a CPA to perform a special audit on the internal controls. The CPA issues an SAS 70 report, so named after the auditing standard that provides guidance on the performance of such an audit. It is normal for the plan's auditor to request this report, as it provides useful information for planning and performing an audit of the plan's financial statements. When a service organization or TPA lacks an SAS 70 report, the plan's auditor should perform procedures for obtaining an understanding of its internal controls. Plan management sometimes obtains and reads this report, since it gives them a sense of how their plan's business is conducted by the service organization.

THE TONE IS SET AT THE TOP

The plan's management (board of trustees, plan administrator, controller, etc.) has an impact on the environment that serves as the backdrop for the internal controls. It is imperative that managers show the same respect for policies and procedures expected from employees. The ethical values and integrity of management, and the attitude of management toward internal controls, filters down to employees. There is no better deterrent to the perpetration of harmful acts against a plan than a management—including the board of trustees—that is proactive and involved. The fact and perception that management pays attention to what is going on increases the likelihood of efficient and effective plan functioning and reduces the risk of fraud.

POLICIES AND PROCEDURES

While a detailed discussion of the various internal control policies and procedures is outside the scope of this chapter, there is one area that should be discussed and that is the segregation of duties. As far as is feasible, certain incompatible duties should not be combined in one person's job. Duties are incompatible when they provide an opportunity for someone to commit an error or fraud and then be able to conceal it. An example is where the employee who collects revenue (cash and checks) does the banking and also maintains the accounting records. Such an individual can commit fraud and then cover it up by "doctoring" the books. In this situation, the employee has custody of assets and maintains the records. Whenever possible, the functions of and responsibility for executing a transaction, recording a transaction and maintaining custody of the assets should be assigned to different employees.

In smaller organizations, it is not possible to have the degree of segregation of duties previously described. In such cases, the procedures below, some of which could also benefit larger plans, should be implemented.

- Plan management should increase its familiarity with operations and thus be better able to spot any anomalies.
- Increase supervision of employees.
- Ensure the accounting software leaves a trail of any bookkeeping entries that are changed or deleted. Once a transaction is recorded, it should only be removed or modified by posting another entry into the accounting records to reflect the deletion or change.
- Promptly prepare monthly bank reconciliations. After preparation, a second plan employee should independently review the bank reconciliations.
- The plan administrator or someone in a comparable position should directly receive and review all correspondence from the bank, including bank statements. That individual should count the canceled checks against the checks listed as cleared on the bank statement and examine canceled checks for any unusual payees and endorsements. Much fraud has been committed by employees writing checks to themselves or to dummy vendors.
- Eliminate or minimize the use of signature stamps. If signature stamps are used, implement adequate safeguards to prevent unauthorized use. Keep signature stamps securely locked with limited access.
- Adequately safeguard unused checks.
- Cancel paid invoices to prevent them from being used again for disbursing cash.
- Make employee vacations mandatory. While one employee is on vacation, have another employee perform the duties of the absent employee.

The above is not an exhaustive list—Your plan's professionals should be able to assist in the identification and implementation of additional procedures and policies.

CONCLUSION

Two other points should be noted: Internal control policies and procedures are only as good as the people carrying them out, and internal controls could become obsolete over time as conditions evolve. Therefore, continuous monitoring should take place to ensure that the entity's objectives are being met.

Chapter 16

Fiduciary Responsibility Issues in Connection With Payment or Reimbursement of Trustee Expenses

Marc Gertner

The Employee Retirement Income Security Act of 1974 (ERISA) has celebrated its 30th birthday as the "bible" of employee benefit plans—be they single employer or multiemployer, be they pension or welfare benefit plans. If one were to review International Foundation Annual Employee Benefits Conference programs from the late 1970s and compare them with the conference programs in the early 2000s, one would be struck with two apparently conflicting thoughts: look how far we have come vs. we are still talking about some of the same issues more than 25 years later. Factually, both conclusions are valid.

The topic of fiduciary responsibility issues in connection with the payment or reimbursement of trustee expenses has been of major interest and concern to both the Department of Labor (DOL) and to trustees of Taft-Hartley employee benefit plans since the enactment of ERISA. Although it has been the subject of numerous talks and articles, it is still an important topic in the prudent and proper operation and administration of employee benefit plans.

The compliance officers and staff of the Employee Benefits Security Administration (EBSA, the ERISA section) of DOL take a very stringent position on this topic. All monies contributed by employers on behalf of their employees pursuant to collective bargaining agreements are plan assets and, as such, are subject to ERISA. The fiduciary responsibility portions of ERISA (Title I, Part 4) are very explicit but very strict on the rules governing the use of plan assets. They must be used "solely in the interest of the participants and beneficiaries." Plan assets shall be expended "within the care, skill, prudence, and diligence . . . that a prudent man acting in a like capacity and familiar with such matters would use . . ." in expending plan assets—either to provide benefits to participants and their beneficiaries or to defray reasonable and necessary expenses of administration. DOL will not permit deviation from these standards.

These general, albeit stringent, principles are then given further meaning in their interpretation and application by the mindset of EBSA personnel. Veteran DOL employees have seen a few examples of flagrant violations of the provisions of Section 404(a) in expenditures by trustees of plans, causing them to be suspicious of most trustees of most Taft-Hartley plans. The guidelines and allowance for their own travel, lodgings, on-assignment meals, etc., are so strict they often tend to measure all similar expenditures by their rules of the game. The compliance officers and other ERISA personnel take their responsibilities very, very seriously and are dedicated to upholding the letter of the law.

In the overwhelming majority of Taft-Hartley plans, educational expenses are a very small part of plan administrative expenses—less than the service providers' annual fees, less than the investment managers' quarterly charges, less than Pension Benefit Guaranty Corporation (PBGC) premiums, less than the plan's annual premium for errors and omissions insurance or bond costs. On the other hand, any expenditure of plan assets is accorded sanctity and the full protection of ERISA. For that reason, DOL is properly concerned with these expenses.

In addition to a general concern, DOL has a number of "hot buttons" in the area of trustees' expenses. Golf while at an educational seminar, in-room movies and cocktails are at or near the top of the list. Spousal expenses are absolutely prohibited. Other DOL hot buttons include first-class airfare, the purchase of alcohol, the personal use of rental cars, personal phone calls and length of reimbursed stay. It is moot to debate the validity of such expenses. The "enforcers" say no! The issue is simply one of prudent compliance with your Section 404(a) general fiduciary duties.

MINDSET OF TRUSTEES

There are several different mindsets that some trustees of Taft-Hartley plans have with regard to payment or reimbursement of expenses incurred by them while attending educational seminars. Some trustees (but fortunately only a very small minority) view it as a paid windfall, a minor hit on the lottery and they are going to enjoy it for all it is worth. More trustees view it as a recompense for the hundreds of hours they spend each year, *without* compensation and away from their primary business, managing the affairs of their plans. They feel, if once every year or so they get a few days in the sun, an educational experience (but with some cocktails and good food, golf and perhaps entertainment), they have earned it. Finally, there are trustees whose position is that if they are expected to attend a seminar, they will do so but will travel as they do for an employer (first-class), stay, eat and relax as they do when they travel on their own (first-class, anything goes!).

Although each of these mindsets is understandable and has some support, none represents the appropriate mindset of a trustee and named fiduciary of an employee benefit plan subject to ERISA. To be legally compliant, the trustees' mindset should start with the concept that they are being afforded an educational opportunity to improve and hone their skills as named fiduciaries of an employee benefit plan subject to ERISA and to thus improve the operation and administration of the plan, solely for the best interests of the plan participants and their beneficiaries. Therefore, they will do anything and everything that can be done to maximize the experience—gain as much educational experience as there is to be gained. This means attending all sessions and using the time outside of sessions to talk with trustees of other comparable plans on how they approach and solve comparable problems.

The other aspect of a trustee's proper mindset deals with the expenditure of money to pay and/or reimburse expenses. If a single trustee traveled from Toledo to Hawaii for the 2005 Annual Employee Benefits Conference of the International Foundation, it probably cost the plan at least $3,500 and perhaps $5,000. If your rate of contribution to the pension plan is $2 per hour, a member had to work 1,750 to 2,500 hours, probably more than a full year, to send one trustee to Hawaii. If the total rate of contributions to all plans is $5 per hour, one electrician had to work 700 to 1,000 hours, almost one-half of total annual benefit contributions, to support the education of one trustee. When cocktails, dinner and tips are translated into hours of pension contribution, it should have a different feel to it, if you have the proper trustee mindset.

PLAN DOCUMENTATION

For trustees to have the legal and proper documentation for the payment and/or reimbursement of trustee expenses in connection with attendance at educational seminars and other like programs, two documents are needed:
1. A written policy statement on attendance at and participation in educational seminars approved by the full board at a duly called meeting
2. A written policy statement on the payment and/or reimbursement of trustees' expenses.

Policy on Attendance and Participation at Educational Seminars

The first step is for your plan(s) and every Taft-Hartley employee benefit plan to adopt a prudent and proper policy statement on the attendance at and participation in educational seminars. This statement would include a clear position on how many seminars each trustee could attend in each plan year. It would make provisions for the number of trustees from the plan who could attend the same seminar. It would set forth the board's rule on obtaining a certificate of attendance and participation at the seminar, in making a report on any and all seminars attended and all other matters pertaining to the attendance and participation at trustee seminars. Strict compliance with the trustees' statement is an absolute condition precedent to a trustee's entitlement to payment or reimbursement of expenses in connection with attendance at that seminar.

Although it is a valid general rule that all plans should have a policy statement on attendance at seminars, since all plans are unique, there is no one statement that will fit all plans. The statement adopted by each separate and distinct plan must be appropriate to that plan and its facts, circumstances and characteristics.

A key issue trustees need to address in their policy statement on attendance at educational seminars is the number of seminars a trustee may attend in any one year. Again, the trustees need to factor in practical and economic conditions. Normally, at least one seminar but not more than two seminars per year would be reasonable, probably not so for a hypothetical small health and welfare plan. In some of our smaller plans, a two- or three-year rotation (i.e., one seminar every two or three years) has been established. Again, for companion pension and welfare plans, with 12,000 to 14,000 participants and $250 million in aggregate assets and a total of only four trustees, attendance at two seminars a year is probably reasonable. Another limitation is that only one trustee should attend a single-program seminar. At the International Foundation's Annual Employee Benefits Conference, with the breadth of its programs, it would be proper for two to four trustees to attend. That intent is to provide coverage at all relevant presentations but to avoid duplication.

Within the general rule, there are several other limitations a prudent and proper policy statement must include. It sounds obvious, but please note pension plan trustees can only attend seminars dealing with pension and pension-related topics and not health and welfare-only programs, and vice versa. A second limitation that should be obvious (but one that has snagged the San Diego Laborers and other plans) is, if the same seminar is being sponsored in multiple locations, the trustees must attend the closest program.

Each trustee seeking to attend an educational seminar, with proper expenses paid and/or reimbursed by the plan(s) on which he or she serves, should have attended at least 75% of the regularly scheduled and specially called meetings of the board(s) of trustees on which he or she serves. This is my opinion and the opinion of the more knowledgeable and respected ERISA fund counsel. There is some support from EBSA, but it is not black-letter law yet.

It is strongly suggested that the policy statement require the trustee attending a seminar to earn a certificate of attendance as a condition of payment and/or reimbursement of expenses by the plan. This is not required, however. In *Dole v. Formica,* 14 EBC 1397 (D.C.N.D.E.D. Ohio, 1991), the court, in considering allegations of breach of fiduciary responsibility in connection with attendance at educational seminars and when a certificate of attendance was not earned, stated:

> The Secretary bears the burden of proving the expenses incurred by the Funds in permitting several Trustees to attend conferences were unreasonable. The Court finds that the Secretary has failed to meet this burden. The Secretary has provided no evidence that such trips to conferences were not common. Mr. Sweeney, the Secretary's own expert witness, stated that attendance was common. The Court finds unpersuasive the Secretary's argument that the conferences were not necessary or helpful because the Trustees did not obtain certificates of attendance. Mr. Sweeney testified that he did not receive certificates of attendance. The Court encourages the Trustees to obtain such certificates in the future in view of this litigation. There is no evidence to show that these conferences were not helpful to Trustees, especially for Trustees, such as these, who are relatively inexperienced in Trust management. Nor has the Secretary provided any testimony that the Trustees in any way manipulated the Funds to cover unlawful expenditures.

Notwithstanding this holding, based on the attitudes and viewpoints of DOL, based upon the source of the money paying for attendance expenses, etc., if a trustee cannot attend enough sessions to earn a certificate, he or she should pay his or her own way. In my opinion, trustees have a duty to adopt and implement such a policy. It obviously needs to be explained to each trustee before he or she leaves to attend an educational conference. It needs to be rigidly enforced, without exception (not even for Mr. Big, owner of the largest employer of union members and the largest contributor to the plans, or for Mr. Popularity, the longtime president of the local union). It may not make the trustees "popular," but it will lead to them being respected!

It is incumbent upon any and all trustees who attend educational seminars at plan expense to come back and report to the other trustees and the advisors on the sessions they attended. A written report is not required, if that is not comfortable for the trustee. A trustee can and should bring back the program materials and his or her notes from the sessions. He or she can tell the other trustees and the advisors what he or she heard. He or she can get the board to talk about the same issues that were on the program, with the attendee as the discussion leader. Again, if a trustee expects a brother to work a year to generate the contributions to cover a seminar, if he or she wants the equivalent of ten members receiving a week of income disability payments of $350 or ten members receiving a $500 monthly pension benefit, then DOL sentiment seems to be that if the trustee cannot report back to the other trustees and share his or her educational experience, that trustee should not attend.

Policy Statement on Payment and/or Reimbursement of Trustees' Expenses

The second document that all trustees of all Taft-Hartley plans should adopt in the discharge of their fiduciary responsibility in the area of trustee expenses is a policy statement on the payment and/or reimbursement of expenses, whether incurred at an educational seminar or otherwise. This document must be in writing, adopted by the trustees at a duly called, convened and held meeting of the trustees and then rigorously followed. Both the statutory enactments and the subsequent regulations to ERISA provide us with insights into the parameters of prudence and reasonableness for this policy statement.

First, Section 404(a) provides that trustees must act solely in the interests of the plan participants. Thus, to send trustees to educational seminars and to pay the expenses thereof requires that plan participants and their beneficiaries must benefit from attendance at the seminar. More importantly, Section 404(a)(1)(A) limits the expenditure of trust assets for the maximization of benefits to plan participants and to defray the reasonable cost of necessary expenses. Please note the trustees must be able to demonstrate the expenses incurred by the plan in connection with the attendance by one or more trustees at a seminar were both:

1. Reasonable in their amount
2. Necessary to the lawful purpose.

Finally, ERISA Section 408(c) allows a fiduciary to receive "reimbursement of expenses properly and actually incurred" in the performance of his or her duties with the plan. Again, note the twin tests:

1. Properly incurred
2. Actually incurred.

DOL Regulation Section 2550.408c-2 is very short but insightful. First, reasonableness is judged on a case-by-case, facts-and-circumstances basis. Thus, reimbursement of $2,500 for expenses in one case in connection with a seminar might be adjudged reasonable, but $500 for expenses in another case might be unreasonable. It is a facts-and-circumstances, case-by-case basis. Second, reimbursement is limited to directly incurred expenses. Thus, a trustee who gets a free ride to a seminar with a trustee of another plan cannot be reimbursed for travel expenses to the seminar.

As you might expect, the regulation clearly states multiple reimbursement for the same expense is illegal, improper and, in one case, confining. A disbarred Miami attorney charged 13 plans $1,500 to defray his expenses to attend a seminar. He served several years in the federal penitentiary at Elgin Air Force Base in Florida, and deservedly so.

Reimbursable expenses shall in no event include expenses of a personal nature or those expenses not related to the operation and administration of the plan. For example, personal recreational expenses such as fishing, golf, tennis, etc., are not deemed reimbursable expenses, nor are expenses incurred by or on behalf of a spouse, companion or associate traveling with the trustee.

Your policy statement should specify the extent of reimbursement of travel expenses. A blanket provision of first-class airfare is neither reasonable nor proper. Can you reimburse for first-class airfare? Yes, if the travel is 1,500 to 2,000 miles or perhaps three to four hours. But to pay first-class airfare to fly from Atlanta to Washington, from New York to Boston or from Los Angeles to San Francisco is silly and a waste of trust assets. If you want to be completely safe, travel the way DOL travels—coach. Perhaps on cross-country trips a first-class policy can be justified, but make it reasonable and proper.

If auto travel is used, it is recommended trustees adopt and use the Internal Revenue Service reimbursement rate. If you do, remember the owner of the car, not the passenger, gets reimbursed. Also, the car travel allowance cannot exceed the applicable air travel allowance.

How about lodging? The proper and reasonable level of reimbursement is a superior room, single occupancy rate. If you want or need a suite, a double or whatever, that is your expense. Superior room, single occupancy meets reasonable and proper tests.

What perhaps is more difficult but what must be addressed in a prudent and proper policy statement is, how many nights of lodging does the plan reimburse? There is a rule of thumb that is believed to be reasonable and proper. If a trustee can leave home at or after 7:00 a.m. and arrive at the seminar one hour before it begins, the trustee cannot be reimbursed for lodging for the night before. If the trustee cannot arrive one hour prior to the seminar, the trustee may go the day before and the plan can reimburse for lodging the night before the seminar. On the other hand, if the trustee can leave the seminar one hour after the conclusion of the seminar and arrive home by 9:00 p.m., he or she should go home. If he or she cannot, the plan can reimburse for postseminar lodging.

A frequently asked question is: May I stay and be reimbursed for my expenses if I go to the seminar site on Saturday before the Monday start to take advantage of my super-saver airfare, which requires a "Saturday night stay"? The answer is incredibly easy. Yes, if the total cost of your expenses incurred is less with a Saturday stay. That is, if you can save more money on the super-saver fare than the extra hotel, food and miscellaneous expenses you incur, you may go on Saturday and be reimbursed. If the cost to the plan is higher (i.e., the extra expenses exceed the super-saver airline savings), the answer, without equivocation, is no.

The other aspects of a proper and prudent policy statement on expenses must deal with meals, surface transportation, etc. There have been as many or more problems in this small dollar area as with car travel and hotels. The cause of the problem is twofold. First, DOL is ultraconservative, bordering on unreasonable, in its approach. DOL will challenge a trustee, who donates 100 or 150 hours a year to serve as a trustee without compensation, over a $3 martini or a $7.95 in-room movie.

A prudent approach is to state in the policy statement that reimbursement will be made for the reasonable cost of necessary expenses actually incurred up to $X per day. The plan does not pay $X per day. The plan reimburses the reasonable cost of necessary expenses actually incurred, not to exceed $X.

There are also some other miscellaneous items that should be included in a policy statement. The first is documentation of expenses. The Internal Revenue Code and the Treasury Department regulations promulgated thereunder clearly state the requisite documentation required for an expense account reimbursement. You are urged to adopt this regulation as your rules and to have your plan's auditor write them for you in language you can understand, to make his or her write-up an exhibit to your policy statement, and to then follow it to the "nth degree." In this regard, it is recommended that someone (the administrative manager, the auditor or counsel) be designated to review and approve all expense accounts vis-à-vis the policy statement and to report thereon either in writing or at a trustees' meeting, which report is then recorded in the minutes.

Another issue to be addressed in your policy statement is that of advances. Trustees should not be expected to front the registration, hotel deposit and/or bill, airline ticket, etc. The better procedure is for the plan to register the trustee and make and pay for hotel, rental car and airline reservations. The fewer dollars the trustees handle, the fewer problems you will have with DOL. Still, it is legal and proper for the plan to advance certain monies to a trustee in connection with his or her attendance at an educational seminar. This topic is addressed in DOL Regulation Section 2550.408c-2, which authorizes the advance *if*:

- The amount advanced is reasonable with respect to the anticipated amount of direct expenses.
- The advance is made no more than 30 days before incurring the actual expense.
- The trustee accounts for the advance against the expenses at the end of the period covered by the advances.

These three rules are simple, reasonable and capable of compliance. Your policy statements should adopt the regulation and spell out the three rules. The sanction, if the trustee does not comply, is no reimbursement at all. He or she must pay back all the money to the plan, with interest.

The issue of per diems is confusing. It is a generally accepted rule that a per diem payment to a trustee in connection with attendance and participation at an educational seminar is per se illegal, because the statute talks about reasonable and necessary "direct expenses actually incurred." A per diem is in lieu of direct expenses actually incurred and is, therefore, illegal. What is being suggested is not a per diem, but a daily cap or maximum; but the basic reimbursement is for reasonable and necessary direct expenses, actually incurred and substantiated. The other area where the concept of per diems is involved is with regard to preseminar advances. Trustees may instruct the administrative manager to make advances based in part upon a daily per diem of $X. However, as the regulation requires, a trustee must account for and substantiate his or her expenses promptly upon return, at which time he or she is reimbursed based upon reasonable and necessary expenses, actually incurred and substantiated. The trustee then receives an additional payment or repays the plan, based upon the final accounting.

It is a prohibited transaction for a trustee to receive reimbursement from the plan for an expense paid for or reimbursed by another party—an association, a union, his or her employer, etc. This is a sensitive area with DOL because of former attorney Seymour Gopman of Miami and others who grossly abused their plans. Please note the mere receipt of monies from the plan that are also paid or reimbursed by another party is a prohibited transaction, even if the next day the trustee repays the plan with interest. Employee benefit plan assets are like your daughter's Girl Scout cookie money or your church assets. You must respect them; you must treat them with care, or you are in for a peck of trouble. In one case where a union trustee took dual advances from the plan and from the union, DOL insisted on a return of the money to the plan, with interest; payment of the penalty for a prohibited transaction; and pursued removal of the trustee. It is not a laughing matter, at least with DOL.

Another topic that must be covered is compensation for lost wages while at a seminar. This topic has created great consternation among some boards of trustees. The rule is set forth in ERISA Section 408(b)(2), as follows:

(c) Nothing in §406 shall be construed to prohibit any fiduciary from—

* * *

(2) receiving any reasonable compensation for services rendered, or for the reimbursement of expenses properly and actually incurred, in the performance of his duties with the plan; except that no person so serving who already receives full-time pay from an employer or an association of employers, whose employees are participants in the plan, or from an employee organization whose members are participants in such plan shall receive compensation from such plan, except for reimbursement of expenses properly and actually incurred; . . .

Applied literally, this can only apply to hourly rated employees, since the statute, the regulations, the case law and common sense all make it clear beyond discussion that a person who is already compensated for his or her time (i.e., salaried union or corporate employees) *cannot be compensated* for the time spent on trustee business, whether it is attendance at a trustees' meeting or at a seminar.

Can plans reimburse an hourly rated trustee attending an educational seminar? Probably. A private letter ruling issued by DOL on March 17, 1976 allowed reimbursement to union trustees who were hourly rated workers, but not for salaried officers or employees of the union. However, plans that wish to avoid a potential challenge from DOL do not reimburse trustees for lost wages. DOL applies a very narrow and strict approach on this issue; understandably so in view of some rather grotesque examples of abuse in the early years. Thus, in some instances, the union reimburses the wages, as it would if the trustees were on a negotiating or grievance committee, or the union may have the member use some vacation time.

For plans to reimburse for lost wages, the trustees must verify the trustee was gainfully employed immediately prior to the seminar, he or she would have worked the days he or she attended the seminar, he or she is reimbursed only for the actual hours of work lost while at the seminar, etc. For example, if a trustee-attendee were a roofer who was gone Monday through Thursday but it rained all day Tuesday and half of Wednesday, he or she cannot properly be reimbursed for those hours because he or she did not actually lose pay while attending the seminar. Also, to reimburse for Thursday the trustee must be able to document he or she could not have reasonably gotten back to his or her hometown in time to work at least part of that day.

An example of the narrow and strict interpretation given to questions of trustee compensation for attendance and participation at trustee meetings, educational seminars and the like involves the legality and propriety of compensating a trustee who is a retired person and, therefore, is not receiving compensation from anyone—save perhaps his or her pension or Social Security entitlement.

On September 26, 1996, DOL issued an information letter to Ira B. Golub, Esquire regarding the S.E.I.U. Local No. 74 employee benefit plans. Golub sought an advisory opinion that James Kosloski, a longtime employer trustee, could receive compensation from the plans for his services as an employer trustee since his company (he owned 99% of the stock, was an officer, director and full-time employee) no longer had a collective bargaining agreement with S.E.I.U. Local No. 74 and no longer made contributions to the plans.

Since the requested opinion was essentially factual in nature, an advisory opinion under ERISA Procedure 76-1, Section 5, was not proper. Instead, an information letter in accordance with Section 11 of the ERISA procedure was issued.

After reviewing Section 406(b)(1) and Section 408(b)(2), DOL concluded as follows:

> In Advisory Opinion 88-13 (Aug. 29, 1988), the Department addressed a situation in which an employer was no longer party to a collective bargaining agreement, was no longer contributing to a welfare benefit plan under the agreement and no longer had participants (either current employees or retirees) in the welfare plan. The Department concluded, under these circumstances, a full-time compensated employee of the employer would not be precluded from receiving compensation from the welfare plan for his services as trustee to the welfare plan. However, the Department distinguished the situation in which former employees of the employer had retired and were continuing to receive benefits under a pension plan to which the employer had formerly contributed, and several current employees had vested rights under the pension plan. Under these circumstances, the Department concluded the trustee was barred from receiving compensation from the pension plan because, with regard to that plan, he was receiving full-time compensation from an employer described in Section 408(c)(2).

In DOL Advisory Opinion 97-03A, DOL held the trustees' decision to pay and/or reimburse expenses out of plan assets is a fiduciary determination subject to the terms of ERISA Section 404(a). As to any particular expense item and as to all expenses, the trustees must consider the following issues:

- Is the payment of the proposed expense by the plan authorized by the plan documents?
- Is the payment of the proposed expense in the interest of the plan participants and beneficiaries?
- Is the amount of the expense reasonable?

Of late, bad-intentioned trustees and well-paid professional service providers have a new ploy to allow trustees of well-administered and well-advised employee benefit plans to enjoy golf, fishing, movies, alcohol, spousal accompaniment and a broad range of personal benefits while attending an educational seminar. The service provider pays for the trustee's round of golf, caddy and souvenir golf shirt, or the trustee's share of the fishing charter, or martinis, or the spouse's food, drink and recreational expenses. There are a sufficient number of court decisions in point to conclude such a practice is illegal. The trustee/plan fiduciary who accepts these economic favors from a service provider is guilty of a breach of fiduciary duty and probably a prohibited transaction. See, for example, *Secretary of Labor v. Carell,* 17 EBC 1159 (M.D.Tenn. 1993); *Brink v. DaLesio,* 496 F.Supp. 1350 (D.C.D.C. 1980). A good rule that will protect the trustees (individually and as a board) and the plan is: If you cannot get a particular expense reimbursed by the plan under its rules and regulations, it cannot be reimbursed to you by anyone and is a personal expense.

Another frequently asked question is: May the plan pay and/or reimburse from plan assets the expenses for registration and attendance at educational seminars for professional, third-party service providers? DOL's answer is generally no. Clearly, the plan cannot pay and/or reimburse the expenses of a service provider to attend an educational seminar to advance the general knowledge of the service provider. If, however, there was a special, single-topic program (i.e., a new federal statute applying to employee benefit plans or a massive revision to ERISA that is directly applicable to action contemplated by the board), it would be permissible. However, I strongly recommend, to avoid possible problems, boards of trustees adopt a rule as part of their payment and/or reimbursement policy statement that service providers' expenses for attendance at seminars *not* be reimbursed and/or paid. You hire a professional because he or she is knowledgeable and experienced. If the law changes, he or she has a professional obligation to stay knowledgeable and experienced. Trustees pay for this in the service providers' hourly rate or monthly fee; and trustees should not be directly obligated to pay for their professionals' continuing education.

In doing research for this chapter, I read an article by Robert Ridley, a well-known and greatly respected Los Angeles ERISA attorney. In his conclusion on the topic of trustee expenses, Ridley stated:

> Reading the prudent man rule makes one realize that there are probably a lot fewer people who possess all of these characteristics than there are positions that must be filled. The result is that the majority of individual trustees are intelligent people of goodwill who find themselves constantly striving to meet the standards established by ERISA.

We are faced not with a shortage of prudent and intelligent persons willing to undertake onerous tasks, but with a definite shortage of individuals who are "familiar with such matters" and with the conduct of enterprises of like character and with like aims. This statement is not an indictment of trustees; rather, it is a recognition of the complexity of the subjects with which the trustees must deal on a day-to-day basis.

***

In sum, problems of trustee expenses are similar to other problems in the field of employee benefits. Their solution depends on the goodwill of dedicated individuals functioning in accordance with both the letter and spirit of the law.

This is an appropriate conclusion to this chapter.

Chapter 17

Trustee Fiduciary Liability Insurance

Jeffrey D. Mamorsky

The failure of those who participate in and provide leadership to the retirement plan system to establish effective retirement plan governance procedures has resulted in a retirement plan crisis of significant proportions. Trustee fiduciary liability has exploded as the result of accounting abuses, mutual fund market timing scandals, hidden investment expense fees, expanding fiduciary litigation, governmental investigations and the alleged "gaming" of pension actuarial assumptions to lower plan contributions and increase benefits.

Trustees now recognize that enormous personal liability comes with the responsibility of being an Employee Retirement Income Security Act (ERISA) fiduciary and only a fiduciary liability policy can indemnify trustees for breaches of fiduciary duty. It is illegal for the plan itself to provide such indemnification.

This liability has increased as the result of new legislation such, as the Sarbanes-Oxley Act of 2002 (SOX) which imposes new ERISA white-collar criminal penalty provisions on trustees for the failure to establish internal control procedures, that assures plan operation in conformance with plan documents and applicable law.

Also, the Internal Revenue Service (IRS) has established a Multiemployer Plans Examination Program that imposes monetary sanctions on trustees for failure to adopt "self-audit" control procedures under the Employee Plans Compliance Resolution System (EPCRS).

Department of Labor (DOL) has also heightened its oversight of ERISA compliance with a Voluntary Fiduciary Correction Program (VFCP) and increased fiduciary and plan expense audits that can result in personal liability and the imposition of ERISA civil penalties. Finally, scandals in the financial and investment community and poor funding of pension plans have spawned an onslaught of participant and government litigation.

RETIREMENT PLAN CRISIS

SOX ERISA White-Collar Crime Penalty Provisions

SOX includes an ERISA white-collar crime penalty provision that amends ERISA so as to enhance the sanctions on multiemployer plan trustees' and other plan fiduciaries' requirements. This could occur, for example, in the case of a certified financial statement of a pension plan where the auditor now requires trustees to represent that the plan is operated pursuant to its terms and applicable law as a result of IRS monetary sanctions. This representation, which appears as a footnote in every plan's financial statement, is likely to be inaccurate in the absence of the establishment of internal control procedures that enable the trustees to identify inconsistencies between administration, plan provisions and IRS qualification requirements to avoid IRS monetary sanctions.

SOX Auditing Standards and Procedures has resulted in the issuance of "SAS No. 99—Consideration of Fraud in a Financial Statement Audit" (SAS 99) by the AICPA. SAS 99 requires the auditor to obtain reasonable assurance that financial statements are free of material misstatements whether caused by error or fraud. According to SAS 99, misrepresenting information in response to audit inquiries may result in fraudulent financial reporting. This could occur, for example, in the absence of internal control procedures that test the integrity of the trustee's representations in the financial report that the plan is operated in accordance with its terms and applicable law.

The SOX enhanced ERISA white-collar crime penalty provisions impose a $100,000 sanction per trustee and up to ten years imprisonment for willful violations of ERISA's financial statements and other reporting and disclosure requirements. Misrepresentation of operational compliance with plan document and IRS qualification requirements in a qualified plan financial statement in the absence of internal control procedures that verify compliance may be considered "willful" behavior resulting in the impositions of such sanctions.

IRS Multiemployer Examination Program

Under the Employee Plans Closing Agreement Program (CAP), IRS imposes CAP monetary sanctions on trustees for failure to operate retirement plans in accordance with IRS qualification requirements and for failure to follow the terms of the plan documents even if plan operation is within compliance with IRS qualification requirements. The IRS EPCRS program requires trustees to establish self-audit internal control procedures to qualify for self-correction and mitigate the amount of IRS monetary sanctions.

Sanctions are imposed by IRS on audit even if failures are unintentional discrepancies between plan operation and plan documents that result in no harm to plan participants. The maximum payment amount (MPA) is the total amount of tax that would apply if the plan were disqualified. For example, the starting point for negotiations with IRS on the amount of the sanction is generally 20% of plan assets.

If an IRS auditor identifies any defects in the plan's operational compliance with the Code's qualification requirements, the auditor will require retroactive correction of the defects and ask the trustees as "responsible fiduciaries" to make a CAP monetary sanction nondeductible payment to IRS, the amount of which is generally based on the total amount of tax that would be imposed on the contributing employers, trust and participants if the plan were disqualified. In many instances, this will be a substantial amount (possibly millions of dollars). IRS has already concluded thousands of CAP audits and has imposed monetary sanctions as high as $10 million in the case of a large multiemployer plan for failure to comply operationally with the Code's qualification requirements. Hundreds of additional cases are currently being negotiated with IRS under CAP.

The issues identified by IRS on audit rarely constitute intentional or blatant violations of the qualification requirements of the Internal Revenue Code. The majority of the problems appear to involve errors that often occur in the administration of qualified plans and are of the type that can easily be discovered on an audit by IRS. For example, in one case the trustees of a large collectively bargained defined benefit plan paid in excess of $5 million in CAP monetary sanctions plus the cost of correction of various service-crediting violations that resulted in vesting and benefit accrual violations. The service-crediting problem was caused by the failure of the employers and plan administrator to maintain a system to track "covered employment" (i.e., employment covered under the terms of the collectively bargained agreement) in an industry in which union shops went in and out of business frequently and there was no system in place to keep track of union members as they moved from one shop to another or from employment status to unemployment status and vice versa.

In another case, a large collectively bargained defined benefit plan did not track service properly and as a result, a large number of employees did not receive service credit under the plan. Moreover, as a result of a failure to adjust employer contributions rates, the plan became vastly overfunded. This resulted in the assessment and collection of a multimillion dollar CAP monetary sanction upon audit by IRS.

There is a new IRS audit initiative targeting "large" retirement plans with 2,500 or more participants. This large retirement plan audit initiative is different in size, scope and intensity than previous audits of qualified plans. An IRS audit team consists of six to eight professionals (including revenue agent, benefits and computer audit specialists, benefits attorney and actuary). The typical large plan IRS audit exam is expected to last 200-300 staff days. Large multiemployer plans and other risk profilers are specifically targeted.

The board of trustees of a multiemployer plan has the ultimate responsibility to maintain the qualified status of the plan. Under an IRS field directive issued March 14, 1995, the trustees are personally liable for any sanctions imposed by IRS under CAP and may also be responsible for certain costs of correcting the disqualifying operational defect. The field directive emphasizes, however, that in the case of a multiemployer plan, IRS may also seek payment of the CAP sanction from responsible fiduciaries (e.g., fund director or other in-house plan administrator), contributing employers or a third party responsible for the disqualifying operational defects such as a professional administrator or other service provider. In such a case, IRS is directed to obtain the assistance of DOL who has "greater leverage to involve the third-party fiduciary in negotiations regarding the source of the CAP sanction."[1]

The field directive provides that if a fiduciary (e.g., trustee) in this situation directs the trust to relieve him of the CAP monetary sanction or other costs of correcting operational defects, the fiduciary may be engaging in a prohibited transaction under Section 4975 of the Internal Revenue Code and Section 406 of ERISA and may also violate the exclusive purpose and prudence requirement of Section 404 of ERISA.

In this regard, in addition to personal liability under ERISA Section 409 for restoring plan losses in the event of a breach of fiduciary duty, as a result of the prohibited transaction the trustees may be assessed a penalty of 15% of the amount involved and 100% of the amount involved for failure to correct within 90 days.

Thus, it is clear IRS considers multiemployer plan trustees responsible for any disqualifying defects and may pursue such persons for payment of the CAP sanction. Indeed, the field directive provides that if IRS has difficulty in obtaining payment of the CAP sanction from the responsible fiduciaries, payment cannot be made from trust assets unless DOL is contacted for help in "bringing fiduciaries to the negotiating table."

VFCP

The VFCP, a DOL program, enables ERISA fiduciaries to identify and correct prohibited transactions and other ERISA violations before an audit by DOL. Such self-correction is important since ERISA Section 502(l) imposes a civil penalty of 20% of the applicable recovery amount in the case of a breach of fiduciary responsibility, including the requirement to administer the plan in accordance with the documents and instruments governing the plan and the requirements of ERISA.

Increased Government and Participant Litigation

Multiemployer plan trustees and union officials face the spectre of participant and member lawsuits by class action plaintiff attorneys such as the so-called "pension police." Moreover, trustees are exposed to civil liability for failure to establish IRS and DOL self-audit compliance programs that require trustees to identify and correct retirement plan violations in order to avoid the imposition of sanctions.

DOL Plan Exposure Audit Initiative

Disclosure of retirement plan expenses to plan participants is the responsibility of multiemployer plan trustees. DOL has established an aggressive plan expense audit initiative that imposes personal liability on trustees for failure to monitor the reasonableness of plan expenses. DOL has also undertaken an audit of plan auditors to make sure that there is an adequate review of internal control procedures.

WHAT CAN BE DONE?

What is surprising is that the current retirement plan crisis has occurred despite the government's establishment of voluntary self-audit programs that enable employers to avoid stiff penalties imposed by IRS and DOL that could equal up to 20% of plan assets. Some trustees have generally been reluctant to establish internal control procedures that identify and correct errors in operational compliance and have instead opted to play the "audit lottery" hoping that they won't get caught by IRS or DOL. This reluctance to self-audit the operational compliance of their retirement plans should change with the enactment of SOX, which for the first time imposes sanctions and imprisonment of trustees and other fiduciaries for failure to establish and monitor internal control procedures that would ascertain operational compliance. For example, a failure to comply with the new SOX ERISA white-collar criminal penalty requirements can result in a penalty of $100,000 per responsible individual and up to ten years imprisonment.

Solutions to the Problem

As a result of these measures, what does a trustee do to make sure that his or her behavior is prudent and adequately protect the trust and himself or herself from personal liability? One answer is to have fund counsel review all relevant insurance policies and report to the trustees on coverage and exclusions (any major changes). Fund counsel should then discuss the protection trustees have (and do not have) under the current policies and meet with the fund's broker and/or consultant to recommend improvements in coverage and/or a lowering of costs. Another answer that will surely result in enhanced coverage on a cost-effective basis is the establishment of self-audit internal control procedures necessary to assure operational and plan document compliance and comply with the IRS Employee Plans Compliance Resolution System, ERISA fiduciary and SOX financial reporting requirements.

Compelling Need for Insurance

As a result of personal liability imposed on trustees for breach of fiduciary duty under ERISA and imposition of monetary sanctions by IRS and DOL for failure to administer plans in accordance with plan documents and applicable law, there is a compelling need for plans and trustees to purchase insurance to cover defense and settlement costs relating to compliance with the bonding requirements of ERISA, ERISA breach of fiduciary and/or prohibited transaction violations, corrections of administrative errors and CAP monetary sanctions imposed by IRS.

Unfortunately, there is often confusion and misunderstanding as to the insurance necessary to cover these four areas of liability. For example, it is not uncommon for trustees to believe that their bonding insurance also covers fiduciary liability, that professional liability "errors and omissions" insurance covers ERISA fiduciary liability, or that their fiduciary liability policy covers not only ERISA breaches of fiduciary duty but also losses relating to errors in the administration of the plan. In reality, it is not uncommon for professional liability "errors and omissions" insurance to exclude wrongful acts relating to breaches of fiduciary responsibility under ERISA and at least one fiduciary liability policy does not cover administrative errors without the purchase of a specific employee benefits liability or "errors and omissions" insurance endorsement.

Moreover, there is limited coverage of fines or penalties such as IRS CAP monetary sanctions which are only covered in certain amounts (no more than $100,000). Only recently has an insurance program been available offering "IRS liability insurance" covering the trustees for expanded CAP monetary sanctions that IRS may impose as a result of a failure to operate the plan in accordance with the Code's qualification requirements, as well as coverage for benefits corrections required by IRS as the result of an audit of the plan, based on the findings of a Fiduciary Audit® Operational Review that has been conducted at the insured's request.

The purpose of this chapter is to sift through the insurance maze, review each type of insurance coverage available to trustees, identify what's covered and what's not covered, and recommend an insurance program that will adequately protect the trust and the trustees' own personal assets which are at risk if the coverage is not there when needed.

THE RIGHT TO PURCHASE FIDUCIARY LIABILITY INSURANCE

ERISA itself generally prohibits the direct payment of trustee litigation expenses out of plan assets (with the exception of claims for benefits discussed earlier). Fortunately, the drafters of ERISA recognized that, even though trustees make a concerted effort to carry out their fiduciary duties, lawsuits may still occur and it is unreasonable to expect fiduciaries to dip into their own pockets to cover defense costs every time someone decides to file a lawsuit.

In recognition of this problem, Section 410(b)(1) of ERISA authorizes fiduciaries (i.e., trustees) to purchase insurance with plan assets "to cover liability or losses occurring by reason of the act or omission of a fiduciary if such insurance permits recourse by the insurer against the fiduciary in the case of a fiduciary obligation by such fiduciary." Such insurance may be purchased with plan assets.

The purchase of fiduciary liability insurance with plan assets has now become a common practice because every fund and its board of trustees face at least some risk of litigation and need coverage of defense costs. However, as noted above, such a policy must include a recourse provision giving the carrier the right to seek reimbursement directly from the trustees for costs incurred by the carrier if the trustees are found by the court to be guilty of breach of fiduciary duty.

The authors of ERISA thought it would be imprudent to allow trustees to purchase fiduciary liability insurance with plan assets and permit the policy to cover defense costs and settlement costs even though the trustees were found guilty of a fiduciary breach. There was a basic concern that, absent a recourse provision, the trustees would have no incentive to take reasonable care in the performance of their fiduciary duties.

Consequently, every fiduciary liability insurance policy is required to include a recourse provision. However, the carriers quickly recognized that it might be difficult to market fiduciary liability insurance policies with the recourse provision because the trustees might think the plan was buying very limited protection if the carrier could turn around under certain conditions and seek recovery directly from the trustees. Carriers also reasoned that, if they selected funds carefully, there would be no need for the recourse provision because the probability of the trustees being found guilty of a breach of fiduciary duty would be relatively low (and, as a result, there would be no legal basis for exercising the recourse provision anyway).

As a result of these considerations, most carriers permit plans to buy a waiver-of-recourse provision, either as part of the basic policy or as an endorsement to it. The charge for this waiver is extremely reasonable, usually no more than $100-$200 a year for each trustee or other insured parties. However, it should be emphasized that this premium may not be paid out of plan assets. The premium must be paid individually by each trustee, or it may be paid by the employer, the employer association or the union on the trustee's behalf.

DOL has expressed concern about this arrangement, which it contends may be a subterfuge of ERISA's requirement that the carrier retain the right of recourse. By letting trustees escape this requirement through the payment of a minimal premium, there is a question as to whether or not this violates the Congressional intent to hold trustees personally liable for their actions when there is a breach of fiduciary duty.

In a policy statement issued in 1975, DOL expressed its concern about the waiver-of-recourse provision as follows:

... the Department will continue to monitor the operation of policies and the reasonableness of premium rates. We anticipate that information on these points will be made available for study. Should experience convince the Secretary of Labor that the policies are unlawful, that position would be publicly stated and any departmental action would be prospective only.[2]

To date, DOL has issued no further statements regarding the waiver-of-recourse provisions and, therefore, purchase of the waiver is still permissible and advisable for every trustee.

WHO IS INSURED?

All fiduciary liability insurance policies cover the trustees as *insureds*. This coverage extends to past, present and future trustees if a claim is filed during the policy period. It is usually not necessary to include the specific name of each trustee in the schedule attached to the policy for coverage to be in effect for each trustee. Consequently, if trustees are replaced during the policy period, coverage is automatically extended to the new trustees.

However, the initial application form usually asks for the names of the present trustees and may also ask for the names of all trustees who have served on the board during the preceding five or six years. This information may become a factor when a carrier is determining whether or not to underwrite coverage for a particular fund, especially if any of the trustees have been involved in prior litigation.

All fiduciary liability insurance policies include the trust or plan under the definition of *insureds*. Such coverage is critical because Section 502(d)(1) of ERISA specifically provides that an "employee benefit plan may sue or be sued as an entity." In most suits filed under ERISA, it is a common practice to sue not only the trustee, but the plan itself. Since the premiums are paid out of plan assets, prudence alone dictates that the plan be protected and not just the trustees. As noted by DOL in an early news release on fiduciary liability insurance, "Fiduciaries must act prudently and solely in the interest of plan participants and beneficiaries when they choose fiduciary liability protection *for the plan*"[3] (emphasis added).

In some cases, the definition of *insureds* may extend to *more than one fund under the same policy* if the various funds (pension, welfare, vacation, etc.) have the same trustees or involve essentially the same contributing employers or union.

Although this arrangement may result in some premium savings compared with insuring each plan separately, it is important to remember that whatever limit of liability is selected applies to all funds *combined* and not to each fund individually. Consequently, if there is a major claim against one of the funds resulting in substantial defense and/or settlement costs, it may leave the other funds covered under the remainder of the policy period. Most carriers do not permit restoration of the liability limit during the policy period, even with the payment of an additional premium.

Another problem with multiple fund coverage under the same policy is that, if a carrier experiences a significant loss on behalf of any one of the funds, the policy may be canceled and, as a result, all funds would be without coverage.

Fund employees are usually included in the definition of *insureds*. If the trustees have a salaried administrator and their own fund office staff, such employees would be protected if they are named in the suit.

DIFFERENT TYPES OF INSURANCE

As mentioned earlier, the insurance coverage that is necessary to adequately protect the plan and its fiduciary trustees is (1) bonding insurance, (2) fiduciary liability insurance, (3) employee benefit liability insurance and (4) IRS liability insurance.

There is often confusion regarding the difference between fiduciary liability coverage, employee benefits liability insurance and the bonding requirements under ERISA. Generally, fiduciary liability insurance covers claims alleging breach of duties specified by ERISA (e.g., engaging in prohibited transactions). Employee benefits liability policies cover claims involving administrative errors pertaining to pension and benefit plans (e.g., failing to name an intended beneficiary on a life insurance policy). ERISA bonding requirements apply to fidelity/dishonesty situations in which fiduciaries illegally appropriate funds.

Bonding Requirements Under ERISA

Under ERISA all fiduciaries and persons who handle plan funds or other plan assets are to be bonded for 10% of the aggregate amount handled, with a minimum bond of $1,000 and a maximum bond of $500,000 (although DOL may raise the $500,000 maximum). It is the trustee's responsibility to make certain that all persons are appropriately bonded. However, bonding is not required of corporate trustees or insurance companies with combined capital and surplus of at least $1 million, if the only assets from which benefits are paid are the general assets of the employer or a union, or if DOL finds that other bonding arrangements or the overall condition of the plan are adequate to protect participants.

Compliance with such rules can be attained by purchasing a pension and welfare fund fiduciary dishonesty policy that pays for losses sustained as a result of fraudulent or dishonest acts (including larceny, theft, embezzlement, forgery, misappropriation or wrongful conversion) committed by an employee while in the service of an employee benefit plan as fiduciary, trustee, administrator or any other person required to be bonded by ERISA.

Fiduciary Liability Versus Employee Benefits Liability

Fiduciary liability insurance covers claims alleging breach of fiduciary duties enumerated by ERISA. In contrast, employee benefits liability coverage applies to claims involving administrative errors.

There are several confusing aspects involved in coordinating fiduciary and employee benefits liability policies. First is the fact that most, although not all, fiduciary liability policies also automatically cover the employee benefits liability exposure. In addition, many of the fiduciary liability insurers that do not cover employee benefits liability within their basic forms will add an endorsement to cover this exposure. Second, employee benefits liability policies do not cover fiduciary liability exposures. However, an insured can obtain fiduciary liability coverage through an endorsement to its employee benefit policy.

IRS Liability Insurance

As mentioned earlier, the plan fiduciary is normally not covered under the standard fiduciary liability or employee benefit liability insurance policy for the CAP monetary sanction since the sanction is considered a penalty and civil penalties are generally excluded from coverage under such policies. Also excluded from coverage under the standard fiduciary liability policy is loss due to administrative expenses, overhead or other charges of employees or plan trustees. This means that the costs of correcting any disqualifying defects for which a plan fiduciary is held responsible will also not be covered by the policy. In both instances, payment of the CAP sanction and payment of costs associated with correction of disqualifying defects, multiemployer plan trustees may be held personally liable.

As a result, trustees should consider purchasing "IRS fiduciary liability insurance" covering the plan and plan sponsor board of trustees for any liability that arises as a result of a failure to operate the plan in accordance with the Code's qualification requirements. While most policies generally exclude fines and penalties, many do offer some CAP coverage albeit in nominal amounts (no more than $100,000). However, as this chapter went to press, an insurance program was being developed that would offer enhanced CAP coverage as well as coverage for the cost of corrections required by IRS as the result of an audit. Such enhanced IRS liability coverage is conditioned upon the completion of a Fiduciary Audit® Operational Review evaluating the plan's administrative procedures for determining compliance with the Code's qualification requirements and identification of operational defects for correction by the trustees and their professional advisors.

This evaluation consists of the completion of a Fiduciary Audit® Investigative Questionnaire (Questionnaire) that tests the fund's compliance with the Code's requirements relating to eligibility, participation and vesting, breaks in service, retired employees, changes in employee status, preretirement survivor benefits, termination of employment, early retirement, normal and postponed retirement, postretirement, joint and survivor benefits, participant and spousal consent, disability benefits, death benefits and other IRS distribution requirements. After a review of the questionnaire, a "pre-IRS audit" is conducted by testing the plans' internal control procedures through a review and analysis of participant data and benefit records and administrative procedures in order to ascertain operational compliance with the qualification requirements of the Code and the regulations issued thereunder and the adequacy of internal control procedures related to such requirements. A Fiduciary Audit® Annual Report is then prepared for the insured recommending corrections of operational defects, if any, and improvements to the plans' internal control procedures.

FIDUCIARY LIABILITY POLICY COVERAGE ANALYSIS

The Big Question Is: What's Covered?

Primary Insuring Clause

The primary insuring clause (which appears at the beginning of the policy) states the carrier's basic intent regarding what actions and costs will be covered. Typically, the primary insuring clause states that the carrier will cover defense costs and settlement costs, up to the limit of liability for any claim *filed during the policy period* alleging that the insureds have committed a "wrongful act" as long as the claimant is seeking monetary damages.

Usually, the primary insuring clause also provides that the carrier has an *obligation to defend* the insureds even though the allegations may be "groundless, false, or fraudulent." Defense costs are *usually included in the limit of liability*. They are not in addition to the limit of liability. For example, if the policy has an aggregate liability of $5 million, that is the total coverage *for both defense costs and settlement costs combined.*

In summary, as long as the claim alleges that the trustees have engaged in a *wrongful act* and the claimant is seeking *damages,* the claim is covered. This raises two obvious questions: (1) What is a wrongful act? and (2) what constitutes damages?

Definition of a Wrongful Act. A *wrongful act* is generally defined as any alleged or actual breach of fiduciary duty committed by the insureds, either jointly or severally, in the discharge of their fiduciary duties. Some policies may also extend to any alleged or actual errors, omissions or negligence on the part of the insureds in the administration of the fund (even if the claimant does not also allege a breach of fiduciary duty). In other words, coverage would extend to claims alleging employee benefits liability such as errors, omissions or negligence related to day-to-day operations of the fund: recordkeeping, collection of delinquencies, providing information to participants, eligibility determination, etc., even if the claim did not allege a breach of fiduciary duty.

It is important to recognize, however, that such outside organizations are not insureds under the policy. Rather, the policies cover only the trustee's liability for the acts of these outside entities. Accordingly, it is important to make sure that outside organizations maintain their own separate professional liability for their activities.

Definition of *Damages.* This is often not clearly defined in the policies but the carriers take the position that for a claim to be covered, the claimant must be seeking some type of monetary settlement that, if paid by the plan, *would result in a loss of plan assets.*

Several types of claims do *not* generally meet this definition: (a) benefit claims and (b) nonpecuniary claims.

Routine benefit claims (e.g., disputes over eligibility, benefit amounts, type of benefit payable, interpretation of plan provisions) are normally *not* covered because such claims often do *not* seek damages. The claimant *merely seeks payment of a benefit* and if the claimant wins, the fund is simply paying an amount that it was *legally obligated to pay in the first place.* Therefore, according to the carriers, the claimant is not seeking damages.

Carriers take the position that if they had to cover defense costs for every benefit claim, their premiums would be prohibitive and that it is far less expensive for the trustees to hire fund counsel to handle benefit claims as such counsel would be most familiar with the issues and with relevant plan provisions. Carriers also justify their exclusion of benefit claims on the grounds that when they used to cover such claims, attorneys sometimes abused the system by increasing fees or prolonging litigation to generate more fees simply because the carrier, rather than the fund, was paying defense costs.

Benefit claims are *not* excluded from coverage if they also request compensatory *damages* and/or *attorney fees* for the claimant. For example, assume that a suit is filed in which the claimant contends that he was entitled to COBRA coverage, was not offered such coverage and as a result he had to sell his home, close out his savings accounts and borrow against his pension plan to pay his medical expenses. As a result, the claimant may seek not only reimbursement of his medical expenses, but compensatory damages for the other monetary losses sustained. In this case, most policies would cover such a benefit claim because compensatory damages are also being sought.

Claims for nonpecuniary relief are also excluded from coverage. This would include actions under Section 502 of ERISA, which specifically authorize participants, beneficiaries, DOL or a fiduciary to take various civil actions to enforce or clarify a participant's rights or to obtain equitable relief for any ERISA violation. Such actions may include a request for an injunction, a declaratory judgment or other court order not involving any monetary relief.

For example, DOL may seek an injunction prohibiting the trustees from making certain real estate investments DOL considers to be imprudent because they do not generate an interest rate equal to the prevailing market rate. DOL may not ask for monetary damages but may ask that these investments be prohibited and may ask for removal of the trustees. Defense costs would not be covered because no damages are being sought.

Please note that the damages provision specifically excludes "fines or penalties imposed by law, taxes, punitive or exemplary damages. . . ." All fiduciary and employee benefit liability policies specifically exclude fines or penalties except for the nominal CAP coverage discussed above. Accordingly, it is extremely important that the trustees also obtain IRS liability insurance covering any monetary sanctions imposed and benefit corrections required by IRS as a result of an IRS audit in which IRS finds that the plan was not operated in accordance with the Code's qualification requirements.

Covered Defense Costs

In addition to covering indemnity payments and settlement amounts associated with claims, fiduciary liability policies also pay the costs involved in investigating, defending and settling claims. These items include attorney fees, adjusters services, court costs, bonds and related expenses required by the claim settlement process.

Under most of the insurer's forms, payment of defense costs reduces the policy's limit of liability. However, a few insurers allow insureds to purchase defense coverage in addition to the policy limits for an additional premium.

All Fiduciary Insurance Policies Are "Claims-Made" Policies

What this means is that claims are covered *during the policy period regardless of when the wrongful act is alleged to have occurred.* In effect, a "claims-made" policy provides coverage of wrongful acts that may have occurred *prior to the current policy period.* For example, assume a real estate investment was made in 2003 and in 2006 DOL files suit alleging that the trustees, including the former trustees, made an imprudent real estate investment because the rate of return was less than the prevailing market rate and the plan had suffered a substantial loss of income as a result. Under a claims-made policy, this claim would be covered *even though the alleged wrongful act occurred prior to the policy period,* assuming that all other terms and conditions of the policy are met.

In effect, trustees have *retroactive coverage,* which is a comforting thought for those trustees who may be *relatively new* and may not be fully aware of earlier decisions made by the board of trustees or other named fiduciary.

Restrictions on Prior Acts Coverage

Prior acts coverage applies provided that: "The Insured, as of the effective date (and subsequent renewal dates) had no knowledge or could not have foreseen any circumstances which might result in a claim."

A carrier's application form or renewal form will invariably ask trustees if they are aware of any potential claim situations. *Failure to answer* this question accurately may result in *no coverage whatsoever* if a claim is later filed and if the carrier can demonstrate that the trustees knew, or should have known, that such claim would be filed.

As a result, this question about potential claim situations should be answered by fund counsel (not the administrative manager or insurance broker) in consultation with the trustees. In fact, when a fiduciary liability policy comes up for renewal, it provides an *excellent opportunity* for fund counsel to review any areas where the fund may be vulnerable to litigation and to suggest appropriate corrective actions to reduce the litigation potential.

Claims-Made Extension Clause

Every policy has a so-called claims-made extension clause that provides that if at any time *during the policy period,* the insureds become aware of a wrongful act that may, later on, lead to a claim and the insureds notify the carrier of the wrongful act, then if a claim related to that wrongful act does occur, coverage is automatically extended as if the claim was first made during the policy period, *even though the policy may no longer be in effect* (canceled or not renewed).

Retroactive Effective Date

The schedule attached to a fiduciary liability policy or an amendatory endorsement to the policy *may* specify *a retroactive effective date* and if the wrongful act occurred before that date, no coverage is provided. In this regard, it is important to note that it is not uncommon for the retroactive date to be defined as the inception date of the policy (a retroactive date prior to inception may require increased premium). Also, an endorsement may exclude claims arising out of *prior or pending litigation* (such an endorsement may be a condition for getting the insurance in the first place).

Suggestion: Check with fund counsel to see if any of these coverage restrictions on prior acts are attached to your policy.

"All-Risk Insurance"

All policies provide *all-risk insurance,* which means that as long as the claim meets the broad definition of a wrongful act and seeks damages, the carrier is obligated to provide coverage unless there is *specific wording* in the policy itself *excluding that particular type of claim.*

Where there is ambiguity in the wording of the policy, the courts generally *favor the policyholder* under an all-risk policy. That is why it is so important to have fund counsel periodically review the *specific exclusions* under your particular policy.

Limits and Deductibles

Nonaccumulation Provisions

Fiduciary liability policies usually include nonaccumulation clauses stipulating that, if a series of claims results from a single wrongful act, error or omission and these claims are made during more than one policy period, the limit of coverage that applies is the one that was in effect at the time the first claim was made. For example, assume that a pension plan is terminated in 2004. As a result, the fiduciaries are sued separately for denial of benefits by three different beneficiaries in 2004, 2005 and 2006, respectively. Under a nonaccumulation clause, the policy limits applying in 2004 represent the total limit available to pay and defend all three claims—regardless of the fact that claims were made against the insureds during the 2005 and 2006 policy years.

Deductible Provisions

Most fiduciary liability policies include "antistacking" clauses in their deductible provisions. They state that the policy deductible applies per wrongful act rather than to each separate claim. For instance, in the example above that illustrated the application of nonaccumulation clauses, only one deductible would apply because all three of the claims arose from a single wrongful act.

Fiduciary liability policy deductible clauses normally state that the deductible applies to both indemnity payments and claims expenses, regardless of whether an indemnity payment is made. In effect, such wording does not provide "first dollar" defense coverage. To illustrate, assume that an insurer expends $100,000 to defend a fiduciary but is not ultimately required to pay a judgment or settlement on the fiduciary's behalf. If the policy contains a $10,000 deductible, the insurer would seek reimbursement from the insured in the amount of $10,000, to satisfy the policy's deductible provision—irrespective of the fact that no indemnity payments were made on the insured's behalf.

On the other hand, a few insurers do cover defense on a first dollar basis. Thus, in the example in the previous paragraph, under a policy covering defense on a first dollar basis, the insurer would not have sought reimbursement of the $10,000 deductible.

Subrogation/Recourse

One unusual aspect of fiduciary liability policies is that, unless specified, underwriters ordinarily have what is known as a *right of recourse,* i.e., the right to subrogate against an insured. This is because if the premium for the fiduciary policy in question is paid out of plan assets, Section 410(b)(1) of ERISA requires that the policy permit recourse by the insurer against the fiduciary in the case of a breach of fiduciary obligation by such fiduciary. Such a procedure represents a distinct departure from the approach used in most other types of professional liability insurance where subrogation against insureds is typically barred by the policy language. However, the logic of the ERISA provision is apparent. That is, a fiduciary should not be financially absolved from the consequences of his or her wrongful acts when premiums for liability coverage are being paid from the assets of the benefit plans he or she is administering to the detriment of the beneficiaries of those plans.

Despite recourse provisions, most fiduciary liability policies also indicate that, by payment of a specified additional premium, the insurer will not be permitted the right of recourse. This is, of course, favorable because if the insurer maintains the right of recourse, it could subrogate against an insured whose nonwillful error caused a loss. Therefore, it is usually a good idea to purchase such an endorsement, especially since the additional premium is generally less than $100 per covered fiduciary.

What Is Not Covered?

Exclusions in fiduciary liability policies can have a significant effect on the scope of coverage the policies provide. Given that policy forms vary considerably as respects their exclusionary language, it is necessary to examine this section of the policy carefully.

While certain exposures may not be specifically excluded under fiduciary liability policies, many insurers would nevertheless refuse to provide coverage for claims produced by these exposures. For example, although not all of the policies contain an exclusion for claims involving libel/slander situations, it is obviously not the intent of any fiduciary liability insurer to cover such claims.

There are many common exclusions in every policy. These exclusions may result from: (1) a definition of terms, (2) specific enumeration in the basic policy or (3) riders or endorsements attached to the basic policy.

Exclusions by Definition

Normally, *loss* is defined as not including:
1. Routine benefit claims unless the claimant seeks compensatory damages and/or the trustees are held personally liable
2. Nonpecuniary claims based on ERISA §502 (e.g., DOL injunction)
3. Civil or criminal fines or penalties. Federal agencies are relying more heavily on fines, penalties and excise taxes as the principal sanctions for enforcement. Examples of such fines or penalties are:
   a. IRS CAP monetary sanctions for failure to operate a pension fund or 401(k) plan in accordance with the Code's qualification requirements
   b. *$100 a day* for failing to provide required information to a participant within 30 days after the request is made
   c. *$1,000 a day* for late or incomplete filing of a Form 5500 (unless revised Form 5500 is filed within 45 days)
   d. *100%* excise tax penalty on the amount involved in any prohibited transaction (same insurers specifically cover the 5% penalty for "inadvertent" violation of Section 406 of ERISA)
   e. *$100/$2,500 a day* for COBRA violations under certain conditions
   f. *Double damages* for certain violations of the "Medicare as secondary payer" rules.
4. Punitive or exemplary damages or the two-thirds portion of any treble damage award (e.g., civil RICO claims) or the portion of any compensatory award that is enhanced or multiplied in any way. Certain policies cover the defense of RICO claims and/or specify that the "multiplier" exclusion does not apply to the award of attorney fees under ERISA.
5. Defense costs in any proceeding before or audit or investigation by a governmental agency such as DOL or IRS.

Exclusions by Enumeration

The exclusions most often found in a typical fiduciary liability policy are set forth below.

Contractual Liability

Fiduciary liability policies often preclude coverage in situations where an insured must hold a third party harmless in conjunction with the operation of a pension or welfare benefit fund. For instance, assume that a CPA firm requests that the trustees hold the CPA firm harmless if the CPA firm is sued in connection with the auditing services it performs for the plan. Also suppose that the CPA certifies that the plan's financial statements have been prepared according to generally accepted accounting principles and fairly represent the plan's true financial condition. Six months later, the plan is declared insolvent by the PBGC. The plan participants sue the CPA firm, which in turn seeks to be held harmless by the trustees of the plan.

Contractual liability exclusions eliminate coverage for hold harmless agreements of this type because outside service providers should maintain their own professional liability coverage. Also, underwriters are averse to assuming liability for hold harmless agreements exposures unless they are aware of them at the inception of a policy. Accordingly, if the trustees must hold another entity harmless, the underwriter should be advised prior to policy inception. This allows the insurer time to evaluate the exposure and assess an appropriate additional premium if the underwriter is willing to cover such an agreement.

Some insurers contain a version of this exclusion that does provide coverage for certain hold harmless agreements. More specifically, if, according to the documents governing the insured plans, a fiduciary is required to hold others harmless, some policies will provide coverage under these circumstances. Underwriters are willing to cover hold harmless agreements of this type because such requirements are stated in plan documents that insurers presumably have had an opportunity to review prior to binding coverage.

Known Circumstances Surrounding a Claim

If an insured is aware prior to policy inception of circumstances or events that may, in the future, give rise to a claim, coverage is excluded by virtually all policies. This is because such claims fall more properly within the purview of the prior insurer.

Claims Reported to Prior Insurers

Most fiduciary liability policies also contain a similar exclusion that precludes coverage if a claim, or circumstances surrounding one, has already been reported to another insurer.

Discrimination

The majority of policies contain exclusions that restrict coverage in situations where acts of discrimination are alleged against fiduciaries. This is an unfavorable policy feature because a fiduciary liability claim could very well involve an allegation of discrimination. Some policies preclude coverage only when discrimination is on the basis of race, creed, age or sex. Others eliminate coverage for discrimination claims on an across-the-board basis. The former more limited version is clearly preferable and should also include an explicit grant of defense cost coverage for allegations of discrimination.

Failure to Collect Contributions Owed to an Employee Benefit Plan

The majority of the policies do not cover claims stemming from the failure of fiduciaries to collect contributions owed to a pension or welfare benefit fund. This is because the collection of pension and welfare benefit fund contributions from employers and/or employees is an activity that is basically within the control of insureds. Thus, the policies will not cover such claims because insurers do not intend to provide what would in effect be "financial guarantee insurance."

Other Insurance

Most other insurance provisions in fiduciary liability insurance policies state that if other insurance is available, the other policy will function automatically as excess coverage (unless the other insurance is specifically issued as excess insurance) in the event that any other valid and collectible insurance policy also applies to a given claim.

Benefits Payable to a Beneficiary

Most policies preclude coverage for payment of benefits owed to a claimant if monies are available within the plan to make such a payment. This is logical because it is not the purpose of an insurance policy to make such payment if such monies can actually be paid from the plan.

Bankruptcy of Bank/Broker

This exclusion precludes coverage when benefits cannot be paid because the bank or broker that holds pension or welfare benefit plan funds is insolvent. Thus, under this exclusion, coverage is not available if the trustees fail to adequately evaluate the solvency and financial strength of a bank or broker. The rationale underlying the exclusion is that, since banks and brokers usually carry their own separate fiduciary or professional liability coverage, a claimant would ordinarily have direct recourse against the broker or bank.

Failure to Fund in Accordance With ERISA

This exclusion is contained in virtually all policies because it would be contrary to public policy to provide insurance coverage for intentional violations of federal law (although providing defense coverage when allegations to this effect are made would not).

Dishonesty

Insuring people for their individual liability arising out of the intentional commission of illegal acts is not permitted as a matter of public policy. However, nearly all policies qualify the exclusion by stipulating that defense coverage applies if, after final adjudication, it is proven that the insured did not commit the alleged dishonest act. Even when a policy does not include this exception, an insurer's duty to defend is generally construed as being broader than its duty to indemnify and, in practice, insurers typically provide coverage of defense costs as long as dishonest acts are alleged yet not proven. Finally, it is important to note that the policies provide defense coverage against allegations of dishonesty only in *civil claims* as opposed to *criminal court cases*.

Personal Profit

Liability of fiduciaries who attain personal profit or financial advantage to which they were not legally entitled is another exposure considered to be uninsurable (e.g., a claim that a trustee of a pension fund made a stock investment on behalf of the fund and at the same time purchased the same stock for himself or herself at a sharply reduced broker's commission). However, most fiduciary liability policies do not apply this exclusion unless the claim of personal profit is factually established. Therefore, it is important to ascertain that policies do contain such exception language and to negotiate with underwriters for its inclusion in the event that they do not.

Failure to Purchase or Maintain Insurance or Bonds

As noted earlier, ERISA requires that certain types of surety bonds be purchased to protect the assets of pension and welfare plans. Claims arising from the insured's failure to comply with such regulations is uninsurable because avoidance of such claims is clearly within the control of the insured.

Workers' Compensation, Unemployment Insurance, Social Security, Disability Benefits

Nearly all fiduciary liability policies preclude claims produced by obligations stemming from workers' compensation, unemployment insurance and disability laws. This is because the purpose of fiduciary liability insurance is to cover only those duties that arise in conjunction with ERISA-covered employee pension and welfare benefit programs. Nevertheless, since workers' compensation, unemployment insurance and disability plans are closely related to those falling within the scope of ERISA, many insurers will, by endorsement, grant coverage for them in return for a nominal premium. It is prudent to broaden coverage in this manner if an underwriter makes this endorsement available.

Bodily Injury, Property Damage, Libel and Slander

Coverage of claims alleging bodily injury, property damage, libel and slander are also beyond the scope of fiduciary liability insurance because normally they fall within the purview of commercial general liability insurance.

Willful or Reckless Violation of Any Statute, Rule or Law

This is a *troublesome exclusion*. It is not uncommon for a suit to allege that the trustees have not only engaged in a breach of fiduciary duty but that the violation of ERISA or other laws was "willful or reckless."

What is *not clear* in some of the policies is *whether the mere allegation* that the trustees were "willful or reckless" in their conduct is sufficient for the carrier to exclude any coverage of defense costs or whether defense costs will be covered until the guilt or innocence of the trustees has been determined by the court. This is a matter that fund counsel should clarify with the carrier.

Policies also contain specific language excluding "any deliberate or intentional acts in which the insured participated, or of which the insured had actual knowledge and with respect to which the insured failed to take appropriate action, knowing such conduct, in either case, to have been a violation of the responsibilities, obligations or duties imposed upon fiduciaries by ERISA."

Other Exclusions by Enumeration

- Liability of any insured to any other insured
- The rendering or failure to render services contracted for with any service provider
- Any professional services, (e.g., legal, accounting, actuarial, investment counseling, fund managing) rendered or that should have been rendered by an insured or third party
- Any wrongful act alleged by PBGC or any person or entity against whom PBGC has asserted any claim or demand
- Defects and potential defects in the operation of the plan that were identified in a Fiduciary Audit® Operational Review conducted at the insured's request for the purpose of obtaining enhanced IRS liability insurance coverage.

Suggestion: Trustees should ask fund counsel to review these and other exclusions enumerated in their particular fiduciary liability insurance policy.

Exclusions by Amendatory Endorsements and/or Riders

Not all exclusions may be stated in the basic policy. Some exclusions may be attached to the basic policy as amendatory endorsements or riders. Some examples are these.

Real Estate Investments

DOL has made no secret of the fact that it has targeted Taft-Hartley funds for continuing investigations regarding their real estate investments.[4] Accordingly, some *policies* exclude real estate unless such investments are directed or *managed* by a qualified professional asset manager (QPAM) as defined under DOL Class Exemption 84-14.[5] If you are a trustee of a pension fund and your pension fund has real estate investments of any kind (such as construction loans, mortgage loans or joint real estate investment with other multiemployer plans), this endorsement should be of special concern.

This endorsement (which several carriers usually include if a pension fund has real estate investments) excludes from coverage any claim related to the investment of plan assets in real estate or mortgages *unless* certain conditions are met:

1. A *major condition* is that the real estate or mortgage investment must be "directed or managed by" a QPAM (with substantial experience

in real estate and/or mortgages), as defined under DOL Class Exemption 84-14.
2. Generally, this Class Exemption relieves trustees of any personal liability for real estate and mortgage decisions if they delegate responsibility for these decisions to a QPAM or if they invest in government-backed mortgages.
3. A QPAM includes banks, savings and loans, insurance companies and other registered investment advisors if they meet certain criteria in terms of net worth, working capital and/or total assets of managed funds.

Under this endorsement, if the trustees utilize a QPAM and are sued for a real estate decision made by, or recommended by the QPAM, the carrier will cover defense costs and settlement costs up to the limit of liability. On the other hand, if trustees make real estate or mortgage decisions *without the professional assistance of a QPAM,* then the endorsement *would preclude coverage of defense costs for any litigation arising out of such decisions.*

One of the reasons why this endorsement is being included by certain carriers is that in recent years DOL has stepped up its litigation against Taft-Hartley pension funds for making construction loans or mortgage loans *at below* prevailing *market rates* or for investing in "union only" construction projects at rates of return *less than the prevailing market rate.* Funds usually end up with *substantial defense costs* for this type of litigation. Moreover, DOL has made no secret of the fact that it has "targeted" Taft-Hartley funds for continuing investigation regarding their real estate investments. *So it is not surprising* that some of the carriers want to limit their liability exposure in this area and one way to do that is for the carrier to insist, under the endorsement, that the trustees utilize the services of a QPAM when making any real estate decisions and not to rely solely on their own judgment.

Whether or not this particular endorsement is unduly *restrictive* is a matter that trustees should discuss with fund counsel if this endorsement is attached to your policy. If so, check to make sure that you are currently employing a QPAM to direct or manage your real estate investments because if you are not, you have no coverage for litigation related to those investments.

Other Exclusions by Amendatory Endorsement or Riders

- Alleged discrimination under any municipal, state or federal law. Such an exclusion may be applied to apprenticeship training funds.
- Bankruptcy, insolvency or inability to pay benefits due to insufficient contributions. This endorsement may be added if the fund has major delinquency collection problems and/or inadequate delinquency control procedures.
- Alleged actuarial errors, omissions, assumptions or projections. This exclusion may be applied if there have been withdrawal liability claims challenging the actuarial interest rate assumption used to calculate withdrawal liability.
- Any legal action between or among the insureds (e.g., a suit filed by one group of trustees against another group of trustees)
- Any alleged violation of the Racketeer Influenced and Corrupt Organizations Act (RICO)
- Items of noncompliance identified in a Fiduciary Audit® Operational Review conducted at the insured's request for the purpose of obtaining enhanced IRS liability insurance coverage.

What to Do: Ask fund counsel if there are any endorsements attached to your policy and if there are, what types of claims are excluded by such endorsements. It is important to know in advance what these exclusions are because you may be able to take certain actions designed to minimize the risk of litigation *in those areas where you have little or no coverage* as a result of an amendatory endorsement(s).

Ask fund counsel about any amendatory endorsements attached to your policy and what restrictions they impose on your coverage.

If your fund counsel is not sure whether or not a particular type of claim is excluded because the wording of the policy is not clear, it would seem appropriate *to seek clarification* directly from the insurance broker or from someone at the carrier's home office who can speak with authority.

You may find that carriers are sometimes reluctant to get "pinned down" and they generally do not like to deal with hypothetical situations. However, your plan is probably paying a healthy premium and you *have a right to know* what that premium is or *is not* buying in terms of coverage. Besides, as trustees, you are not just concerned about protecting the plan's assets; you are concerned about protecting *your own personal assets* that are at risk if the coverage is not there when you need it.

A Final Suggestion: If you can not get clarification on what your policy covers or if you have experienced significant premium increases, *do not hesitate to shop around.* It is well worth the time and effort to fill out an application and obtain competitive premium quotes. You may be pleasantly surprised to find out you can purchase the same or better coverage with another carrier at a lower rate.

HOW MUCH IS THE DEDUCTIBLE AND HOW IS IT APPLIED?

Most fiduciary liability insurance policies have a deductible amount specified in the schedule attached to the basic policy. However, the amount of the deductible and the conditions under which the deductible will be applied vary among different policies. Trustees should know what the deductible amount is and when it will be applied.

As mentioned earlier, the deductible may or may not apply to defense costs. Most carriers require that the deductible be paid each time a new claim is filed against the insured during the policy period (unless the claim is related to an earlier claim involving the same wrongful act), regardless of whether or not the claimant is successful with the suit. As a result, the deductible applies to the defense costs incurred for any claim.

A few carriers require the payment of the deductible only if damages are actually awarded to the claimant. In other words, the deductible does not apply to the defense costs. This latter arrangement may be preferred, but trustees should carefully evaluate the total premium being paid. Waiver of the deductible unless damages are awarded may end up costing the plan a significantly higher premium solely to obtain a waiver of the deductible to defense costs.

A typical deductible charged by most carriers is $1,000 per claim or $1,000 for a claim involving a class action suit or a series of related claims. This is an aggregate amount and is not affected by the number of trustees, the type of benefits being provided by the fund (welfare, pension or other) or by the type of funding method used (insured vs. self-funded). In some cases, a carrier may offer a higher deductible—such as $5,000, $10,000 or $25,000—in exchange for a lower premium, or a carrier may require a higher deductible as a condition of insurability if the carrier believes that a particular fund represents an above-average risk for the carrier. In the latter case, this higher deductible may sometimes be reduced to $1,000 by the plan paying the difference between the higher deductible and the $1,000 deductible as part of the basic premium charge. For example, if a $5,000 deductible is required, the fund may be permitted to reduce the deductible to $1,000 if it adds another $4,000 to the established premium charge.

As the foregoing discussion suggests, there is considerable variation among the carriers with respect to the dollar amounts charged as a deductible and the way the deductible is applied (i.e., whether applied to every claim filed or only applied if damages are awarded to the claimant). For this reason, trustees should check to see what the deductible is under their particular plan and whether or not it would apply to defense costs.

It may also be advisable to periodically ask the current carrier what premium savings, if any, would result if the trustees opted for a higher deductible. If a plan has had no litigation over a number of years and if fund counsel believes the potential for litigation is minimal, it may be appropriate for trustees to consider the election of a higher deductible in order to reduce premium costs.

WHAT FACTORS SHOULD BE CONSIDERED IN SELECTING A LIABILITY LIMIT? WHAT LIMITS ARE AVAILABLE?

Selecting an appropriate liability limit for coverage of defense and settlement costs is a difficult decision for trustees because it requires balancing the need for protection against what the plan can afford to pay.

The first step in this process is for the trustees to obtain an assessment from their fund counsel as to what the risks of litigation and IRS monetary sanctions may be for the trustees and their particular fund, because the primary reason to purchase a fiduciary liability insurance policy is to cover defense costs and sanctions that IRS may impose as a result of a failure to operate the plan in accordance with the Code's qualification requirements. If the trustees are diligent in the performance of their fiduciary duties, and if the trustees employ competent professional advisors and follow their advice, the risk of litigation and sanctions may be fairly minimal under normal circumstances and the liability limit selected should take that into account.

The risk of litigation and sanctions may also depend on the type of fund involved (welfare, pension, apprenticeship training, vacation). IRS monetary sanctions only apply to a qualified pension fund. Moreover, it is reasonable to expect few suits against an apprenticeship training fund or vacation fund (although they have occurred). On the other hand, welfare funds often have exposure to claims involving benefit disputes. However, as noted earlier, such claims are not usually covered by most fiduciary liability insurance policies unless they seek compensatory damages. As a result, it will be the welfare fund, not the carrier, that will end up absorbing the defense costs for most benefit claims, and this fact should be recognized when selecting an appropriate liability limit. It should also be noted that most welfare fund investments are in short-term, fixed income media and, as a result, the risk of litigation (and, therefore, the need for liability protection) related to investment decisions made by welfare fund trustees should be minimal.

This is not to say that welfare funds have no liability exposure just because most benefit claims are not covered and investment claims are unlikely. Many other types of claims may be filed against a welfare fund, such as claims alleging failure to adequately fund health care benefits, failure to collect delinquencies, failure to maintain adequate records to determine eligibility, failure to provide participants with information required by ERISA, and so on. Welfare fund trustees should ask fund counsel what the potential risks of litigation are for the types of claims that would be covered under their fiduciary liability insurance policy and to use that evaluation as a basis for selecting an adequate liability limit.

By contrast, a pension fund would generally have a

higher risk of litigation than a welfare fund due to the long-term nature of pension fund investments and the wider range of investment options available to a pension fund. The risk of litigation for a pension fund might also be greater if a significant percentage of plan assets is invested in real estate and mortgages.

It is also important to note that DOL gives top priority in its enforcement efforts to the examination of real estate investments made by Taft-Hartley trustees, especially if it appears that such investments have been made at below prevailing market rates. Even if the responsibility for making these decisions has been delegated to a professional asset manager, this does not mean that DOL will back off from filing a lawsuit if it thinks violation of ERISA's prudent man rule has occurred. Such litigation can precipitate significant defense costs even though the trustees are not held personally liable for their actions, and this is a factor for pension fund trustees to consider when selecting a liability limit.

There are many other factors in addition to the type of fund and the amount and types of fund investments that may affect the risk of litigation. Trustees should ask their own fund counsel to assess such risks for their particular fund and to rely on that assessment for determining what an appropriate liability limit might be.

There is considerable choice in the limits of liability available from various carriers. Most carriers offer a minimum limit of $250,000. Maximum liability limits range from $5 million to $10 million (although higher limits are available from some carriers through a reinsurance arrangement).

These limits are usually applied on a policy-year basis, regardless of the number of claims filed during the policy period; once the limit is exhausted by one or more claims during the policy period, coverage ceases. As a general rule, carriers are not willing to restore the liability limit for the remainder of the policy period once the original limit has been exceeded. Moreover, if the full liability limit has been paid out by the carrier, there is a high probability that the policy will be canceled.

In selecting an appropriate liability limit, a major consideration is whether or not the liability limit offered by a carrier includes or excludes defense costs. Defense costs are normally included in the liability limit. As a result, it is always possible that the liability limit could be exceeded by defense costs, in which case there would be no money left over to pay damages if they are awarded by the court. Although most fiduciary liability insurance policies are purchased primarily to cover defense costs, it should be recognized that, if the trustees are held personally liable for their actions, settlement costs would not be covered if the liability limit is exhausted by defense costs already paid out by the carrier during the course of the trial.

Trustees may wish to ask fund counsel what they might anticipate in the way of defense costs if a major claim were filed against the trustees and use that amount as a starting point for determining a minimum liability limit. However, a judgment would still have to be made upon advice of fund counsel as to how much additional cushion, if any, should be added to cover settlement costs in the event that the trustees and/or the plan is assessed damages.

HOW IS THE PREMIUM DETERMINED? WHAT IS A REASONABLE PREMIUM?

Determination of the premium by any carrier involves consideration of certain factors that are quantifiable, but it also may involve a wide range of other factors.

Most carriers give considerable weight to the sheer size of the fund in setting their premiums. In the case of a pension fund, size is determined by the number of plan participants, number of retirees and total assets. In the case of a welfare fund, size is determined on the basis of number of plan participants and total annual contributions.

However, carriers are quick to acknowledge that there are many other factors that enter into their premium determination decision. These factors include, but are not limited to:

1. Liability limit selected
2. Deductible selected (if choice is available)
3. Annual amount of benefit claims paid
4. Whether the benefits are insured or self-funded (with higher premiums usually charged if self-funded)
5. Litigation experience of the fund and its trustees before and after the policy was first put into effect
6. Extent to which the trustees delegate investment responsibility to a professional asset manager within written guidelines provided by the trustees
7. Professional reputation of the fund's service providers (e.g., fund counsel, administrative manager and fund consultant)
8. Trade, craft or industry involved
9. Geographic area covered by the fund's jurisdiction
10. The specific union(s) represented on the board of trustees.

In addition to being used for premium determination purposes, many of these same factors are also used for determining the insurability of a particular fund.

It is not known how much weight a particular carrier gives to each of these factors in setting the premium, but there is no doubt that any one of these factors may have a significant effect on how the carrier perceives its liability risk, and that perception will have an effect on the premium charged. For this reason, if a fund has been experiencing significant premium increases in recent years (especially if no claims have been filed with the carrier), it would be advisable to ask the carrier what factors are being used to set the premium. Once those factors are known, the trustees can determine whether or not there are any actions they can take to reduce any of the risk factors that may be affecting their premium adversely.

Every board of trustees is concerned about whether it is paying too much for its fiduciary liability insurance coverage. This concern has intensified in recent years because many Taft-Hartley funds have experienced significant increases in their fiduciary liability insurance policies premiums (even though they may have filed no claims with the carrier). As fiduciaries, trustees have a legal obligation under ERISA to act prudently in the expenditure of fund assets for fiduciary liability insurance. This point is emphasized in a DOL news release on fiduciary liability insurance which states that:

> ... any plan fiduciary who is involved in buying insurance must do his best to secure the most suitable coverage for the plan *at no greater expense of plan assets than is necessary.*[6] [Emphasis added]

This statement suggests that trustees are obligated to determine whether or not their current fiduciary liability insurance premium is reasonable in today's marketplace.

This is not an easy assignment because there are no comparable data readily available at a single source that trustees can use to determine how their premium stacks up against those being charged other funds of similar size (in terms of number of participants, total assets or annual contributions). Moreover, as noted earlier, carriers take so many factors into consideration in addition to plan size that direct comparisons of premiums among funds of similar size are of limited value.

The best way to find out whether the fund's premium is in the ballpark is for the trustees to periodically ask for premium quotes from a number of different carriers, along with a specimen copy of the policy so that fund counsel may evaluate its coverage against the current coverage.

There are at least four major carriers underwriting fiduciary liability insurance for Taft-Hartley funds, and that fact alone suggests some degree of competition.[7] Although carriers may not be pounding down fund office doors trying to sell fiduciary liability insurance, some carriers are interested in new business.

Consequently, it makes sense for the trustees of any well-managed fund (especially one that has experienced no litigation but is experiencing significant increases in its fiduciary liability insurance policy premium) to see what the competition has to offer—in terms of both cost and coverage. Although it takes time and effort to complete the application forms and obtain premium quotes, shopping around is a no-lose proposition. If nothing else, trustees may find their current premium and coverages are in line with those being offered by other carriers—or may even be better. On the other hand, trustees may be surprised to find that they can purchase the same or better coverage at a more reasonable premium from another carrier.

As mentioned earlier, there may soon be a new program offering enhanced IRS liability insurance coverage for liability that arises (e.g., monetary sanctions imposed against the trustees) as a result of an IRS audit in which IRS finds that the plan was not operated in accordance with the Code's qualification requirements. However, an evaluation of the plan's administrative procedures for determining compliance with the Code's qualification requirements and identification of operational defects for correction by the trustees and their professional advisors based upon a Fiduciary Audit® Operational Review conducted at the insured's request is a condition for obtaining such insurance against imposition of the CAP monetary sanction.

The important point to remember is that there are changes occurring in the fiduciary liability insurance marketplace that seem to be encouraging some degree of competition among the carriers. For this reason, trustees should not hesitate to ask fund counsel to periodically request premium quotes from various carriers, compare available coverages and report to the trustees on any new carriers and their coverages.

WHAT TIME PERIOD IS COVERED BY THE POLICY?

The time period covered by a fiduciary liability insurance policy is usually one year.

WHAT IF THE POLICY IS CANCELED?

Trustees are legitimately concerned about what happens to their coverage if the carrier cancels the policy, especially if they are unable to find another carrier willing to underwrite coverage or cannot purchase fiduciary liability insurance from any carrier at an affordable premium. Although trustees undoubtedly hope their policy will never be canceled, it is important to know what can be done to continue coverage in the event of cancellation.

It makes good sense for the trustees and fund counsel to sit down as soon as possible after a cancellation notice is received, *but prior to the cancellation date* (usually a period of 30 days or less), to identify any wrongful acts that may have been committed prior to the cancellation date and report such acts to the carrier.

It would also be appropriate at that time to check with the carrier to find out how much detail must be provided about each potential claim situation in order to assure future coverage if such claims arise. Although this exercise may require some time and effort on the part of trustees and their fund counsel, it is an opportunity that should not be missed. After all, the future coverage provided under the claims-made extension clause costs the plan absolutely nothing.

Most fiduciary liability insurance policies permit funds to purchase extended coverage for another six or 12 months for a premium 25%-75% higher than the premium charged for the most recent policy period. Such coverage extends to a wrongful act that occurred prior to the cancellation date but that was not discovered *until after the policy was canceled.* In effect, the purchase of this extended coverage provides trustees with some additional protection in the event a claim arises that no one anticipated and would not be covered under the claims-made extension clause because the carrier had no advance notification of the wrongful act leading to the claim. No coverage is provided, however, for a claim based on a wrongful act committed *after* the cancellation date.

Policies vary widely in terms of the time allowed to purchase such extended coverage. In some cases, this option must be exercised *prior* to the effective date of cancellation. In other cases, the extended coverage must be purchased no later than ten or 30 days *after* the date of cancellation. Consequently, if the policy is canceled, the trustees should ask fund counsel to check immediately on this time limit.

Whether or not extended coverage is worth the increased premium is a decision trustees, in consultation with their fund attorney, will have to make based on individual circumstances. If coverage is picked up immediately from a new carrier, then there may be limited value to purchasing extended coverage unless the new policy has prior act limitations. However, it probably will take some time before an application for coverage with a new carrier is processed, so purchase of extended coverage may be essential, especially if the trustees anticipate a major claim being filed based on a wrongful act allegedly committed prior to the cancellation date.

CONCLUDING OBSERVATIONS AND SUGGESTIONS

The typical fiduciary liability insurance policy provides no more than a minimum security blanket of protection for trustees. Although the protection it provides is better than no protection at all, the typical policy is loaded with exclusions in one form or another. Moreover, like most insurance policies, a fiduciary liability insurance policy always contains some fuzzy wording and legal mumbo-jumbo, which create uncertainties as to what protection would be provided under a specific set of circumstances.

If a policy is not clear regarding whether or not a particular type of claim would or would not be covered, then fund counsel should be asked to seek further clarification directly from the insurance broker or from someone at the carrier's home office who can speak with authority regarding the carrier's intent to provide coverage under a specific set of circumstances.

Following is a forewarning regarding the carrier's response to these types of inquiries: Carriers often do not want to respond to inquiries involving hypothetical claims situations. They may also say that "the policy speaks for itself" with respect to claims that are covered and those that are not covered. The fact is that often a policy does not speak for itself because it has legal wording subject to varying interpretations. For this reason, trustees and their fund counsel should not hesitate to pin down the carrier with respect to what the policy does and does not cover.

After all, the plan is probably paying a substantial premium for its fiduciary liability insurance policy. For that reason alone, trustees have a right to know what the premium is or is not buying in terms of coverage. Besides, trustees are concerned not only about protecting the plan's assets, but also protecting their personal assets, which are at risk if the coverage isn't there when they need it

As a result, trustees and their fund counsel should not hesitate to seek clarification from the carrier as to what types of claims are covered (or excluded). For example, if the fund has a delinquency control problem, it should be known in advance whether or not defense costs would be covered if participants file suit alleging the trustees failed to collect delinquencies and, therefore, their actions adversely affected the financial soundness of the plan. Or, if a fund sometimes assesses withdrawal liability, the trustees should know whether their fiduciary liability insurance policy would cover defense costs if an employer challenges the withdrawal liability assessment. Or, if a pension fund has substantial real estate investments, the trustees should know in advance whether defense costs would be covered if these investments are challenged by a lawsuit.

There may be many other types of potential claims situations about which a particular board of trustees may be concerned, and trustees should ask their fund counsel whether such claims would be covered under their current fiduciary liability insurance policy. If the policy isn't clear, then fund counsel should seek clarification directly from the carrier. If the carrier fails to provide a clear-cut answer, then it may be time for the trustees and their fund counsel to check out the competition.

Policies vary with respect to the extent of coverage provided. Any fiduciary liability insurance policy may undergo changes with the adoption of a new federal law or related regulations. Every carrier is quick to recognize that these new federal laws and regulations may significantly increase its own liability risk and, if this is the case, it will not be surprising to find new exclusions inserted in the basic policy or added to the policy as an amendatory endorsement. This is why it is so important that trustees encourage their fund counsel to both carefully monitor these changes and keep the trustees up to date on any new restrictions imposed under their particular policy.

It seems likely that, for the foreseeable future, the minimum blanket of protection provided under most fiduciary liability insurance policies will diminish, rather than improve, at the same time that premiums continue their upward climb. Remember: No carrier is out to win a popularity contest among trustees. Carriers are out to make money and will do whatever they believe is necessary to accomplish that objective, including reducing coverage, increasing premiums, and/or tightening the underwriting standards used to determine whether or not they want to insure a particular fund in the first place.

Trustees should not expect to find fiduciary liability insurance that will provide all the protection they think they need at an affordable price. The fact is that all policies have coverage gaps. Nevertheless, some policies do provide better coverage than others, and some carriers have a better reputation than others when it comes to responding to claims covered under their policies. For these reasons, it is extremely important that trustees insist that their fund counsel stay abreast of any new developments that might give them better protection at the same or lesser cost.

Of course, the best protection in the world against trustee liability does not come from the purchase of a fiduciary liability insurance policy but, rather, from trustee actions that are designed to reduce the risk of litigation in the first place. Many of these actions have been described earlier in this handbook including:

1. Hiring a full complement of competent professional advisors
2. Delegating investment responsibility to a professional asset manager or managers, providing the investment manager with a clear statement of the trustees' investment objectives and carefully monitoring his or her performance
3. Participating in an ongoing program of trustee education by attending Foundation meetings, reading Foundation publications and utilizing the Foundation's vast library resources
4. Carefully monitoring the prudence of trustee expenses
5. Maintaining an effective delinquency control program
6. Delegating fiduciary responsibilities to appropriate trustee committees
7. Authorizing fund counsel and/or the fund consultant to undertake periodic compliance audits to assure that the fund is in full compliance with new federal laws and regulations.

Although it may be comforting to have fiduciary liability insurance, the fact remains that trustees must ultimately rely on their own behavior as fiduciaries to protect themselves and the plan against the risk of litigation, IRS monetary sanctions and against the risk of being held personally liable for their actions.

KEY CONCEPTS

The following questions are provided to stimulate trustee thinking regarding fiduciary liability insurance protection.

1. Does fund counsel periodically review with the entire board of trustees the coverages, exclusions, deductible, liability limit and other features of the current fiduciary liability insurance policy?
2. Do the trustees know if the policy would (or would not) cover defense costs for a claim involving the following?
   - A wrongful act allegedly committed before the policy period
   - A dispute over a benefit claim (unless compensatory damages are sought)
   - An allegation that the trustees have engaged in willful or reckless violation of a statute
   - An allegation that the trustees obtained personal profit or advantage to which they were not entitled as fiduciaries under the plan
3. Does the policy cover IRS monetary sanctions imposed against the trustees for failure to operate a pension fund in accordance with the Code's qualification requirements?
4. Has an amendatory endorsement regarding real estate and mortgage investments been attached to the policy? If yes, does the fund meet the conditions set forth in the endorsement in order to assure coverage for claims arising out of real estate and/or mortgage investments?
5. At the time of policy renewal, does fund counsel review with the board of trustees any potential claim situations that should be reported on the renewal form? At the same time, does fund counsel make suggestions as to what the trustees should do to reduce the risks of litigation against the plan and its trustees?
6. Has the fund experienced any significant increases in its fiduciary liability insurance premium during the last several years? If yes:
   - Has fund counsel asked the carrier what factors explain the premium increases?
   - Have the trustees asked fund counsel to obtain premium quotes from other carriers to help the trustees determine whether or not the fund is being overcharged?

7. Has every trustee purchased a waiver-of-recourse provision eliminating the carrier's right to seek reimbursement in the event the trustees are found guilty of a breach of fiduciary duty?

ENDNOTES

1. Internal Revenue Service Employee Plans Division Field Directive Setting Guidelines on Limited Circumstances Under Which Service May Accept Payment of Sanctions Under Closing Agreement Program, Issued March 14, 1995, BNA *Daily Tax Report,* 3-15-95, P.L.-1-1-2.

2. Department of Labor News Release, "Policy on Fiduciary Liability Insurance," USDL-7-127 (March 4, 1975), 4.

3. Bureau of National Affairs, Highlights of the New Pension Law, 122.

4. Dennis Kass, former Assistant Secretary of Labor, remarks made at the 32nd Annual Employee Benefits Conference of the International Foundation of Employee Benefit Plans, published in the *Digest,* February 1987: 3-6.

5. Department of Labor, Class Prohibited Transaction Exemption 84-14, published in the *Federal Register* on March 13, 1984, pp. 9494-9507.

6. Department of Labor News Release, "Policy on Fiduciary Liability Insurance," 4.

7. These carriers include Aetna, Lloyd's, the Chubb Group, Union Labor Life Casualty Company, First State and National Union Insurance Companies.

SECTION III

DESIGN OF WELFARE PLANS

Chapter 18

Managed Prescription Drug Benefit Programs

Sean Brandle

During the last ten years, a number of major changes in the pharmaceutical industry have dramatically transformed the environment in which multiemployer health plan sponsors operate in order to provide pharmacy benefit plans. This chapter will examine some of the driving forces behind these changes and will present strategies designed to control costs and better ensure the delivery of effective pharmacy benefit programs for participants.

RECENT TRENDS IN PRESCRIPTION BENEFITS

The Segal Company's *2005 Health Plan Cost Trend Survey* (see Figure 1) predicted a moderate slowing of rates of increase for pharmacy benefit cost trend. In order to begin to effectively cope with prescription plan cost increases, trustees of multiemployer health plans must examine and understand the key, underlying cost drivers.

TREND DRIVERS

This section lists and describes several of the forces driving prescription plan cost increases[1] experienced by multiemployer health plans in recent years.

Direct to Consumer Advertising

The relaxation (in 1997) of direct-to-consumer advertising regulations created an entirely new avenue through which pharmaceutical companies could promote the benefits of their prescription drug products. By directly communicating with consumers, drug manufacturers created a powerful new mechanism for stimulating demand for prescription drugs. This, combined with the release of several blockbuster medications, drove higher utilization and increased prescription drug trend in the late 1990s. The drugs that were introduced at that time included valuable medications that no health plan would deny to participants, as well as those, it can be argued, that provided benefits geared more toward lifestyle enhancement rather than saving lives.

Prescription Drug Cost Inflation

Inflation has historically played a large role in increasing the costs of prescription drugs. In past years, the inflation rate for prescription drugs outpaced medical and general inflation rates, but data for 2003 and 2004 show (see Figure 2) prescription drug inflation as measured by the Consumer Price Index was more in line with the overall CPI.[2]

Drug Indications

New indications (i.e., new reasons for prescribing a drug) for existing drugs also add to prescription drug plan costs. For example, new, lower guidelines for cholesterol levels caused an increase in the number of individuals receiving cholesterol lowering medication. Cost increases that result from new indications are often acceptable; they can improve the health status of participants and offset potential medical costs resulting from controlling and monitoring existing conditions. In many cases, effective prescription drug treatment for chronic conditions can alleviate medical costs for acute episodes of illness.

New Drugs

The creation and market introduction of new prescription drugs has been a key driver for higher drug plan costs. As new drugs enter the market, it is impor-

Figure 1

**FIVE-YEAR SUMMARY OF PRESCRIPTION DRUG PROJECTED TRENDS:
2001-2005—ACTIVES AND RETIREES UNDER 65**

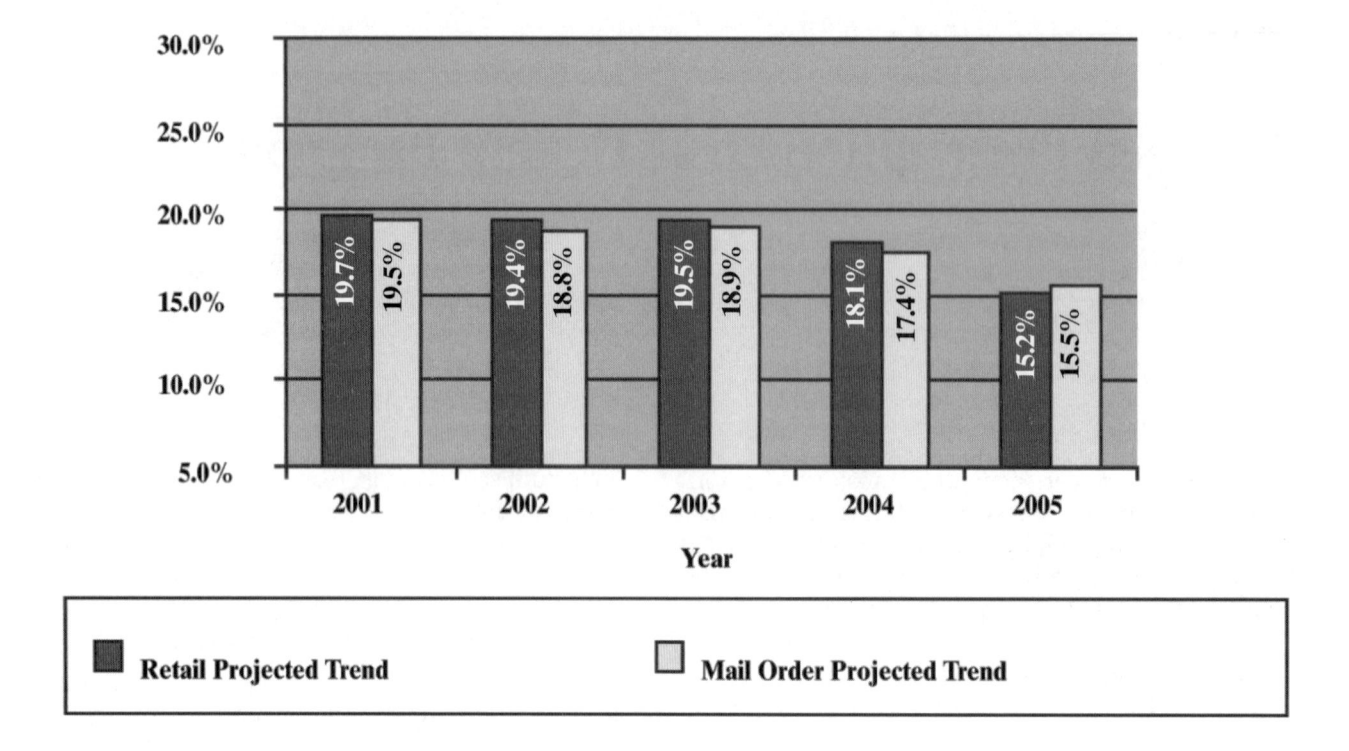

Year	Retail Projected Trend	Mail Order Projected Trend
2001	19.7%	19.5%
2002	19.4%	18.8%
2003	19.5%	18.9%
2004	18.1%	17.4%
2005	15.2%	15.5%

Source: The Segal Company.

Figure 2

CONSUMER PRICE INDEX

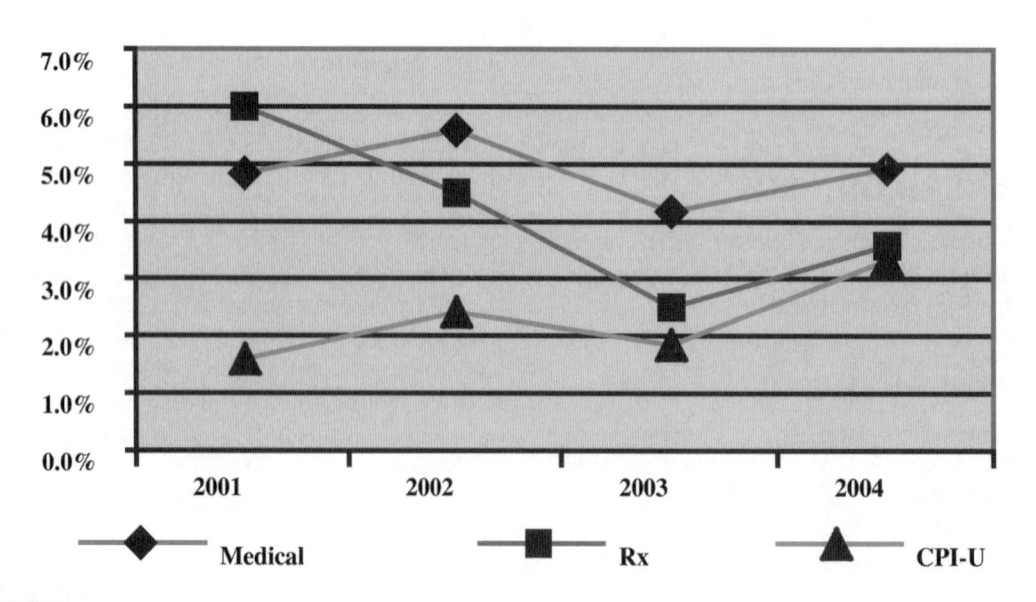

Year	Medical	Rx	CPI-U
2001	4.9%	6.0%	1.7%
2002	5.6%	4.5%	2.5%
2003	4.2%	2.5%	1.9%
2004	5.0%	3.6%	3.3%

Source: Bureau of Labor Statistics.

Table

**COST OF SELECTED BIOTECH DRUGS
APPROVED BY THE FOOD AND DRUG ADMINISTRATION (FDA) IN 2003**

Product	Disease or Condition Treated	Estimated Cost
Aldurazyme®	MPS-1(a rare genetic enzyme deficiency)	$170,000/year
Fabrazyme®	Fabry's disease (a fat storage disorder that causes various health problems)	$165,000/year
Fuzeon®	Advanced HIV	$20,000/year
Iressa®	Lung cancer	$24,000/year
Xolair®	Allergic asthma	$15,000/year

Notes: This list is not inclusive and is provided as a reference only. Please refer to manufacturer's full prescribing information for a complete discussion of these products. Actual costs vary based on treatment cycles.
Source: Caremark Trends Prescription® 2003. Cited with permission.

tant to learn whether they represent truly unique products that provide improvements and advancements in treatment, or whether they are *copycat* therapies. Copycat drugs represent alternatives to existing, effective therapies already on the market. Multiemployer health plan sponsors should work closely with their pharmacy benefit managers (PBMs) and plan advisors to monitor utilization of newly introduced drugs and consider implementing cost and utilization control programs.

Specialty/Bio-Tech Products

Specialty drugs are expensive, bioengineered drug products designed to treat uncommon conditions. Currently, products exist to treat such diseases as hemophilia, multiple sclerosis, Gaucher disease, HIV and various forms of cancer. These drugs are very expensive, are primarily injectable and require close patient monitoring to ensure appropriate outcomes and cost effective utilization. The table lists some of the biotech drug products that were approved in 2003 and provides estimated annual patient medication costs.

A complicating factor associated with biotech medications is their distribution and availability. Due to cost, special handling and distribution requirements, these drugs are not widely available at neighborhood pharmacies and are only provided to select pharmacies. As a result, specialty pharmacies have arisen to facilitate the effective distribution and utilization of these medications. This creates a situation where plan sponsors must actively monitor plan drug utilization to keep abreast of specialty drug spending.

Currently, there are a number of organizations whose sole function is the purchase, distribution, and patient management associated with specialty drugs. Major PBMs have also recently become interested in the distribution of these medications and are acquiring specialty drug distribution companies to help them manage the emerging cost.

Expanding Role of the PBMs

PBMs are playing an increasingly important role for plan sponsors. Formerly serving primarily as claims processors, PBMs are now being looked to as entities that can provide assistance in navigating the increasingly complex maze of pharmacy program management. PBMs are positioned to assume this role because of their historically close proximity to drug manufacturers and retail and mail order drug distributors. This new role for PBMs creates opportunities as well as complexities for plan sponsors.

As PBMs become more involved in managing prescription drug benefits and associated costs, plan sponsors must be more vigilant in their oversight of the PBM. Measuring and monitoring a PBM's performance—and routinely renegotiating contractual, financial and service terms—has become crucial to ensuring appropriate management of overall plan cost

It is important to remember that all PBMs utilize the same national data file components in the claim adjudication process. This claim file contains many details regarding the patient, the prescriber and the drug being dispensed. The complex, yet consistent nature of prescription drug data and the adjudication process involved make pharmacy claims management possible. All PBMs provide pharmacists access to this nationally consistent data through their individual electronic claim adjudication systems. This enables the pharmacist to simultaneously fill a prescription and adjudicate the claim on the PBM's system. This also presents the PBM with the opportunity to collect valuable patient data and engage the pharmacist in cost and utilization control activities.

Figure 3

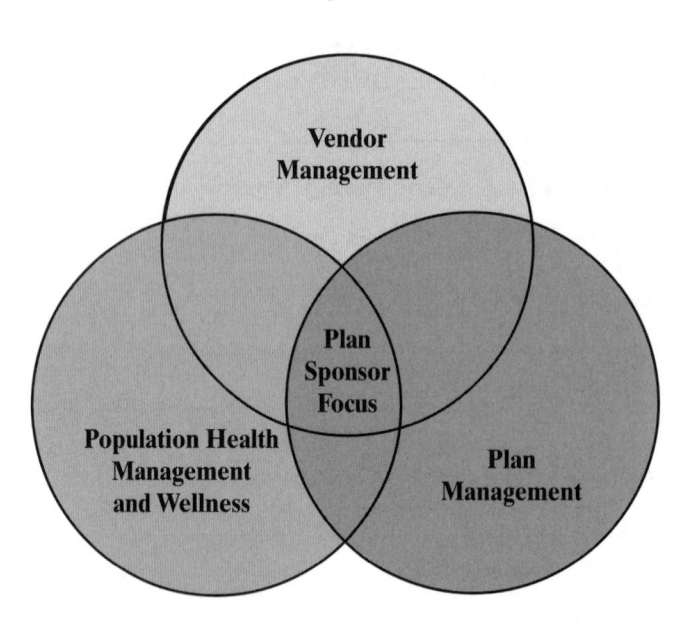

[Venn diagram with three overlapping circles labeled "Vendor Management", "Population Health Management and Wellness", and "Plan Management", with "Plan Sponsor Focus" at the center intersection.]

Three-Prong Approach to Controlling Prescription Drug Costs

A successful strategy designed to control costs and maintain quality of a prescription drug benefit plan consists of the three main components shown in Figure 3.

Plan sponsors should focus initially on the vendor management aspect in order to provide savings that may be available without causing any participant disruption. Subsequent examination of plan and population health management and wellness can result in actions that should be based on a number of issues, including:

- Plan sponsor goals and benefit delivery philosophy
- Perceived participant response to potentially disruptive PBM programs
- Plan sponsor and participant cost sensitivities.

The rest of this section will examine the actions that sponsors of multiemployer health plans should consider when utilizing the three-pronged approach to controlling prescription plan costs.

Vendor Management: Putting PBMs to Work for Your Plan

Given the evolution of the prescription drug and PBM market, plan sponsors must actively monitor and manage their PBM's performance. The same data that is available to assist plan sponsors with crafting plan design can be used to gauge a PBM's performance. Further, the power of conducting an independent review of a PBM's financial performance cannot be underestimated as a cost control mechanism. As experienced buyers of health insurance, most sponsors of multiemployer health have done a commendable job of seeking out PBM arrangements with the most advantageous financial terms and the most robust support services. But, it may be possible to reduce costs by managing and negotiating terms more aggressively. Here are some examples:

- **Closely inspect PBM contracts.** In our experience, PBM financial terms can vary dramatically among competing organizations. Evaluation of financial delivery terms should include valid benchmark data to illustrate the financial terms available to a given plan sponsor, based on demographics and the mix of drugs being dispensed. Further, plan sponsors should obtain guarantees that represent dollar for dollar reimbursement from any PBMs that do not attain the guaranteed financial terms previously negotiated.
- **Reduce drug cost expenses.** Benchmarking can be used as a guideline for determining whether the contractual discounts are appropriate based on program cost and utilization characteristics.
- **Reduce administrative expenses.** Benchmarking can be also used as a guideline for determining whether these administrative expenses represent an appropriate percentage of total program costs.
- **Evaluate the PBM's efforts regarding programs designed to control costs and improve patient care and outcomes.** For example, some PBM clinical intervention programs (paid for by plan sponsors)

have provided little evidence of savings or improved outcomes and may actually promote alternative drug products and therapies that produce greater revenue for the PBM.
- **Review claims processing results.** Claims reviews have uncovered situations wherein the claims payers misinterpreted existing or changed plan provisions and were paying benefits improperly. Such reviews enable a plan sponsor to rectify the problem and ensure administration of the plan as originally intended.
- **Require vendors to agree to performance guarantees.** Guarantees can be tied to efforts to detect fraud, as well as to improve accuracy and timeliness of payments. These also have the advantage of contributing to participant satisfaction. Of course, performance guarantees are only of value if periodic reviews are performed to validate that the guarantees are being met.
- **Closely review vendor contracts and subject them to competitive bids periodically to reduce program costs and/or upgrade services.** We have found a wide discrepancy in the fees charged to plan sponsors among vendors offering similar services. Drug manufacturer rebate payments are an important cost offset for any self-insured prescription drug program. Rebate levels should be firmly guaranteed.

Plan Management: Considering Changes in Designs and Features

Plan design is probably the most controllable factor affecting prescription benefit plan costs. The types and number of plan offerings are key variables. How the benefits are designed and delivered also has a profound effect on total costs. How a plan sponsor ultimately crafts plan design is a direct reflection of sponsor's goals. Plan sponsors are typically balancing the desire to continue providing meaningful benefits while encouraging appropriate behavior from the plan participants. Plan sponsors must also make decisions about providing first dollar coverage versus providing catastrophic coverage. Much of a plan sponsor's approach depends on the particular characteristics of a group, including demographic profile, industry and the participant's ability to pay. Plan sponsors should review the following features when designing their prescription drug plans:
- **Establish appropriate cost sharing (i.e., deductibles, copayments and coinsurance).** Cost sharing should be designed to balance the plan sponsor's need to discourage overuse of the plan with making sure that participants seek essential care. The goal of meaningful cost sharing is to encourage the appropriate behavior—not to ask plan participants to pay more than the plan sponsor determines is suitable given the unique characteristics of the group.
- **Encourage use of generics.** Generic drugs are, on average, 30% to 60% less costly than brand-name drugs. Some plan sponsors have introduced a "mandatory generic" plan—a feature that will only reimburse the generic drug cost, when a generic equivalent exists. Another common approach is to create copay differentials between coverage for brand-name and generic prescriptions that are significant enough to encourage the use of generic drugs.
- **Establish appropriate cost-sharing differentials among treatment options so plan participants are encouraged to seek appropriate courses of treatment in the most advantageous settings.** Different payment levels between competing therapies and inpatient/outpatient settings can help drive the desired behavior. Plans that encourage less expensive treatment options can change patients' behavior, benefiting both plan participants and plan sponsors.
- **Provide coverage incentives for support services and complementary care to motivate plan participants to improve their health.** Educational material about treatment options, home health aides and access to support groups are examples of support services and complementary care.
- **Focus on and enforce precertification and utilization review rules.** Broad-based, nonspecific, precertification rules that ultimately result in approval of all requests are a waste of time and money. To be most effective, precertification rules should be targeted to treatments and services that are subject to overuse or abuse. For example, some people with minor, acute conditions may improperly use narcotic painkillers on an ongoing basis, indicating potential addiction. Requiring precertification can identify these cases and often stop the abuse before it begins. However, precertification could raise additional administrative issues for plan sponsors under the claims and appeals regulations. Of course, all plan sponsors should obtain the advice of counsel when adopting new plan rules.

Population Health Management and Wellness: Educating Participants and Supporting Them With Tools and Resources to Influence Plan Costs

Evidence exists suggesting that some health care delivery systems are inefficient, often delivering care of questionable quality. Some health care services are overused or ineffective; some are not being properly adhered to by patients. This could be avoided through prevention and health promotion. Yet, few plan sponsors evaluate the effectiveness of the treatments being rendered to plan participants, and fewer still create wellness programs that educate patients and provide access to alternative, effective treatment options.

Following are several strategies that encourage participant involvement in their own care and also work to control costs, especially over the long-term:

- **Introduce disease management programs for chronic conditions, such as diabetes, hypertension and depression.** These programs, which identify providers, facilities and treatments that have the best track records for improved outcomes, can produce long-term returns on investment by reducing the frequency and levels of future high-cost claims.
- **Promote compliance with prescribed treatments.** If a PBM detects that a patient has neglected to refill a prescription for an essential drug treatment and informs the patient's physician, the physician will be better able to manage and monitor the patient's condition.
- **Use education and financial incentives to encourage plan participants with weight problems and poor eating habits to change their diets and exercise more.** Health care costs tend to be higher for obese individuals, and there is a strong link between obesity and expensive, chronic conditions, such as heart disease and diabetes. A major study sponsored by the American Diabetes Association found that patients with Type II diabetes were able to control their blood sugar levels through diet and exercise at equal or better levels than those patients taking oral diabetes medications.
- **Reduce the frequency of costly and questionable claims and services by educating plan participants and encouraging appropriate behavior through plan design.** For example, the Centers for Disease Control determined that over 50% of children for whom antibiotics were prescribed did not test positive for any bacterial infection. Some strategies to address this include providing plan participants with easy-to-read information about the success of competing treatments (e.g., surgery, rest and pharmaceutical therapy) and/or asking participants to pay for a reasonable portion of the cost of treatment.

DATA IS POWER: DETERMINING THE MOST APPROPRIATE ACTIONS

One of the main benefits of using PBMs is taking advantage of the timely and accurate data PBMs capture. Based on the "point of sale" nature of current systems in which pharmacists utilize the PBM claim system to adjudicate claims, the problems that were often associated with paper claim processing are virtually eliminated. PBMs' electronic data can help plan sponsors easily identify and address problem areas and opportunities. Plan sponsors can then develop strategies to address the vendor, plan design and population health management aspects of effective prescription benefit plan management mentioned earlier in this chapter. Meaningful cost reduction is attainable for plan sponsors willing to dig into the details of their programs.

Plan sponsors can identify savings opportunities by reviewing vendor contracts and competitive information and by drawing comparisons to industry benchmarks. The most important task health plan sponsors can undertake is to perform a detailed claims analysis on a periodic basis. This will ensure that their health care cost-management activity targets the sources of particular problem areas. A detailed claims analysis enables plan sponsors to develop targeted plan design changes and patient management services that address "critical" areas in need of plan sponsor attention.

CONCLUSION

Given the current rate of health care inflation, sponsors of multiemployer health plans that want to rein in spending—while preserving attractive prescription coverage—need to take aggressive and comprehensive steps in all three categories of cost management (vendor management, plan design management and population health management and wellness) discussed in this chapter. Please keep in mind that these strategies will not necessarily yield a solution for all the problems in every multiemployer health plan.

Before pursuing one or more of these strategies, trustees should ensure that they are consistent with their overall goals and should weigh the potential costs and benefits of a particular approach. The extremely difficult choices involving coverage and cost management that plan sponsors are facing are expected to continue in the foreseeable future. Isolated actions will likely fall short of delivering sustained plan cost savings. However, a comprehensive approach that is monitored and adjusted over time can increase the chances of plan sponsor success.

ENDNOTES

1. Trend is the forecast change in health plans' per capita claims cost determined by insurance carriers, managed care organizations (MCOs) and third party administrators (TPAs).
2. A measure of the average change in consumer prices over time in a fixed market basket of goods and services.

Chapter 19

Retiree Health Benefits

Michael I. Helmer and Thomas F. Del Fiacco

This chapter will examine the evolution of multiemployer retiree health benefits from their origination as a relatively inexpensive component of the benefit program to their current status as a growing financial concern for most multiemployer health and welfare funds. We also will look at some plan design and funding strategies that trustees can employ in their efforts to continue providing postretirement health benefits while prudently managing related costs. First, here is a look at how retiree health benefit plans have evolved.

A BRIEF HISTORY OF RETIREE HEALTH BENEFITS AND THE REGULATORY ENVIRONMENT

During the middle of the 20th century, employer-sponsored health care coverage gained popularity as a tool for attracting and retaining employees without increasing payroll expense. The federal government enhanced the attractiveness of providing health care benefits by passing legislation that made the costs associated with providing health insurance exempt from federal taxes. Then, in 1965, Medicare, the federally subsidized insurance program offered to older and disabled Americans, was enacted. The result was that many employers added retiree benefits "because they needed them to make their retirement packages work, because they were attractive to labor in competitive labor markets, and because the costs were rarely significant."[1]

Partly because of the relatively low cost of providing postretirement health benefits throughout most of their history (and also because of tax policy), they have never been subject to any regulatory funding requirement. Consequently, unlike qualified defined benefit (DB) pension plans, which are required to be funded during the working careers of the plan participants to help ensure actuarial solvency, retiree health benefits historically have been financed on a pay-as-you-go basis. That is, they have been paid from general assets rather than from carefully crafted and specifically allocated reserves.

In December 1990, the Financial Accounting Standards Board (FASB) issued Statement of Financial Accounting Standards No. 106 (FAS 106), which addressed "accounting issues related to measuring and recognizing the exchange that takes place between an employer that provides postretirement benefits and employees who render services in exchange for these benefits."[2] In other words, FASB decided that an employer's accounting for the cost of postretirement health benefits should recognize these benefits are accrued during employees' working careers even if they are not so funded.

Subsequently, the American Institute of Certified Public Accountants (AICPA) Statement of Position 92-6 (SOP 92-6) required funded welfare benefit plans (including multiemployer health and welfare funds) to disclose the postretirement benefit obligation calculated in accordance with FAS 106. The postretirement benefit obligation is to be "measured as the actuarial present value of the future benefits attributed to plan participants' services rendered to the measurement date."[3] The postretirement benefit obligation is determined by an actuary who projects the size of a specific active and retiree population into the future and then assesses the value of the future cost of providing postretirement benefits in current dollars by making assumptions regarding such future events as health care inflation, retirement, mortality and the relationship of increased costs and utilization of health care expenses at older ages.

DEVELOPMENT OF THE PERFECT STORM

During the mid-1990s, medical inflation rates fell to single digits as plan sponsors began addressing two key components of health care inflation: utilization and unit cost. Utilization was reduced by implementing elements of managed care, such as pre-authorization review, case management and gatekeeping. Unit costs were reduced by leveraging membership volume to obtain pricing discounts, as well as by prescription drug advances that helped to prevent acute and more expensive conditions requiring hospitalization and other medical treatment.

These trend-reducing strategies were effective for a short time only and in the early 2000s, health care inflation returned to double-digit rates. A major contributor to the recent high health care inflation rates is the increasing average age of the population—the older the population gets, the more health care services are required. By 2020, the number of individuals ages 55 to 65 is projected to increase by 75% and, by 2030, the number of those over age 65 is expected to double.[4]

To make matters worse, the impending retirement of the baby boomers means those remaining in the workforce will need to subsidize more retirees. As the ratio of retirees to active lives increases, the subsidy burden per active increases. For example, consider a welfare fund that currently maintains a retiree per active ratio of one retiree for every two actives and a retiree subsidy of 50¢ per hour. If, in five years, the retiree per active ratio increases to one retiree for every 1½ actives, the hourly subsidy will have to increase 33% from 50¢ to 67¢ per hour even before health care inflation is taken into account. If we assume that health care inflation will continue to grow, even modestly, at 8% per year over the same five-year period, the subsidy will need to nearly double from 50¢ to 98¢ per hour. These challenges have been compounded by the difficult investment environment of the early 2000s, resulting in the "perfect storm."

IDENTIFYING POSTRETIREMENT SUBSIDIES

Typically, welfare funds that offer postretirement health benefits provide coverage to early retirees who are not yet eligible for Medicare. Although benefits for pre-age-65 retirees are typically paid for a shorter period and to a younger population than the post-age-65 group, the costs per retiree can be twice or more than that of the cost of a Medicare-eligible retiree. This relationship exists because once a retiree reaches age 65, Medicare will typically cover 65% to 75% of the costs the fund would have otherwise incurred in the absence of Medicare.

Many multiemployer welfare funds provide postretirement health coverage benefits to Medicare-eligible retirees. Until now, much of the cost associated with post-age-65 retirees was paid for by Medicare, but prescription drugs were not covered. In fact, prescription drugs have accounted for the largest and fastest growing component of post-age-65 cost. Now, as a result of the Medicare Prescription Drug, Improvement, and Modernization Act of 2003, beginning on January 1, 2006, Medicare will provide a limited, voluntary benefit for outpatient prescription drugs.

The MMA has far-reaching implications for the Medicare program, health plans that coordinate with Medicare and health plans in general. Individuals entitled to benefits under Part A or enrolled in Part B of Medicare could elect to join a new Medicare program—Part D—to be delivered by Medicare Advantage plans and stand-alone commercial prescription drug plans. A temporary Medicare prescription drug discount card program was implemented to cover the period until the new Part D program begins. Additional Medicare changes include Part B and reimbursement procedure changes and other key provisions.

STRATEGIC PLANNING—FUNDING CONSIDERATIONS

When considering how to manage retiree health subsidies provided through multiemployer health funds, trustees need to make prudent and sometimes difficult decisions about plan design and financing. When considering plan design, trustees usually consider the three sources of financing available for postretirement health benefits:
- Employer contributions derived from hours worked by active employees
- Self-pay contributions from retired participants
- Investment returns on fund assets.

Most postretirement benefits have historically been financed on a pay-as-you-go basis. Welfare funds may hold reserves, but typically no portion of the reserve is specifically designated for postretirement obligations.

When considering retiree benefits, the issue of reserves takes on new dimensions. Even though the accounting disclosure requirements for pension and retiree health benefits are quite similar, the appropriate financing strategies may be quite different. A pension plan has a legal obligation to pay certain future benefits (those that "vest") to current active participants. Retiree health benefit plans have no corresponding funding requirements. There is no established legal requirement that welfare plans must be continued at their current level of benefits or that they must be continued at all.

Therefore, a welfare plan is not legally required to fully, or even partially, prefund benefits by the time participants reach retirement age. (Of course, fund counsel must always be consulted in these matters.) As a result, the possible levels of reserves can vary significantly. A pay-as-you-go funding strategy where retiree benefits are paid from the surplus of the plan generated by a combination of favorable experience, investment return and employer contributions from current active partic-

Table

DB VERSUS DC RETIREE HEALTH PLANS

Advantages	Defined Benefit	Defined Contribution
	• Ensures a specified level of benefits to retirees	• Financing level established and maintained
	• Allows for significant benefits to those nearing retirement	• No actuarial valuation required
Disadvantages	• Requires regular actuarial valuations	• Participants approaching retirement may not be able to accrue a sufficient benefit.
	• Welfare fund at risk for assets and demographics not meeting expectations	• Level of postretirement subsidy is unknown before retirement.

ipants may have a zero reserve. Alternatively, trustees may elect to earmark portions of a welfare fund's reserves to fulfill part or all of the plan's SOP 92-6 obligations.

If trustees are committed to providing postretirement subsidies but are concerned about the impact that escalating subsidies will have on their future active population, they may establish a retiree-only reserve either within the existing fund or as a separate trust fund. Assets that are set aside for postretirement benefits are referred to as the *retiree reserve* and all other assets as the *general fund*. The fund would then enter a "build-up period" during which annual contributions are made to the retiree reserve (in addition to general fund contributions), coincident with and followed by a "paydown period" where all benefit payments are made from a combination of the retiree reserve and retiree self-payments.

There are many types of cost-sharing arrangements. Here are two potential approaches that trustees may consider (see table):

- **DB approach**—The DB approach is similar to a DB pension plan. Under this approach, retirees are provided with credits that are based on years of service and/or age. For example, retirees would receive $10 per year of service or 2% of the expected cost per year of service.
- **Defined contribution (DC) approach**—The DC approach awards an allocation to participants' individual accounts that, with interest, will grow. At retirement, the value of the individual account can be used to defray the cost of postretirement health care coverage.

For both DB and DC approaches, age and service will affect the level of the postretirement subsidy. Until recently, it was common to provide a full postretirement health benefits package to those participants who retired at age 55 with ten years of service. However, unlike a pension benefit that is reduced to account for early retirement or few years of service, the postretirement health benefit obligation does not get adjusted the same way. Therefore, trustees should carefully consider participant demographics when setting financial strategy.

PLAN DESIGN CONSIDERATIONS

Once trustees have concluded what type of postretirement health benefits can be afforded for whom and for what duration, they can begin to design and adopt specific levels of benefits to coincide with the postretirement benefit financing. Recently, trustees have focused on the following key areas to provide a level of benefits that fit the available resources:

- **Eligibility**—In an effort to both contain postretirement benefit costs as well as promote longer active service and corresponding hourly contributions, welfare funds have either restricted the eligibility age for receiving postretirement benefits by increasing the minimum age and/or service requirement, or provided a reduced subsidy for early retirees with fewer service credits. The subsidy has typically been reduced by increasing the self-pay requirement for those individuals.
- **Coinsurance Versus Copays**—Many welfare plans are moving away from copays to coinsurance, because under a copay structure, unless copay amounts are indexed annually through plan amendments, the entire impact of health care inflation is borne by the fund. In fact, because of leveraging, year-to-year expense increases to the fund will exceed actual trend. For example: A $100 prescription with a $20 copay costs the fund $80 in a year. If

trend is 15%, the same prescription will cost the fund $95 in the following year ($115 Rx cost − $20 copay). This is actually an 18.75% increase in expense to the fund versus the actual 15% trend. But, by charging a coinsurance amount, the effect of trend is shared by both the participants and the fund. Here's how: A $100 prescription with a 20% coinsurance costs the fund $80 in a year. If trend is 15%, the prescription costs the fund $92 in the following year, exactly 15% more than in the first year. The participant pays $23 (20% of $115), also 15% more than the participant paid in the previous year.

- **Retiree Contributions**—Funds should examine the methodology currently being used to establish self-pay rates. Contributions can be set to help control active subsidy levels and reward longer service participants. Retiree contributions can also be set to adjust for tier status (single vs. family) and level of benefits (pre- vs. post-age 65).
- **Coordination of Benefits (COB) with Medicare**—Plans that offer medical benefits to retirees should regularly review their Coordination of Benefits with Medicare provision. Self-funded post-age-65 benefits are typically coordinated through one of the following methodologies:
  - **Full Coordination of Benefits**—The fund pays the lesser of the amount it would have paid in the absence of Medicare and the remaining expenses after Medicare has paid its portion. This method is the most generous to the participant and the most expensive to the fund.
  - **Exclusion**—The balance of expenses after Medicare's payment are adjudicated and split between the participant and the welfare fund according to the plan's deductible and coinsurance provisions. This methodology shares the savings from Medicare between the participant and the fund.
  - **Carve-Out**—The fund's responsibility toward paying benefits is reduced by the Medicare payment. This is the least expensive coordination method for the fund and therefore provides more savings to the fund than full COB or exclusion.

In lieu of self-funding post-age-65 medical benefits, trustees may find financial opportunities to contract with Medicare Advantage or other fully insured, supplemental products.

CONCLUSION

Welfare fund trustees are beginning to examine and understand their funds' SOP 92-6 obligations as a result of an aging workforce and impending baby boomer retirements. Trustees must pay particular attention to how providing postretirement health benefits will affect their funds' abilities to provide a level of benefits that match participants' needs. Reviewing financial issues and demographics can allow trustees to determine the funding and plan design strategies that will enable both short- and long-term success.

ENDNOTES

1. G. Lawrence Atkins, "The Employer Role in Financing Health Care for Retirees," in Judith Mazo, Anna Rappaport and Sylvester Schieber, eds., *"Providing Health Care Benefits in Retirement,"* p. 108.
2. "Statement of Financial Accounting Standards No. 106," paragraph 4.
3. Amendment to AICPA Audit and Accounting Guide, "Audits of Employee Benefit Plans," and SOP 92-6, "Accounting and Reporting by Health and Welfare Benefit Plans," paragraph 12.
4. General Accounting Office (GAO)—01-374.

Chapter 20

Next Generation Health Plan Solutions: Trends in Multiemployer Health Plan Design

Edward A. Kaplan

INTRODUCTION

With health care trend continuing to increase at double-digit rates, the pressure on sponsors of multiemployer health plans is unrelenting. Based on the notion that necessity is the mother of invention, plan sponsors are introducing an unprecedented level of new benefit strategies to help control spending, including the implementation of innovative medical plan designs. Many trustees have made plan changes that affect participant coverage. Changes range from the minor, limiting annual physical therapy visits, to the major, replacing first dollar medical coverage with high deductible catastrophic coverage. This chapter will focus on some new trends in plan design that are being adopted by increasing numbers of multi-employer health fund boards of trustees.

THE PROBLEM: HEALTH CARE SPENDING

Health plan trends (annual rate of plan claim cost increases) are steadily rising at a rate that is four to five times the level of the general consumer price index (CPI). (See Table I.)

Further, the health care delivery system is plagued with an aging workforce that has chronic health problems often caused by behavioral issues (smoking, obesity, stress), expensive new technology, inflation in the cost of treatments, overutilization of services (frequently resulting from the practice of defensive medicine), direct-to-consumer prescription drug advertising and cost-shifting by providers from uninsured and underinsured individuals to health plans. At the current pace, the cost to provide health care coverage for participants will exceed 25% of wages in less than five years.

NEXT GENERATION COST-MANAGEMENT STRATEGIES

Despite this, trustees can try to manage health care costs in a number of ways. Some solutions we suggest in this chapter are new, while others borrow from the past. No single approach is likely to solve the problem for either the short or the long term. Success will require a combination of strategies and actions that are uniquely developed for each plan sponsor that will have to be continually revisited and revised as conditions change going forward. Today, we recommend plan sponsors approach health care cost-containment by utilizing a three-pronged strategy:
1. Vendor management
2. Plan management
3. Population health management and wellness programs.

Although many plan sponsors have aggressively managed their vendors over the last few years, less attention has been given to creative plan management and effective wellness programs. With this in mind, plan

Table I

	2001	2003	2005 est.
PPO	11.0%	13.0%	12.0%
HMO	10.0	14.0	11.0
Rx	15.0	19.0	14.0
CPI	2.0	2.5	3.0

sponsors should introduce more creative plan designs and features that significantly reduce the cost of providing adequate health coverage to plan participants and their dependents. The plans that apply an aggressive and innovative three-pronged approach are seeing results. In fact, in our experience, using all three approaches has helped one in five health plans to trend well below 10% per year on a consistent basis.

IT ALL BEGINS WITH DATA

Meaningful cost reduction is attainable for those plan sponsors willing to dig into the details of their programs. Trustees should begin to consider the following questions when they seek to address the primary cost-drivers within their current health program:
- Does the plan balance the needs of participants with the plan's financial resources?
- Is the plan design (copays and cost-sharing) steering participants to cost-effective therapies, treatments and settings?
- Which major conditions and illnesses consume the greatest portion of claim costs?
- Are there atypical claim patterns around specific illnesses or providers?
- Does the current plan design encourage overuse of inappropriate services?
- Can plan rules be designed that steer participants to the most effective health care facilities and treatments?
- Does coverage have adequate controls for tampering, fraud and abuse?
- Does the plan discourage proper treatment because of high amounts of participant cost-sharing that exceeds participants' ability to pay?
- What tools and programs are provided to participants to help them manage chronic conditions, improve health, become knowledgeable of all treatment options and improve compliance with effective treatment protocols?

Plan sponsors can answer many of these questions by gathering data from claim history, vendor contracts, review of competitive information and comparisons to industry benchmarks. The good news is there is a tremendous amount of data that plans can now access. By carefully examining the data available, plan sponsors can identify the problem areas. Then, armed with this information, they can chart a course that will help better manage health care costs and improve participants' health.

Data that should be examined includes history for medical, drug and laboratory claims by provider type, setting (inpatient or outpatient), treatment or procedure, primary diagnosis, disease and condition.

Data can then be used to:
- Determine the medical conditions and diseases that consume the largest percentages of the fund's health plan budget
- Benchmark cost and utilization results to those of other plan sponsors
- Determine levels of participant out-of-pocket costs.
- Ensure the plan is paying claims according to plan design
- More precisely measure savings from plan modifications
- Profile cost and quality by provider and/or facility
- Assess the competitiveness of vendor discounts and fees
- Perform predictive modeling regarding the likelihood and level of future claims and intervene to help patients navigate their health care treatment options more effectively.

EXAMPLES OF PLAN DESIGN FEATURES

Probably the most influential element of health plan costs, other than the age of the covered population, is plan design. The major elements to consider, in regard to plan design, are:
- Eligibility and coordination of benefit rules for actives, retirees and dependents
- Active, retiree and dependent premiums (if any)
- Network arrangements (such as PPOs or high-performance networks)
- Patient out-of-pocket costs (copays, deductibles, coinsurance requirements, health care reimbursement arrangements, health savings accounts)
- Use of gatekeepers, precertification and utilization review rules
- Prescription drug plan design, including use of generics, step therapy, copays, coinsurance, deductibles, formularies, mail service, limited supplies for targeted substances and precertification
- Differentials in payment levels between competing therapies and settings, for example:
  —Emergency room copays versus office visit copays
  —In-network versus out-of-network benefits
  —Brand-name versus generic prescription drugs
- Benefits exclusions and limitations.

In addition, for plan sponsors to preserve effective levels of coverage, plan designs must have the following five characteristics:

1. ***Appropriate levels of participant cost-sharing.*** Cost-sharing decisions should take into account the ability of a particular population to pay and should balance the desire of trustees to encourage participants to seek appropriate care, while at the same time encouraging participants to make responsible decisions when accessing health care services.

2. *Effective financial differentials between treatment options and settings.* These differentials should be set in order to reward those patients who seek the most cost-effective course of treatment and the most efficient providers (e.g., seeking physical therapy as opposed to surgery, when appropriate).
3. *Motivate participants to improve health.* Coverage incentives for support services and complementary care should be provided.
4. *Eliminate coverage for abused and ineffective treatments.* An increasing number of surgeries are being performed with questionable appropriateness and/or outcomes.
5. *Set appropriate limits on participant out-of-pocket costs.* In order to relieve participants of financial burdens when they need to focus on nonfinancial matters, out-of-pocket costs should be aligned with a participant's realistic ability to pay. Catastrophic events and illnesses should not be an undue burden.

Some plans may see positive effects from modestly tweaking current offerings, but for others, more dramatic changes may be required. Regardless of the approach taken, plan sponsors must attack the treatments that consume the greatest dollars and should benchmark the plan with the level of benefits offered by other plans in the same industry in order to remain competitive.

RECENT TRENDS IN ADOPTING NEW PLAN DESIGN STRATEGIES AND FEATURES

Following are three case studies that illustrate how changing plan design can help lower costs.

Case One, Addressing Eligibility

A multiemployer plan located in New England with significant costs attributed to extended medical coverage eligibility decided to make some changes in order to help reverse deficit spending. The original rule extended coverage for six months for those who met eligibility rules. After several options were considered, the trustees adopted a vested eligibility rule. For those with five or more years of service, the extension of medical coverage was six months. For those workers with fewer than five years, the extension was reduced to 30 days. The change in rules resulted in a noticeable reduction in claim liability.

Case Two, Adopting Participant Choice

A West Coast multiemployer health plan sought to control costs by adding multiple medical plan options from which participants could select. The options ranged from HMOs to PPOs and included a high deductible PPO plan with a health savings account feature. Some options had no participant contributions while others required a participant contribution. Annual open enrollment election periods were set up to allow participants to reselect options. As this chapter was written, financial savings had not yet been measured, but early signs were positive and participant acceptance was high.

Case Three, Three-Tier Coinsurance

A Midwest health plan adopted a PPO plan design that provides for improved coverage as participant out-of-pocket costs escalate. Table II illustrates the plan features.

Although this plan has coinsurance that varies by the

Table II

Treatment Category	Network	Nonnetwork
Deductible	$300 per individual 2 × per family	$600 per individual 2 × per family
Tier One—First $2,000 in Eligible Expenses	70% after deductibles	50%
Tier Two—Next $2,000 in Eligible Expenses	90%	60%
Tier Three—100% Coverage	100% after deductible and $4,000 in allowed expenses were submitted	70%
Prevention and Wellness	$500 annual limit for exam, weight loss, etc.	$500 annual limit for exam, weight loss, etc.
Inside Limits and Copays	$50 ER visits Visit limits on chiro, PT, rehab, etc.	$100 per ER visit Visit limits on chiro, PT, rehab, etc.

Table III

Drug Class	Retail Network	Mail Service
Generic	$5 copay, 30-day supply limit	$10, 90-day supply limit
Formulary Brand	20% copay to a $35 maximum	20% to a $75 maximum
Nonformulary Brand	30% copay to a $50 maximum	$30% to a $100 maximum
Other Features	Preauthorization for select drugs $1,000 out-of-pocket maximum	
Network Restrictions	Custom network	Mail covered after 2nd fill at retail

dollar amounts incurred and not by specific procedure, it provides similar levels of coverage compared to plans with typical fixed dollar copays. Participant out-of-pocket costs are $1,100 per year if network providers are used, which is not that different from most plans today. Furthermore, such a plan creates improved coverage as claim liabilities increase for participants. This plan design reduced plan costs dramatically over the prior plan. In the first year after adoption, costs were nearly 20% below prior levels.

PRESCRIPTION DRUG PLANS

Prescription plans have seen the greatest amount of change over the last few years. Plan sponsors are adopting many new features to contain costs, including:
- Multiple, tiered levels of copays by drug type
- Percentage copay plans that replace fixed dollar co-pay plans
- Front-end deductibles specifically for prescription drugs
- Lower benefits for nonformulary brand drugs
- Mandated use of generic drugs and/or mail service
- Restricted day supply rules (e.g., 21-day supply for initial Rx—new therapy)
- Step therapy (i.e., initial mandatory use of lower cost drug therapies)
- Expanding coverage to select over-the-counter drugs
- Therapy class maximum allowances
- Managing specialty drugs.

The following case study shows how changing prescription drug plan design can save a plan money, and the accompanying chapter on prescription benefit plans provides a more in-depth review of this issue.

CASE STUDY— CONVERTING TO A PERCENT COPAY PRESCRIPTION PLAN

A New England multiemployer health fund had been running a significant deficit, with prescription costs reaching close to $80 per participant per month (or about 16% of the total plan cost). After considering several plan design modifications, the trustees adopted the three-tier design illustrated in Table III with percent copays for brand-name drugs.

This new design cut prescription costs by over 30% in the first year and helped to close the gap between fund income and expenses. The design increased the use of generic drugs and reduced utilization of nonformulary drugs. Although participants had an increase in out-of-pocket costs, for most, the increases were modest.

WELLNESS AND DISEASE MANAGEMENT

Evidence is building that suggests many of today's health care services are overused, ineffective and not being properly adhered to by patients. Many of these issues could be avoided through plan designs that encourage disease prevention and health promotion. Consider the following:
- The Centers for Disease Control has determined that over 50% of children for whom antibiotics were prescribed did not test positive for any bacterial infection.
- A major teaching hospital conducted a study on patients with arthritis in their knees. Some patients received surgery while others were prepared for surgery and anesthetized but did not actually undergo surgery. Those receiving the placebo treatment had results that were similar to those for patients who underwent the surgical procedure.
- A major study sponsored by the American Diabetes Association showed that patients with Type II diabetes were able to control their blood sugar levels through diet and exercise at equal or better levels than those patients taking oral diabetes medications.

The point of these studies (and others) is that much can be done to change patient behaviors and treatment options and to avoid costly claims and invasive services that may produce results that are no better than noninvasive treatments.

There are savings opportunities for plan sponsors that address the issues of obesity, depression, noncompliant patients and other manageable conditions. Few plans evaluate the effectiveness of the treatments being rendered to their participants and fewer still create wellness programs that educate patients and provide access to all treatment options. In an age where benefit reductions are becoming commonplace, trustees may be able to add new coverage and programs that produce savings and reduce future high-cost claims.

CONCLUSION

With no cost relief in sight, difficult choices lie ahead for most health plan sponsors. However, trustees of multiemployer health plans can look at creative new plan designs to contain future spending. Some health funds are already taking these steps and are seeing results. In addition, the plan sponsors that dig into their claims data and aggressively manage all three cost-management prongs (vendor management, plan management and population health management and wellness programs) will succeed in preserving effective health coverage for plan participants.

Chapter 21

Recent Regulations in Compliance: HIPAA and COBRA

Kathryn Bakich and Kaye Pestaina

In this chapter we will discuss recent regulations issued under two federal statutes—the Health Insurance Portability and Accountability Act of 1996 (HIPAA) and the Consolidated Omnibus Budget Reconciliation Act of 1986 (COBRA) that trustees of multiemployer health plans should be aware of and pay attention to. Both statutes require extensive administrative procedures designed to increase portability of an individual's employment-based health insurance. HIPAA prohibits certain preexisting condition exclusions, prohibits discrimination on the basis of health status, requires that plans "specially enroll" individuals who have certain qualifying events and requires that plans issue a notice of creditable coverage when an individual's coverage terminates. COBRA requires that plans offer individuals the right to purchase an extension of coverage upon the occurrence of certain qualifying events. Finally, HIPAA's administrative simplification provisions require that plans use standard transactions for transmitting data electronically, and assure the security and privacy of individually identifiable health information.

HIPAA PORTABILITY

On December 30, 2004, the Employee Benefits Security Administration (EBSA), the Internal Revenue Service (IRS) and the Centers for Medicare and Medicaid Services (CMS) published final regulations governing HIPAA's portability of health insurance coverage. This regulation finalizes interim rules issued in 1997, which have been implemented by all affected group health plans. The final rules will become effective for group health plans and health insurers for plan years beginning on or after July 1, 2005. The U.S. Department of Labor (through EBSA) has been actively auditing group health plans for compliance with these standards.

SPECIAL ENROLLMENT OBLIGATIONS

HIPAA requires that group health plans allow individuals to enroll without having to wait for late or open enrollment if (1) a current employee or dependent with other health coverage loses eligibility for coverage (loss of coverage special enrollment) or (2) if a person becomes a dependent through marriage, birth, adoption or placement for adoption (dependent special enrollment).

The final regulations elaborate on and clarify some of the circumstances where special enrollment would apply. Sponsors of multiemployer health plans should be aware that special enrollment goes beyond merely adding a dependent to the plan under certain circumstances. Here are some examples of what the special enrollment rules require:

- *A Current Employee Not Enrolled in the Plan May Specially Enroll.* A current employee does not have to be enrolled in the plan to exercise his or her special enrollment rights. If the employee has a new dependent or their dependent loses other coverage, the employee can enroll himself and his dependents in the plan.
- *Plans Must Allow Enrollment in Any Available Benefit Option.* The plan must allow special enrollment for the current employee, spouse and dependent in any available benefit package.
- *"Declining" Coverage Occurs Every Time the Employee or Dependent has an Opportunity to Enroll in the Plan and Does Not.* Under HIPAA, an employee's ability to special enroll herself and her dependents under loss-of-coverage special enrollment is limited to situations where the employee and dependent declined coverage when it was previously offered because they had other health coverage. The final rules clarify that the initial opportunity for en-

rollment (usually occurring when employment begins) is not the only time when an individual could decline coverage because they had other coverage.
- **Reaching a Lifetime Limit Triggers Special Enrollment.** A plan is generally required to allow a dependent to specially enroll if that dependent reached a lifetime limit on all benefits under the dependent's plan.
- **Termination of Employer Contributions Triggers Special Enrollment.** A special enrollment right could also occur when employer contributions toward other coverage terminates.

The final HIPAA Portability regulation also restates the requirement from the statute and interim rule that plans must provide all employees (both those that enroll in the plan and those that do not) with a notice describing the special enrollment rights "at or before" the time an employee is initially offered the opportunity to enroll in the plan. The final rules contain model language for this notice. Plans should include this language in their enrollment materials.

The final rules also clarify that plans must special enroll an individual where a request for special enrollment is "requested" within 30 days of the relevant event. Some plans may be improperly requiring individuals to complete all enrollment materials within the 30 days. Only a request for special enrollment is required within this timeframe.

NEW MODEL FOR CERTIFICATES OF CREDITABLE COVERAGE

Creditable coverage is defined as coverage under most health benefit programs including employer or multiemployer group health plans, individual health insurance policies, Medicare, Medicaid, state and local governmental programs, etc.[1] Individuals with creditable coverage receive an offset against a new plan's preexisting condition exclusion limitations based on the length of their coverage.

Certificates of creditable coverage must meet specific content requirements. Plans will be deemed to satisfy these content requirements if they use a new model certificate provided in the final regulation. The final rules also require that plans have written procedures for individuals to request and receive certificates of creditable coverage.

HIDDEN PREEXISTING CONDITION EXCLUSIONS

HIPAA places specific limits on the use of preexisting condition exclusions, so instead of meeting all the requirements, many group health plans eliminated preexisting condition exclusions years ago. However, the final regulations point out that certain provisions will be considered preexisting condition exclusions if they condition benefits on when a condition or injury arose relative to the effective date of coverage under the plan. Plans are not prohibited from having these kinds of provisions, but any such exclusions must meet all of the limitations set out in HIPAA (e.g., exclude only conditions treated within six months of the enrollment date).

Hidden preexisting condition exclusions include the following:
- A lifetime limit on coverage for the treatment of diabetes for those diagnosed with diabetes before the effective date of coverage under a plan
- Coverage for an accidental injury only if the injury occurred while covered under the plan
- Excluding benefits for a congenital condition (such as a congenital heart problem) when it otherwise provides benefits for the condition when it is not congenital.

OTHER REQUIREMENTS IN THE FINAL RULES

The final regulations also clarify and update rules concerning what is "excepted" from HIPAA's portability requirements, including:
- Plans that have *fewer than two participants who are current employees.* Thus, retiree-only plans probably do not have to comply with HIPAA portability.
- *"Limited scope" dental and vision benefits.* HIPAA portability will not apply to these benefits if the benefit is either provided under a separate policy, certificate or contract of insurance, or if participants both have the right not to elect to receive coverage for the benefit and must pay an additional premium or contribution if they choose to elect the coverage.
- *Health flexible spending accounts.* Portability does not apply if an employer makes other benefits not excepted by HIPAA available to participants and the maximum benefits payable to the participant under the FSA does not exceed two times the participant's salary reduction election (or, if greater, does not exceed $500 plus the amount of the participant's salary reduction).[2]
- *Supplemental insurance* provided to coverage under a group health plan that is provided under a separate policy, certificate or contract of insurance. The final rules clarify that supplemental insurance includes Medigap policies but does not include coverage that becomes secondary or supplemental only under coordination of benefits provisions. This generally means that group health plans covering both actives and retirees, but that limit coverage for retirees to coverage that supplements Medicare benefits do not meet the requirements of this exception and must comply with the HIPAA portability requirements.

Plan sponsors should also be aware that additional portability requirements might be added to these final regulations in the future. Along with the final HIPAA regulation, the three agencies also issued proposed rules and a request for information seeking comments on specific portability issues. Plans are not now required to comply with these proposed standards. The agencies seek comment on these proposed standards and will issue final rules on these issues at a later date. These proposed standards include tolling certain time periods that affect HIPAA's 63-day break rule and rules concerning HIPAA's interaction with the Family and Medical Leave law.

The request for information asks interested parties to provide input on whether a benefit-specific waiting period is a preexisting condition exclusion under HIPAA. An example of a benefit-specific waiting period is a one-year waiting period before an individual could receive covered benefits for weight-reduction surgery. The agencies have not yet determined whether this type of waiting period is a HIPAA violation.

HIPAA ADMINISTRATIVE SIMPLIFICATION

In addition to portability rules, HIPAA required that group health plans transmit electronic data related to claims payment and eligibility using standard transactions. To facilitate these electronic transactions, plans were required to keep individually identifiable health information, including demographic information, private and secure. The electronic data interchange rules of HIPAA (EDI) were implemented in 2002. Privacy rules, which were the most detailed of the three, were implemented in 2003, and the security rules went into effect in 2005. Small health plans (those with under $5 million in annual receipts) had an extra year to comply.

HIPAA PRIVACY RULES

The Department of Health and Human Services (HHS) is responsible for HIPAA privacy implementation. HHS has issued extensive procedures to safeguard and internally police the use and disclosure of private health information. The rules apply to all ERISA-governed self-insured plans, multiemployer plans, insured plans, individual insurance policies, church plans and state and local governmental plans. The regulations would not apply directly to employers, but an employer that self-administers a health plan would be required to comply. The rules do not apply to other types of insurance, such as workers' compensation, automobile insurance, other property and casualty insurance and certain limited benefits coverage.

Health plans may use private health information without written authorization from the individual for plan administration purposes, including payment, treatment, utilization review and case management, audit and other health care operations.

Plans must make all reasonable efforts to use the minimum amount of information necessary to accomplish these functions. There are several additional categories of protected health information that may be disclosed and used without written authorization. These include but are not limited to public health activities; health oversight activities; certain judicial and law enforcement purposes; research; emergency circumstances; disclosure to next-of-kin; other specialized uses, such as for military purposes; and other uses or disclosures required by law. For all other uses of information, plans would have to obtain a written authorization from the individual.

A health plan cannot give protected health information to a business associate, such as an administrator, lawyer or consultant, unless there is a contract between the health plan and the business associate that establishes how the business associate can use and disclose protected health information. The regulations also create new individual rights to medical information. Individuals receive a notice of health information practices from the plan informing them how the plan will use their medical information. Individuals have the right to inspect, get copies of and propose corrections to medical records.

Plans would be obligated to have administrative, technical and physical procedures in place to protect the security of medical records. This includes maintaining the physical security of electronic records, training plan employees on privacy policies and procedures and assuring that business associates also protect the privacy of health information. Plans would have to designate a privacy official to be responsible for developing and implementing privacy policies.

HIPAA provides for significant civil and criminal penalties for failure to comply with the regulations. HHS may inspect a plan's procedures for compliance with the rules and may impose civil monetary penalties of not more than $100 per person per violation, with a $25,000 annual maximum for violations of a single rule. HIPAA also established a criminal penalty for any person who wrongfully discloses individually identifiable health information. This crime would lead to a fine of not more than $50,000 and/or imprisonment of not more than one year, with even higher penalties for offenses committed with intent to use the information for commercial advantage, personal gain, or malicious harm. There is no individual right to sue a plan for violation of the privacy regulations. The first criminal prosecution for a HIPAA privacy violation occurred in 2004 and resulted in a jail sentence and restitution.

HIPAA SECURITY RULES

The security rules were issued by the Centers for Medicare and Medicaid (CMS), an agency of the Department of Health and Human Services (HHS). CMS will also have responsibility for enforcing the rules. The same set of civil and criminal penalties that apply to the privacy and electronic data interchange (EDI) rules will apply for violations of the security rules.

Generally, a *covered entity* (including health plans, health care clearinghouses and certain health care providers) must ensure the confidentiality, integrity and availability of electronic protected health information (PHI) it creates or maintains, and protect it from reasonably anticipated threats or improper use or disclosure.

The exact security measures are detailed in a matrix that lists the general standards and the implementation specification(s). The matrix, which is summarized in Table I at the end of this chapter, also lists whether the implementation specification is required (indicated in the second column of the table by the letter R) or addressable (indicated in the second column of the table by the letter A).

COBRA NOTICE RULES FINALIZED

On May 26, 2004, the Department of Labor (DOL) issued final rules concerning notification requirements for continuation of health coverage under the Consolidated Omnibus Budget Reconciliation Act of 1985 (COBRA).[3] The final rules provide, for the first time since COBRA was enacted in 1985, comprehensive standards regarding the timing and content of notices relating to the implementation of COBRA for private health plans. The final rules are summarized in Table II at the end of this chapter. They include the following:

- *Amended Model General and Election Notices.* These notices include a change that incorporates new guidance from the Internal Revenue Service concerning when a second qualifying event will result in extended COBRA coverage.
- *Two New Notices.* Two notices first mentioned in the proposed rule will now be required: a notice that COBRA is not available and a notice of the early termination of COBRA coverage.
- *Amended Content Requirements for the General and Election Notices.* Plans will not have to include certain information in these notices. For example, a general notice need not explain the requirement to provide notice when there is a second qualifying event (QE). An election notice need not explain alternative coverage to COBRA or conversion rights.
- *Stop using the out-of-date model notice found in Technical Release 86-2,* issued by DOL in 1986. Since May 28, 2003, use of that model has not been considered good faith compliance with COBRA.
- *Prepare a reasonable, written procedure for participants and beneficiaries to provide notice of certain QEs.* Inadequate notice from qualified beneficiaries often leads to complaints from individuals who claim they should have been eligible for COBRA (e.g., a divorced spouse). The final rule requires that plans have a written procedure that allows plan-qualified beneficiaries to provide notice of QEs. Moreover, without a written procedure, the rules "deem" informal communications to certain entities to meet the notice requirements.

HIPAA and COBRA place extensive requirements on group health plans that did not exist when ERISA was passed in 1974. This chapter provides only a broad overview of the very technical standards contained in HIPAA and COBRA. Trustees of multiemployer health plans should make sure fund administrators and staff have been properly trained on the rules and how they apply in the multiemployer context. In recent years, DOL has increased its auditing of group health plans, especially multiemployer funds. Plans should not only make sure they have complied with all of the HIPAA and COBRA requirements but also should document their compliance efforts and be prepared to demonstrate compliance if DOL audits the plan.

ENDNOTES

1. The final regulations add a few new types of health benefits to the list of creditable coverage including health coverage provided by a foreign government.

2. Although not discussed in the final rules, the preamble to the final rules states that to the extent that health savings accounts (HSAs) are not employee welfare benefit plans, they will not be subject to the HIPAA portability requirements. DOL issued a Field Assistance Bulletin early this year stating that HSAs are generally not employee welfare benefit plans. The preamble to the final HIPAA rules does state that the high deductible health plan that must be coupled with an HSA is an employee welfare benefit plan covered by the HIPAA portability requirements. *69 Fed. Reg. 78734.*

3. The final rules were published in the May 26, 2004 issue of the *Federal Register.*

Table I

THE HIPAA SECURITY STANDARDS AND IMPLEMENTATION SPECIFICATION(S)

Standards (in **Bold**) and Implementation Specification(s)	*	Brief Explanation
Security Management Process: ☐ Risk Analysis ☐ Risk Management ☐ Sanction Policy ☐ Information System Activity Review	R R R R	Conducting the required risk analysis is one of the most important elements of the security rules. Risk management covers, among other things, the implementation of security measures to eliminate or reduce the risks and vulnerabilities identified in the risk analysis. The sanction policy should apply to all benefits staff who have access to ePHI. An information system activity review entails regularly reviewing all "non-software" systems logs (*e.g.*, audit logs, access card reader reports and security incident tracking reports).
Assigned Security Responsibility	R	Employers must delegate a person to be the health plan's security officer. This can be the same individual assigned as the HIPAA privacy officer.
Workforce Security: ☐ Authorization and/or Supervision ☐ Workforce Clearance Procedure ☐ Termination Procedures	A A A	Employers must implement policies and procedures to ensure that only authorized members of the workforce have access to ePHI.
Information Access Management: ☐ Access Authorization ☐ Access Establishment & Modification	A A	Policies and procedures should be in place for granting access to ePHI (*e.g.*, through access to a particular workstation or software program) and for documenting, reviewing and modifying a user's right of access.
Security Awareness & Training: ☐ Security Reminders ☐ Protection from Malicious Software ☐ Log-in Monitoring ☐ Password Management	A A A A	Although all of the implementation specifications for this standard are addressable, it is important to note that security and awareness training is required. However, employers do not need to conduct this training themselves.
Security Incident Procedures: ☐ Response & Reporting	R	Employers must implement formal, documented report and response procedures so security incidents would be reported and handled promptly.
Contingency Plan: ☐ Data Backup Plan ☐ Disaster Recovery Plan ☐ Emergency Mode Operation Plan ☐ Testing & Revision Procedures ☐ Applications & Data Criticality Analysis	R R R A A	Employers must establish and document a formal data backup plan that establishes procedures for backing up and retrieving data. Employers must also develop a disaster recovery plan with procedures for restoring any loss of data. The emergency operation plan must describe how the employers will keep critical business processes operational in the event of a disaster or emergency. To develop a contingency plan, employers will need some method of identifying critical data and systems applications.
Evaluation of Security Policies: ☐ Periodic Technical & Non-Technical Evaluation	R	These evaluations must be undertaken in response to an *environmental or operational change* that could compromise the security of ePHI (*e.g.*, allowing benefits staff to access the plan's network from home with a remote connection for the first time or the addition of a health benefits software system).
Business Associate Contracts & Other Arrangements: ☐ Written Contract or Other Arrangement	R	Business associates are permitted to receive, use or transmit ePHI only after providing satisfactory assurances that they will appropriately safeguard ePHI.

(All rows above are under **ADMINISTRATIVE SAFEGUARDS**.)

* This column indicates whether each standard or implementation specification is required (R) or addressable (A)

Table continues on next page.

Continuation of table from previous page.

THE HIPAA SECURITY STANDARDS AND IMPLEMENTATION SPECIFICATION(S)

Standards (in **Bold**) and Implementation Specification(s) * Brief Explanation

	Standard / Specification	*	Brief Explanation
TECHNICAL SAFEGUARDS	**Access Controls:** ☐ Unique User Identification ☐ Emergency Access Procedure ☐ Automatic Logoff ☐ Encryption & Decryption	R R A A	Employers must create unique user identifications for everyone who has access to their software systems that store or transmit ePHI. Employers must also have an emergency access process that documents all possible means by which benefits staff can access software systems containing ePHI if "business as usual" is interrupted. An automatic logoff terminates an electronic session after a predetermined amount of inactivity. Encryption and decryption are mechanisms to prevent unauthorized access to ePHI.
	Audit Controls	R	This standard requires employers to have procedures to record and examine activity in information systems that contain or use ePHI. A sample procedure might call for review, every two months, of the log showing who has logged onto the network or has attempted to log into the primary software for managing the health plan's participant data.
	Integrity: ☐ Mechanism to Authenticate ePHI	A	This standard requires the implementation of mechanisms to assure that ePHI has not been improperly altered or destroyed. This standard may be met with error-correcting memory and magnetic disk storage, which are mechanisms found in most hardware and operating systems existing at benefit offices.
	Person or Entity Authentication	R	Employers must implement procedures to verify the identity of anyone seeking access to ePHI.
	Transmission Security: ☐ Integrity Controls ☐ Encryption	A A	Employers are required to ensure the confidentiality and integrity (*i.e.*, that data was not altered or destroyed) of ePHI while it is being transmitted over an electronic network. The regulations encourage some form of encryption for the transmission of ePHI, particularly over the Internet.
PHYSICAL SAFEGUARDS	**Facility Access Controls:** ☐ Contingency Operations ☐ Facility Security Plan ☐ Access Control & Validation Procedures ☐ Maintenance Records	A A A A	This standard encompasses the security of the benefit office's premises, ensuring that only properly authorized access is permitted (including during an emergency when staff may need to restore lost data or continue critical operations). Repairs or modifications to physical structures (*e.g.*, changing locks) can have security implications.
	Workstation Use	R	All workstations used to store, work with and/or transmit ePHI must be protected by a "proper use" policy that covers the proper functions to be performed on the workstation (*e.g.*, it may only be used to view and update participant eligibility), the manner in which those functions are to be performed (*e.g.*, accessing data with a unique password) and the attributes of the physical surroundings of a specific workstation (*e.g.*, monitors may only be viewed by benefits office staff).
	Workstation Security	R	This standard requires that access to all workstations used to store, work with and/or transmit ePHI be restricted to authorized users only. For example, if a secure separate/lockable room is unavailable, workstations could be grouped behind partitions at one end of a room in the benefits office.
	Device & Media Controls: ☐ Disposal ☐ Media Re-use ☐ Accountability ☐ Data Backup & Storage	R R A A	Employers are required to implement policies and procedures that manage the receipt and removal of hardware and electronic media that contain ePHI into and out of a facility, as well as the movement of these items within the facility. Employers must document the disposal and re-use of diskettes, old workstations, magnetic tapes and any other media containing ePHI.

* This column indicates whether each standard or implementation specification is required (R) or addressable (A)

Table II

Group health plans that are covered by COBRA were required to comply with this regulation no later than the first day of the first plan year beginning on or after November 26, 2004.* For calendar year plans, this meant compliance by January 1, 2005.

COBRA NOTICE REQUIREMENTS

NOTICE	To/From	Content	Timing	DOL Model?
General (or Initial) Notice	Plan administrator to covered employee and spouse	Minimum requirements (listed in the final rule)	Generally, within 90 days after coverage begins	Yes
Employer Qualifying Event (QE) Notice	Employer to plan administrator	Information about plan, covered employee, QE and date of QE	30 days after QE	No
Employee QE Notices	Covered employee or qualified beneficiary to plan administrator	What the plan provides under a reasonable notice procedure	60 days after QE	No
Election Notice	Plan administrator to covered employees and qualified beneficiaries	Minimum requirements (listed in the final rule)	14 days after notice of QE *or* 44 days (for certain QEs) after receipt of notice of QE if employer is administrator	Yes
New: **Notice of COBRA Unavailability**	Plan administrator to employees and beneficiaries who provide notice of QE	Explanation of why individual is not entitled to COBRA	Same time frame as plan would have had to send election notice	No
New: **Notice of Early Termination of COBRA**	Plan administrator to covered employees and qualified beneficiaries	Reason for and date of termination; any rights individual has to elect alternative group or individual coverage	"As soon as practicable" after administrator determines COBRA must terminate	No

---

*Penalties can be imposed for failure to observe COBRA's notice requirements. COBRA penalties can include excise taxes imposed under the Internal Revenue Code ($100 per day per qualified individual, not more than $200 per day per family), a court-imposed discretionary $110 per day penalty for failure to provide certain required notices under ERISA and participant lawsuits for continuation coverage.

SECTION IV

FINANCING OF HEALTH AND WELFARE PLANS

Chapter 22

Traditional Insurance Financing Methods

Arthur L. Wilmes

INTRODUCTION

This chapter and those following will discuss the primary means through which welfare plans are financed. This chapter focuses on traditional methods of financing welfare plans, while the subsequent chapters discuss nontraditional or alternative financing methods.

This chapter will define traditional insurance financing methods. It will also compare and contrast the two primary providers of traditional insurance: insurance companies and Blue Cross and Blue Shield organizations. The remainder of the chapter will be devoted to a discussion of the various methods used by these two providers to finance welfare plans.

WHAT IS A TRADITIONAL INSURANCE PLAN?

A *traditional insurance plan* can be defined as a method that contains the following characteristics:
1. The welfare benefits are financed through an insurance carrier.
2. The financing is done by means of premium payments.
3. The welfare benefits are administered by the insurance carriers.
4. The insurance carrier guarantees that the welfare benefits will be provided.

Traditional insurance benefits can be obtained from two primary providers: (1) insurance companies and (2) Blue Cross and Blue Shield organizations. These two insurance carriers have a substantial portion of the traditional insurance market.

Insurance companies and Blue Cross and Blue Shield organizations have historically differed in their approach to financing welfare benefits. These historic differences, however, have narrowed over time. Despite this narrowing, there still remain some traditional differences between these two providers of traditional insurance benefits.

Insurance Companies

Insurance companies are large providers of welfare benefits. Financing can be provided by either a life insurance company or a property and casualty insurance company.

The insurance company may also be a stock insurance company (owned by public shareholders) or a mutual insurance company (owned by the company's policyholders).

Insurance companies provide a wide range of welfare benefits, including term life insurance, accidental death and dismemberment insurance, disability (short-term and long-term) insurance, hospital and surgical insurance, major medical insurance and ancillary benefits, such as vision and dental insurance. These welfare benefits are generally available in states in which the insurance company is licensed to sell insurance.

Blue Cross and Blue Shield Organizations

Blue Cross and Blue Shield organizations are also large providers of traditional insurance. The origin of Blue Cross and Blue Shield organizations differs from insurance companies.

Blue Cross and Blue Shield organizations traditionally have operated in specific geographic areas. They are organized on a nonprofit basis in cooperation with the hospitals within the Blue Cross and Blue Shield service area. These area hospitals become members of the organization's plan. The members are under contract with the organization to provide hospital services to the organization's subscribers or members. Reimbursements to the member hospitals, for the services that are provided, are generally based upon a reimbursement formula that is negotiated by the member hospital and the Blue Cross and Blue Shield organization.

The benefits offered by Blue Cross and Blue Shield plans are similar to insurance company plans. Blue Cross and Blue Shield plans have traditionally provided full hospital benefits, with additional benefits provided through a supplemental major medical plan. As comprehensive major medical plans have become more popular through their use by insurance companies, Blue Cross and Blue Shield organizations have begun writing their own comprehensive major medical contracts in order to remain competitive with insurance companies.

KEY DIFFERENCES BETWEEN INSURANCE COMPANIES AND BLUE CROSS AND BLUE SHIELD ORGANIZATIONS

Competition between insurance companies and Blue Cross and Blue Shield organizations has tended to diminish the distinctions between the two types of welfare benefit providers. As the distinctions between the two insurers narrow, the choice between an insurance company and a Blue Cross and Blue Shield association becomes more difficult for trustees. Despite this narrowing of distinctions, there are two key differences between insurance companies and Blue Cross and Blue Shield associations: (1) type of benefit and (2) tax status.

The characteristics of these organizations continue to evolve. Trustees should be aware that the distinctions discussed in this chapter may diminish in the future as competition further blurs the differences between the organizations.

Type of Benefit

Hospital Services

Insurance companies provide two general types of hospital benefits:
1. Specified/scheduled limits. The scheduled limit benefit plans provide a specific or scheduled dollar reimbursement to an insured member while the member is in the hospital. The specified dollar amount is usually expressed as a fixed dollar amount per day (for example, $50 per day). In addition to the scheduled per diem, scheduled limit benefit designs generally place a maximum limit on the number of days for which the per diem scheduled amount will be paid.
2. Usual and customary charges. (A *usual charge* is defined as a charge that is usually submitted for a particular service. A *charge* is defined as *customary* when it is within a specified range of the usual charges submitted by similar providers in the same geographic area.) A usual and customary charge benefit design is one that provides for reimbursement (subject to interior policy limits, deductibles and coinsurance) of charges up to but not exceeding the usual and customary charge levels for the area in which the services are provided.

Blue Cross plans have traditionally provided service type hospital benefits to their insured members. For example, the Blue Cross plan may provide for 100 days of semiprivate hospital care per year to its members. This traditional benefit design results from the provider arrangements established between the Blue Cross plan and its member hospitals.

The advantages of a Blue Cross service type hospital benefit is that the insured members are not billed for hospital charges that may exceed the contractual fees established between the member hospital and the Blue Cross organization. By contrast, the insurance company (scheduled benefit or usual and customary) hospital benefit design may result in additional costs for the insured member if billed charges exceed either the scheduled daily limit or the usual and customary charges.

A disadvantage of the Blue Cross organization service type hospital benefit is that the insured member must use a Blue Cross member hospital to receive the full-service benefits. In contrast, an insurance company member is free to receive hospital services from any hospital provider. The member hospital restriction used by the Blue Cross plan design could limit the insured member's provider selection in areas that have a limited number of Blue Cross member hospitals.

Physician Services

Insurance companies generally provide physician benefits on a usual and customary basis. The benefits are reimbursed in a manner similar to the hospital benefits in that only charges (within the policy limits, deductible and coinsurance) not exceeding the usual and customary levels will be reimbursed.

Blue Shield plans provide for reimbursement of physician expenses by means of three different methods:
1. Usual and customary benefits. Blue Shield plans generally reimburse physician expenses on a usual and customary basis. This basis is similar to the insurance company method of providing physician benefits. As with all usual and customary methods, the insured member may be balance billed by the physician if the Blue Shield usual and customary charge limit provides for a payment that is less than the charge submitted by the physician.
2. Scheduled benefits. Scheduled benefits are a second method used by Blue Shield providers to reimburse physicians. Under this method, the

physician reimbursement is based upon a scheduled charge limit that is assigned to a specific type of service that is provided. Similar to the usual and customary charge method, the insured member will likely be balance billed for the physician charges that exceed the scheduled insurance amount.

3. Income-based benefits. Income-based benefits provide for a "floating" physician reimbursement. The reimbursement is based upon the insured member's annual income. The amount of benefit reimbursed decreases as the annual income of the insured member increases. Therefore, this method resembles usual and customary benefits for low-income members and scheduled benefits for higher income members. Income-based benefits are not as prevalent as they were when Blue Shield plans first began providing benefits. Generally, the reimbursement does not vary relative to the annual income of the insured.

Tax Status

Insurance companies are generally subject to local, state and federal income taxation. In addition, the premiums charged by insurance companies are subject to any applicable state premium taxes.

Blue Cross and Blue Shield organizations, by contrast, are generally incorporated on a not-for-profit basis, which enables them to be totally or partially exempt from taxation. A few states do impose premium taxes upon Blue Cross and Blue Shield organizations. For those states that impose a premium tax, the tax level is generally less than the level imposed on insurance companies.

ALTERNATIVE METHODS OF TRADITIONAL INSURANCE FINANCING

Insurance companies and Blue Cross and Blue Shield organizations finance insurance programs through a variety of different financing methods. The remainder of this chapter will define the different methods that are available from these insurers and will discuss some of the advantages and disadvantages related to each method.

Fixed Premium Group Insurance

With fixed premium group insurance, a group that is being insured receives a premium rate developed from the insurer's experience for similar groups. In other words, the insurer combines (or pools) similar groups and charges each with its pro rata share of what is projected to be its total claims, administration expenses, selling expenses, taxes and other charges. The pro rata share is not affected by the actual claim or expense experience for an individual group within a pooling category.

Fixed premium group insurance is used primarily for small groups that, due to their small size, may not be eligible for another type of insurance financing method. This method is also used for insurers for newly issued groups that, due to their size, may be eligible for alternative insurance financing methods, but have not accumulated sufficient prior claims experience to make them initially eligible.

The advantage of this financing method is that the claim exposure for a particular group is limited to its pro rata share of the claim experience for all groups in the pool. Any adverse claim and expense experience for one group is spread among all groups in the pool.

The disadvantages of this insurance financing method is that groups with above-average claim experience do not have their favorable experience fully reflected in their premium rate.

Experience Rating

An experience rating financing method fully or partially reflects the claim and expense experience in the premium rates that are ultimately paid by a particular group. In other words, for groups that are sufficiently large, the claim and expense experience for the group is believed to be a more credible actuarial basis from which premiums can be developed.

Insurers often apply an experience rating method to groups whose claim experience, due to the group size, may not be actuarially credible. The use of experience rating for these types of groups is generally done for competitive reasons. Insurance companies and Blue Cross and Blue Shield organizations would find it difficult to compete with a self-insurance alternative if experience rating was not used. By using experience rating, the insurance company or Blue Cross and Blue Shield organization can offer a less costly alternative to fixed premium group insurance to groups with favorable claim and expense experience.

Experience rating can be done either prospectively or retrospectively. Under a *prospective experience-rated financing method,* prospective premium rates for specific groups are calculated based upon past claims and expense experience. In other words, the group's actual prior claim experience is partially or fully reflected in its renewal premium rate.

Prospective premium rates will generally be higher for groups with less favorable past experience since the experience is reflected in the premium rate. An exception may occur if the unfavorable past claims and expense experience resulted from a characteristic that is not expected to carry forward into the future. For example, if adverse claim experience resulted from the birth of a premature baby, a prospective experience-rated premium would generally exclude from its premium development the prior claim experience associated with the birth.

The second experience rating method is called *retrospective experience rating*. Retrospective rating credits or charges a group with its favorable or unfavorable claim experience in the insurance period that the experience was incurred. A retrospective insurance rating formula is generally used to credit or charge a group for its actual claim and expense experience.

A typical retrospective experience rating formula is illustrated in the table. The key elements of a retrospective experience rating formula are as follows:

1. Earned premiums. Earned premiums are equal to premiums paid by the policyholder, less any increase in the unearned premium reserve.
2. Investment income. Retrospective experience rating formulas generally credit investment income earned on reserves that are held on deposit with the insurer. Examples of reserves for which investment income would be credited include unearned premium reserves, claim reserves and claim stabilization reserves.
3. Incurred claims. Incurred claims are composed of claims paid during the insurance period, the change in claim reserves held for the group and any pooling charges related to the group. Paid claims are equal to the amounts paid in benefits during the insurance period. The change in claim reserve is equal to the claim reserve held at the end of the insurance period less the claim reserve held at the beginning of the insurance period. This amount is added to paid claims. The pooling charges are equal to the group's claims subject to pooling provisions less the group's share of the claim pool. This item is deducted from paid claims.
4. Conversion charges. Insurance companies and Blue Cross and Blue Shield organizations generally provide a conversion policy for employees or members who terminate from the group. Individuals accepting the conversion privilege are generally in poorer health than an average insured because the conversion privilege is extended irrespective of whether the individual would normally qualify for insurance with the insurance company. Insurance companies and Blue Cross and Blue Shield organizations generally charge the group policyholder with a conversion charge for each group conversion reflective of the extra costs associated with them.
5. Commissions. Commissions are generally paid to the agent or broker who sells the group contract.
6. Administrative expenses. The insurance company and Blue Cross and Blue Shield organization will charge for the expense of administering the group insurance contract. The administration charge is generally based upon a fixed percentage of earned premium.
7. Risk/profit charge. Insurance companies and Blue Cross and Blue Shield organizations generally do not show an explicit profit charge in their experience rating formula. The profit charge, rather, is combined with a risk charge. A risk charge is assessed to develop a risk surplus that is available to offset losses incurred on groups that cancel in a deficit position with respect to their retrospective fund.
8. Premium tax. The retrospective premium formula generally passes premium tax payments directly to the insured group.

The example in the table calculates an experience surplus for the group with favorable claim experience and an experience deficit for a group with unfavorable claim experience.

The payment of experience surpluses or deficits is based upon the method negotiated by the insurer and the insured group. Surpluses may be fully or partially held, at interest, by the insurer as a claims stabilization reserve. Deficits may be carried forward to future insurance periods to be offset with future experience surpluses. Deficits that are carried forward generally incur interest until repaid.

Experience rating provides a cost advantage, relative to a fixed premium method, to a group with favorable claim experience.

Minimum Premium Arrangement

A *minimum premium arrangement* is a modification made to a fixed premium method. Under a minimum premium arrangement, a rider is attached to a fixed premium contract to modify the way that claims are paid. Typical rider provisions would require that a portion of the premium paid under the fixed premium contract be allocated to a special trust fund through which claims for the group are paid. The portion of premium allocated to the trust fund is commonly 90%. If claim payments fully deplete the amounts in the trust fund, the remaining claims are paid directly by the insurer through the fixed premium plan.

The advantage of a minimum premium arrangement is that the amounts deposited in the trust fund escape state premium tax. This may be a significant cost advantage for large groups. The disadvantage of a minimum premium arrangement is that some states (California, for example) do not exclude trust fund accounts from premium tax.

Table

RETROSPECTIVE EXPERIENCE RATING

FORMULA EXAMPLE

	Claim Experience Scenario	
	90% of Projected	110% of Projected
Income		
Earned premiums	$1,000,000	$1,000,000
Investment income	22,500	22,500
Total income	$1,022,500	$1,022,500
Expenses		
Incurred claims	$792,000	$968,000
Conversion charges	2,400	2,400
Commissions	15,000	15,000
Administration expenses	60,000	60,000
Risk/profit charge	25,000	25,000
Premium tax	20,000	20,000
Total expenses	$914,400	$1,090,400
Retrospective credit/(charge)	$108,100	$(67,900)

Note: Two claim scenarios are provided to illustrate the experience refund calculation for a surplus and a deficit.

Retrospective Premium Arrangement

A *retrospective premium arrangement* is a modification of a retrospective experience rating formula. Under a retrospective arrangement, an insurer charges less than the normal insurance premium. For example, an insurer might agree to a premium that is 90% of the amount normally charged. At the end of the insurance period, an additional premium (or retrospective premium) is payable if incurred claims plus other expenses exceed the initial premium that was paid. A retrospective premium arrangement generally limits the total premium liability for the group to a percentage (for example, 125%) of the initial premium that is paid. Amounts due in excess of this limiting percentage are the liability of the insurer.

The advantage of a retrospective premium arrangement is the reduced initial premium payment. The reduced premium allows a group to retain a portion of the premium that it normally would have paid under a fixed premium arrangement. Cash flow and investment income are improved for the group as a result. The disadvantage to a retrospective premium arrangement is that the group is liable for claims experience up to the retrospective limit, which may exceed the premium that would have been paid under a fixed premium arrangement.

Premium Drag Arrangement

Group insurance plans generally provide a 30-day grace period in which to pay premiums due. A *premium drag arrangement* extends the grace period for an additional 30 to 60 days. By extending the grace period, the insurer is allowing the group policyholder to temporarily hold up to 25% (90 days) of the annual premium.

Cash flow for the group policyholder is improved since, through the premium drag arrangement, a portion of the premium normally due is withheld. The disadvantage of a premium drag arrangement is that the insurer may charge a higher risk fee to the group. In addition, the insurer may charge interest on the premium that is withheld.

No-Reserve Arrangement

A premium drag arrangement implicitly allows the group policyholder to hold a portion of the funds normally paid to the insurer. A *no-reserve arrangement* explicitly allows a group policyholder to withhold funds normally paid to an insurer since the reserves normally held by the insurer are held by the policyholder.

The advantage of a no-reserve arrangement is improved cash flow for the group policyholder because the funds normally paid to the insurer are reduced. The disadvantage of a no-reserve arrangement is that the insurer may increase the risk charge for the group.

The group policyholder is responsible for the reserve funds normally held by the insurer. The group policyholder must ensure that it has sufficient assets to pay the amounts that will ultimately need to be paid to the insurer.

GUIDELINES FOR EVALUATION OF TRADITIONAL INSURANCE FINANCING METHODS

Trustees will need to go through a careful evaluation process to determine which traditional insurance financing method is most appropriate for their group. In practice, a combination of financing methods may be most suitable. For example, accidental death and dismemberment plans or group term life insurance plans may be financed through a fixed premium financing method. Other plans, such as group medical expense insurance or short-term disability insurance, may be financed through a modified traditional insurance financing method. This section contains some general guidelines for trustees to reflect upon in their evaluation of traditional insurance financing methods.

1. Cash flow. Trustees may wish to improve their cash flow position by retaining some of the assets normally held by an insurer. Opportunities for holding these assets are available through a premium drag arrangement and a no-reserve arrangement. Cash flow is enhanced by these arrangements, however, only if the interest earned by the fund exceeds the interest credits of the insurer.

2. Asset position. Funds with a healthy asset position will be better positioned to absorb unexpected fluctuations in claim experience that may occur under some modified insurance arrangements. If a fund's asset position is weak, it may not be advisable to finance the welfare benefits through anything other than a fixed premium plan.

3. Group size. The size of the plan's group and the credibility of its prior claim experience will limit or enhance its ability to obtain a modified insurance arrangement. Smaller groups or groups with little prior loss experience may have no option other than a fixed premium method.

4. Benefit type. The type of benefit to be financed affects the financing decision. Benefits subject to low claim frequency but high claim amount (for example, accidental death and dismemberment insurance) may be more suitably financed through a fixed premium plan. More stable benefits, such as medical expense, may be more feasibly financed through a modified insurance arrangement.

5. Trustees' risk aversion. Trustees may not be willing to accept the potential for wide variances in year-to-year financial results that could occur with modified insurance arrangements. Fixed premium arrangements tend to provide for more stable and predictable results.

Chapter 23

Health Care Management Programs

Arthur L. Wilmes

INTRODUCTION

The increase in the cost of providing health care benefits through employee benefit plans has meant that employer expenditures for health benefits have become an increasingly larger portion of total employee benefit dollars.

Employers and health insurance carriers have responded by developing health care management programs in an attempt to reduce the rate of growth in health care costs. The term *health care management program* is defined here as a program that seeks to reduce the rate of growth in health care costs by means of a structured management approach. Health maintenance organizations and preferred provider organizations, which are discussed in this chapter, may be described as forms of health care management programs.

By way of introduction, this chapter begins by providing a background or history of the growth in health care costs. Health care management programs are then discussed. In addition, an overview of the effectiveness of these programs is provided. A brief discussion of the legal aspects related to health care management programs is also provided. The chapter includes a set of guidelines that can be used by trustees to help them analyze the feasibility of incorporating some form of health care management program in their health and welfare fund.

GROWTH IN THE COST OF HEALTH CARE

Prior to 1970, there was a consistent one-to-one relationship between the increase in the medical care component of the Consumer Price Index (CPI) and the increase in the CPI for all goods and services. Beginning in 1970, however, the increase in the medical care CPI began to diverge from the CPI for all items.

The difference between the two annualized growth rates has steadily increased since 1970.

There is a need to develop health care management programs to reduce the future rate of growth in medical care costs as we well know in 2005.

The recent increases in the cost of medical care are not directly attributable to one single factor. There are numerous factors that affect the growth in the cost of medical services. The following list summarizes the primary causes of growth in medical care costs.

1. *Inflation.* Medical care costs are subject to inflationary pressure much like any other component of the gross national product (GNP). For example, hospital room and board and ancillary charges are based upon an estimate of nursing salaries, hospital operating costs, hospital debt retirement and other items that are sensitive to inflation. Likewise, a physician determines his or her schedule of fees reflective of an inflationary load that is intended to at least maintain his or her current standard of living. These examples illustrate that medical care cost increases reflect the general rate of inflation in the U.S. economy.
2. *Utilization.* Medical care costs are also influenced by utilization trends. If the usage of services increases, the total cost of providing those services will increase irrespective of whether the cost per rendered service increases. Therefore, an increase in the utilization of medical care services has a leveraging effect upon the medical care trend. The rate of growth is affected not only by general inflation increases, but also by

increases in the usage rate of medical care services.
3. *Medical technology.* Evolutionary changes in medical care practice patterns and technology also have an impact on the increase in medical service costs. For example, the introduction of CAT scans resulted in an additional treatment modality that carried an expensive price tag. Providers of medical services generally purchase new technology to remain competitive. The fixed costs of these new technologies must then be passed to the provider's patients.
4. *Defensive medicine.* Trends in malpractice suits and the establishment of more refined institutional policies have increased the amount of defensive medicine or conservative medicine currently practiced by today's physicians. Defensive medicine is a corollary to increased utilization in that there is a greater likelihood that more medical services will be ordered by an attending physician in order to reduce malpractice risk.
5. *Plan design.* Plan designs have, historically, been benefit rich. In other words, the plans were designed to require very little out-of-pocket payment by the insured member. With the passage of time, these low out-of-pocket plan designs have not kept pace with medical cost inflation. The out-of-pocket payments that may have been meaningful when first designed have had their effectiveness eroded by inflation. See Cost Transfer Methods later in this chapter.
6. *Third party payers.* The growth in commercial and Blue Cross and Blue Shield insurers subsequent to World War II and the growth in employer-provided insurance benefits have resulted in an environment in which the receiver of medical care services often is removed from the cost of providing those services. Third party payers, such as insurance companies or employers, pay for most of the cost of providing medical services. Because the costs often are passed on to the third parties, there are no direct financial incentives for the receivers of medical services to use those services more prudently or to use less costly treatment alternatives.
7. *Medical care economics.* The economic laws of supply and demand do not generally apply to medical care. The supply of medical care services and the demand for those services tend to move parallel to each other. In other words, as the supply of physicians and hospitals increases, the demand or use of physicians and hospitals also tends to increase. As a result, the growth in medical care costs may also be affected by the increase in medical care providers.
8. *Cost shifting.* The per capita revenue provided to hospitals and physicians from government insurance programs has decreased. These hospitals and physicians may seek to replace their lost revenue by increasing the service costs for individuals who are insured by employers and insurance carriers.

TYPES OF HEALTH CARE MANAGEMENT PROGRAMS

In response to the increased growth in the cost of providing medical care services, employers and insurance companies have developed a number of health care management programs. These programs have been established to reduce the increase in the cost of providing medical care services.

A summary of some of the different types of health care management programs that have been developed is shown in Table I.

Cost Transfer Methods

Cost transfer methods are health care management programs that directly pass health care costs to the receiver of medical services by means of benefit plan design. The following list summarizes some of the primary cost transfer methods:
1. *Deductibles.* Deductibles represent the amount of front end cost that is paid by the receiver of medical care services. As deductibles increase, the out-of-pocket expenses for the employee increase. The increased out-of-pocket payments reduce the employer or insurance company cost for the program. In addition, higher deductibles provide an economic incentive for more prudent use of medical services.
2. *Coinsurance.* Coinsurance represents the percentage of medical care costs (in excess of the initial deductible level) that is provided by a third party payer or employer. Similar to deductibles, a lower coinsurance percentage not only reduces direct insurance costs, but also provides an economic incentive for more prudent medical benefit use.
3. *Interior limits/maximums.* Interior limits are the caps that are placed upon the amount of benefits that will be provided through an insurance contract to an employee. The interior maximums are generally used for benefits where benefit utilization is more discretionary on the part of the insured in an effort to encourage more prudent usage of certain benefit services. Examples would include treatment of mental and nervous conditions and alcohol and drug abuse treatment.

Table I

HEALTH CARE MANAGEMENT PROGRAMS

Cost Transfer Methods
- —Deductibles
- —Coinsurance
- —Interior limits/maximums
- —Employee contributions
- —Medical expense budget

Utilization Management Methods
- —Preadmission testing
- —Second surgical opinion
- —Outpatient surgery
- —Preadmission certification
- —Concurrent hospital stay review
- —Retrospective hospital stay review
- —Physician profiling

Alternative Care Management Methods
- —Large case management
- —Disease management
- —Hospice care
- —Extended care facilities
- —Home health care

Preventive Care Management Methods
- —Wellness programs
- —Periodic health examinations
- —Employee communications
- —Health risk appraisals
- —Demand management

Financial Management Methods
- —Negotiated provider reimbursements
- —Hospital bill audits
- —Employee audits
- —Employee bonus programs

---

4. *Employee contributions.* Employee contributions not only reduce the employer's medical benefit costs, they also increase the employee's awareness as to the total cost of the health insurance program.

5. *Medical expense budget.* Some employers have gone to a medical expense budget approach for providing health insurance benefits. Under this method, an employer allocates a specified dollar amount that can be used by the employee to provide for health insurance benefits. The budget approach is often used in conjunction with a benefit program that allows for a choice among various health insurance alternatives. With a medical expense budget program, the employee is free to choose a benefit rich health insurance plan. If the cost of the selected health insurance plan exceeds the medical expense budget, the employee must provide the difference from his or her own pocket. The employer controls its medical benefit cost increases because it controls the increases in the expense budget level.

Utilization Management Methods

Utilization management methods are health care management programs that focus their cost reduction methods on the utilization of medical services. The primary goal of utilization management methods is to reduce the amount of unnecessary or inefficient utilization of services in a medical insurance program. The following list summarizes some of the primary utilization management methods.

1. *Preadmission testing.* Under a preadmission testing program, pathology and radiology tests and examinations that formerly were done on an inpatient basis subsequent to hospital admission are completed prior to admission to the hospital. By requiring preadmission testing, hospital days and their resulting costs are reduced because preliminary tests are done prior to entry into the hospital.

2. *Second surgical opinion.* Second surgical opinion programs are established to reduce the amount of unnecessary surgeries. Second surgical opinion programs may be either voluntary or mandatory. In either situation, the second surgical opinion is usually reimbursed at a full "usual and customary" value.

3. *Outpatient surgery.* Outpatient surgery programs seek to reduce health care costs by requiring that certain procedures be performed on an outpatient basis. Outpatient surgery is generally performed in either an ambulatory surgery clinic or a doctor's office. Most outpatient surgery programs require certain surgical procedures to be performed on an outpatient basis unless inpatient surgery is medically necessary.

4. *Preadmission certification.* Under a preadmission certification program, an insured is required

to prequalify or precertify his or her admission into a hospital. Preadmission certification is only required on nonemergency hospital admissions. The preadmission certification is generally handled by the insured's attending physician. When a hospital preadmission certification application is made, the attending physician will discuss the diagnosis and recommended course of treatment with a preadmission certification specialist. The specialist is generally either a registered nurse or a medical doctor. If the admission is approved, the preadmission certification specialist will also authorize a hospital length of stay. If the hospital length of stay extends beyond the preauthorized limit, an additional request must be made to the precertification specialist for the extra hospital days. Hospital admissions not approved by the preadmission certification specialist are subject to an appeal procedure.

5. *Concurrent review.* Concurrent review programs generally monitor a patient while he or she is in the hospital. The monitoring may be done by an onsite registered nurse or via phone conversations with the attending physician. The purpose of the concurrent review program is to ensure that the patient's care program is following the program that was preauthorized. By staying abreast of the treatment provided the patient, the concurrent review program can assist the patient and doctor to ensure that the patient is being treated in a medically appropriate yet cost-effective manner.

6. *Retrospective review.* Retrospective review programs track the care and treatment of an insured subsequent to a hospital discharge. The retrospective review is similar to an audit whereby inappropriate services or errors can be corrected and a bill adjustment made. Another form of retrospective review involves the monitoring of physician practice patterns and hospital length-of-stay averages. This monitoring allows the insurance program to isolate physicians and providers that consistently deliver cost-effective and quality health care. In addition, it provides an opportunity to suggest alternative treatment patterns to physicians whose practice patterns appear to be outside of the norm established by their professional peers.

7. *Physician profiling.* Physician profiling programs review medical utilization data to determine if certain patterns of use result for individual physicians. The purpose of physician profiling is to determine if certain physicians practice and prescribe in ways that significantly differ from a particular physician's peer group. Examples of outlier patterns may be frequent or infrequent use of basic diagnostic testing, radiology and pathology services. Other examples may include higher costs of total patient treatment or variance referral patterns. The results of the profile information is sent to each physician in a report that compares that individual physician's profile to his or her peer group of physicians. The reason for variations in practice patterns are investigated and authenticated. The use of physician profiling information varies. Some programs provide the information to the physicians and rely upon that individual physician to recognize his or her variation and to modify behavior. Some programs are more comprehensive in that the information is used by medical directors for corrective action or possible removal from a physician panel. The ultimate goal of a well-constructed profiling system is consistency in patient care.

Alternative Care Management Methods

Alternative care management methods are health care management programs that ensure that the most cost-effective and highest quality method of treatment is used. These programs generally make use of alternative treatment centers and philosophies. The following list summarizes some of the primary alternative care management methods.

1. *Large case management.* Large case management programs generally apply to catastrophic cases such as AIDS, burn victims, premature babies or injuries of the central nervous system. With these programs, a case manager or treatment specialist consults with the primary physician at the onset of the catastrophic claim to assure that the highest quality and most cost-effective treatment is provided to the patient. A characteristic of large case management is that often contractual limits or restrictions are waived in order to provide the most cost-effective and highest quality benefits to the patient.

2. *Disease management.* Disease management is a special form of large case management. Disease management focuses on a group of clinical conditions and designs patient-specific programs intended to control the course of a specific disease. The hope is that a more proactive patient approach will result in improved patient results. Typically, disease management programs have been designed around diabetes, asthma, chronic obstructive pulmonary disease or depression. Disease management involves many clinical professionals such as physicians, pharmacists, social workers and therapists.

3. *Hospice care.* Traditional medical benefit programs generally do not cover hospice care bene-

fits. Current medical plans recognize the cost-effective nature of hospice programs and now may include them as a covered benefit. To be cost-effective, *hospice care benefits* are generally defined as treatment programs available in the last six months of life of a terminally ill patient. In addition, the benefits generally are required to be provided as a substitute for inpatient hospital benefits.

4. *Extended care facilities.* Extended care facilities are often used in conjunction with large concurrent review programs. Since extended care facility daily charges are generally less than daily charges for inpatient hospital stays, physicians are encouraged to transfer patients to an extended care facility as soon as it becomes medically appropriate.

5. *Home health care.* Home health care is an alternative care management program comparable to an extended care facility program. Under home health care, the attending physician is encouraged to discharge the patient to a home setting as soon as medically appropriate. Home health care generally is a viable alternative as long as an at-home caregiver is available for the patient.

Preventive Care Management Methods

Preventive care management methods are health care management programs that seek to reduce health care costs through prevention. The following list summarizes some of the primary preventive care management methods.

1. *Wellness programs.* Wellness programs are health care management methods that seek to improve the quality of the insured's health through lifestyle change techniques. Examples of wellness programs include smoking cessation programs, weight loss programs, onsite exercise facilities and blood pressure and cholesterol screenings. Wellness programs are an effective means of reducing the long-term growth in health care costs. Residual benefits of a wellness program are that it may also improve employee productivity and reduce employee absenteeism. This results from the lifestyle improvements inherent in the wellness program.

2. *Periodic health examinations.* Periodic health examinations are often used in conjunction with wellness programs. The goals of a periodic health examination program are twofold: early detection of illnesses and employee education by a physician on preventive care strategies. Periodic health risk appraisals are sometimes used in conjunction with periodic health examinations. A health risk appraisal is an individualized profile prepared for an employee to make him or her more aware of his or her chance of death, illness or injury. Information gathered from a health risk appraisal can be used by an employer to help institute programs specifically tailored to employees to improve their health and lifestyle.

3. *Employee communications.* Employee communications are a third form of preventive care management method. In an employee communication program, an employer educates employees on prudent medical care services and wellness programs by means of mass communication campaigns.

4. *Health risk appraisal.* Health risk appraisals traditionally were used by physicians to assess the medical conditions and risk factors associated with a new patient. In current practice, health risk appraisals produce the same information; however, the information is proactively used to determine chronic risk factors in order to develop patient-specific treatment plans. The goal of the appraisal is a reduction in the total treatment costs for the chronic patient. Areas reviewed by a health risk appraisal include a patient history, physical exam, nutritional assessment, current medications and existence of or propensity for chronic diseases such as diabetes or heart problems.

5. *Demand management.* Demand management programs are intended to provide patients with sufficient information to make intelligent health maintenance decisions. Common forms of demand management are home care manuals, expanded preventive service programs and expanded clinic/office hours. More advanced programs include a 24-hour nurse advice line. The intent of demand management is to reduce inefficient utilization. Programs that have implemented demand management, particularly the 24-hour nurse phone line, report a reduction in emergency room visits.

Financial Management Methods

Financial management methods are health care management programs that seek to reduce the cost of health care by means of financial methods. The following list summarizes some of the primary financial management methods.

1. *Negotiated reimbursement arrangements.* Negotiated reimbursement arrangements reduce the cost of health care by means of specific contractual arrangements between an insurer or an employer and a health care provider. Examples of negotiated reimbursement arrange-

ments are discount arrangements with hospitals and physicians, preestablished per diem rates for hospitals, contractual fee arrangements with physicians and prescription drug card programs. Cost reduction is accomplished because provider services are obtained at below market prices.
2. *Hospital audits.* Hospital audits are generally applied on large claims to ensure that no accounting errors in billing have occurred. Hospital audits generally seek to reduce accounting errors in order to ensure that all services for which bills were received were delivered and that the billed charges are usual and customary.
3. *Employee audits.* Employee audits are voluntary programs in which employees are encouraged to review their hospital and physician bills prior to submission to an insurer for payment. Financial incentives are used to encourage employee audits of provider bills. Examples of incentives that are used include a fixed dollar reward or a percentage of billing error subject to correction.
4. *Employee bonus programs.* Employee bonus programs encourage prudent utilization of medical services. The bonus usually takes the form of profit sharing with all employees who participate in the insurance program. "Profits" result if the total health care costs incurred under the insurance program are less than the amount that was projected for the program. Generally, not all of the profit is shared with the employees. Some of the profit is retained by the employer as a contingency reserve.

EFFECTIVENESS OF HEALTH CARE MANAGEMENT PROGRAMS

The savings resulting from health care management programs are difficult to estimate. Often, accurate records of claim experience prior to implementation of health care management programs are not kept. This makes before and after comparisons difficult. In addition, when multiple programs are implemented, the savings that occur in one area may be offset by cost increases occurring in another area.

The amount of savings resulting from a health care management program depends upon a number of factors, as follows.
1. *Current utilization levels.* Utilization management programs achieve savings by encouraging more prudent utilization of health care services. The savings potential for these programs is directly related to current utilization levels. If current utilization levels are high (with respect to national utilization norms), relatively large savings can be expected. Lower savings can be expected if current utilization levels are relatively low.
2. *Voluntary vs. mandatory programs.* The expected cost savings from health care management programs may vary depending upon whether or not the program is voluntary or mandatory. Voluntary programs provide a financial incentive to use alternative services. Under these programs, some of the savings achieved by these programs is given back to the insured member. Mandatory programs generally do not provide financial rewards for compliance but, rather, use financial penalties as incentives for program compliance. With mandatory programs, savings are achieved not only through program compliance, but also through the assessment of penalties.
3. *Multiple programs.* When multiple health care management programs are used, it is difficult to isolate the savings associated with each specific program. The savings for multiple programs are generally not additive since the programs tend to overlap. For example, preadmission certification programs may reduce or totally eliminate any potential savings resulting from an outpatient surgery program since some surgery admissions may be denied and referred to an outpatient facility.
4. *Negotiated reimbursement arrangement.* The savings expected from a negotiated reimbursement arrangement will vary depending upon the type of arrangement that is negotiated. Discount programs, for example, may or may not result in significant savings, depending upon the quality of the discount that is negotiated.
5. *Cost of administration.* Cost-management programs typically increase the insurance program's administrative costs. These costs should be recognized in evaluating the net effect the programs will have on the overall health care costs.

It is reasonable to expect savings from health care management programs in the range of 0-10%. A cost savings range is estimated due to the many factors that affect the potential for health care cost savings. This savings estimate reflects an estimate of the cost reduction resulting in the year in which the health care programs are first implemented. It is important to realize that programs that encourage prudent health care utilization affect not only current health care costs, but also health care costs in the future. For example, a utilization management program will not only reduce unnecessary utilization in the current year, but it will also eliminate the unnecessary utilization in subsequent years.

MANAGEMENT INFORMATION SYSTEMS

An integral component of a health care management program is the development of an advanced management information system (MIS). A sophisticated MIS is used not only for evaluating the feasibility of implementing a health care management program, but also for subsequent monitoring of the effects of the health care management program. An advanced MIS will make the trustees more effective managers of the health care benefits provided to their members.

An effective MIS should produce periodic reports to allow the trustees to review and compare the following types of claim information:

1. Hospital days per thousand (by type of hospital admission)
2. Effects of outpatient surgery-, radiology- and pathology-incurred charges and office visit utilization
3. Psychiatric benefit claims (frequency and total charges)
4. Chiropractor claims (frequency and total charges)
5. Prescription drug claims (reported separately for generic and brand prescriptions)
6. Wellness program costs.

To develop proper comparisons of the information provided, the claim frequencies and hospital days should be shown on an age- and sex-adjusted basis. In other words, the data should be normalized to a standard population basis so that valid comparisons can be made.

LEGAL ASPECTS OF HEALTH CARE MANAGEMENT PROGRAMS

Trustees should be aware of potential liability exposures resulting from implementation of a health care management program. Examples of this potential liability exposure include:

1. Employer or sponsor exposure resulting from a plan design that encourages certain delivery systems
2. Preadmission certification exposure that results when a certain number of days are precertified when additional days may actually be needed
3. Punitive risks resulting from physician errors where the physician is involved in a risk sharing or financial incentive arrangement with the health care program
4. The fiduciary responsibility under ERISA may also apply to the trustees' responsibility for selecting only the most qualified hospital providers and physicians.

The trustees should have their legal counsel review the health care management programs that are proposed, any contracts that the plan may have with health care management vendors and providers, the disclaimers used in any employee communication material, and the liability limits established in the provider contracts. Legal counsel is encouraged to constantly monitor the health care management programs to ensure that liability exposure is minimized.

GUIDELINES FOR TRUSTEES

Trustees reviewing the feasibility of implementing a health care management program should go through a careful evaluation process prior to making a final decision. The following general guidelines have been prepared to assist trustees in their evaluation.

1. *Analysis of current data.* Trustees should review their current utilization levels and medical practice patterns. Their current utilization levels should be compared to national standards on an age- and sex-adjusted basis. In addition, the data should also be compared to groups comparable to their fund members. This analysis will indicate to the trustees what areas can be improved and what cost savings can be reasonably expected.
2. *Management approach.* Trustees should outline a management approach for the health care management program. The management approach will concentrate on what programs can feasibly be implemented. It should include an analysis of the program's estimated "bang per buck" vs. an estimate of the employee satisfaction or lack of satisfaction that will result from implementation of a health care management program.
3. *Cost analysis.* An estimate should be made of the reasonable cost reductions that can be expected from the implementation of a health care management program. The cost analysis should reflect any extra administration costs associated with the health care management program. This cost analysis will indicate whether there is significant savings potential associated with the health care management program. The cost analysis should not only estimate the cost savings for the next plan year, but also should estimate the savings potential for the program over the next three to five years.
4. *Management information systems.* Management information systems should be developed in order to effectively monitor the effects of the health care management program. The MIS should be capable of producing utilization reports on an age- and sex-adjusted basis, as well as reports summarizing hospital and physician/provider treatment patterns.
5. *Legal exposure.* The trustees' analysis should

include a report from the plan's legal counsel reviewing the potential for liability exposure associated with a health care management program. The report should provide recommendations as to how the liability exposure may be minimized.

HEALTH MAINTENANCE ORGANIZATIONS

The financing of medical expense benefits and employee benefits by means of health maintenance organizations (HMOs) has been increasing. Growth in the HMO industry has been spurred by the need to control the rapid rate of increase in health care costs and the desire by health and welfare fund sponsors to provide a more comprehensive package of benefits with an emphasis on preventive care.

This section is designed to provide trustees with an overview of HMOs. The term *HMO* will be defined, and various types of HMO structures will be discussed. The section will also summarize the key differences between an HMO and traditional group insurance. This section provides an overview of the various HMO premium rate structures. This is important since HMOs tend to rate in a manner different from traditional group insurance. Also included in this section is a set of guidelines or checklists to help trustees select among various HMO offerings. Since some HMOs are federally qualified by the Department of Health and Human Services, federally qualified HMOs are discussed later in this section.

WHAT IS AN HMO?

The term *HMO* has been used to define many types of organizations. HMOs generally share the following characteristics:
1. Deliver comprehensive health care services (including preventive services).
2. Operate and provide services in a limited geographic area.
3. Provide services for a fixed or prepaid fee rather than payments being made when services are rendered.
4. Place restrictions as to which providers can be used by HMO members.

HMOs fall into general categories based upon the methods used to contract or affiliate with their provider physicians. Understanding the nature of these categories, or *models* as they are often called, is an important concern for trustees who are faced with decisions regarding which type of HMO is most appropriate for their members. For the purposes of this chapter, we have categorized HMOs into four basic types or models. These models and definitions are consistent with those used by the research organization InterStudy in its annual HMO census.

The traditional HMO categories are as follows:
1. Group practice model
2. Network model
3. Staff model
4. Individual practice model.

Even though HMOs fall into these four basic categories, it is not uncommon for an HMO in one category to share certain characteristics with HMOs in other categories.

Group Practice Model

Early HMOs were developed as group practice models. Under this HMO model, an independent group of physicians practices medicine as a group and contracts with an HMO plan to provide medical services. The physician group generally represents many medical specialties. Kaiser Permanente Medical Group is an example of a group practice model.

This HMO model is sometimes called a *closed panel plan* in that physician's services can be received only from physicians who are members of the group practice. Services are provided outside of the group only if a referral is made by a group practice physician to an outside physician.

With a group practice model, members or employer groups subscribing to the HMO pay a fixed level payment or capitation amount. In return for the capitation fee, the HMO provides services through its affiliated physician and hospital providers. Since the HMO provides the services in exchange for a fixed prepaid capitation payment, it assumes the risk that the cost of the services it is providing will not exceed the capitation amounts. This risk feature provides the HMO with an incentive to provide quality health care services through the most efficient means feasible.

Physicians in a group practice model sometimes provide services exclusively to HMO members. Oftentimes, however, the medical group in a group HMO model has a significant amount of non-HMO or fee-for-service business.

Network Model

The network model is a variation on the group practice model. Its structure is similar to a group model with the exception that the HMO contracts with more than one independent group practice.

Network models are often not defined as clearly as previously stated. Frequently, the network model description has been applied to HMOs that have characteristics of two or more of the other models described in this chapter. For example, an HMO that contracts with both independent practice physicians and multispecialty physician groups may be called a *network model*. This hybrid contracting arrangement frequently occurs for well-established group or staff models that are interested in expanding their HMO network area.

Staff Model

In a staff model, an HMO delivers medical services through its own group of salaried physicians. Rather than contracting with the HMO, the physicians are paid directly by the HMO. This arrangement contracts with the group model in which physicians contract or affiliate with an HMO. In staff models, the medical services are usually provided at HMO facilities or health centers. Services are generally provided exclusively to HMO members, although some staff models do participate in a small amount of fee-for-service business.

The size and number of specialties represented in the staff model HMO tend to vary. Very large HMOs, for example, may have many specialists employed as staff physicians. Smaller models may employ only primary care physicians, such as family practitioners, general practitioners, pediatricians or internists. In the case of small staff models, the HMOs generally contract with independent physicians for specialties that are not represented by their staff group.

Individual Practice Model

An HMO that contracts with a number of independent physicians who are practicing individually or in single specialty groups is referred to as an *individual practice model* HMO. This model does not have centralized or integrated facilities.

Generally, the physicians in this type of HMO operate in solo practices and are not under the direct management or control of the HMO. Physicians participating in this model are generally paid on a modified fee-for-service basis, although some may be compensated on a capitated basis and share in some of the financial risk of the HMO.

NONSTANDARD HMO PRODUCTS

The traditional HMO benefit plan design is one that subjects the patient to certain control features that are viewed by consumers as limiting choices or access. The traditional design, for example, will not allow patient self-referral. If a patient desires to see a certain specialist, the visit must be authorized by the patient's primary care physician. Another perceived limitation is that the patient can only receive "covered" benefits from health care providers either within the network or authorized by the network.

These perceived limits to choice and access have placed limitations upon HMOs' market share. To increase their market opportunities, HMOs have developed expanded product offerings. Two primary expansions to the traditional HMO offering are open access plans and point-of-service plans.

Point-of-Service Plans

Point-of-service plans expand the open access concept in that freedom of choice extends to non-HMO physicians and providers.

A typical point-of-service design provides a base set of plan benefits if HMO network providers are used by a member. These base benefits tend to be comparable to "typical" HMO benefits from the standpoint of low or limited member cost sharing. The member has the choice of non-HMO physicians if desired; however, the plan benefits are reduced, resulting in greater out-of-pocket costs to the individual member.

The term *point of service* developed from the freedom that a member had with respect to provider selection "at the point in time when the service was desired."

In general, the point-of-service design requires referral authorization and other patient management features in order to qualify for network benefits.

HMOs VS. TRADITIONAL GROUP INSURANCE PLANS

Key Differences

HMOs have historically represented a distinctly different approach to financing and delivering medical care. Although both types of delivery systems are constantly evolving, and there is some overlap, HMOs tend to differ from traditional health insurance programs in the following areas.

Provider Choice

HMOs generally contract with a limited number of providers in their service area. Any nonemergency and nonreferral services must be provided through participating HMO providers if the cost of care is to be paid by the HMO. Under traditional group insurance, an employee is generally free to go to the physician of his or her choice.

Comprehensive Benefit Package

HMOs generally offer a relatively complete or comprehensive package of health care services. In addition, HMOs traditionally have placed a high priority on preventive medical care, early detection of illness and early treatment of conditions. This emphasis on preventive services stands as an important distinction between HMOs and traditional insurance carriers.

Negotiated Fees

Most HMOs reimburse their medical care providers

according to fees negotiated in advance between the two parties. The negotiated fees can be based upon a percentage discount to regularly billed charges, a fixed amount per service, a maximum fee per service or on a capitated or "at risk" basis. In most situations, the negotiated fee is accepted by the providers as payment in full with no balance billing to the HMO member for the difference between the provider's usual billed charge and the HMO negotiated amount.

Geographic Concentration

As part of their formula for success, HMOs generally service specific and limited geographic areas. These areas tend to be metropolitan. Because of this tendency to be geographically concentrated, one HMO may not be sufficient to provide medical benefits to a decentralized or diverse set of members. This contrasts with traditional group insurance, which can provide medical coverage to all members irrespective of geographic location.

Periodic Flat Fee

Services of an HMO are purchased in exchange for a periodic flat fee or premium payment. In exchange for this fee, the HMO generally provides comprehensive benefit services with little or no cost sharing by the member.

Provider Control

Traditional group insurance programs generally do not exercise a great deal of control over the providers of health care. In contrast, HMOs generally exercise a great deal of control over their health care providers. In addition, HMOs may even own and operate their own hospitals and other medical care facilities.

Quality Assurance Programs

A major emphasis for HMOs is to provide quality care by means of the most cost-efficient method available. Because of the comprehensive nature of their benefit designs, an HMO must significantly reduce patient utilization to be competitive. This is particularly true for inpatient hospitalization stays. Most HMOs incorporate preadmission certification and concurrent review of all hospital admissions. Before a member is admitted to the hospital, the hospital admission must be certified as appropriate. An appropriate length of stay is established in advance and reviewed subsequent to admission. With regard to outpatient services, most HMOs require that specialty referrals be approved in advance by the member's primary care physician. Although traditional insurance programs have begun to incorporate HMO type utilization and quality assurance programs, their programs are generally not as stringent or effective as their HMO counterparts.

Advantages and Disadvantages

HMOs differ from traditional group insurance with respect to providing health care services. As such, there are certain advantages and disadvantages associated with HMOs as compared to traditional group insurance plans.

In general, the advantages of an HMO delivery system can be summarized as follows:
1. Comprehensive package of benefits with little or no deductible or copayment provisions
2. Emphasis on preventive care
3. More cost-effective delivery of health care benefits
4. Minimal use of claim forms
5. Continuity of medical care for the member resulting from the primary care physician format.

The disadvantages of an HMO can be summarized as follows:
1. HMO members lose free choice of physician and other medical care providers.
2. Comprehensive nature of the services provided by an HMO may result in more expensive costs per member than traditional insurance programs.
3. HMO facilities may not be conveniently located for all members.
4. The HMO's structure of primary care physicians and specialty referrals contrasts with the less rigid nature of traditional group insurance.
5. The nature of the HMO system has led to concerns over the quality of care received.

HMO PREMIUM RATES

Premium rates charged by an HMO are developed in accordance with methodologies used by traditional group insurance carriers. In other words, it must charge premiums sufficient to cover its incurred operational expenses and administrative costs, including its target profit margin. Although an HMO's premium development methodology is similar to traditional group insurance, the philosophy of the premium rates for HMOs tends to differ.

Three basic premium rating methods are used by HMOs:
1. Community rating
2. Community rating by class
3. Experience rating.

Community Rating

Community rating began with the early Blue Cross and Blue Shield plans. These plans typically charged the same premium for single or family contract members who were covered in a certain geographic area. Early

HMOs developed premiums based upon this community rating philosophy. They spread their costs equally among all HMO members rather than providing for variances based upon utilization by individual members or groups.

Federally qualified HMOs must abide by certain community rating requirements. Community rates for federally qualified HMOs must be determined by one of three community rating bases:
1. Rates for all employer groups and individual enrollees must be based upon a fixed schedule.
2. Rates may vary by employer group, but the same per-member-per-month revenue must be charged to all employer groups.
3. Rates may vary by employer group, but the same revenue per subscriber (single or family contract) per month must be charged for all employer groups.

Community rating has been very practical for many HMOs. Its simplicity is especially useful for staff models that may have difficulty in defining a group's actual experience, because the cost of the health center facility and physicians' salaries are generally fixed and do not vary by group utilization patterns. Community rating is also more feasible for HMOs that may enroll only a portion of a group's employees or small groups because their claim experience may not be credible enough for anything other than a community rating method.

Community Rating by Class

Federally qualified HMOs formerly could community rate only within rigid specifications. These specifications were expanded in 1981 for federally qualified HMOs in an attempt to provide them with greater flexibility in rating and to allow them to be more competitive when marketing against nonqualified HMOs and traditional group carriers. The enhancements to the rating system made in 1981 are referred to as *community rating by class*.

Under a community rating by class system, the HMO separates its members into classes based upon factors that are reflective of their utilization of health services, thereby allowing for subsets of community rates to be developed for different categories of employee groups. Common separations are based upon age, sex, family status and industry.

Experience Rating

Traditionally, experience rating has been used by insurance companies and Blue Cross and Blue Shield organizations. Experience rating has generally not been widely used by HMOs, since it is difficult for them to separate experience by employer group. For example, a staff model HMO may not be able to allocate the costs of its salaried physician by specific employer group. In addition, medical group capitation or the rate at which an HMO compensates its affiliated physicians would need to vary by employer group under an experience rating system. Despite these administrative complexities, employers are continuing to pressure HMOs to experience rate.

GUIDELINES FOR EVALUATION OF HMOs

When trustees are provided with an opportunity to select among various soliciting HMOs, they may need to go through a careful evaluation process in order to select only the most qualified HMO programs. The following general guidelines have been prepared to assist trustees in their evaluation process.

HMO Type

The different types of HMOs were discussed earlier in this chapter. The trustees will need to evaluate which type of HMO model is most suitable for the members.

Along with the type of HMO, the trustees should consider the sponsor of the HMO. Typical sponsors of HMOs would include Blue Cross and Blue Shield plans, insurance companies, hospitals and physician groups. Each of these owner types brings different managerial skills to the HMO. The trustees should evaluate which sponsor type is most compatible with their members.

Also related to HMO type is the quality of the top executive officers of the HMO. Part of the evaluation process by the trustee should involve analysis of the qualifications and experience of the persons who will be providing most of the management to the HMO.

Benefit Package

An important consideration for the trustees is the benefit offering provided by the different HMOs. Important points to consider include the basic medical benefits to be provided, the out-of-pocket costs for the HMO members relative to the premium charged, the extent of preventive services, the gatekeeper or primary care physician system for the HMO, and the availability of ancillary insurance benefits such as group life insurance, accidental death and dismemberment insurance or disability insurance. Trustees should also evaluate whether the HMO allows the HMO member to choose, at the point of service, to receive benefits through the HMO network. Such an HMO option is referred to as an *open-ended* HMO. An open-ended HMO allows the HMO member to receive medical services from non-HMO providers, usually at a greater out-of-pocket cost.

Premium Structure

Trustees should evaluate the premium structure of the HMO. For example, small groups may benefit from pooling their claim experience with other groups of a similar type, especially if the group cannot sustain large fluctuations in its claim experience. For groups of this type, a community-rated structure may be more appropriate. Larger groups, or those that can sustain fluctuations in claim experience, may find it more advantageous to select an HMO that uses some form of experience rating.

Quality Assurance Program

Trustees should screen and review the quality assurance programs for the various HMOs in advance. Of particular interest are the assurance programs covering inpatient utilization and outpatient utilization services.

As part of the quality assurance program review, trustees may wish to request from the HMO its targeted hospital utilization rates for the group. These utilization rates are generally expressed as an average number of hospital days per thousand members. The trustees should review the HMO's utilization targets for reasonableness as compared with the current hospital utilization. In addition, they should also consider whether the utilization target is too extreme for their group. This is especially important for a group that was not previously subject to utilization controls.

Network Service Area

An important selection criterion is the proximity of the HMO provider facilities (including the primary care clinics and hospitals) to the work location and residence of the majority of members.

Physician Specialties

Trustees should request the various medical specialties to be provided by the HMO. In addition, the trustees should evaluate the qualifications and experience of the various specialty heads. Smaller staff models, for example, may not provide a large number of specialty services. For these types of HMOs, the trustees should request the credentials of the specialty physicians that would be used through a referral system.

HMO Membership Size

The membership size for an HMO is another characteristic to be analyzed by trustees. Larger HMOs, with large membership enrollment, may be able to negotiate more favorable fees with their various providers and, therefore, pass on this reduced cost of medical services to the HMO members. The trustees should evaluate not only current membership size, but also recent growth or declines in membership enrollment. This may help the trustees assess the viability or stability of the HMO.

Management Information Systems

The types of management information systems of the HMO should be evaluated. The HMOs should be requested to provide sample management reports that are typical of what they provide on a periodic basis. The management information reports will help the trustees understand how their health care dollars are being spent. Advanced information systems will help the trustees assess the effectiveness of the HMO and will make them better managers of their health care costs.

PREFERRED PROVIDER ORGANIZATIONS

Following is an overview of preferred provider organizations (PPOs). The term *PPO* will be defined, and common features and characteristics of PPOs will be discussed. For trustees to understand more fully the differences between PPOs and other methods of financing health insurance benefits, PPOs will be contrasted with both traditional group insurance plans and HMOs. Also reviewed in this chapter are some of the more common methods used by PPOs to contract with health care providers since, like HMOs, PPOs use different methods to contract with health care providers. This chapter will conclude with a set of guidelines to assist trustees when evaluating PPOs.

WHAT IS A PPO?

PPOs generally do not fall into one precise category or definition. Among different PPOs there may be critical differences in key characteristics that may tend to make them similar in name only. Irrespective of the differences among PPOs, they share a common focus that is based upon the following general characteristics:

1. *Provider/purchaser arrangement.* PPOs are arrangements between providers of health care and purchasers of health care whereby the providers make their services available at a reduced cost.
2. *Preferred status.* In exchange for providing health care services on a discounted or reduced cost basis, the providers are granted preferred status with respect to the health care purchasers. Employees are encouraged to use the preferred health care providers through incentives such as more liberal plan benefits. In exchange for the reduced cost, the preferred providers anticipate greater patient volume.

3. *Quality assurance/utilization review programs.* Preferred provider arrangements generally include utilization review guidelines or other cost-control systems. Generally, the controls and systems used by PPOs are not as advanced as HMOs.
4. *Point-of-service choice.* Employees who are enrolled in the PPO may receive their medical benefits from either the preferred providers or the nonpreferred providers. As mentioned in item 2, however, employees are generally provided with some form of incentive to use the preferred panel of providers.
5. *Financial risk.* Traditional PPOs assume no financial risk for providing medical services. The financial risk is still retained by the health care purchaser.

PRIMARY FEATURES OF PPOs

PPOs share common goals. The means by which they accomplish their goals, however, sometimes differ. Trustees need to be aware that all PPOs are not similar. PPOs may vary among themselves with regard to how they approach the following features of PPO design:
1. Negotiated fees
2. Benefit design
3. Quality assurance programs
4. Risk sharing
5. Provider choice.

Negotiated Fees

One of the key features of PPOs is their direct contracts with health care providers such as hospitals and physicians. Although PPOs contract with hospitals and physician providers, there is generally no typical contract or arrangement used. The arrangements and terms are usually developed to meet the needs of the two parties involved.

One of the more traditional negotiated reimbursement methods for hospitals and physicians is a percentage discount to regularly charged fees. Under this method, the hospital or physician agrees to provide services at a discount or percentage reduction to their regularly charged fees. This type of arrangement is advantageous if the discount by the provider is meaningful. Prior to the rise in the use of negotiated fees with providers, this approach may have resulted in substantial discounts to the "real" cost of providing health care services. As negotiated reimbursement arrangements have become more prevalent, the advantage of a provider discount has diminished. Discounts are generally only used for hospital inpatient and outpatient services.

As the use of discounts increases, the income base for providers tends to decrease, meaning the regular billed fees charged by them will likely rise to compensate for the higher discounts. The increase in providers' regular fees results in percentage discounts that are more apparent than real. If trustees are considering a PPO that uses percentage discounts, they may wish to have an independent cost analysis developed to determine the "true" discount being offered through the PPO network.

A second method of provider contracting is a per diem payment arrangement. This method relates to hospital services. With a per diem payment arrangement, a hospital provider agrees to provide hospital services for a predetermined daily charge. The per diem charge may vary by type of hospital stay. For example, a medical stay per diem may differ from a surgical stay per diem. A per diem arrangement has the advantage of locking the provider into a fixed daily cost. The disadvantage of a per diem arrangement is that the total hospital cost could increase if overall lengths of hospital stay are not governed by an efficient utilization and concurrent review program.

A less common method of contracting with hospitals is an arrangement where the reimbursement is based upon the diagnosis-related group (DRG). This method is patterned after the DRG system used by the Health Care Financing Administration for Medicare. The advantage of a DRG reimbursement system is that the health care purchaser is locked into a fixed cost per hospital admission (based upon a specific diagnosis) regardless of the length of hospital stay. The disadvantage of a DRG contract is that it may be difficult to obtain from hospitals if the DRG levels reflect cost and length-of-stay assumptions considerably less than the hospital's current levels.

A negotiated reimbursement method commonly used for physicians is a fee schedule. A fee schedule allows for physician reimbursement up to a fixed dollar fee, which varies by the types of the medical service provided. The advantage of a fee schedule is that some effective cost savings may be realized if the fee schedule is set at a level that is less than the usual and customary prevailing physician charge levels. A disadvantage of the fee schedule method is that the schedule may be set at an excessive level so that most physician charges fall at or below the scheduled amount. In addition, a fee schedule may provide physicians with an opportunity to break apart or unbundle their claim submissions in order to increase their return. Trustees may wish to have an independent cost analysis developed to assess the effective impact of a PPO's physician fee schedule.

Benefit Design

Benefit designs tend to vary from PPO to PPO. Despite this variance, PPOs share a common benefit design characteristic in that benefits received through preferred providers are richer than the benefits provided through nonpreferred providers.

The first generation of PPOs tended to design their benefits with positive incentives. In other words, there was a positive incentive to use the preferred providers. An example of a positive incentive would be a PPO that replaces a traditional comprehensive major medical plan. A positive incentive design would reimburse incurred expenses at a more generous level if preferred providers were used. The benefits received by nonpreferred providers would be reimbursed at the same deductible and coinsurance percentages as the comprehensive plan. For example, if the nonpreferred provider coinsurance was 80%, the preferred provider coinsurance percentage may be increased to 90%, or possibly even 100%, for certain benefits.

The primary disadvantage of a positive incentive benefit design is that the cost reductions realized through utilization controls are reduced or even eliminated by the extra expense incurred when preferred providers are used and richer benefits are provided.

Recent generations of PPO benefit designs have made use of negative incentives. Using the previous example in which a PPO replaces a traditional comprehensive major medical plan, benefits received from preferred providers would be reimbursed at the same deductible and coinsurance percentage as the comprehensive medical plan it replaced. Plan reimbursements would be reduced if nonpreferred providers are used. In other words, the preferred provider coinsurance would be 80%, while the nonpreferred provider coinsurance percentage may be reduced to 70% or less.

Trustees should be aware that provider contracts may vary relative to the PPO benefit design. For example, a hospital may provide its services at a 10% discount if a positive incentive design is used but only provide a 5% discount if a negative incentive design is used.

Quality Assurance Programs

Quality assurance programs are used by nearly all PPOs. The level of intensity in the program, however, varies from PPO to PPO. Generally, the quality assurance programs used by PPOs are not as effective as those used by HMOs because PPOs inherently lack the HMO's financial incentives and risk.

Trustees will need to sort through the features of the various quality assurance programs that will be offered by different PPOs in order to assess their relative effectiveness. The following question may help trustees in their analysis:

1. Who provides the service? The quality assurance program may be internally delegated to a health care provider, contracted to a third party organization or jointly administered by a health care provider and a third party organization. Internally delegated quality assurance programs are generally less costly. They suffer, however, from inherent conflicts of interest because the provider is being asked to balance the purchaser's need for cost-effectiveness with the provider's need for revenue. Quality assurance programs administered by third party organizations may eliminate the conflict-of-interest dilemma. They may, however, result in increased costs for program administration.
2. What health care services are subject to the program? PPOs generally concentrate their quality assurance programs on hospital services. Trustees should determine whether or not the programs deal solely with hospital services or whether they also cover ambulatory care. In general, a quality assurance program that deals with both hospital and ambulatory care is more effective than a program that deals solely with hospital inpatient services.
3. What are the screening criteria? The trustees should request the screening criteria that will be used by the quality assurance program to determine whether the most appropriate medical care is being provided. A quality assurance program should not unduly slow the health care delivery process. An optimal program would be one that provides for quick approval screening techniques that are effective at flagging specific cases that may need to be evaluated further.
4. How are the physicians involved? The quality assurance program should provide for physician support for the screening process. The program should provide for meaningful dialog between the assurance program administrator and the attending physician. Trustees should review the procedures used by the program to resolve differences of opinion regarding treatment modes.
5. How qualified is the program administrator? The trustees should request the credentials and years of experience of the key managers of the program.
6. What are the management information systems' capabilities? The management information systems used by the quality assurance program should be capable of supporting the preadmission and utilization review programs. They should also produce accurate and comprehensive data with respect to the utilization profiles of individual health care providers.

Risk Sharing

Unlike HMOs, PPOs generally do not assume any financial risk. Their primary focus is organizing a network of providers. They do not underwrite risk because they generally lack the assets to do so, and they are restricted from doing so unless licensed as a risk taker. Without financial risk, the PPO may become nothing more than an intermediary that receives a commission or administration fee for organizing a provider network.

To make themselves more unique, some PPOs have undertaken modified risk sharing arrangements. The PPOs do not directly take the underwriting or claims risk but will place some portion of their administration fees at risk based upon the underwriting or claims performance. This arrangement provides the PPO with some incentive to manage the delivery of health care more effectively because there is an opportunity for a loss or gain of a percentage of their administration fee.

To make the risk sharing mechanism feasible, an independent third party may be used to establish reasonable targets upon which the risk incentives will be based. If the targets are exceeded, the PPO will be penalized for a percentage of the administration fee. Likewise, if actual results are less than the targets, the PPO's compensation will be increased by a percentage of the administration fee. It may not be prudent to attempt to negotiate risk sharing arrangements that place the entire administration fee at risk.

Provider Choice

Traditional PPOs allow employees to elect their health care provider at the point of service. In other words, until an employee has a need to see a physician, he or she does not have to decide whether a preferred provider will be used.

A recent trend in benefit design is to require an employee to elect the provider at the time of enrollment in the PPO program. This type of provider election is more restrictive than the traditional approach.

Trustees should take into consideration the type of provider choice options available for each PPO. They may decide to grade into a more restrictive choice system over time. This gradual changeover will allow the employees to acclimate themselves not only to a new delivery system but also to a new set of physicians and hospitals.

PPOs VS. TRADITIONAL GROUP INSURANCE

PPOs differ from traditional group insurance. The first key difference between PPOs and traditional group insurance relates to provider choice. Under a traditional insurance plan, the plan enrollee is free to use any health care provider. Regardless of which provider is used, the enrollee will be reimbursed on the same basis.

In a PPO, the enrollee is free to use any provider. The benefits provided through a preferred provider, however, will be reimbursed on a preferential basis. This restriction in the choice of providers relates to a second key difference between a PPO and traditional group insurance—the use of negotiated arrangements with providers. This difference will be reduced as traditional group insurers make greater use of negotiated reimbursement arrangements.

A third key difference between PPOs and traditional insurance programs is that PPOs generally do not assume any financial risk. Traditional group insurance generally acts as a financial intermediary; PPOs do not. PPOs are not responsible for collecting premiums, nor are they financially responsible for reimbursing medical claims.

PPOs vs. HMOs

PPOs differ from HMOs in a number of areas. For example, HMOs are risk takers while PPOs generally do not accept risk.

HMOs usually place greater restrictions on the enrollee's choice of provider. In contrast, a PPO enrollee (with some exceptions) is free to use his or her provider of choice. To expand their market share, some HMOs have begun to offer a product that includes a point-of-service selection option.

HMOs also differ from PPOs in that HMOs typically provide a more comprehensive package of health benefits. HMOs may include not only traditional indemnity type benefits like hospital and physician coverages but also preventive benefits such as physical exams, immunizations, well-baby care, and vision and hearing screenings. PPO benefit designs tend to be more like traditional group insurance indemnity programs, with the exception that incentives are included to use the preferred provider.

GUIDELINES FOR EVALUATION OF PPOs

When trustees are provided with an opportunity to select among various soliciting PPOs, they will need to go through a careful evaluation process in order to select only the most qualified PPO systems. This section contains some general guidelines for trustees to reflect in their evaluation process.

PPO Sponsor

PPOs may be sponsored by hospitals, Blue Cross and Blue Shield plans, physician groups, insurance companies or even HMOs or employers. When evaluating a PPO, the trustees should ensure that they understand the motivations of the sponsoring organization as it relates to the PPO.

Benefit Design

The trustees should determine whether a positive or negative incentive benefit design will work best for their group. Positive incentive designs may make the PPO more appealing to the employees initially, in that the employees are not penalized if they do not use the preferred providers. A negative incentive may result in less initial employee satisfaction, but the combination of favorable negotiated reimbursements, utilization controls and benefit design results in a greater potential for initial cost savings.

Provider Contracting Arrangements

PPOs may vary in the methods used to reimburse hospitals and physicians. To assist in the decision making process, the trustees may wish to have an independent analysis done to estimate the reduction in cost that will result from the actual reimbursement method used by each of the different PPOs.

Provider Choice

PPOs may differ with respect to the provider choice available to an employee. Trustees will need to determine whether a point-of-service provider choice or a point-of-enrollment provider choice design is feasible for their group.

Quality Assurance Program

The intensity of the quality assurance program tends to vary among PPOs. Trustees should review the screening procedures used by the quality assurance program. In addition, the trustees should determine whether the program covers only hospital benefits or both hospital and ambulatory care benefits. The trustees should request actual utilization results achieved for comparable groups in order to estimate reasonable utilization targets for their own group.

Provider Network Area

Traditional PPOs tended to have very concentrated service areas. As PPOs become more prevalent, their network areas have begun to expand. Trustees should compare the location of the PPO providers with the work location and residence of the majority of their members.

Provider Selection Criteria

The trustees may wish to review the criteria used by the PPO to select physicians and hospitals that will become members of the preferred network. With respect to hospitals, it is important to review the PPO's criteria for (1) location, (2) services that can be provided, (3) state license, (4) liability insurance coverage, (5) accreditation and (6) the number of board-certified physicians by specialty type.

With respect to physicians, it is important to review criteria for (1) location, (2) state license, (3) liability insurance, (4) pending and/or awarded malpractice claims, (5) board specialty and (6) experience in working in an alternative delivery system.

The trustees should place special emphasis upon such measurable selection standards as clinical quality and cost-effective practice patterns when evaluating the criteria used by the PPO.

Management Information Systems

With respect to management information systems, the PPO should have the capability to produce accurate and comprehensive provider cost and utilization profiles for individual providers. Additionally, the PPO should be able to support the preadmission and concurrent hospital review programs and ambulatory review programs associated with its quality assurance program.

CASE STUDY—PPO EVALUATION

The financial evaluation of a PPO proposal involves the total projected revenue impact expected for the PPO. This includes a comparison of the direct fees charged by the PPO as well as the effect that the PPO's physician and hospital fee contracts will have upon the expected cost of claims. Frequently, it is assumed that the "claims will be claims" and the PPO will not impact them. This is not necessarily true. Higher PPO fees may be acceptable if lower claims are expected to result.

The following case study summarizes the major elements and results of a PPO proposal analysis. The sample encompasses a number of issues itemized above.

Review of PPO Proposals— Recommendation and Analysis

The trustees of Local #000 (fund) directed the fund consultant to send requests for proposals (RFPs) to five PPOs for the purpose of reviewing PPO options available to the fund. This letter documents the recommendation to the trustees and provides a summary of the analysis that was performed on the RFP responses that were received.

Prospective PPOs

The following PPOs and contacts were sent an RFP.
    PPO A
    Street
    City, State, Zip
Contact: John/Jane Doe, Title

PPO B
Street
City, State, Zip
Contact: John/Jane Doe, Title
PPO C
Street
City, State, Zip
Contact: John/Jane Doe, Title
PPO D
Street
City, State, Zip
Contact: John/Jane Doe, Title
PPO E
Street
City, State, Zip
Contact: John/Jane Doe, Title

The RFPs requested responses by DD/MM/YY. Table II summarizes the information that was provided by each PPO contact.

Table II

PPO	Response
1. PPO A	All RFPs addressed
2. PPO B	All RFPs addressed
3. PPO C	All RFPs addressed
4. PPO D	All RFPs addressed
5. PPO E	Did not submit response

Copies of materials provided by each PPO are available.

Recommendations

Based upon the analysis of the proposals, the fund consultant recommends that the trustees retain PPO D as its PPO. The recommendation of PPO D is based upon (a) ease of transition, (b) fee structure for fund participation, (c) net fund cost (monthly fees combined with the effect of provider discounts) and (d) the current working relationship with the fund.

PPO A provided a strong proposal, but it is the fund consultant's opinion that PPO D has more strength in the areas related to (a) monthly fees, (b) interaction with the fund's insurance carrier and (c) litigation history. The litigation history limited the credibility of the discount information supplied by PPO A.

PPO B and PPO C were not recommended largely because the combined effect of monthly fees and estimated provider discounts were not as competitive as PPO D.

Analysis Process and Criteria

The RFP that was sent to prospective PPOs was presented to the trustees at the DD/MM/YY trustee meeting.

At that meeting, the fund consultant presented the key areas upon which the analysis and recommendation would be based:

1. Ease of transition for fund members, fund office personnel and plan administrator
2. Fee structure proposed for fund participation
3. Network service coverage area and consistency with the location of fund members
4. Benefit plan design requirements that the PPO may impose upon the fund
5. Proposed interaction by the PPO with plan administrator and the fund office
6. Actuarial value of the hospital and physician contracting arrangements and the projected impact on the fund's benefit costs
7. PPO's general operational and financial status and any litigation history for the PPO or its affiliates
8. Provider profiling, quality assurance and patient treatment protocols.

The letters requesting a proposal were sent to each prospective PPO. The RFP specified various questions, which were intended to provide the information necessary to fully analyze the responses as they related to above decision criteria.

Summary of Analysis

The results of the analysis are summarized as follows.

Fee Structure. Each PPO submitted a monthly fee for (a) participation in the PPO, (b) utilization review and management, and (c) other miscellaneous functions. Table III summarizes the monthly fees per employee and estimates the annual cost to the fund based upon an average number of covered employees per month equal to 1,304.

The PPO D proposal is the lowest proposal with annual costs of approximately $40,000.

Network Service Area. Each PPO was provided with a current listing of member's ZIP codes and was asked to map the location of their providers to the ZIP codes to determine the coverage area of the PPO. The fund consultant requested that each PPO define the maximum driving distance to be considered within a network service area. Table IV summarizes the coverage area information provided by each PPO.

Actuarial Value of Provider Contracts. Each PPO was provided with a sample of hospital claims to be repriced. In addition, each PPO provided its physician fees for sample physician services. The purpose of this information was to estimate the effective discount of each PPO's provider contracts.

To analyze the fees, the fund consultant developed an approximate distribution of current benefit costs by service category as shown in Table V.

Table III

PPO	Monthly Fee	# Months	Avg. Members	Estimated Annual Cost
PPO A	$5.25	12	1,304	$ 82,152
PPO B	7.10	12	1,304	111,101
PPO C	5.12	12	1,304	80,118
PPO D	2.50	12	1,304	39,120

Notes: 1. PPO A fee quote does not include a percent of savings provision. Monthly costs are equal to the quoted monthly fee plus 10% of savings on all claims. The "10% savings" fee is reflected in the analysis related to hospital and physician costs.
2. PPO D fee includes optimal ambulatory care review monthly costs of $.60. The proposal without this option is $1.90 per month.

Table IV

PPO	Provider Coverage Percent	Maximum Mileage Definition
PPO A	97.7%	20 miles
PPO B	88.7	25 miles
PPO C	99.5	25 miles
PPO D	79.9	35 miles

Table V

Benefit Service	Estimated Cost Allocation	Estimated Annual Savings
Hospital	45.0%	$2,160,000
Physician—Medicine	26.2	1,257,600
Physician—Surgery	6.0	288,000
Physician—Obstetrics	3.1	148,800
Physician—Pathology	4.5	216,000
Physician—Radiology	5.2	249,600
Other	10.0	480,000
Total	100.0%	$4,800,000

Notes: 1. Estimated cost allocations are based up Milliman & Robertson, Inc. *Health Cost Guidelines.*
2. Estimated annual fund costs were approximated by annualizing current claims paid through MMYY.

The costs in Table V were assumed to be reflective of costs associated with PPO D since that is the current PPO. To analyze the impact of the provider contracts by other PPOs, we compared the actuarial value of their contracts to PPO D and, based upon the ratio, estimated cost savings (deficits) that would result from each proposal. These estimates are summarized in Table VI.

The hospital component was estimated based upon repriced hospital claims. The PPO A fee proposal is based upon a fixed monthly fee plus 10% of savings. As such, the estimated hospital discount for PPO A was adjusted to net the 10% savings, which would be retained by PPO A.

The estimated physician savings or deficit was estimated based upon physician fee information provided by each PPO. As with the hospital component, the PPO A values were adjusted to net the additional access fee equal to 10% of the discount.

Operational and Financial Status. Each PPO supplied information related to its operational and financial status. All PPOs were able to provide a list of Taft-Hartley clients, indicating experience with plans such as the fund.

Each PPO carries per occurrence liability protection of $1 million or higher.

Each PPO proposed an implementation plan that would result in closure within two months. Since PPO D is the current PPO, no implementation is needed.

Litigation History. PPO D and PPO B reported no litigation with respect to their organizations. Both PPO C and PPO A provided information regarding litigation history.

Table VI

ESTIMATED PPO SAVINGS/(DEFICIT)

Benefit Service	PPO A	PPO B	PPO C	PPO D
Hospital	$190,810	($88,424)	$997,681	$0
Physician—Medicine	(163,148)	91,510	(446,875)	0
Physician—Surgery	48,777	23,247	(128,254)	0
Physician—Obstetrics	20,747	24,368	(15,001)	0
Physician—Pathology	0	(4,561)	(125,149)	0
Physician—Radiology	21,054	8,849	(99,626)	0
Other	0	0	0	0
Estimated Total	$118,240	$54,989	($715,137)	$0

Notes: 1. Values are estimated based upon provider fee information provided in each PPO's proposal.
2. The PPO A fees have been adjusted to approximate the return of 10% of savings to PPO A.
3. No savings or deficit is assumed for PPO D since this is the base scenario.

There are two lawsuits currently pending against PPO C. One lawsuit involves medical malpractice. No specifics were provided. A second lawsuit involves a contractual dispute. Since its inception in 19YY, PPO C has been involved in nine lawsuits that were dismissed, eight lawsuits that resulted in settlement, and two lawsuits in which judgment was entered against PPO C.

PPO A indicated no litigation history with respect to the PPO but noted various actions against its parent company. No details were provided. The fund consultant has heard that PPO A has pending litigation with respect to the return of provider discounts. This is important since its proposal includes additional fees based upon the discount. The fund consultant's understanding is that the litigation is similar to current class action suits against sister companies. These suits allege that PPO A failed to pass on to members the discounts that it negotiated with hospitals and providers.

Benefit Plan Design Requirements. PPO B and PPO D would not require a benefit plan design change. PPO C and PPO A encourage a 5% incentive for Plan 4.

Interaction With Plan Administrator. We requested that the plan administrator directly contact the PPOs to discuss interaction and data transfer arrangements. The plan administrator states that interaction will be feasible with each PPO; however, it would not be feasible to accommodate the preferred claim processing method proposed by PPO A. The preferred method of claim processing by PPO A would involve the following steps:

1. Gross claims sent to plan administrator for adjudication
2. Adjudicated claims returned to PPO A
3. PPO A applies discount to adjudicated claims and claim checks issued by PPO A.

We do not recommend this payment method for the fund.

Provider Profiling. All PPOs submitted information related to provider profiling, quality assurance and patient treatment protocols. The procedures employed by each PPO are consistent with standard practices and guidelines used in the industry.

Data Reliance. In preparing the analysis, the fund consultant reviewed information provided by each PPO. The fund consultant relied upon them for the accuracy of the information provided.

Chapter 24

Self-Financing of Welfare Plans

Arthur L. Wilmes

INTRODUCTION

Self-financing[1] is an alternative to conventional insurance for financing welfare plans. The roots of self-financing lie in the areas of pension plans and workers' compensation. Over time, the self-financing mechanisms used for pension plans and workers' compensation have been extended to welfare plans.

This chapter provides a generalized definition of *self-financing*. The feasibility of self-financing as it relates to welfare benefit plans is also discussed. In addition, the advantages and disadvantages of self-financing are reviewed. Included in this chapter is a self-financing analysis case study. The case study can be used by trustees as an example of a cost analysis that may be done if a self-financing alternative is under consideration. This chapter concludes with a set of guidelines that can be used by trustees to help them analyze the feasibility of self-financing as it relates to their welfare fund.

WHAT IS SELF-FINANCING?

A welfare fund that self-finances assumes all the duties and liabilities of a convention insurer. In a sense, this is a reasonable definition of *self-financing*. The self-financing welfare fund must, therefore, be prepared to perform the following operations:

1. *Total liability.* The total liability for all claims incurred must be assumed. The liability can be reduced by the purchase of stop-loss insurance, which will place a limit on the overall liability assumed.
2. *Employee communications.* In the case of welfare benefits, self-financing does not eliminate the need to provide employees with a handbook and other materials necessary for a genuine understanding of the welfare fund's benefits. The self-financing welfare fund is responsible for all design, printing and distribution costs associated with these materials. To the extent the self-financed plan duplicates the coverages that existed under the previous plan, some design and legal costs may be reduced.
3. *Claims administration.* A method of handling claims must be developed. Claims handling involves the development of claims forms, claims filing procedures, claims adjudication procedures, procedures for claims analysis, a system to pay valid claims that are submitted, the establishment of usual and customary guidelines, monitoring procedures for claims that exceed the usual and customary guidelines, and procedures for coordinating benefits with other insurers. This list is not exhaustive, but it does illustrate some of the vital components of an efficient claims system.
4. *General administration.* An administration system must be developed to maintain appropriate records. Such an administration system would include a premium collection process for plans that are contributory. To the extent that payroll is administered in-house, the development and maintenance cost of an administration system may be reduced. An alternative to in-house administration would be the purchase of administrative services from an insurance company via an administrative services only (ASO) contract or from a third party administrator (TPA).
5. *Other traditional duties of an insurance company must be assumed as well.* Responsibilities regarding loss prevention, actuarial, legal, investment and accounting functions must be performed in-house or be contracted to outside consultants.

SELF-FINANCING OF WELFARE BENEFITS

General

Most types of welfare benefits can be self-financed. Self-financing of some welfare benefits, however, is more feasible than others. Generally, medical expense benefits are the most common form of self-financed welfare benefits, followed by disability income benefits. Life insurance benefits, for example, are self-financed by very few welfare funds.

Self-Financed Plans

Medical expense coverages are good candidates for full or partial self-financing. Most refined conventional group insurance coverages generally provide that group policyholders receive a premium refund by means of an experience rating formula.[2] The major component in an experience rating formula is actual claims paid. Smaller components consist of policy expenses and the increase in reserves.

Through the experience rating process, employee groups in or near the "jumbo" category (1,000 lives or more) can expect to pay the full cost of their claim experience because the experience rating method usually gives full credibility to their actual experience. As a result, the group insurer assumes very little risk for the current claim expenses, and the policyholder effectively pays all the benefit costs and associated expenses of the policy.

Since claim experience for larger groups may remain reasonably stable from year to year, some form of self-financing may be sought since the anticipated economic advantages of self-financing far outweigh the risk of substantial financial hardship that could result from adverse fluctuations in claim experience.

The tax treatment of benefits received from a self-financed medical expense plan does not affect the self-financing decision since medical expense benefits provided by such a plan are not taxable as income. Self-financed medical expense plans are, however, subject to state requirements mandating conversion privileges to an individual plan of insurance upon employment termination.

Disability income benefits may also be effectively provided through a full or partial self-financing mechanism. Qualifications for benefits, as well as the disability benefit payments, may be efficiently handled through the current payroll system. The tax treatment of benefits paid to the disabled employee does not affect the self-financing decision since benefits received from either an employer-pay-all conventional group contract or a self-financed welfare plan receive the same income tax treatment.

Life insurance and accidental death benefits are generally not self-financed by welfare plans. A self-financed life insurance benefit in excess of $5,000 is taxable income to the recipient of the proceeds. Additionally, life and accidental death benefit claim experience is subject to volatile fluctuations resulting in more risk than is acceptable for welfare plans.

Types of Self-Financing

Welfare plans may choose to self-finance their benefits under one of two funding methods. The first method is classified as *unfunded* self-financing. An unfunded self-financed welfare plan uses no specific trust instrument to fully fund the benefit costs incurred by the welfare fund. Rather, cash benefits are paid when due from either the fund's assets or cash flow.

A second method of self-financing is classified as *funded* self-financing. A funded self-financed welfare plan funds its cash benefit costs, as well as its accrued-but-unpaid benefits costs, through a specific trust instrument. The trust instrument most often used by a funded plan is a voluntary employees' beneficiary association (VEBA).[3]

If an unfunded self-financed program is used, the liabilities for the welfare plan should be calculated on a period basis. By developing an estimate of the plan's liabilities, trustees can determine whether their assets are adequate to fully fund the plan's incurred benefit obligations if the plan were to terminate on the date the liabilities were estimated.

THE SELF-FINANCING DECISION

Advantages of Self-Financing

There are several major motivations or perceived advantages to self-financing as it relates to welfare plans.

Cost Reduction

Self-financing can eliminate certain costs that are part of a conventional group insurance contract. One such cost is state premium tax, which may make up to 20-30% of an insurer's total retention charges. This advantage is not applicable to states that subject self-financed plans to premium tax.

A second area of cost savings involves the profit and contingency charge assessed by an insurer. The profit charge not only compensates the insurer for its services and assumption of risk but also provides it with a return on its business investment. The contingency charge for an insurer represents an additional margin to cover fluctuations in claim experience.

A third element of cost savings is the elimination of commissions paid to an insurer's agents or brokers. Since self-financing does not involve the sale of a product by compensated agents, a cost savings can be realized.

Improved Investment Return

Unpaid claim reserves are established by an insurer to provide an account to pay claims that have been accrued but not yet been paid. This is usually referred to as the report for claims that have been incurred but not reported (IBNR) at the end of an accounting period. The insurer generally sets the IBNR reserve equal to two to three months' premiums or 20-30% of incurred claims.

A self-financed plan may receive a better investment return, net of investment expenses and taxes, if it holds or controls the reserves. This advantage may be diminished if the insurer credits a competitive rate of investment return on the reserves it establishes.

Improved Cash Flow

Any realized cost savings that result from self-financing can be used for the plan's investment. Improved cash flow is also a corollary to improved investment return. Cash flow may also be improved if the self-financing plan is responsible for setting the reserves for the welfare benefit plan.

Insulation From Market Conditions

Insurance pricing practices tend to be cyclical. Market conditions tend to dictate the level of rate increases. The market gets soft when the drive for market share influences the product price. Small rate increases result. When underwriting results worsen and the industry's balance sheets begin to reflect the extended period of underpricing, the market hardens. As a result, large rate increases are not uncommon. Self-financing may provide some insulation from these types of cyclical pricing patterns.

Disadvantages of Self-Financing

Self-financing may result in some cost savings due to the elimination of premium taxes, sales commissions, profit and risk charges, and retention of the reserve. The magnitude of the cost savings can sometimes be overstated, however, if not properly balanced against the costs incurred by the self-financed plan. Some of these costs are not incurred under a conventionally insured plan. A self-financing analysis should reflect the expenses removed by self-financing, as well as the expenses added by self-financing.

The level of claims will not necessarily be unchanged under a self-financed plan. For example, a self-financed plan that liberally interprets its benefits will result in higher total claim costs as compared to the replaced conventional plan that had stricter benefit interpretations. For example, a self-financing plan may lack the sophistication to interpret the benefits as detailed in the policy form; it may not be able to adjudicate borderline claims to its advantage; or it may unknowingly duplicate coverages from other insurances. Finally, additional costs may result with respect to medical claims if the claims analysis system does not limit claims to the usual and customary charge levels.

In addition to increased benefit costs, there may be other disadvantages related to self-financing:

1. A self-financed welfare plan may not be able to provide a terminating employee with a conversion privilege to an individual plan.
2. A self-financed welfare benefit plan may shift the insurance risk to the insured employee. Without stop-loss coverage, the self-financed plan can run the risk of not having sufficient funds to pay for large claims, making the unpaid claim the responsibility of the employee.
3. Considerable trustee time must be spent to ensure that benefits remain competitive with the current employee benefits market.
4. There will be development and maintenance costs for a self-financed plan. Loss prevention, actuarial, legal, accounting and administrative duties must not be performed by the welfare plan or contracted to outside providers.
5. A self-financed plan is responsible for the settlement of its claims. This places the burden of adjudication and resulting employee complaints on the trustees rather than an impartial third party. This disadvantage occurs to a lesser degree through the trustee appeal process.

The Self-Financing Decision

Despite the economic advantages of self-financing, funds generally do not totally self-finance. Rather, a modified insurance arrangement or partial self-financing[4] is used for the following reasons:

1. Self-financing can result in fluctuations in insurance costs from year to year. Modified arrangements that may involve stop-loss reinsurance provide for more consistent financial results, as they tend to stabilize yearly benefit costs.
2. A self-financed plan must essentially maintain a miniature insurance company. A substantial investment is required just to establish the necessary operational departments. After the initial setup, a great deal of trustees' time and talent is needed to maintain the operations. Administrative services may be contracted via an ASO or a TPA.
3. Self-financing requires a sufficient number of homogeneous exposure units. This is necessary to project a reasonable range of annual benefit costs. With a small workforce or limited exposure to risk, it may be difficult to develop such projections with confidence. Insured programs that partially pool the benefit risk may be used by smaller groups.

Table

HEALTH AND WELFARE FUND

Restated Financial Statement—1989

		Insured	Self-Financed
Contribution income			
Major medical	$239,018		
Other	898,550	$1,137,568	$1,137,568
Interest income		7,000	31,939
Total income		$1,144,568	$1,169,507
Claims		$ 946,505	$ 946,505
Change in reserve			
Beginning	$446,771		
Ending	441,164	(5,607)	(5,607)
Premium tax		22,751	0
Insurer expense		33,558	0
Insurer risk charge		22,751	0
Claims and general administration		34,127	34,127
Stop-loss		0	31,852
Actuarial fees		0	10,000
Total expenses		$1,054,085	$1,016,877
Surplus (deficit)		$ 90,483	$ 152,630
Estimated gain (deficit) from self-funding			$ 62,147
As a percent of end-of-year assets			4.6%

4. Equitable settlement of claims is a major element of employee satisfaction for a self-financed welfare benefit plan. Utilization of an impartial third party claims administrator may transfer a majority of the adjudication decisions from the trustees to the administrator.
5. Self-financed plans, in general, lack the internal expertise and necessary capital to develop an efficient claims administration system. This leads to inefficient claim settlement practices resulting from poor benefit coordination with other insurers, payments in excess of usual and customary levels, and liberal interpretation of borderline cases. A self-financed plan, therefore, may find itself with claim costs larger than a comparable modified insured plan. Third parties are generally used to take advantage of their claim payment expertise.

Self-Financing Analysis— Case Study

Trustees considering self-financing as an alternative to conventional insurance should have an actuarial analysis prepared to study the impact of self-financing on the welfare plan.

An example of a partial self-financing[5] actuarial analysis is summarized in the table. The table compares the actual financial results under an insured plan with the results projected as if the plan were partially self-financed. The analysis assumes that contributions, claims, changes in reserves and administration expenses do not change if the plan is self-financed. This assumption may not be valid for all funds.

Under the self-financed projection, investment income is projected to increase because the plan receives a higher investment return on the reserves that are held.

Additional investment income is earned on the cash flow gain achieved by the self-financed plan.

Expenses for the self-financed plan are reduced because premium taxes and the insurer's expense, risk and profit charge are eliminated. Additional expenses are incurred by the self-financed plan due to the purchase of stop-loss reinsurance and actuarial services. Administration is assumed to be provided at no change in cost.

This case study indicates that the welfare plan would have reduced its total insurance costs by $62,147 or 4.6% of end-of-year assets.

It should be noted that this example is a retrospective analysis. It provides the actual savings based upon no change in the cost of claims. A complete actuarial analysis would also include a prospective review of projected claim costs for the next one to three years. The prospective analysis would involve a scenario of reasonable claim results in order to test the sensitivity of self-financing underwriting results to deviations in the expected claims. In other words, the expected prospective self-financing results and the volatility of the results to deviations in claim experience should be compared to the prospective conventional insurance results.

GUIDELINES FOR TRUSTEES

Trustees faced with a self-financing alternative should go through a careful evaluation process prior to making a final decision. The following general guidelines have been prepared to assist trustees in their evaluation.

1. *Asset strength.* A strong asset base may increase the feasibility of self-financing since it increases the plan's ability to deal with random fluctuations in claim experience. The need for asset strength may be reduced if the plan is able to purchase some form of excess loss reinsurance at an equitable price.
2. *Administration capability.* Plan administration becomes the responsibility of the plan if it self-finances. The trustees need to decide whether it is feasible for the plan administration to be done internally or whether it should be purchased from an external administration agency.
3. *Risk aversion.* Trustees may not be willing to accept the potential for wide variances in year-to-year financial results that could occur with self-financing. Conventional insurance arrangements tend to provide for more stable and predictable results.
4. *Claim experience.* Self-financing may be more feasible for groups that have a demonstrated consistency in year-to-year claim experience. Consistency, generally, is inherent in larger groups.
5. *Benefit types.* A corollary to stable claim experience is the types of benefits that are proposed for self-financing. Generally, medical expense benefits and disability benefits are better candidates for self-financing because their experience tends to be more stable. Benefits such as life insurance are lesser candidates for self-financing since these benefits have a low frequency of claim occurrence, but a high cost per claim potential.
6. *Tax considerations.* Benefits received from a self-financed welfare plan are, in general, subject to the same income tax treatment as conventionally insured benefits. An exception is a self-financed life insurance benefit. Self-financed life insurance benefits in excess of $5,000 are taxable as income.
7. *Actuarial analysis.* A self-financing decision should include an actuarial analysis or cost impact study in order to estimate the potential gain or loss expected under a self-financed plan. The actuarial analysis should estimate the risk to a self-financed plan resulting from random fluctuations in claim experience.

ENDNOTES

1. Many different terms have been used to describe a welfare plan that provides benefits directly from its cash flow, assets or a segregated trust rather than through an insurer. The author prefers to use the term *self-financing*. Trustees, however, should be aware that other terms are frequently used. Examples include *self-insurance* and *self-funding*.
2. Experience rating formulas are discussed in chapter 21.
3. VEBAs are also called *501(c)(9) trusts* since that is the section of the Internal Revenue Code that exempts VEBAs from income tax.
4. Under partial self-financing, the welfare fund does not fully assume the duties and obligations of an insurance company. Rather, plan administration may be contracted through a third party or part of the insurance risk may be transferred via stop-loss insurance. It should be noted that full self-financing is feasible for only a few large plans.
5. In this example, administration is provided by a TPA, and aggregate stop-loss reinsurance is proposed.

Chapter 25

Savings Accounts and Consumer-Directed Health Plans

Arthur L. Wilmes

INTRODUCTION

The annual rise in health care benefit costs has vexed the best professionals in the industry for over 40 years. The nexus of the problem began in the late 1970s and has progressed from the proverbial gnat on the elephant's buttocks to the proverbial elephant in the middle of the room. The topic consumes most political debates, confounds benefits administrators and has produced numerous "fixes for the problem." The problem, however, is that the problem continues. Solutions tend to have temporary life spans. The problem has been transferred from the payer to the provider and back to the payer. The latest iteration appears to be a transfer from the payer and the provider to the consumer.

The most recent proposal to reduce health care benefit costs comes in the form of consumer-directed health plans (CDHPs), flexible spending accounts (FSAs), medical savings accounts (MSAs), health savings accounts (HSAs) and health reimbursement accounts (HRAs).

INNOVATION OR COST TRANSFER?

The literal million-dollar question is whether these new plan approaches benefit the consumer and abate medical cost inflation. It is too early to understand if either of these premises is true.

CDHPs are sometimes viewed as the lead step to converting defined medical benefits, the current standard for medical benefit plans, to defined contribution plans. In the former, the benefit plan design is defined and the funding level rises and falls to meet the level of ultimate medical benefit consumption. In the latter, the dollar contribution or cost is defined and the level of ultimate medical benefit rises and falls to meet the level of funds available for paying for services. This view demonstrates how a CDHP could be used to control the employee benefit expense and leave the balance of unpaid expenses to the covered employee.

Despite the view taken of CDHPs, it appears that both the single employer market and the multiple employer market are looking at these new financing approaches for medical benefits.

CURRENT ENROLLMENT TRENDS

Data specific to multiple employer plans is not readily available; however, these plans are either reviewing the feasibility of CDHPs or have actually put such plans into place. The general market trends for CDHPs, specifically HSAs, have increased dramatically. The top 21 financial firms involved in the HSA administration business report that approximately 425,000 HSAs have been established since January 1, 2004. The current rate of new HSAs is reported to be 50,000 a month.

Figure 1 is an excerpt from research conducted by Forrester Research that indicates a steep increase in CDHP annual premiums.

It would appear from Figure 2 that CDHPs are projected to grow at the expense of traditional HMOs and PPOs.

It remains to be seen if the promise of reduced cost, improved quality and increased access result from CDHPs. An innovative idea that offers potential for enhancing care and quality while reducing costs should be encouraged and given an opportunity to demonstrate its viability. The benefit industry has been in this position in the past, however. Some professionals have expressed concerns that CDHPs may only provoke the

Figure 1

CONSUMER-DIRECTED HEALTH PLANS ON THE RISE
Total Annual Revenue From CDHP Premiums (in billions)

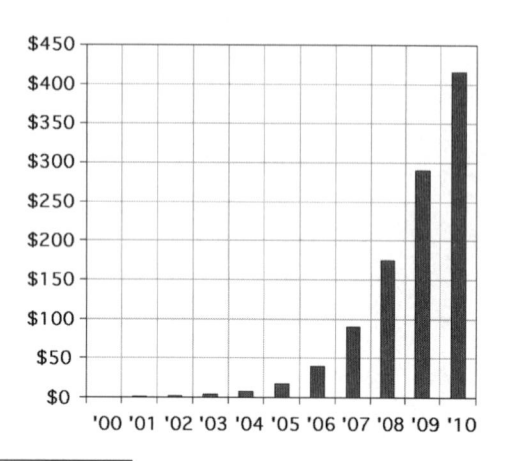

Source: Forrester Research.

Figure 2

CDHPs PROJECTED TO EXPAND AT EXPENSE OF PPO, POS, HMO PLANS' MARKET SHARE*

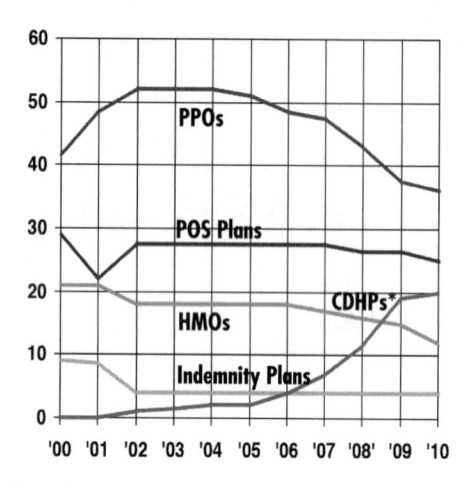

*Numbers may not equal 100% due to rounding.
Source: Forrester Research.

---

type of backlash experienced by the managed care industry.

Long-term success will depend upon how well the CDHPs will address the following issues.

- **Cost-Sharing Strategies.** CDHPs should be structured to require the highest cost sharing for services where the member's decisions can make a difference. Examples include elective services, choices among different treatments (for the same diagnosis) with differing costs and outcomes, and choice of providers with different efficiencies and outcomes.
- **Provider Choice.** CDHPs should align incentives for choice of provider where possible, using price and quality measures as differentiating value factors.
- **Treatment Price.** CDHPs should align incentives for choice of treatment using price. Choice of services and treatments can be sharply distinguished by price, and such pricing differentiation can influence members to make more responsible decisions.
- **Lifestyle Incentives.** CDHPs should include incentives for members to engage in healthy behaviors.
- **Communication.** CDHPs require various communication means to convey choices, medical counsel and other decision support services to members. It should be understood that members will have varying needs and means for receiving information.
- **Available Information.** CDHPs should make pricing information available to members and providers at or before point of care. This information should link the member's deductible, copay, coinsurance and spending account status to network pricing of services. This can be handled most efficiently through real-time access to information electronically such as through secure Web portals or telephone.
- **Availability of Quality Data.** Providers should be encouraged (via incentives) to submit clinical quality data to CDHPs and to reputable third parties using Health Insurance Portability and Accountability Act (HIPAA)- and state privacy law-compliant approaches for analysis and presentation to the public.
- **Lower-Wage Earners.** CDHPs should consider steps for reducing the likelihood that lower-wage employees will be offered and will select plan designs with unaffordable out-of-pocket maximums.
- **Chronic Illness.** CDHPs should consider several options for assuring that the special needs of the chronically ill are met.
- **Health Risk Assessment.** CDHPs should consider including a health risk assessment tool and provide effective consumer information concerning preventive services.
- **Catastrophic Coverage.** CDHPs should continue to include a catastrophic policy.

Early results suggest the CDHP approach can produce savings, despite the current lack of full price transparency and the availability of only relatively rudimentary quality measures. (See Table I, data from Aetna HealthFund.) There are no reliable multiyear studies looking at the impact on medical expenditures and premiums under CDHPs, whether savings are replicable

Table I

**ESTIMATED TRENDS FOR CDHP OPTIONS
2003-2004
Aetna HealthFund Results (2003)***

Overall Medical Cost Trend 2003-2004
Aetna HealthFund (CDHP)
As option	3.7% increase
As full replacement	11% decrease
Aetna comparison group	11% decrease

Factors in HealthFund Results
Primary care office visits	11% decrease
Specialist office visits	3% increase
ER visits	3% decrease
Outpatient cases	14% decrease
Inpatient admissions	5% decrease
Pharmacy costs	5% decrease
Prescriptions filled	13% decrease
Generic prescriptions	7% increase

*Numbers may not equal 100% due to rounding.
Source: Aetna HealthFund.

and sustainable, or how such savings might compare to savings under managed care plans. The Society of Actuaries has formed a work group that is gathering data on CDHPs to perform more rigorous actuarial analysis of these issues.

HOW DO THE VARIOUS SAVINGS ACCOUNTS COMPARE?

The various savings account options historically have been developed for different reasons and purposes. There is not necessarily a one-size-fits-all account. Table II compares general features of the four more common accounts: flexible savings accounts (FSAs), medical savings accounts (MSAs), health savings accounts (HSAs) and health reimbursement accounts (HRAs).

GUIDELINES FOR TRUSTEES

Trustees reviewing a CDHP option should evaluate how certain features of the CDHP will affect their fund and covered members. The following general guidelines have been prepared to assist trustees in their evaluation.

- **Affordability.** CDHP members may be faced with the risk of high out-of-pocket expenses if the cost of the health care they need exceeds the amount of funding in the health reimbursement account. Deductibles for consumer-directed plans are relatively high—generally between $2,000 and $4,000 annually. The difference between the amount in the HRA and the deductible could leave members with several thousand dollars in out-of-pocket costs.
- **Health Incentives.** CDHPs make members responsible for the difference between the amount in the HRA and the deductible. This design feature is not only for containing costs for the fund, but also for creating financial incentives for members to be more cost-conscious in making medical decisions. The trustees need to understand how the plan can be designed to assist the members in this effort.
- **Adverse Risk Selection.** A concern for CDHPs is the potential for disrupting the medical risk pool by segmenting the pool into low- and high-risk populations. This separation, it is feared, may eliminate or greatly reduce the cross-subsidization that allows individuals—especially those with high health risks—to have affordable benefits.
  —*Low-risk individuals*—typically the young and healthy—may be attracted to these low-cost, high-deductible benefit plans. They may be more willing to gamble on the probability of not getting sick or injured.
  —*High-risk individuals*—generally older workers with more extensive health care needs—may be less likely to be drawn to high-deductible insurance plans out of fear they will be forced to incur substantial health costs before the insurance benefits take effect.
- **Education.** The theory of CDHPs is that, with a fixed amount of funding to use for medical services, members will be more aware of the costs of medical services, such as physician visits, hospital stays and diagnostic procedures. Members, it is believed, will have an incentive to compare the prices and quality of different service providers before making decisions about accessing care.

There are concerns that members will shop around for the lowest cost of care without investigating the quality of that care. The lower cost medical procedure, treatment or diagnostic procedure may reduce costs, but it does not necessarily represent high-quality care. There needs to be a way for members to receive education as to the complexities of health care—specifically, health care quality and costs.

Internet-based technology can be an important tool for disseminating information to members on health care costs and quality. Telephone advice lines staffed by medical professionals to provide consumers with guidance in deciding where and how to seek care are also essential.

Table II
COMPARISON OF SAVINGS ACCOUNT PROVISIONS

	Flexible Savings Account—FSA	Medical Savings Account—MSA	Health Savings Account—HSA	Health Reimbursement Arrangement—HRA
Account Funding	Employee and/or employer	Employee or employer but not both	Employee and/or employer	Employer only
Eligibility	All employees, but not self-employed	Self-employed or small business. Must be covered by HDHP.	Insured under qualified HDHP. Not covered by other insurance (some exceptions). Not participating in an HRA or FSA (some exceptions).	Employer determined—subject to non-discrimination rules
Contributions 1. Limits	Employer specified		Lesser of 100% of annual deductible or $2,650 for single coverage and $5,250 for family coverage (in total).* Makes no difference who contributes (employee or employer).	Employer specified
2. Tax treatment	Deductions excluded from gross income	Single—65% of deductible Family—75% of deductible	Employee: Contributions are deductible. Employer: Treated as employer-provided coverage, excluded from gross income. Not subject to income tax or FICA. State tax treatment may vary.	Coverage/reimbursements are generally excluded from employee's gross income. State tax treatment may vary.
Funding Requirements	None/pay-as-you-go allowed	Prefunded trust	Prefunded trust	None/pay-as-you-go allowed
Account Information	No account is necessary. Typically only an employer bookkeeping account.	Trust created for the sole purpose of paying medical expenses. Employee is the sole owner (employer has no say).	Trust created for the sole purpose of paying medical expenses. Employee is the sole owner (employer has no say).	No account is necessary. Typically only an employer bookkeeping account.
Vesting of Account	Employer specified	100% vested/nonforfeitable	100% vested/nonforfeitable	Employer specified
Administration of Account	Generally administered by the employer	Qualified trustee or custodian; not the employer	Qualified trustee or custodian; not the employer	Generally administered by the employer
Portability/Carryover	Subject to use-it-or-lose-it rules	Employee owned; no employer responsibility.	Employee owned; no employer responsibility.	Employer specified, but generally participants may carry forward amounts to increase the maximum reimbursement in subsequent periods.
Distributions 1. Qualified medical expenses	Unreimbursed qualified medical expenses	Unreimbursed qualified medical expenses	Unreimbursed medical expenses for employee, spouse and dependents. Uninsured benefits qualify. OTC medications qualify. Premium payments do not qualify (some exceptions.)	Employer can limit reimbursed expenses, but generally: Unreimbursed medical expenses for employee, spouse and dependents. Uninsured benefits qualify. OTC medications qualify.
2. Tax treatment	Only payments of qualified medical expenses are nontaxable.	Only payments of qualified medical expenses are nontaxable. Other withdrawals are possible, but are taxed/penalized. No employer responsibility.	Only payments of qualified medical expenses are nontaxable. Other withdrawals are possible, but are taxed/penalized.	Qualified medical expenses are nontaxable.
High-Deductible Health Plan (HDHP) Requirements	N/A	Minimum deductible $1,700-$2,600/single* $3,450-$5,150 family* First-dollar preventive care allowed	Minimum deductible $1,000 single/ $2,000 family* Maximum out of pocket $5,100 single/ $10,200 family* All benefits subject to deductible (including Rx) First-dollar preventive care allowed	None

*Contribution limits, deductibles and out-of-pocket maximums are at 2005 levels. Future years will be indexed to inflation.

REFERENCES

Brudenheim, Milt. "A New Health Plan May Raise Expenses for Sickest Workers." *New York Times*, December 2001.

Cross, Margaret Ann. "Consumer-Directed Health Care: Too Good to Be True?" *MultiMedia*, September 2003.

Martinez, Barbara. "Health Plan That Puts Employees in Charge of Spending Catches On." *Wall Street Journal*, January 2002.

PR Newswire. "$460 Million Now Held in Health Savings Accounts per Inside Consumer-Directed Health Care." *Atlantic Information Services*, May 2005.

Quinn, Jane Bryant. "Paying Up for Quality Care." *Newsweek*, May 2002.

Saleem, Haneefa T. *Health Spending Accounts.* December 2003.

U.S. Department of the Treasury. Medicare Prescription Drug, Improvement, and Modernization Act of 2003.

U.S. Department of the Treasury, Office of Division Counsel. Section 223—Health Savings Accounts—Interaction With Other Health Arrangements, Revenue Ruling 2004-45, June 2002.

Chapter 26

Actuarial Analytics—A Technical Explanation

Arthur L. Wilmes

INTRODUCTION

Some statistical texts have used the metaphor of a wandering drunk to describe the activity of certain statistical systems. The image generally presented describes the activity of a drunk staggering from lamppost to lamppost in a random manner, sometimes backtracking, sometimes moving forward and sometimes moving from side to side. The pattern, though discernible, may not follow a consistent or expected route, given that the navigator is in an inebriated state of mind.

Such a metaphor also may be used to describe the behavior of group medical claims experience. Like our intoxicated friend, health claims seem to move in a random and unpredictable manner. Each new move is seemingly unrelated to the last. Catastrophic results may occur for which no advance warning was indicated (for example, suddenly landing face down in the curb).

A system describing the potential actions of the drunk can be developed. The outcome of each lamppost encounter can be modeled since each street has a limited number of lampposts. As such, the drunk has only so many opportunities to grab onto a balance point. While group health claims may represent a system with significantly more "lampposts," the potential path can be estimated by means of a statistical system that has been developed from an observation of prior claims experience. Such a system can be used as the basis for certain critical actuarial analytics that can provide trustees an understanding of health plan risk.

SIMULATION

An actuary, given access to unlimited resources, could develop parametric models that account for the many factors affecting group health claims experience. Unfortunately, expending unlimited resources to develop parametric models is not always prudent, nor is it an efficient use of resources. Very often, an actual claims database can provide sufficient information in lieu of advanced parametric models.

Stochastic Processes

A *stochastic process* can be described as a random sum of random variables. The totality of a group's health claims experience would fall within the definition of a stochastic process. The composition of the claims experience is an accumulation of discrete points that represent the actual claims experience of each individual receiving health benefits. When these discrete points are accumulated, the result is a *distribution of claims* for the group.

The development of a distribution is a major first step for any actuarial analytical process. It becomes the primary tool from which the analytics are built. Simulations would not be possible without the construction of this basic actuarial building block.

Stochastic and Deterministic Analysis

Actuaries primarily prepare both deterministic and stochastic analyses for trustees of funds. A *deterministic analysis* provides a discrete answer or evaluation result. The result of a deterministic analysis is generally the mean or average value for a distribution. Contributions, for example, result from a deterministic analysis. Projections of net assets available for benefits, claim reserve

---

Note: This technical chapter is included for trustees who would like to delve into actuarial analytics. Please see Guidelines for Trustees at the conclusion for advice on practical application.

values, or average claim values are also examples of values resulting from a deterministic analysis.

Deterministic results are necessary when one value is needed, as in the example of contribution rates. While this type of analysis has a very useful utility, an important bit of information is missing. The probability or likelihood that the deterministic value will occur is not known. The only information that we can provide for certainty is that, provided we can observe an unlimited number of trials, the average result will be that which is estimated through a deterministic analysis.

What is the Risk?

A stochastic analysis is necessary to supplement the deterministic analysis. "What is the likelihood that my claim reserve estimate will be adequate?" "What is our level of confidence that the contribution rate will be adequate?" These questions address the risk associated with decisions that result in a single point estimate. The analysis of the risk requires a stochastic model combined with a simulation process.

Stochastic Simulation

A *stochastic simulation* is composed of many runs or trials. Each trial requires the generation of a random number, which is paired with a random variable or potential outcome. In the example of a group's health claims, the distribution is composed of an infinite number of claim outcomes, each with an associated probability or likelihood of occurrence. The distribution generally includes a probability point for no claims. There are various claim levels and probabilities beyond the no-claims point with generally a long tail of claim values that exhibit high cost, but very low probability.

The generalized form of a stochastic analysis involves a series of random trials involving an underlying distribution intended to simulate random claims outcomes for a group of covered lives. The process is repeated such that one trial is performed for each life in the risk pool. For example, if it is assumed that the pool contains 5,000 lives, the process will generate 5,000 random trials. One set of trials represents one outcome for the group of lives.

The second series of random trials is generated to simulate a second set of outcomes. This process is repeated (generally 1,000 or more times) to create a distribution of potential outcomes for a group of 5,000 lives. The average of the distribution of the series of outcomes represents a point estimate of the average risk. There generally is an approximately even chance that actual risk results (assuming that the underlying distribution is appropriate) will be less than the average risk point estimate. Likewise, there generally is an approximately even chance that actual risk results will be greater than the average risk point estimate.

A series of claim outcomes will result from the simulation. The example discussed earlier assumed 1,000 trials or simulation outcomes. As such, each trial outcome can be placed in an order that is ranked from the least expensive claim outcome to the most expensive claim outcome. The average claim result is the mean value of all 1,000 trial outcomes. Since all claim outcomes are ordered, however, the analysis can be used to determine the point where a certain percentage of outcomes occur. Such is the process that can be used to determine the percentage probability that actual claims outcomes will be less than or equal to a certain point estimate. This point can be determined by reviewing the outcomes of the simulations and determining the point estimate where the desired percentage appears. For example, an 80% probability would select the point estimate associated with ordered trial number 801. All outcomes below this point represent the 800 simulations that are less than simulation 801.

CASE STUDY— USING SIMULATION TO EVALUATE EXCESS LOSS REINSURANCE

Excess loss insurance or reinsurance is also known as stop-loss or medical stop-loss. The difference between the terms *insurance* and *reinsurance* is whether the fund is fully insured or self-insured. The description *excess loss insurance* is generally used to define the transaction for a self-insured fund.

Two Types

Excess loss coverage consists of two types:
- **Individual**—Protects against large individual claims for single (or individual) members
- **Aggregate**—Protects against an excessive amount of total claims for all members combined.

Excess loss is a financial arrangement that assumes customers with budget management and protection of surplus and reserves. Both forms of stop-loss limit the risk of claims volatility due to large individual claims or a variance in aggregate claims experience. Over time, and if the risk has been evaluated appropriately, the stop-loss insurer expects to collect sufficient revenue to pay all claim obligations plus a gain/return for providing budget stability to its customers. It can be considered to be a line of credit to cover surprise financial demands, so that the surprises can be amortized over a number of risk cycles. The excess loss insurer is the intermediary responsible for organizing a risk pool for spreading excess loss risk among groups of paying customers.

Figure 1 illustrates how a $50,000 excess individual insurance arrangement limits the effect of large claims. The contrasting "peaks" are flattened into "mesas" by the excess insurance. One can visualize the amortizing nature

Figure 1

CLAIMS EXPERIENCE EXAMPLE

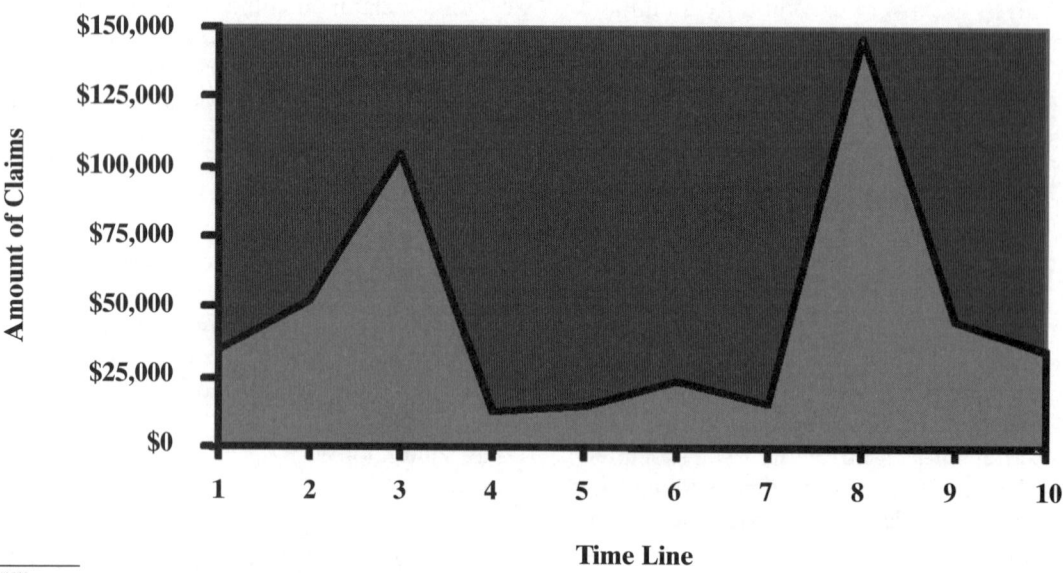

Source: Milliman.

of excess loss insurance if these peaks were used to fill in the contrasting valleys that occur between the peaks.

ACTUARIAL TOOLS FOR EXCESS LOSS ANALYSIS

An actuarial analysis of excess loss insurance, in part, includes a self-analysis of the risk specific to the group. The purpose of this analysis is to estimate the base risk for claim volatility so as to better assess the relative financial value (or fairness) of the excess loss proposal.

The basic actuarial tool for a risk analysis is a claims probability distribution (CPD). The CPD provides, for select groups of claim levels, the frequency (or probability) that the claim level will occur, as well as the estimated financial value of the average claim occurring at that probability level. The table illustrates a sample CPD.

The first column in the chart provides the range of the claims levels; in other words, the average claim falling within the range endpoints shown in the range. The remaining columns are numbered and defined as follows:

1. **Members.** This column "counts" the number of covered members with annual claims within each corresponding claim range in the adjacent column. The total number of lives appears at the bottom of the column.
2. **Annual Frequency.** This column summarizes the percent of total members that appear in Column 1.
3. **Total Claim Amount.** This column is the sum of all eligible claims associated with the members in each row.
4. **Total Annual Claim.** This column is the average annual claim per member and is equal to Column 3 divided by Column 1.
5. **Annual Cost of Claims.** This column is the "expected value" of the average claim. It is equal to Column 4 times Column 2. It can be viewed as the probability adjusted value of the average claim.
6. **Probability Claims Are Greater Than or Equal to Column 4.** This column is the inverse sum of Column 2.
7. **Annual Cost of Claims Greater Than or Equal to Column 4.** This column is the inverse sum of Column 5.

There are many uses for a CPD. One basic purpose is to estimate the value of claims that exceed a specific excess loss level.

The estimates developed from a CPD represent an average value or outcome. Actual results, unfortunately, are not average as they are subject to variance risk. An additional actuarial tool is needed to assess the volatility of claim estimates derived from a CPD.

A second actuarial tool is a *Monte Carlo* simulation. In effect, a Monte Carlo simulation creates a distribution of outcomes for a CPD. Particular values in a CPD have an estimated probability of occurrence. This means that some claim values (those with a higher frequency) are more likely to occur than others.

Table

CLAIM PROBABILITY DISTRIBUTION

Total Annual Paid Claim Range	(1) Members	(2) Annual Frequency	(3) Total Claim Amount	(4) Total Annual Claim	(5) Annual Cost of Claims	(6) Probability Claims Are Greater Than or Equal to Column 4	(7) Annual Cost of Claims Greater Than or Equal to Column 4
0	575,137	0.2197	$ -	$ -	$ -	1.000	$ 2,529.57
1 - 50	82,261	0.0314	2,243,033	27.27	0.86	0.780	2,529.57
51 - 100	117,469	0.0449	8,753,661	74.52	3.34	0.749	2,528.72
101 - 150	99,380	0.0380	12,415,819	124.93	4.74	0.704	2,525.37
151 - 200	86,525	0.0331	15,133,136	174.90	5.78	0.666	2,520.63
201 - 250	75,662	0.0289	17,023,944	225.00	6.50	0.633	2,514.84
251 - 500	281,180	0.1074	103,012,470	366.36	39.36	0.604	2,508.34
501 - 750	191,081	0.0730	118,191,570	618.54	45.16	0.497	2,468.98
751 - 1,000	139,159	0.0532	120,971,160	869.30	46.22	0.424	2,423.82
1,001 - 1,500	192,428	0.0735	237,127,259	1,232.29	90.60	0.370	2,377.60
1,501 - 2,000	130,791	0.0500	227,006,308	1,735.64	86.73	0.297	2,287.00
2,001 - 2,500	94,830	0.0362	212,240,539	2,238.12	81.09	0.247	2,200.27
2,501 - 3,000	73,308	0.0280	200,839,551	2,739.67	76.74	0.211	2,119.17
3,001 - 4,000	104,920	0.0401	363,735,723	3,466.79	138.98	0.183	2,042.44
4,001 - 5,000	71,344	0.0273	318,933,923	4,470.37	121.86	0.14	1,903.46
5,001 - 7,500	107,045	0.0409	653,914,518	6,108.78	249.85	0.115	1,781.60
7,501 - 10,000	59,418	0.0227	513,390,130	8,640.31	196.16	0.074	1,531.76
10,001 - 12,500	35,673	0.0136	397,853,292	11,152.78	152.01	0.05	1,335.60
12,501 - 15,000	23,358	0.0089	319,032,662	13,658.39	121.90	0.038	1,183.59
15,001 - 20,000	26,402	0.0101	454,107,853	17,199.75	173.51	0.029	1,061.69
20,001 - 25,000	14,013	0.0054	312,407,056	22,294.09	119.36	0.019	888.19
25,001 - 30,000	8,538	0.0033	233,193,080	27,312.38	89.10	0.014	768.82
30,001 - 35,000	5,762	0.0022	186,490,892	32,365.65	71.25	0.01	679.73
35,001 - 40,000	3,996	0.0015	149,158,744	37,327.01	56.99	0.008	608.47
40,001 - 45,000	3,002	0.0011	127,238,954	42,384.73	48.62	0.007	551.48
45,001 - 50,000	2,279	0.0009	108,033,079	47,403.72	41.28	0.006	502.86
50,001 - 60,000	3,218	0.0012	175,813,015	54,634.25	67.17	0.00	461.59
60,001 - 70,000	2,173	0.0008	140,511,021	64,662.23	53.69	0.003	394.41
70,001 - 80,000	1,497	0.0006	111,871,387	74,730.39	42.74	0.00	340.73
80,001 - 90,000	1,106	0.0004	93,545,026	84,579.59	35.74	0.002	297.98
90,001 - 100,000	766	0.0003	72,508,431	94,658.53	27.70	0.00	262.24
100,001 - 125,000	1,256	0.0005	139,496,341	111,063.97	53.30	0.001	234.54
125,001 - 150,000	734	0.0003	100,287,848	136,631.95	38.32	0.001	181.24
150,001 - 175,000	450	0.0002	72,585,533	161,301.18	27.73	0.00	142.92
175,001 - 200,000	319	0.0001	59,814,490	187,506.24	22.85	0.000	115.19
200,001 - 225,000	206	0.0001	43,688,612	212,080.64	16.69	0.00	92.33
225,001 - 250,000	128	0.0000	30,389,956	237,421.53	11.61	0.000	75.64
250,001 - 300,000	187	0.0001	51,280,673	274,228.20	19.59	0.000	64.03
300,001 - 400,000	146	0.0001	49,274,920	337,499.45	18.83	0.00	44.44
400,001 - 500,000	53	0.0000	23,466,769	442,769.23	8.97	0.000	25.61
500,001 - 1,000,000	49	0.0000	31,113,968	634,978.94	11.89	0.000	16.64
> 1,000,000	9	0.0000	12,446,285	1,382,920.56	4.76	0.000	4.76
Totals	2,617,258	1.0000	$ 6,620,542,632	$ 2,529.57	$ 2,529.57		

Annual Claims $ 2,529.57

PMPM $ 210.80

Source: Milliman.

A Monte Carlo simulation iteratively creates an outcome, using a random selection process, for one simulation of a claim outcome. Each simulation is recorded and repeated. The process may be repeated up to 1,000 times or more to create 1,000 or more outcomes of a CPD simulation. The process involving 1,000 simulations can be summarized by Figure 2. The chart shows that there are times that the simulation outcome exceeds the average. This chart summarizes the volatility for the claims outcomes. The reader will note that it takes the familiar "bell curve shape," even though the outcomes are not a typical bell type.

Figure 3 summarizes the cumulative distribution of Monte Carlo simulations. The chart indicates that approximately 900 trials had outcomes that were up to 150% of the expected claims level.

This figure provides the following inferences:

- The 900 trials represent the 90th percentile or a 90% confidence. This can be interpreted as, out of ten chances, nine are estimated to result in outcomes less than or equal to 150% of expected cost.
- A surplus reserve fund equal to 50% of the expected cost would be needed to ensure that base fund assets are protected with a 90% confidence.
- There is an approximate 10%-12% chance that aggregate claims will exceed 125% of expected claims.
- A "fair" base price for aggregate insurance, with a 125% attachment point, would be estimated with the following formula:

(Probability that claims >125% × (Average claims in excess of expected claims) of 125% of expected claims)

assuming a 12% probability and an average excess claim equal to 175% of expected; the estimated "fair" base price would be:

(12%) × (175% − 125%) = 6% of expected claims.

Figure 2

MEDICAL STOP-LOSS EXAMPLE

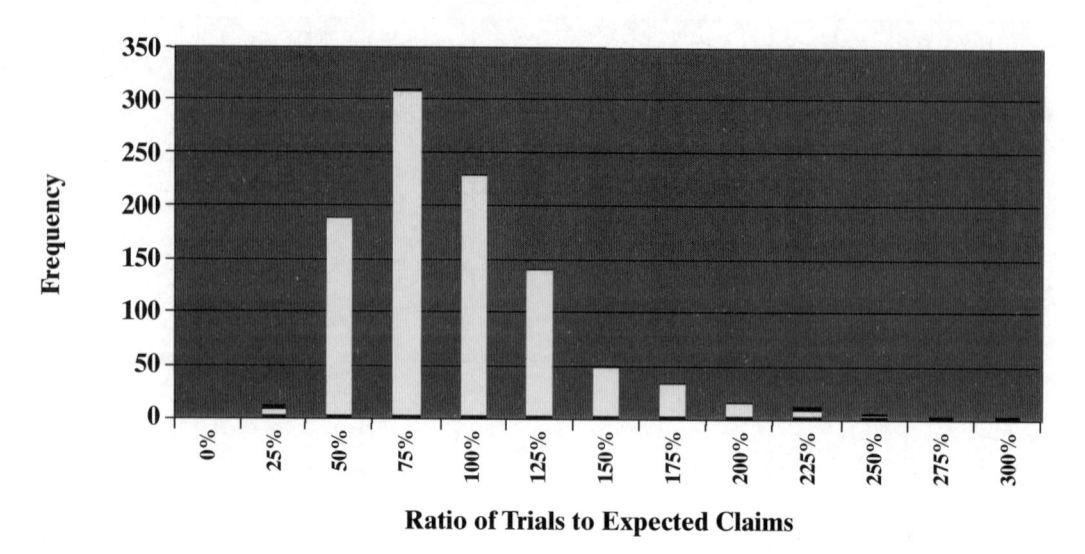

[Bar chart: Frequency vs. Ratio of Trials to Expected Claims (0% to 300%). Y-axis: Frequency 0 to 350. Bars approximately: 0%: 0, 25%: 10, 50%: 190, 75%: 310, 100%: 230, 125%: 140, 150%: 45, 175%: 30, 200%: 10, 225%: 5, 250%: 2, 275%: 1, 300%: 1.]

Ratio of Trials to Expected Claims

Source: Milliman.

Figure 3

MEDICAL STOP-LOSS EXAMPLE

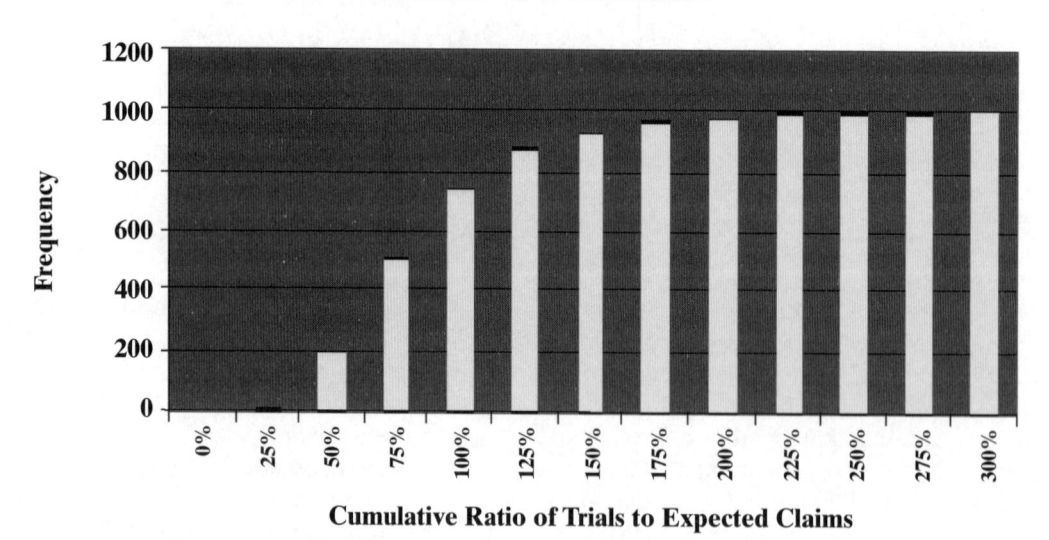

[Bar chart: Frequency vs. Cumulative Ratio of Trials to Expected Claims (0% to 300%). Y-axis: Frequency 0 to 1200. Bars approximately: 0%: 0, 25%: 10, 50%: 190, 75%: 500, 100%: 740, 125%: 870, 150%: 920, 175%: 955, 200%: 970, 225%: 985, 250%: 990, 275%: 990, 300%: 990.]

Cumulative Ratio of Trials to Expected Claims

Source: Milliman.

GUIDELINES FOR TRUSTEES

Trustees should be aware that simple deterministic actuarial techniques may not be sufficient to analyze the risk associated with health and welfare funds. Advances in computer simulation techniques now allow for more advanced risk assessment. Database management has also become more efficient, providing for more advanced deterministic actuarial models.

Trustees should assure themselves that the actuarial analytics for their health and welfare funds include all or more of the following actuarial tools:

1. **Actuarial Cost Model.** Deterministic model that summarizes utilization and cost statistics for a health and welfare fund. The level of detail varies, but generally includes hospital inpatient services (by admission/discharge type); hospital outpatient services (by service type); physician services (by primary service type); and prescription drugs (separately for brand/generic and retail/mail).
2. **Claim Lag Tables.** Deterministic data used to estimate incurred but not reported claims liability.
3. **Claims Probability Distribution.** Statistical table that segregates claims by size and probability.
4. **Monte Carlo Simulations.** Stochastic model that may be used to assess the degree of confidence associated with actuarial estimates.

REFERENCES

Chang, Kai Lai. *Elementary Probability Theory with Stochastic Processes.* Springer-Verlag New York, Inc., 1975.

Pindyck, Robert S. and Daniel L. Rubinfield. *Economic Models and Econometric Forecasts.* Irwin McGraw-Hill, 1998.

Hoel, Paul G., *Introduction to Mathematical Statistics.* John Wiley & Sons, Inc., 1971.

SECTION V

MULTIEMPLOYER PENSION PLAN DESIGN

Foreword

Daniel F. McGinn

A significant array of economic, social and political factors affect the design of multiemployer retirement plans. Bargaining parties and trustees face great challenges as single industry plans struggle to fund retirement programs while the industry is altered gradually by employers that shift business locations out of the country and produce goods with nonunion labor. Other bargaining parties and trustees struggle to accommodate the ever-changing faces of industries that are affected dramatically by computerization, robotics and fierce international competition. Some industries are disappearing while others are being sharply modified. Finally, the massive investment losses experienced by most plans in the early years of this century have caused unprecedented funding problems.

These combined influences have de-funded many plans, causing major reductions in, and sometimes elimination of, benefit accruals. Often, workers are forced to retire while they are still able-bodied and need continued employment; sometimes, they must move into a different industry and work at a lower level of compensation. Then again, individuals with substantial seniority in their union employment often must accept nonunion work.

In light of these issues, employers often are pressed to agree to significant contribution increases to a traditional defined benefit (DB) retirement plan to retain a reasonable level of benefit accrual for active participants. However, before agreeing to contribution increase demands, employers often need assurance from plan trustees that such contributions will not precipitate a growth in unfunded vested benefit liabilities (UVBLs). An increased UVBL could be a basis for withdrawal liabilities being assessed against such employer(s) if economic conditions require the employer(s) to cease making plan contributions. Sometimes, if trustees are unable or unwilling to restructure their traditional DB plan to achieve and maintain fully funded vested benefit liabilities, employers will press for agreement by union representatives to allocate contribution increases to a *defined contribution (DC) or 401(k)* plan that is always fully funded. However, in such instances, the plight of the older plan participant who is exposed to job loss on account of mechanization, plant relocation and so forth, will obtain little financial assistance. A *DC* plan primarily benefits the younger employees who often can be retrained for computerized operations and who also have sufficient future employment years during which invested contributions can accumulate in value to an amount adequate to fund a reasonable retirement income.

The chapters of Section V address the topics outlined below.
- Basic characteristics of DB plans are explored, including alternative plan designs. IRS rules governing benefit accruals are examined and discussed.
- Minimum participation and vesting rules, benefit adjustments upon reemployment after payments commence and mandatory benefit distribution rules
- Joint and survivor pensions, including a brief discussion of payments under qualified domestic relations orders (QDROs)
- Minimum and maximum funding of DB plans
- Other plan design considerations, including a discussion of rules governing normal, early and deferred retirement are reviewed. Finally, pre- and postretirement death benefits are evaluated.
- DC plans, available as alternatives to traditional DB retirement plans, are reviewed and evaluated.

ACKNOWLEDGMENTS

This Section V reflects several technical suggestions of Rick G. Mayo, FSA. Additionally, secretarial support for the numerous drafts was provided by one of our company secretaries, Mrs. Vivian M. Shokry. I sincerely thank them for their efforts.

Chapter 27

Design of Multiemployer Plans

Daniel F. McGinn

In current times, few multiemployer defined benefit (DB) plans are being established. Rather, many small plans are merging with larger plans to reduce costs and to benefit from increased asset diversification after funds are pooled. Whether a plan is being established or merged, trustees need to understand DB plan design issues and funding practices and how such plans differ from defined contribution (DC) plans.

In the following paragraphs, the basic characteristics of DB plans are explored. Then, alternative plan designs are reviewed and benefit accrual rules are examined.

BASIC CHARACTERISTICS OF DB PLANS

The two major characteristics of a multiemployer DB plan are (1) a benefit formula, fixed in advance, that definitely determines benefits earned by plan participants and (2) specified employer contributions made pursuant to the collective bargaining process intended to fund such benefits.

The definitely determinable benefit features of DB plans insulate employees from investment risk; that risk is borne primarily by the trust fund in which contributions are invested. Also, employers may bear some of the risk because of minimum funding requirements or, upon withdrawal from plan participation, through the assessment of withdrawal liabilities. As a consequence, actuarial assumptions and methods must be selected by actuaries so the definitely determinable benefit levels can be supported by negotiated contributions made on a "best estimate" basis of expected future experience. As experience evolves, actuarial assumptions and contribution requirements may require change to reflect actual investment results, employee turnover, age retirement patterns, the incidence of deaths and administrative expenses.

DESIGNING A DB PLAN

Generally, one of three principal categories of formulas is used in calculating benefits to determine a participant's monthly pension. The formulas may determine the monthly lifetime pension as:
- A unit (in dollars) per year of service
- A unit of benefit based on *final contributions rate* and years of service or
- A percentage of annual employer contributions.

For each category, a wide variety of formulas may be used. The formulas are structured to reflect the anticipated retirement needs of the covered participants, the level of contributions, the demographic characteristics of the participants and the enrolled actuary's assumptions and methods.

The perceived need of participants generally will guide the trustees in the design of a DB plan as they evaluate the answers to these basic questions:
- What should the normal retirement age be? Age 65? Should retirement be allowed and considered "normal" after 25 or 30 years of contributory service regardless of participant age?
- Should employee service with the contributing employers before plan participation be recognized and, if so, how many years should be counted?
- How many years of service should be required for early retirement and at what age should early retirement be allowed? Should benefits earned up to the date of early retirement be actuarially reduced to limit the cost of early retirement?
- How might subsidized early retirement benefits be granted while
  —Limiting increases in unfunded vested benefit liabilities
  —Minimizing additional funding charges?

- Should a participant be granted a monthly benefit if he or she becomes disabled? If so, should minimum conditions be met before the participant is entitled to the benefit (e.g., entitlement to a Social Security disability award)? How should the benefit be determined? Should the benefit be the full earned benefit or should it be actuarially reduced, subject to some minimum amount (for example, 50% of the earned benefit)?
- Should a spouse be protected if the participant dies before or after retirement? Both the Employee Retirement Income Security Act of 1974 (ERISA) and the Retirement Equity Act of 1984 (REA) mandate a certain form of spouse protection. However, there are several ways to provide such benefits. Consequently, in lieu of a lifetime monthly income, a lump sum might be allowed to be paid under certain conditions. Trustees may wish to evaluate whether or not to allow such arrangements. Also, they may decide that some of the cost of the protection should be borne by the participants rather than being absorbed entirely by the trust fund.
- After a covered employee begins to participate in a retirement plan, how many years of vesting service should be required before benefits earned become fully or partially nonforfeitable? Most multiemployer plans currently use a five-year cliff vesting schedule, but a graded vesting schedule might be advantageous.
- Should postretirement benefits be protected from erosion by inflation in some manner? What are the cost implications and funding requirements of any form of cost-of-living protection?

The trustees will address these questions, depending on the pressures from the bargaining parties and will rely on both legal counsel and the actuary to evolve a plan structure that reflects the responses to these questions while satisfying the requirements of an IRS-qualified plan. Nevertheless, in designing the plan to satisfy IRS qualification requirements, numerous provisions are mandatory.

In the following several paragraphs, three classifications of benefit formulas are discussed, and the ERISA rules governing how participants accrue (earn) benefits under these DB plan formulas are explored. In following chapters, other basic plan design matters are examined.

ALTERNATIVE BENEFIT FORMULAS

Unit Benefit

Under this type of formula, a monthly pension unit of, say, $25 per month is earned for each year of benefit service. A year of benefit service is normally granted for a specified number of covered hours (e.g., 1,500 or 1,800 covered hours), but past service is sometimes based on elapsed time if it is difficult or impossible to get records of hours before the establishment of the plan. Sometimes, if a retiring employee with substantial past service and little future service would otherwise receive a monthly pension of less than $200 or $300 per month, a flat minimum benefit is provided.

Initially, the unit often was the same for both past and future service, where past service is covered employment rendered before the establishment of the plan and future service is subsequent covered employment. As time elapsed and contribution rates escalated, many plans substantially increased the benefit unit for past service or only allowed moderate increases in the benefit unit for past service.

For example, when the monthly pension benefit per year of service was at a level of $10, $20 or some smaller amount, usually no distinction was made between past and future service benefits. However, as contributions increased and the number of pensioners and covered participants nearing retirement age grew, trustees began to realize that future service benefits might be seriously curtailed if past service benefits were kept at the same level as future service benefits.

Currently, many pension plans that provide a benefit unit per year of service and reflect relatively high contribution rates also provide past service benefits of, perhaps, $10 to $15 per year of service. On the other hand, numerous plans have retained the concept of equal benefit rates for both past and future service even though the practice may limit the level of benefits that can be earned by newly entering plan participants.

As years have passed and contribution rates have been increased periodically, trustees have also realized that, *if the benefit unit for all future service is constantly increased,* the plan's unfunded liabilities likewise increase dramatically even when the past service benefit unit has not been improved. In other words, it's just as much a problem to continually increase all benefit credits earned after the establishment of the plan as it is to continually increase past service benefits.

To control the proportion of employer contributions required to amortize unfunded liabilities, some plans decided to improve only future service benefits attributable to service rendered after a contribution increase, rather than all future (contributory) service benefits. Under this arrangement, there would be one benefit unit for original past service and two or more different future service benefit units. The past service benefit unit might be $10; the initial benefit unit for future service (up to the plan anniversary when contributions are increased) might be $20; and the future service benefit unit thereafter might be $50.

Another element considered in this type of unit benefit formula is the number of past service credits that are allowed and, perhaps, the total combined number of past and future service benefit credits granted under the plan. For example, a limit of ten or 15 years of past service credit is often imposed, but some plans count all past service credits with essentially no limit.

When plans are established for industries where employees usually work for a single employer, past service benefits may be limited to only the continuous employment of the participant with the employer that makes the first contribution on the participant's behalf. Occasionally, a maximum number of benefit units will be imposed under a plan so that no more than 25 or 30 benefit units, whether they are past service units or future service units, will be allowed.

Final Contribution Rate Benefit

The majority of benefit formulas are established to provide specified benefit units per year of service, and increased benefits are only granted by positive trustee action from time to time as contribution rates change or favorable experience dictates a need for an increase. There are formulas that gear pension benefits to the final contribution rate or final average contribution rate. The contributions may be expressed in dollars and cents per hour or in dollars per week or month.

Under this type of formula, the hours worked or weeks worked are accumulated and a year of benefit service is granted for, say, 1,800 hours or 50 weeks worked, depending upon the particular plan's basis of required contributions. For example, an employee who worked 18,000 hours over a number of years would have earned ten benefit service years. Thus, under this method, the number of years of contributory service is determined and a specified benefit unit will be multiplied by that number of years. The benefit unit will be directly related to the final contribution rate or final average contribution rate.

The *final contribution rate* will often be defined as the contribution rate applicable to the bargaining unit in which covered employees worked the majority of their hours or weeks during the last three to five years of covered employment. With this formula, the benefit unit for past service is frequently the same as the unit applicable to future service, but the benefit unit for past service could be a single specified benefit dollar amount, such as $10 per year of past service, independent of the final contribution rate.

If the benefit unit is based on the *final average contribution rate,* the average may be determined as the average rate applicable to the bargaining units in which covered employees worked during their last five or ten years of service. Under both of these formulas, every time the contribution rate increases, all prior contributory service benefits (and sometimes past service benefits) are automatically increased, creating substantial increases in unfunded liabilities.

This type of benefit formula may be funded on a sound basis if the actuary establishes the benefit formula by taking into account the probable increases in contribution rates in the future. Consequently, if the benefit unit is expressed as a percentage of contributions, adjusted to reflect the expected final contribution rate (or final average contribution rate), the percentage will generally be substantially lower than the percentage that would apply in a career average plan where the benefit unit is related to actual career employer contributions made on behalf of a participant.

For example, if the percentage applied under a plan to a participant's career employer contributions were 3%, then the percentage applicable under a final rate formula might be 2%, since the final contribution rate would be used to establish the benefit unit payable on account of the participant's career hours worked.

Percentage-of-Employer-Contributions Benefit

Another formula, which has come into frequent use in recent years, establishes the monthly pension benefit for an employee as a percentage of the employer contributions; for example, the formula might be 1.5%, 2% or 2.5% of employer contributions. Sometimes, "step-rate" percentages are applied, granting a higher percentage after an individual has accumulated 15 or 20 years of service.

The specific percentage factor(s) would be established according to the actuary's cost calculations that would reflect, among other matters, the age, service, projected turnover, incidence of early retirement (and early retirement subsidies, if any), and employer contribution rate characteristics of the covered employees. This type of formula establishes the future service benefit under a plan, and the past service benefit is often fixed as a benefit unit of, say, $10 or $20 per year of past service credit. On the other hand, the past service benefit unit granted might reflect the level(s) of plan coverage available in the initial years(s) of plan coverage.

When a wide variety of contribution rates are payable under the plan, this percentage-of-employer-contributions formula is very convenient. For example, if contributions on behalf of one group of employees could be as little as $500 per year and for other groups could be $3,000 or more per year, this formula is convenient not only for recordkeeping purposes, but also for purposes of communicating benefits to employees. For a specified hourly contribution rate, this formula produces a unit pension benefit for a single plan year, and the unit benefit earned is directly proportional to the hours of service on which contributions are made.

A disadvantage to this type of benefit formula is that the past service benefit may not be adequately supported by extremely low contribution rates for some of the groups. For example, if the past service benefit unit were $25 per year of past service, it might require a minimum contribution rate of at least 50¢ or 60¢ per hour to fund both the future service benefits and the past service benefits.

ACCRUAL OF BENEFITS

Various benefits may become available if the employee's service under the plan is severed before the plan's normal retirement age. These benefits may include a vested pension if the employee terminates, a spouse pension if the employee dies, a disability pension if the employee becomes disabled, or either a reduced or unreduced pension if the employee retires early. The amount of these benefits is rarely based on the full pension benefit projected to be payable at the normal retirement age; it's more likely based on the pension *accrued* for the employee's service to the date of severance of employment. However, in the current years of corporate mergers, sometimes special contributions are negotiated to fund full, unreduced pensions for individuals who satisfy certain age and long-service conditions. In a multiemployer pension plan, a unit of benefit is usually granted for each full year of future service. Therefore, if only future service is considered and if an individual has been fully employed for each of 20 years by the time retirement age is reached, the individual typically accrues one-twentieth of the full pension payable at the age of 65 for each year of service.

Under ERISA, a plan must be designed so that the *benefits accrued for contributory service* by any single employee will at least satisfy one of the three alternative benefit accrual rules, referred to as the 3% rule, the fractional rule and the 133⅓% rule.

Under the 3% rule, the normal retirement pension must accrue at a rate of at least 3% of the maximum normal pension benefit for each year of service so that, after 33⅓ years of service, a full pension can be earned. This 3% benefit accrual alternative may be useful when a flat dollar benefit is provided at a specified retirement age. For example, if the normal retirement pension were $1,000 per month, then this accrual rule would require that an employee earn at least $30 per month (future service credit) for each full year of future service.

Under the fractional rule, the benefit earned each year must not be less than the pro-rata share of the full benefit payable at the normal retirement age. In other words, a terminating participant's benefits are computed by multiplying the participant's projected benefit by a fraction: the actual number of years of plan participation over the total number of service years that would be accumulated if the participant remained covered by the plan until normal retirement age. To illustrate, if a participant were employed at the age of 25 and a $1,000 monthly pension would be payable at normal retirement age 65, then after, say, ten years of service, the participant must accrue at least ten-fortieths of the $1,000 monthly pension, or $250. The participant would have completed ten of the 40 years of expected service.

Under the 133⅓% rule, a limit is imposed on the extent of difference between the levels of benefit units a participant can earn each year. Increases in salary, contribution rates and hours are not factored into the benefit accrual rates. Under this alternative, a plan cannot be designed so that the benefit unit accrued by a participant in a single year can exceed 133⅓% of the benefit unit accrued in any preceding year. For example, a participant would not satisfy this rule if a benefit unit could be accrued of, say, $10 per year of service for the first ten years of service and $20 per year of service thereafter. If there is to be a step-rate benefit accrual, under this rule the increase cannot exceed 33⅓%. Thus, in this latter instance, the benefit unit could not exceed $13.33 (= $10 × 133⅓%) for service after the first ten years. If a plan's level of benefits is revised by amendment for service through a specified date due to a contribution increase or otherwise, then a new threshold for measuring prospective benefits may be established under this rule.

ERISA's accrual rules do not apply to past service benefit credits since, during that period of time, a contributing employer did not maintain the pension plan. ERISA recognizes for a multiemployer pension plan that the employer *maintains the plan* only during the periods when the employer contributes to the plan pursuant to a pension contribution agreement.

As will be discussed later in this section, ERISA requires that an employee be granted a year of vesting service if 1,000 or more hours of service are accrued during a 12-month period or year. Under ERISA's benefit accruals rules, a pro-rata portion of the future service benefit credit must be granted to each individual who accrues a vesting service year during a plan year.

For example, if a plan requires 1,800 hours of future (contributory) service to earn a full benefit credit, then an employee who earns a vesting service year and works 1,000 covered hours must accrue at least 1,000/1,800 of a benefit credit; that is, 55.6% of a full future service benefit credit must be accrued for the 1,000 covered hours.

In most plans, a full year of future service credit is earned if an employee works 1,500 to 1,800 hours in a year, and fractional credit is granted if less than 300 to 500 hours, respectively, are worked in a single year. However, the number of hours required for a full year of future service should reflect the average work year of the covered group. In some construction trades, 1,200 hours may be appropriate, and a smaller number of hours probably would be used for seasonally employed groups.

Many plans provide that no more than one benefit unit may be earned in any one plan year. For example, if an individual worked 2,000 hours for a full benefit unit, such an individual would be credited with only a single benefit unit.

This situation has troubled a great many of the union employees covered by multiemployer pension plans who believe a plan should be designed so that the benefit credit would reflect every hour worked. The plan previously mentioned could be modified to grant every covered employee a benefit credit of 1/1,500 of a full year's benefit credit for each covered hour; a *covered hour* being an hour for which a contribution is required to be made on behalf of a covered employee. With this revised formula, an individual who worked 1,800 hours would receive 1,800/1,500 of a full year's full benefit credit; that is, the individual would earn 1.2 benefit units for the 1,800 hours worked. On the other hand, if the benefit is determined as a percentage of contributions, the plan automatically gives benefit credit for every hour of service for which contributions are required.

Some bargaining agreements require contributions to be made on every hour worked, while other agreements restrict contributions to straight-time hours only or to hours of employment after a 30- or 60-day probationary period for new employees. The actual hours used for benefit accrual purposes should reflect the conditions stipulated by bargaining agreements, even though a different basis may be required for purposes of measuring vesting service.

Future benefit service also may be related to contributory weeks, and a full week of service may be granted when at least one hour of employment in a week has been rendered. The benefit accrual rules should reflect the plan under the bargaining agreements.

Regarding the accrual of past service credits, there probably are as many bases for determining the amount of benefit earned as there are multiemployer pension plans. For example, one-quarter of a past service credit may be granted for each consecutive calendar quarter immediately preceding an employee's first covered hour during which time an employer in the industry made contributions on the employee's behalf to the Social Security system.

On the other hand, another plan might grant a full year of service for each year of an unbroken series of calendar years during which the employee was at work or available for work *in the industry* immediately preceding his or her first covered hour under the plan.

Still another plan might require a minimum number of hours or weeks of employment in each past service year in order to be granted past service benefit credit. There are, of course, numerous other methods employed to determine a covered employee's past service benefit accruals.

In virtually all situations, the trustees will generally require that a minimum number of contributory future service years be earned within a short period following an employee's first covered hour in order for an employee to be eligible for past service benefit credits.

BENEFIT ACCRUALS— SPECIAL CONSIDERATIONS

The definition of an *hour of service* for purposes of benefit accrual need not be the same as the definition used for vesting service purposes. For vesting purposes, service for which compensation is paid directly or indirectly must be counted; for benefit accrual purposes, only contributions made or required to be made under a bargaining agreement need to be recognized.

The phrase *required to be made,* as it applies to benefit accrual, is very important because it implies that contributions may not actually be made for such hours of service. In other words, any period of time when hours of service are rendered by an employee and for which employer contributions are required under an acceptable written agreement must be counted for benefit accrual purposes, even though the employer may have become bankrupt and the plan may never receive such contributions.

With this fact in mind, it is important to establish rules that determine the period of time a written agreement is acceptable while an employer is delinquent so that a limit is placed on the extent of the benefit accrual. In other words, when an employer is delinquent in contributions for a period of three to six months, the plan may deem that the written agreement is no longer acceptable and contributions are no longer required so benefits will not continue to accrue. This safeguard is necessary to maintain the sound funding of a multiemployer pension plan—primarily because of the danger that the required contributions will not be recovered from a bankrupt employer.

Another matter of great importance to a multiemployer pension plan relates to the conditions that apply if past service benefits are increased from time to time as contribution rates rise; a plan could sustain a substantial and unanticipated increased financial burden if those benefits could not be canceled if the employer withdraws prematurely. Under ERISA, past service credits earned attributable to service with an employer that withdraws from a plan may be canceled under certain circumstances if that employer ceases making contributions to the plan.

However, it is important that the trustees carefully evaluate the granting of additional past service credits as contribution rates increase. Perhaps, in lieu of past service benefit improvements, trustees might decide to grant for past service only *supplemental benefits* for active employees who retire directly from service and who have originally earned past service credits.

Under ERISA's 3% accrual rate, as long as each contributory year's benefit credit earned is at least 3% of the maximum benefit payable for the specified level of employer contributions, and a participant has the opportunity to earn 33⅓ years of contributory service, such supplemental benefits would not have to be accrued by any individual.

The supplemental benefits (for past service) might be payable only to employees who retire from active participation. Employees who become vested either before or after the employer ceases to contribute to the multi-employer pension plan might not be entitled to such supplemental benefits.

Chapter 28

Minimum Participation and Vesting, Postretirement Age Benefit Adjustments and General Benefit Distribution Rules

Daniel F. McGinn

PLAN COVERAGE CHARACTERISTICS

A multiemployer retirement plan can cover any type of employee group such as hourly employees, part-time or seasonal employees and employees in many sectors of the economy. The particular type of employee group covered will—to the extent required or allowed under ERISA—be reflected in the plan's eligibility requirements for participation. In the balance of this chapter, the general philosophy of trustees will be examined vis-à-vis plan coverage, the service requirements for participation, and the general and specific treatment accorded certain employee groups.

A multiemployer retirement plan must at least meet the same participation requirements as a single employer corporate plan. However, because of the unique characteristics of multiemployer plans, the eligibility provisions often are different from and more liberal than corporate retirement plans. ERISA generally requires that a plan maintained by an employer include all employees who have reached the age of 18 and have completed one year of service. Few, if any, multiemployer retirement plans incorporate these limits in establishing plan participation requirements. The reason is simple: The many collective bargaining agreements between employers and a union require that contributions be made for all employees within a bargaining unit, regardless of age. Sometimes bargaining agreements require contributions on all hours worked. Since employer contributions to multiemployer retirement plans have been considered by employees to be a form of deferred wages, participation in most pre-ERISA plans normally had been either immediate or deferred only until contri-butions were required. Occasionally, under defined benefit (DB) plans, when an employer group has a high level of turnover, employer contributions are deferred or made at a reduced level for up to three or six months for newly hired employees under a bargaining agreement. Under a defined contribution (DC) plan, participation is generally immediate regardless of employee turnover, and a portion of the forfeitures (limited to one or two months) might be applied to pay administrative and operating expenses. Although rare, if a multiemployer retirement plan requires *employee* contributions, the plan participation would commence when the employee contributions commence—often after a three-month or other probationary employment period.

SERVICE REQUIREMENT FOR PARTICIPATION—GENERAL

Employees covered by multiemployer retirement plans may, during a single year, work for several employers that contribute to the plan. For this reason alone, service under these retirement plans is measured according to the number of hours, days, weeks or months of service with *all* contributing employers in a plan year, depending on the terms of the plan and the bargaining agreements. Consequently, this combined employer service is counted in determining when an employee becomes a participant. As can be recognized, due to the nature of multiemployer retirement plans, the requirements for plan participation involve considerations quite different from those of a single employer, corporate retirement plan.

ERISA specifically provides that an employee who is

over age 18 must be eligible to participate in a retirement plan no later than the earlier of (1) the first day of the first plan year commencing after the completion of a year of service or (2) six months after the completion of a year of service. A standard year of service is earned when an employee accumulates 1,000 hours of service within a continuous 12-month period from the date of hire. If an employee fails to earn 1,000 hours of service within this 12-month period, then the 12-month period may be measured from the anniversary of the *date of hire* or may be based on plan years for the purpose of determining eligibility for participation. If the employee then earns 1,000 hours of service during such period, he or she must become a participant no later than stated above. This rule can apply continually from one employment anniversary date to the next anniversary date or from plan year to plan year.

For DB plans, if the minimum participation requirements of ERISA, exclusive of the age requirement, are incorporated into a multiemployer retirement plan's eligibility provisions, 1,000 hours of service would be required within the 12-month period immediately following an employee's date of hire. If this tack is followed, the hours of service records of a covered employee would have to be examined for the initial 12-month period following his or her first covered hour, and an employee who satisfies this eligibility requirement would have to be allowed to commence plan participation no later than the earlier of (1) the first day of the first plan year beginning after the date on which the employee first satisfied such requirement or (2) six months after the employee first satisfied such requirement. The record of an employee who continues in covered employment but fails initially to meet the 1,000 hours of service requirement would have to be tested in successive 12-month periods based on either anniversaries of hire date or plan years to establish whether or not the employee has met the participation requirements.

Following these specific ERISA eligibility rules can be somewhat complicated. Consequently, the effective date of a covered employee's plan participation may not require any hours of service for establishing plan participation; that is, an employee may be allowed to become a participant when the employee first has a contribution made on his or her behalf. On the other hand, one of the principal reasons plans require a minimum number of hours of contributory service for an employee to become a participant is to avoid having to distribute a great volume of materials to employees shortly after their employment and before the administrator has established adequate records for these newly entering employees. Usually, newly hired employees are subject to a high rate of turnover, and many trustees have established minimum participation requirements to limit the extent to which the administrator must obtain and maintain name and address files for transient employees who are hired and work a very short time but who do not remain in employment for at least 1,000 hours of service.

Administration of a participation requirement can be simplified by allowing entrance into plan participation at six-month intervals during a plan year. For example, if a plan is on a calendar-year basis, plan participation might be allowed on January 1 or July 1 of the plan year for any covered employee who met the 1,000 hours of service requirement during the immediately preceding 12-month period. Alternatively, an even more simplified approach might be adopted to reduce administrative efforts. For instance, the effective date of participation under a multiemployer retirement plan might be established as of the first day of the month immediately following an employee's accumulation of 1,000 hours of service with all contributing employers in any two consecutive plan years. This technique for determining the effective date of an employee's participation under the plan eliminates the complexities inherent in the literal application of ERISA's eligibility rules and will generally allow an earlier date of plan participation at little additional administrative cost.

Although multiemployer DB retirement plans may follow the precise ERISA participation rules, under the simplified participation rule previously suggested, a plan administrator need only accumulate the hours of service reported for each employee from month to month and then establish when and if the employee first participates in the plan. Using the standard year of service rule, an employee who never works 1,000 hours in any two consecutive plan years will not participate in the plan. When an employee's participation date is defined by the simplified participation rule, any past service credits may be limited to those employees whose contributory service began within the 24-month period *immediately preceding* the date when the employee first meets this participation requirement. This technique controls the extent to which past service benefits are allowed under a plan by limiting past service benefits to those employees who are in substantial employment immediately following the date when an employer first contributes to the plan. For example, if an employee earns 300 hours of service in the first plan year that contributions are made on his or her behalf and 700 or more hours of service in the next plan year, the employee may be granted past service credit for unbroken service before the date of the first contributory hour. On the other hand, if 300 hours of service are earned in the first year, 500 hours of service in the second year, and 600 hours of service by the end of the third year, the employee would become a plan participant in the third plan year but may not be granted past service credits because the period of noncontributory service ended (at the time of the first contributory hour) more than 24 months before the employee became a plan participant.

Certain exceptions may be made to the regular eligibility rules for plan participation when a new employer unit is first covered under the plan. Under the latter circumstance, all bargaining unit employees may be covered immediately as plan participants with the effective date of the employer's first contribution on their behalf. One of the principal reasons for this exception to the regular eligibility rules is that the plan should not require long-service existing employees to meet normal eligibility requirements.

HOURS OF SERVICE FOR PARTICIPATION

Under ERISA the standard rule is that not more than 1,000 hours of service can be required to qualify for the one year of service which, as a minimum, may be required as one of the conditions for participation in a retirement plan. The hours of service counted must be hours for which compensation is paid by an employer *directly or indirectly*. An hour of service must include time for which an employee was compensated while on a leave of absence, jury duty, disability, layoff, vacation, holiday, in military service (when the employee's rights are protected by law) and, of course, all hours worked for which compensation was actually paid. In addition, if an employee is granted a back payment award, the value of the award must be converted into an equivalent number of hours of service for which the payment was made. These requirements, which fix the determination of service on a more liberal basis than "hours for which employer contributions to the plan are required to be made," adds complexity to plan administration.

In recognition of the administrative complexity of these types of hours of service, Department of Labor regulations allow, among others, the following several alternatives to the standard 1,000 hours of service requirement:
1. 870 hours of service, in which case hours of service relating to leaves of absence, jury duty, disability, vacation, holiday, layoff and military service may be disregarded (i.e., only hours worked for which compensation is received and certain hours for which back pay is awarded need be included).
2. 750 hours of service in which case overtime hours may be disregarded in addition to the service omitted in item 1 above.
3. Elapsed time, under which one year of service is granted for each 12-month period of unbroken employment.
4. An alternative year of service may be established under which each month or partial month of employment is deemed to include 190 hours of service. Under this alternative an employee who is employed for five months and one day is deemed to have worked for six months and, therefore, achieves the 1,000 hours of service required for plan participation.

In addition to these several alternatives, special rules apply to the maritime industry because of its unique problems.

Thus, in order to avoid the administrative burdens of counting hours of service for periods when no contributions are required, the alternatives generally provide for more liberal conditions for participation than the basic ERISA rules. For most plans, there is little cost impact resulting from adoption of these liberal rules. The reason is that a marginal member of a covered employee group (one whose employment is sporadic or minimal) who becomes a participant due *solely* to the use of these more liberal participation rules, is quite unlikely to accrue sufficient service to ultimately receive a benefit.

Employment rendered by an employee with the same employer outside of the bargaining unit covered by the plan may have to be recognized for participation purposes. If an employee is employed with an employer on or after the date the employer first contributes to a multiemployer retirement plan, that service must be counted for participation purposes if the employee later becomes part of a bargaining unit for which contributions to the plan are negotiated. Thus, an employee's service outside of a bargaining unit that is *contiguous* to the employee's bargaining unit service must be counted to the extent an employer contributes to the plan during such period.

For example, assume an employer commenced contributions to a multiemployer retirement plan under a bargaining agreement in 1995 and a supervisory employee of that employer in 1995 was not included in a bargaining unit until 2004. Assume also that supervisory employees were first organized and represented by the union and the employer commenced contributions to the plan for the supervisory bargaining unit during 2004. In this circumstance, the supervisory employee's service from 1995 through 2004, inclusive, must be counted for eligibility and vesting purposes under the plan as soon as the employer contributes to the plan on behalf of the supervisory employees. In other words, as soon as the first employer contribution is made on behalf of such employee, the employee may not only become a plan participant but may also have earned sufficient vesting service to be 100% vested in all benefits.

A similar situation can occur when an employee is employed in a division of an employer that is not represented by the union and the employee is transferred to another division of the same employer and becomes an employee in a bargaining unit for which contributions are required. The nonbargaining unit service rendered before the transfer is contiguous and must likewise be counted for participation and vesting purposes. This nonbargaining unit service does not have to apply to the calculation of benefit credits.

Both types of *contiguous service* could cause administrative difficulties for a multiemployer retirement plan since information relating to such hours of service is not a natural by-product of the administration of the plan. Generally, the administrator bills an employer for an employee's hours worked in *covered employment*, but the administrator has no knowledge of the hours of service rendered by an employee not included in the bargaining unit. In fact, the administrator generally will not know which, if any, employees have this type of uncovered vesting employment.

VESTING AND BREAK-IN-SERVICE PROVISIONS

Minimum Vesting Standards

In general, multiemployer DB plans provide that a plan member's accrued benefit must vest (become nonforfeitable) under one of two alternative vesting schedules, as follows:

- *Five-year cliff vesting.* A plan member who has accumulated at least five years of vesting service must have a nonforfeitable right to 100% of his or her accrued benefit derived from employer contributions. Prior to the vesting point, the plan member would be nonvested.
- *Three to seven-year graded vesting.* A plan member must have a nonforfeitable right after three years of service to a percentage of his or her accrued benefit derived from employer contributions. For instance, after three years of service, the plan member would have a 30% right, grading up 10% per year until he or she is 100% vested after an additional seven years.

Note

1. For plan member service before 1997, the accrued benefit under a multiemployer plan must have been vested after ten years of vesting service.
2. Technically, a plan could require two years of service before a covered employee begins participation, provided that such person is immediately vested upon participation. However, such arrangement is not practical for most multiemployer plans.

Definition of *Vesting Service*

Service for the purpose of determining an employee's progress along a vesting schedule is measured according to the same rules that apply to eligibility for participation in the plan. Essentially, a year of vesting service is earned by a participant according to the particular rules of a multiemployer retirement plan and will be based on the 1,000-hour, 870-hour, 750-hour or other alternative rules, but more liberal rules may be adopted by the trustees under regulations published by the Department of Labor.

Vesting and Break-in-Service Provisions

ERISA allows a plan to establish a standard one-year break in service to be suffered by a participant who earns no more than one half of the hours of service specified in the law or regulations for one year of vesting service. For example, if the standard 1,000 hours of service is used to measure a year of service for participation and vesting, then an employee may suffer a one-year break in service if 500 or fewer hours of service are earned. If an employee incurs a one-year break in service, the employee no longer has to be considered an active participant in the plan and may forfeit all earned service and benefit credits unless he or she is already partially or fully vested in plan benefits. Whether or not an employee is vested, after a one-year break in service is incurred, a plan may again require the employee to meet its participation requirements after reemployment before again becoming an active participant.

If an employee who has incurred a one-year break in service is reemployed by a contributing employer before the accumulated number of consecutive one-year breaks in service equals the greater of five or number of vesting service years, all of the employee's vesting service years and all earned benefit credits under the plan must be reinstated upon becoming an active participant. If such employee recommences participation after the number of consecutive one-year breaks in service has equaled or exceeded the greater of five and the accumulated number of vesting service years (the rule of parity), and if the employee has no vested interest in plan benefits, all accrued vesting service and benefits are permanently forfeited, and he or she becomes an active participant just as any new employee. If the employee is vested, benefits can be forfeited because of a break in service.

The operation of this rule of parity probably has a significant impact on individual industries in which employees work sporadically; that is, a great number of hours of service in one, two or three years and very few hours of service in one or two following years. It is possible for employees under this rule to have worked continually for the same employer, have sharply fluctuating hours of service and a few years of very little service and still become vested in their accrued benefit credits. This fact can be very important in industries where the product tends to be somewhat cyclical in nature. For example, in the fish canning industry, there are years when an abundance of fish is harvested and, consequently, a great amount of work is available. However, periodically very little work is available and employees far down on the union seniority list are temporarily out of employment.

MANDATORY DISTRIBUTIONS

Federal law requires that a participant's vested benefits commence no later than April 1 following the calendar year when he or she reaches age 70½ (the mandatory commencement date) whether or not the participant is still working. If benefits are not commenced by the mandatory commencement date, the plan can be disqualified by the IRS, and the participant can suffer an excise tax of 50% on all payments due.

This mandatory commencement date does not complicate a plan's administration severely and has little or no actuarial impact on a plan's funding. Most participants do not continue working beyond age 70½. Conversely, most participants retire before the normal retirement age (usually age 65). This mandatory commencement rule requires a plan to attempt to locate vested terminated participants who have not applied for benefits so they can begin on or before the mandatory commencement date. This can be difficult for plans with incomplete records of participant dates of birth. Also, certain procedures have to be adopted including assumption that the spouse is ten years younger than the pensioner when determining the joint life expectancy (the expected payment period) of the participant and spouse if such use reduces the required minimum distribution.

SUSPENSION OF BENEFITS

Before and After Normal Retirement Date

Benefits payable to a pensioner or a participant who has reached the plan's normal retirement age may be suspended upon reemployment when the individual earns 40 or more hours of service and the plan gives appropriate advance notice of benefit suspension. Under DOL regulations, *suspendible employment* is generally considered to be work either as a regular employee or a self-employed person in

- Any industry covered by the plan
- An industry that employed the retiree when he was covered by the plan
- A trade or craft in which the retiree was employed in the geographical area covered by the plan.

Upon the plan's appropriate advance written notice of benefit suspension, a plan may provide for the suspension of pension payments that begin before the attainment of normal retirement age under relatively liberal conditions, but the suspension of benefits after the normal retirement age can only be for *suspendible employment*. Suspendible employment occurs when a participant completes 40 or more hours of service in a month in the same trade or craft in the geographical area of the plan. Before the normal retirement date, benefits may be suspended without regard to the definition of suspendible employment. Also, prior to the normal retirement date a plan can suspend benefits for service in a geographical area covered by a reciprocal agreement, or it can limit suspension of benefits to nonunion employment in the plan's geographical area. However, when suspension before the normal retirement date is not suspendible employment (e.g., employment is in a geographical area covered by a reciprocating plan), the suspended benefits must be actuarially increased once the individual reaches the plan's normal retirement age. In other words, the suspended payments must be accumulated with interest and applied to increase the individual's retirement benefit.

CASHOUT OF ANNUITY BENEFITS

A plan may provide for immediate distribution of the present value of the nonforfeitable accrued benefit under either a qualified joint and survivor annuity or a qualified preretirement survivor annuity if the present value does not exceed $5,000. However, no distribution may be made after the annuity starting date unless the participant and his or her spouse (or his or her surviving spouse) consent in writing to the distribution.

In addition, if the present value of the nonforfeitable accrued benefit under the qualified joint and survivor annuity or the qualified preretirement survivor annuity exceeds $5,000, the participant and the spouse (or the surviving spouse if the participant has died) must consent in writing before the plan can immediately distribute the present value of the annuity. Written consent of the participant and/or the participant's spouse to the distribution must be given 90 days before the annuity starting date. An accrued benefit is immediately distributable if any part of the benefit could be distributed to the participant or beneficiary before the participant attains (or would have attained if not deceased) the later of normal retirement age or age 62. The failure of a participant or spouse to consent to a distribution while a benefit is immediately distributable is deemed to be an election to defer commencement of payment of any benefit for purposes of IRC Section 401 (a)(14) (relating to when benefit payments must begin).

In determining the present value of a qualified joint and survivor annuity or a qualified preretirement survivor annuity as of the distribution date, the plan is required to use an interest rate no greater than the applicable interest rate used by the PBGC in valuing a lump-sum distribution upon plan termination. The PBGC applicable interest rate is the immediate interest rate if an immediate annuity is being valued, and is a set of interest rates computed for varying time periods if a deferred annuity is being valued.

ELECTION PERIOD FOR OPTIONAL BENEFITS

Usually, DB plans are designed so a participant has options that he or she may exercise at retirement. Often, the normal form of pension is a lifetime-only pension but, sometimes, the form of pension may include a guaranteed number of payments. For example, payments may be guaranteed for 60 months. If the pensioner retires under this type of retirement form, his or her designated beneficiary receives benefits if he or she doesn't live to collect 60 guaranteed payments. The qualified joint and survivor annuity must, of course, be paid to a married retiree unless both the participant and spouse opt out of this benefit form. Finally, it is not unusual for a plan to provide one or more additional optional benefit forms.

Under current regulations, a retirement plan must provide automatic survivor benefits to the surviving spouse of a retiree under a qualified joint and survivor annuity or to the surviving spouse of a vested participant who dies before retirement under a preretirement survivor annuity. In order for a participant to elect out of joint and survivor annuity or preretirement survivor annuity coverage, the participant must obtain the consent of his or her spouse. The period for opting out of the joint and survivor annuity is called the *election period*, and it begins not more than 90 days and not less than 30 days before the participant's retirement date. If a participant does not receive a description of the optional benefit forms offered under the plan at least 30 days before his or her elected benefit commencement date, then the election period is extended. Also, if a participant requests additional information during his or her original election period, then a new election period is established. The new election period extends for an additional 90-day period from the date of requested information.

In some respects, the plan's design, including the number of optional forms of retirement benefits, can have considerable administrative impact on the plan's operation. The number of optional retirement forms requires more communication with retiring participants to explain available alternatives, and these explanations may tend to increase the number of election periods as participants attempt to decide upon the form of their retirement benefits.

Chapter 29

Joint and Survivor Pensions

Daniel F. McGinn

JOINT AND SURVIVOR AND PRERETIREMENT SURVIVOR ANNUITY REQUIREMENTS

In general, a plan must provide for survivor annuity protection both before and after retirement in order to qualify under the Internal Revenue Code (IRC). A plan is required to provide automatic survivor benefits in the form of a qualified joint and survivor annuity when a vested participant reaches his or her annuity starting date, and when a vested participant dies before the annuity starting date and has a surviving spouse.

Benefits earned to the date of retirement under defined benefit (DB) plans can be reduced to reflect the longer period of expected payment to a person who retires early. Then, again, the reduced amount can be adjusted downward to compensate for the longer period of payment and the greater total amount of payments otherwise expected to be paid to both a pensioner and spouse when retirement benefits commence early. For instance, if an unreduced single lifetime pension were payable at the normal retirement age of 65, upon the death of the participant at the plan's early retirement age of 55, the full actuarial reduction in the participant's earned benefit might be as much as 80% to 85% to provide the survivor benefit at the survivor age of 55. This generally would allow a surviving spouse a benefit equal to 15% to 20% of the participant's earned benefits.

The actual adjustment depends on specific plan features. For example, if an unreduced single lifetime pension benefit were payable at age 60, the total reduction might be 60% or 65% if the pension for the surviving spouse were payable upon the participant's death at age 55. In other words, the pension for the survivor might be 35% or 40% of the participant's earned benefits.

The adjustment generally will be based on whether the spouse is older or younger than the participant. Federal law allows a plan sponsor to require employees to pay for the cost of the pension for the surviving spouse, but notice and election requirements, together with the resulting administrative complexity, usually prompt plans to absorb the relatively small additional costs of these death benefits.

If a vested, married participant dies before he or she is eligible for retirement under a DB plan, the retirement benefits payable to the spouse can be deferred until the time at which the participant would have been eligible to retire. If deferred, the cost of this federally required surviving spouse benefit is low. Few vested participants die before the most common early retirement age of 55. Even when a death occurs, on the average, payment of a pension to the surviving spouse is deferred for many years (however, no later than the date the participant would have been eligible for early retirement, unless additional deferral of pension payments is elected by the spouse)—automatically resulting in low costs.

As discussed, a plan must allow a married participant to elect spouse pension protection if he or she is vested and will be eligible to retire before normal retirement age. Also, automatic spouse pension protection is mandated for a married participant who retires from active service, remains in service on or after normal retirement age or terminates service after eligibility for commencement of benefits—unless the plan member and spouse elect otherwise. The following sections discuss the administrative concerns regarding each of these important requirements.

Preretirement Spouse Protection

Under a plan that grants early retirement benefits, a married participant who is vested must be able to elect spouse survivor annuity protection that will apply when the plan member would qualify for early retirement. If the married participant were to elect the preretirement spouse protection, a spouse pension would become payable if the participant dies while in active employment after the coverage becomes effective and before normal retirement age.

The complexity of administration of this preretirement death benefit *on an elective basis* has prompted many boards of trustees to provide the required protection to spouses on an automatic basis *at no cost to the participants*. In this case, the administrative burden is reduced to the processing of claims for deaths that actually occur.

Postretirement Spouse Protection

ERISA requires that the pension be paid on the joint and survivor form *automatically* for a participant who retires on or after the normal retirement age unless the plan member and spouse opt out of this benefit form.

If a multiemployer plan has no early retirement provisions, information concerning this automatic joint and survivor annuity form of pension and any elections available must be communicated to a participant nine months before normal retirement age. The information provided must indicate the financial effect of any election. In lieu of delivery by mail or in person, this information can be published in an employee newsletter or can be disseminated by arranging with employers and the union to permanently post a notice if (1) all participants have reasonable assurance of seeing it and (2) the information is distributed regularly and continually.

If early retirement is allowed and the preretirement spouse pension protection is granted *automatically* to active participants, then the information concerning the automatic joint and survivor annuity form of pension must also be communicated to an active participant nine months before the qualified early retirement age.

Since many plans offer optional forms of pension at retirement, this requirement to provide information to prospective pensioners on postretirement spouse protection does not add substantially to the administrative burden of processing retirements.

QUALIFIED DOMESTIC RELATIONS ORDER (QDRO)

Another important form of survivor benefits relates to the portion of a plan member's retirement benefit that may be payable to a former spouse (or multiple spouses) under one or more qualified domestic relations orders (QDROs). Although a QDRO governing certain rights of a participant's former spouse(s) is not a plan design feature, its existence does influence the operations of every DB plan. The following brief discussion is intended to acquaint the reader with the manner in which a QDRO influences a plan's operation.

Most states currently recognize that a nonemployee spouse has a marital property interest in retirement benefits earned by a participating employee during marriage. The rules governing joint and survivor annuities discussed previously protect the nonemployee spouse's interest in retirement benefits earned by the participant during marriage. However, what happens if the marriage is dissolved? Is the participant's former spouse afforded any protection? The general rule is the plan must provide that a participant's earned benefits may not be assigned or alienated. However, the creation, assignment or recognition of a right to any benefit payable with respect to a participant pursuant to a court's QDRO is not treated as an assignment or alienation prohibited by ERISA. Thus, a QDRO may require the distribution of all or part of a participant's benefits under a retirement plan to an alternate payee.

A QDRO must satisfy the following conditions:
- The alternate payee(s) entitled to benefits, the plan participant, the name of the plan(s) to which the order applies, the date when entitlement applies and the last known mailing addresses of the alternate payee(s) and the plan participant *must be identified*.
- The amount, percentage or method of determining the amount or percentage of a participant's benefits payable to the alternate payee *must be stipulated*.
- The order must not require the plan to pay increased benefits.
- The period of payment or number of payments to which the order is applicable must be stated.
- The type or form of benefit or option required to be paid must be currently available under the plan (i.e., the order cannot require the plan to pay a type or form of benefit or option that is not provided under the plan).

The administrator of a plan that receives a domestic relations order must promptly notify the participant and alternate payee of receipt of the order and the plan's procedures for determining whether the order is qualified. Each plan is to establish reasonable procedures to determine the qualified status of domestic relations orders and to administer distributions under such qualified orders. Ordinarily, a plan need not be amended to implement the domestic relations provisions of such legislation. However, ERISA Section 206(d)(3)(G)(ii) requires *established procedures to be in writing*. If the plan administrator determines the domestic relations order is qualified, then the plan must abide by the order and pay the participant's former spouse the specified portion of the participant's pension.

One effect of a QDRO on a multiemployer plan is the possible commencement of pension benefits to a former spouse before the participant actually retires. For instance, if a former spouse is granted the right to receive a portion of a participant's benefits (the portion of a plan member's monthly pension earned while a marriage existed), the spouse can commence those benefits at the time when the participant would be eligible to retire early. The plan member could, in fact, be working in covered employment and earning additional pension credits while his or her former spouse (or spouses, if there were several marriages and divorces while covered by the pension plan) is receiving a court-ordered share of his or her pension.

Chapter 30

Minimum and Maximum Funding of Defined Benefit (DB) Plans

Daniel F. McGinn

The Internal Revenue Code (IRC) limits the tax deductibility of employer contributions to DB plans in two main methods:
1. By limiting the rate at which actuarial liabilities may be funded
2. By imposing full funding limitations (FFLs).

There are tests that need to be examined to determine the contribution limit for a particular plan.

Under ERISA, the original *maximum* tax-deductible contributions for a year were equal to the current service benefit costs plus amounts necessary to pay off certain unfunded actuarial values (including gains/losses) in level payments over ten-year periods. These contributions were further limited by a full funding limitation (FFL), measured by the excess of actuarial liabilities over plan assets, subject to *normal rules* governing tax-deductible contributions. For example, if liabilities were $5 million and assets amounted to $4.9 million, contributions would be limited to $100,000 if the $100,000 difference did not exceed the calculated maximum contribution under the first method listed above.

The Retirement Protection Act of 1994 (RPA '94) defined a new kind of current liability. The RPA '94 current liability is an expected actuarial present value of accrued benefits at the end of the year, taking account of expected benefit accruals and of expected liability releases due to disbursements during the year. It is also calculated using a liability interest rate within a specified range of the rates for 30-year Treasury bonds. (At this time such bonds are not being issued, and IRS is specifying the rates to be used for this purpose. A new index will probably be specified at some time.) The RPA '94 current liability must be calculated based on specified mortality tables.

This RPA '94 current liability has a number of funding applications. In the FFL context, 90% of the RPA '94 current liability provides a minimum FFL amount. In particular, regardless of ERISA, the FFL for a plan will not be less than 90% of the end-of-year RPA '94 current liability, minus the actuarial asset value (also projected to the end of the year).

When contributions are not limited by the FFL, the RPA '94 current liability can increase tax-deductible contribution amounts since multiemployer plans may receive tax-deductible contributions up to the amount needed to fully fund the RPA '94 current liability even if these contributions exceed the standard tax-deductible amount of the current service cost plus allowable amortization of unfunded actuarial values, gains/losses, etc., as previously mentioned. The RPA '94 liability is also used to increase the minimum required contributions for corporate (but not multiemployer) plans that do not meet specified funding levels.

CALCULATING THE MAXIMUM TAX-DEDUCTIBLE CONTRIBUTIONS FOR ANY YEAR

In general, the maximum tax-deductible contribution under IRC Section 404 is an amount equal to the normal cost (or current service cost) for the plan year, plus an amount necessary to amortize all unfunded actuarial liabilities or actuarial gains or losses in equal annual payments over a period of ten years from the establishment of the amortizable amount. However, the maximum tax-deductible contribution cannot be less than the minimum funding required by IRC Section 412.

The maximum deduction so calculated is then compared with the FFL; i.e., the amount of contribution that would cause a plan to be considered fully funded by the end of the year under IRS rules and regulations. The FFL serves as the ceiling for the maximum tax-deductible contribution calculated as described above. In the final step, the maximum deductible contribution is increased to the amount necessary to fully fund the RPA '94 current liability, if greater.

The calculation of the basic maximum tax-deductible contribution includes the items summarized below.

- *Normal Cost Plus Limit Adjustment*
  (a) Normal cost (including expenses) at the beginning of calculation year *plus*
  (b) Limit adjustment (maximum amount of contributions allowed to amortize unfunded actuarial liabilities) *plus*
  (c) Interest to end of year equals
  (d) Maximum tax-deductible contribution (= sum of a, b and c).
- *Full Funding Limitation*
  (a) ERISA FFL (standard unfunded actuarial liability projected to end of year)
  (b) RPA '94 FFL floor (unfunded portion of 90% of RPA current liability at end of year)
  (c) Full funding limitation (= greater of a and b).
- *RPA Funding Override* (= unfunded RPA current liability at end of year)
- *Maximum Tax-Deductible Contribution* (= lesser of normal cost plus limit adjustment and FFL, but not less than RPA funding override).

NOTES:
- To determine the Funding Standard Account adjustments when full funding limitations apply, the ERISA full funding limitation is adjusted by the funding standard account credit balance.
- For any plan year when employer contributions would not be tax-deductible due to the FFLs, IRC Section 412(c)(8) allows the plan to make a benefit adjustment, by plan amendment, adjusted no later than two years after the close of the plan year and retroactive to the beginning of the year of the initial overfunding, so that all employer contributions will be fully tax-deductible.

CALCULATING THE RPA '94 CURRENT LIABILITY

A calculation of current liability required under RPA '94 uses the 1983 Group Annuity Mortality tables, as specified by IRC and an interest rate that can be selected from a range of rates published by IRS.

RPA '94 current liability information *as of the beginning of each year* must include actuarial liability information broken down for each category shown below, but including the number of plan members, vested benefit liability and total benefit liability, for:

- Pensioners and beneficiaries
- Inactive vested participants
- Active participants
- Total.

The following information also must be reported:

- Expected increase in RPA '94 current liability as of January 1, 200X for benefits accruing during 200X
- Expected benefit payments during 200X
- Interest used for determining RPA '94 current liability
- Interest adjustment amount to December 31, 200X, after reflecting these amounts
- RPA current liability projected to December 31, 200X
- Actuarial value of assets projected to December 31, 200X
- Unfunded RPA current liability projected to December 31, 200X.

Chapter 31

Other Plan Design Considerations

Daniel F. McGinn

RETIREMENT BENEFITS

Throughout the prior four chapters, there has been frequent reference to a plan's normal retirement age and occasional mention of early retirement. The next several paragraphs discuss the conditions and circumstances affecting retirements. After these retirement benefits matters are discussed, there is a brief review of retirement benefit options and the conditions in which disability benefits can be paid under a plan. Finally, there is a review of both preretirement and postretirement benefits.

NORMAL RETIREMENT

The normal retirement age of most pension plans has been established at the age of 65. In some industries, the normal retirement age has been reduced to the age of 62, when Social Security benefits are first available on an actuarially reduced basis. Also, some plans have reduced the normal retirement age to 60 or even 55. Of course, when airline pilots are involved, the normal retirement age has long been set at the age of 60 because that is the latest age at which a pilot is considered to be physically able to endure the stress of that occupation. Likewise, in the fields where other risks exist, retirement ages have been set at the age of 50 or 55; for example, the public safety employees of state and municipal retirement systems (police, firefighters and guards at correctional institutions) often have a normal retirement age of 55 or 60. The underlying concept that justifies these lower retirement ages is the risk of the occupation.

In the construction trades, sometimes the retirement age has been changed primarily because of the difficulties in maintaining work opportunities for younger workers. Some plan trustees have agreed to reduce the normal retirement age not only to 60 or 55 but also to allow unreduced pensions to be payable when an active participant retires with 25 to 30 years of credited service.

One difficulty that has arisen as a by-product of reducing the normal retirement age is the fact that the benefits that become vested under a plan are due and payable to participants at the reduced *normal retirement age*. Therefore, if the normal retirement age is set at 55, 60 or 62, a *participant's vested rights* become linked to the substantially more expensive benefits of such reduced normal retirement age.

EARLY RETIREMENT

If available, early retirement rights must be extended to both active vested participants and the inactive vested participants. In general, there cannot be different treatment for active vested and vested terminated employees since the benefit to be payable at normal retirement age must be computed using the same benefit formula for all participants; i.e., for those entering retirement from *active service* and those entering from a *terminated vested status*. There is no requirement that any *special unreduced or subsidized pension benefits* payable to participants who retire early *directly from service* have to be paid to vested employees who retire early from terminated vested status. This distinction can be very important if a board of trustees wishes to allow participants who *retire early directly from service* to receive a pension benefit that is not actuarially reduced. For example, plans may allow early pension benefits to be payable in unreduced amounts to those who retire directly from service at the age of 55 or 60 or under a Rule of 85 or 80 (where the combined age and service equals either 85 or 80, respectively).

Early retirement in most plans is set at about ten years prior to the normal retirement age. In other words, most plans have age 55 as the age when early retirement may first occur. However, for early retirement benefits to be payable, many plans will require a participant to have at least ten years of vesting service (contributory service).

Under construction trade plans, the early retirement benefits may be payable at the age of 55 with, say, ten years of vesting service or at any age after 25 years or 30 years of total credited service. The benefit amount payable is often more favorable than an actuarially reduced benefit and, sometimes, is unreduced.

From a practical point of view, unless the benefit level is quite substantial, experience has shown that many employees will not retire until they qualify for Social Security benefits. Since Social Security benefits are payable in a reduced amount at the age of 62, a substantial number of early retirements under a retirement plan will occur at the age of 62. Some plans have attempted to encourage employees to retire even earlier than age 62 by introducing an early retirement benefit option that allows a temporarily increased pension until age 62 or age 65 when Social Security benefits generally are scheduled to commence and, thereafter, a reduced pension. This option is designed so the reduced pension, payable when Social Security benefits commence, will, in combination with Social Security benefits, provide total monthly payments that are approximately equal to the increased pension payable before Social Security payments begin.

DEFERRED RETIREMENT

In many instances, employees have the right to retire at the normal retirement age but they continue in service because the income they earn while employed is so much greater than their expected pension, and they are sufficiently healthy to perform their jobs well. When such an employee remains in the plan's covered employment, the benefits payable at the normal retirement age are actuarially increased during the term of the plan member's continued employment. Pension benefits earned at normal retirement age are actuarially increased to reflect both the additional investment income earned on the actuarial reserve for the earned benefits and the shorter expected lifetime over which the payments will be made once the deferred retirement age has been reached. If an employee defers retirement, death benefits normally paid upon death before the normal retirement age are often reduced or eliminated. If a retired employee reenters covered employment, pension benefits usually may be suspended if he or she works in "suspendible employment" for more than 40 hours per month. Under the latter circumstances, the employee often would receive no additional pension credits during such reemployment even though contributions may be made on his or her behalf.

DISABILITY RETIREMENT BENEFITS

Most multiemployer DB pension plans have adopted some form of disability income protection for plan participants. Sometimes, these benefits become available after a participant has accumulated at least ten or 15 years of total credited service, including several years of future credited service. Often, the benefit becomes available only after a participant has become vested under the plan. With the general adoption of a five-year vesting schedule by multiemployer DB pension plans, many plans now allow disability benefits to be payable only when an individual becomes vested under the plan.

The more common form of disability benefit is a monthly pension of 50% of the participant's unreduced earned pension benefit or, if greater, the benefit that a participant could receive if he or she were to retire early. In a number of multiemployer pension plans with relatively high contribution rates, the full accrued pension benefit without actuarial reduction may be paid upon a participant's disability. Sometimes, the full accrued pension benefit will be payable if a participant is totally and permanently disabled and unable to perform work of any kind.

For most multiemployer DB pension plans, it is impractical for the trustees to establish whether a participant is, in fact, eligible for a disability pension. Consequently, many multiemployer DB pension plans rely exclusively upon the Social Security Administration's determination of whether or not an individual is disabled. In general, SSA requires that an employee be totally disabled and that the disablement be expected to last at least one year. In addition, before any disability benefit award is granted, SSA requires that the disability be deemed permanent and that the employee not be capable of being rehabilitated to perform other work.

Because of these several conditions, many employees who are disabled sufficiently so that they can no longer perform the tasks required of their trade or craft are not, nonetheless, granted a Social Security disability award. If an employee is, in effect, disabled from performing work required of his or her trade or craft but is unable to receive a Social Security disability award, sometimes multiemployer DB pension plans allow a *partial disability pension* and will require objective evidence that the participant is disabled. The evidence may involve medical and/or psychological examination by one or more physicians designated by the plan administrator. Sometimes a board of trustees will retain a physician as a consultant and will require certification of disability by a physician who is designated by the local medical board of review as qualified to perform the examination and to give an informed professional opinion.

In general, a plan must provide for survivor annuity

protection both before and after retirement in order to qualify under IRC. The cost of the preretirement death benefit protection can be borne by the participant (usually by a reduction in benefits at retirement), but most multiemployer plans absorb the relatively small cost of this important benefit. As discussed previously, a DB plan is required to provide automatic survivor benefits in the form of a qualified joint and survivor annuity when a vested participant reaches his or her annuity starting date, and when a vested participant dies before the annuity starting date and has a surviving spouse.

NOTE

Under a DC plan (discussed in the next chapter), the automatic survivor coverage rule also applies unless:

1. The plan is not subject to federal minimum funding standards (e.g., a profit-sharing plan); DC plans generally are subject to minimum funding standards.
2. The plan provides that the participant's entire nonforfeitable accrued benefit will be paid to the spouse on the participant's death. An exception would be acceptable if the spouse consents to the participant's designation of a different beneficiary.
3. The participant does not elect payments in the form of a life annuity.
4. The plan is not a transferee plan with respect to the participant. A plan is a *transferee plan* if it has received a transfer of benefit value(s) that were held under a DB plan, a DC plan subject to minimum funding or a DC plan subject to automatic surviving spouse benefits.

If a DC plan is subject to the qualified joint and survivor annuity rules, it must provide an annuity to the surviving spouse with an actuarial equivalent of not less than 50% of the participant's nonforfeitable account balance unless the spouse consents to a different form of distribution.

POSTRETIREMENT DEATH BENEFITS

A common postretirement death benefit, payable upon the death of an unmarried participant, guarantees the plan would pay the remaining balance of, say, 60 monthly benefit payments if the participant dies before that number of payments has been made. This type of benefit may be payable under either a normal or optional form of pension. Many plans provide only a straight life pension (life only) with no form of death benefit protection. Regardless of the normal form of pension (life only, 60 months certain and life, etc.), a married participant jointly with his or her spouse must opt out of the automatic qualified joint and survivor annuity pension for any form of optional death benefit to be payable.

For a plan to satisfy the requirements of the IRC, if a participant is married at the time of retirement, the participant must receive the earned normal pension benefit *in a reduced amount* in the form of a qualified joint and survivor annuity *unless* the plan member and the spouse elect to receive either the normal form of pension or an optional form of pension available under the plan. The qualified joint and survivor annuity is the actuarially reduced equivalent of the participant's earned normal pension. Upon the retired participant's death, his or her surviving spouse must be provided with a lifetime pension of at least 50% of the participant's reduced pension. The participant must have the right to make an alternative pension option election, jointly with his or her spouse within a reasonable period of time prior to actual retirement. In general, if this automatic joint and survivor form of pension becomes effective, there may be a 10% to 15% reduction in the participant's normal pension benefit to pay for the cost of the death benefit (the reduced survivor pension) provided to the spouse if the normal form of pension does not provide for a guaranteed number of payments. The reduction will be smaller if a special number of pension payments are guaranteed under the basic plan. Most plans do not subsidize this actuarial reduction at retirement, and probably few participants will allow this reduced joint and survivor pension form to become effective unless the amount of their monthly pension is substantial or either the spouse or participant have a health impairment. In other words, unless a participant determines that the reduced joint and survivor pension and the participant's Social Security benefits will allow him or her to receive a reasonable retirement income, most participants would elect not to receive this joint and survivor pension.

Chapter 32

Defined Contribution (DC) Retirement Plans—An Alternative to Defined Benefit (DB) Plans

Daniel F. McGinn

INTRODUCTION

Until the passage of the Multiemployer Pension Plan Amendments Act (MPPAA) in 1980, in general, there was little interest expressed during the collective bargaining process in DC plans because they do not provide a guaranteed monthly income at retirement. With the advent of MPPAA and the imposition of employer withdrawal liability when an employer ceases contributions to a DB retirement plan with an unfunded vested benefit liability, DC plans took on a new attractiveness to contributing employers. Since DC plans are designed to be fully funded and there is no guaranteed pension benefit, a contributing employer's liability is limited to the required contributions.

Since 1980, there has been a significant growth in the number of multiemployer DC plans. In the following paragraphs, the features of money purchase, profit-sharing and 401(k) programs are explored as they exist in the multiemployer plan environment. A brief description of a target benefit plan is included later in this chapter (essentially a variation of a money purchase plan).

GENERAL OVERVIEW OF DC PLANS

The primary characteristic of a DC plan is that the plan sponsor makes no commitment to provide employees with a predetermined (or guaranteed) level of retirement income. Benefits payable under a DC plan are always equal in value to the participant's individual account value unless a minimum benefit is provided through coordination with a DB plan. Stated simply, unless a "floor" of benefits is provided by a DB plan, benefits payable at retirement, employment termination or death are identical, i.e., they are merely the account value. By converting the account value to an annuity, a guaranteed monthly income can be provided, all subject to qualified joint and survivor annuity requirements.

Employer contributions and, in many instances, employee contributions (or employee pretax salary deferrals under 401(k) programs) are invested and an employee's retirement benefits are determined by the value of the account maintained on his or her behalf. Each employee bears the risk that the plan's investment performance may be unfavorable. Sometimes, the level of contributions initially is set to provide a desired level of retirement income, but no employee is assured that a preset benefit goal will be achieved.

ALTERNATIVE DC PLAN DESIGN

In the multiemployer plan environment, there are several types of DC arrangements available, as follows:
- Money purchase plans
- Profit-sharing plans
- 401(k) plans
- Target benefit plans.

MONEY PURCHASE PLANS

When an employer makes contributions to a multiemployer money purchase plan, the individual participant contributions are pooled for investment purposes, and individual accounts are established and maintained. Contributions are often expressed as a percentage of covered payroll, but sometimes contributions vary with the employee's age when participation begins. Employer contributions might be 10% of the employee's current W-2 wages or 50¢, 75¢, $1 or more per covered hour. In theory, the employer's contributions may be at a lower rate on the portion of the employee's wages subject to Social Security taxes. However, such a basis for employer contributions would not be found in the pension clause of the collective bargaining agreement because all covered employees are treated equally.

Generally, DC plan contributions are invested according to the provisions of a trust agreement under trustee general direction, pursuant to a stated investment policy. Investments generally will include stocks, bonds and sometimes mutual funds. The contributions might also be invested under various forms of life insurance company group annuity contracts, individual annuity contracts or guaranteed investment contracts.

Investment results are allocated periodically to each participant's account balance. The allocations of employer contributions are made monthly, and valuations of participant accounts are made annually, semiannually, quarterly, monthly, weekly or daily. Monthly valuations are the most frequent and practical arrangements for multiemployer plans.

Each participant's rights to his or her account value (resulting from employer contributions) are determined by the vesting provisions of the plans. Under a typical multiemployer DC plan, vesting would be initially deferred for only two or three months since contributions to such plans are often considered a form of deferred wages.

Perhaps the most attractive features of a money purchase plan are its simplicity of operation, ease of communication to employees and the lack of actuarial complexity intrinsic in a DB plan. No actuarial computations are required since retirement income benefits are usually provided by the purchase of annuities from an insurance company. The most important requirements for a successful money purchase plan are a reasonable level of employer contributions, favorable investment results, timely and accurate maintenance of individual participant account records and proper allocations of investment results. Forfeited account balances might be applied to reduce employer contributions, but generally are reallocated to continuing plan participants, using the same basis as for allocating employer contributions.

From a participant's perspective, a most important feature of a money purchase plan is its fully funded status. That is, the cost of all benefits is always paid for when the employer's contributions are made. No actuarial estimates of costs are required; no premiums are imposed by PBGC for plan termination insurance, and there is no employer withdrawal liability if an employer ceases contributions.

As with all types of DC plans, the participant is never certain of the actual retirement benefits to be provided until he or she retires, becomes disabled or terminates with a vested right, at which time the lump-sum value of benefits is fixed. Historically, most plans have provided for the conversion of the lump-sum value to an annuity, but retirees were able to opt for a single-sum distribution. If a vested participant receives a lump-sum distribution before age 59½, a 10% penalty tax is imposed unless, within 60 days from the date of distribution, the funds are rolled over to another IRS-qualified plan or transferred to an individual retirement account (IRA).

When evaluating the ability of a money purchase plan to provide an adequate retirement income, not only is the adequacy of favorable investment results important, but the age when participation commenced and the level of contributions are critical. For instance, if contributions began when a participant was age 25, 30 or 35, there would have been an adequate period of time to accumulate a significant account value and to have weathered economic cycles that impact investment results.

On the other hand, if contributions began at the age of 50 or over, there often is not an adequate period to accumulate a substantial account value and provide a reasonable level of retirement income. (Some individuals consider investment results as favorable when the investment return outpaces the average rate of compensation increases during plan participation while others use the Consumer Price Index as a measuring rod to evaluate investment success.) Many DC plan participants are disillusioned with their prospects of having an adequate retirement benefit due to the devastating effect of stock market value declines in the 2000 to 2002 period. This experience demonstrates the investment risk borne by the participants who participate in DC plans!

PROFIT-SHARING PLANS

In many respects, the technical operation of a profit-sharing plan is similar to a money purchase plan and every other type of DC plan. The principal difference between a profit-sharing plan and other DC plans is that an employer does not need to make contributions every year. However, in the multiemployer plan environment, if there is a joint labor-management sponsorship of a profit-sharing plan, the purpose generally might be to provide a vehicle for also sponsoring a 401(k) retirement savings arrangement. The latter would accommodate the investment of employee pretax 401(k) contributions and the maintenance of the resulting individual investment accounts. The employer's basic contributions and, perhaps, matching contributions equal to 25% or 50% of employee pretax contributions might be made and invested, subject to special plan and trust provisions. For instance, unlike money purchase plans, profit-sharing plans can be designed so delinquent employer contributions are not required to be credited to individual participant accounts.[1] This feature reduces the complexities caused by employer delinquencies that do not become collectible.

IRS regulations allow the employer contributions to a profit-sharing plan to be allocated to participants in a manner that takes into account the employer contributions under OASDI so that contributions may be integrated with the Social Security benefit program. This practice would allow a lower percentage of contributions to apply to compensation up to the Social Security taxable wage base and a higher contribution rate to apply to the excess. Also, IRC Section 415 limits the amount of aggregate contributions and allocated forfeitures made on behalf of any individual. These matters do not affect the operation of a typical multiemployer program since the program will not be integrated with the Social Security benefit program, and the covered employees generally are not classified as highly compensated. Rather, the same level of contributions (e.g., 5% of compensation or $1 per covered hour) generally applies to all individuals in a bargaining unit.

401(k) PLANS

The 401(k) plan is an incentive savings program that has become a most popular form of DC plan—principally when sponsored by a single employer. IRS rules and regulations have allowed employees who participate in such plans to make substantial contributions by accepting a reduction in compensation so that contributions may be made on a pretax basis. If an employer were to negotiate to provide this type of program, he generally would also negotiate to make contributions to a profit-sharing plan and trust. Such contributions do not have to be based on "profits" since the Tax Reform Act of 1986 eliminated that condition. The covered employees would always be 100% vested in their accounts based on their pretax contributions, but any employer-funded participant accounts maintained under the profit-sharing plan would be subject to normal vesting conditions. As stated previously, DC plan contributions made by the employer are generally credited to participant accounts, and such account values may be vested after a very short period of time.

Sometimes, 401(k) programs may allow hardship withdrawals or loans from an individual's own account. Such arrangements complicate the administration of these programs in many ways. For instance, to satisfy Treasury regulations, rigorous standards must be followed, and such distributions may be granted only in very extreme circumstances. Likewise, loans must be secured by a participant's account value, and the amount of loan is limited under the IRC. Also, ERISA sets forth specific rules governing the loan arrangement. Both types of plan features complicate the program's administration and can lead to a substantial reduction in a participant's ultimate distribution if the amounts received are not repaid in full. With participants likely to move among different employers and to be employed outside a participating bargaining unit, these arrangements generally are avoided by multiemployer plans.

For most employees, 401(k) plans represent an attractive savings vehicle. For instance, employees who cannot make tax-deductible IRA contributions can defer compensation under this type of plan. Also, older employees who may have earned a very small pension or anticipate a need to supplement Social Security benefits also might find these programs quite useful. Even employees who expect to remain with an employer and in covered employment for only a few years can use a 401(k) program to accumulate savings under a tax-deferred arrangement, and such an arrangement continues to provide a very valuable savings vehicle for the long-term employee. At the time of this writing, there are very few "true" multiemployer 401(k) plans. Often, a plan that is really a money purchase plan may be referred to as a 401(k) plan as a convenient way to describe the plan.

TARGET BENEFIT PLANS

A fourth plan is a target benefit program. Its essential features are that it is designed to "look like" a DB plan even though it is a form of DC plan; and, at the start, individual allocations to participant accounts are calculated like the individual costs of a DB plan. In other words, a benefit goal or target benefit is established, generally recognizing projected service and current contribution rates.

By making a few assumptions, we can illustrate simply both the individual costs and the plan design features common to many target benefit plans. For example, assume the plan's retirement benefit target is to provide an annual pension benefit of $250 for each year of service and also that a new participant is 25 years old and normal retirement is fixed at the age of 65.

If the cost of a lifetime pension of $1 annually, beginning at the age of 65, is $12 and the plan is never changed, we calculate the following results:

- Target benefit: $10,000 annually (= $250 per year × 40 years)
- At the age of 65, the value of the target benefit is $120,000 (= $10,000 × 12)
- The level annual cost at 6% is about $731. This amount will accumulate to approximately $120,000 over the 40-year period from age 25 to age 65.

If $731 is contributed to an individual's account at the beginning of each year (i.e., contributions equivalent to about 35¢ per hour for a 2,076 hour year) and all monies are invested and earn 6% annually, the account balance will accumulate to about $120,000. Annually, actual investment results are allocated directly to the account. The participant's ultimate value is determined by actual investment experience, not the assumed 6% rate used to fix the contribution. That is, if the fund earns 8% each year, the account balance could grow to equal about $205,000 after 40 years. On the other hand, if a participant's account balance is heavily invested in equities and market values are subjected to periodic and significant downturns, as experienced in the 2000 to 2002 period, actual investment results might produce a value less than $120,000 after 40 years. Such a risk of investment loss is a fundamental characteristic of DC plans.

Under this plan arrangement, when changes in contributions occur, the changes result in a revised target benefit amount. Upon death, disability, retirement or termination in vested status, the account value is paid. The account value will be close to the target benefit at the age of 65 only if, over the period of investment, the average rate of investment results is close to the rate (e.g., 6%) assumed in establishing the initial (and, perhaps, revised) target benefit.

ALLOCATIONS OF CONTRIBUTIONS AND INVESTMENT RESULTS

There are several factors that influence how employer contributions (and pretax 401(k) participant contributions) and investment results are allocated to individual participant accounts. For instance,

- Employer contributions and participant pretax contributions generally will be remitted to the administrative office by the middle of the month immediately following the month of covered employment for which contributions are made. This practice usually would be spelled out in the collective bargaining agreement (CBA). As a consequence, the contributions often will be credited to a participant's account and invested one month after the month for which contributions are made.
- Allocations of investment results from trust-directed investments may be made in numerous ways, depending upon the cost constraints imposed by the size of the covered employee population. When there is no self-directed investment arrangement, the valuation of assets may be performed on an annual, semiannual, quarterly, monthly, weekly or daily basis. A portion of the total investment results may be applied to cover administrative and operational expense *before* net investment results are allocated to individual accounts. On the other hand, the allocation may be made on a pro-rata basis to all individual accounts. To illustrate, if one participant's account has a value of $5,000 on the date of allocation and the aggregate value of all accounts is $1 million, then that participant's account might be allocated 0.5% of the investment results (including dividends, interest, and realized and unrealized capital value changes).

If self-directed investment arrangements were allowed (e.g., when pretax 401(k) plan investments are made), then a practical and inexpensive alternative for the trustees would be to make a group of diversified mutual funds available to participants to provide the investment vehicles (options). A simple by-product of mutual fund investments is the periodic account statements that are provided for the participants by the mutual fund organization(s). Such statements include all relative information on the individual account balances (including investment results).

COMMENTS

The benefits payable when there is a retirement, a vested termination, a death or a disability covered by a DC plan are identical, i.e., the account value(s) of the participant as of the appropriate valuation date. The account value will include the sum of all contributions made, adjusted for investment results and allocated forfeitures due to employment termination of participants who were not fully vested. A plan may have provisions to allow a participant or beneficiary, as applicable, to convert the account value into a form of life annuity or joint and survivor annuity provided by an insurance company, and such an arrangement tends to make DC plans more like true retirement income plans, not cash severance programs.

OBSERVATIONS

These suggested DC plan designs have real, but limited, future value—all problems are not resolved. However, the target benefit plan may offer a relatively new way to solve some difficult problems, from the perspectives of both employers and covered employees. Reliance solely on DC account-type plans tends to misallocate funds. Often, too much is credited to younger, shorter service employees who generally will spend the accumulated account balances just as soon as they receive a distribution. This practice reduces the funds available for the older, longer service employees, diminishing the retirement incomes that could be provided by their account balances.

Perhaps the best solution is a balanced mix of DB (traditional pension) and DC plans. A combination of both types of plans is most likely to satisfy the needs of a majority of covered employees—young and old.

ENDNOTE

1. Barry S. Slevin, "Defined Contribution Plans: Obligations and Options," *Employee Benefit Issues: The Multiemployer Prospective* (Brookfield: International Foundation of Employee Benefit Plans, 1998), 513.

Checklist for Trustees on Key Points in Section V

The following is a step-by-step procedure trustees should use in formulating a pension plan design policy.

1. Articulate objectives clearly, taking into account the current pension landscape, younger as well as older employees' desires, employer pressure to restrain the growth of unfunded vested benefit liabilities and the potential occurrence of funding deficiencies.
2. Choose between the two basic plan types—defined benefit and defined contribution—only after examining the ability of each type of plan to provide adequacy and security of benefits. The legal, actuarial, investment and administrative issues unique to each type must be identified and evaluated.
3. Adopt covered employee participation rule and vesting schedule, keeping in mind the administrative ramifications of the 1,000-hour rule standard under ERISA and more liberal alternatives allowable by DOL.
4. Decide the method by which benefits are to be calculated in light of ERISA's benefit accrual rules.
5. Review the minimum and maximum funding limitations to ensure 100% tax deductibility of employer contributions.
6. Keep in mind the several recent legislative developments affecting plan design: the mandatory commencement rules, benefit suspension (before and after normal retirement date) rules and the option election period requirements.
7. Be continuously apprised of all recent legal, as well as legislative, developments that may aid or hinder plan objectives.

SECTION VI
ACTUARIAL CONSIDERATIONS

Chapter 33

The Actuarial Process

Ralph M. Weinberg

INTRODUCTION

The trustees of a multiemployer, defined benefit pension plan engage the services of a group of professionals who work together to assist in the operation of the plan. In addition to an actuary and a plan administrator, virtually all plans require the services of an attorney, accountant, one or more investment managers and an investment consultant. This chapter focuses on the role of the actuary and the actuarial process. The actuary's primary function is to assist the trustees in maintaining the financial integrity of the plan. The primary tool for doing so is the annual actuarial valuation, which is needed to determine accrued and projected future benefits payable from the plan. The results of the valuation form the basis for the information that is provided annually to the Internal Revenue Service, which is responsible for confirming that the plan is being properly funded under the rules of ERISA and the Internal Revenue Code. The actuarial valuation is also the source for information on the accumulated value of plan benefits for all participants, which must be included in audited financial statements for multiemployer plans covering at least 100 participants. The actuary is also called upon to provide assistance in a number of other ways, most notably in projecting the assets and liabilities of the plan many years into the future. This chapter will also touch briefly on the importance of such projections and also on the determination of unfunded vested benefit liabilities, which form the basis for assessing withdrawal liability to employers who leave the plan. Such an assessment is required under the Multiemployer Pension Plan Amendments Act.

THE ACTUARIAL VALUATION

Each year an enrolled actuary[1] completes an actuarial valuation of the assets and liabilities of the plan. The valuation is needed to determine the minimum required employer contribution under ERISA, the maximum allowable deductible contribution under the Internal Revenue Code, the present value of vested benefits for withdrawal liability purposes and the present value of accumulated benefits (whether vested or not) for the plan auditor. One of the major differences between single employer and multiemployer pension plans is that the employer in a single employer plan makes a decision on how much to contribute to the plan for a given year, where in virtually all multiemployer plans, the contribution rate is determined by the bargaining parties and is set forth in the collective bargaining agreement.

In order to complete an actuarial valuation, the actuary must receive participant and financial data from the plan administrator. For each active participant in the plan, the information should include date of birth, date of employment, earnings information (for plans with pay-related formulas), accrued benefit and vesting credits and the most recent year of hours/contributions required to be made on the participant's behalf. For inactive participants eligible for but not yet receiving benefits (vested terminations), the information needed is simply date of birth and the amount of the participant's accrued benefit. For retirees currently receiving benefits, the actuary needs the date of birth, the amount of benefit being paid, the form of benefit payment (life only, joint and survivor benefit, five-year certain benefit, etc.) and date of birth of any contingent annuitant. It is quite common these days for the data to include working retirees, which may require special handling by the actuary depending on the plan's rules for paying pensions when a retiree returns to perform work covered by the plan. There also may be a need to perform special calculations for benefits that have been awarded to participants' former spouses under Qualified Domestic Relations Orders (QDROs). In addition, the actuary must be provided with detailed financial information regarding the plan's assets. In most plans, the actuary uses a smoothing method to determine the "actuarial value" of assets. Doing so avoids the volatility associated with using the market value of assets.

Once the actuary is provided with the participant and financial information, the *actuarial valuation* can be completed. This valuation consists of determining the amount of fund assets required as of the valuation date to pay current and future benefits as they become due.

Inherent in these calculations is the concept of *present value*, which is best described by example: If the fund had an obligation to pay $107 one year from now, the amount of money needed today (the present value) is that amount that would earn enough interest to accumulate to $107 one year hence. If a 7% interest assumption were used, the present value of this obligation today would be $100, because $100 invested for one year at 7% would accumulate to $107.

The actual calculations the actuary completes are much more complicated than the above example because of the additional *actuarial assumptions* used in the valuation. Actuarial assumptions are needed to make reasonable estimates of the future obligations of a plan. In addition to the assumption of future investment return, the actuary must consider the following:

- Withdrawal or turnover rates—the probability that an active participant may terminate employment during a year
- Mortality rates—the probability that a participant (active, terminated vested or retired) may die during a year
- Disability rates—the probability that a participant may become disabled during a year
- Retirement rates—the probability that a participant may retire during a year
- Expenses—the estimated amount of plan expenses paid out of the fund during a year
- Benefit accrual during the year—the amount of benefits earned during the year (and future years) by a plan participant
- Rate of salary increase—if the benefit formula is based on salary levels, an assumption regarding future salary increases may also be appropriate in the actuarial valuation.

The actuarial assumptions determine the overall present value of future liabilities for the plan. However, the value is not required to be on hand nor is it required to be paid in a single year. Therefore, an allocation of the liabilities into periodic payments is developed through an *actuarial funding method*. There are a variety of acceptable actuarial funding methods that develop different schedules of funding requirements.

Under all actuarial funding methods, a *normal cost* is determined, which is the theoretical cost of benefits accruing during the year to pay for the annual benefit earned during that year when it becomes due.

An *actuarial accrued liability* is also calculated under most funding methods. This amount represents the present value of benefits earned to the valuation date under the actuarial funding method. The actuarial accrued liability less the value of assets already on hand on the valuation date is the *unfunded actuarial accrued liability*. As described later in this chapter, ERISA requires that the unfunded actuarial accrued liability be amortized over a period of years to ensure that the minimum contribution requirements are met.

The actuarial funding method and assumptions develop the expected periodic costs of the plan. However, the true costs of the plan are based on the actual benefits earned. Differences between the actual experience of the plan and the assumptions become actuarial *gains or losses*.

Under most actuarial funding methods, these gains or losses are calculated each year and become a separate component of valuation results. However, there are some methods in which gains or losses become part of the future normal cost requirements and are not separately calculated. The two most common actuarial funding methods that do not require annual gain/loss calculations are the aggregate and frozen entry age methods. Separate annual gain/loss calculations are completed for the entry age normal and unit credit methods.

Another aspect of the actuarial funding method is the *asset valuation method*. Depending upon the plan's investment policy and the types and characteristics of the plan's investments, the actuary may recommend the use of a method of valuing assets other than market value, to mitigate large fluctuations in asset values from year to year. This method may be as simple as using book value, averaging realized and unrealized gains and losses over a certain period of time or may be a method that is significantly more complex. In no event can the asset value used in the actuarial valuation be less than 80% or greater than 120% of the market value of assets, nor may the method determine a value that is consistently above or below the market value of assets.

The enrolled actuary normally recommends which actuarial funding method to use for a pension plan. Trustees should be aware of which method is employed in order to fully understand the relationship between the contribution requirements determined under the selected funding method and the actual contributions expected to be made to the plan.

IRS monitors the level of contributions made to the plan by comparing the annual contributions to a minimum and maximum requirement. (The minimum requirement is discussed in the next section on the funding standard account.)

Contributions must equal or exceed the minimum requirement or funding deficiencies will occur. A funding deficiency indicates that the plan is being funded too slowly—insufficient monies are being remitted to pay for benefits when due. A funding deficiency could subject contributing employees to potentially severe penalties.

If contributions are greater than the maximum annual requirement, the excess over the limitation will not be deductible by participating employers (in the multi-employer setting). In addition, if the plan is being funded too rapidly, trustees will need to assess whether the plan of benefits should be improved, contribution levels should be adjusted, or both, since contributions are more than sufficient to support the plan's benefit requirements. However, trustees should be aware that only current benefit levels can be reflected in the requirements. Anticipated increases in benefits cannot be funded until adopted and effective, although the rules are different for single employer plans.

To best gauge the relationship between funding requirements and actual contributions, many boards adopt a funding policy. This policy typically sets an annual funding amount that generally falls between the minimum and maximum requirements. (However, because of differing amortization requirements for minimum and maximum funding, this is not always the case.) A funding policy usually requires payment of the normal cost and expenses plus an amortization payment of the unfunded liabilities over a specified number of years over which unfunded liabilities are being amortized. In any event, it is a good idea for trustees to monitor the level of contributions compared to funding requirements to anticipate under- or overfunding before it occurs.

When the valuation is completed, the results are summarized in an *actuarial valuation report*. This report includes the development of contribution and funding policy requirements, a summary of the actuarial methods and assumptions employed and a summary of plan provisions valued by the actuary. This report is required by ERISA and includes a statement by the enrolled actuary certifying that the report is complete and accurate and that the assumptions reflect the actuary's best estimate of future experience.

MINIMUM FUNDING

Under ERISA, plan sponsors are required to meet annual minimum contribution requirements. Development of the minimum requirement and the actual contributions made to the plan are documented on the Schedule B attachment to the annual IRS reporting Form 5500. Schedule B must be signed by the enrolled actuary employed by the trustees, certifying the results as detailed in the actuarial valuation report.

A portion of the minimum requirement is developed as part of what is known as the *funding standard account* (FSA). The FSA is a historical financial account of the funding requirements since the ERISA effective date (usually 1976, for plans in effect prior to 1974).

The FSA operates very much like a bank account, where annual charges and credits are determined, resulting in a credit or deficit at the end of each year. An end-of-year credit is known as an *FSA credit balance*, which can be used to offset future minimum requirements. A deficit at the end of the year is known as an *FSA funding deficiency*, which can result in certain excise taxes and additional reporting requirements. (Funding deficiencies are discussed in more detail later.)

The actual credits and charges developed annually in the FSA are as follows:

1. Credits
   - Prior year credit balance plus interest
   - Contributions plus interest
   - Amortization of actuarial gains
   - Amortization of decreases in the unfunded actuarial accrued liability resulting from changes in actuarial assumptions, funding methods or plan provisions.
2. Charges
   - Prior year funding deficiency plus interest
   - Normal cost for the year
   - Amortization of the initial unfunded actuarial accrued liability, determined as of the date the FSA started
   - Amortization of actuarial losses
   - Amortization of increases in the unfunded actuarial accrued liability due to changes in actuarial assumptions, funding methods or plan provisions.

The difference between the charges and credits becomes the credit balance or funding deficiency.

The amortization payments of the FSA are determined in a manner similar to mortgage payments, where a specific base amount is required to be amortized over a certain period of years by annual principal and interest payments. The specific periods for the various amortization bases are as follows for multiemployer plans:

- Initial unfunded or overfunded actuarial accrued liability: 40 years
- Actuarial gains and losses: 20 years for amounts arising prior to 1980, 15 years for amounts arising during 1980 and later
- Changes in actuarial funding methods: 30 years if change results in a credit, 40 years minus number of years FSA is in effect if change results in a charge, prior to 1995; ten years for changes during 1995 and later that result in charges or credits
- Changes in plan provisions: 30 years
- Changes in actuarial assumptions: 30 years.

Under certain circumstances, extensions of certain

amortization periods may be granted by the IRS to lower minimum requirements.

In addition to the basic charges and credits described above, extra components of the FSA may be required, as follows:

- Full funding credit: When a plan is well funded, the IRS allows for a credit to the FSA where the annual minimum requirement for a plan becomes the amount necessary to fully fund current obligations. When the full funding credit applies, the amortization bases are eliminated. In future years, only new amortization bases will be recognized.
- Waived funding deficiency: If the plan reported a funding deficiency for a past year, in some cases IRS may have waived immediate payment of the deficit. If a waiver is received, the amount of the deficiency is amortized over 15 years as a charge to the FSA. No more than five waivers in any 15-year period can be received.
- Shortfall charge: Some multiemployer plans may periodically employ a funding method known as the *shortfall method*. Simply described, the contribution requirement under the FSA becomes the expected contribution for the year using the prevailing contribution rate times expected reported units (hours, weeks, months, etc.). The difference between the actual FSA requirement and the expected contributions becomes an additional adjustment to the FSA.

OTHER CONSIDERATIONS

Maximum Contribution Requirements

Contributions in excess of the maximum IRS limitations are not deductible in the current tax year by participating employers. In addition, excess contributions are subject to a 10% excise tax. Therefore, trustees must be cognizant of the limitation, as well as ensuring that minimum requirements are met.

The maximum limitation is the sum of the normal cost and expenses plus a ten-year amortization of the initial unfunded actuarial accrued liability and the bases described under the FSA. However, this limit may not be less than the FSA minimum requirement. An additional limitation is imposed on the maximum, which is the amount necessary to fully fund current obligations. Well-funded plans may be subject to this limit.

In 2002, the rules were changed to allow employer contributions to be fully deductible if in a given year, they are less than the "unfunded current liability" of the plan. The unfunded current liability is equal to the value of all accrued benefits of the plan, determined by using an interest rate that approximates current interest rate levels and a mortality table specified by the Internal Revenue Service. The prescribed mortality table may or may not be the same as the one the actuary is using as the plan's mortality assumption, but it would be a coincidence if the interest rate used for determining the "current liability" was the same as the investment return assumption used by the actuary for funding purposes. The current liability interest rate used by the actuary must fall within the permissible range of rates published by the Internal Revenue Service.

In the current relatively low interest rate environment, the contributions made by employers to almost all multiemployer plans will be fully deductible. However, if contributions are anticipated to exceed the maximum limitation, to avoid having nondeductible contributions and excise taxes trustees must either decrease contributions or increase benefit eligibility and/or levels so that the contribution requirements increase. This poses a dilemma for trustees, since contributions are governed under collective bargaining agreements. Correspondingly, improving benefits generally means a contribution requirement increase, not only for the year in question, but for future years also. However, there is a possibility of adopting certain types of improvements that do not automatically impact future years, such as a one-time lump-sum (13th check) increase to retirees. Depending on the timing of when the actuary notifies trustees of this situation, there may be other solutions, such as a temporary reduction in contributions, diverting the contributions to fund other participant benefits or temporarily parking excess contributions in an escrow fund.

Funded Status and Employer Withdrawal Liability

The actuarial accrued liability, discussed earlier, is used for funding purposes. This liability may be different from the liability for accrued benefits earned as of the valuation date because of the way the actuarial funding method allocates the total present value of benefits to the past and future. The liability for accrued benefits earned as of the valuation date is usually reported in separate categories for retirees and beneficiaries, terminated vesteds and actives. The accrued liability for actives is further split between vested and nonvested benefits.

The relationship between assets as of the valuation date and total accrued liabilities is known as the *funded status*. The difference between vested accrued liabilities and assets is the *unfunded vested benefit liability* used to calculate employer withdrawal liability. Different actuarial assumptions may be used to calculate employer withdrawal liabilities from those used for funding purposes.

The Multiemployer Pension Plan Amendments Act of 1980 (MPPAA) imposed certain liabilities on employers that withdraw from a multiemployer plan. Employer withdrawal liability is determined by an allocation of the plan's unfunded vested benefits liability to each participating employer. Except for certain industries, like construction, there are as many as four allocation methods. In certain circumstances, a different method can be employed, if approval is received from the Pension Benefit Guaranty Corporation (PBGC).

Although the calculation of withdrawal liability is complicated, the rationale for withdrawal liability is quite simple. When an employer withdraws, vested liabilities for employees of that employer remain an obligation of the plan. If the liability is not fully funded, remaining current and future employers are left with the obligation. Not only does this lower the potential to use future contributions as a means to improve benefits, but it leaves remaining employers with an obligation to pay vested benefits earned by employees of employers that withdraw. Assessment of withdrawal liability helps to mitigate these results.

Trustees must be aware of the plan's unfunded vested benefits liability to ensure that appropriate assessments are made when an employer withdraws. In addition, the trustees must understand the effects of plan changes on vested liabilities. Generally, with the exception of future service benefit improvements, most benefit improvements increase the plan's vested benefits liability, thereby increasing potential employer withdrawal liability.

Setting Benefit/Contribution Levels

The collective bargaining process is critical in determining the ultimate funded position of the plan. Under almost all collective bargaining agreements, it is the contribution rate that is negotiated. Contributions are made by participating employers based on work units such as hours, months, jobs and so on. These contributions pay for the benefits and expenses of the plan.

Under a few collective bargaining agreements, the benefit level is negotiated. Here the bargaining agreement should normally require that the contribution be determined by the plan's actuary. In a few rare instances, the bargaining parties negotiate both the contribution rate and the plan benefits. Trustees must be extremely careful to ensure that the contributions and benefit levels set correspond to funding policies and fall within the minimum and maximum IRS requirements.

In many instances, the parties involved in the collective bargaining process may be interested in what an increase in contributions can buy with respect to plan improvements. The plan's actuary can determine this by completing an actuarial valuation and determining the effects of various benefit improvements on contribution requirements.

Sometimes, changes in the collective bargaining agreement are made that do not seem to directly affect the plan. Modifications to the group covered, changes in the timing of when contributions are made, extensions on probationary periods and deferrals of contributions all affect the overall contribution dollars paid to the plan. The trustees must monitor these changes, and the plan's actuary should be kept informed so that appropriate adjustments in the valuation process can be made.

Throughout the period from 1970 through 1999, plan assets tended to grow percentage-wise in an amount at least equal to (and in most years well in excess of) the actuary's investment return assumption. There would be an occasional year like 1974 and 1994, where the assumption may not have been met but, by and large, most plans have had a steady if not spectacular rise in the level of plan assets for 30 years or more. Very few plans needed to be concerned about meeting minimum funding requirements or worrying about the plan's Funding Standard Account credit balance. When an actuarial gain due to good investment performance in 1980 became fully amortized in 1995, it tended to be replaced by a new gain due to good asset performance in 1995. Thus, the cycle continued and there was always a series of amortization gain bases being created to replace earlier gain bases that became fully amortized. During this period of growth, almost all plans increased their benefits because the plan was able to support those increases and, in many cases, benefit improvements were needed to make all employer contributions fully deductible. Unfortunately, the world changed dramatically in the years 2000-2002 where the asset performance of almost all plans fell short of meeting the underlying investment return assumption. In many cases, the plan assets actually earned a negative rate of return. If the actual investment return of the plan's assets in 2002 was -10% and the actuary was using a 7.50% investment return assumption, the plan suffered an actuarial loss on assets of 17.50%! Suddenly and unexpectedly, the cycle of replenishing fully amortized gains with newly created gains had been broken.

This turn of events has caused the role of the plan's actuary to change dramatically. The failure to regenerate new gain bases and their replacement with loss bases has put many plans into financial stress to a point where the actuary is projecting that a funding deficiency will occur at some point in the future. Virtually all actuaries serving multiemployer plans are now providing their clients with projections of whether a funding deficiency is expected to occur and, if so, when. Because there are a limited number of solutions to the problem, it is important that such projections be provided sooner rather than later. Trustees who choose to wait until a funding deficiency is just around the corner, and who are hoping that superior investment performance alone will solve the problem, are likely to find that they have simply run out of time, at which point more drastic action will be needed. The most common approaches used to address such a projected funding deficiency are contribution increases and benefit reductions. However, as a practical matter, it may take time to negotiate contribution increases due to the collective bargaining process. It is important to note that benefit cuts, in general, can only apply to benefits to be earned in the future, since generally accrued benefits are protected under ERISA. Sophisticated projection models have been developed by actuaries to allow trustees to examine the impact of various future investment performance, contribution increases and benefit changes.

ENDNOTE

1. The person signing the filing made to the Internal Revenue Service must be an enrolled actuary. The Joint Board for the Enrollment of Actuaries is responsible for setting the requirements for initial and continued enrollment, conferring the designation of enrolled actuary on qualified candidates and administering the continuing education requirements needed to maintain the designation.

Checklist for Trustees on Key Points in Section VI

1. Is the proper participant and asset data being provided to the fund's actuary on a timely basis?
2. Are the trustees keeping the fund's actuary informed on investment decisions and other issues, such as changes in collective bargaining agreements and participant age/service characteristics?
3. Do the trustees monitor the level of contributions compared to minimum and maximum IRS requirements either by use of a funding policy or annual review?
4. When changing benefit levels, do the trustees review both current and prospective contribution levels compared to the new funding requirements and the effects on employer withdrawal liability?
5. Are the trustees aware of the funding method and actuarial assumptions used to determine funding requirements? To determine vested benefit liabilities for withdrawal liability purposes?
6. Have the trustees examined both the short- and long-term implications of changes to the plan's demographics, the plan of benefits, the plan's investment policy and the funding policy?

Chapter 34

Pension Fund Mergers

Barry S. Slevin

Consideration of merging multiemployer pension funds (which I will refer to as a fund) is on the increase as a result of a number of factors impacting the operations of these funds. This chapter will focus on the process of considering a merger from the board of trustees' perspective.[1]

REASONS FOR A MERGER

There are a variety of reasons why a fund may be interested in a merger.

A key reason involves the funding status of the respective funds. In many cases, the combination of two funds can result in a merged fund that is stronger than the sum of its parts. For instance, one fund may be well-funded on a current basis, but face an uncertain or problematic future. Another fund may have current funding problems, but have strong prospects for the future. A merger of two such funds might take advantage of the strong current funding status of one and the future prospects of the other, to create a single fund that is better able to withstand short-term and long-term funding problems.

This example highlights the importance of industry trends in making a merger attractive. Many funds find themselves in declining industries, with resulting decreases in the number of active participants covered by the fund or an aging population, calling into question its long-term financial future. In such situations, it may be possible to merge with a fund covering a different industry, even one that is growing. Just like diversification in investments lowers risk, covering a number of different industries could lower the merged fund's risk of decline.

Another reason for considering a merger is the cost savings that might result. As is true with operating most financial institutions, larger multiemployer funds benefit from economies of scale. Some of the costs of operating a multiemployer fund are fixed, or do not increase proportionately based on the number of participants. For instance, measured on a per participant basis, larger funds typically have lower administration costs—whether under in-house or third party administration—as well as lower accounting, legal and actuarial costs. Custodial and investment management fees are also generally lower, since these fees are often based on the amount of assets, and therefore a larger pool of assets will result in lower overall investment fees. The cost savings attributable to lower overall administrative expenses generally is not a sufficient reason alone to merge, but it is a beneficial result of a merger.

External factors may also create conditions that make a merger beneficial. For instance, the merger of unions may create opportunities for mergers, based on some of the considerations I have mentioned. When unions merge, they may find they now have more than one fund covering their membership and it therefore makes sense to merge the funds. The increasingly common merger of international unions may present opportunities to take advantage of industry diversification, since a single international union may cover more than one industry.

With or without a merger, retirements by trustees, and difficulty in replacing their expertise, may be another reason why a merger makes sense. Many funds have difficulty finding qualified trustees who are willing to serve, and a merger may be the best way to ensure the fund will continue to be administered by competent trustees.

It is not permissible for one fund to merge to subsidize another, or, to put it more bluntly, to bail out a fund in trouble. While subsidization may be a consequence of a merger, it cannot be the purpose of the merger. The trustees of each fund must act solely and for the exclusive purpose of their own fund's participants and beneficiaries, and therefore it would be a breach of fiduciary duty for a board of trustees of a "healthy" fund to merge to benefit a weaker fund and its participants. However, that is not to say any subsidization is impermissible. By the very nature of multiemployer funds, no two funds will ever be funded on the same basis at the time of the merger or have the same future prospects. As I have noted, combining two funds may make sense based on the profile of the merged fund.

STEPS TO A MERGER

There are steps that take place when considering and implementing a merger. They may not be identified as separate tasks, and some may take place contemporaneously, but typically, a well-organized merger project involves making sure each task is performed. In some situations—a small fund merging into a large fund—a fund may not have the bargaining power to negotiate changes in the way the merged fund will operate. However, even in that situation, taking the appropriate steps to investigate the merger will uncover issues about the larger fund for the trustees of the smaller fund to consider. Similarly, if the smaller fund can make well-considered suggestions to improve how the larger fund operates, those suggestions may be adopted if the board of trustees of the larger fund agrees, acting consistently with its fiduciary duties, that the suggestions are good ones.

INITIAL EXPLORATION

To see whether it is worth the time and expense to seriously explore a merger, there is typically a period of initial exploration to see whether a merger may make sense. The first issue that needs to be addressed is the funding status of the respective funds and the benefits they provide. If the difference in funding levels is too great, then the better funded fund may not be interested in merging despite the other benefits of a merger. If the benefit designs are too different, then a merger may not make sense (although I have been involved in a number of mergers in which the merged fund retained both benefit designs). The funding of the funds, both on a separate and merged basis, is the most important issue to be considered as part of a merger, and therefore it is important the funds' actuaries analyze this issue in depth, and report to the board of trustees on the strengths and weaknesses of a potential merger. While it is beyond the scope of this chapter to address the actuarial issues that will be encountered by the board of trustees, suffice it to say it is important the actuary be involved early in the process. The actuary should communicate with the board of trustees about the implications of a merger from a number of actuarial viewpoints, such as the status of the fund viewed from the perspective of ERISA's minimum funding requirements, the current funding status, the long-term expected funding status and the impact on withdrawal liability.

Another important issue that has to be investigated early is the collective bargaining relationships and the specific language of the collective bargaining agreements calling for participation in the two funds. Again, it is beyond the scope of this article to fully discuss all the problems that can arise in the context of the collective bargaining relationships. However, it is important to note, if the collective bargaining parties do not agree that a merger should take place, they may be able to block it, depending on the language of the collective bargaining agreements. Indeed, an initial question that will have to be determined by fund counsel is who has the power to merge—the collective bargaining parties or the trustees? Obviously, if the power to merge is left with the collective bargaining parties, then the trustees can only investigate a merger and make recommendations to the collective bargaining parties—They cannot actually agree to a merger.

Governance issues also have to be addressed at an early stage, to see whether a merger can be accomplished. As a practical matter, incumbent trustees may not want to give up control over administration and therefore there should be an early discussion as to who will be on the board of trustees of the merged fund. While many funds deal with this issue by creating an expanded board of trustees, they should be aware of the pitfalls of having a large board of trustees and deal with the implications early, by agreeing, for instance, on the establishment of committees and delegating authority to committees.

Another issue that needs to be addressed early in the process is which providers will be involved in the merger and which providers will serve the merged fund. Sometimes some of the same providers serve both funds. However, when they do not, this can be a problem, especially if a provider losing a client is allowed to slow down or derail the merger process. Thus, the trustees have to analyze this issue at an early stage of the consideration of the merger, and maintain control of the process to ensure that it moves forward.

MERGER TEAM AND TIMETABLE

I have found what works best in moving a merger forward is for the trustees of the two funds considering a merger to designate a team with responsibility for moving the merger process forward. The team typically consists of at least one union and one employer trustee from each fund, as well as a designated administrative officer, counsel, accountant and actuary. Creation of such a team also leads to accountability, so the trustees can get reports on the progress of the investigation of the merger and be assured actions that need to be taken are actually performed. As part of this process, it usually helps to agree on a timetable for considering the merger, including a proposed effective date. By targeting an effective date, the trustees can establish a time line for actions to be taken. Of course, this timetable is for planning purposes only and can be revised as necessary, or abandoned completely if it is determined a merger doesn't make sense. However, targeting a specific effective date can create the incentive and accountability necessary to make sure the process moves forward.

DUE DILIGENCE

If, based on the initial exploration, it seems a merger may make sense, the next step is a more extensive investigation of each fund by the other. All aspects of the funds should be reviewed, so there are no surprises in implementing the merger. Thorough investigation also minimizes the likelihood of surprises after the merger.

The investigative stage is key to satisfying the trustees' obligation to act prudently, as required by Section 404(a)(1)(B) of ERISA (assuming it applies). The duty to act prudently requires the fiduciaries investigate all appropriate facts bearing on their decision, consider available alternative courses of action and consult with appropriate professionals as may be necessary in making their decision. The investigation of each fund by the other is the foundation of satisfying this prudence requirement.

Once the respective boards of trustees have decided to pursue a merger, there should be no limit on the information exchanged, since each fund should fully understand the implications of the merger. It is surprising what may be found in the context of such an investigation. Some of the issues we have uncovered during the due diligence process for a merger include:
- No determination of tax qualification from the IRS
- Failure to follow ERISA's reporting and disclosure rules
- Insurance contracts that are not worth the amount understood at the time of the initial merger discussions
- Funding status significantly different from what was originally represented due to different actuarial assumptions, data problems and the like
- Plan documents or amendments never adopted by the board of trustees.
- Unsigned contracts with providers, including providers supposedly acting as investment managers without any signed agreement acknowledging they are a fiduciary, as required by ERISA to create investment manager status.

While these issues can be resolved, they have to be identified before the trustees can take corrective action and move forward with the merger.

PLAN DESIGN AND FUNDING
Plan of Benefits

Clearly, one of the key discussions addresses what benefits will be provided by the merged plan. One of the greatest challenges facing trustees, even trustees who have decided that a merger should take place, is determining the merged fund's plan of benefits. The differences in benefits can be slight, or they can be so different that a merged plan seems unworkable. Indeed, one of the first tasks in considering the merger from a funding viewpoint is analyzing the cost of each plan and making sure all the differences are taken into account when comparing the two.

There are a variety of ways to deal with the differences in the benefit accruals of the respective plans. For instance, I have been involved in at least one situation in which the plans were so different the trustees decided to retain both sets of benefits intact in the merged plan. As long as all the assets of the merged fund are available to pay all the benefits, the fund will be considered a single plan under ERISA and, therefore, the fund will have the benefits of a merger. However, the fund will sacrifice some of the administrative simplicity that typically results from having a unified, single plan of benefits. Over time, the plan may become more uniform, if future amendments are applied to both programs of benefits to make them more similar.

Another way to deal with this issue is to lock in or "freeze" the benefits earned as of the date of the merger, based on the provisions of the prior plans, and adopt a different plan going forward under which all participants will earn their future benefits. In this situation, when a participant retires, his or her benefit would be the sum of the benefit earned prior to the merger plus the benefit earned after the merger, paid in a single check.

A related area of complexity involves the benefit options available to participants. When combining plans, trustees will have to decide whether to extend all of the benefit options previously provided under each plan to all participants or, as I have described in the context of benefit accruals, lock in the benefit options under which benefits have been earned as of the merger date, and have a simplified plan with one set of benefit options for post-merger accruals. Such an approach may make sense to avoid a multiplicity of benefit options going forward, but it creates administrative complexity since the merged fund will have to keep track of the separate components of the benefits that have been earned.

Trustees have to face these difficult decisions because the law has an anticutback rule that prohibits plans from reducing benefits or eliminating benefit options for benefits that have accrued already. In the recent case of *Central Laborers' Pension Fund v. Heinz,* 541 U.S. 739

(2004), the Supreme Court had occasion to address the scope of this rule in the context of a multiemployer pension plan's adoption of an amendment expanding the circumstances under which retirees' benefits would be suspended. The Supreme Court gave an expansive reading to the anticutback rule, finding that the new rule could not be applied to suspend the benefits of participants who had already retired with benefits earned under the less restrictive suspension-of-benefits rule. Thus, in considering a merger, the safest course is for the trustees to assume benefits earned to date, as well as the benefit options and rules relating to the payment of those benefits, must be preserved and may only be reduced or eliminated for benefits earned in the future. Specific features of the plan should be reviewed with fund counsel.

Withdrawal Liability

Another important issue that needs to be addressed is what withdrawal liability rules will govern the merged fund. For instance, there are a number of options under ERISA for implementing the withdrawal liability provisions, including what method will be used to determine withdrawal liability and which de minimis rule will apply. These should be addressed in the context of the merger, so there is an agreement on which withdrawal liability rule will apply after the merger.

The difference in the funded status of the two funds may lead to the conclusion that a determination of withdrawal liability based on the funding status of the merged fund would be unfair. This can take place, for instance, when one of the funds has no unfunded vested benefits, and therefore no withdrawal liability, and the other has unfunded vested benefits. In this type of situation, the merged fund may elect a special withdrawal liability rule that has the effect of preserving the separateness of the two funds solely for the purpose of determining withdrawal liability. Such a rule is not specifically enumerated in ERISA, but may be approved by the Pension Benefit Guaranty Corporation (PBGC) under ERISA Section 4211(c)(5).

GOVERNANCE AND OPERATIONS

In addition to deciding on a merged plan, the trustees also need to address other issues affecting the governance of the fund.

The issue of who will be the surviving fund's trustees is an important one. Once it is known that a merger is going forward, the trustees need to make the final decision on this issue. In some cases, the full board of trustees has delegated final decision-making authority to a committee, and in other cases the committee only has the power to make recommendations to the board. The trustees need to decide whether existing committees will continue and the scope of their authority. As I noted, even if the merging funds did not have committees, committees may make sense as a result of an expanded board of trustees resulting from the merger. The trustees should address these issues before the merger takes place, to avoid any surprises after the merger has been implemented.

Similarly, the trustees should review what policies govern the operations of the fund. A well-run fund will typically have, at a minimum, an investment policy, a delinquency policy and a trustee expense policy governing fund operations. These policies should be reviewed as part of the due diligence process, and which policies will govern the merged fund should be discussed.

Final decisions also have to be made on fund providers. Typically, the trustees will have agreed preliminarily on which outside providers will be retained by the surviving fund. If the fund has in-house administration, difficult personnel issues may have to be addressed if the merged fund wants to take full advantage of the economies of scale resulting from a merger. A merged fund office may mean that fewer personnel are needed, and the trustees need to discuss with the administrative manager of the merged fund how to deal with those issues. If personnel have to be terminated, the trustees need to decide how that is going to be accomplished, consult with counsel about the fund's obligations as an employer and decide on what benefits will be provided to terminated employees.

Addressing the issue of providers is particularly knotty when it comes to the investment arena. The trustees have to arrive at an overall investment program for the surviving fund, in consultation with the investment consultant for the merged fund. Economies of scale can be achieved through larger portfolios given that many investment managers' fees are lower for a larger portfolio. However, these economies of scale can only be enjoyed if portfolios are combined. If a fund has separate managers by style (for instance, large cap value and growth or international equities and the like) the trustees will have to review, in consultation with the investment consultant, which managers have overlapping styles and which managers complement each other. Then the trustees will have to decide which firms will manage the assets of the surviving fund. This may be an opportunity to renegotiate fees, since the surviving investment manager may end up with a portfolio larger than was contemplated when the manager was first retained.

A related issue is whether transition managers should be retained to liquidate portfolios, to reduce costs in transitioning the portfolios. This too should be addressed with the investment consultant, and fund counsel will have to negotiate a contract if one is retained.

OPERATIONS

Although I have alluded to the need to have every aspect of fund operations involved in the due diligence process, it is worth stressing the need to involve the administrative manager of each fund very early in the discussions and investigation of the merger. Trustees and other professionals sometimes do not appreciate the complications that can arise from combining funds that are maintained with different computer systems, different data and different procedures for communicating with employers and participants. It is important these differences be identified and addressed. While many of the issues involved in the merger will not impact participants, if the administrative issues are not dealt with appropriately, this increases the likelihood of disruption in implementing the merger, with attendant loss of confidence in the fund by participants and participating employers.

THE MERGER AGREEMENT

A comprehensive merger agreement is key to documenting the merger in a number of respects. First, the merger agreement is the document that formalizes the exchange of information that has taken place. Therefore, it will typically include the key documents that have been exchanged as exhibits. It also will include representations made by each board of trustees to the other regarding the fund, its status and its compliance with law. These aspects of the merger agreement are important to document the process that has been undertaken by the board of trustees in investigating the merger and serve as a record of the prudent procedures that have been undertaken. Another important benefit of such a merger agreement is that it preserves in one place documentation relating to the merged fund, in case reference to the prior trust agreement, plan and participant data is needed at a future date.

The third key benefit of a formal merger agreement is documentation of the trustees' decisions on the various issues I have discussed. Reducing these decisions to writing to create the merger agreement helps avoid any misunderstandings; indeed, the process of drafting the agreement and negotiating the language typically helps uncover issues on which there may not be a complete understanding, so they can be resolved in advance.

In addition to formalizing the exchange of information and the agreements that have been reached, there are three key issues that we typically encounter in drafting a merger agreement.

The first important issue is the liability of trustees of the fund that is going out of existence, and of former trustees who may resign in the context of the merger. The level of importance of this issue may be determined by what was uncovered in the due diligence process; if no potential problems were uncovered, the issue of indemnification and insurance may be viewed as less important, as opposed to mergers in the context of identified legal and regulatory problems. However, even if the trustees are not aware of any problems involving either of the funds, the trustees still will want to be assured of protection from legal liability.

One way to deal with this issue is to have the surviving fund indemnify any former trustees from liability. This is a helpful first step, but it is limited because Section 410 of ERISA generally prohibits a fund from indemnifying trustees against fiduciary breach. That means the total solution to the problem will typically involve ensuring that fiduciary insurance is in place to cover any claims that may be made. This is usually implemented by adding the former trustees to the fiduciary insurance of the surviving fund, or by purchasing a separate policy to cover the liability, either under a new policy or a continuation of the policy formerly held by the fund going out of existence. The relative merits of the options should be discussed with fund counsel and the fund's fiduciary insurance broker.

A second issue involves obtaining a determination of tax qualification after the merger. Clearly it is crucial that the merged fund retain its tax qualification. We typically condition the merger on the surviving fund obtaining a determination of tax qualification from the Internal Revenue Service (IRS). The merger agreement should provide specificity regarding who will obtain the determination of tax qualification and what will occur in the unlikely event it is not obtained.

Third, the merger agreement should clearly specify who will be responsible for filing the required governmental forms for the fund that is going out of existence. Unless there is a clear delineation of responsibilities, for example, retention of the former accountant specifically for that purpose as part of the merger procedures, there is a risk the final Form 5500 and other required forms will not be filed.

IMPLEMENTATION

Even after both funds agree to the merger and the merger agreement has been negotiated and signed, there is still work to be done to implement the merger. However, most of this work already should have been accomplished during the merger process, and therefore the steps to implementation should be more mechanical than discretionary at that point.

For instance, a new agreement and declaration of trust may need to be adopted, as well as the new plan and new withdrawal liability rules. A new summary plan description will have to be drafted and adopted. The fund's assets may have to be retitled to the name of the surviving entity. All the contracts will need to be amended to ensure the fund's contractual relationships are clear and in the name of the surviving fund. Notifications have to be sent to employees, employers and providers to advise them of the effective date of the merger and its impact on them. The fiduciary insurance carrier needs to be notified as well. Finally, collective bargaining agreements may have to be amended to reflect the merged entity. While it is the fund administrative personnel and professionals who should be taking these steps, it is important the trustees monitor the completion of these transitional tasks.

LEGAL CONSIDERATIONS

The purpose of this chapter has been to outline the procedural steps that should be taken to properly investigate, negotiate and implement a merger. However, it is worth briefly touching on other legal considerations of which trustees should be aware in considering a merger.

Authority to Merge and Capacity of Decision Maker

A crucial starting point when considering a merger is determining who has the authority to merge. However, even if the board of trustees has the power to decide on a merger, that does not end the inquiry. There is still a question as to the capacity in which the board of trustees is acting.

There is a split of authority on the issue of whether a board of trustees of a multiemployer plan is a settlor or fiduciary when it takes actions that, in a single employer plan context, would be considered actions by the settlor. Some courts, including in the more recent cases, have held plan design decisions are settlor functions and not fiduciary acts, even when accomplished by the trustees rather than the bargaining parties. *Gard v. Blankenburg,* 2002 U.S. App. LEXIS 2963, 27 E.B.C. 1776 (6th Cir. 2002) (amendment of a multiemployer defined benefit plan is not a fiduciary act); *Pope v. Central States Southeast and Southwest Areas Health and Welfare Fund,* 27 F.3d 211, 213 (6th Cir. 1994) (amendment of multiemployer welfare fund by trustees is a settlor act); *Walling v. Brady,* 125 F.3d 114, 120 (3d Cir. 1997) (amending multiemployer pension plan is a settlor, not a fiduciary, function); *Hartline v. Sheet Metal Workers' Nat'l Pension Fund,* 134 F.Supp. 2d 1, 12 (D.D.C. 2000) (concluding that trustees "do not engage in a fiduciary function when they design or amend a pension plan, whether or not it is a multiemployer plan"). Other courts, however, have held that trustees of multiemployer funds are fiduciaries when they amend the plan because the trustees are allocating finite trust resources. See, e.g., *Musto v. Am. General Corp.,* 861 F.2d 897 (6th Cir. 1988), *cert. denied,* 490 U.S. 1020 (1989) (referred to as dictum and not followed in *Gard and Pope*);

Chambless v. Masters, Mates & Pilots Pension Plan, 772 F.2d 1032 (2d Cir. 1985), *cert. denied,* 475 U.S. 1012 (1986) (plan amendment adopted by trustees breached trustees' fiduciary duty to act solely in interest of participants and beneficiaries).

The Department of Labor's (DOL) apparent position is that a fund's documents can designate the role in which the trustees are acting, but if the trustees are designed as settlors, they cannot use fund assets for expenses incurred in that capacity. See *Department of Labor Field Assistance Bulletin 2002-2* (November 4, 2002) (FAB). Further litigation on this issue can be expected.

In a single employer plan merger context, it is clear the employer's decision to merge plans is not a fiduciary decision and the plan sponsor is subject to liability for breach of fiduciary duty only if it does not comply with the requirement that a participant's accrued benefits must not be lower after a merger than immediately before the merger. See *John Blair Communications, Inc. Profit Sharing Plan v. Telemundo Group, Inc., Profit Sharing Plan,* 26 F.3d 360, 364 (2d Cir. 1994); *Blaw Knox Ret. Income Plan v. White Consol. Ind.,* 998 F.2d 1185, 1189 (3d Cir. 1993), *cert. denied,* 510 U.S. 1042 (1994); *United Steelworkers, Local 2116 v. Cyclops Corp.,* 860 F.2d 189 (6th Cir. 1988); *Bigger v. Am. Commercial Lines,* 862 F.2d 1341 (8th Cir. 1988).

Other than in the FAB, DOL has not addressed the issue in a multiemployer context. In Opinion 89-29A, DOL considered the fiduciary considerations under ERISA Sections 403(c) and 404(a)(1) that trustees who decide to merge plans must take into account. However, DOL did not discuss (because the question was not presented) whether those considerations apply to fiduciaries who merge plans at the direction of the plans' settlors. A district court has held that a board of trustees' decision to terminate a plan and merge it into another (without satisfying all of the merging plan's pre-merger obligations) could not be reviewed for breach of fiduciary duty because ERISA's fiduciary provisions "generally do not govern a plan sponsor's decision to terminate a welfare plan." *Jackson v. Truck Drivers' Union Local 42 Health & Welfare Fund,* 933 F.Supp. 1124, 1142 (D.Mass. 1996). However, the court drew a distinction between "the decision to terminate a plan and the manner in which that decision is implemented" and found the trustees breached their fiduciary duty by implementing a merger in contravention of the terms of the merging fund's trust agreement. *Id.* at 1143.

In a similar case, a court analyzed a merger directed by the bargaining parties and implemented by the trustees. *Bd. of Tr. of Container Mechanics Welfare/Pension Fund v. Universal Enter.,* 5 E.B.C. 1199 (S.D. Ga. 1983), aff'd, 751 F.2d 1177 (11th Cir. 1985). Where the bargaining parties negotiated a merger subject to final approval and implementation by the trustees of the funds, the court found the trustees were obligated to approve the merger absent conflict with applicable federal law, citing *UMWA Health & Ret. Funds v. Robinson,* 455 U.S. 562 (1982). Since the court found the bargaining parties' merger directive did not violate federal law, it held the trustees "breached no fiduciary duties in approving and administering the merger in accordance with the agreement between the [bargaining parties]." *Id.* at 1214.

Required Procedures

Section 4231 of ERISA contains procedures that apply to the merger of multiemployer pension plans. They include a 120-day advance notice to PBGC; the protection of accrued benefits; a determination that there is no likelihood of plan insolvency (as discussed in Section 4225 of ERISA) as a result of the merger; and required actuarial valuations. Obviously, fund counsel and the actuary should be charged with ensuring these requirements are met.

Fiduciary Responsibility

I have reviewed the key general fiduciary rules governing the trustees' consideration of a merger if they are treated as fiduciaries. They must act solely in the interests of participants and beneficiaries in deciding on whether to merge and they must act prudently, by investigating the facts, considering all reasonable alternatives and consulting with professionals as appropriate.

Prohibited Transactions

If the merger is going forward for the purpose of benefiting participants and beneficiaries, there should be no problem with the prohibited transaction rules as they relate to benefiting parties other than the participants and beneficiaries. However, one prohibited transaction problem can arise even if the transaction is in the best interests of participants and beneficiaries and does not benefit any third parties. Section 406(b)(2) of ERISA prohibits fiduciaries from acting in any transaction involving the fund on behalf of an adverse party. If there are trustees that serve on both funds considering a merger, this section can be implicated.

However, there are a variety of ways to deal with this issue, if it arises. First, if there are overlapping, but not identical, trustees, then the overlapping trustees can recuse themselves from considering and acting on the merger, leaving the nonconflicted trustees to decide on the merger. If overlapping trustees must act on the merger, then the fund can obtain a determination from PBGC, which provides an exemption under Section 408(b)(11) of ERISA. Finally, if there are other prohibited transaction concerns, the board of trustees can appoint an independent fiduciary to act on the merger.

Withdrawal Liability

Finally, there are significant withdrawal liability implications to a merger, which should be dealt with by the trustees by adopting rules that will apply after the merger. However, under Section 4211(f) of ERISA, if a withdrawal occurs in the first plan year after the merger, the withdrawal liability rules of the premerged fund will apply.

Conclusion

A merger of two multiemployer pension plans is a complicated undertaking. However, there are a number of advantages to merging, and therefore it may be in the best interests of participants and beneficiaries to do so. If the board of trustees assembles the right team and carefully investigates the merger and its implications through a methodical process, it can result in a smooth, beneficial merger that is to the benefit of everyone—trustees, participating employers and, most important, the participants and beneficiaries.

ENDNOTE

1. This article is adapted from a session on pension fund mergers presented by Mr. Slevin at the International Foundation's December 2004 Annual Conference.

SECTION VIII

INVESTMENT OF PLAN ASSETS

Chapter 35

Investment Fundamentals

Eugene B. Burroughs

The purpose of establishing a pension fund is to accumulate assets to meet current and future payments to retirees. A small increase in the rate of return on investments may have a significant impact upon benefit levels over the long run. A rule of thumb is that a consistent increase of only one-half of 1% in the annual rate of return can provide the means for increasing benefits 10-12%.

Before looking into the more complex issues connected with investing the money of a trust, it is appropriate to recognize two investment principles that are fundamental to achieving success in the investment funding process.

First, *return and risk are related.* The level of risk assumed by the trustees will determine the level of return achieved (see Figure 1).

Second, adopting and adhering to the longest investment planning horizon permissible tends to reduce overall portfolio risk since the longer holding period increases the probability that the historically expected returns from the various asset classes will, in fact, be achieved (see Figure 2).

The ultimate funding goal of the investment operations is to assure that an adequate amount of dollars will be available on a timely basis to meet the accrued benefit payments. The trustees must balance their desire to enhance the values of the trust fund with a prudent regard for the protection of the accumulated principal. With their desire to control the overall risk posture of the fund, the trustees should adopt a program that will facilitate the achievement of their long-term objectives.

To assist them in this process, the trustees ordinarily engage one or more investment managers that engage in activities targeted to achieve the trustees' investment goals. Thus, it becomes the *joint* task of the trustees and retained managers to adopt and implement policy that will lead to the creation of a diversified investment portfolio with a risk/reward posture deemed to be the most appropriate given the funding needs of the plan. To do this, the trustees must identify the funding planning horizon of their plan and stay the course.

Trustees are in the risk management business. With counsel from their actuary and perhaps an investment consultant, they must examine how the various dimensions of risk may have an impact on their fund's funding process over time. The various dimensions of risk are:
1. Financial (business) risk
2. Interest rate (market) risk
3. Purchasing power (inflation) risk
4. Manager selection risk
5. Benefits payment risk.

Financial (business) risk is the uncertainty embraced by a plan in its selection of the quality of the securities permitted for inclusion in the portfolio. What is the level of assurance that rents will be received, principal returned, dividends declared and interest payments collected?

Interest rate (market) risk is the uncertainty that the plan embraces related to the values of the securities in the portfolio during the holding period and opportunity levels upon reinvestment of those securities. Price changes in the future positively and negatively affect the value of the securities already in the portfolio.

Purchasing power (inflation) risk is the uncertainty that the plan faces in its ability to preserve the purchasing power of its accumulated assets. This is particularly important for a pension plan, since it is deemed socially desirable to assure that the participants and beneficiaries will be able to maintain a standard of living throughout their retirement years not too distant from what they enjoyed in their first year of retirement. Even a "modest" level of inflation, say 3%, over a ten-year period can reduce the purchasing power of a retirement benefit payment by almost 50%! (See Figure 3.)

Figure 1

**LEVEL OF RISK ASSUMED DETERMINES
LEVEL OF RETURN ACHIEVED**

HIGH

R
E
T
U
R
N

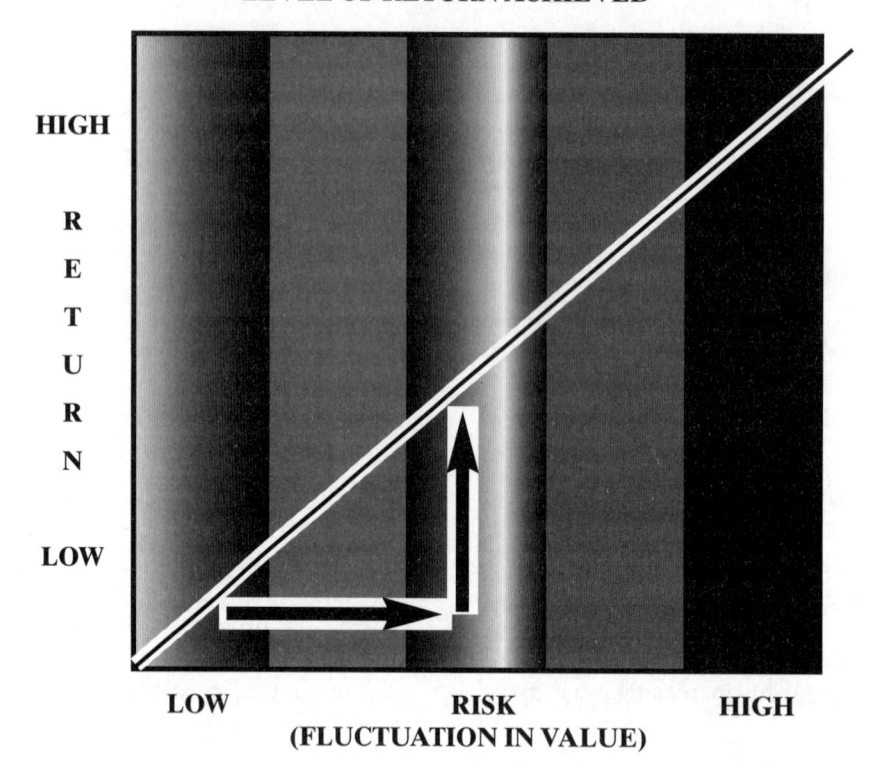

LOW

LOW   RISK   HIGH
(FLUCTUATION IN VALUE)

Figure 2

RETURN

**EXPECTED VERSUS REALIZED
VARIABLE ASSETS
(STOCKS, LONG BONDS, REAL ESTATE)**

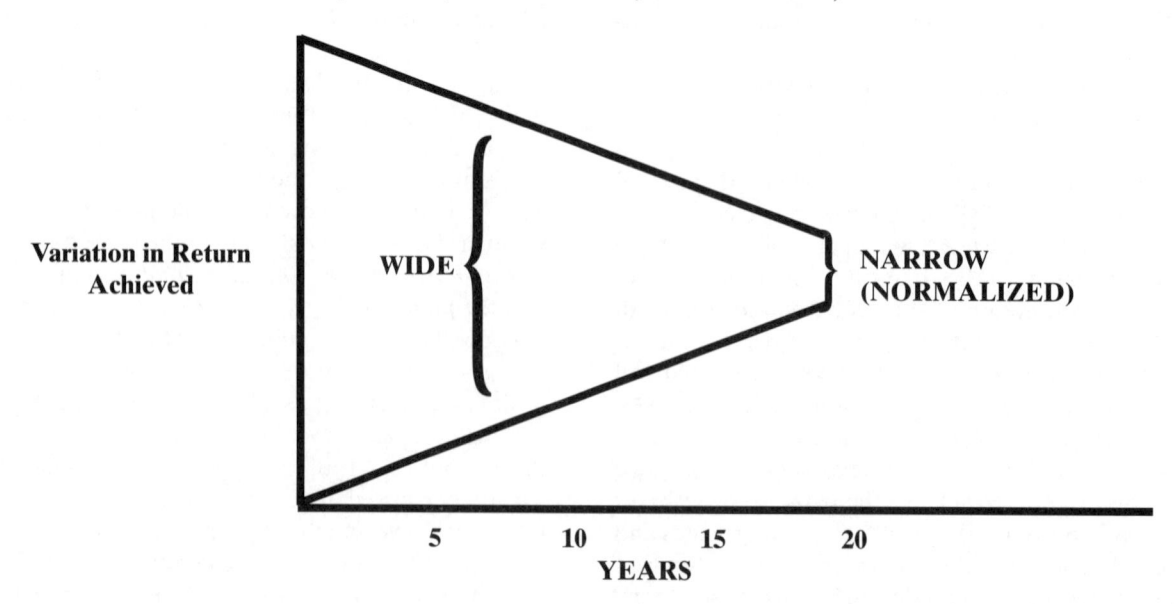

Variation in Return Achieved   WIDE   NARROW (NORMALIZED)

5   10   15   20
YEARS

Figure 3

THE "HIDDEN" RISK—INFLATION
LOSS OF PURCHASING POWER VALUE OF $1

Number of Years	3%	4%	6%	8%
5	$ .086	$ .082	$0.75	$ .068
10	0.74	0.68	0.56	0.46
15	0.64	0.56	0.42	0.32
20	0.55	0.46	0.31	0.21
25	0.48	0.38	0.23	0.15
30	0.41	0.31	0.17	0.10

Manager selection risk is the uncertainty embraced by trustees as they grant to investment professionals the discretionary supervision of the assets. The decisions made by the manager over time either positively or negatively affect plan valuations.

Finally, the *benefits payment risk* is the uncertainty related to the ability of the plan, through investment management operations to augment, as expected, the plan's overall funding operations in order to make timely payments of benefits. It is a concern for these and other risks that has prompted fiduciaries as they face the uncertain future to seek out ways to reduce the overall risks in their portfolios primarily through creating *diversified* portfolios.

As the investment markets have become more volatile, trustees have gradually broadened the diversification in their portfolios, which tends to increase the probability of producing less volatile (and thus, less risky) results. Although the asset class most dominant historically among the Taft-Hartley plans has been bonds, recent surveys have reflected that many plans are including, to a greater degree, other asset classes in their portfolios.

Benefits derived from portfolio diversification include:

- Permits positive impact from assets experiencing *unanticipated* explosive returns
- Permits exposure to some *high return/high risk* assets
- Permits *contrarian* approach with some of the assets.

Building the plan's diversified investment portfolio involves the selection, among a wide menu of alternatives, of those classes whose inherent characteristics combine to achieve a collective appropriateness as to quality, return and volatility (see Figure 4).

Asset allocation decisions are important in the task of building the diversified portfolio. Answers to the following questions will have the biggest impact on the performance of the plan's portfolio:

1. Which asset classes should be included in the portfolio?
2. What policy weights should be assigned to those classes over the long term?
3. What short-term strategic weights should be assigned to these classes?
4. Which manager(s) and management strategies should be used within and/or across asset classes?

Thus the trustees, together with their professional advisors, endeavor to create an investment program for the purpose of facilitating portfolio management operations that will result in achieving success in the benefit funding process (see Figure 5).

In summary, the ultimate objective of this procedural quest for successful funding through a prudent stewardship of the accumulated assets is to adopt an appropriate long-term investment policy and, if so inclined, to permit periodic strategic shifts within the overall policy constraints.

The investment funding process begins with the trustees, who are charged with the overall stewardship responsibility. Determined to ask the right questions and resourcefully armed with a knowledge of basic investment principles, the trustees can add significant value to a plan's portfolio. With such determination, knowledge and insight, the trustees begin by an examination of the plan's internal factors to adopt investment objectives appropriate to the plan's requirements and to examine the long-term historical risk/reward characteristics of the various investment classes. Then, with the performance objectives in mind, and with an awareness of which classes and subclasses of securities can best facilitate the attainment of those objectives, they can next turn to the selection of the funding vehicles.

The trustee may very well choose to retain professionals to assist them in this arduous process, but they are ultimately responsible to see that each step is performed in an effective manner.

Figure 4

INVESTMENT OPPORTUNITIES

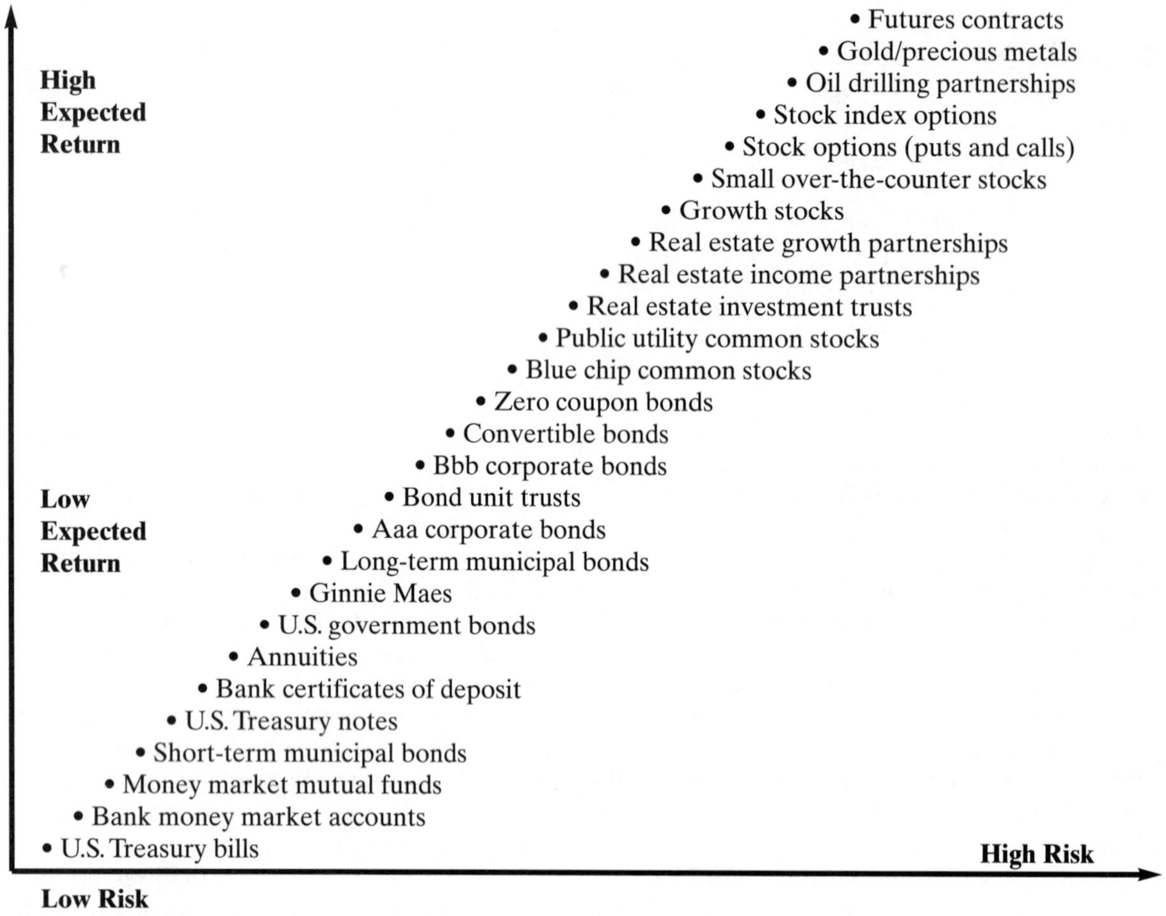

```
↑
|                                          • Futures contracts
|                                          • Gold/precious metals
High                                       • Oil drilling partnerships
Expected                                   • Stock index options
Return                                     • Stock options (puts and calls)
|                                        • Small over-the-counter stocks
|                                      • Growth stocks
|                                    • Real estate growth partnerships
|                                   • Real estate income partnerships
|                                  • Real estate investment trusts
|                                 • Public utility common stocks
|                                • Blue chip common stocks
|                              • Zero coupon bonds
|                            • Convertible bonds
|                           • Bbb corporate bonds
Low                         • Bond unit trusts
Expected                   • Aaa corporate bonds
Return                    • Long-term municipal bonds
|                        • Ginnie Maes
|                       • U.S. government bonds
|                      • Annuities
|                     • Bank certificates of deposit
|                    • U.S. Treasury notes
|                   • Short-term municipal bonds
|                  • Money market mutual funds
|                 • Bank money market accounts
| • U.S. Treasury bills                                       **High Risk**
+─────────────────────────────────────────────────────────────→
**Low Risk**
```

Source: The Complete Investor, Hirt & Block.

Figure 5

PORTFOLIO MANAGEMENT OPERATIONS

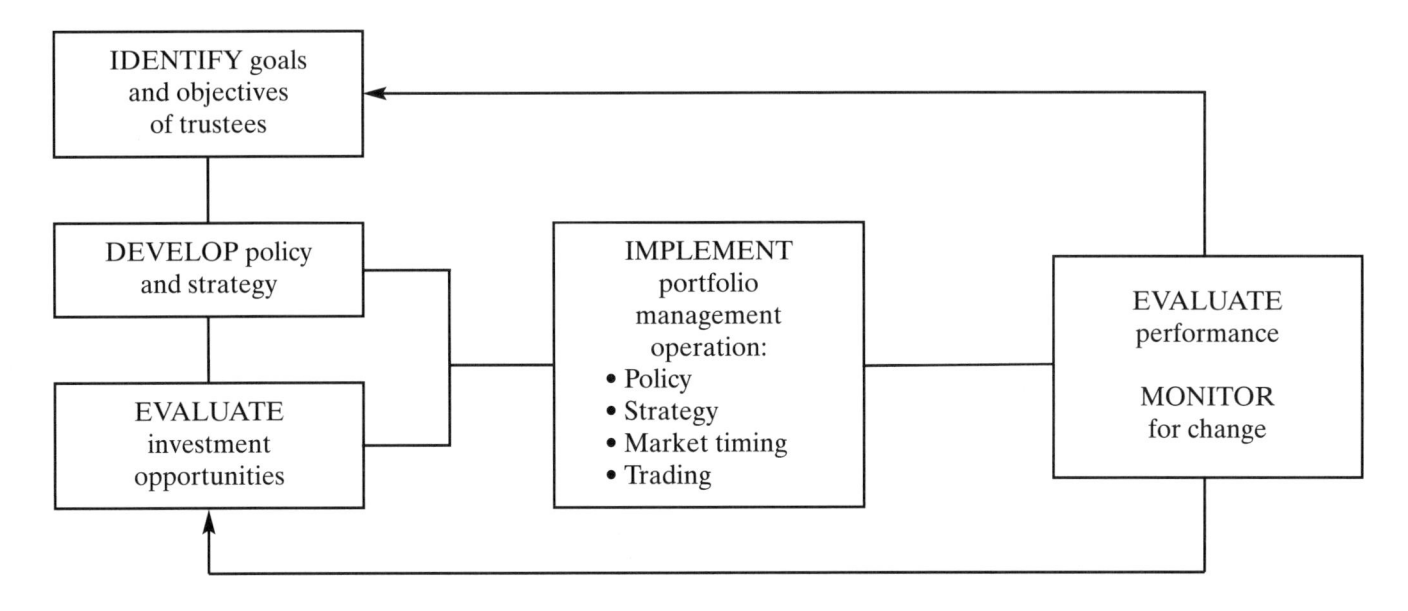

```
┌──────────────────┐
│ IDENTIFY goals   │
│ and objectives   │←──────────────────────────────┐
│ of trustees      │                               │
└────────┬─────────┘                               │
         │                                         │
┌────────┴─────────┐      ┌──────────────┐    ┌────┴─────────┐
│ DEVELOP policy   │      │ IMPLEMENT    │    │ EVALUATE     │
│ and strategy     │      │ portfolio    │    │ performance  │
└────────┬─────────┘      │ management   │    │              │
         │                │ operation:   │    │ MONITOR      │
┌────────┴─────────┐      │ • Policy     │    │ for change   │
│ EVALUATE         ├─────→│ • Strategy   ├───→│              │
│ investment       │      │ • Market     │    │              │
│ opportunities    │      │   timing     │    │              │
└────────▲─────────┘      │ • Trading    │    └──────┬───────┘
         │                └──────────────┘           │
         └─────────────────────────────────────────────┘
```

INVESTMENT FUNDAMENTALS   287

SECTION VIII
INVESTMENT OF PLAN ASSETS

Chapter 36

Investment Vehicles

Eugene B. Burroughs

Under the Employee Retirement Income Security Act of 1974 (ERISA), trustees and other fiduciaries associated with pension plans have the duty to ensure investment decisions are made with the care, skill, prudence and diligence a prudent person familiar with such matters would use. A plan fiduciary must also diversify plan investments so as to minimize risk. To accomplish these duties, it is important for trustees to be familiar with the basic investment vehicles in the marketplace.

COMMON STOCKS

The characteristic that most attracts the employee benefit plan investor to common stock is its ability to add real value to a portfolio. Since one of the long-range goals for many employee benefit plans is to pay benefits in inflation-adjusted dollars, the choice of common stock has proven to be a productive funding facility.

Stock evidences ownership of a corporation represented by shares. Pension funds are interested in owning stock for several reasons, including capital appreciation, dividends and voting rights. When the price of a stock increases above its purchase price, the stock has experienced capital appreciation. A stock price may increase when the underlying company is economically successful or when there is demand for the stock in the market. When the stock price increases, the investor may either sell the stock at a profit or hold it, hoping it will continue to appreciate.

Stocks are either common or preferred. Common stockholders participate in the earnings of a corporation through dividends. Corporations are not required to pay dividends, and the dividend amount is discretionary. Still, many expend these funds to reward stockholders and to enhance the corporate image.

Another less tangible stockholder right is participation in the management of the corporation through voting. As owners of the corporation, stockholders elect the directors and decide other corporate issues through the voting process. A stockholder can attend the corporation annual meeting or other special meeting to vote the shares, or can give written authorization to someone else to vote the shares. This is called a *proxy*. In the event of a liquidation, common stock owners also have a claim upon the corporation's remaining assets after all debts have been paid.

Preferred stockholders have the same ownership interest as common stockholders, but ordinarily do not have voting rights. Owners of preferred stock have a *superior* claim to dividends over common stock owners. If dividends are declared by the issuing corporation, preferred stockholders will receive their dividends first, and only then will the remaining earnings pass through to the common stockholders. Also, unlike dividends on common stock, preferred stock dividends usually are fixed by the corporation and cumulative. When a corporation liquidates, preferred stockholders also have a superior claim over common stockholders to any remaining assets.

Descriptive names have developed in the market to describe groups of stocks sharing similar characteristics:
- *Blue chip stocks* are high-grade stocks from leading companies that have a long history of earnings.
- *Growth stocks* are issues from companies whose sales, earnings and market share are increasing faster than the economy and faster than the average for the industry.
- *Value stocks* are issues from companies whose prices reflect *lower* relative price-to-earnings ratios and *higher* dividend payout ratios.
- *Cyclical stocks* are from companies whose earnings shift with business cycles. Industries generally regarded as cyclical include steel, cement, paper, machinery, airlines, railroads and automobiles.

- *Defensive stocks* are stable stocks that perform well during periods of uncertainty or recessions. Utilities, food and drug companies, and gold mining companies are considered to be defensive stocks.
- *Interest-sensitive stocks* relate to companies whose production is closely associated to interest rates. Examples are building and construction companies, banks and life insurance companies.

The driving forces behind stock prices are earnings, return on equity and the issuing firm's dividend policy. Increased earnings influence the company's board of directors to increase dividend payouts, which in turn influence stock analysts to pay a higher price for the shares. As demand for the shares increases, at some point the stock becomes fully valued, or overvalued, which should lead the investment manager to sell the shares, take the profits and reinvest the proceeds in a stock that is still passing through the undervalued part of its pricing cycle. Such portfolio management should produce the historical 6% real return expected from common stock ownership.

The rewards of stock ownership, resulting from a combination of an increasing dividend stream and appreciation in the value of the shares, can be unlimited. These rewards accrue from the investors' willingness to pay a higher multiple for the increased earnings and the ability of the firm to "manage its store" successfully.

The increases in the price/earnings (P/E) multiple and dividend payout stream flow in part from the firm's ability to capitalize on its research and development activity. This, in turn, fosters consumer acceptance of its products or services and eventually leads to increased sales. If costs are efficiently controlled, increasing sales should lead to growing earning power, profitable reinvestment opportunities for the earnings and, ultimately, increased confidence shown by the investment community in the firm's ability to manage its affairs successfully in the future. Investors, reflecting their increased confidence in the future fortunes of the firm, will increase their activity in accumulating the stock that, in turn, will bid up the P/E multiple. Thus, the P/E multiple becomes a measure of the attractiveness of a particular security versus all other available securities as determined by the investing public.

Even though common stock as a class has proven to be an attractive funding facility, plan sponsors need to identify stock managers that have developed and can apply superior selection techniques. Unless the manager can consistently buy stock with a present price at or below its intrinsic value, the sponsor may have to forsake active management and resort to dollar-cost averaging into a passively managed index fund.

The sponsor, in turn, must exercise patience while longer term investment trends overcome the shorter term cyclical influences in the determination of share value. Actively managing a portfolio of common stock can achieve superior results, but the results do not come automatically. It takes a combination of superior stock selection, successful market timing or both, all of which result from superior forecasting ability.

Charles Ellis of Greenwich Research Associates sums it up well when he says that the "keys to successful common stock management are (1) adopt a policy (style) and apply it consistently; (2) strive for excellence in a few areas; (3) concentrate on when to sell; and (4) maintain modest expectations."

Trustees have been more frequently adopting passive stock management (a style of management that seeks to attain average risk-adjusted performance) because the hurdle rate required from active management is so high. To justify the use of active management, the return from active management must exceed the return from a comparable market index plus a recoupment return for the higher relative transaction costs.

Trustees are also adopting passive strategies to implement asset redeployment moves to complement their existing active managers and as a temporary parking place for equity-destined monies while undertaking a management search.

Common stock has evolved over time to become a favored investment medium of the funds because it offers the possibility of providing the most attractive real rate of return. However, before that possibility becomes a reality, trustees have two options. They can find a manager that can recognize change early, select those stocks whose emerging positive attributes will be discovered by other analysts and pay attention to the price paid for stocks as a class and for its stocks in particular. Or, in the absence of finding such a manager, the trustees can participate in a passively supervised stock index portfolio.

BONDS

A *bond* is a debt security issued by the government, a government agency, municipality or corporation. Unlike the stockholder, who has an ownership interest in the corporation, a bond purchaser is lending money to the issuer. In return, the purchaser of the bond has a contractual right to receive the principal on the maturity date and periodic interest payments (usually twice a year) from the bond issuer. Reinvesting these periodic stated interest payments, known as *coupon payments,* can result in a substantial accumulation over time.

Alternatively, many debt instruments contain no coupon payments. These instruments, known as *pure discount* or *zero coupon instruments,* promise to pay the face amount at maturity and are sold for less than the promised future payment.

Bonds issued by corporations are either secured or unsecured. A *secured* bond is backed by the assets or property of the issuing corporation. Under a mortgage bond, for example, the lender's (bondholder's) investment is backed by the property of the issuing corporation. If the corporation fails to pay the coupon payments or fails to return the principal upon maturity, the bondholder may acquire the underlying property.

An *unsecured* bond is not backed by any assets but, rather, by the general credit of the issuer. An unsecured corporate bond is known as a *debenture*. The owner of a debenture has a subordinate claim to corporation assets in the event of liquidation.

Other types of bonds are convertible bonds, which can be exchanged for common stock by bondholders; income bonds, which require the issuing company to pay interest only when earned; and tax-exempt bonds, which pay interest that is not subject to federal, state and/or local income tax.

Many pension funds indicate a certain minimum rating a bond must achieve to be considered appropriate for a prudent investor to purchase. Several organizations have developed bond rating systems that assess the credit worthiness of a bond issuer in regard to a specific bond issue. The ratings are based on the likelihood of default, the nature of the obligation and the relative position of the obligation in the event of bankruptcy or reorganization. Standard & Poor's Corporation, for example, has developed the following corporate and municipal bond rating system:

- AAA—extremely strong capacity to pay interest and repay principal
- AA—very strong capacity to pay interest and repay principal
- A—strong capacity to pay interest and repay principal, although susceptible to adverse economic conditions
- BBB—adequate capacity to pay interest and principal
- BB, B, CCC, CC (speculative issues)—uncertain payment of interest and repayment of principal
- C—income bonds on which no interest is being paid
- D—payments currently in arrears.

Junk bonds refers to bonds with a speculative credit rating (BB or lower). The high yields available on junk bonds are due to the greater risk of default on interest and principal repayment.

The federal government also issues debt obligations. The Treasury Department sells bills, notes and bonds, which are backed by the faith and credit of the government and are exempt from state and local taxes. Treasury bills (or T-bills, as they are often called) have maturities of one year or less and require a minimum investment of $10,000. Treasury notes have maturities ranging from one to ten years, and Treasury bonds have maturities of ten years or more. Both notes and bonds can be purchased for as little as $1,000.

Another investment medium has been recently created by the U.S. Treasury; *inflation-linked* (I/L) U.S. Treasury notes and bonds. Whether they will actually find a place in trust fund portfolios will be decided by the trustees and/or their bond managers, but their potential efficacy should be explored, and their introduction and early experience in the marketplace should be watched and evaluated. Inflation-linked bonds may offer for the first time an alternative in the fixed income side of pension fund portfolios that can effectively provide an inflation hedge.

During the growth period of our economy following the Depression (1936-1995), U.S. Treasury bonds have provided 5.2% per year, in an inflationary environment of 4.1% per year. Thus, over this 60-year period of *economic growth,* the bond investor has been left with only a *1.1% real* rate of return. The strategic use of I/L bonds just may provide a higher real rate of return than this.

The U.S. Treasury issued in January 1997 the first ten-year "inflation-indexed" bonds, the principal of which will increase annually equal to the increase in the Consumer Price Index (CPI). Thus, if the interest rate is set at 3% each year, investors will receive interest equal to 3% of the bond's ever larger principal value. For example, if the Consumer Price Index rose 3% in the year after an investor purchased a $1,000 bond, the principal value of the investment would be $1,030. If the interest rate were 3%, the investor would receive interest payments during the year totaling $30.90, or 3% of $1,030.

It is anticipated that the Treasury will serially, over time, issue I/L bonds, including 30-year maturities. If inflation is stable, or declines over the life of an I/L bond, the Treasury "wins." Conversely, if inflation escalates during the investor's holding period, the investor "wins." Thus, the ideal is to hold I/L bonds during inflationary cycles and traditional bonds during stable and disinflationary cycles.

Since inflation cycles are longer in duration and more consistent in their direction than the cycles of the securities markets, they can be more confidently exploited. Although it would be imprudent to attempt large scale redeployments, trustees may decide to at least "tilt" their fixed income portfolio toward or away from I/L bonds, as the inflationary cycles evolve over time.

Bonds have traditionally been the bellwether asset in employee benefit plan portfolios. Unfortunately, the increasing rate of inflation has reduced the real rate of return from bond investments to levels *significantly* below the returns from common stock. Bond managers have developed a number of strategies and products to effectively control the risk in bond portfolios and otherwise constructively exploit this asset class.

A bond manager can make active bets on interest rate movements while also engaging in sector swaps and so on; can forgo (or limit) interest rate anticipation moves while still actively trading the portfolio with arbitrage moves; or can immunize or dedicate the portfolio and forgo shorter term upside potential (or limit downside risk) through a wholly passive approach (indexing).

These strategies can be implemented using governments, corporates and utilities or the more recent market entrants—mortgage-backed securities and derivative instruments. The newest entrant is the accounts receivable-backed bond, which securitizes credit card and automobile purchases.

Why would trustees include bonds as a part of their plan's funding mechanism? First, the plan (the lender) has a preferred claim on the income and assets of the issuer (the borrower). The lender has a contractual right to return of stated principal and a contractual right to receive the periodic stated interest payments.

From this right springs a plan's expectation of receiving and cultivating an income stream. It is the periodic reinvestment of this income stream that permits a plan to exploit the principle of the power of compounding interest. In just 20 years, $100 growing at 7% (i.e., 4% inflation plus 3% rent for loaning money) results in an accumulation of $386. The tax-exempt status of the plan increases all the more the efficacy of compounding interest.

The success of a bond investment depends upon whether the financial accumulation from ownership compares favorably to the original expectations at purchase. If a plan's objective is to produce a real rate of return, the income stream from the bond should exceed the loss due to inflation in purchasing power of the principal. Unfortunately, this is only one of the risks faced in bond investment. Others are credit (default) risk (if the issuer goes bankrupt), interest rate risk (if bonds must be sold below the price paid), call risk (if the issuer calls in the bond in a lower interest rate environment) and reinvestment risk (if comparable, creditworthy bonds are paying a lower rate of interest when principal or coupons are being reinvested).

Bond risk can be controlled. Besides the use of interest rate futures, there are many portfolio management techniques that can provide comfort to the trustees. Inflation risk can be reduced by buying bonds only when the real spread (interest rates minus probable inflation) is at a historical premium. Correctly assessing when a premium spread is available takes a combination of astute historical perspective, forecasting ability and luck. The phenomenon of lagging return premiums probably exists because bond buyers, having previously erred in their forecasting of inflation's rise, demand high rates long after inflation has subsided in intensity.

Credit risk can be controlled through the exercise of superior credit analysis and adequate quality threshold guidelines. Interest rate risk can be reduced by keeping maturities short, dollar-cost averaging purchases and adopting the various immunization and dedication strategies. To manage call risk, one must simply read the fine print. Reinvestment risk can be eliminated by purchasing zero coupon bonds or laddering the bond maturities.

MONEY MARKET INSTRUMENTS

A *money market instrument* is a short-term debt security (generally with a maturity of less than one year) that is highly liquid and virtually risk free. Pension plans invest in these instruments to receive interest payments on cash holdings rather than let money remain idle. Money market instruments include Treasury bills, U.S. government agency issues, certificates of deposit and commercial paper.

The following is a review of the most frequently used short-term investment instruments:

- *Repurchase agreements* are evidence of the sale of securities together with a related agreement to repurchase the same securities at some future time for a set price.
- *Commercial paper notes* are unsecured promissory notes of specific maturities and principal amounts supported by the general credit of the issuing business corporations.
- *Eurodollar time deposits* are interest-bearing deposits of specific amounts and maturities at a foreign financial or savings institution, including overseas branches of U.S. banks.
- *Eurodollar certificates of deposit* evidence time deposits of U.S. dollars in U.S. bank branches or foreign banks located outside the United States. They specify principal amount, rate of interest and maturity.
- *U.S. Treasury bills* are noninterest-bearing discount securities issued by the U.S. Treasury to finance a portion of the national debt.
- *Bankers acceptances* are drafts or bills of exchange accepted by banks or trust companies, with the accepting institution thereby assuming primary liability for payment in full of principal and interest at maturity.
- *Federal National Mortgage Association (FNMA) discount notes* are noninterest-bearing securities issued for the purpose of financing, in part, the secondary mortgage market operations of FNMA, a government-sponsored corporation.
- *Farm Credit Banks consolidated systemwide discount notes* are noninterest-bearing discount securities issued by the Farm Credit System, an independent federal agency, to finance its interim credit needs.
- *Federal Home Loan consolidated discount notes* are noninterest-bearing discount securities issued by the Federal Home Loan Banks to support short-term credit operations on behalf of the savings in-

dustry. The difference between the discounted purchasing price and par at maturity reflects the interest received.
- *Negotiable certificates of deposit* evidence time deposits with commercial banks at specific rates of interest for specific periods of time and in stated principal amounts.
- *"Yankee" certificates of deposit* are evidence of time deposits issued by the U.S. branches of foreign banks.
- *Bank short-term investment funds* are commercial bank common trust funds invested in money market instruments.
- *Bank master notes* are variable rate notes of corporate issuers held by commercial trust departments for participation by trust department customers.
- *Money market mutual funds* are commingled funds invested exclusively in short-term instruments.

GUARANTEED INVESTMENT CONTRACTS

A *guaranteed investment contract (GIC)* is a deposit arrangement with an insurance company. Basically, the investor deposits money with the insurance company over a specified period of time (either one lump sum or a series of payments). On the maturity date, the insurance company repays the total amount deposited, along with the interest guaranteed to the investor, in a lump sum or a series of payments. Unlike stocks or bonds, GICs are not marketable securities.

GICs consist of two types: individual and pooled contracts. Individual contracts are single contracts between one investor and one issuer. Individual contracts are sometimes sold for millions of dollars per contract to keep administrative costs down and, therefore, are out of range for many small investors.

Alternatively, pooled contracts (or funds) are more accessible to smaller investors. Pooled funds combine assets of several smaller investors to purchase larger contracts. Pooled funds can be either open end or closed end. An open-end pool is a continuous fund that investors may enter or leave by contract. A closed-end pool is designed for a specific group of investors that commit in advance.

INDEX FUNDS

An *index fund* is a mix of securities that replicates the portfolio of a broad based index, such as the Standard & Poor's 500 (S&P 500). The S&P 500 is a measurement of changes in stock market conditions based on the performance of 500 widely held industrial, transportation and financial companies and public utility common stocks. Index funds have recently been developed for fixed income investments.

Although a number of active managers have demonstrated their ability over the long term to add value above a benchmark index, it is difficult for the trustees to determine which managers will continue to so perform in the future. Since the market's rate of return swamps the sector and company decisions of the managers, allocating a portion of the pension fund to one or more index funds improves the risk/reward posture of the pension fund in the aggregate.

Although the risk (volatility) is demonstrably reduced in a 50:50 index fund/active manager mix, the reward is not reduced to the same degree. Index funds have become very popular, in part because studies have revealed that almost 90% of a manager's portfolio is influenced by the market portfolio.

Evolution of Indexing

Indexing started as an academic theory, was initially labeled a "fad," has been used extensively as a supplement to active management (in some cases a substitution) and more recently has evolved to the "new generation" of funds, enhanced index funds. In each decade (starting in 1960 with the Renshaw/Feldstein Study) indexing has been validated by academic studies, and yet trustees have been slow to accept it as a viable alternative.

Over the years, the popular press has "discovered" the power of indexing, as evidenced by *Money Magazine* declaring "The Triumph of Indexing" in its August 1995 issues. *Money* concluded:

Since the S&P 500 index topped 83% of all general equity funds over the past decade; and since only three times in the past dozen years through 1994 have more than 50% of diversified equity funds outpaced the S&P 500, index funds should be the core (holding) of most portfolios today.

Indexing has proven itself to be a viable alternative to actively managed accounts for the following reasons:
1. It lowers investment management fees.
2. It provides high liquidity.
3. It has provided strong relative performance when compared to active management.
4. It lowers transactions and commissions costs.
5. It provides broad diversification.
6. It increases certainty that the return received will be commensurate with the risk taken.
7. It is not affected by personnel changes at the investment management firm.
8. It can provide a *core holding* around which you can build your overall portfolio.

An index fund has certain advantages over active managers:
1. The index fund is fully invested at market bottoms (the typical manager has 8% or more *all the time* in cash).

2. The index fund eliminates the risk of "shorting" the wrong stocks; it's invested in *all* of the stocks in the benchmark.
3. Active managers have an additional "hurdle-rate" to overcome of 150-175 basis points resulting from the accumulation of various costs:
   a. Higher portfolio turnover
   b. Higher round-trip transactions costs (brokerage and market impact)
   c. Higher custody costs
   d. Higher investment management fee.

The New Generation of Indexing— Enhanced Index Funds

There is a new generation of index funds; *enhanced index funds*. By embracing enhanced indexing, trustees hold the manager to a "short leash," permitting him or her to apply a proprietary strategy seeking a controlled, modest, return advantage over a "plain vanilla" index fund. If you can be assured that your investment will "substantially replicate" the return of a chosen index, you may be willing to take a modest amount of "manager induced" risk, which provides the potential to enhance the portfolio's return above the benchmark return.

Types of Enhanced Strategies
1. Fundamental
   - Company focused
   - Based on identification and exploitation of undervalued and overvalued securities
   - Often limit industry and sector weights to the same as found in the index
2. Quantitative
   - Company focused
   - Also employ computer screens and optimization models to build portfolios
3. Synthetic
   - Employ a futures position with debt instruments to create a "synthetic" S&P 500 return plus an increment
4. Mathematical
   - Do not use financial criteria
   - Rely on principles and theorems well known in mathematics, physics and engineering

The higher commitment to indexing in the portfolio, the greater need there is to diversify the portfolio into alternative asset classes whose returns are not highly correlated with the returns and variability of the indexed assets.

REAL ESTATE

Real estate investments refers to an entire market that is composed of a multitude of different types of properties, positions, structures and vehicles. The common characteristics binding them together to form a market is that all are investment interests in real property. One study counted 880 different types of real estate equity investment vehicles. When debt options also are counted, the magnitude of the marketplace is immense.

While real estate investments have many characteristics in common with stocks and bonds, they do not share an efficient market mechanism. To the contrary, the real estate market is an inefficient marketplace. There is no central collection point where a consensus of opinions on value is recorded. Rather, it is a marketplace of private, individual transactions. The value of a particular property depends essentially upon the decision of the buyer and seller, who will value the property through their transaction.

The class of equity real estate is added to a portfolio within the context of a pension plan's objectives to (1) exploit its long-term horizon, (2) defend against the possibility that higher inflationary periods may reappear (repeat of the 1976-1981 environment), (3) add a third asset class that offers the potential to produce real rates of return in all price environments and (4) contribute to a smoothing of portfolio returns over time when combined with stocks and bonds in a portfolio because of its noncovariance characteristics.

Like common stock, equity real estate has the potential to add significant real value over time. Its hybrid nature of being both financial (leases) and tangible (bricks and mortar) in character enables its owner to hedge effectively against either a low- or high-inflation scenario. Overage rents, net leases, expense escalation clauses, equity equivalent loans and so on all result in the investor being assured that his or her principal will stay competitive with inflation. The hybrid nature of convertible participating mortgages enables the pension fund sponsor to hedge against an unknown future.

Real Estate Manager

Successful real estate investing requires attention to location, product and management. Therefore, a fund must retain a real estate manager with a resourceful research staff. Since real estate is a relatively inefficient market, a real estate management organization should, by processing information in an effective manner, ultimately acquire those properties whose configurations of attributes will assure relatively high demand.

Building on a firm base of research capability, the manager must have developed a strategic approach compatible with the plan and demonstrated the ability to acquire properties astutely through analytical talent and negotiating skills.

An underrated resource of a manager is his or her property (asset) management capability, whether developed in-house or successfully retained and monitored.

It also is important to determine that the principals of the firm have formed a team that enjoys industry peer group respect. It takes time and effort to develop marketing packages for complex properties. Those management teams that (1) have attracted sufficient client base to provide continuing cash flow availability, (2) have available the diverse disciplines to evaluate a deal effectively and (3) can quickly respond to the offer to capitalize on a market opportunity will be afforded priority in being shown the more desirable properties.

Other caveats that must be considered are:
1. The properties acquired must be well conceived, well located and well managed.
2. The sponsor must be willing to undergo "income only" years in anticipation of the slower emerging capital appreciation years.
3. The manager must purchase the properties using the current effective rents as the basis for determination of value.
4. A plan just beginning in real estate may be well advised to dollar-cost average into the market over several years.
5. If a plan is going into open-end funds that use net asset valuations supported by yearly appraisals of the portfolio properties, due diligence should be performed by the plan sponsor to assure that the net asset valuation currently used reflects the realities of the current marketplace. One would not want to place new dollars indirectly into real estate assets at inflated valuations resulting from a lagging recognition of deteriorating portfolio values.

COMMINGLED FUNDS

A *commingled fund* is an investment entity composed of more than one investor. Several investors agree to pool their money for investment purposes. In the real estate industry, the term *commingled funds* specifically refers to investment entities that have been established to serve as investment vehicles primarily for employee benefit plans.

Real estate commingled funds, as we know them today, came into existence in 1969. Such funds provide investors with experienced real estate investment management services and a high degree of diversification.

Commingled funds may use any of several legal entities as an operational vehicle. The entity selected should not have an impact on the performance results of a fund. The main point here is to make certain the type of entity utilized is an allowable investment for the plan.

Some of the common entities utilized are:
- Insurance company separate account
- Group trust
- Limited partnership
- Real estate investment trust (public or private).

Because of the legal requirements, the type of entity utilized is most commonly a function of the nature of the fund manager. Only insurance companies may use a separate account structure, and only banks and trust companies may use a common trust structure. Other types of fund managers are usually limited to the group trust, limited partnership or real estate investment trust structure.

As in other investment areas, there are different types of commingled funds with differing investment objectives. There are two main types of funds: open end and closed end.

Open-End Commingled Funds

Such funds are analogous to open-end securities mutual funds. They are, at least theoretically, always "open" for new contributions or redemptions. Such funds normally reinvest all earnings. Profits are reflected in terms of increases in the value of the funds' shares. To realize a profit, the shares must be redeemed by the fund.

Share values in the open-end commingled real estate funds are a combination of the appraised fair market value of the assets plus retained earnings. Most funds report on a quarterly basis and allow redemptions or new contributions based on the reported share values. The investor should ensure that the reported value of the shares is at least a reasonable value upon which to base a purchase or sale.

The advantage of the open-end structure is that it provides a certain level of liquidity for an asset that is relatively illiquid. One of the reasons many employee benefit plans give for not investing in real estate is its perceived illiquidity. The open-end funds were structured to resolve that issue.

However, the liquidity of some funds may be more theoretical than real in many cases. As of the date of this writing, none of the sponsors of such funds *guarantee* the redemption of shares. The capital for redemption comes from the fund itself. If there is capital available to redeem shares, they will be redeemed. If not, shareholders must wait until there is sufficient capital available to do so.

Open-end funds reinvest earnings. Thus, they take on the nature of an index fund if they continue to buy based on the same investment strategy through all cycles of the market. There is also the potential for dilution due to new contributions coming into the fund, which will be reinvested at current market rates. Open-end funds, by nature, are large. Thus, they can provide an investor with a much greater degree of diversification than smaller closed-end funds.

Closed-End Commingled Funds

Closed-end commingled funds are structured to allow

a one-time infusion of capital at their formation and then are "closed" to new investors. These funds are *blind pools* in the sense that there are no assets in the fund prior to capital contributions by the investors.

Usually, such funds have a specific term, such as ten years, and earnings and proceeds from sale are distributed rather than reinvested. Investors buy the assets at cost, rather than on appraised values, since the assets are acquired after the formation of the fund and no new shares are sold thereafter.

Closed-end funds may target their investment strategy much more precisely than open-end funds because closed-end funds do not reinvest earnings or bring in new contributions. They may select a specific opportunity at a particular point in a market cycle, make the investment and then not dilute that position by investing in other phases of the cycle. For this reason, such a structure is more adaptable to a market timing approach than is an open-end structure.

The closed-end structure was not designed with liquidity as its prime objective, even though all such funds have some form of redemption mechanism. Rather, it was based on the premise that real estate is a long-term investment.

An investor should examine a closed-end fund's investment strategy carefully because it will tend to be more specialized than that of an open-end fund. The investor should also consider whether the amount of the diversification offered is reasonable in light of the plan's overall real estate investment position.

REAL ESTATE INVESTMENT TRUSTS (REITS)

A *REIT* is a corporation that engages primarily in the ownership of income producing real estate or real estate-related loans or interests. A REIT does not pay taxes if it complies with several requirements relating to its organization, ownership, assets and income and a requirement that it distribute to its shareholders at least 95% of its taxable income in the form of dividends. REITs can generally be classified as *equity, hybrid* or *mortgage*.
- Equity REIT—A REIT that owns, invests, manages and/or develops real property directly, deriving its revenue principally from rent payments
- Hybrid REIT—A REIT that owns a mixture of equity and mortgage interests in properties
- Mortgage REIT—A REIT that invests in the underlying liens on property, essentially loaning money to real estate owners.

MORTGAGES

Whereas equity real estate investments represent *ownership* of the asset, mortgage investments are *claims* against an asset and its stream of income. These instruments are loans to the owner of a property, who pledges the property as collateral for securing the loan. Thus, the mortgagor's position is that of a creditor, just as in any other loan transaction.

Historically, mortgages have not provided an investor with the potential of hedging against inflation because they did not represent ownership of assets or their underlying income stream. More recently, there are many types of mortgages that provide some type of equity "kicker" or interest rate adjustment. Additionally, real estate provides an indirect offset against inflation by virtue of the increasing value of the collateral securing the loan. This feature, in terms of security, makes mortgages an attractive debt alternative during periods of inflation.

Mortgages may be made during all phases of the life cycle, for example:
- Land loans
- Land improvement loans
- Construction loans
- Tenant improvement loans
- Bridge loans
- Long-term first mortgage loans
- Second mortgage loans.

Yields, loan-to-value ratios and underwriting criteria obviously vary greatly, depending on the specific set of circumstances and the nature of the borrower. A unique characteristic of most forms of real estate loans is that they are placed on a nonrecourse basis, i.e., the lender agrees to look solely to the property in the event of default. This feature has obvious benefits for the borrower, but it also highlights the lender's opinion of the inherent value of real estate assets. At the same time, it places a heavy burden on the lender to value the property appropriately.

Loans made on a direct property-by-property basis, looking only to the borrower and property for recovery, are called *conventional loans*. Those debts are by far the most typical loan form in the commercial sector of the market.

Loans that carry a guarantee of a governmental agency or private insurer are termed *insured loans*. As such, they have an added degree of security because the lender has recourse against the insurer as well as the property. These loans are most prevalent in the residential markets. Because of the insured feature, generally they have lower yields than conventional loans. On the other hand, they are more liquid because there are active secondary markets for insured loans.

Due to the negative impact of inflation on long-term, fixed interest rate mortgages, a number of hybrid debt/equity structures have been devised to afford lenders some degree of inflation protection. All of these structures provide for increased yield in the event that inflation increases by sharing in the underlying value of the real estate asset. The following discussion illustrates some of the means by which this sharing is accomplished:

- Participating mortgages: This structure is utilized in the commercial sector and is applicable only to income producing assets. Such loans are structured to pay the lender a fixed interest rate (usually below the market rate for a fixed rate loan), plus participation in any increase in gross (or net) revenues for the property. Some participating loans also share in any capital gains achieved when a property is sold.
- Variable rate mortgages: This form is employed mainly with nonincome producing properties, such as single family houses. Since there is no income stream in which to participate, lenders peg increases in yield to another index, such as the Consumer Price Index (CPI), Gross Domestic Product (GDP) deflator or Treasury bills. If the selected index increases, the interest rate also increases. Normally, these loans have a maximum allowable rate of increase (a cap) to enhance their acceptance by borrowers.
- Shared appreciation mortgages: In this form, lenders make loans and receive not only an interest rate, but a percentage of the increase in the value of the asset. This structure creates a joint venture between the lender and the borrower, at least in effect, if not in form. This type of loan was designed for single family residences, but has not yet been widely accepted in that market.

Trustees may participate in mortgage investments through commingled funds, similar to those available for equity real estate investing.

VENTURE CAPITAL

Venture capital is investment in new or expanding businesses that contain substantial risks. These risks are offset by potential high returns. High-tech, health care and service companies are examples of venture capital possibilities. If new products or services offered by these companies are successful, the investor may receive a considerable return. However, if the new business fails, the investor may lose the entire amount contributed.

A pension plan may invest in venture capital through one of the following methods:

1. A fund can make a private placement of securities with a new, emerging company. This alternative presents the highest possible returns but also the most risk.
2. A private placement can be made through a limited partnership arrangement. This type of investment requires management fees and override charges.
3. Publicly traded securities of companies with smaller-than-normal market capitalization for traditional equity investment.
4. Certain mutual funds invest in venture capital opportunities. These funds offer the greatest liquidity and diversification for high-level returns.

INTERNATIONAL INVESTMENTS

No longer is the United States as dominant in the world's financial markets. European and Asian markets are increasing market share. Therefore, with the recent reapportionment of the world's wealth, the addition of some international securities to a portfolio can more efficiently diversify the portfolio.

Including international securities in a portfolio with domestic securities may reduce the volatility of returns. This is possible because the different economic, social, political and legal climates present in foreign countries cause their assets to react differently to world events than domestic assets. Therefore, including foreign securities in a portfolio will allow an investor to diversify to an extent not possible with only domestic securities.

A problem facing all international investors is administrative barriers. Before any investment can transpire, an investor may have to overcome reports in foreign languages, financial statements in foreign currencies, legal restrictions, lack of data and the poor quality of available information. The investor also faces higher-than-average transaction costs.

One solution to these problems is an international index fund. Such an index fund mirrors an international marketplace, such as Europe, Australia and the Far East. International (EAFE) index funds offer impressive returns at a risk equal to that of the market and are also relatively liquid. More recently, to enhance returns *and* diversification, trustees have been reaching beyond the developed countries that are included in the EAFE index and allocating small amounts of money into stocks of the *emerging markets*. An *emerging market* is a securities market in a developing country. The investment attraction is that these markets are deemed to offer the opportunities for high returns and may provide opportunities for portfolio return/risk relationships superior to those of portfolios limited to investments in developed markets.

Relatively high-economic growth translates into superior equity returns. Driving this economic growth is:

1. By definition, a developing country is starting from a low economic base.
2. Turning toward more open, democratic, opportunistic society
3. Desire to "catch up" with the developed countries
4. High personal savings and business investment rates

5. Progressive monetary, fiscal and social welfare systems
6. Reduced global trade barriers.

It is projected that many of the developing countries will experience growth rates *three times* that of the developed countries. This growth should be reflected in their respective securities markets.

All developing countries do not qualify as an opportunistic "emerging market." There must be constructive "change" taking place:
- Increasing political stability
- Fiscal policies that encourage growth
- Strengthened financial institutions
- Open securities markets, supported by increasing liquidity and an improving regulatory environment.

When viewed in isolation, emerging market investments are *very risky*. Political uncertainties, natural disasters, trading hurdles, volatile prices, currency fluctuations, etc., coalesce to influence the prices of individual securities resulting in significant swings in values from year to year. An example of such resulting volatility is the swing from the +72% (1993) to −11% (1994) that the emerging markets mutual funds, as a group, experienced.

However, although the price swings can be dramatic, emerging markets are *less* correlated to the U.S. markets than are the larger developed countries, and thus adding emerging markets securities to a portfolio *lowers overall risk*.

Broadening the portfolio beyond the larger, developed countries to include some exposure to the emerging markets results in a more efficiently diversified portfolio; returns over the years should be accompanied by slightly lower risk (volatility).

Taft-Hartley Funds and International Investments

All but a few Taft-Hartley (T/H) plans have historically avoided investing in the securities issued by foreign-domiciled companies. The few plans that have invested have done so predominantly through ADRs (American depository receipts) or through participating in commingled accounts containing foreign securities and managed by their domestic investment managers.

The motivation for T/H trustees to exclude foreign securities from their portfolios has been primarily their understandable interest in protecting the domestic job market. After all, any decrease in domestic employment results in a decrease in funding to the pension plans. Trustees are also concerned about the workplace environment at overseas companies and about companies that are domiciled in countries that represent security risks to the United States.

If a T/H fund decides to gain access to the international markets through an index account, a collective trust or a mutual fund, the allocation among countries and companies is, of course, at the discretion of the investment manager. If trustees prefer to "target" their investing, then a separate account must be established, accompanied by policy guidelines adopted by the trustees and acceptable to the manager.

"Targeting" international investments is a complicated issue, raising such questions as: Which companies are really "foreign"; which companies are engaged in "net exporting" of domestic jobs; does the purchase or nonpurchase of securities in the *secondary* market have any impact on the issuing companies; given the minuscule amount of T/H dollars committed to emerging markets securities, do "targeting" policies significantly influence foreign commerce?

Because of the inherent limitations to influence portfolio allocations when using commingled accounts, and the many issues complicating "targeting" foreign investments, some have suggested that perhaps trustees' efforts to preserve and promote domestic jobs is more effective by funding domestic investment vehicles that provide the ancillary benefit of *domestic job creation*.

OPTION CONTRACTS

Stock option contracts can provide a combination of important investment characteristics that can improve a manager's ability to meet the objectives of the portfolio. These advantages include return enhancement and risk reduction. The use of options in employee benefit plans has been limited primarily to writing so-called covered calls against stocks held already in the portfolio.

Calls permit the buyers of the contract to buy stock at a specified quote (strike price) on or before the specified expiration date. For granting this privilege, the seller of the call receives a "premium" from the buyer.

The primary result of an option transaction is to reallocate the risk in common stock ownership. The buyer pays a premium, which represents the expected risk of loss, as well as the interest cost of holding the underlying stock. For this fee, the buyer obtains the opportunity to gain the upside price potential in the stock. Conversely, the seller of the call receives a premium, which cushions the downside risk to some degree, but also limits the seller's potential for gain during the contract period.

Historically, option contracts had not been used extensively by employee benefit plans. However, the inclusion of option contracts in their portfolios may permit plans in search of higher returns to utilize greater proportions of common stock as a class than they might have without the cushioning effect provided by options. Also, the pension fund can transfer short-term market risk to those who are willing to speculate on shorter term movements. The success of such hedging activity is dependent upon the insight of the particular investment manager. Those trustees interested in using derivative instruments as risk hedging devices should be open to recommendations from their investment managers.

PRIVATE PLACEMENTS

A substantial amount of all debt securities issued annually in America are placed privately through direct sales to large institutional lenders. By definition, private placements are not offered to the general public and, as such, do not have to be cleared by the Securities and Exchange Commission (SEC).

There are advantages to both the issuer and the purchaser of private placements. The issuer saves considerable expense by virtue of bypassing the SEC's screening procedures and is able to offer such securities at a higher yield to the investor. Additionally, purchasers of private placements generally are large buyers, which enables issuers to service debt at lower cost than public issues.

Buyers of private placements may be able to negotiate an issue's maturity date, call features, sinking fund requirements and so on, thus providing an opportunity to purchase securities tailor-made for cash flow and liquidity requirements. During periods of capital shortages, the buyer frequently is able to negotiate "equity kickers" in the form of warrants, conversions to common stock and so on, which provide the chance for considerably higher rates of return than just the coupon rate. However, when considering private placements, buyers should recognize their limited marketability in comparison to publicly issued securities.

A small portion of a plan invested in a private placements commingled fund can:
1. Eliminate the "trading activities" risk of active bond management and maximize return potential through the internal compounding effect of the more passive private placement account
2. Avoid full rate sensitivity to the marketable securities market
3. Provide increased return from exploiting the credit risk of the individual positions through the commingled account's diversification.

Commingled private placement accounts, supervised by qualified investment managers, have frequently produced returns in excess of long-term corporates, long-term Treasuries and the Shearson Lehman Government/Corporate Bond Index.

INSURANCE COMPANY PRODUCTS AND SERVICES

Some life insurance companies provide investors with participation across the spectrum of the financial markets. Life insurance companies may invest in any and all markets, but they differ from other investment facilities in their emphasis on the pooling of funds for investment. Generally, life insurance companies maintain separate pools for each sector of the investment spectrum—i.e., one for common stocks, one for short-term paper and so on. The largest carriers may have more than one large pool or separate account for the same investment sector to accommodate different investment orientations or different plan characteristics.

For example, common stock accounts might be designed to match one of the market indexes. Others with a somewhat more aggressive philosophy could utilize foreign stocks. In all, however, the pooling principle remains a hallmark of life insurance company investment facilities.

Separate Accounts

Most separate accounts are of the open-end variety. Participants can buy and sell at a unit price based on appraised value of total assets, and they can enter and leave at quarterly (or monthly) valuation dates. In addition, some companies maintain closed-end accounts.

Because open-end separate accounts generally are run on a unit value basis, the mechanics are similar to those of mutual funds. Clients buy into and sell out of these accounts at market value. In some cases, restrictions are placed on selling units in open-end separate accounts, especially where the underlying assets are relatively illiquid, like private placements or real estate.

The investment pooling approach has the following consequences:
- Buying into a large existing pool of investments provides immediate diversification across a broader range of individual issues than normally would be possible for a fund purchasing individual securities.
- Selling out of a large pool can usually be accommodated by new money entering the pool, as well as by selected sales of securities chosen from a broad range of existing holdings.
- Insurance companies utilize investment personnel with specialized skills that may offer investment expertise for large and small funds alike.

Occasionally, where a client has a special investment viewpoint, life insurance companies will manage a separate account for a single client. This accommodation is economically feasible only for a client with substantial funds, say, more than $25 million.

The pooled accounts, as well as special accounts for single clients, are called *separate accounts* to distinguish them from the insurance company's general account, which normally is run quite differently. Funds placed in a separate account are invested solely on a "best effort" basis; there is usually no guarantee (although some companies will overlay a minimum guarantee) of principal or rate of return. The resulting track record of actual performance is the only basis for evaluating the attractiveness of the medium.

General Accounts

The general account of most life insurance companies consists of a broad collection of debt securities—primarily mortgages and direct placements—with relatively small participation in common stocks and equity real estate. There is no established market for ready disposition of the principal types of investments—and no need to dispose of them. Therefore, the general account does not operate on a market-value basis.

The general account is by far the largest pool of capital invested by most insurance companies. It is the asset base supporting life insurance and annuity guarantees and, as such, it represents the carrier's own best judgment of mix of alternative investment outlets consistent with maintaining a substantial participation in major investment sectors.

However, state insurance laws restrict the amount of investment of general account assets in certain classes of investments—e.g., common stocks. Some plans, especially smaller ones, may utilize individual insurance and annuity policies (backed by the general account) for some or all of their investments. Through the purchase of annuities, the trustees can transfer the plan's mortality and investment risk to the insuring company. They can also eliminate the requirement for any further funding in the future since the underwriting insurance company is responsible for the timely payment of benefits.

All money received in a given calendar year for general account investment generally is credited then and thereafter with the rates of return actually experienced on the investments made in that calendar year. This rate of return is the sum of actual investment income plus any actual capital gains (or losses) realized from sales of assets.

When funds are withdrawn subsequently from an insurance company, the amount accumulated on the carrier's books—the so-called book value—is marked to a fair value that recognizes the current worth of the client's share of original investments relative to the rate of return available on investments made at the time of withdrawal. Alternatively, withdrawal may be made at book value over an extended period, such as ten years.

Annuities

Life insurance companies also issue contracts under which they guarantee annuities. For example, a plan sponsor may wish to purchase annuities for a group of pensioners. This program involves removing sufficient assets to cover the liabilities for a specific group of plan participants (e.g., retirees) and can result in a substantial gain in overall investment flexibility. The purchase of annuities for the retired lives portion of the plan permits increased flexibility in the management of the remaining assets, if the trustees so desire.

Alternatively, when a plan terminates, this type of contract can be used to guarantee accrued benefits to pensioners and nonpensioners alike. In this case, if the plan so provides, any excess funds can be returned to the employer. Under these contracts, the insurance company guarantees the interest rate, mortality table for the pensioners and expenses that will be incurred to pay the annuities.

MUTUAL FUNDS

Mutual funds are pools of assets belonging to many shareholders and are used to acquire collections of investments, such as stocks, bonds and other publicly traded securities. As pension fund investments, mutual funds are utilized particularly, although not exclusively, by the sponsors of small retirement plans. Mutual funds can achieve the investment objectives and meet the diversification requirements of ERISA.

Traditionally, plan sponsors of small funds have taken one of the three following approaches to ensure adequate investment diversification:

- They have used lower risk investments, such as certificates of deposit, time deposit accounts or guaranteed insurance contracts.
- They have entered pooled accounts with bank trust departments or insurance company separate accounts.
- They have invested in several different mutual funds, either with different mutual fund managers or within the same management organization.

The two major types of mutual funds—open end and closed end—are described below. Open-end funds comprise the greater part of the industry and may be the appropriate type for most pension funds.

Open-End Funds

Open-end funds stand ready to sell shares to new investors and redeem shares from participants on an ongoing basis. Shares are bought and sold at the so-called net asset value, plus sales load if applicable. The net asset value (NAV) of an open-end mutual fund is computed daily and is determined by dividing the total market value of the securities held in the fund by the total number of shares of that fund held by shareholders. For example, an open-end mutual fund valued at $75,735,000 and having 20,250,000 shares outstanding would have a net asset value of $3.74 on that day.

The major advantage of investing in an open-end fund versus a closed-end fund is purchasing and selling liquidity at net asset value. In other words, the investor has an unrestricted opportunity to buy or to sell, and at a known price (i.e., the net asset value)—an opportunity that is not characteristic of closed-end funds.

Closed-End Funds

The opportunity to buy and sell shares at net asset value is not continuous. A specific initial underwriting creates the fund and, from that point, no new shares are created, nor are existing shares redeemed. Frequently, shares of closed-end mutual funds are bought and sold in auction markets, such as the over-the-counter (OTC) market.

Shares of closed-end mutual funds may be transferred from one shareholder to another, but the price may not be equal to the net asset value of the fund at that time. For example, on a day when the net asset value of a closed-end mutual fund is $20, shares might trade at prices higher or lower than $20. The sale is made to a third party buyer and is not restricted to a transaction between the shareholder and the mutual fund. Therefore, the sale price is influenced by the same marketplace factors that govern the auction market for stocks and bonds generally.

One disadvantage of a closed-end fund is poor liquidity. Investors wishing to buy, or shareholders wishing to sell, may pay more or sell for less than net asset value. The advantage of a closed-end fund is that the fund cannot be diluted with a heavy influx of new cash (new shares created) or drained by an unexpected withdrawal of capital (redemption). This gives both the mutual fund manager and shareholders comfort that pursuit of the investment objectives will not be compromised by sudden and unexpected influxes or withdrawals of capital.

Load vs. No-Load Funds

One distinction between closed-end and open-end funds is that many open-end funds charge a sales fee. In the case of a so-called load fund, the offering price for shares is equal to the net asset value *plus* a sales charge. There is no initial sales charge on a no-load fund; therefore, the shares are sold at their net asset value. However, when establishing positions of institutional size, the sales charge of load funds declines proportionately at prescribed breakpoints, generally reaching a 1% sales load for purchases of $1 million or more.

Benefits of Mutual Funds

Mutual funds offer plan sponsors diversification, flexibility, liquidity, a means of specialization, cost efficiencies and, in certain instances, superior performance. In addition, the mutual fund industry is regulated by the Investment Company Act of 1940, which states that a mutual fund must set forth clearly in its prospectus (updated annually and whenever necessary) its investment objectives, a report of its holdings, and its performance and frequency of dividend distribution. Thus, performance information is updated and reported quarterly.

Diversification

By owning shares of mutual funds, investors purchase a representative participation in a broad range of industries and/or companies. Diversification can be accomplished within specific investment objectives—for example, large growth companies or specific industries. The number of equity issues owned by a particular mutual fund and, thus, the degree of diversification generally varies between 25 and 200 companies, depending on investment philosophy and style.

Since a variety of mutual funds is available, the objective of many plan sponsors can be accomplished by blending various fund types, although choosing the proper blend requires some sophistication. Many mutual fund management companies manage several funds with different stated investment objectives and risk/reward characteristics.

Specialization

Mutual funds may also specialize in a particular sector of the market or type of investment. By way of illustration, a mutual fund may be classified as a growth fund, yet its portfolio may contain only medical technology stocks, insurance stocks or energy-related stocks. Other growth funds may emphasize changes in international trade relationships and may have up to 40% of assets invested in stocks outside the United States. All in all, in recent years, management companies have expanded their offering of mutual funds that invest in selected stock market sectors, such as technology, health care, utilities, energy, precious metals and minerals.

Flexibility

Since most mutual funds stand ready to redeem their shares at the net asset value, timely moves can be executed quickly and efficiently. Major changes in the policy group's investment strategy, involving substantial shifting of assets from one market sector to another, often can be accomplished quickly. Additionally, new capital contributions can be invested within a day's time. Third, in contrast to the delays associated with severing ties with a poorly performing independent investment manager, holding of mutual funds can be liquidated and reinvested elsewhere within 24 hours.

Cost Efficiencies

With no-load mutual funds, each dollar contributed represents a dollar of invested assets. With load funds, a contributed dollar represents a range of 92¢ to 99¢ of invested assets. Acquisition costs for new capital contributions, if invested in load funds, can be reduced via cumulative purchase privileges.

Transaction costs incurred within a particular mutual fund through its own portfolio activity may be relatively small because mutual funds generally are large institutional investors that can affect economies of size. There is no need to employ custodial and portfolio recordkeeping services when using mutual funds because such services are provided by the mutual funds themselves.

Mutual Funds for Large Plans

In large pension plans (here defined as those plan sponsors with internal control of the asset allocation process), mutual funds can be used to accomplish specific, or highly specialized, investment objectives. For example, large plan sponsors, employing specialized equity and fixed income investment managers, can use mutual funds to capture specific specialized investment objectives, such as emerging growth companies, international, medical technology, energy, precious metals and turnarounds. Because the sponsor may wish to invest only a small portion of the plan's assets in a given investment category, mutual funds offer the benefits of diversification within each.

Mutual Funds for Small Plans

A particular benefit to the small pension plan sponsor in using mutual funds is the ability to create the kind of multimanager investment system commonly used by large plan sponsors. This program can be accomplished either by utilizing an investment advisory firm, whose responsibilities include asset allocation decisions as well as specific mutual fund investments, or by investing through a mutual fund management company offering different types of mutual funds.

In the first case, the separate advisory company should be willing to assume responsibility for asset allocation adjustments, both as a function of that firm's market outlook and the sponsor's tolerance for risk and reward. In the second case (use of multiple funds within a mutual fund management company), the plan sponsor itself generally is responsible for asset allocation readjustments over time. In either case, mutual funds offer smaller plan sponsors diversification, liquidity and the opportunity to create a "multimanager" system.

Disadvantages of Mutual Funds

While mutual funds offer the pension fund sponsor many potential benefits, this form of investing, like all others, carries potential disadvantages. Among these disadvantages is an absence of individual account servicing. Usually, there is no direct communication relationship between the investor and the mutual fund manager. However, independent mutual fund investment counseling firms can serve to bridge this gap.

Chapter 37

Developing Investment Policy

Eugene B. Burroughs

To produce a cohesive, well-organized investment policy statement, the trustees—assisted by the plan's legal counsel, actuary, administrator, investment manager and other consultants (as deemed appropriate)—must identify, and debate, the relevant issues for the ultimate goal of identifying the investment objectives that will complement and augment the overall funding process.

The policy development process includes the identification and analysis of various internal compelling forces:
- Financial characteristics of the plan's contributing sponsors
- Trends within the sponsors' industries
- The current funding level of the plan's obligations
- The cash flow projection.

The trustees' attitude toward risk, the industry and company trends, the plan's status (underfunded, fully funded or overfunded) and the prospective cash flow needs all have an impact on investment policy choices because they have an impact on funding requirements. Funding policies necessarily influence investment policies since the return from investments over the life of the plan plays such an important part in the benefit payment delivery process.

After examining the internal plan factors, the trustees can then consider the external factors, an examination of the capital markets themselves. Risk and reward tradeoffs are considered: Will the fiduciaries be satisfied with achieving the markets' rates of return? Or do they want to attempt to achieve returns, with the accompanying volatility, above the markets' returns? This decision affects the investment management structure adopted. The range of choices includes:
1. Using only accounts that replicate the markets' returns (passive approach)
2. Using accounts that replicate the return of a chosen referenced (benchmark) portfolio (passive-plus approach)
3. Using accounts that are managed within the discretion of an investment management organization (active approach)
4. Using a combination of the above (passive/active approach).

The trustees' attitude toward risk will affect the degree of flexibility in policy. Is the board willing to achieve slower growth in value in exchange for less volatile returns, or does it seek faster growth in value accompanied by higher volatility? The former would constrain the portfolio to include, at the riskiest level, balanced growth and income stocks and real estate vehicles; the latter would permit moving out further on the risk spectrum and include the use of growth and capital appreciation stocks and small company growth stocks.

How much management risk is the board willing to embrace? The answer to this question indicates how much of the portfolio can be deployed to value adding active managers. Fiduciaries desiring to eliminate investment management risk completely have to content themselves with the markets' rates of return and endure the accompanying short-term volatility. The group, in reality, trades off investment manager vulnerability for market vulnerability. It accepts prices set by the masses versus the assessment of value by a professional.

Adoption of investment performance objectives is influenced by the conflicting goals to preserve principal value, produce current income, enhance principal value, preserve purchasing power, produce capital gains and enhance purchasing power. To the degree one emphasizes the performance objective of value enhancement over value preservation, one must be willing to move out on the risk/reward spectrum. The wider the range of alternatives granted the investment managers, the less control the trustees have over the stability in portfolio values.

Objectives to preserve and enhance principal value,

produce current income and preserve purchasing power would most probably encourage the use of money market accounts, fixed income accounts, equity income accounts and real estate accounts. Performance objectives to enhance purchasing power and produce capital gains would most probably encourage the use of real estate accounts, balanced (stock and bond) accounts, growth and income accounts, growth stock accounts, capital appreciation accounts and small company growth stock accounts, and even venture capital.

Very few boards still express their performance objectives using a single absolute number. Since most fiduciaries are aware that the investment earnings assumption used by the actuary for planning purposes is an inappropriate performance target (it should follow, not lead, the investment experience), any other single absolute number chosen is even more of an arbitrary target. An 8% absolute target return would seem reasonable and attainable in a disinflationary environment; it would be less meaningful and attainable in higher inflation periods.

More funds seem to be favoring the adoption of relative return objectives: returns relative to the Consumer Price Index (CPI), returns relative to chosen referenced benchmarks, and so on. The acceptance of relative return objectives recognizes the inherent environmental limitations that exist in the management of institutional portfolios.

It is axiomatic that every employee benefit plan has investment objectives unique to its own set of characteristics. These differing characteristics affect the planning horizon, the types of investments that are appropriate and the mix of those investments. However, one can generalize about the differing conclusions in objective setting when addressing the three types of funds (health and welfare plans, defined benefit plans and defined contribution plans). The table examines these three plans and the differences in objectives when the factors of liquidity, liability matching, market risk and financial risk are also examined.

To protect a fund's future valuations from being overly vulnerable to the fortunes of any one asset class, trustees are encouraged to adopt policies that will lead to the construction of diversified portfolios. An employee benefit plan portfolio's value is the sum of its component parts. If the plan is to reach its ultimate performance objectives, these component parts must, each in its own way, make a contribution to the whole fund. No class of assets exists in isolation. Such an orderly blending of related investment components is not happenstance, but must be carefully orchestrated to produce a harmonious conclusion. Thus, a cardinal rule in plan investing is *diversify, diversify, diversify*.

If trustees were ever tempted in the past to ignore the wisdom of diversifying their plan's portfolio, the Black Monday experience in October 1987—when the market lost in excess of 20% of its value in one day—should have once and for all assured attention to this

Table

FACTORS IN OBJECTIVE SETTING

Risk Factor	Health and Welfare	Defined Benefit	Defined Contribution
Need for liquidity	High priority due to potential for adverse claims experience	Minimum required, unless it is a matured plan	Uncertain benefit payout demands require liquidity reserves
Need to match liabilities with maturing assets	Potentially shortened payment schedule requires liquidity	Deemed desirable to protect surplus—some matching is desirable	There are no surplus/deficit constraints
Need to control market risk	Highly desirable to provide redemption, if needed, at little or no loss of principal	Largely a decision of trustees, since they are "responsible" for any shortfall	Participants/beneficiaries bear the risk; they generally opt for limited fluctuations in their accounts
Need to control financial (credit) risk	Highly desirable to forgo return from credit risk exposure to preserve principal value	*Prudence* generally requires high quality portfolio	Participants/beneficiaries generally opt for *very high* quality portfolios to assure principal protection

principle. Any employee benefit plan committed solely to common stock during October 1987 would have seen as much as one-fifth of the value of its portfolio vanish in one month's time.

Such significant downside deterioration is not easily accepted by the plan's participants. After all, their retirement security is at stake. Thus, given the utility curve of the participants in the plan and the comfort level of all fiduciaries party to the process, it is generally considered wise to diversify the portfolio over more than one asset class.

Although collectively the classes of common stock, bonds and equity real estate represent the preponderance of allocations in employee benefit plan portfolios, other vehicles used in the funding process include guaranteed investment contracts (GICs), mortgages and venture capital. Deciding to use these various asset classes in the same portfolio requires an additional decision—the asset allocation decision.

What is the asset allocation process? It is a methodology that ultimately leads to a determination of the optimum distribution of a portfolio among the various classes of assets so as to offer the highest probability of consistently achieving the investment return objectives deemed appropriate for the fund given its overall funding objectives.

The optimal distribution of the portfolio is decided upon after consideration is given to both return and risk characteristics of alternative portfolios. Return and risk are related; the asset mix chosen will consider the incidence, magnitude and level of returns and portfolio ratability. Often the process includes the use of computer support to access, examine and evaluate the substantial amount of data related to the decision. The asset mix decided upon can be predicated upon long-term policy objectives or short-term strategic objectives. In most instances, plan fiduciaries include both policy and strategy asset allocation redeployment activities in their investment operations.

With the advent of index funds, once the trustees have decided on the appropriate mix, they may then merely choose index accounts that replicate the market's returns, i.e., passive investing. Most funds, however, opt for an active management program wherein redeployment decisions are made that lead to deviations from the market's returns. Of course, it is hoped that the manager's expertise produces positive deviations. In addition to allocating the assets among different classes, assets can be rotated based upon sector, industry, term, quality and coupon characteristics.

Several studies have concluded that the asset allocation choice is the primary determinant of long-run risk and return. One such study concluded that 93% of the long-term total account performance resulted from asset deployment activities. Security selection decisions had an impact on only 7% of the long-term total account performance. It would appear from such studies that fund fiduciaries would be well advised to spend time, effort and money in the search for the most effective asset allocation for their fund. Unfortunately, the record shows that supervising fiduciaries have spent the bulk of their investment management fees on management that emphasizes security selection activities, not asset allocation activities.

In investing, the way one approaches the process is just as important as the choice of vehicles themselves. Thus, the policy statement becomes the necessary road map to successful funding. The absence of a cohesive written statement results in an investment approach composed of a loose aggregation of ideas, which usually results in a fuzzy understanding of the objectives. The investment manager may be seeking objectives incompatible with the needs of the plan, or the investment vehicles selected for the plan may be inappropriate, given its needs. If a policy is not in writing, it cannot be mutually understood, and the absence of understanding between the trustees and professionals is the most significant cause of poor investment results.

The investment policy statement becomes the overall game plan from which all substrategies and implementation of those strategies evolve. Investment decisions will then be in concert with the needs of the plan, and the group's stewardship role will have been fulfilled as the "management of risk" directives have been effectively articulated. Cohesive investment policy fosters good understanding among all participants in the process. Lines of demarcation are carefully drawn, permitting appropriate accountability and adjustments in the review, reevaluation and modification process.

Diverse areas—the requirements of the Employee Retirement Income Security Act of 1974 (ERISA), fiduciary liability, acceptable performance, diversification, the discretion delegated to managers and attitudes toward economically targeted investing—need to be addressed. Without the development of policy and its subsequent reduction to a written statement, the portfolio, like a ship without a rudder, may founder in the changing economic environments.

Such an empirical process is an ongoing effort. The policy and evolving strategies of the plan must respond to the dynamic political, social and economic environment. The policy statement for the plan in the aggregate then becomes the stepping stone for the individual policy statements for the separate investment managers.

Reducing a plan's investment policy to a written statement provides legal protection, improves communication and supplies instructions to investment managers. The statement prepared for the fund in the aggregate generally includes at least the following elements:

1. Background information on the fund
2. Identification of fiduciaries

3. Organizational structure
4. Cash flow requirements
5. Lines of authority and delegation
6. Diversification of the portfolio
7. Active/passive strategies
8. Definition of *assets*
9. Performance objectives
10. Guidelines
11. Brokerage
12. Voting of proxies
13. Trusteeship/custodianship.

The statement related to each investment manager would include background information; future funding and cash flow projections; investment objectives; policies related to the voting of proxies; portfolio guidelines; report requirements; and review, evaluation and modification methods.

Monitoring, reevaluation and modification of the investment funding process is an unending task because of the dynamic spheres of influence affecting policy selection. Characteristics of the plan sponsors change, plan demographics change, markets change and investing facilities change. Thus, an ongoing ability to effectively monitor and modify, if necessary, is important to long-term success. Independent performance measurement services assist in objective evaluation. Plan liability studies assist in achieving objective-setting precision. Analysis of expected rates of return helps in portfolio tilting activities. The exercise of patience on the part of the trustees is important to assure that counterproductive changes do not unnecessarily squander portfolio values.

In summary, the ultimate result of this procedural quest for successful funding techniques through successful stewardship of accumulated assets is to adopt an appropriate long-term investment policy and, if so inclined, to limited tactical portfolio moves within the overall policy constraints.

Chapter 38

Selecting an Investment Manager

Eugene B. Burroughs

Portfolios of pension funds may be invested in any number of financial instruments, as well as in tangible assets such as real estate. Responsibility for all the investment decisions may be retained by the trustees—which is called in-house management—or it may be delegated to other organizations, such as insurance companies or the trust departments of banks or firms specializing primarily in investment management. Mutual funds are also popular investment vehicles, particularly with the trustees of smaller employee benefit plans.

Because the buy and sell decisions in investment management operations are so technically demanding, trustees are generally advised to retain investment managers to provide discretionary supervision of the portfolio within the policy adopted by the board.

The term *investment manager* refers to a fiduciary that:
1. Has the power to manage, acquire or dispose of any assets of a plan
2. Is a registered investment advisor under the Investment Advisers Act of 1940, or a bank as defined in that act, or is an insurance company qualified to perform investment services in any state
3. Has acknowledged in writing that he or she is a fiduciary with respect to the plan.

An early interpretation of the Employee Retirement Income Security Act of 1974 (ERISA) and its fiduciary standards suggested the need for outside professional investment management. As a result, many plan sponsors opted for the designation of an investment manager to obtain the safe harbor of ERISA Section 405(d)(1). Section 405 provides that, if an investment manager is appointed, the trustees are not liable for any act or omission of the investment manager, nor are they obligated to invest or manage plan assets assigned to the investment manager.

However, plan sponsors that appoint investment managers must be prudent in the following ways: selection of the investment manager, establishment of investment objectives and monitoring the performance of the investment manager. With the alternative of index funds being available to trustees, it is now incumbent upon them to seek out managers that show promise of being able to provide returns superior to the markets' returns.

What distinguishes the *superior* investment management organization? First, it should be recognized that success in investment decision making is indifferent to the structure of the organization, its size or location. Whether the firm is organized as a bank, insurance company, mutual fund organization or independent counsel firm, the keys to its success are the people and the process. Of course, to the degree that any one of these four organizational types becomes more successful in attracting, compensating and motivating the best and brightest professionals, this type of organization will eventually produce superior performance.

If structure is unimportant, what about size? Some studies support the conclusion that smaller firms (as measured by money under management) produce higher returns than do larger firms. Yet we all know of firms managing billions of dollars that have done very well. The higher relative returns attributed to the smaller firms may be more related to the risk/reward profile of the securities the firms have chosen to emphasize, rather than the firms themselves.

The smart manager, however, will limit the assets he or she attempts to supervise if the marketplace for the manager's set of securities imposes volume limitations on success. In any event, any size criteria used in selection of the manager should be carefully considered before automatically eliminating the larger management firms.

What about location? The location of the management firm is probably the least significant factor in the selection process. A manager in the trustees' own neighborhood may, over the longer term, provide them with the most resourceful counsel. At one time, a close proximity to Wall Street was considered important. Now, with improved global communication, a manager can be wired to receive whatever information is deemed important at any location. Some managers are successful, in part, because they have distanced themselves from the financial centers and cultivated a more objective environment for processing information.

What are the characteristics of a superior manager? He or she should have developed an approach to investing that has proven successful in the past. The manager should consistently apply that approach and understandably articulate it. The firm should have highly intelligent, insightful, well-trained, experienced professionals and motivate them with performance incentives. The firm should cultivate an environment conducive to creativity and innovation. It should target the investment management activities to attain the client's objectives and goals. And finally, it should have resourceful quantitative support systems and should maintain a high standard of internal quality control in the delivery of the firm's investment management services.

It is not sufficient, however, for trustees to have identified the superior manager and allocated the trust fund monies to his or her discretion. Professionalism begets professionalism. Managers work harder (and more successfully) for those fund fiduciaries who comprehend and are supportive of the manager's efforts to add value. Becoming an insightful client should be the personal goal of each trustee. Instead of attempting to "manage the manager," the trustees need to lead the manager in the identification of the most critical issues related to the needs of the fund. Then the manager, with the professional support of the trustees, is free to strategically exploit his or her investment universe to the extent permissible within the guidelines established for the account.

The science (art?) of investing is a complex discipline. It involves collecting and analyzing a myriad of variables. Culled from these variables are data the manager deems to be the most relevant in the quest to add value. Thus, to render the best service, the manager must be emotionally free to exercise his or her skills. Informed trustees acting professionally can bring out the best in the manager.

In *Managing Your Investment Manager* (Dow Jones-Irwin, 1986), Arthur Williams III offers the following practical advice to fiduciaries who aspire to be good clients:

1. State your goals.
2. State your goals precisely.
3. Don't change your goals too frequently.
4. Don't compare yourself to others with different goals.
5. Provide your manager with cash flow projections.
6. Don't make surprise contributions or withdrawals.
7. Confide in your manager about internal preferences and (fund management) politics.
8. Don't fall for every fad.
9. Don't believe the performance figures of every person who walks in the door.
10. Don't expect miracles.

THE PROCESS OF SELECTING INVESTMENT MANAGERS

From the outset, the essential characteristics of a pension fund itself, as well as those of its sponsors, should provide the main guidelines for choosing investment management firms. Managers that pursue aggressive investment approaches could be appropriate for large and rapidly growing pension funds, especially for those with relatively small near-term payout requirements. By contrast, a conservative management approach may be more appropriate for smaller and/or more stable plans, especially for those that have heavy payout commitments.

Presumably, all these items have been considered during formulation of the statement of investment policy, which itself should be a major determinant in the manager selection process. Nevertheless, the main human and economic influences bearing on a particular pension plan should be reviewed before initiating a search for investment firms.

HOW TO CONTACT AND APPRAISE INVESTMENT MANAGERS

Perhaps the best way to initiate a search for investment management is to delegate the responsibility for assembling and screening initial candidates to a smaller group among the trustees. Of course, many other people, both inside and outside the board, may suggest investment firms for consideration. However, progress should not be slowed by the inclusion of candidates that are inappropriate for the special needs of a particular fund.

Once organized, a review of investment firms may be conducted by the smaller group designated for the task, working independently or together with outside consultants. Such outside consulting services are provided by brokerage firms, many actuarial and accounting organizations, and independent pension consulting firms, a number of which specialize in assisting with the selection and monitoring of investment management firms. Advice about whom to employ as a consultant can be obtained from attorneys familiar with the pension fund area, accountants and actuaries, or even the management of investment firms.

It may be wise to work with a consultant for several

reasons. First of all, consultants can provide the trustees with a better understanding of the kinds of investment firms that would serve the trustees' needs and be suitable to the characteristics of the fund as well. Second, consultants can pinpoint the specific information needed from investment management candidates, frame the questionnaire and help organize the subsequent interviews. Finally, consultants can help construct the initial list so that these firms may be screened efficiently without the entire board having to waste its time and effort.

Nevertheless, trustees should keep in mind that it is they—and not their consultant—who must be comfortable with who the managers finally selected.

Moreover, no matter how much expertise is brought to bear in this process, the relationship is not likely to prove wholly satisfactory, or even lasting, unless the interpersonal chemistry is good. Finally, trustees must remember that it is they and not consultants who bear ultimate responsibility for the investment results, which may prove disappointing no matter how carefully the portfolio managers have been chosen.

After the initial list has been culled and reduced to those firms for more intensive investigation, the next step is to send them detailed questionnaires. These documents should ask for specific information on such matters as portfolio strategies and tactics, ownership as well as employee compensation, decision making procedures, a list of current clients and specific people to contact for references, names of accounts lost as well as those gained in recent years, historic performance for each class of assets managed, and—this is crucial—an explanation of exactly how the firm's performance statistics have been computed.

Meetings with the finalists should not be scheduled until the answers to these questionnaires—plus related materials—have been reviewed thoroughly and references have been checked. Several trustees may be designated to visit the offices of the candidates for first hand impressions of their organizations. In all probability, visits made on their "home turf" are likely to yield more accurate assessments of investment style and capabilities than "staged" presentations made in the offices of potential clients.

Interviews with prospective investment firms should be structured with great care. Otherwise, these sessions may wind up being little more than sales pitches. The following guidelines may help.

First, the presentations of prospective managers should be contained within limited time frames, unless it is necessary to explain some highly unusual investment strategy. In any event, all introductory remarks should be monitored closely for depth of content, and special care should be taken to avoid being swayed by either eloquence or clever graphics. By analogy, remember that it is the flavor of the steak, and not its sizzle on the platter, that really matters.

Second, the main questions asked of prospects should be designed to elicit specific information on research procedures, decision making routines, strategies and tactics employed, control disciplines, transaction guidelines, levels of salaries and other incentives for employees, key personnel as well as major client turnover, differences in fees among clients, the computation of investment performance statistics and the degree of performance variation among accounts. Representatives of the sponsor should ask for an accounting of exactly how portfolio executives function daily and should review sample portfolios to assess whether the firm actually utilizes the methods described by its literature and spokesperson.

Third, after the initial interviews have been completed, the written questionnaires should be reviewed for inconsistencies with oral statements.

Provided the third step proves satisfactory, further checks with clients and other references should be pursued. This combination of reviewing the answers to questions, checking references, talking to *former* clients and making field trips to visit candidate firms should enable the search team to condense the list to no more than two or four finalists.

These finalists then appear before the full board for the final selection. All appear to offer good potential; it is up to the board to select the manager that appears to offer the chemistry that will foster good client-manager relationships. Choosing a manager is really an *elimination* process; the trustees can't hope to pick the very best manager (only time will reveal that), but the trustees can hope that their insightful review process will have eliminated those managers who have the least potential to successfully supervise the portfolio. Thus, the lone remaining candidate represents the best hope for successful execution. A few things to evaluate during the manager presentations are:

1. The *people*—Do they appear trustworthy, credible, resourceful and understandable?
2. The *portfolio management process*—Is it clear what *types of securities* will be included in the portfolio and how it is decided when to *buy* and *sell* those securities?
3. Which firm gives evidence that:
   a. Their process can add value above a given benchmark (index) and
   b. Their process has safeguards sufficient to assure that the portfolio will not substantially underperform the benchmark.

A minimum of an hour should be allocated to each manager candidate.

Finally, upon selection of the manager (or managers) that is granted full discretionary authority to manage the assets, the trustees should recognize that they must now exercise patience and adopt *reasonable expectations* as the manager repositions the portfolio to conform to its management style.

After the selected manager begins to assume responsibility for the discretionary supervision of the portfolio, the trustees must monitor his activities. To facilitate this ongoing process, several committees and the board of directors of the International Foundation of Employee Benefit Plans have jointly recommended a *Prototype Money Manager Report* (see Exhibit A at the end of this chapter). Trustees adopting this suggested reporting format may want to consider the following modifications/additions that have been suggested by investment consultants who have reviewed the suggested reporting format:

1. Add year-to-date investment returns as well as dollar amounts.
2. Add total equity commissions, brokers, cents-per-share information, any off exchange trading practices.
3. Include both gross of management fee rates of return, as well as net of management fee rates of return.
4. Include annual report of how proxies were voted.
5. Request information on soft dollar and commission recapture arrangements.

Exhibit A

PROTOTYPE

MONEY MANAGER REPORT

NAME OF FUND: _____

DATE OF MEETING: _____

NAME OF MANAGER: _____

ADDRESS AND PHONE NUMBER: _____
    (OF INVESTMENT MANAGER)

TABLE OF CONTENTS

I. Fund's Investment Policy and Objectives

II. Summary of Asset Allocation, Cash Flows and Returns

III. Portfolio Holdings

IV. Economic and Market Overview

V. Portfolio Rates of Return

SECTION I

FUND'S STATEMENT OF INVESTMENT POLICY AND OBJECTIVES

This section is a copy of the fund's statement of investment policy and objectives.

It should, at a minimum, include:

- Total portfolio return objective and its time horizon

- Total portfolio return performance benchmarks
  (such as a % mix of an equity and fixed income index
  that matches the target mix of total portfolio
  between stocks and bonds)

- Equity return objective and time horizon

- Equity risk parameters

- Equity diversification guidelines

- Equity performance benchmark

- Bond return objective and time horizon

- Bond risk parameters

- Bond performance benchmarks

- Reporting frequency/content

- Prohibitions

- Proxy voting

SECTION II

SUMMARY OF ASSET ALLOCATION, CASH FLOWS AND RETURNS
ENDING CURRENT QUARTER FOR "SAMPLE" FUND—BALANCED PORTFOLIO

Asset Allocation (Current Qtr. End)	Target %	As of Current Qtr. End Actual %	Prior Qtr. End Actual %
U.S. Stocks			
U.S. Bonds			
Short-Term			
Other			
	100%	100%	100%

Cash Flows (for Current Qtr.)

Beginning Market Value Start of Quarter

Net Contributions/(Withdrawals)

Investment Income (Dividends and Interest)

Net Realized Gains (Losses)

Change in Unrealized Gains (Losses)

Ending Market Value

Rates of Return: (Net Offers)	Current Qtr.	Year to Date	1 Yr.	3 Yrs.	5 Yrs.	10 Yrs.*
Total Portfolio Returns**						
Total Portfolio Benchmark Returns (e.g., S&P Return or Solomon Inv. Grade Bond Index or Some Other Index)						

*Or since inception, provided it falls within measurable time frames.

**Balanced portfolios may include return information on the "stock only" and/or "bond only" portions of the portfolio, if relevant.

SECTION III

PORTFOLIO HOLDINGS

List of all securities held, organized by asset class (equities, bonds, short-term), to include, at a minimum:

    Security name/description

    Number of shares or par value

    Current price

    Cost value

    Market value

    Percentage of portfolio

SECTION IV

ECONOMIC AND MARKET OVERVIEW

Manager should discuss the economic/investment climate as it relates to the portfolio. This might include such items as:

- General economic commentary
- U.S. equity market perspective
- U.S. bond market perspective
- Other

This material should be concise and probably on no more than one to two pages.

SECTION V

PORTFOLIO RATES OF RETURN

(NAME OF FUND)

Qtr. End Date*	Portfolio Rate of Return**	Benchmark Return***
Year 2005		
12/31/05		
9/30/05		
6/30/05		
3/31/05		
Year 2004		
12/31/04		
9/30/04		
6/30/04		
3/31/04		
Year 2003		
12/31/03		
9/30/03		
6/30/03		
3/31/03		
Year 2002		
12/31/02		
9/30/02		
6/30/02		
3/31/02		
Year 2001		
12/31/01		
9/30/01		
6/30/01		
3/31/01		

*Up to trailing five years
**One year returns where indicated; otherwise quarterly returns
***Benchmark return—S&P 500, Solomon Index, etc.

Chapter 39

Performance Measurement

Eugene B. Burroughs

To insightfully monitor the plan's investment program, the trustee should retain an organization to objectively measure, and assist in the evaluation of, the investment performance of the aggregate portfolio and its components. The several objectives of this ongoing measurement process include the following:

- Comparing the fund's returns with actuarial earnings assumptions to estimate the potential for underfunding or overfunding. This return is most appropriate in the measurement of the fund's total portfolio for it measures the *internal* rate of return. This is the return used when comparing the plan's investment performance to the investment return assumed by the plan's actuary in his or her calculations.
- Evaluating the performance of the in-house and/or outside manager(s) to determine the need to replace managers or reallocate assets among managers
- Comparing the fund's performance with that of funds with similar and different policies to evaluate the wisdom of the fund's investment policy and strategy.

The two most common types of rate-of-return calculations are dollar weighted and time weighted. The dollar-weighted rate of return is the simple return per unit of assets. However, when comparing the fund's returns with its long-term nominal and/or real rate-of-return objectives, this calculation can lead to spurious conclusions when used for making comparisons of managers' performance. For example, if a large capital contribution is committed to a fund at a market peak, a subsequent decline will erode both the original and the newly committed assets. Thus, the rate of return might be negative *at that time*.

The time-weighted rate of return, on the other hand, is computed to measure the relative performance in a way so as to "neutralize" the effect of cash flows. This technique recognizes that the timing of cash flow into a pension fund is usually outside the control of investment managers. Therefore, the effect of this flow can be either helpful or injurious to the fund's performance and should not be attributed to actions of the manager.

For example, assume an investor purchases two shares of a mutual fund—share A on January 1 at $100 per share and share B on July 1 at $90 per share. Assume further that the mutual fund declined 10% in the first six months and increased 20% in the latter six months. That is, the original share A purchased for $100 dropped in value to $90 by July 1 and rose subsequently to $108 by the end of the year. On the other hand, share B, purchased for $90 and held for six months, enjoyed 20% appreciation from $90 per share to $108 per share. (An even more favorable return of 40% can be attributed to the purchase of share B if we extrapolate an annual rate of return.)

The dollar-weighted rate of return recognizes:
1. $100 invested for one year at 8%
2. $90 invested for one-half year at 20%
3. Ending investment (shares A and B) equals $216
4. Dollar-weighted rate of return "r" equals
   - $100 (1 + r1) + $90 (1 + r½) = $216
   - r = 18.2% per annum.

The calculation shown above accurately expresses the investor's true return, that is, the dollar-weighted return. However, it does not express the return of the mutual fund itself, i.e., the time-weighted rate of return. This would be computed in the first six months and the second six months independently of the midyear investment of share B because this purchase was not related to the mutual fund manager. Therefore, the time-weighted rate of return would be calculated as follows:

1. Share value dropped 10% for six months

2. Share value increased 20% for six months
3. Time-weighted rate of return "r"
4. Calculation for the fund is:
   - Rate = $(1 + r1)(1 + r2) - 1$
   - r = 10%
   - r = 20%
   - $(1 - .10)(1 + .20) - 1$ @
   - $(0.90)(1.20) - 1$ @ $1.08 - 1 = 8\%$.

The time-weighted rate of return more accurately describes the performance of the mutual fund manager. The manager achieved an 8% return for the year. The dollar-weighted rate of return more accurately describes the impact on return of the investor's cash flow timing.

Comparing and evaluating a pension fund's investment performance goes beyond simply assessing the rate of return as either *good* or *bad*. The trustees should attempt to identify those factors that contributed to the returns generated, i.e., sector factors, security selection, industry weightings and market timing decisions. Performance measurement activities should be a "schoolmaster" to the trustees, enabling them to make more insightful policy, strategy and manager selection decisions over time.

Chapter 40

The Role of the Investment Consultant

Thomas A. Mitchell Sr., CEBS

INTRODUCTION

The business of pension fund consulting traces its origins to several events that occurred in the late 1960s. Some say that the first pension fund consultant was George Russell Jr., who changed the company founded by his father, Frank Russell Co., from a mutual fund and insurance sales firm into the first pension fund consulting firm. Others consider the brokerage firm A. G. Becker, the first to offer investment performance measurement charts and graphs via the Becker "green books," to be the true originator.

Whatever its origins, the pension fund consulting industry of today is a multimillion dollar industry serving funds with over $4 trillion in assets. A Barron's article published in 1988 estimated that there were more than 90 firms in the field at the time. Today, pension fund consulting services are offered by a large number of generalists that serve many types of clients, and specialists that focus on only certain types of funds, such as union-oriented Taft-Hartley funds or public employee funds. Some consultants are independent, in that they provide only performance evaluation, money manager search services and advice. In addition to these independents, some of the actuarial firms, as well as a number of brokerage houses, engage in pension fund consulting.

For the most part, pension fund consultants serve a useful role. They serve pension fund managers and trustees as independent advisors, offering a number of useful tools and services that help plan fiduciaries, who often lack investment expertise, do their jobs better.

THE CONSULTANT RELATIONSHIP

In some instances consultants are hired for specific one-time projects such as a single money manager search or an asset allocation study, but most consulting relationships are ongoing general relationships.

The ongoing general relationship puts the consultant in the position of a key advisor to the pension fund manager or board of trustees. As a key advisor, the consultant utilizes a number of tools that help fiduciaries make decisions, but often the most useful tool is independent and objective advice. In order for this advice to be taken seriously, the consultant and the client must develop a relationship of mutual trust.

From the client perspective, selecting a pension fund consultant is one of the most important decisions to be made. Thus, the selection process must be thorough and based on criteria designed to identify a firm and an individual that possess the resources, reputation, experience, integrity and philosophy consistent with the needs of the plan and its fiduciaries.

SELECTING THE CONSULTANT

In selecting an investment consultant, you will be selecting both a firm and a specific individual who will serve as the primary contact with the pension fund manager or board of trustees. A good starting point in the selection process is to define the proposed role and duties of the consultant. Will this be a single, one-time project or an ongoing general relationship? If this is to be an ongoing general relationship, is there a specific issue or problem that needs to be addressed immediately?

Each firm should be evaluated in terms of its resources, reputation, support staff and backup personnel, independence and potential for conflicts of interest. You'll need to know where each firm is located, its staffing level by function, number and type of clients served, the ownership structure and length of time in business.

Request a complete description of the services provided and the percent of annual revenue generated by each service. Each candidate should describe its fee structure, whether paid in cash or through directed brokerage, hourly or fee for service, etc. A current list of clients, with contact names and telephone numbers, is helpful for checking a candidate's reputation.

The individual consultant who will serve as the primary contact between the client and the pension fund must also be evaluated. Key issues such as background, knowledge, experience and relationship skills can be determined during the interview process. Availability is important. Determine the number of client relationships for which the individual has primary responsibility. Discuss the number and timing of meetings he or she will be required to attend each year.

Attached is a Pension Investment Consultant Questionnaire that was developed by Bernard M. Baum, counsel to a large number of pension funds. This questionnaire can be quite useful in the selection process.

EVALUATING CONSULTING SERVICES

Most pension fund investment consulting firms provide asset allocation analysis, investment manager structure and selection services, and performance measurement and evaluation services. Some firms also provide custodian bank reviews, proxy voting services, and most will undertake special research projects.

Asset allocation is the most important factor contributing to the long-term investment success of a pension fund. A number of research studies have concluded that asset mix (the percentage of fund assets allocated to stocks, bonds, real estate, etc.) determines approximately 90% of the investment return. All other decisions such as active or passive management, the investment managers utilized, the securities selected, contribute just 10% of the long-term investment return.

Diversification among investments is not only mandated by ERISA; it is the best tool for achieving an appropriate balance between investment risk and return. Asset allocation studies and periodic reviews often include a discussion of the annual returns of various asset classes, with emphasis on short-term and long-term variability measures.

A discussion of correlation between asset classes helps trustees understand how blending asset types with different patterns of return can actually reduce volatility and increase investment return.

Important inputs to the asset allocation discussion must be provided by the client. What is the interest assumption used in the fund actuary's projections? What is the outlook for the industry served by the pension fund? Is this a growing industry or is the employment level stagnant or declining? What are the near-term and longer term cash flow projections? Do contributions cover monthly benefit and administrative outflows? When are contribution levels expected to increase? What is the funding status of the plan?

Trustees should stress test different asset mixes and agree on a maximum exposure to stocks that will serve as both the target allocation and the maximum allocation to this most volatile asset class. A formal or informal agreement to rebalance whenever stock exposure is significantly above or below the target maximum helps to keep risk in check. Keep in mind that allowing investment managers to control the asset mix may lead to more risk than is necessary to achieve your investment goals or could result in a shortfall. When several investment managers are managing plan assets, each individual manager has only a narrow view of the whole plan and the many factors that influence it. The trustees, working with the consultant, are in the best position to monitor and control overall investment risk through asset allocation.

No single asset mix is appropriate for all pension funds. An asset mix that may be appropriate for one pension fund may be inappropriate for another. An appropriate asset mix is one that offers a high likelihood of achieving an investment return that is expected to fund the benefit levels promised by the plan and does so with a high degree of diversification, at the lowest possible risk level. This is the goal of asset allocation.

Once the asset allocation decisions have been made, a statement of investment policy should be drafted. The statement of investment policy outlines the asset mix selected by the pension fund manager or board of trustees. Each allowable asset class is defined in detail, identifying which security types are allowable and which are prohibited. Minimum credit quality levels are stated and risk controls are outlined. One very important aspect of the statement of investment policy involves defining the specific performance benchmarks and time periods that will be used to measure investment performance. The statement of investment policy will become the road map guiding the pension fund's investment program.

Investment manager structure and selection steps follow the asset allocation decision. The asset mix adopted by the trustees and outlined in the statement of investment policy will set the stage for determining the number and types of investment managers needed to fill the various roles. Trustees will need to weigh the pros and cons of several different alternatives, and the investment consultant plays a key role in these discussions.

Some of these issues are the following.
1. Should the fund utilize investment managers serving in generalist roles, managing stocks and bonds in a single portfolio, or use a specialist structure where manager assignments such as large capitalization stocks, small capitalization stocks, domestic fixed income, non-U.S. stocks or

bonds, etc., are assigned to firms with specific expertise in those areas?
2. Should the fund utilize passively managed index funds such as S&P 500 Index funds instead of active managers or in combination with active managers?
3. To what degree do the fund's existing investment managers possess the expertise required to fill the investment roles defined above?

The investment consulting firm usually has a separately staffed department assigned to investment manager evaluation and selection. The manager search staff's job is to collect detailed information on hundreds of investment management firms, verify the investment results of each firm and interview firm representatives. This research provides a universe of investment firms within many disciplines that may be available for consideration by trustees when new roles are added or existing investment firms need to be replaced.

An important consideration from the client's perspective should be whether the investment consultant is truly independent and without conflicts of interest relative to any recommendations being made concerning investment management firms to be considered. In some cases, investment consultants will have business relationships with investment management firms. Investment management firms may purchase performance-ranking services from investment consultants to be used in marketing material. You may be familiar with certain investment firms that advertise they rank in the "top quartile" of some investment consultant's universe. In other cases, the consultant may actually be a subsidiary of or partially owned by an investment firm.

Just because a consultant has a relationship with one or more investment firms does not automatically imply anything improper has occurred, but pension fund managers and trustees should be aware of the potential for conflicts of interest and carefully question the consultant concerning these issues. Discussing these issues openly, in advance, will promote a level of trust that is necessary for a successful relationship with the consultant.

Performance measurement and evaluation services are an integral part of the ongoing relationship with the consultant. Pension fund managers and trustees must have a reliable, objective and independent method of measuring and evaluating the fund's overall investment performance and each manager's performance relative to the benchmarks outlined in the statement of investment policy.

The collection of asset and transaction data from the fund's custodian bank, editing the data, accounting for all securities and calculating rates of return usually consume the largest part of the investment consultant's overhead. This is a detail-oriented, time-consuming operation.

Pension fund managers and trustees will use performance measurement and the investment consultant's evaluation of those results as the basis for a number of key decisions during the life of the fund. It is critical that these calculations be completed accurately and in a timely manner.

Consultants base their calculations on data provided by the fund's custodian bank rather than data available from the investment managers. While the consultant should complete these calculations independently, it is appropriate to compare these results to the investment returns calculated by the investment manager and to reconcile differences in advance. Where unreconciled differences still exist, these differences should also be reported to the pension fund manager or trustees.

In order to be clearly understood and acted upon, performance results should be presented in an easy-to-understand report format. Trustees should view the performance report as a tool to be used to trigger further analysis rather than the absolute determinant for decision making. In other words, performance evaluation is a process that uses the consultant's performance reports, the consultant's independent advice and discussions with the investment managers to develop an overall picture of the fund and its investment managers. From time to time, investment managers will underperform relative to their benchmarks. This should be expected, since even the very best investment managers underperform periodically. Diversification among asset classes and among investment managers will usually prevent the fund's total performance from missing its target. In certain instances, it will be necessary to replace an underperforming investment manager, but this decision should be based on considerable objective analysis using appropriate time periods.

Custodian bank monitoring is a service that is not offered by all consultants, but nevertheless is an important part of monitoring all aspects of the pension fund. The custodian bank operates, to a large degree, in the background. The custodian is responsible for the safekeeping of fund assets, accurately pricing all securities at the end of each month, collecting all dividend and interest payments in a timely manner, settling all trades that were initiated by the investment managers, investing any idle cash within each investment manager's account and providing the fund with verified accounting reports.

Since all of these operations go on behind the scenes, it is very difficult to know if the custodian is performing all of these assignments in an accurate and timely manner. The consultant is in the best position to police the custodian, but to do so requires quite a bit of work.

The consultant must have the resources to verify that all securities have been accounted for by the bank, that the bank's pricing of the securities is accurate, that all dividend and interest payments have indeed been posted accurately on time, that all trades were settled on their contractual settlement date and all idle cash was invested in short-term funds. This is a time-consuming, detail-oriented task, but it is worthwhile since even the biggest and best custodian banks do make mistakes that may cost the fund. Monitoring the custodian bank can be worthwhile if the investment consultant has the necessary systems and resources.

Proxy voting is a service provided by just a small number of investment consulting firms, but this too can be quite useful to the pension fund manager or board of trustees. The U.S. Department of Labor has made it clear that voting the proxy ballots associated with common stocks owned by the fund is a fiduciary act. The responsibility for researching the issues and voting the proxies may be delegated to the fund's investment managers or another registered investment advisor, but the process must be monitored by the trustees. The adoption of a statement of policy concerning the voting of proxy ballots, together with an annual review of all proxy issues addressed and how the proxy ballots were cast, can be an important part of the monitoring process.

The investment consultant is perhaps in a better position than the investment managers to research and vote the proxies on behalf of the trustees, for a couple of reasons. Investment firms serve many different clients; these include many single employer plans as well as jointly trusteed plans. Oftentimes, the investment manager will have a relationship with the same corporations whose stock is owned by the pension fund, and voting the proxies in a completely objective manner might be difficult.

Another problem occurs when more than one investment manager working for the fund will own the same stock, yet vote the proxy ballots differently. This may result in votes being nullified by the other manager. One solution is to have a single entity, the investment consultant, which is in a position to be completely objective, vote all proxy ballots on behalf of the plan.

Special research projects may be elicited by discussions between the pension fund manager or trustees and the investment consultant. New investment vehicles are being constructed by Wall Street technicians regularly and are often presented as the next "better mouse trap" by investment managers. Understanding the investment risks associated with their use is often difficult. The investment consultant is often in the best position to research these offerings and objectively advise trustees on their potential.

CONCLUSION

The investment consultant can be an invaluable resource to pension fund managers and boards of trustees. Finding a consultant that "fits" is important because the advice provided by the investment consultant will have a dramatic impact on the long-term success of the pension fund's investment program. When undertaking a search for an investment consultant, do your homework, pay attention, build a relationship based on mutual trust. Good luck!

PENSION INVESTMENT
CONSULTANT QUESTIONNAIRE

Name of Respondent: _____

Title: _____

Address: _____

Telephone: _____

Questionnaire provided by Bernard M. Baum, Director, Baum, Sigman, Auerbach, Pierson & Neuman, Ltd., Chicago, Illinois.

I. ORGANIZATION

A. GENERAL

1. When was your firm founded?

2. What is the present ownership of your organization? Please be specific.

3. a. Has your firm merged with, been acquired by or acquired another organization within the past three years?

   b. Does your firm or any affiliate of your firm provide trust, investment management or securities brokerage services? If yes, please explain.

B. PENSION INVESTMENT CONSULTING

1. When did your firm begin providing investment consulting?

2. a. What were the revenues attributable to your investment consulting practice during your last fiscal year?

   b. What percentage of your organization's revenues were attributable to the investment consulting practice?

   c. What has been the compound growth rate in investment consulting revenues during the past three fiscal years?

3. Besides consulting, what other investment-related services do you provide to pension clients?

4. Does your firm provide investment-related services to investment managers? If yes, please describe them.

The remainder of this questionnaire applies to your firm's investment consulting practice unless otherwise indicated.

II. STAFFING

1. a. What is the total size of your staff?

   b. How many of these are consultants?

2. Please attach biographic information on your five most senior consultants.

3. Please list all consultants who have left your staff during the past three years. Include their reasons for leaving and present employer (if known).

4. Based on what you know at this point, what consultant would you expect to assign to the Stone Makers Industry Retirement's relationship? Please provide biographic information below.

III. CLIENTS

1. a. Please provide on an attachment a representative list of your investment consulting clients.

   b. Please list your Taft-Hartley clients and the size of the portfolios you manage for them.

2. a. How many clients pay you an agreed-upon retainer fee?

   b. Are you willing to accept nonretainer clients for specific assignments?

3. Of your retainer clients, how many are in each of the following categories?

Taft-Hartley	_____
Corporate	_____
Public Funds	_____
Foundation and Endowment	_____
Other	_____

4. Please list clients that have terminated your firm's services during the past three years. Indicate their reasons for terminating your services.

5. Please provide five references below. To the extent you have them, include Taft-Hartley clients for whom you provide performance measurement/evaluation services. Please indicate contact name, address and telephone number.

IV. SERVICES

A. GENERAL

1. Please indicate with an "X" which of the services listed below your firm provides.

Service	
Investment policy development	_____
Asset mix modeling	_____
Asset/liability modeling	_____
Investment manager selection	_____
Domestic equity	_____
Domestic fixed income	_____
International equity	_____
International fixed income	_____
Real estate	_____
Other: _____	_____
_____	_____
Insurance contract selection/negotiation	_____
Performance measurement/evaluation	_____
Analysis of trading	_____
Proxy voting	_____

Please respond to the following questions regarding specific services.

B. INVESTMENT POLICY DEVELOPMENT

1. a. Describe briefly the processes and tools your firm uses to help clients develop investment policies and objectives.

   b. To what extent do you use models or quantitative techniques? Please describe them.

2. Does your firm assist clients in making shorter term tactical asset allocation decisions? If yes, please describe the process you use.

C. MANAGER SELECTION

1. a. How many investment managers are in your manager database?

   b. Please indicate how many are in the following categories?

   USA equity   _____

   USA fixed income   _____

2. What process do you use to evaluate investment managers? Do you conduct on-site visits? Please explain.

3. a. Do you classify equity managers by style? If yes, please indicate the style categories you use.

   b. What process do you use to determine a manager's style?

4. How do you verify the validity of managers' performance records?

D. PERFORMANCE MEASUREMENT AND EVALUATION

1. a. How frequently do you produce performance evaluation reports for your clients?

   b. How frequently do you meet with your performance evaluation clients?

2. a. Do you purchase universe data or do you maintain your own? If purchased, from whom?

   b. Please specify the universes you have available.

   c. Do you maintain a separate universe of Taft-Hartley funds?

3. Besides your performance universes, what other databases do you use in your performance evaluation and analysis?

4. a. Describe the types of analysis included in a typical performance evaluation report.

   b. Please enclose a sample performance report.

5. To what extent can your performance reports be customized to meet a particular client's needs? Please explain.

6. What do you believe sets your performance evaluation services apart from the competition?

V. FEES

1. How are your fees normally determined?

2. a. To the extent your firm has agreed-upon retainer fees, what services are typically covered by the retainer?

   b. Does your firm offer an all-inclusive retainer?

   c. What is the range of the annual retainer fees currently being paid by your clients?

3. Do you accept "soft-dollar" payments? Please explain.

4. Please estimate your annual fee for providing performance evaluation consulting to the Stone Makers Industry Retirement Fund. You may use the following assumptions:

   Defined Contribution Plan   ($77,476,470.75)

   The portfolios include: Two balanced managers

   Quarterly reports

   Quarterly meetings

5. Please estimate additional fees, if any, for:

   Selecting investment manager(s)   _____

   Developing/reevaluating investment policies   _____

VI. LEGAL

1. Is your firm registered as an investment advisor with the Securities and Exchange Commission?

2. Does your firm consider itself to be a fiduciary in its role as pension investment consultant?

3. Has your firm or a principal of your firm ever been investigated by the SEC or another regulatory agency? If yes, please explain.

4. Has your firm or a principal of your firm ever been charged by the SEC or any other regulatory agency of any violation of applicable law? If yes, please explain.

5. Do you have any clients or associations that could present a conflict of interest and preclude you from representing this fund? If yes, please explain.

6. At the present time, does your firm have any lawsuits pending against it concerning the performance of investing consulting services for any client? If yes, please explain.

Chapter 41

The Utilization of Commission Dollars

Thomas A. Mitchell Sr., CEBS

INTRODUCTION

The commission dollars generated by the active management of equity portfolios represents annual revenues to brokerage firms totaling hundreds of millions of dollars. Commissions are plan expenses, yet money managers have had complete control over how these millions are spent.

With the advent of fully negotiated commissions in 1975, commission rates have fallen from $.20 to $.30 per share to $.04 to $.05 per share, a reduction of about 85%. This change dramatically reduced revenues to brokers. Prior to negotiated commissions, brokerage firms offered proprietary research and third-party research free of charge to those money managers with whom they did business. Once commission rates fell, brokers found that they could no longer provide these services to money managers free. Money managers were told that in order to pay for this research they would be given credits for each dollar of commission revenue. These credits would then be used to pay for the research services.

This practice of purchasing research services using commission dollars is generally referred to as *soft dollar* purchases. Today, most institutional money managers buy research services using soft dollars, spending from one-quarter to one-half of all commission dollars in this manner.

Since not all commission dollars need to be directed to brokers for the purchase of research services, plan sponsors found that they could "direct" their money managers to use certain other brokers. In return, the plan could use a portion of its commission dollars to reduce other plan expenses such as investment consulting fees, or the plan could receive direct rebates of a portion of the commission dollars directed in this manner. These are referred to as *directed brokerage* trades, or *commission recapture* trades.

Since every expense associated with the investment of plan assets tends to reduce the overall investment return, reducing commissions or reducing other plan expenses through the use of directed commission programs or commission recapture programs can result in better overall investment performance.

TRADING STOCKS

Money managers can trade shares of stock in a number of ways. In most instances, they use either the stock exchanges, such as the New York Stock Exchange (also known as the *auction* market), or other non-exchange-based systems such as NASDAQ (also known as the *over-the-counter* market).

The brokers trading shares for customers on the exchanges charge commissions for each share traded. The non-exchange-based systems are networks of dealers linked by computer. These networks, such as NASDAQ, do not charge commissions as such, but investors pay the *spread* between what these dealers will pay to buy shares or will accept for the purchase of shares. For example, a bid price of 25¼ and an ask price of 25¾ reveals that a dealer will buy shares for $25.25 each but will sell shares for $25.75 each. The $.50 difference between the bid and the ask price is dealer profit.

While commissions have historically not been charged for these over-the-counter market trades between dealers, the charging of commissions by intermediaries is beginning to become more common.

Another, less common, resource used by index fund managers and other portfolio managers and traders is collectively referred to as the *crossing networks* or "electronic trading networks." These networks, such as Instinet, offer a service that matches natural buyers and sellers by computer. Both the buyer and seller agree to accept or pay share prices that are unknown prior to the actual execution of the trade. That is, they usually pay or receive a price that is between the bid and ask price at the close of the trading day, or the price in existence at a certain time of the day. The commissions charged for trades on these crossing networks generally range between $.015 and $.025 (one and one-half to two and one-half cents per share). Not all common stocks are readily available on these matching systems, and personal service is not part of the package. Also, because these trades are computer based, they may not benefit from the *auction process* that takes place on the exchanges. Pension fund portfolio managers may use these services for a small percentage of their trades.

Crossing network trades are part of a broader category of trades referred to as *execution-only* trades. Execution-only trades may take place either on an exchange or on one of the crossing networks. What differentiates this type of trade is that the broker does not offer the research or other services and products associated with soft dollar trades, and as a result, brokers charge lower commissions, generally in the range of $.015 to $.04 (one and one-half to four cents per share).

Exchange-based trading is by far the medium of choice for institutional money managers. For the most part, whether a trade is 50,000 shares or 500,000 shares, large capitalization stocks such as those included in the Dow Jones Industrial Average or the S&P 500 Index trade at an average of $.04 to $.05 per share. Quite often, these large blocks are handled by *block traders* who will commit their own capital by purchasing blocks of shares from the money manager, thus providing liquidity that may not be immediately available in the market. This liquidity can help reduce price impact that can occur when a large block of shares is revealed to the market all at once.

Soft dollar trades are those where the money manager, on behalf of its clients, arranges with a broker to use a portion of the commissions generated to purchase products or services that will be utilized by the investment manager in the investment decision-making process.

When ERISA was passed, there was concern that the use of soft dollars would violate its fiduciary responsibility provisions because the manager may be paying more than just the true cost of execution. Prior to the elimination of fixed commission rates on stock exchange transactions, money managers often purchased additional services with commission dollars beyond simple execution, clearance and settlement. After the elimination of fixed commission rates in May 1975, Congress amended the Securities Exchange Act of 1934 to add Section 28(e).

Section 28(e) allows the use of soft dollars for the purchase of research services as long as all of the section's stipulations are met. Specifically, Section 28(e) provides a safe harbor with respect to the use of commissions in connection with securities transactions. Commissions paid to acquire brokerage and investment services that are provided through a broker are allowed if the investment manager has investment discretion and determines in good faith that the amount of commission paid is reasonable.

The SEC has indicated that if the investment manager uses soft dollars to pay for nonresearch-related services, the transaction falls outside the protection afforded by Section 28(e) and may be in violation of securities laws. Therefore, if the services purchased by the investment manager are only partially related to investment decision making, an appropriate allocation must be made between payment using commissions and cash payment directly from the investment manager.

The Department of Labor, in Technical Release 86-1, issued in May 1986, acknowledged that these soft dollar (research trade) arrangements that meet the requirements of Section 28(e) do not violate ERISA.

TRUSTEE OVERSIGHT RESPONSIBILITY

When investment management responsibility has been properly delegated by plan trustees to an investment manager, the investment manager has fiduciary responsibility for trading decisions. The plan trustees have oversight responsibility to monitor the investment manager to assure that the manager has secured best execution[1] and to assure that the commissions are reasonable in relation to the value of the brokerage and research services provided to the plan.

This oversight process can be accomplished by asking each investment manager to provide information about its brokerage allocation policies and practices. The investment manager should describe:

- The products, research and services received
- Whether clients may be paying commissions higher than those obtainable from other brokers for the same products and services
- Whether the research benefits all of the investment manager's clients
- The procedures the investment manager used to direct client securities transactions to a particular broker in return for products and research services received.

Directed brokerage refers to an arrangement where a plan sponsor requests that its investment managers, subject to best execution, direct commissions to a particular broker who will provide services, pay obligations of the plan or make cash rebates to the plan. These arrangements are outside of Section 28(e), since Section 28(e) is only applicable to persons exercising investment discretion.

When an investment manager directs transactions through a designated broker-dealer for the exclusive benefit of the plan, provided that the amount paid for brokerage and other goods and services is reasonable, and the investment manager has fulfilled its obligation to obtain best execution, such transactions do not violate the fiduciary provisions of ERISA.

In order to fulfill fiduciary obligations to the plan, the trustees, when they instruct an investment manager to use a particular broker should:

- Initially determine that the broker is capable of providing best execution and evaluate whether the commissions are reasonable relative to the services provided
- Periodically monitor the broker's execution of transactions for the plan.

The investment manager must make sure that securities transactions of one plan are not used to pay for services or expenses attributable to another plan.

USING DIRECTED BROKERAGE TO PAY INVESTMENT CONSULTANTS

In years past, it was a fairly common practice for plans to pay for investment consulting services through the use of a directed brokerage or commission recapture service. At one time most investment consultants offered this service since the consultant was often already a broker dealer registered with the SEC and regulated by the National Association of Securities Dealers. Today it is less common for investment consultants to offer commission recapture services, and virtually all consultants charge a cash fee for consulting services, even if they offer commission recapture services as an adjunct to investment consultant services. When trades are directed through the investment consultant, the investment consultant becomes the broker of record and is legally responsible for the trade; however, the investment consultant does not actually execute the trade. The investment consultant will usually have a *correspondent* relationship with one or more large brokers that will execute, clear and settle these trades on their behalf. The consultant, as the broker of record, will pay the broker for the execution of the trade and must pay any other associated costs.

When utilizing a directed brokerage program, it is important to make sure that the consultant provides a regular accounting of the commissions that are directed through the program. If directed commissions are to be applied to the consultant's fees for investment consulting services, those fees, as well as the formula for crediting directed commissions to those consulting fees, should be specified in advance. Typically, a ratio of 2:1 is used in these formulas, where for every two dollars of commissions, one dollar is applied to the consulting fee.

The cents-per-share cost of directed brokerage trades should be no more than the cost of research trades, approximately $.04 to $.05 per share. Be sure to get a complete accounting of all trades for all investment managers serving the fund. This accounting should include all trades through all brokers as well as those trades that were directed through the consultant.

Trustees should be aware of the potential for conflicts of interest between an investment consultant and investment management firms when trades are directed through the investment consultant. Investment consultants may market performance ranking services to investment firms and therefore have a business relationship with those firms.

This relationship could be viewed as a potential conflict of interest if the investment consultant is also expected to advise the trustees concerning an investment firm's investment performance or suitability for retention. Other similar concerns address the practice of some investment firms that direct trades through consultants, without being asked to do so by clients, in the hope of being viewed in a more favorable light by the consultant.

Since participation in directed brokerage and commission recapture programs has the potential to substantially reduce commission costs for a fund, trustees should give these programs due consideration. Part of this consideration is to discuss these issues with the consultant before entering into a directed brokerage or commission recapture program. While there exists the potential for conflicts of interest, this does not automatically imply that there will be such conflicts. Full disclosure appears to be the best remedy.

FACTORS THAT INFLUENCE TRADING COSTS

When investment firms trade, they usually trade in large blocks that include shares for each portfolio they manage. A block trade may represent several hundred thousand shares earmarked for hundreds of client accounts. The money manager's trader begins to work the trade by contacting the institutional trading desk of those brokers that have expertise with the issue being traded. The cents-per-share commission is determined upfront by the investment manager and is agreed to by the broker executing the trade.

Additionally, the investment firm communicates special instructions such as the maximum or minimum price per share, timing considerations and whether a portion of the trade should be directed through the consultant acting as the broker of record.

One question often asked is why the broker is willing to reduce the total commissions received by giving up a portion of the commissions to another broker of record such as the investment consultant. One of the reasons for this accommodation is the fact that institutional brokers are interested in trade volume. Large block trades of liquid stocks represent the lifeblood of these firms, which have high overhead expenses and high personnel costs. A continual flow of trades from these large block trades is a primary source of revenue.

Another aspect to consider is that the brokerage firm may get to see both sides of the trade. One side of the trade is the large block being traded by the money manager, but the other side of the trade (the buyer if this is a sell order, or seller if this is a buy order) may be made up of many smaller blocks traded on behalf of other clients of the institutional broker. Participating on both sides of the trade may double the revenue to the broker.

Trustees have asked, "If the investment firm is setting the cents-per-share commission rate, why don't they set it at $.02 to $.03 per share, rather than the more typical $.04 to $.05?" This answer goes back to the relationships that develop between the investment firm and the institutional brokers. Traders at the institutional trading desks of the broker firms are compensated by sharing in commission revenue. Commissions that are set too low provide little incentive to actively work the trade or commit the firm's capital, nor is there incentive to contact the money manager when traders become aware of sought-after shares becoming available from another trade. A commission rate of $.04 to $.05 seems to be the level at which brokers are reasonably compensated.

BEST EXECUTION

The Department of Labor charges plan sponsors with the responsibility of assuring *best execution* for all trading done under their fiduciary authority. But best execution is very hard to measure, given the fact that each trade is dependent on so many factors that are often impossible to measure by looking after the fact at transactions.

The money manager has the responsibility to seek best execution because it is the one making the investment decisions and can control (to some degree) the cost impact of each decision. The total cost of a trade includes commissions, price impact costs and opportunity costs. Price impact costs result from price movements between the time a portfolio manager decides to trade and the final execution of the complete order. Opportunity costs represent the cost of failing to find enough shares to complete the trade. These price impact and opportunity costs can dwarf the $.04 to $.05 per share paid in commissions. In order to achieve best execution, the investment manager must consider all of these costs.

The implementation of investment ideas is an integral part of the investment process. The key is that all implementation costs affect performance. There is no fundamental difference between a dollar lost in excessive commissions or a dollar lost to timing costs. All implementation costs need attention. The optimal procedure is one that minimizes total cost and maximizes portfolio performance.

ENDNOTE

1. Neither the Department of Labor nor the Securities and Exchange Commission has provided a complete definition of *best execution*.

Chapter 42

Participant-Directed Investing in Defined Contribution Plans

Thomas A. Mitchell Sr., CEBS

INTRODUCTION

Most trustees understand the fundamental differences between defined benefit pension plans and defined contribution annuity plans.

In *defined benefit* pension plans, monthly pension benefit levels are calculated using a predetermined formula described in the plan. Investment returns are important to the funding of these benefit promises, but retirement benefits are not directly linked to a participant's account balance, nor are benefits directly tied to an actual investment return.

In *defined contribution* annuity plans, each participant has an account to which employer contributions as well as investment earnings or losses are posted. The participant's account balance equals his or her retirement benefit. There is a direct link between a participant's final benefit amount and investment performance.

In multiemployer plan circles, defined benefit pension plans have been negotiated as the primary vehicle for funding retirement benefits. Defined contribution annuity plans came later, most often as supplements to the defined benefit pension plans rather than replacements for them. There are cases where the only jointly negotiated retirement plan is a defined contribution annuity plan, but this is the exception rather than the rule.

Boards of trustees, acting in the best interest of all plan participants, have traditionally made the investment decisions for both pension and annuity plans. In recent years, however, a number of annuity plan participants have expressed interest in having more control over their individual accounts. This participant-directed investment decision process presents a number of challenges to those funds considering such a change. In this chapter, we'll investigate a number of these challenges.

DEFINED CONTRIBUTION PLAN STRUCTURES

There are two basic types of defined contribution plans available under the U.S. Tax Code. These are the *money purchase* plan and the *profit-sharing* plan. Both types have several common attributes, but the main difference has been the availability of a 401(k) option under the profit-sharing plan form. This option was not previously available under the money purchase plan form.

A good way to understand the relationship between the defined contribution plan and the 401(k) option is to remember that the tax-qualified structure of defined contribution plans allows employer contributions to the plan to be a deductible expense to the employer. The 401(k) option allows the participant to defer wages on a pretax basis, providing tax-advantaged savings.

When multiemployer groups began to implement defined contribution annuity plans, the only form available was the money purchase plan. Use of the profit-sharing plan form required that all participating employers be profitable before contributions could be deemed deductible. Beginning in 1986, following regulatory changes, the profit-sharing plan structure became available to multiemployer groups.

In both forms, contributions required through collective bargaining are posted to each participant's account. Investment returns, minus investment fees and administrative costs, are also added to each account balance. Plan participants periodically receive statements showing contributions and investment returns.

In some cases, a plan will permit limited withdrawals prior to termination of employment, and many plans permit loans. For the most part, since these plans supplement a defined benefit pension plan, they are viewed by many plan participants as savings plans.

Among multiemployer plans, the decisions concerning the investment of plan assets have traditionally been made by the plan's board of trustees. Trustees have done a good job of balancing the needs of both older and younger plan participants and have developed investment programs that are generally more aggressive than savings accounts, yet they are more conservatively invested than pension plans.

PARTICIPANT-DIRECTED INVESTING

Instead of deciding themselves how to invest the dollars accumulating in participants' defined contribution accounts, trustees can permit participants to make their own investment decisions by choosing among several options selected by the trustees. When participants make these decisions instead of the trustees, the term *participant-directed* is used to describe how investment decisions are made. In recent years there has been a new focus on participant-directed investing. This new focus has been driven by a number of factors, including the following.

The growth and availability of 401(k) plans. Most people are at least somewhat familiar with 401(k) plans since they are offered by a large number of corporations. Union members may have a spouse or other family member whose employer offers a 401(k) plan. The investment decisions necessary for these plans are often discussed over the kitchen table.

The growth of mutual funds. Mutual funds have enjoyed phenomenal growth in a short time. In 1980 there were barely 500 stock, bond and money market funds. Today there are over 7,000 funds of all types. Most of us are inundated by advertisements for mutual funds and retirement planning seminars. Almost every newspaper and business magazine includes mutual fund advertising.

Peer pressure within companies. A number of employers have been offering participant-directed plans to their nonbargaining unit employees while contributing to trustee-directed defined contribution plans for the bargaining unit employees. In some cases the bargaining unit employees are now asking their employers for the same participant-directed decision-making ability.

ERISA Section 404(c). One incentive for trustees to offer participant-directed investing comes from recent clarifying regulations concerning Section 404(c) of ERISA. Section 404(c) limits trustees' fiduciary liability for investment decisions, when those decisions are made by participants who *exercise control over their individual accounts.*

ERISA Section 404(c) regulations set out a series of provisions that, if followed completely, can limit trustees' fiduciary liability.
1. Trustees must provide participants with at least three investment options with substantially different risk and return characteristics for each.
2. Trustees must provide sufficient information (education) that will enable participants to make informed choices from among the options available. There is an important distinction between information and *advice.* If the information is considered *advice,* fiduciary liability could revert back to the trustees.
3. Participants must have the opportunity to reallocate account balances or direct new contributions, or both, among the available options at least every three months.
4. Trustees must continue to monitor the investment choices being offered to participants and must add or replace investment options that do not meet expectations.

RECORDKEEPING REQUIREMENTS

With the introduction of participant-directed investing, recordkeeping becomes quite a bit more complex. Considering that each participant may have a different allocation among the various investment options and may change allocations among the investment options each quarter, the recordkeeping system requirements can be daunting.

In some cases, third-party administrators or in-house administration teams possess these recordkeeping capabilities. In other cases, the administrator does not have the systems in place to handle the influx of calls and paperwork that participant-directed investing entails. A common alternative to in-house recordkeeping is the selection of an independent contractor such as a mutual fund company or investment firm, a benefits consulting firm or a bank.

The independent recordkeeper works with the administrator, investment managers, custodian bank and trustees to make the participant-directed investment program run smoothly.

Typical responsibilities of the recordkeeper are:
1. Recordkeeping
   - Posting contributions and investment earnings to participant accounts
   - Recording participant directions for investment of new contributions and account balances, and providing instructions for transfers to investment vehicles
   - Preparation of accounting reports and reconciling plan assets to participant balances.
2. Providing information
   - Distribution of prospectuses and other legally required fund information to participants at enrollment
   - Creating participant investment education and communications material

- Preparation of periodic statements of participants' account balances
- Distributing Summary Annual Reports and Summary Plan Descriptions.
3. Distributions
    - In-service withdrawals, participant loans, lump-sum payouts and annuity purchases are formally administered by the fund office, then communicated to the recordkeeper.
    - Tax-related withholding (20%) and penalties for early withdrawals (10%) are calculated and a Form 1099R is prepared for withdrawals and payouts as required.
    - Inactive accounts may be subject to forced distribution if the participant's account balance is less than $5,000.
4. 401(k) testing
    - The recordkeeper assists the fund office with the comparative deferral (nondiscrimination) testing required by the IRS.
5. Compliance
    - The recordkeeper can prepare certain financial portions of Form 5500 and its schedules and assist in other government filings.

INVESTMENT ISSUES

There are a number of generally accepted advantages and disadvantages associated with participant-directed investing.

Advantages

1. Participants can tailor their investment choices based on age, expected retirement date, other family resources for retirement income and risk tolerance.
2. With the availability of a number of investment options, participants can further diversify the risk and return characteristics of their personalized investment programs.
3. Participant-directed investing can teach investment skills and may encourage individual savings.

Disadvantages

1. Adding participant-directed investing can increase a plan's complexity, administrative costs and investment-related expenses.
2. If participants choose investment choices that are too conservative, retirement needs may not be met. If participants concentrate investments in higher risk assets, investment losses may be discouraging, or retirement benefits could be reduced if losses occur close to retirement.
3. Allowing participants to reallocate their account balances among different investment options may encourage "market timing."
4. Trustees have developed investment policies that quantify their risk and return expectations, and through regular meetings with portfolio managers they communicate their expectations. The use of mutual funds in participant-directed plans limits the trustees' control over the investment policy, perhaps exposing them to unforeseen investment risks. Also, trustees should not expect to meet with the investment professionals responsible for managing the mutual funds.

INCREASED COSTS

Since I've mentioned the increased costs associated with participant-directed investing, let's look at some of them.

Recordkeeping expenses are already being paid by all retirement plans. Both defined benefit and defined contribution plans have detailed recordkeeping requirements with which most trustees are familiar. These expenses will continue. When trustees decide to offer participant-directed investment options, the plan's recordkeeping expenses will increase.

Based on data from the Investment Company Institute (an association of mutual fund companies), annual per participant recordkeeping fees ranged from a median of $47 for services offered by mutual fund companies to a median of $82 for other providers. This was based on 1995 data. These costs have been coming down and, in certain instances when plans agree to utilize the investment options offered by the recordkeeper, the recordkeeping services are provided free of charge. Keep in mind that, even though recordkeeping fees may appear to be free from certain providers, their other investment-related fees can more than make up for this give-up.

The recordkeeping fees charged by mutual fund companies are often lower than those charged by other providers because mutual funds must include a portion of their common recordkeeping expenses in the "expense ratio" deducted from all mutual fund investors' accounts each year.

Annual recordkeeping fees do not include startup costs for designing and drafting investment programs, designing communication material, etc. Startup costs can be quite low for off-the-shelf programs but can rise to several hundred thousand dollars for custom-designed investment programs and associated communication materials and seminars.

OTHER INVESTMENT-RELATED FEES

Since many participant-directed plans and most

401(k) plans utilize mutual funds, we should take a look at some of the other costs associated with their use.

Some mutual funds charge a sales commission and are referred to as *load* funds, and others, which do not charge these commissions, are referred to as *no-load* funds. The *load* funds charge their sales commission either upfront, specified as a percentage of each new investment dollar, or on the way out, specified as a percentage of each dollar withdrawn. These commissions are paid to the broker or financial planner who directed the investor to the mutual fund. These front end or back end load charges can range up to 8.5%.

As you might imagine, these sales loads were not well received by most investors, and many mutual funds reduced or eliminated sales loads in favor of another, less visible, method of passing on costs to investors, the *12b-1 fee*.

Section 12b-1 allows mutual funds to charge investors an annual fee to offset distribution expenses and to compensate brokers selling their funds. The 12b-1 fees can be charged in addition to front end or back end loads, or may be levied in place of loads. The SEC allows mutual funds to charge annual 12b-1 fees up to a maximum of 1% of assets. Some mutual fund companies charge neither sales loads nor 12b-1 fees; others charge just 12b-1 fees, often at less than the full 1% allowed.

Consider how much an investor can give up in terms of retirement resources when a mutual fund company charges front end or back end sales loads, then reduces the investor's account balance by up to 1% every year. Even when commission loads are not charged, a 12b-1 fee can erode investment returns.

INVESTMENT-RELATED EXPENSES

Investment management fees are a fact of life for all investors. These fees are paid to the investment advisor or subadvisor who is responsible for making the investment decisions for the separate portfolio or mutual fund. Trustees of annuity funds that use separate account management rather than mutual funds are used to paying between 0.4% and 0.8% for equity portfolio management, and 0.2% to 0.5% for fixed income portfolio management. Index funds, which match the return of broad market indexes such as the S&P 500 Stock Index, generally have the lowest investment management fees, often in the range of 0.05% (five basis points) to 0.2% (20 basis points). Added to the separate account management fees are the bank custody fees. These average from three to six basis points.

Mutual fund expenses are most often much higher than separate account management fees plus custody charges. Equity mutual fund expenses average 1.5% per year, and range from 0.2% to 2.2% or more. Balanced funds carry average annual expenses of 1.0%, and range from 0.3% to 1.9%.

These higher costs reduce investment returns. A study of 741 domestic equity mutual funds conducted by John Bogle, the retired chairman of Vanguard Mutual Funds, noted that the lowest cost mutual fund annual expenses reduced average equity investment returns (equities returned 11% on average over the last 70 years) by about 22 basis points (a basis point is one one-hundredth of 1%) but the highest cost mutual fund expenses reduced average equity returns by 242 basis points.

Another revealing aspect of this study addressed investment risk, finding that a long-term investment return expectation of 7.5% per year might be achieved with less risk using low-cost funds but would require higher risk taking when high-cost mutual funds are used. An asset mix of 40% stocks/60% bonds invested in the lowest cost mutual funds would average approximately 7.5% over long periods, after deducting expenses. Using the highest cost mutual funds would require a ratio of 80% stocks/20% bonds to achieve the same results after expenses.

Clearly, the ease of investing in mutual funds, which offer daily valuations and daily liquidity, is appealing. Investors don't always consider what the true cost of this convenience might be.

Mutual funds deduct their operating expenses from each investor's account balance throughout the year based on an annual expense ratio. This *annual expense ratio* is deducted from each investor's account, and it includes 12b-1 fees, investment advisory fees, administrative expenses and those recordkeeping fees associated with all investors. This percentage can vary from year to year. Certain investment advisory or other fees may be waived in the startup years of a mutual fund but may reappear later.

OTHER ISSUES TO BE CONSIDERED

Are there too many choices? Recent surveys indicate that plan sponsors (primarily 401(k) plans are being surveyed) are offering more and more investment options. A report by Fidelity Investments is insightful. Based on eight million participants enrolled in 10,000 plans at the end of 2003, the report noted the average number of investment options available to plan participants in 2003 increased to 18 (the median was 16), continuing a trend among Fidelity record-kept plans to add an average of two options per year. The average number of investment options was lower at 13 for smaller plans and higher with an average of 49 options for large plans.

The Vanguard Group's recent report covering over 2.5 million participants in 1,500 plans showed similar numbers. At the end of 2003 the average number of investment options offered was 16.4. This number is similar to the average of 16.8 investment options reported by the Profit Sharing/401(k) Council of America.

Ninety-nine percent (99%) of the Fidelity-administered plans offered domestic equity funds, 93% offered fixed income funds and 91% offered blended funds, while 76% offered short-term funds and 29% offered stable-value funds. The number of plans offering international equity funds increased to 89%. Interestingly, within the domestic equity category plan sponsors offered an average of nine different funds, with a low of 7.5 domestic equity fund options for small plans and a high of 24.9 domestic equity funds for large plans.

It is difficult to imagine how the typical plan participant would be able to select from this multitude of investment choices. This presents a challenge to the trustees of plans transitioning to participant-directed investing. Too many investment options may overwhelm plan participants, resulting in poor investment choices. Plan participants will sometimes allocate equal percentages to all fund options offered thinking they will end up with a more diversified portfolio.

Even though plans are offering an ever-growing list of investment options, plan participants appear to be selecting a manageable number. The Fidelity report noted 25% of plan participants held just one option, 45% held between two and four options, and 29% held five or more investment options, with the overall average at 3.6. The Vanguard Group report noted a similar average of 3.4 investment options held by participants at the end of 2003, with 26.5% holding five or more funds.

One of the best ways for plan participants to make asset allocation decisions is to utilize life-cycle or life-stage blended funds that allocate among stocks, bonds and short-term investments in ratios that are based on the participant's current age or expected retirement age. These options are designed to serve participants wanting a single diversified investment option. Within the Fidelity fund offerings, the life-stage funds were offered by 72% of plan sponsors. The Vanguard Group report noted half of the plans they administer offered life-cycle options to participants. The Vanguard Group reports twice as many plans offered life-cycle options in 2003 as did in the beginning of 2000. The Vanguard report also noted only 30% of plan participants used the life-cycle option as the intended "one-stop shopping" investment choice.

Are participant investment choices too conservative? Conservative investment options designed to protect principal continue to play a role. When considering those plans that make the conservative investment options available, 22% of assets were allocated to the stable-value option, 8% was allocated to the short-term option, and 5% was allocated to the fixed income options.

For plans with fewer participants the percentage allocation to short-term and fixed income options was higher, and for plans with large numbers of participants the allocation to short-term and fixed income options was lower. This may have something to do with the level of education offered by large plans. Allocations to stable-value options were more consistent across plans of all sizes.

Company stock continues to play a significant role in 401(k) plans (but not in multiemployer plans), representing 17% of assets overall, according to the Fidelity report. Vanguard reports 14% of assets were invested in company stock.

Considering the equity market decline during 2000-2002, participants reacted by exchanging out of equity investment options into the conservative options during 2000, 2001 and 2002, then gravitated back to equities during the recovery in 2003. At the end of 2003, Fidelity reported the overall percentage allocation to domestic and international equities was 52%, down from 56% in 2002. The Vanguard report notes 77% of assets were invested in equities in 2000; this percentage dropped to 64% in 2002, then went back to 69% in 2003. The Vanguard equity exposure percentage is similar to the Fidelity percentage when company stock is considered. Individual allocations vary considerably. Vanguard reported 14% of participants held no equity exposure, and at the other extreme 21% of participants held their entire account balance in equities.

It's important that younger participants with many years to invest before retirement make asset allocation decisions that are appropriate. The Fidelity report showed younger plan participants are indeed allocating a smaller percentage of assets to the conservative options and a higher percentage to equities. Participants under age 50 held approximately 70% in equities. As would be expected, participants over age 65 had generally opposite allocations with 60% to 70% in conservative investment options and 30% to 40% in equities. According to Vanguard, participants aged 65 and older held 47% in equity investments, while participants under age 55 held between 72% and 78% in equity investments.

Overall, these results suggest while some individual participants are either too conservative, or too aggressive in their asset allocation decisions, for the most part participants are making appropriate investment option decisions.

ARE PARTICIPANT-DIRECTED INVESTMENTS DELIVERING ACCEPTABLE INVESTMENT RETURNS?

A Watson Wyatt Company article published in October 1994 concluded that, for a variety of reasons, investment decisions made by employees tended to produce lower rates of return. Using 1991 Form 5500 annual reports, Wyatt reported that returns for participant-directed plans were 2-3% lower than returns from plans where trustees made the investment decisions.

An article in the *Journal of Portfolio Management*

examined the impact of market timing on investment returns from mutual funds. The authors concluded that poor market timing and dollar cost averaging have cost mutual fund investors about 1% per year since 1984. This market timing, plus the extra costs associated with mutual fund investing, may be among the reasons for mutual funds generally underperforming relative to the broad market index returns.

CONCLUSION

Converting a plan to participant-directed investing requires a great deal of involvement by trustees and other professionals. Administrative costs will surely increase with the introduction of more frequent valuations, new investment options and participant education. If mutual funds are utilized, expenses may be much higher, and trustees give up the right to vote proxies and impose investment restrictions on managers. Even when ERISA 404(c) regulations are closely followed, trustees continue to shoulder fiduciary liability; and it's not clear whether plan participants will end up with a larger retirement nest egg.

Nevertheless, trustees may be faced with having to offer participant-directed investing to plan participants, so here are a few thoughts to consider.

1. Be prepared to spend quite a bit of time reviewing options and making decisions, and allow plenty of time to implement those decisions.
2. Carefully consider who will provide the account administration and investment education. Poor implementation and communication can result in a public relations nightmare.
3. Costs can vary widely and can be hard to measure on an "apples-to-apples" basis. Mutual funds might be perceived as the low-cost, easy-to-use alternative, but their expenses can be quite high, and these costs ultimately reduce investment earnings.
4. In a perfect world, participants would have enough investment knowledge to choose a well-diversified mix of investment options, resulting in the right balance between risk and return, and tailored to their specific needs. Since we don't live in that perfect world, consider the creation of three or four lifestyle options. Each option would include stocks, bonds, GICs, etc., in varying percentages. The risk posture of each option would increase from reasonably low to moderately high.

Participants can choose an option that is consistent with their age, financial status, tolerance for risk, etc. Every option would have some exposure to every asset class, ensuring diversification. This could be implemented using separate account management, index funds or mutual funds in combination.

This approach offers diversification, reasonably low costs and a greater expectation of long-term investment success and retains control over a number of important aspects of the investment program.

Bibliography

Burroughs, Eugene B. *Investment Policy Guidebook for Trustees.* Brookfield, Wis.: International Foundation of Employee Benefit Plans, 1995.

Burroughs, Eugene B., editor. *Trustees and Their Professional Advisors.* Brookfield, Wis.: International Foundation of Employee Benefit Plans, 1996.

Davidson, Terence S. "Investment Options for Private Trusteed Pension Funds." *Employee Benefits Basics,* Third Quarter 1989. International Foundation of Employee Benefit Plans.

Ellis, Charles D. *Investment Policy: How to Win the Loser's Game.* Homewood, Ill.: Dow Jones-Irwin, 1985.

Malkiel, Burton G. *A Random Walk Down Wall Street.*

Mennis, Edmund A. *How the Economy Works.* New York, N.Y.: New York Institute of Finance, Simon and Schuster, 1991.

Owen, James P. *The Prudent Investor.* Chicago, Ill.: Prabus Publishing Co., 1990.

Rosenberg, Claude N. Jr. *Investing With the Best.* New York, N.Y.: John Wiley and Sons, 1986.

Tobias, Andrew. *The Only Investment Guide You'll Ever Need.* Orlando, Fla.: Harcourt Brace & Co., 1996.

Trone, Allbright and Taylor. *The Management of Investment Decisions.* Chicago, Ill.: Irwin, 1996.

Wurman, Richard S. *The Wall Street Journal Guide to Understanding Money & Markets.* New York, N.Y.: Access Press, 1990.

Checklist for Trustees on Key Points in Section VIII

The following questions are provided to stimulate thinking of a trustee concerning the investment function.

1. Is the board of trustees familiar with fundamentals of investing money? Do the trustees understand investment terminology? Do the trustees understand the alternative types of investment vehicles available to the fund with which they are involved? Do the trustees understand alternative investment management agencies available to trust funds?
2. Does the trust fund regularly measure the investment performance of its portfolio?
3. Is the performance of the portfolio measured against other funds and market indexes?
4. Has the board of trustees reviewed the implications of the fiduciary standards under the Employee Retirement Income Security Act of 1974 (ERISA) as these standards might apply to their particular fund?
5. Has the trust fund established specific investment objectives? Have these objectives been reduced to writing in an investment policy statement?
6. Has the board of trustees recognized the importance of the asset allocation decision?
7. Does the board of trustees regularly communicate with their investment manager to review performance versus objectives?
8. Has the board of trustees specifically discussed such matters as risk definition and the trustees' attitude toward risk?
9. Has the board of trustees discussed the ways in which the fund might wish to diversify assets as required under the act? Has the board explored the use of alternatives to stocks, bonds and real estate?
10. Has the board of trustees reviewed the pension investment alternatives offered by agencies other than the kind currently being used?
11. Has the board of trustees familiarized itself with index funds as an alternative means of investing?
12. Has the board of trustees reviewed from time to time the way cash flow is managed to determine whether available monies may be left uninvested for significant periods of time?

SECTION IX

COLLECTIONS

Chapter 43

Collections

Ira R. Mitzner

INTRODUCTION

The poor investment returns during 2000, 2001 and 2002 had a devastating impact on many Taft-Hartley funds. The downturn in the stock market resulted in the failure of funds to meet their actuarial assumptions and, in some cases, trustees were forced to make benefit cuts. These unusual economic conditions, which have had a long-term detrimental effect, have made it more important than ever for funds to ensure a steady flow of contributions from participating employers by pursuing employer delinquencies.

It is the responsibility of trustees to ensure those monies are collected—and collected on time. There are many pressures on trustees that make the task more daunting. Multiemployer trustees wear "two hats" and have obligations both to the fund participants and to those who appointed them (union or employer). There is the need to create a collection system that works automatically and chronologically because, otherwise, trustees may be pressured to create exceptions for the "good union employer." Trustees today are increasingly faced with the disappearance of signatory employers and the emergence of "new" employers—the alter ego dilemma. Funds are constantly in search of new and effective weapons to deal with delinquencies, including liens, bonds and collateral assignments.

This chapter on collections hopefully will provide guidance to resolve some of these issues. Trustees must understand their responsibilities under the Employee Retirement Income Security Act of 1974 (ERISA), as amended, as those obligations have been interpreted by the Department of Labor (DOL) and the courts. They also must be aware of the "two-hat" problem and make efforts to ensure the actions they take recognize the distinction between their union or employer "hat" and their trustee "hat." They must enact written collection procedures and create a system that works on "automatic pilot" rather than unnecessarily injecting the trustee into the collection process. They should use every available weapon, aggressive collections and settlements backed up by "stipulated judgments" or "collateral assignments."

The purpose of this chapter is not to transform trustees into legal experts in collections, but to provide sufficient information for them to know whether the fund is meeting the basic requirements and whether fund counsel is doing what needs to be done to protect the trustees.[1]

LEGAL PRINCIPLES UNDERLYING THE DUTY TO COLLECT DELINQUENCIES

Statutory and Legislative Authority for Enforcing the Duty to Collect

Every employer obligated to make contributions to a multiemployer plan is required to make those contributions according to the terms of the plan or applicable collective bargaining agreement. ERISA Section 502(g)(2), passed as part of the 1980 amendments to ERISA in the Multiemployer Pension Plan Amendments Act (MPPAA), is the key to collection of employer delinquencies.

Congress passed the 1980 amendments pertaining to delinquent employer contributions because it "intended that [ERISA's] enforcement provisions should have teeth." MPPAA was enacted to counteract

> the serious problem created by the "[f]ailure of employers to make promised contribution [s] in a timely fashion [,which] imposes a variety of costs on plans[.] . . . The intent of this section is to promote the prompt payment of contributions and assist plans in recovering the costs incurred in connection with delinquencies.

343

Congress made clear that MPPAA was intended to compensate funds for the loss of use of delinquent payments and for the costs of collecting delinquencies.

Statutory and Regulatory Authority Governing the Trustees' Duty to Collect

There are no regulatory guidelines specifically directed to collection of employer delinquencies. However, regulations promulgated under the *Prohibited Transactions* section of ERISA provide guidance as to the duty to collect employer delinquencies. The prohibited transactions provisions of ERISA make it per se unlawful for certain parties to engage in transactions with certain other parties and define the prohibition not by the nature of the transaction but by the relationship of the parties. One such prohibited transaction is a loan or extension of credit granted by a plan to a *party in interest*. Under ERISA, contributing employers are defined as parties in interest and therefore are precluded from receiving loans or extensions of credit from a plan. When a plan fails to collect delinquencies from an employer, that failure to collect is deemed a prohibited transaction within the meaning of ERISA.

Under Prohibited Transaction Class Exemption 76-1, DOL set forth the circumstances under which the plan may extend credit or permit a delinquent employer to meet its obligations under an extended payment schedule without committing a prohibited transaction. While PTE 76-1 permits trustees to settle cases pursuant to a "written" settlement agreement, its first tenet is that a plan must make reasonable, "systematic" and "diligent" efforts to collect employer delinquencies.

Fiduciary Responsibilities of Trustees for Failing to Collect Employer Delinquencies

The duty to collect employer delinquencies rests squarely on the shoulders of the trustees. The United States Supreme Court articulated this principle in *Central States, Southeast & Southwest Areas Pension Fund v. Central Transport, Inc.*, and rejected the notion that responsibility for collection of delinquencies rests primarily on the shoulders of the union, DOL or the beneficiaries.[2] The cases on fiduciary responsibility in collections show ERISA gives broad powers to trustees to collect delinquencies and places a heavy burden on those trustees if the power is not properly exercised. Thus, the themes of expansive power and extensive duties on trustees recur in the collections arena.

Trustees who fail to comply with their fiduciary duties can be held personally liable under ERISA. A court may order a trustee to make good all losses to the plan, post a cash or surety bond to cover potential losses and disgorge any "compensation" received from the plan without any setoff for services actually performed by the trustee. A court also can remove an individual from a trustee position or prohibit the trustee from serving as a fiduciary in the future.

COLLECTION BY THE FUND

The best way to ensure compliance with a trustee's fiduciary duties and to resolve conflicts of responsibility is to create a collection system set on "automatic pilot." Each plan should have written collection procedures that eliminate discretion, as much discretion as possible, from the collection process. It is important the procedure work automatically and without discretion in order to insulate trustees from pressures exerted on them by delinquent employers and those speaking on their behalf (which often include union business agents). A trustee can find at least some protection in a system that is written, clear and free from politics.

The procedure should work both chronologically and automatically. All participating employers should be notified as to when contributions are due so they understand their obligations. If the contributions are not paid in a timely manner, a notice should go out warning that interest and liquidated damages will be assessed. If the delinquency is still not satisfied, the matter should automatically be referred to counsel. By requiring referrals to the next steps on specific dates and removing discretion from the process, these procedures will work both chronologically and automatically. For employers that repeatedly fall delinquent, the fund may require a cash or surety bond for protection. Health funds will want procedures that allow benefits to be cut off following notice to the delinquent employer and the employees. Such a notice to employees will bring substantial pressure on the employer to cure the delinquency.

In a typical example of a collection procedure, contributions may be due on January 15 for work performed in December. If contributions are not received, a reminder notice is issued on February 1. On February 15, a notice of delinquency is issued and on March 1, interest is assessed and liquidated damages are imposed. However, it is important to remember the timing of the collection procedures will vary with the needs of the industry.

The responses by employers to such a collection system will vary. Some employers receive the initial reminder and pay automatically. Others do not respond until the word *counsel* appears in the letter and there is the threat of litigation. Experience has shown if an employer has the money to pay, business sense compels payment before interest and liquidated damages are imposed. However, some employers will still attempt to use the fund as a "bank."

A collection system will work best if the plan's collection philosophy is to be tough but fair, and to impose progressive discipline on delinquent employers. *Pro-*

gressive discipline means, for example, that on day 15 a delinquency warning letter is issued, on day 30 interest is assessed and on day 45 liquidated damages are assessed—all automatically. Participating employers will not look to the plan for loans if the system works chronologically and automatically and imposes this type of increasing penalties.

COLLECTION LITIGATION

Tactics

Trustees have a duty to ensure the collection mechanism works at the plan level and after referral to counsel. Counsel's role in the process begins where the plan's role ends. When a delinquent employer fails to make payment, the matter automatically is referred to plan counsel by the fund under the timetable set forth in the collection procedures. The collection procedures should specify that counsel's letter to the delinquent employer will be issued within a given number of days from referral. Typically, counsel's letter will warn that the full ERISA remedies will be brought to bear if payment is not received within a given time (e.g., ten days). If payment is not received, suit should be filed promptly.

There are certain tactical advantages available to ERISA funds. If the delinquent employer is located in a federal district different from the fund, suit may be brought where the fund is "administered." A large national fund can process delinquencies on an assembly line basis and meet little resistance obtaining and enforcing default judgments from employers who ignore counsel's letter of warning. Once a default judgment is obtained, the judgment must be referred to local counsel for collection, which will turn upon the remedies available in each state.

A debate has been raging for years as to whether arbitration or litigation is the better course in pursuing delinquencies. The choice depends predominantly upon the circumstances in a particular jurisdiction. Years of litigation experience have led the author to conclude that, in most circumstances, it is strategically advantageous for a plan to bring suit under ERISA rather than have the union obtain an arbitration award and then move to enforce it. The litigation method ensures recovery of all ERISA remedies, including legal fees. The most significant exception to using this method is the case in which a judge would be called upon to interpret provisions of the collective bargaining agreement. For example, an employer may claim that particular work does not fall within the "jurisdictional clause" of the collective bargaining agreement; e.g., his workers are merely "helpers," not "tile setters." In these circumstances, it may be better to obtain an interpretation of work jurisdiction under the collective bargaining agreement from the arbitrator who is versed in the "law of the shop," rather than from a federal judge who is not.

The Complaint and Available Remedies

While ERISA appears to permit suit in the name of the plan, the safest course is to sue in the names of the trustees on behalf of the fund. It is important to ensure the current trustees are named as plaintiffs.

The actions should be brought using the proper name of the delinquent employer. If there is a basis for naming an alter ego corporation or an individual, that defendant should be added separately. Counsel should err on the side of including all possible entities, since it may be difficult to name them as defendants at a later time. However, counsel must have a good faith, factual basis for naming each defendant.

ERISA provides that the court "shall" award damages for contributions, interest, liquidated damages and attorney fees. The statute further provides that interest may be set at a reasonable rate established by the fund trustees. Assuming there is a basis for it in the plan, liquidated damages may be imposed (1) up to 20% of contributions or (2) an additional computation of interest, whichever is higher. Unlike other parts of ERISA, which make attorney fees "discretionary," the collection provisions make the imposition of attorney fees *mandatory*. However, such fees must be "reasonable," and some courts are quite stringent about the manner and form of fee applications. Recovery of costs (such as filing fees) also is permitted. Most federal courts also are willing to award the costs associated with service of the complaint. The complaint should, in separate paragraphs, seek recovery for interest, liquidated damages, attorney fees and costs. In the unusual case involving a "willful, wanton and malicious" refusal to pay monies owed, punitive damages also may be sought.

It is often very difficult to know the amount to be included in the complaint because the employer has failed to file reports and/or refused to permit an audit. In such circumstances, the best tactic is to estimate damages (erring on the high side) rather than waste time just seeking to compel an audit. Once the case is under way, the fund can require the production of documents necessary for the audit, rather than risk an injunction. The law is clear that if the defendant refuses to turn over documents that would allow precise calculation, estimates are permissible and all doubts are resolved in favor of the plaintiff.

The Audit Weapon

Every employee benefit plan should have a policy regarding the conducting of payroll audits. Some audits may be carried out on a random basis, and others are implemented only for "problem" employers. While the subject of audits is beyond the scope of this chapter, a few guidelines can be followed in using audits as part of ERISA litigation tactics.

First, the fund's collection procedures should address the subject of audits, and the trust documents should make clear that audits are sanctioned by the trust.[3] Second, the fund must locate an auditor knowledgeable in payroll audits and the industry. Many good CPA firms have no idea how to conduct a payroll audit well and on a cost-effective basis for the fund. An experienced auditor also can provide useful information to counsel about alter ego relationships. (One auditor heard the alter ego business being run from the back of the employer's office.) Third, the fund may wish to impose the cost of the audit on an employer when the audit reveals a delinquency. Authorization for the imposition of such costs should be contained in the fund's documents. Problems may arise when the cost of the audit fees exceeds the amount of the delinquency. Finally, if an employer does not permit the fund access, application can be made to the court for injunctive relief. However, as explained previously, an "estimate" or document production demand may be superior weapons.

Some contracts in the construction industry contain a traveling contractor clause—meaning that if a Florida employer works in New York, it must comply with the terms of the New York contract, although it did not sign it. Recently, such a clause was upheld in *Flynn v. Beeler* in the United States District Court for the District of Columbia. An auditor must be familiar with the workings of such a contract in order to properly examine the books and records of the employer.

Pursuing Alter Ego Entities and Piercing the Corporate Veil

One of the most difficult and frustrating problems faced by plans today occurs when they discover their participating employer who has ceased making contributions is defunct and without assets. Or perhaps the participating employer has "disappeared," leaving behind a new company that is purportedly unrelated to the former but nevertheless is run by one of the family members of the former employer. A variation on that theme is that an old employer obligated to contribute to the plan suddenly becomes a "new" employer that claims no such obligation. This section is intended to provide trustees with enough information to spot the situations in which contractors are "cheating" and avoiding obligations to plans by changing corporate form or hiding behind corporate form without abiding by corporate formalities. Plan counsel then may pursue a strategy that ensures collections from these entities or individuals.

As a general rule, a corporation will be looked upon as a legal entity that is liable for only its own debts; and the personal liability of its officers, directors and shareholders for the debts of the corporate entity is quite limited. One of the major problems faced today by employee benefit plans is that judges across the United States often come from "Corporate America" and are extremely reluctant to impose personal liability on the individuals or hold one corporation accountable for the debts of another. For example, in *International Brotherhood of Painters & Allied Trades Union v. George A. Kracher, Inc.*, the court stressed:

> [L]imited liability is a hallmark of corporate law. Surely if Congress had decided to alter such a universal and time-honored concept, it would have signaled that resolve somehow in the legislative history [of ERISA].

A plan may encounter a similar reaction by a court any time it seeks to impose alter ego liability or to pierce the corporate veil.

Piercing the Corporate Veil

Under the common law doctrine of piercing the corporate veil, a court will prevent a corporate entity from being used as a mere instrumentality or business conduit of another person or corporation in order to commit a wrong or a fraud. When a party improperly attempts to use a corporate veil, the law will treat the corporation as an association of persons and impose liability accordingly. In sum, the court "pierces" through the corporate protections and imposes liability on the individual.

For example, in *Alman v. Danin,* two individuals, Danin and Fredella, manufactured raincoats and bought a company, B&S, to sew these raincoats. They then formed a new corporation named Mohawk. Mohawk, represented by Danin, entered into a collective bargaining contract that, among other things, required Mohawk to make weekly contributions to several union-operated employee benefit funds. When Mohawk failed to make the payments, the union obtained a judgment against Mohawk. Upon discovering that Mohawk was defunct, the union sued Danin and Fredella (and another corporation owned by them) for recovery of the judgment. In holding Danin and Fredella liable for the debts of Mohawk, the court said:

> In concluding that Danin and Fredella had not respected Mohawk's separate existence even minimally, the district court pointed out that Mohak's board of directors had never formally met, that Mohawk kept no corporate records, and that Danin and Fredella did not charge Mohawk for its use of B&S' former equipment and facilities. From the outset, Mohawk was inadequately capitalized. The judge noted deposition testimony indicating that the only asset Danin and Fredella provided Mohawk was the use of the former B&S facilities; beyond that, the company never received any liquid assets or working capital. Since Danin and Fredella could not have expected Mohawk to be

able to pay its debts, the court inferred that both men, being Mohawk's principles [sic], had acted in bad faith in their dealings with the union.

Courts thus look to many factors to determine whether a corporate veil should be pierced, including the factors addressed in *Alman,* such as whether there are formal meetings of corporate officers and proper maintenance of corporate records; whether equipment and facilities are shared without adequate consideration; whether the entity is adequately capitalized; and whether it is expected that the corporation will be able to pay its debts.

Another important factor examined by the court is fraud or wrongdoing. If there is evidence that a corporation has been established to avoid meeting corporate contractual obligations, with no reasonable ability to meet its debts, liability may be found. In *Leddy v. Standard Drywall, Inc.,* the court held a controlling officer personally liable for deliberately defrauding and conspiring to defraud the fund. In proving motivation to avoid obligations, counsel also should pursue evidence of antiunion animus on the part of management.

As stated, the capitalization of a corporation also may be a significant indicator of whether a corporate shell has been established to avoid certain mandatory corporate obligations. Courts often have looked to the incorporators' failure to adequately capitalize the corporation and the making of interest-free loans from one corporate affiliate to another. Additionally, plans should look for the sale of corporate assets for less than fair market value, particularly sales of assets at book value.

Alter Ego

A related doctrine, the alter ego doctrine, also has been employed against fraudulently formed corporate subsidiaries and affiliates, as well as "double-breasted" situations in which a new employer springs up from an old employer and is no longer included under the collective bargaining agreement. The alter ego doctrine permits courts to disregard a corporation that is the mere alter ego, or business conduct, of another corporation. The rationale behind the doctrine is that if shareholders or corporations disregard legal formalities, the law also will disregard them so far as is necessary to protect individual and corporate creditors. In such cases, specific evidentiary factors considered by courts include the complete control of one corporation over another, the substantial identity between companies and the failure to observe corporate formalities.

For example, in *NLRB v. Omnitest Inspection Services, Inc.,* Omnitest was a company formed by McCool that specialized in pipeline testing. McCool owned 205 of Omnitest's total number of shares and was its president. He negotiated a collective bargaining agreement with a local union. In early 1986, Omnitest began experiencing financial problems, and the European entity that owned 60% of Omnitest's stock directed McCool to cease operations. Instead, McCool chose to continue to run the company for a two-month period before ultimately closing its doors.

In the meantime, McCool formed a partnership called Amspec Technical Services that began business the day after Omnitest closed its doors. (This scenario may seem quite familiar to many trustees.) Amspec also was in the business of nondestructive testing and performed some nonpipeline tests for Omnitest's former clients.

After Omnitest ceased operations, McCool met with the union in response to a complaint that Omnitest had failed to make payments to the employees' health, welfare and pension funds. Instead of telling the union Omnitest had ceased operations, McCool stated that Omnitest might go out of business because it was in dire financial straits. McCool threatened to form a new company and sign a collective bargaining agreement with a different union if the union would not settle its claim for employees' unpaid benefits.

The district court enforced the National Labor Relations Board's determination that Amspec was the alter ego of Omnitest and therefore was liable to the union for Omnitest's delinquent contributions. The court ruled that the factors to be evaluated to determine whether two employers are the same business in the same market include whether the old and new employers share substantially identical management, business purpose, operation, equipment, customers and supervision, as well as ownership. The court was persuaded by the facts that McCool controlled the formation, operations and labor relations of both Omnitest and Amspec, and that both companies had substantially the same management, business purpose, supervisor, employees, location, equipment and customers. Significantly, the court rejected McCool's argument that because he had owned only 20% of Omnitest, he could not have controlled Omnitest as he controlled Amspec.

The courts also will find alter ego when family members are used to circumvent the collective bargaining agreement. In *Flynn v. R.C. Tile,* a union company owned by one family member disappeared and a new company, with a similar name, was formed by a related family member. The Court of Appeals for the D.C. Circuit found alter ego and held it was unnecessary for the fund to prove antiunion animus.

No criteria alone is the determining factor of alter ego status. Plans may find information from union representatives helpful in detecting business fluctuations. A quick outline of how to prove a plan's case against an alter ego entity includes:
- Advise business agents and employees of alter ego/piercing the corporate veil factors.
- Observe the business.

- Examine documents (report forms, financial documents, etc.).
- Examine records on file with the state.
- Check the telephone book. (Do both companies have the same phone number?)
- Learn about other lawsuits filed against the employer.
- Examine payroll audits: Your auditor should be your eyes and ears.

The plan can obtain information concerning alter ego situations by being vigilant for circumstances in which there is an initial cessation of business by an employer but a later resumption of business under the same ownership, workforce, etc. Relationships between parent and subsidiary corporations, and between individual officers and shareholders and their corporations, also must be examined carefully in order to determine whether the veil may be pierced.

CHEATERS CHECKLIST

Business agents, auditors and employees often are anxious to help the fund to establish evidence of alter ego and to accomplish piercing the corporate veil. Below is a cheaters checklist that sets forth the type of evidence that is helpful:

1. Common directors and officers
2. Same place of business
3. Common control of the business
4. Common control of labor relations
5. Sharing of equipment
6. Sale of business for less than fair market value
7. Sale of equipment for less than fair market value
8. Common administrative services
9. Intermingling of financial affairs
10. Undercapitalization of the business
11. Similar customers
12. One business is a shell of the other.
13. Disappearance of one business and sudden emergence of another
14. Similar type of business
15. Failure to follow corporate formalities
16. Failure to issue stock, pay dividends or keep corporate records
17. Family members perpetuating a fraud.

SETTLEMENT TACTICS

As discussed above, under PTE 76-1, after the trustees employ reasonable, diligent and systematic efforts to collect employer delinquencies, trustees may settle cases pursuant to "written" settlement agreements. All settlements must be reasonable and prudent in view of the likelihood of collections and the cost of collection. Under the exemption, it is therefore permissible for a fund to settle a claim for only a percentage of its value if warranted by the costs of collection versus the prospects of recovery. Collection efforts may not be abandoned unless collection costs exceed probable recoveries.

In light of these regulations, just as a fund must adopt a uniform policy to govern the processing of delinquencies through the pre-litigation and litigation phases, so must it adopt a uniform policy for settlement of delinquent cases. That policy should, at a minimum, set forth the criteria for determining when a contribution claim can be settled, when a delinquency due from an employer is uncollectible, and when liquidated damages, statutory interest and/or attorney fees may be waived.

FIDUCIARY THEORY

Funds have long been frustrated by the difficult task of piercing the corporate veil to impose personal liability. For a short time, there was the hope that the definition of *employer* in ERISA could be expanded to encompass corporate owners. The theory was not embraced by the courts.

Then a new theory arose with regard to "contributory" funds—where the contribution was deducted from the individual's paycheck. The courts held that because this money belonged to the employee, the employer became a "fiduciary"[4] when it unlawfully took control of the monies. Thus began suits against employers for breach of fiduciary duty.

In an effort to extend this rationale to noncontributory funds, some trusts were amended to provide that contributions due that are held by the employer constitute *fund assets*. This theory has now been adopted in a number of jurisdictions. However, in order to impose individual liability on corporate owners, the fund must show a particular individual made the decision (the exercise of fiduciary discretion) not to pay contributions to the fund.

BANKRUPTCY, LIENS AND BONDS

Any effort to collect money from delinquent contractors raises the specter of bankruptcy litigation, a subject beyond the scope of this chapter. For present purposes, the following rules should be followed if the delinquent employer files for protection. The fund should note whether the petition is for liquidation (Chapter 7) or reorganization (usually Chapter 11). If it is for reorganization and the fund has a substantial claim, the fund should attempt to become a member of the creditors committee, which will give it a say in important matters. The fund should file the proof of claim on time, and remember that fund delinquencies enjoy a priority over many other types of claims. If delinquencies persist for monies owed after the filing of a Chapter 11 petition (post-petition claims), the fund may obtain relief directly from the bankruptcy court. Those responsible for collection should not be afraid to use the processes of bankruptcy court (including depositions) to examine vigorously the delinquent employer to uncover all assets and all related companies.

The law regarding liens and bonds is problematic because it varies from state to state, and there have been some recent changes in the law. It has now been established in most jurisdictions that performance bonds are enforceable and not "preempted" by ERISA. There is still a split of authority over whether mechanic's liens can be enforced by a fund directly. If liens or bonds are available, a claim should be made quickly because a short time period for notice is usually provided.

CONCLUSION

Collection of employer delinquencies presents a formidable task. Trustees face pressures not to "put the employer out of business" and challenges from chameleon employers who evade their obligations using "corporate veils" or "alter egos." It is a challenge for trustees to carry out their duties under ERISA without destroying the "good" employers who are going through difficult economic times.

Trustees can meet the challenge by creating a collection system that works, hunting down the "cheaters" (using the cheaters checklist) and employing flexible remedies that fulfill fiduciary requirements.

ENDNOTES

1. This chapter borrows liberally from Chapter 8 of Mitzner, *ERISA Litigation: A Basic Guide,* (Brookfield, WI: International Foundation of Employee Benefit Plans, 1993).

2. In the term before *Central Transport,* the Supreme Court held a trust may sue under ERISA and need not defer to the grievance procedure of the collective bargaining agreement. *Schneider Moving & Storage Co. v. Robbins.*

3. The documents should cover both "problem" audits (where there is a basis to believe there is a delinquency) and "random" audits.

4. Fiduciary status can result from having "discretion" or "control" over fund assets.

SECTION X

ADMINISTRATION OF TAFT-HARTLEY PLANS

Foreword

Today's multiemployer plan finds as its genesis Section 302 of the Labor-Management Relations Act of 1947, commonly referred to as the Taft-Hartley Act. This provision of the law specifically bars employers from giving or contributing anything of value to any representative or labor organization, or any officer or employee thereof, which represents or seeks to represent, or who would admit to membership any employees of that employer. Were plans to be solely administered by unions, Section 302 would prohibit the existence of such plans if they are financed by employers.

An important exception to this ban is found in Section 302(c)(5) of the Taft-Hartley Act. This provision provides the legal framework for the creation of a jointly trusteed employee benefit plan administered by a board of trustees on which labor and management are equally represented with equal voting power. Within that general framework, certain other requirements must be met, including:

- Any employer payments must be made to a separate trust.
- The trust must be established for the sole and exclusive benefit of the employees of the employer, their families and dependents.
- Payments from the trust must be made for the benefit of employees, their families and dependents for medical or hospital care, pensions on retirement or death of employees, compensation for injuries or illnesses resulting from occupational activities or insurance to provide any of these forms of benefits, or unemployment benefits or life insurance, disability and sickness insurance, or accident insurance, as well as for industry advancement or promotion, apprenticeship training, scholarship, day care or group legal service benefits.
- The basis on which employer contributions are to be made to the benefit fund/trust must be detailed in a written agreement.
- The basis on which payments from the trust are to be made must be set forth in a written agreement.
- A procedure for selecting an impartial umpire to handle deadlocked issues must be provided.
- The trust document must also contain provisions for an annual audit of the trust fund, the results of which must be made available for inspection by interested persons at the principal office of the trust fund or at another designated location.

Prior to January 1, 1976, the effective date of the Employee Retirement Income Security Act of 1974 (ERISA), the administration of trust funds was generally governed by the common law of trusts and/or state statutes. These principles of common law state statutes assigned major responsibility to trustees within the scope of their fiduciary relationship with regard to the trust. The trustees were required to administer the trust solely in the interest of beneficiaries, to deal fairly with beneficiaries and to make known all material facts in connection with any transaction. The major responsibilities assigned to trustees included:

- General administration of the trust
- Acquisition, ownership and protection of trust property
- Provision of benefits for beneficiaries
- Taking such steps as necessary to ensure trust property is productive
- Collecting all monies due the trust fund
- Accounting for the handling of all funds.

With the passage of ERISA, provision was made for participation, vesting and funding rules for pension plans, pension termination insurance, the guarantee of pension benefits, as well as the establishment of a body of federal statutory law governing fiduciary responsibilities of persons who have the authority to control and manage benefit plans.

More specifically, Section 3(21) of ERISA provides a person is a *fiduciary* if that person exercises any discretionary authority or control with respect to the management of the plan, or with respect to the management or disposition of plan assets, or has any discretionary authority or responsibility in the administration of the plan. Clearly, all named trustees of jointly managed plans are fiduciaries and, in the general sense, are administrators.

As described elsewhere in this treatise, ERISA also provides for strict reporting and disclosure requirements for all plans; sets forth certain prohibited transactions; and imposes sanctions and excise taxes as components of an elaborate enforcement procedure.

In many situations, distinctions have been made between *Administrator* and *administrator,* the former being a fiduciary and the latter a nonfiduciary who performs merely ministerial actions at the direction and control of the trustees. In general usage, many Taft-Hartley jointly managed plans continue to use the term administrator for the title of the person who may be the head of staff or of the organization that is charged with responsibility of everyday activities and operations of a benefit plan. Perhaps this person or entity might more aptly be titled the *administrative manager.* While it may be more technically correct to deem the trustees of the funds as the *Administrators* and the person or persons involved in the day-to-day administrative operations as the *administrative managers,* we will, in this section, use the title *administrator* to refer to the party assigned the responsibility for handling day-to-day operations, as differentiated from the statutory designation.

The first chapter of this section (Chapter 43) will provide an overview of administrative functions, as well as the various and varying forms of administrative management that have evolved since the birth of the modern Taft-Hartley plan in 1947. Chapter 44 will review the relationship between the administrator or administrative manager with trustees, plan professionals, the public and governmental authorities, as well as with plan participants, participating unions and contributing employers. In Chapter 45, we will discuss how plan administrative costs might be calculated and measured.

Acknowledgment: This particular section of previous editions of the *Trustees Handbook* were authored by Bernard Handel. In that much of the format and reference material in this edition was derived from Mr. Handel's work, the author wishes to credit him for his ongoing role and guidance in making this section of the *Trustees Handbook* possible.

William J. Einhorn

Chapter 44

The Various Forms and Functions of Plan Administration

William J. Einhorn

The current era of multiemployer benefit plans has existed for less than 60 years. Throughout that period of time, these types of benefit plans continue to evolve at a revolutionary and meteoric pace. During their relatively short history, these plans have evolved from common law trusts to highly complex and highly federally regulated entities.

Since the effective date of ERISA in 1976, myriad legislation that affects employee benefits has been passed by Congress. This legislation includes, among others, the Tax Equity and Fiscal Responsibility Act of 1982 (TEFRA), the Deficit Reduction Act of 1984 (DEFRA), the Retirement Equity Act of 1984 (REA), the Tax Reform Act of 1986 (TRA '86), the Consolidated Omnibus Budget Reconciliation Act of 1985 (COBRA), the Omnibus Reconciliation Acts (OBRA '85, '86, '87 and '89) and more recently, the Economic Growth and Tax Relief Reconciliation Act of 2001 (EGTRRA). These virtually annual reconciliation acts implement almost annual revisions of the Internal Revenue Code or other statutes with a significant effect on employee benefit plans.

Interspersed among all of these tax reconciliation acts came a variety of other laws that directly impacted employee benefit plans with profound effects on administration of these plans. Consider the following:
- Health Insurance Portability and Accountability Act (HIPAA) and the subsequent Privacy and Security Regulations promulgated thereunder
- The Small Business Job Protection Act
- Mental Health Parity Act
- Newborns' and Mothers' Health Protection Act
- The Women's Health and Cancer Rights Act of 1998
- The Medicare Prescription Drug, Improvement, and Modernization Act of 2003
- The Veterans Benefits Improvement Act of 2004 (modifying and amending portions of the Uniformed Services Employment and Reemployment Rights Act of 1994 (USERRA)).

This annual bombardment resulted in significant changes in the employee benefit industry and placed an even greater responsibility on those entrusted with the administration of Taft-Hartley plans. It should be noted, of course, that not all of the legislation solely affected multiemployer, Taft-Hartley trust funds. Most of the legislation affected single employer plans as well. Traditionally, collectively bargained employee benefits have been, to say the least, dynamic. Parties involved in collective bargaining, trustees and administrative managers continue to find much of their work is concerned with adapting administrative methods and internal plan regulations to conform to constant changes in federal laws and regulations, as well as the workplace realities and the "give and take" inherent in collective bargaining. There has been a notable increase in federal reporting and disclosure requirements in recent years, as well as additional mandated communication with plan participants. Administrators are required to work closely with their attorneys, accountants and actuaries in implementing annual changes to meet, at times, major revisions in the operational methods of plans caused by federal legislation and regulation. The most recent example, as will be discussed later in this chapter, is the implementation of the HIPAA Privacy Regulations in April 2003 and HIPAA Security Regulations in April 2005.

As a result of significant federal and state legislation, regulations resulting from that legislation and countless volumes of federal and state litigation over the period since ERISA's enactment, no one could argue that jointly managed employee benefit trusts are highly regulated. The regulatory forces have produced a strong stimulus to the emergence of professional administrative managers employed by plan trustees.

Trustees of Taft-Hartley plans were quick to recognize that, even though they were legally responsible for fund administration as fiduciaries, they could not personally handle the numerous administrative tasks that needed to be performed.

Administration of multiemployer plans, with all the involved regulations and activities, is an impossible workload for trustees, who generally fill full-time occupations in their own enterprises. In addition, trustees are not generally compensated for their work as trustees, so there is little incentive to take on the responsibility associated with the daily operation of a trust fund.

Finally, it was never intended the trustees would individually or collectively possess the specialized skills and experience required for effective fund administration. It was logical, therefore, for trustees to seek assistance through employment of professional administrative managers or delegate administrative responsibilities to a third party to the extent possible. This reliance on third parties has helped produce a professional administrative manager who is employed on either a salaried or a contractual basis.

DELEGATION OF ADMINISTRATIVE RESPONSIBILITY

Within the general framework of Taft-Hartley, the trustees can employ third parties to handle the everyday activities of the plan. Obviously, agents employed for this purpose must be selected with reasonable and prudent care, and any delegation of responsibility must be specifically authorized by the legal documents establishing the trust and federal and state regulations. Despite appropriate and lawful delegation, the trustees are charged with the responsibility of constantly monitoring the performance of such agents to determine if they are performing in accordance with their contractual obligations and in the sole, exclusive and best interests of plan participants.

Proper delegation of administrative tasks by the trustees generally requires that independent third parties be employed for this purpose. In accordance with the spirit of the Taft-Hartley Act, courts have generally held fund operations must be kept separate from union or management operations. The trust fund must separate its operations completely from the activities of union and management in connection with the administration of Taft-Hartley plans. This principle was expressly recognized on a number of occasions by the U.S. Supreme Court, beginning with its decision in *NLRB v. Amax Coal Company.*

MAJOR FUNCTIONS OF A TAFT-HARTLEY PLAN

The fiduciary duties specified in Section 404 of ERISA require, among other things, that the trust be administered "in accordance with the documents and instruments governing the plan." Further delineating that global responsibility, the major functions of a Taft-Hartley fund include, but are never limited to, the following major classifications:

1. Establishing an office for the effective operation of the fund
2. Maintaining a workflow to ascertain that the activities of the fund are performed in a businesslike, efficient manner
3. Collection of fund revenue and property
4. Investment of plan assets and managing cash
5. Accounting for assets, income and expenses of the fund
6. Maintaining data and other recordkeeping for the trust fund
7. Processing claims for benefits submitted by or on behalf of plan participants
8. Communication with plan participants, trustees, participating local unions and employers
9. Ascertaining the plan complies with federal and state laws and regulations
10. Retention and maintenance of records and control of property
11. Security and internal control of records and assets.

The establishment of policy to fulfill these major functions is a primary responsibility of the board of trustees. This requires the careful selection of the fund administrative manager to implement the decisions made by the board. In addition, the trustees will generally arrange for the continuous services of legal counsel, a plan auditor, a plan actuary/consultant and other advisors when deemed necessary. In most instances, particularly for larger plans, one or more investment managers may be retained. In very large plans, there may even be a monitoring service that will measure the performance of investment advisors. Many plans also contract with consultants in such fields as communications, data processing, health care utilization and disease management.

The trustees are responsible for establishing the site and form of plan recordkeeping and the procedures to be effectuated to serve the needs of the trust. Orderly records must be maintained so that proper benefits are paid to plan participants. Modern accounting equipment and methodologies must be provided to ensure timely and efficient performance of routine operations.

There can be many structural administrative forms for multiemployer benefit plans. For example, a health and welfare plan that directly pays benefits from the fund office using fund personnel will require a much more involved office structure than a plan that pays premiums to an insurance company which, in turn, pays claims. Similarly, the procedures for the operation of a health and welfare plan may differ vastly from those necessary for a pension or vacation plan.

The Need for an Administrative Manager

The administrative manager, whether salaried or contract, is vital to the operations of the employee benefit program. As Taft-Hartley jointly managed plans grew in scope and number, a demand arose for professional administrative managers who would either be full- or part-time employees of the fund on a contract basis. The increase in fund activity, as well as assets and income, requires qualified full-time staff capable of working with the administrative manager to handle the large number of necessary operational tasks.

As a generalist with knowledge and expertise, the administrative manager provides services that cover all aspects of plan operations, including general management, finance, personnel administration, recordkeeping, economics, benefit processing and data processing, communications, collections, coordination with professionals, investments, insurance, advising participants, as well as dealing with outside vendors, the public and governmental agencies. Today's administrative managers vary from persons who have worked their way up to manager from clerical positions in benefit plans, to rank-and-file union members, to professionals who are certified public accountants (CPAs), master's of business administration degree holders (M.B.A.s), lawyers, economists and computer experts.

Forms of Trust Administration

One of the first decisions of a newly established fund is the determination of how the trust should be administered. In other words, where will the "back office" be located and who will run it?

Throughout the history of these jointly trusteed trust funds, administrative functions were delegated to either a salaried administrator, a contract administrator, a bank or an insurance company. The great majority of plans today have delegated the administrative operations of these plans to salaried or contract administrators. The majority of funds today are self-administered and hire a salaried administrator and supporting full- and part-time personnel. However, a significant number of funds continue to utilize the services of contract administrators that combine the operations of a number of Taft-Hartley funds in the same office environment in the interest of efficiency and cost economy. Even today, a small number of plans continue to use banks or insurance companies for administrative purposes.

Although the primary function remains the same, there are differences between contract and salaried administrative managers. For the most part, salaried administration suggests the administrator is employed on a full-time basis, and is concerned only with the administration of a single fund or a single group of related funds without any conflicting arrangements. The trustees will arrange for the engagement, retention and replacement of one person who will be deemed the plan administrator and to whom is delegated the responsibility to handle the day-to-day operations at the permanent office(s) of the fund.

Contract administration, sometimes referred to as third-party administration (TPA), offers potentially substantial cost advantages resulting from the spreading of fixed costs for office and operational expenses, including executive salaries, data processing, claims processing, computerization and communication, among a number of Taft-Hartley funds and, in some cases, single employer benefit plans. Smaller funds may also benefit from contract administration in being able to participate in the joint use of sophisticated systems that would not otherwise be economically appropriate or available.

Clearly, there are advantages in either type of arrangement. The decision of what form of "back office" would be appropriate is one for the trustees to make based upon the many times unique requirements and circumstances are involved. On the one hand, a full-time salaried administrator would owe allegiance and responsibility only to a particular fund and its participants. This might ensure the continuity of plan operations, direct responsibility to the trustees and the avoidance of conflict with other benefit plans. On the other hand, contract administrators or TPAs provide a high level of expertise, experience, training and capabilities equal to or exceeding those of a salaried administrative office, particularly in the case of smaller plans. Further, the contract administrator may claim the major advantage of limiting trustees' liability. Certainly, the errors and omissions and professional liability insurance of the contract administrator could serve as a reassuring, added protection for boards of trustees in this area.

Combined Arrangements

One other form of administration, other than by banks or insurance companies, is a combination or hybrid arrangement. This can be an amalgamation of several trusts—either one industry or related industries. For example, building trades funds, stemming from a number of collective bargaining agreements spread over a large geographical area could be administered by a corporation that is a creation of the respective trusts. It operates a nonprofit organization. This type of hybrid organization may have some of the advantages of contract administration—particularly in the area of spreading fixed costs, the ability to engage in more sophisticated data processing, the ability to handle peak loads and the minimal effect of changes in personnel—while retaining the advantages of self-administration on a relative local level, with elements of direct contact, no profit margin and a central location.

Another hybrid arrangement that has emerged, particularly in the health and welfare arena, is a welfare trust that is partially insured and partially self-insured. For example, a fund may provide medical benefits through an insurance company, but "carve out" mental health benefits and provide such benefits on a self-insured basis with the fund office personnel paying claims. Other funds may be fully self-insured, except for death benefits so beneficiaries may take advantage of the full Internal Revenue Code income exclusion in the case of life insurance benefits.

Use of TPA for Paying Claims

Another variation of self-administration occurs frequently in health and welfare plans. The welfare plan may operate entirely on a self-administered basis with full-time personnel handling all aspects of administration other than the processing of benefit claims. A specialized third-party administrator may be utilized strictly to provide claims processing services (and also, frequently, stop-loss insurance to provide a maximum limitation of the claims liability of the self-insured health and welfare fund). TPAs have become one of the fastest growing elements in employee benefit plan administration throughout the country, particularly with respect to corporate and institutional health and welfare clients.

It should be noted welfare plans utilizing an insurance company on a fully insured basis or only to pay claims are functioning in the identical manner as a fund engaging a TPA. The self-administered health and welfare plan will pay insurance premiums to the carrier, which will in turn, provide claims services.

Insurance Companies as Administrative Agents

In their role as administrators, insurance companies function, in effect, as contract administrators; that is, a pool of talent, sophisticated data processing equipment, the ability to handle peak workloads and the spreading of fixed costs over a body of customers.

Historically, insurance companies have not focused their activities toward administrative functions related to the processing of contributions and eligibility recordkeeping. Most have offered assistance in claims control to health and welfare plans in addition to processing claims. More recently, some carriers have branched out to provide a wide variety of administrative and investment services for both health and welfare and pension plans.

An important innovation that has become somewhat commonplace in the last decade has been the *administrative services only* or *ASO* arrangement for noninsured health and welfare plans. The arrangement is not unlike that offered by carriers in the pension area that contract directly to provide investment custodial and administrative services.

ASO contracts are tailored on a case-by-case basis to the particular coverages plan trustees have developed. Such contracts include services such as claims processing, payment and control; management reports, tabulation of data for governmental reports; actuarial and underwriting services; and assistance in preparing plan booklets.

Under a typical ASO arrangement, the insurance carrier will pay claims using its checking account or the checking account of the fund and bill the fund for the reimbursement of the claims paid plus an administrative services contract charge. A variation of the ASO procedure has been incorporated in what are called minimum premium insurance arrangements in which the insurance carrier primarily pays claims, and a large portion of the risk is assumed by the benefit plan. Since the latter part of the 1990s, managed care entities and preferred provider organizations (PPOs) have offered contract services to Taft-Hartley funds. The functions delegated to those organizations include arrangement of fiscal remuneration contracts with medical, dental and prescription drug providers; actual payment of claims; furnishing of health care services to plan participants; data collection and analysis; utilization management; and other health treatment activities, including disease management programs.

Administrative Services by Banks

A small number of banks provide benefit plan services, including receiving and recording the receipt of employer contributions and other income; general reporting and account procedures; claims processing and payments; preparation of governmental reports; safeguarding of records and assets; and, of course, investment services. To the very largest extent, banks performing these services are more likely to do so in the pension plan area than in the health and welfare plan arena.

Many of the characteristics of contract administrative managers and insurance companies also apply to banks. Like insurance companies with their ASO contracts, banks may enter into arrangements to provide only specific services such as handling receipts and recordkeeping and/or claims processing and payment.

Whatever the form of administration—be it salaried, contract or handled by a bank or insurance company or some hybrid—the fundamental tasks to be performed remain the same.

Overall Administrative Mission

Irrespective of the size of the trust fund, whether insured or self-insured, the fund administrator will be required to ascertain whether the correct amount of revenue is received from employers and other sources; proper records are maintained, benefits are processed and paid as required by the plan documents; communications are maintained on a current basis with all parties in interest; governmental reporting and disclosure requirements are met; and the overall benefit plan is operated efficiently and in a cost-effective manner. Every effort must be made to collect and receive plan assets and earn the highest possible return while operating solely and exclusively in the best interests of plan participants.

While all trustees may not be actively involved in the day-to-day details of administration, they should understand the operational systems of the fund. It is their duty to ascertain that the trust is administered in the most efficient manner possible and in accordance with the plan documents.

The complexity of the administration procedures for a particular fund depends upon a number of factors, including the size of the fund (number of participating employees, beneficiaries and contributing employers), the purpose of the fund, the nature in which benefits are provided and the form of administration.

Each of the primary administrative functions is described in the following sections.

PRIMARY ADMINISTRATIVE FUNCTIONS

Accounting Controls

Effective and efficient plan administration requires financial records be maintained in accordance with generally accepted accounting principles, applicable to any business enterprise, as specifically tailored for a jointly managed employee benefit plan. The account records of a benefit plan would include the general types of financial data and journals maintained by any similar organization.

These records might be maintained in a variety of formats, ranging from manual records, to the use of specialized accounting machines, to the utilization of off-the-shelf personal computer programs, to a complete, automated computerized data processing mode. In today's business world, it is more likely most medium to large benefit plans would use computerized systems ranging from personal computers expanded for this purpose to networks of workstations and mainframes to handle all facets of plan administration.

In any event, the records maintained by an employee benefit trust must be designed thoughtfully to produce the information necessary to assure effective internal control over handling of fund assets and to generate the data needed for preparation of audit reports and periodic financial reports to trustees, as well as separate reports to governmental agencies and professionals serving the fund.

In larger funds, segregation of functions over several departments may be necessary to provide sufficient internal controls to prevent fraud or material misstatement in the financial records of the trust. As explained elsewhere in this treatise, independent auditors consider these internal controls as part of their audit for the purpose of expressing their opinion on the financial statements. In the parlance of the auditor world, "a material weakness is a condition in which the design or operation of the specific internal control elements does not reduce to a relatively low level the risk that errors or irregularities in amounts that would be material in relation to the financial statements being audited may occur and not be detected within a timely period by employees in the normal course of performing their assigned functions." In layman's terms, auditors look to see that procedures are in place that reduce the risk of someone cheating the fund or "cooking the books."

It is particularly significant that the accounting system include proper records to maintain control over the contributions of participating employers. In addition, controls must be established to monitor the collection of income on investments, both on a long- and short-term basis; self-payment made by plan participants (if permitted under the plan document); and other types of income.

What are the basic records that are required? As in any business entity, accounting for fund activities requires a basic set of accounting records with extensive supporting records to guarantee accurate and timely reporting. The basic account records—whether in a manual, electric accounting machine or computerized form—would normally include:

- Cash receipts and disbursement records
- General journal records for all noncash transactions
- General ledger summary accounts of income, expenses, assets and liabilities
- Subsidiary records, including detailed accounts of individual transactions, individual employer contributions, employee eligibility, employee service credit, investment register, claim register, and investment dividend and interest income register.

It is important detailed records be maintained with respect to individual employee credits for the purpose of determining the eligibility of an individual to receive benefits from a plan. This may require short-term records on a monthly, quarterly or annual basis for health and welfare and vacation fund credits. For defined benefit (DB) pension and defined contribution (DC) annuity fund purposes, however, permanent records are required to accumulate and substantiate career and lifetime data.

Accurate accounting control must be maintained with respect to fund investments. There should be a permanent record maintained for each investment by type (stocks, bonds, mortgages, etc.), principal amounts, cost market value, earnings, dividends, and interest received, brokerage costs, proxy voting, etc.

The records maintained by each benefit plan will vary based upon its own idiosyncrasies and nature. The fund's certified public accountant (CPA), working with the trustees and the administrative manager, will usually design the accounting system. In this process, the system must be designed to produce information that will assist the trustees. The trustees will need data on the general administration of the plan and in making important decisions with respect to employee eligibility rules, projection of budgets, costs of benefits, etc.

Another function of proper accounting records is to ensure proper handling of funds and property and to enable the preparation of financial statements for the trustees, as well as the preparation of government-required reports. Trustees often look to the fund's independent auditor to provide comments on the fund's internal controls through the medium of a "no material weakness" letter accompanying the annual audited financial statements.

Security and retention of accounting records is another important consideration for trustees. Most funds either engage a custodian to hold valuable property, or store such material in a safe deposit vault at an outside location with access limited to authorized persons. In view of the long-term significance of certain records, most benefit plans make some arrangement for permanent record retention.

In the absence of a trustee resolution regarding record retention, it is usually the administrative manager that determines which records should be maintained for specific lengths of time. This author recommends that every plan adopt a record retention policy, keeping in mind that the policies will differ with regard to pension and welfare funds. For example, records of individual employer contributions might be held for a period of six years for a welfare fund but, in the case of a pension plan, it may be important to retain such records permanently to enable the trustees to furnish proper credits to employees upon retirement many years after the date the employer contribution reports and contributions are received. Similarly, it may be necessary to store government reports and annual financial statements permanently so they would be available for government review and inspection by proper parties in accordance with federal law.

Data Processing Systems

In today's technological era, an important and, indeed, indispensable function in the administrative arena is the establishment and maintenance of a sophisticated data system. The scope and extent of a computerized data record system will vary with the size of the fund, diversity of assets and income. Other practical considerations dictated, perhaps, by the peculiarities of the industry in which plan participants work, will determine the design, nature and scope of such a system.

Most benefit plans, and contract administrators, generally provide or engage data processing consultants to help design and install the appropriate system for a benefit fund. Such services include system maintenance and periodic upgrades to meet advancements in the technological world, as well as changes required by plan operations, new legislation and regulations.

When the trustees resolve to consider the possibility of data processing, a feasibility study would normally be undertaken by a data processing consultant. The consultant's report would generally be reviewed by the administrator. Based upon the review and recommendation of administrative management, the trustees would authorize the appropriate type of system and equipment to be utilized. The decision made by the trustees would include the determination of whether the fund would use in-house equipment or a service bureau. The use of the service bureau involves an arrangement by which the computer hardware and software is maintained at a location separate and apart from the fund office. The fund office personnel access the system remotely via some form of telecommunications/modem. Hardware and software updates, enhancements and improvements are made by the service bureau provider. In this fashion, the fund has the use of the "latest and greatest" technology. Whether in-house or service bureau, the chosen system should permit future expansion and provide ready access to data and data extracts as required.

Much thought and planning in system design is essential to a successful implementation and ongoing operation. Careful, upfront design will avoid costly changes later down the road. An appropriate adage to remember in this regard is "garbage in, garbage out." What information is retrievable is dictated by the data elements inputted into the system.

The administrative manager usually works with the data processing consultant to validate and document software (as well as hardware), makes certain the system will produce the reports and end results desired, and trains employees to use the system for administrative tasks. The manager usually monitors the effectiveness of the computer hardware and software and determines when to recommend updating of equipment or programs.

The essential elements in the recordkeeping procedure are the verification and control of employer contributions, as well as investment and other income of the fund. (These matters are discussed in detail in preceding sections of this Handbook.) A key element is the establishment of procedures to maintain security and internal controls in the system in the interest of preserving confidentiality, as well as the permanence and safety of the information stored. This has become particularly critical in the last several years with the advent of the HIPAA Privacy and Security Regulations, a topic that will be discussed later in this chapter.

The accounting system should be sufficient in scope to furnish the significant data that will be required by the trustees. Some of the information that should be readily available includes:

- The status of employer contributions; the amount of any contribution delinquencies, aging of delinquencies and efforts made for the collection thereof
- The normal cash flow requirements needed to meet current benefit claims and operating expenditures
- The balance of monies available for the purposes of meeting expenses and allocations for investment purposes; the amount of assets allocated for short-term investment purposes; and analysis of long-term investments
- The performance of the investment portfolio in terms of investment return and capital gains or losses
- The amount of professional fees and expenses paid to professional advisors for services rendered
- The amount of liabilities of the benefit fund, including insurance premiums payable, benefits payable, general liabilities, reserve for future benefits, liability for future eligibility of participants and liability for claims processed but unpaid.

For the trustees to determine the status of the fund at any particular time, it is essential that timely financial statements be available and furnished as expeditiously as possible. Interim, unaudited financial statements may be prepared by the administrative manager based upon the records maintained by the fund. An annual report (and, frequently, periodic interim reports) is prepared by the independent CPA serving the fund.

Annual financial statements are required under ERISA Section 103(b). These statements are generally included in the annual report furnished to the Department of Labor and the Internal Revenue Service. The annual financial statements furnished to trustees usually include the opinion of the qualified public accountant as to whether the statements fairly reflect, in all material respects, the financial positions of the fund, and conform to generally accepted accounting principles applied on a consistent basis. For this purpose, *qualified public accountant* means a CPA or a licensed public accountant certified by regulatory authority in states with such licensing procedures.

The Taft-Hartley Act, particularly in Section 302(c)(5), requires an annual audit of the trust fund, the results of which must be "available for inspection by interested persons at the principal office of the trust fund and at such other place as may be designated in such written agreement."

In addition to these legal requirements, an annual audit of the books of account and the records of the trust fund by an independent public accountant assures the trustees that records are being kept accurately and may be relied upon as part of the decision-making process. Generally after the annual audit is completed, the independent accountants will usually furnish to the board of trustees a separate letter that comments on and perhaps suggests changes in internal controls and the record-keeping maintained by the plan.

A trustee has a duty and responsibility to review financial statements, understand the meaning of the data reported and make inquiries when in doubt about particular matters.

COLLECTION OF EMPLOYER CONTRIBUTIONS AND OTHER INCOME

The primary source of revenue for a benefit fund is employer contributions. These contributions finance benefits and administrative costs. In addition, investment income from both short- and long-term investments is also of material significance. Because employer contributions represent the majority of income of most trust funds, efficient administration of the collection function is basic to the successful operation of any benefit plan. Proper procedures and records must be established to account for all cash receipts and amounts receivable and to monitor whether all income is properly received on a timely basis.

It should be noted that one of the first pronouncements of the U.S. Department of Labor after the effective date of ERISA was Prohibited Transaction Exemption (PTE) 76-1. This particular pronouncement detailed it was clearly part of a trustee's fiduciary obligation to ensure a policy was in place to provide for the systematic, reasonable and diligent identification of employer delinquencies and the collection thereof.

In Taft-Hartley jointly managed funds, the amount of required employer contributions is generally set forth in the collective bargaining agreement, and is usually expressed in terms of a fixed amount per hour, percentage of payroll or flat weekly or monthly amounts per employee. Under some conditions, the amount of contributions may be established on the basis of payment for each shift or production unit, tonnage, etc.

The administrative manager must establish a system of reporting and accounting to make certain the trust receives proper contributions in full, and that proper credits are given to each employer, as well as individual employees for eligibility for benefits under each type of benefit program.

Most benefit plans provide employers with remittance forms accompanied by specific instruction for reporting and payment of contributions. In some instances, these contribution reports will indicate the names and identification numbers of employees reported in the previous contribution period to facilitate payment by the employer. Contributions are normally reported and paid on a weekly or monthly basis. In recent years, it has become more commonplace for these remittance reports to be forwarded to the contributing employer electronically with the employer reporting in a like fashion and wiring funds from its bank account to the fund's bank account.

Although the type of remittance form varies substantially from fund to fund, it generally includes a listing of employees, Social Security numbers and hours worked or the unit on which contributions are based. In many instances, a number of employee benefit plans to which contributions are required by the collective bargaining agreement are handled by the identical benefit office, and one remittance form will cover contributions for several funds, such as welfare, pension, apprenticeship training, vacation, legal services, scholarship and annuity. When the benefit fund supplies prelisted forms, usually on a monthly basis, the employers are asked to include employees who were not employed the previous month, and to delete those who were terminated. Most plans request the employer furnish the date of termination in such instances to facilitate proper administration of COBRA continuation programs.

When the reports and remittances from employers are received, the administrative manager's staff generally reviews the mathematical accuracy of the form, monitors the accuracy of the employer's contribution and arranges for updating permanent records with respect to the employer's remittances and individual employee credits.

Based upon a review of employer contributions, the administration office normally reports delinquencies to the trustees and counsel for the fund and follows a procedure to expedite collection. In this connection, trust funds generally establish criteria by which an employer is deemed delinquent. These criteria might include:

1. An employer that fails to submit a report or payment on the due date
2. An employer that submits a report without commensurate contributions or with a check that does not clear the bank
3. An employer that submits a report and payment, but does not include all employees, all hours or all contributions required under the collective bargaining agreement.

Frequently, the administrative manager's responsibilities will include notifying not only the trustees when an employer falls into delinquency status, but also parties to the collective bargaining agreement, such as the union and management associations. The administrative manager is usually given considerable authority to pursue the collection of delinquencies in accordance with the procedures adopted by the board of trustees and to eventually transfer the matter to legal counsel for further action when authorized.

To ensure proper administration of contributions, it is necessary for most funds to establish a procedure relating to payroll audits. As noted earlier, a routine and systematic auditing procedure is contemplated in PTE 76-1 issued by the U.S. Department of Labor. Many funds will arrange to audit employers on a random basis over a period of years, on a regularly scheduled basis under which all employers may be audited, or on a selective basis when specific employers with questionable contributions or delinquencies are chosen to be audited. The trustees may arrange for such examinations to be conducted by the CPA auditors of the fund or a separate payroll auditing firm. In some instances, larger benefit funds may employ their own internal staff for this purpose.

In addition to employer contributions, some trust funds may provide for self-payment by individual employees under certain conditions. These payments may be designed to continue an employee's eligibility during periods of layoff or disability or upon termination. Also, contributions may be submitted under continuation of health insurance protection programs required by federal law, specifically, COBRA. If self-payments are made, a reporting system must assure accurate timing and crediting of appropriate amounts to individual employee accounts. In addition, a procedure has to be established to notify employees when their payments are overdue and when their grace periods are about to expire to enable them to maintain their benefit qualification. To be sure, such notification procedures must be in place to comply with the very specific notice requirements of the COBRA regulations.

In addition to payroll audits, some funds may use other outside means to verify the accuracy of employer contributions. Funds may require an independent report from employees as to the name of their employer and time worked on a weekly or monthly basis, which can be compared to actual employer remittances. Other funds may use shop stewards' reports or information from the union that lists hours worked by subject employees. Still other funds provide reports to the individual employees on a monthly or quarterly basis of hours reported so those employees might independently verify the remitted information. Still others provide Web site access to this information on a "24 hour per day/7 day per week" basis.

Other issues related to collection of employer contributions are discussed in Section IX of this Handbook.

Investment Earnings

Earnings on investments represent an important source of fund income. In many long-established pension funds, it is possible that, as a result of the accumulation of pension reserves, investment income may actually exceed employer contributions, but in more recent times (given significant market downturns at the start of the 21st century), such investment income may be needed to meet current benefit and administrative expenditures. This is particularly true in maturing pension funds where retirees equal or exceed the number of active employees.

In the same fashion as with employer and employee contributions, investment earnings must be received on time, accounted for and monitored. The administrative manager's responsibility includes verification of earnings received and reported by the fund's corporate trustee, custodian or investment manager when such organizations are used as collection agencies for investment income.

Many trusts maintain their own data records as a cross check on the periodic reports of investment managers and custodians with respect to investment earnings received. Others may rely on the annual audit conducted by their CPA to verify the accuracy of income and physical existence of documents of ownership.

Cash Management

Many funds prepare, on a yearly basis, a cash management projection, usually arranged in the form developed by the plan administrator in conjunction with the independent accountant and/or benefit consultant. Under such a method, a projection would be made of contribution and investment income, budgeted expenses, benefit payment estimates and provisions for contingencies; and a plan arranged for the short-term, as well as long-term, investment of funds. An effective cash management projection will maximize investment income and the proper disposition of income receipts by the fund.

The importance of proper administration as an effective means to control, receive and monitor all revenues of the plan cannot be overemphasized. Unless the maximum income from contributions and investment earnings is received, the goals of the fund will be jeopardized, with a serious impact upon funds available to cover benefit payments and administrative expenses.

MAINTENANCE OF INDIVIDUAL DATA RECORDS

The primary purpose of a jointly managed trust benefit plan is to provide specific benefits to those who meet the qualification rules. Qualification requires meeting certain eligibility rules for initial participation, continued participation and attainment of eligibility. These rules are generally based upon some quantitative measure of work, such as the number of hours actually worked by an employee that were reported through employer contributions. In addition, many plans may give credit for time lost because of disability, military service, jury duty and other acceptable absences from employment.

The administrative manager is responsible for developing a recordkeeping system that can generate the work experience to determine an individual's employment/eligibility status. The type of information and the form in which the data is maintained and made available may vary significantly among various types of benefit plans based upon classification of benefits provided (e.g., welfare or pension), number of employees and contributing employers involved, etc.

Health and Welfare Plans

For welfare fund purposes, eligibility is usually based upon the cumulative number of hours worked by an employee during a stipulated period, as reflected on the individual's record. The typical database would indicate the employee's aggregate credits, status as to eligibility for welfare fund benefits, date of initial eligibility, the class of benefits for which the employee and his or her dependents are eligible, and an appropriate statistical body of information delineating the birth dates, Social Security numbers and identity of covered dependents.

The system should possess the ability to signal situations that might lead to a loss of benefits, such as failure to meet certain minimal work requirements, disability or failure to make self-payments. The data should enable the plan to meet its requirements under the federal COBRA law of notifying employees and their dependents of their rights to continue health insurance by making direct payments to the fund for stipulated periods (usually 18- or 36-month periods).

Adequate records will also enable compliance with HIPAA. This statute requires welfare plans to furnish certificates to each terminating participant that indicate:
- The date on which the waiting period for benefits began
- The date coverage began
- The date coverage ended.

The data records required for welfare fund eligibility should be geared to the rules established by each particular fund. Funds require varying initial qualification periods before the effective date of employee eligibility; some may continue persons in the eligible category for a period of time after the date of last employment by a contributing employer. Others may permit "banking" of past credited hours, which would enable individuals to retain eligibility for a stipulated period based on the number of banked hours and even prior years of continuous service.

Provision must be made to protect the database records against fire, theft, vandalism, tampering and other contingencies that could result in the loss of, or damage to, valuable records. Welfare eligibility records should be retained for at least a six-year period. In reality, however, because in many funds work-hour records are reported in conjunction with pension hours and contributions, most funds retain this information permanently.

HIPAA Privacy and Security Regulations

Beginning in April 2003, far beyond the enactment of HIPAA into law, a complex set of regulations, promulgated by the U.S. Department of Health and Human Services aimed to protect the confidentiality of a participant's health information, came into play. Although these Privacy Regulations delineate those circumstances under which "protected health information" (PHI) may and may not be disclosed and the circumstances under which it may be used internally, these regulations were followed by the HIPAA Security Regulations, which took effect in April 2005. The Security Regulations delineate a plan's obligation to protect the confidentiality, integrity and accessibility of PHI. The HIPAA Privacy Regulations set forth requirements for record retention and a participant's access to this type of PHI. A plan is required to account for certain types of disclosure of a participant's PHI and is under an obligation to consider adjusting or correcting that information upon a participant's claim of inaccuracy of such data.

As one might imagine, these regulations have required each and every health plan to develop specific and comprehensive procedures governing:

- Who within the organization may access and use PHI and why and to what extent that person must use PHI
- With whom, how and for what purpose(s) the health plan may share PHI (i.e., fund auditors, attorneys, actuaries, consultants, service providers, specialized vendors, etc.), all of which must be memorialized in a separate "business associate" agreement
- Participant-authorized disclosures of PHI
- Accounting for authorized disclosures of PHI, as well as disclosures incident to judicial proceedings and other governmental activities
- Accounting for participant requests for corrections to PHI and special requests for confidential communications
- Training and periodic retraining of fund office staff relating to the requirements of the Privacy and Security Regulations
- Sanctions for violations of fund policies relating thereto
- Assessments of potential security breaches, disasters, loss of records and procedures aimed at preventing same
- Designation of a person or persons to serve as the entity's Privacy Officer and Security Official.

Handling of PHI has become a critical concern in a fund office. The civil and criminal fines, as well as private causes of action, have raised legitimate concerns to protect the fund from what could easily amount to significant liability.

DB Pension Funds

In view of the long-term nature of DB pension plans, data for determination of eligibility and service credits should be stored in a permanent form and available throughout the working career of an employee. This information will be needed to substantiate and determine eligibility and pension entitlement at the date the employee becomes eligible for benefit payment.

Because such data will be accumulated over a 20- to 30-year period of time (and even more in some cases), it is important to guarantee the retention of this information in some protective form that will avoid any problem of loss from fire, damage, tampering or other disasters. There must also be some means of verifying past credits for employment prior to the effective date of participation (when and if such credit is given under the terms of the plan), because claims for benefits will occur many years after credits are actually earned and/or reported to the fund. More important, protection of this data in the short term is critical to the periodic actuarial valuation of the plan. Without accurate data, the actuarial report may prove to be unreliable to the trustees in the ongoing planning and operation of the trust.

At the time of retirement, an employee's pension eligibility is usually based upon the history accumulated in the fund's database. When an employee claims additional credits, it may be necessary for the administrative office to obtain additional information from past employers, the Social Security Administration, the union (in those cases where a history of employment is maintained), reciprocal credits from other funds and other possible sources of information relating to an employee's work history.

Pension eligibility records, as with welfare records, should be structured to signal certain danger points at which eligibility might be jeopardized. In the case of pension credits, these danger points often include a break in service, failure to file a claim or an appeal within the time period specified by the plan, or a return to work in the craft or industry after retirement.

ERISA and subsequent regulations contain specific requirements with respect to breaks in service and, under certain circumstances, reemployment after retirement. Because these circumstances and others may lead to suspension, termination or loss of benefits, it is essential that the data system provides for the signaling of such danger points.

DC and Annuity Plans

The individual eligibility records for employees in DC and annuity plans are similar to those for DB pension plans. However, in lieu of work records, the credits are usually based upon the crediting of actual employer contributions to each employee's account. The aggregate amounts credited to such annuity or DC account, together with some pro-rata share of annual net investment income after expenses, usually serves as the basis for determining the benefits on retirement or lump-sum payment available to employees upon termination of employment.

Vacation Funds

As in annuity plans and DC plans, actual employer contributions are usually the basis of recordkeeping for vacation funds. A vacation program essentially is a revolving fund in that the amounts accumulated for each employee are usually paid out to the individual at a specified point in time or upon application.

Other Employee Data Records

In addition to maintaining basic eligible credits for each employee, the fund's database should include the employee's identity by name and address, Social Security number, union affiliation, birth date and name of employer. In addition, the data should include the marital status and names and birth dates of dependents. It may be desirable to obtain the Social Security identification number for each employee's spouse and each child. This will facilitate eligibility verification at the time of claim. Identification by Social Security number for eligible dependents, although not required at present, may be required by federal law eventually.

Particularly for welfare fund purposes, data may include certain particular restrictions or legal assignments pertaining to benefit payments and eligibility, such as a qualified domestic relations order (QDRO) for a pension plan or survivor option and restrictions; for welfare purposes, there may be identification of employment status of other family members if the plan has a coordination of benefits (COB) procedure, identification of college students, designation of beneficiaries, etc. More recently, qualified medical child support orders (QMCSOs), sometimes affectionately known as "kiddy QDROs," are required to be recognized by a fund. Such orders typically require enrollment of dependents in a plan even though the employee had not done so.

Information Furnished to Plan Participants as to Benefit Status

Historically, many trust funds, particularly those with data processing capabilities, provide annual (and sometimes more frequent) statements to employees that reflect eligibility status and credited service under benefit plans. Under the terms of ERISA, such reports must be furnished as to pension status and credits when requested by plan participants.

This type of report usually indicates pension credits accredited to date, total amount contributed to an individual account for an annuity plan or DC account, and the value of benefits that could be obtained from present accumulated contributions. An individual DB pension statement may also indicate the amount of vested benefits. For welfare fund purposes, statements may be offered on an optional basis that indicate the status of welfare fund eligibility for the employee and dependents, as well as a summary of banked hours when that feature exists in a particular plan.

Data reporting to plan participants requires the administrative manager design the database system so the necessary data may be generated at the proper time and issued in an economical and efficient manner to plan participants.

It should also be noted that there has been pending for some years a proposed ERISA regulation that would require an annual statement to plan participants with respect to their pension status. While this mandatory reporting has never been finalized, many pension plans voluntarily report accumulated and vesting credits to plan participants. Moreover, regulations will soon take effect mandating the relative value of each pension benefit option be calculated and disclosed/described to the plan participant. Systems must be in place to meet these required challenges.

PROCESSING AND CONTROL OF BENEFIT CLAIMS

Multiemployer funds exist for the purpose of paying benefits for those who qualify under conditions deemed appropriate under the terms of the benefit program developed by the fund's board of trustees. Processing of claims involves the determination of eligibility, calculation of amounts payable and actual payment of those claims. The manner in which claims paying functions are performed is dependent upon the nature of the plan (welfare, pension, vacation, etc.) and the form in which the fund is administered (contract or self-administration, ASO, etc.).

Welfare Fund Claims

If premiums are paid to an insurance carrier that assumes full or partial risk, either the insurance company or the fund office will issue benefit checks. Certification of eligibility would normally be a function of the administrative office. This certification may be effected on an individual claim basis or, in the insured situation, by periodic mass certification, which requires eligibility data to be fed to the carrier in the form of computer printouts, tapes, disks, lists or electronic transmittal.

When the insurance carrier makes payment, the administrative office certifies eligibility in advance and may review actual claims paid to ascertain that benefits have not been paid for ineligible persons and that benefits were paid in accordance with plan terms and conditions.

When the fund office itself pays claims using checks or drafts of the insurance carrier, an internal audit should be performed to make certain quality assurance is maintained as to the accuracy and propriety of claim payment; in addition, an external postaudit may be performed by the insurance carrier, as well as by the plan accountant, to verify the accuracy of benefit payments.

In a self-insured situation, the fund office handles all phases of claims processing—from initial certification of eligibility to adjudication and payment of the claim. In some instances, a self-insured fund may perform exactly the same function as it would if insured, that is, certifying the eligibility of the claimant and forwarding the claim to a third-party payer (either an independent TPA or an insurance carrier operating on an ASO basis, or to a PPO network for repricing). In all circumstances, identical provisions as to postpayment review by the fund office and outside audit would apply. The self-administered fund paying its own claims must establish internal control procedures and standards of quality assurance and arrange for its public accountant to test or verify claim payments during the course of an annual or other periodic examination.

When a COB provision is in place in the insurance contract or in the plan relating to an employee or one or more dependents covered by other insurance contracts, certain controls must be established to determine the fund's liability as compared to the possible obligation of other benefit payers. Whatever system prevails, the methods and controls should be the most economical and feasible system available to the trustees in the overall interest of preserving maximum dollars for benefit payments for all participants.

Whether the plan is insured or self-insured, and regardless of which party is designated as claims processor, the following tasks must be performed:

1. Determining whether employees and/or their dependents are individually eligible for plan benefits for the particular claim submitted
2. Verifying that the participant, whether employee or dependent, is eligible on the date that the claim was incurred
3. Ascertaining the actual type of claim is one covered by the benefit program and the degree to which it is subject to reimbursement of actual costs incurred
4. Verifying that all claim control procedures have been performed to ascertain that treatment is for necessary medical conditions and charges are reasonable, usual and customary for the medical condition
5. Paying claims to the participant or the assignee (hospital or other medical provider), including issuing appropriate explanation of benefits statements
6. Preparing required annual reports for federal and state governments indicating payments made for tax purposes
7. Accumulating data for claims analysis purposes and submitting claim experience reports to the trustees
8. Complying with HIPAA privacy and security regulations with regard to PHI of plan participants.

An important element in claims processing is the determination of whether the employee is eligible. That determination is facilitated if the rules are reasonable and clearly stated and communicated to participants in a manner that will assist comprehension.

Trustees are usually granted considerable authority under the collective bargaining or trust agreements to formulate eligibility requirements and decide questions of eligibility. The trustees bear the ultimate responsibility for deciding whether a participant is eligible for benefits and to hear and rule on appeals that may be made in this regard.

Courts and arbitrators have generally given trustees broad discretionary powers in the adoption and application of eligibility rules. However, they have also sustained claimant appeals in cases where the trustees have exceeded the scope of authority as specified in the trust agreement, or if the trustees have adopted unreasonable eligibility rules or applied reasonable eligibility requirements in a discriminatory or capricious manner. Trustees must notify employees when a claim is declined, rejected or partially denied; reference the plan provisions under which the claim was denied and why; and give the employees an opportunity to furnish additional information in accordance with the appeal procedures specified in ERISA.

Pension Benefit Claims

Whether retirement benefits are insured or self-insured, the administrative office usually bears the initial responsibility for compiling data and determining an applicant's eligibility. The result of such data accumulation is subject to review and determination by the trustees.

If the plan uses an insurance company to handle pension claims, the carrier will review the eligibility and data accumulation by the fund office and establish the benefits for purposes of the issuance of an annuity contract or making direct, periodic (usually monthly) pension payments.

In the self-insured situation, the administration office is responsible for the preparation of application forms for pension benefits; review of the application; retrieval of documentary records assembled/compiled over a long period of time to establish not only eligibility, but also the level of benefits; final approval of the application; and establishing the benefit level, subject to review and approval by the trustees. The pension office would then normally issue the pension certificate and arrange for the monthly payment of benefit checks directly from the pension fund. The fund office arranges for the distribution of appropriate forms detailing optional forms of retirement benefits and the procedures for tax reporting of payments made to pensioners.

A similar procedure would be followed for annuity fund payments, as well as for benefits under a DC pension plan. The accumulated annuity or DC account would become the basis of benefits paid to retirees and the beneficiaries, and the procedure for filing applications, certification thereof and approval by the trustees would be similar to that for a DB pension plan. Once benefit payments commence, an entirely separate set of data must be maintained by the fund office or its designee (such as an insurance company, TPA, etc.). Such data is necessary for the yearly actuarial valuation in a defined benefit pension situation.

Vacation Fund Payouts

In some vacation funds, individual applications are required before distribution of vacation fund accumulations to participants. In other plans, as provided in the trust and collective bargaining agreements, payments will be made on a regular basis to participants. Some plans provide for vacation money to be paid on certain designated dates on a uniform basis; others require application by employees with the approval of the employers in order to avoid mass vacations by all employees simultaneously.

CLAIMS CONTROLS AND HEALTH CARE COST-CONTAINMENT

The upward surge in health care costs in recent years has highlighted the importance of maintaining adequate controls over health insurance claims. It has dramatized the need for health care cost-containment. Health care claims are by far the largest component of a welfare fund's expenditures. The high rate of medical inflation (compared to overall inflation) and the explosion in utilization of health services in recent years mandates claims control and cost-containment as a means of maintaining the financial solvency of health and welfare benefit programs.

The major objectives in effective claims control are to identify excessive and unnecessary services and charges by hospitals and other medical service providers, avoid abnormal charges for services and detect and prevent the payment of fraudulent claims.

As discussed in the next chapter (regarding communication with plan participants), it is essential that employees be adequately and properly informed of their health care benefits and the role they can play in controlling overutilization and excessive charges. Many forms of participant communication have been developed and are useful to assist employees in becoming better health care consumers so they will be able to avoid the unnecessary use of medical services that may be prescribed by medical service providers. A well-designed educational program is an important factor in making employees aware of how they can assist in keeping health care costs at the lowest possible level.

There is a close relationship between monitoring and implementing cost-containment innovations and the entire claims processing procedure. Data collection is a natural by-product of claims processing. Therefore, the burden of collecting, comparing and analyzing data generally falls on the plan administrator, assisted by plan consultants. This responsibility is particularly significant if the benefit plan itself pays claims. The responsibility may also fall on third-party claims administrators that process those claims. If an insurance carrier pays claims, the data obtained from the carrier will usually be adequate, but not always enough, to meet the needs of the fund. Many benefit plans maintain their own databank of their claims to supplement or supersede reports received from the insurance company.

The Importance of Reliable Data

A vital prerequisite in the cost-containment effort is the need to accumulate meaningful data that will be of assistance in the proper analysis of the causes of ever-increasing health care costs. Cost-containment has become a significant factor because health care costs have risen faster than any other segment in the American economy. The nation spends almost four times as much for health care today as it did in the 1970s.

Reliable data allows a plan to identify, break down and analyze the components of health cost increases and to consider less expensive alternatives to traditional delivery systems. Competition for health care dollars by providers has reached almost epidemic proportions. Although such competition has not always resulted in the reduction of prices, it does open an opportunity to seek less costly alternatives. Almost every benefit plan is attempting to limit and control its health care expenditures. Many have experienced some success at least in managing costs, if not reducing them.

The key to controlling costs is the availability of

meaningful data. Data will identify the forces and elements at work in the health industry that affect the claim payments of a benefit plan. Trustees need to review summaries of such data, which must be accurate, complete, understandable and timely.

The minimum data generally needed by trustees and consultants for the purpose of developing health care cost-containment strategies include the following:

1. Summary reports by claims paid by type of claim, with aggregation of deductible and co-insurance costs incurred by plan participants. This may include a comparison of charges submitted by providers compared to amounts paid by the fund, as well as savings gained through effective administration of COB and subrogation recoveries.
2. Claims lag studies showing the length of time between the date medical treatment is rendered and the date the plan makes benefit payments. This helps determine the reserves required by the fund.
3. Analysis of benefits paid by type, such as hospitalization, outpatient ambulatory surgery, inpatient surgery, medical, dental, diagnostic, x-ray and prescription drug
4. Analysis of claims by major classification of illness using a standard type of medical coding, such as "major diagnostic category"
5. Analysis of medical and dental claims by procedures reflecting the average of charges and the payments for specific procedures
6. Analysis of hospital average length of stay, cost of average confinement and comparison with other published indicators of hospital costs and utilization trends.

Such data will enable the trustees to compare the experience of their plan to others in the industry and region, as well as to national indices. Another purpose is to enable the consultant and trustees to prepare projections of future costs and comparison to prospective sources of revenue. Adequate data also enables the board of trustees, plan consultants and the fund administrator to monitor the effectiveness of cost-containment strategies that may have been implemented, such as disease management programs (as discussed below).

Meaningful data may be extremely helpful in enabling a plan to enter into a preferred provider organization (PPO) arrangement with selected providers. Under such an arrangement, the plan would contract directly with certain health providers based on established negotiated fees for specific services rendered to plan participants. Normally there would be a discount or reduction in fees in connection with such an arrangement. It is important that the plan monitor the effectiveness of the PPO through ongoing data analysis.

Claim Audits

Actual auditing of the records of health providers represents a means for controlling and avoiding unnecessary payment of claims. A claim audit may include a visit to a hospital and/or doctor's office to review medical records to determine that services were necessary, services were properly administered, and charges, therefore, were appropriate in accordance with reasonable and customary levels and the price lists of the health provider.

The administrative office should implement controls to prevent abuse and excessive payment of health care claims. Some items of abuse to which administrators and their staff become sensitive include:

1. Longer than necessary hospital confinements
2. Longer absence from work than medically necessary in connection with disability claims
3. Unnecessary medical services rendered, such as x-rays and laboratory tests
4. Reporting hospital confinement under converge circumstances when in reality the confinement was for a noncovered situation (for example, cosmetic surgery)
5. Returning to work, earning compensation from other employment although receiving disability benefits from the plan.

Many plans use a precertification method by which an independent party will use peer review to ascertain the need for hospital or other medical/dental services. A utilization review organization will frequently be employed to monitor hospital admissions and length of stay in hospitals.

Coordination of Benefits (COB)

One element in the control of claims is the use of COB. Such a provision is designed to prevent a situation in which multiple group health insurance coverage of the same person or members of a participant's family results in a claim payment greater than the insured's actual medical expenses. This may occur if an employee's spouse is covered under another employer's program.

When a COB provision is in effect, one plan will be deemed the primary carrier, and the other will be the secondary carrier. The secondary carrier only pays to the extent that covered charges are incurred in excess of the amounts paid by the primary carrier. There are various methods in determining which carrier is primary and which is secondary.

The National Association of Insurance Commissioners (NAIC) has established a "birthday rule" for COB regulations. Although self-insured ERISA plans are not bound by NAIC dictates, the purpose of the NAIC regulation is to establish uniformity and avoid delays in processing and paying claims.

Under the birthday rule, the earliest birthday (month and day) occurring during the calendar year replaces gender as the means of determining whether a father's or mother's insurance plan is the primary payer for a dependent child's medical claim. Thus, the plan of the husband's employer would be used for the husband's claim, initially, as the primary carrier; the insurance carrier for the employer providing insurance for the mother would be used for the mother's claims as primary carrier; then the birthday rule, based on the actual birthdays of the husband and wife, would determine the liability for the claims of the children. To the extent reasonable and necessary health care expenses exceed the amount paid by the primary carrier, the secondary carrier would become partially responsible.

It should be noted federal criminal statutes could be interpreted to require the disclosure of the availability of other insurance or health benefits in those cases in which a benefit plan has a COB provision. More specifically, 18 U.S.C. §1027 makes it a federal crime to make a false statement or representation of fact or knowingly conceal any fact necessary to verify, explain, clarify or check for the accuracy and completeness of any report or document required to be kept as part of the records of any welfare benefit plan. This statute has been used to federally prosecute a plan participant for failing to disclose COB information in a case in which the plan paid out more in benefits than it would have had the COB information been disclosed.

To encourage the disclosure of COB information, many plans have incorporated within their plan design a "COB savings bank." Under such an arrangement, COB savings are credited to a participant and may be used during the remainder of the plan year to cover otherwise uncovered medical expenses. Typically, the savings are not carried forward after the plan year.

Subrogation

Subrogation is a concept under which the fund "stands in the shoes" of a participant with respect to a right of recovery against a third party who is responsible for causing the condition requiring medical treatment. In a typical case, the fund's plan document will require the execution of a subrogation/reimbursement agreement as a condition of providing benefits in a case where third-party liability may exist. Should the participant recover from the third party, part of the proceeds of that recovery (limited to the extent the plan has provided benefits) would then be reimbursed to the plan.

In order to have a successful subrogation recovery program, the administrative manager must have in place a range of specific procedures to:
- Identify claims representing potential subrogation.
- Gather information from the participant and/or his or her attorney regarding other parties and coverages involved, the particulars of the accident/incident, etc.
- Secure signed subrogation/reimbursement agreements from participants.
- Update and communicate the extent of the fund's subrogation lien to the participant's attorney and/or the fund's attorney.
- Track notice and collection efforts.
- Flag claims and eligibility in the event the participant refuses to honor the subrogation/reimbursement agreement.

Fraudulent Claims

One of the functions of the administrative office and/or claims payer is to prevent fraud with respect to submitted claims. The incidence of fraud does not appear to be as prevalent as other abuses. Nevertheless, trustees, administrative managers and claims personnel know that fraud, in fact, has been committed against employee benefit plans by participants, providers and others. The potential for loss to funds exists through numerous fraudulent acts: identity of the claimant, patient or provider; statements of service provided or supplies furnished; statements regarding the cause of illness or injury; and failure to advise of the existence of other coverage.

Susan P. Weaver, a member of an independent auditing firm specializing in employee benefit plan audits, in a recently published article in the International Foundation's *Benefit & Compensation Digest* (Vol. 42, No 4, April 2005), detailed the many ways in which fraud might be committed against a multiemployer fund. This comprehensive listing is most worthy of reproduction here.

Benefit Disbursements
- Pension funds
  —Deceased pensioners
  —Phony pensioners
  —Manipulation of pension calculation
- Health and welfare funds
  —Unbundling and upcoding of services
  —Sweetheart deals with network providers
  —General kickbacks
    –Monetary
    –Things of value
  —Fictitious services
    –Physician
    –Service provider
  —Nontransmittal of appropriate rebates and discounts
  —Claims
    –Fictitious claims by service providers
      *Billing for services not rendered
      *Upgrade in services provided
      *Performance of unnecessary services
      *Referral kickbacks from providers

–Fictitious claims by participants
　*Claims for invalid dependents
　*Phony out-of-pocket expenses
　*Duplicate claims
　*Abuse
—Duplicate coverage
- Apprenticeship funds
—Fund buying tools for personal use
—Service to homes of officers
—Payment to fictitious instructors
—Registration fees never turned in
- Annuity funds
—Fictitious annuitants
—Theft of unclaimed annuity benefits
—Interception of annuity checks
- Legal Services funds
—Service provider bills for incorrect case type
—Improper continuation of case
—Billings in excess of plan limitation
—Inflated hours or fictitious case work

Employer Contributions
- Alter egos
- Omission of covered employees
- Omission of covered pay types
- Omission of covered wages
- Improper inclusion of owners/relatives
- Delinquency
- Deficiency
- Diversion of employer contributions

Administrative Expenses
- Inflated professional fees
- Fictitious employees
- Unreasonable allocation of shared expenses
- Inflated purchase prices
- Fictitious payments for goods and services
- Inflated travel expenses
- Kickbacks
- Inflated payroll tax deposits
- Personal use of computer equipment
- Inflated salaries
- Personal expenses paid by fund
- Diversion of rental and other income

Investments
- Unauthorized transfer from investment accounts
- Diversion of investment income
- Investments with no substance
- Kickbacks
- Self-dealing investment transactions.

Clearly, there are any number of ways a fraud might be perpetrated upon a trust fund. Administrative procedures must be put in place to minimize the risk of such fraudulent acts.

A fraudulent claim can be submitted without a participant's knowledge. This may be particularly true with respect to prescription card plans and minor claims in which assigned claims are submitted directly to a benefit plan for payment to the health provider. In such a case, the participant may not be aware that someone has assumed his or her identity and obtained free health care, or an unscrupulous provider has submitted claims for services never rendered. Thus, the importance of urging participants to review explanation of benefits statements to help combat such fraud is critical.

Fraud may also be conducted with the knowledge of the participant who assists an ineligible participant or a nonparticipant in obtaining hospital, surgical, prescription drug or other medical care. A claim may be submitted with the signature of a fictitious provider or a forged signature of a bona fide provider. A more common fraud involves false answers to questions on claim forms about other coverage with which the plan coordinates or subrogates. Participants frequently leave questions unanswered about other group health insurance. This information must be obtained during claims processing.

Participants may have to be educated to the fact that false answers constitute fraud and are not merely another way of obtaining what some believe is their right. For example, participants and employees may make fraudulent statements about the cause of illness or injury and indicate there is no liability under workers' compensation insurance; the same is true for an occupational disease, as well as whether the injury or illness is job related.

Federal Regulations Governing Claims Processing

Federal law imposes certain requirements on parties that process employee benefit claims. If the fund itself is responsible for part or all of claims processing, the administrative office must provide procedures to comply with the regulations; assure trustees they are in compliance; and implement those procedures to avoid unnecessary and costly legal problems that could result from noncompliance.

Section 503 of ERISA requires that, subject to regulations published by the secretary of labor, every employee benefit plan shall adopt claim procedures designed to assure the participants are properly notified if their claim is denied and are given specific reasons for such denial and afforded a "reasonable opportunity for a full and fair review."

Regulations issued by the U.S. Department of Labor in the last several years differentiate between pre- and postservice claims appeals. Preservice claim determination appeals are further differentiated between urgent and nonurgent matters. Very strict time limits, as short as 72 hours, apply and appropriate reviews by medical peers are required in some cases.

With regard to the initial processing of a claim, federal regulations stipulate that a claim must be replied to or paid within a certain period of time. The period of time for processing claims is considered reasonable if the processing is completed within 90 days after the plan receives the claim. There may be an extension if written notice is given to the claimant. In no event may the extension exceed a second 90-day period.

The trustees, or the party to whom the trustees have delegated the responsibility of claims processing, must provide to every claimant who is denied a claim for benefits a written notice setting forth, in a manner calculated to be understood by the claimant: the specific reason or reasons for the denial; specific reference to the pertinent plan provisions on which the denial was based; a description of any additional material or information necessary to complete the claim, with an explanation of why such information or material is necessary; and appropriate information as to the steps to be taken if the participant/beneficiary wishes to submit his or her claim for review. Every plan is required to establish a procedure by which a claimant, or the claimant's duly authorized representative, has a reasonable opportunity to appeal the denial of the claim to an appropriate named fiduciary or person designated by the fiduciaries of the plan. The procedure must provide that a claimant may request review upon written application to the plan and have the right to review pertinent documents and submit issues and comments in writing.

This review may be assumed by an insurance company, managed care organization, insurance service or other similar organization. In such case, the company or service organization is said to be the appropriate named fiduciary for purposes of claim review. Trustees of insured plans or those that use a service or other organization subject to state insurance laws may retain authority for review and do not delegate this function to the insurance company.

The trustees' claims review and appeal procedure may include a limited period under which the claimant must file a request for review of a denied claim. The regulations provide that the time limit must be reasonable and related to the nature of the benefit and other related circumstances. In no event may a claimant be given less than 60 days to request a review, which is measured from the date the claimant receives written notification of denial.

The trustees' decision or review must be made promptly, and in the case of postservice reviews, ordinarily within 60 days after the plan receives the request for review unless special circumstances exist. If circumstances exist requiring an extension of time for processing the review, a decision must be rendered as soon as possible, but not later than 120 days after the plan received the request for review.

Other Cost-Containment Strategies

In addition to review of treatment to ascertain that submitted claims represent necessary and reasonable care at usual, customary and reasonable charges, many plans have initiated other cost-containment efforts. These may include the following:

- Plan design revisions to encourage the use of less costly alternatives and to discourage excessive use of health services. This may include a certain amount of cost-sharing by plan participants through coinsurance, deductibles, inside benefit limits and scheduled coverages (e.g., examinations covered once every year, two years, etc.).
- The encouragement of lower cost alternatives by providing incentives for the use of such services as outpatient surgery, preadmission testing, second surgical opinion or specific procedures, home health care, hospice care, nonphysician practitioners, free-standing centers and ambulatory rather than inpatient care.
- Administrative changes to restrain health care cost increases by review of funding methods and possible use of self-insurance or third-party administrators rather than insurance companies in the interest of reducing administrative costs
- Tightened COB and subrogation efforts resulting in significant and substantial savings to the fund's "bottom line"
- The introduction of disease management programs to identify, at an early stage, the onset of potentially chronic conditions involving diabetes, asthma, hypertension, chronic obstructive pulmonary disease, chronic heart failure, HIV/AIDS and Hepatitis C.

As to the last bulleted item, in recent years, there has been a great emphasis on health education, health promotion and employee assistance programs. Many plans are actively involved in these efforts in an attempt to develop long-term approaches for health and lifestyle improvements. This may include working with employees to control or reduce hazards caused by alcoholism, smoking, mental stress, hypertension, substance abuse, overweight, lack of physical fitness, back problems, and family and financial problems. Many plans have arranged such educational and counseling programs with private counseling firms, local charitable organizations, local hospitals and medical teaching institutions. Data collection gathered through claims processing is essential to the success of these efforts.

Still other plans have found it necessary to tighten eligibility rules to require a higher level of work in covered employment and higher employer contributions more closely coordinated to the actual cost of health care incurred by plan participants each year. Others have instituted aggressive means of utilization review, using peer organizations to monitor the type of hospital facilities utilized, length of stay, the need for admission and actual services rendered to plan participants.

Many plans audit provider charges and billings to ascertain that billings are proper. They engage medical and dental consultants who review actual claims submitted to detect inappropriate charges or treatment that is unreasonable or unnecessary. Some funds use case management techniques in which they engage health professionals to review the sequence and type of treatment of people with major conditions from the viewpoint of making certain the most appropriate, efficient and economical form of treatment is rendered. Plans may review alternative means of health delivery in their area and encourage employees to use PPOs (based on negotiated fee arrangements), which may result in lower charges and costs to the health plan. Finally, plans have found it necessary to revisit their overall plan design and have expanded their offerings from a traditional indemnity, fee-for-service-type plan to PPO and HMO alternative plans.

ROLE OF THE ADMINISTRATIVE OFFICE IN PARTICIPATING IN TRUSTEES' DECISION MAKING

Virtually all administrative managers are involved in establishing the dates and procedures for meetings of the board of trustees. Generally, the administrative manager will handle the notice of such meetings, the determination of which parties are to be invited other than the members of the board of trustees, the site and date of meetings and so forth. The administrative manager may frequently maintain the minutes of trustees meetings. In some instances, the administrative manager may prepare drafts of minutes of such meetings that are forwarded to legal counsel for final approval. In any event, the administrative manager will be responsible for reviewing the final minutes and assuring they reflect the accurate record of the meetings.

An administrative manager will generally be the party primarily involved in developing the data and information the trustees will need or request at the trustees meetings or in the decision-making process in general.

Frequently, the administrative manager will be the source of the specific issues and problems to be addressed by trustees. Based upon the day-to-day operations of the fund by administrative staff, the manager is the agent in the organization most likely to understand and know which problems require action by the board of trustees, and to present the issues, background, supporting data and a meaningful explanation of the problem. Similarly, the administrative manager will develop and propose alternative solutions. Also, he or she will generally be the party responsible for implementing decisions made at trustees meetings.

To assist the trustees in making decisions, the administrative manager usually prepares many reports, possibly including (but not limited to) the following:
1. Summary of employer contributions
2. Summary of investment results
3. Interim financial statements and cash projections
4. Listing of delinquent employers
5. Recommendation for matters to be submitted to legal counsel
6. Summary of claims paid
7. Claim trends
8. Proposed capita costs
9. Changes in personnel
10. Budget of internal operations and administrative expenses
11. Approval of expenditures.

In this connection, and as discussed in Chapter 44, the administrative manager may also be involved in engaging and coordinating activities of plan professionals. Almost invariably, the administrative manager acts as the coordinating agent between the trustees and professionals such as the fund's independent public accountant, attorney, employee benefit plan consultant, pension actuary, investment manager(s), investment consultant, investment custodian and insurance representatives.

As health care cost-containment activity has expanded in recent years in many funds, the administrative manager is also involved in dealing with additional consultants, including:
1. Utilization review firms (hospitalization and ambulatory claims)
2. Those engaged for second surgical opinions for certain procedures
3. Prescription drug service providers
4. Representatives of PPOs and HMOs
5. Data processing consultants
6. Medical consultants
7. Dental consultants
8. Case management/disease management specialists.

The administrative manager may also be requested not only to coordinate the various reports and services of such professionals, but also to comment on their performance and efficiency. In many instances, the administrative manager will aid the trustees in the selection of the professionals and consulting firms and will help monitor and evaluate their performance.

GENERAL FUND ADMINISTRATION

The term *administration,* in the broadest sense, can be used to cover all aspects of operating the fund—from policy setting to implementation. The trustees are the policy makers of the funds. The trustees establish the goals and objectives and delegate the day-to-day operations to the administrative manager.

Day-to-Day Functions of the Administrative Manager

The administrator's job is to run the day-to-day operations of the plan for the trustees as they direct. Whether the administrator is salaried or contract, the administrator has a professional role calling for a high degree of skill, years of experience, detailed technical knowledge of many disciplines and, last but certainly not least, the ability to get along with other people.

Abbreviated into essential functions, the administrator/administrative manager is responsible to:
1. Accept, process and account for employer reports and contributions.
2. Carry out the established procedures involved in handling delinquent and incomplete accounts.
3. Control employer contributions through annual confirmation of contributions to employees and periodic reports to trustees. Also, if directed by the trustees, audit employer records.
4. Implement trust policy on collection of delinquent contributions, and assist the trust fund attorney with the processing of legal matters involving delinquencies.
5. Allocate contributions to employee accounts, handle self-payments (including COBRA administration), carry out the provisions of any reciprocity agreements, determine eligibility and send periodic eligibility notices to employees.
6. Issue claim forms, receive and process claims, and calculate and pay benefits.
7. Establish financial controls, maintain the fund records and furnish the trustees with periodic financial statements.
8. Keep close track of the claims experience of the fund, analyze trends and make periodic reports to the trustees.
9. Maintain investment schedules.
10. Keep the rough minutes of the meetings and committees as directed by the board of trustees.
11. Prepare the various federal, state and insurance department forms and reports and amendments thereto.
12. Handle plan communications (a critical area in the operations of the modern day Taft-Hartley trust fund).

Administrator's Role in Office Procedures and Workflow

A considerable amount of an administrative manager's time and energy is spent on what many would call ministerial functions, that is, putting together the raw materials needed to implement various policies of the board of trustees. The manager's job is to mobilize the physical and human resources needed to carry out the basic administrative functions described earlier in this chapter. This mobilization of resources requires numerous decisions regarding personnel, office facilities and equipment, recordkeeping systems and security measures. The trustees sometimes look on these decisions casually, as if they were always made with relative ease and then automatically implemented without effort.

However, the breadth of these duties is almost endless given their variations from fund to fund. Completing these ministerial duties is an ongoing and sometimes Herculean task. Although no attempt is made here to provide an exhaustive listing, the major areas of responsibilities for these "ministerial" duties include:
1. Personnel management
   - Evaluation of present and future personnel needs, including preparation of job descriptions
   - Formulation of personnel policies pertaining to work conditions, compensation levels and employee benefits
   - Recruiting, hiring and training of staff
   - Supervision and coordination of staff activities
   - Periodic evaluation of staff performance
2. Office management
   - Continuous evaluation of the adequacy of administrative housing (location and available space)
   - Allocation of floor space to staff and equipment to facilitate work flow
   - Projection of future space needs
   - Selection and procurement of supplies, equipment, fixtures, furniture and other hardware
   - Maintenance of an inventory of the fund's personal property
3. Recordkeeping and security of records
   - Evaluation and selection of a recordkeeping system (manual, mechanized, electronic data processing or a combination of all three)
   - Provision for physical security of records against loss
   - Selection of a method for record storage and duplication (microfilm, microfiche, carbon copies, magnetic tapes and disk, photocopy, scanning, etc.)
   - Formulation of a policy regarding accessibility of records to staff, trustees, participants and others
   - Establishment of a policy to preserve the confidentiality of records
   - Maintenance of general fund records
4. Protection of premises and personnel
   - Selection and placement of insurance and bonds:

—To protect the trust fund against general public liability

—To protect the trustees and employees of the fund against personal liability for errors or omissions

—To have in place the necessary workers' compensation and related coverages

—To protect fund property against losses due to fire, theft and other hazards

5. Implementation of policies and procedures adopted by the trustees, including investment policies, recordkeeping and record retention policies, personnel and contribution overpayment policies

6. Publish and file all required governmental reports and notices (e.g., Forms 5500, Summary Annual Reports, Annual WHCRA notice, etc.).

Although these are the most basic ministerial functions, the range may be much broader. Much depends on what the trustees expect from their administrative manager and what services he or she is qualified to perform on their behalf. For example, in some cases, the administrative manager is the secretary to the board of trustees or secretary of the fund and prepares and maintains board minutes and agendas. Frequently, the administrator is asked to prepare, produce and distribute plan booklets. In some cases, he or she manages real property where the fund owns the property in which the fund office is located and rents space in the same or other buildings to other parties.

Although ministerial duties vary, every administrative manager must be concerned about the mobilization of resources to get the job done. For example, the administrative manager must consider:

- The number of people needed to perform various administrative tasks, such as eligibility and claims processing
- The best place to recruit personnel that might be needed for fund operations
- The recruitment techniques most likely to be successful
- The level of on-the-job training necessary for fund personnel; the standards which apply in evaluation of staff performance
- The adequacy of office facilities over the short and longer term
- The need, if any, to improve the accessibility of the fund office to plan participants, employees, contributing employers and participating local unions
- The manner in which the fund office is furnished and the image the office should convey to plan participants
- The equipment needed for the maintenance of employee, employer and accounting records
- Whether equipment should be rented or purchased
- Provisions that should be made to prevent the loss of records due to fire, theft and other hazards
- Limitations on access to employee and employer records
- Insurance, bonding and fiduciary coverages needed to protect the fund assets, employees, trustees and personal or real property.

Decisions on these issues ultimately determine the level of service received by plan participants. Obviously, the administrative manager does not make these decisions alone, nor does he or she always have the broadest possible range of choice. It is reasonable to assume the trustees would be involved in some phases of the internal management processing, especially when it involves the expenditure of trust fund monies. In some instances, an outside consultant may be retained to evaluate personnel, equipment, space requirements or other aspects of fund administration.

Nevertheless, the administrative manager must keep the trustees informed about what resources he or she believes are necessary to carry out his or her responsibilities. The initiative rests with the manager because he or she has to get the job done within the limits of available resources.

As has been described in this chapter, multiemployer trust fund administration is not as simple and straightforward as one might initially believe. Collective bargaining, changes in trades and industries, technological advances, participant expectations and the dictates of an ever-growing body of federal law and regulation have all contributed to the evolution of today's trust fund office into a complex, multifaceted business operation.

Chapter 45

The Administrative Manager's Relationship With Plan Trustees, Plan Professionals, Participants and Others

William J. Einhorn

In the previous chapter, we reviewed the forms and functions of administrative management and the major activities undertaken in the administrative process.

To fulfill all of the obligations of administrative management of a Taft-Hartley benefit plan, the administrator wears many hats and fulfills many roles, such as:
1. Executive director or manager
2. Designer of administrative and physical systems for plan operations
3. Designer, manager or monitor of data systems
4. Administrator of the benefit program and overseer of the payment of benefit claims
5. Coordinator of office staff
6. "Point person" for plan participants, outside professionals, trustees, the public and government
7. Policy executor
8. Educator and communicator
9. Advisor and initiator of policy.

The degree to which the administrative manager fulfills all or any of these roles varies due to the individual factors of any particular benefit plan. In some plans, the administrator actively participates in the decision-making process. In others, the administrative manager will be solely responsible for a portion of these activities, while the trustees take an active, direct role in certain specific administrative functions and the determination of fund policy. Although the roles are not mutually exclusive, they fall along a continuum leading to an expanded range of responsibilities for the administrative manager. In Chapter 44, the activities of the administrative manager in fulfilling these tasks were detailed. In this chapter, we will discuss the coordinating role of the administrator with all parties.

The manager is involved with the engagement and retention of staff, whether on a contract administration basis or for that of a self-administered trust fund. The manager is also the agent of the trustees with respect to their interaction with outside professionals. This delegated coordination will involve attorneys, accountants, actuaries and benefit consultants, investment advisors, investment consultants, insurance and managed care companies, and other types of consultants, as well as providers of services and the general public. Most importantly, the administrator is the agent of the trustees in dealing with plan participants, participating unions and contributing employers.

RELATIONSHIP OF ADMINISTRATIVE MANAGER WITH TRUSTEES

In Chapter 44, we discussed the role of the administrator in working with the trustees in the decision-making process and as their agent in the daily operation of the trust.

The decision-making process usually involves meetings of the board of trustees. The administrator generally makes the arrangements for the dates, site, amenities and the agenda for such meetings. The administrator normally sends out the notice of meetings and determines the outside parties to be invited.

The administrative manager usually maintains the minutes of the trustees meetings, either by directly writing such minutes or holding the permanent minutes, which may be written by counsel or the secretary of the board of trustees. In some instances, the administrator may prepare a draft of minutes that will be forwarded to counsel for final review.

The administrator is the party primarily responsible

for developing the information to be made available to the trustees at meetings or during other stages of the decision-making process. Frequently, the administrator will be the source of the list of issues and problems to be addressed. The manager generally prepares the meeting agenda after consultation with the fund's staff, trustees, counsel and other plan professionals.

The manager is the agent most involved in the day-to-day operations and is most aware of problems and issues faced by benefit plan employees. As a consequence, the administrative manager is the one person most likely to understand which matters require action by the board. Based on such knowledge, the administrator presents the issues, background, supporting data and explanation of the problem. Often trustees look to the administrative manager to develop and propose alternative solutions to problems.

After the resolution of the problems at the trustees meeting and determination of future policy, the administrator is the party responsible for implementing such decisions. In this role, the administrator may work with plan professionals with respect to litigation, communications, announcement material and instituting changes in benefit plan policy and procedure.

In addition to the day-to-day interrelationship with individual members of the board of trustees and the board as an entity, the administrative manager usually acts as the conduit for communications among the trustees, plan professionals and participants. Overall, the administrator coordinates all activities of plan professionals to avoid duplication and needless expenditures. In many plans, the administrator also is involved in the engagement of plan professionals, as well as the acquisition of all needed services and supplies.

In recent years, as the activities of benefit plans have expanded, particularly with respect to health care cost containment, the manager may also deal regularly with new types of service providers such as hospital utilization review organizations, second surgical opinion firms, prescription drug service plans, drug utilization review vendors, preferred provider organizations (PPOs), health maintenance organizations (HMOs), physician-hospital organizations, data processing consultants, medical and dental consultants, nurses and communication consultants.

In addition to coordinating the various reports and services of outside professionals and providers, the administrator may also be involved in the process of evaluating such services.

The role of the administrative manager in the decision-making process may be summarized as follows:

1. Accumulating information relating to an issue or problem
2. Providing insight as to the extent and nature of the issue, taking into consideration input received from staff
3. Defining the issue
4. Determining the cause of the problem
5. Developing alternative solutions
6. Evaluating the alternatives
7. Selecting the best solution
8. Implementing the solution determined and decided by the trustees.

The administrator may participate in all of these phases except for perhaps the final determination of the solution. It should be noted that in many instances, the board of trustees expects a recommendation from the administrator. In such cases, the administrator would be involved to a greater extent in the final choice of alternatives and may advocate a specific solution as the best method of resolving the particular problem.

The role of the administrator as an advocate varies from fund to fund. In many plans, the trustees expect the administrator to take an aggressive position with respect to policy issues; in others, the trustees expect the administrator to be neutral and the policy decisions are made exclusively by the board. In the latter case, the administrator would present the issue and alternatives, augmented by input from outside professionals (particularly fund counsel when the matter is of a legal nature).

Accumulating the Information

The administrator has access to information from fund records, experience and the actual details of the matter involved in the decision-making process. By accumulating such information and presenting it to the board of trustees in an efficient and concise form, the administrator plays a vital role in enabling the board to make an appropriate decision. In the process of presenting the problem, the administrator provides information based upon the particulars of the matter as gained from the experiences of the entire administrative staff.

Defining the Problem

By submitting, in written form, a concise and clear explanation of the problem and its causes, the administrator can avoid wasted time and effort by the trustees and other parties attending trustees meetings. This summary can be a key element in shortening what can be extremely long trustees' meetings.

It is important for the administrator to clarify whether the problem is common to many participants or one that is remote and applicable to only a small number of employees.

Developing Alternatives

The key element in the resolution of any problem is

the presentation of clearly applicable alternatives to the board of trustees. If the problem is primarily an administrative one, the administrative manager usually develops the alternatives.

If the problem is one of plan policy, financial stability, governmental requirements, investment changes and other major considerations, the administrator will generally seek the input of plan professionals in advance to provide the alternatives to the trustees.

The degree to which the administrative manager will be involved in evaluating alternatives generally varies with the nature of the issue. If the problem is primarily administrative, the input of the administrator is vital and perhaps serves as the exclusive voice in explaining the alternatives to the board. If, on the other hand, the matter is a matter of policy extending far beyond routine administrative matters, the input as to alternatives would probably be furnished by the plan professionals most involved in that particular field.

General Information Brought to the Attention of the Trustees

The administrator generally is the person responsible for reporting to the trustees the effects of economic, legislative or regulatory changes on the trust fund. If changes occur that require revision of administrative practice or should be brought to the attention of the trustees, the administrator reports at the next board meeting or uses other means of communicating with them.

The administrator may receive information from specific employers and/or unions with respect to matters that may involve possible changes in fund practices. To that extent, the administrative manager is the conduit for information made available to the board of trustees that is furnished to parties in interest.

Because one of the main roles of the administrative manager and staff is to maintain constant communication with plan participants, the feedback from participants can be of vital importance and significance to the trustees. Listening to and understanding the significance of participants' comments, inquiries and complaints can provide the administrator with input for decisions by the trustees that might not otherwise be available.

This is particularly true when more participants contact the fund office instead of the union office, or when the manager makes presentations to participant groups at local union meetings. Such contact can bring to light real problems from employees that were not foreseen and that, if known by the trustees, can be remedied.

Exchanges of information and ideas in conversation, discussion groups or other educational sessions provide background about experience of others. The International Foundation of Employee Benefit Plans has done a particularly fine job in creating this kind of learning environment. Sessions in educational programs are presented by practitioners and are relevant to the manager's general daily concerns. The administrator will frequently advise the trustees at meetings of vital information that may have been acquired during such exchanges.

The administrator is also responsible for keeping informed about services and technology related to fund administration. Based on information that the administrator may obtain from reporting services, trade journals, periodicals, presentations by vendors and educational programs, this type of information can be relayed to the trustees and serve a vital purpose in ongoing efforts to provide the highest level of quality service to plan participants and parties in interest in the most efficient and economical fashion.

Trustees Meeting Procedures

In addition to the day-to-day contact that may occur between the members of the board of trustees and the administrator, there is a formal relationship that occurs at scheduled or special meetings of the board of trustees. The frequency of such meetings depends upon the nature of the plan, trust agreement requirements, complexity of operations and occurrence of special events. The administrator may also coordinate and participate in special committee meetings (for boards of trustees that establish committees or subcommittees to do background work on behalf of the entire board).

The agenda for a typical meeting includes the following:

1. Review and approval of the minutes of the prior meeting
2. Review of fund finances, including independent accountant's report (when available)
3. Review of employer collections and delinquencies
4. Review of any reports of committees of the board
5. Review of reports and recommendations of legal counsel and other professionals
6. Administrative manager's report and recommendations
7. Consideration of items raised in the administrative manager's report not previously covered
8. Review of special matters and issues that may have arisen
9. Consideration of unfinished business
10. Claim appeals or committee reports on appeals
11. Review of benefit applications, if not covered in the administrative manager's report
12. Establishment of the date and location of the next meeting of the board and/or committees.

The discussion of reports of consultants and the administrative manager generally include review of investments, investment performance, claims experience, attorney's report on collections and litigation, recommendations from the actuary, cash and certificate of deposit management and changes in eligibility rules.

ADMINISTRATIVE MANAGER'S RELATIONSHIP WITH PLAN PARTICIPANTS

The key contact between plan participants and the plan is the administrative manager and staff, whether salaried or contract. In the area of employee benefits, communication emphasizes the conveying of benefit plan information in an understandable, intelligent and interesting way to plan participants and beneficiaries. Effective communications create goodwill through a clear and concise summary of the plan benefits available to participants and their families when a claim arises or retirement approaches. In addition, the manner in which participants and their families are treated by the administration office has much to do with the attitudes these parties have toward the fund and the trustees.

After the enactment of ERISA, the area of communication became even more important to the fund, particularly as it applies to plan participants. The emphasis was on the communication and disclosure of information involving employee and beneficiary rights under the plan, most notably through the publication and timely update of a summary plan description.

One of the administrator's first responsibilities is to properly and adequately communicate with participants and their dependents and beneficiaries with respect to benefit structures, the extent and limitation of coverages, and requirements of qualification, and to advise of danger areas that might adversely affect ultimate eligibility for benefits.

Information about the level of benefits must be made available—to the greatest extent possible—to every potential beneficiary in sufficiently precise language to meet legal requirements. Communications must be in a language the average participant can readily understand. To the typical board of trustees, this responsibility falls on the administrative manager.

Communication with participants includes such items as eligibility status, potential loss of eligibility, dependent coverage, effect of new legislation that may alter existing coverages, tax aspects of benefits and general advice. Communication in the employee benefits field encompasses preparation, printing and distribution of descriptive material, including plan booklets; notification of eligibility and current accumulation of pension, annuity and vacation fund credits; notification of potential loss of eligibility or breaks in service; issuance of identification cards; issuance of informational brochures, such as summary plan descriptions and summary annual reports; and contact by telephone and in person.

In the welfare area, one of the key strategies of health care cost containment is communication with plan participants as well as providers of health care. The purpose of such communication is aimed at helping plan participants develop a sense of consumerism and become prudent purchasers of health care. To be sure, the communication responsibilities of the administrative office have greatly expanded.

The same may be said with respect to the retirement area. In Section 401(k) benefit plans, communication becomes of even greater significance and importance than in all other defined benefit (DB) and defined contribution (DC) plans. Communication is required with participants in some of the following areas:

- Detailing types of choices available to participants as to investments
- Furnishing means of taking advantage of withdrawal and loan features of these plans
- Availability of current account balances and investment returns. Some plans have instituted voice technology and Internet capabilities in which plan participants may obtain the current account balances on a daily, weekly or monthly basis.
- Details as to the available investments and choices
- Providing information by the trustees to plan participants to assist them in making investment decisions
- Communicating changes in investment programs, beneficiaries, loans, withdrawals, etc.
- In those plans allowing for self-directed investments, advising and arranging appropriate educational seminars for plan participants regarding investment strategies, appropriate asset allocations and options.

ADMINISTRATIVE MANAGER'S RELATIONSHIP WITH PLAN PROFESSIONALS

The relationship between the administrative manager and plan professionals takes on many themes and variations. The individual characteristics and practices of a particular benefit plan determine the trustees' method of using the services of professional advisors in the day-to-day operations of the fund.

In fulfilling their fiduciary role, boards of trustees will normally rely on such advisors as attorneys, investment consultants, investment managers, benefit consultant actuaries, certified public accountants (CPAs), computer consultants and insurance brokers; in certain special types of funds, additional advisors may be required, such as preretirement planning counselors, medical and dental consultants, nurses, instructors and supervisors of education for training and retraining programs (especially in the area of 401(k) retirement programs with participant self-directed options) and bank advisors.

Some boards require attorneys and specific consultants to attend every meeting, and other advisors by invitation; in other funds, the trustees may require written consultants' recommendations and documentation on issues with infrequent appearances at meetings.

The trustees typically look to and assign the responsibility for coordination with plan professionals to the administrative manager. In dealing with such consultants, the manager is required to furnish relevant data to them to help fulfill their responsibilities.

In addition, the administrator will generally identify meaningful matters that raise issues to be referred to the consultants. The manager may work with the professionals in deciding the amount and type of information needed to help resolve issues. The administrative manager is usually involved in developing the information being prepared by the consultants for the trustees. Frequently, the administrative manager will receive the report and recommendation of a consultant for the purpose of initial review and analysis and preliminary comments to the advisor. This may enable the consultant to measure the effect of the report and make corrections when and where applicable.

In summary, the administrative manager's function with respect to the interrelationship and communication with plan professionals is to identify and shape issues and solutions; understand the information provided by professionals and its impact on administrative operations; furnish professionals with information from fund records; react to the reports and recommendations of professionals; review and comment upon reports and responses from professionals; and submit their reports to the board of trustees.

After the trustees have resolved an issue and finalized a policy position with the assistance of plan professionals, the administrative manager usually has the responsibility to implement the decision.

Overall, the administrative manager serves a vital and pivotal role in the communication and relationship between the board of trustees and plan professionals. The manager arranges, coordinates and implements the reports and recommendations of the professionals and serves as the "hub of the wheel," driving the overall functioning of the trust fund in the best interests of its participants and their beneficiaries.

The interrelationship of the administrative manager with each of the major professional disciplines will be reviewed in the following sections.

Attorneys

Virtually every jointly managed multiemployer benefit fund engages legal counsel. Attorneys are usually engaged at the inception of the trust fund to help develop legal documents and assist in the application to the Internal Revenue Service (IRS) for approval of the fund as a tax-exempt qualified entity. Attorneys work with benefit plan consultants and actuaries to help formulate plan rules and regulations, plan documents governing benefits and the rights of participants, and summary plan descriptions and announcement materials.

After the inception of the trust fund, counsel are usually engaged on an ongoing basis to serve as general legal consultants. The firm engaged to fulfill such a capacity may also handle collections of employer delinquencies and other routine legal matters. Some funds will use one legal firm for general counsel and another firm for collection of delinquencies.

General counsel for the fund usually attends trustees meetings and may prepare the minutes of such meetings. They will be involved with the development of contracts with insurance companies, contract and/or salaried administrators, other professionals, vendors, preferred health care providers, and other consultants and suppliers providing services to the fund. In addition to the specific services uniquely characteristic of employee benefit plans, counsel also perform routine activities, such as contracts, lease of space and equipment, employment, mortgage and real estate contracts and investment documents.

Depending upon the practice of the fund, counsel may prepare the actual wording of notices to plan participants and employers, summary plan descriptions, summary annual reports, reports to the government, investment guidelines and promulgation and publication of administrative policy. In some funds, the administrative manager and benefit consultants may draft the text of such documents and procedures subject to the review of legal counsel.

In every fund, however, the trustees require counsel to interpret federal and state laws governing the operation of the plan, as well as regulations that may be issued and court decisions that may affect trustee policy and plan operations. The trustees and administrative manager will rely on counsel for advice relating to the fulfillment of fiduciary obligations and the legal consequences of trustees' actions (or avoidance of action in certain circumstances).

Counsel represents the trustees collectively in their relationship with the IRS and the U.S. Department of Labor (DOL); in litigation with participants, employers and others; and with respect to contracts with service providers, such as insurance companies, investment advisors, computer consultants, vendors, medical groups and hospitals.

When an independent attorney represents plan participants in a legal action with respect to appeals and claims or a question of eligibility or pension status, the administrator and the trustees refer such matter to fund counsel. When other problems arise that appear to be a substantial prospect for litigation, it is prudent for the administrator and trustees to turn over such matters to counsel at the earliest possible time. In some funds, this time sequence begins with the internal plan appeal; that is, some plans require that counsel attend the initial claims review/appeal meetings before the matter is elevated to full-blown litigation.

Counsel may also serve a unique role in representing the board of trustees in relationship to other professionals. The trustees may delegate to counsel the responsibility to negotiate contracts or renewals with the administrator (whether salaried or contract), the CPA, the investment consultant, investment advisors, benefit plan consultants, actuaries and other service providers.

The role of counsel with respect to the everyday operations of the trust fund varies with the style of the trustees, administrator and the attorney. For example, a fund may delegate to the attorney the sole responsibility for the preparation and periodic review of governing documents, written policies, contracts and minutes of the meetings. Under another format, the attorney may retain primary responsibility, but confer with a benefit consultant and administrator with respect to such instruments. In another form, the consultant may take primary responsibility for drafting and maintaining the plan and related documents and work with the administrator in developing operating policy. Minutes, summary plan descriptions and other notices might be prepared by the consultant or administrative manager and reviewed by fund counsel, which may offer recommendations relating to these matters.

Attorneys may initiate original reports and information directly for the board of trustees or respond to requests for specific information with opinions and recommendations. Frequently, a portion of the attorney's assignments may include analysis of the effect of judicial decisions or proposed regulatory or legislative changes, and advising trustees of the prospective impact of such matters on fund policy and operations. In addition, much of the attorneys' work may develop at trustees meetings as problems emerge during discussions.

As a result of changes on eligibility rules, benefit provisions and limitations, revisions may be required in formal plan documents and even in the trust agreement itself. Counsel will prepare amendments to plan documents, contracts and eligibility rules, as well as related summary plan descriptions and announcements for plan participants.

In the event of a particular participant's appeal of a claim or denial, counsel may prepare detailed memoranda for the board of trustees to support its opinion or the findings of the trustees.

With respect to inquiries raised by governmental agencies, the fund administrator usually refers such matters to counsel so the attorney can research the matter and develop a formal reply on behalf of the board.

The attorneys handling collection of delinquent employer contributions are in frequent contact with the administrative manager. After the manager and/or the board of trustees has determined which accounts are to be forwarded to counsel, the attorneys obtain information from the fund office to determine the amount due the trust from the employer and commence collection procedures. When payments are received on a partial or full basis, the manager notifies counsel of such collection and the possibility of obviating or modifying legal action.

Attorneys are also involved in the negotiation and arrangement of reciprocal agreements with other welfare and pension funds in the same industries. These agreements are usually complicated and vary considerably in nature. After input from the administrator and trustees, counsel prepares new agreements or proposed agreements and/or perhaps negotiates with counsel for other funds to conclude contracts to protect reciprocal credits for plan participants who work under more than one collective bargaining agreement from time to time.

The relationship between the fund administrative manager and the attorneys is generally close. When there is mutual respect for the integrity and professionalism of each party, a team effort normally develops and ensures the smooth coordination of the attorneys' work on behalf of the trust fund. An efficient administrative manager can reduce the work load of legal counsel and facilitate the manner in which counsel's recommendations are acted upon by the board of trustees and incorporated in administrative policies. Similarly, attorneys who maintain and develop a close working relationship with the administrative manager may benefit considerably from this harmonious relationship in the performance of their duties.

The compensation of legal counsel is usually arranged directly with the board of trustees. Compensation may consist of an annual retainer to cover specific legal services detailed in the legal engagement agreement. There may be provision for additional compensation in the event of litigation or collection efforts.

The administrative manager may be involved in the selection process by which legal counsel is chosen. If a change is contemplated by the board of trustees, the administrative manager may be requested to develop a list of available, experienced attorneys with background in jointly managed employee benefit trusts. The administrative manager may be authorized to contact selected attorneys from such lists, request proposals and arrangements and participate in the interview and final selection process.

Similarly, counsel may be involved in the selection and recruitment of other professionals. Normally, if there is an opening for the position of contract administrator, counsel might be involved in the process of recruiting and interviewing applicants and developing a final contract with the candidates selected by the board.

When a salaried administrator is sought, a lesser role may be played by the fund counsel. In such instances, the board of trustees (or a subcommittee of the board) may be directly involved in recruiting and interviewing prospective administrators. Legal counsel would generally prepare the final contract of employment with the administrator.

Benefit Consultants/Actuaries

With the exception of a minority of relatively small jointly managed benefit plans that utilize insurance companies for providing welfare and pension benefits and related counsel services, virtually all trust funds engage employee benefit plan consultants; pension and annuity plans engage actuaries. Frequently the actuary and benefit consultant represent the same consulting firm.

In recent years, as escalating health care costs have become a critical issue to welfare plans, many funds have contracted for the services of health cost-management consultants. The long-term costs of retired employees' health coverage have caused some welfare benefit funds to undertake actuarial studies of this prospective liability. Because the American Institute of Certified Public Accountants (AICPA) and the Financial Accounting Standards Board (FASB) now require disclosure of postretirement health care liabilities in the financial statements of welfare plans, it has become commonplace for welfare funds to undertake yearly actuarial studies of a plan's prospective liability for long-term costs of retired employees.

The functions of consultants include providing information to the trustees on policy issues and costs affecting benefits, preparation of written documents relating to reporting and disclosure requirements, and helping in the development and fulfillment of administrative procedures.

Benefit consultants usually prepare an annual report summarizing the operations of the plan from the viewpoint of the benefits program, including a possible budget projection of costs of plan improvements and methods of funding. The actuaries prepare an actuarial valuation of a DB pension plan to meet necessary governmental requirements and enable trustees to make decisions as to benefit improvements and adjustments.

In addition to being available as consultants on everyday problems (such as claims appeals, eligibility rules and reporting and disclosure requirements), consultants normally furnish information on the following matters:
1. Funding methods for either a pension or health care plan
2. Alternatives for plan design
3. Input as to plan administration and rules
4. Cost controls with respect to benefits
5. Claim processing procedures and controls
6. The impact of legislation, regulations, court decisions, changes in accounting rules, public policy, etc.

Benefit plan consultants furnish an annual report or more frequent interim reports as such items as:
1. Projection of contribution income compared to prospective benefit claims and operating expenses
2. Cost of maintaining, changing or improving benefits
3. Review of eligibility rules and self-payment programs
4. Technical developments, such as methods of handling conversion and continuation of health insurance by terminated participants under COBRA
5. Recommendations for the establishment of financial reserves with respect to claims (reserve for incurred and unreported claims, liability for received and unpaid claims, liability for continued eligibility established under trustee rules, etc.)
6. Reserves that might be required for postretirement health care and death benefits
7. Review of insurance carriers' contracts, rates, administrative charges and renewal actions
8. Determination of reasonableness of claim and premium reserves established by insurance carriers
9. Change in policy to an administrative services only (ASO) or minimum premium type of funding
10. Change to self-insurance
11. Expanding benefit options and programs to better manage participants' health care
12. Establishment of annual self-pay and COBRA premium rates
13. Reasonableness and appropriateness of reciprocity agreements.

With respect to arrangements with insurance carriers, consultants usually prepare specifications for requests for bids by insurance companies. The consultants obtain and review responses from carriers, prepare a summary for the trustees, and issue and report comparing the proposals of the respective bidders. In some instances, the consultants may make a recommendation for choice of carrier. In any event, the consultants are involved in the implementation of insurance arrangements with a new carrier, as well as finalization of the administrative procedures that might be required in connection with such a change.

Similarly, consultants would be involved in the negotiation and arrangement of contracts with preferred providers, HMOs, closed panels of medical/dental providers, prescription drug service vendors, medical and dental consultants, utilization review companies, disease management vendors and many of the other services that have developed to assist the fund in claims administration and cost containment.

The trustees often look to benefit consultants for assistance in reviewing administrative procedures and the efficacy of the administrative arrangement. The consultants may be helpful in the evaluation of the administrative manager and may be asked to develop specifications for a change in administrative manager and even for a recommendation as to the use of a contract vs. salary administration mode. Most consultants attend a number of trustees meetings during the year and have always attended the meeting when their annual report is reviewed by the board.

Benefit consultants serve a vital role to the board of trustees in apprising them of the latest technology and changes that may affect the delivery of benefits to plan participants. Based upon their wide knowledge and acquaintance with many benefit programs from both a multiemployer and single employer point of view, they may be in a position to make meaningful recommendations that would assist the trustees in fulfilling their goal to deliver significant benefits on a cost-effective basis. They are in the best position to know available options and appropriate "players," while the administrative manager provides insight on the particular needs of the trust fund and its participants.

In most funds, the consultant has full or shared responsibility for drafting plan documents, announcements, notices and summary plan descriptions subject to review by counsel and the administrator.

The administrative manager fills a significant role in enabling the benefit consultant and actuary to meet their respective responsibilities. These professionals depend upon the administrator to furnish necessary and accurate data to be utilized in their reports or the development of responses to particular inquiries raised by the trustees.

The consultants/actuaries rely upon the administrative manager to obtain vital data as to participant census, pension vesting status, health and pension benefit payments by type and amount, employee turnover and eligibility, mortality statistics, aggregate totals of hours of employment, type of claim by nature and classification of participant, analysis of claims by medical/dental procedure, etc. Depending upon the report/recommendation requested by the trustees, the types of requested data spans a wide spectrum.

The accuracy and completeness of such data enables consultants to perform services in an efficient and meaningful manner. Absent such information, the reports of the consultants will be less specific and based more on generalities, thereby diluting the accuracy and reliability.

DB pension plans are required by ERISA to engage an enrolled actuary for the purpose of preparing an annual actuarial valuation. Pension actuaries and consultants fill the same role for pension funds as employee benefit consultants do for other funds. In addition to performing an annual valuation, they submit information on the cost of proposed and mandated benefit changes and may certify individual pension applications.

The pension actuary needs annual updated service credit and demographic data to perform a valuation. This information is usually furnished by the administrator in a form compatible with the procedure used by the actuary to perform valuations. In many instances, the actuary will request the data in a digitized, computerized format. When supplied by the administrative manager in this format, both the time to complete the valuation and, perhaps, the cost of doing so, are greatly reduced.

In fulfilling their duties, the benefit consultant/actuary works exclusively and closely with the administrator in all funds. For pension plans, the actuary works with the administrative manager to determine the withdrawal liability of an employer upon such employer's termination from a DB plan in accordance with the federal Multiemployer Pension Plan Amendments Act (MPPAA).

In some pension plans, the administrative manager will obtain pension applications from prospective pensioners, review the applications in detail and submit the entire file to the actuary for certification before approval by the board of trustees. This procedure is used by pension funds to reduce the possibility of an inadvertent error and to assure the board of trustees of the propriety of pension approvals. In other funds, this function may be handled exclusively by the administrative manager and fund staff subject to an annual review/audit by the fund actuary in preparing the valuation.

In addition to compiling the data to enable the consultants/actuaries to prepare such reports, the administrator serves as the conduit for communications between the trustees and these types of consultants. The manager reviews and distributes the reports, coordinates the exchange of information between consultants and the independent CPA necessary for mutual preparation of required governmental reports, and collects the consultants' information needed by counsel to reply to governmental requests. The collective accumulation of input from and to all professionals is coordinated by the administrator. The administrator and consultants are usually in frequent, verbal and personal contact with respect to everyday problems relating to claims, eligibility and routine matters involving administration of the plan.

Investment Advisors

The typical jointly-trusteed Taft-Hartley trust fund may utilize a wide variety of investment advisors. Regardless of the type or size of the fund, or its method of administration (salaried, contract, TPA), it is the administrator who almost always serves as the coordinator between the board of trustees and these advisors.

The investments of benefit trust funds are discussed separately in this handbook. As indicated therein, the characteristics of the type of individual fund will determine the investment program that may be selected. Welfare and vacation funds may adopt less complicated investment guidelines and tend to invest in a short-term mode. Pension and annuity funds, on the other hand, adopt a diversified long-term program, including corporate and government bonds, balanced investment portfolios, real estate and mortgages, common stocks, private placements, venture capital and, more recently, hedge funds.

Virtually all trust funds engage a professional investment manager to help the board understand investments, develop investment guidelines and goals, and gain the highest possible return on a prudent basis. The investment advisor furnishes information, helps trustees in addressing key issues and finalizes investment guidelines and programs. The advisor may be given discretionary authority to make investments and is responsible to the board of trustees for his or her success in meeting investment objectives.

In some plans, a multiple number of investment advisors may be utilized. This is particularly true of larger funds. In that event, the investment results of each manager are compared, generally annually. To aid the trustees in monitoring the individual investment manager's performance and adherence to guidelines, funds also utilize the services of an investment evaluation firm, either on an ad hoc periodic or regular basis, whose function is to measure and compare the performance of the investment managers. These investment consultants also assist the board in a variety of related matters including periodic review of investment policy guidelines, asset allocation and appropriate searches for investment managers to invest fund assets.

The administrative manager's relationship and communications with the investment consultants, managers and ancillary firms (brokers' custodians, etc.) are constant and ongoing. By receiving daily reports of investment changes, the administrator is responsible to an extent to make certain that the manager follows guidelines established by the trustees.

The administrator maintains the accounting books and records with respect to investments, monitors the receipt of interest and dividends, and ascertains that errors are not inadvertently made that would result in the loss of investment income. In addition, the administrative manager coordinates necessary related reports from, and contact with, the investment consultants, managers, custodians, bankers and other parties involved in the investment process.

The administrative manager may work with the investment manager (and in larger funds, the investment consultant) and fund auditor to develop a short-term cash management program to meet the needs of the benefit program and to allocate amounts to be used for long-term investment. When specific cash needs arise, the administrator notifies the investment manager to liquidate sufficient investments accordingly. This may be particularly true in health and welfare funds when an increase in claims over budget results in a temporary cash shortfall.

Some benefit plans (usually pension funds) may make mortgage or other large loans directly to particular borrowers. The administrative manager is then involved with counsel in developing and executing various documents and contracts, such as a service agreement with a mortgage service company; commitment letter issued with respect to a mortgage; and an agreement for a purchase lease or mortgage participation agreement. The administrator additionally becomes involved in communications, collections and accountings involving mortgages if the trustees do not delegate this authority to an outside party. In that case, the administrator would not only handle all the duties normally provided by mortgage servicing companies and custodians, but would also be responsible for recording and following up on payment of principal and interest, handling communications with borrowers and furnishing information to the trustees with respect to defaults, arrears, unpaid taxes, inadequate insurance, lack of maintenance and other related matters.

Banks

Normally, the administrator represents the board of trustees completely in relations with banks and their trust departments. This could include:
- Establishment of a lock box arrangement to receive employer contributions and direct bank deposits
- Receiving and sending wire transfers of funds
- Maintenance of checking and savings accounts with banks, including arrangements for $0 balance accounts replenished as needed to cover expenditures as authorized by the administrator
- Implementing "positive pay" features and procedures to prevent check fraud
- Short-term investments and cash management.

The administrator may also coordinate arrangements between the investment managers and banks to provide necessary funds for investment purposes, as well as the handling of interest, dividends and other income from investments owned by the trust.

Administrative managers also participate in the designation of depository banks and relations with employees of such institutions. Because bank representatives rarely attend trustees meetings, they depend upon the administrator to handle their recommendations and reports. The manager forwards instructions from the trustees directly to the bank; receives, reviews and records bank reports on a regular basis; and verifies the action and propriety of banking transactions.

Health Care Professionals and Providers

Many health and welfare trust funds employ medical and dental consultants to assist in plan design, as well as processing claims. The coordination between the board of trustees and such consultants is usually handled exclusively by the administrative manager and fund staff. The trustees, working through the fund manager, will expect this cadre of consultants to give them assurance that claim dollars are being spent appropriately; access to quality care is maintained on behalf of plan participants; and monitoring is maintained over the necessity of medical services and fees charged.

The medical consultants help establish parameters for reasonable charges, type and length of treatment based upon experience and public sources. They help the administrator and the fund office determine whether particularly complex and innovative medical procedures are covered by plan provisions; the procedures are appropriate and necessary; and fees are reasonable and customary. The administrative manager may submit specific claims to the consultants for their review or establish a procedure under which particular types of claims will be automatically forwarded. The administrator will use the responses of the medical/dental examiners in processing the payment of claims and/or communications with participants and health providers as to the amounts deemed eligible for payment. In addition, the administrative manager may arrange for the review by medical/dental examiners of claims paid on a random basis to test the accuracy of claim payment.

In some instances, when the possibility of fraud may arise or when medical charges appear totally unreasonable, the administrative manager may submit the claim to the medical examiners and request them to obtain medical and hospital records for a detailed review. This may involve requesting x-rays and results of diagnostic tests, and even arranging for the examination of the patient by the medical consultant of the fund.

With the proliferation of popular drug card plans, the administrator is charged with the responsibility of working with the service firm to develop:

- Eligibility, cost and quality controls
- Types of prescription drugs to be covered
- Identification and utilization of participating pharmacies
- Recommendations for plan design, changes and modifications in response to ever-changing technologies and pharmaceutical advances.

The administrator furnishes the names of eligible participants to the card service firm, which will make such information known to participating pharmacies, arrange for identification cards, receive and process claims electronically, etc.

With respect to claims for disability pensions, the administrative manager usually works with the fund medical consultant to determine whether the applicant meets plan requirements. Often, it is the administrative manager who arranges for medical examinations for that purpose.

With respect to mandatory and/or voluntary second surgical opinion programs, which are used by many health and welfare funds in the cases of elective surgeries for certain specific conditions, the fund office frequently coordinates and arranges for the availability of board-certified specialists, appointments and confirmation reports.

In light of the relatively recent U.S. DOL regulations dealing with claims appeals, participants may seek an expedited preservice claim review of an initial denial of coverage for a particular medical procedure. The provider of service may characterize the need as "urgent," thus triggering relatively short time frames in which an appropriate peer review must take place. The responsibility for arranging such expedited reviews typically falls on the administrative manager.

In many trust funds, the administrator and/or benefit consultant has arranged for contracts with preferred health providers under which a participant has the right, at the time of treatment, to select between a provider of his or her own choice and a preferred provider. If the participant uses a PPO, there may be a reduction in charges made to the fund, as well as to the participant, in the form of a reduced copayment or the avoidance of any form of balance billing between the charges submitted and the amounts paid by the fund.

Some funds have extended this concept to include an exclusive provider organization (EPO) arrangement. Under an EPO, a participant chooses for a limited period of time (such as one year) between freedom of choice of all providers, and a limited panel of exclusive providers. Incentives may be furnished to participants to select exclusive coverage by EPO providers, including full payment by the fund and no copayments or other charges to the participant.

In either case, be it PPO or EPO, it is the responsibility of the administrator to make available to the participants their options as to the use of the PPO or EPO and follow through to ascertain that proper charges are made by such providers, with some assurance of quality of care. The board of trustees will rely on the administrative manager to implement these programs, usually with considerable input from legal counsel and the benefit plan consultant.

Health Care Cost-Containment Consultants

As health care costs have escalated with adverse financial results to many welfare funds, trustees have instituted cost-management procedures designed to assure, to the greatest extent possible, that medical care is provided in a necessary and cost-effective manner. Many funds have contracted with utilization review firms to monitor the necessity and appropriateness of medical care at hospitals and at outpatient facilities. These organizations may also review the propriety of provider charges.

Other significant innovations have included the development of case management and disease management. *Case management* is concerned with major or large claims. *Disease management* focuses on participants with conditions that, if left unchecked, will develop into costly and chronic medical problems. The trustees will arrange to utilize the services of a case management firm to:
- Intervene
- Review the proposed method, type and sequence of treatment
- Ascertain that the most cost-effective procedures are utilized.

Similarly, a disease management firm will be engaged to:
- Identify patients with potentially chronic conditions, such as asthma, diabetes, congestive heart failure, hypertension, HIV/AIDS and Hepatitis C
- Contact the patient to ascertain current medical status and lifestyle
- Provide the participant with advice and educational material for recommended lifestyle changes
- Provide guidance for treatment options with his or her physician
- Follow up and work closely with the participant's treating physician to maximize favorable outcomes and to avoid escalation of the medical problem to a chronic condition.

In both the case management and disease management situations, the administrative manager must provide the necessary information to identify prospective patients and arrange for the transmittal of all needed information to these service providers.

Other innovations that have increased the work load of the administrative manager are the development of a multiple number of alternative health care delivery options. In one plan, a participant may choose a traditional fee-for-service plan, a PPO, an EPO, an HMO, a closed panel of medical/dental groups, individual practice associations (IPAs), as well as particular hospitals and other medical providers who have negotiated special arrangements with the trust fund. Working with the benefit consultant and legal counsel in many instances, the administrative manager spends considerable time and effort finalizing such arrangements, including the preparation and delivery of announcements and descriptive information to plan participants to facilitate their choices at the time of a periodic open enrollment or at the time of required treatment.

Insurance Brokers

Some funds utilize the services of insurance brokers to obtain services from insurance companies relating to death and health care benefits, guaranteed investment contracts or general pension services. In addition, brokers are used to obtain insurance for the normal risks and hazards of operating a benefit fund office. The latter category would include general insurance to include property, liability, workers' compensation, fidelity bonds and trustees' fiduciary liability coverage. The administrator serves as the coordinating link between the trustees and the insurance broker.

As many health and welfare funds adopted self-insurance of benefits, there has been a need to obtain specific and aggregate risk (stop-loss) insurance to cover large amounts of individual, specific and catastrophic claims or a large increase in the number of total annual claims. The fund may work through an insurance broker and/or risk manager. Frequently, the benefit plan consultant to the fund may assist in this role.

Other Providers of Service

In the course of general administration, the trustees will deal with many vendors to obtain the facilities, services and supplies necessary for the conduct of fund business. Invariably, such arrangements are handled by the administrator. The administrator seeks and receives information on available needed products and services and submits proposals to the trustees with appropriate comments, evaluation and recommendations. These providers could span the spectrum of real estate agents needed to secure office facilities, to consultants needed for upgrades to computer hardware and software, to firms providing payroll and other interim auditing services.

Overall, these newly developed techniques by boards of trustees have placed added responsibilities on the administrator. The administrative manager is called upon to produce ever-increasing types and quantities of data to help monitor and evaluate these innovations. As new professions and consultants are engaged, the administrator must relay information to and from those parties and coordinate and often comment upon and expand on their reports and recommendations. A major effort is required by the administrative manager to integrate the work product, reports and performance of all outside consultants into the data made available to the board of trustees for subsequent review, consideration and action.

Independent Auditors

With the exception of the presentation of his or her annual report, the fund's independent auditor is rarely involved in direct communication with the trustees. It is the administrative manager that typically has direct communication with the CPA. The communication and coordination are extensive and continual. The administrative manager coordinates preparation of financial and other records with the accountant's schedule so the audit is available as required by the trustees. Timely preparation of the audited financial statements is required to meet filing requirements of governmental reports.

The administrator will prepare the data and preliminary financial statements made available to the auditor for examination. In addition, supporting data will be assembled. Generally, the independent auditors will request outside verification through correspondence of any aspects of the financial statements, including accounts receivable, accounts payable, liabilities to be reported by the benefit consultant, the actuarial report, verification of cash, investments held by custodians and amounts due from brokers.

In addition, contributions receivable from employers are verified by outside correspondents. The fund manager arranges to prepare the requests for outside verification and the names of the firms to which they are mailed. The verification requests are sent directly to the CPA firm.

The fund manager makes available all the minutes, copies of governmental reports filed during the year and all documents requested by the independent auditor during the course of the examination. In addition, the administrative manager makes available documentation with respect to eligibility, claims payments and experience, insurance contracts, premium reports and other administrative matters supporting the financial results and reflected in the financial books and records of the fund.

The auditing firm also serves as a support organization for the administrative manager in furnishing day-to-day routine information as to regulatory and tax law changes that may influence the method by which the fund is operated, as well as the reporting and tax treatment of benefits paid to plan participants.

The independent auditors rely on the accounting standards developed by AICPA. Most recently, AICPA has established within its organization an "Employee Benefit Plan Audit Quality Center." The purpose of the quality center is to help CPAs meet the challenges of performing quality audits in the unique and complex area of employee benefit plans. Through its Quality Center, AICPA seeks to ensure adherence to not only AICPA guidelines, but standards issued by the Financial Accounting Standards Board (FASB) relating to accounting, reporting and disclosure by DB pension plans and health and welfare plans. FASB guidelines establish the standards for accounting of all employee benefit plans and the necessary records. Administrative managers refer to these types of guidelines and work closely with the auditors to efficiently and effectively implement established standards.

Overall, the independent auditors play a vital role in the function of employee benefit plans. The auditors serve not only a statutory purpose, but also as a valuable professional advisor to the board of trustees and the administrative manager. The administrator normally maintains a close working relationship with the fund auditor in a mutual effort to ensure records are properly kept in the best interest of plan participants and to safeguard assets and resources.

Employers, Employer Associations and Unions

In addition to dealing with numerous plan professionals, service providers, vendors and the entire class of plan participants, the administrative manager and office staff serve as the central point for employers, employer associations and participating unions.

Employers

The amount of time required by the administrator to communicate and interact with employers is usually less than the time devoted to participants and beneficiaries. Nevertheless, the quality of this interaction with employers can influence the administrative work load and the ease of providing benefits. It is therefore important for the administrator to ascertain that the staff develop attitudes and techniques that will assist in relaying information to and from employers. This interaction, verbal and written, relates to any one or all of the following:

1. Contribution rates, effective dates and procedures for making payments
2. Continuation of the employers' obligation to contribute after the expiration of an agreement and during periods of negotiations
3. Delinquency of the signatory employer
4. Obtaining signatures of new employers to become parties to the trust document
5. Responses to questions by employers relating to individual participants (new employees, terminated or disabled employees, employees on leave of absence, etc.)
6. Reports to employers to furnish payroll information
7. Arranging payroll audits
8. Providing information on the pension or welfare eligibility status of a particular participant and family (subject, of course, to HIPAA privacy guidelines in the case of welfare coverage)

9. Discussion with and notification to employers relating to particular contractual requirements
10. Arrangement for employees to self-pay or for the continuation of health insurance after termination under COBRA regulations
11. Inquiries by employers on the status of employees' claims
12. Requests by employers for reporting forms, plan booklets, claim forms, retirement applications, etc.
13. Notices required by ERISA
14. Notice to employers of liability for unfunded withdrawal liability after withdrawal from a multiemployer DB pension plan
15. Receipt from employers of information on terminated employees to facilitate the transmittal of appropriate COBRA notices to participants
16. Sending confirmation requests to employers for verifying employer contributions for annual audit purposes.

Often representatives from the employer's human resources department will act as a "go-between," "ombudsman," "advocate," etc., on behalf of a plan participant. It is not unusual for the plan participant not to understand a particular plan provision or plan determination for a particular claim and to seek the aid of another employee on the employer's staff to obtain answers to inquiries. Before HIPAA and HIPAA privacy regulations, the flow of communication was, in most cases, simple and smooth. However, because some of this information would be considered "protected health information" of a plan participant, very specific, signed authorizations must be obtained before any information can be released to anyone other than the plan participant. Many funds have adopted a policy and procedure by which information from the employer concerning a plan participant's claim may be received and the inquiry logged, but the answer given only to the plan participant. Understandably, this has caused much frustration in the process, has inhibited the communication and has delayed the transmittal of ultimate answers to plan participants.

The fund office may frequently, at the request of the trustees, communicate directly with employer associations with respect to some of the items discussed above. Notably, when employer members of an employer association are delinquent to the trust, the trustees may direct that the association be advised of the delinquency so that payment might be expedited. Similarly, the fund office may communicate with the employer association to determine whether an employer has withdrawn from the industry in the particular geographic area served by the fund. Finally, especially in the case of industrywide bargaining, the administrative manager might have significant direct communication with representatives of the employer association.

In addition, many employers cooperate with benefit funds to distribute plan materials in the form of payroll stuffers and brochures with an employee's paycheck.

Participating Unions

The labor union that negotiates the collective bargaining agreement providing for contributions to the plan must be involved in the everyday function of the benefit trust. The union's need for information from a benefit fund office is predetermined by the union's function in the operation of the benefit plan, the nature of the service to its members regarding the benefit plan and its responsibilities for enforcing the labor agreement.

The members of the union look to the union, its offices and staff for information and assistance. It is not unusual for employees to seek information and interpretation of the benefit programs and individual eligibility under various benefit plans from the union, rather than the fund office. This occasionally leads to difficulties, and many unions instruct their business agents and office staff not to furnish interpretations of the benefit plan, but to refer the individual participant and beneficiary to the fund office. Trustees of several plans have gone so far as to put very specific disclaimers at the beginning of plan booklets, advising that reliance on advice from anyone other than the plan administrator is at the participant's risk.

The union must take precautions when it attempts to act or give the appearance of acting on behalf of the trustees or with the authority of the trustees. It is possible that both the benefit plan and the union may incur unknown liabilities when agents of the union provide participants with unauthorized, incomplete or inaccurate information or interpretations and the participants and/or beneficiaries rely on such incorrect input to their detriment.

Because the union is responsible for policing and enforcing an employer's contractual commitments, including the correct and timely report and payment to benefit funds, it is vital that the fund office notify unions when employers fail to meet their obligations under the collective bargaining agreement.

As a party in interest to the collective bargaining agreement, the union has an obligation to enforce the agreement's terms with respect to contribution delinquencies. In a typical case, with the advice of legal counsel for the fund, the fund trustees develop a policy and procedure that involves the union in collecting delinquent contributions and the imposition of sanctions under the collective bargaining agreement when that occurs. The fund office will arrange with the union to establish a procedure in which it will relay information about employer contributions, variances, payroll audit discoveries, delinquencies, legal actions and collections.

Another area to be handled with great care, and with advice from counsel, relates to the circumstances under which the fund office furnishes information to collective bargaining parties during the negotiation process. During that process, the fund office may be requested to obtain from the consultants and fund records an estimate of additional costs for improvement in the plan or changes in eligibility rules, which may be the subject of collective bargaining. It is important that this information be furnished to all parties and that the release be authorized by the board of trustees. An issue discussed elsewhere in this handbook is the delicate question of who must pay for such studies or data retrievals.

Most trustees develop a formal board policy for the distribution of reports and studies. The compilation of such data may be expensive and time-consuming; the administrator should insist on specific, advance authorization by the board of trustees. There must be a balance of interest between information that a union, association or employer would like to have and the primary purpose of the trust, which is to provide benefits to employee participants and their dependents.

Obviously, there will be a constant interchange of information between the fund office and a participating union. General, day-to-day communication between the fund office and local unions includes:

- Names of employers that are parties to the collective bargaining agreement
- Effective date an employer becomes party to the agreement
- Changes in contribution rates for individual employers
- Changes in agreements that may affect the liability or contributions for particular types of employees
- The result of collection efforts by unions with respect to delinquencies and whether liquidated damages or employer bonds are to be obtained
- The need to initiate collection efforts for pension withdrawal liability
- The need to obtain information to meet the requirements of COBRA, the Family and Medical Leave Act and HIPAA
- Names and addresses of new union members/plan participants
- Identity of employees who have obtained employment in the jurisdiction of other benefit funds with which there may be a reciprocity agreement
- Results of payroll audits.

Frequently, the union or employer association may publish a newsletter, newspaper or other periodical that is distributed to plan participants and contributing employers. The benefit fund may use such media as a means of sending announcement materials to members and employers. In addition, the benefit fund may publish posters and notices that are distributed to employers for posting at job sites conveying information about prescribed policies and procedures, including:

- Toll-free telephone numbers and voice technology/Internet procedures
- Procedures for making self-payments
- New benefit options and programs available to plan participants.

Such posters and notices may also be displayed in union meeting halls, hiring halls, the union bulletin board at the employer's location and at work sites, all to ensure maximum exposure.

As detailed in this chapter, in order for a trust fund to operate in an efficient and cost-effective manner, the administrative manager and fund staff must act as the central hub of the exchange of ideas and data between all parties in interest—plan participants, contributing employers, participating local unions, attorneys, actuaries, benefit consultants, auditors, medical/dental consultants, case management vendors, disease management vendors, utilization review specialists and on and on. To ensure the success of operations, the administrative manager must not be complacent and assume the communication between the plan and parties in interest is acceptable "because it's always been done that way." If they do not already have one in place, benefit funds should consider a formal or informal procedure of feedback to enhance communications and relationships with unions, employer associations and plan participants. Such feedback can take the form of full-blown surveys or merely regular meetings with union representatives, as well as representatives of the employers and employer associations, to discuss problems that may have been encountered between plan participants or other parties and the fund office. In that manner, trustees can be assured of an ever-evolving and improving fund office operation.

Chapter 46

Measuring and Evaluating the Cost of Plan Administration

William J. Einhorn

Few subjects in the employee benefits field have created as much controversy as attempts to quantify and compare the costs of administrative services for jointly managed multiemployer benefit programs.

Some of the problems that have caused difficulties in such efforts to compare relative costs include the following:
1. *Demographics.*
    - Should quantitative per capita figures and ratios be based on active and fully eligible employees only, or include employees for whom contributions are made to the fund but who do not become eligible?
    - How should retired employees be handled? Should they be included in the total figure for per capita calculations since there may be little (or no) contribution effort or expense applicable to self-payments?
    - How should adjustments be made if there are different contribution rates for specific classifications of employees and different classes of benefits applicable to certain groups?
    - Under all these circumstances, how would one fund be compared to another?
2. *Geographical variations.* There are problems in quantifying costs for funds that cover large geographical areas and have many offices to service participants and employers in comparison to smaller funds with one office location and limited staff. Another problem in comparing geographical areas is a possible large region variance in the cost of services, rentals, personnel and operating expenses.
3. *Size of plan.* In addition to the demographic problems, a simple matter that creates problems in comparison is the fact that large funds with a high number of plan participants and employers may indicate far lower per capita costs than smaller funds. Funds with a small number of participants are likely to reflect high per capita costs.
4. *Functions assumed by administrative offices vary drastically among benefit funds.*
    - Some funds may farm out or use independent providers for many of the administrative services provided to plan participants. A welfare plan, for example, can be fully insured and claims can be paid by an insurance company. The insurance company might issue all claim forms to participants and directly receive applications for benefits and pay claims. The only function of the benefit office would be to notify the insurance company of the eligibility of the plan participants. This plan would obviously show far lower expenses than a similar fund of exactly the same size that was self-administered and processed and paid its own claims, requiring a larger staff with resulting greater personnel, data processing and other office expenses.
    - A similar discrepancy would occur if certain functions were performed by fund office personnel rather than by outside parties. For example, some funds employ their own collection agents and payroll auditors, rather than utilizing the services of outside attorneys and payroll servicing firms. Other funds might use data processing consultants and outside servicing bureaus to perform some information processing tasks. Some funds accept long-distance calls from employers and claimants; some others do not. There is a great variety in the scope

and type of tasks and duties fulfilled by benefit funds. Without a detailed investigation of specific functions and activities of every particular fund, it is difficult to compare one to another in terms of administrative costs.

5. *Working styles of trustees in particular funds.* Some trustees ask their administrative office to handle virtually all phases of administration; thus, all minutes, reports and studies would be prepared by the administrative manager after consultation with outside professionals and forwarded to the trustees. This might result in lower costs than if outside professionals and consultants directly handled such functions.

6. *Type of fund.* It is impossible to compare the administrative costs of a health and welfare fund to those of a pension fund. Each type of plan must be compared to a similar fund performing the same overall functions. Obviously, a welfare fund involved with day-to-day eligibility of participants and their families and payment of a large number of claims during the year would reflect far greater operating expenses than a pension fund that accumulates monies over a long period of time to pay claims only upon retirement, death or termination.

7. *Joint administration of a multiple number of related plans and trust funds.* If a plan is the only benefit fund created by collective bargaining and administered without any relationship to any other fund, its expenses may be far in excess of a benefit trust that is one of a multiple number of jointly managed plans established by a labor union with affiliated employers. In the construction and other industries in which the multiemployer fund model is traditional, a union may negotiate with an employer association and/or group of employers for participation in a number of benefit funds, including health and welfare, defined benefit pension, defined contribution, annuity, training, vacation and holiday, scholarship, industry advancement, group legal services and even day care. If all these funds were administered by the one benefit office in which the respective trusts' expenses are shared, it should result in a proportionately reduced expenditure by each particular fund in accordance with the method used to apportion expenses among participating funds.

Overall, the missions of benefit funds and trustees are similar. Whether administered by office personnel directly hired and responsible to the board of trustees or by a contract administrator, the mission of the administrative office is to fulfill the goals of the board of trustees to efficiently operate the fund for the sole and exclusive benefit of plan participants by providing benefits to participants while operating at the lowest possible expense.

In fulfilling this mission, the administration of benefit funds will include the functions described in previous chapters in this section. Some of the functions are common to all funds. Others are optional and may be assumed by the fund, not performed at all or delegated to others. The optional functions vary widely in cost in the same manner the common functions performed by all funds vary according to the individual idiosyncrasies of the plan, the working styles of the trustees and administrator, demographics and geography. Thus, it is virtually impossible to arrive at a precise comparison. It is, however, important to do so to continually monitor the efficiencies of the fund office.

Some of the common functions that would be basically assumed by all benefit funds include:

1. A database for contributing employers and participating employees
2. General accounting and recordkeeping
3. Individual recordkeeping for employer contributions and delinquency
4. Determination of employee eligibility and credits applicable to each participant
5. Arranging for reporting forms for employer contributions (there may be substantial savings in administrative costs if the contributions of more than one fund are reported and paid jointly)
6. Collection efforts by fund personnel
7. Eligibility determinations by fund personnel
8. Determination of amounts available for investment and transfer to investment resources
9. Record retention
10. Reports to trustees and outside professionals
11. Communication with employees, employers and unions
12. The common daily activities of employee benefit funds that have been previously discussed.

With respect to optional functions that may or may not be performed by a benefit office, examples include:

1. Minutes of trustees meetings and distribution to trustees and professionals
2. Sophisticated data computerization of claim payments, supporting data, eligibility and so on. In many funds, this information is maintained by a service bureau rather than the internal fund office.
3. Preparation and communication of announcements, summary plan descriptions, newsletters and other reporting and disclosure documents. In some funds, this task is assumed completely by the fund manager and personnel. In others, outside communication specialists and insurance companies may prepare these documents and even arrange for distribution to plan participants.

4. Claims processing and payment. The payment of claims by health and welfare funds is a function that may be fulfilled in any number of ways. As discussed in Chapter 44, some funds use an insurance company for the purpose of processing and paying claims to participants. The insurance company may also be at risk for the claim liability or may serve only in a service capacity. Other funds will use the services of an outside third-party administrator to pay claims. Lastly, self-administered funds process claims using their own personnel and data processing techniques; it is likely that this type of fund would show the highest amount of administrative costs, although there may be a substantial savings in reduced insurance and benefit costs.
5. Health and welfare fund cost-containment activities. Many "insured" funds utilize the services of their insurance company to arrange for hospitalization preapproval, predetermination of necessity of medical services, utilization review, case management, second surgical opinion, health provider audits and other techniques of cost-management. On the other hand, self-administered funds incur substantial expenses to arrange similar services. In addition, if a benefit fund itself assumed responsibility for some of these procedures, there would be substantial additional internal personnel, telephone, printing and other expenses to provide such services as utilization review, case management and communication with plan participants and health providers.
6. When the fund is involved with a number of alternative service delivery systems (including health maintenance organizations (HMOs), individual practitioner associations (IPAs), preferred provider organizations (PPOs), exclusive provider organizations (EPOs), physician hospital organizations (PHOs), closed panels, etc)., higher administrative expenses will result to arrange and deal with such health care providers and to serve as an intermediary with plan participants in making arrangements for such alternative treatment.
7. Plans use different methods in handling certain aspects of the reporting and disclosure requirements of COBRA and other federal laws, state insurance conversion laws, termination notices, certification notices required by HIPAA, self-pay arrangements and related required communications.
8. Pension plans. As is the case with health and welfare plans, practices are not consistent. Many pension plans arrange for a bank custodian, insurance company or other servicing organization to issue and process pension checks. Other funds will directly issue pension checks to plan participants. Issuing checks is also accompanied by a substantial amount of tax reporting, which adds to administrative costs.
9. Investments. Many plans do not keep accounting records for investments, accepting the reports of custodians and advisors. Other plans maintain a complex system of recordkeeping and monitoring of investment income and assets to establish checks and balances and to compare the performance of various investment managers.
10. Internal controls. Some plans (particularly larger funds) have developed a broad system of checks and balances and internal controls to monitor and control all aspects of fund operations. In smaller funds with fewer employees, it may not be as necessary or practical to set up a system for quality assurance and internal control over all operations. A plan with one employee handling all bookkeeping, for example, would not hire another employee for the sole purpose of internal control. Large funds establish a control system to maintain a high standard of recordkeeping to protect plan assets and avoid losses to the fund.

It is obvious, therefore, that there is a great variety of services performed by different types of funds with varying numbers of involved employees. For these reasons, it is difficult to measure the effectiveness of administration in a quantitative manner.

Two other aspects of administration should be considered. One is the quality of service rendered. The other is the determination of whether the prospective size of a fund should be considered in determining whether it should exist as a separate operational unit for measurement purposes.

QUALITY OF ADMINISTRATIVE SERVICE

In reviewing this section on administration of Taft-Hartley jointly managed funds, it is easy to overlook the fact that the prime objective of the trustees is to fulfill the needs of plan participants within the scope of the hopes of the parties that negotiated the collective bargaining agreement. Quality of service, therefore, is an important aspect of plan operations. This is also extremely difficult to measure.

Perhaps the most effective method of peer review of the internal operations of a benefit fund is to establish a team consisting of the administrator, benefit consultant and certified public accountant (and attorney, possibly) to study the administration of the fund from time to time. In some cases, particularly for larger plans that perform such periodic evaluations, it may be advantageous to engage a consultant. A person or firm with extensive knowledge, experience and administrative background in the employee benefit field may be best qualified to assist in such an objective evaluation.

It is important that the procedures in claim payments by benefit plans be carefully scrutinized each year by the independent certified public accountants and the benefit consultant. Their aim should be reassuring the board of trustees that every effort is made to pay claims in as expeditious a period of time as possible after careful review, taking into consideration the needs of participants to obtain the benefits of the fund in a manner that safeguards the interest of the trustees and other parties to the trust.

Periodic evaluations of the performance of the contract and/or salaried administrator should be made by a committee of the board of trustees or the entire board. It is important such evaluations take into consideration the ever-changing nature and structure of employee benefit plans and the need by administrators and their staff to adjust to endless regulations and changes.

Trustees should establish the highest possible standards of service within the scope of the operations of the plan and the practical aspects of budgetary appropriation compatible with the income and expenses of the trust. Administrators should seek a higher degree of excellence in the performance of their services. Participants, employers and unions have a right to expect the highest level of service. The trustees should make certain they reaffirm this mission to the administrator and take every possible step to ascertain that the standards are being met on a regular basis.

SIZE OF THE FUND

One of the major problem areas in comparing funds and determining relative costs is the relatively small number of employees working under a collective bargaining agreement. In a plan with fewer than 500 employees, for example, costs would be spread over a small number of employees, resulting in an apparent high percentage of total income being utilized for administrative expense and high per capita costs. This may be acceptable to the board of trustees as meeting the objectives of the union and employers, as well as serving the interests of participants. However, constant scrutiny should be maintained by small funds to make certain that every effort is made to arrange the most economical and efficient type of administration so that the greatest possible portion of employer contributions is available for benefits.

In some instances, smaller funds have merged with others so costs may be spread over a larger body of employees. In other instances, smaller funds have been able to survive with an acceptable per employee cost by arranging multiple plan administration in one joint administrative entity—welfare, pension, annuity, vacation, training and so on. Funds jointly managed can reduce aggregate and individual expenses.

A growing problem with respect to demographics is the ratio of active to retired employees. In many older funds, particularly as this ratio decreases, there may be a large number of retired employees for whom little or no contributions are being made (other than by retired employees themselves) as compared to a diminishing number of active employees. This may increase the costs of administration spread among a decreasing number of active employees. Accompanied by a usual increase in per capita claims for such retired employees, this could jeopardize the fund by the trend toward high benefits as well as administrative costs.

This situation may be particularly applicable to those funds that have a high rate of early retirement before participants become eligible for federal Medicare benefits; in many cases, the trust will provide the same benefits for such retired employees under age 65 as for all other active, working employees. This may lead to considerable financial difficulties for the fund.

ATTEMPTS TO MEASURE ADMINISTRATIVE COSTS ON A COMPARATIVE BASIS

The problem in identifying and comparing administrative costs can be illustrated by a comparison of the operational methods of a hypothetical health and welfare fund.

For Tables I and II, we have prepared some data for a hypothetical health and welfare fund. The assumptions for both tables are as follows:
1. 2,500 active, eligible participants
2. 500 retired, eligible participants
3. Average number of employees reported who do not meet eligibility rules is 500, including 100 subject to reciprocity transfers
4. Average number of hours worked by all active employees in categories A and C is 1,300
5. Employer contribution rates:
   • Two-thirds of hours at $2
   • One-third of hours at $1.50.

Based on such assumptions, Table I reflects the operating income and expenses of such fund in a typical year. In Fund A, we are assuming that this health and welfare fund obtains its insurance coverage through an insurance company that pays claims, issues booklets, investigates claims and handles all phases of benefit processing.

As illustrated in Table I, benefit payments consist entirely of insurance premiums paid to the carrier in the amount of $6 million. This represents 83.9% of the employer and employee contributions under the hypothetical example. Taking investment income into consideration, this premium represents approximately 75.9% of total income.

Table I

FUND A
(Benefits Are Fully Insured; Insurance Carrier Processes Claims)

			Percentage of		Per Capita (Annual)		
			Contrb. Inc.	Total Inc.	Active (2,500)	Act/Retired (3,000)	All (3,500)
Income							
Employer and employee contributions (3,900,000 hours)							
2/3 (2,600,000 × $2)	$5,200,000						
1/3 (1,300,000 × $1.50)	$1,950,000						
Total Contribution Income		$7,150,000	100.0%	90.4%	$2,860	$2,383	$2,043
Investment income							
($10 million portfolio @ 8%)	$800,000						
Less investment advisor and custodian expense	$60,000						
	$740,000						
Unrealized investment income	$20,000	$760,000		9.6%	$304	$253	$217
Total Income		$7,910,000		100.0%	$3,164	$2,637	$2,260
Benefit Payments							
Insurance premiums for benefits	$6,000,000						
Self-insured benefits	$0						
Stop-loss insurance premiums	$0						
Total Benefit Cost		$6,000,000	83.9%	75.9%	$2,400	$2,000	$1,714
Administrative Costs							
Direct costs (personnel, fringes, office, data processing, etc.)	$600,000						
Claims processing expense	$0						
Cost-containment expenses	$0						
Total direct administrative costs		$600,000	8.4%	7.6%	$240	$200	$171
Plan Professionals	$60,000						
Trustees' liability insurance	$10,000						
Trustees' meeting and educational expenses	$10,000						
		$80,000	1.1%	1.0%	$32	$27	$23
Total Expenses		$680,000	9.5%	8.6%	$272	$227	$194
Total benefits and administrative expenses		$6,680,000	93.4%	84.5%	$2,672	$2,227	$1,909
Surplus (Deficit)		$1,230,000		15.5%			

Administrative costs, excluding plan professionals and trustees' expenses, are $600,000, representing 8.4% of employer and employee contributions and 7.6% of total income. The costs for plan professionals and trustees' liability and bonding insurance and meeting educational expenses are approximately $80,000, adding another 1.1% of contributions or 1% of total income to the combined total of expenses and benefits. Thus, it would appear that total administrative expenses were approximately 9.5% of employer contributions or 8.6% of total income. This might be considered to be a highly acceptable and efficient operating fund—And it is.

However, if one were to compare this to a self-insured fund, one would think this fund was operating much more efficiently than a self-insured fund because it is not required to incur substantial expenses necessary for the administration of a self-insured fund. In addition, an insured fund tends to distort comparative operating results since the figure for insurance premiums includes a substantial amount of administrative expenses incurred by the insurance company for the printing of booklets, underwriting claim forms, claim processing, claim draft preparation, supplies, data processing costs, stop-loss insurance and many other features.

Thus, if one were to assume that 8.33% of the total premiums represented insurer administration, this would add approximately $500,000 to the administration costs of $680,000. This would raise percentages and per capita as shown in Table III.

It should be noted that the percentage method is the most likely way to distort the overall expenses of a fund. A percentage of employer contributions is not meaningful unless the same relative amount of employer contributions were constant in all funds being compared. Collective bargaining in an individual fund determines the amount of employer contribution, not any action taken by the trustees directly. For example, in Fund A, Table I, employer contributions were $7,150,000; if the rate of employer contributions had been twice that amount based on collective bargaining, would that really mean that administrative costs decreased by 50%? Clearly, they did not. Thus, the percentile method is hardly a measure of the efficiency of a fund.

A more accurate measure would be per capita costs.

In the case of Table I, it is noted that there is a summary of per capita cost using three different methodologies:

1. Based on the eligible employees for whom contributions are made (2,500)
2. The average number of active and retired employees who are eligible for benefits (3,000)
3. The average number of active and retired eligible employees and the average number of reported employees who never became eligible because they did not meet the eligibility standards or are subject to reciprocity transfer (3,500).

Which is the proper per capita amount to use? All three standards are used regularly in determining per capita costs. Some consultants and funds spread all expenses among active eligible employees as the most consistent way of comparing costs. That method is not really applicable if retired employees are provided with benefits and make self-payments; some part of cost should be allocated for retired employees.

The third method of including employees for whom contributions are received, but who never become insured, in the quantification methodology seems to be reasonable. However, because there are no claims for such employees, is it really fair to spread all administrative costs ratably among such employees on a per capita basis?

A more objective method in expressing per capita cost would be to arrive at the specific value for each function in every fund and then apply that to actual costs and each class of employees. While theoretically sound, it hardly seems practical for application in a consistent manner for funds throughout the country.

In summary, there is a constant problem of how to measure per capita costs in comparison to other trust funds.

Table II presents the similar operating results of Fund B. Fund B has exactly the same income, expenses and characteristics as Fund A except that it is self-administered and self-insured, providing all benefits directly to insured participants and acquiring stop loss and specific insurance to cover major and catastrophic claims.

When one looks at the comparative operating costs of Fund B as compared to Fund A, it appears Fund B's expenses are approximately $990,000 as compared to $680,000 for Fund A. The per capita cost for expenses is considerably higher for Fund B than for Fund A. Based upon the average number of active, insured, eligible employees, the per capita cost has increased from $272 in Fund A to $396 in Fund B. Based upon active and retired employees, the per capita cost increased from $227 in Fund A to $330 in Fund B; based upon employees reported to the fund, active and retired and those not eligible, the per capita cost increased from $194 for Fund A to $283 for Fund B.

These are substantial variations of costs, but is Fund A more efficient than Fund B? Note that in Fund B, claims of $5,400,000 and a $100,000 premium for stop loss and specific excess insurance yields total benefit costs of $5,500,000. This is a reduction of about $500,000 in benefit payments compared to Fund A. However, this $500,000 represents the same dollars of administrative costs included in the insurance company's premium. Adding the $500,000 back into Fund A's adjusted administrative expense changes the landscape as in Table III.

Note the increase in administrative costs by Fund B: Direct administrative costs increased $50,000, representing the additional cost of printing, supplies, claim checks, recordkeeping, telephone calls and correspondence relating to the claim processing effort. In addition, there is a new expense for direct claim processing of $150,000, representing labor and other costs of direct processing of claims, including data processing, recordkeeping, correspondence and postage. Last, there is a cost-containment expenditure of $80,000 for second surgical opinion arrangements, utilization review, predetermination of claims, use of medical and dental consultants, audit of health provider bills and other cost-management efforts. Thus, direct administrative expenses have increased $280,000. In addition, legal, accounting and consulting services increased by $20,000 to take into consideration the change to self-insurance. Finally, trustees' liability and bonding insurance doubled because of the higher hazards faced by the fund with respect to assuming the responsibility of processing its own claims, hiring more employees and necessary increased bonding limits. Thus, there is an overall increase of $310,000 in administrative costs.

This increase of $310,000 causes a substantial increase in per capita expenses. However, as indicated, it is more than offset by the $500,000 reduction in benefit costs as a result of the elimination of the insurance carrier's administrative expenses and retention. The net effect is an increased fund gain for the year of $190,000.

Table II

FUND B
(Self-Insured Fund Processing Claims Directly)

			Percentage of		Per Capita (Annual)		
			Contrb. Inc.	Total Inc.	Active (2,500)	Act/Retired (3,000)	All (3,500)
Income							
Employer and employee contributions (3,900,000 hours)							
2/3 (2,600,000 × $2)	$5,200,000						
1/3 (1,300,000 × $1.50)	$1,950,000						
Total Contribution Income		$7,150,000	100.0%	90.4%	$2,860	$2,383	$2,043
Investment income							
($10 million portfolio @ 8%)	$800,000						
Less investment advisor and custodian expense	$60,000						
	$740,000						
Unrealized investment income	$20,000	$760,000		9.6%	$304	$253	$217
Total Income		$7,910,000		100.0%	$3,164	$2,637	$2,260
Benefit Payments							
Insurance premiums for benefits	$0						
Self-insured benefits	$5,400,000						
Stop-loss insurance premiums	$100,000						
Total Benefit Cost		$5,500,000	76.9%	69.5%	$2,200	$1,833	$1,571
Administrative Costs							
Direct costs (personnel, fringes, office, data processing, etc.)	$650,000						
Claims processing expense	$150,000						
Cost-containment expenses	$80,000						
Total direct administrative costs		$880,000	12.3%	11.1%	$352	$293	$251
Plan Professionals	$80,000						
Trustees' liability insurance	$20,000						
Trustees' meeting and educational expenses	$10,000						
		$110,000	1.5%	1.4%	$44	$37	$31
Total Expenses		$990,000	13.8%	12.5%	$396	$330	$283
Total benefits and administrative expenses		$6,490,000	90.8%	82.0%	$2,596	$2,163	$1,854
Surplus (Deficit)		$1,420,000		18.0%			

Table IV compares Fund A to Fund B on a more "apples-to-apples" basis.

From an overall income and expense perspective, Fund B is the more efficient on a per capita basis, taking into consideration the real administrative costs of Fund A (including the substantial portion included in insurance premiums).

It should be noted that these are hypothetical assumptions and not every plan would benefit as greatly from changing to self-insurance. The purpose of these illustrations is not necessarily to show the advantages of self-insurance compared to insured arrangements, but merely to show the disparity in measurement figures in comparing the operations of health and welfare funds.

Fund B is more efficient in showing a greater gain for the year, even though its expenses rose; it also had the effect of the variation in percentile method if that were to be seriously considered. Because of the change in the means of paying claims, benefit costs decreased from 84% to 77% and administrative costs increased from 9.5% to 13.8%; yet the exact result was quite different. The fund improved its efficiency and effectiveness, even though its per capita costs went up.

There are many characteristics and idiosyncrasies of

Table III

	Fund A	Fund A Adjusted for Insurance Carrier Admin. Expenses
Administrative costs	$680,000	$1,180,000
Percentage of contribution income	9.5%	16.5%
Percentage of total income	8.6%	14.9%
Annual per capita cost for 2,500 actives	$272	$472

Table IV

	Fund B	Fund A	Fund A Adjusted for Insurance Carrier Admin. Expenses
Administrative costs	$990,000	$680,000	$1,180,000
Percentage of contribution income	13.8%	9.5%	16.5%
Percentage of total income	12.5%	8.6%	14.9%
Annual per capita cost for 2,500 actives	$396	$272	$472

benefit funds to be considered in attempting to determine comparative costs and efficiencies. Because of variations in procedures, methods and styles of benefit programs, it is increasingly difficult to compare funds. Even if an adjustment is made for services provided by insurance companies, it is still impractical to attempt to make sheer mathematical comparisons.

Adjustments must be made for:
- Size of the fund
- Number of offices and geographical area serviced
- Type of fund (i.e., welfare vs. pension, vacation vs. annuity, etc.)
- Whether the fund is one of a multiple number of funds being jointly managed
- Cost variations by geographical area
- Scope of the fund—local, statewide or national
- Difference in work styles of trustees
- Amount of employer contributions, number of participants and employers and varying contribution rates
- Functions assumed by fund offices.

As indicated in an earlier edition of the *Trustees Handbook* published by the International Foundation of Employee Benefit Plans in 1979, an eminent administrator, William C. Earhart, stated:

When the thinking processes began as to what functions are common to all funds, it became apparent that few functions are, without exception, common to all funds.

Mr. Earhart closed by stating:

It is regrettable that the variations in administrative functions required by various trusts do not lend themselves to the establishment of guidelines as to administrative costs, even on plans that appear to be very similar.

All attempts over the years to establish quantitative measurement of funds have been unsuccessful. The best index of the effectiveness and efficiency of any benefit fund is a review of fund procedures, costs and the quality of service. It is incumbent upon the board of trustees and administrative office of the fund to ascertain that the fund is operating on the most efficient and cost-effective basis for the best interest of participants.

This may not be easily measured mathematically. However, a detailed investigation through a periodic valuation by a committee or subcommittee of trustees with the assistance of various professionals is valuable in evaluating the performance of the administrative operation, taking into consideration the goals of the trustees. While it may be difficult to compare funds, it is not difficult to evaluate whether a particular fund is or is not efficient and cost-effective in fulfilling its mission.

Checklist for Trustees on Key Points in Section IX

- Recordkeeping
  —Plan's governing documents (trust agreement, plan of benefits, SPDs, collective bargaining agreements, etc.) maintained and readily available?
  —Service provider agreements (in writing) maintained and available?
  —Financial records maintained in good order?
  　–Accounting controls in place?
  　–Adequate and appropriate internal controls in place to reduce risk of fraud in collections, eligibility determinations, benefit approvals and payments?
  　–Adequate and appropriate accounting for/tracking of investments?
  —Trustees' policies and directives followed?
  　–Delinquency/collection policy
  　–Record retention policy
  　–Travel reimbursement/educational policy
  　–Investment policy guidelines
- Claim processing and claims records
  —Timely?
  —Accurate?
  —Appeals handled in accordance with mandated procedures?
  —Claims experience available for ongoing analysis?
  　–Data processing/database sufficient for plan's needs?
  　–Individuals' records adequately maintained?
  　　*In compliance with HIPAA Privacy Regulations with regard to an individual's "protected health information?"
  —Cost controls in place to prevent unnecessary expenditure of benefit dollars?
  　–Utilization review?
  　–Large case management?
  　–Disease management?
  　–Coordination of benefits?
  　–Subrogation?
  　–Antifraud procedures and controls?
- Trustees meetings
  —Materials to be covered at the meeting sent out in advance, when possible?
  —Meetings effectively organized?
  —Reliable, timely and comprehensive reports provided by fund administration?
- Coordination with plan professionals
  —Administrator understands and can relate content of reports of plan's professionals?
  —Flow of information between administrative office and plan professionals smooth and efficient?
  —Any problems with plan professionals not getting the information they require to perform the services for which they were engaged?
- Communication with plan participants
  —SPDs up to date?
  —Notices/announcements/program materials disseminated and available?
  —Helpful, effective, accurate and courteous service rendered by fund office?
  —Benefit statements/information provided to participants readily understandable?

- Communication with union/employers
  - Plan rules clearly explained?
  - Helpful, effective, accurate and courteous service rendered by fund office?
  - Appropriate assistance given by fund office in area of collective bargaining?
  - Notice(s) of delinquencies given by fund office to all appropriate parties?
- Governmental reporting and compliance
  - Annual tax returns accurate and timely filed?
  - Summary annual reports (SARs) published when required?
  - Required notices published (e.g., WHCRA annual notice)?
  - Compliance with COBRA, FMLA, HIPAA, USERRA, etc.?
  - Appeals handled within time frames dictated by federal regulations?
- Fund office
  - Appropriate location to service parties in interest, especially participants?
  - Properly equipped to fulfill scope of needed operations?
- Staffing
  - Smooth and efficient workflow?
  - Personnel practices and policies clearly defined?
  - Economical and efficient?
  - HIPAA trained?
- Security issues
  - HIPAA security—in compliance?
  - Insurance and bonding in place?
  - Internal control of assets, records and other property sufficient?
- Administrative costs
  - Periodically reviewed?
  - Reasonable, given established norms?

SECTION XI

COMMUNICATIONS

Chapter 47

Reporting and Disclosure Under ERISA

Lonie A. Hassel

The Employee Retirement Income Security Act of 1974 (ERISA) requires plan administrators to provide certain types of information to plan participants. Some disclosure requirements are clearly spelled out in ERISA, such as the duty to provide summary plan descriptions. Other disclosure requirements are more generally described. And some courts have found that ERISA's fiduciary duty of loyalty requires certain disclosures that are not expressly stated in ERISA.

Compliance with disclosure requirements is important to ensure that plan participants and beneficiaries have the information they need to obtain the benefits they are entitled to receive. Failure to comply with these requirements not only can shortchange participants, but it also can put plan fiduciaries at risk of legal action for monetary penalties and breach of fiduciary duty.

This chapter will serve as a guide to identifying information that must be provided and determining whether disclosure should be made even where not expressly required by ERISA.[1] In addition, the chapter discusses the risks of miscommunication and inadvertent vesting of retiree welfare benefits.

I. REQUIRED DISCLOSURES

A. Pension and Welfare Plans

1. Summary Plan Description

Within 90 days after a participant becomes covered by a plan or a beneficiary begins receiving benefits under a plan, the plan must give the participant or beneficiary a summary plan description and all modifications and changes to the summary plan description. ERISA §104b. Every five years (or ten years if there have been no changes to the plan) an updated summary plan description must be provided to each participant covered by the plan and each beneficiary receiving benefits under the plan. ERISA §104(b).

Department of Labor regulations describe the specific information that must be included in the SPD. 29 C.F.R. §2520.102-3.

2. Summary of Material Modifications

Within 210 days after the end of a plan year in which any material modification is adopted, the plan must distribute to each participant covered by the plan and each beneficiary receiving benefits under the plan a summary description of the modification. ERISA §104(b)(1)(B).

3. Summary Annual Report

Within nine months after the end of the plan year, the plan administrator must distribute a summary annual report to each participant and to each beneficiary receiving benefits under the plan (other than beneficiaries under a welfare plan). The summary annual report must include statements and schedules for the fiscal year, and any other material necessary to fairly summarize the latest annual report. 29 C.F.R. §2520.104b-10.

B. Pension Plans

1. Benefit Statement

The plan administrator must give participants who terminate service, participants who incur a one-year break in service, and participants or beneficiaries who request it in writing a statement showing the individual's accrued benefits and nonforfeitable benefits and, if applicable, the earliest date on which benefits will become nonforfeitable. ERISA §§105, 209(a).

2. Annual Funding Notice to Participants

Section 101(f) of ERISA requires the plan administrator of a defined benefit multiemployer pension plan to issue a plan funding notice each year to plan participants and beneficiaries, labor organizations representing them, contributing employers and the Pension Benefit Guaranty Corporation (PBGC) describing the funded level of the plan, the benefits that would be guaranteed by PBGC in the event the plan became insolvent and other financial information about the plan. A Department of Labor (DOL) regulation implementing this requirement was proposed in February 2005 to apply to plan years beginning on and after December 31, 2004.

3. Notice of Significant Reduction in Benefit Accruals

The plan administrator must provide written notice to participants, alternate payees and unions representing participants before the effective date of a plan amendment that significantly reduces benefit accruals. ERISA §204(h). Generally, the notice must be provided 15 days in advance. In the event of an egregious failure to comply with the notice requirement, participants may receive the greater of the benefits they would have been entitled to receive with and without the amendment.

C. Group Health Plans

1. Within 60 days after the adoption of a material modification resulting in a material reduction in covered services or benefits under a group health plan, the plan administrator must distribute a summary description of such modifications to each participant covered by the plan and each beneficiary receiving benefits under the plan. ERISA §104(b); 29 C.F.R. §2520.104b-3(d). This requirement may be satisfied by publishing the modification in a regular communication with participants that is issued at least every 90 days. 29 C.F.R. §2520.104b-3(d).
2. Notice of Special Enrollment Rights: The plan must give enrolling employees a written notice of enrollment rights describing the circumstances under which an employee who declines coverage may later enroll himself or herself or family members. 29 C.F.R. §2590.701-6(c).
3. Certificate of Coverage: Group health plans must issue a certificate of creditable coverage to individuals who lose coverage under the plan, become covered by COBRA, lose COBRA coverage or request a certificate within 24 months after losing plan or COBRA coverage. ERISA §701(e)(1). An individual's period of creditable coverage identified in the certificate offsets any preexisting condition periods in the individual's subsequent group health plan. ERISA §701(a)(3).
4. Women's Health and Cancer Rights Act Notice: Upon enrollment and annually thereafter, group health plans must notify participants that, under the Women's Health and Cancer Rights Act of 1998, the plan provides benefits for certain mastectomy-related services. ERISA §713.
5. COBRA Rights Notice: Within 90 days after coverage under a group health plan, the plan administrator must notify participants and their spouses of their rights to continuation coverage under COBRA. ERISA §606. The notice may be provided in the SPD. Other notice requirements apply when an individual becomes entitled to elect COBRA coverage or COBRA coverage is denied.

II. DISCLOSURES THAT MUST BE MADE UPON REQUEST OF A PLAN PARTICIPANT OR BENEFICIARY

ERISA requires the plan administrator, "upon written request of a participant or beneficiary, to furnish a copy of the latest updated summary plan description, plan description, and the latest annual report, any terminal report, the bargaining agreement, trust agreement, contract, or other instruments under which the plan is established or operated." ERISA §104(b)(4). The plan administrator may charge a reasonable copying fee, which may not exceed $0.25 per page, for the requested documents.

A court may, in its discretion, assess personal liability against a plan administrator who fails to provide the requested documents within 30 days after receiving a written request from a plan participant or beneficiary, in an amount up to $110 per day for each day from the date of the failure. ERISA §502(c)(1). In deciding whether and how much liability to assess, the court considers factors such as the plan administrator's bad faith or intentional conduct, the length of the delay, number of requests made, the documents withheld and any prejudice to the participant or beneficiary.

While the requirement to furnish certain documents is plainly stated, the limits of the requirement to provide, upon written request, *"other instruments under which the plan is established or operated,"* is not as clear. Stretched to its logical limits, this could require a plan administrator to provide virtually every document it possesses. Fortunately for our forests, courts interpreting this provision have read it fairly narrowly, but it is difficult to discern a consistent standard from the court opinions that govern disclosure. For example, courts have found that this provision requires the plan administrator to supply a copy of the plan's actuarial report, procedure for calculating benefits, and plan funding and investment policies. Courts also have found that this provision does not require disclosure of the plan's actuarial report, IRS determination letter, bonding policy, physician compensation agreements, participant lists and certain trustee meeting minutes. Given the lack of consistent guidance, it may be necessary to consult with legal counsel when a participant or beneficiary submits a written request for a document that is not expressly required to be provided under Section 104(b)(4) of ERISA.

III. OTHER FIDUCIARY DISCLOSURE

The Supreme Court has found that fiduciaries of ERISA plans violate their duty of loyalty if they knowingly and significantly mislead plan participants. *Varity Corporation v. Howe,* 516 U.S. 489, 506 (1996). Other courts similarly have found fiduciary disclosure duties beyond the express disclosure requirements in ERISA. While fiduciaries are not required to be clairvoyant in response to participant questions, they are required to answer questions forthrightly, and may be found liable for material misrepresentations. A misrepresentation is material if there is a substantial likelihood that it would mislead a reasonable employee in making an adequately informed retirement decision. For example, a fiduciary's affirmative, systematic representations that retiree benefits would continue, even though the plan sponsor had reserved the right to terminate retiree benefits, has been found to be a breach of fiduciary duty.

A fiduciary may have duty to provide information to a participant that a participant does not ask for if the fiduciary knows the participant does not have the information he or she needs. This could occur, for example, where a participant with a terminal illness asks a general question about his or her benefits and the plan administrator knows that in the participant's circumstances, a particular benefit option could maximize the amounts payable to the participant and beneficiary under the plan.

IV. CONSEQUENCES OF MISCOMMUNICATION AND HOW TO AVOID THEM

Trustees of a multiemployer plan are plan fiduciaries, and often are designated as the plan administrator. In communications with plan participants and beneficiaries, therefore, trustees, acting as such, generally are bound by ERISA's fiduciary requirements. But trustees usually do not engage in day-to-day communications with participants and beneficiaries concerning benefits. This function may be performed by plan employees or contractors hired to provide this service. Whether these individuals also are fiduciaries depends upon whether they have been delegated discretionary authority in the administration of the plan. Plan employees who perform ministerial tasks, such as responding to telephone questions concerning the plan, generally would not be fiduciaries and their communications to participants and beneficiaries therefore should not give rise to a fiduciary breach.

Even a fiduciary is not subject to absolute liability in communications with participants. Fiduciaries can and do make mistakes and, so long as the mistakes are honest, not made willfully or in bad faith, they should not constitute a fiduciary breach. *Frahm v. Equitable Life Assurance Soc'y of the United States,* 137 F.3d 955, 960 (7th Cir. 1998), *cert. denied,* 525 U.S. 817 (1998); *Burke v. Latrobe Steel Co.,* 775 F.2d 88, 91 (3d Cir. 1985).

In some circumstances, however, a miscommunication can bind the plan and result in the payment of promised benefits to the participant or beneficiary who relied on the miscommunication. Under the doctrine of *estoppel,* a court will require a party to make good on a statement, if the statement was an intentional misrepresentation and if the party to whom the statement was made reasonably relied on the statement to his or her detriment. With respect to defined benefit pension plans, some courts refuse to recognize estoppel because it would undermine the plan's actuarial soundness by requiring the plan to pay benefits that are not funded. Courts usually are reluctant to apply the doctrine of estoppel, even with respect to welfare plans, because it is inconsistent with ERISA's basic requirement that plan documents be in writing. Courts therefore have adopted various tests such as requiring "extraordinary circumstances" before applying the doctrine of estoppel.

Union representatives are another source of information for multiemployer plan participants. Often, plan participants do not distinguish between the union and the plan. To avoid misunderstandings and help to ensure that participants receive accurate information, it is important to notify them that questions about plan benefits should be addressed to plan representatives, not union representatives.

V. COMMUNICATIONS ABOUT RETIREE WELFARE BENEFITS

Unlike pension benefits, ERISA does not expressly provide that retiree welfare benefits, such as retiree health benefits, are nonforfeitable (i.e., are *vested*) upon completion of a minimum period of service. In light of this statutory distinction, the United States Supreme Court has concluded that ERISA generally permits welfare plans to be modified or terminated at any time. *Curtiss-Wright Corp. v. Schoonejongen,* 514 U.S. 73, 78 (1995). By the same token, ERISA also does not expressly forbid vesting of health and welfare benefits. To determine whether retirees are entitled to continued welfare benefits, courts look at the representations that have been made in prior collective bargaining agreements, plan documents, summary plan descriptions and other related documents. *U.A.W. v. Skinner Engine Co.,*

188 F.3d 130, 139 (3rd Cir. 1999) (retiree welfare benefits may vest "under a collective bargaining agreement, SPD [summary plan description], or other plan document"); *United Food & Commercial Workers Int'l Union Local 150-A v. Dubuque Packing Co.,* 756 F.2d 66, 70 (8th Cir. 1985) (despite plant closing and termination of collective bargaining agreement, retiree health and welfare benefits had vested because there were "many indications in the agreements and course of dealing that the parties intended the right to benefits would vest upon retirement"); *United Steelworkers of America v. Connors Steel Co.,* 855 F.2d 1499 (11th Cir. 1988) (employer obligated to provide retiree benefits under an expired collective bargaining agreement); *Jensen v. SIPCO, Inc.,* 38 F.3d 945, 949-52 (8th Cir. 1994) (retiree health benefits are vested under the terms of summary plan descriptions).

There are no special words that need be used in order to turn retiree health benefits into vested benefits. The courts look for a manifestation in the language of the plan document, summary plan description or collective bargaining agreement that signifies the employer's intent to provide benefits throughout a participant's retirement. A written statement that benefits in retirement "will be continued for the rest of your life" has been found to communicate such a promise. *Helwig v. Kelsey-Hayes Co.,* 93 F.3d 243, 248 (6th Cir. 1996). So too have contractual provisions saying that the company "will provide insurance benefits [to retirees] equal to the active group," *International Union, UAW v. Yard-Man, Inc.,* 716 F.2d 1476, 1480 (6th Cir. 1983), or that retired employees "after completion of twenty years of full-time permanent service and at least age 55 will be insured." *Devlin v. Empire Blue Cross & Blue Shield,* 274 F.3d 76, 79 (2nd Cir. 2001), *cert. denied,* 123 S.Ct. 1015 (2003).

In many cases, however, the courts focus on the presence or absence of language in the plan documents that specifically reserves to the employer the power to amend, modify, or terminate the plan benefits. Such reservation-of-rights clauses are often treated as powerful evidence that the employer neither intended nor communicated any intention to vest retiree benefits, e.g., *In re Unisys Corp. Retiree Med. Benefit Litig.,* 58 F.3d 896, 904 (3rd Cir. 1996); *Sprague v. General Motors Corp.,* 133 F.3d 388 (6th Cir. 1998) *(en banc); Chiles v. Certain Corp.,* 95 F.3d 1505 (10th Cir. 1996); *Alday v. Container Corp. of America,* 906 F.2d 660 (11th Cir. 1990). The presence of a reservation of rights clause may not automatically demonstrate that benefits are not vested, however. *In re Unisys Corp.,* 58 F.3d at 904 n.11 ("each case must be considered fact specific and the court must make its determination of the benefits provided based on the language of the particular plan . . .").

To avoid inadvertently vesting costly welfare benefits, it is important to review carefully the summary plan description, plan document and notices provided to participants for promises of lifetime benefits or unqualified promises to continue benefits.

ENDNOTE

1. This chapter does not address disclosures required under the Internal Revenue Code or Health Insurance Portability and Accountability Act security provisions.

Chapter 48

Benefit Claims

Lonie A. Hassel

Communication is vital to an effective benefit claim administration process. In addition to the specific communications required under the Employee Retirement Income Security Act of 1974 (ERISA) and the Department of Labor (DOL) claims regulation, this chapter highlights practices that plans should consider in their communications concerning benefit claims.

REQUIRED BENEFIT CLAIM COMMUNICATIONS

ERISA and DOL claims regulations require plans to establish and follow reasonable claims procedures. This requires the plan to describe the claims procedures and time limits in the summary plan description and in any adverse claim decision. 29 C.F.R. §§2560.503-1(b)(2), (g)(1)(iv). If a plan does not establish and follow claims procedures in accordance with the regulation, a claimant "shall be deemed to have exhausted the administrative remedies" under the plan. 29 C.F.R. §2560.503-1(l). Later guidance indicates that, in DOL's view, the claimant must demonstrate that the plan did not meet its duty to establish and follow reasonable claims procedures, and not every deviation from the regulation requirements gives rise to a failure to establish and maintain reasonable claim procedures.

As explained by DOL, a plan that establishes procedures in conformity with the regulation might, in processing a particular claim, inadvertently deviate from its procedures. If the plan's procedures provide an opportunity to remedy the inadvertent deviation without prejudice to the claimant, through the internal appeal process or otherwise, then there ordinarily will not have been a failure to establish or follow reasonable procedures.

INITIAL CLAIM DECISION

For all plans, an adverse claim decision must (i) state the specific reason for the denial; (ii) refer to specific plan provisions; (iii) describe additional information necessary to perfect the claim and why the information is necessary; and (iv) describe plan procedures, time limits and the claimant's right to sue. 29 C.F.R. §2560.503-1(g)(1). For group health plans and disability plans, the notice also must disclose any internal rule, guideline or protocol relied on in making an adverse determination (or state that such information is available free of charge). If a claim is denied based on medical necessity or an experimental care exclusion, the notice must explain the scientific or clinical basis of the determination (or state that such information is available free of charge).

REVIEW OF ADVERSE CLAIM DECISION

Plans must offer claimants the opportunity for a full and fair review of their claims. This means giving the claimant the opportunity to submit written information concerning the claim, and if the claimant asks, giving the claimant access to and copies of documents that are "relevant" to the claim. 29 C.F.R. §2560.503-1(h)(2). A document is relevant if it was relied on in making the claim decision, was submitted, considered or generated in the course of the benefit decision (whether or not relied upon), demonstrates compliance with the plan's procedures for assuring consistent treatment of similarly situated claimants, and, in the case of a group health plan or plan that provides disability benefits, is a statement of policy concerning the denied treatment option or benefit (whether or not relied upon). 29 C.F.R. §2560.503-1(m)(8).

The claims regulation does not specify a particular method for demonstrating consistent treatment of similarly situated claimants. In guidance issued after publication of the regulation, DOL explained that consistency in deciding benefit claims could be ensured by applying protocols, guidelines, criteria, rate tables, fee schedules and the like. Consistent decisions could be verified by periodic examinations, reviews or audits of benefit claims to determine whether the appropriate protocols, guidelines, criteria, rate tables and fee schedules were applied in the claims determination process. The claims regulation, moreover, does not contemplate the development of new documents solely to comply with this disclosure requirement. Instead, DOL has stated that claimants will be provided with the documents actually used in deciding the claim, such as the plan rules or guidelines governing the application of specific protocols, criteria, rate tables and fee schedules to claims like the claim at issue, or a specific checklist or cross-checking document demonstrating that the plan rules or guidelines were applied to the claimant's claim. Further, DOL has explained that, while information from individual claim files may be compiled for developing the criteria and guidelines to ensure consistent application of plan rules, plans are not required to disclose other claimants' individual records or information specific to the resolution of other claims in order to comply with this requirement.

BENEFIT CLAIM COMMUNICATIONS

Know your plan. To communicate accurate information, the plan administrator must have accurate information. Plan documents often include provisions that are to be applied "in accordance with procedures adopted by the plan administrator." Often, however, no such procedures exist. Review the plan document for references to procedures and adopt procedures where necessary.

Know your beneficiary. An increasing amount of benefit litigation involves disputes over who is the beneficiary of a deceased participant's benefit. Disputes arise for many reasons, including divorce issues, beneficiaries who are minors, partially completed beneficiary forms, completed forms that were not submitted or apparently not received and the like. Communication with participants can help to protect the plan in these types of situations. Helpful communications include sending an acknowledgement letter upon receipt of a properly completed (or other) beneficiary designation and notifying participants that a beneficiary designation is not automatically changed upon divorce (unless the plan provides that spousal beneficiary designations are invalid upon divorce).

Know your forms. Develop and issue standardized forms for participants to use for filing claims and appeals, designating an authorized representative. This will help to streamline the claims process and reduce ambiguity concerning whether a claim or appeal has been filed, or whether a representative has been appointed.

Similarly, standardized language should be used where possible in notices to participants of claim and appeal decisions, recognizing that additional details that are unique to a participant also should be added.

Identify nonroutine claims. Written claim decisions in cases that are factually complicated or otherwise out of the ordinary may need additional explanation, beyond that required under ERISA. Clear and persuasive decision letters in these types of cases can help the plan to prevail in litigation or to avoid litigation in the first place.

Exhaustion. In deciding benefit claims under ERISA, courts have developed the requirement that a participant exhaust administrative remedies under the plan before commencing a court action. This rule is not found in ERISA, and therefore should be clearly communicated to participants in the summary plan description and other claim-related documents.

Limitations. ERISA does not include a "statute of limitations" for bringing claims to court. If not otherwise specified, courts generally have applied the applicable state law limitations period for contract actions. A plan may, however, adopt its own limitations period as short as one year or less, which must be communicated to participants.

Finders are not keepers. Plan fiduciaries have an obligation to take appropriate steps to collect amounts owed to the plan, including overpayments. Overpayment errors occur even in the best-run plans, raising a variety of issues, including whether to charge interest, how hard to pursue repayment and whether to offset future benefits to collect the overpayment. Written procedures communicated to all plan participants and beneficiaries will put participants on notice that benefit overpayments are not theirs to keep (any more than the plan is entitled to keep underpayments).

Private communications. A union representative or other individual may act as a liaison between a participant and a health plan. The participant is free to tell the union representative his or her own health information, but the plan should not discuss the participant's claim with anyone other than the participant without a written authorization from the participant.

Communicate during the administrative process. Communication with the participant during the administrative process can help to assure a complete administrative record. The claimant should be allowed to submit any information he or she believes is relevant in support of the claim. During the administrative review process, the claimant also should be given reports of the plan's medical experts. A court recently declined to uphold a plan's decision on a disability claim because the plan had obtained a report from a medical expert and had not given the participant the opportunity to review the report or provide rebuttal evidence.

SECTION XIII

TRUSTEE EFFECTIVENESS

Chapter 49

Trustees Meetings

Timothy J. Parsons

INTRODUCTION

To properly fulfill their responsibilities to the participants in employee benefit plans, the individuals who are fiduciaries or trustees of such plans must understand how to conduct the necessary business of the plan in an efficient and appropriate manner. This chapter discusses both the practical and legal aspects of how the trustees of a fund should conduct the fund's business.

Practical Considerations

- Effective service to plan participants and beneficiaries
- Effective use of plan assets
- Avoidance of possible personal liability.

Legal Considerations

Members of boards of trustees of multiemployer benefit plans must carry out their duties in accordance with statutory requirements in order to avoid potential criminal liability. Sections 302(a) and (b) of the Labor-Management Relations Act of 1947 (LMRA) provide that it is a crime for an employer to pay money or any other thing of value to a labor organization that represents its employees. The statute provides that the criminal prohibitions do not apply to an employer's payment of:

> ... money or other thing of value ... to a trust fund established by such representative, for the sole and exclusive benefit of the employees of such employer, and their families and dependents (or of such employees, families and dependents jointly with the employees of other employers making similar payments, and their families and dependents); *provided,* that (A) such payments are held in trust ... ; (B) the detailed basis on which ... payments [of contributions] are to be made is specified in a written agreement with the employer, and employees and employers are equally represented in the administration of such fund, together with such neutral persons as the representatives of the employers and the representatives of employees may agree upon. . . .

Section 302(c) of LMRA, 29 U.S.C. §186(c).

Under the Employee Retirement Income Security Act of 1974 (ERISA), the fiduciaries or trustees of an employee benefit plan must know how to conduct the necessary business of the plan because they have the exclusive responsibility and authority to do so. ERISA requires that the written document of an employee benefit plan "shall provide for one or more named fiduciaries who jointly and severally shall have authority to control and manage the operation and administration of the plan." ERISA §402(a)(l).

In general, ". . . all assets of an employee benefit plan shall be held in trust by one or more trustees . . . the trustee or trustees shall have exclusive authority and discretion to manage and control the assets of the plan, . . . " ERISA §403(a).

The assets of an employee benefit plan ". . . shall never inure to the benefit of any employer and shall be held for the exclusive purposes of providing benefits to participants in the plan and then beneficiaries and defraying the reasonable expenses of administering the plan." ERISA §403(c)(l); see also §404(a)(l)(A).

Fiduciaries are required to meet a high standard of care—". . . the care, skill, prudence, and diligence under the circumstances then prevailing that a prudent man acting in a like capacity and familiar with such matters would use in the conduct of an enterprise of a like character and with like aims. . . . " ERISA §404(a)(l)(B).

Fiduciaries cannot, directly or indirectly, engage in what they know *or should know* are prohibited transactions with parties in interest. ERISA §406(a)(l).

Knowledge of how to properly conduct the business of a plan is also essential to protect the fiduciaries from possible personal liability. If fiduciaries breach "... any of the responsibilities, obligations, or duties imposed upon fiduciaries ..." they "... shall be personally liable to make good to such plan any losses resulting from each such breach," ERISA §409(a), and also may be held liable for payment of potential 10% civil penalties under ERISA §502(1)(1).

Plan fiduciaries may also be sued by individual participants under ERISA §502(a)(3) for "other appropriate equitable relief to remedy breaches of fiduciary duties or violations of other provisions of ERISA, e.g., *Ream v. Frey,* 107 F.3d 147, 20 EBC 2657 (3rd Cir. 1997), although the weight of authority now holds that "equitable relief" does not include any awards of compensatory damages or other types of monetary relief. See *Great-West Life & Annuity Ins. Co. v. Knudson,* 534 U.S. 204 (2002).

In addition, although a participant can maintain an action for recovery of damages resulting from breaches of fiduciary duty that recovery must, under ERISA §409(a), must be sought for the plan as a whole. Plan participants cannot seek individual recoveries of monetary damages on a claim for breach of fiduciary duty, e.g., *Milofsky v. American Airlines, Inc.,* 2005 U.S. App. LEXIS 4449 (5th Cir. 2005).

Plan fiduciaries may also be sued by their co-fiduciaries with respect to issues of co-fiduciary responsibility and indemnification under ERISA §405(a). *Youngberg v. The Bekins Co.,* 20 EBC 1650 (E.D.Calif. 1996). Also, present fiduciaries may be sued by former fiduciaries.

Regardless of whether individual fiduciaries have been appointed by a union or by an employer group, all fiduciaries have exactly the same duty to the participants of the plan, *NLRB v. AMAX Coal Company,* 453 U.S. 322, 834 (1981), and this duty is not the same as that of a representative for purposes of collective bargaining.

Plan advisors, such as attorneys, actuaries and accountants, and service providers, such as third-party administrators, are usually *not* found to be fiduciaries; see, e.g., *Custer v. Sweeney,* 20 EBC 1569 (4th Cir. 1996) (former attorneys for Sheet Metal Workers National Pension Fund were held to not be fiduciaries where there was no showing that the attorneys exercised sufficient discretionary authority or control over the plan's assets), and fiduciary responsibilities cannot be delegated to such advisors.

In the view of the Department of Labor (DOL), the authority to appoint and, presumably, to remove, a fiduciary is an exercise of discretionary authority or control over management of a plan and, therefore, is a fiduciary function. See 29 CFR §2509.75-8 at Q&A D-4. The DOL regulations also indicate that there is an ongoing fiduciary duty on the part of the appointing entity to review the performance of appointed trustees at "reasonable intervals." See 29 CFR §2509.75-8, Q&A FR-17 and D-4.

In briefs filed in the WorldCom, Inc. and Enron ERISA lawsuits, DOL asserted the position that not only is the appointment of plan fiduciaries itself a fiduciary act, but also that the appointing fiduciaries have "ongoing responsibilities," at reasonable intervals, to review the performance of appointed fiduciaries "in such a manner as may be reasonably expected to ensure that their performance has been in compliance with the terms of the plan and statutory standards," citing 29 CFR §2509.75-8 at FR-17.

The DOL position was adopted by the court in the Enron litigation, *In re Enron Corp. Sec., Derivative & ERISA Litigation,* 284 F.Supp. 2d 511, 552-53 (S.D.Tex. 2003), although it has been rejected in other cases such as *In re Williams Cos. ERISA Litigation,* 2003 WL 22794417 (N.D.Okla. 2003).

DOL stated in its WorldCom brief that the duty to monitor does not require "... the appointing fiduciary to second-guess every decision of its appointee, or to guarantee the wisdom of the appointee's decisions," but it is hard to see where and how the line will be drawn as plaintiffs' attorneys are arguing a "guarantee" theory and, given the potential unlimited personal liability of a fiduciary under ERISA Section 409(a), the potential stakes are very high.

THE SETTLOR FUNCTION RULE

Decisions of boards of trustees of multiemployer plans to amend the terms of a benefit plan are not subject to the fiduciary responsibility provisions of ERISA, e.g., *Gard v. Blankenburg,* 2002 U.S. App. LEXIS 2963, 27 EBC 1776 (6th Cir. 2002); *Walling v. Brady,* 125 F.3d 114, 21 EBC 1437 (3d Cir. 1997); *Lockheed Corp. v. Spink,* 517 U.S. 882 (1996).

This broad authority, however, is not unlimited. Statutory provisions may preclude certain types of amendments, e.g., ERISA §204(g) which prohibits plan amendments that would eliminate or reduce accrued pension benefits, discussed in *Board of Trustees of the Sheet Metal Workers National Pension Fund v. Commissioner of Internal Revenue,* 318 F.3d 599, 29 EBC 2377 (4th Cir. 2003).

Plan trustees also cannot adopt or amend plan provisions that are inconsistent with the terms of the applicable collective bargaining agreements. See *La Barbera v. J.D. Collyer Equipment Corp.,* 337 F.3d 132 (2d Cir. 2003) and DOL Advisory Opinion 2002-06A (July 3, 2002).

Plan trustees must also be aware, however, that if their actions are not fiduciary or plan administration activities, then plan assets may not be able to be used to pay for expenses that are incurred in the course of such activities. See DOL Field Assistance Bulletin 2002-2

(November 4, 2002), DOL Advisory Opinion 2001-01A (January 18, 2001), DOL "Guidance on Settlor v. Plan Expenses."

APPOINTMENT AND REMOVAL OF TRUSTEES

Under the trust agreements of virtually all multi-employer benefit plans, the members of the employer or management group of fiduciaries are appointed by an association or other group composed of or representing the employers that are signatory to collective bargaining agreements with the union. Correspondingly, the members of the employee or labor group of fiduciaries are appointed by officers of the appropriate local or regional labor organization. One group has no authority to appoint the representatives of the other group.

The terms of trust agreements and/or plan documents concerning which group or entity has the authority to appoint or remove trustees or the composition of the board of trustees in terms of which local unions or employer groups will be represented, unless stated to be irrevocable, are themselves subject to amendment, e.g., *Worthy v. International Longshoremen's Association,* 342 F.3d 422, 31 EBC.1050 (5th Cir. 2003), *Detroit Terrazzo Contractors Assoc. v. Board of Trustees of the B.A.C. Local 32 Insurance Fund,* 2003 U.S. App. LEXIS 16284, 30 EBC 2883 (6th Cir. 2003).

Of course, persons who have been convicted of or imprisoned for certain types of crimes are not eligible to serve as fiduciaries of employee benefit plans or to act in certain other capacities with respect to a plan. See ERISA §411(a).

The group or entity that has the power or authority to appoint fiduciaries also has the authority to remove fiduciaries. No reasons need be given but, particularly in situations of labor union reform, dissension or changes in leadership, the constitutional procedures of the labor organization must be followed. See *International Union of Bricklayers and Allied Craftsmen v. Gallante,* 912 F.Supp. 695 (S.D.N.Y. 1996).

Trust agreements customarily provide that, once appointed, fiduciaries are to serve until they die, resign or are removed. There is no limitation in either ERISA or LMRA on the length of time a fiduciary may serve, and there is also no limitation on a trust agreement provision that would provide that fiduciaries serve for a fixed term of years. DOL has, however, indicated its disagreement with plan or trust terms that would effectively allow fiduciaries to serve on a "permanent" basis or for an unlimited term. In Advisory Opinion No. 85-41A (December 5, 1985), DOL stated that it was ". . . generally of the view that a life time term of appointment for a . . . fund trustee would be inconsistent with ERISA's fiduciary responsibility provisions."

The Advisory Opinion also states DOL's view that ". . . the conduct of fiduciaries should be subject to effective oversight on behalf of plan participants and beneficiaries." Indeed, in a lawsuit seeking relief from breach of fiduciary duties, a federal court has authority under Section 409(a) of ERISA to order the removal of a fiduciary.

DISCLOSURES CONCERNING REASONS FOR REMOVAL

When fiduciaries of an employee benefit plan resign or are removed, the reasons for the resignation or removal or other material information may need to be disclosed, at least to the other fiduciaries, particularly if the information is material to the person's previous service as a fiduciary, and the plan or other fiduciaries are not aware of the information, but need to know it for their own protection. *Glaziers & Glassworkers Union Local No. 252 Annuity Fund,* 93 F.3d 1171 (3rd Cir. 1996), see also *Ream v. Frey,* 20 EBC 2657 (3d Cir. 1997) (a trustee has a fiduciary duty to disclose its reasons for resignation if the resignation and subsequent appointment of a successor trustee could result in potential harm to the beneficiaries of the trust).

In *Ream,* the court also discussed that the resignation of a fiduciary was subject to the fiduciary standard of care of Section 404(a) of ERISA and must also be in accordance with the procedures and requirements stated in the plan documents.

HOW TO RUN A TRUSTEES MEETING

Procedures in the plan and/or trust documents, e.g., procedure for plan amendments (required by ERISA §402(b)(3)), must be reviewed and followed to assure proper trustee action *and* as a matter of fiduciary responsibility under ERISA §404(a)(l)(D) (fiduciaries must discharge their duties "in accordance with the documents and instruments governing the plan").

The trustees should generally meet at least quarterly, see Consent Order with Eighth District Electrical Workers Pension Fund, entered on April 4, 2002, in *Chao v. Legino,* (D.Oreg.), at part II H, or otherwise as required by the terms of the plan and trust documents.

Agenda/Planning

- Notices of regular meetings
- Notices of specially called meetings

Parliamentary Procedure

A fund trust agreement will usually specify a quorum, i.e., the number of fiduciaries who are required to be in attendance at a meeting so that valid action can be taken, sometimes in terms of the minimum number of trustees, subject to a requirement of equal representation. Example: A board of trustees consists of eight members, four appointed by employers and four by union. The required quorum could consist of at least four trustees present in person, provided there are at least two employer trustees and two union trustees present.

If a quorum is not present, a meeting may still proceed, but any action taken is subject to ratification (approval) by the absent trustees. As with corporations, a trust agreement can also provide that trustees can act without a meeting, if they do so by unanimous written consent.

What happens if a proper quorum is present at the start of a meeting but, before the end of the meeting, one or more trustees must leave? *Robert's Rules of Order* (9th edition), suggests in §39 that the meeting cannot continue further at that point and is subject to adjournment if a member/trustee raises the question by means of a point of order or else business could continue, but any decisions would be subject to ratification by the other trustees.

Privileged motions—which are always in order:
- Lay on the table (*Roberts*, §17)
- Recess (*Roberts*, §20)
- Adjourn (*Roberts*, §21)
- To fix the time to which to adjourn (*Roberts*, §22).

Who Should Attend Trustees Meetings? Who Can Attend?

- Plan participants (active and/or retired)?
- Nontrustee representatives of unions and employers?
- Service providers?

The trustees should consider adoption of a statement of policy on attendance at meetings (see example included as an appendix to this chapter).

Protection of Attorney-Client Privilege

When legal advice is given, particularly on current or anticipated litigation, the meeting should be limited to only the clients, i.e., the fiduciaries, in an executive session, and the matters discussed should not be disclosed in the regular meeting minutes. Some form of minutes or a summary should be prepared and retained by the attorney.

Trustees' Obligation of Monitoring and Oversight

The fiduciaries of an employee benefit plan can delegate administrative authority to either designated fiduciaries, such as an investment manager or to nonfiduciaries, subject to a requirement of regular monitoring, oversight and reports by either the full board of trustees or a designated committee. Delegation of authority is not abandonment; the delegating fiduciaries must be aware of what is going on and have an ongoing duty to monitor the actions of appointed fiduciaries.

In the view of DOL, a benefit plan must establish, implement and maintain internal controls and procedures so that plan fiduciaries will, on a regular and ongoing basis, monitor and evaluate all services rendered to the plan, the performance of each service provider, and the compensation arrangements for such services, and also review and monitor the conduct of the plan's trustees. Consent Order, *supra*, at parts II D and I.

Voting

The procedure for voting should be specified in the plan documents and, once specified, must be followed in order to assure proper decisions and as a matter of fiduciary responsibility under ERISA §404(a)(l)(D).

The most common types of actions taken by boards of trustees are plan amendments. Even though they may not be regarded as fiduciary actions (see the discussion of the "settlor function" rule, supra), in order to be valid they must be in written form and the approval process "must be conducted" in accord with the terms of the plan documents, e.g., *Depenbrock v. CIGNA Corp.*, 389 F.3d 78 (3d Cir. 2004); *Curtiss-Wright Corp. v. Schoonejongen*, 514 U.S. 713 (1995).

Thus, oral or informal amendments to employee benefit plans are ineffective and the notice requirements of either the plan documents or ERISA must be satisfied, e.g., the last sentence of ERISA §104(b)(1) now requires that if there is a modification to the terms of a welfare benefit plan that ". . . is a material reduction in covered services or benefits" then a written summary description of the modification or change must be given to the plan's participants not later than 60 days after the date of adoption of the modification or change. Similarly, ERISA §204(h) requires "reasonable" advance written notice of amendments to pension plans that will cause significant reductions in the rate of future benefit accruals.

Improperly authorized plan amendments generally cannot be ratified by subsequent acts. *Depenbrock, supra*. Similarly, plan amendments cannot be applied on a retroactive basis where the effect of the amendment would be to reduce the intervening rights of third parties, such as plan participants. *id.*

Common plan provisions on voting may include a prohibition of proxy voting and a limitation that official action can be taken only by a majority vote of the trustees present at a meeting for which there was a proper quorum and for which proper notice was given.

Some plan documents may require that specific advance notice be given if certain types of action will be discussed at a meeting, e.g., plan or trust amendments.

The LMRA requirement of "equal representation" of labor and management on joint boards of trustees has generally been construed to mean or require that each group of trustees must have *equal voting power* even if there are not *equal numbers* of trustees present. In other words, each side should have "veto power" on any proposed action. *Associated Contractors of Essex County, Inc., v. LIUNA,* 559 F.2d 222 (3d Cir. 1977). For example, board of trustees consists of eight members, four appointed by employers and four by union. Quorum requires that at least four trustees be present in person, provided there are at least two employer trustees and two union trustees present. Trust agreement provides that each group of trustees has equal voting power and can cast an equal number of *votes,* even if an equal *number* of trustees is not present. If four employer trustees and two union trustees were present, then each employer trustee could cast a vote with a weight of one and each union trustee could cast a vote with a weight of two.

An alternative procedure is called *unit voting.* Under this type of arrangement, each group of trustees can caucus, decide how to vote and then, as a group, cast a single vote. The vote of each group is determined by a majority vote of the individual trustees within each group and official action can be taken only if there is a unanimous vote by each group of trustees.

In Advisory Opinion 92-11A (March 31, 1992), DOL ruled that a unit voting procedure such as that discussed above was not in violation of ERISA, since there is nothing in ERISA §§403(a) or 404(a)(1) "which expressly prohibits or limits the exercise of any particular method of decision making by plan trustees." DOL expressly stated, however, that the fiduciaries ". . . should be aware that compliance with unit voting procedures will not operate to relieve individual trustees of liability . . . in any particular instance," under ERISA §§403(a) or 404(a)(l).

DOL also discussed the issue of possible co-fiduciary liability under ERISA §405(a) and noted that under ERISA §410 ". . . provisions in a plan document that purport to relieve a fiduciary from responsibility or liability under the fiduciary responsibility provisions of Title I of ERISA are void as against public policy."

Trustee Recusal From Voting

From time to time, individual trustees may encounter situations where their own personal or business interests may be in conflict with their fiduciary responsibility under ERISA §404(a)(1) to act "solely in the interest of the [plan] participants and beneficiaries" and may place them in situations of potential prohibited transactions under ERISA §§406(b)(1)-(3).

In these types of situations, DOL regulations provide that a trustee can avoid prohibited transaction issues by "removing him or herself from all consideration" of the particular issue or transaction and "by not otherwise exercising" any fiduciary authority, control or responsibility. 29 CFR §2550.408b-2(e).

In an Information Letter to William Lindsay issued on February 23, 2005, DOL also pointed out, however, that if a plan trustee who has recused himself or herself "has material information" concerning a particular transaction "that would be necessary in order for other plan fiduciaries to make an appropriate and prudent decision," then the recused fiduciary's duties under ERISA §404 "would require informing the deciding fiduciaries" of that information.

If Trustees Cannot Reach Agreement, What Steps Should Dissenting Trustees Take?

In Advisory Opinion 92-11A (March 31, 1992), DOL pointed out that ". . . the steps minority trustees must take to protect themselves from liability under [ERISA] sections 409 and 405(b)l(A). . . ." are discussed in 29 CFR §2509.75-5, FR-10, and that those steps ". . . would be relevant regardless of whether plan documents provide for decision making by majority vote or unit voting."

In 29 CFR §2509.75-5, at FR-10, DOL considered a situation where "a majority of the trustees appear ready to take action which would clearly be contrary to the prudence requirement of ERISA §404(a)(l)(B)." In such a situation, it is the view of DOL that:

> . . . it is incumbent on the minority trustees to take all reasonable and legal steps to prevent the action. Such steps might include preparations to obtain an injunction from a Federal District court under section 502(a)(3) of the Act, to notify the Labor Department, or to publicize the vote if the decision is to proceed as proposed. If, having taken all reasonable and legal steps to prevent the imprudent action, the minority trustees have not succeeded, they will not incur liability for the action of the majority. Mere resignation, however, without taking steps to prevent the imprudent action, will not suffice to avoid liability for the minority trustees once they have knowledge that the imprudent action is under consideration.

More generally, trustees should take great care to document adequately all meetings where actions are taken with respect to management and control of plan assets. Written minutes of all actions taken should be kept describing the action taken, and stating how each trustee voted on each matter. If, as in the case above, trustees object to a proposed action on the grounds of possible violation of the fiduciary responsibility provisions of the act, the trustees so objecting should insist that their objections and the responses to such objections be included in the record of the meeting. It should be noted that, where a trustee believes that a co-trustee has already committed a breach, resignation by the trustee as a protest against such breach will not generally be considered sufficient to discharge the trustee's positive duty under Section 405(a)(3) to make reasonable efforts under the circumstances to remedy the breach.

All fiduciaries must be aware that abstention from voting or resignation will not protect an individual from potential liability for actions taken or decisions made while the individual was serving as a fiduciary. See ERISA §405(d)(2). If a trustee seriously disagrees with action that was taken by the majority, the trustee should consider how to fulfill his or her co-fiduciary responsibilities or should resign. ERISA §409(b) expressly states that "[n]o fiduciary shall be liable with respect to a breach of fiduciary duty . . . if such breach was committed before he became a fiduciary or after he ceased to be a fiduciary."

Can Trustees Be Compensated for Service as Trustees?

Under ERISA §408(c)(3), an individual may serve as a fiduciary in addition to being an officer, employee, agent or other representative of a party in interest.

If a fiduciary of an employee benefit plan "already receives full-time pay" from an employer, employer association or union whose employees or members are participants in an employee benefit plan, then such a fiduciary *cannot* receive compensation from the plan for service as a fiduciary, *but* can receive ". . . reimbursement of expenses properly and actually incurred in the performance of his duties with the plan; . . ." ERISA §408(c)(2).

If a fiduciary does not "already receive full-time pay" from an employer, employer association or union involved with the plan, then such a fiduciary can receive "reasonable compensation for services rendered."

If fiduciaries are hourly paid employees who have to miss work to attend plan meetings and, therefore, will lose pay for periods when they are serving as a fiduciary, they can receive reimbursement from the plan for identifiable lost wages, in addition to reimbursement of expenses. See DOL Advisory Opinions 76-03 and 76-57 (1976).

USE OF COMMITTEES

Scope of Permissible Delegation to Committees

The ability of the full board of trustees to delegate authority to either individual fiduciaries or to committees consisting of appointed members of the full board must be provided for in the plan documents. ERISA §§403(b)(2) and 405(c)(1).

If the plan document "expressly provides" for the delegation or allocation of fiduciary responsibilities "among named fiduciaries," then ERISA §405(c)(2) states that, if any fiduciary responsibility is allocated to another person, such as investment manager who meets the requirements of ERISA §3(38), by a named fiduciary, . . . then such named fiduciary shall not be liable for an act or omission of such person in carrying out such responsibility except to the extent that—

(A) the named fiduciary violated Section 1104(a)(1) of this title—
  (i) with respect to such allocation or designation,
  (ii) with respect to the establishment or implementation of the [allocation] procedure . . . , or
  (iii) in continuing the allocation or designation; or
(B) the named fiduciary would otherwise be liable in accordance with subsection (a) of this section.

See also 29 CFR §2509.75-8 at FR-12 to FR-17.

To avoid fiduciary liability concerns, the delegating fiduciaries must monitor the activities of the appointed fiduciary on a regular basis so as to be certain that the delegated functions are being properly performed.

Should the Officers of the Board of Trustees Attend All Committee Meetings?

Yes, but if officers of a plan are not designated members of committees, they should attend the meetings only for purposes of obtaining information and participating in discussion, not for voting.

What Types of Reports Need to Go to the Full Board of Trustees?

If the delegation or assignment to a committee is to study a certain issue or make a recommendation to the full board of trustees, e.g., claim appeals or termination of an investment manager, then the committee should report its recommendations with reasons to the full board of trustees for its concurrence or disagreement.

If the delegation or assignment to a committee is to make a decision on a particular issue, then the committee should report its decision to the full board of trustees, preferably in the form of approved minutes from its meeting(s).

If the delegation or assignment to a committee is to monitor or have oversight over certain service providers, e.g., investment managers, hospital precertification providers, etc., the committee should provide a report to the full board of trustees on its activities with any recommendations that are thought to be necessary. The full board can accept the report and take action on any recommendations.

MINUTES OF MEETINGS

What Must or Should Be Included?

Minutes are intended to be a brief statement of what occurred at a meeting, not a transcript of all that was said by every person on every topic. In the view of DOL, minutes are to be prepared in written form and are to provide "a complete and accurate report of what transpired at each meeting, including all persons present, presentations made, opinions presented, discussions held, and votes taken." Consent Order, *supra,* at part II H.

The general rule with respect to minutes of corporate meetings, e.g., board of directors or shareholders, is that minutes are prima facie evidence of what they purport to show as to business transacted at a meeting, but they are by no means conclusive. In order to avoid possible ambiguity or subsequent dispute, it is good practice, when feasible, to have all persons participating in the meeting sign the minutes to acknowledge their approval or to have the written minutes of a meeting prepared and distributed in advance of the next meeting and then have them reviewed and approved as one of the first items of business of the next meeting. See, generally, W. M. Fletcher, *Cyclopedia on the Law of Private Corporations* (Perm. Ed.) at §3:23.

What About Tape Recordings of Meetings?

Tape recordings are not required. If they are allowed, they should be utilized only as a reference source to assist in preparation of written minutes. After the written minutes have been prepared and approved, any tape recordings should be destroyed. If this procedure is adopted, it is essential that the tapes be destroyed on a regular basis. Otherwise, in the event of litigation the tapes are subject to discovery and can be utilized as evidence, particularly to the extent that issues are raised with respect to the trustees' intent or motivation in taking certain actions. E.g., *Walker v. Board of Trustees,* 2003 U.S. App. LEXIS 14603 at **25-**29, 31 EBC 1706 (10th Cir. 2003) (finding transcripts prepared from tapes of meetings admissible on issue of whether trustees of a governmental pension plan had acted "willfully and wantonly").

Can Participants Obtain Disclosure of Minutes of Trustees Meetings?

Under ERISA §104(b)(2), the administrator of a plan, i.e., the joint board of trustees in the case of a multiemployer plan, see ERISA §3(16)(B)(iii), must make copies of the following documents available *for examination* "by any plan participant" without charge:

- Plan description
- Latest annual report
- Latest bargaining agreement
- Trust agreement
- Contract
- "Other instruments under which the plan was established or is operated."

ERISA §104(b)(4) requires that the administrator of a plan must, upon the *written* request of any participant, *also furnish copies* of the following documents to the participant, subject to "a reasonable charge to cover the cost of furnishing complete copies" (not more than $.25 per page under DOL regulations 29 CFR §2520.104b-30(b)):

- Latest updated SPD
- Plan description
- Latest annual report
- Any terminal report
- Bargaining agreement
- Trust agreement
- Contracts
- "Other instruments under which the plan is established or operated."

Failure to respond to a participant's written request within 30 days can subject a plan administrator to *personal* liability for payment of a civil penalty in an amount of up to $100 per day and such other relief as a court "deems proper" under ERISA §§502(a)(l)(A) and 502(c)(2), as well as a possible award of reasonable attorney fees and costs under ERISA §502(g)(l).

The types of plan documents that *must* be provided to participants upon request have been held to include items such as plan actuarial valuation reports, *Bartling v. Fruehauf Corp.,* 29 F.3d 1062 (6th Cir. 1994), and charts needed for the calculation of amounts of retirement benefits, *Lee v. Dayton Power and Light Co.,* 604 F.Supp. 987 (S.D.Ohio 1985), but to *not* include copies of minutes of trustees meetings or prior decisions of the trustees. *Chambless v. Masters, Mates & Pilots Pension Plan,* 571 F.Supp. 1430 (S.D.N.Y. 1983). See also DOL Advisory Opinions 82-21A (April 21, 1982) and 82-33A (July 21, 1982), both of which state that minutes of trustees meeting are not required to be produced under ERISA §104(b)(4), unless the minutes themselves became an instrument under which the plan was established or operated, e.g., if the minutes of a meeting established a claims procedure.

In Advisory Opinion 96-14A (July 31, 1996), DOL stated that, under ERISA §104(b)(2), participants "should have access to documents that directly affect their benefit entitlement under an employee benefit plan" such as a schedule of "usual and customary" fees for medical procedures. Therefore, DOL ruled that participants in a welfare benefit plan were entitled to request copies of:

> . . . any document or instrument that specifies procedures, formulas, methodologies, or schedules to

be applied in determining or calculating a participant's or beneficiary's benefit entitlement under an employee benefit plan..., regardless of whether such information is contained in a document designated as the "plan document."

However, in the case of *Board of Trustees of the CWA/ITU Negotiated Pension Plan v. Weinstein,* 107 F.3d 139 (2d Cir. 1997), the court held that the reasoning of DOL Advisory Opinion 96-14A was not persuasive and that a plan participant was not entitled to demand production of copies of a pension plan's actuarial reports.

Similarly, in DOL Advisory Opinion Letter 97-11A (April 10, 1997), DOL ruled that, generally, plan participants are not entitled to demand production of copies of a plan's contract with its third-party administrator.

ARBITRATION OF TRUSTEE DISPUTES

Required Under Section 302(c)(5)(B) of LMRA, But Not Under ERISA

LMRA Section 302(c)(5)(B) provides that if the employer and employee trustee groups "deadlock on the administration" of a fund, they may, but are not required to, seek arbitration.

Arbitration can be had only over issues of "administration" that the trustees have authority under the plan documents to decide. *Hodges v. Holzer,* 707 F.Supp. 232 (M.D.La. 1988) (court could not appoint an umpire to arbitrate a dispute among trustees of an ERISA benefit fund over whether local fund should merge with an international fund because, under trust agreement, power of trustees to agree to a merger was conditioned upon approval of union and employer association). If, however, the board of trustees does not have authority to perform a certain act, e.g., amendment of a trust agreement, arbitration cannot be compelled on such an issue. *Employee Trustees of the Eighth District Electrical Pension Fund v. Employer Trustees of the Eighth District Electrical Pension Fund,* 959 F.2d 176 (10th Cir. 1992).

Avoid Arbitration by Adding a Permanent "Neutral" Trustee?

Expressly permitted under LMRA, not prohibited by ERISA.

CONCLUSION

The proper and orderly conduct of business at trustees meetings is vital to both the best interests of plan participants and beneficiaries and protection of plan trustees from allegations of breach of their fiduciary responsibilities.

APPENDIX

STATEMENT OF POLICY ON PARTICIPANT ATTENDANCE AT MEETINGS OF BOARDS OF TRUSTEES AND COMMITTEES

1. The meetings of the boards of trustees and of committees of the boards of trustees are private business meetings, not public meetings.

2. Attendance at meetings of the boards of trustees is generally limited to only the members of the boards of trustees, the funds' administrative staff and the trustees' professional advisors.

3. The business matters discussed at meetings of the boards of trustees generally involve discussion of confidential financial, claim and legal issues. Therefore, participants in the benefits funds, as well as representatives of signatory employers, are not permitted to attend the meetings as observers.

4. Unless it is necessary for proper discussion of particular issues, service providers such as investment managers, performance monitors, auditors, should attend only that portion of a meeting which is necessary for presentation of their report.

5. Upon advance written request submitted to the funds' administrator that identifies the participant's interest in a particular issue or subject, a participant may be allowed to attend a specific meeting of a board of trustees for the portion of the meeting that involves discussion and/or consideration of the particular issue or subject. When they are permitted to attend a meeting, participants are in the status of an observer and, unless specifically requested to do so by the chairman of the board of trustees, are not permitted to ask questions, to participate in discussions, or to vote on any matter.

6. Participants are not permitted to attend any meetings of committee of the boards of trustees, except for meetings of the Claim Appeals Committee where a participant has made an advance request to the funds' administrator to make a personal appearance before the committee concerning his or her own appeal. If a personal appearance is permitted, the participant's attendance shall be limited to the time that is necessary for making of a personal presentation of the appeal to the committee and for answering any questions that members of the committee and/or the trustees' advisors may have.

7. The boards of trustees, through the chairmen of each board and of each committee, reserve the right to reject any or all requests for attendance at meetings of the board of trustees or committees.

8. This Statement of Policy may be amended or rescinded at any time by action of the Board of Trustees.

Chapter 50

Required Trustee Action Where Trustees Don't Agree on a Decision

Vivian C. Folk

INTRODUCTION

From time to time, trustees don't agree on a course of action. This is often healthy, prompting additional dialogue, debate and compromise—leading to good decision making. In rare circumstances, however, a deadlock results. Or a dissenting trustee honestly believes that the majority of trustees have taken action that violates their fiduciary responsibilities to the plan they represent.

Trustees placed in this sensitive position invariably ask about their responsibilities.

DISCUSSION

Discretion vs. Responsibility

At the risk of oversimplification, there are two types of decisions made by trustees: discretionary decisions and those decisions where particular results are mandated by the fiduciary responsibility or other provisions of applicable law.

Discretionary decisions are *fence sitters,* those decisions that could have different results without violating law. For example, should we hire this well-qualified individual to be our administrative manager, or should we hire another well-qualified individual? If the trust and other plan documents declare the trust settlors' intent that the trustees be vested with broad discretion, courts will not interfere with trustees' judgment. The only exception is where the trustees' decision is "arbitrary or capricious" or an "abuse of discretion."[1] Because there is broad latitude in discretionary decision making, the dissenting trustee's actions and reactions should be much different than where the trustee believes a particular course of action would violate applicable law.

An example of fiduciary responsibility and other nondiscretionary decision making is furnished in Department of Labor regulations:

FR-10 Q: An employee benefit plan is considering the construction of a building to house the administration of the plan. One trustee has proposed that the building be constructed on a cost plus basis by a particular contractor without competitive bidding. When the trustee was questioned by another trustee as to the basis of choice of the contract, the impact of the building on the plan's administrative costs, whether a cost plus contract would yield a better price to the plan than a fixed price basis, and why a negotiated contract would be better than letting the contract for competitive bidding, no satisfactory answers were provided.[2]

In such circumstances, where possible violation of law is an issue, the dissenting trustee must be concerned with co-fiduciary liability.

Co-Fiduciary Liability

Under ERISA Section 405(a), a fiduciary is responsible for another fiduciary's breach if:

- He participates knowingly, or knowingly undertakes to conceal, an act or omission of such other fiduciary, knowing such act or omission is a breach (participation violation)
- By his failure to comply with Section 405(a)(1) . . . in the administration of his specific responsibilities which give rise to his status as a fiduciary, he has enabled such other fiduciary to commit a breach (enablement violation)
- He has knowledge of a breach by such other fiduciary, unless he makes reasonable efforts under the circumstances to remedy the breach (guilty knowledge violation).[3]

Co-fiduciary liability will generally be determined based on whether the trustee addresses the decision directly, or whether the trustee attempts to run and hide from the decision-making process. Inaction will result in co-fiduciary liability.[4] By contrast, and as stated by the Department of Labor:

> If, having *taken all reasonable* and legal *steps* to prevent the imprudent action, the minority trustees have not succeeded, they will not incur liability for the action of the majority.[5]

In short, neither the courts nor the Department of Labor will tolerate a co-fiduciary's abdication of responsibility, by inaction or otherwise.

Documenting Decision Making, Through Minutes and Otherwise

Where a question arises as to whether a decision is legal or appropriate, the minutes are almost invariably consulted for decisions made by the trustees and the rationale for such decisions. Where a trustee disagrees with a decision, he or she should make certain his or her dissenting vote and reasons are reflected in the minutes. The Department of Labor has made this clear in regulations:

> Trustees should take great care to document adequately all meetings where actions are taken with respect to management and control of plan assets. Written minutes of all actions taken should be kept, describing the action taken, and stating how each trustee voted on each matter. If . . . trustees object to a proposed action on the grounds of possible violation of the fiduciary responsibility provisions of the Act, the trustees so objecting should insist that their objections and the responses to such objections be included *in the record of the meeting.*[6]

The dissenting trustee should insist that the minutes provide a "full and complete" record of the trustee meeting.

The trustee should make certain that:
- The minutes reflect the *date, time* and *place* at which the meeting was called to order.
- The minutes state *who was present* for the meeting—trustees and other persons present (e.g., administrative manager, certified public accountant, investment manager, consultant and counsel).
- The minutes state whether a *quorum* existed to conduct all business to come before the board of trustees.
- The minutes reflect *each and every topic* that was discussed at the meeting.
- In regard to each and every topic discussed, the minutes answer the following questions—*who, what, when, where* and *why.* For example, *who* gave the report on investments? *What* course of action did the investment manager recommend? *What* questions did the trustees ask the investment manager about his recommendation? *Why* did the trustees decide to adopt the investment manager's recommendation? By asking who, what, when, where and why, you create a record, establishing that the trustees' decisions are based on a thorough decision-making process consistent with ERISA's prudent man rule.
- Motions that are made should be stated with completeness and accuracy.

Where minutes are inadequate, incomplete or inaccurate, the dissenting trustee should note his or her proposed changes and additions in writing and communicate them. This will help protect the trustee if there are subsequent legal proceedings.

Arbitration

Section 302 of the Taft-Hartley Act contains guidelines for resolving disputes where there is a "deadlock" in the "administration" of the fund. That section provides:

> in the event the employer and employee groups *deadlock* on the *administration* of such fund . . . the two groups shall agree on an impartial umpire to decide such dispute, or in the event of their failure to agree within a reasonable length of time, an impartial umpire to decide such disputes shall, on petition of either group, be appointed by the District Court of the United States for the District where the Trust Fund has its principal office . . . (emphasis added)[7]

Your plan's trust agreement should contain provisions on deadlock consistent with the Taft-Hartley Act, and you should consult those provisions.

Not every deadlocked dispute is subject to arbitration—only those suits involving a plan's "administration." The term *administration* has been construed as being limited to day-to-day practical questions.[8] The term has been interpreted as excluding, however, legal disputes and issues.[9] Accordingly, issues regarding breach of ERISA's fiduciary responsibility provisions would fall outside the Taft-Hartley Act's arbitration provision.

Even if a deadlocked dispute is subject to arbitration, I encourage trustees to resolve their disputes without recourse to an arbitrator. Trustees have a better understanding of the management and administration of their plans than an arbitrator who is an "outsider." More importantly, the hard feelings that can remain from a hard-fought arbitration can affect trustees' relations and plan management for years to come. Disputes are best resolved by the trustees themselves.

Litigation and Other Action

Fiduciary violations and other legal issues must generally be determined by the courts or in another forum. Using the example recited earlier in this article of awarding a contract without competitive bidding, the Department of Labor provided the following guidance:

> Several of the trustees have argued that letting such a contract would be a violation of their general fiduciary responsibilities. Despite their arguments, a majority of the trustees appear to be ready to vote to construct the building as proposed. What should the minority trustees do to protect themselves from liability under section 409(a) of the Act and section 405(b)(1)(A) of the Act?
>
> A: Here, where a majority of trustees appear ready to take action which would clearly be contrary to the prudence requirements of section 404(a)(1)(B) of the Act, it is incumbent on the minority trustees to take all reasonable and legal steps to prevent the action. Such steps might include preparations to obtain an injunction from a Federal District court under section 502(a)(3) of the Act, to notify the Labor Department, or to publicize the vote if the decision is to proceed as proposed.[10]

The courts agree with the Department of Labor that trustees must from time to time challenge fiduciary conduct in a judicial proceeding.[11]

Resignation as a Trustee

There is some temptation, when faced with actions with which we don't agree, to simply walk away from the situation. But the Department of Labor has suggested that trustees generally cannot avoid liability by resignation:

> Mere resignation, however, without taking steps to prevent the imprudent action, will not suffice to avoid liability for the minority trustees once they have knowledge that the imprudent action is under consideration.[12]

In fact, such resignation might be construed as inconsistent with the trustees' duty to remedy the breach:

> It should be noted that, where a trustee believes that a trustee has already committed a breach, resignation by the trustee as a protest against such breach will not generally be considered sufficient to discharge the trustee's positive duty under section 405(a)(3) to make reasonable efforts under the circumstances to remedy the breach.[13]

In short, resigning may create additional liability.

Where a trustee resigns with no successor, an additional breach of fiduciary responsibility may result. Having accepted the appointment as trustee, that trustee cannot simply walk away without adequate provision for successors and management of plan affairs.[14]

CONCLUSION

Much of the satisfaction of serving as a trustee can be derived from the lively dialogue, debate and give and take among fellow trustees of prudent trustee decision-making processes. Occasionally, however, an economic motive, or bargaining or other hidden agenda can threaten to derail a prudent decision-making process. Strong views can prompt deadlock in the administration of a plan's affairs. In rare circumstances, the trustees' compliance with ERISA's fiduciary responsibility provisions or other law is an issue.

In deciding how to react to a dispute, the trustee must determine whether a dispute involves a "discretionary" issue where numerous results are all appropriate, or whether the dispute involves legal issues with fewer acceptable courses of action available. Inaction and/or "flight" are inappropriate and dangerous responses. At a minimum, a trustee must make certain his or her actions and dissent to the action of other fiduciaries are recorded in the minutes or otherwise. In extreme circumstances, a trustee may be required to institute an action for declaratory or injunctive relief.

In most circumstances, however, the same dialogue, debate and give and take among trustees that eventually leads to good decision making will also eventually prompt a resolution of the trustee dispute.

ENDNOTES

1. *Firestone Tire and Rubber Co. v. Bruch,* 489 U.S. 101, 109 S.Ct. 948, 103 L.Ed. 2d 80 (1989).
2. 29 CFR §2509.75-5, FR-10.
3. 29 U.S.C. §1105.
4. *Free v. Briody,* 732 F.2d 1331 (7th Cir. 1984). See also *Tittle v. Enron Corp. (In re Enron Corp. Sec. Derivative & ERISA Litig.),* 284 F.Supp. 2d 511, 2003 U.S. Dist. LEXIS 17492, 31 Employee Benefits Cas. (BNA) 2281 (S.D.Tex. 2003) (co-fiduciaries' failure to inform plan fiduciaries about employer's actual financial status and/or failure to monitor fiduciaries); *Kling v. Fid. Mgmt. Trust Co.,* 323 F.Supp. 2d 132, 2004 U.S. Dist. LEXIS 12634, 33 Employee Benefits Cas. (BNA) 1035 (D.Mass. 2004) (directed trustee may be liable for failing to disclose material information to plan fiduciaries and participants regarding imprudence of investing in company stock).
5. 29 CFR §2509.75-5, FR-10.
6. Id.
7. 29 U.S.C. §186(c)(5).
8. *Mahoney v. Fisher,* 277 F.2d 5 (2d Cir. 1960) (question was whether present or former broker could be paid $600 compensation for services). See also *Bueno v. Gill,* 237 F.Supp. 2d 447, 2002 U.S. Dist. LEXIS 22206, 29 Employee Benefits Cas. (BNA) 1932 (S.D.N.Y. 2004) (issues are not arbitrable where they are outside the trustees' power, absent amendment of the plan's trust agreement).
9. See *Bath v. Pixler,* 283 F.Supp. 632, at 635 (D.C.Colo. 1968) ("The dispute among the trustees is a legal controversy, not a dispute over the practical administration of the trust.")

10. 29 CFR §2509.75-5, FR-10.

11. *Cf. Modern Woodcrafts, Inc. v. Hawley,* 534 F.Supp. 1000 (D.Conn. 1982). See also *Weiler v. Lapkof,* 2002 U.S. Dist. LEXIS 23485, 29 Employee Benefits Cas. (BNA) 2219 (N.D.Ill. Dec. 5, 2002) (Trustees have standing to sue original plan's trustees for failing to credit split-off plan with demutualization compensation).

12. 29 CFR §2509.75-5, FR-10.

13. *Id.*

14. See, e.g., *Freund et al. v. Marshall & Ilsley Bank et al. and Marshall v. R.W. DeKeyser et al.,* 485 F.Supp. 629 (W.D.Wisc. 1979); *Usery v. Conser et al.* No. C77-61, *sub nom Marshall v. Conser et al.* (N.D.Oh. March 2, 1977); *Lane v. Marshall,* Civ. Action No. 779-0868, ____ F.Supp. ____ (N.D.Cal. 1979).

APPENDIX A

SECTIONS OF EMPLOYEE RETIREMENT INCOME SECURITY ACT OF 1974

Title I – Protection of Employee Benefit Rights

Subtitle A – General Provisions

SEC. 3. DEFINITIONS.

For purposes of this title:

(1) The terms "employee welfare benefit plan" and "welfare plan" mean any plan, fund, or program which was heretofore or is hereafter established or maintained by an employer or by an employee organization, or by both, to the extent that such plan, fund, or program was established or is maintained for the purpose of providing for its participants or their beneficiaries, through the purchase of insurance or otherwise, (A) medical, surgical, or hospital care or benefits, or benefits in the event of sickness, accident, disability, death or unemployment, or vacation benefits, apprenticeship or other training programs, or day care centers, scholarship funds, or prepaid legal services, or (B) any benefit described in §302(c) of the Labor Management Relations Act, 1947 (other than pensions on retirement or death, and insurance to provide such pensions).

(2)(A) Except as provided in subparagraph (B), the terms "employee pension benefit plan" and "pension plan" mean any plan, fund, or program which was heretofore or is hereafter established or maintained by an employer or by an employee organization, or by both, to the extent that by its express terms or as a result of surrounding circumstances such plan, fund, or program—

    (i) provides retirement income to employees, or

    (ii) results in a deferral of income by employees for periods extending to the termination of covered employment or beyond,

regardless of the method of calculating the contributions made to the plan, the method of calculating the benefits under the plan or the method of distributing benefits from the plan.

(B) The Secretary may by regulation prescribe rules consistent with the standards and purposes of this Act providing one or more exempt categories under which—

    (i) severance pay arrangements, and

    (ii) supplemental retirement income payments, under which the pension benefits of retirees or their beneficiaries are supplemented to take into account some portion or all of the increases in the cost of living (as determined by the Secretary of Labor) since retirement,

shall, for purposes of this title, be treated as welfare plans rather than pension plans. In the case of any arrangement or payment a principal effect of which is the evasion of the standards or purposes of this Act applicable to pension plans, such arrangement or payment shall be treated as a pension plan.

(3) The term "employee benefit plan" or "plan" means an employee welfare benefit plan or an employee pension benefit plan or a plan which is both an employee welfare benefit plan and an employee pension benefit plan.

* * *

(14) The term "party in interest" means, as to an employee benefit plan—

(A) any fiduciary (including, but not limited to, any administrator, officer, trustee, or custodian), counsel, or employee of such employee benefit plan;

(B) a person providing services to such plan;

(C) an employer any of whose employees are covered by such plan;

(D) an employee organization any of whose members are covered by such plan;

(E) an owner, direct or indirect, of 50 percent or more of—

(i) the combined voting power of all classes of stock entitled to vote or the total value of shares of all classes of stock of a corporation,

(ii) the capital interest or the profits interest of a partnership; or

(iii) the beneficial interest of a trust or unincorporated enterprise,

which is an employer of an employee organization described in subparagraph (C) or (D);

(F) a relative (as defined in paragraph (15)) of any individual described in subparagraph (A), (B), (C), or (E);

(G) a corporation, partnership, or trust or estate of which (or in which) 50 percent or more of—

(i) the combined voting power of all classes of stock entitled to vote or the total value of shares of all classes of stock of such corporation,

(ii) the capital interest or profits interest of such partnership, or

(iii) the beneficial interest of such trust or estate,

is owned directly or indirectly, or held by persons described in subparagraph (A), (B), (C), (D), or (E);

(H) an employee, officer, director (or an individual having powers or responsibilities similar to those of officers or directors), or a 10 percent or more shareholder directly or indirectly, of a person described in subparagraph (B), (C), (D), (E), or (G), or of the employee benefit plan; or

(I) a 10 percent or more (directly or indirectly in capital or profits) partner or joint venturer of a person described in subparagraph (B), (C), (D), (E), or (G).

The Secretary, after consultation and coordination with the Secretary of the Treasury, may by regulation prescribe a percentage lower than 50 percent for subparagraph (E) and (G) and lower than 10 percent for subparagraph (H) or (I). The Secretary may prescribe regulations for determining the ownership (direct or indirect) of profits and beneficial interests, and the manner in which indirect stockholdings are taken into account. Any person who is a party in interest with respect to a plan to which a trust described in §501(c)(22) of the Internal Revenue Code of 1954 is permitted to make payments under §4223 shall be treated as a party in interest with respect to such trust.

(15) The term "relative" means a spouse, ancestor, lineal descendant, or spouse of a lineal descendant.

(16)(A) The term "administrator" means—

(i) the person specifically so designated by the terms of the instrument under which the plan is operated;

(ii) if an administrator is not so designated, the plan sponsor; or

(iii) in the case of a plan for which an administrator is not designated and a plan sponsor cannot be identified, such other person as the Secretary may by regulation prescribe.

(B) The term "plan sponsor" means—

(i) the employer in the case of an employee benefit plan established or maintained by a single employer,

(ii) the employee organization in the case of a plan established or maintained by an employee organization, or

(iii) in the case of a plan established or maintained by two or more employers or jointly by one or more employers and one or more employee organizations, the association, committee, joint board of trustees, or other similar group of representatives of the parties who establish or maintain the plan.

* * *

(21)(A) Except as otherwise provided in subparagraph (B), a person is a fiduciary with respect to a plan to the extent (i) he exercises any discretionary authority or discretionary control respecting management of such plan or exercises any authority or control respecting management or disposition of its assets, (ii) he renders investment advice for a fee or other compensation, direct or indirect, with respect to any moneys or other property of such plan, or has any authority or responsibility to do so, or (iii) he has any discretionary authority or discretionary responsibility in the administration of such plan. Such term includes any person designated under §405(c)(1)(B).

(B) If any money or other property of an employee benefit plan is invested in securities issued by an investment company registered under the Investment Company Act of 1940, such investment shall not by itself cause such investment company or such investment company's investment adviser or principal underwriter to be deemed to be a fiduciary or a party in interest as those terms are defined in this title, except insofar as such investment company or its investment adviser or principal underwriter acts in connection with an employee benefit plan covering employees of the investment company, the investment adviser, or its principal underwriter. Nothing contained in this subparagraph shall limit the duties imposed on such investment company, investment adviser, or principal underwriter by any other law.

* * *

(38) The term "investment manager" means any fiduciary (other than a trustee or named fiduciary, as defined in §402(a)(2))—

    (A) who has the power to manage, acquire, or dispose of any asset of a plan;

    (B) who is (i) registered as an investment adviser under the Investment Advisers Act of 1940; (ii) is not registered as an investment adviser under such Act by reason of paragraph (1) of §203(A)(a) of such Act, is registered as an investment adviser under the laws of the State (referred to in such paragraph (1)) in which it mains its principal office and place of business, and, at the time the fiduciary last filed the registration form most recently filed by the fiduciary with such State in order to maintain the fiduciary's registration under the laws of such State, also filed a copy of such form with the Secretary; (iii) is a bank, as defined in that Act; or (iv) is an insurance company qualified to perform services described in subparagraph (A) under the laws of more than one State; and

    (C) has acknowledged in writing that he is a fiduciary with respect to the plan.

* * *

SEC. 4. COVERAGE.

(a) Except as provided in subsection (b) or (c) and in §§201, 301, and 401, this title shall apply to any employee benefit plan if it is established or maintained—

    (1) by any employer engaged in commerce or in any industry or activity affecting commerce; or

    (2) by any employee organization or organizations representing employees engaged in commerce or in any industry or activity affecting commerce; or

    (3) by both.

(b) The provisions of this title shall not apply to any employee benefit plan if—

    (1) such plan is a governmental plan (as defined in §3(32));

    (2) such plan is a church plan (as defined in §3(33)) with respect to which no election has been made under §410(d) of the Internal Revenue Code of 1954;

    (3) such plan is maintained solely for the purpose of complying with applicable workmen's compensation laws or unemployment compensation or disability insurance laws;

    (4) such plan is maintained outside of the United States primarily for the benefit of persons substantially all of whom are nonresident aliens; or

    (5) such plan is an excess benefit plan (as defined in §3(36)) and is unfunded.

The provisions of part 7 of subtitle B shall not apply to a health insurance issuer (as defined in §733(b)(2)) solely by reason of health insurance coverage (as defined in §733(b)(1)) provided by such issuer in connection with a group health plan (as defined in §733(a)(1)) if the provisions of this title do not apply to such group health plan.

(c) If a pension plan allows an employee to elect to make voluntary employee contributions to accounts and annuities as provided in §408(q) of the Internal Revenue Code of 1986, such accounts and annuities (and contributions thereto) shall not be treated as part of such plan (or as a separate pension plan) for purposes of any provision of this title other than §403(c), 404, or 405 (relating to administration and enforcement). Such provisions shall apply to such accounts and annuities in a manner similar to their application to a simplified employee pension under §408(k) of the Internal Revenue Code of 1986.

* * *

Subtitle B – Regulatory Provisions

Part 1 – Reporting and Disclosure

SEC. 101. DUTY OF DISCLOSURE AND REPORTING.

(a) **Summary Plan Description and Information to be Furnished to Participants and Beneficiaries.**—The administrator of each employee benefit plan shall cause to be furnished in accordance with §104(b) to each participant covered under the plan and to each beneficiary who is receiving benefits under the plan—

(1) a summary plan description described in §102(a)(1); and

(2) the information described in §§104(b)(3) and 105(a) and (c).

(b) **Plan Description, Modifications and Changes, and Reports to be Filed with Secretary of Labor.**—The administrator shall, in accordance with §104(a), file with the Secretary—

(1) the annual report containing information required by §103;

(2) terminal and supplementary reports as required by subsection (c) of this section.

(c) **Terminal and Supplementary Reports.**—

(1) Each administrator of an employee pension benefit plan which is winding up its affairs (without regard to the number of participants remaining in the plan) shall, in accordance with regulations prescribed by the Secretary, file such terminal reports as the Secretary may consider necessary. A copy of such report shall also be filed with the Pension Benefit Guaranty Corporation.

(2) The Secretary may require terminal reports to be filed with regard to any employee welfare benefit plan which is winding up its affairs in accordance with regulations promulgated by the Secretary.

(3) The Secretary may require that a plan described in paragraph (1) or (2) file a supplementary or terminal report with the annual report in the year such plan is terminated and that a copy of such supplementary or terminal report in the case of a plan described in paragraph (1) be also filed with the Pension Benefit Guaranty Corporation.

(d) **Notice of Failure to Meet Minimum Funding Standards.—**

(1) **In general.—**If an employer maintaining a plan other than a multiemployer plan fails to make a required installment or other payment required to meet the minimum funding standard under §302 to a plan before the 60th day following the due date for such installment or other payment, the employer shall notify each participant and beneficiary (including an alternate payee as defined in §206(d)(3)(K)) of such plan of such failure. Such notice shall be made at such time and in such manner as the Secretary may prescribe.

(2) **Subsection not to apply if waiver pending.—**This subsection shall not apply to any failure if the employer has filed a waiver request under §1083 of this title with respect to the plan year to which the required installment relates, except that if the waiver request is denied, notice under paragraph (1) shall be provided within 60 days after the date of such denial.

(3) **Definitions.—**For purposes of this subsection, the terms "required installment" and "due date" have the same meanings given such terms by §1082(e) of this title.

(e) **Notice of Transfer of Excess Pension Assets to Health Benefits Accounts.—**

(1) **Notice to participants.—**Not later than 60 days before the date of a qualified transfer by an employee pension benefit plan of excess pension assets to a health benefits account, the administrator of the plan shall notify (in such manner as the Secretary may prescribe) each participant and beneficiary under the plan of such transfer. Such notice shall include information with respect to the amount of excess pension assets, the portion to be transferred, the amount of health benefits liabilities expected to be provided with the assets transferred, and the amount of pension benefits of the participant which will be nonforfeitable immediately after the transfer.

(2) **Notice to secretaries, administrator, and employee organizations.—**

(A) In general.—Not later than 60 days before the date of any qualified transfer by an employee pension benefit plan of excess pension assets to a health benefits account, the employer maintaining the plan from which the transfer is made shall provide the Secretary, the Secretary of the Treasury, the administrator, and each employee organization representing participants in the plan a written notice of such transfer. A copy of such notice shall be available for inspection in the principal office the administrator.

(B) Information relating to transfer.—Such notice shall identify the plan from which the transfer is made, the amount of the transfer, a detailed accounting of assets projected to be held by the plan immediately before and immediately after the transfer, and the current liabilities under the plan at the time of the transfer.

(C) Authority for additional reporting requirements.—The Secretary may prescribe such additional reporting requirements as may be necessary to carry out the purposes of this section.

(3) **Definitions.—**For purposes of paragraph (1), any term used in such paragraph which is also used in §420 of the Internal Revenue Code of 1986 (as in effect on the date of the enactment of the Pension Funding Equity Act of 2004) shall have the same meaning as used in such section.

(f) **Multiemployer Defined Benefit Plan Funding Notices.—**

(1) **In general.—**The administrator of a defined benefit plan which is a multiemployer plan shall for each year provide a plan funding notice to each plan participant and beneficiary, to

each labor organization representing such participants or beneficiaries, to each employer that has an obligation to contribute under the plan, and to the Pension Benefit Guaranty Corporation.

(2) **Information contained in notices.**—

(A) Identifying information.—Each notice required under paragraph (1) shall contain identifying information, including the name of the plan, the address and phone number of the plan administrator and the plan's principal administrative officer, each plan sponsor's employer identification number, and the plan number of the plan.

(B) Specific information.—A plan funding notice under paragraph (1) shall include—

(i) a statement as to whether the plan's funded current liability percentage (as defined in §302(d)(8)(B)) for the plan year to which the notice relates is at least 100 percent (and, if not, the actual percentage);

(ii) a statement of the value of the plan's assets, the amount of benefit payments, and the ratio of the assets to the payments for the plan year to which the notice relates;

(iii) a summary of the rules governing insolvent multiemployer plans, including the limitations on benefit payments and any potential benefit reductions and suspensions (and the potential effects of such limitations, reductions, and suspensions on the plan); and

(iv) a general description of the benefits under the plan which are eligible to be guaranteed by the Pension Benefit Guaranty Corporation, along with an explanation of the limitations on the guarantee and the circumstances under which such limitations apply.

(C) Other information.—Each notice under paragraph (1) shall include any additional information which the plan administrator elects to include to the extent not inconsistent with regulations prescribed by the Secretary.

(3) **Time for providing notice.**—Any notice under paragraph (1) shall be provided no later than two months after the deadline (including extensions) for filing the annual report for the plan year to which the notice relates.

(4) **Form and manner.**—Any notice under paragraph (1)—

(A) shall be provided in a form and manner prescribed in regulations of the Secretary,

(B) shall be written in a manner so as to be understood by the average plan participant, and

(C) may be provided in written, electronic, or other appropriate form to the extent such form is reasonably accessible to persons to whom the notice is required to be provided.

(g) **Reporting by Certain Arrangements.**—The Secretary may, by regulation, require multiple employer welfare arrangements providing benefits consisting of medical care (within the meaning of §733(a)(2)) which are not group health plans to report, not more frequently than annually, in such form and such manner as the Secretary may require for the purpose of determining the extent to which the requirements of part 7 are being carried out in connection with such benefits.

(h) **Simple Retirement Accounts.** —

(1) **No employer reports.** — Except as provided in this subsection, no report shall be required under this section by an employer maintaining a qualified salary reduction arrangement under §408(p) of the Internal Revenue Code of 1986.

(2) **Summary description.** — The trustee of any simple retirement account established pursuant to a qualified salary reduction arrangement under §408(p) of such Code shall provide to the employer maintaining the arrangement each year a description containing the following information:

(A) The name and address of the employer and the trustee.

(B) The requirements for eligibility for participation.

(C) The benefits provided with respect to the arrangement.

(D) The time and method of making elections with respect to the arrangement.

(E) The procedures for, and effects of, withdrawals (including rollovers) from the arrangement.

(3) **Employee notification.** — The employer shall notify each employee immediately before the period for which an election described in §408(p)(5)(C) of such Code may be made of the employee's opportunity to make such election. Such notice shall include a copy of the description described in paragraph (2).

(i) **Notice of Blackout Periods to Participant or Beneficiary Under Individual Account Plan.** —

(1) **Duties of plan administrator.** — In advance of the commencement of any blackout period with respect to an individual account plan, the administrator shall notify the plan participants and beneficiaries who are affected by such action in accordance with this subsection.

(2) **Notice requirements.** —

(A) In general. — The notices described in paragraph (2) shall be written in a manner calculated to be understood by the average plan participant and shall include —

(i) the reasons for the blackout period,

(ii) an identification of the investments and other rights affected,

(iii) the expected beginning date and length of the blackout period,

(iv) in the case of investments affected, a statement that the participant or beneficiary should evaluate the appropriateness of their current investment decisions in light of their inability to direct or diversify assets credited to their accounts during the blackout period, and

(v) such other matters as the Secretary may require by regulation.

(B) Notice to participants and beneficiaries.—Except as otherwise provided in this subsection, notices described in paragraph (1) shall be furnished to all participants and beneficiaries under the plan to whom the blackout period applies at least 30 days in advance of the blackout period.

(C) Exception to 30-day notice requirement.—In any case in which—

(i) a deferral of the blackout period would violate the requirements of subparagraph (A) or (B) of §404(a)(1), and a fiduciary of the plan reasonably so determines in writing, or

(ii) the inability to provide the 30-day advance notice is due to events that were unforeseeable or circumstances beyond the reasonable control of the plan administrator, and a fiduciary of the plan reasonably so determines in writing,

subparagraph (B) shall not apply, and the notice shall be furnished to all participants and beneficiaries under the plan to whom the blackout period applies as soon as reasonably possible under the circumstances unless such a notice in advance of the termination of the blackout period is impracticable.

(D) Written notice.—The notice required to be provided under this subsection shall be in writing, except that such notice may be in electronic or other form to the extent that such form is reasonably accessible to the recipient.

(E) Notice to issuers of employer securities subject to blackout period.—In the case of any blackout period in connection with an individual account plan, the plan administrator shall provide timely notice of such blackout period to the issuer of any employer securities subject to such blackout period.

(3) **Exception for blackout periods with limited applicability.**—In any case in which the blackout period applies only to 1 or more participants or beneficiaries in connection with a merger, acquisition, divestiture, or similar transaction involving the plan or plan sponsor and occurs solely in connection with becoming or ceasing to be a participant or beneficiary under the plan by reason of such merger, acquisition, divestiture, or transaction, the requirement of this subsection that the notice be provided to all participants and beneficiaries shall be treated as met if the notice required under paragraph (1) is provided to such participants or beneficiaries to whom the blackout period applies as soon as reasonably practicable.

(4) **Changes in length of blackout period.**—If, following the furnishing of the notice pursuant to this subsection, there is a change in the beginning date or length of the blackout period (specified in such notice pursuant to paragraph (2)(A)(iii)), the administrator shall provide affected participants and beneficiaries notice of the change as soon as reasonably practicable. In relation to the extended blackout period, such notice shall meet the requirements of paragraph (2)(D) and shall specify any material change in the matters referred to in clauses (i) through (v) of paragraph (2)(A).

(5) **Regulatory Exceptions.**—The Secretary may provide by regulation for additional exceptions to the requirements of this subsection which the Secretary determines are in the interests of participants and beneficiaries.

(6) **Guidance and model notices.**—The Secretary shall issue guidance and model notices which meet the requirements of this subsection.

(7) **Blackout period.**—For purposes of this subsection—

(A) In general.—The term "blackout period" means, in connection with an individual account plan, any period for which any ability of participants or beneficiaries under the plan, which is otherwise available under the terms of such plan, to direct or diversify assets credited to their accounts, to obtain loans from the plan, or to obtain distributions from the plan is temporarily suspended, limited, or restricted, if such suspension, limitation, or restriction is for any period of more than 3 consecutive business days.

(B) Exclusions.—The term "blackout period" does not include a suspension, limitation, or restriction—

(i) which occurs by reason of the application of the securities laws (as defined in §3(a)(47) of the Securities Exchange Act of 1934),

(ii) which is a change to the plan which provides for a regularly scheduled suspension, limitation, or restriction which is disclosed to participants or beneficiaries through any summary of material modifications, any materials describing specific investment alternatives under the plan, or any changes thereto, or

(iii) which applies only to 1 or more individuals, each of whom is the participant, an alternate payee (as defined in §206(d)(3)(K)), or any other beneficiary pursuant to a qualified domestic relations order (as defined in §206(d)(3)(B)(i)).

(8) **Individual account plan.**—

(A) In general.—For purposes of this subsection, the term "individual account plan" shall have the meaning provided such term in §3(34), except that such term shall not include a one-participant retirement plan.

(B) One-participant retirement plan.—For purposes of subparagraph (A), the term "one-participant retirement plan" means a retirement plan that—

(i) on the first day of the plan year—

(I) covered only the employer (and the employer's spouse) and the employer owned the entire business (whether or not incorporated), or

(II) covered only one or more partners (and their spouses) in a business partnership (including partners in an S or C corporation (as defined in §1361(a) of the Internal Revenue Code of 1986)),

(ii) meets the minimum coverage requirements of §410(b) of the Internal Revenue Code of 1986 (as in effect on the date of the enactment of this paragraph) without being combined with any other plan of the business that covers the employees of the business,

(iii) does not provide benefits to anyone except the employer (and the employer's spouse) or the partners (and their spouses),

(iv) does not cover a business that is a member of an affiliated service group, a controlled group of corporations, or a group of businesses under common control, and

(v) does not cover a business that leases employees.

(j) **Cross References.**—For regulations relating to coordination of reports to the Secretaries of Labor and the Treasury, see §3004.

* * *

SEC. 102. SUMMARY PLAN DESCRIPTION.

(a) A summary plan description of any employee benefit plan shall be furnished to participants and beneficiaries as provided in §104(b). The summary plan description shall include the information described in subsection (b), shall be written in a manner calculated to be understood by the average plan participant, and shall be sufficiently accurate and comprehensive to reasonably apprise such participants and beneficiaries of their rights and obligations under the plan. A summary of any material modification in the terms of the plan and any change in the information required under subsection (b) shall be written in a manner calculated to be understood by the average plan participant and shall be furnished in accordance with §104(b)(1).

(b) The summary plan description shall contain the following information: The name and type of administration of the plan; in the case of a group health plan; in the case of a group health plan (as defined in §733(a)(1)), whether a health insurance issuer (as defined in §733(b)(2)) is responsible for the financing or administration (including payment of claims) of the plan and (if so) the name and address of such issuer; the name and address of the person designated as agent for the service of legal process, if such person is not the administrator; the name and address of the administrator; names, titles and addresses of any trustee or trustees (if they are persons different from the administrator); a description of the relevant provisions of any applicable collective bargaining agreement; the plan's requirements respecting eligibility for participation and benefits; a description of the provisions providing for nonforfeitable pension benefits; circumstances which may result in disqualification, ineligibility, or denial or loss of benefits; the source of financing of the plan and the identity of any organization through which benefits are provided; the date of the end of the plan year and whether the records of the plan are kept on a calendar, policy, or fiscal year basis; the procedures to be followed in presenting claims for benefits under the plan including the office at the Department of Labor through which participants and beneficiaries may seek assistance or information regarding their rights under this Act and the Health Insurance Portability and Accountability Act of 1996 with respect to health benefits that are offered through a group health plan (as defined in §733(a)(1)) and the remedies available under the plan for the redress of claims which are denied in whole or in part (including procedures required under §503 of this Act).

* * *

SEC. 103. ANNUAL REPORTS.

(a) **Publication and Filing.**—

(1)(A) An annual report shall be published with respect to every employee benefit plan to which this part applies. Such report shall be filed with the Secretary in accordance with §104(a), and shall be made available and furnished to participants in accordance with §104(b).

(B) The annual report shall include the information described in subsections (b) and (c) and where applicable subsections (d) and (e) and shall also include—

(i) a financial statement and opinion, as required by paragraph (3) of this subsection, and

(ii) an actuarial statement and opinion, as required by paragraph (4) of this subsection.

(2) If some or all of the information necessary to enable the administrator to comply with the requirements of this title is maintained by—

(A) an insurance carrier or other organization which provides some or all of the benefits under the plan, or holds assets of the plan in a separate account,

(B) a bank or similar institution which holds some or all of the assets of the plan in a common or collective trust or a separate trust, or custodial account, or

(C) a plan sponsor as defined in §3(16)(B),

such carrier, organization, bank, institution, or plan sponsor shall transmit and certify the accuracy of such information to the administrator within 120 days after the end of the plan year (or such other date as may be prescribed under regulations of the Secretary).

(3)(A) Except as provided in subparagraph (C), the administrator of an employee benefit plan shall engage, on behalf of all plan participants, an independent qualified public accountant, who shall conduct such an examination of any financial statements of the plan, and of other books and records of the plan, as the accountant may deem necessary to enable the accountant to form an opinion as to whether the financial statements and schedules required to be included in the annual report by subsection (b) of this section are presented fairly in conformity with generally accepted accounting principles applied on a basis consistent with that of the preceding year. Such examination shall be conducted in accordance with generally accepted auditing standards, and shall involve such tests of the books and records of the plan as are considered necessary by the independent qualified public accountant. The independent qualified public accountant shall also offer his opinion as to whether the separate schedules specified in subsection (b)(3) of this section and the summary material required under §104(b)(3) present fairly and in all material respects the information contained therein when considered in conjunction with the financial statements taken as a whole. The opinion by the independent qualified public accountant shall be made a part of the annual report. In a case where a plan is not required to file an annual report, the requirements of this paragraph shall not apply. In a case where by reason of §104(a)(2) a plan is required only to file a simplified annual report, the Secretary may waive the requirements of this paragraph.

(B) In offering his opinion under this section the accountant may rely on the correctness of any actuarial matter certified to by an enrolled actuary, if he so states his reliance.

(C) The opinion required by subparagraph (A) need not be expressed as to any statements required by subsection (b)(3)(G) prepared by a bank or similar institution or insurance carrier regulated and supervised and subject to periodic examination by a State or Federal agency if such statements are certified by the bank, similar institution, or insurance carrier as accurate and are made a part of the annual report.

(D) For purposes of this title, the term "qualified public accountant" means—

(i) a person who is a certified public accountant, certified by a regulatory authority of a State;

(ii) a person who is a licensed public accountant, licensed by a regulatory authority of a State; or

(iii) a person certified by the Secretary as a qualified public accountant in accordance with regulations published by him for a person who practices in States where there is no certification or licensing procedure for accountants.

(4)(A) The administrator of an employee pension benefit plan subject to the reporting requirement of subsection (d) of this section shall engage, on behalf of all plan participants, an enrolled actuary who shall be responsible for the preparation of the materials comprising the actuarial statement required under subsection (d) of this section. In a case where a plan is not required to file an annual report, the requirement of this paragraph shall not apply, and, in a case where by reason of §104(a)(2), a plan is required only to file a simplified report, the Secretary may waive the requirement of this paragraph.

(B) The enrolled actuary shall utilize such assumptions and techniques as are necessary to enable him to form an opinion as to whether the contents of the matters reported under subsection (d) of this section—

(i) are in the aggregate reasonably related to the experience of the plan and to reasonable expectations; and

(ii) represent his best estimate of anticipated experience under the plan.

The opinion by the enrolled actuary shall be made with respect to, and shall be a part of, each annual report.

(C) For purposes of this title, the term "enrolled actuary" means an actuary enrolled under subtitle C of title III of this Act.

(D) In making a certification under this section the enrolled actuary may rely on the correctness of any accounting matter under §103(b) as to which any qualified public accountant has expressed an opinion, if he so states his reliance.

(b) **Financial Statement.**—An annual report under this section shall include a financial statement containing the following information:

(1) With respect to an employee welfare benefit plan: a statement of assets and liabilities; a statement of changes in fund balance; and a statement of changes in financial position. In the notes to financial statements, disclosures concerning the following items shall be considered by the accountant: a description of the plan including any significant changes in the plan made during the period and the impact of such changes on benefits; a description of material lease commitments, other commitments, and contingent liabilities; a description of agreements and transactions with persons known to be parties in interest; a general description of priorities upon termination of the plan; information concerning whether or not a tax ruling or determination letter has been obtained; and any other matters necessary to fully and fairly present the financial statements of the plan.

(2) With respect to an employee pension benefit plan: a statement of assets and liabilities, and a statement of changes in net assets available for plan benefits which shall include details of revenues and expenses and other changes aggregated by general source and application. In the notes to financial statements, disclosures concerning the following items shall be considered by the accountant: a description of the plan including any significant changes in the plan made during the period and the impact of such changes on benefits; the funding policy (including policy with respect to prior service cost), and any changes in such policies during the year; a description of any significant changes in plan benefits made during the period; a description of material lease commitments, other commitments, and contingent liabilities; a description of agreements and transactions with persons known to be parties in interest; a general description of priorities upon termination of the plan; information concerning whether or not a tax ruling or determination letter has been obtained; and any other matters necessary to fully and fairly present the financial statements of such pension plan.

(3) With respect to all employee benefit plans, the statement required under paragraph (1) or (2) shall have attached the following information in separate schedules:

(A) a statement of the assets and liabilities of the plan aggregated by categories and valued at their current value, and the same data displayed in comparative form for the end of the previous fiscal year of the plan,

(B) a statement of receipts and disbursements during the preceding twelve-month period aggregated by general sources and applications;

(C) a schedule of all assets held for investment purposes aggregated and identified by issuer, borrower, or lessor, or similar party to the transaction (including a notation as to whether such party is known to be a party in interest), maturity date, rate of interest, collateral, par or maturity value, cost, and current value;

(D) a schedule of each transaction involving a person known to be party in interest, the identity of such party in interest and his relationship or that of any other party in interest to the plan, a description of each asset to which the transaction relates; the purchase or selling price in case of a sale or purchase, the rental in case of a lease, or the interest rate and maturity date in case of a loan; expenses incurred in connection with the transaction; the cost of the asset, the current value of the asset, and the net gain (or loss) on each transaction;

(E) a schedule of all loans or fixed income obligations which were in default as of the close of the plan's fiscal year or were classified during the year as uncollectible and the following information with respect to each loan on such schedule (including a notation as to whether parties involved are known to be parties in interest): the original principal amount of the loan, the amount of principal and interest received during the reporting year, the unpaid balance, the identity and address of the obligor, a detailed description of the loan (including date of making and maturity, interest rate, the type and value of collateral, and other material terms), the amount of principal and interest overdue (if any) and an explanation thereof;

(F) a list of all leases which were in default or were classified during the year as uncollectible; and the following information with respect to each lease on such schedule (including a notation as to whether parties involved are known to be parties in interest): the type of property leased (and, in the case of fixed assets such as land, buildings, leasehold, and so forth, the location of the property), the identity of the lessor or lessee from or to whom the plan is leasing, the relationship of such lessors and lessees, if any, to the plan, the employer, employee organization, or any other party in interest, the terms of the lease regarding rent, taxes, insurance, repairs, expenses, and renewal options; the date the leased property was purchased and its cost, the date the property was leased and its approximate value at such date, the gross rental receipts during the reporting period, expenses paid for the leased property during the reporting period, the net receipts from the lease, the amounts in arrears, and a statement as to what steps have been taken to collect amounts due or otherwise remedy the default;

(G) if some or all of the assets of a plan or plans are held in a common or collective trust maintained by a bank or similar institution or in a separate account maintained by an insurance carrier or a separate trust maintained by a bank as trustee, the report shall include the most recent annual statement of assets and liabilities of such common or collective trust, and in the case of a separate account or a separate trust, such other information as is required by the administrator in order to comply with this subsection; and

(H) a schedule of each reportable transaction, the name of each party to the transaction (except that, in the case of an acquisition or sale of a security on the market, the report need not identify the person from whom the security was acquired or to whom it was sold) and a description of each asset to which the transaction applies; the purchase or selling price in case of a sale or purchase, the rental in case of a lease, or the interest rate and maturity date in case of a loan; expenses incurred in connection with the transaction; the cost of the asset, the current value of the asset, and the net gain (or loss) on each transaction. For purposes of the preceding sentence, the term "reportable transaction" means a transaction to which the plan is a party if such transaction is—

(i) a transaction involving an amount in excess of 3 percent of the current value of the assets of the plan;

(ii) any transaction (other than a transaction respecting a security) which is part of a series of transactions with or in conjunction with a person in a plan year, if the aggregate amount of such transactions exceeds 3 percent of the current value of the assets of the plan;

(iii) a transaction which is part of a series of transactions respecting one or more securities of the same issuer, if the aggregate amount of such transactions in the plan year exceeds 3 percent of the current value of the assets of the plan; or

(iv) a transaction with or in conjunction with a person respecting a security, if any other transaction with or in conjunction with such person in the plan year respecting a security is required to be reported by reason of clause (i).

(4) The Secretary may, by regulation, relieve any plan from filing a copy of a statement of assets and liabilities (or other information) described in paragraph (3)(G) if such statement and other information is filed with the Secretary by the bank or insurance carrier which maintains the common or collective trust or separate account.

(c) **Information to be Furnished by Administrator.**—The administrator shall furnish as a part of a report under this section the following information:

(1) The number of employees covered by the plan.

(2) The name and address of each fiduciary.

(3) Except in the case of a person whose compensation is minimal (determined under regulations of the Secretary) and who performs solely ministerial duties (determined under such regulations), the name of each person (including but not limited to, any consultant, broker, trustee, accountant, insurance carrier, actuary, administrator, investment manager, or custodian who rendered services to the plan or who had transactions with the plan) who received directly or indirectly compensation from the plan during the preceding year for services rendered to the plan or its participants, the amount of such compensation, the nature of his services to the plan or its participants, his relationship to the employer of the employees covered by the plan, or the employee organization, and any other office, position, or employment he holds with any party in interest.

(4) An explanation of the reason for any change in appointment of trustee, accountant, insurance carrier, enrolled actuary, administrator, investment manager, or custodian.

(5) Such financial and actuarial information including but not limited to the material described in subsections (b) and (d) of this section as the Secretary may find necessary or appropriate.

(d) **Actuarial Statement.**—With respect to an employee pension benefit plan (other than (A) a profit sharing, savings, or other plan, which is an individual account plan, (B) a plan described in §301(b), or (C) a plan described both in §4021(b) and in paragraph (1), (2), (3), (4), (5), (6), or (7) of §301(a)) an annual report under this section for a plan year shall include a complete actuarial statement applicable to the plan year which shall include the following:

(1) The date of the plan year, and the date of the actuarial valuation applicable to the plan year for which the report is filed.

(2) The date and amount of the contribution (or contributions) received by the plan for the plan year for which the report is filed and contributions for prior plan years not previously reported.

(3) The following information applicable to the plan year for which the report is filed: the normal costs, the accrued liabilities, an identification of benefits not included in the calculation; a statement of the other facts and actuarial assumptions and methods used to determine costs, and a justification for any change in actuarial assumptions or cost methods; and the minimum contribution required under §302.

(4) The number of participants and beneficiaries, both retired and nonretired, covered by the plan.

(5) The current value of the assets accumulated in the plan, and the present value of the assets of the plan used by the actuary in any computation of the amount of contributions to the plan required under §302 and a statement explaining the basis of such valuation of present value of assets.

(6) Information required in regulations of the Pension Benefit Guaranty Corporation with respect to:

(A) the current value of the assets of the plan,

(B) the present value of all nonforfeitable benefits for participants and beneficiaries receiving payments under the plan,

(C) the present value of all nonforfeitable benefits for all other participants and beneficiaries,

(D) the present value of all accrued benefits which are not nonforfeitable (including a separate accounting of such benefits which are benefit commitments, as defined in §4001(a)(16)), and

(E) the actuarial assumptions and techniques used in determining the values described in subparagraphs (A) through (D).

(7) A certification of the contribution necessary to reduce the accumulated funding deficiency to zero.

(8) A statement by the enrolled actuary—

(A) that to the best of his knowledge the report is complete and accurate, and

(B) the requirements of §302(c)(3) (relating to reasonable actuarial assumptions and methods) have been complied with.

(9) A copy of the opinion required by subsection (a)(4).

(10) A statement by the actuary which discloses—

(A) any event which the actuary has not taken into account, and

(B) any trend which, for purposes of the actuarial assumptions used, was not assumed to continue in the future,

but only if, to the best of the actuary's knowledge, such event or trend may require a material increase in plan costs or required contribution rates.

(11) If the current value of the assets of the plan is less than 70 percent of the current liability under the plan (within the meaning of §302(d)(7)), the percentage which such value is of such liability.

(12) Such other information regarding the plan as the Secretary may by regulation require.

(13) Such other information as may be necessary to fully and fairly disclose the actuarial position of the plan.

Such actuary shall make an actuarial valuation of the plan for every third plan year, unless he determines that a more frequent valuation is necessary to support his opinion under subsection (a)(4) of this section.

(e) **Statement From Insurance Company, Insurance Service, or Other Similar Organizations Which Sell or Guarantee Plan Benefits.**—If some or all of the benefits under the plan are purchased from and guaranteed by an insurance company, insurance service, or other similar organization, a report under this section shall include a statement from such insurance company, service, or other similar organization covering the plan year and enumerating—

(1) the premium rate or subscription charge and the total premium or subscription charges paid to each such carrier, insurance service, or other similar organization and the approximate number of persons covered by each class of such benefits; and

(2) the total amount of premiums received, the approximate number of persons covered by each class of benefits, and the total claims paid by such company, service, or other organization; dividends or retroactive rate adjustments, commissions, and administrative service or other fees or other specific acquisition costs paid by such company, service, or other organization; any amounts held to provide benefits after retirement; the remainder of such premiums; and the names and addresses of the brokers, agents, or other persons to whom commissions or fees were paid, the amount paid to each, and for what purpose. If any such company, service, or other organization does not maintain separate experience records covering the specific groups it serves, the report shall include in lieu of the information required by the foregoing provisions of this paragraph (A) a statement as to the basis of its premium rate or subscription charge, the total amount of premiums or subscription charges received from the plan, and a copy of the financial report of the company, service, or other organization and (B) if such company, service, or organization incurs specific costs in connection with the acquisition or retention of any particular plan or plans, a detailed statement of such costs.

* * *

SEC. 104. FILING AND FURNISHING OF INFORMATION.

(a) **Filing of Annual Report, Plan Description, and Modifications and Changes with Secretary.—**

(1) The administrator of any employee benefit plan subject to this part shall file with the Secretary the annual report for a plan year within 210 days after the close of such year (or within such time as may be required by regulations promulgated by the Secretary in order to reduce duplicative filing). The Secretary shall make copies of such annual reports available for inspection in the public document room of the Department of Labor.

(2)(A) With respect to annual reports required to be filed with the Secretary under this part, he may by regulation prescribe simplified annual reports for any pension plan which covers less than 100 participants.

(B) Nothing contained in this paragraph shall preclude the Secretary from requiring any information or data from any such plan to which this part applies where he finds such data or information is necessary to carry out the purposes of this title nor shall the Secretary be precluded from revoking provisions for simplified reports for any such plan if he finds it necessary to do so in order to carry out the objectives of this title.

(3) The Secretary may by regulation exempt any welfare benefit plan from all or part of the reporting and disclosure requirements of this title, or may provide for simplified reporting and disclosure if he finds that such requirements are inappropriate as applied to welfare benefit plans.

(4) The Secretary may reject any filing under this section—

(A) if he determines that such filing is incomplete for purposes of this part; or

(B) if he determines that there is any material qualification by an accountant or actuary contained in an opinion submitted pursuant to §103(a)(3)(A) or §103(a)(4)(B).

(5) If the Secretary rejects a filing of a report under paragraph (4) and if a revised filing satisfactory to the Secretary is not submitted within 45 days after the Secretary makes his determination under paragraph (4) to reject the filing, and if the Secretary deems it in the best interest of the participants, he may take any one or more of the following actions—

(A) retain an independent qualified public accountant (as defined in §103(a)(3)(D)) on behalf of the participants to perform an audit,

(B) retain an enrolled actuary (as defined in §103(a)(4)(C) of this Act) on behalf of the plan participants, to prepare an actuarial statement,

(C) bring a civil action for such legal or equitable relief as may be appropriate to enforce the provisions of this part, or

(D) take any other action authorized by this title.

The administrator shall permit such accountant or actuary to inspect whatever books and records of the plan are necessary for such audit. The plan shall be liable to the Secretary for the expenses for such audit or report, and the Secretary may bring an action against the plan in any court of competent jurisdiction to recover such expenses.

(6) The administrator of any employee benefit plan subject to this part shall furnish to the Secretary, upon request, any documents relating to the employee benefit plan, including but not limited to, the latest summary plan description (including any summaries of plan changes not contained in the summary plan description), and the bargaining agreement, trust agreement, contract, or other instrument under which the plan is established or operated.

(b) **Publication of Summary Plan Description and Annual Report to Participants and Beneficiaries of Plan.**—Publication of the summary plan descriptions and annual reports shall be made to participants and beneficiaries of the particular plan as follows:

(1) The administrator shall furnish to each participant, and each beneficiary receiving benefits under the plan, a copy of the summary plan description, and all modifications and changes referred to in §102(a)—

(A) within 90 days after he becomes a participant, or (in the case of a beneficiary) within 90 days after he first receives benefits, or

(B) if later, within 120 days after the plan becomes subject to this part.

The administrator shall furnish to each participant, and each beneficiary receiving benefits under the plan, every fifth year after the pan becomes subject to this part an updated summary plan description described in §102(a) which integrates all plan amendments made within such five-year period, except that in a case where no amendments have been made to a plan during such five-year period this sentence shall not apply. Notwithstanding the foregoing, the administrator shall furnish to each participant, and to each beneficiary receiving benefits under the plan, the summary plan description described in §102 every tenth year after the plan becomes subject to this part. If there is a modification or change described in 102(a) (other than a material reduction in covered services or benefits provided in the case of a group health plan (as defined in §733(a)(1)), a summary description of such modification or change shall be furnished not later than 210 days after the end of the plan year in which the change is adopted to each participant, and to each beneficiary who is receiving benefits under the plan. If there is a modification or change described in §102(a) that is a material reduction in covered services or benefits provided under a group health plan (as defined in §733(a)(1)), a summary description of such modification or change shall be furnished to participants and beneficiaries not later than 60 days after the date of the adoption of the modification or change. In the alternative, the plan sponsors may provide such description at regular intervals of not more than 90 days. The Secretary shall issue regulations within 180 days after the date of enactment of the Health Insurance Portability and Accountability Act of 1996, providing alternative mechanisms to delivery by mail through which group health plans (as so defined) may notify participants and beneficiaries of material reductions in covered services or benefits.

(2) The administrator shall make copies of the latest updated summary plan description and the latest annual report and the bargaining agreement, trust agreement, contract, or other instruments under which the plan was established or is operated available for examination by any plan participant or beneficiary in the principal office of the administrator and in such other places as may be necessary to make available all pertinent information to all participants (including such places as the Secretary may prescribe by regulations).

(3) Within 210 days after the close of the fiscal year of the plan, the administrator shall furnish to each participant, and to each beneficiary receiving benefits under the plan, a copy of the statements and schedules, for such fiscal year, described in subparagraphs (A) and (B) of §103(b)(3) and such other material (including the percentage determined under §103(d)(11)) as is necessary to fairly summarize the latest annual report.

(4) The administrator shall, upon written request of any participant or beneficiary, furnish a copy of the latest updated summary plan description, and the latest annual report, any terminal report, the bargaining agreement, trust agreement, contract, or other instruments under which the plan is established or operated. The administrator may make a reasonable charge to cover the cost of furnishing such complete copies. The Secretary may by regulation prescribe the maximum amount which will constitute a reasonable charge under the preceding sentence.

(c) **Statement of Rights.**—The Secretary may by regulation require that the administrator of any employee benefit plan furnish to each participant and to each beneficiary receiving benefits under the plan a statement of the rights of participants and beneficiaries under this title.

(d) **Cross References.**—For regulations respecting coordination of reports to the Secretaries of Labor and Treasury, see §3004.

* * *

SEC. 105. REPORTING OF PARTICIPANT'S BENEFIT RIGHTS.

(a) **Statement Furnished by Administrator to Participants and Beneficiaries.**—Each administrator of an employee pension benefit plan shall furnish to any plan participant or beneficiary who so requests in writing, a statement indicating, on the basis of the latest available information—

(1) the total benefits accrued, and

(2) the nonforfeitable pension benefits, if any, which have accrued, or the earliest date on which benefits will become nonforfeitable.

(b) **One-per-Year Limit on Reports.**—In no case shall a participant or beneficiary be entitled under this section to receive more than one report described in subsection (a) during any one 12-month period.

(c) **Individual Statement Furnished by Administrator to Participants Setting Forth Information in Administrator's Internal Revenue Registration Statement and Notification of Forfeitable Benefits.**—Each administrator required to register under §6057 of the Internal Revenue Code of 1954 shall, before the expiration of the time prescribed for such registration, furnish to each participant described in subsection (a)(2)(C) of such section, an individual statement setting forth the information with respect to such participant required to be contained in the registration statement required by §6057(a)(2) of such Code. Such statement shall also include a notice to the participant of any benefits which are forfeitable if the participant dies before a certain date.

(d) **Plans to Which More Than One Unaffiliated Employer is Required to Contribute; Regulations.**—Subsection (a) of this section shall apply to a plan to which more than one unaffiliated employer is required to contribute only to the extent provided in regulations prescribed by the Secretary in coordination with the Secretary of the Treasury.

* * *

SEC. 107. RETENTION OF RECORDS.

Every person subject to a requirement to file any report or to certify any information therefor under this title or who would be subject to such a requirement but for an exemption or simplified reporting requirement but for an exemption or simplified reporting requirement under §104(a)(2) or (3) of this title shall maintain records on the matters of which disclosure is required which will provide in sufficient detail the necessary basic information and data from which the documents thus required may be verified, explained, or clarified, and checked for accuracy and completeness, and shall include vouchers, worksheets, receipts, and applicable resolutions, and shall keep such records available for examination for a period of not less than six years after the filing date of the documents based on the information which they contain, or six years after the date on which such documents would have been filed but for an exemption or simplified reporting requirement under §104(a)(2) or (3).

* * *

SEC. 402. ESTABLISHMENT OF PLAN.

(a) **Named Fiduciaries.**—

(1) Every employee benefit plan shall be established and maintained pursuant to a written instrument. Such instrument shall provide for one or more named fiduciaries who jointly or severally shall have authority to control and manage the operation and administration of the plan.

(2) For purposes of this title, the term "named fiduciary" means a fiduciary who is named in the plan instrument, or who, pursuant to a procedure specified in the plan, is identified as a fiduciary (A) by a person who is an employer or employee organization with respect to the plan or (B) by such employer and such an employee organization acting jointly.

(b) **Requisite Features of Plan.**—Every employee benefit plan shall—

(1) provide a procedure for establishing and carrying out a funding policy and method consistent with the objectives of the plan and the requirements of this title,

(2) describe any procedure under the plan for the allocation of responsibilities for the operation and administration of the plan (including any procedure described in §405(c)(1)),

(3) provide a procedure for amending such plan, and for identifying the persons who have authority to amend the plan, and

(4) specify the basis on which payments are made to and from the plan.

(c) **Optional Features of Plan.**—Any employee benefit plan may provide—

(1) that any person or group of persons may serve in more than one fiduciary capacity with respect to the plan (including service both as trustee and administrator);

(2) that a named fiduciary, or a fiduciary designated by a named fiduciary pursuant to a plan procedure described in §405(c)(1), may employ one or more persons to render advice with regard to any responsibility such fiduciary has under the plan; or

(3) that a person who is a named fiduciary with respect to control or management of the assets of the plan may appoint an investment manager or managers to manage (including the power to acquire and dispose of) any assets of a plan.

* * *

SEC. 403. ESTABLISHMENT OF TRUST.

(a) **Benefit Plan Assets to be Held in Trust; Authority of Trustees.**—Except as provided in subsection (b), all assets of an employee benefit plan shall be held in trust by one or more trustees. Such trustee or trustees shall be either named in the trust instrument or in the plan instrument described in §402(a) or appointed by a person who is a named fiduciary, and upon acceptance of being named or appointed, the trustee or trustees shall have exclusive authority and discretion to manage and control the assets of the plan, except to the extent that—

(1) the plan expressly provides that the trustee or trustees are subject to the direction of a named fiduciary who is not a trustee, in which case the trustees shall be subject to proper directions of such fiduciary which are made in accordance with the terms of the plan and which are not contrary to this Act, or

(2) authority to manage, acquire, or dispose of assets of the plan is delegated to one or more investment managers pursuant to §402(c)(3).

(b) **Exceptions.**—The requirements of subsection (a) of this section shall not apply—

(1) to any assets of a plan which consist of insurance contracts or policies issued by an insurance company qualified to do business in a State;

(2) to any assets of such an insurance company or any assets of a plan which are held by such an insurance company;

(3) to a plan—

(A) some or all of the participants of which are employees of described in §401(c)(1) of the Internal Revenue Code of 1986; or

(B) which consists of one or more individual retirement accounts described in §408 of the Internal Revenue Code of 1986,

to the extent that such plan's assets are held in one or more custodial accounts which qualify under §401(f) or 408(h) of such Code, whichever is applicable;

(4) to a plan which the Secretary exempts from the requirement of subsection (a) and which is not subject to any of the following provisions of this Act;

(A) part 2 of this subtitle,

(B) part 3 of this subtitle, or

(C) title IV of this Act; or

(5) to a contract established and maintained under §403(b) of the Internal Revenue Code of 1954 to the extent that the assets of the contract are held in one or more custodial accounts pursuant to §403(b)(7) of such Code.

(6) Any plan, fund or program under which an employer, any of whose stock is directly or indirectly owned by employees, former employees or their beneficiaries, proposes through an unfunded arrangement to compensate retired employees for benefits which were forfeited by such employees under a pension plan maintained by a former employer prior to the date such pension plan became subject to this Act.

(c) **Assets of Plan Not to Inure to Benefit of Employer; Allowable Purposes of Holding Plan Assets.—**

(1) Except as provided in paragraph (2), (3), or (4) or subsection (d), or under §4042 and 4044 (relating to termination of insured plans), or under §420 of the Internal Revenue Code of 1986 (as in effect on the date of enactment of the Pension Funding Equity Act of 2004), the assets of a plan shall never inure to the benefit of any employer and shall be held for the exclusive purposes of providing benefits to participants in the plan and their beneficiaries and defraying reasonable expenses of administering the plan.

(2)(A) In the case of a contribution, or a payment of withdrawal liability under part 1 of subtitle E of title IV—

(i) if such contribution or payment is made by an employer to a plan (other than a multiemployer plan) by a mistake of fact, paragraph (1) shall not prohibit the return of such contribution to the employer within one year after the payment of the contribution, and

(ii) if such contribution or payment is made by an employer to a multiemployer plan by a mistake of fact or law (other than a mistake relating to whether the plan is described in §401(a) of the Internal Revenue Code of 1954 or the trust which is part of such plan is exempt from taxation under §501(a) of such Code), paragraph (1) shall not prohibit the return of such contribution or payment to the employer within 6 months after the plan administrator determines that the contribution was made by such a mistake.

(B) If a contribution is conditioned on initial qualification of the plan under §401 or 403(a) of the Internal Revenue Code of 1986, and if the plan receives an adverse determination with respect to its initial qualification, then paragraph (1) shall not prohibit the return of such contribution to the employer within one year after such determination, but only if the application for the determination is made by the time prescribed by law for filing the employer's return for the taxable year in which such plan was adopted, or such later date as the Secretary of the Treasury may prescribe.

(C) If a contribution is conditioned upon the deductibility of the contribution under §404 of the Internal Revenue Code of 1954, then, to the extent the deduction is disallowed, paragraph (1) shall not prohibit the return to the employer of such contribution (to the extent disallowed) within one year after the disallowance of the deduction.

(3) In the case of a withdrawal liability payment which has been determined to be an overpayment, paragraph (1) shall not prohibit the return of such payment to the employer within 6 months after the date of such determination.

(d) **Termination of Plan.**—

(1) Upon termination of a pension plan to which §4021 does not apply at the time of termination and to which this part applies (other than a plan to which no employer contributions have been made) the assets of the plan shall be allocated in accordance with the provisions of §4044 of this Act, except as otherwise provided in regulations of the Secretary.

(2) The assets of a welfare plan which terminates shall be distributed in accordance with the terms of the plan, except as otherwise provided in regulations of the Secretary.

* * *

SEC. 404. FIDUCIARY DUTIES.

(a) **Prudent Man Standard of Care.**—

(1) Subject to §§403(c) and (d), 4042, and 4044, a fiduciary shall discharge his duties with respect to a plan solely in the interest of the participants and beneficiaries and—

(A) for the exclusive purpose of:

(i) providing benefits to participants and their beneficiaries; and

(ii) defraying reasonable expenses of administering the plan;

(B) with the care, skill, prudence, and diligence under the circumstances then prevailing that a prudent man acting in a like capacity and familiar with such matters would use in the conduct of an enterprise of a like character and with like aims;

(C) by diversifying the investments of the plan so as to minimize the risk of large losses, unless under the circumstances it is clearly prudent not to do so; and

(D) in accordance with the documents and instruments governing the plan insofar as such documents and instruments are consistent with the provisions of this title and title IV.

(2) In the case of an eligible individual account plan (as defined in §407(d)(3)), the diversification requirement of paragraph (1)(C) and the prudence requirement (only to the extent that it requires diversification) of paragraph (1)(B) is not violated by acquisition or holding of qualifying employer real property or qualifying employer securities (as defined in §407(d)(4) and (5)).

(b) **Indicia of Ownership of Assets Outside Jurisdiction of District Courts.**— Except as authorized by the Secretary by regulation, no fiduciary may maintain the indicia of ownership of any assets of a plan outside the jurisdiction of the district courts of the United States.

(c) **Control of Assets by Participant or Beneficiary.**—

(1) In the case of a pension plan which provides for individual accounts and permits a participant or beneficiary to exercise control over assets in his account, if a participant or beneficiary exercises control over the assets in his account (as determined under regulations of the Secretary)—

(A) such participant or beneficiary shall not be deemed to be a fiduciary by reason of such exercise, and

(B) no person who is otherwise a fiduciary shall be liable under this part for any loss, or by reason of any breach, which results from such participant's, or beneficiary's exercise of control.

(2) In the case of a simple retirement account established pursuant to a qualified salary reduction arrangement under §408(p) of the Internal Revenue Code of 1986, a participant or beneficiary shall, for purposes of paragraph (1), be treated as exercising control over the assets in the account upon the earliest of—

(A) an affirmative election among investment options with respect to the initial investment of any contribution,

(B) a rollover to any other simple retirement account or individual retirement plan, or

(C) one year after the simple retirement account is established.

No reports, other than those required under §101(g), shall be required with respect to a simple retirement account established pursuant to such a qualified salary reduction arrangement.

(3) In the case of a pension plan which makes a transfer to an individual retirement account or annuity of a designated trustee or issuer under §401(a)(31)(B) of the Internal Revenue Code of 1986, the participant or beneficiary shall, for purposes of paragraph (1), be treated as exercising control over the assets in the account or annuity upon—

(A) the earlier of—

(i) a rollover of all or a portion of the amount to another individual retirement account or annuity; or

(ii) one year after the transfer is made; or

(B) a transfer that is made in a manner consistent with guidance provided by the Secretary.

(d)(1) If, in connection with the termination of a pension plan which is a single-employer plan, there is an election to establish or maintain a qualified replacement plan, or to increase benefits, as provided under §4980(d) of the Internal Revenue Code of 1986, a fiduciary shall discharge the fiduciary's duties under this title and title IV in accordance with the following requirements:

(A) In the case of a fiduciary of the terminated plan, any requirement—

(i) under §4980(d)(2)(B) of such Code with respect to the transfer of assets from the terminated plan to a qualified replacement plan, and

(ii) under §4080(d)(2)(B)(ii) or 4980(d)(3) of such Code with respect to any increase in benefits under the terminated plan.

(B) In the case of a fiduciary of a qualified replacement plan, any requirement—

(i) under §4980(d)(2)(A) of such Code with respect to participation in the qualified replacement plan of active participants in the terminated plan,

(ii) under §4980(d)(2)(B) of such Code with respect to the receipt of assets from the terminated plan, and

(iii) under §4980(d)(2)(C) of such Code with respect to the allocation of assets to participants of the qualified replacement plan.

(2) For purposes of this subsection—

(A) any term used in this subsection which is also then used in §4980(d) of the Internal Revenue Code of 1986 shall have the same meaning as when used in such section, and

(B) any reference to this subsection in the Internal Revenue Code of 1986 should be a reference to such Code as in effect immediately after the enactment of the Omnibus Budget Reconciliation Act of 1990.

* * *

SEC. 405. LIABILITY FOR BREACH BY CO-FIDUCIARY.

(a) **Circumstances Giving to Liability.**—In addition to any liability which he may have under any other provision of this part, a fiduciary with respect to a plan shall be liable for a breach of fiduciary responsibility of another fiduciary with respect to the same plan in the following circumstances:

(1) if he participates knowingly in, or knowingly undertakes to conceal, an act or omission of such other fiduciary, knowing such act or omission is a breach;

(2) if, by his failure to comply with §404(a)(1) in the administration of his specific responsibilities which give rise to his status as a fiduciary, he has enabled such other fiduciary to commit a breach; or

(3) if he has knowledge of a breach by such other fiduciary, unless he makes reasonable efforts under the circumstances to remedy the breach.

(b) **Assets Held by Two or More Trustees.**—

(1) Except as otherwise provided in subsection (d) and in §403(a)(1) and (2), if the assets of a plan are held by two or more trustees—

(A) each shall use reasonable care to prevent a co-trustee from committing a breach; and

(B) they shall jointly manage and control the assets of the plan, except that nothing in this subparagraph (B) shall preclude any agreement, authorized by the trust instrument, allocating specific responsibilities, obligations, or duties among trustees, in which event a trustee to whom certain responsibilities, obligations, or duties have not been allocated shall not be liable by reason of this subparagraph (B) either individually or as a trustee for any loss resulting to the plan arising from the acts or omissions on the part of another trustee to whom such responsibilities, obligations, or duties have been allocated.

(2) Nothing in this subsection shall limit any liability that a fiduciary may have under subsection (a) or any other provision of this part.

(3)(A) In the case of a plan the assets of which are held in more than one trust, a trustee shall not be liable under paragraph (1) except with respect to an act or omission of a trustee of a trust of which he is a trustee.

(B) No trustee shall be liable under this subsection for following instructions referred to in §403(a)(1).

(c) **Allocation of Fiduciary Responsibility; Designated Persons to Carry Out Fiduciary Responsibilities.—**

(1) The instrument under which a plan is maintained may expressly provide for procedures (A) for allocating fiduciary responsibilities (other than trustee responsibilities) among named fiduciaries, and (B) for named fiduciaries to designate persons other than named fiduciaries to carry out fiduciary responsibilities (other than trustee responsibilities) under the plan.

(2) If a plan expressly provides for a procedure described in paragraph (1), and pursuant to such procedure any fiduciary responsibility of a named fiduciary is allocated to any person, or a person is designated to carry out any such responsibility, then such named fiduciary shall not be liable for any act or omission of such person in carrying out such responsibility except to the extent that—

(A) the named fiduciary violated §404(a)(1)—

(i) with respect to such allocation or designation,

(ii) with respect to the establishment or implementation of the procedure under paragraph (1), or

(iii) in continuing the allocation or designation; or

(B) the named fiduciary would otherwise be liable in accordance with subsection (a).

(3) For purposes of this subsection, the term "trustee responsibility" means any responsibility provided in the plan's trust instrument (if any) to manage or control the assets of the plan, other than a power under the trust instrument of a named fiduciary to appoint an investment manager in accordance with §402(c)(3).

(d) **Investment Managers.—**

(1) If an investment manager or managers have been appointed under §402(c)(3), then, notwithstanding subsections (a)(2) and (3) and subsection (b), no trustee shall be liable for the acts or omissions of such investment manager or managers, or be under an obligation to invest or otherwise manage any asset of the plan which is subject to the management of such investment manager.

(2) Nothing in this subsection shall relieve any trustee of any liability under this part for any act of such trustee.

* * *

SEC. 406. PROHIBITED TRANSACTIONS.

(a) **Transactions Between Plan and Party In Interest.**—Except as provided in §408:

(1) A fiduciary with respect to a plan shall not cause the plan to engage in a transaction, if he knows or should know that such transaction constitutes a direct or indirect—

(A) sale or exchange, or leasing, of any property between the plan and a party in interest;

(B) lending of money or other extension of credit between the plan and a party in interest;

(C) furnishing of goods, services, or facilities between the plan and a party in interest;

(D) transfer to, or use by or for the benefit of, a party in interest, of any assets of the plan; or

(E) acquisition, on behalf of the plan, of any employer security or employer real property in violation of §407(a).

(2) No fiduciary who has authority or discretion to control or manage the assets of a plan shall permit the plan to hold any employer security or employer real property if he knows or should know that holding such security or real property violates §407(a).

(b) **Transactions Between Plan and Fiduciary.**—A fiduciary with respect to a plan shall not—

(1) deal with the assets of the plan in his own interest or for his own account,

(2) in his individual or in any other capacity act in any transaction involving the plan on behalf of a party (or represent a party) whose interests are adverse to the interests of the plan or the interests of its participants or beneficiaries, or

(3) receive any consideration for his own personal account from any party dealing with such plan in connection with a transaction involving the assets of the plan.

(c) **Transfer of Real or Personal Property to Plan by Party in Interest.**—A transfer of real or personal property by a party in interest to a plan shall be treated as a sale or exchange if the property is subject to a mortgage or similar lien which the plan assumes or if it is subject to a mortgage or similar lien which a party-in-interest placed on the property within the 10-year period ending on the date of the transfer.

* * *

SEC. 408. EXEMPTIONS FROM PROHIBITED TRANSACTIONS.

(a) **Grant of Exemptions.**—The Secretary shall establish an exemption procedure for purposes of this subsection. Pursuant to such procedure, he may grant a conditional or unconditional exemption of any fiduciary or transaction, or class of fiduciaries or transactions, from all or part of the restrictions imposed by §§406 and 407(a). Action under this subsection may be taken only after consultation and coordination with the Secretary of the Treasury. An exemption granted under this section shall not relieve a fiduciary from any other applicable provision of this Act. The Secretary may not grant an exemption under this subsection unless he finds that such exemption is—

(1) administratively feasible,

(2) in the interests of the plan and of its participants and beneficiaries, and

(3) protective of the rights of participants and beneficiaries of such plan.

Before granting an exemption under this subsection from §406(a) or 407(a), the Secretary shall publish notice in the Federal Register of the pendency of the exemption, shall require that adequate notice be given to interested persons, and shall afford interested persons opportunity to present views. The Secretary may not grant an exemption under this subsection from §406(b) unless he affords an opportunity for a hearing and makes a determination on the record with respect to the findings required by paragraphs (1), (2), and (3) of this subsection.

(b) **Enumeration of Transactions Exempted From Section 1106 Prohibitions.**—The prohibitions provided in §406 shall not apply to any of the following transactions:

(1) Any loans made by the plan to parties in interest who are participants or beneficiaries of the plan if such loans (A) are available to all such participants and beneficiaries on a reasonably equivalent basis, (B) are not made available to highly compensated employees (within the meaning of §414(q) of the Internal Revenue Code of 1986) in an amount greater than the amount made available to other employees, (C) are made in accordance with specific provisions regarding such loans set forth in the plan, (D) bear a reasonable rate of interest, and (E) are adequately secured.

(2) Contracting or making reasonable arrangements with a party in interest for office space, or legal, accounting, or other services necessary for the establishment or operation of the plan, if no more than reasonable compensation is paid therefor.

(3) A loan to an employee stock ownership plan (as defined in §407(d)(6)), if—

(A) such loan is primarily for the benefit of participants and beneficiaries of the plan, and

(B) such loan is at an interest rate which is not in excess of a reasonable rate.

If the plan gives collateral to a party in interest for such loan, such collateral may consist only of qualifying employer securities (as defined in §407(d)(5)).

(4) The investment of all or part of a plan's assets in deposits which bear a reasonable interest rate in a bank or similar financial institution supervised by the United States or a State, if such bank or other institution is a fiduciary of such plan and if—

(A) the plan covers only employees of such bank or other institution and employees of affiliates of such bank or other institution, or

(B) such investment is expressly authorized by a provision of the plan or by a fiduciary (other than such bank or institution or affiliate thereof) who is expressly empowered by the plan to so instruct the trustee with respect to such investment.

(5) Any contract for life insurance, health insurance, or annuities with one or more insurers which are qualified to do business in a State, if the plan pays no more than adequate consideration, and if each such insurer or insurers is—

(A) the employer maintaining the plan, or

(B) a party in interest which is wholly owned (directly or indirectly) by the employer maintaining the plan, or by any person which is a party in interest with respect to the plan, or by any person which is a party in interest with respect to the plan, but only if the total premiums and annuity considerations written by such insurers for life insurance, health insurance, or annuities for all plans (and their employers) with respect to which such insurers are parties in interest (not including premiums or annuity considerations written by the employer maintaining the plan) do not exceed 5 percent of the total premiums and annuity considerations written for all lines of insurance in that year by such insurers (not including premiums or annuity considerations written by the employer maintaining the plan).

(6) The providing of any ancillary service by a bank or similar financial institution supervised by the United States or a State, if such bank or other institution is a fiduciary of such plan, and if—

(A) such bank or similar financial institution has adopted adequate internal safeguards which assure that the providing of such ancillary service is consistent with sound banking and financial practice, as determined by Federal or State supervisory authority, and

(B) the extent to which such ancillary service is provided is subject to specific guidelines issued by such bank or similar financial institution (as determined by the Secretary after consultation with Federal and State supervisory authority), and adherence to such guidelines would reasonably preclude such bank or similar financial institution from providing such ancillary service (i) in an excessive or unreasonable manner, and (ii) in a manner that would be inconsistent with the best interests of participants and beneficiaries of employee benefit plans.

Such ancillary services shall not be provided at more than reasonable compensation.

(7) The exercise of a privilege to convert securities, to the extent provided in regulations of the Secretary, but only if the plan receives no less than adequate consideration pursuant to such conversion.

(8) Any transaction between a plan and (i) a common or collective trust fund or pooled investment fund maintained by a party in interest which is a bank or trust company supervised by a State or Federal agency or (ii) a pooled investment fund of an insurance company qualified to do business in a State, if—

(A) the transaction is a sale or purchase of an interest in the fund,

(B) the bank, trust company, or insurance company receives not more than reasonable compensation, and

(C) such transaction is expressly permitted by the instrument under which the plan is maintained, or by a fiduciary (other than the bank, trust company, or insurance company, or an affiliate thereof) who has authority to manage and control the assets of the plan.

(9) The making by a fiduciary of a distribution of the assets of the plan in accordance with the terms of the plan if such assets are distributed in the same manner as provided under §4044 of this Act (relating to allocation of assets).

(10) Any transaction required or permitted under part 1 of subtitle E of title IV.

(11) A merger of multiemployer plans, or the transfer of assets or liabilities between multiemployer plans, determined by the Pension Benefit Guaranty Corporation to meet the requirements of §4231.

(12) The sale by a plan to a party in interest on or after December 18, 1987, of any stock, if—

(A) the requirements of paragraphs (1) and (2) of subsection (e) are met with respect to such stock,

(B) on the later of the date on which the stock was acquired by the plan, or January 1, 1975, such stock constituted a qualifying employer security (as defined in §407(d)(5) as then in effect), and

(C) such stock does not constitute a qualifying employer security (as defined in §407(d)(5) as in effect at the time of the sale).

(13) Any transfer made before January 1, 2014, of excess pension assets from a defined benefit plan to a retiree health account in a qualified transfer permitted under §420 of the Internal Revenue Code of 1986 (as in effect on the date of the enactment of the Pension Funding Equity Act of 2004).

(c) Nothing in §406 shall be construed to prohibit any fiduciary from—

(1) receiving any benefit to which he may be entitled as a participant or beneficiary in the plan, so long as the benefit is computed and paid on a basis which is consistent with the terms of the plan as applied to all other participants and beneficiaries;

(2) receiving any reasonable compensation for services rendered, or for the reimbursement of expenses properly and actually incurred, in the performance of his duties with the plan; except that no person so serving who already receives full-time pay from an employer or an association of employers, whose employees are participants in the plan, or from an employee organization whose members are participants in such plan shall receive compensation from such plan, except for reimbursement of expenses properly and actually incurred; or

(3) serving as a fiduciary in addition to being an officer, employee, agent, or other representative of a party in interest.

(d) **Owner-Employees; Family Members; Shareholder Employees.—**

(1) Section 407(b) and subsections (b), (c), and (e) of this section shall not apply to any transaction in which a plan directly or indirectly—

    (A) lends any part of the corpus or income of the plan to,

    (B) pays any compensation for personal services rendered to the plan to, or

    (C) acquires for the plan any property from, or sells any property to,

any person who is with respect to the plan an owner-employee (as defined in §401(c)(3) of the Internal Revenue Code of 1986), a member of the family (as defined in §267(c)(4) of such Code) of any such owner-employee, or any corporation in which any such owner-employee owns, directly or indirectly, 50 percent or more of the total combined voting power of all classes of stock entitled to vote or 50 percent or more of the total value of shares of all classes of stock of the corporation.

(2)(A) For purposes of paragraph (1), the following shall be treated as owner-employees:

    (i) A shareholder-employee.

    (ii) A participant or beneficiary of an individual retirement plan (as defined in §7701(a)(37) of the Internal Revenue Code of 1986).

    (iii) An employer or association of employees which establishes such an individual retirement plan under §408(c) of such Code.

    (B) Paragraph (1)(C) shall not apply to a transaction which consists of a sale of employer securities to an employee stock ownership plan (as defined in §407(d)(6)) by a shareholder-employee, a member of the family (as defined in §267(c)(4) of such Code) of any such owner-employee, or a corporation in which such a shareholder-employee owns stock representing a 50 percent or greater interest described in paragraph (1).

    (C) For purposes of paragraph (1)(A), the term "owner-employee" shall only include a person described in clause (ii) or (iii) of subparagraph (A).

(3) For purposes of paragraph (2), the term "shareholder-employee" means an employee or officer of an S corporation (as defined in §1361(a)(1) of such Code) who owns (or is considered as owning within the meaning of §318(a)(1) of such Code) more than 5 percent of the outstanding stock of the corporation on any day during the taxable year of such corporation.

(e) **Acquisition or Sale by Plan of Qualifying Employer Securities; Acquisition, Sale, or Lease by Plan of Qualifying Employer Real Property.—** Sections 406 and 407 shall not apply to the acquisition or sale by a plan of qualifying employer securities (as defined in §407(d)(5)) or acquisition, sale or lease by a plan of qualifying employer real property (as defined in §407(d)(4))—

(1) if such acquisition, sale, or lease is for adequate consideration (or in the case of a marketable obligation, at a price not less favorable to the plan than the price determined under §407(e)(1)),

(2) if no commission is charged with respect thereto, and

(3) if—

    (A) the plan is an eligible individual account plan (as defined in §407(d)(3)), or

    (B) in the case of an acquisition or lease of qualifying employer real property by a plan which is not an eligible individual account plan, or of an acquisition of qualifying employer securities by such a plan, the lease or acquisition is not prohibited by §407(a).

(f) **Applicability of Statutory Prohibitions to Mergers or Transfers.—** Section 406(b)(2) shall not apply to any merger or transfer described in subsection (b)(11).

* * *

SEC. 409. LIABILITY FOR BREACH OF FIDUCIARY DUTY.

(a) Any person who is a fiduciary with respect to a plan who breaches any of the responsibilities, obligations, or duties imposed upon fiduciaries by this title shall be personally liable to make good to such plan any losses to the plan resulting from each such breach, and to restore to such plan any profits of such fiduciary which have been made through use of assets of the plan by the fiduciary, and shall be subject to such other equitable or remedial relief as the court may deem appropriate, including removal of such fiduciary. A fiduciary may also be removed for a violation of §411 of this Act.

(b) No fiduciary shall be liable with respect to a breach of fiduciary duty under this title if such breach was committed before he became a fiduciary or after he ceased to be a fiduciary.

* * *

SEC. 410. EXCULPATORY PROVISIONS; INSURANCE.

(a) Except as provided in §§405(b)(1) and 405(d), any provision in an agreement or instrument which purports to relieve a fiduciary from responsibility or liability for any responsibility, obligation, or duty under this part shall be void as against public policy.

(b) Nothing in this subpart shall preclude—

(1) a plan from purchasing insurance for its fiduciaries or for itself to cover liability or losses occurring by reason of the act or omission of a fiduciary, if such insurance permits recourse by the insurer against the fiduciary in the case of a breach of a fiduciary obligation by such fiduciary;

(2) a fiduciary from purchasing insurance to cover liability under this part from and for his own account; or

(3) an employer or an employee organization from purchasing insurance to cover potential liability of one or more persons who serve in a fiduciary capacity with regard to an employee benefit plan.

* * *

SEC. 412. BONDING.

(a) **Requisite Bonding of Plan Officials.**—Every fiduciary of an employee benefit plan and every person who handles funds or other property of such a plan (hereafter in this section referred to as "plan official") shall be bonded as provided in this section; except that—

(1) where such plan is one under which the only assets from which benefits are paid are the general assets of a union or of an employer, the administrator, officers, and employees of such plan shall be exempt from the bonding requirements of this section, and

(2) no bond shall be required of a fiduciary (or of any director, officer, or employee of such fiduciary) if such fiduciary—

(A) is a corporation organized and doing business under the laws of the United States or of any State;

(B) is authorized under such laws to exercise trust powers or to conduct an insurance business;

(C) is subject to supervision or examination by Federal or State authority; and

(D) has at all times a combined capital and surplus in excess of such a minimum amount as may be established by regulations issued by the Secretary, which amount shall be at least $1,000,000. Paragraph (2) shall apply to a bank or other financial institution which is authorized to exercise trust powers and the deposits of which are not insured by the Federal Deposit Insurance Corporation, only if such bank or institution meets bonding or similar requirements under State law which the Secretary determines are at least equivalent to those imposed on banks by Federal law.

The amount of such bond shall be fixed at the beginning of each fiscal year of the plan. Such amount shall be not less than 10 per centum of the amount of funds handled. In no case shall such bond be less than $1,000 nor more than $500,000, except that the Secretary, after due notice and opportunity for hearing to all interested parties, and after consideration of the record, may prescribe an amount in excess of $500,000, subject to the 10 per centum limitation of the preceding sentence. For purposes of fixing the amount of such bond, the amount of funds handled shall be determined by the funds handled by the person, group, or class to be covered by such bond and by their predecessor or predecessors, if any, during the preceding reporting year, or if the plan has no preceding reporting year, the amount of funds to be handled during the current reporting year by such person, group, or class, estimated as provided in regulations of the Secretary. Such bond shall provide protection to the plan against loss by reason of acts of fraud or dishonesty on the part of the plan official, directly or through connivance with others. Any bond shall have as surety thereon a corporate surety company which is an acceptable surety on Federal bonds under authority granted by the Secretary of the Treasury pursuant to §§6 through 13 of title 6, United States Code. Any bond shall be in a form or of a type approved by the Secretary, including individual bonds or schedule or blanket forms of bonds which cover a group or class.

(b) **Unlawful Acts.**—It shall be unlawful for any plan official to whom subsection (a) applies, to receive, handle, disburse, or otherwise exercise custody or control of any of the funds or other property of any employee benefit plan, without being bonded as required by subsection (a) and it shall be unlawful for any plan official of such plan, or any other person having authority to direct the performance of such functions, to permit such functions, or any of them, to be performed by any plan official, with respect to whom the requirements of subsection (a) have not been met.

(c) **Conflict of Interest Prohibited in Procuring Bonds.**—It shall be unlawful for any person to procure any bond required by subsection (a) from any surety or other company or through any agent or broker in whose business operations such plan or any party in interest in such plan has any control or significant financial interest, direct or indirect.

(d) **Exclusiveness of Statutory Basis for Bonding Requirement for Persons Handling Funds or Other Property of Employee Benefit Plans.**—Nothing in any other provision of law shall require any person, required to be bonded as provided in subsection (a) because he handles funds or other property of an employee benefit plan, to be bonded insofar as the handling by such person of the funds or other property of such plan is concerned.

(e) **Regulations.**—The Secretary shall prescribe such regulations as may be necessary to carry out the provisions of this section including exempting a plan from the requirements of this section where he finds that (1) other bonding arrangements or (2) the overall financial condition of the plan would be adequate to protect the interests of the beneficiaries and participants. When, in the opinion of the Secretary, the administrator of a plan offers adequate evidence of the financial responsibility of the plan, or that other bonding arrangements would provide adequate protection of the beneficiaries and participants, he may exempt such plan from the requirements of this section.

* * *

SEC. 502. CIVIL ENFORCEMENT.

(a) **Persons Empowered to Bring Civil Action.**—A civil action may be brought—

(1) by a participant or beneficiary—

(A) for the relief provided for in subsection (c) of this section, or

(B) to recover benefits due to him under the terms of his plan, to enforce his rights under the terms of the plan, or to clarify his rights to future benefits under the terms of the plan;

(2) by the Secretary, or by a participant, beneficiary or fiduciary for appropriate relief under §409;

(3) by a participant, beneficiary, or fiduciary, (A) to enjoin any act or practice which violates any provision of this title or the terms of the plan, or (B) to obtain other appropriate equitable relief (i) to redress such violations or (ii) to enforce any provisions of this title or the terms of the plan;

(4) by the Secretary, or by a participant, or beneficiary for appropriate relief in the case of a violation of 105(c);

(5) except as otherwise provided in subsection (b), by the Secretary (A) to enjoin any act or practice which violates any provision of this title, or (B) to obtain other appropriate equitable relief (i) to redress such violation or (ii) to enforce any provision of this title;

(6) by the Secretary to collect any civil penalty under paragraph (2), (4), (5), (6) or (7) of subsection (c) or under subsection (i) or (l);

(7) by a State to enforce compliance with a qualified medical child support order (as defined in §609(a)(2)(A));

(8) by the Secretary, or by an employer or other person referred to in §101(f)(1), (A) to enjoin any act or practice which violates subsection (f) of §101, or (B) to obtain appropriate equitable relief (i) to -redress such violation or (ii) to enforce such subsection; or

(9) in the event that the purchase of an insurance contract or insurance annuity in connection with termination of an individual's status as a participant covered under a pension plan with respect to all or any portion of the participant's pension benefit under such plan constitutes a violation of part 4 of this title or the terms of the plan, by the Secretary, by any individual who was a participant or beneficiary at the time of the alleged violation, or by a fiduciary, to obtain appropriate relief, including the posting of security if necessary, to assure receipt by the participant or beneficiary of the amounts provided or to be provided by such insurance contract or annuity, plus reasonable prejudgment interest on such amounts.

(b) **Plans Qualified Under Internal Revenue Code; Maintenance of Actions Involving Delinquent Contributions.—**

(1) In the case of a plan which is qualified under §401(a), 403(a), or 405(a) of the Internal Revenue Code of 1954 (or with respect to which an application to so qualify has been filed and has not been finally determined) the Secretary may exercise his authority under subsection (a)(5) with respect to a violation of, or the enforcement of, parts 2 and 3 of this subtitle (relating to participation, vesting, and funding) only if—

(A) requested by the Secretary of the Treasury, or

(B) one or more participants, beneficiaries, or fiduciaries, of such plan request in writing (in such manner as the Secretary shall prescribe by regulation) that he exercise such authority on their behalf.

In the case of such a request under this paragraph he may exercise such authority only if he determines that such violation affects, or such enforcement is necessary to protect, claims of participants or beneficiaries to benefits under the plan.

(2) The Secretary shall not initiate an action to enforce §515.

(3) The Secretary is not authorized to enforce under this part any requirement of part 7 against a health insurance issuer offering health insurance coverage in connection with a group health plan (as defined in §733(a)(1)). Nothing in this paragraph shall affect the authority of the Secretary to issue regulations to carry out such part.

(c) **Administrator's Refusal to Supply Requested Information; Penalty for Failure to Provide Annual Report in Complete Form.—**

(1) Any administrator (A) who fails to meet the requirements of paragraph (1) or (4) of §606, §101(e)(1), or §101(f) with respect to a participant or beneficiary, or (B) who fails or refuses to comply with a request for any information which such administrator is required by this title to furnish to a participant or beneficiary (unless such failure or refusal results from matters reasonably beyond the control of the administrator) by mailing the material requested to the last known address of the requesting participant or beneficiary within 30 days after such request may in the court's discretion be personally liable to such participant or beneficiary in the amount of up to $100 a day from the date of such failure or refusal, and the court may in its discretion order such other relief as it deems proper. For purposes of this paragraph, each violation described in subparagraph (A) with respect to any single participant, and each violation described in subparagraph (B) with respect to any single participant or beneficiary, shall be treated as a separate violation.

(2) The Secretary may assess a civil penalty against any plan administrator of up to $1,000 a day from the date of such plan administrator's failure or refusal to file the annual report required to be filed with the Secretary under §101(b)(4). For purposes of this paragraph, an annual report that has been rejected under §104(a)(4) for failure to provide material information shall not be treated as having been filed with the Secretary.

(3) Any employer maintaining a plan who fails to meet the notice requirement of §101(d) with respect to any participant or beneficiary or who fails to meet the requirements of §101(e)(2) with respect to any person or who fails to meet the requirements of §302(d)(12)(E) with respect to any person may in the court's discretion be liable to such participant or beneficiary or to such person in the amount of up to $100 a day from the date of such failure, and the court may in its discretion order such other relief as it deems proper.

(4) The Secretary may assess a civil penalty of not more than $1,000 a day for each violation by any person of §302(b)(7)(F)(vi).

(5) The Secretary may assess a civil penalty against any person of up to $1,000 a day from the date of the person's failure or refusal to file the information required to be filed by such person with the Secretary under regulations prescribed pursuant to §101(g).

(6) If, within 30 days of a request by the Secretary to a plan administrator for documents under §104(a)(6), the plan administrator fails to furnish the material requested to the Secretary, the Secretary may assess civil penalty against the plan administrator of up to $100 a day from the date of such failure (but in no event in excess of $1,000 per request). No penalty shall be imposed under this paragraph for any failure resulting from matters reasonably beyond the control of the plan administrator.

(7) The Secretary may assess a civil penalty against a plan administrator of up to $100 a day from the date of the plan administrator's failure or refusal to provide notice to participants and beneficiaries in accordance with §101(i). For purposes of this paragraph, each violation with respect to any single participant or beneficiary shall be treated as a separate violation.

(8) The Secretary and the Secretary of Health and Human Services shall maintain such ongoing consultation as may be necessary and appropriate to coordinate enforcement under this subsection with enforcement under §1144(c)(8) of the Social Security Act.

(d) **Status of Employee Benefit Plan as Entity.—**

(1) An employee benefit plan may sue or be sued under this title as an entity. Service of summons, subpoena, or other legal process of a court upon a trustee or an administrator of an employee benefit plan in his capacity as such shall constitute service upon the employee benefit plan. In a case where a plan has not designated in the summary plan description of the plan an individual as agent for the service of legal process, service upon the Secretary shall constitute such service. The Secretary, not later than 15 days after receipt of service under the preceding sentence, shall notify the administrator or any trustee of the plan of receipt of such service.

(2) Any money judgment under this title against an employee benefit plan shall be enforceable only against the plan as an entity and shall not be enforceable against any other person unless liability against such person is established in his individual capacity under this title.

(e) **Jurisdiction.—**

(1) Except for actions under subsection (a)(1)(B) of this section, the district courts of the United States shall have exclusive jurisdiction of civil actions under this title brought by the

Secretary or by a participant, beneficiary, fiduciary, or any person referred to in §101(f)(1). State courts of competent jurisdiction and district courts of the United States shall have concurrent jurisdiction of actions under paragraphs (1)(B) and (7) of subsection (a).

(2) Where an action under this title is brought in a district court of the United States, it may be brought in the district where the plan is administered, where the breach took place, or where a defendant resides or may be found, and process may be served in any other district where a defendant resides or may be found.

(f) **Amount in Controversy; Citizenship of Parties.**—The district courts of the United States shall have jurisdiction, without respect to the amount in controversy or the citizenship of the parties, to grant the relief provided for in subsection (a) of this section in any action.

(g) **Attorney's Fees and Costs; Awards in Actions Involving Delinquent Contributions.**—

(1) In any action under this title (other than an action described in paragraph (2)) by a participant, beneficiary, or fiduciary, the court in its discretion may allow a reasonable attorney's fee and costs of action to either party.

(2) In any action under this title by a fiduciary for or on behalf of a plan to enforce §515 in which a judgment in favor of the plan is awarded, the court shall award the plan—

    (A) the unpaid contributions,

    (B) interest on the unpaid contributions,

    (C) an amount equal to the greater of—

        (i) interest on the unpaid contributions, or

        (ii) liquidated damages provided for under the plan in an amount not in excess of 20 percent (or such higher percentage as may be permitted under Federal or State law) of the amount determined by the court under subparagraph (A),

    (D) reasonable attorney's fees and costs of the action, to be paid by the defendant, and

    (E) such other legal or equitable relief as the court deems appropriate.

For purposes of this paragraph, interest on unpaid contributions shall be determined by using the rate provided under the plan, or, if none, the rate prescribed under §6621 of the Internal Revenue Code of 1954.

(h) **Service Upon Secretary of Labor and Secretary of the Treasury.**—A copy of the complaint in any action under this title by a participant, beneficiary, or fiduciary (other than an action brought by one or more participants or beneficiaries under subsection (a)(1)(B) which is solely for the purpose of recovering benefits due such participants under the terms of the plan) shall be served upon the Secretary and the Secretary of the Treasury by certified mail. Either Secretary shall have the right in his discretion to intervene in any action, except that the Secretary of the Treasury may not intervene in any action under part 4 of this subtitle. If the Secretary brings an action under subsection (a) on behalf of a participant or beneficiary, he shall notify the Secretary of the Treasury.

(i) **Administrative Assessment of Civil Penalty.**—In the case of a transaction prohibited by §406 by a party in interest with respect to a plan to which this part applies, the Secretary may assess a civil penalty against such party in interest. The amount of such penalty may not exceed 5 percent of the amount involved in each such transaction (as defined in §4975(f)(4) of the Internal Revenue Code of 1986) for each year or part thereof during which the prohibited transaction continues, except that, if the transaction is not corrected (in such manner as the Secretary shall prescribe in regulations which shall be consistent with §4975(f)(5) of such Code) within 90 days after notice from the Secretary (or such longer period as the Secretary may permit), such penalty may be in an amount not more than 100 percent of the amount involved. This subsection shall not apply to a transaction with respect to a plan described in §4975(e)(1) of such Code.

(j) **Direction and Control of Litigation by Attorney General.**—In all civil actions under this title, attorneys appointed by the Secretary may represent the Secretary (except as provided in §518(a) of title 28, United States Code), but all such litigation shall be subject to the direction and control of the Attorney General.

(k) **Jurisdiction of Action Against Secretary of Labor.**—Suits by an administrator, fiduciary, participant, or beneficiary of an employee benefit plan to review a final order of the Secretary, to restrain the Secretary from taking any action contrary to the provisions of this Act, or to compel him to take action required under this title, may be brought in the district court of the United States for the district where the plan has its principal office, or in the United States District Court for the District of Columbia.

(l) **Civil Penalties on Violations by Fiduciaries.**—

(1) In the case of—

(A) any breach of fiduciary responsibility under (or other violation of) part 4 by a fiduciary, or

(B) any knowing participation in such a breach or violation by any other person,

the Secretary shall assess a civil penalty against such fiduciary or other person in an amount equal to 20 percent of the applicable recovery amount.

(2) For purposes of paragraph (1), the term "applicable recovery amount" means any amount which is recovered from a fiduciary or other person with respect to a breach or violation described in paragraph (1)—

(A) pursuant to any settlement agreement with the Secretary, or

(B) ordered by a court to be paid by such fiduciary or other person to a plan or its participants and beneficiaries in a judicial proceeding instituted by the Secretary under subsection (a)(2) or (a)(5).

(3) The Secretary may, in the Secretary's sole discretion, waive or reduce the penalty under paragraph (1) if the Secretary determines in writing that—

(A) the fiduciary or other person acted reasonably and in good faith, or

(B) it is reasonable to expect that the fiduciary or other person will not be able to restore all losses to the plan (or to provide the relief ordered pursuant to subsection (a)(9)) without severe financial hardship unless such waiver or reduction is granted.

(4) The penalty imposed on a fiduciary or other person under this subsection with respect to any transaction shall be reduced by the amount of any penalty or tax imposed on such fiduciary or other person with respect to such transaction under subsection (i) of this section and §4975 of the Internal Revenue Code of 1986.

(m) **Penalty for Improper Distribution.**—In the case of a distribution to a pension plan participant or beneficiary in violation of §206(e) by a plan fiduciary, the Secretary shall assess a penalty against such fiduciary in an amount equal to the value of the distribution. Such penalty shall not exceed $10,000 for each such distribution.

* * *

SEC. 503. CLAIMS PROCEDURE.

In accordance with regulations of the Secretary, every employee benefit plan shall—

(1) provide adequate notice in writing to any participant or beneficiary whose claim for benefits under the plan has been denied, setting forth the specific reasons for such denial, written in a manner calculated to be understood by the participant, and

(2) afford a reasonable opportunity to any participant whose claim for benefits has been denied for a full and fair review by the appropriate named fiduciary of the decision denying the claim.

* * *

SEC. 514. OTHER LAWS.

(a) **Supersedure; Effective Date.**—Except as provided in subsection (b) of this section, the provisions of this title and title IV shall supersede any and all State laws insofar as they may now or hereafter relate to any employee benefit plan described in §4(a) and not exempt under §4(b). This section shall take effect on January 1, 1975.

(b) **Construction and Application.**—

(1) This section shall not apply with respect to any cause of action which arose, or any act or omission which occurred, before January 1, 1975.

(2)(A) Except as provided in subparagraph (B), nothing in this title shall be construed to exempt or relieve any person from any law of any State which regulates insurance, banking, or securities.

(B) Neither an employee benefit plan described in §4(a), which is not exempt under §4(b) (other than a plan established primarily for the purpose of providing death benefits), nor any trust established under such a plan, shall be deemed to be an insurance company or other insurer, bank, trust company, or investment company or to be engaged in the business of insurance or banking for purposes of any law of any State purporting to regulate insurance companies, insurance contracts, banks, trust companies, or investment companies.

(3) Nothing in this section shall be construed to prohibit use by the Secretary of services or facilities of a State agency as permitted under §506 of this Act.

(4) Subsection (a) shall not apply to any generally applicable criminal law of a State.

(5)(A) Except as provided in subparagraph (B), subsection (a) shall not apply to the Hawaii Prepaid Health Care Act (Haw. Rev. Stat. §§393-1 through 393-51).

(B) Nothing in subparagraph (A) shall be construed to exempt from subsection (a)—

(i) any State tax law relating to employee benefit plans, or

(ii) any amendment to the Hawaii Prepaid Health Care Act enacted after September 2, 1974, to the extent it provides for more than the effective administration of such Act as in effect on such date.

(C) Notwithstanding subparagraph (A), parts 1 and 4 of this subtitle, and the preceding sections of this part to the extent they govern matters which are governed by the provisions of such parts 1 and 4, shall supersede the Hawaii Prepaid Health Care Act (as in effect on or after the date of the enactment of this paragraph), but the Secretary may enter into cooperative arrangements under this paragraph and §506 with officials of the State of Hawaii to assist them in effectuating the policies of provisions of such Act which are superseded by such parts 1 and 4 and the preceding sections of this part.

(6)(A) Notwithstanding any other provision of this section—

(i) in the case of an employee welfare benefit plan which is a multiple employer welfare arrangement and is fully insured (or which is a multiple employer welfare arrangement subject to an exemption under subparagraph (B)), any law of any State which regulates insurance may apply to such arrangement to the extent that such law provides—

(I) standards, requiring the maintenance of specified levels of reserves and specified levels of contributions, which any such plan, or any trust established under such a plan, must meet in order to be considered under such law able to pay benefits in full when due, and

(II) provisions to enforce such standards, and

(ii) in the case of any other employee welfare benefit plan which is a multiple employer welfare arrangement, in addition to this title, any law of any State which regulates insurance may apply to the extent not inconsistent with the preceding sections of this title.

(B) The Secretary may, under regulations which may be prescribed by the Secretary, exempt from subparagraph (A)(ii), individually or by class, multiple employer welfare arrangements which are not fully insured. Any such exemption may be granted with respect to any arrangement or class of arrangements only if such arrangement or each arrangement which is a member of such class meets the requirements of §3(1) and §4 necessary to be considered an employee welfare benefit plan to which this title applies.

(C) Nothing in subparagraph (A) shall affect the manner or extent to which the provisions of this title apply to an employee welfare benefit plan which is not a multiple employer welfare arrangement and which is a plan, fund, or program participating in, subscribing to, or otherwise using a multiple employer welfare arrangement to fund or administer benefits to such plan's participants and beneficiaries.

(D) For purposes of this paragraph, a multiple employer welfare arrangement shall be considered fully insured only if the terms of the arrangement provide for benefits the amount of all of which the Secretary determines are guaranteed under a contract, or policy of insurance, issued by an insurance company, insurance service, or insurance organization, qualified to conduct business in a State.

(7) Subsection (a) shall not apply to qualified domestic relations orders (within the meaning of §206(d)(3)(B)(i)), qualified medical child support orders (within the meaning of §609(a)(2)(A)), and the provisions of law referred to in §609(a)(2)(B)(ii) to the extent they apply to qualified medical child support orders.

(8) Subsection (a) of this section shall not be construed to preclude any State cause of action—

(A) with respect to which the State exercises its acquired rights under §609(b)(3) with respect to a group health plan (as defined in §607(l)), or

(B) for recoupment of payment with respect to items or services pursuant to a State plan for medical assistance approved under title XIX of the Social Security Act which would not have been payable if such acquired rights had been executed before payment with respect to such items or services by the group health plan.

(9) For additional provisions relating to group health plans, see §731.

(c) **Definitions.**—For purposes of this section:

(1) The term "State law" includes all laws, decisions, rules, regulations, or other State action having the effect of law, of any State. A law of the United States applicable only to the District of Columbia shall be treated as a State law rather than a law of the United States.

(2) The term "State" includes a State, any political subdivisions thereof, or any agency or instrumentality of either, which purports to regulate, directly or indirectly, the terms and conditions of employee benefit plans covered by this title.

(d) **Alteration, Amendment, Modification, Invalidation, Impairment, or Supersedure of Any Law of the United States Prohibited.**—Nothing in this title shall be construed to alter, amend, modify, invalidate, impair, or supersede any law of the United States (except as provided in §§111 and 507(b)) or any rule or regulation issued under any such law.

* * *

SEC. 601. PLANS MUST PROVIDE CONTINUATION COVERAGE TO CERTAIN INDIVIDUALS.

(a) **In General.**—The plan sponsor of each group health plan shall provide, in accordance with this part, that each qualified beneficiary who would lose coverage under the plan as a result of a qualifying event is entitled, under the plan, to elect, within the election period, continuation coverage under the plan.

(b) **Exception for Certain Plans.**—Subsection (a) shall not apply to any group health plan for any calendar year if all employers maintaining such plan normally employed fewer than 20 employees on a typical business day during the preceding calendar year.

* * *

SEC. 602. CONTINUATION COVERAGE.

For purposes of §601, the term "continuation coverage" means coverage under the plan which meets the following requirements:

(1) **Type of benefit coverage.**—The coverage must consist of coverage which, as of the time the coverage is being provided, is identical to the coverage provided under the plan to similarly situated beneficiaries under the plan with respect to whom a qualifying event has not occurred. If coverage is modified under the plan for any group of similarly situated beneficiaries, such coverage shall also be modified in the same manner for all individuals who are qualified beneficiaries under the plan pursuant to this part in connection with such group.

(2) **Period of coverage.**—The coverage must extend for at least the period beginning on the date of the qualifying event and ending not earlier than the earliest of the following:

(A) Maximum required period.—

(i) General rule for terminations and reduced hours.—In the case of a qualifying event described in §603(2), except as provided in clause (ii), the date which is 18 months after the date of the qualifying event.

(ii) Special rule for multiple qualifying events.—If a qualifying event (other than a qualifying event described in §603(6)) occurs during the 18 months after the date of a qualifying event described in §603(2), the date which is 36 months after the date of the qualifying event described in §603(2).

(iii) Special rule for certain bankruptcy proceedings.—In the case of a qualifying event described in §603(6) (relating to bankruptcy proceedings), the date of the death of the covered employee or qualified beneficiary (described in §607(3)(C)(iii)), or in the case of the surviving spouse or dependent children of the covered employee, 36 months after the date of the death of the covered employee.

(iv) General rule for other qualifying events.—In the case of a qualifying event not described in §603(2) or 603(6), the date which is 36 months after the date of the qualifying event.

(v) Medicare entitlement followed by qualifying event.—In the case of a qualifying event described in §603(4) that occurs less than 18 months after the date the covered employee became entitled to benefits under title XVIII of the Social Security Act, the period of coverage for qualified beneficiaries other than covered employees shall not terminate under this subparagraph before the close of the 36-month period beginning on the date the covered employee became so entitled.

In the case of a qualified beneficiary who is determined, under title II or XVI of the Social Security Act, to have been disabled at any time during the first 60 days of continuation coverage under this part, any reference in clause (i) or (ii) to 18 months is deemed a reference to 29 months (with respect to all qualified beneficiaries), but only if the qualified beneficiary has provided notice of such determination under §606(3) before the end of such 18 months.

(B) End of plan.—The date on which the employer ceases to provide any group health plan to any employee.

(C) Failure to pay premium.—The date on which coverage ceases under the plan by reason of a failure to make timely payment of any premium required under the plan with respect to the qualified beneficiary. The payment of any premium (other than any payment referred to in the last sentence of paragraph (3)) shall be considered to be timely if made within 30 days after the date due or within such longer period as applies to or under the plan.

(D) Group health plan coverage or Medicare entitlement.—The date on which the qualified beneficiary first becomes, after the date of the election—

(i) covered under any other group health plan (as an employee or otherwise) which does not contain any exclusion, or limitation with respect to any preexisting condition of such beneficiary (other than such an exclusion or limitation which does not apply to (or is satisfied by) such beneficiary by reason of chapter 100 of the Internal Revenue Code of 1986, part 7 of this subtitle, or title XXVII of the Public Health Service Act), or

(ii) in the case of a qualified beneficiary other than a qualified beneficiary described in §607(3)(C), entitled to benefits under title XVIII of the Social Security Act.

(E) Termination of extended coverage for disability.—In the case of a qualified beneficiary who is disabled at any time during the first 60 days of continuation coverage under this part, the month that begins more than 30 days after the date of the final determination under title II or XVI of the Social Security Act that the qualified beneficiary is no longer disabled.

(3) **Premium requirements.**—The plan may require payment of a premium for any period of continuation coverage, except that such premium—

(A) shall not exceed 102 percent of the applicable premium for such period, and

(B) may, at the election of the payor, be made in monthly installments.

In no event may the plan require the payment of any premium before the day which is 45 days after the day on which the qualified beneficiary made the initial election for continuation coverage. In the case of an individual described in the last sentence of paragraph (2)(A), any reference in subparagraph (A) of this paragraph to "102 percent" is deemed a reference to "150 percent" for any month after the 18th month of continuation coverage described in clause (i) or (ii) of paragraph (2)(A).

(4) **No requirement of insurability.**—The coverage may not be conditioned upon, or discriminate on the basis of lack of, evidence of insurability.

(5) **Conversion option.**—In the case of a qualified beneficiary whose period of continuation coverage expires under paragraph (2)(A), the plan must, during the 180-day period ending on such expiration date, provide to the qualified beneficiary the option of enrollment under a conversion health plan otherwise generally available under the plan.

* * *

SEC. 603. QUALIFYING EVENT.

For purposes of this part, the term "qualifying event" means, with respect to any covered employee, any of the following events which, but for the continuation coverage required under this part, would result in the loss of coverage of a qualified beneficiary:

(1) The death of the covered employee.

(2) The termination (other than by reason of such employee's gross misconduct), or reduction of hours, of the covered employee's employment.

(3) The divorce or legal separation of the covered employee from the employee's spouse.

(4) The covered employee becoming entitled to benefits under title XVIII of the Social Security Act.

(5) A dependent child ceasing to be a dependent child under the generally applicable requirements of the plan.

(6) A proceeding in a case under title II, United States Code, commencing on or after July 1, 1986, with respect to the employer from whose employment the covered employee retired at any time.

In the case of an event described in paragraph (6), a loss of coverage includes a substantial elimination of coverage with respect to a qualified beneficiary described in §607(3)(C) within one year before or after the date of commencement of the proceeding.

* * *

SEC. 604. APPLICABLE PREMIUM.

For purposes of this part—

(1) **In general.**—The term "applicable premium" means, with respect to any period of continuation coverage of qualified beneficiaries, the cost to the plan for such period of the coverage for similarly situated beneficiaries with respect to whom a qualifying event has not occurred (without regard to whether such cost is paid by the employer or employee).

(2) **Special rule for self-insured plans.**—To the extent that a plan is a self-insured plan—

(A) In general.—Except as provided in subparagraph (B), the applicable premium for any period of continuation coverage of qualified beneficiaries shall be equal to a reasonable estimate of the cost of providing coverage for such period for similarly situated beneficiaries which—

(i) is determined on an actuarial basis, and

(ii) takes into account such factors as the Secretary may prescribe in regulations.

(B) Determination on the basis of past cost.—If an administrator elects to have this subparagraph apply, the applicable premium for any period of continuation coverage of qualified beneficiaries shall be equal to—

(i) the cost to the plan for similarly situated beneficiaries for the same period occurring during the preceding determination period under paragraph (3), adjusted by

(ii) the percentage increase or decrease in the implicit price deflator of the gross national product (calculated by the Department of Commerce and published in the Survey of Current Business) for the 12-month period ending on the last day of the sixth month of such preceding determination period.

(C) Subparagraph (B) not to apply where significant change.—An administrator may not elect to have subparagraph (B) apply in any case in which there is any significant difference, between the determination period and the preceding determination period, in coverage under, or in employees covered by, the plan. The determination under the preceding sentence for any determination period shall be made at the same time as the determination under paragraph (3).

(3) **Determination period.**—The determination of any applicable premium shall be made for a period of 12 months and shall be made before the beginning of such period.

* * *

SEC. 605. ELECTION.

(a) **In General.**—For purposes of this part—

(1) **Election period.**—The term "election period" means the period which—

(A) begins not later than the date on which coverage terminates under the plan by reason of a qualifying event,

(B) is of at least 60 days' duration, and

(C) ends not earlier than 60 days after the later of—

(i) the date described in subparagraph (A), or

(ii) in the case of any qualified beneficiary who receives notice under §606(4), the date of such notice.

(2) **Effect of election on other beneficiaries.**—Except as otherwise specified in an election, any election of continuation coverage by a qualified beneficiary described in subparagraph (A)(i) or (B) of §607(3) shall be deemed to include an election of continuation coverage on behalf of any other qualified beneficiary who would lose coverage under the plan by reason of the qualifying event. If there is a choice among types of coverage under the plan, each qualified beneficiary is entitled to make a separate selection among such types of coverage.

(b) **Temporary Extension of COBRA Election Period for Certain Individuals.**—

(1) **In general.**—In the case of a nonelecting TAA-eligible individual and notwithstanding subsection (a), such individual may elect continuation coverage under this part during the 60-day period that begins on the first day of the month in which the individual becomes a TAA-eligible individual, but only if such election is made not later than 6 months after the date of the TAA-related loss of coverage.

(2) **Commencement of coverage; no reach-back.**—Any continuation coverage elected by a TAA-eligible individual under paragraph (1) shall commence at the beginning of the 60-day election period described in such paragraph and shall not include any period prior to such 60-day election period.

(3) **Preexisting conditions.**—With respect to an individual who elects continuation coverage pursuant to paragraph (1), the period—

(A) beginning on the date of the TAA-related loss of coverage, and

(B) ending on the first day of the 60-day election period described in paragraph (1),

shall be disregarded for purposes of determining the 63-day periods referred to in §701(c)(2), §2701(c)(2) of the Public Health Service Act, and §9801(c)(2) of the Internal Revenue Code of 1986.

(4) **Definitions.**—For purposes of this subsection:

(A) Nonelecting TAA-eligible individual.—The term "nonelecting TAA-eligible individual" means a TAA eligible individual who—

(i) has a TAA-related loss of coverage; and

(ii) did not elect continuation coverage under this part during the TAA-related election period.

(B) TAA-eligible individual.—The term "TAA-eligible individual" means—

(i) an eligible TAA recipient (as defined in paragraph (2) of §35(c) of the Internal Revenue Code of 1986), and

(ii) an eligible alternative TAA recipient (as defined in paragraph (3) of such section).

(C) TAA-related election period.—The term "TAA-related election period" means, with respect to a TAA-related loss of coverage, the 60-day election period under this part which is a direct consequence of such loss.

(D) TAA-related loss of coverage.—The term "TAA-related loss of coverage" means, with respect to an individual whose separation from employment gives rise to being an TAA-eligible individual, the loss of health benefits coverage associated with such separation.

* * *

SEC. 606. NOTICE REQUIREMENTS.

(a) **In General.**—In accordance with regulations prescribed by the Secretary—

(1) the group health plan shall provide, at the time of commencement of coverage under the plan, written notice of each covered employee and spouse of the employee (if any) of the rights provided under this subsection,

(2) the employer of an employee under a plan must notify the administrator of a qualifying event described in paragraph (1), (2), (4), or (6) of §603 within 30 days (or, in the case of a group health plan which is a multiemployer plan, such longer period of time as may be provided in the terms of the plan) of the date of the qualifying event,

(3) each covered employee or qualified beneficiary is responsible for notifying the administrator of the occurrence of any qualifying event described in paragraph (3) or (5) of §603 within 60 days after the date of the qualifying event and each qualified beneficiary who is determined, under title II or XVI of the Social Security Act, to have been disabled at any time during the first 60 days of continuation coverage under this part is responsible for notifying the plan administrator of such determination within 60 days after the date of the determination and for notifying the plan administrator within 30 days after the date of any final determination under such title or titles that the qualified beneficiary is no longer disabled, and

(4) the administrator shall notify—

(A) in the case of a qualifying event described in paragraph (1), (2), (4), or (6) of §603, any qualified beneficiary with respect to such event, and

(B) in the case of a qualifying event described in paragraph (3) or (5) of §603 where the covered employee notifies the administrator under paragraph (3), any qualified beneficiary with respect to such event,

of such beneficiary's rights under this subsection.

(b) **Alternative Means of Compliance with Requirement for Notification of Multiemployer Plans by Employers.**—The requirements of subsection (a)(2) shall be considered satisfied in the case of a multiemployer plan in connection with a qualifying event described in paragraph (2) of §603 if the plan provides that the determination of the occurrence of such qualifying event will be made by the plan administrator.

(c) **Rules Relating to Notification of Qualified Beneficiaries by Plan Administrator.**—For purposes of subsection (a)(4), any notification shall be made within 14 days (or, in the case of a group health plan which is a multiemployer plan, such longer period of time as may be provided in the terms of the plan) of the date on which the administrator is notified under paragraph (2) or (3), whichever is applicable, and any such notification to an individual who is a qualified beneficiary as the spouse of the covered employee shall be treated as notification to all other qualified beneficiaries residing with such spouse at the time such notification is made.

* * *

SEC. 607. DEFINITIONS AND SPECIAL RULES.

For purposes of this part—

(1) **Group health plan.**—The term "group health plan" means an employee welfare benefit plan providing medical care (as defined in §213(d) of the Internal Revenue Code of 1954) to participants or beneficiaries directly or through insurance, reimbursement, or otherwise. Such term shall not include any plan substantially all of the coverage under which is for qualified long-term care services as defined in §7702(B) of such Code.

(2) **Covered employee.**—The term "covered employee" means an individual who is (or was) provided coverage under a group health plan by virtue of the performance of services by the individual for one or more persons maintaining the plan (including as an employee defined in §401(c)(1) of the Internal Revenue Code of 1986).

(3) **Qualified beneficiary.**—

(A) In general.—The term "qualified beneficiary" means, with respect to a covered employee under a group health plan, any other individual who, on the day before the qualifying event for that employee, is a beneficiary under the plan—

(i) as the spouse of the covered employee, or

(ii) as the dependent child of the employee.

Such term shall also include a child who is born to or placed for adoption with the covered employee during the period of continuation coverage under this part.

(B) Special rule for terminations and reduced employment.—In the case of a qualifying event described in §603(2), the term "qualified beneficiary" includes the covered employee.

(C) Special rule for retirees and widows.—In the case of a qualifying event described in §603(6), the term "qualified beneficiary" includes a covered employee who had retired on or before the date of substantial elimination of coverage and any other individual who, on the day before such qualifying event, is a beneficiary under the plan—

(i) as the spouse of the covered employee,

(ii) as the dependent child of the employee, or

(iii) as the surviving spouse of the covered employee.

(4) **Employer.**—Subsection (n) (relating to leased employees) and subsection (t) (relating to application of controlled group rules to certain employee benefits) of §414 of the Internal Revenue Code of 1986 shall apply for purposes of this part in the same manner and to the same extent as such subsections apply for purposes of §106 of such Code. Any regulations prescribed by the Secretary pursuant to the preceding sentence shall be consistent and coextensive with any regulations prescribed for similar purposes by the Secretary of the Treasury (or such Secretary's delegate) under such subsections.

(5) **Optional extension of required period.**—A group health plan shall not be treated as failing to meet the requirements of this part solely because the plan provides both—

(A) that the period of extended coverage referred to in §602(2) commences with the date of the loss of coverage, and

(B) that the applicable notice period provided under §606(a)(2) commences with the date of the loss of coverage.

* * *

APPENDIX B

LABOR-MANAGEMENT RELATIONS ACT
SECTION 302(c) [18 U.S.C. §186(c)]

§186. Restrictions on financial transactions

* * *

(c) **Exceptions**

The provisions of this section shall not be applicable (1) in respect to any money or other thing of value payable by an employer to any of his employees whose established duties include acting openly for such employer in matters of labor relations or personnel administration or to any representative of his employees, or to any officer or employee of a labor organization, who is also an employee or former employee of such employer, as compensation for, or by reason of, his service as an employee of such employer; (2) with respect to the payment or delivery of any money or other thing of value in satisfaction of a judgment of any court or a decision or award of any arbitrator or impartial chairman or in compromise, adjustment, settlement, or release of any claim, complaint, grievance, or dispute in the absence of fraud or duress; (3) with respect to the sale or purchase of an article or commodity at the prevailing market price in the regular course of business; (4) with respect to money deducted from the wages of employees in payment of membership dues in a labor organization: *Provided*, That the employer has received from each employee, on whose account such deductions are made, a written assignment which shall not be irrevocable for a period of more than one year, or beyond the termination date of the applicable collective agreement, whichever occurs sooner; (5) with respect to money or other thing of value paid to a trust fund established by such representative, for the sole and exclusive benefit of the employees of such employer, and their families and dependents (or of such employees, families, and dependents jointly with the employees of other employers making similar payments, and their families and dependents): *Provided*, That (A) such payments are held in trust for the purpose of paying, either from principal or income or both, for the benefit of employees, their families and dependents, for medical or hospital care, pensions on retirement or death of employees, compensation for injuries or illness resulting from occupational activity or insurance to provide any of the foregoing, or unemployment benefits or life insurance, disability or sickness insurance, or accident insurance; (B) the detailed basis on which such payments are to be made is specified in a written agreement with the employer, and employees and employers are equally represented in the administration of such fund, together with such neutral persons as the representatives of the employers and the representatives of employees may agree upon and in the event the employer and employee groups deadlock on the administration of such fund and there are no neutral persons empowered to break such deadlock, such agreement provides that the two groups shall agree on an impartial umpire to decide such dispute, or in event of their failure to agree within a reasonable length of time, an impartial umpire to decide such dispute shall, on petition of either group, be appointed by the district court of the United States for the district where the trust fund has its principal office, and shall also contain provisions for an annual audit of the trust fund, a statement of the results of which shall be available for inspection by interested persons at the principal office of the trust fund and at such other places as may be designated in such written agreement; and (C) such payments as are intended to be used for the purpose of providing pensions or annuities for employees are made to a separate trust which provides that the funds held therein cannot be used for any purpose other than paying such pensions or annuities; (6) with respect to money or other thing of value paid by any employer to a trust fund established by such representative for the purpose of pooled vacation, holiday, severance or similar benefits, or defraying costs of apprenticeship or other training programs: *Provided*, That the requirements of clause (B) of the proviso to clause (5) of this subsection shall apply to such trust funds; (7) with respect to money or other thing of value paid by any employer to a pooled or individual trust fund established by such representative for the purpose of (A) scholarships for the benefit of employees, their families, and dependents for study at educational institutions, (B) child care centers for preschool and school age dependents of employees, or (C) financial assistance for employee housing: *Provided*, That no labor organization or employer shall be required to bargain on the establishment of any such trust fund, and refusal to do so shall not constitute an unfair labor practice: *Provided further*, That the requirements of clause (B) of the proviso to clause (5) of this subsection shall apply to such trust funds; (8) with respect to money or any other thing of value paid by any employer to a trust fund established by such representative for the purpose of defraying the costs of legal services for employees, their families, and dependents for counsel or plan of their choice: *Provided*, That the requirements of clause (B) of the proviso to clause (5) of this subsection shall apply to such trust funds: *Provided further*, That no such legal services shall be furnished: (A) to initiate any proceeding directed (i) against any such employer or its officers or agents except in workman's compensation cases, or (ii) against such labor organization, or its parent or subordinate bodies, or their officers or agents, or (iii) against any other employer or labor organization, or their officers or agents, in any matter arising under subchapter II of this chapter or this chapter; and (B) in any proceeding where a labor organization would be prohibited from defraying the costs of legal services by the provisions of the Labor-Management Reporting and Disclosure Act of 1959 [29 U.S.C.A. §401 et seq.]; or (9) with respect to money or other things of value paid by an employer to a plant, area or industrywide labor management committee established for one or more of the purposes set forth in section 5(b) of the Labor Management Cooperation Act of 1978.

APPENDIX C

INTERNAL REVENUE CODE SECTIONS

SEC. 401. QUALIFIED PENSION, PROFIT-SHARING, AND STOCK BONUS PLANS.

(a) REQUIREMENTS FOR QUALIFICATION.—A trust created or organized in the United States and forming part of a stock bonus, pension, or profit-sharing plan of an employer for the exclusive benefit of his employees or their beneficiaries shall constitute a qualified trust under this section—

(1) if contributions are made to the trust by such employer, or employees, or both, or by another employer who is entitled to deduct his contributions under section 404(a)(3)(B) (relating to deduction for contributions to profit-sharing and stock bonus plans), or by a charitable remainder trust pursuant to a qualified gratuitous transfer (as defined in section 664(g)(1)) for the purpose of distributing to such employees or their beneficiaries the corpus and income of the fund accumulated by the trust in accordance with such plan;

(2) if under the trust instrument it is impossible, at any time prior to the satisfaction of all liabilities with respect to employees and their beneficiaries under the trust, for any part of the corpus or income to be (within the taxable year or thereafter) used for, or diverted to, purposes other than for the exclusive benefit of his employees or their beneficiaries but this paragraph shall not be construed, in the case of a multiemployer plan, to prohibit the return of a contribution within 6 months after the plan administrator determines that the contribution was made by a mistake of fact or law (other than a mistake relating to whether the plan is described in section 401(a) or the trust which is part of such plan is exempt from taxation under section 501(a), or the return of any withdrawal liability payment determined to be an overpayment within 6 months of such determination);

(3) if the plan of which such trust is a part satisfies the requirements of section 410 (relating to minimum participation standards); and

(4) if the contributions or benefits provided under the plan do not discriminate in favor of highly compensated employees (within the meaning of section 414(q)). For purposes of this paragraph, there shall be excluded from consideration employees described in section 410(b)(3)(A) and (C).

(5) SPECIAL RULES RELATING TO NONDISCRIMINATION REQUIREMENTS.—

(A) SALARIED OR CLERICAL EMPLOYEES.—A classification shall not be considered discriminatory within the meaning of paragraph (4) or section 410(b)(2)(A)(i) merely because it is limited to salaried or clerical employees.

(B) CONTRIBUTIONS AND BENEFITS MAY BEAR UNIFORM RELATIONSHIP TO COMPENSATION.—A plan shall not be considered discriminatory within the meaning of paragraph (4) merely because the contributions or benefits of, or on behalf of, the employees under the plan bear a uniform relationship to the compensation (within the meaning of section 414(s)) of such employees.

(C) CERTAIN DISPARITY PERMITTED.—A plan shall not be considered discriminatory within the meaning of paragraph (4) merely because the contributions or benefits of, or on behalf of, the employees under the plan favor highly compensated employees (as defined in section 414(q)) in the manner permitted under subsection (l).

(D) INTEGRATED DEFINED BENEFIT PLAN.—

(i) IN GENERAL.—A defined benefit plan shall not be considered discriminatory within the meaning of paragraph (4) merely because the plan provides that the employer-derived accrued retirement benefit for any participant under the plan may not exceed the excess (if any) of—

(I) the participant's final pay with the employer, over

(II) the employer-derived retirement benefit created under Federal law attributable to service by the participant with the employer.

For purposes of this clause, the employer-derived retirement benefit created under Federal law shall be treated as accruing ratably over 35 years.

(ii) FINAL PAY.—For purposes of this subparagraph, the participant's final pay is the compensation (as defined in section 414(q)(4)) paid to the participant by the employer for any year—

(I) which ends during the 5-year period ending with the year in which the participant separated from service for the employer, and

(II) for which the participant's total compensation from the employer was highest.

(E) 2 OR MORE PLANS TREATED AS SINGLE PLAN.—For purposes of determining whether 2 or more plans of an employer satisfy the requirements of paragraph (4) when considered as a single plan—

(i) CONTRIBUTIONS.—If the amount of contributions on behalf of the employees allowed as a deduction under section 404 for the taxable year with respect to such plans, taken together, bears a uniform relationship to the compensation (within the meaning of section 414(s)) of such employees, the plans shall not be considered discriminatory merely because the rights of employees to, or derived from, the employer contributions under the separate plans do not become nonforfeitable at the same rate.

(ii) BENEFITS.—If the employees' rights to benefits under the separate plans do not become nonforfeitable at the same rate, but the levels of benefits provided by the separate plans satisfy the requirements of regulations prescribed by the Secretary to take account of the differences in such rates, the plans shall not be considered discriminatory merely because of the difference in such rates.

(F) SOCIAL SECURITY RETIREMENT AGE.—For purposes of testing for discrimination under paragraph (4)—

(i) the social security retirement age (as defined in section 415(b)(8)) shall be treated as a uniform retirement age, and

(ii) subsidized early retirement benefits and joint and survivor annuities shall not be treated as being unavailable to employees on the same terms merely because such benefits or annuities are based in whole or in part on an employee's social security retirement age (as so defined).

(G) STATE AND LOCAL GOVERNMENTAL PLANS.—Paragraphs (3) and (4) shall not apply to a governmental plan (within the meaning of section 414(d)) maintained by a State or local government or political subdivision thereof (or agency or instrumentality thereof).

(6) A plan shall be considered as meeting the requirements of paragraph (3) during the whole of any taxable year of the plan if on one day in each quarter it satisfied such requirements.

(7) A trust shall not constitute a qualified trust under this section unless the plan of which such trust is a part satisfies the requirements of section 411 (relating to minimum vesting standards).

(8) A trust forming part of a defined benefit plan shall not constitute a qualified trust under this section unless the plan provides that forfeitures must not be applied to increase the benefits any employee would otherwise receive under the plan.

(9) REQUIRED DISTRIBUTIONS.—

(A) IN GENERAL.—A trust shall not constitute a qualified trust under this subsection unless the plan provides that the entire interest of each employee—

(i) will be distributed to such employee not later than the required beginning date, or

(ii) will be distributed, beginning not later than the required beginning date, in accordance with regulations, over the life of such employee or over the lives of such employee and a designated beneficiary (or over a period not extending beyond the life expectancy of such employee or the life expectancy of such employee and a designated beneficiary).

(B) REQUIRED DISTRIBUTION WHERE EMPLOYEE DIES BEFORE INTEREST IS DISTRIBUTED.—

(i) WHERE DISTRIBUTIONS HAVE BEGUN UNDER SUBPARAGRAPH (A)(ii).—A trust shall not constitute a qualified trust under this section unless the plan provides that if—

(I) the distribution of the employee's interest has begun in accordance with subparagraph (A)(ii), and

(II) the employee dies before his entire interest has been distributed to him,

the remaining portion of such interest will be distributed at least as rapidly as under the method of distribution being used under subparagraph (A)(ii) as of the date of his death.

(ii) 5-YEAR RULE FOR OTHER CASES.—A trust shall not constitute a qualified trust under this section unless the plan provides that, if an employee dies before the distribution of the employee's interest has begun in accordance with subparagraph (A)(ii), the entire interest of the employee will be distributed within 5 years after the death of such employee.

(iii) EXCEPTION TO THE 5-YEAR RULE FOR CERTAIN AMOUNTS PAYABLE OVER LIFE OF BENEFICIARY.—If—

(I) any portion of the employee's interest is payable to (or for the benefit of) a designated beneficiary,

(II) such portion will be distributed (in accordance with regulations) over the life of such designated beneficiary (or over a period not extending beyond the life expectancy of such beneficiary), and

(III) such distributions begin not later than 1 year after the date of the employee's death or such later date as the Secretary may by regulations prescribe,

for purposes of clause (ii), the portion referred to in subclause (I) shall be treated as distributed on the date on which such distributions began.

(iv) SPECIAL RULES FOR SURVIVING SPOUSE OF EMPLOYEE.—If the designated beneficiary referred to in clause (iii)(I) is the surviving spouse of the employee—

(I) the date on which the distributions are required to begin under clause (iii)(III) shall not be earlier than the date on which the employee would have attained age 70 , and

(II) if the surviving spouse dies before the distributions to such spouse begin, this subparagraph shall be applied as if the surviving spouse were the employee.

(C) REQUIRED BEGINNING DATE.—For purposes of this paragraph—

(i) IN GENERAL.—The term "required beginning date" means April 1 of the calendar year following the later of—

(I) the calendar year in which the employee attains age 70 , or

(II) the calendar year in which the employee retires.

(ii) EXCEPTION.—Subclause (II) of clause (i) shall not apply—

(I) except as provided in section 409(d), in the case of an employee who is a 5-percent owner (as defined in section 416) with respect to the plan year ending in the calendar year in which the employee attains age 70 , or

(II) for purposes of section 408(a)(6) or (b)(3).

(iii) ACTUARIAL ADJUSTMENT.—In the case of an employee to whom clause (i)(II) applies who retires in a calendar year after the calendar year in which the employee attains age 70 , the employee's accrued benefit shall be actuarially increased to take into account the period after age 70 in which the employee was not receiving any benefits under the plan.

(iv) EXCEPTION FOR GOVERNMENTAL AND CHURCH PLANS.— Clauses (ii) and (iii) shall not apply in the case of a governmental plan or church plan. For purposes of this clause, the term "church plan" means a plan maintained by a church for church employees, and the term "church" means any church (as defined in section 3121(w)(3)(A)) or qualified church-controlled organization (as defined in section 3121(w)(3)(B)).

(D) LIFE EXPECTANCY.—For purposes of this paragraph, the life expectancy of an employee and the employee's spouse (other than in the case of a life annuity) may be redetermined but not more frequently than annually.

(E) DESIGNATED BENEFICIARY.—For purposes of this paragraph, the term "designated beneficiary" means any individual designated as a beneficiary by the employee.

(F) TREATMENT OF PAYMENTS TO CHILDREN.—Under regulations prescribed by the Secretary, for purposes of this paragraph, any amount paid to a child shall be treated as if it had been paid to the surviving spouse if such amount will become payable to the surviving spouse upon such child reaching majority (or other designated event permitted under regulations).

(G) TREATMENT OF INCIDENTAL DEATH BENEFIT DISTRIBUTIONS.— For purposes of this title, any distribution required under the incidental death benefit requirements of this subsection shall be treated as a distribution required under this paragraph.

(10) OTHER REQUIREMENTS.—

(A) PLANS BENEFITING OWNER-EMPLOYEES.—In the case of any plan which provides contributions or benefits for employees some or all of whom are owner-employees (as defined in subsection (c)(3)), a trust forming part of such plan shall constitute a qualified trust under this section only if the requirements of subsection (d) are also met.

(B) TOP-HEAVY PLANS.—

(i) IN GENERAL.—In the case of any top-heavy plan, a trust forming part of such plan shall constitute a qualified trust under this section only if the requirements of section 416 are met.

(ii) PLANS WHICH MAY BECOME TOP-HEAVY.—Except to the extent provided in regulations, a trust forming part of a plan (whether or not a top-heavy plan) shall constitute a qualified trust under this section only if such plan contains provisions—

(I) which will take effect if such plan becomes a top-heavy plan, and

(II) which meet the requirements of section 416.

(iii) EXEMPTION FOR GOVERNMENTAL PLANS.—This subparagraph shall not apply to any governmental plan.

(11) REQUIREMENT OF JOINT AND SURVIVOR ANNUITY AND PRERETIREMENT SURVIVOR ANNUITY.—

(A) IN GENERAL.—In the case of any plan to which this paragraph applies, except as provided in section 417, a trust forming part of such plan shall not constitute a qualified trust under this section unless—

    (i) in the case of a vested participant who does not die before the annuity starting date, the accrued benefit payable to such participant is provided in the form of a qualified joint and survivor annuity, and

    (ii) in the case of a vested participant who dies before the annuity starting date and who has a surviving spouse, a qualified preretirement survivor annuity is provided to the surviving spouse of such participant.

(B) PLANS TO WHICH PARAGRAPH APPLIES.—This paragraph shall apply to—

    (i) any defined benefit plan,

    (ii) any defined contribution plan which is subject to the funding standards of section 412, and

    (iii) any participant under any other defined contribution plan unless—

        (I) such plan provides that the participant's nonforfeitable accrued benefit (reduced by any security interest held by the plan by reason of a loan outstanding to such participant) is payable in full, on the death of the participant, to the participant's surviving spouse (or, if there is no surviving spouse or the surviving spouse consents in the manner required under section 417(a)(2), to a designated beneficiary),

        (II) such participant does not elect a payment of benefits in the form of a life annuity, and

        (III) with respect to such participant, such plan is not a direct or indirect transferee (in a transfer after December 31, 1984) of a plan which is described in clause (i) or (ii) or to which this clause applied with respect to the participant.

Clause (iii)(III) shall apply only with respect to the transferred assets (and income therefrom) if the plan separately accounts for such assets and any income therefrom.

(C) EXCEPTION FOR CERTAIN ESOP BENEFITS.—

    (i) IN GENERAL.—If the case of—

        (I) a tax credit employee stock ownership plan (as defined in section 409(a)), or

        (II) an employee stock ownership plan (as defined in section 4975(e)(7)),

subparagraph (A) shall not apply to that portion of the employee's accrued benefit to which the requirements of section 409(h) apply.

(ii) NONFORFEITABLE BENEFIT MUST BE PAID IN FULL, ETC.—In the case of any participant, clause (i) shall apply only if the requirements of subclauses (I), (II), and (III) of subparagraph (B)(iii) are met with respect to such participant.

(D) SPECIAL RULE WHERE PARTICIPANT AND SPOUSE MARRIED LESS THAN 1 YEAR.—A plan shall not be treated as failing to meet the requirements of subparagraphs (B)(iii) or (C) merely because the plan provides that benefits will not be payable to the surviving spouse of the participant unless the participant and such spouse had been married throughout the 1-year period ending on the earlier of the participant's annuity starting date or the date of the participant's death.

(E) EXCEPTION FOR PLANS DESCRIBED IN SECTION 404(C).—This paragraph shall not apply to a plan which the Secretary has determined is a plan described in section 404(c) (or a continuation thereof) in which participation is substantially limited to individuals who, before January 1, 1976, ceased employment covered by the plan.

(F) CROSS REFERENCE.—For—

(i) provisions under which participants may elect to waive the requirements of this paragraph, and

(ii) other definitions and special rules for purposes of this paragraph,

see section 417.

(12) A trust shall not constitute a qualified trust under this section unless the plan of which such trust is a part provides that in the case of any merger or consolidation with, or transfer of assets or liabilities, to any other plan after September 2, 1974, each participant in the plan would (if the plan then terminated) receive a benefit immediately after the merger, consolidation, or transfer which is equal to or greater than the benefit he would have been entitled to receive immediately before the merger, consolidation, or transfer (if the plan had then terminated). The preceding sentence does not apply to any multiemployer plan with respect to any transaction to the extent that participants either before or after the transaction are covered under a multiemployer plan to which title IV of the Employee Retirement Income Security Act of 1974 applies.

(13) ASSIGNMENT AND ALIENATION.—

(A) IN GENERAL.—A trust shall not constitute a qualified trust under this section unless the plan of which such trust is a part provides that benefits provided under the plan may not be assigned or alienated. For purposes of the preceding sentence, there shall not be taken into account any voluntary and revocable assignment of not to exceed 10 percent of any benefit payment made by any participant who is receiving benefits under the plan unless the assignment or alienation is made for purposes of defraying plan administration costs. For purposes of this paragraph a loan made to a participant or beneficiary shall not be treated as an assignment or alienation if such loan is secured by the participant's accrued nonforfeitable benefit and is exempt from the tax imposed by section 4975 (relating to tax on prohibited transactions) by reason of section 4975(d)(1). This paragraph shall take effect on January 1, 1976 and shall not apply to assignments which were irrevocable on September 2, 1974.

(B) SPECIAL RULES FOR DOMESTIC RELATIONS ORDERS.—Subparagraph (A) shall apply to the creation, assignment, or recognition of a right to any benefit payable with respect to a participant pursuant to a domestic relations order, except that subparagraph (A) shall not apply if the order is determined to be a qualified domestic relations order.

(C) SPECIAL RULE FOR CERTAIN JUDGMENTS AND SETTLEMENTS.—Subparagraph (A) shall not apply to any offset of a participant's benefits provided under a plan against an amount that the participant is ordered or required to pay to the plan if—

(i) the order or requirement to pay arises—

(I) under a judgment of conviction for a crime involving such plan,

(II) under a civil judgment (including a consent order or decree) entered by a court in an action brought in connection with a violation (or alleged violation) of part 4 of subtitle B of title I of the Employee Retirement Income Security Act of 1974, or

(iii) pursuant to a settlement agreement between the Secretary of Labor and the participant, or a settlement agreement between the Pension Benefit Guaranty Corporation and the participant, in connection with a violation (or alleged violation) of part 4 of such subtitle by a fiduciary or any other person,

(ii) the judgment, order, decree, or settlement agreement expressly provides for the offset of all or part of the amount ordered or required to be paid to the plan against the participant's benefits provided under the plan, and

(iii) in a case in which the survivor annuity requirements of section 401(a)(11) apply with respect to distributions from the plan to the participant, if the participant has a spouse at the time at which the offset is to be made—

(I) either such spouse has consented in writing to such offset and such consent is witnessed by a notary public or representative of the plan (or it is established to the satisfaction of a plan representative that such consent may not be obtained by reason of circumstances described in section 417(a)(2)(B)), or an election to waive the right of the spouse to either a qualified joint and survivor annuity or a qualified preretirement survivor annuity is in effect in accordance with the requirements of section 417(a),

(II) such spouse is ordered or required in such judgment, order, decree, or settlement to pay an amount to the plan in connection with a violation of part 4 of such subtitle, or

(III) in such judgment, order, decree, or settlement, such spouse retains the right to receive the survivor annuity under a qualified joint and survivor annuity provided pursuant to section 401(a)(11)(A)(i) and under a qualified preretirement survivor annuity provided pursuant to section 401(a)(11)(A)(ii), determined in accordance with subparagraph (D).

A plan shall not be treated as failing to meet the requirements of this subsection, subsection (k), section 403(b), or section 409(d) solely by reason of an offset described in this subparagraph.

(D) SURVIVOR ANNUITY.—

(i) IN GENERAL.—The survivor annuity described in subparagraph (C)(iii)(III) shall be determined as if—

(I) the participant terminated employment on the date of the offset,

(II) there was no offset,

(III) the plan permitted commencement of benefits only on or after normal retirement age,

(IV) the plan provided only the minimum-required qualified joint and survivor annuity, and

(V) the amount of the qualified preretirement survivor annuity under the plan is equal to the amount of the survivor annuity payable under the minimum-required qualified joint and survivor annuity.

(ii) DEFINITION.—For purposes of this subparagraph, the term "minimum-required qualified joint and survivor annuity" means the qualified joint and survivor annuity which is the actuarial equivalent of the participant's accrued benefit (within the meaning of section 411(a)(7)) and under which the survivor annuity is 50 percent of the amount of the annuity which is payable during the joint lives of the participant and the spouse.

(14) A trust shall not constitute a qualified trust under this section unless the plan of which such trust is a part provides that, unless the participant otherwise elects, the payment of benefits under the plan to the participant will begin not later than the 60th day after the latest of the close of the plan year in which—

(A) the date on which the participant attains the earlier of age 65 or the normal retirement age specified under the plan,

(B) occurs the 10th anniversary of the year in which the participant commenced participation in the plan, or

(C) the participant terminates his service with the employer.

In the case of a plan which provides for the payment of an early retirement benefit, a trust forming a part of such plan shall not constitute a qualified trust under this section unless a participant who satisfied the service requirements for such early retirement benefit, but separated from the service (with any nonforfeitable right to an accrued benefit) before satisfying the age requirement for such early retirement benefit, is entitled upon satisfaction of such age requirement to receive a benefit not less than the benefit to which he would be entitled at the normal retirement age, actuarially reduced under regulations prescribed by the Secretary.

(15) A trust shall not constitute a qualified trust under this section unless under the plan of which such trust is a part—

(A) in the case of a participant or beneficiary who is receiving benefits under such plan, or

(B) in the case of a participant who is separated from the service and who has nonforfeitable rights to benefits,

such benefits are not decreased by reason of any increase in the benefit levels payable under title II of the Social Security Act or any increase in the wage base under such title II, if such increase takes place after September 2, 1974, or (if later) the earlier of the date of first receipt of such benefits or the date of such separation, as the case may be.

(16) A trust shall not constitute a qualified trust under this section if the plan of which such trust is a part provides for benefits or contributions which exceed the limitations of section 415.

(17) COMPENSATION LIMIT.—

(A) IN GENERAL.—A trust shall not constitute a qualified trust under this section unless, under the plan of which such trust is a part, the annual compensation of each employee taken into account under the plan for any year does not exceed $200,000.

(B) COST-OF-LIVING ADJUSTMENT.—The Secretary shall adjust annually the $200,000 amount in subparagraph (A) for increases in the cost-of-living at the same time and in the same manner as adjustments under section 415(d); except that the base period shall be the calendar quarter beginning July 1, 2001, and any increase which is not a multiple of $5,000 shall be rounded to the next lowest multiple of $5,000.

(18) [Repealed.]

(19) A trust shall not constitute a qualified trust under this section if under the plan of which such trust is a part any part of a participant's accrued benefit derived from employer contributions (whether or not otherwise nonforfeitable), is forfeitable solely because of withdrawal by such participant of any amount attributable to the benefit derived from contributions made by such participant. The preceding sentence shall not apply to the accrued benefit of any participant unless, at the time of such withdrawal, such participant has a nonforfeitable right to at least 50 percent of such accrued benefit (as determined under section 411). The first sentence of this paragraph shall not apply to the extent that an accrued benefit is permitted to be forfeited in accordance with section 411(a)(3)(D)(iii) (relating to proportional forfeitures of benefits accrued before September 2, 1974, in the event of withdrawal of certain mandatory contributions).

(20) A trust forming part of a pension plan shall not be treated as failing to constitute a qualified trust under this section merely because the pension plan of which such trust is a part makes 1 or more distributions within 1 taxable year to a distributee on account of a termination of the plan of which the trust is a part, or in the case of a profit-sharing or stock bonus plan, a complete discontinuance of contributions under such plan. This paragraph shall not apply to a defined benefit plan unless the employer maintaining such plan files a notice with the Pension Benefit Guaranty Corporation (at the time and in the manner prescribed by the Pension Benefit Guaranty Corporation) notifying the Corporation of such payment or distribution and the Corporation has approved such payment or distribution or, within 90 days after the date on which such notice was filed, has failed to disapprove such payment or distribution. For purposes of this paragraph, rules similar to the rules of section 402(a)(6)(B) (as in effect before its repeal by section 521 of the Unemployment Compensation Amendments of 1992) shall apply.

(21) [Repealed.]

(22) If a defined contribution plan (other than a profit-sharing plan)—

(A) is established by an employer whose stock is not readily tradable on an established market, and

(B) after acquiring securities of the employer, more than 10 percent of the total assets of the plan are securities of the employer, any trust forming part of such plan shall not constitute a qualified trust under this section unless the plan meets the requirements of subsection (e) of section 409. The requirements of subsection (e) of section 409 shall not apply to any employees of an employer who are participants in any defined contribution plan established and maintained by such employer if the stock of such employer is not readily tradable on an established market and the trade or business of such employer consists of publishing on a regular basis a newspaper for general circulation. For purposes of the preceding sentence, subsections (b), (c), (m), and (o) of section 414 shall not apply except for determining whether stock of the employer is not readily tradable on an established market.

(23) A stock bonus plan shall not be treated as meeting the requirements of this section unless such plan meets the requirements of subsections (h) and (o) of section 409, except that in applying section 409(h) for purposes of this paragraph, the term "employer securities" shall include any securities of the employer held by the plan.

(24) Any group trust which otherwise meets the requirements of this section shall not be treated as not meeting such requirements on account of the participation or inclusion in such trust of the moneys of any plan or governmental unit described in section 818(a)(6).

(25) REQUIREMENT THAT ACTUARIAL ASSUMPTIONS BE SPECIFIED.—A defined benefit plan shall not be treated as providing definitely determinable benefits unless, whenever the amount of any benefit is to be determined on the basis of actuarial assumptions, such assumptions are specified in the plan in a way which precludes employer discretion.

(26) ADDITIONAL PARTICIPATION REQUIREMENTS.—

(A) IN GENERAL.—In the case of a trust which is a part of a defined benefit plan, such trust shall not constitute a qualified trust under this subsection unless on each day of the plan year such trust benefits at least the lesser of—

(i) 50 employees of the employer, or

(ii) the greater of—

(I) 40 percent of all employees of the employer, or

(II) 2 employees (or if there is only 1 employee, such employee).

(B) TREATMENT OF EXCLUDABLE EMPLOYEES.—

(i) IN GENERAL.—A plan may exclude from consideration under this paragraph employees described in paragraphs (3) and (4)(A) of section 410(b).

(ii) SEPARATE APPLICATION FOR CERTAIN EXCLUDABLE EMPLOYEES.—If employees described in section 410(b)(4)(B) are covered under a plan which meets the requirements of subparagraph (A) separately with respect to such employees, such employees may be excluded from consideration in determining whether any plan of the employer meets such requirements if—

(I) the benefits for such employees are provided under the same plan as benefits for other employees,

(II) the benefits provided to such employees are not greater than comparable benefits provided to other employees under the plan, and

(III) no highly compensated employee (within the meaning of section 414(q)) is included in the group of such employees for more than 1 year.

(C) ELIGIBILITY TO PARTICIPATE.—In the case of contributions under section 401(k) or 401(m), employees who are eligible to contribute (or may elect to have contributions made on their behalf) shall be treated as benefiting under the plan.

(D) SPECIAL RULE FOR COLLECTIVE BARGAINING UNITS.—Except to the extent provided in regulations, a plan covering only employees described in section 410(b)(3)(A) may exclude from consideration any employees who are not included in the unit or units in which the covered employees are included.

(E) PARAGRAPH NOT TO APPLY TO MULTIEMPLOYER PLANS.—Except to the extent provided in regulations, this paragraph shall not apply to employees in a multiemployer plan (within the meaning of section 414(f)) who are covered by collective bargaining agreements.

(F) SPECIAL RULE FOR CERTAIN DISPOSITIONS OR ACQUISITIONS.—Rules similar to the rules of section 410(b)(6)(C) shall apply for purposes of this paragraph.

(G) SEPARATE LINES OF BUSINESS.—At the election of the employer and with the consent of the Secretary, this paragraph may be applied separately with respect to each separate line of business of the employer. For purposes of this paragraph, the term "separate line of business" has the meaning given such term by section 414(r) (without regard to paragraph (2)(A) or (7) thereof).

(H) EXCEPTION FOR STATE AND LOCAL GOVERNMENTAL PLANS.—This paragraph shall not apply to a governmental plan (within the meaning of section 414(d)) maintained by a State or local government or political subdivision thereof (or agency or instrumentality thereof).

(I) REGULATIONS.—The Secretary may by regulation provide that any separate benefit structure, any separate trust, or any other separate arrangement is to be treated as a separate plan for purposes of applying this paragraph.

(27) DETERMINATION AS TO PROFIT-SHARING PLANS.—

(A) CONTRIBUTIONS NEED NOT BE BASED ON PROFITS.—The determination of whether the plan under which any contributions are made is a profit-sharing plan shall be made without regard to current or accumulated profits of the employer and without regard to whether the employer is a tax-exempt organization.

(B) PLAN MUST DESIGNATE TYPE.—In the case of a plan which is intended to be a money purchase pension plan or a profit-sharing plan, a trust forming part of such plan shall not constitute a qualified trust under this subsection unless the plan designates such intent at such time and in such manner as the Secretary may prescribe.

(28) ADDITIONAL REQUIREMENTS RELATING TO EMPLOYEE STOCK OWNERSHIP PLANS.—

(A) IN GENERAL.—In the case of a trust which is part of an employee stock ownership plan (within the meaning of section 4975(e)(7)) or a plan which meets the requirements of section 409(a), such trust shall not constitute a qualified trust under this section unless such plan meets the requirements of subparagraphs (B) and (C).

(B) DIVERSIFICATION OF INVESTMENTS.—

(i) IN GENERAL.—A plan meets the requirements of this subparagraph if each qualified participant in the plan may elect within 90 days after the close of each plan year in the qualified election period to direct the plan as to the investment of at least 25 percent of the participant's account in the plan (to the extent such portion exceeds the amount of which a prior election under this subparagraph applies). In the case of the election year in which the participant can make his last election, the preceding sentence shall be applied by substituting "50 percent" for "25 percent".

(ii) METHOD OF MEETING REQUIREMENTS.—A plan shall be treated as meeting the requirements of clause (i) if—

(I) the portion of the participant's account covered by the election under clause (i) is distributed within 90 days after the period during which the election may be made, or

(II) the plan offers at least 3 investment options (not inconsistent with regulations prescribed by the Secretary) to each participant making an election under clause (i) and within 90 days after the period during which the election may be made, the plan invests the portion of the participant's account covered by the election in accordance with such election.

(iii) QUALIFIED PARTICIPANT.—For purposes of this subparagraph, the term "qualified participant" means any employee who has completed at least 10 years of participation under the plan and has attained age 55.

(iv) QUALIFIED ELECTION PERIOD.—For purposes of this subparagraph, the term "qualified election period" means the 6-plan-year period beginning with the later of—

(I) the 1st plan year in which the individual first became a qualified participant, or

(II) the 1st plan year beginning after December 31, 1986.

For purposes of the preceding sentence, an employer may elect to treat an individual first becoming a qualified participant in the 1st plan year beginning in 1987 as having become a participant in the 1st plan year beginning in 1988.

(C) USE OF INDEPENDENT APPRAISER.—A plan meets the requirements of this subparagraph if all valuations of employer securities which are not readily tradable on an established securities market with respect to activities carried on by the plan are by an independent appraiser. For purposes of the preceding sentence, the term "independent appraiser" means any appraiser meeting requirements similar to the requirements of the regulations prescribed under section 170(a)(1).

(29) SECURITY REQUIRED UPON ADOPTION OF PLAN AMENDMENT RESULTING IN SIGNIFICANT UNDERFUNDING.

(A) IN GENERAL.—If—

(i) a defined benefit plan (other than a multiemployer plan) to which the requirements of section 412 apply adopts an amendment an effect of which is to increase current liability under the plan for a plan year, and

(ii) the funded current liability percentage of the plan for the plan year in which the amendment takes effect is less than 60 percent, including the amount of the unfunded current liability under the plan attributable to the plan amendment,

the trust of which such plan is a part shall not constitute a qualified trust under this subsection unless such amendment does not take effect until the contributing sponsor (or any member of the controlled group of the contributing sponsor) provides security to the plan.

(B) FORM OF SECURITY.—The security required under subparagraph (A) shall consist of—

(i) a bond issued by a corporate surety company that is an acceptable surety for purposes of section 412 of the Employee Retirement Income Security Act of 1974,

(ii) cash, or United States obligations which mature in 3 years or less, held in escrow by a bank or similar financial institution, or

(iii) such other form of security as is satisfactory to the Secretary and the parties involved.

(C) AMOUNT OF SECURITY.—The security shall be in an amount equal to the excess of—

(i) the lesser of—

(I) the amount of additional plan assets which would be necessary to increase the funded current liability percentage under the plan to 60 percent, including the amount of the unfunded current liability under the plan attributable to the plan amendment, or

(II) the amount of the increase in current liability under the plan attributable to the plan amendment and any other plan amendments adopted after December 22, 1987, and before such plan amendment, over

(ii) $10,000,000.

(D) RELEASE OF SECURITY.—The security shall be released (and any amounts thereunder shall be refunded together with any interest accrued thereon) at the end of the first plan year which ends after the provision of the security and for which the funded current liability percentage under the plan is not less than 60 percent. The Secretary may prescribe regulations for partial releases of the security by reason of increases in the funded current liability percentage.

(E) DEFINITIONS.—For purposes of this paragraph, the terms "current liability", "funded current liability percentage", and "unfunded current liability" shall have the meanings given such terms by section 412(l), except that in computing unfunded current liability there shall not be taken into account any unamortized portion of the unfunded old liability amount as of the close of the plan year.

(30) LIMITATIONS ON ELECTIVE DEFERRALS.—In the case of a trust which is part of a plan under which elective deferrals (within the meaning of section 402(g)(3)) may be made with respect to any individual during a calendar year, such trust shall not constitute a qualified trust under this subsection unless the plan provides that the amount of such deferrals under such plan and all other plans, contracts, or arrangements of an employer maintaining such plan may not exceed the amount of the limitation in effect under section 402(g)(1)(A) for taxable years beginning in such calendar year.

Caution: The heading for Code Sec. 401(a)(31), below, prior to amendment by P.L. 107-16, applies to distributions made before final regulations implementing §657(c)(2)(A) are prescribed.

(31) OPTIONAL DIRECT TRANSFER OF ELIGIBLE ROLLOVER DISTRIBUTIONS.—

Caution: The heading for Code Sec. 401(a)(31), below, as amended by P.L. 107-16, applies to distributions made after final regulations implementing §657(c)(2)(A) are prescribed. For sunset provision, see P.L. 107-16, 901, in the amendment notes.

(31) DIRECT TRANSFER OF ELIGIBLE ROLLOVER DISTRIBUTIONS.—

(A) IN GENERAL.—A trust shall not constitute a qualified trust under this section unless the plan of which such trust is a part provides that if the distributee of any eligible rollover distribution—

(i) elects to have such distribution paid directly to an eligible retirement plan, and

(ii) specifies the eligible retirement plan to which such distribution is to be paid (in such form and at such time as the plan administrator may prescribe),

such distribution shall be made in the form of a direct trustee-to-trustee transfer to the eligible retirement plan so specified.

Caution: Code Sec. 401(a)(31)(B), below, prior to amendment by P.L. 107-16, generally applies to distributions on or before December 31, 2001, and before final regulations implementing P.L. 107-16, §657(c)(2)(A), are prescribed.

(B) LIMITATION.—Subparagraph (A) shall apply only to the extent that the eligible rollover distribution would be includible in gross income if not transferred as provided in subparagraph (A) (determined without regard to sections 402(c) and 403(a)(4)).

Caution: Code Sec. 401(a)(31)(B), below, as amended by P.L. 107-16, §641(e)(3) and §643(b) but prior to redesignation and amendment by §657(a), generally applies to distributions made after December 31, 2001 and before final regulations implementing §657(c)(2)(A) are prescribed. For sunset provision, see P.L. 107-16, §901, in the amendment notes.

(B) LIMITATION.—Subparagraph (A) shall apply only to the extent that the eligible rollover distribution would be includible in gross income if not transferred as provided in subparagraph (A) (determined without regard to sections 402(c), 403(a)(4), 403(b)(8), and 457(e)(16)). The preceding sentence shall not apply to such distribution if the plan to which such distribution is transferred—

(i) agrees to separately account for amounts so transferred, including separately accounting for the portion of such distribution which is includible in gross income and the portion of such distribution which is not so includible, or

(ii) is an eligible retirement plan described in clause (i) or (ii) of section 402(c)(8)(B).

Caution: Code Sec. 401(a)(31)(B), below, as added by P.L. 107-16, §657(a)(1), applies to distributions made after final regulations implementing §657(c)(2)(A) are prescribed. For sunset provision, see P.L. 107-16, §901, in the amendment notes.

(B) CERTAIN MANDATORY DISTRIBUTIONS.—

(i) IN GENERAL.—In case of a trust which is part of an eligible plan, such trust shall not constitute a qualified trust under this section unless the plan of which such trust is a part provides that if—

(I) a distribution described in clause (ii) in excess of $1,000 is made, and

(II) the distributee does not make an election under subparagraph (A) and does not elect to receive the distribution directly,

the plan administrator shall make such transfer to an individual retirement plan of a designated trustee or issuer and shall notify the distribute in writing (either separately or as part of the notice under section 402(f)) that the distribution may be transferred to another individual retirement plan.

(ii) ELIGIBLE PLAN.—For purposes of clause (i), the term "eligible plan" means a plan which provides that any nonforfeitable accrued benefit for which the present value (as determined under section 411(a)(11)) does not exceed $5,000 shall be immediately distributed to the participant.

Caution: Code Sec. 401(a)(31)(C), below, as redesignated and amended by P.L. 107-16 and P.L. 107-147, applies generally to distributions after December 31, 2001, and after final regulations implementing P.L. 107-16, §657(c)(2)(A), are prescribed. For sunset provision, see P.L. 107-16, §901, in the amendment notes.

(C) LIMITATION.—Subparagraphs (A) and (B) shall apply only to the extent that the eligible rollover distribution would be includible in gross income if not transferred as provided in subparagraph (A) (determined without regard to sections 402(c), 403(a)(4), 403(b)(8), and 457(e)(16)). The preceding sentence shall not apply to such distribution if the plan to which such distribution is transferred—

(i) is a qualified trust which is part of a plan which is a defined contribution plan and agrees to separately account for amounts so transferred, including separately accounting for the portion of such distribution which is includible in gross income and the portion of such distribution which is not so includible, or

(ii) is an eligible retirement plan described in clause (i) or (ii) of section 402(c)(8)(B).

Caution: Code Sec. 401(a)(31)(D)-(E), below, as redesignated by P.L. 107-16, applies to distributions made after final regulations implementing P.L. 107-16, §657(c)(2)(A), are prescribed. For sunset provision, see P.L. 107-16, §901, in the amendment notes.

(D) ELIGIBLE ROLLOVER DISTRIBUTION.—For purposes of this paragraph, the term "eligible rollover distribution" has the meaning given such term by section 402(f)(2)(A).

(E) ELIGIBLE RETIREMENT PLAN.—For purposes of this paragraph, the term "eligible retirement plan" has the meaning given such term by section 402(c)(8)(B), except that a qualified trust shall be considered an eligible retirement plan only if it is a defined contribution plan, the terms of which permit the acceptance of rollover distributions.

(32) TREATMENT OF FAILURE TO MAKE CERTAIN PAYMENTS IF PLAN HAS LIQUIDITY SHORTFALL.—

(A) IN GENERAL.—A trust forming part of a pension plan to which section 412(m)(5) applies shall not be treated as failing to constitute a qualified trust under this section merely because such plan ceases to make any payment described in subparagraph (B) during any period that such plan has a liquidity shortfall (as defined in section 412(m)(5)).

(B) PAYMENTS DESCRIBED.—A payment is described in this subparagraph if such payment is—

(i) any payment, in excess of the monthly amount paid under a single life annuity (plus any social security supplements described in the last sentence of section 411(a)(9)), to a participant or beneficiary whose annuity starting date (as defined in section 417(f)(2)) occurs during the period referred to in subparagraph (A),

(ii) any payment for the purchase of an irrevocable commitment from an insurer to pay benefits, and

(iii) any other payment specified by the Secretary by regulations.

(C) PERIOD OF SHORTFALL.—For purposes of this paragraph, a plan has a liquidity shortfall during the period that there is an underpayment of an installment under section 412(m) by reason of paragraph (5)(A) thereof.

(33) PROHIBITION ON BENEFIT INCREASES WHILE SPONSOR IS IN BANKRUPTCY.—

(A) IN GENERAL.—A trust which is part of a plan to which this paragraph applies shall not constitute a qualified trust under this section if an amendment to such plan is adopted while the employer is a debtor in a case under title 11, United States Code, or similar Federal or State law, if such amendment increases liabilities of the plan by reason of—

(i) any increase in benefits,

(ii) any change in the accrual of benefits, or

(iii) any change in the rate at which benefits become nonforfeitable under the plan,

with respect to employees of the debtor, and such amendment is effective prior to the effective date of such employer's plan of reorganization.

(B) EXCEPTIONS.—This paragraph shall not apply to any plan amendment if—

(i) the plan, were such amendment to take effect, would have a funded current liability percentage (as defined in section 412(l)(8)) of 100 percent or more,

(ii) the Secretary determines that such amendment is reasonable and provides for only de minimis increases in the liabilities of the plan with respect to employees of the debtor,

(iii) such amendment only repeals an amendment described in subsection 412(c)(8), or

(iv) such amendment is required as a condition of qualification under this part.

(C) PLANS TO WHICH THIS PARAGRAPH APPLIES.—This paragraph shall apply only to plans (other than multiemployer plans) covered under section 4021 of the Employee Retirement Income Security Act of 1974.

(D) EMPLOYER.—For purposes of this paragraph, the term "employer" means the employer referred to in section 412(c)(11) (without regard to subparagraph (B) thereof).

(34) BENEFITS OF MISSING PARTICIPANTS ON PLAN TERMINATION.—In the case of a plan covered by title IV of the Employee Retirement Income Security Act of 1974, a trust forming part of such plan shall not be treated as failing to constitute a qualified trust under this section merely because the pension plan of which such trust is a part, upon its termination, transfers benefits of missing participants to the Pension Benefit Guaranty Corporation in accordance with section 4050 of such Act.

Paragraphs (11), (12), (13), (14), (15), (19), and (20) shall apply only in the case of a plan to which section 411 (relating to minimum vesting standards) applies without regard to subsection (e)(2) of such section.

(b) CERTAIN RETROACTIVE CHANGES IN PLAN.—A stock bonus, pension, profit-sharing, or annuity plan shall be considered as satisfying the requirements of subsection (a) for the period beginning with the date on which it was put into effect, or for the period beginning with the earlier of the date on which there was adopted or put into effect any amendment which caused the plan to fail to satisfy such requirements, and ending with the time prescribed by law for filing the return of the employer for his taxable year in which such plan or amendment was adopted (including extensions thereof) or such later time as the Secretary may designate, if all provisions of the plan which are necessary to satisfy such requirements are in effect by the end of such period and have been made effective for all purposes for the whole of such period.

(c) DEFINITIONS AND RULES RELATING TO SELF-EMPLOYED INDIVIDUALS AND OWNER-EMPLOYEES.—For purposes of this section—

(1) SELF-EMPLOYED INDIVIDUAL TREATED AS EMPLOYEE.—

(A) IN GENERAL.—The term "employee" includes, for any taxable year, an individual who is a self-employed individual for such taxable year.

(B) SELF-EMPLOYED INDIVIDUAL.—The term "self-employed individual" means, with respect to any taxable year, an individual who has earned income (as defined in paragraph (2)) for such taxable year. To the extent provided in regulations prescribed by the Secretary, such term also includes, for any taxable year—

(i) an individual who would be a self-employed individual within the meaning of the preceding sentence but for the fact that the trade or business carried on by such individual did not have net profits for the taxable year, and

(ii) an individual who has been a self-employed individual within the meaning of the preceding sentence for any prior taxable year.

(2) EARNED INCOME.—

Caution: The flush text at the end of Code Sec. 401(c)(2)(A), below, was amended by P.L. 107-16. For sunset provision, see P.L. 107-16, §901, in the amendment notes.

(A) IN GENERAL.—The term "earned income" means the net earnings from self-employment (as defined in section 1402(a)), but such net earnings shall be determined—

(i) only with respect to a trade or business in which personal services of the taxpayer are a material income-producing factor,

(ii) without regard to paragraphs (4) and (5) of section 1402(c),

(iii) in the case of any individual who is treated as an employee under sections 3121(d)(3)(A), (C), or (D), without regard to paragraph (2) of section 1402(c),

(iv) without regard to items which are not included in gross income for purposes of this chapter, and the deductions properly allocable to or chargeable against such items,

(v) with regard to the deductions allowed by section 404 to the taxpayer, and

(vi) with regard to the deduction allowed to the taxpayer by section 164(f).

For purposes of this subparagraph, section 1402, as in effect for a taxable year ending on December 31, 1962, shall be treated as having been in effect for all taxable years ending before such date. For purposes of this part only (other than sections 419 and 419A), this subparagraph shall be applied as if the term "trade or business" for purposes of section 1402 included service described in section 1402(c)(6).

(C) [B] INCOME FROM DISPOSITION OF CERTAIN PROPERTY.—For purposes of this section, the term "earned income" includes gains (other than any gain which is treated under any provision of this chapter as gain from the sale or exchange of a capital asset) and net earnings derived from the sale or other disposition of, the transfer of any interest in, or the licensing of the use of property (other than good will) by an individual whose personal efforts created such property.

(3) OWNER-EMPLOYEE.—The term "owner-employee" means an employee who—

(A) owns the entire interest in an unincorporated trade or business, or

(B) in the case of a partnership, is a partner who owns more than 10 percent of either the capital interest or the profits interest in such partnership.

To the extent provided in regulations prescribed by the Secretary, such term also means an individual who has been an owner-employee within the meaning of the preceding sentence.

(4) EMPLOYER.—An individual who owns the entire interest in an unincorporated trade or business shall be treated as his own employer. A partnership shall be treated as the employer of each partner who is an employee within the meaning of paragraph (l).

(5) CONTRIBUTIONS ON BEHALF OF OWNER-EMPLOYEES.—The term "contribution on behalf of an owner-employee" includes, except as the context otherwise requires, a contribution under a plan—

(A) by the employer for an owner-employee, and

(B) by an owner-employee as an employee.

(6) SPECIAL RULE FOR CERTAIN FISHERMEN.—For purposes of this subsection, the term "self-employed individual" includes an individual described in section 3121(b)(20) (relating to certain fishermen).

(d) CONTRIBUTION LIMIT ON OWNER-EMPLOYEES.—A trust forming part of a pension or profit-sharing plan which provides contributions or benefits for employees some or all of whom are owner-employees shall constitute a qualified trust under this section only if, in addition to meeting the requirements of subsection (a), the plan provides that contributions on behalf of any owner-employee may be made only with respect to the earned income of such owner-employee which is derived from the trade or business with respect to which such plan is established.

(e) [Repealed.]

(f) CERTAIN CUSTODIAL ACCOUNTS AND CONTRACTS.—For purposes of this title, a custodial account, an annuity contract, or a contract (other than a life, health or accident, property, casualty, or liability insurance contract) issued by an insurance company qualified to do business in a State shall be treated as a qualified trust under this section if—

(1) the custodial account or contract would, except for the fact that it is not a trust, constitute a qualified trust under this section, and

(2) in the case of a custodial account the assets thereof are held by a bank (as defined in section 408(n)) or another person who demonstrates, to the satisfaction of the Secretary,

that the manner in which he will hold the assets will be consistent with the requirements of this section.

For purposes of this title, in the case of a custodial account or contract treated as a qualified trust under this section by reason of this subsection, the person holding the assets of such account or holding such contract shall be treated as the trustee thereof.

(g) ANNUITY DEFINED.—For purposes of this section and sections 402, 403, and 404, the term "annuity" includes a face-amount certificate, as defined in section 2(a)(15) of the Investment Company Act of 1940 (15 U.S.C., sec. 80a-2); but does not include any contract or certificate issued after December 31, 1962, which is transferable, if any person other than the trustee of a trust described in section 401(a) which is exempt from tax under section 501(a) is the owner of such contract or certificate.

(h) MEDICAL, ETC., BENEFITS FOR RETIRED EMPLOYEES AND THEIR SPOUSES AND DEPENDENTS.—Under regulations prescribed by the Secretary, and subject to the provisions of section 420, a pension or annuity plan may provide for the payment of benefits for sickness, accident, hospitalization, and medical expenses of retired employees, their spouses and their dependents, but only if—

(1) such benefits are subordinate to the retirement benefits provided by the plan,

(2) a separate account is established and maintained for such benefits,

(3) the employer's contributions to such separate account are reasonable and ascertainable,

(4) it is impossible, at any time prior to the satisfaction of all liabilities under the plan to provide such benefits, for any part of the corpus or income of such separate account to be (within the taxable year or thereafter) used for, or diverted to, any purpose other than the providing of such benefits,

(5) notwithstanding the provisions of subsection (a)(2), upon the satisfaction of all liabilities under the plan to provide such benefits, any amount remaining in such separate account must, under the terms of the plan, be returned to the employer, and

(6) in the case of an employee who is a key employee, a separate account is established and maintained for such benefits payable to such employee (and his spouse and dependents) and such benefits (to the extent attributable to plan years beginning after March 31, 1984, for which the employee is a key employee) are only payable to such employee (and his spouse and dependents) from such separate account.

For purposes of paragraph (6), the term "key employee" means any employee, who at any time during the plan year or any preceding plan year during which contributions were made on behalf of such employee, is or was a key employee as defined in section 416(i). In no event shall the requirements of paragraph (1) be treated as met if the aggregate actual contributions for medical benefits, when added to actual contributions for life insurance protection under the plan, exceed 25 percent of the total actual contributions to the plan (other than contributions to fund past service credits) after the date on which the account is established.

(i) CERTAIN UNION-NEGOTIATED PENSION PLANS.—In the case of a trust forming part of a pension plan which has been determined by the Secretary to constitute a qualified trust under subsection (a) and to be exempt from taxation under section 501(a) for a period beginning after contributions were first made to or for such trust, if it is shown to the satisfaction of the Secretary that—

(1) such trust was created pursuant to a collective bargaining agreement between employee representatives and one or more employers,

(2) any disbursements of contributions, made to or for such trust before the time as of which the Secretary determined that the trust constituted a qualified trust, substantially complied with the terms of the trust, and the plan of which the trust is a part, as subsequently qualified, and

(3) before the time as of which the Secretary determined that the trust constitutes a qualified trust, the contributions to or for such trust were not used in a manner which would jeopardize the interests of its beneficiaries,

the such trust shall be considered as having constituted a qualified trust under subsection (a) and as having been exempt from taxation under section 501(a) for the period beginning on the date on which contributions were first made to or for such trust and ending on the date such trust first constituted (without regard to this subsection) a qualified trust under subsection (a).

(j) [Repealed.]

(k) CASH OR DEFERRED ARRANGEMENTS.—

(1) GENERAL RULE.—A profit-sharing or stock bonus plan, a pre-ERISA money purchase plan, or a rural cooperative plan shall not be considered as not satisfying the requirements of subsection (a) merely because the plan includes a qualified cash or deferred arrangement.

(2) QUALIFIED CASH OR DEFERRED ARRANGEMENT.—A qualified cash or deferred arrangement is any arrangement which is part of a profit-sharing or stock bonus plan, a pre-ERISA money purchase plan, or a rural cooperative plan which meets the requirements of subsection (a)—

(A) under which a covered employee may elect to have the employer make payments as contributions to a trust under the plan on behalf of the employee, or to the employee directly in cash;

(B) under which amounts held by the trust which are attributable to employer contributions made pursuant to the employee's election—

(i) may not be distributable to participants or other beneficiaries earlier than—

Caution: Code Sec. 401(k)(2)(B)(i)(I), below, was amended by P.L. 107-16. For sunset provision, see P.L. 107-16, §901, in the amendment notes.

(I) severance from employment, death, or disability,

(II) an event described in paragraph (10),

(III) in the case of a profit-sharing or stock bonus plan, the attainment of age 59 , or

(IV) in the case of contributions to a profit-sharing or stock bonus plan to which section 402(e)(3) applies, upon hardship of the employee, and

(ii) will not be distributable merely by reason of the completion of a stated period of participation or the lapse of a fixed number of years;

(C) which provides that an employee's right to his accrued benefit derived from employer contributions made to the trust pursuant to his election is nonforfeitable, and

(D) which does not require, as a condition of participation in the arrangement, that an employee complete a period of service with the employer (or employers) maintaining the plan extending beyond the period permitted under section 410(a)(1) (determined without regard to subparagraph (B)(i) thereof).

(3) APPLICATION OF PARTICIPATION AND DISCRIMINATION STANDARDS.—

(A) A cash or deferred arrangement shall not be treated as a qualified cash or deferred arrangement unless—

(i) those employees eligible to benefit under the arrangement satisfy the provisions of section 410(b)(1), and

(ii) the actual deferral percentage for eligible highly compensated employees (as defined in paragraph (5)) for the plan year bears a relationship to the actual deferral percentage for all other eligible employees for the preceding plan year which meets either of the following tests:

(I) The actual deferral percentage for the group of eligible highly compensated employees is not more than the actual deferral percentage of all other eligible employees multiplied by 1.25.

(II) The excess of the actual deferral percentage for the group of eligible highly compensated employees over that of all other eligible employees is not more than 2 percentage points, and the actual deferral percentage for the group of eligible highly compensated employees is not more than the actual deferral percentage of all other eligible employees multiplied by 2.

If 2 or more plans which include cash or deferred arrangements are considered as 1 plan for purposes of section 401(a)(4) or 410(b), the cash or deferred arrangements included in such plans shall be treated as 1 arrangement for purposes of this subparagraph.

If any highly compensated employee is a participant under 2 or more cash or deferred arrangements of the employer, for purposes of determining the deferral percentage with respect to such employee, all such cash or deferred arrangements shall be treated as 1 cash or deferred arrangement. An arrangement may apply clause (ii) by using the plan year rather than the preceding plan year if the employer so elects, except that if such an election is made, it may not be changed except as provided by the Secretary.

(B) For purposes of subparagraph (A), the actual deferral percentage for a specified group of employees for a plan year shall be the average of the ratios (calculated separately for each employee in such group) of—

(i) the amount of employer contributions actually paid over to the trust on behalf of each such employee for such plan year, to

(ii) the employee's compensation for such plan year.

(C) A cash or deferred arrangement shall be treated as meeting the requirements of subsection (a)(4) with respect to contributions if the requirements of subparagraph (A)(ii) are met.

(D) For purposes of subparagraph (B), the employer contributions on behalf of any employee—

(i) shall include any employer contributions made pursuant to the employee's election under paragraph (2), and

(ii) under such rules as the Secretary may prescribe, may, at the election of employer, include—

(I) matching contributions (as defined in section 401(m)(4)(A)) which meet the requirements of paragraph (2)(B) and (C), and

(II) qualified nonelective contributions (within the meaning of section 401(m)(4)(C)).

(E) For purposes of this paragraph, in the case of the first plan year of any plan (other than a successor plan), the amount taken into account as the actual deferral percentage of nonhighly compensated employees for the preceding plan year shall be—

(i) 3 percent, or

(ii) if the employer makes an election under this subclause, the actual deferral percentage of nonhighly compensated employees determined for such first plan year.

(F) SPECIAL RULE FOR EARLY PARTICIPATION.—If an employer elects to apply section 410(b)(4)(B) in determining whether a cash or deferred arrangement meets the requirements of subparagraph (A)(i), the employer may, in determining whether the arrangement meets the requirements of subparagraph (A)(ii), exclude from consideration all eligible employees (other than highly compensated employees) who have not met the minimum age and service requirements of section 410(a)(1)(A).

(G) A governmental plan (within the meaning of section 414(d)) maintained by a State or local government or political subdivision thereof (or agency or instrumentality thereof) shall be treated as meeting the requirements of this paragraph.

(4) OTHER REQUIREMENTS.—

(A) BENEFITS (OTHER THAN MATCHING CONTRIBUTIONS) MUST NOT BE CONTINGENT ON ELECTION TO DEFER.—A cash or deferred arrangement of any employee shall not be treated as a qualified cash or deferred arrangement if any other benefit is conditioned (directly or indirectly) on the employee electing to have the employer make or not make contributions under the arrangement in lieu of receiving cash. The preceding sentence shall not apply to any matching contribution (as defined in section 401(m)) made by reason of such an election.

(B) ELIGIBILITY OF STATE AND LOCAL GOVERNMENTS AND TAX-EXEMPT ORGANIZATIONS.—

(i) TAX-EXEMPTS ELIGIBLE.—Except as provided in clause (ii), any organization exempt from tax under this subtitle may include a qualified cash or deferred arrangement as part of a plan maintained by it.

(ii) GOVERNMENTS INELIGIBLE.—A cash or deferred arrangement shall not be treated as a qualified cash or deferred arrangement if it is part of a plan maintained by a State or local government or political subdivision thereof, or any agency or instrumentality thereof. This clause shall not apply to a rural cooperative plan or to a plan of an employer described in clause (iii).

(iii) TREATMENT OF INDIAN TRIBAL GOVERNMENTS.—An employer which is an Indian tribal government (as defined in section 7701(a)(40)), a subdivision of an Indian tribal government (determined in accordance with section 7871(d)), an agency or instrumentality of an Indian tribal government or subdivision thereof, or a corporation chartered under Federal, State, or tribal law which is owned in whole or in part by any of the foregoing may include a qualified cash or deferred arrangement as part of a plan maintained by the employer.

(C) COORDINATION WITH OTHER PLANS.—Except as provided in section 401(m), any employer contribution made pursuant to an employee's election under a qualified cash or deferred arrangement shall not be taken into account for purposes of determining whether any other plan meets the requirements of section 401(a) or 410(b). This subparagraph shall not apply for purposes of determining whether a plan meets the average benefit requirement of section 410(b)(2)(A)(ii).

(5) HIGHLY COMPENSATED EMPLOYEE.—For purposes of this subsection, the term "highly compensated employee" has the meaning given such term by section 414(q).

(6) PRE-ERISA MONEY PURCHASE PLAN.—For purposes of this subsection, the term "pre-ERISA money purchase plan" means a pension plan—

(A) which is a defined contribution plan (as defined in section 414(i)),

(B) which was in existence on June 27, 1974, and which, on such date, included a salary reduction arrangement, and

(C) under which neither the employee contributions nor the employer contributions may exceed the levels provided for by the contribution formula in effect under the plan on such date.

(7) RURAL COOPERATIVE PLAN.—For purposes of this subsection—

(A) IN GENERAL.—The term "rural cooperative plan" means any pension plan—

(i) which is a defined contribution plan (as defined in section 414(i)), and

(ii) which is established and maintained by a rural cooperative.

(B) RURAL COOPERATIVE DEFINED.—For purposes of subparagraph (A), the term "rural cooperative" means—

(i) any organization which—

(I) is engaged primarily in providing electric service on a mutual or cooperative basis, or

(II) is engaged primarily in providing electric service to the public in its area of service and which is exempt from tax under this subtitle or which is a State or local government (or an agency or instrumentality thereof), other than a municipality (or an agency or instrumentality thereof),

(ii) any organization described in paragraph (4) or (6) of section 501(c) and at least 80 percent of the members of which are organizations described in clause (i),

(iii) a cooperative telephone company described in section 501(c)(12), and

(iv) an organization which—

(I) is a mutual irrigation or ditch company described in section 501(c)(12) (without regard to the 85 percent requirement thereof), or

(II) is a district organized under the laws of a State as a municipal corporation for the purpose of irrigation, water conservation, or drainage, and

(v) an organization which is a national association of organizations described in clause (i), (ii), (iii), or (iv).

(C) SPECIAL RULE FOR CERTAIN DISTRIBUTIONS.—A rural cooperative plan which includes a qualified cash or deferred arrangement shall not be treated as violating the requirements of section 401(a) or of paragraph (2) merely by reason of a hardship distribution or a distribution to a participant after attainment of age 59 . For purposes of this section, the term "hardship distribution" means a distribution described in paragraph (2)(B)(i)(IV) (without regard to the limitation of its application to profit-sharing or stock bonus plans).

(8) ARRANGEMENT NOT DISQUALIFIED IF EXCESS CONTRIBUTIONS DISTRIBUTED.—

(A) IN GENERAL.—A cash or deferred arrangement shall not be treated as failing to meet the requirements of clause (ii) of paragraph (3)(A) for any plan year if, before the close of the following plan year—

(i) the amount of excess contributions for such plan year (and any income allocable to such contributions) is distributed, or

(ii) to the extent provided in regulations, the employee elects to treat the amount of the excess contributions as an amount distributed to the employee and then contributed by the employee to the plan.

Any distribution of excess contributions (and income) may be made without regard to any other provision of law.

(B) EXCESS CONTRIBUTIONS.—For purposes of subparagraph (A), the term "excess contributions" means, with respect to any plan year, the excess of—

(i) the aggregate amount of employer contributions actually paid over to the trust on behalf of highly compensated employees for such plan year, over

(ii) the maximum amount of such contributions permitted under the limitations of clause (ii) of paragraph (3)(A) (determined by reducing contributions made on behalf of highly compensated employees in order of the actual deferral percentages beginning with the highest of such percentages).

(C) METHOD OF DISTRIBUTING EXCESS CONTRIBUTIONS.—Any distribution of the excess contributions for any plan year shall be made to highly compensated employees on the basis of the amount of contributions by, or on behalf of, each of such employees.

(D) ADDITIONAL TAX UNDER SECTION 72(t) NOT TO APPLY.—No tax shall be imposed under section 72(t) on any amount required to be distributed under this paragraph.

(E) TREATMENT OF MATCHING CONTRIBUTIONS FORFEITED BY REASON OF EXCESS DEFERRAL OR CONTRIBUTION.—For purposes of paragraph (2)(C), a matching contribution (within the meaning of subsection (m)) shall not be treated as forfeitable merely because such contribution is forfeitable if the contribution to which the matching contribution relates is treated as an excess contribution under subparagraph (B), an excess deferral under section 401(g)(2)(A), or an excess aggregate contribution under section 401(m)(6)(B).

(F) CROSS REFERENCE.—

For excise tax on certain excess contributions, see section 4979.

(9) COMPENSATION.—For purposes of this subsection, the term "compensation" has the meaning given such term by section 414(s).

Caution: Code Sec. 410(k)(10), below, was amended by P.L. 107-16. For sunset provision, see P.L. 107-16, §901, in the amendment notes.

(10) DISTRIBUTIONS UPON TERMINATION OF PLAN.—

(A) IN GENERAL.—An event described in this subparagraph is the termination of the plan without establishment or maintenance of another defined contribution plan (other than an employee stock ownership plan as defined in section 4975(e)(7)).

(B) DISTRIBUTIONS MUST BE LUMP SUM DISTRIBUTIONS.—

(i) IN GENERAL.—An event shall not be treated as described in subparagraph (A) with respect to any employee unless the employee receives a lump sum distribution by reason of the termination.

(ii) LUMP SUM DISTRIBUTION.—For purposes of this subparagraph, the term "lump-sum distribution" has the meaning given such term by section 402(e)(4)(D) (without regard to subclauses (I), (II), (III), and (IV) of clause (i) thereof). Such term includes a distribution of an annuity contract from—

(I) a trust which forms a part of a plan described in section 401(a) and which is exempt from tax under section 501(a), or

(II) an annuity plan described in section 403(a).

(11) ADOPTION OF SIMPLE PLAN TO MEET NONDISCRIMINATION TESTS.—

(A) IN GENERAL.—A cash or deferred arrangement maintained by an eligible employer shall be treated as meeting the requirements of paragraph (3)(A)(ii) if such arrangement meets—

(i) the contribution requirements of subparagraph (B),

(ii) the exclusive plan requirements of subparagraph (C), and

(iii) the vesting requirements of section 408(p)(3).

(B) CONTRIBUTION REQUIREMENTS.—

(i) IN GENERAL.—The requirements of this subparagraph are met if, under the arrangement—

Caution: Code Sec. 410(k)(11(B)(i)(I), below, was amended by P.L. 107-16. For sunset provision, see P.L. 107-16, §901, in the amendment notes.

(I) an employee may elect to have the employer make elective contributions for the year on behalf of the employee to a trust under the plan in an amount which is expressed as a percentage of compensation of the employee but which in no event exceeds the amount in effect under section 408(p)(2)(A)(ii).

(II) the employer is required to make a matching contribution to the trust for the year in an amount equal to so much of the amount the employee elects under subclause (I) as does not exceed 3 percent of compensation for the year, and

(III) no other contributions may be made other than contributions described in subclause (I) or (II).

(ii) EMPLOYER MAY ELECT 2-PERCENT NONELECTIVE CONTRIBUTION.—An employer shall be treated as meeting the requirements of clause (i)(II) for any year if, in lieu of the contributions described in such clause, the employer elects (pursuant to the terms of the arrangement) to make nonelective contributions of 2 percent of compensation for each employee who is eligible to participate in the arrangement and who has at least $5,000 of compensation from the employer for the year. If an employer makes an election under this subparagraph for any year, the employer shall notify employees of such election within a reasonable period of time before the 60th day before the beginning of such year.

(iii) ADMINISTRATIVE REQUIREMENTS.—

(I) IN GENERAL.—Rules similar to the rules of subparagraphs (B) and (C) of section 408(p)(5) shall apply for purposes of this subparagraph.

(II) NOTICE OF ELECTION PERIOD.—The requirements of this subparagraph shall not be treated as met with respect to any year unless the employer notifies each employee eligible to participate, within a reasonable period of time before the 60th day before the beginning of such year (and, for the first year the employee is so eligible, the 60th day before the first day such employee is so eligible), of the rules similar to the rules of section 408(p)(5)(C) which apply by reason of subclause (I).

(C) EXCLUSIVE PLAN REQUIREMENT.—The requirements of this subparagraph are met for any year to which this paragraph applies if no contributions were made, or benefits were accrued, for services during such year under any qualified plan of the employer on behalf of any employee eligible to participate in the cash or deferred arrangement, other than contributions described in subparagraph (B).

(D) DEFINITIONS AND SPECIAL RULE.—

(i) DEFINITIONS.—For purposes of this paragraph, any term used in this paragraph which is also used in section 408(p) shall have the meaning given such term by such section.

(ii) COORDINATION WITH TOP-HEAVY RULES.—A plan meeting the requirements of this paragraph for any year shall not be treated as a top-heavy plan under section 416 for such year if such plan allows only contributions required under this paragraph.

(E) [Stricken.]

(12) ALTERNATIVE METHODS OF MEETING NONDISCRIMINATION REQUIREMENTS.—

(A) IN GENERAL.—A cash or deferred arrangement shall be treated as meeting the requirements of paragraph (3)(A)(ii) if such arrangement—

(i) meets the contribution requirements of subparagraph (B) or (C), and

(ii) meets the notice requirements of subparagraph (D).

(B) MATCHING CONTRIBUTIONS.—

(i) IN GENERAL.—The requirements of this subparagraph are met if, under the arrangement, the employer makes matching contributions on behalf of each employee who is not a highly compensated employee in an amount equal to—

(I) 100 percent of the elective contributions of the employee to the extent such elective contributions do not exceed 3 percent of the employee's compensation, and

(II) 50 percent of the elective contributions of the employee to the extent that such elective contributions exceed 3 percent but do not exceed 5 percent of the employee's compensation.

(ii) RATE FOR HIGHLY COMPENSATED EMPLOYEES.—The requirements of this subparagraph are not met if, under the arrangement, the rate of matching contribution with respect to any elective contribution of a highly compensated employee at any rate of elective contribution is greater than that with respect to an employee who is not a highly compensated employee.

(iii) ALTERNATIVE PLAN DESIGNS.—If the rate of any matching contribution with respect to any rate of elective contribution is not equal to the percentage required under clause (i), an arrangement shall not be treated as failing to meet the requirements of clause (i) if—

(I) the rate of an employer's matching contribution does not increase as an employee's rate of elective contributions increase, and

(II) the aggregate amount of matching contributions at such rate of elective contribution is at least equal to the aggregate amount of matching contributions which would be made if matching contributions were made on the basis of the percentages described in clause (i).

(C) NONELECTIVE CONTRIBUTIONS.—The requirements of this subparagraph are met if, under the arrangement, the employer is required, without regard to whether the employee makes an elective contribution or employee contribution, to make a contribution to a defined contribution plan on behalf of each employee who is not a highly compensated employee and who is eligible to participate in the arrangement in an amount equal to at least 3 percent of the employee's compensation.

(D) NOTICE REQUIREMENT.—An arrangement meets the requirements of this paragraph if, under the arrangement, each employee eligible to participate is, within a reasonable period before any year, given written notice of the employee's rights and obligations under the arrangement which—

(i) is sufficiently accurate and comprehensive to appraise the employee of such rights and obligations, and

(ii) is written in a manner calculated to be understood by the average employee eligible to participate.

(E) OTHER REQUIREMENTS.—

(i) WITHDRAWAL AND VESTING RESTRICTIONS.—An arrangement shall not be treated as meeting the requirements of subparagraph (B) or (C) of this paragraph unless the requirements of subparagraphs (B) and (C) of paragraph (2) are met with respect to all employer contributions (including matching contributions) taken into account in determining whether the requirements of subparagraphs (B) and (C) of this paragraph are met.

(ii) SOCIAL SECURITY AND SIMILAR CONTRIBUTIONS NOT TAKEN INTO ACCOUNT.—An arrangement shall not be treated as meeting the requirements of subparagraph (B) or (C) unless such requirements are met without regard to subsection (l), and, for purposes of subsection (l), employer contributions under subparagraph (B) or (C) shall not be taken into account.

(F) OTHER PLANS.—An arrangement shall be treated as meeting the requirements under subparagraph (A)(i) if any other plan maintained by the employer meets such requirements with respect to employees eligible under the arrangement.

(l) PERMITTED DISPARITY IN PLAN CONTRIBUTIONS OR BENEFITS.—

(1) IN GENERAL.—The requirements of this subsection are met with respect to a plan if—

(A) in the case of a defined contribution plan, the requirements of paragraph (2) are met, and

(B) in the case of a defined benefit plan, the requirements of paragraph (3) are met.

(2) DEFINED CONTRIBUTION PLAN.—

(A) IN GENERAL.—A defined contribution plan meets the requirements of this paragraph if the excess contribution percentage does not exceed the base contribution percentage by more than the lesser of—

(i) the base contribution percentage, or

(ii) the greater of—

(I) 5.7 percentage points, or

(II) the percentage equal to the portion of the rate of tax under section 3111(a) (in effect as of the beginning of the year) which is attributable to old-age insurance.

(B) CONTRIBUTION PERCENTAGES.—For purposes of this paragraph—

(i) EXCESS CONTRIBUTION PERCENTAGE.—The term "excess contribution percentage" means the percentage of compensation which is contributed by the employer under the plan with respect to that portion of each participant's compensation in excess of the integration level.

(ii) BASE CONTRIBUTION PERCENTAGE.—The term "base contribution percentage" means the percentage of compensation contributed by the employer under the plan with respect to that portion of each participant's compensation not in excess of the integration level.

(3) DEFINED BENEFIT PLAN.—A defined benefit plan meets the requirements of this paragraph if—

(A) EXCESS PLANS.—

(i) IN GENERAL.—In the case of a plan other than an offset plan—

(I) the excess benefit percentage does not exceed the base benefit percentage by more than the maximum excess allowance,

(II) any optional form of benefit, preretirement benefit, actuarial factor, or other benefit or feature provided with respect to compensation in excess of the integration level is provided with respect to compensation not in excess of such level, and

(III) benefits are based on average annual compensation.

(ii) BENEFIT PERCENTAGES.—For purposes of this subparagraph, the excess and base benefit percentages shall be computed in the same manner as the excess and base contribution percentages under paragraph (2)(B), except that such determination shall be made on the basis of benefits attributable to employer contributions rather than contributions.

(B) OFFSET PLANS.—In the case of an offset plan, the plan provides that—

(i) a participant's accrued benefit attributable to employer contributions (within the meaning of section 411(c)(1)) may not be reduced (by reason of the offset) by more than the maximum offset allowance, and

(ii) benefits are based on average annual compensation.

(4) DEFINITIONS RELATING TO PARAGRAPH (3).—For purposes of paragraph (3)—

(A) MAXIMUM EXCESS ALLOWANCE.—The maximum excess allowance is equal to—

(i) in the case of benefits attributable to any year of service with the employer taken into account under the plan, of a percentage point, and

(ii) in the case of total benefits, of a percentage point, multiplied by the participant's years of service (not in excess of 35) with the employer taken into account under the plan.

In no event shall the maximum excess allowance exceed the base benefit percentage.

(B) MAXIMUM OFFSET ALLOWANCE.—The maximum offset allowance is equal to—

(i) in the case of benefits attributable to any year of service with the employer taken into account under the plan, percent of the participant's final average compensation, and

(ii) in the case of total benefits, percent of the participant's final average compensation, multiplied by the participant's years of service (not in excess of 35) with the employer taken into account under the plan.

In no event shall the maximum offset allowance exceed 50 percent of the benefit which would have accrued without regard to the offset reduction.

(C) REDUCTIONS.—

(i) IN GENERAL.—The Secretary shall prescribe regulations requiring the reduction of the percentage factor under subparagraph (A) or (B)—

(I) in the case of a plan other than an offset plan which has an integration level in excess of covered compensation, or

(II) with respect to any participant in an offset plan who has final average compensation in excess of covered compensation.

(ii) BASIS OF REDUCTIONS.—Any reductions under clause (i) shall be based on the percentages of compensation replaced by the employer-derived portions of primary insurance amounts under the Social Security Act for participants with compensation in excess of covered compensation.

(D) OFFSET PLAN.—The term "offset plan" means any plan with respect to which the benefit attributable to employer contributions for each participant is reduced by an amount specified in the plan.

(5) OTHER DEFINITIONS AND SPECIAL RULES.—For purposes of this subsection—

(A) INTEGRATION LEVEL.—

(i) IN GENERAL.—The term "integration level" means the amount of compensation specified under the plan (by dollar amount or formula) at or below which the rate at which contributions or benefits are provided (expressed as a percentage) is less than such rate above such amount.

(ii) LIMITATION.—The integration level for any year may not exceed the contribution and benefit base in effect under section 230 of the Social Security Act for such year.

(iii) LEVEL TO APPLY TO ALL PARTICIPANTS.—A plan's integration level shall apply with respect to all participants in the plan.

(iv) MULTIPLE INTEGRATION LEVELS.—Under rules prescribed by the Secretary, a defined benefit plan may specify multiple integration levels.

(B) COMPENSATION.—The term "compensation" has the meaning given such term by section 414(s).

(C) AVERAGE ANNUAL COMPENSATION.—The term "average annual compensation" means the participant's highest average annual compensation for—

(i) any period of at least 3 consecutive years, or

(ii) if shorter, the participant's full period of service.

(D) FINAL AVERAGE COMPENSATION.—

(i) IN GENERAL.—The term "final average compensation" means the participant's average annual compensation for—

(I) the 3-consecutive year period ending with the current year, or

(II) if shorter, the participant's full period of service.

(ii) LIMITATION.—A participant's final average compensation shall be determined by not taking into account in any year compensation in excess of the contribution and benefit base in effect under section 230 of the Social Security Act for such year.

(E) COVERED COMPENSATION.—

(i) IN GENERAL.—The term "covered compensation" means, with respect to an employee, the average of the contribution and benefit bases in effect under section 230 of the Social Security Act for each year in the 35-year period ending with the year in which the employee attains the social security retirement age.

(ii) COMPUTATION FOR ANY YEAR.—For purposes of clause (i), the determination for any year preceding the year in which the employee attains the social security retirement age shall be made by assuming that there is no increase in the bases described in clause (i) after the determination year and before the employee attains the social security retirement age.

(iii) SOCIAL SECURITY RETIREMENT AGE.—For purposes of this subparagraph, the term "social security retirement age" has the meaning given such term by section 415(b)(8).

(F) REGULATIONS.—The Secretary shall prescribe such regulations as are necessary or appropriate to carry out the purposes of this subsection, including—

(i) in the case of a defined benefit plan which provides for unreduced benefits commencing before the social security retirement age (as defined in section 415(b)(8)), rules providing for the reduction of the maximum excess allowance and the maximum offset allowance, and

(ii) in the case of an employee covered by 2 or more plans of the employer which fail to meet the requirements of subsection (a)(4) (without regard to this subsection), rules preventing the multiple use of the disparity permitted under this subsection with respect to any employee.

For purposes of clause (i), unreduced benefits shall not include benefits for disability (within the meaning of section 223(d) of the Social Security Act).

(6) SPECIAL RULE FOR PLAN MAINTAINED BY RAILROADS.—In determining whether a plan which includes employees of a railroad employer who are entitled to benefits under the Railroad Retirement Act of 1974 meets the requirements of this subsection, rules similar to the rules set forth in this subsection shall apply. Such rules shall take into account the employer-derived portion of the employees' tier 2 railroad retirement benefits and any supplemental annuity under the Railroad Retirement Act of 1974.

(m) NONDISCRIMINATION TEST FOR MATCHING CONTRIBUTIONS AND EMPLOYEE CONTRIBUTIONS.—

(1) IN GENERAL.—A defined contribution plan shall be treated as meeting the requirements of subsection (a)(4) with respect to the amount of any matching contribution or employee contribution for any plan year only if the contribution percentage requirement of paragraph (2) of this subsection is met for such plan year.

(2) REQUIREMENTS.—

(A) CONTRIBUTION PERCENTAGE REQUIREMENT.—A plan meets the contribution percentage requirement of this paragraph for any plan year only if the contribution percentage for eligible highly compensated employees for such plan year does not exceed the greater of—

(i) 125 percent of such percentage for all other employees for the preceding plan year, or

(ii) the lesser of 200 percent of such percentage for all other eligible employees for the preceding plan year, or such percentage for all other eligible employees for the preceding plan year plus 2 percentage points.

This subparagraph may be applied by using the plan year rather than the preceding plan year if the employer so elects, except that if such an election is made, it may not be changed except as provided the Secretary.

(B) MULTIPLE PLANS TREATED AS A SINGLE PLAN.—If two or more plans of an employer to which matching contributions, employee contributions, or elective deferrals are made are treated as one plan for purposes of section 410(b), such plans shall be treated as one plan for purposes of this subsection. If a highly compensated employee participates in two or more plans of an employer to which contributions to which this subsection applies are made, all such contributions shall be aggregated for purposes of this subsection.

(3) CONTRIBUTION PERCENTAGE.—For purposes of paragraph (2), the contribution percentage for a specified group of employees for a plan year shall be the average for the ratios (calculated separately for each employee in such group) of—

(A) the sum of the matching contributions and employee contributions paid under the plan on behalf of each such employee for such plan year, to

(B) the employee's compensation (within the meaning of section 414(s)) for such plan year.

Under regulations, an employer may elect to take into account (in computing the contribution percentage) elective deferrals and qualified nonelective contributions under the plan or any other plan of the employer. If matching contributions are taken into account for purposes of subsection (k)(3)(A)(ii) for any plan year, such contributions shall not be taken into account under subparagraph (A) for such year. Rules similar to the rules of subsection (k)(3)(E) shall apply for purposes of this subsection.

(4) DEFINITIONS.—For purposes of this subsection—

(A) MATCHING CONTRIBUTION.—The term "matching contribution" means—

(i) any employer contribution made to a defined contribution plan on behalf of an employee on account of an employee contribution made by such employee, and

(ii) any employer contribution made to a defined contribution plan on behalf of an employee on account of an employee's elective deferral.

(B) ELECTIVE DEFERRAL.—The term "elective deferral" means any employer contribution described in section 402(g)(3).

(C) QUALIFIED NONELECTIVE CONTRIBUTIONS.—The term "qualified nonelective contributions" means any employer contribution (other than a matching contribution) with respect to which—

(i) the employee may not elect to have the contribution paid to the employee in cash instead of being contributed to the plan, and

(ii) the requirements of subparagraphs (B) and (C) of subsection (k)(2) are met.

(5) EMPLOYEES TAKEN INTO CONSIDERATION.—

(A) IN GENERAL.—Any employee who is eligible to make an employee contribution (or, if the employer takes elective contributions into account, elective contributions) or to receive a matching contribution under the plan being tested under paragraph (1) shall be considered an eligible employee for purposes of this subsection.

(B) CERTAIN NONPARTICIPANTS.—If an employee contribution is required as a condition of participation in the plan, any employee who would be a participant in the plan if such employee made such a contribution shall be treated as an eligible employee on behalf of whom no employer contributions are made.

(C) SPECIAL RULE FOR EARLY PARTICIPATION.—If an employer elects to apply section 410(b)(4)(B) in determining whether a plan meets the requirements of section 410(b), the employer may, in determining whether the plan meets the requirements of paragraph (2), exclude from consideration all eligible employees (other than highly compensated employees) who have not met the minimum age and service requirements of section 410(a)(1)(A).

(6) PLAN NOT DISQUALIFIED IF EXCESS AGGREGATE CONTRIBUTIONS DISTRIBUTED BEFORE END OF FOLLOWING PLAN YEAR.—

(A) IN GENERAL.—A plan shall not be treated as failing to meet the requirements of paragraph (1) for any plan year if, before the close of the following plan year, the amount of the excess aggregate contributions for such plan year (and any income allocable to such contributions) is distributed (or, if forfeitable, is forfeited). Such contributions (and such income) may be distributed without regard to any other provision of law.

(B) EXCESS AGGREGATE CONTRIBUTIONS.—For purposes of subparagraph (A), the term "excess aggregate contributions" means, with respect to any plan year, the excess of—

(i) the aggregate amount of the matching contributions and employee contributions (and any qualified nonelective contribution or elective contribution taken into account in computing the contribution percentage) actually made on behalf of highly compensated employees for such plan year, over

(ii) the maximum amount of such contributions permitted under the limitations of paragraph (2)(A) (determined by reducing contributions made on behalf of highly compensated employees in order of their contribution percentages beginning with the highest of such percentages).

(C) METHOD OF DISTRIBUTING EXCESS AGGREGATE CONTRIBUTIONS.—Any distribution of excess aggregate contributions for any plan year shall be made to highly compensated employees on the basis of the amount of contributions on behalf of or by each such employee. Forfeitures of excess aggregate contributions may not be allocated to participants whose contributions are reduced under this paragraph.

(D) COORDINATION WITH SUBSECTION (k) AND 402(g).—The determination of the amount of excess aggregate contributions with respect to a plan shall be made after—

(i) first determining the excess deferrals (within the meaning of section 402(g)), and

(ii) then determining the excess contributions under subsection (k).

(7) TREATMENT OF DISTRIBUTIONS.—

(A) ADDITIONAL TAX OF SECTION 72(t) NOT APPLICABLE.—No tax shall be imposed under section 72(t) on any amount required to be distributed under paragraph (6).

(B) EXCLUSION OF EMPLOYEE CONTRIBUTIONS.—Any distribution attributable to employee contributions shall not be included in gross income except to the extent attributable to income on such contributions.

(8) HIGHLY COMPENSATED EMPLOYEE.—For purposes of this subsection, the term "highly compensated employee" has the meaning given to such term by section 414(q).

Caution: Code Sec. 401(m)(9), below, was amended by P.L. 107-16. For sunset provision, see P.L. 107-16, §901, in the amendment notes.

(9) REGULATIONS.—The Secretary shall prescribe such regulations as may be necessary to carry out the purposes of this subsection and subsection (k), including regulations permitting appropriate aggregation of plans and contributions.

(10) ALTERNATIVE METHOD OF SATISFYING TESTS.—A defined contribution plan shall be treated as meeting the requirements of paragraph (2) with respect to matching contributions if the plan—

(A) meets the contribution requirements of subparagraph (B) of subsection (k)(11),

(B) meets the exclusive plan requirements of subsection (k)(11)(C), and

(C) meets the vesting requirements of section 408(p)(3).

(11) ADDITIONAL ALTERNATIVE METHOD OF SATISFYING TESTS.—

(A) IN GENERAL.—A defined contribution plan shall be treated as meeting the requirements of paragraph (2) with respect to matching contributions if the plan—

(i) meets the contribution requirements of subparagraph (B) or (C) of subsection (k)(12),

(ii) meets the notice requirements of subsection (k)(12)(D), and

(iii) meets the requirements of subparagraph (B).

(B) LIMITATION ON MATCHING CONTRIBUTIONS.—The requirements of this subparagraph are met if—

(i) matching contributions on behalf of any employee may not be made with respect to an employee's contributions or elective deferrals in excess of 6 percent of the employee's compensation,

(ii) the rate of an employer's matching contribution does not increase as the rate of an employee's contributions or elective deferrals increase, and

(iii) the matching contribution with respect to any highly compensated employee at any rate of an employee contribution or rate of elective deferral is not greater than that with respect to an employee who is not a highly compensated employee.

(12) CROSS REFERENCE.—

For excise tax on certain excess contributions, see section 4979.

(n) COORDINATION WITH QUALIFIED DOMESTIC RELATIONS ORDERS.—The Secretary shall prescribe such rules or regulations as may be necessary to coordinate the requirements of subsection (a)(13)(B) and section 414(p) (and the regulations issued by the Secretary of Labor thereunder) with the other provisions of this chapter.

(o) CROSS REFERENCE.—

For exemption from tax of a trust qualified under this section, see section 501(a).

SEC. 402. TAXABILITY OF BENEFICIARY OF EMPLOYEES' TRUST.

(a) TAXABILITY OF BENEFICIARY OF EXEMPT TRUST.—Except as otherwise provided in this section, any amount actually distributed to any distributee by any employees' trust described in section 401(a) which is exempt from tax under section 501(a) shall be taxable to the distributee, in the taxable year of the distributee in which distributed, under section 72 (relating to annuities).

(b) TAXABILITY OF BENEFICIARY OF NONEXEMPT TRUST.—

(1) CONTRIBUTIONS.—Contributions to an employees' trust made by an employer during a taxable year of the employer which ends with or within a taxable year of the trust for which the trust is not exempt from tax under section 501(a) shall be included in the gross income of the employee in accordance with section 83 (relating to property transferred in connection with performance of services), except that the value of the employee's interest in the trust shall be substituted for the fair market value of the property for purposes of applying such section.

(2) DISTRIBUTIONS.—The amount actually distributed or made available to any distributee by any trust described in paragraph (1) shall be taxable to the distributee, in the taxable year in which so distributed or made available, under section 72 (relating to annuities), except that distributions of income of such trust before the annuity starting date (as defined in section 72(c)(4)) shall be included in the gross income of the employee without regard to section 72(e)(5) (relating to amounts not received as annuities.)

(3) GRANTOR TRUSTS.—A beneficiary of any trust described in paragraph (1) shall not be considered the owner of any portion of such trust under subpart E of part I of subchapter J (relating to grantors and others treated as substantial owners).

(4) FAILURE TO MEET REQUIREMENTS OF SECTION 410(b).—

(A) HIGHLY COMPENSATED EMPLOYEES.—If 1 of the reasons a trust is not exempt from tax under section 501(a) is the failure of the plan of which it is a part to meet the requirements of section 401(a)(26) or 410(b), then a highly compensated employee shall, in lieu of the amount determined under paragraph (1) or (2) include in gross income for the taxable year with or within which the taxable year of the trust ends an amount equal to the vested accrued benefit of such employee (other than the employee's investment in the contract) as of the close of such taxable year of the trust.

(B) FAILURE TO MEET COVERAGE TESTS.—If a trust is not exempt from tax under section 501(a) for any taxable year solely because such trust is part of a plan which fails to meet the requirements of section 401(a)(26) or 410(b), paragraphs (1) and (2) shall not apply by reason of such failure to any employee who was not a highly compensated employee during—

(i) such taxable year, or

(ii) any preceding period for which service was creditable to such employee under the plan.

(C) HIGHLY COMPENSATED EMPLOYEE.—For purposes of this paragraph, the term "highly compensated employee" has the meaning given such term by section 414(q).

(c) RULES APPLICABLE TO ROLLOVERS FROM EXEMPT TRUSTS.—

(1) EXCLUSION FROM INCOME.—If—

(A) any portion of the balance to the credit of an employee in a qualified trust is paid to the employee in an eligible rollover distribution,

(B) the distributee transfers any portion of the property received in such distribution to an eligible retirement plan, and

(C) in the case of a distribution of property other than money, the amount so transferred consists of the property distributed,

then such distribution (to the extent so transferred) shall not be includible in gross income for the taxable year in which paid.

Caution: Code Sec. 402(c)(2)-(3), below, was amended by P.L. 107-16. For sunset provision, see P.L. 107-16, §901, in the amendment notes.

(2) MAXIMUM AMOUNT WHICH MAY BE ROLLED OVER.—In the case of any eligible rollover distribution, the maximum amount transferred to which paragraph (1) applies shall not exceed the portion of such distribution which is includible in gross income (determined without regard to paragraph (1)). The preceding sentence shall not apply to such distribution to the extent—

(A) such portion is transferred in a direct trustee-to-trustee transfer to a qualified trust which is part of a plan which is a defined contribution plan and which agrees to separately account for amounts so transferred, including separately accounting for the portion of such distribution which is includible in gross income and the portion of such distribution which is not so includible, or

(B) such portion is transferred to an eligible retirement plan described in clause (i) or (ii) of paragraph (8)(B).

In the case of a transfer described in subparagraph (A) or (B), the amount transferred shall be treated as consisting first of the portion of such distribution that is includible in gross income (determined without regard to paragraph (1)).

  (3) TRANSFER MUST BE MADE WITHIN 60 DAYS OF RECEIPT.—

    (A) IN GENERAL.—Except as provided in subparagraph (B), paragraph (1) shall not apply to any transfer of a distribution made after the 60th day following the day on which the distributee received the property distributed.

    (B) HARDSHIP EXCEPTION.—The Secretary may waive the 60-day requirement under subparagraph (A) where the failure to waive such requirement would be against equity or good conscience, including casualty, disaster, or other events beyond the reasonable control of the individual subject to such requirement.

  (4) ELIGIBLE ROLLOVER DISTRIBUTION.—For purposes of this subsection, the term "eligible rollover distribution" means any distribution to an employee of all or any portion of the balance to the credit of the employee in a qualified trust; except that such term shall not include—

    (A) any distribution which is one of a series of substantially equal periodic payments (not less frequently than annually) made—

      (i) for the life (or life expectancy) of the employee or the joint lives (or joint life expectancies) of the employee and the employee's designated beneficiary, or

      (ii) for a specified period of 10 years or more,

    (B) any distribution to the extent such distribution is required under section 401(a)(9), and

  Caution: Code Sec. 402(c)(4)(C), below, was amended by P.L. 107-16. For sunset provision, see P.L. 107-16, §901, in the amendment notes.

    (C) any distribution which is made upon hardship of the employee.

  (5) TRANSFER TREATED AS ROLLOVER CONTRIBUTION UNDER SECTION 408.—For purposes of this title, a transfer to an eligible retirement plan described in clause (i) or (ii) of paragraph (8)(B) resulting in any portion of a distribution being excluded from gross income under paragraph (1) shall be treated as a rollover contribution described in section 408(d)(3).

  (6) SALES OF DISTRIBUTED PROPERTY.—For purposes of this subsection—

    (A) TRANSFER OF PROCEEDS FROM SALE OF DISTRIBUTED PROPERTY TREATED AS TRANSFER OF DISTRIBUTED PROPERTY.—The transfer of an amount equal to any portion of the proceeds from the sale of property received in the distribution shall be treated as the transfer of property received in the distribution.

    (B) PROCEEDS ATTRIBUTABLE TO INCREASE IN VALUE.—The excess of fair market value of property on sale over its fair market value on distribution shall be treated as property received in the distribution.

(C) DESIGNATION WHERE AMOUNT OF DISTRIBUTION EXCEEDS ROLLOVER CONTRIBUTION.—In any case where part or all of the distribution consists of property other than money—

    (i) the portion of the money or other property which is to be treated as attributable to amounts not included in gross income, and

    (ii) the portion of the money or other property which is to be treated as included in the rollover contribution,

shall be determined on a ratable basis unless the taxpayer designates otherwise. Any designation under this subparagraph for a taxable year shall be made not later than the time prescribed by law for filing the return for such taxable year (including extensions thereof). Any such law for designation, once made, shall be irrevocable.

(D) NONRECOGNITION OF GAIN OR LOSS.—No gain or loss shall be recognized on any sale described in subparagraph (A) to the extent that an amount equal to the proceeds is transferred pursuant to paragraph (1).

(7) SPECIAL RULE FOR FROZEN DEPOSITS.—

(A) IN GENERAL.—The 60-day period described in paragraph (3) shall not—

    (i) include any period during which the amount transferred to the employee is a frozen deposit, or

    (ii) end earlier than 10 days after such amount ceases to be a frozen deposit.

(B) FROZEN DEPOSITS.—For purposes of this subparagraph, the term "frozen deposit" means any deposit which may not be withdrawn because of—

    (i) the bankruptcy or insolvency of any financial institution, or

    (ii) any requirement imposed by the State in which such institution is located by reason of the bankruptcy or insolvency (or threat thereof) of 1 or more financial institutions in such State.

A deposit shall not be treated as a frozen deposit unless on at least 1 day during the 60-day period described in paragraph (3) (without regard to this paragraph) such deposit is described in the preceding sentence.

(8) DEFINITIONS.—For purposes of this subsection—

(A) QUALIFIED TRUST.—The term "qualified trust" means an employees' trust described in section 401(a) which is exempt from tax under section 501(a).

Caution: Code Sec. 402(c)(8)(B), below, as amended by P.L. 107-16, §641, but prior to amendment by §617(c), generally applies to distributions after December 31, 2001, and to tax years beginning on or before December 31, 2005. For sunset provision, see P.L. 107-16, §901, in the amendment notes.

(B) ELIGIBLE RETIREMENT PLAN.—The term "eligible retirement plan" means—

(i) an individual retirement account described in section 408(a),

(ii) an individual retirement annuity described in section 408(b) (other than an endowment contract),

(iii) a qualified trust,

(iv) an annuity plan described in section 403(a),

(v) an eligible deferred compensation plan described in section 457(b) which is maintained by an eligible employer described in section 457(e)(1)(A), and

(vi) an annuity contract described in section 403(b).

Caution: Code Sec. 402(c)(8)(B), below, as amended by P.L. 107-16, §§617(c) and 641, applies to tax years beginning after December 31, 2005. For sunset provision, see P.L. 107-16, §901, in the amendment notes.

(B) ELIGIBLE RETIREMENT PLAN.—The term "eligible retirement plan" means—

(i) an individual retirement account described in section 408(a),

(ii) an individual retirement annuity described in section 408(b) (other than an endowment contract),

(iii) a qualified trust,

(iv) an annuity plan described in section 403(a),

(v) an eligible deferred compensation plan described in section 457(b) which is maintained by an eligible employer described in section 457(e)(1)(A), and

(vi) an annuity contract described in section 403(b).

If any portion of an eligible rollover distribution is attributable to payments or distributions from a designated Roth account (as defined in section 402A), an eligible retirement plan with respect to such portion shall include only another designated Roth account and a Roth IRA.

Caution: Code Sec. 402(c)(9), below, was amended by P.L. 107-16. For sunset provision, see P.L. 107-16, §901, in the amendment notes.

(9) ROLLOVER WHERE SPOUSE RECEIVES DISTRIBUTION AFTER DEATH OF EMPLOYEE.—If any distribution attributable to an employee is paid to the spouse of the employee after the employee's death, the preceding provisions of this subsection shall apply to such distribution in the same manner as if the spouse were the employee.

Caution: Code Sec. 402(c)(10), below, was added by P.L. 107-16. For sunset provision, see P.L. 107-16, §901, in the amendment notes.

(10) SEPARATE ACCOUNTING.—Unless a plan described in clause (v) of paragraph (8)(B) agrees to separately account for amounts rolled into such plan from eligible retirement plans not described in such clause, the plan described in such clause may not accept transfers or rollovers from such retirement plans.

(d) TAXABILITY OF BENEFICIARY OF CERTAIN FOREIGN SITUS TRUSTS.—For purposes of subsections (a), (b), and (c), a stock bonus, pension, or profit-sharing trust which would qualify for exemption from tax under section 501(a) except for the fact that it is a trust created or organized outside the United States shall be treated as if it were a trust exempt from tax under section 501(a).

(e) OTHER RULES APPLICABLE TO EXEMPT TRUSTS.—

(1) ALTERNATE PAYEES.—

(A) ALTERNATE PAYEE TREATED AS DISTRIBUTEE.—For purposes of subsection (a) and section 72, an alternate payee who is the spouse or former spouse of the participant shall be treated as the distributee of any distribution or payment made to the alternate payee under a qualified domestic relations order (as defined in section 414(p)).

(B) ROLLOVERS.—If any amount is paid or distributed to an alternate payee who is the spouse or former spouse of the participant by reason of any qualified domestic relations order (within the meaning of section 414(p)), subsection (c) shall apply to such distribution in the same manner as if such alternate payee were the employee.

(2) DISTRIBUTIONS BY UNITED STATES TO NONRESIDENT ALIENS.—The amount includible under subsection (a) in the gross income of a nonresident alien with respect to a distribution made by the United States in respect of services performed by an employee of the United States shall not exceed an amount which bears the same ratio to the amount includible in gross income without regard to this paragraph as—

(A) the aggregate basic pay paid by the United States to such employee for such services, reduced by the amount of such basic pay which was not includible in gross income by reason of being from sources without the United States, bears to

(B) the aggregate basic pay paid by the United States to such employee for such services.

In the case of distributions under the civil service retirement laws, the term "basic pay" shall have the meaning provided in section 8331(3) of title 5, United States Code.

(3) CASH OR DEFERRED ARRANGEMENTS.—For purposes of this title, contributions made by an employer on behalf of an employee to a trust which is a part of a qualified cash or deferred arrangement (as defined in section 401(k)(2)) or which is part of a salary reduction agreement under section 403(b) shall not be treated as distributed or made available to the employee nor as contributions made to the trust by the employee merely because the arrangement includes provisions under which the employee has an election whether the contribution will be made to the trust or received by the employee in cash.

(4) NET UNREALIZED APPRECIATION.—

(A) AMOUNTS ATTRIBUTABLE TO EMPLOYEE CONTRIBUTIONS.—For purposes of subsection (a) and section 72, in the case of a distribution other than a lump sum distribution, the amount actually distributed to any distributee from a trust described in subsection (a) shall not include any net unrealized appreciation in securities of the employer corporation attributable to amounts contributed by the employee (other than deductible employee contributions within the meaning of section 72(o)(5)). This subparagraph shall not apply to a distribution to which subsection (c) applies.

(B) AMOUNTS ATTRIBUTABLE TO EMPLOYER CONTRIBUTIONS.—For purposes of subsection (a) and section 72, in the case of any lump sum distribution which includes securities of the employer corporation, there shall be excluded from gross income the net unrealized appreciation attributable to that part of the distribution which consists of securities of the employer corporation. In accordance with rules prescribed by the Secretary, a taxpayer may elect, on the return of tax on which a lump sum distribution is required to be included, not to have this subparagraph apply to such distribution.

(C) DETERMINATION OF AMOUNTS AND ADJUSTMENTS.—For purposes of subparagraphs (A) and (B), net unrealized appreciation and the resulting adjustments to basis shall be determined in accordance with regulations prescribed by the Secretary.

(D) LUMP-SUM DISTRIBUTION.—For purposes of this paragraph—

(i) IN GENERAL.—The term "lump sum distribution" means the distribution or payment within one taxable year of the recipient of the balance to the credit of an employee which becomes payable to the recipient—

(I) on account of the employee's death,

(II) after the employee attains age 59 ,

(III) on account of the employee's separation from service, or

(IV) after the employee has become disabled (within the meaning of section 72(m)(7)),

from a trust which forms a part of a plan described in section 401(a) and which is exempt from tax under section 501 or from a plan described in section 403(a). Subclause (III) of this clause shall be applied only with respect to an individual who is an employee without regard to section 401(c)(1), and subclause (IV) shall be applied only with respect to an employee within the meaning of section 401(c)(1). For purposes of this clause, a distribution to two or more trusts shall be treated as a distribution to one recipient. For purposes of this paragraph, the balance to the credit of the employee does not include the accumulated deductible employee contributions under the plan (within the meaning of section 72(o)(5)).

(ii) AGGREGATION OF CERTAIN TRUSTS AND PLANS.—For purposes of determining the balance to the credit of an employee under clause (i)—

(I) all trusts which are part of a plan shall be treated as a single trust, all pension plans maintained by the employer shall be treated as a single plan, all profit-sharing plans maintained by the employer shall be treated as a single plan, and all stock bonus plans maintained by the employer shall be treated as a single plan, and

(II) trusts which are not qualified trusts under section 401(a) and annuity contracts which do not satisfy the requirements of section 404(a)(2) shall not be taken into account.

(iii) COMMUNITY PROPERTY LAWS.—The provisions of this paragraph shall be applied without regard to community property laws.

(iv) AMOUNTS SUBJECT TO PENALTY.—This paragraph shall not apply to amounts described in subparagraph (A) of section 72(m)(5) to the extent that section 72(m)(5) applies to such amounts.

(v) BALANCE TO CREDIT OF EMPLOYEE NOT TO INCLUDE AMOUNTS PAYABLE UNDER QUALIFIED DOMESTIC RELATIONS ORDER.—For purposes of this paragraph, the balance to the credit of an employee shall not include any amount payable to an alternate payee under a qualified domestic relations order (within the meaning of section 414(p)).

(vi) TRANSFERS TO COST-OF-LIVING ARRANGEMENT NOT TREATED AS DISTRIBUTION.—For purposes of this paragraph, the balance to the credit of an employee under a defined contribution plan shall not include any amount transferred from such defined contribution plan to a qualified cost-of-living arrangement (within the meaning of section 415(k)(2)) under a defined benefit plan.

(vii) LUMP-SUM DISTRIBUTIONS OF ALTERNATE PAYEES.—If any distribution or payment of the balance to the credit of an employee would be treated as a lump-sum distribution, then, for purposes of this paragraph, the payment under a qualified domestic relations order (within the meaning of section 414(p)) of the balance to the credit of an alternate payee who is the spouse or former spouse of the employee shall be treated as a lump-sum distribution. For purposes of this clause, the balance to the credit of the alternate payee shall not include any amount payable to the employee.

(E) DEFINITIONS RELATING TO SECURITIES.—For purposes of this paragraph—

(i) SECURITIES.—The term "securities" means only shares of stock and bonds or debentures issued by a corporation with interest coupons or in registered form.

(ii) SECURITIES OF THE EMPLOYER.—The term "securities of the employer corporation" includes securities of a parent or subsidiary corporation (as defined in subsections (e) and (f) of section 424) of the employer corporation.

(5) [Stricken.]

(6) DIRECT TRUSTEE-TO-TRUSTEE TRANSFERS.—Any amount transferred in a direct trustee-to-trustee transfer in accordance with section 401(a)(31) shall not be includible in gross income for the taxable year of such transfer.

(f) WRITTEN EXPLANATION TO RECIPIENTS OF DISTRIBUTIONS ELIGIBLE FOR ROLLOVER TREATMENT.—

Caution: Code Sec. 402(f)(1), below, as amended by P.L. 107-16, §641, but prior to amendment by §657(b), applies generally to distributions after December 31, 2001, and before final regulations implementing §657(c)(2)(A) are prescribed. For sunset provision, see P.L. 107-16, §901, in the amendment notes.

(1) IN GENERAL.—The plan administrator of any plan shall, within a reasonable period of time before making an eligible rollover distribution, provide a written explanation to the recipient—

(A) of the provisions under which the recipient may have the distribution directly transferred to another eligible retirement plan,

(B) of the provision which requires the withholding of tax on the distribution if it is not directly transferred to another eligible retirement plan,

(C) of the provisions under which the distribution will not be subject to tax if transferred to an eligible retirement plan within 60 days after the date on which the recipient received the distribution,

(D) if applicable, of the provisions of subsections (d) and (e) of this section, and

(E) of the provisions under which distributions from the eligible retirement plan receiving the distribution may be subject to restrictions and tax consequences which are different from those applicable to distributions from the plan making such distribution.

Caution: Code Sec. 402(f)(1), below, as amended by P.L. 107-16, §§641 and 657(b), applies to distributions made after final regulations implementing §657(c)(2)(A) are prescribed. For sunset provision, see P.L. 107-16, §901, in the amendment notes.

(1) IN GENERAL.—The plan administrator of any plan shall, within a reasonable period of time before making an eligible rollover distribution, provide a written explanation to the recipient—

(A) of the provisions under which the recipient may have the distribution directly transferred to an eligible retirement plan and that the automatic distribution by direct transfer applies to certain distributions in accordance with section 401(a)(31)(B),

(B) of the provision which requires the withholding of tax on the distribution if it is not directly transferred to an eligible retirement plan,

(C) of the provisions under which the distribution will not be subject to tax if transferred to an eligible retirement plan within 60 days after the date on which the recipient received the distribution,

(D) if applicable, of the provisions of subsections (d) and (e) of this section, and

(E) of the provisions under which distributions from the eligible retirement plan receiving the distribution may be subject to restrictions and tax consequences which are different from those applicable to distributions from the plan making such distribution.

(2) DEFINITIONS.—For purposes of this subsection—

Caution: Code Sec. 402(f)(2)(A), below, was amended by P.L. 107-16. For sunset provision, see P.L. 107-16, §901, in the amendment notes.

(A) ELIGIBLE ROLLOVER DISTRIBUTION.—The term "eligible rollover distribution" has the same meaning as when used in subsection (c) of this section, paragraph (4) of section 403(a), subparagraph (A) of section 403(b)(8), or subparagraph (A) of section 457(e)(16).

(B) ELIGIBLE RETIREMENT PLAN.—The term "eligible retirement plan" has the meaning given such term by subsection (c)(8)(B).

(g) LIMITATION ON EXCLUSION FOR ELECTIVE DEFERRALS.—

Caution: Code Sec. 402(g)(1), below, as amended by P.L. 107-16, §611(d)(1), but prior to amendment by §617(b)(1), and as amended by P.L. 107-147, applies generally to years beginning after December 31, 2001, and to tax years beginning on or before December 31, 2005. For sunset provision, see P.L. 107-16, §901, in the amendment notes.

(1) IN GENERAL.—

(A) LIMITATION.—Notwithstanding subsections (e)(3) and (h)(1)(B), the elective deferrals of any individual for any taxable year shall be included in such individual's gross income to the extent the amount of such deferrals for the taxable year exceeds the applicable dollar amount.

(B) APPLICABLE DOLLAR AMOUNT.—For purposes of subparagraph (A), the applicable dollar amount shall be the amount determined in accordance with the following table:

For taxable years beginning in calendar year:	The applicable dollar amount:
2002	$11,000
2003	$12,000
2004	$13,000
2005	$14,000
2006 or thereafter	$15,000.

(C) CATCH-UP CONTRIBUTIONS.—In addition to subparagraph (A), in the case of an eligible participant (as defined in section 414(v)), gross income shall not include elective deferrals in excess of the applicable dollar amount under subparagraph (B) to the extent that the amount of such elective deferrals does not exceed the applicable dollar amount under section 414(v)(2)(B)(i) for the taxable year (without regard to the treatment of the elective deferrals by an applicable employer plan under section 414(v)).

Caution: Code Sec. 402(g)(1), below, as amended by P.L. 107-16, §611(d)(1) and §617(b)(1), and by P.L. 107-147, applies generally to years beginning after December 31, 2001, and to tax years beginning after December 31, 2005. For sunset provision, see P.L. 107-16, §901, in the amendment notes.

(1) IN GENERAL.—

(A) LIMITATION.—Notwithstanding subsections (e)(3) and (h)(1)(B), the elective deferrals of any individual for any taxable year shall be included in such individual's gross income to the extent the amount of such deferrals for the taxable year exceeds the applicable dollar amount. The preceding sentence shall not apply [to] the portion of such excess as does not exceed the designated Roth contributions of the individuals for the taxable year.

(B) APPLICABLE DOLLAR AMOUNT.—For purposes of subparagraph (A), the applicable dollar amount shall be the amount determined in accordance with the following table:

For taxable years beginning in calendar year:	The applicable dollar amount:
2002	$11,000
2003	$12,000
2004	$13,000
2005	$14,000
2006 or thereafter	$15,000.

(C) CATCH-UP CONTRIBUTIONS.—In addition to subparagraph (A), in the case of an eligible participant (as defined in section 414(v)), gross income shall not include elective deferrals in excess of the applicable dollar amount under subparagraph (B) to the extent that the amount of such elective deferrals does not exceed the applicable dollar amount under section 414(v)(2)(B)(i) for the taxable year (without regard to the treatment of the elective deferrals by an applicable employer plan under section 414(v)).

(2) DISTRIBUTION OF EXCESS DEFERRALS.—

Caution: Code Sec. 402(g)(2)(A), below, prior to amendment by P.L. 107-16, applies to tax years beginning on or before December 31, 2005.

(A) IN GENERAL.—If any amount (hereinafter in this paragraph referred to as "excess deferrals") is included in the gross income of an individual under paragraph (1) for any taxable year—

(i) not later than the 1st March 1 following the close of the taxable year, the individual may allocate the amount of such excess deferrals among the plans under which the deferrals were made and may notify each such plan of the portion allocated to it, and

(ii) not later than the 1st April 15 following the close of the taxable year, each such plan may distribute to the individual the amount allocated to it under clause (i) (and any income allocable to such amount).

The distribution described in clause (ii) may be made notwithstanding any other provision of law.

Caution: Code Sec. 402(g)(2)(A), below, as amended by P.L. 107-16, applies to tax years beginning after December 31, 2005. For sunset provision, see P.L. 107-16, §901, in the amendment notes.

(A) IN GENERAL.—If any amount (hereinafter in this paragraph referred to as "excess deferrals") is included in the gross income of an individual under paragraph (1) (or would be included but for the last sentence thereof) for any taxable year—

(i) not later than the 1st March 1 following the close of the taxable year, the individual may allocate the amount of such excess deferrals among the plans under which the deferrals were made and may notify each such plan of the portion allocated to it, and

(ii) not later than the 1st April 15 following the close of the taxable year, each such plan may distribute to the individual the amount allocated to it under clause (i) (and any income allocable to such amount).

The distribution described in clause (ii) may be made notwithstanding any other provision of law.

(B) TREATMENT OF DISTRIBUTION UNDER SECTION 401(k).—Except to the extent provided under rules prescribed by the Secretary, notwithstanding the distribution of any portion of an excess deferral from a plan under subparagraph (A)(ii), such portion shall, for purposes of applying section 401(k)(3)(A)(ii), be treated as an employer contribution.

(C) TAXATION OF DISTRIBUTION.—In the case of a distribution to which subparagraph (A) applies—

(i) except as provided in clause (ii), such distribution shall not be included in gross income, and

(ii) any income on the excess deferral shall, for purposes of this chapter, be treated as earned and received in the taxable year in which such income is distributed.

No tax shall be imposed under section 72(t) on any distribution described in the preceding sentence.

(D) PARTIAL DISTRIBUTIONS.—If a plan distributes only a portion of any excess deferral and income allocable thereto, such portion shall be treated as having been distributed ratably from the excess deferral and the income.

(3) ELECTIVE DEFERRALS.—For purposes of this subsection, the term "elective deferrals" means, with respect to any taxable year, the sum of—

(A) any employer contribution under a qualified cash or deferred arrangement (as defined in section 401(k)) to the extent not includible in gross income for the taxable year under subsection (e)(3) (determined without regard to this subsection),

(B) any employer contribution to the extent not includible in gross income for the taxable year under subsection (h)(1)(B) (determined without regard to this subsection),

(C) any employer contribution to purchase an annuity contract under section 403(b) under a salary reduction agreement (within the meaning of section 3121(a)(5)(D)), and

(D) any elective employer contribution under section 408(p)(2)(A)(i).

An employer contribution shall not be treated as an elective deferral described in subparagraph (C) if under the salary reduction agreement such contribution is made pursuant to a one-time irrevocable election made by the employee at the time of initial eligibility to participate in the agreement or is made pursuant to a similar arrangement involving a one-time irrevocable election specified in regulations.

Caution: Code Sec. 402(g)(4), below, was amended and redesignated by P.L. 107-16. For sunset provision, see P.L. 107-16, §901, in the amendment notes.

(4) COST-OF-LIVING ADJUSTMENT.—In the case of taxable years beginning after December 31, 2006, the Secretary shall adjust the $15,000 amount under paragraph (1)(B) at the same time and in the same manner as under section 415(d), except that the base period shall be the

calendar quarter beginning July 1, 2005, and any increase under this paragraph which is not a multiple of $500 shall be rounded to the next lowest multiple of $500.

Caution: Code Sec. 402(g)(5-(7)), below, was redesignated by P.L. 107-16. For sunset provision, see P.L. 107-16, §901, in the amendment notes.

(5) DISREGARD OF COMMUNITY PROPERTY LAWS.—This subsection shall be applied without regard to community property laws.

(6) COORDINATION WITH SECTION 72.—For purposes of applying section 72, any amount includible in gross income for any taxable year under this subsection but which is not distributed from the plan during such taxable year shall not be treated as investment in the contract.

(7) SPECIAL RULE FOR CERTAIN ORGANIZATIONS.—

(A) IN GENERAL.—In the case of a qualified employee of a qualified organization, with respect to employer contributions described in paragraph (3)(C) made by such organization, the limitation of paragraph (1) for any taxable year shall be increased by whichever of the following is the least:

(i) $3,000,

(ii) $15,000 reduced by amounts not included in gross income for prior taxable years by reason of this paragraph, or

(iii) the excess of $5,000 multiplied by the number of years of service of the employee with the qualified organization over the employer contributions described in paragraph (3) made by the organization on behalf of such employee for prior taxable years (determined in the manner prescribed by the Secretary).

Caution: Code Sec. 402(g)(7)(B), below, was amended by P.L. 107-16 and P.L. 107-147. For sunset provision, see P.L. 107-16, §901, in the amendment notes.

(B) QUALIFIED ORGANIZATION.—For purposes of this paragraph, the term "qualified organization" means any educational organization, hospital, home health service agency, health and welfare service agency, church, or convention or association of churches. Such term includes any organization described in section 414(e)(3)(B)(ii). Terms used in this subparagraph shall have the same meaning as when used in section 415(c)(4) (as in effect before the enactment of the Economic Growth and Tax Relief Reconciliation Act of 2001).

(C) QUALIFIED EMPLOYEE.—For purposes of this paragraph, the term "qualified employee" means any employee who has completed 15 years of service with the qualified organization.

(D) YEARS OF SERVICE.—For purposes of this paragraph, the term "years of service" has the meaning given such term by section 403(b).

Caution: Code Sec. 402(g)(8), below, was redesignated by P.L. 107-16. For sunset provision, see P.L. 107-16, §901, in the amendment notes.

(8) MATCHING CONTRIBUTIONS ON BEHALF OF SELF-EMPLOYED INDIVIDUALS NOT TREATED AS ELECTIVE EMPLOYER CONTRIBUTIONS.—Except as provided in section 401(k)(3)(D)(ii),

any matching contribution described in section 401(m)(4)(A) which is made on behalf of a self-employed individual (as defined in section 401(c)) shall not be treated as an elective employer contribution under a qualified cash or deferred arrangement (as defined in section 401(k)) for purposes of this title.

(h) SPECIAL RULES FOR SIMPLIFIED EMPLOYEE PENSIONS.—For purposes of this chapter—

(1) IN GENERAL.—Except as provided in paragraph (2), contributions made by an employer on behalf of an employee to an individual retirement plan pursuant to a simplified employee pension (as defined in section 408(k))—

(A) shall not be treated as distributed or made available to the employee or as contributions made by the employee, and

(B) if such contributions are made pursuant to an arrangement under section 408(k)(6) under which an employee may elect to have the employer make contributions to the simplified employer pension on behalf of the employee, shall not be treated as distributed or made available or as contributions made by the employee merely because the simplified employee pension includes provisions for such election.

(2) LIMITATIONS ON EMPLOYER CONTRIBUTIONS.—Contributions made by an employer to a simplified employee pension with respect to an employee for any year shall be treated as distributed or made available to such employee and as contributions made by the employee to the extent such contributions exceed the lesser of—

Caution: Code Sec. 402(h)(2)(A), below, was amended by P.L. 107-147, effective as if included in P.L. 107-16. For sunset provision, see P.L. 107-16, §901, in the amendment notes.

(A) 25 percent of the compensation (within the meaning of section 414(s)) from such employer includible in the employee's gross income for the year (determined without regard to the employer contributions to the simplified employee pension), or

(B) the limitation in effect under section 415(c)(1)(A), reduced in the case of any highly compensated employee (within the meaning of section 414(q)) by the amount taken into account with respect to such employee under section 408(k)(3)(D).

(3) DISTRIBUTIONS.—Any amount paid or distributed out of an individual retirement plan pursuant to a simplified employee pension shall be included in gross income by the payee or distributee, as the case may be, in accordance with the provisions of section 408(d).

(i) TREATMENT OF SELF-EMPLOYED INDIVIDUALS.—For purposes of this section, except as otherwise provided in subparagraph (A) of subsection (d)(4), the term "employee" includes a self-employed individual (as defined in section 401(c)(1)(B)) and the employer of such individual shall be the person treated as his employer under section 401(c)(4).

(j) EFFECT OF DISPOSITION OF STOCK BY PLAN ON NET UNREALIZED APPRECIATION.—

(1) IN GENERAL.—For purposes of subsection (e)(4), in the case of any transaction to which this subsection applies, the determination of net unrealized appreciation shall be made without regard to such transaction.

(2) Transaction to which Subsection Applies.—This subsection shall apply to any transaction in which—

 (A) the plan trustee exchanges the plan's securities of the employer corporation for other such securities, or

 (B) the plan trustee disposes of securities of the employer corporation and uses the proceeds of such disposition to acquire securities of the employer corporation within 90 days (or such longer period as the Secretary may prescribe), except that this subparagraph shall not apply to any employee with respect to whom a distribution of money was made during the period after such disposition and before such acquisition.

(k) Treatment of Simple Retirement Accounts.—Rules similar to the rules of paragraphs (1) and (3) of subsection (h) shall apply to contributions and distributions with respect to a simple retirement account under section 408(p).

Caution: Code Sec. 402A, below, as added by P.L. 107-16, applies to tax years beginning after December 31, 2005. For sunset provision, see P.L. 107-16, §901, in the amendment notes.

SEC. 402A. OPTIONAL TREATMENT OF ELECTIVE DEFERRALS AS ROTH CONTRIBUTIONS.

(a) General Rule.—If an applicable retirement plan includes a qualified Roth contribution program—

 (1) any designated Roth contribution made by an employee pursuant to the program shall be treated as an elective deferral for purposes of this chapter, except that such contribution shall not be excludable from gross income, and

 (2) such plan (and any arrangement which is part of such plan) shall not be treated as failing to meet any requirement of this chapter solely by reason of including such program.

(b) Qualified Roth Contribution Program.—For purposes of this section—

 (1) In general.—The term "qualified Roth contribution program" means a program under which an employee may elect to make designated Roth contributions in lieu of all or a portion of elective deferrals the employee is otherwise eligible to make under the applicable retirement plan.

 (2) Separate Accounting Required.—A program shall not be treated as a qualified Roth contribution program unless the applicable retirement plan—

  (A) establishes separate accounts ("designated Roth account") for the designated Roth contributions of each employee and any earnings properly allocable to the contributions, and

  (B) maintains separate recordkeeping with respect to each account.

(c) Definitions and Rules Relating to Designated Roth Contributions.—For purposes of this section—

(1) DESIGNATED ROTH CONTRIBUTION.—The term "designated Roth contribution" means any elective deferral which—

(A) is excludable from gross income of an employee without regard to this section, and

(B) the employee designates (at such time and in such manner as the Secretary may prescribe) as not being so excludable.

(2) DESIGNATION LIMITS.—The amount of elective deferrals which an employee may designate under paragraph (1) shall not exceed the excess (if any) of—

(A) the maximum amount of elective deferrals excludable from gross income of the employee for the taxable year (without regard to this section), over

(B) the aggregate amount of elective deferrals of the employee for the taxable year which the employee does not designate under paragraph (1).

(3) ROLLOVER CONTRIBUTIONS.—

(A) IN GENERAL.—A rollover contribution of any payment or distribution from a designated Roth account which is otherwise allowable under this chapter may be made only if the contribution is to—

(i) another designated Roth account of the individual from whose account the payment or distribution was made, or

(ii) a Roth IRA of such individual.

(B) COORDINATION WITH LIMIT.—Any rollover contribution to a designated Roth account under subparagraph (A) shall not be taken into account for purposes of paragraph (1).

(d) DISTRIBUTION RULES.—For purposes of this title—

(1) EXCLUSION.—Any qualified distribution from a designated Roth account shall not be includible in gross income.

(2) QUALIFIED DISTRIBUTION.—For purposes of this subsection—

(A) IN GENERAL.—The term "qualified distribution" has the meaning given such term by section 408A(d)(2)(A) (without regard to clause (iv) thereof).

(B) DISTRIBUTIONS WITH NONEXCLUSION PERIOD.—A payment or distribution from a designated Roth account shall not be treated as a qualified distribution if such payment or distribution is made within the 5-taxable-year period beginning with the earlier of—

(i) the first taxable year for which the individual made a designated Roth contribution to any designated Roth account established for such individual under the same applicable retirement plan, or

(ii) if a rollover contribution was made to such designated Roth account from a designated Roth account previously established for such individual under another applicable retirement plan, the first taxable year for which the individual made a designated Roth contribution to such previously established account.

(C) DISTRIBUTIONS OF EXCESS DEFERRALS AND CONTRIBUTIONS AND EARNINGS THEREON.—The term "qualified distribution" shall not include any distribution of any excess deferral under section 402(g)(2) or any excess contribution under section 401(k)(8), and any income on the excess deferral or contribution.

(3) TREATMENT OF DISTRIBUTIONS OF CERTAIN EXCESS DEFERRALS.—Notwithstanding section 72, if any excess deferral under section 402(g)(2) attributable to a designated Roth contribution is not distributed on o before the 1st April 15 following the close of the taxable year in which such excess deferral is made, the amount of such excess deferral shall—

(A) not be treated as investment in the contract, and

(B) be included in gross income for the taxable year in which such excess is distributed.

(4) AGGREGATION RULES.—Section 72 shall be applied separately with respect to distributions and payments from a designated Roth account and other distributions and payments from the plan.

(e) OTHER DEFINITIONS.—For purposes of this section—

(1) APPLICABLE RETIREMENT PLAN.—The term "applicable retirement plan" means—

(A) an employees' trust described in section 401(a) which is exempt from tax under section 501(a), and

(B) a plan under which amounts are contributed by an individual's employer for an annuity contract described in section 403(b).

(2) ELECTIVE DEFERRAL.—The term "elective deferral" means any elective deferral described in subparagraph (A) or (C) of section 402(g)(3).

SEC. 403. TAXATION OF EMPLOYEE ANNUITIES.

(a) TAXABILITY OF BENEFICIARY UNDER A QUALIFIED ANNUITY PLAN.—

(1) DISTRIBUTEE TAXABLE UNDER SECTION 72.—If an annuity contract is purchased by an employer for an employee under a plan which meets the requirements of section 404(a)(2) (whether or not the employer deducts the amounts paid for the contract under such section), the amount actually distributed to any distributee under the contract shall be taxable to the distributee (in the year in which so distributed) under section 72 (relating to annuities).

(2) [Repealed.]

(3) SELF-EMPLOYED INDIVIDUALS.—For purposes of this subsection, the term "employee" includes an individual who is an employee within the meaning of section 401(c)(1), and the employer of such individual is the person treated as his employer under section 401(c)(4).

(4) ROLLOVER AMOUNTS.—

(A) GENERAL RULE.—If—

(i) any portion of the balance to the credit of an employee in an employee annuity described in paragraph (1) is paid to him in an eligible rollover distribution (within the meaning of section 402(c)(4)),

(ii) the employee transfers any portion of the property he receives in such distribution to an eligible retirement plan, and

(iii) in the case of a distribution of property other than money, the amount so transferred consists of the property distributed,

then such distribution (to the extent so transferred) shall not be includible in gross income for the taxable year in which paid.

(B) CERTAIN RULES MADE APPLICABLE.—Rules similar to the rules of paragraphs (2) through (7) of section 402(c) shall apply for purposes of subparagraph (A).

(5) DIRECT TRUSTEE-TO-TRUSTEE TRANSFER.—Any amount transferred in a direct trustee-to-trustee transfer in accordance with section 401(a)(31) shall not be includible in gross income for the taxable year of such transfer.

(b) TAXABILITY OF BENEFICIARY UNDER ANNUITY PURCHASED BY SECTION 501(c)(3) ORGANIZATION OR PUBLIC SCHOOL.—

Caution: Code Sec. 403(b)(1)-(3), below, was amended by P.L. 107-16 and P.L. 107-147. For sunset provision, see P.L. 107-16, §901, in the amendment notes.

(1) GENERAL RULE.—If—

(A) an annuity contract is purchased—

(i) for an employee by an employer described in section 501(c)(3) which is exempt from tax under section 501(a),

(ii) for an employee (other than an employee described in clause (ii)), who performs services for an educational organization described in section 170(b)(1)(A)(ii), by an employer which is a State, a political subdivision of a State, or an agency or instrumentality of any one or more of the foregoing, or

(iii) for the minister described in section 414(e)(5)(A) by the minister or by an employer,

(B) such annuity contract is not subject to subsection (a),

(C) the employee's rights under the contract are nonforfeitable, except for failure to pay future premiums,

(D) except in the case of a contract purchased by a church, such contract is purchased under a plan which meets the nondiscrimination requirements of paragraph 12, and

(E) in the case of a contract purchased under a salary reduction agreement, the contract meets the requirements of section 401(a)(30),

then contributions and other additions by such employer for such annuity contract shall be excluded from the gross income of the employee for the taxable year to the extent that the aggregate of such contributions and additions (when expressed as an annual addition (within the meaning of section 415(c)(2))) does not exceed the applicable limit under section 415. The amount actually distributed to any distributee under such contract shall be taxable to the distributee (in the year in which so distributed) under section 72 (relating to annuities). For purposes of applying the rules of this subsection to contributions and other additions by an employer for a taxable year, amounts transferred to a contract described in this paragraph by reason of a rollover contribution described in paragraph (8) of this subsection or section 408(d)(3)(A)(ii) shall not be considered contributed by such employer.

(2) [Stricken.]

(3) INCLUDIBLE COMPENSATION.—For purposes of this subsection, the term "includible compensation" means, in the case of any employee, the amount of compensation which is received from the employer described in paragraph (1)(A), and which is includible in gross income (computed without regard to section 911) for the most recent period (ending not later than the close of the taxable year) which under paragraph (4) may be counted as one year of service, and which precedes the taxable year by no more than five years. Such term does not include any amount contributed by the employer for any annuity contract to which this subsection applies. Such term includes—

(A) any elective deferral (as defined in section 402(g)(3)), and

(B) any amount which is contributed or deferred by the employer at the election of the employee, and which is not includible in the gross income of the employee by reason of section 125, 132(f)(4), or 457.

(4) YEARS OF SERVICE.—In determining the number of years of service for purposes of this subsection, there shall be included—

(A) one year for each full year during which the individual was a full-time employee of the organization purchasing the annuity for him, and

(B) a fraction of a year (determined in accordance with regulations prescribed by the Secretary) for each full year during which such individual was a part-time employee of such organization and for each part of a year during which such individual was a full-time or part-time employee of such organization.

In no case shall the number of years of service be less than one.

(5) APPLICATION TO MORE THAN ONE ANNUITY CONTRACT.—If for any taxable year of the employee this subsection applies to 2 or more annuity contracts purchased by the employer, such contracts shall be treated as one contract.

Caution: Code Sec. 403(b)(6), below, was stricken by P.L. 107-147, effective as if included in P.L. 107-16. For sunset provision, see P.L. 107-16, §901, in the amendment notes.

(6) [Stricken.]

(7) CUSTODIAL ACCOUNTS FOR REGULATED INVESTMENT COMPANY STOCK.—

(A) AMOUNTS PAID TREATED AS CONTRIBUTIONS.—For purposes of this title, amounts paid by an employer described in paragraph (1)(A) to a custodial account which satisfies the requirements of section 401(f)(2) shall be treated as amounts contributed by him for an annuity contract for his employee if—

(i) the amounts are to be invested in regulated investment company stock to be held in that custodial account, and

Caution: Code Sec. 403(b)(7)(A)(ii), below, was amended by P.L. 107-16. For sunset provision, see P.L. 107-16, §901, in the amendment notes.

(ii) under the custodial account no such amounts may be paid or made available to any distributee before the employee dies, attains age 59 , has a severance from employment, becomes disabled (within the meaning of section 72(m)(7)), or in the case of contributions made pursuant to a salary reduction agreement (within the meaning of section 3121(a)(1)(D)), encounters financial hardship.

(B) ACCOUNT TREATED AS PLAN.—For purposes of this title, a custodial account which satisfies the requirements of section 401(f)(2) shall be treated as an organization described in section 401(a) solely for purposes of subchapter F and subtitle F with respect to amounts received by it (and income from investment thereof.)

(C) REGULATED INVESTMENT COMPANY.—For purposes of this paragraph, the term "regulated investment company" means a domestic corporation which is a regulated investment company within the meaning of section 851(a).

(8) ROLLOVER AMOUNTS.—

Caution: Code Sec. 403(b)(8)(A)(B), below, was amended by P.L. 107-16. For sunset provision, see P.L. 107-16, §901, in the amendment notes.

(A) GENERAL RULE.—If—

(i) any portion of the balance to the credit of an employee in an annuity contract described in paragraph (1) is paid to him in an eligible rollover distribution (within the meaning of section 402(c)(4)),

(ii) the employee transfers any portion of the property he receives in such distribution to an eligible retirement plan described in section 402(c)(8)(B), and

(iii) in the case of a distribution of property other than money, the property so transferred consists of the property distributed,

then such distribution (to the extent so transferred) shall not be includible in gross income for the taxable year in which paid.

(B) CERTAIN RULES MADE APPLICABLE.—The rules of paragraphs (2) through (7) and (9) of section 402(c) and section 402(f) shall apply for purposes of subparagraph (A), except that section 402(f) shall be applied to the payor in lieu of the plan administrator.

(9) RETIREMENT INCOME ACCOUNTS PROVIDED BY CHURCHES, ETC.—

(A) AMOUNTS PAID TREATED AS CONTRIBUTIONS.—For purposes of this title—

(i) a retirement income account shall be treated as an annuity contract described in this subsection, and

(ii) amounts paid by an employer described in paragraph (1)(A) to a retirement income account shall be treated as amounts contributed by the employer for an annuity contract for the employee on whose behalf such account is maintained.

(B) RETIREMENT INCOME ACCOUNT.—For purposes of this paragraph, the term "retirement income account" means a defined contribution program established or maintained by a church, a convention or association of churches, including an organization described in section 414(e)(3)(A), to provide benefits under section 403(b) for an employee described in paragraph (1) or his beneficiaries.

(10) DISTRIBUTION REQUIREMENTS.—Under regulations prescribed by the Secretary, this subsection shall not apply to any annuity contract (or to any custodial account described in paragraph (7) or retirement income account described in paragraph (9)) unless requirements similar to the requirements of sections 401(a)(9) and 401(a)(31) are met (and requirements similar to the incidental death benefit requirements of section 401(a) are met) with respect to such annuity contract (or custodial account or retirement income account). Any amount transferred in a direct trustee-to-trustee transfer in accordance with section 401(a)(31) shall not be includible in gross income for the taxable year of the transfer.

Caution: Code Sec. 403(b)(11), below, was amended by P.L. 107-16. For sunset provision, see P.L. 107-16, §901, in the amendment notes.

(11) REQUIREMENT THAT DISTRIBUTIONS NOT BEGIN BEFORE AGE 59 , SEPARATION FROM EMPLOYMENT, DEATH, OR DISABILITY.—This subsection shall not apply to any annuity contract unless under such contract distributions attributable to contributions made pursuant to a salary reduction agreement (within the meaning of section 402(g)(3)(C)) may be paid only—

(A) when the employee attains age 59 , has a severance from employment, dies, or becomes disabled (within the meaning of section 72(m)(7)), or

(B) in the case of hardship.

Such contract may not provide for the distribution of any income attributable to such contributions in the case of hardship.

(12) NONDISCRIMINATION REQUIREMENTS.—

(A) IN GENERAL.—For purposes of paragraph (1)(D), a plan meets the nondiscrimination requirements of this paragraph if—

(i) with respect to contributions not made pursuant to a salary reduction agreement, such plan meets the requirements of paragraphs (4), (5), (17), and (26) of section 401(a), section 401(m), and section 410(b) in the same manner as if such plan were described in section 401(a), and

(ii) all employees of the organization may elect to have the employer make contributions of more than $200 pursuant to a salary reduction agreement if any employee of the organization may elect to have the organization make contributions for such contracts pursuant to such agreement.

For purposes of clause (i), a contribution shall be treated as not made pursuant to a salary reduction agreement if under the agreement it is made pursuant to a 1-time irrevocable election made by the employee at the time of initial eligibility to participate in the agreement or is made pursuant to a similar arrangement involving a one-time irrevocable election specified in regulations. For purposes of clause (ii), there may be excluded any employee who is a participant in an eligible deferred compensation plan (within the meaning of section 457) or a qualified cash or deferred arrangement of the organization or another annuity contract described in this subsection. Any nonresident alien described in section 410(b)(3)(C) may also be excluded. Subject to the conditions applicable under section 410(b)(4), there may be excluded for purposes of this subparagraph employees who are students performing services described in section 3121(b)(10) and employees who normally work less than 20 hours per week.

(B) CHURCH.—For purposes of paragraph (1)(D), the term "church" has the meaning given to such term by section 3121(w)(3)(A). Such term shall include any qualified church-controlled organization (as defined in section 3121(w)(3)(B)).

(C) STATE AND LOCAL GOVERNMENTAL PLANS.—For purposes of paragraph (1)(D), the requirements of subparagraph (A)(i) (other than those relating to section 401(a)(17)) shall not apply to a governmental plan (within the meaning of section 414(d)) maintained by a State or local government or political subdivision thereof (or agency or instrumentality thereof).

Caution: Code Sec. 403(b)(13), below, was added by P.L. 107-16. For sunset provision, see P.L. 107-16, §901, in the amendment notes.

(13) TRUSTEE-TO-TRUSTEE TRANSFERS TO PURCHASE PERMISSIVE SERVICE CREDIT.—No amount shall be includible in gross income by reason of a direct trustee-to-trustee transfer to a defined benefit governmental plan (as defined in section 414(d)) if such transfer is—

(A) for the purchase of permissive service credit (as defined in section 415(n)(3)(A)) under such plan, or

(B) a repayment to which section 415 does not apply by reason of subsection (k)(3) thereof.

(c) TAXABILITY OF BENEFICIARY UNDER NONQUALIFIED ANNUITIES OR UNDER ANNUITIES PURCHASED BY EXEMPT ORGANIZATIONS.—Premiums paid by an employer for an annuity contract which is not subject to subsection (a) shall be included in the gross income of the employee in accordance with section 83 (relating to property transferred in connection with performance of services), except that the value of such contract shall be substituted for the fair market value of the property for purposes of applying such section. The preceding sentence shall not apply to that portion of the premiums paid which is excluded from gross income under subsection (b). In the case of any portion of any contract which is attributable to premiums to which this subsection applies, the amount actually paid or made available under such contract to any beneficiary which is attributable to such premiums shall be taxable to the beneficiary (in the year in which so paid or made available) under section 72 (relating to annuities).

SEC. 404. DEDUCTION FOR CONTRIBUTIONS OF AN EMPLOYER TO AN EMPLOYEES' TRUST OR ANNUITY PLAN AND COMPENSATION UNDER A DEFERRED-PAYMENT PLAN.

(a) GENERAL RULE.—If contributions are paid by an employer to or under a stock bonus, pension, profit-sharing, or annuity plan, or if compensation is paid or accrued on account of any employee under a plan deferring the receipt of such compensation, such contributions or compensation shall not be deductible under this chapter; but if they would otherwise be deductible, they shall be deductible under this section, subject, however, to the following limitations as to the amounts deductible in any year:

(1) PENSION TRUSTS.—

Caution: Code Sec. 404(a)(1)(A), below, was amended by P.L. 107-16. For sunset provision, see P.L. 107-16, §901, in the amendment notes.

(A) IN GENERAL.—In the taxable year when paid, if the contributions are paid into a pension trust (other than a trust to which paragraph (3) applies), and if such taxable year ends within or with a taxable year of the trust for which the trust is exempt under section 501(a), in an amount determined as follows:

(i) the amount necessary to satisfy the minimum funding standard provided by section 412(a) for plan years ending within or with such taxable year (or for any prior plan year), if such amount is greater than the amount determined under clause (ii) or (iii) (whichever is applicable with respect to the plan),

(ii) the amount necessary to provide with respect to all of the employees under the trust the remaining unfunded cost of their past and current service credits distributed as a level amount, or a level percentage of compensation, over the remaining future service of each such employee, as determined under regulations prescribed by the Secretary, but if such remaining unfunded cost with respect to any 3 individuals is more than 50 percent of such remaining unfunded cost, the amount of such unfunded cost attributable to such individuals shall be distributed over a period of at least 5 taxable years,

(iii) an amount equal to the normal cost of the plan, as determined under regulations prescribed by the Secretary, plus, if past service or other supplementary pension or annuity credits are provided by the plan, an amount necessary to amortize the unfunded costs attributable to such credits in equal annual payments (until fully amortized) over 10 years, as determined under regulations prescribed by the Secretary.

In determining the amount deductible in such year under the foregoing limitations the funding method and the actuarial assumptions used shall be those used for such year under section 412, and the maximum amount deductible for such year shall be an amount equal to the full funding limitation for such year determined under section 412.

(B) SPECIAL RULE IN CASE OF CERTAIN AMENDMENTS.—In the case of a plan which the Secretary of Labor finds to be collectively bargained which makes an election under this subparagraph (in such manner and at such time as may be provided under regulations prescribed by the Secretary), if the full funding limitation determined under section 412(c)(7) for such year is zero, if as a result of any plan amendment applying to such plan year, the amount determined under section 412(c)(7)(B) exceeds the amount determined under section 412(c)(7)(A), and if the funding method and the actuarial assumptions used are those used for such year under section 412, the maximum amount deductible in such year under the limitations of this paragraph shall be an amount equal to the lesser of—

  (i) the full funding limitation for such year determined by applying section 412(c)(7) but increasing the amount referred to in subparagraph (A) thereof by the decrease in the present value of all unamortized liabilities resulting from such amendment, or

  (ii) the normal cost under the plan reduced by the amount necessary to amortize in equal annual installments over 10 years (until fully amortized) the decrease described in clause (i).

In the case of any election under this subparagraph, the amount deductible under the limitations of this paragraph with respect to any of the plan years following the plan year for which such election was made shall be determined as provided under such regulations as may be prescribed by the Secretary to carry out the purposes of this subparagraph.

  (C) CERTAIN COLLECTIVELY-BARGAINED PLANS.—In the case of a plan which the Secretary of Labor finds to be collectively bargained, established or maintained by an employer doing business in not less than 40 States and engaged in the trade or business of furnishing or selling services described in section 168(i)(10)(C), with respect to which the rates have been established or approved by a State or political subdivision thereof, by any agency or instrumentality of the United States, or by a public service or public utility commission or other similar body of any State or political subdivision thereof, and in the case of any employer which is a member of a controlled group with such employer, subparagraph (B) shall be applied by substituting for the words "plan amendment" the words "plan amendment or increase in benefits payable under title II of the Social Security Act". For purposes of this subparagraph, the term "controlled group" has the meaning provided by section 1563(a), determined without regard to section 1563(a)(4) and (e)(3)(C).

Caution: Code Sec. 404(a)(1)(D), below, was amended by P.L. 107-16 and P.L. 107-147. For sunset provision, see P.L. 107-16, §901, in the amendment notes.

  (D) SPECIAL RULE IN CASE OF CERTAIN PLANS.—

   (i) IN GENERAL.—In the case of any defined benefit plan, except as provided in regulations, the maximum amount deductible under the limitations of this paragraph shall not be less than the unfunded current liability determined under section 412(l).

   (ii) PLANS WITH 100 OR LESS PARTICIPANTS.—For purposes of this subparagraph, in the case of a plan which has 100 or less participants for the plan year, unfunded current liability shall not include the liability attributable to benefit increases for highly compensated employees (as defined in section 414(q)) resulting from a plan amendment which is made or becomes effective, whichever is later, within the last 2 years.

   (iii) RULE FOR DETERMINING NUMBER OF PARTICIPANTS.—For purposes of determining the number of plan participants, all defined benefit plans maintained by the same employer (or any member of such employer's controlled group (within the meaning of section 412(l)(8)(C))) shall be treated as one plan, but only employees of such member or employer shall be taken into account.

(iv) SPECIAL RULE FOR TERMINATING PLANS.—In the case of a plan which, subject to section 4041 of the Employee Retirement Income Security Act of 1974, terminates during the plan year, clause (i) shall be applied by substituting for unfunded current liability the amount required to make the plan sufficient for benefit liabilities (within the meaning of section 4041(d) of such Act).

(E) CARRYOVER.—Any amount paid in a taxable year in excess of the amount deductible in such year under the foregoing limitations shall be deductible in the succeeding taxable years in order of time to the extent of the difference between the amount paid and deductible in each such succeeding year and the maximum amount deductible for such year under the foregoing limitations.

(F) ELECTION TO DISREGARD MODIFIED INTEREST RATE.—An employer may elect to disregard subsections (b)(5)(B)(ii)(II) and (l)(7)(C)(i)(IV) of section 412 solely for purposes of determining the interest rate used in calculating the maximum amount of the deduction allowable under this paragraph.

(2) EMPLOYEES' ANNUITIES.—In the taxable year when paid, in an amount determined in accordance with paragraph (1), if the contributions are paid toward the purchase of retirement annuities, or retirement annuities and medical benefits as described in section 401(h), and such purchase is a part of a plan which meets the requirements of section 401(a)(3), (4), (5), (6), (7), (8), (9), (11), (12), (13), (14), (15), (16), (17), (19), (20), (22), (26), (27), and (31), and, if applicable, the requirements of section 401(a)(10) and of section 401(d), and if refunds of premiums, if any, are applied within the current taxable year or next succeeding taxable year towards the purchase of such retirement annuities, or such retirement annuities and medical benefits.

(3) STOCK BONUS AND PROFIT-SHARING TRUSTS.—

(A) LIMITS ON DEDUCTIBLE CONTRIBUTIONS.—

(i) IN GENERAL.—In the taxable year when paid, if the contributions are paid into a stock bonus or profit-sharing trust, and if such taxable year ends within or with a taxable year of the trust with respect to which the trust is exempt under section 501(a), in an amount not in excess of the greater of—

Caution: Code Sec. 404(a)(3)(A)(i)(I), below, was amended by P.L. 107-16. For sunset provision, see P.L. 107-16, §901, in the amendment notes.

(I) 25 percent of the compensation otherwise paid or accrued during the taxable year to the beneficiaries under the stock bonus or profit-sharing plan, or

(II) the amount such employer is required to contribute to such trust under section 401(k)(11) for such year.

(ii) CARRYOVER OF EXCESS CONTRIBUTIONS.—Any amount paid into the trust in any taxable year in excess of the limitation of clause (i) (or the corresponding provision of prior law) shall be deductible in the succeeding taxable years in order of time, but the amount so deductible under this clause in any 1 such succeeding taxable year together with the amount allowable under clause (i) shall not exceed the amount described subclause (I) or (II) of clause (i), whichever is greater,, with respect to such taxable year.

(iii) CERTAIN RETIREMENT PLANS EXCLUDED.—For purposes of this subparagraph, the term "stock bonus or profit-sharing trust" shall not include any trust designed to provide benefits upon retirement and covering a period of years, if under the plan the amounts to be contributed by the employer can be determined actuarially as provided in paragraph (1).

(iv) 2 OR MORE TRUSTS TREATED AS 1 TRUST.—If the contributions are made to 2 or more stock bonus or profit-sharing trusts, such trusts shall be considered a single trust for purposes of applying the limitations in this subparagraph.

Caution: Code Sec. 404(a)(3)(A)(v), below, was amended by P.L. 107-16 and P.L. 107-147. For sunset provision, see P.L. 107-16, §901, in the amendment notes.

(v) DEFINED CONTRIBUTION PLANS SUBJECT TO THE FUNDING STANDARDS.—Except as provided by the Secretary, a defined contribution plan which is subject to the funding standards of section 412 shall be treated in the same manner as a stock bonus or profit-sharing plan for purposes of this subparagraph.

Caution: Code Sec. 404(a)(3)(B), below, was amended by P.L. 107-16 and P.L. 107-147. For sunset provision, see P.L. 107-16, §901, in the amendment notes.

(B) PROFIT-SHARING PLAN OF AFFILIATED GROUP.—In the case of a profit-sharing plan, or a stock bonus plan in which contributions are determined with reference to profits, of a group of corporations which is an affiliated group within the meaning of section 1504, if any member of such affiliated group is prevented from making a contribution which it would otherwise have made under the plan, by reason of having no current or accumulated earnings or profits or because such earnings or profits are less than the contributions which it would otherwise have made, then so much of the contribution which such member was so prevented from making may be made for the benefit of the employees of such member, by the other members of the group, to the extent of current or accumulated earnings or profits, except that such contribution by each such other member shall be limited, where the group does not file a consolidated return, to that proportion of its total current and accumulated earnings or profits remaining after adjustment for its contribution deductible without regard to this subparagraph which the total prevented contribution bears to the total current and accumulated earnings or profits of all the members of the group remaining after adjustment for all contributions deductible without regard to this subparagraph. Contributions made under the preceding sentence shall be deductible under subparagraph (A) of this paragraph by the employer making such contribution, and, for the purpose of determining amounts which may be carried forward and deducted under the second sentence of subparagraph (A) of this paragraph in succeeding taxable years, shall be deemed to have been made by the employer on behalf of whose employees such contributions were made.

(4) TRUSTS CREATED OR ORGANIZED OUTSIDE THE UNITED STATES.—If a stock bonus, pension, or profit-sharing trust would qualify for exemption under section 501(a) except for the fact that it is a trust created or organized outside the United States, contributions to such a trust by an employer which is a resident, or corporation, or other entity of the United States, shall be deductible under the preceding paragraphs.

(5) OTHER PLANS.—If the plan is not one included in paragraph (1), (2), or (3), in the taxable year in which an amount attributable to the contribution is includible in the gross income of employees participating in the plan, but, in the case of a plan in which more than one

employee participates only if separate accounts are maintained for each employee. For purposes of this section, any vacation pay which is treated as deferred compensation shall be deductible for the taxable year of the employer in which paid to the employee.

(6) TIME WHEN CONTRIBUTIONS DEEMED MADE.—For purposes of paragraphs (1), (2), and (3), a taxpayer shall be deemed to have made a payment on the last day of the preceding taxable year if the payment is on account of such taxable year and is made not later than the time prescribed by law for filing the return for such taxable year (including extensions thereof).

(7) LIMITATION ON DEDUCTIONS WHERE COMBINATION OF DEFINED CONTRIBUTION PLAN AND DEFINED BENEFIT PLAN.—

(A) IN GENERAL.—If amounts are deductible under the foregoing paragraphs of this subsection (other than paragraph (5)) in connection with 1 or more defined contribution plans and 1 or more defined benefit plans or in connection with trusts or plans described in 2 or more of such paragraphs, the total amount deductible in a taxable year under such plans shall not exceed the greater of—

(i) 25 percent of the compensation otherwise paid or accrued during the taxable year to the beneficiaries under such plans, or

(ii) the amount of contributions made to or under the defined benefit plans to the extent such contributions do not exceed the amount of employer contributions necessary to satisfy the minimum funding standard provided by section 412 with respect to any such defined benefit plans for the plan year which ends with or within such taxable year (or for any prior plan year).

A defined contribution plan which is a pension plan shall not be treated as failing to provide definitely determinable benefits merely by limited employer contributions to amounts deductible under this section. For purposes of clause (ii), if paragraph (1)(D) applies to a defined benefit plan for any plan year, the amount necessary to satisfy the minimum funding standard provided by section 412 with respect to such plan for such plan year shall not be less than the unfunded current liability of such plan under section 412(l).

(B) CARRYOVER OF CONTRIBUTIONS IN EXCESS OF THE DEDUCTIBLE LIMIT.—Any amount paid under the plans in any taxable year in excess of the limitation of subparagraph (A) shall be deductible in the succeeding taxable years in order of time, but the amount so deductible under this subparagraph in any 1 such succeeding taxable year together with the amount allowable under subparagraph (A) shall not exceed 25 percent of the compensation otherwise paid or accrued during such taxable year to the beneficiaries under the plans.

Caution: Code Sec. 404(a)(7)(C), below, was amended by P.L. 107-147, effective as if included in and P.L. 107-16. For sunset provision, see P.L. 107-16, §901, in the amendment notes.

(C) PARAGRAPH NOT TO APPLY IN CERTAIN CASES.—

(i) BENEFICIARY TEST.—This paragraph shall not have the effect of reducing the amount otherwise deductible under paragraphs (1), (2), and (3), if no employee is a beneficiary under more than 1 trust or under a trust and an annuity plan.

(ii) ELECTIVE DEFERRALS.—If, in connection with 1 or more defined contribution plans and 1 or more defined benefit plans, no amounts (other than elective deferrals (as defined in section 402(g)(3))) are contributed to any of the defined contribution plans for the taxable year, then subparagraph (A) shall not apply with respect to any of such defined contribution plans and defined benefit plans.

(D) SECTION 412(i) PLANS.—For purposes of this paragraph, any plan described in section 412(i) shall be treated as a defined benefit plan.

(8) SELF-EMPLOYED INDIVIDUALS.—In the case of a plan included in paragraph (1), (2), or (3) which provides contributions or benefits for employees some or all of whom are employees within the meaning of section 401(c)(1), for purposes of this section—

(A) the term "employee" includes an individual who is an employee within the meaning of section 401(c)(1), and the employer of such individual is the person treated as his employer under section 401(c)(4);

(B) the term "earned income" has the meaning assigned to it by section 401(c)(2);

(C) the contributions to such plan on behalf of an individual who is an employee within the meaning of section 401(c)(1) shall be considered to satisfy the conditions of section 162 or 212 to the extent that such contributions do not exceed the earned income of such individual (determined without regard to the deductions allowed by this section) derived from the trade or business with respect to which such plan is established, and to the extent that such contributions are not allocable (determined in accordance with regulations prescribed by the Secretary) to the purchase of life, accident, health, or other insurance; and

(D) any reference to compensation shall, in the case of an individual who is an employee within the meaning of section 401(c)(1), be considered to be a reference to the earned income of such individual derived from the trade or business with respect to which the plan is established.

(9) CERTAIN CONTRIBUTIONS TO EMPLOYEE STOCK OWNERSHIP PLANS.—

(A) PRINCIPAL PAYMENTS.—Notwithstanding the provisions of paragraphs (3) and (7), if contributions are paid into a trust which forms a part of an employee stock ownership plan (as described in section 4975(e)(7)), and such contributions are, on or before the time prescribed in paragraph (6), applied by the plan to the repayment of the principal of a loan incurred for the purpose of acquiring qualifying employer securities (as described in section 4975(e)(8)), such contributions shall be deductible under this paragraph for the taxable year determined under paragraph (6). The amount deductible under this paragraph shall not, however, exceed 25 percent of the compensation otherwise paid or accrued during the taxable year to the employees under such employee stock ownership plan. Any amount paid into such trust in any taxable year in excess of the amount deductible under this paragraph shall be deductible in the succeeding taxable years in order of time to the extent of the difference between the amount paid and deductible in each such succeeding year and the maximum amount deductible for such year under the preceding sentence.

(B) INTEREST PAYMENT.—Notwithstanding the provisions of paragraphs (3) and (7), if contributions are made to an employee stock ownership plan (described in subparagraph (A)) and such contributions are applied by the plan to the repayment of interest on a loan incurred for the purpose of acquiring qualifying employer securities (as described in subparagraph (A)), such contributions shall be deductible for the taxable year with respect to which such contributions are made as determined under paragraph (6).

 (C) S CORPORATIONS.—This paragraph shall not apply to an S corporation.

 (D) QUALIFIED GRATUITOUS TRANSFERS.—A qualified gratuitous transfer (as defined in section 664(g)(1)) shall have no effect on the amount or amounts otherwise deductible under paragraph (3) or (7) or under this paragraph.

(10) CONTRIBUTIONS BY CERTAIN MINISTERS TO RETIREMENT INCOME ACCOUNTS.—In the case of contributions made by a minister described in section 414(e)(5) to a retirement income account described in section 403(b)(9) and not by a person other than such minister, such contributions—

 (A) shall be treated as made to a trust which is exempt from tax under section 501(a) and which is part of a plan which is described in section 401(a), and

Caution: Code Sec. 404(a)(10)(B), below, was amended by P.L. 107-16. For sunset provision, see P.L. 107-16, §901, in the amendment notes.

 (B) shall be deductible under this subsection to the extent such contributions do not exceed the limit on elective deferrals under section 402(g) or the limit on annual additions under section 415.

For purposes of this paragraph, all plans in which the minister is a participant shall be treated as one plan.

(11) DETERMINATIONS RELATING TO DEFERRED COMPENSATION.—For purposes of determining under this section—

 (A) whether compensation of an employee is deferred compensation; and

 (B) when deferred compensation is paid,

no amount shall be treated as received by the employee, or paid, until it is actually received by the employee.

Caution: Code Sec. 404(a)(12), below, was added by P.L. 107-16 and amended by P.L. 107-147. For sunset provision, see P.L. 107-16, §901, in the amendment notes.

(12) DEFINITION OF COMPENSATION.—For purposes of paragraphs (3), (7), (8), and (9) and subsection (h)(1)(C), the term "compensation" shall include amounts treated as "participant's compensation" under subparagraph (C) or (D) of section 415(c)(3).

(b) METHOD OF CONTRIBUTIONS, ETC., HAVING THE EFFECT OF A PLAN; CERTAIN DEFERRED BENEFITS.—

 (1) METHOD OF CONTRIBUTIONS, ETC., HAVING THE EFFECT OF A PLAN.—If—

  (A) there is no plan, but

(B) there is a method or arrangement of employer contributions or compensation which has the effect of a stock bonus, pension, profit-sharing, or annuity plan, or other plan deferring the receipt of compensation (including a plan described in paragraph (2)),

subsection (a) shall apply as if there were such a plan.

(2) PLANS PROVIDING CERTAIN DEFERRED BENEFITS.—

(A) IN GENERAL.—For purposes of this section, any plan providing for deferred benefits (other than compensation) for employees, their spouses, or their dependents shall be treated as a plan deferring the receipt of compensation. In the case of such a plan, for purposes of this section, the determination of when an amount is includible in gross income shall be made without regard to any provisions of this chapter excluding such benefits from gross income.

(B) EXCEPTION.—Subparagraph (A) shall not apply to any benefit provided through a welfare benefit fund (as defined in section 419(e)).

(c) CERTAIN NEGOTIATED PLANS.—If contributions are paid by an employer—

(1) under a plan under which such contributions are held in trust for the purpose of paying (either from principal or income or both) for the benefit of employees and their families and dependents at least medical or hospital care, or pensions on retirement or death of employees; and

(2) such plan was established prior to January 1, 1954, as a result of an agreement between employee representatives and the Government of the United States during a period of Government operation, under seizure powers, of a major part of the productive facilities of the industry in which such employer is engaged,

such contributions shall not be deductible under this section nor be made nondeductible by this section, but the deductibility thereof shall be governed solely by section 162 (relating to trade or business expenses). For purposes of this chapter and subtitle B, in the case of any individual who before July 1, 1974, was a participant in a plan described in the preceding sentence—

(A) such individual, if he is or was an employee within the meaning of section 401(c)(1), shall be treated (with respect to service covered by the plan) as being an employee other than an employee within the meaning of section 401(c)(1) and as being an employee of a participating employer under the plan,

(B) earnings derived from service covered by the plan shall be treated as not being earned income within the meaning of section 401(c)(2), and

(C) such individual shall be treated as an employee of a participating employer under the plan with respect to service before July 1, 1975, covered by the plan.

Section 277 (relating to deductions incurred by certain membership organizations in transactions with members) does not apply to any trust described in this subsection. The first and third sentences of this subsection shall have no application with respect to amounts contributed to a trust on or after any date on which such trust is qualified for exemption from tax under section 501(a).

(d) DEDUCTIBILITY OF PAYMENTS OF DEFERRED COMPENSATION, ETC., TO INDEPENDENT CONTRACTORS.—If a plan would be described in so much of subsection (a) as precedes paragraph

(1) thereof (as modified by subsection (b)) but for the fact that there is no employer-employee relationship, the contributions or compensation—

 (1) shall not be deductible by the payor thereof under this chapter, but

 (2) shall (if they would be deductible under this chapter but for paragraph (1)) be deductible under this subsection for the taxable year in which an amount attributable to the contribution or compensation is includible in the gross income of the persons participating in the plan.

 (e) CONTRIBUTIONS ALLOCABLE TO LIFE INSURANCE PROTECTION FOR SELF-EMPLOYED INDIVIDUALS.—In the case of a self-employed individual described in section 401(c)(1), contributions which are allocable (determined under regulations prescribed by the Secretary) to the purchase of life, accident, health, or other insurance shall not be taken into account under paragraph (1), (2), or (3) of subsection (a).

[Sec. 404(f)—Repealed]

 (g) CERTAIN EMPLOYER LIABILITY PAYMENTS CONSIDERED AS CONTRIBUTIONS.—

 (1) IN GENERAL.—For purposes of this section, any amount paid by an employer under section 4041(b), 4062, 4063, or 4064, or part 1 of subtitle E of title IV of the Employee Retirement Income Security Act of 1974 shall be treated as a contribution to which this section applies by such employer to or under a stock bonus, pension, profit-sharing, or annuity plan.

 (2) CONTROLLED GROUP DEDUCTIONS.—In the case of a payment described in paragraph (1) made by an entity which is liable because it is a member of a commonly controlled group of corporations, trades, or businesses, within the meaning of subsection (b) or (c) of section 414, the fact that the entity did not directly employ participants of the plan with respect to which the liability payment was made shall not affect the deductibility of a payment which otherwise satisfies the conditions of section 162 (relating to trade or business expenses) or section 212 (relating to expenses for the production of income).

 (3) TIMING OF DEDUCTION OF CONTRIBUTIONS.—

 (A) IN GENERAL.—Except as otherwise provided in this paragraph, any payment described in paragraph (1) shall (subject to the last sentence of subsection (a)(1)(A)) be deductible under this section when paid.

 (B) CONTRIBUTIONS UNDER STANDARD TERMINATIONS.— Subparagraph (A) shall not apply (and subsection (a)(1)(A) shall apply) to any payments described in paragraph (1) which are paid to terminate a plan under section 4041(b) of the Employee Retirement Income Security Act of 1974 to the extent such payments result in the assets of the plan being in excess of the total amount of benefits under such plan which are guaranteed by the Pension Benefit Guaranty Corporation under section 4022 of such Act.

 (C) CONTRIBUTIONS TO CERTAIN TRUSTS.—Subparagraph (A) shall not apply to any payment described in paragraph (1) which is made under section 4062(c) of such Act and such payment shall be deductible at such time as may be prescribed in regulations which are based on principles similar to the principles of subsection (a)(1)(A).

 (4) REFERENCES TO EMPLOYEE RETIREMENT INCOME SECURITY ACT OF 1974.— For purposes of this subsection, any reference to a section of the Employee Retirement Income

Security Act of 1974 shall be treated as a reference to such section as in effect on the date of the enactment of the Retirement Protection Act of 1994.

    (h)   SPECIAL RULES FOR SIMPLIFIED EMPLOYEE PENSIONS.—

Caution: Code Sec. 404(h)(1)-(2), below, was amended by P.L. 107-16. For sunset provision, see P.L. 107-16, §901, in the amendment notes.

    (1)   IN GENERAL.—Employer contributions to a simplified employee pension shall be treated as if they are made to a plan subject to the requirements of this section. Employer contributions to a simplified employee pension are subject to the following limitations:

    (A)   Contributions made for a year are deductible—

    (i)   in the case of a simplified employee pension maintained on a calendar year basis, for the taxable year with or within which the calendar year ends, or

    (ii)   in the case of a simplified employee pension which is maintained on the basis of the taxable year of the employer, for such taxable year.

    (B)   Contributions shall be treated for purposes of this subsection as if they were made for a taxable year if such contributions are made on account of such taxable year and are made not later than the time prescribed by law for filing the return for such taxable year (including extensions thereof).

    (C)   The amount deductible in a taxable year for a simplified employee pension shall not exceed 25 percent of the compensation paid to the employees during the calendar year ending with or within the taxable year (or during the taxable year in the case of a taxable year described in subparagraph (A)(ii)). The excess of the amount contributed over the amount deductible for a taxable year shall be deductible in the succeeding taxable years in order of time, subject to the 25 percent limit of the preceding sentence.

    (2)   EFFECT ON CERTAIN TRUSTS.—For any taxable year for which the employer has a deduction under paragraph (1), the otherwise applicable limitations in subsection (a)(3)(A) shall be reduced by the amount of the allowable deductions under paragraph (1) with respect to participants in the trust subject to subsection (a)(3)(A).

    (3)   COORDINATION WITH SUBSECTION (a)(7).—For purposes of subsection (a)(7), a simplified employee pension shall be treated as if it were a separate stock bonus or profit-sharing trust.

[Sec. 404(i)—Repealed.]

    (j)   SPECIAL RULES RELATING TO APPLICATION WITH SECTION 415.—

    (1)   NO DEDUCTION IN EXCESS OF SECTION 415 LIMITATION.—In computing the amount of any deduction allowable under paragraph (1), (2), (3), (4), (7), or (9) of subsection (a) for any year—

    (A)   in the case of a defined benefit plan, there shall not be taken into account any benefits for any year in excess of any limitation on such benefits under section 415 for such year, or

(B) in the case of a defined contribution plan, the amount of any contributions otherwise taken into account shall be reduced by any annual additions in excess of the limitation under section 415 for such year.

(2) NO ADVANCE FUNDING OF COST-OF-LIVING ADJUSTMENTS.—For purposes of clause (i), (ii) or (iii) of subsection (a)(1)(A), and in computing the full funding limitation, there shall not be taken into account any adjustments under section 415(d)(1) for any year before the year for which such adjustment first takes effect.

(k) DEDUCTION FOR DIVIDENDS PAID ON CERTAIN EMPLOYER SECURITIES.—

Caution: Code Sec. 404(k)(1), below, was amended by P.L. 107-147, effective as if included in P.L. 107-16. For sunset provision, see P.L. 107-16, §901, in the amendment notes.

(1) GENERAL RULE.—In the case of a C corporation, there shall be allowed as a deduction for a taxable year the amount of any applicable dividend paid in cash by such corporation with respect to applicable employer securities. Such deduction shall be in addition to the deductions allowed under subsection (a).

(2) APPLICABLE DIVIDEND.—For purposes of this subsection—

Caution: Code Sec. 404(k)(2)(A), below, was amended by P.L. 107-16. For sunset provision, see P.L. 107-16, §901, in the amendment notes.

(A) IN GENERAL.—The term "applicable dividend" means any dividend which, in accordance with the plan provisions—

(i) is paid in cash to the participants in the plan or their beneficiaries,

(ii) is paid to the plan and is distributed in cash to participants in the plan or their beneficiaries not later than 90 days after the close of the plan year in which paid,

(iii) is, at the election of such participants or their beneficiaries—

(I) payable as provided in clause (i) or (ii), or

(II) paid to the plan and reinvested in qualifying employer securities, or

(iv) is used to make payments on a loan described in subsection (a)(9) the proceeds of which were used to acquire the employer securities (whether or not allocated to participants) with respect to which the dividend is paid.

Caution: Code Sec. 404(k)(2)(B), below, was amended by P.L. 107-147, effective as if included in P.L. 107-16. For sunset provision, see P.L. 107-16, §901, in the amendment notes.

(B) LIMITATION ON CERTAIN DIVIDENDS.—A dividend described in subparagraph (A)(iv) which is paid with respect to any employer security which is allocated to a participant shall not be treated as an applicable dividend unless the plan provides that employer securities with a fair market value of not less than the amount of such dividend are allocated to such participant for the year which (but for subparagraph (A)) such dividend would have been allocated to such participant.

(3) APPLICABLE EMPLOYER SECURITIES.—For purposes of this subsection, the term "applicable employer securities" means, with respect to any dividend, employer securities which are held on the record date for such dividend by an employee stock ownership plan which is maintained by—

(A) the corporation paying such dividend, or

(B) any other corporation which is a member of a controlled group of corporations (within the meaning of section 409(l)(4)) which includes such corporation.

(4) TIME FOR DEDUCTION.—

(A) IN GENERAL.—The deduction under paragraph (1) shall be allowable in the taxable year of the corporation in which the dividend is paid or distributed to a participant or his beneficiary.

Caution: Code Sec. 404(k)(4)(B)-(C), below, was amended by P.L. 107-147, effective as if included in P.L. 107-16. For sunset provision, see P.L. 107-16, §901, in the amendment notes.

(B) REINVESTMENT DIVIDENDS.—For purposes of subparagraph (A), an applicable dividend reinvested pursuant to clause (iii)(II) of paragraph (2)(A) shall be treated as paid in the taxable year of the corporation in which such dividend is reinvested in qualifying employer securities or in which the election under clause (iii) of paragraph (2)(A) is made, whichever is later.

(C) REPAYMENT OF LOANS.—In the case of an applicable dividend described in clause (iv) of paragraph (2)(A), the deduction under paragraph (1) shall be allowable in the taxable year of the corporation in which such dividend is used to repay the loan described in such clause.

(5) OTHER RULES.—For purposes of this subsection—

Caution: Code Sec. 404(k)(5)(A), below, was amended by P.L. 107-16. For sunset provision, see P.L. 107-16, §901, in the amendment notes.

(A) DISALLOWANCE OF DEDUCTION.—The Secretary may disallow the deduction under paragraph (1) for any dividend if the Secretary determines that such dividend constitutes, in substance, an avoidance or evasion of taxation.

(B) PLAN QUALIFICATION.—A plan shall not be treated as violating the requirements of section 401, 409, or 4975(e)(7), or as engaging in a prohibited transaction for purposes of section 4975(d)(3), merely by reason of any payment or distribution described in paragraph (2)(A).

(6) DEFINITIONS.—For purposes of this subsection—

(A) EMPLOYER SECURITIES.—The term "employer securities" has the meaning given such term by section 409(1).

(B) EMPLOYEE STOCK OWNERSHIP PLAN.—The term "employee stock ownership plan" has the meaning given such term by section 4975(e)(7). Such term includes a tax credit employee stock ownership plan (as defined in section 409).

Caution: Code Sec. 404(k)(7), below, was amended by P.L. 107-147, effective as if included in P.L. 107-16. For sunset provision, see P.L. 107-16, §901, in the amendment notes.

(7) FULL VESTING.—In accordance with section 411, an applicable dividend described in clause (iii)(II) of paragraph (2)(A) shall be subject to the requirements of section 411(a)(1).

Caution: Code Sec. 404(l), below, was amended by P.L. 107-16. For sunset provision, see P.L. 107-16, §901, in the amendment notes.

(l) LIMITATION ON AMOUNT OF ANNUAL COMPENSATION TAKEN INTO ACCOUNT.—For purposes of applying the limitations of this section, the amount of annual compensation of each employee taken into account under the plan for any year shall not exceed $200,000. The Secretary shall adjust the $200,000 amount at the same time, and by the same amount, as the adjustment under section 401(a)(17)(B). For purposes of clause (i), (ii), or (iii) of subsection (a)(1)(A), and in computing the full finding limitation, any adjustment under the preceding sentence shall not be taken into account for any year before the year for which such adjustment first takes effect.

(m) SPECIAL RULES FOR SIMPLE RETIREMENT ACCOUNTS.—

(1) IN GENERAL.—Employer contributions to a simple retirement account shall be treated as if they are made to a plan subject to the requirements of this section.

(2) TIMING.—

(A) DEDUCTION.—Contributions described in paragraph (1) shall be deductible in the taxable year of the employer with or within the calendar year for which the contributions were made ends.

(B) CONTRIBUTIONS AFTER END OF YEAR.—For purposes of this subsection, contributions shall be treated as made for a taxable year if they are made on account of the taxable year and are made not later than the time prescribed by law for filing the return for the taxable year (including extensions thereof).

Caution: Code Sec. 404(n), below, was added by P.L. 107-16 and amended by P.L. 107-147. For sunset provision, see P.L. 107-16, §901, in the amendment notes.

(n) ELECTIVE DEFERRALS NOT TAKEN INTO ACCOUNT FOR PURPOSES OF DEDUCTION LIMITS.—Elective deferrals (as defined in section 402(g)(3)) shall not be subject to any limitation contained in paragraph (3), (7), or (9) of subsection (a) or paragraph (1)(C) of subsection (h), and such elective deferrals shall not be taken into account in applying any such limitation to any other contributions.

SEC. 404A. DEDUCTION FOR CERTAIN FOREIGN DEFERRED COMPENSATION PLANS.

(a) GENERAL RULE.—Amounts paid or accrued by an employer under a qualified foreign plan—

(1) shall not be allowable as a deduction under this chapter, but

(2) if they would otherwise be deductible, shall be allowed as a deduction under this section for the taxable year for which such amounts are properly taken into account under this section.

(b) RULES FOR QUALIFIED FUNDED PLANS.—For purposes of this section—

(1) IN GENERAL.—Except as otherwise provided in this section, in the case of a qualified funded plan contributions are properly taken into account for the taxable year in which paid.

(2) PAYMENT AFTER CLOSE OF TAXABLE YEAR.—For purposes of paragraph (1), a payment made after the close of a taxable year shall be treated as made on the last day of such year if the payment is made—

(A) on account of such year, and

(B) not later than the time prescribed by law for filing the return for such year (including extensions thereof).

(3) LIMITATIONS.—In the case of a qualified funded plan, the amount allowable as a deduction for the taxable year shall be subject to—

(A) in the case of—

(i) a plan under which the benefits are fixed or determinable, limitations similar to those contained in clauses (ii) and (iii) of subparagraph (A) of section 404(a)(1) (determined without regard to the last sentence of such subparagraph (A)), or

(ii) any other plan, limitations similar to the limitations contained in paragraph (3) of section 404(a), and

(B) limitations similar to those contained in paragraph (7) of section 404(a).

(4) CARRYOVER.—If—

(A) the aggregate of the contributions paid during the taxable year reduced by any contributions not allowable as a deduction under paragraphs (1) and (2) of subsection (g), exceeds

(B) the amount allowable as a deduction under subsection (a) (determined without regard to subsection (d)),

such excess shall be treated as an amount paid in the succeeding taxable year.

(5) AMOUNTS MUST BE PAID TO QUALIFIED TRUST, ETC.—In the case of a qualified funded plan, a contribution shall be taken into account only if it is paid—

 (A) to a trust (or the equivalent of a trust) which meets the requirements of section 401(a)(2),

 (B) for a retirement annuity, or

 (C) to a participant or beneficiary.

(c) RULES RELATING TO QUALIFIED RESERVE PLANS.—For purposes of this section—

 (1) IN GENERAL.—In the case of a qualified reserve plan, the amount properly taken into account for the taxable year is the reasonable addition for such year to a reserve for the taxpayer's liability under the plan. Unless otherwise required or permitted in regulations prescribed by the Secretary, the reserve for the taxpayer's liability shall be determined under the unit credit method modified to reflect the requirements of paragraphs (3) and (4). All benefits paid under the plan shall be charged to the reserve.

 (2) INCOME ITEM.—In the case of a plan which is or has been a qualified reserve plan, an amount equal to that portion of any decrease for the taxable year in the reserve which is not attributable to the payment of benefits shall be included in gross income.

 (3) RIGHTS MUST BE NONFORFEITABLE, ETC.—In the case of a qualified reserve plan, an item shall be taken into account for a taxable year only if—

  (A) there is no substantial risk that the rights of the employee will be forfeited, and

  (B) such item meets such additional requirements as the Secretary may by regulations prescribe as necessary or appropriate to ensure that the liability will be satisfied.

 (4) SPREADING OF CERTAIN INCREASES AND DECREASES IN RESERVES.—There shall be amortized over a 10-year period any increase or decrease to the reserve on account of—

  (A) the adoption of the plan or a plan amendment,

  (B) experience gains and losses, and

  (C) any change in actuarial assumptions,

  (D) changes in the interest rate under subsection (g)(3)(B), and

  (E) such other factors as may be prescribed by regulations.

(d) AMOUNTS TAKEN INTO ACCOUNT MUST BE CONSISTENT WITH AMOUNTS ALLOWED UNDER FOREIGN LAW.—

 (1) GENERAL RULE.—In the case of any plan, the amount allowed as a deduction under subsection (a) for any taxable year shall equal—

  (A) the lesser of—

   (i) the cumulative United States amount, or

(ii) the cumulative foreign amount, reduced by

(B) the aggregate amount determined under this section for all prior taxable years.

(2) CUMULATIVE AMOUNTS DEFINED.—For purposes of paragraph (1)—

(A) CUMULATIVE UNITED STATES AMOUNT.—The term "cumulative United States amount" means the aggregate amount determined with respect to the plan under this section for the taxable year and for all prior taxable years to which this section applies. Such determination shall be made for each taxable year without regard to the application of paragraph (1).

(B) CUMULATIVE FOREIGN AMOUNT.—The term "cumulative foreign amount" means the aggregate amount allowed as a deduction under the appropriate foreign tax laws for the taxable year and all prior taxable years to which this section applies.

(3) EFFECT ON EARNINGS AND PROFITS, ETC.—In determining the earnings and profits and accumulated profits of any foreign corporation with respect to a qualified foreign plan, except as provided in regulations, the amount determined under paragraph (1) with respect to any plan for any taxable year shall in no event exceed the amount allowed as a deduction under the appropriate foreign tax laws for such taxable year.

(e) QUALIFIED FOREIGN PLAN.—For purposes of this section, the term "qualified foreign plan" means any written plan of an employer for deferring the receipt of compensation but only if—

(1) such plan is for the exclusive benefit of the employer's employees or their beneficiaries,

(2) 90 percent or more of the amounts taken into account for the taxable year under the plan are attributable to services—

(A) performed by nonresident aliens, and

(B) the compensation for which is not subject to tax under this chapter, and

(3) the employer elects (at such time and in such manner as the Secretary shall by regulations prescribe) to have this section apply to such plan.

(f) FUNDED AND RESERVE PLANS.—For purposes of this section—

(1) QUALIFIED FUNDED PLAN.—The term "qualified funded plan" means a qualified foreign plan which is not a qualified reserve plan.

(2) QUALIFIED RESERVE PLAN.—The term "qualified reserve plan" means a qualified foreign plan with respect to which an election made by the taxpayer is in effect for the taxable year. An election under the preceding sentence shall be made in such manner and form as the Secretary may by regulations prescribe and, once made, may be revoked only with the consent of the Secretary.

(g) OTHER SPECIAL RULES.—

(1) NO DEDUCTION FOR CERTAIN AMOUNTS.—Except as provided in section 404(a)(5), no deduction shall be allowed under this section for any item to the extent such item is attributable to services—

(A) performed by a citizen or resident of the United States who is a highly compensated employee (within the meaning of section 414(q)), or

(B) performed in the United States the compensation for which is subject to tax under this chapter.

(2) TAXPAYER MUST FURNISH INFORMATION.—

(A) IN GENERAL.—No deduction shall be allowed under this section with respect to any plan for any taxable year unless the taxpayer furnishes to the Secretary with respect to such plan (at such time as the Secretary may by regulations prescribe)—

(i) a statement from the foreign tax authorities specifying the amount of the deduction allowed in computing taxable income under foreign law for such year with respect to such plan,

(ii) if the return under foreign tax law shows the deduction for plan contributions or reserves as a separate, identifiable item, a copy of the foreign tax return for the taxable year, or

(iii) such other statement, return, or other evidence as the Secretary prescribes by regulation as being sufficient to establish the amount of the deduction under foreign law.

(B) REDETERMINATION WHERE FOREIGN TAX DEDUCTION IS ADJUSTED.—If the deduction under foreign tax law is adjusted, the taxpayer shall notify the Secretary of such adjustment on or before the date prescribed by regulations, and the Secretary shall redetermine the amount of the tax year or years affected. In any case described in the preceding sentence, rules similar to the rules of subsection (c) of section 905 shall apply.

(3) ACTUARIAL ASSUMPTIONS MUST BE REASONABLE; FULL FUNDING.—

(A) IN GENERAL.—Except as provided in subparagraph (B), principles similar to those set forth in paragraphs (3) and (7) of section 412(c) shall apply for purposes of this section.

(B) INTEREST RATE FOR RESERVE PLAN.—

(i) IN GENERAL.—In the case of a qualified reserve plan, in lieu of taking rates of interest into account under subparagraph (A), the rate of interest for the plan shall be the rate selected by the taxpayer which is within the permissible range.

(ii) RATE REMAINS IN EFFECT SO LONG AS IT FALLS WITHIN PERMISSIBLE RANGE.—Any rate selected by the taxpayer for the plan under this subparagraph shall remain in effect for such plan until the first taxable year for which such rate is no longer within the permissible range. At such time, the taxpayer shall select a new rate of interest which is within the permissible range applicable at such time.

(iii) PERMISSIBLE RANGE.—For purposes of this subparagraph, the term "permissible range" means a rate of interest which is not more than 20 percent above, and not more than 20 percent below, the average rate of interest for long-term corporate bonds in the appropriate country for the 15-year period ending on the last day before the beginning of the taxable year.

(4) ACCOUNTING METHOD.—Any change in the method (but not the actuarial assumptions) used to determine the amount allowed as a deduction under subsection (a) shall be treated as a change in accounting method under section 446(e).

(5) SECTION 481 APPLIES TO ELECTION.—For purposes of section 481, any election under this section shall be treated as a change in the taxpayer's method of accounting. In applying section 481 with respect to any such election, the period for taking into account any increase or decrease in accumulated profits, earnings and profits or taxable income resulting from the application of section 481(a)(2) shall be the year for which the election is made and the fourteen succeeding years.

(h) REGULATIONS.—The Secretary shall prescribe such regulations as may be necessary to carry out the purposes of this section (including regulations providing for the coordination of the provisions of this section with section 404 in the case of a plan which has been subject to both of such sections).

SEC. 501. EXEMPTION FROM TAX ON CORPORATIONS, CERTAIN TRUSTS, ETC.

(a) EXEMPTION FROM TAXATION.—An organization described in subsection (c) or (d) or section 401(a) shall be exempt from taxation under this subtitle unless such exemption is denied under section 502 or 503.

(b) TAX ON UNRELATED BUSINESS INCOME AND CERTAIN OTHER ACTIVITIES.—An organization exempt from taxation under subsection (a) shall be subject to tax to the extent provided in parts II, III, and VI of this subchapter, but (notwithstanding parts II, III and VI of this subchapter) shall be considered an organization exempt from income taxes for the purpose of any law which refers to organizations exempt from income taxes.

(c) LIST OF EXEMPT ORGANIZATIONS.—The following organizations are referred to in subsection (a):

(1) Any corporation organized under Act of Congress which is an instrumentality of the United States but only if such corporation—

(A) is exempt from Federal income taxes—

(i) under such Act as amended and supplemented before July 18, 1984, or

(ii) under this title without regard to any provision of law which is not contained in this title and which is not contained in a revenue Act, or

(B) is described in subsection (l).

(2) Corporations organized for the exclusive purpose of holding title to property, collecting income therefrom, and turning over the entire amount thereof, less expenses, to an organization which itself is exempt under this section. Rules similar to the rules of subparagraph (G) of paragraph (25) shall apply for purposes of this paragraph.

(3) Corporations, and any community chest, fund, or foundation, organized and operated exclusively for religious, charitable, scientific, testing for public safety, literary, or educational purposes, or to foster national or international amateur sports competition (but only if no part of its activities involve the provision of athletic facilities or equipment), or for the prevention of cruelty to children or animals, no part of the net earnings of which inures to the benefit of any private shareholder or individual, no substantial part of the activities of which is carrying on propaganda, or otherwise attempting, to influence legislation (except as otherwise provided in subsection (h)), and which does not participate in, or intervene in (including the publishing or distributing of statements), any political campaign on behalf of (or in opposition to) any candidate for public office.

(4)(A) Civic leagues or organizations not organized for profit but operated exclusively for the promotion of social welfare, or local associations of employees, the membership of which is limited to the employees of a designated person or persons in a particular municipality, and the net earnings of which are devoted exclusively to charitable, educational, or recreational purposes.

(B) Subparagraph (A) shall not apply to an entity unless no part of the net earnings of such entity inures to the benefit of any private shareholder or individual.

(5) Labor, agricultural, or horticultural organizations.

(6) Business leagues, chambers of commerce, real-estate boards, boards of trade, or professional football leagues (whether or not administering a pension fund for football players), not organized for profit and no part of the net earnings of which inures to the benefit of any private shareholder or individual.

(7) Clubs organized for pleasure, recreation, and other nonprofitable purposes, substantially all of the activities of which are for such purposes and no part of the net earnings of which inures to the benefit of any private shareholder.

(8) Fraternal beneficiary societies, orders, or associations—

(A) operating under the lodge system or for the exclusive benefit of the members of a fraternity itself operating under the lodge system, and

(B) providing for the payment of life, sick, accident, or other benefits to the members of such society, order, or association or their dependents.

(9) Voluntary employees' beneficiary associations providing for the payment of life, sick, accident, or other benefits to the members of such association or their dependents or designated beneficiaries, if no part of the net earnings of such association inures (other than through such payments) to the benefit of any private shareholder or individual.

(10) Domestic fraternal societies, orders, or associations, operating under the lodge system—

(A) the net earnings of which are devoted exclusively to religious, charitable, scientific, literary, educational, and fraternal purposes, and

(B) which do not provide for the payment of life, sick, accident, or other benefits.

(11) Teachers' retirement fund associations of a purely local character, if—

(A) no part of their net earnings inures (other than through payment of retirement benefits) to the benefit of any private shareholder or individual, and

(B) the income consists solely of amounts received from public taxation, amounts received from assessments on the teaching salaries of members, and income in respect of investments.

(12)(A) Benevolent life insurance associations of a purely local character, mutual ditch or irrigation companies, mutual or cooperative telephone companies, or like organizations; but only if 85 percent or more of the income consists of amounts collected from members for the sole purpose of meeting losses and expenses.

(B) In the case of a mutual or cooperative telephone company subparagraph (A) shall be applied without taking into account any income received or accrued—

(i) from a nonmember telephone company for the performance of communication services which involve members of the mutual or cooperative telephone company,

(ii) from qualified pole rentals,

(iii) from the sale of display listings in a directory furnished to the members of the mutual or cooperative telephone company, or

(iv) from the prepayment of a loan under section 306A, 306B, or 311 of the Rural Electrification Act of 1936 (as in effect on January 1, 1987).

(C) In the case of a mutual or cooperative electric company, subparagraph (A) shall be applied without taking into account any income received or accrued—

(i) from qualified pole rentals, or

(ii) from the prepayment of a loan under section 306A, 306B, or 311 of the Rural Electrification Act of 1936 (as in effect on January 1, 1987).

(D) For purposes of this paragraph, the term "qualified pole rental" means any rental of a pole (or other structure used to support wires) if such pole (or other structure)—

(i) is used by the telephone or electric company to support one or more wires which are used by such company in providing telephone or electric services to its members, and

(ii) is used pursuant to the rental to support one or more wires (in addition to the wires described in clause (i)) for use in connection with the transmission by wire of electricity or of telephone or other communications.

For purposes of the preceding sentence, the term "rental" includes any sale of the right to use the pole (or other structure).

(13) Cemetery companies owned and operated exclusively for the benefit of their members or which are not operated for profit; and any corporation chartered solely for the purpose of the disposal of bodies by burial or cremation which is not permitted by its charter to engage in any business not necessarily incident to that purpose and no part of the net earnings of which inures to the benefit of any private shareholder or individual.

(14)(A) Credit unions without capital stock organized and operated for mutual purposes and without profit.

(B) Corporations or associations without capital stock organized before September 1, 1957, and operated for mutual purposes and without profit for the purpose of providing reserve funds for, and insurance of shares or deposits in—

(i) domestic building and loan associations,

(ii) cooperative banks without capital stock organized and operated for mutual purposes and without profit,

(iii) mutual savings banks not having capital stock represented by shares, or

(iv) mutual savings banks described in section 591(b).

(C) Corporations or associations organized before September 1, 1957, and operated for mutual purposes and without profit for the purpose of providing reserve funds for associations or banks described in clause (i), (ii), or (iii) of subparagraph (B); but only if 85 percent or more of the income is attributable to providing such reserve funds and to investments. This subparagraph shall not apply to any corporation or association entitled to exemption under subparagraph (B).

(15)(A) Insurance companies (as defined in section 916(a)) other than life (including interinsurers and reciprocal underwriters) if—

(i)(I) the gross receipts for the taxable year do not exceed $600,000, and

(II) more than 50 percent of such gross receipts consist of premiums, or

(ii) in the case of a mutual insurance company—

(I) the gross receipts of which for the taxable year do not exceed $150,000, and

(II) more than 35 percent of such gross receipts consist of premiums.

Clause (ii) shall not apply to a company if any employee of the company, or a member of the employee's family (as defined in section 2032A(e)(2)), is an employee of another company exempt from taxation by reason of this paragraph (or would be so exempt but for this sentence).

(B) For purposes of subparagraph (A), in determining whether any company or association is described in subparagraph (A), such company or association shall be treated as receiving during the taxable year amounts described in subparagraph (A) which are received during such year by all other companies or associations which are members of the same controlled group as the insurance company or association for which the determination is being made.

(C) For purposes of subparagraph (B), the term "controlled group" has the meaning given such term by section 831(b)(2)(B)(ii), except that in applying section

831(b)(2)(B)(ii) for purposes of this subparagraph, subparagraphs (B) and (C) of section 1563(b)(2) shall be disregarded.

(16) Corporations organized by an association subject to part IV of this subchapter or members thereof, for the purpose of financing the ordinary crop operations of such members or other producers, and operated in conjunction with such association. Exemption shall not be denied any such corporation because it has capital stock, if the dividend rate of such stock is fixed at not to exceed the legal rate of interest in the State of incorporation or 8 percent per annum, whichever is greater, on the value of the consideration for which the stock was issued, and if substantially all such stock (other than nonvoting preferred stock, the owners of which are not entitled or permitted to participate, directly or indirectly, in the profits of the corporation, on dissolution or otherwise, beyond the fixed dividends) is owned by such association, or members thereof; nor shall exemption be denied any such corporation because there is accumulated and maintained by it a reserve required by State law or a reasonable reserve for any necessary purpose.

(17)(A) A trust or trusts forming part of a plan providing for the payment of supplemental unemployment compensation benefits, if—

(i) under the plan, it is impossible, at any time prior to the satisfaction of all liabilities with respect to employees under the plan, for any part of the corpus or income to be (within the taxable year or thereafter) used for, or diverted to, any purpose other than the providing of supplemental unemployment compensation benefits,

(ii) such benefits are payable to employees under a classification which is set forth in the plan and which is found by the Secretary not to be discriminatory in favor of employees who are highly compensated employees (within the meaning of section 414(q)), and

(iii) such benefits do not discriminate in favor of employees who are highly compensated employees (within the meaning of section 414(q)). A plan shall not be considered discriminatory within the meaning of this clause merely because the benefits received under the plan bear a uniform relationship to the total compensation, or the basic or regular rate of compensation, of the employees covered by the plan.

(B) In determining whether a plan meets the requirements of subparagraph (A), any benefits provided under any other plan shall not be taken into consideration, except that a plan shall not be considered discriminatory—

(i) merely because the benefits under the plan which are first determined in a nondiscriminatory manner within the meaning of subparagraph (A) are then reduced by any sick, accident, or unemployment compensation benefits received under State or Federal law (or reduced by a portion of such benefits if determined in a nondiscriminatory manner), or

(ii) merely because the plan provides only for employees who are not eligible to receive sick, accident, or unemployment compensation benefits under State or Federal law the same benefits (or a portion of such benefits if determined in a nondiscriminatory manner) which such employees would receive under such laws if such employees were eligible for such benefits, or

(iii) merely because the plan provides only for employees who are not eligible under another plan (which meets the requirements of subparagraph (A)) of supplemental unemployment compensation benefits provided wholly by the employer the same benefits (or a portion of such benefits if determined in a nondiscriminatory manner) which such employees would receive under such other plan if such employees were eligible under such other plan, but only if the employees eligible under both plans would make a classification which would be nondiscriminatory within the meaning of subparagraph (A).

(C) A plan shall be considered to meet the requirements of subparagraph (A) during the whole of any year of the plan if on one day in each quarter it satisfies such requirements.

(D) The term "supplemental unemployment compensation benefits" means only—

(i) benefits which are paid to an employee because of his involuntary separation from the employment of the employer (whether or not such separation is temporary) resulting directly from a reduction in force, the discontinuance of a plant or operation, or other similar conditions, and

(ii) sick and accident benefits subordinate to the benefits described in clause (i).

(E) Exemption shall not be denied under subsection (a) to any organization entitled to such exemption as an association described in paragraph (9) of this subsection merely because such organization provides for the payment of supplemental unemployment benefits (as defined in subparagraph (D)(i)).

(18) A trust or trusts created before June 25, 1959, forming part of a plan providing for the payment of benefits under a pension plan funded only by contributions of employees, if—

(A) under the plan, it is impossible, at any time prior to the satisfaction of all liabilities with respect to employees under the plan, for any part of the corpus or income to be (within the taxable year or thereafter) used for, or diverted to, any purpose other than the providing of benefits under the plan,

(B) such benefits are payable to employees under a classification which is set forth in the plan and which is found by the Secretary not to be discriminatory in favor of employees who are highly compensated employees (within the meaning of section 414(q)),

(C) such benefits do not discriminate in favor of employees who are highly compensated employees (within the meaning of section 414(q)). A plan shall not be considered discriminatory within the meaning of this subparagraph merely because the benefits received under the plan bear a uniform relationship to the total compensation, or the basic or regular rate of compensation, of the employees covered by the plan, and

(D) in the case of a plan under which an employee may designate certain contributions as deductible—

(i) such contributions do not exceed the amount with respect to which a deduction is allowable under section 219(b)(3),

(ii) requirements similar to the requirements of section 401(k)(3)(A)(ii) are met with respect to such elective contributions,

Caution: Code Sec. 501(c)(18)(D)(iii), below, was amended by P.L. 107-16. For sunset provision, see P.L. 107-16, §901, in the amendment notes.

    (iii) such contributions are treated as elective deferrals for purposes of section 402(g), and

    (iv) the requirements of section 401(a)(30) are met.

For purposes of subparagraph (D)(ii), rules similar to the rules of section 401(k)(8) shall apply. For purposes of section 4979, any excess contribution under clause (ii) shall be treated as an excess contribution under a cash or deferred arrangement.

  (19) A post or organization of past or present members of the Armed Forces of the United States, or an auxiliary unit or society of, or a trust or foundation for, any such post or organization—

   (A) organized in the United States or any of its possessions,

   (B) at least 75 percent of the members of which are past or present members of the Armed Forces of the United States and substantially all of the other members of which are individuals who are cadets or are spouses, widows, widowers, ancestors, or lineal descendents of past or present members of the Armed Forces of the United States or of cadets, and

   (C) no part of the net earnings of which inures to the benefit of any private shareholder or individual.

  (20) An organization or trust created or organized in the United States, the exclusive function of which is to form part of a qualified group legal services plan or plans, within the meaning of section 120. An organization or trust which receives contributions because of section 120(c)(5)(C) shall not be prevented from qualifying as an organization described in this paragraph merely because it provides legal services or indemnification against the cost of legal services unassociated with a qualified group legal services plan.

  (21)(A) A trust or trusts established in writing, created or organized in the United States, and contributed to by any person (except an insurance company) if—

    (i) the purpose of such trust or trusts is exclusively—

     (I) to satisfy, in whole or in part, the liability of such person for, or with respect to, claims for compensation for disability or death due to pneumoconiosis under Black Lung Acts,

     (II) to pay premiums for insurance exclusively covering such liability,

     (III) to pay administrative and other incidental expenses of such trust in connection with the operation of the trust and the processing of claims against such person under Black Lung Acts, and

     (IV) to pay accident or health benefits for retired miners and their spouses and dependents (including administrative and other incidental expenses of such trust in connection therewith) or premiums for insurance exclusively covering such benefits; and

(ii) no part of the assets of the trust may be used for, or diverted to, any purpose other than—

(I) the purposes described in clause (i),

(II) investment (but only to the extent that the trustee determines that a portion of the assets is not currently needed for the purposes described in clause (i)) in qualified investments, or

(III) payment into the Black Lung Disability Trust Fund established under section 9501, or into the general fund of the United States Treasury (other than in satisfaction of any tax or other civil or criminal liability of the person who established or contributed to the trust).

(B) No deduction shall be allowed under this chapter for any payment described in subparagraph (A)(i)(IV) from such trust.

(C) Payments described in subparagraph (A)(i)(IV) may be made from such trust during a taxable year only to the extent that the aggregate amount of such payments during such taxable year does not exceed the lesser of—

(i) the excess (if any) (as of the close of the preceding taxable year) of—

(I) the fair market value of the assets of the trust, over

(II) 110 percent of the present value of the liability described in subparagraph (A)(i)(I) of such person, or

(ii) the excess (if any) of—

(I) the sum of a similar excess determined as of the close of the last taxable year ending before the date of the enactment of this subparagraph plus earnings thereon as of the close of the taxable year preceding the taxable year involved, over

(II) the aggregate payments described in subparagraph (A)(i)(IV) made from the trust during all taxable years beginning after the date of the enactment of this subparagraph.

The determinations under the preceding sentence shall be made by an independent actuary using actuarial methods and assumptions (not inconsistent with the regulations prescribed under section 192(c)(1)(A)) each of which is reasonable and which are reasonable in the aggregate.

(D) For purposes of this paragraph:

(i) The term "Black Lung Acts" means part C of title IV of the Federal Mine Safety and Health Act of 1977, and any State law providing compensation for disability or death due to that pneumoconiosis.

(ii) The term "qualified investments" means—

(I) public debt securities of the United States,

(II) obligations of a State or local government which are not in default as to principal or interest, and

(III) time or demand deposits in a bank (as defined in section 581) or an insured credit union (within the meaning of section 101(7) of the Federal Credit Union Act, 12 U.S.C. 1752(7)) located in the United States.

(iii) The term "miner" has the same meaning as such term has when used in section 402(d) of the Black Lung Benefits Act (30 U.S.C. 902(d)).

(iv) The term "incidental expenses" includes legal, accounting, actuarial, and trustee expenses.

(22) A trust created or organized in the United States and established in writing by the plan sponsors of multiemployer plans if—

(A) the purpose of such trust is exclusively—

(i) to pay any amount described in section 4223(c) or (h) of the Employee Retirement Income Security Act of 1974, and

(ii) to pay reasonable and necessary administrative expenses in connection with the establishment and operation of the trust and the processing of claims against the trust,

(B) no part of the assets of the trust may be used for, or diverted to, any purpose other than—

(i) the purposes described in subparagraph (A), or

(ii) the investment in securities, obligations, or time or demand deposits described in clause (ii) of paragraph (21)(B),

(C) such trust meets the requirements of paragraphs (2), (3), and (4) of section 4223(b), 4223(h), or, if applicable, section 4223(c) of the Employee Retirement Income Security Act of 1974, and

(D) the trust instrument provides that, on dissolution of the trust, assets of the trust may not be paid other than to plans which have participated in the plan or, in the case of a trust established under section 4223(h) of such Act, to plans with respect to which employers have participated in the fund.

(23) Any association organized before 1880 more than 75 percent of the members of which are present or past members of the Armed Forces and a principal purpose of which is to provide insurance and other benefits to veterans or their dependents.

(24) A trust described in section 4049 of the Employee Retirement Income Security Act of 1974 (as in effect on the date of the enactment of the Single-Employer Pension Plan Amendments Act of 1986).

(25)(A) Any corporation or trust which—

(i) has no more than 35 shareholders or beneficiaries,

(ii) has only 1 class of stock or beneficial interest, and

(iii) is organized for the exclusive purposes of—

(I) acquiring real property and holding title to, and collecting income from, such property, and

(II) remitting the entire amount of income from such property (less expenses) to 1 or more organizations described in subparagraph (C) which are shareholders of such corporation or beneficiaries of such trust.

For purposes of clause (iii), the term "real property" shall not include any interest as a tenant in common (or similar interest) and shall not include any indirect interest.

(B) A corporation or trust shall be described in subparagraph (A) without regard to whether the corporation or trust is organized by 1 or more organizations described in subparagraph (C).

(C) An organization is described in this subparagraph if such organization is—

(i) a qualified pension, profit sharing, or stock bonus plan that meets the requirements of section 401(a),

(ii) a governmental plan (within the meaning of section 414(d)),

(iii) the United States, any State or political subdivision thereof, or any agency or instrumentality of any of the foregoing, or

(iv) any organization described in paragraph (3).

(D) A corporation or trust shall in no event be treated as described in subparagraph (A) unless such corporation or trust permits its shareholders or beneficiaries—

(i) to dismiss the corporation's or trust's investment adviser, following reasonable notice, upon a vote of the shareholders or beneficiaries holding a majority of interest in the corporation or trust, and

(ii) to terminate their interest in the corporation or trust by either, or both, of the following alternatives, as determined by the corporation or trust:

(I) by selling or exchanging their stock in the corporation or interest in the trust (subject to any Federal or State securities law) to any organization described in subparagraph (C) so long as the sale or exchange does not increase the number of shareholders or beneficiaries in such corporation or trust above 35, or

(II) by having their stock or interest redeemed by the corporation or trust after the shareholder or beneficiary has provided 90 days notice to such corporation or trust.

(E)(i) For purposes of this title—

(I) a corporation which is a qualified subsidiary shall not be treated as a separate corporation, and

(II) all assets, liabilities, and items of income, deduction, and credit of a qualified subsidiary shall be treated as assets, liabilities, and such items (as the case may be) of the corporation or trust described in subparagraph (A).

(ii) For purposes of this subparagraph, the term "qualified subsidiary" means any corporation if, at all times during the period such corporation was in existence, 100 percent of the stock of such corporation is held by the corporation or trust described in subparagraph (A).

(iii) For purposes of this subtitle, if any corporation which was a qualified subsidiary ceases to meet the requirements of clause (ii), such corporation shall be treated as a new corporation acquiring all of its assets (and assuming all of its liabilities) immediately before such cessation from the corporation or trust described in subparagraph (A) in exchange for its the stock.

(F) For purposes of subparagraph (A), the term "real property" includes any personal property which is leased under, or in connection with, a lease of real property, but only if the rent attributable to such personal property (determined under the rules of section 856(d)(1)) for the taxable year does not exceed 15 percent of the total rent for the taxable year attributable to both the real and personal property leased under, or in connection with, such lease.

(G)(i) An organization shall not be treated as failing to be described in this paragraph merely by reason of the receipt of any otherwise disqualifying income which is incidentally derived from the holding of real property.

(ii) Clause (i) shall not apply if the amount of gross income described in such clause exceeds 10 percent of the organization's gross income for the taxable year unless the organization establishes to the satisfaction of the Secretary that the receipt of gross income described in clause (i) in excess of such limitation was inadvertent and reasonable steps are being taken to correct the circumstances giving rise to such income.

(26) Any membership organization if—

(A) such organization is established by a State exclusively to provide coverage for medical care (as defined in section 213(d)) on a not-for-profit basis to individuals described in subparagraph (B) through—

(i) insurance issued by the organization, or

(ii) a health maintenance organization under an arrangement with the organization,

(B) the only individuals receiving such coverage through the organization are individuals—

(i) who are residents of such State, and

(ii) who, by reason of the existence or history of a medical condition—

(I) are unable to acquire medical care coverage for such condition through insurance or from a health maintenance organization, or

(II) are able to acquire such coverage only at a rate which is substantially in excess of the rate for such coverage through the membership organization,

(C) the composition of the membership in such organization is specified by such State, and

(D) no part of the net earnings of the organization inures to the benefit of any private shareholder or individual.

A spouse and any qualifying child (as defined in section 24(c)) of an individual described in subparagraph (B) (without regard to this sentence) shall be treated as described in subparagraph (B).

(27)(A) Any membership organization if—

(i) such organization is established before June 1, 1996, by a State exclusively to reimburse its members for losses arising under workmen's compensation acts,

(ii) such State requires that the membership of such organization consist of—

(I) all persons who issue insurance covering workmen's compensation losses in such State, and

(II) all persons and governmental entities who self-insure against such losses, and

(iii) such organization operates as a non-profit organization by—

(I) returning surplus income to its members or workmen's compensation policyholders on a periodic basis, and

(II) reducing initial premiums in anticipation of investment income.

(B) Any organization (including a mutual insurance company) if—

(i) such organization is created by State law and is organized and operated under State law exclusively to—

(I) provide workmen's compensation insurance which is required by State law or with respect to which State law provides significant disincentives if such insurance is not purchased by an employer, and

(II) provide related coverage which is incidental to workmen's compensation insurance,

(ii) such organization must provide workmen's compensation insurance to any employer in the State (for employees in the State or temporarily assigned out-of-State) which seeks such insurance and meets other reasonable requirements relating thereto,

(iii) (I) the State makes a financial commitment with respect to such organization either by extending the full faith and credit of the State to the initial debt of such organization or by providing the initial operating capital of such organization, and (II) in the case of periods after the date of enactment of this subparagraph, the assets of such organization revert to the State upon dissolution or State law does not permit the dissolution of such organization, and

(iv) the majority of the board of directors or oversight body of such organization are appointed by the chief executive officer or other executive branch official of the State, by the State legislature, or by both.

(28) The National Railroad Retirement Investment Trust established under section 15(j) of the Railroad Retirement Act of 1974.

(d) RELIGIOUS AND APOSTOLIC ORGANIZATIONS.—The following organizations are referred to in subsection (a): religious or apostolic associations or organizations, if such associations or corporations have a common treasury or community treasury, even if such associations or corporations engage in business for the common benefit of the members, but only if the members thereof include (at the time of filing their returns) in their gross income their entire pro rata shares, whether distributed or not, of the taxable income of the association or corporation for such year. Any amount so included in the gross income of a member shall be treated as a dividend received.

(e) COOPERATIVE HOSPITAL SERVICE ORGANIZATIONS.—For purposes of this title, an organization shall be treated as an organization organized and operated exclusively for charitable purposes, if—

(1) such organization is organized and operated solely—

(A) to perform, on a centralized basis, one or more of the following services which, if performed on its own behalf by a hospital which is an organization described in subsection (c)(3) and exempt from taxation under subsection (a), would constitute activities in exercising or performing the purpose or function constituting the basis for its exemption: data processing, purchasing (including the purchasing of insurance on a group basis), warehousing, billing and collection (including the purchase of patron accounts receivable on a recourse basis), food, clinical, industrial engineering, laboratory, printing, communications, record center, and personnel (including selection, testing, training, and education of personnel) services; and

(B) to perform such services solely for two or more hospitals each of which is—

(i) an organization described in subsection (c)(3) which is exempt from taxation under subsection (a),

(ii) a constituent part of an organization described in subsection (c)(3) which is exempt from taxation under subsection (a) and which, if organized and operated as a separate entity, would constitute an organization described in subsection (c)(3), or

(iii) owned and operated by the United States, a State, the District of Columbia, or a possession of the United States, or a political subdivision or an agency or instrumentality of any of the foregoing;

(2) such organization is organized and operated on a cooperative basis and allocates or pays, within 8 months after the close of its taxable year, all net earnings to patrons on the basis of services performed for them; and

(3) if such organization has capital stock, all of such stock outstanding is owned by its patrons.

For purposes of this title, any organization which, by reason of the preceding sentence, is an organization described in subsection (c)(3) and exempt from taxation under subsection (a), shall be treated as a hospital and as an organization referred to in section 170(b)(1)(A)(iii).

(f) COOPERATIVE SERVICE ORGANIZATIONS OF OPERATING EDUCATIONAL ORGANIZATIONS.—For purposes of this title, if an organization is—

(1) organized and operated solely to hold, commingle, and collectively invest and reinvest (including arranging for and supervising the performance by independent contractors of investment services related thereto) in stocks and securities, the moneys contributed thereto by each of the members of such organization, and to collect income therefrom and turn over the entire amount thereof, less expenses, to such members,

(2) organized and controlled by one or more such members, and

(3) comprised solely of members that are organizations described in clause (ii) or (iv) of section 170(b)(1)(A)—

(A) which are exempt from taxation under subsection (a), or

(B) the income of which is excluded from taxation under section 115(a),

then such organization shall be treated as an organization organized and operated exclusively for charitable purposes.

(g) DEFINITION OF AGRICULTURAL.—For purposes of subsection (c)(5), the term "agricultural" includes the art or science of cultivating land, harvesting crops or aquatic resources, or raising livestock.

(h) EXPENDITURES BY PUBLIC CHARITIES TO INFLUENCE LEGISLATION.—

(1) GENERAL RULE.—In the case of an organization to which this subsection applies, exemption from taxation under subsection (a) shall be denied because a substantial part of the activities of such organization consists of carrying on propaganda, or otherwise attempting, to influence legislation, but only if such organization normally—

(A) makes lobbying expenditures in excess of the lobbying ceiling amount for such organization for each taxable year, or

(B) makes grass roots expenditures in excess of the grass roots ceiling amount for such organization for each taxable year.

(2) DEFINITIONS.—For purposes of this subsection—

(A) LOBBYING EXPENDITURES.—The term "lobbying expenditures" means expenditures for the purpose of influencing legislation (as defined in section 4911(d)).

(B) LOBBYING CEILING AMOUNT.—The lobbying ceiling amount for any organization for any taxable year is 150 percent of the lobbying nontaxable amount for such organization for such taxable year, determined under section 4911.

(C) GRASS ROOTS EXPENDITURES.—The term "gross roots expenditures" means expenditures for the purpose of influencing legislation (as defined in section 4911(d) without regard to paragraph (1)(B) thereof).

(D) GRASS ROOTS CEILING AMOUNT.—The grass roots ceiling amount for any organization for any taxable year is 150 percent of the grass roots nontaxable amount for such organization for such taxable year, determined under section 4911.

(3) ORGANIZATIONS TO WHICH THIS SUBSECTION APPLIES.—This subsection shall apply to any organization which has elected (in such manner and at such time as the Secretary may prescribe) to have the provisions of this subsection apply to such organization and which, for the taxable year which includes the date the election is made, is described in subsection (c)(3) and—

(A) is described in paragraph (4), and

(B) is not a disqualified organization under paragraph (5).

(4) ORGANIZATIONS PERMITTED TO ELECT TO HAVE THIS SUBSECTION APPLY.—An organization is described in this paragraph if it is described in—

(A) section 170(b)(1)(A)(ii) (relating to educational institutions),

(B) section 170(b)(1)(A)(iii) (relating to hospitals and medical research organizations),

(C) section 170(b)(1)(A)(iv) (relating to organizations supporting government schools),

(D) section 170(b)(1)(A)(vi) (relating to organizations publicly supported by charitable contributions),

(E) section 509(a)(2) (relating to organizations publicly supported by admissions, sales, etc.), or

(F) section 509(a)(3) (relating to organizations supporting certain types of public charities) except that for purposes of this subparagraph, section 509(a)(3) shall be applied without regard to the last sentence of section 509(a).

(5) DISQUALIFIED ORGANIZATIONS.—For purposes of paragraph (3) an organization is a disqualified organization if it is—

(A) described in section 170(b)(1)(A)(i) (relating to churches),

(B) an integrated auxiliary of a church or of a convention or association of churches, or

(C) a member of an affiliated group of organizations (within the meaning of section 4911(f)(2)) if one or more members of such group is described in subparagraph (A) or (B).

(6) YEARS FOR WHICH ELECTION IS EFFECTIVE.—An election by an organization under this subsection shall be effective for all taxable years of such organization which—

(A) end after the date the election is made, and

(B) begin before the date the election is revoked by such organization (under regulations prescribed by the Secretary).

(7) NO EFFECT ON CERTAIN ORGANIZATIONS.—With respect to any organization for a taxable year for which—

(A) such organization is a disqualified organization (within the meaning of paragraph (5)), or

(B) an election under this subsection is not in effect for such organization,

nothing in this subsection or in section 4911 shall be construed to affect the interpretation of the phrase, "no substantial part of the activities of which is carrying on propaganda, or otherwise attempting, to influence legislation," under subsection (c)(3).

(8) AFFILIATED ORGANIZATIONS.—

For rules regarding affiliated organizations, see section 4911(f).

(i) PROHIBITION OF DISCRIMINATION BY CERTAIN SOCIAL CLUBS.— Notwithstanding subsection (a), an organization which is described in subsection (c)(7) shall not be exempt from taxation under subsection (a) for any taxable year if, at any time during such taxable year, the charter, bylaws, or other governing instrument, of such organization or any written policy statement of such organization contains a provision which provides for discrimination against any person on the basis of race, color, or religion. The preceding sentence to the extent it relates to discrimination on the basis of religion shall not apply to—

(1) an auxiliary of a fraternal beneficiary society if such society—

(A) is described in subsection (c)(8) and exempt from tax under subsection (a), and

(B) limits its membership to the members of a particular religion, or

(2) a club which in good faith limits its membership to the members of a particular religion in order to further the teachings or principles of that religion, and not to exclude individuals of a particular race or color.

(j) SPECIAL RULES FOR CERTAIN AMATEUR SPORTS ORGANIZATIONS.—

(1) IN GENERAL.—In the case of a qualified amateur sports organization—

(A) the requirement of subsection (c)(3) that no part of its activities involve the provision of athletic facilities or equipment shall not apply, and

(B) such organization shall not fail to meet the requirements of subsection (c)(3) merely because its membership is local or regional in nature.

(2) QUALIFIED AMATEUR SPORTS ORGANIZATION DEFINED.—For purposes of this subsection, the term "qualified amateur sports organization" means any organization organized and operated exclusively to foster national or international amateur sports competition if such organization is also organized and operated primarily to conduct national or international competition in sports or to support and develop amateur athletes for national or international competition in sports.

(k) TREATMENT OF CERTAIN ORGANIZATIONS PROVIDING CHILD CARE.—For purposes of subsection (c)(3) of this section and sections 170(c)(2), 2055(a)(2), and 2522(a)(2), the term "educational purposes" includes the providing of care of children away from their homes if—

(1) substantially all of the care provided by the organization is for purposes of enabling individuals to be gainfully employed, and

(2) the services provided by the organization are available to the general public.

(l) GOVERNMENT CORPORATIONS EXEMPT UNDER SUBSECTION (c)(1).—For purposes of subsection (c)(1), the following organizations are described in this subsection:

(1) The Central Liquidity Facility established under title III of the Federal Credit Union Act (12 U.S.C. 1795 et seq.).

(2) The Resolution Trust Corporation established under section 21A of the Federal Home Loan Bank Act.

(3) The Resolution Funding Corporation established under section 21B of the Federal Home Loan Bank Act.

(m) CERTAIN ORGANIZATIONS PROVIDING COMMERCIAL-TYPE INSURANCE NOT EXEMPT FROM TAX.—

(1) DENIAL OF TAX EXEMPTION WHERE PROVIDING COMMERCIAL-TYPE INSURANCE IS SUBSTANTIAL PART OF ACTIVITIES.—An organization described in paragraph (3) or (4) of subsection (c) shall be exempt from tax under subsection (a) only if no substantial part of its activities consists of providing commercial-type insurance.

(2) OTHER ORGANIZATIONS TAXED AS INSURANCE COMPANIES ON INSURANCE BUSINESS.—In the case of an organization described in paragraph (3) or (4) of subsection (c) which is exempt from tax under subsection (a) after the application of paragraph (1) of this subsection—

(A) the activity of providing commercial-type insurance shall be treated as an unrelated trade or business (as defined in section 513), and

(B) in lieu of the tax imposed by section 511 with respect to such activity, such organization shall be treated as an insurance company for purposes of applying subchapter L with respect to such activity.

(3) COMMERCIAL-TYPE INSURANCE.—For purposes of this subsection, the term "commercial-type insurance" shall not include—

(A) insurance provided at substantially below cost to a class of charitable recipients,

(B) incidental health insurance provided by a health maintenance organization of a kind customarily provided by such organizations,

(C) property or casualty insurance provided (directly or through an organization described in section 414(e)(3)(B)(ii)) by a church or convention or association of churches for such church or convention or association of churches,

(D) providing retirement or welfare benefits (or both) by a church or a convention or association of churches (directly or through an organization described in section 414(e)(3)(A) or 414(e)(3)(B)(ii)) for the employees (including employees described in section 414(e)(3)(B)) of such church or convention or association of churches or the beneficiaries of such employees, and

(E) charitable gift annuities.

(4) INSURANCE INCLUDES ANNUITIES.—For purposes of this subsection, the issuance of annuity contracts shall be treated as providing insurance.

(5) CHARITABLE GIFT ANNUITY.—For purposes of paragraph (3)(E), the term "charitable gift annuity" means an annuity if—

(A) a portion of the amount paid in connection with the issuance of the annuity is allowable as a deduction under section 170 or 2055, and

(B) the annuity is described in section 514(c)(5) (determined as if any amount paid in cash in connection with such issuance were property).

(n) CHARITABLE RISK POOLS.—

(1) IN GENERAL.—For purposes of this title—

(A) a qualified charitable risk pool shall be treated as an organization organized and operated exclusively for charitable purposes, and

(B) subsection (m) shall not apply to a qualified charitable risk pool.

(2) QUALIFIED CHARITABLE RISK POOL.—For purposes of this subsection, the term "qualified charitable risk pool" means any organization—

(A) which is organized and operated solely to pool insurable risks of its members (other than risks related to medical malpractice) and to provide information to its members with respect to loss control and risk management,

(B) which is comprised solely of members that are organizations described in subsection (c)(3) and exempt from tax under subsection (a), and

(C) which meets the organizational requirements of paragraph (3).

(3) ORGANIZATIONAL REQUIREMENTS.—An organization (hereinafter in this subsection referred to as the "risk pool") meets the organizational requirements of this paragraph if—

(A) such risk pool is organized as a nonprofit organization under State law provisions authorizing risk pooling arrangements for charitable organizations,

(B) such risk pool is exempt from any income tax imposed by the State (or will be so exempt after such pool qualifies as an organization exempt from tax under this title),

(C) such risk pool has obtained at least $1,000,000 in startup capital from nonmember charitable organizations,

(D) such risk pool is controlled by a board of directors elected by its members, and

(E) the organizational documents of such risk pool require that—

(i) each member of such pool shall at all times be an organization described in subsection (c)(3) and exempt from tax under subsection (a),

(ii) any member which receives a final determination that it no longer qualifies as an organization described in subsection (c)(3) shall immediately notify the pool of such determination and the effective date of such determination, and

(iii) each policy of insurance issued by the risk pool shall provide that such policy will not cover the insured with respect to events occurring after the date such final determination was issued to the insured.

An organization shall not cease to qualify as a qualified charitable risk pool solely by reason of the failure of any of its members to continue to be an organization described in subsection (c)(3) if, within a reasonable period of time after such pool is notified as required under subparagraph (E)(ii), such pool takes such action as may be reasonably necessary to remove such member from such pool.

(4) OTHER DEFINITIONS.—For purposes of this subsection—

(A) STARTUP CAPITAL.—The term "startup capital" means any capital contributed to, and any program-related investments (within the meaning of section 4944(c)) made in, the risk pool before such pool commences operations.

(B) NONMEMBER CHARITABLE ORGANIZATION.—The term "nonmember charitable organization" means any organization which is described in subsection (c)(3) and exempt from tax under subsection (a) and which is not a member of the risk pool and does not benefit (directly or indirectly) from the insurance coverage provided by the pool to its members.

(o) TREATMENT OF HOSPITALS PARTICIPATING IN PROVIDER-SPONSORED ORGANIZATIONS.—An organization shall not fail to be treated as organized and operated exclusively for a charitable purpose for purposes of subsection (c)(3) solely because a hospital which is owned and operated by such organization participates in a provider-sponsored organization (as defined in section 1855(d) of the Social Security Act), whether or not the provider-sponsored organization is exempt from tax. For purposes of subsection (c)(3), any person with a material financial interest in such a provider-sponsored organization shall be treated as a private shareholder or individual with respect to the hospital.

(p) SUSPENSION OF TAX-EXEMPT STATUS OF TERRORIST ORGANIZATIONS.—

(1) IN GENERAL.—The exemption from tax under subsection (a) with respect to any organization described in paragraph (2), and the eligibility of any organization described in paragraph (2) to apply for recognition of exemption under subsection (a), shall be suspended during the period described in paragraph (3).

(2) TERRORIST ORGANIZATIONS.—An organization is described in this paragraph if such organization is designated or otherwise individually identified—

(A) under section 212(a)(3)(B)(vi)(II) or 219 of the Immigration and Nationality Act as a terrorist organization or foreign terrorist organization,

(B) in or pursuant to an Executive order which is related to terrorism and issued under the authority of the International Emergency Economic Powers Act or section 5 of the United Nations Participation Act of 1945 for the purpose of imposing on such organization an economic or other sanction, or

(C) in or pursuant to an Executive order issued under the authority of any Federal law if—

(i) the organization is designated or otherwise individually identified in or pursuant to such Executive order as supporting or engaging in terrorist activity (as defined in section 212(a)(3)(B) of the Immigration and Nationality Act) or supporting terrorism (as defined in section 140(d)(2) of the Foreign Relations Authorization Act, Fiscal Years 1988 and 1989); and

(ii) such Executive order refers to this subsection.

(3) PERIOD OF SUSPENSION.—With respect to any organization described in paragraph (2), the period of suspension—

(A) begins on the later of—

(i) the date of the first publication of a designation or identification described in paragraph (2) with respect to such organization, or

(ii) the date of the enactment of this subsection, and

(B) ends on the first date that all designations and identifications described in paragraph (2) with respect to such organization are rescinded pursuant to the law or Executive order under which such designation or identification was made.

(4) DENIAL OF DEDUCTION.—No deduction shall be allowed under any provision of this title, including sections 170, 545(b)(2), 556(b)(2), 642(c), 2055, 2106(a)(2), and 2522, with respect to any contribution to an organization described in paragraph (2) during the period described in paragraph (3).

(5) DENIAL OF ADMINISTRATIVE OR JUDICIAL CHALLENGE OF SUSPENSION OR DENIAL OF DEDUCTION.—Notwithstanding section 7428 or any other provision of law, no organization or other person may challenge a suspension under paragraph (1), a designation or identification described in paragraph (2), the period of suspension described in paragraph (3), or a denial of a deduction under paragraph (4) in any administrative or judicial proceeding relating to the Federal tax liability of such organization or other person.

(6) ERRONEOUS DESIGNATION.—

(A) IN GENERAL.—If—

(i) the tax exemption of any organization described in paragraph (2) is suspended under paragraph (1),

(ii) each designation and identification described in paragraph (2) which has been made with respect to such organization is determined to be erroneous pursuant to the law or Executive order under which such designation or identification was made, and

(iii) the erroneous designations and identifications result in an overpayment of income tax for any taxable year by such organization,

credit or refund (with interest) with respect to such overpayment shall be made.

(B) WAIVER OF LIMITATIONS.—If the credit or refund of any overpayment of tax described in subparagraph (A)(iii) is prevented at any time by the operation of any law or rule of law (including res judicata), such credit or refund may nevertheless be allowed or made if the claim therefor is filed before the close of the 1-year period beginning on the date of the last determination described in subparagraph (A)(ii).

(7) NOTICE OF SUSPENSIONS.—If the tax exemption of any organization is suspended under this subsection, the Internal Revenue Service shall update the listings of tax-exempt organizations and shall publish appropriate notice to taxpayers of such suspension and of the fact that contributions to such organization are not deductible during the period of such suspension.

(q) CROSS REFERENCE.—

For nonexemption of Communist-controlled organizations, see section 11(b) of the Internal Security Act of 1950 (64 Stat. 997; 50 U.S.C. 790(b)).

SEC. 502. FEEDER ORGANIZATIONS.

(a) GENERAL RULE.—An organization operated for the primary purpose of carrying on a trade or business for profit shall not be exempt from taxation under section 501 on the ground that all of its profits are payable to one or more organizations exempt from taxation under section 501.

(b) SPECIAL RULE.—For purposes of this section, the term "trade or business" shall not include—

(1) the deriving of rents which would be excluded under section 512(b)(3), if section 512 applied to the organization,

(2) any trade or business in which substantially all the work in carrying on such trade or business is performed for the organization without compensation, or

(3) any trade or business which is the selling of merchandise, substantially all of which has been received by the organization as gifts or contributions.

APPENDIX D

LABOR-MANAGEMENT REPORTING AND DISCLOSURE ACT OF 1959, AS AMENDED

Editor's Note: The National Labor Relations Act (NLRA), enacted on July 5, 1935 is the main private sector federal labor law in the United States. Public employers are not covered under the NLRA.

The original statute was amended by subsequent legislation, mainly the Labor-Management Relations Act of 1947, sometimes called the Taft-Hartley Act, and the Labor-Management Reporting and Disclosure Act of 1959, also known as the Landrum-Griffin Act.

```
[Revised text[1] shows new or amended language in boldface type.]

Public Law 86-257, September 14, 1959, 73 Stat. 519-546, as amended by:

Public Law 89-216, September 29, 1965, 79 Stat. 888

Public Law 98-473, October 12, 1984, 98 Stat. 2031, 2133, 2134

Public Law 99-217, December 26, 1985, 99 Stat. 1728

Public Law 100-182, December 7, 1987, 101 Stat. 1266, 1269
```

AN ACT

To provide for the reporting and disclosure of certain financial transactions and administrative practices of labor organizations and employers, to prevent abuses in the administration of trusteeships by labor organizations, to provide standards with respect to the election of officers of labor organizations, and for other purposes.

Be it enacted by the Senate and House of Representatives of the United States of America in Congress assembled, That this Act may be cited as the "Labor-Management Reporting and Disclosure Act of 1959."

Declaration of Findings, Purposes, and Policy

(29 U.S.C. 401)

SEC. 2. (a) The Congress finds that, in the public interest, it continues to be the responsibility of the Federal Government to protect employees' rights to organize, choose their own representatives, bargain collectively, and otherwise engage in concerted activities for their mutual aid or protection; that the relations between employers and labor organizations and the millions of workers they represent have a substantial impact on the commerce of the Nation; and that in order to accomplish the objective of a free flow of commerce it is essential that labor organizations, employers, and their officials adhere to the highest standards of responsibility and ethical conduct in administering the affairs of their organizations, particularly as they affect labor-management relations.

(b) The Congress further finds, from recent investigations in the labor and management fields, that there have been a number of instances of breach of trust, corruption, disregard of the rights of individual employees, and other failures to observe high standards of responsibility and ethical conduct which require further and supplementary legislation that will afford necessary protection of the rights and interests of employees and the public generally as they relate to the activities of labor organizations, employers, labor relations consultants, and their officers and representatives.

(c) The Congress, therefore, further finds and declares that the enactment of this Act is necessary to eliminate or prevent improper practices on the part of labor organizations, employers, labor relations consultants, and their officers and representatives which distort and defeat the policies of the Labor Management Relations Act, 1947, as amended, and the Railway Labor Act, as amended, and have the tendency or necessary effect of burdening or obstructing commerce by (1) impairing the efficiency, safety, or operation of the instrumentalities of commerce; (2) occurring in the current of commerce; (3) materially affecting, restraining, or controlling the flow of raw materials or manufactured or processed goods into or from the channels of commerce, or the prices of such materials or goods in commerce; or (4) causing diminution of employment and wages in such volume as substantially to impair or disrupt the market for goods flowing into or from the channels of commerce.

Definitions

(29 U.S.C. 402)

SEC. 3. For the purposes of titles I, II, III, IV, V (except section 505), and VI of this Act-

(a) "Commerce" means trade, traffic, commerce, transportation, transmission, or communication among the several States or between any State and any place outside thereof.

(b) "State" includes any State of the United States, the District of Columbia, Puerto Rico, the Virgin Islands, American Samoa, Guam, Wake Island, the Canal Zone, and Outer Continental Shelf lands defined in the Outer Continental Shelf Lands Act (43 U.S.C. 1331-1343).

(c) "Industry affecting commerce" means any activity, business, or industry in commerce or in which a labor dispute would hinder or obstruct commerce or the free flow of commerce and includes any activity or industry "affecting commerce" within the meaning of the Labor Management Relations Act, 1947, as amended, or the Railway Labor Act, as amended.

(d) "Person" includes one or more individuals, labor organizations, partnerships, associations, corporations, legal representatives, mutual companies, joint-stock companies, trusts, unincorporated organizations, trustees, trustees in cases under Title 11 of the United States Code, [2] or receivers.

(e) "Employer" means any employer or any group or association of employers engaged in an industry affecting commerce (1) which is, with respect to employees engaged in an industry affecting commerce, an employer within the meaning of any law of the United States relating to the employment of any employees or (2) which may deal with any labor organization concerning grievances, labor disputes, wages, rates of pay, hours of employment, or conditions of work, and includes any person acting directly or indirectly as an employer or as an agent of an employer in relation to an employee but does not include the United States or any corporation wholly owned by the Government of the United States or any State or political subdivision thereof.

(f) "Employee" means any individual employed by an employer, and includes any individual whose work has ceased as a consequence of, or in connection with, any current labor dispute or because of any unfair labor practice or because of exclusion or expulsion from a labor organization in any manner or for any reason inconsistent with the requirements of this Act.

(g) "Labor dispute" includes any controversy concerning terms, tenure, or conditions of employment, or concerning the association or representation of persons in negotiating, fixing, maintaining, changing, or seeking to arrange terms or conditions of employment, regardless of whether the disputants stand in the proximate relation of employer and employee.

(h) "Trusteeship" means any receivership, trusteeship, or other method of supervision or control whereby a labor organization suspends the autonomy otherwise available to a subordinate body under its constitution or bylaws.

(i) "Labor organization" means a labor organization engaged in an industry affecting commerce and includes any organization of any kind, any agency, or employee representation committee, group, association, or plan so engaged in which employees participate and which exists for the purpose, in whole or in part, of dealing with employers concerning grievances, labor disputes, wages, rates of pay, hours, or other terms or conditions of employment, and any conference, general committee, joint or system board, or joint council so engaged which is subordinate to a national or international labor organization, other than a State or local central body.

(j) A labor organization shall be deemed to be engaged in an industry affecting commerce if it -

> (1) is the certified representative of employees under the provisions of the National Labor Relations Act, as amended, or the Railway Labor Act, as amended; or

> (2) although not certified, is a national or international labor organization or a local labor organization recognized or acting as the representative of employees of an employer or employers engaged in an industry affecting commerce; or

> (3) has chartered a local labor organization or subsidiary body which is representing or actively seeking to represent employees of employers within the meaning of paragraph (1) or (2); or

> (4) has been chartered by a labor organization representing or actively seeking to represent employees within the meaning of paragraph (1) or (2) as the local or subordinate body through which such employees may enjoy membership or become affiliated with such labor organization; or

> (5) is a conference, general committee, joint or system board, or joint council, subordinate to a national or international labor organization, which includes a labor organization engaged in an industry affecting commerce within the meaning of any of the preceding paragraphs of this subsection, other than a State or local central body.

(k) "Secret ballot" means the expression by ballot, voting machine, or otherwise, but in no event by proxy, of a choice with respect to any election or vote taken upon any matter, which is cast in such a manner that the person expressing such choice cannot be identified with the choice expressed.

(1) "Trust in which a labor organization is interested" means a trust or other fund or organization (1) which was created or established by a labor organization, or one or more of the trustees or one or more members of the governing body of which is selected or appointed by a labor organization, and (2) a primary purpose of which is to provide benefits for the members of such labor organization or their beneficiaries.

(m) "Labor relations consultant" means any person who, for compensation, advises or represents an employer, employer organization, or labor organization concerning employee organizing, concerted activities, or collective bargaining activities.

(n) "Officer" means any constitutional officer, any person authorized to perform the functions of president, vice president, secretary, treasurer, or other executive functions of a labor organization, and any member of its executive board or similar governing body.

(o) "Member" or "member in good standing", when used in reference to a labor organization, includes any person who has fulfilled the requirements for membership in such organization, and who neither has voluntarily withdrawn from membership nor has been expelled or suspended from membership after appropriate proceedings consistent with lawful provisions of the constitution and bylaws of such organization.

(p) "Secretary" means the Secretary of Labor.

(q) "Officer, agent, shop steward, or other representative", when used with respect to a labor organization, includes elected officials and key administrative personnel, whether elected or appointed (such as business agents, heads of departments or major units, and organizers who exercise substantial independent authority), but does not include salaried nonsupervisory professional staff, stenographic, and service personnel.

(r) "District court of the United States" means a United States district court and a United States court of any place subject to the jurisdiction of the United States.

TITLE I -- BILL OF RIGHTS OF MEMBERS OF LABOR ORGANIZATIONS

Bill of Rights

(29 U.S.C. 411)

SEC. 101. (a)(1) EQUAL RIGHTS.-- Every member of a labor organization shall have equal rights and privileges within such organization to nominate candidates, to vote in elections or referendums of the labor organization, to attend membership meetings and to participate in the deliberations and voting upon the business of such meetings, subject to reasonable rules and regulations in such organization's constitution and bylaws.

(2) FREEDOM OF SPEECH AND ASSEMBLY.-- Every member of any labor organization shall have the right to meet and assemble freely with other members; and to express any views, arguments, or opinions; and to express at meetings of the labor organization his views, upon candidates in an election of the labor organization or upon any business properly before the meeting, subject to the organization's established and reasonable rules pertaining to the conduct of meetings: *Provided,* That nothing herein shall be construed to impair the right of a labor organization to adopt and enforce reasonable rules as to the responsibility of every member toward the organization as an institution and to his refraining from conduct that would interfere with its performance of its legal or contractual obligations.

(3) DUES, INITIATION FEES, AND ASSESSMENTS.-- Except in the case of a federation of national or international labor organizations, the rates of dues and initiation fees payable by members of any labor organization in effect on the date of enactment of this Act shall not be increased, and no general or special assessment shall be levied upon such members, except-

(A) in the case of a local organization, (i) by majority vote by secret ballot of the members in good standing voting at a general or special membership meeting, after reasonable notice of the intention to vote upon such question, or (ii) by majority vote of the members in good standing voting in a membership referendum conducted by secret ballot; or

(B) in the case of a labor organization, other than a local labor organization or a federation of national or international labor organizations, (i) by majority vote of the delegates voting at a regular convention, or at a special convention of such labor organization held upon not less than thirty days' written notice to the principal office of each local or constituent labor organization entitled to such notice, or (ii) by majority vote of the members in good standing of such labor organization voting in a membership referendum conducted by secret ballot, or (iii) by majority vote of the members of the executive board or similar governing body of such labor organization, pursuant to express authority contained in the constitution and bylaws of such labor organization: *Provided,* That such action on the part of the executive board or similar governing body shall be effective only until the next regular convention of such labor organization.

(4) PROTECTION OF THE RIGHT TO SUE.-- No labor organization shall limit the right of any member thereof to institute an action in any court, or in a proceeding before any administrative agency, irrespective of whether or not the labor organization or its officers are named as defendants or respondents in such action or proceeding, or the right of any member of a labor organization to appear as a witness in any judicial, administrative, or legislative proceeding, or to petition any legislature or to communicate with any legislator: *Provided,* That any such member may be required to exhaust reasonable hearing procedures (but not to exceed a four-month lapse of time) within such organization, before instituting legal or administrative proceedings against such organizations or any officer thereof: *And provided further,* That no interested employer or employer association shall directly or indirectly finance, encourage, or participate in, except as a party, any such action, proceeding, appearance, or petition.

(5) SAFEGUARDS AGAINST IMPROPER DISCIPLINARY ACTION.-- No member of any labor organization may be fined, suspended, expelled, or otherwise disciplined except

for nonpayment of dues by such organization or by any officer thereof unless such member has been (A) served with written specific charges; (B) given a reasonable time to prepare his defense; (C) afforded a full and fair hearing.

(b) Any provision of the constitution and bylaws of any labor organization which is inconsistent with the provisions of this section shall be of no force or effect.

Civil Enforcement

(29 U.S.C. 412)

SEC. 102. Any person whose rights secured by the provisions of this title have been infringed by any violation of this title may bring a civil action in a district court of the United States for such relief (including injunctions) as may be appropriate. Any such action against a labor organization shall be brought in the district court of the United States for the district where the alleged violation occurred, or where the principal office of such labor organization is located.

Retention of Existing Rights

(29 U.S.C. 413)

SEC. 103. Nothing contained in this title shall limit the rights and remedies of any member of a labor organization under any State or Federal law or before any court or other tribunal, or under the constitution and bylaws of any labor organization.

Right to Copies of Collective Bargaining Agreements

(29 U.S.C. 414)

SEC. 104. It shall be the duty of the secretary or corresponding principal officer of each labor organization, in the case of a local labor organization, to forward a copy of each collective bargaining agreement made by such labor organization with any employer to any employee who requests such a copy and whose rights as such employee are directly affected by such agreement, and in the case of a labor organization other than a local labor organization, to forward a copy of any such agreement to each constituent unit which has members directly affected by such agreement; and such officer shall maintain at the principal office of the labor organization of which he is an officer copies of any such agreement made or received by such labor organization, which copies shall be available for inspection by any member or by any employee whose rights are affected by such agreement. The provisions of section 210 shall be applicable in the enforcement of this section.

Information as to Act

(29 U.S.C. 415)

SEC. 105. Every labor organization shall inform its members concerning the provisions of this Act.

TITLE II -- REPORTING BY LABOR ORGANIZATIONS, OFFICERS AND EMPLOYEES OF LABOR ORGANIZATIONS, AND EMPLOYERS

Report of Labor Organizations

(29 U.S.C. 431)

SEC. 201. (a) Every labor organization shall adopt a constitution and bylaws and shall file a copy thereof with the Secretary, together with a report, signed by its president and secretary or corresponding principal officers, containing the following information-

(1) the name of the labor organization, its mailing address, and any other address at which it maintains its principal office or at which it keeps the records referred to in this title;

(2) the name and title of each of its officers;

(3) the initiation fee or fees required from a new or transferred member and fees for work permits required by the reporting labor organization;

(4) the regular dues or fees or other periodic payments required to remain a member of the reporting labor organization; and

(5) detailed statements, or references to specific provisions of documents filed under this subsection which contain such statements, showing the provisions made and procedures followed with respect to each of the following: (A) qualifications for or restrictions on membership, (B) levying of assessments, (C) participation in insurance or other benefit plans, (D) authorization for disbursement of funds of the labor organization, (E) audit of financial transactions of the labor organization, (F) the calling of regular and special meetings, (G) the selection of officers and stewards and of any representatives to other bodies composed of labor organizations' representatives, with a specific statement of the manner in which each officer was elected, appointed, or otherwise selected, (H) discipline or removal of officers or agents for breaches of their trust, (I) imposition of fines, suspensions, and expulsions of members, including the grounds for such action and any provision made for notice, hearing, judgment on the evidence, and appeal procedures, (J) authorization for bargaining demands, (K) ratification of contract terms, (L) authorization for strikes, and (M) issuance of work permits. Any change in the information required by this subsection shall be reported to the Secretary at the time the reporting labor organization files with the Secretary the annual financial report required by subsection (b).

(b) Every labor organization shall file annually with the Secretary a financial report signed by its president and treasurer or corresponding principal officers containing the following information in such detail as may be necessary accurately to disclose its financial condition and operations for its preceding fiscal year-

(1) assets and liabilities at the beginning and end of the fiscal year;

(2) receipts of any kind and the sources thereof,

(3) salary, allowances, and other direct or indirect disbursements (including reimbursed expenses) to each officer and also to each employee who, during such fiscal year, received more than $10,000 in the aggregate from such labor organization and any other labor organization affiliated with it or with which it is affiliated, or which is affiliated with the same national or international labor organization;

(4) direct and indirect loans made to any officer, employee, or member, which aggregated more than $250 during the fiscal year, together with a statement of the purpose, security, if any, and arrangements for repayment;

(5) direct and indirect loans to any business enterprise, together with a statement of the purpose, security, if any, and arrangements for repayment; and

(6) other disbursements made by it including the purposes thereof, all in such categories as the Secretary may prescribe.

(c) Every labor organization required to submit a report under this title shall make available the information required to be contained in such report to all of its members, and every such labor organization and its officers shall be under a duty enforceable at the suit of any member of such organization in any State court of competent jurisdiction or in the district court of the United States for the district in which such labor organization maintains its principal office, to permit such member for just cause to examine any books, records, and accounts necessary to verify such report. The court in such action may, in its discretion, in addition to any judgment awarded to the plaintiff or plaintiffs, allow a reasonable attorney's fee to be paid by the defendant, and costs of the action.

(d) Subsections (f), (g), and (h) of section 9 of the National Labor Relations Act, as amended, are hereby repealed.

(e) Clause (i) of section 8(a)(3) of the National Labor Relations Act, as amended, is amended by striking out the following: "and has at the time the agreement was made or within the preceding twelve months received from the Board a notice of compliance with section 9(f), (g), (h)".

Report of Officers and Employees of Labor Organizations

(29 U.S.C. 432)

SEC. 202. (a) Every officer of a labor organization and every employee of a labor organization (other than an employee performing exclusively clerical or custodial services) shall file with the Secretary a signed report listing and describing for his preceding fiscal year-

(1) any stock, bond, security, or other interest, legal or equitable, which he or his spouse or minor child directly or indirectly held in, and any income or any other benefit with monetary value (including reimbursed expenses) which he or his spouse or minor child derived directly or indirectly from, an employer whose employees such labor organization represents or is actively seeking to represent, except payments and other benefits received as a bona fide employee of such employer;

(2) any transaction in which he or his spouse or minor child engaged, directly or indirectly, involving any stock, bond, security, or loan to or from, or other legal or equitable interest in the business of an employer whose employees such labor organization represents or is actively seeking to represent;

(3) any stock, bond, security, or other interest, legal or equitable, which he or his spouse or minor child directly or indirectly held in, and any income or any other benefit with monetary value (including reimbursed expenses) which he or his spouse or minor child directly or indirectly derived from, any business a substantial part of which consists of buying from, selling or leasing to, or otherwise dealing with, the business of an employer whose employees such labor organization represents or is actively seeking to represent;

(4) any stock, bond, security, or other interest, legal or equitable, which he or his spouse or minor child directly or indirectly held in, and any income or any other benefit with monetary value (including reimbursed expenses) which he or his spouse or minor child directly or indirectly derived from, a business any part of which consists of buying from, or selling or leasing directly or indirectly to, or otherwise dealing with such labor organization;

(5) any direct or indirect business transaction or arrangement between him or his spouse or minor child and any employer whose employees his organization represents or is actively seeking to represent, except work performed and payments and benefits received as a bona fide employee of such employer and except purchases and sales of goods or services in the regular course of business at prices generally available to any employee of such employer; and

(6) any payment of money or other thing of value (including reimbursed expenses) which he or his spouse or minor child received directly or indirectly from any employer or any person who acts as a labor relations consultant to an employer, except payments of the kinds referred to in section 302(c) of the Labor Management Relations Act, 1947, as amended.

(b) The provisions of paragraphs (1), (2), (3), (4), and (5) of subsection (a) shall not be construed to require any such officer or employee to report his bona fide investments in securities traded on a securities exchange registered as a national securities exchange under the Securities Exchange Act of 1934, in shares in an investment company registered under the Investment Company Act or in securities of a public utility holding company registered under the Public Utility Holding Company Act of 1935, or to report any income derived therefrom.

(c) Nothing contained in this section shall be construed to require any officer or employee of a labor organization to file a report under subsection (a) unless he or his spouse or minor child holds or has held an interest, has received income or any other benefit with monetary value or a loan, or has engaged in a transaction described therein.

Report of Employers

(29 U.S.C. 433)

SEC. 203. (a) Every employer who in any fiscal year made—

(1) any payment or loan, direct or indirect, of money or other thing of value (including reimbursed expenses), or any promise or agreement therefor, to any labor organization or officer, agent, shop steward, or other representative of a labor organization, or employee of any labor organization, except (A) payments or loans made by any national or State bank, credit union, insurance company, savings and loan association or other credit institution and (B) payments of the kind referred to in section 302(c) of the Labor Management Relations Act, 1947, as amended;

(2) any payment (including reimbursed expenses) to any of his employees, or any group or committee of such employees, for the purpose of causing such employee or group or committee of employees to persuade other employees to exercise or not to exercise, or as the manner of exercising, the right to organize and bargain collectively through representatives of their own choosing unless such payments were contemporaneously or previously disclosed to such other employees;

(3) any expenditure, during the fiscal year, where an object thereof, directly or indirectly, is to interfere with, restrain, or coerce employees in the exercise of the right to organize and bargain collectively through representatives of their own choosing, or is to obtain information concerning the activities of employees or a labor organization in connection with a labor dispute involving such employer, except for use solely in conjunction with an administrative or arbitral proceeding or a criminal or civil judicial proceeding;

(4) any agreement or arrangement with a labor relations consultant or other independent contractor or organization pursuant to which such person undertakes activities where an object thereof, directly or indirectly, is to persuade employees to exercise or not to exercise, or persuade employees as to the manner of exercising, the right to organize and bargain collectively through representatives of their own choosing, or undertakes to supply such employer with information concerning the activities of employees or a labor organization in connection with a labor dispute involving such employer, except information for use solely in conjunction with an administrative or arbitral proceeding or a criminal or civil judicial proceeding; or

(5) any payment (including reimbursed expenses) pursuant to an agreement or arrangement described in subdivision (4);

shall file with the Secretary a report, in a form prescribed by him, signed by its president and treasurer or corresponding principal officers showing in detail the date and amount of each such payment, loan, promise, agreement, or arrangement and the name, address, and position, if any, in any firm or labor organization of the person to whom it was made and a full explanation of the circumstances of all such payments, including the terms of any agreement or understanding pursuant to which they were made.

(b) Every person who pursuant to any agreement or arrangement with an employer undertakes activities where an object thereof is, directly or indirectly-

(1) to persuade employees to exercise or not to exercise, or persuade employees as to the manner of exercising, the right to organize and bargain collectively through representatives of their own choosing; or

(2) to supply an employer with information concerning the activities of employees or a labor organization in connection with a labor dispute involving such employer, except information for use solely in conjunction with an administrative or arbitral proceeding or a criminal or civil judicial proceeding;

shall file within thirty days after entering into such agreement or arrangement a report with the Secretary, signed by its president and treasurer or corresponding principal officers, containing the name under which such person is engaged in doing business and the address of its principal office, and a detailed statement of the terms and conditions of such agreement or arrangement. Every such person shall file annually, with respect to each fiscal year during which payments were made as a result of such an agreement or arrangement, a report with the Secretary, signed by its president and treasurer or corresponding principal officers, containing a statement (A) of its receipts of any kind from employers on account of labor relations advice or services, designating the sources thereof, and (B) of its disbursements of any kind, in connection with such services and the purposes thereof. In each such case such information shall be set forth in such categories as the Secretary may prescribe.

(c) Nothing in this section shall be construed to require any employer or other person to file a report covering the services of such person by reason of his giving or agreeing to give advice to such employer or representing or agreeing to represent such employer before any court, administrative agency, or tribunal of arbitration or engaging or agreeing to engage in collective bargaining on behalf of such employer with respect to wages, hours, or other terms or conditions of employment or the negotiation of an agreement or any question arising thereunder.

(d) Nothing contained in this section shall be construed to require an employer to file a report under subsection (a) unless he has made an expenditure, payment, loan, agreement, or arrangement of the kind described therein. Nothing contained in this section shall be construed to require any other person to file a report under subsection (b) unless he was a party to an agreement or arrangement of the kind described therein.

(e) Nothing contained in this section shall be construed to require any regular officer, supervisor, or employee of an employer to file a report in connection with services rendered to such employer nor shall any employer be required to file a report covering expenditures made to any regular officer, supervisor, or employee of an employer as compensation for service as a regular officer, supervisor, or employee of such employer.

(f) Nothing contained in this section shall be construed as an amendment to, or modification of the rights protected by, section 8(c) of the National Labor Relations Act, as amended.

(g) The term "interfere with, restrain, or coerce" as used in this section means interference, restraint, and coercion which, if done with respect to the exercise of rights guaranteed in section 7 of the National Labor Relations Act, as amended, would, under section 8(a) of such Act, constitute an unfair labor practice.

Attorney-Client Communications Exempted

(29 U.S.C. 434)

SEC. 204. Nothing contained in this Act shall be construed to require an attorney who is a member in good standing of the bar of any State, to include in any report required to be filed pursuant to the provisions of this Act any information which was lawfully communicated to such attorney by any of his clients in the course of a legitimate attorney-client relationship.

Reports Made Public Information

(29 U.S.C. 435)

SEC. 205. (a)[3] The contents of the reports and documents filed with the Secretary pursuant to sections 201, 202, **203, and 211** shall be public information, and the Secretary may publish any information and data which he obtains pursuant to the provisions of this title. The Secretary may use the information and data for statistical and research purposes, and compile and publish such studies, analyses, reports, and surveys based thereon as he may deem appropriate.

(b)[4] The Secretary shall by regulation make reasonable provision for the inspection and examination, on the request of any person, of the information and data contained in any report or other document filed with him pursuant to section 201, 202, **203, or 211.**

(c)[5] The Secretary shall by regulation provide for the furnishing by the Department of Labor of copies of reports or other documents filed with the Secretary pursuant to this title, upon payment of a charge based upon the cost of the service. The Secretary shall make available without payment of a charge, or require any person to furnish, to such State agency as is designated by law or by the Governor of the State in which such person has his principal place of business or headquarters, upon request of the Governor of such State, copies of any reports and documents filed by such person with the Secretary pursuant to section 201, 202, **203, or 211,** or of information and data contained therein. No person shall be required by reason of any law of any State to furnish to any officer or agency of such State any information included in a report filed by such person with the Secretary pursuant to the provisions of this title, if a copy of such report, or of the portion thereof containing such information, is furnished to such officer or agency. All moneys received in payment of such charges fixed by the Secretary pursuant to this subsection shall be deposited in the general fund of the Treasury.

Retention of Records

(29 U.S.C. 436)

SEC. 206. Every person required to file any report under this title shall maintain records on the matters required to be reported which will provide in sufficient detail the necessary basic information and data from which the

documents filed with the Secretary may be verified, explained or clarified, and
checked for accuracy and completeness, and shall include vouchers, worksheets,
receipts, and applicable resolutions, and shall keep such records available for
examination for a period of not less than five years after the filing of the
documents based on the information which they contain.

Effective Date

(29 U.S.C. 437)

SEC. 207. (a) Each labor organization shall file the initial report required
under section 201(a) within ninety days after the date on which it first becomes
subject to this Act.

(b)[6]Each person required to file a report under section 201(b), 202, 203(a), **the
second sentence of section 203(b), or section 211** shall file such report within
ninety days after the end of each of its fiscal years; except that where such
person is subject to section 201(b), 202, 203(a), **the second sentence of section
203(b), or section 211,** as the case may be, for only a portion of such a fiscal
year (because the date of enactment of this Act occurs during such person's
fiscal year or such person becomes subject to this Act during its fiscal year)
such person may consider that portion as the entire fiscal year in making such
report.

Rules and Regulations

(29 U.S.C. 438)

SEC. 208. The Secretary shall have authority to issue, amend, and rescind rules
and regulations prescribing the form and publication of reports required to be
filed under this title and such other reasonable rules and regulations (including
rules prescribing reports concerning trusts in which a labor organization is
interested) as he may find necessary to prevent the circumvention or evasion of
such reporting requirements. In exercising his power under this section the
Secretary shall prescribe by general rule simplified reports for labor
organizations or employers for whom he finds that by virtue of their size a
detailed report would be unduly burdensome, but the Secretary may revoke such
provision for simplified forms of any labor organization or employer if he
determines, after such investigation as he deems proper and due notice and
opportunity for a hearing, that the purposes of this section would be served
thereby.

Criminal Provisions

(29 U.S.C. 439)

SEC. 209. (a) Any person who willfully violates this title shall be fined not
more than $10,000 or imprisoned for not more than one year, or both.

(b) Any person who makes a false statement or representation of a material fact,
knowing it to be false, or who knowingly fails to disclose a material fact, in
any document, report, or other information required under the provisions of this

title shall be fined not more than $10,000 or imprisoned for not more than one year, or both.

(c) Any person who willfully makes a false entry in or willfully conceals, withholds, or destroys any books, records, reports, or statements required to be kept by any provision of this title shall be fined not more than $10,000 or imprisoned for not more than one year, or both.

(d) Each individual required to sign reports under sections 201 and 203 shall be personally responsible for the filing of such reports and for any statement contained therein which he knows to be false.

Civil Enforcement

(29 U.S.C. 440)

SEC. 210. Whenever it shall appear that any person has violated or is about to violate any of the provisions of this title, the Secretary may bring a civil action for such relief (including injunctions) as may be appropriate. Any such action may be brought in the district court of the United States where the violation occurred or, at the option of the parties, in the United States District Court for the District of Columbia.

Surety Company Reports[1]

(29 U.S.C. 441)

SEC. 211. Each surety company which issues any bond required by this Act or the Employee Retirement Income Security Act of 1974 shall file annually with the Secretary, with respect to each fiscal year during which any such bond was in force, a report, in such form and detail as he may prescribe by regulation, filed by the president and treasurer or corresponding principal officers of the surety company, describing its bond experience under each such Act, including information as to the premiums received, total claims paid, amounts recovered by way of subrogation, administrative and legal expenses and such related data and information as the Secretary shall determine to be necessary in the public interest and to carry out the policy of the Act. Notwithstanding the foregoing, if the Secretary finds that any such specific information cannot be practicably ascertained or would be uninformative, the Secretary may modify or waive the requirement for such information.

TITLE III -- TRUSTEESHIPS

Reports

(29 U.S.C. 461)

SEC. 301. (a) Every labor organization which has or assumes trusteeship over any subordinate labor organization shall file with the Secretary within thirty days after the date of the enactment of this Act or the imposition of any such trusteeship, and semiannually thereafter, a report, signed by its president and treasurer or corresponding principal officers, as well as by the trustees of such subordinate labor organization, containing the following information: (1) the name and address of the subordinate organization; (2) the date of establishing the trusteeship; (3) a detailed statement of the reason or reasons for establishing or continuing the trusteeship; and (4) the nature and extent of participation by the membership of the subordinate organization in the selection of delegates to represent such organization in regular or special conventions or other policy-determining bodies and in the election of officers of the labor organization which has assumed trusteeship over such subordinate organization. The initial report shall also include a full and complete account of the financial condition of such subordinate organization as of the time trusteeship was assumed over it. During the continuance of a trusteeship the labor organization which has assumed trusteeship over a subordinate labor organization shall file on behalf of the subordinate labor organization the annual financial report required by section 201(b) signed by the president and treasurer or corresponding principal officers of the labor organization which has assumed such trusteeship and the trustees of the subordinate labor organization.

(b) The provisions of section 201(c), 205, 206, 208, and 210 shall be applicable to reports filed under this title.

(c) Any person who willfully violates this section shall be fined not more than $10,000 or imprisoned for not more than one year, or both.

(d) Any person who makes a false statement or representation of a material fact, knowing it to be false, or who knowingly fails to disclose a material fact, in any report required under the provisions of this section or willfully makes any false entry in or willfully withholds, conceals, or destroys any documents, books, records, reports, or statements upon which such report is based, shall be fined not more than $10,000 or imprisoned for not more than one year, or both.

(e) Each individual required to sign a report under this section shall be personally responsible for the filing of such report and for any statement contained therein which he knows to be false.

Purposes for Which a Trusteeship May Be Established

(29 U.S.C. 462)

SEC. 302. Trusteeships shall be established and administered by a labor organization over a subordinate body only in accordance with the constitution and bylaws of the organization which has assumed trusteeship over the subordinate body and for the purpose of correcting corruption or financial malpractice, assuring the performance of collective bargaining agreements or other duties of a bargaining representative, restoring democratic procedures, or otherwise carrying out the legitimate objects of such labor organization.

Unlawful Acts Relating to Labor Organization Under Trusteeship

(29 U.S.C. 463)

SEC. 303. (a) During any period when a subordinate body of a labor organization is in trusteeship, it shall be unlawful (1) to count the vote of delegates from such body in any convention or election of officers of the labor organization unless the delegates have been chosen by secret ballot in an election in which all the members in good standing of such subordinate body were eligible to participate or (2) to transfer to such organization any current receipts or other funds of the subordinate body except the normal per capita tax and assessments payable by subordinate bodies not in trusteeship: *Provided,* That nothing herein contained shall prevent the distribution of the assets of a labor organization in accordance with its constitution and bylaws upon the bona fide dissolution thereof.

(b) Any person who willfully violates this section shall be fined not more than $10,000 or imprisoned for not more than one year, or both.

Enforcement

(29 U.S.C. 464)

SEC. 304. (a) Upon the written complaint of any member or subordinate body of a labor organization alleging that such organization has violated the provisions of this title (except section 301) the Secretary shall investigate the complaint and if the Secretary finds probable cause to believe that such violation has occurred and has not been remedied he shall, without disclosing the identity of the complainant, bring a civil action in any district court of the United States having jurisdiction of the labor organization for such relief (including injunctions) as may be appropriate. Any member or subordinate body of a labor organization affected by any violation of this title (except section 301) may bring a civil action in any district court of the United States having jurisdiction of the labor organization for such relief (including injunctions) as may be appropriate.

(b) For the purpose of actions under this section, district courts of the United States shall be deemed to have jurisdiction of a labor organization (1) in the district in which the principal office of such labor organization is located, or (2) in any district in which its duly authorized officers or agents are engaged in conducting the affairs of the trusteeship.

(c) In any proceeding pursuant to this section a trusteeship established by a labor organization in conformity with the procedural requirements of its constitution and bylaws and authorized or ratified after a fair hearing either before the executive board or before such other body as may be provided in accordance with its constitution or bylaws shall be presumed valid for a period of eighteen months from the date of its establishment and shall not be subject to attack during such period except upon clear and convincing proof that the trusteeship was not established or maintained in good faith for a purpose allowable under section 302. After the expiration of eighteen months the trusteeship shall be presumed invalid in any such proceeding and its discontinuance shall be decreed unless the labor organization shall show by clear and convincing proof that the continuation of the trusteeship is necessary for a purpose allowable under section 302. In the latter event the court may dismiss the complaint or retain jurisdiction of the cause on such conditions and for such period as it deems appropriate.

Report to Congress

(29 U.S.C. 465)

SEC. 305. The Secretary shall submit to the Congress at the expiration of three years from the date of enactment of this Act a report upon the operation of this title.

Complaint by Secretary

(29 U.S.C. 466)

SEC. 306. The rights and remedies provided by this title shall be in addition to any and all other rights and remedies at law or in equity: *Provided,* That upon the filing of a complaint by the Secretary the jurisdiction of the district court over such trusteeship shall be exclusive and the final judgment shall be res judicata.

TITLE IV - ELECTIONS

Terms of Office; Election Procedures

(29 U.S.C. 481)

SEC. 401. (a) Every national or international labor organization, except a federation of national or international labor organizations, shall elect its officers not less often than once every five years either by secret ballot among the members in good standing or at a convention of delegates chosen by secret ballot.

(b) Every local labor organization shall elect its officers not less often than once every three years by secret ballot among the members in good standing.

(c) Every national or international labor organization, except a federation of national or international labor organizations, and every local labor organization, and its officers, shall be under a duty, enforceable at the suit of any bona fide candidate for office in such labor organization in the district court of the United States in which such labor organization maintains its principal office, to comply with all reasonable requests of any candidate to distribute by mail or otherwise at the candidate's expense campaign literature in aid of such person's candidacy to all members in good standing of such labor organization and to refrain from discrimination in favor of or against any candidate with respect to the use of lists of members, and whenever such labor organizations or its officers authorize the distribution by mail or otherwise to members of campaign literature on behalf of any candidate or of the labor organization itself with reference to such election, similar distribution at the request of any other bona fide candidate shall be made by such labor organization and its officers, with equal treatment as to the expense of such distribution. Every bona fide candidate shall have the right, once within 30 days prior to an election of a labor organization in which he is a candidate, to inspect a list containing the names and last known addresses of all members of the labor organization who are subject to a collective bargaining agreement requiring membership therein as a condition of employment, which list shall be maintained and kept at the principal office of such labor organization by a designated official thereof. Adequate safeguards to insure a fair election shall be provided, including the right of any candidate to have an observer at the polls and at the counting of the ballots.

(d) Officers of intermediate bodies, such as general committees, system boards, joint boards, or joint councils, shall be elected not less often than once every four years by secret ballot among the members in good standing or by labor organization officers representative of such members who have been elected by secret ballot.

(e) In any election required by this section which is to be held by secret ballot a reasonable opportunity shall be given for the nomination of candidates and every member in good standing shall be eligible to be a candidate and to hold office (subject to section 504 and to reasonable qualifications uniformly imposed) and shall have the right to vote for or otherwise support the candidate or candidates of his choice, without being subject to penalty, discipline, or improper interference or reprisal of any kind by such organization or any member thereof. Not less than fifteen days prior to the election notice thereof shall be mailed to each member at his last known home address. Each member in good standing shall be entitled to one vote. No member whose dues have been withheld by his employer for payment to such organization pursuant to his voluntary authorization provided for in a collective bargaining agreement shall be declared ineligible to vote or be a candidate for office in such organization by reason of alleged delay or default in the payment of dues. The votes cast by members of each local labor organization shall be counted, and the results published, separately. The election officials designated in the constitution and bylaws or the secretary, if no other official is designated, shall preserve for one year the ballots and all other records pertaining to the election. The election shall be conducted in accordance with the constitution and bylaws of such organization insofar as they are not inconsistent with the provisions of this title.

(f) When officers are chosen by a convention of delegates elected by secret ballot, the convention shall be conducted in accordance with the constitution and bylaws of the labor organization insofar as they are not inconsistent with the provisions of this title. The officials designated in the constitution and bylaws or the secretary, if no other is designated, shall preserve for one year the credentials of the delegates and all minutes and other records of the convention pertaining to the election of officers.

(g) No moneys received by any labor organization by way of dues, assessment, or similar levy, and no moneys of an employer shall be contributed or applied to promote the candidacy of any person in an election subject to the provisions of this title. Such moneys of a labor organization may be utilized for notices, factual statements of issues not involving candidates, and other expenses necessary for the holding of an election.

(h) If the Secretary, upon application of any member of a local labor organization, finds after hearing in accordance with the Administrative Procedure Act that the constitution and bylaws of such labor organization do not provide an adequate procedure for the removal of an elected officer guilty of serious misconduct, such officer may be removed, for cause shown and after notice and hearing, by the members in good standing voting in a secret ballot conducted by the officers of such labor organization in accordance with its constitution and bylaws insofar as they are not inconsistent with the provisions of this title.

(i) The Secretary shall promulgate rules and regulations prescribing minimum standards and procedures for determining the adequacy of the removal procedures to which reference is made in subsection (h).

Enforcement

(29 U.S.C. 482)

SEC. 402. (a) A member of a labor organization—

(1) who has exhausted the remedies available under the constitution and bylaws of such organization and of any parent body, or

(2) who has invoked such available remedies without obtaining a final decision within three calendar months after their invocation,

may file a complaint with the Secretary within one calendar month thereafter alleging the violation of any provision of section 401 (including violation of the constitution and bylaws of the labor organization pertaining to the election and removal of officers). The challenged election shall be presumed valid pending a final decision thereon (as hereinafter provided) and in the interim the affairs of the organization shall be conducted by the officers elected or in such other manner as its constitution and bylaws may provide.

(b) The Secretary shall investigate such complaint and, if he finds probable cause to believe that a violation of this title has occurred and has not been remedied, he shall, within sixty days after the filing of such complaint, bring a civil action against the labor organization as an entity in the district court of the United States in which such labor organization maintains its principal office to set aside the invalid election, if any, and to direct the conduct of an election or hearing and vote upon the removal of officers under the supervision of the Secretary and in accordance with the provisions of this title and such rules and regulations as the Secretary may prescribe. The court shall have power to take such action as it deems proper to preserve the assets of the labor organization.

(c) If, upon a preponderance of the evidence after a trial upon the merits, the court finds—

(1) that an election has not been held within the time prescribed by

section 401, or

(2) that the violation of section 401 may have affected the outcome of an election,

the court shall declare the election, if any, to be void and direct the conduct of a new election under supervision of the Secretary and, so far as lawful and practicable, in conformity with the constitution and bylaws of the labor organization. The Secretary shall promptly certify to the court the names of the persons elected, and the court shall thereupon enter a decree declaring such persons to be the officers of the labor organization. If the proceeding is for the removal of officers pursuant to subsection (h) of section 401, the Secretary shall certify the results of the vote and the court shall enter a decree declaring whether such persons have been removed as officers of the labor organization.

(d) An order directing an election, dismissing a complaint, or designating elected officers of a labor organization shall be appealable in the same manner as the final judgment in a civil action, but an order directing an election shall not be stayed pending appeal.

Application of Other Laws

(29 U.S.C. 483)

SEC. 403. No labor organization shall be required by law to conduct elections of officers with greater frequency or in a different form or manner than is required by its own constitution or bylaws, except as otherwise provided by this title. Existing rights and remedies to enforce the constitution and bylaws of a labor organization with respect to elections prior to the conduct thereof shall not be affected by the provisions of this title. The remedy provided by this title for challenging an election already conducted shall be exclusive.

Effective Date

(29 U.S.C. 484)

SEC. 404. The provisions of this title shall become applicable-

(1) ninety days after the date of enactment of this Act in the case of a labor organization whose constitution and bylaws can lawfully be modified or amended by action of its constitutional officers or governing body, or

(2) where such modification can only be made by a constitutional convention of the labor organization, not later than the next constitutional convention of such labor organization after the date of enactment of this Act, or one year after such date, whichever is sooner. If no such convention is held within such one-year period, the executive board or similar governing body empowered to act for such labor organization between conventions is empowered to make such interim constitutional changes as are necessary to carry out the provisions of this title.

TITLE V-SAFEGUARDS FOR LABOR ORGANIZATIONS

Fiduciary Responsibility of Officers of Labor Organizations

(29 U.S.C. 501)

SEC. 501. (a) The officers, agents, shop stewards, and other representatives of a labor organization occupy positions of trust in relation to such organization and its members as a group. It is, therefore, the duty of each such person, taking into account the special problems and functions of a labor organization, to hold its money and property solely for the benefit of the organization and its members and to manage, invest, and expend the same in accordance with its constitution and bylaws and any resolutions of the governing bodies adopted thereunder, to refrain from dealing with such organization as an adverse party or in behalf of an adverse party in any matter connected with his duties and from holding or acquiring any pecuniary or personal interest which conflicts with the interests of such organization, and to account to the organization for any profit received by him in whatever capacity in connection with transactions conducted by him or under his direction on behalf of the organization. A general exculpatory provision in the constitution and bylaws of such a labor organization or a general exculpatory resolution of a governing body purporting to relieve any such person of liability for breach of the duties declared by this section shall be void as against public policy.

(b) When any officer, agent, shop steward, or representative of any labor organization is alleged to have violated the duties declared in subsection (a) and the labor organization or its governing board or officers refuse or fail to sue or recover damages or secure an accounting or other appropriate relief within a reasonable time after being requested to do so by any member of the labor organization, such member may sue such officer, agent, shop steward, or representative in any district court of the United States or in any State court of competent jurisdiction to recover damages or secure an accounting or other appropriate relief for the benefit of the labor organization. No such proceeding shall be brought except upon leave of the court obtained upon verified application and for good cause shown which application may be made ex parte. The trial judge may allot a reasonable part of the recovery in any action under this subsection to pay the fees of counsel prosecuting the suit at the instance of the member of the labor organization and to compensate such member for any expenses necessarily paid or incurred by him in connection with the litigation.

(c) Any person who embezzles, steals, or unlawfully and willfully abstracts or converts to his own use, or the use of another, any of the moneys, funds, securities, property, or other assets of a labor organization of which he is an officer, or by which he is employed, directly or indirectly, shall be fined not more than $10,000 or imprisoned for not more than five years, or both.

Bonding

(29 U.S.C. 502)

SEC. 502. (a)[8] Every officer, agent, shop steward, or other representative or employee of any labor organization (other than a labor organization whose property and annual financial receipts do not exceed $5,000 in value), or of a trust in which a labor organization is interested, who handles funds or other property thereof shall be bonded **to provide protection against loss by reason of acts of fraud or dishonesty on his part directly or through connivance with others.** The bond of each such person shall be fixed at the beginning of the organization's fiscal year and shall be in an amount not less than 10 per centum of the funds handled by him and his predecessor or predecessors, if any, during the preceding fiscal year, but in no case more than $500,000. If the labor organization or the trust in which a labor organization is interested does not have a preceding fiscal year, the amount of the bond shall be, in the case of a local labor organization, not less than $1,000, and in the case of any other labor organization or of a trust in which a labor organization is interested, not less than $10,000. Such bonds shall be individual or schedule in form, and shall have a corporate surety company as surety thereon. Any person who is not covered by such bonds shall not be permitted to receive, handle, disburse, or otherwise exercise custody or control of the funds or other property of a labor organization or of a trust in which a labor organization is interested. No such bond shall be placed through an agent or broker or with a surety company in which any labor organization or any officer, agent, shop steward, or other representative of a labor organization has any direct or indirect interest. Such surety company shall be a corporate surety which holds a grant of authority from the Secretary of the Treasury under the Act of July 30, 1947 (6 U.S.C. 6-13), as an acceptable surety on Federal bonds: **Provided, That when in the opinion of the Secretary a labor organization has made other bonding arrangements which would provide the protection required by this section at comparable cost or less, he may exempt such labor organization from placing a bond through a surety company holding such grant of authority.**

(b) Any person who willfully violates this section shall be fined not more than $10,000 or imprisoned for not more than one year, or both.

Making of Loans; Payment of Fines

(29 U.S.C. 503)

SEC. 503. (a) No labor organization shall make directly or indirectly any loan or loans to any officer or employee of such organization which results in a total indebtedness on the part of such officer or employee to the labor organization in excess of $2,000.

(b) No labor organization or employer shall directly or indirectly pay the fine of any officer or employee convicted of any willful violation of this Act.

(c) Any person who willfully violates this section shall be fined not more than $5,000 or imprisoned for not more than one year, or both.

Prohibition Against Certain Persons Holding Office

(29 U.S.C. 504)

SEC. 504. (a) No person who is or has been a member of the Communist Party [9] or who has been convicted of, or served any part of a prison term resulting from his conviction of, robbery, bribery, extortion, embezzlement, grand larceny, burglary, arson, violation of narcotics laws, murder, rape, assault with intent to kill, assault which inflicts grievous bodily injury, or a violation of title II or III of this Act,[10] **any felony involving abuse or misuse of such person's position or employment in a labor organization or employee benefit plan to seek or obtain an illegal gain at the expense of the members of the labor organization or the beneficiaries of the employee benefit plan, or conspiracy to commit any such crimes or attempt to commit any such crimes, or a crime in which any of the foregoing crimes is an element,** shall serve or be permitted to serve -

> (1) as a consultant or adviser to any labor organization,
> (2) as an officer, director, trustee, member of any executive board or similar governing body, business agent, manager, organizer, employee, or representative in any capacity of any labor organization,
> (3) as a labor relations consultant or adviser to a person engaged in an industry or activity affecting commerce, or as an officer, director, agent, or employee of any group or association of employers dealing with any labor organization, or in a position having specific collective bargaining authority or direct responsibility in the area of labor-management relations in any corporation or association engaged in an industry or

activity affecting commerce, or
   (4) in a position which entitles its occupant to a share of the proceeds
   of, or as an officer or executive or administrative employee of, any entity
   whose activities are in whole or substantial part devoted to providing
   goods or services to any labor organization, or
   (5) in any capacity, other than in his capacity as a member of such labor
   organization, that involves decisionmaking authority concerning, or
   decisionmaking authority over, or custody of, or control of the moneys,
   funds, assets, or property of any labor organization,

during or for the period of thirteen years after such conviction or after the end
of such imprisonment, whichever is later, unless the sentencing court on the
motion of the person convicted sets a lesser period of at least three years after
such conviction or after the end of such imprisonment, whichever is later, or
unless prior to the end of such period, in the case of a person so convicted or
imprisoned, (A) his citizenship rights, having been revoked as a result of such
conviction, have been fully restored, or (B) if the offense is a Federal offense,
the sentencing judge or, if the offense is a State or local offense, the United
States district court for the district in which the offense was committed,
pursuant to sentencing guidelines and policy statements under section 994(a) of
title 28, United States Code, determines that such person's service in any
capacity referred to in clauses (1) through (5) would not be contrary to the
purposes of this Act. Prior to making any such determination the court shall hold
a hearing and shall give notice of such proceeding by certified mail to the
Secretary of Labor and to State, county, and Federal prosecuting officials in the
jurisdiction or jurisdictions in which such person was convicted. The court's
determination in any such proceeding shall be final. No person shall knowingly
hire, retain, employ, or otherwise place any other person to serve in any
capacity in violation of this subsection.

(b) Any person who willfully violates this section shall be fined not more than
$10,000 or imprisoned for not more than five years, or both.

(c) For the purpose of this section-

   (1) A person shall be deemed to have been "convicted" and under the
   disability of "conviction" from the date of the judgment of the trial
   court, regardless of whether that judgment remains under appeal.
   (2) A period of parole shall not be considered as part of a period of
   imprisonment.

(d) Whenever any person-

   (1) by operation of this section, has been barred from office or other
   position in a labor organization as a result of a conviction, and
   (2) has filed an appeal of that conviction,

any salary which would be otherwise due such person by virtue of such office or
position, shall be placed in escrow by the individual employer or organization
responsible for payment of such salary. Payment of such salary into escrow shall
continue for the duration of the appeal or for the period of time during which
such salary would be otherwise due, whichever period is shorter. Upon the final
reversal of such person's conviction on appeal, the amounts in escrow shall be
paid to such person. Upon the final sustaining of such person's conviction on

appeal, the amounts in escrow shall be returned to the individual employer or organization responsible for payments of those amounts. Upon final reversal of such person's conviction, such person shall no longer be barred by this statute from assuming any position from which such person was previously barred.

Amendment to Section 302, Labor Management Relations Act, 1947

SEC. 505. Subsections (a), (b), and (c) of section 302 of the Labor Management Relations Act, 1947, as amended, are amended to read as follows:

[11]SEC. 302. (a) It shall be unlawful for any employer or association of employers or any person who acts as a labor relations expert, adviser, or consultant to an employer or who acts in the interest of an employer to pay, lend, or deliver, or agree to pay, lend, or deliver, any money or other thing of value—

> (1) to any representative of any of his employees who are employed in an industry affecting commerce; or
> (2) to any labor organization, or any officer or employee thereof, which represents, seeks to represent, or would admit to membership, any of the employees of such employer who are employed in an industry affecting commerce; or
> (3) to any employee or group or committee of employees of such employer employed in an industry affecting commerce in excess of their normal compensation for the purpose of causing such employee or group or committee directly or indirectly to influence any other employees in the exercise of the right to organize and bargain collectively through representatives of their own choosing; or
> (4) to any officer or employee of a labor organization engaged in an industry affecting commerce with intent to influence him in respect to any of his actions, decisions, or duties as a representative of employees or as such officer or employee of such labor organization.

(b)(1) It shall be unlawful for any person to request, demand, receive, or accept, or agree to receive or accept, any payment, loan, or delivery of any money or other thing of value prohibited by subsection (a).

(2) It shall be unlawful for any labor organization, or for any person acting as an officer, agent, representative, or employee of such labor organization, to demand or accept from the operator of any motor vehicle (as defined in section 10101 of Title 49)[12] employed in the transportation of property in commerce, or the employer of any such operator, any money or other thing of value payable to such organization or to an officer, agent, representative or employee thereof as a fee or charge for the unloading, or in connection with the unloading, of the cargo of such vehicle: *Provided*, That nothing in this paragraph shall be construed to make unlawful any payment by an employer to any of his employees as compensation for their services as employees.

(c) The provisions of this section shall not be applicable (1) in respect to any money or other thing of value payable by an employer to any of his employees whose established duties include acting openly for such employer in matters of labor relations or personnel administration or to any representative of his employees, or to any officer or employee of a labor organization, who is also an employee or former employee of such employer, as compensation for, or by reason of, his service as an employee of such employer; (2) with respect to the payment or delivery of any money or other thing of value in satisfaction of a judgment of any court or a decision or award of an arbitrator or impartial chairman or in compromise, adjustment, settlement, or release of any claim, complaint, grievance, or dispute in the absence of fraud or duress; (3) with respect to the sale or purchase of an article or commodity at the prevailing market price in the regular course of business; (4) with respect to money deducted from the wages of employees in payment of membership dues in a labor organization: *Provided,* That the employer has received from each employee, on whose account such deductions are made, a written assignment which shall not be irrevocable for a period of more than one year, or beyond the termination date of the applicable collective agreement, whichever occurs sooner; (5) with respect to money or other thing of value paid to a trust fund established by such representative, for the sole and exclusive benefit of the employees of such employer, and their families and dependents (or of such employees, families, and dependents jointly with the employees of other employers making similar payments, and their families and dependents): *Provided,* That (A) such payments are held in trust for the purpose of paying, either from principal or income or both, for the benefit of employees, their families and dependents, for medical or hospital care, pensions on retirement or death of employees, compensation for injuries or illness resulting from occupational activity or insurance to provide any of the foregoing, or unemployment benefits or life insurance, disability and sickness insurance, or accident insurance; (B) the detailed basis on which such payments are to be made is specified in a written agreement with the employer, and employees and employers are equally represented in the administration of such fund, together with such neutral persons as the representatives of the employers and the representatives of employees may agree upon and in the event the employer and employee groups deadlock on the administration of such fund and there are no neutral persons empowered to break such deadlock, such agreement provides that the two groups shall agree on an impartial umpire to decide such dispute, or in event of their failure to agree within a reasonable length of time, an impartial umpire to decide such dispute shall, on petition of either group, be appointed by the district court of the United States for the district where the trust fund has its principal office, and shall also contain provisions for an annual audit of the trust fund, a statement of the results of which shall be available for inspection by interested persons at the principal office of the trust fund and at such other places as may be designated in such written agreement; and (C) such payments as are intended to be used for the purpose of providing pensions or annuities for employees are made to a separate trust which provides that the funds held therein cannot be used for any purpose other than paying such pensions or annuities; (6) with respect to money or other thing of value paid by any employer to a trust fund established by such representative for the purpose of pooled vacation, holiday, severance or similar benefits, or defraying costs of apprenticeship or other training programs: *Provided,* That the requirements of clause (B) of the proviso to clause (5) of this subsection shall apply to such trust funds; (7) with respect to money or other thing of value paid by any employer to a pooled or individual trust fund established by such representative for the purpose of (A) scholarships for the benefit of employees, their families, and dependents for study at educational institutions, (B) child care centers for preschool and school age dependents of employees, or (C) financial assistance for employee housing:[13] *Provided,* That no labor organization or employer shall be required to bargain on the establishment of any such trust fund, and refusal to do so shall not constitute an unfair labor practice: *Provided further,* That the requirements of clause (B) of the proviso to clause (5) of this subsection shall apply to such trust funds; (8) with respect to money or any other thing of value paid by any employer to a trust fund established by such representative for the purpose of defraying the costs of legal services for employees, their families, and dependents for counsel or plan of their choice: *Provided,* That the requirements of clause (B) of the proviso to clause (5) of this subsection shall apply to such trust funds: *Provided further,* That no such legal services shall be furnished: (A) to initiate any proceeding directed (i) against any such employer or its officers or agents except in workman's compensation cases, or (ii) against such labor organization, or its parent or subordinate bodies, or their officers or agents, or (iii) against any other employer or labor organization, or their officers or agents, in any matter arising under the National Labor Relations Act, as amended, or this Act; and (B) in any proceeding where a labor organization would be prohibited from defraying the costs of legal services by the provisions of the Labor-Management Reporting and Disclosure Act of 1959; or (9) with respect to money or other things of value paid by an employer to a plant, area or industrywide labor management committee established for one or more of the purposes set forth in section 5(b) [14] of the Labor Management Cooperation Act of 1978.[15]

[The remaining subsections, (d) through (g), of section 302 of the Labor Management Relations Act, 1947, are found at 29 U.S.C. 186(d) through (g).]

TITLE VI -- MISCELLANEOUS PROVISIONS

Investigations

(29 U.S.C. 521)

SEC. 601. (a) The Secretary shall have power when he believes it necessary in order to determine whether any person has violated or is about to violate any provision of this Act (except title I or amendments made by this Act to other statutes) to make an investigation and in connection therewith he may enter such places and inspect such records and accounts and question such persons as he may deem necessary to enable him to determine the facts relative thereto. The Secretary may report to interested persons or officials concerning the facts required to be shown in any report required by this Act and concerning the reasons for failure or refusal to file such a report or any other matter which he deems to be appropriate as a result of such an investigation.

(b) For the purpose of any investigation provided for in this Act, the provisions of sections 9 and 10 (relating to the attendance of witnesses and the production of books, papers, and documents) of the Federal Trade Commission Act of September 16, 1914, as amended (15 U.S.C. 49, 50), are hereby made applicable to the jurisdiction, powers, and duties of the Secretary or any officers designated by him.

Extortionate Picketing

(29 U.S.C. 522)

SEC. 602. (a) It shall be unlawful to carry on picketing on or about the premises of any employer for the purpose of, or as part of any conspiracy or in furtherance of any plan or purpose for, the personal profit or enrichment of any individual (except a bona fide increase in wages or other employee benefits) by taking or obtaining any money or other thing of value from such employer against his will or with his consent.

(b) Any person who willfully violates this section shall be fined not more than $10,000 or imprisoned not more than twenty years, or both.

Retention of Rights Under Other Federal and State Laws

(29 U.S.C. 523)

SEC. 603. (a) Except as explicitly provided to the contrary, nothing in this Act shall reduce or limit the responsibilities of any labor organization or any officer, agent, shop steward, or other representative of a labor organization, or of any trust in which a labor organization is interested, under any other Federal law or under the laws of any State, and, except as explicitly provided to the contrary, nothing in this Act shall take away any right or bar any remedy to which members of a labor organization are entitled under such other Federal law or law of any State.

(b) Nothing contained in titles I, II, III, IV, V, or VI of this Act shall be construed to supersede or impair or otherwise affect the provisions of the Railway Labor Act, as amended, or any of the obligations, rights, benefits, privileges, or immunities of any carrier, employee, organization, representative, or person subject thereto; nor shall anything contained in said titles (except section *505*) of this Act be construed to confer any rights, privileges, immunities, or defenses upon employers, or to impair or otherwise affect the rights of any person under the National Labor Relations Act, as amended.

Effect on State Laws

(29 U.S.C. 524)

SEC. 604. Nothing in this Act shall be construed to impair or diminish the authority of any State to enact and enforce general criminal laws with respect to robbery, bribery, extortion, embezzlement, grand larceny, burglary, arson, violation of narcotics laws, murder, rape, assault with intent to kill, or assault which inflicts grievous bodily injury, or conspiracy to commit any of such crimes.

Service of Process

29 U.S.C. 525)

SEC. 605. For the purposes of this Act, service of summons, subpena, or other legal process of a court of the United States upon an officer or agent of a labor organization in his capacity as such shall constitute service upon the labor organization.

Administrative Procedure Act

(29 U.S.C. 526)

SEC. 606. The provisions of the Administrative Procedure Act shall be applicable to the issuance, amendment, or rescission of any rules or regulations or any adjudication, authorized or required pursuant to the provisions of this Act.

Other Agencies and Departments

(29 U.S.C. 527)

SEC. 607. In order to avoid unnecessary expense and duplication of functions among Government agencies, the Secretary may make such arrangements or agreements for cooperation or mutual assistance in the performance of his functions under this Act and the functions of any such agency as he may find to be practicable and consistent with law. The Secretary may utilize the facilities or services of any department, agency, or establishment of the United States or of any State or political subdivision of a State, including the services of any of its employees, with the lawful consent of such department, agency, or establishment; and each department, agency, or establishment of the United States is authorized and directed to cooperate with the Secretary and, to the extent permitted by law, to provide such information and facilities as he may request for his assistance in the performance of his functions under this Act. The Attorney General or his representative shall receive from the Secretary for appropriate action such evidence developed in the performance of his functions under this Act as may be found to warrant consideration for criminal prosecution under the provisions of this Act or other Federal law.

Criminal Contempt

(29 U.S.C. 528)

SEC. 608. No person shall be punished for any criminal contempt allegedly committed outside the immediate presence of the court in connection with any civil action prosecuted by the Secretary or any other person in any court of the United States under the provisions of this Act unless the facts constituting such criminal contempt are established by the verdict of the jury in a proceeding in the district court of the United States, which jury shall be chosen and empaneled in the manner prescribed by the law governing trial juries in criminal prosecutions in the district courts of the United States.

Prohibition on Certain Discipline by Labor Organization

(29 U.S.C. 529)

SEC. 609. It shall be unlawful for any labor organization, or any officer, agent, shop steward, or other representative of a labor organization, or any employee thereof to fine, suspend, expel, or otherwise discipline any of its members for exercising any right to which he is entitled under the provisions of this Act. The provisions of section 102 shall be applicable in the enforcement of this section.

Deprivation of Rights Under Act by Violence

(29 U.S.C. 530)

SEC. 610. It shall be unlawful for any person through the use of force or violence, or threat of the use of force or violence, to restrain, coerce, or intimidate, or attempt to restrain, coerce, or intimidate any member of a labor organization for the purpose of interfering with or preventing the exercise of any right to which he is entitled under the provisions of this Act. Any person who willfully violates this section shall be fined not more than $1,000 or imprisoned for not more than one year, or both.

Separability Provisions

(29 U.S.C. 531)

SEC. 611. If any provision of this Act, or the application of such provision to any person or circumstances, shall be held invalid, the remainder of this Act or the application of such provision to persons or circumstances other than those as to which it is held invalid, shall not be affected thereby.

TITLE VII -- AMENDMENTS TO THE LABOR MANAGEMENT RELATIONS ACT, 1947, AS AMENDED

[The text of sections 701 through 707 is not included here. However, the complete text of Title VII, Amendments to the Labor Management Relations Act, 1947, As Amended, may be found in Public Law 86-257.]

Endnotes

[1] This revised text has been prepared by the U.S. Department of Labor.

[2] Section 320 of Public Law 95-598 (92 Stat. 2678), Nov. 6, 1978, substituted "cases under Title 11 of the United States Code" for "bankruptcy".

[3] Prior to amendment by section 2(a) of Public Law 89-216, the first sentence of section 205(a) read as follows: "Sec. 205. (a) The contents of the reports and documents filed with the Secretary pursuant to sections 201, 202, and 203 shall be public information, and the Secretary may publish any information and data which he obtains pursuant to the provisions of this title."

[4] Prior to amendment by section 2(b) of Public Law 89-216, section 205(b) read as follows: "(b) The Secretary shall by regulation make reasonable provision for the inspection and examination, on the request of any person, of the information and data contained in any report or other document filed with him pursuant to section 201, 202, or 203."

[5] Prior to amendment by section 2(c) of Public Law 89-216, the second sentence of section 205(c) read as follows: "The Secretary shall make available without payment of a charge, or require any person to furnish, to such State agency as is designated by law or by the Governor of the State in which such person has his principal place of business or headquarters upon request of the Governor of such State, copies of any reports and documents filed by such person with the Secretary pursuant to section 201, 202, or 203, or of information and data contained therein."

(6) Prior to amendment by section 2(d) of Public Law 89-216, section 207(b) read as follows: "(b) Each person required to file a report under section 201(b), 202, 203(a), or the second sentence of 203(b) shall file such report within ninety days after the end of each of its fiscal years; except that where such person is subject to section 201(b), 202, 203(a), or the second section of 203(b), as the case may be, for only a portion of such a fiscal year (because the date of enactment of this Act occurs during such person's fiscal year or such person becomes subject to this Act during its fiscal year) such person may consider that portion as the entire fiscal year in making such report."

(7) Section 211 was added by section 3 of Public Law 99-216 (79 Stat. 888); section 111(a)(2)(D) of Public Law 93-406 (88 Stat. 852), Sept. 2, 1974, substituted "Employee Retirement Income Security Act of 1974" for "Welfare and Pension Plans Disclosure Act".

(8) Prior to amendment by section 1 of Public Law 89-216, the first sentence of section 502(a) read as follows: "Sec. 502(a). Every officer, agent, shop steward, or other representative or employee of any labor organization (other than a labor organization whose property and annual financial receipts do not exceed $5,000 in value), or of a trust in which a labor organization is interested, who handles funds or other property thereof shall be bonded for the faithful discharge of his duties." Section 1 of Public Law 89-216 also added the proviso at the end of section 502(a).

(9) The U.S. Supreme Court, on June 7, 1965, held unconstitutional as a bill of attainder the section 504 provision which imposes criminal sanctions on Communist Party members for holding union office (*U.S. v. Brown*, 381 U.S. 437, 85 S. Ct. 1707).

(10) The following text shows changes made by Public Law 98-473, Oct. 12, 1984, 98 Stat. 2031, 2133, 2134 and by Public Law 100-182, Dec. 7, 1987, 101 Stat. 1266, 1269. Public Law 99-217, Dec. 26, 1985, 99 Stat. 1728, changed the effective date for the amendment made by Public Law 98-473, 98 Stat. 2031, from Nov. 1, 1986, to Nov. 1, 1987; Public Law 100-182, 101 Stat. 1266, made that amendment applicable only to crimes committed after Nov. 1, 1987.

(11) This reprinted text of subsections (a), (b), and (c) of section 302 of the Labor Management Relations Act, 1947, does not reflect the amended text as originally found in the Labor-Management Reporting and Disclosure Act of 1959. It does, however, reflect the legislative changes which have occurred to those subsections from 1959 through October 1991.

(12) In subsection (b)(2) of section 302 of the Labor Management Relations Act, 1947, the phrase "section 10101 of Title 49" was substituted for the phrase "part II of the Interstate Commerce Act [49 U.S.C. 301 et. seq.]" by section 3(b) of Public Law 95-473, October 17, 1978.

(13) Subsection (c)(7)(C) of section 302 of the Labor Management Relations Act, 1947, was added by section 1 of Public Law 101-273, April 18, 1990.

(14) Section 5(b) of the Labor Management Cooperation Act of 1978 probably means section 6(b) of Public Law 95-524 (92 Stat. 2020; 29 U.S.C. 175a note).

(15) Subsection (b)(7) of section 302 of the Labor Management Relations Act, 1947 was added by Public Law 91-86, Oct. 14, 1969; subsection (b)(8) by Public Law 93-95, Aug. 15, 1973; and subsection (b)(9) by section 6(d) of Public Law 95-524, Oct. 27, 1978.

Index

A

Actuarial assumptions, 268
Actuarial process, 267
Administrative services only (ASO), 149, 222, 356, 379
Administrators, 128, 352, 355, 370-372, 389
American Institute of Certified Public Accountants (AICPA), 128, 139, 140, 157, 181, 379, 384
Asset allocation, 321
Audit, 135, 140
Auditor, role of, 138

B

Bankruptcy, 348
Birthday rule, 366
Bond, 289
    debenture, 290
    unsecured bond, 290

C

Carve-out, 356
Centers for Medicare and Medicaid Services (CMS), 190
Certificate of creditable coverage, 398
Change agents, 21-22
    demographics, 22
    growth of small business, 22
    information, 22
    technology, 21
Collection procedures, 344
Commingled funds, 294
    closed-end commingled funds, 294
    open-end commingled funds, 294
Common stocks, 288
Consolidated Omnibus Budget Reconciliation Act (COBRA), 4, 163, 190, 193, 353, 379, 386, 398
Consumer-directed health plans (CDHPs), 227
Consumer price index, 303
Coordination of benefits (COB), 366
Cost-management strategies, 185-188
Creditable coverage, definition of, 191

D

Deficit Reduction Act of 1984 (DEFRA), 353
Defined benefit plans
    accrual of benefits, 244
    cashout, 251
    characteristics, 241
    contributions, 256
    design, 241
    hours of service, 249
    investments, 334
    minimum and maximum funding, 256
    service requirement, 247
    suspension of benefits, 251
    vesting, 250
Defined contribution plans
    401(k) plans, 263
    investments, 334
    money purchase plans, 261, 334
    profit-sharing plans, 262, 334
    target benefit plans, 263
Delinquencies, 343
Delinquent Filer Voluntary Compliance Program (DFVC), 135, 139
Department of Health and Human Services (HHS), 192
Department of Labor (DOL), 15, 30, 33, 34, 35, 36, 37, 41, 42, 64, 65, 66, 72, 73, 77, 78, 79, 91, 93, 95, 96, 99, 100, 103, 111, 114, 119, 122, 125, 134, 142, 150, 157, 249, 280, 343, 359, 368, 377, 398, 401, 404, 413
Deterministic analysis, 232, 333
Discretionary decisions, 412
Disease management, 188

E

Economic Growth and Tax Relief Reconciliation Act of 2001 (EGTRRA), 353
Employee Benefit Security Administration (EBSA), 134, 190
Employee Plans Compliance Resolution System (EPCRS), 136, 157
Employee Retirement Income Security Act of 1974 (ERISA), 4, 8, 59, 122, 134, 138, 142, 150, 157, 242, 288, 306, 343, 351, 397, 401, 403
    Section 3(21)(A), 13
    Section 3(21)(A)(ii), 30
    Section 103(a)(3)(A), 139

Section 103(b), 359
Section 104(b)(1), 406
Section 204(g), 404
Section 204(h), 406
Section 402(a), 13
Section 402(c)(2), 123
Section 402(c)(3), 123
Section 403(a), 403
Section 403(c), 280
Section 403(c)(1), 403
Section 404, 52, 123, 158, 354
Section 404(a), 13, 31, 150, 152
Section 404(a)(1), 61, 280, 403
Section 404(a)(1)(A), 13, 31, 32, 117, 152, 403
Section 404(a)(1)(B), 14, 31, 62, 68, 95-98, 117, 277, 403
Section 404(a)(1)(C), 31, 67, 98
Section 404(a)(1)(D), 31, 36, 405, 406
Section 404(c)(1), 31, 32
Section 405, 53
Section 405(a), 123, 412
Section 405(c), 124
Section 405(d)(1), 306
Section 405(d)(2), 408
Section 406, 53, 123, 158
Section 406(a), 14, 37
Section 406(a)(1), 403
Section 406(a)(1)(c), 72
Section 406(a)(1)(D), 101
Section 406(b), 14, 15, 105
Section 406(b)(1), 39
Section 406(b)(2), 39, 281
Section 406(b)(3), 39
Section 406(d)(5), 104
Section 408(b), 15
Section 408(b)(2), 35, 101, 154
Section 408(b)(8), 41
Section 408(b)(11), 281
Section 408(c), 15, 153
Section 408(c)(3), 408
Section 409, 123, 158
Section 409(a), 404, 405
Section 410(b)(1), 160, 279
Section 411(a), 405
Section 502(a)(1)(B), 115
Section 502(a)(3), 51, 120, 404
Section 502(d)(1), 161
Section 502(g)(2), 343
Section 503, 368

Enrolled actuary, 272, 380
ERISA maximum age, 11
ERISA minimum participation, 11
ERISA minimum vesting schedules for employer contributions, 11
ERISA vesting of participant contributions, 11
ERISA year of service/hour of service, 11
Excess loss coverage, 233
Exclusive provider organization (EPO), 382
Exclusive purpose rule, 32
Experience rating, 199

F

Family and Medical Leave Act, 386
Fiduciary, definition of, 29, 61, 352
    fiduciary liability, 62
    fiduciary liability insurance, 15, 157, 159
    liability limit, 169
    premium, 170
Fiduciary responsibilities, 13-14, 52, 150, 404
Fiduciary responsibility, definition of, 43
Fiduciary status, 29
Financial Accounting Standards Board (FASB), 138, 379
Fixed premium group insurance, 199
Flexible savings accounts, 229
Form 5500, 135, 137, 139, 142, 147, 279, 338
Full funding limitations (FFLs), 256
Funding standard account (FSA), 268

G

General fiduciaries, 13
Generally accepted auditing principles (GAAP), 138, 144
Generally accepted auditing standards (GAAS), 138, 142
Guaranteed investment contracts (GICs), 75-77, 292

H

Health care cost management, 204-206, 365, 369
   case management, 383
   disease management, 383
   utilization review, 383
Health Insurance Portability and Accountability Act (HIPAA), 4, 190, 193, 353, 359, 362, 386
Health maintenance organizations (HMOs), 210-214
Health reimbursement accounts (HRAs), 223
Health savings accounts (HSAs), 223

I

Independent qualified public accountant (IQPA), 139
Index fund, 292
In-house asset managers (INHAMs), 103
Insurance companies, 197
Internal controls, 146, 357
Internal Revenue Code (IRC), 256, 353
   Section 404, 256
   Section 411(c)(2)(C)(iii), 11
   Section 412, 256
   Section 412(c)(8), 257
Internal Revenue Service (IRS), 136-137, 190, 279, 359
Investment Advisers Act of 1940, 69, 124
Investment considerations, 65-68
Investment consultant, 320
Investment manager, definition of, 14, 129, 306
IRS Restructuring and Reform Act of 1998, 136

J

Joint and survivor pensions, 253-255

K

Kickbacks, 119

L

Labor-Management Relations Act of 1947 (LMRA), 3, 9, 50, 88, 351, 359, 403, 410, 413
   see also Taft-Hartley Act

M

Medical savings accounts, 223
Medicare, 181, 182
Medicare Prescription Drug, Improvement, and Modernization Act of 2003, 182
Money market instruments, 291
Monte Carlo simulation, 234
Multiemployer Pension Plan Amendments Act of 1980 (MPPAA), 4, 138, 261, 267, 343, 380
Mutual funds, 299
   advantages, 300
   disadvantages, 301

N

Named fiduciary, 29, 123, 151
National Association of Insurance Commissioners (NAIC), 366
National Association of Securities Dealers, 332

O

Omnibus Budget Reconciliation Act of 1985 (OBRA '85, '86, '87, '89), 353

P

Parliamentary procedure, 405
Parties in interest, 13, 101, 344
Pension Annuitants Protection Act of 1994, 75
Pension Benefit Guaranty Corporation (PBGC), 74, 134-136, 271, 278, 398
Pension benefits, design, 16
Pension fund mergers, 275
Pharmacy benefit managers (PBMs), 114, 148
Plan administrator, 30
Preferred provider organizations (PPOs), 214-221, 382
Prescription drug benefits, 175-180
Procedural prudence, 125
Prohibited Transaction Class Exemption (PTCE), 101
Prohibited transactions, 14, 101, 136
Protected health information, 192, 362
Proxy voting, 73
Prudence standard, 34, 44, 59, 61-62, 123, 129
Prudent expert standard, 123, 131
Prudent man rule, 14, 95, 156

Q

Qualified domestic relations orders (QDROs), 239, 254, 268
Qualified professional asset managers (QPAMs), 102, 167, 168
Qualifying employer real property, 35
Qualifying employer securities, 35

R

Real estate investment trusts (REITs), 87, 295
Retiree benefits, 181-184
Retirement benefits, 258
    deferred retirement, 259
    early retirement, 258
    normal retirement, 258
Retirement Equity Act of 1984 (REA), 242, 353
Retirement Protection Act of 1994 (RPA), 256
Revenue Act of 1978, 23
Risk management, 283

S

Safe harbor, 72
SAS 70 report, 148
Securities and Exchange Commission, 298, 332
Securities Exchange Act of 1934, 331
Self-financing, definition of, 222
Settlor function, 113, 404
Social investing, 77
Stochastic process, 232
Subrogation, 120, 368
Summary Annual Reports, 336
Summary Plan Descriptions, 336

T

Taft-Hartley Act of 1947
    see also Labor-Management Relations Act
Tax Equity and Fiscal Responsibility Act of 1982 (TEFRA), 353
Third-party administrator (TPA), 128, 222
Travel expenses, 153
Trustee responsibilities, 30, 43
Trustees
    appointment and removal, 107
    monitoring, 111
Trusteeship, 15
Two-hatted trustee, 50, 343

U

Unfunded vested benefit liabilities (UVBLs), 239

V

Venture capital, 296
Voluntary employees beneficiary association (VEBA), 140, 223
Voluntary Fiduciary Correction Program, 135, 157, 159

W

Wagner Act, 3
Welfare benefits, design, 16
Wellness, 188
Withdrawal liability, 12, 261, 270, 278